Health Care Administration
Managing Organized Delivery Systems

Fifth Edition

Lawrence F. Wolper

JONES AND BARTLETT PUBLISHERS

Sudbury, Massachusetts

BOSTON   TORONTO   LONDON   SINGAPORE

World Headquarters

Jones and Bartlett Publishers	Jones and Bartlett Publishers	Jones and Bartlett Publishers
40 Tall Pine Drive	Canada	International
Sudbury, MA 01776	6339 Ormindale Way	Barb House, Barb Mews
978-443-5000	Mississauga, Ontario L5V 1J2	London W6 7PA
info@jbpub.com	Canada	United Kingdom
www.jbpub.com		

Jones and Bartlett's books and products are available through most bookstores and online booksellers. To contact Jones and Bartlett Publishers directly, call 800-832-0034, fax 978-443-8000, or visit our website www.jbpub.com.

Substantial discounts on bulk quantities of Jones and Bartlett's publications are available to corporations, professional associations, and other qualified organizations. For details and specific discount information, contact the special sales department at Jones and Bartlett via the above contact information or send an email to specialsales@jbpub.com.

This publication is designed to provide accurate and authoritative information in regard to the Subject Matter covered. It is sold with the understanding that the publisher is not engaged in rendering legal, accounting, or other professional service. If legal advice or other expert assistance is required, the service of a competent professional person should be sought.

Production Credits
Publisher: Michael Brown
Editorial Assistant: Catie Heverling
Editorial Assistant: Teresa Reilly
Production Manager: Tracey Chapman
Senior Marketing Manager: Sophie Fleck
Manufacturing and Inventory Control Supervisor: Amy Bacus
Composition: Cape Cod Compositors, Inc.
Cover Design: Scott Moden
Printing and Binding: Malloy, Inc.
Cover Printing: Malloy, Inc.

Library of Congress Cataloging-in-Publication Data
Health care administration : managing organized delivery systems / [edited by] Lawrence F. Wolper. — 5th ed.
    p. ; cm.
    Prev. ed. has subtitle: planning, implementing, and managing organized delivery.
    Includes bibliographical references and index.
    ISBN-13: 978-0-7637-5791-5 (pbk.)
    ISBN-10: 0-7637-5791-8 (pbk.)
  1. Hospitals—Administration.   2. Health services administration.   I. Wolper, Lawrence F.
  [DNLM: 1. Hospital Administration.   2. Delivery of Health Care—organization & administration.
3. Health Services Administration.   WX 150 H4335 2011]
    RA971.H384 2011
    362.1068—dc22

                                                                                    2009044579

6048
Printed in the United States of America
14 13 12 11 10   10 9 8 7 6 5 4 3 2 1

To Maxine, Emily, and Lisa

Table of Contents

About the Author/Editor

Lawrence F. Wolper, MBA, FACMPE, is president of L. Wolper, Inc., with offices in New York and New Jersey. The firm is a full-service consulting organization specializing in all aspects of physician group practice, faculty practice, and ambulatory care. In addition, L. Wolper, Inc. has experience in contract-managing physician group practices and ambulatory surgery centers, as well as in practice turnarounds. The firm also conducts civil and health industry mediation.

Mr. Wolper has more than 25 years of consulting and senior executive experience and has been the advisor to, or managed, major group practices, faculty practice plans, ambulatory surgery centers, and integrated networks. Prior to founding his firm in 1987, he was a partner in KPMG International, LLP, with New York–area and national responsibility for physician practice and ambulatory care consulting. At that time, he was involved in the development of large group practices, faculty practice plans, and provider networks. Prior to his partnership in KPMG, he was a consulting partner with Ingram, Weitzman, Mertens & Co, a large regional healthcare accounting and consulting firm.

He has published more than 35 professional journal articles and 8 texts on a variety of subjects germane to physician and faculty practice and to healthcare administration.

Mr. Wolper received an MBA in healthcare administration from Bernard M. Baruch College–Mount Sinai School of Medicine and a BA in advertising/marketing from Hofstra University. He was a Robert Wood Johnson Foundation Fellow in HMO Management at the Wharton School, University of Pennsylvania, and an Association of University Programs in Hospital Administration (AUPHA) Fellow studying the British National Health System at the King's Fund College of Hospital Management in London, England. He is a Fellow in the American College of Medical Practice Executives.

Preface and Acknowledgments

The idea for the first edition of this book occurred many years ago when I was completing my master's degree in business and healthcare administration. I came across a text titled *Hospital Organization and Management* by Dr. Malcolm Thomas MacEachern. A well-respected text found on every administrator's bookshelf, it was out of touch with the changes that had occurred in the industry since its first printing in 1935 and the editions that occurred thereafter. I decided at that time that I would like to produce a book that would encompass nearly all the topics relevant to the healthcare industry.

The first edition of this book was published in 1987, 23 years ago. Consistent with the times, the focus was on the hospital, and it was organized to include sections on departmental operations, as well as one encompassing the functional/technical areas pertaining to hospitals and the industry in general. It included sections on information systems, management engineering, and marketing, among others.

The second edition of the text was modified as a result of major regulatory, delivery system, and technological changes. In addition, trends toward managed care and the acquisition of physician practices necessitated the inclusion of several entirely new chapters on topics such as managed care, ambulatory care, physician practice, and international healthcare systems. In light of the fact that many graduate programs in healthcare administration use this book, the revisions in that edition added more technical detail to give students a complete understanding of information systems, inpatient and outpatient Medicare reimbursement, physician practice, ambulatory care, and other topics. The second edition recognized the emergence of organized delivery systems and the changing role of the hospital within those emerging systems. Ambulatory care, increased care in doctors' offices, decreasing hospital reimbursement, managed care and utilization review, and other factors were reducing the long-standing role of the hospital as the major locus of care.

Although the second edition recognized the emergence of organized delivery systems, the theme of the third edition *was* the organized delivery system. There no longer were three parts in the book, but two. The first, and dominant part of the book, "Planning, Implementing, and Managing Organized Delivery Systems," broadly began with international health care. Other chapters in Part I covered a range of detailed functional, technical, and organizational matters that pertained to organized delivery systems from the system and corporate (i.e., not hospital) perspective. Part II of the book, "The Hospital in an Organized Delivery System," was devoted to matters that relate to the hospital or functions that occur at the hospital level, particularly those in an organized delivery system.

The fourth edition of this text remained consistent with the prior edition, and, as such, continued to focus on organized delivery systems and the role of the hospital within a system environment. Most of the long-standing chapters in the text were updated, and new chapters were added covering labor law, designing and implementing a hospital compliance program, implementing a physician practice compliance program, biomedical ethics, and, in response to changing times, a chapter on bioterrorism preparedness. In recognition of the continuing presence and changing character of managed care, the chapter on this subject was expanded.

Now, 23 years after the first edition, the fifth edition comes at a time when there may be broad healthcare reform at hand. Not merely a change in the type of insurance methodology (i.e., from indemnity to managed care, or from cost-plus based to DRGs), but change that is intended to insure millions of uninsured, promote integrated and electronic health records, trim costs that do not contribute more directly to the health status of Americans, and to make insurance more affordable. After decades of attempting broad healthcare reform by at least four US presidents, such reform may be achievable in some form. The fifth edition of the book is shorter, with the existing chapters largely all modified. The chapters retain their technical detail, particularly in those such as "Healthcare Information Technologies in an Era of Healthcare Reform: A Complex Adaptive System Perspective," "The Management of Nursing Services," "Facility Design and Planning for Ambulatory Care Centers," "Organized Delivery Systems," and "International Health Care," which is now a comparison of 12 countries.

I would like to acknowledge all authors, and the many coauthors and researchers who assisted them. In particular, I acknowledge Myron Fottler and Donna Malvey for updating an already excellent chapter; Gabe Imperato and staff for keeping the legal issues as up-to-date as possible in a fast-paced industry; Leslie Eldenburg, Eldon Schafer, and Dwight Zulauf for keeping their chapter always contemporary; Wilhelmina Manzano and Gina Bufe who accepted the challenge of rewriting the nursing chapter and did an exemplary job; Roberta Clarke, who, in the area of marketing in the healthcare industry, always seems to introduce new ideas and challenges to those of us in the industry; Richard Sprow, Sonya Dufner, and Chris Bormann, who wrote an excellent chapter on facility design; Eliot Lazar and his coauthors for rewriting the chapter on quality and patient safety; and to Michael Kelley and his coauthors for keeping the chapter on physician practice on pace with the rapid changes in that sector of the industry.

I am grateful to my daughters Emily and Lisa, and my wife Maxine, because they have provided me with a great deal of the energy and enthusiasm required to conceive of, plan, and produce a comprehensive text. As young adults, my daughters and their generation will, I hope, benefit from the industry changes that will occur in the coming years without being the beneficiaries of an onerous tax burden. On the other hand, relating to my wife and I, as we approach

Medicare coverage in the years to come, our hope is that the program remains as comprehensive and vital as it has for prior generations.

In spite of the weaknesses in our healthcare system and the high costs associated with it, there are strengths to which other countries aspire. It is hoped that in our drive to reduce healthcare expenditures, extend insurance to millions of uninsured, and to restructure a vibrant industry, we do not move so far and fast that the high quality of care always associated with our system will be subordinated. If such conditions appear to be materializing, I expect that the public will intervene politically. Consumerism remains an expanding influence in the healthcare and other industries. It is hoped that we make better use of healthcare dollars, and that the United States begins to catch up with many countries in terms of improving healthcare outcomes in which we do not compare favorably to many other advanced countries. Those countries have continued to modify their systems for many decades. The impending healthcare legislation will not likely "get it right" the first time. Many legislative modifications will be required in the decades to come.

—Lawrence F. Wolper, MBA, FACMPE

Contributors

Kevin W. Barr, MBA
Chief Executive Officer
Bon Secours Virginia HealthSource, Inc.
Richmond, Virginia

Karl Bartscht, MSE, FAAHC
Former CEO
The Chi Group, Inc.
Ann Arbor, Michigan

John D. Blair, PhD
Trinity Company Professor of Management
Center for Health Care Leadership & Strategy
Rawls College of Business
Texas Tech University
Lubbock, Texas

Christian F. Bormann, AIA, NCARB, LEED® AP
Principal, Healthcare Market Sector Leader
Perkins+Will
New York, New York

Charles L. Breindel, PhD
Former Professor
Medical College of Virginia
Virginia Commonwealth University
Richmond, Virginia

Paul J. Brzozowski, MT (ASCP), MPA
Partner
Applied Management Systems, Inc.
Burlington, Massachusetts

Gina M. Bufe, PhD, RN
New York-Presbyterian Hospital
New York, New York

Paul D. Camara, MS
Manager
Applied Management Systems, Inc.
Burlington, Massachusetts

Roberta N. Clarke, MBA, DBA
Associate Professor
School of Management
Boston University
Boston, Massachusetts

Karen Scott Collins, MD, MPH
Vice President
New York-Presbyterian Hospital
New York, New York

Patrick M. Collins, JD
Counsel, Labor and Employment Practice Group
Greenberg Traurig, LLP
New York, New York

Anthony Dawson, RN, MSN
Vice President
Operations at the Milstein Pavilion
New York-Presbyterian/Columbia
New York, New York

Sonya Dufner, ASID, LEED AP
Perkins+Will
New York, New York

Leslie G. Eldenburg, PhD, CPA
Associate Professor of Accounting
Eller School of Management
University of Arizona
Tucson, Arizona

Steven Falcone, MD
Leonard M. Miller School of Medicine
University of Miami
Boca Raton, Florida

Harry Feirman, PhD
Rocheport, Missouri

Myron D. Fottler, MBA, PhD
Professor and Director
Health Services Administration Programs
University of Central Florida
Orlando, Florida

Barbara B. Friedman, MA, MPA, FAHRM
Consultant
Forest Hills, New York

Cynthia A. Holubik, RN, BSN, MSM
Director
Bioterrorism Preparedness Project
Center for Health Care Leadership and Strategy
College of Business Administration
Texas Tech University
Lubbock, Texas

Daniel Hyman, MD, MMB
The Children's Hospital
Aurora, Colorado

Gabriel L. Imperato, JD
Managing Partner
Broad and Cassel
Ft. Lauderdale, Florida

Robert K. Keel, BS, MA
Research Assistant
Texas Tech University
Lubbock, Texas

Michael J. Kelley, MBA
Vice Chair for Administration
Office of the Executive Clinical Dean at FAU
University of Miami
Miller School of Medicine at FAU
Miami, Florida

Eliot J. Lazar, MD, MBA
Senior Vice President, Chief Quality and Patient Safety Officer,
   New York-Presbyterian Hospital
Chief Medical Officer
New York-Presbyterian Healthcare System
New York, New York

Donna Malvey, PhD, MHSA
Visiting Assistant Professor
University of Central Florida, Cocoa Campus
College of Health and Public Affairs
Cocoa, Florida

Wilhelmina M. Manzano, MA, RN, NEA-BC
New York-Presbyterian Hospital
New York, New York

David Moxley
University of Missouri School of Medicine
Health Management & Informatics Department
Columbia, Missouri

Amy Myers
University of Missouri School of Medicine
Health Management & Informatics Department
Columbia, Missouri

Jesus J. Peña, MPA, Esq.
Jesus J. Peña & Associates, Jackson Heights, New York
Attorney
Saint Michael's Medical Center
Newark, New Jersey
Jackson Heights, New York

Ephraim Perez

Lester J. Perling
Partner
Broad and Cassel
Ft. Lauderdale, Florida

Brian K. Regan, PhD
Director, Clinical Affairs
New York-Presbyterian Healthcare System
New York, New York

Angela M. Roberson, MBA
Administrative Fellow
MD Anderson Cancer Center
Houston, Texas

Keila Rooney
Administrative Resident
Health First, Inc.
Rockledge, Florida

Aimee Sato

Grant T. Savage, PhD
Professor
Department of Management and Marketing
University of Alabama
Tuscaloosa, Alabama

Eldon L. Schafer, PhD, CPA
Professor Emeritus
University of Arizona
Tucson, Arizona

William L. Scheyer
City Administrator
Erlanger, Kentucky

Stephen G. Schwartz, MD, MBA
Bascom Palmer Eye Institute
Naples, Florida

Mike Segal, BA, JD, LLM
Partner
Broad and Cassel
Miami, Florida

Richard Sprow, AIA
Architect
Perkins+Will
New York, New York

Peter D. Stergios, BA, JD
Greenberg Traurig
New York, New York

Joseph Tan, PhD
Professor
Business Department
School of Business Administration
Wayne State University
Detroit, Michigan

Joshia Tan
Student
Olin Business School
Washington University
St. Louis, Missouri

Steven R. Tomlinson
Department of Chemistry & Biochemistry
Texas Tech University
Lubbock, Texas

Leo van der Reis, MD
Adjunct Professor
Clinical Professor
Department of Management and Marketing
University of Alabama
Tuscaloosa, Alabama

Andrew L. Wilson, PharmD, FASHP
Director of Pharmacy Services
Department of Pharmacy
Virginia Commonwealth University Health System
Richmond, Virginia

Karol Wollenburg
Pharmacy Department
New York-Presbyterian Hospital
New York, New York

Dwight J. Zulauf, BS, MS, PhD, CPA
Professor and Dean Emeritus
School of Business
Pacific Lutheran University
Tacoma, Washington

The "Corporate" View of Organized Delivery Systems

International Health Care:
A Twelve Country Comparison

*Grant T. Savage, Harry Feirman, Leo van der Reis,
Amy Myers, and David Moxley*

Within the United States and among other high-income countries, health care has become an international topic of major concern. One reason for this interest is pragmatic: National health risks such as AIDS, flu, and bioterrorism have global impact, affecting international health, politics, and commerce.[1] Another reason is ethical: Even within countries with high per capita incomes, inequities in the access, financing, and delivery of health services often mean the poor are sicker and pay proportionately more for care than the rich.[2] In fact, making financial access to and provision of health care both equitable and cost-effective are the predominant values driving most ethical and political arguments for changing national healthcare systems.[3]

Beginning during the 1990s, market-driven changes and the commercialization of health services—strengthening the role of the private sector, encouraging user fees, providing pay-for-performance, and separating the financing and service provision functions—have transformed the financing and organization of health care both in the United States[4,5] and around the world.[6] Although some researchers believed these changes would address the US healthcare system's shortcomings,[7] other researchers since the early 1990s have been looking toward the healthcare systems in Canada[8-11] and in Western Europe[12,13] for solutions. Given the United States's reliance on voluntary, employer-based insurance, lessons can also be drawn from other countries that employ a broad mix of health financing options, including compulsory and voluntary individual or employment-based health insurance. Such comparisons should help inform the debate on changing the healthcare system in the United States, a debate that now has added urgency with President Obama's pledge to make health care more accessible and affordable for all citizens.

In this chapter, 12 national healthcare systems are compared: Argentina, Brazil, Canada, Germany, Greece, Indonesia, Mexico, the Netherlands, Sweden, Turkey, the United Kingdom, and the United States. This is a diverse set of nations, representing a range of low-, middle-, and high-income nations, with per capita incomes in 2006 ranging from $3,310 (Indonesia) to $44,070 (United States) in international dollars adjusted for purchasing parity.[14] Whatever the level of per capita income, national healthcare systems can be characterized and evaluated in terms of who may be treated, for how much money, and with what expected outcome. Every healthcare system must deal with the trade-off among issues of financial access, cost, and quality. In the first section, the focus is on two factors that influence these issues: (1) Financing, that is, how monies are mobilized and allocated for the provision of health care; and (2) how health services are organized, that is, who provides services and the relative weights placed on the provision of primary and tertiary care. We seek to answer the question, "How and to whom is health care provided, and with what effect?" The following sections provide a brief review of the historical development and current organization and financing within each national health system, focusing on three prototypes for achieving universal access. The final section provides a set of lessons learned from comparing these 12 national health systems, which will help inform the debate on reforming health care in the United States.

The Financing, Organization, and Outcomes from the Provision of Health Care

Table 1.1 compares 12 national health systems on simple measures of financial access to, cost of, and quality of health care. The left-hand column lists each country according to its quality and cost performance. Within the 12-country comparison, Sweden anchors the high end, while Indonesia anchors the low end.

Table 1.1 Comparisons among 12 Nations on the Financial Access, Cost, and Quality of Health Care

Country	Financial Access	Cost (2006)	Quality (2003)
Listed by Quality and Cost Results	Degree and Form of Insurance Coverage	Percentage of GDP for Health Care	Health-Adjusted Life Expectancy at Birth (HALE)
Sweden	Universal access via a devolved national health service with supplementary, private insurance	8.9% 0.3% Δ avg.	73 years 6.0 Δ avg.
Canada	Universal access within a devolved, single-payer system with supplementary, private insurance	10.0% 1.4% Δ avg.	72 years 4.6 Δ avg.

Table 1.1   *(Continued)*

Country	Financial Access	Cost (2006)	Quality (2003)
Germany	Universal access within a compulsory system of social insurance and substitutive, private insurance	10.4% 1.8% Δ avg.	72 years 4.6 Δ avg.
United Kingdom	Universal access via a devolved national health service with supplementary, private insurance	8.4% –0.3% Δ avg.	71 years 3.6 Δ avg.
Netherlands	Universal access via a compulsory system of private insurance with supplementary, private insurance and government subsidies	9.3% 0.7% Δ avg.	71 years 3.6 Δ avg.
Greece	Universal rights and variable access within a system of national health services (ESY), social insurance, and private insurance	9.9% 1.3% Δ avg.	71 years 3.6 Δ avg.
United States	Variable access within a system of employment-based, voluntary insurance, social insurance, and public programs and services	15.3% 6.7% Δ avg.	69 years 1.6 Δ avg.
Argentina	Variable access within a multipayer system of employment-based social insurance, private insurance, and public health services	10.1% 1.5% Δ avg.	65 years (2.4) Δ avg.
Mexico	Universal rights but variable access within a system of employment-based social insurance, public health services, and private insurance	6.2% –2.5% Δ avg.	65 years (2.4) Δ avg.
Turkey	Universal access within a single-payer system that includes both publicly and privately owned health services	5.6% –3.1% Δ avg.	62 years (5.6) Δ avg.
Brazil	Universal rights but variable access within a system of national and contracted services, along with substitutive, private insurance	7.5% –1.2% Δ avg.	60 years (7.4) Δ avg.
Indonesia	Variable access within a system of employment-based social insurance and private insurance, with public health services	2.2% –6.5% Δ avg.	58 years (9.4) Δ avg.
		8.79% avg.	67.4 avg.

Source: WHOSIS: WHO Statistical Information System, World Health Organization, retrieved November 24, 2008, from http://www.who.int/whosis/en/.

Financial Access to Health Care

The access column in Table 1.1 incorporates information about how each nation organizes and finances its healthcare system. The assessments of access are based primarily on financial access because it is the most amenable to policy interventions and because comparative data are most readily available on this aspect of access. National healthcare systems display three distinct configurations for ensuring universal access: (1) a government-owned, national health service (Sweden and the United Kingdom); (2) a national, compulsory social or private insurance (Canada and the Netherlands, respectively); or (3) a mixture of compulsory social and private insurance (Germany). Interestingly, both Greece and Turkey combine a national health service with a mixture of compulsory social and private health insurance. The lack of universal financial access in the United States is and has been the focus for most of its health reform debates.

Financing can be broken out into two aspects: the direct versus indirect provision of health services by various national governments.[15] Direct financing of health services occurs if the main health insurer or government—whether national, regional, or local—owns healthcare facilities and employs healthcare professionals, as in Greece, Sweden, and the United Kingdom. Indirect financing, in contrast, occurs if the main insurer or government contracts for the provision of various health services. For example, the provincial and regional governments in Canada, the sickness funds in Germany, and the insurance companies in the Netherlands contract with providers for health services.

Costs of Health Care

The percentage of gross domestic product (GDP) devoted to healthcare expenditures provides a convenient and meaningful ratio for comparing healthcare costs (see Table 1.1). Due, in part, to lower transaction costs,[16] the direct financing of health care in Sweden and the United Kingdom averages 8.65% of the GDP and is less costly than the indirect financing in Canada, Germany, and the Netherlands, which averages 9.9% of the GDP. **Figure 1.1** expands upon this point and shows both the level of GDP and the international dollars (adjusted for purchasing power parity) per capita devoted to health care by each of the 12 nations in 2006. Taking into account the dollars per capita for health care is important, as less wealthy nations have to spend a greater percentage of their GDP in order to achieve comparable levels of funding. Nonetheless, the United States clearly spent much more on health care than any other country in 2006 (15.3% GDP; $6,714 per capita). Indeed, even when taking the influence of per capita GDP on health expenditures—i.e., wealthy nations typically spend more on health than poor nations—the United States spends far more than other nations of comparable wealth. This holds true even when taking into account the increased demand for health services from an aging population within the United States and is most likely due to the prices for services.[17]

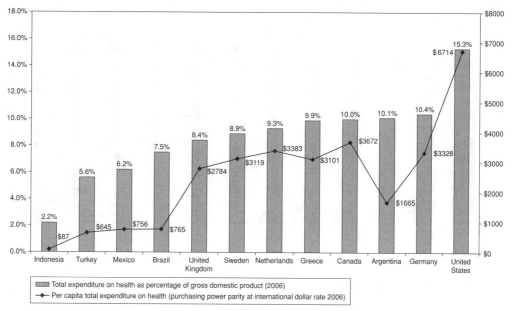

FIGURE 1.1   Comparisons among 12 Nations on the Percentage of Gross Domestic Product and Per Capita Spending on Health Care in 2006. Data from *WHOSIS: WHO Statistical Information System*, World Health Organization, retrieved November 24, 2008, from http://www.who.int/whosis/en/.

Quality of Health Care

Although the total cost of health in the United States and other high-income countries is a focus of many attempts at reform, the focus of recent efforts in the United States is on obtaining greater value for the money spent. Ideally one would like to compare national healthcare systems on the basis of clinical outcomes and quality of life. The right-hand column in Table 1.1 shows quality, based on a population measure of health-adjusted life expectancy (HALE); this is probably the single best proxy available for assessing health outcomes across the 12 countries in the comparisons. HALE estimates the average number of years that a person can expect to live in "full health" by taking into account years lived in less than full health due to disease and/or injury. For example, the average HALE for the six countries with universal financial access is 71.7 years; in contrast, the average HALE for the United States is 69 years, while the average HALE for the five middle- and low-income countries is 62 years.

Figure 1.2 shows how the United States fares in comparisons across the 12 countries on two measures of HALE when compared to two preventable healthcare outcomes—infant mortality and maternal mortality at birth. The health quality outcome index in Figure 1.2 subtracts the sum of the standardized scores for preventable deaths (infant and maternal) from the sum of the standardized scores for female HALE and male HALE. While this is a crude measure of

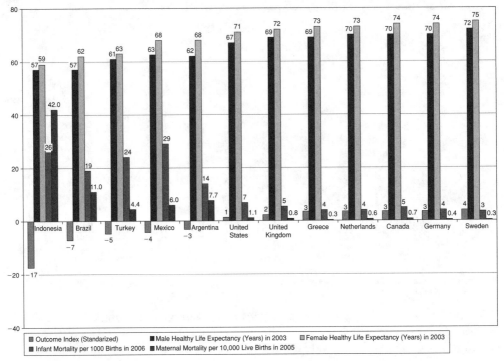

FIGURE 1.2   Comparisons among 12 Nations on Four Health Care Outcome
Measures, Ordered by Standardized Outcome Index. Data from *WHOSIS: WHO
Statistical Information System*, World Health Organization, retrieved November 24, 2008,
from http://www.who.int/whosis/en/.

amenable healthcare quality, it does take into account both healthy life expectancy and the
provision of maternal and infant care. Based on this outcome index, the United States is
ranked 7th out of the 12 national health systems under comparison, the same point as the
United States ranking in Table 1.1. All of the countries with higher rankings provide universal financial access to their citizens. Interestingly, the health quality outcome index also suggests changes to the rankings listed in Table 1.1, with Germany, the Netherlands, and Greece
moving up in the rankings by one or two places, and Canada and the United Kingdom
falling in the rankings by one and two places, respectively. These changes undoubtedly reflect
the addition of infant and maternal mortality in the health outcome index. Taken together,
infant and maternal mortality is an important proxy for health system quality since most
birth-related deaths are preventable, assuming diet, living conditions, and healthcare provision are adequate. Significantly, that set of presumptions may be questionable not only in
low- and middle-income countries with large inequities in family income such as Argentina,
Brazil, and Mexico,[18] but also in the United States, which has had increasing inequities in
family income distribution.[19]

Toward an Institutional Framework for Understanding Health System Constraints

Clearly, the United States should be able to obtain far better value for the amount of money it spends on health care. Given that countries such as Sweden, Germany, and Canada obtain better healthcare outcomes (see Figure 1.2) and spend less than the United States (see Figure 1.1), we should be able to learn some lessons from examining their healthcare systems, as well as the systems in Greece, the Netherlands, and the United Kingdom that obtain better cost-benefit ratios than the United States. At the same time, it would be wise to look at those middle- and low-income nations that are also addressing healthcare financial access, cost, and quality issues, particularly Indonesia, Mexico, and Turkey, which are all undergoing major healthcare reforms.

At the national level, both the allocation of healthcare resources and the funding sources for health care establish institutional constraints on health system efficiency and effectiveness. For example, three health resource indicators, along with a health outcome indicator, help illuminate not only the diverse ways in which health care is organized, but also how the configuration of these resources impacts effectiveness and efficiency. **Figure 1.3** displays the density of hospital beds, nurses and midwifes, and physicians in each of the 12 countries, ordered by the total (combined) density of these three resources. The country with the highest combined density of

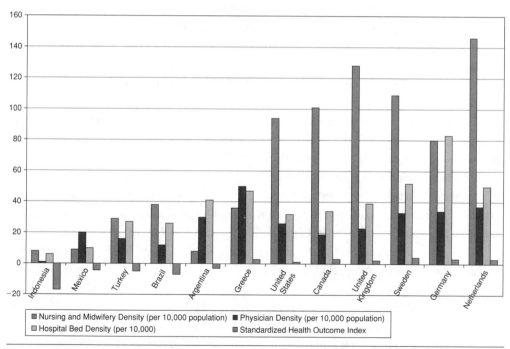

FIGURE 1.3   Comparisons among 12 Nations on Density of Hospital Beds, Nursing and Midwifery, and Physicians, Ordered by Combined Density. Data from *WHOSIS: WHO Statistical Information System*, World Health Organization, retrieved November 24, 2008, from http://www.who.int/whosis/.

these three resources is the Netherlands, while Indonesia has the lowest density. The outcome index reported in Figure 1.3 is the same standardized health outcome displayed in Figure 1.2. Not surprisingly, improved health outcomes correlate with increases in the allocation of health resources, illustrating that effectiveness improves as more total resources are devoted to health care.

More interestingly, the four countries with established, high-performing primary care networks—Canada, the Netherlands, Sweden, and the United Kingdom—display a greater reliance on nursing and midwifery in relationship to both physicians and hospitals than do other countries. This configuration of resources is more efficient than others. For example, among the high-income countries, this difference is particularly pronounced in comparison to Germany and Greece, both of which have relatively higher numbers of hospital beds per capita. In addition, Argentina, Greece, and Mexico are the only countries that have proportionately more physicians than nurses and midwives, a clearly high-cost configuration. Moreover, with the exception of Canada, the four countries with a primary care configuration of resources also devote lower levels of their gross domestic product to health care (see Figure 1.1) while obtaining comparable or better health outcomes. However, taking into account only Figure 1.3, both Canada and Sweden obtain the best health outcomes given the health resources they allocate to health care. Next, we turn to a discussion of the ways in which health care is financed, further illuminating a key constraint on health system performance.

Figure 1.4 compares the sources of revenue for health expenditures in each of the 12 national health systems. Taking into consideration the organization of these national health systems, these sources of revenue for health expenditures help explain both the flexibility and constraints facing each country. Only the three countries at the top (UK, Sweden, and Canada) and the two countries at the bottom (Germany and the Netherlands) of Figure 1.4 offer universal financial access. The United Kingdom, Sweden, and Canada rely primarily on taxation; in contrast, Germany achieves universal financial access through compulsory social insurance, as did the Netherlands in 2006. (Currently, the Netherlands achieves universal financial access via compulsory private insurance.) On one hand, financial access to health care within these national health systems does not come without rationing and limiting access to secondary and, especially, tertiary health care.[20] On the other hand, mixing sources of funding and types of financing often leads not only to high costs, but also to limited financial access and poor quality outcomes. For example, the mixture of public services and social and voluntary private insurance within the Mexican and US health systems, along with the fragmentation among the various subsystems of care, effectively limits access to health care. In 2000, approximately 38.4 million US citizens (13.7%) were without health insurance,[21] while roughly 57 million Mexicans (58.7%) were without health insurance in 2000.[22,23] However, since 2004, the Mexican government has expanded its public health insurance and public assistance for the poor, while the United States has not. Consequently, in 2007, approximately 45.7 million US citizens (15.3%) were without health insurance,[21] while about 35 million Mexicans (30%) were without health insurance.[24]

Synthesizing the discussion to this point, **Table 1.2** displays a framework for describing the primary, secondary, and tertiary means of financing and organizing health care that have been

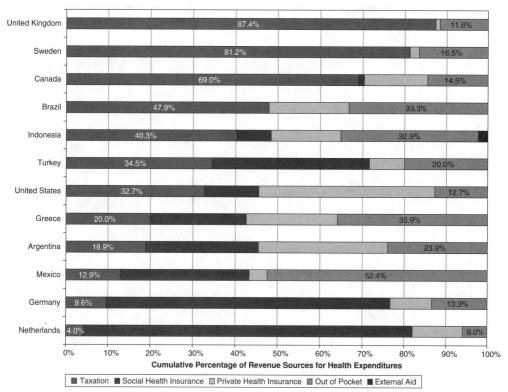

FIGURE 1.4   Comparisons among 12 Nations on Sources of Revenue for Health
Expenditures, Ordered by Reliance on Taxation (2006). Data from *WHOSIS: WHO Statistical
Information System*, World Health Organization, retrieved November 26, 2008, from
http://www.who.int/whosis/.

adopted by the 12 nations. Clearly, every nation relies on at least three means to finance and
two means to organize health services.

Caution must be used, however, when interpreting Table 1.2. First, the percentage of the
population covered, rather than the magnitude of the source of revenue is the main factor in determining the categorization. Second, the categorization is not directly linked to health system
performance; for example, Greece, Sweden, Turkey, and the United Kingdom rely primarily on
taxation to support national or public health services, and each country also relies on out-of-
pocket payments as a secondary or tertiary means to fund the indirect provision of health services. However, these countries do so with different levels of funding (see Figure 1.1) and
achieve varying levels of access (see Table 1.1) and quality (see Figure 1.2).

The next section reviews the historical development and current organization and financing within selected national health systems. This section is organized around three health
system prototypes, depending upon their primary means of financing and organizing health
care. The United Kingdom and Sweden exemplify the tax-funded, direct provision of health
services prototype. Each of these countries has achieved universal access, relatively low costs,

Table 1.2 Primary, Secondary, and Tertiary Means of Financing and Organizing Health Care in 12 Countries

	Direct Provision of Health Services	Indirect Provision of Health Services
Taxation	GREECE, SWEDEN, TURKEY, UNITED KINGDOM INDONESIA *Argentina, Mexico*	BRAZIL, CANADA *United States*
Social Health Insurance		ARGENTINA, GERMANY MEXICO, TURKEY, UNITED STATES, GREECE *Indonesia*
Private Compulsory Insurance		NETHERLANDS GERMANY
Private Voluntary Insurance		UNITED STATES CANADA *Brazil, Sweden, United Kingdom*
Out-of-Pocket Payments		MEXICO ARGENTINA, BRAZIL, GREECE, SWEDEN, UNITED KINGDOM *Canada, Germany, Netherlands, Turkey*

Key
Primary: LARGE CAPITALIZATION; Secondary: SMALL CAPITALIZATION; Tertiary: *Italicized*

and moderate- to high-quality outcomes with their national health services. Canada's system of compulsory national insurance exemplifies a tax-funded prototype with indirect provision of health services. This system has achieved universal access, with moderate- to high-quality outcomes. The compulsory insurance prototype is exemplified by the German and the Dutch systems, which indirectly provide health services funded by mandatory social and private insurance, respectively; these prototypes have achieved universal access and moderate to high quality, albeit with slightly higher costs. Lastly, we will discuss those countries pursuing mixed models, including Argentina, Brazil, Greece, Indonesia, Mexico, Turkey, and the United States.

Tax-Funded Models for Direct Provision of Health Services

While both Sweden and the United Kingdom make use of national health services that provide universal access to health care to all of their citizens, they differ in the degree to which those services are decentralized and locally controlled. Nonetheless, each country recently has engaged in reforms to control expenses, reduce waiting times for specialized services, ensure the quality of care, and develop national health information networks.

The United Kingdom's National Health Service

While formally implemented in 1948, the UK's National Health Service (NHS) has its roots both in the laws for aiding the poor established in the 1600s and in the mutual aid societies that flourished in Great Britain during the 1840s. Well-to-do employers lent support to these societies in order to help sick, but lowly paid, employees. While such measures in combination with the Poor Law system reduced the demand on general tax revenues, public outrage over the poor condition of recruits for the Boer War (nearly one half of whom were considered unfit for service) led to the School Medical Service Act of 1907 and to an investigation by the Royal Commission on the Poor Laws and Relief of Distress. This commission issued two reports in 1909—a majority report, advocating better charity care, and a minority report, advocating a unified medical service. The reports laid out the issues involved in establishing a national system of health care.[25]

Based on the Royal Commission's reports, the National Health Insurance Act of 1911, introduced to Parliament by Lloyd George, and virtually unopposed except by physicians, established statutory insurance for all manual workers earning less than £160 (about $780) per year. (Interestingly, most physicians supported a mixture of voluntary health insurance and government-funded medical services for the poor, thus advocating a system similar to that in the United States today.) Contributions from both employees and employers were required, with the government funding the administration of the insurance and covering exceptionally low-income and indigent persons' contributions.[26]

The period from World War I through 1938 established many of the values and the concepts on which the NHS would be based. Several significant documents emerged during this time, including the 1920 Dawson Report on healthcare policy, which advocated a hospital-centered integrated system of care; the 1920 Cave Report on saving voluntary hospitals; the 1926 Report of the Royal Commission on National Health Insurance; and the 1930 and 1938 Reports of the British Medical Association on national medical care policy that increased its public stature and enabled it to have considerable voice in health policy.[25] By the late 1930s, the number of people covered under mandatory (and voluntary) health insurance had steadily increased, especially as income thresholds for mandatory insurability were raised. Nonetheless, during the Depression, dissatisfaction with the national health insurance's "means-tested" coverage and limited benefits reached a level requiring major reforms.[27] Under Winston Churchill's Conservative government and the chairmanship of Sir William Beveridge, an Interdepartmental Committee on Social Insurance and Allied Services was created and charged with surveying the existing national policies of social insurance, including healthcare insurance. The Beveridge Report, issued in 1942, made sweeping recommendations to expand all branches of social insurance, from old-age pensions to disability benefits. In particular, it set the stage for the NHS by recommending the establishment of a national health service to provide medical and rehabilitation treatment to all citizens.

After World War II, the Labour Party won control of the government and sponsored the National Health Services Act of 1946. This draft legislation for creating a national health service was the target of fiery debates between the British Medical Association and the Minister of

Health, Aneurin Bevan, a Welshman and former coal miner. The final legislation for the NHS, implemented in July 1948, contained a number of compromises: (1) universal coverage was financed primarily by general revenues, with social insurance contributions limited to a small percentage of the total; (2) GPs were paid via capitation; (3) nearly all public and voluntary hospitals were put under the control of the national government; (4) public hospitals were permitted to maintain up to 5% of beds for private patients of consultants, that is, senior hospital physician specialists; and (5) health centers were limited to a few experimental facilities.[26]

The basic structure of the NHS, as Roemer underscores, was balanced across the four primary stakeholders providing health care, including the general practitioners, the community hospitals and their staffs of specialists, the medical school–affiliated teaching hospitals, and the local public health authorities. This four-fold structure within the NHS was maintained until 1974, even though problems of coordinating care across the four branches and the increasing dominance of specialized hospital care led to calls for reform during the 1960s. To enhance local control, in April 1974, the NHS was reorganized to include 90 area health authorities (AHAs) and 14 regional health authorities (RHAs). By the late 1970s, the usefulness of the AHAs for coordinating and responding to local needs was brought into question. Rather than adding a fourth level of bureaucracy into the NHS, it was decided that the District Health Authorities (DHAs) would be consolidated into units serving populations of about 250,000. Thus, the former AHAs' responsibilities were devolved to DHAs.[26]

During the 1980s, the Thatcher-led Conservative government tried to control rising healthcare costs through cutbacks on the global budgets to the RHAs and the expansion of the private medical sector. Not only were physicians encouraged to devote part of their practice to private patients, but also employers and employees were allowed tax deductions for private insurance. Hence, the private market for health care expanded rapidly, from less than 2% of the population being covered by voluntary insurance in 1969 to about 6.3% in 1980[26] and to more than 10% in 1990.[28] Even though only 6% of the total healthcare expenditures during 1987 occurred in the private sector, both the public and the medical professions became increasingly disenchanted with the NHS. Indeed, 1987–1988 was a year of crisis for the NHS, with hospitals closing down thousands of beds to meet budget constraints, long queues forming for all types of care, delays and cancellations for critical surgery, and DHAs running out of money.

In response to this turmoil, the Conservative government considered radical changes to the NHS, resulting in a white paper in 1989 that set out the reforms implemented between 1990 and 1991.[27] These reforms instituted an internal market, separating purchasers (e.g., district and local authorities) from providers (e.g., GPs and hospitals). The intent was to decentralize the NHS, encourage internal competition, and improve efficiency. This effort was redirected when the Labour government gained control and launched its own plans for the NHS in 1997.[29] Under Prime Minister Tony Blair, the separation between providers and purchasers continued, along with the devolution of services and their management to the departments of health under the leadership of the secretaries of state in England, Northern Ireland, Scotland, and Wales. However, the NHS initially underwent recentralization of funding and programs within each of these ministries,[30] while the responsibility for purchasing health services was devolved to various entities in England, Scotland, Wales, and Northern Ireland.[31]

Ambitious reforms—The NHS Plan—were announced during the summer of 2000 to reduce waiting times, increase access to care, improve the quality of care, upgrade and expand hospitals and primary care facilities, and develop a responsive internal market with clear financial incentives for providing value to patients.[32] Major changes in the NHS system structure and its financing were introduced in a series of steps, ranging from a new consultant (specialist physician) contract in 2003 and a new general practitioner (primary care physician) contract in 2004, to a payment by result (PbR) scheme for acute and specialist hospital services in 2004, to an 18-week limit on all waits for treatment referrals by the end of 2008.[33]

Current System Structure and Financing

All residents of the United Kingdom (England, Wales, Scotland, Northern Ireland, as well as the island states of Guernsey, Isle of Man, and Jersey) are covered under the National Health Service, which is funded through national taxes. Within England, the Department of Health (DH) is in overall charge of the NHS, with a cabinet minister reporting as secretary of state for health to the prime minister. The department controls England's 10 Strategic Health Authorities (SHAs), which oversee all NHS activities in England. In turn, each SHA is responsible for the strategic supervision of all the NHS trusts in its area. The devolved NHS administrations of Northern Ireland (Health and Social Care, HSC[34]), Scotland (NHS Scotland[35]), and Wales (NHS Wales[36]) plan, organize, and manage their services separately.[37] In other words, as purchasers and providers of health care, the government entities for England, Northern Ireland, Scotland, and Wales retain the responsibility for health legislation and general policy. Healthcare expenditure planning takes place within each government's general public expenditure planning process. NHS funding for the following year is established during this process.

In 2006, taxes raised by the national government accounted for 87.4% of total expenditures on health care. Out-of-pocket payments include payment for nonprescription medications, ophthalmic and dental services, and private health care (although the latter may be covered through private health insurance). In 2006, out-of-pocket expenditures accounted for 11.6% of total healthcare expenditures. Both for-profit and nonprofit companies provide private health insurance, which accounted for about 1.0% of total health expenditures in 2006.[14]

Comprehensive health services are provided by the NHS, ranging from preventive to primary to acute to rehabilitative care. Within the NHS England, these services include inpatient and outpatient hospital care, physician services, inpatient and outpatient drugs, dental care, and mental health care. Citizens may choose a general practitioner within their locale, as well as have a choice for specialist care. All hospital and specialist services are supplied without charge to the patient; however, user charges occur for outpatient drugs, dentistry, and ophthalmology. These charges are regulated, depending on treatment, and may be waived (e.g., sight test) or subsidized based on income and other criteria.[38]

The following discussion of health system structuring, including hospitals and physicians, focuses only on the NHS in England, which provides services to the largest population segment in the United Kingdom. On one hand, secondary and tertiary care services are overseen by 175 acute trusts, which manage hospitals. There are also 60 mental health trusts and 12 ambulance trusts.[37] On the other hand, primary care trusts (PCTs) not only organize and provide primary care services via general practitioners, dentists, opticians, and pharmacists but also commission hospital and other specialist services for local populations. Currently, the 152 PCTs in England control about 80% of the total NHS budget.[33,37] Foundation trusts (FTs) were first established in April 2004, and they have greater financial and operational oversight than do other acute trusts and mental health trusts within the NHS. The 117 FTs, including 33 mental health trusts, are subject to NHS performance inspection, but are independently regulated by Monitor, rather than by the SHAs.[39] Another recent innovation are care trusts, which provide both health and social services; there are currently eight pilot care trusts. Taken together, there are 235 acute trusts, specialist trusts, and foundation trusts.[37]

Hospitals.

The 1600 NHS hospitals and specialty centers are managed by the 235 NHS trusts and FT noted earlier. Secondary and tertiary care services are provided in these locations; a subset of hospitals offer emergency care services, while specialty hospitals and centers offer mental health services.[37] In 2004, there were 3.9 hospital beds per 1000 people.[14]

Physicians.

The British Medical Association negotiates with the Department of Health to determine the NHS payment systems for both general practitioners (GPs/primary care physicians) and consultants (physician specialists). The NHS has a well-developed primary care system made up of GPs, midlevel providers (e.g., midwives and practice nurses), and other healthcare professionals. General practitioners may be independent contractors or salaried employees. However, most GPs are independent, self-employed professionals within partnership-based group medical practices. Whether as a member of a group medical practice, as a solo practitioner, or as a salaried employee, the GP provides preventive and primary care, acts as a gatekeeper to specialized care, and receives payments from a PCT. These payments include a mix of capitation fees, fixed allowances for practice costs, fees linked to quality processes and outcomes, and specific fees for enhanced services and the dispensing of drugs. Acute trusts and foundation trusts employ consultants on either a full-time (~40 hours) or part-time basis and pay them on a set salary scale based on seniority, with additional payments for extended services and clinical skills. As has been the tradition, both full-time and part-time consultants may supplement their salary by treating private patients.[40]

Present Problems and Initiatives

The NHS Plan of 2000 introduced a myriad of reforms,[32] and the NHS has made many improvements to problems the health system faced just a few short years ago. One past critical issue for the NHS was queues, or waiting lists. Patients could potentially wait more than a year for treatment. Today, most patients wait only a few weeks for specialist referrals. Moreover, the introduction of walk-in centers for urgent ambulatory care, along with the extension of practice hours for GPs by PCTs, has made it possible for most people to access primary care within 48 hours or less. Additionally, the Quality Outcomes Framework for paying GPs has increased the quality of care for patients, especially those with chronic conditions, and has improved their outcomes and satisfaction with treatment.[33]

Critical problems facing the UK's health system include higher expectations because of greater wealth across the nation and the continuous improvement and development of information technology, changes in demand because of an aging demographic, ease of access to information for the general public, changes in the types of diseases and health conditions being treated, new and advancing treatment options, and finally, a new work environment that features increased complexity and a greater emphasis on quality work. In 2008, a review of the NHS was conducted to determine the next steps for improving quality of care. The initial steps that were identified include incorporating population-specific wellness and prevention services. To accomplish this task, such services will be incorporated into PCTs. Also, a Coalition for Better Health (replacing the Health Commission) has been created to involve the government, private sector organizations, and other entities in the pursuit of improved health outcomes, with an initial focus on reducing obesity and creating a healthy workforce.[41]

One of the most dramatic initiatives set forth by this review is the implementation of the first National Health Service Constitution. The NHS Constitution was developed by a group of stakeholders that included patients, employees, community members, and policy experts. The main purpose of this document is to guarantee the existence of the NHS, with reexamination of its premises to occur every 10 years. It also summarizes patient rights and outlines what the NHS promises to provide to its employees. The constitution clarifies national standards of care that have been set forth by Parliament, as well as local standards of accountability.[41]

Overall, the UK's National Health Service provides universal access to basic health services at low cost relative to other high-income countries (see Figure 1.1), with moderate- to high-quality outcomes (see Figure 1.2). To address the problems of waiting lists for specialized services, an undercapitalized and aging infrastructure, and quality of care problems, the Labour government decentralized the NHS, devoting more resources to both specialized services and hospital infrastructures, and implementing performance management initiatives. These initiatives have, by and large, had some success. To build on these changes, the latest report from the NHS sets out important goals pertaining to both patient-centered, quality care and the improvement of workplace culture and conditions.

Sweden's National Health Service

The roots of governmental involvement in Swedish health care go back at least to the mid-18th century when the monarchy paid provincial doctors to see indigent patients without charge. Similarly, in the mid-19th century the monarchy required county councils to provide hospital care for indigents. By the mid-20th century, a national health insurance fund had been created to pay for primary care.[42] In 1975, faced with growing concerns about rising costs, fragmented yet ever increasing demands for care, and an inflexible, centralized system, the Swedish cabinet appointed a Commission of Inquiry to develop new legislation for medical care.[43] The commission was directed to specify overall goals and criteria for all aspects of health and sickness care under the guiding principle that everyone living in the country has an equal right to such care.

The commission's recommendations were reviewed by the Parliament in 1981, and the legislation took effect in 1982. This act set general guidelines and parameters for the organization of medical care following four basic tenets:

- equality of care and the promotion of good health;
- counties would have total responsibility and accountability for medical care;
- physicians were to direct all medical activity and delegate responsibility to others as much as possible;
- the national government would be responsible for setting regulations to protect individuals and stating conditions for employment in medical care settings.

In accord with Swedish culture, details concerning planning and implementation were left to the county councils and local authorities.[44]

As a result, Swedish citizens' home addresses determined the hospitals, primary healthcare centers, and the physicians from which they could seek healthcare services. This decentralized system, however, led to the inequitable distribution of providers and resources during the 1980s. As in the United Kingdom, Swedes faced waiting lists and limited access to certain services, depending upon locale. Moreover, Sweden had intensive resource constraints based on a faltering economy and an aging population. Beginning in the early 1990s, Sweden embarked on a series of changes to health policy—known as the ADEL reforms—which were heavily influenced by the British NHS internal market reforms. While the two best-known efforts were the "Dala model" in Kopparberg County and the experiments in Stockholm County, at least a third of Sweden's counties also introduced innovations in service delivery.[45] For example, patient choice was emphasized through the separation of purchasers and providers, an internal market regulated by contracts, competitive tendering, and the encouragement of the private sector.[46] Despite sustained criticisms[47–49] and changes in policy direction toward cooperation and long-term contracting,[50] an assessment of the Stockholm County reforms indicated that performance-based incentives have improved physicians' productivity and efficiency, while maintaining their satisfaction with working conditions.[51]

After 1992, the role of financing changed for county councils. With the ADEL reform, local municipalities were held responsible for social welfare services to elderly individuals, as well as the disabled. They also became responsible for long-term inpatient care. These changes significantly reduced the long-term care costs within the NHS, shifting these expenses against the tax revenues devoted to local social welfare.[52] The reforms of the 1990s addressed the problems of cost containment within a decentralized National Health Service with universal access and high-quality outcomes. Since 1995, each county council has rationed care using the principles of human rights, individual need, solidarity, and cost-effectiveness. Many elective procedures (e.g., in vitro fertilization) were not performed unless the patient directly paid for the service.[52] To further control utilization and costs, Sweden's central government managed physician training, capital expenditures, and equalization and incentive grants to the county councils. County councils and municipalities imposed tight fiscal controls on the number of healthcare personnel and on their salaries. During the 1990s, overall employment in health care was reduced by 25%.[48] Other cost-control mechanisms that were introduced include rationing based on evidence-based care, as well as comparative effectiveness evaluations of medical technologies.[53] These cost-control measures were very effective in the 1990s, as Sweden was the only Organization for Economic Cooperation and Development (OECD) country to continually reduce health expenditures during that decade.[54] However, the rationing introduced in the 1990s resulted in high out-of-pocket costs and reduced services.

The 1992 Guarantee of Care Act attempted to balance fiscal restrictions with consumer responsiveness, mandating that patients placed on a waiting list for nonacute, low-priority problems should have services provided within three months.[55] Moreover, the National Board of Health and Welfare produced a set of guidelines concerning quality in 1994. These guidelines were updated in 1997 by a law requiring the health services to implement a system of continuous quality improvement (CQI). During this period, guidelines were developed for prioritizing the treatment of patients according to the severity of their injury, illness, or disease.[54] Several national organizations were involved in this effort to diffuse CQI methods and tools throughout Swedish health care, with most of the actual CQI work performed at the local level.[56] The Federation of County Councils, which, as a result of a merger with the Federation of County Councils become the Association for Local Authorities and Regions) developed 50 healthcare quality registers to implement and benchmark CQI systems in health care. The Federation also promoted a competition for a Swedish Health Services Quality Award.[57] Currently, the Swedish Association for Local Authorities and Regions and the National Board of Health and Welfare provide regional comparisons of quality and efficiency in Swedish health care. This work relies on multiple measures of medical-care outcomes, patient experiences, care availability, and costs.[58]

During 1997 and 1998, drug reform was implemented in two phases. The first phase of the reform included a new National Drug Benefit Scheme that regulated co-payments and was kept separate from the cost ceiling applied to medical treatments. The second phase, in 1998, placed all responsibility for the costs of drug treatments in the hands of the county councils.[54] Beginning in 1999, additions were made to the 1982 Health Care Act that required more from the city council on behalf of patients. These changes dramatically enhanced and increased patient rights. Under these additions, patients have the right to choose their primary care provider as well as what treatment option they will pursue if multiple options are available. Patients are also free to request a second opinion from anywhere in the country.[54]

Current System Structure and Financing

The National Health Service covers all Swedish citizens, as well as immigrants and foreign residents. Although a basic package of care services is not set, the NHS typically provides preventive care, public health care, prescription drugs, inpatient and outpatient care, dental care, long-term care and rehabilitation, and mental health care services.[59] The NHS has three levels of organization: national (Ministry of Health and Social Affairs, National Board of Health and Welfare, as well as other regulatory agencies), regional (Swedish Association of Local Authorities and Regions), and local (20 county councils, the island of Gotland, and 200 municipalities). At the national level, the government sets forth principles and policies either through laws and regulation or through negotiation. The National Board of Health and Welfare typically represents the central government in negotiations with the Swedish Association of Local Authorities and

Regions.[60] It also acts as the supervisory and advisory agency for health and social services, as well as licensing agency for all healthcare personnel. On one hand, county councils have authority over primary and inpatient care, including public health and preventive care. On the other hand, the municipalities determine the housing, social support, and health care for the elderly and disabled.[59]

Patients are able to choose their principal healthcare provider. Choices may also be made concerning outpatient facilities and health centers in the county council. A referral may be necessary for care outside the individual's county council.[59] Income taxes are levied on residents with rates determined by county councils and municipalities. The average collective rate of taxation of local income is around 30%. Health care accounts for about 85% of total county expenditures.

In 2006, national, county, and municipal taxes accounted for 81.2% of total expenditures on health care. Out-of-pocket expenditures accounted for 16.5% of total healthcare expenditures. Dental and pharmaceutical co-payments, as well as supplemental charges for private physicians, are the major costs associated with out-of-pocket expenses. Private health insurance accounted for about 2.3% of total health expenditures in 2006.[14]

Hospitals

Sweden has 73 hospitals. Specialty care is provided by 65 district/county hospitals; 60 of these hospitals provide 24-hour emergency care and are owned by county councils. Both secondary and tertiary care are provided by eight regional, academic medical hospitals.[60]

Physicians

More than 90% of physicians belong to the Swedish Medical Association, a union and professional organization for medical practitioners. The SMA negotiates general employment conditions (e.g., salaries, benefits, working hours) for its members through collective agreements, primarily with county councils.[61] In 2004, a total of 26,400 licensed physicians were employed in Sweden, with 21,900 employed within the NHS. Most physicians are specialists employed in hospitals (12,500 plus 5000 licensed residents). The 4400 general practitioners within the NHS serve as family doctors, but not as gatekeepers, and are employed by the county councils. Physicians employed within the NHS typically are paid a salary if they are specialists; general practitioners may be remunerated prospectively via capitation. Physicians in private practice (2000 in 2004) may set their own fee-for-service rates, but must adhere to county and national guidelines if they are to be reimbursed by the NHS and must have a contract with the county council. Otherwise these private practice physicians must use the regulated fee schedule or receive payment directly from the patient.[62,63] Basic care—preventive, primary, and public health—is provided at 1000 public health centers. In addition to physicians, patients may receive care from district nurses and other midlevel providers.[60]

Present Problems and Initiatives

The decentralized Swedish NHS has used rationing to maintain high-quality care, to contain costs, and to uphold universal access to basic health services. One result of rationing is that citizens face both out-of-pocket costs for some health services and delays in accessing needed health services. On the one hand, to address the equity problems created by out-of-pocket charges, there are caps on both yearly out-of-pocket charges for health services and for pharmaceutical products. On the other hand, to address the chronic problem of patient wait lists, Sweden enhanced its national patient care guarantee in 2005, and it has allowed county and municipal councils to shift toward more contractual agreements with private providers, which now account for about 10% of all healthcare services. The care guarantee states that no patient should have to wait for more than three months once it has been determined what care is needed. If this time limit is exceeded, the county council is obligated to pay for services elsewhere, including the patient's travel costs.[60]

Another problem of a decentralized system is the lack of systemwide data for comparing, and improving, performance at the county and municipal levels. However, the National Board of Health and Welfare and the Swedish Association of Local Authorities and Regions have recently established a model for comparing and evaluating healthcare outcomes. This effort has resulted in yearly reports "to stimulate and support local and regional efforts to improve healthcare services, both in terms of clinical quality and medical outcomes, and in terms of patient experience and efficient use of resources."[58,252] Moreover, these two entities, along with other national stakeholders, are committed to creating a robust system for health information exchange for both healthcare providers and patients.[64]

Summary Lessons: Using Tax-Funded Models for Direct Provision of Health Care

While the United Kingdom and Sweden provide universal access to health care by relying primarily on taxes to fund the direct provision of care, each country has followed different paths and encountered different problems. The UK's NHS is a historically centralized system of care, which from the start had a network of primary care providers. These GPs acted as gatekeepers, implicitly rationing and limiting access to specialists and hospitals, thus containing costs that Sweden has struggled to reduce. However, until recently, the United Kingdom experienced long waiting lists for specialized services and an undercapitalized and aging infrastructure. To address these problems, the United Kingdom decentralized the NHS, devoting more resources to primary care trusts and allowing them to direct patients to those specialized services within hospitals where access was available. To ensure quality, the NHS has implemented performance management initiatives, established a Care Quality Commission, and invested in its infrastructure, including a national health information system linking ambulatory and acute care providers.

In contrast, the already decentralized Swedish NHS has drawn on evidence-based medicine and explicitly rationed health services for almost two decades. It has done so while maintaining high-quality care, containing costs, and upholding universal access to basic health services. These efforts have been complemented both by a focus on quality improvement and by the development of a national health information network. Nonetheless, Swedish citizens have faced high out-of-pocket costs and delays in specialty care. As a result, the Swedish NHS has established caps on out-of-pocket expenses, established a patient care guarantee, and expanded contracting with both public and private providers to ensure timely access to health services.

Tax-Funded Model for Indirect Provision of Health Services

While Canada shares with Sweden and the United Kingdom a single-payer model of funding health services, it differs in that health providers are not employed by the state, and the federal or provincial governments typically do not own healthcare facilities. Ten provinces and three territories administer the Canadian system of Medicare, with the federal government recently instituting reforms to ensure equitable funding for, and access to, health services.

The Canadian Healthcare System

Canadian public health insurance has always resembled a quilt more than a uniform blanket covering the nation.[65] Beginning as far back as 1909—when the province of Saskatchewan enacted the Rural Municipalities Act, leading to the creation of local medical care insurance schemes—the provision of medical care to its citizens has been of major concern for Canada.[25,66] Various initiatives to provide medical care were instituted individually by some of the provinces, but it was not until 1943, after examining about 40 plans from other countries, that proposals to provide federal subsidies to provincially administered health insurance programs were first presented to the Canadian House of Commons.[67] Despite much discussion and endorsement, the provinces were unable to reach agreement on a specific proposal and several provinces proceeded with universal hospital insurance on their own.[26]

By the 1950s, provinces that provided insurance were being compared to provinces without such plans, as well as to early regionally organized capitation plans in the United States. Only the three provinces that had developed state-supported plans were judged to be adequately supplying medical care to their residents, and with costs comparable to—or less than—those provinces without such systems.[25] Moreover, during the 1950s, Canadian leaders and physicians began to actively support the premise that there should be reasonable access to quality health care for all Canadians independent of financial means. By 1959, a fully universal government-operated hospital insurance system, providing 50% federal funding for provincial expenditures on medically necessary hospital care, was in place.[68,69] However, when Saskatchewan implemented government-run insurance for physicians' services in 1962, physicians were strongly opposed and a bitter and unsuccessful 23-day strike by physicians ensued. As their worst fears failed to materialize and as they quickly became the highest-paid physicians in the country, professional opposition to the program decreased, and by 1971, all provinces and territories operated physician insurance programs.[25,70]

As Canada moved into the highly inflationary 1970s, problems began to develop with the program. The provinces were unable to control their individual health services priorities and the federal government lost control of its health budget since it was forced to match whatever the provinces spent.[68] During 1977, the matching formulas were abandoned and the federal contribution was changed to an indexed per capita block grant. Additionally, the Extended Health Care Services Program was initiated to entice the provinces to develop less expensive support services such as home and ambulatory health care. The Canadian Health Act was passed in 1984 to consolidate all the earlier laws that authorized federal subsidies to the various insurance plans. As a result, there is a single, government-operated provincial health plan that is the sole payer for hospital and physician care in each of the 12 provinces/territories. The 1984 Health Act also eliminated (1) all user charges for physician and hospital services, (2) any extra billing by physicians, and (3) private insurance for covering services available under the provincial health plans; moreover, the Health Act increased eligibility to all residents regardless of their employment status.[25,67,70] Additions made to the Canada Health Act in 1996 and 1997 made provisions for federal contributions to health and social services. The 1996 and 1997 revisions consolidated contributions into the Canada Health Transfer (CHT) and Canada Social Transfer (CST). The combined CHT and CST transfers of taxes and cash payments equalizes funding and allows territories and provinces to control their systems of health care and social programs in accord with their own priorities.[71] Nonetheless, the provincial and territorial health systems must meet the dictates of the Canada Health Act and provide social assistance with no minimum residency.

Current System Structure and Financing

Canada indirectly provides health services through a tax-funded public system, which is accessible by all Canadians.[72] Citizens receive coverage for ambulatory services, inpatient services, prescription medications, physician services, community health services, disease prevention programs, and health protection programs. Home care is covered at varying levels.[73] While the provincial and territorial governments oversee the provision of health services in their jurisdictions, the federal government is directly in charge of the healthcare services for the following groups: Royal Canadian Mounted Police, veterans, members of the armed forces, inmates in federal jails, Inuit, and status Indians.

Federal, territorial, provincial, and municipal governments share the costs of health care. In 2006, taxes accounted for 70.4% of total expenditures on health care. Supplementary private insurance accounted for 15.1%, and out-of-pocket payments for 14.5%, of total health expenditures; these sources were used primarily for drugs and dental care. Social security accounted for the remaining 2% of public expenditures on health in 2006.[14]

Hospitals

Canadians were served by 535 general hospitals (61,906 beds; about 3.4 hospital beds per 1000 people) in 2005.[14,74] Most hospitals are nonprofit, autonomous entities that provide inpatient and ambulatory services and diagnostic testing, as well as other services. Hospitals are staffed with physicians, registered nurses, licensed practical nurses, registered psychiatric nurses, aides, and various other healthcare professionals. In many hospitals, the staff works to provide patient care through a primary care team.

Physicians

In 2007, there were 63,682 physicians (1.92 physicians per 1000 people) in Canada.[75] About half of all physicians are general practitioners, who act as gatekeepers for secondary and tertiary health services.[18,76] Most GPs and specialists are paid on a fee-for-service basis; their fee schedules vary based on provincial and territorial government negotiations with regional medical associations. Some GPs, such as community clinic physicians, and a few specialists, such as hospitalists, are salaried. Recently, some provinces have been shifting toward a mixed payment method for both GPs and specialists, combining fee-for-service with a salary or capitation component.[77]

For example, the provincial government of Ontario revised its physician services agreement with the Ontario Medical Association. This new agreement not only increases base payments to physicians, but also incentivizes physicians to enroll unattached patients, to work collaboratively with other healthcare providers to coordinate patient care, to increase on-call coverage, to reduce avoidable emergency department admissions, to manage diabetic patient care, to increase psychiatric care services, and to enhance interdisciplinary care service for the frail elderly.[78]

Present Problems and Initiatives

Like Sweden, Canada provides universal access with high-quality care, but struggles to contain costs. Like the United Kingdom, Canada implicitly rations care through primary care gatekeeping and by imposing waiting lists for specialized care. Recent reforms have focused on maintaining high quality and reducing waiting times while controlling costs. In addition to federal and provincial oversight of healthcare budgets, a variety of methods are used to control costs, including technology evaluations and rationalization and hospital budgets administered by local or regional health authorities. At the hospital, provincial, and national levels, Canada monitors health performance and quality. Significantly, in 1999, all first ministers (except the premier of Quebec) signed a Social Union Framework, which provided a collaborative structure for social policy, including assurances for collecting and sharing healthcare data. In addition, two other entities have contributed to this national effort: the Canadian Institute for Health Information and the Canadian Council on Health Services Accreditation.

Since 2000, the Canadian Institute for Health Information has produced annual reports on health indicators.[79] It has worked cooperatively with Accreditation Canada (formerly the Canadian Council on Health Services Accreditation), which accredits the entire range of healthcare services, from Regional Health Authorities to hospitals to home care. In 1995, it introduced Client-Centered Accreditation, thereby ensuring principles of quality improvement were incorporated into accreditation standards. In 2000, its AIM (Achieving Improved Measurement) Project updated the accreditation process with standardized performance indicators based on four quality dimensions: responsiveness, system competency, client/community focus, and work life.[80] Beginning in 2008, it launched the Qmentum Accreditation Program, with special focus on quality improvement and patient safety.[81]

Canada's recent health reforms increased spending on public health and measures to maintain fiscal sustainability of the public health sector. In 2003, the prime minister and the provincial and territorial leaders agreed to an Accord on Health Care Renewal. This policy dedicates the government to a sustainable public healthcare system and provides for an action plan through which leaders agreed to provide first-dollar coverage for certain short-term and acute home care needs. At the same time, the leadership declared that by 2011, 50% of the Canadian population would have access to a primary care provider. An addition to the accord in 2004 provided for home care, catastrophic drug coverage, and pharmaceutical management. In September 2004, a 10-Year Plan to Strengthen Health Care was released and called for the reduction of wait times and a greater focus on primary healthcare reform.[18]

Another issue that the Canadian health system is facing, along with many other countries, is its aging population. Although the healthcare system in Canada appears sustainable now, the fear is that once the population ages and the expectations for care change, that it will lose its sustainability. Increased life expectancy, along with a lower birth rate and the retirement of the baby boomer generation, will contribute to the change in utilization of care and an increase in spending on health care.[82]

Overall, the decentralized Canadian healthcare system achieves universal access, high quality, and moderate costs through implicit and explicit rationing of services. Its efforts to maintain this balanced approach to health deserves continued scrutiny by other health systems.

Compulsory Insurance Model for Indirect Provision of Health Services

Both Germany and the Netherlands rely on compulsory health insurance that is used to purchase health services from various health providers. Recent legislation in both countries has reformed how and by whom health insurance is purchased. On one hand, the Dutch have implemented an individual mandate for health insurance; on the other hand, the Germans have made access to health insurance both a right and a requirement within an employment-based insurance system. Significantly, as part of these reforms, both countries have also implemented risk equalization schemes to incentivize health insurers to compete on the basis of health quality and efficiency, while ensuring equitable and affordable access to a basic package of health services for all.

The German Healthcare System

The German healthcare system has its roots in cooperative organizations, called sickness funds, which were sponsored by guilds during medieval times. These sickness funds provided financial security to guild members and their families in the event of illnesses or injuries, usually by levying fixed fees two or three times a year on all guild members. Importantly, the sickness funds operated on the basis of maximizing social solidarity (group cohesion) rather than on the basis of minimizing individual losses. (Individualistic self-interest, by contrast, is the basis for the current US system of indemnity insurance, which attempts to spread risk across individuals and exclude those with exceptionally high risk potential.) As the German states became more mercantile between the 16th and mid-19th centuries, the sickness funds were extended by various communities to include not just craftsmen, but also miners, foundry workers, and other artisans.[83]

However, the rapid industrialization of the newly unified Germany in the late 19th century created a large urban population of factory workers who were no longer adequately covered by the community-based and craft-centered sickness funds. Under the urging of chancellor Otto von Bismarck, the Parliament (Reichstag) in 1883 enacted compulsory national health insurance for all hourly laborers in order to secure social stability. The Health Insurance Act of 1883 and other acts to extend accident insurance for factory workers (1884) and agricultural workers (1886), as well as old-age and disability pensions (1899), established Europe's first social welfare state.[84] During the ensuing years from 1883 to 1975, statutory health insurance was expanded to include not only blue-collar workers, but also the following categories: transport and commercial workers (1901), agriculture and forestry workers and domestic servants (1911), civil service employees (1914), unemployed people (1918), seamen (1927), dependents of fund members (1930), voluntary participants earning wages above the statutory limits (1941), pensioners (1941), farm workers and salesmen (1966), self-employed agricultural workers and dependents (1972), and students and disabled persons (1975).[85] The results of this expansion included exponential growth in sickness fund enrollment, steady consolidation of the sickness funds,[83] and a large increase in the number of physicians.[85]

During the first three decades of this expansion, the sickness funds exercised a great deal of power. Each fund was free to hire anyone to provide health care, often negotiating extremely low fees from doctors who had not passed their board exams, and typically restricted fund members from seeing physicians who did not hold a contract with a fund. During the hyper inflationary period following World War I, cost pressures and physician dissatisfaction with the worker-dominated sickness funds resulted in businesses joining physicians in calls for healthcare reform. The balance of power began to swing more to the physicians' side as the Weimar Republic issued a series of decrees to meet the demands of this stakeholder coalition, culminating in the Weimar Settlement of 1931. This decree increased the ratio of physicians to fund members, recognized medicine as a profession, and created sickness fund physician associations (*Kassenärztliche Vereinigungen*–KVs). Significantly, each physician was now legally bound to join a KV in order to receive payments from a sickness fund. Most importantly, each KV established a bargaining monopoly for local physicians vis-à-vis the numerous sickness funds with whom physicians previously had to arrange separate contracts. From this point forward, the KVs have served as the primary mechanism through which physician charges flow to sickness funds and fund payments flow to physicians.

The fall of the Third Reich divided Germany, creating two distinct health systems: (1) the Federal Republic of Germany, initially under Allied occupation, continued with the decentralized, sickness fund–based system begun under Bismarck and (2) the German Democratic Republic, under Soviet oversight, developed a centralized, state-directed health system similar to the former USSR's command-and-control model. These separate healthcare systems were conjoined after the 1990 reunification, with major reforms occurring in East Germany in order to make it similar to the West German system. In Western Germany, the period after the occupation through the 1960s was one of growth driven by the increasing prosperity of the newly reconstructed Germany. However, during the 1970s, the growth of healthcare expenditures began to exceed the growth in GDP to such a degree that a series of reforms were instituted to contain costs.[83] One of the most notable elements of these acts was the establishment in 1987 of the Council for Concerted Action in Health Care—a panel of 70 representatives from the interested parties in health care—to set a ceiling on the rate of growth for ambulatory and dental care and pharmaceutical and other medical supplies.[12] Since that time there have been five more notable attempts at reform: the 1992 Health Care Structure Act, the 1996 Hospital Expenditure Stabilizing Act, the Second Statutory Health Insurance Restructuring Act of 1997, the 2004 Statutory Health Insurance Modernization Act, and, most recently, the 2007 Strengthen Competition in the Statutory Health Insurance Act.[86]

In 2004, the Statutory Health Insurance Modernization Act was passed, ending a five-year struggle between the two major political parties in Germany: the Social Democratic Party (SDP) and the Christian Democratic Party (CDU). The act was intended to stabilize social health insurance contribution rates and to improve overall quality and efficiency. In order to achieve these goals, several actions were taken. Among other things, some benefits were excluded from the social health insurance (SHI) package, co-payment requirements were restructured, and new sources of income for SHI were created through budget subsidies. The Federal Joint Committee was introduced, combining several federal committees already in existence in order to create one source of coordinated decision making.[87]

The 2007 reforms revolved around several key issues within the German healthcare system. This new legislation addressed prevention and improving the coordination of activities among the various players in the system. Other changes included adjustments to long-term care insurance contributions and fundamental changes to the compensation and financing portion of SHI.

Current System Structure and Financing

Every German is eligible to participate in the statutory, social insurance system. Individuals above a determined income level have the right to obtain private health insurance. Because of the 2007 reforms, every individual must obtain either statutory (beginning in 2007) or private health insurance (beginning in 2009).[88] In 2006, social health insurance accounted for 67%, while private health insurance accounted for 10.1% of health expenditures. Government taxes covered 9.6%, with out-of-pocket costs accounting for the remaining 13.3% of health expenditures.[14]

The chief system for financing health care is through contributions toward statutory, social health insurance (SHIs) funds, which included about 220 funds in 2009.[86] In 2002, the average contribution rate was 14% of an employee's salary, with that cost being shared between employee and employer. The unemployed, the homeless, and immigrants are covered through a special sickness fund financed through general revenues. The benefits covered include health screening and prevention, nonphysician care, ambulatory medical services, inpatient care, home nursing care, dental care, and some types of rehabilitation. Early reforms during this decade shifted costs to patients via user charges. Co-payments exist for pharmaceuticals, non-physician care, dental treatments, ambulance transportation, and initial hospitalization or rehabilitation. Nonetheless, these charges are limited or exempted for those with low incomes or chronic illnesses, or those who are under 18 years.[87]

The Federal Ministry for Health and the Parliament are in charge of health care at the national level. Decision-making authority is shared between the federal government and the 16 Lander (states). One of their most significant roles is to oversee the sickness funds and voluntary insurance companies, ensuring a level playing field for competition. Because sickness funds vary in their income and expenditures depending upon their pools of insured people, a compensation scheme operates to equalize these differences, requiring transfers of income from low-cost sickness funds to sickness funds with high expenditures based on age, gender, and disability. Beginning in 2009, the risk equalization scheme also takes into account the morbidity of the insured population using 106 morbidity groups based on 80 diseases. The intent of this reform is to prevent risk selection by sickness funds, to improve care for patients with chronic or catastrophic illnesses, and to provide a level playing field in which sickness funds may compete based on quality and efficiency.[89]

Hospitals

In 2009, Germany had about 2200 general hospitals,[86] and about 8.3 hospital beds per 1000 people in 2006.[14] Private for-profit hospitals account for around 20% of the total, with non-profit private hospitals accounting for more than 40%.[90] However, all of these hospitals contract with the social insurance funds. Sources for hospital funding include operating costs from the sickness funds and investment costs from the Lander. The 1992 Health Care Structure Act and subsequent pieces of legislation introduced an inpatient prospective payment system. Representatives of the sickness funds negotiate with individual hospitals over prospective payment rates.

Physicians

In 2009, Germany had about 300,000 doctors,[86] and about 3.4 physicians per 1000 people in 2006.[14] Most GPs and specialists are self-employed and paid based on fee-for-service with budget ceilings. For services to patients covered by social health insurance funds (SHIs), the fee-for-service reimbursement is subject to some controls. SHIs and regional physicians' associations negotiate the total amount to be distributed to physicians under the fee-for-service payments. SHIs make the payment to regional physicians' associations for all their affiliate physicians, and physicians' associations distribute the payments among affiliated physicians based on the Uniform Value Scale and other additional rules. The 2007 reform abolishes the aforementioned prospective fee-setting mechanism, and a fixed fee schedule with performance bonuses for high-quality care is expected to come into effect in 2009. For services to private patients, physicians are paid on a fee-for-service basis by private health insurance and receive out-of-pocket payments. Some GPs and specialists are salaried employees and work in hospitals. Both salaried GPs and specialists can also treat and bill private patients based on a fee schedule for private patients.[77]

Present Problems and Initiatives

The German model of indirectly providing health services funded by mandatory social and private insurance has achieved universal access and high quality, but historically has struggled to contain costs for hospital and ambulatory care. Various techniques have been used to control costs, including prospective payment systems, global budgets, and uniform value scales. The 1992 Health Care Structure Act and subsequent legislation introduced an inpatient prospective payment system. Representatives of the sickness funds negotiate with individual hospitals over prospective payment rates. Interestingly, because of competition among funds, selective purchasing for inpatient services (similar to preferred provider contracts in the United States) has recently become an issue. Based on negotiations on per capita rates, physicians' associations receive global budgets from the sickness funds. The associations, in turn, use a Uniform Value Scale (EBM) to reimburse their physician members. To prevent false claims or overutilization, the physicians' associations closely monitor physician reimbursement claims and sanction with fines and other measures those physicians who abuse or defraud the associations.[90]

Similarly, physician specialty societies have monitored and attempted to improve the quality of medical care through structural means. However, after passage of a revised social security act on quality assurance, physicians' associations have started quality management projects. The Social Code Book V (SGB V) introduced the Federal Coordination Committee (FCC) and the Federal Committee Hospital as well as determining the duties of the Federal Committee for the Improvement of Quality Assurance (FCIQA). The responsibility of these committees is to ensure use of quality assurance measures. Many institutions and commissions have also developed quality assessment activities focusing on evidence-based medicine.[91,92]

Immediate issues facing Germany's SHI system begin with demographic changes. Due to a low birthrate and a longer life expectancy, the German population is getting increasingly older. As a result, there are fewer citizens of working age to replace individuals that retire. In 1995, there were 4.4 working individuals for every 1 retiree, but by 2020 this will be reduced to 2.1 for every 1. Additionally, Germany has challenging unemployment rates and income erosion, which makes cost containment even more difficult.[93] Another challenge is the rising cost of health care. Germany ranks below only the United States, France, and Switzerland in annual healthcare spending,[94] so keeping up with the latest in technology and medical advances might become difficult if costs need to be reduced.

In summary, the German model of compulsory health insurance has achieved universal access while containing costs by creating competition among health insurers, by reducing benefits, and by shifting costs to the insured. In doing so, the Germans have adopted many US managed care techniques to provide incentives for efficient care provision by providers. Germany has also addressed concerns about quality by engaging in comparative effectiveness research via its Institute for Quality and Efficiency in Health Care.[95]

The Dutch Healthcare System

Prior to World War II, health care in the Netherlands was provided largely through private enterprise and charity, with the government's role limited to monitoring the quality of care and ensuring the provision of preventive care. During the postwar years, however, the government took an increasingly more central role in the financing and regulation of primary through tertiary care, creating a complex mixture of private enterprise and government oversight.[96,97]

The Sickness Funds Decree of 1941 and 1948 mandated that sickness funds must contract with all physicians in their region, simultaneously guaranteeing free choice of doctor by patients and eliminating competition among physicians.[97] The Decree of 1948 also created guidelines for social insurance to ensure financial access to health care among the poor while the Netherlands underwent a decade-long period of tightly planned reconstruction.[96] The Sickness Funds Insurance Act (Ziekenfondswet—ZFW) of 1964 replaced the Decree of 1948. The ZFW specified the level of income under which social insurance was compulsory for acute and short-term illnesses, and it obligated sickness funds to contract with all providers in their regions.[97]

The General Special Sickness Expenses Act (Algemene Wet Bijzondere Ziektekosten— AWBZ) of 1967 provides universal insurance for catastrophic and long-term illnesses, including physical and mental handicaps. The Health Care Tariffs Act (WTG) of 1980, implemented in 1982, allows a special government office to set the parameters for a bargaining process between providers—hospitals, physicians, and other medical professionals—and buyers, including both sickness funds and private insurers, for determining tariffs. This legislation strengthened the power of the associations both for providers (especially GPs and specialists) and for insurers by institutionalizing a bilateral monopoly.[96,97]

The Health Insurance Access Act (WTZ) of 1986 required private insurers to provide "specified risk groups a comprehensive benefits package for a legally determined maximum premium."[97,1446] The purpose of this legislation was to counteract the premium differentiation and market segmentation that since the 1970s had eroded the preservation of universal coverage for the elderly and other high-risk groups. In 1989, these benefits were extended to all people over 65; in 1991, they were mandated for all people who were privately insured who paid more than the maximum standard premium.

While price controls and government restrictions on hospital capacity and physician supply certainly had an impact during the 1980s, their total effect was disappointing.[98] Neither sickness funds nor physicians had any incentives to improve efficiency, while sickness funds and private insurers were unable to direct patients to the most cost-effective providers. At the same time, universal access to acute care was being threatened by the growing market segmentation and premium differentiation by private insurers. Within this context, the Dutch government set up an advisory Committee on the Structure and Financing of Health Care, chaired by Dr. W. Dekker. The Dekker Report, published in March 1987, proposed major changes in the healthcare system that were subsequently endorsed by two coalition cabinets in 1988 and 1990.[97,99] However, the managed competition envisioned in the Dekker Report did not become a reality until the 2006 Health Insurance Act (ZVW). Up until 2006, all citizens with an annual income below a set level were required to enroll under the Ziekenfondswet (Medical Insurance Access Act, or ZFW) into a public social insurance fund for acute and short-term health care (65% of the population in 2004). Those with an annual income above the determined level were required to purchase private social health insurance for medical care.[100]

Current System Structure and Financing

On one hand, all citizens are covered under the Algemene Wet Bijzondere Ziektekosten (Exceptional Medical Expenses Act, or AWBZ) that provides funding for long-term, disability, and chronic psychiatric care. On the other hand, in 2006, the ZVW reforms were passed, which altered the structure of the sickness funds and private insurance for acute and primary care. Under the new financing scheme, individuals are no longer automatically enrolled in a health insurance plan. Rather, they are required by law to enroll in a plan of their choosing. This reform attempts to shift the Dutch system from supply- to demand-driven care. To attract members, insurance companies can offer competitive premiums for the basic benefits mandated by the government; many companies also offer extra voluntary benefit packages for services not covered under the base package. Regulation of the system is provided for in the ZVW and is performed by two entities, the Health Care Insurance Board (CVZ) and the Health Insurance Monitoring Board (CTZ). When the Health Market Regulation Act was passed in July 2006, the CTZ merged with the Health Care Tariffs Board to form the Netherlands Health Care Authority (NZa).[101]

Hospitals

In 2007, there were 3.0 acute hospitals beds per 1000 people.[102] For-profit and not-for-profit hospitals may be either privately or publicly owned. In 2006, the Dutch government passed legislation (Wet Toelating Zorinstellingen—WTZi) that deregulates planning for hospitals and other providers, allowing them more autonomy for building and capacity decisions. However, the high-tech hospitals associated with academic medical centers remain centrally regulated.[103]

Physicians

In 2005, there were 60,519 physicians, or about 3.7 physicians per 1000 people.[14] About a third of all physicians are general practitioners who provide preventive and primary care and serve as gatekeepers for secondary and tertiary care services. GPs may be paid via a combination of capitation and fee-for-service, with performance bonuses for preventive care services and managing chronic diseases. Most specialists are self-employed and paid on a fee-for-service basis. However, specialists working in university or municipality hospitals and physicians-in-training are paid salaries. They supplement their incomes by working at night or during the weekend.[77] With the reforms of the health insurance system, selective contracting with health providers has also started to occur, which will undoubtedly change the physician payment system.[104]

Present Problems and Initiatives

The Dutch health system of indirect provision of care funded through compulsory health insurance offers universal access and has produced high quality at moderate costs. The system differs most markedly from the German system in the use of primary care providers as gatekeepers. Current problems include delays in accessing GPs, waiting lists for specialty care, and security and privacy concerns about the introduction of electronic health records.[105] The last is a new problem, while the former have been recurring. The recurring problems are discussed first.

To address the delays and waiting list problem, the Dutch are relying on the expansion of after-hours care and on managed competition. After-hours care (defined as care from 5 P.M. to 8 A.M. and on weekends) is provided by primary care cooperatives that integrate telephone consultations with nursing triage, face-to-face consultations with GPs, and house calls by GPs.[106] Both physician and patient satisfaction with this approach is high; in comparison to other models, it has "scale advantages with characteristics of strong primary care, such as high accessibility, continuity and coordination of care."[107]

To encourage efficiency and greater access for medically necessary tertiary care, a system based on Diagnosis Treatment Combinations (DBC) is now used to reimburse hospitals and medical specialists, replacing per diem rates. This prospective payment system takes into account the degree to which the demand for care falls to the hospital and the medical specialists, how demand for care should be handled, and the costs associated with this service. It differs from DRGs in that the entire episode of care, including outpatient treatment, is included.[108] Although the payments associated with this prospective payment system initially were set by the Dutch Ministry of Health, beginning in 2005 hospitals could negotiate prices with health insurers for a growing subset of DBCs. In 2005 these negotiations affected about 10% of the DBCs; by 2009 that had grown to 34% of the DBCs. This segment of services has seen faster growth than the government-regulated DBCs, alleviating some of the waiting list pressures.[103, 104]

However, both the after-hours care primary care cooperatives and managed competition via use of the DBCs rely on the implementation of electronic health records linking not only healthcare providers but also patients. The Dutch Ministry of Health is establishing a national infrastructure for data exchange of electronic health records (EHRs) among both providers and patients. The core of this infrastructure is an index that connects all EHRs of a patient. Because of concerns with patient confidentiality and liability, the launch of this EHR initiative has been more difficult than anticipated.[105]

One of the successes in the Netherlands has been its focus on quality outcomes through health technology assessment and evidence-based medicine.[109] Based on 1989 legislation, quality management is the responsibility of both healthcare professionals and management, with input from insurers and patients. Three different approaches have been undertaken to manage healthcare quality.[110] The National Organization for Quality Assurance in Hospitals (CBO) not only conducts peer review activities of physician practices, but also supports efforts aimed at quality assurance in hospitals. In addition, 28 scientific societies accredit various medical specialties, conducting site visits that assess quality process management, use of guidelines, and the evaluation of patient satisfaction and treatment outcomes. Medical specialty and general practice associations have developed numerous consensus guidelines and evidence-based medicine protocols for treatment and diagnosis, with input from patient organizations and third-party payers.[111]

Overall, the Dutch healthcare system, with its primary care gatekeeping, has shared with the United Kingdom the problem of waiting lists for specialty care. Like Germany, it also has struggled to contain costs and sought to implement managed competition and managed-care techniques. The Dutch system, arguably, has been more effective in containing costs because of its history and focus on primary care, health technology assessment, and evidence-based medicine; it has also established a risk equalization pool that allows private insurers to compete based on price and service, rather than competing based on risk avoidance.

Summary Lessons: Using Compulsory Insurance for Indirect Provision of Health Care

Both the German and Dutch models of compulsory health insurance provide universal access to basic health services and achieve very good to excellent quality as measured by a variety of health outcomes. However, both systems have struggled to contain costs, and both have either adopted or independently developed certain managed care techniques, ranging from primary care gatekeeping and capitation to DRGs and disease management. Both health systems also have introduced various forms of managed competition between insurers and providers to increase efficiency. While the Dutch reforms are too recent to assess their overall effectiveness, they show promise as a way to reduce governmental payments for health care, but do require serious governmental regulation to ensure that managed competition benefits Dutch citizens. The German approach to managed competition has many similarities, albeit within a system of employer-based health insurance. Both Germany and the Netherlands have introduced risk equalization schemes for health insurers, an approach that has great merit for the United States and other countries.

Mixed Models for Provision of Health Services

With the exception of Greece and Turkey, all of the national health systems that follow mixed models for the funding and provision of health services have not yet achieved universal access to health insurance. Those nations include Argentina, Brazil, Indonesia, Mexico, and the United States. Many of these countries have declared health care as a right, but rely on both public and private systems of care. The most common mix is one of social health insurance combined with tax-funded, direct, and indirect provision of care. Regardless of the funding mix, all of these countries are attempting to reform health care to expand insurance coverage and access to care. First, we ponder, a brief review of each national healthcare system and its problems, beginning with Argentina and ending with the United States. We then suggest the most likely prototype and path that would stabilize each health system while ensuring universal access to health insurance.

The Argentine Healthcare System

The main forces in Argentina's health services sector have historically been large labor unions, large federations representing individual professionals, and private hospitals. Between 1960 and 1990, the public health sector serving the poor declined, while the social security sector grew. At this time, a multitude of these social insurance organizations (*obras sociales*) grew under trade union control. The government played little, if any, role in health care. Rather, the health services sector was negotiated between the *obras sociales* from the demand side and the medical federations and private hospitals on the supply side. In 1970, health coverage was mandated by law for employees/employers within the various trade unions, and unsuccessful attempts were made to equalize coverage among the multitude of *obras sociales* throughout the 1980s.[112]

After the hyperinflationary years of the 1980s and the transfer of political power to a new regime with extraordinary powers, reforms favored deregulation/privatization. Many of the *obras sociales* suffered from financial deficits and were ripe for reform at this point. Their financial trouble prompted providers to require higher co-payments from beneficiaries and flooded the public health system. The new government attempted to centralize social security contributions into a single fund (SUSS) in 1991. A series of reforms during the 1990s attempted to promote competition among *obras sociales* by allowing some freedom of choice to beneficiaries and mandating minimum coverage. In addition, reforms focused on funding by promising the *obras sociales* that the government would pay the difference between contributions received and the actual cost of services and dictating that the *obras sociales* pay for services provided to their beneficiaries at public hospitals. Estimates from 2001 indicate that 52% of the population was covered by some kind of health insurance, dropping more than 10% from 1991 estimates.[113] Despite insurance reforms aimed at achieving universal coverage,[114] the dependence on employment-based social insurance (*obras sociales*) probably decreased the percentage of the population with coverage.[115,116]

Current System Structure and Financing

The Argentine health system combines tax-funded, direct provision of health services with compulsory social and private health insurance with indirect provision of services. Around 10% of the population purchases private, substitutive health insurance. Treatment services, especially inpatient care, are emphasized. Other coverage available includes transplants, dental care, services for hemophiliacs, dialysis for chronic patients, and psychological care, but these are covered with variability among different *obras sociales*. Employees gained some freedom to choose among insurance plans in 1997. The reforms that have introduced managed care also have increased the burden of co-payments (20–30%) by those covered by *obras sociales*.[117]

During 2006, private expenditures accounted for 54.5% of the total expenditure on health, of which 23.9% was out-of-pocket. Social health insurance plans (*obras sociales*) accounted for 26.6% of health expenditures, while taxation accounted for the remaining 18.9% of health expenditures.[14] Despite the creation of a National Health Services Superintendency under the Ministry of Health and Social Action,[116,118] the federal government does not play the central role in regulating health care. Rather, that regulation is the result of contracts between payers, intermediaries, and direct providers.[119]

Hospitals

Beginning in the 1990s, attempts were made to decentralize public hospitals; 20 hospitals and some specialized centers or social programs became the responsibility of provinces. Several public hospitals were created as self-managed entities. Public hospitals receive funding from their jurisdiction and insurance like *obras sociales*, as well as from private insurance and out-of-pocket payments; however, they have suffered from poor reimbursements from these third-party payers.[119] In 2000, there were about 4.1 hospital beds per 1000 people.[14]

Physicians

In 1998, there were 108,800 physicians, or about 3.0 physicians per 1000 people.[14] General practitioners in private practice work on a per capita basis, while private specialists or physicians providing ambulatory services are paid on either a fee-for-service or per capita basis. Public physicians are paid salaries.[120]

Present Problems and Initiatives

At the start of the 21st century, Argentina faced severe economic problems, and in 2002 it devalued its currency. While this action eventually reinvigorated the economy, it created immediate and severe disparities in access to health care. Many low-income workers lost their social health insurance benefits and became reliant upon publicly provided services, which became increasingly underfunded. As a result, adequate and balanced funding of the public health (direct provision of care) system and the *obras sociales* (indirect provision of care) system continues to be major challenges. At the same time, there have been many unintended consequences from the introduction of managed care during the 1990s. On the one hand, price competition among providers was introduced into the system with the reforms of the early 1990s in which the *obras sociales* were free to contract with providers without scheduled fee restrictions. The new managed-care funding system discouraged overprovision or overcharging. With the reforms of 1993, *obras sociales* could mandate accreditation or other criteria for categorizing healthcare providers in order to enhance quality. On the other hand, managed care cost containment, along with inadequate monitoring and regulation from the public health system, has encouraged the transfer of expensive private insurance and *obras sociales* patients from private to public hospitals. Increased income testing at public hospitals has also decreased access by the working poor, who increasingly pay out-of-pocket for services.[121]

Despite efforts to reform, the Argentinean healthcare system in 2006 was characterized by financial segmentation among those with social health insurance and/or private health insurance, and those reliant on publicly provided services. As a result of the varied sources of financing, the decentralization of the public provision of care, and discrepancies in wealth across regions, access to health services is fragmented, with those reliant on the public provision of care typically receiving fewer services, with more delays, and with uneven quality. Thus, the system of public provision of health services to the poor in conjunction with the purchasing of privately provided health services by those with social health insurance (*obras sociales*) and/or private health insurance, has led to inequitable access and quality of care across the population as a whole. However, this is not out of the ordinary as health care in Argentina has historically been known for operating under high degrees of inefficiency and inequity.[120]

In summary, Argentina's mixture of indirect and direct public provision of care based on taxes, along with both a compulsory social health insurance (*obras sociales*) and a voluntary private insurance market, remains both inefficient and inequitable. Recent reforms have had some positive results, for example, in reducing the impact of catastrophic illnesses on the poor.

However, additional reforms such as extending risk-pooling mechanisms, improving the benefit package, and regulating the private sector would improve the equity of care and reduce costs.[117] Without such changes, Argentina will continue to have difficulty in providing access, controlling costs, and improving healthcare quality.

The Brazilian Healthcare System

The Brazilian government has funded the indirect provision of health services through social security insurance from both public and private employers since the 1930s. Under social security, access was limited based on participation in the formal labor market and rationed according to categorization within that market. At the same time, chronic care facilities were funded directly through the Ministry of Health.

As the authoritarian regime took control of Brazil in 1964, the government took an increasingly central role in the health sector, both to stimulate economic growth of the private sector and to legitimize political control. Social security was unified into a single national institution and coverage was expanded to more and more employees. However, those in the informal labor market were still excluded. In the 1970s, medical care became the responsibility of the Instituto Nacional de Assistencia Medica da Previdencia Social (INAMPS). Both public and private health services were based on fee-for-service payments, with no control over the kind of medical care provided. This encouraged high-cost, specialized, hospital-based treatment and discouraged preventive and primary care. From the 1970s, access was expanded to include workers in all segments of the economy (with variable benefits based on contributions) and universal emergency services. Increased demand for health services during this period, as well as subsidies from the military regime, spurred the growth of the private health sector. However, funding continued to be supported by compulsory payroll contributions. Thus, funding levels were variable and problematic during the economic recession of the 1980s.[122]

Capitalizing on problems during the 1980s, the Health Movement (a group of intellectuals, health professionals, and left-wing militants from opposition parties) succeeded in associating the demand for healthcare services with the demand for a democratic regime. The 1988 constitution defines health care as a right for all citizens and a responsibility of the state. The Unified Health System (SUS) was created at this time. The national, state, and municipal governments share responsibility for health care. However, the private health system is not integrated with the public system and has been regulated by public health authorities for only a short time. Beginning in 1993, municipal governments began to take on more responsibility for health care.[123]

Current System Structure and Financing

Brazil relies on both a public and a private subsystem, and covers about 75% of the population through the public health sector. The public health system relies on taxes to provide or contract for health services. In 2003, about 24.5% of the population had private health insurance.[124]

The Ministry of Health is responsible for regulating standards of care. The public system provides most primary and secondary care, as well as emergency services. There are several types of private, supplementary health insurance with varying types of coverage. However, most affluent Brazilians opt for substitutive private health insurance, provided either through employment or directly purchased. Employer-managed health plans provide services for employees of large public or private organizations and offer a wide variety of services, including dental care. Both group medical companies and medical cooperatives cover substitutive services based on prepaid arrangements.[123]

Taxes at the federal, state, and municipal levels accounted for 47.9% of total health expenditures in 2006. Private expenditures on health accounted for 52.1% of total health expenditures in 2006, of which out-of-pocket expenditures accounted for 33.3% of all healthcare expenditures.[14]

Hospitals

In 2002, there were 2.6 hospital beds per 1000 Brazilians.[14] Inpatient care occurs mostly within private hospitals with reimbursement from public funds. In contrast, most outpatient care occurs in public institutions. In 2002, public hospitals accounted for only 31% of all hospital beds in Brazil. Most secondary and tertiary care is located in the most affluent and populated regions of Brazil. The federal government uses a prospective payment mechanism to reimburse both public and private hospitals. Each state receives funds based on quotas and is subject to financial caps.[124]

Physicians

In 2000, there were 198,153 physicians, or about 1.2 physicians per 1000 people.[14] General practitioners do not play a gatekeeping role; specialist care is emphasized. Starting in 1998, financing of ambulatory services began to be distributed on a per capita basis to municipalities. Health insurance companies incorporate both reimbursement and delivery of services within health provider networks, similar to preferred provider organizations in the United States. The number of doctors has increased dramatically over the past 30 years, with the number in private practice growing most rapidly.[125]

Present Problems and Initiatives

Brazil faces both market pressures to privatize its public system from an affluent middle and upper class, and political pressure to extend public access to all of its population from a disenfranchised lower-middle and lower class.[123] This tension often results in equivocal health policies. For example, Brazil represents one of the largest markets in the world for drugs, many of which are banned within the countries producing them because of the lack of regulation and inspection. The primary problems within the Brazilian healthcare system have included insufficient financing and mechanisms to control expenses; conflicts between the public and private health systems and between levels of government; and the prevailing curative care model.[122] Reforms to decentralize the SUS have addressed both its financing and governance issues, placing both more control and more funding responsibilities onto states and municipalities.[125]

The activities of the federal government in Brazil are guided by a multiyear plan (PPA) that determines the issues of importance for the next four years. Within the PPA for 2004 to 2007, approximately 18 priorities were related to health, including increased access to low-cost prescription medication, quality improvement throughout the healthcare system, greater oversight of health activities and financial resources, decentralization of the system to the regional level, and approval of the National Health Plan. In 2006, a new commitment was developed entitled "Pact for Life: Strengthening the SUS and its Management." This pact changed the way the federal, state, and municipal levels of government interact with one another. Specifically, part of the pact outlined a commitment to solidarity on the regional level as the system worked toward decentralization.[124] Underscoring this commitment, the Organisation for Economic Co-operation and Development recommends that Brazil's success with inter-municipal initiatives for procurement and its success with flexible arrangements for hospital administration and human resource management should be broadly disseminated at the state and municipal level.[126]

The SUS also continues to focus on the importance of primary care. This strategy includes promoting health and working with Brazilians to encourage preventive medicine. The Family Health Programme created in 1994 has proven to be one of the most effective programs for providing care for families in health clinics, hospitals, or even their homes.[127] It has also significantly reduced the level of infant mortality during the past decade.[128]

Overall, Brazil's mixture of indirect and direct public provision of care based on taxes, along with a private system supported by employers has made significant steps toward providing universal access to primary care. Challenges facing Brazil include not only controlling costs and improving healthcare quality, but also sustaining and continuing to improve access to care within its public system.

The Greek Healthcare System

Until the establishment of the Ministry of Hygiene and Social Welfare in 1922, Greeks had very limited financial access to care, with about 10% of the population covered. The first serious attempt to increase access to health care in Greece occurred in 1934 with the creation of the social security organization, IKA, which covered about 30% of the Greek population. After an unsuccessful attempt to establish a national health system in the 1950s, social health insurance coverage expanded to include employees in the public and financial services sectors, self-employed professionals, and agricultural workers. IKA established its own infrastructure for providing health services, while public and private insurance contracted with private physicians for primary care and both public and private providers of secondary and tertiary care. This system remained throughout the political turmoil of the 1970s.[129]

A national health system (ESY) was finally established in 1983 to make good on a promise that all citizens have "equal rights to high quality social and health care, and treatment."[130] A fundamental goal with the establishment of ESY was to clearly separate public and private health systems with the intent that the private system would disappear; hence, publicly employed physicians were prohibited from private practice. The Ministry of Health and Welfare was tasked with leading massive reforms of the public healthcare system in the 1980s. Plans were to consolidate all social insurance funds into one: place all publicly funded hospitals under the ESY and to expand their functions; prohibit new, as well as the expansion of existing, private hospitals; establish a network of urban and rural primary care centers; and devolve decisions to 10 health regions. Only a portion of these reforms was accomplished. The most significant was the establishment in rural areas of 176 clinics for preventive and primary care, 19 small hospitals, and 3 large university hospitals. Additionally, since 1983, the number of social insurance funds funded by employers has been cut in half, from around 80 to 30.[130,131]

Plans to establish urban clinics, consolidate social insurance funds, and decentralize the ESY's administration, however, did not materialize. Although prohibitions on private hospital facilities were loosened in the 1990s, the private market has flourished by providing ambulatory diagnostic and therapeutic care.[132] Also, private, substitutive, and supplementary insurance has actually grown since the establishment of ESY.[130]

Current System Structure and Financing

Presently, the Greek healthcare system is a combination of tax-funded, direct provision and social insurance–funded, indirect provision of care. All citizens have access to physician services, outpatient and inpatient care, health promotion and disease prevention, prescription drugs, and dental care. However, variations in coverage still exist based on the social insurance fund. Most social insurance covers lost income due to illness or maternity, while the largest four social insurers cover nearly every possible healthcare service or product, short of cosmetic surgery. Long-term care is covered almost exclusively by private funds and is relatively rare. Co-payments for pharmaceuticals are 25%, while out-of-pocket payments for private physicians, outpatient, and inpatient services vary.[130]

State and national taxes fund ESY. In 2006, taxation accounted for 20% of total health expenditures. National and employer-sponsored funds like IKA and the other social insurance accounted for 22.5% of the health expenditures in 2006.[14] Private funding in the form of both insurance and out-of-pocket money funded the remaining 30% of the healthcare system in 1992, growing from 2.9% (GDP) in 1980 to 5% (GDP) in 2004.[133] As of 2006, out-of-pocket payments accounted for 35.9% of total health expenditures, while private insurance accounted for 21.6% of total expenditures.[14]

Hospitals

Although the hope was to strangle private hospitals with reforms in 1983, both private and public hospitals remain. Public hospitals are financed primarily by tax revenue, with the addition of social insurance funds and user fees. Because hospitals are concentrated in urban areas, Greek citizens receive less overall inpatient care than do other European citizens. As of 2000, there were 139 public and 218 private facilities.[130] In 2005, there were about 4.7 hospital beds per 1000 people.[14]

Physicians

In 2005, there were 55,556 physicians, or about 5 physicians per 1000 people.[14] In 1996, the relative distribution of specialized doctors was 81:19 between public and private hospitals. In addition, only 5% of all specialists served rural citizens, who made up 25% of the Greek population. General practitioners are supposed to serve a gatekeeping function by referring patients to specialized primary or other secondary care; however, that has not been the case. Relatively few physicians choose general practice.[129]

Present Problems and Initiatives

Greece's ESY, unlike the NHS in the United Kingdom or Sweden, is still in the process of absorbing its social health insurance subsystem of care. As a result, it faces a unique set of problems in controlling health service costs and ensuring equitable quality of care. While the ESY directly provides both health facilities and employs physicians, nurses, and other health professionals, funding comes both from taxation and compulsory social health insurance. Moreover, the ESY does not have the capacity to provide health services to all citizens, nor restrain the overutilization of hospital services. The IKA and other social health insurers contract with both public and private providers, maintaining the vitality of the private sector. In addition, the largest social health insurer, IKA, provides a network of primary care polyclinics in urban areas, undercutting the ESY's gatekeeping efforts at the primary care level.

At the same time, insufficient pay for public physicians and inefficient management of public hospitals has encouraged a "black market" of informal payments for physician services and preferential treatment.[130] Public funds pay for all hospital expenses not covered by social insurance. Thus, the system is demand-led, with no incentives for cost control. Public physicians are paid a salary with public and social insurance funds. While these salaries increased dramatically after 1983, they were still comparatively low. Thus, methods for paying physicians encourage the long-established practice of unofficial payments. Some estimate these "black market" payments supplement physician salaries by about 40%.[129] The Greek healthcare system has displayed issues with resource allocation due in part to transactions that take place between the public and private sectors. This system has also had difficulty with efficiency measures, and the implementation of health information systems has been slow. Additionally, very little performance monitoring is done and there is no mapping of health conditions within the country's population.[133]

In 2002, reforms established a public organization (ODIPY) for financially managing health resources of all major social insurance funds. The various social insurance funds are to be consolidated into one main fund in an attempt to separate purchasing from the provision of healthcare services. On the provider side, 17 semiautonomous health regions have been established to decentralize the ESY, improve its decision making and accountability, and enhance its ability to invest in primary care centers in urban areas.[130] This movement toward an internal managed market was designed to emphasize prevention and health promotion and also to deal with the overutilization of health services, especially by urban hospitals.[134] Reforms also sought to remedy the problems with informal payments. The government agreed to pay physicians in three ways: a monthly payment, an annual capitation fee, and a productivity bonus. However, physicians would also be allowed to work additional hours in private practice under a fee-for-service system.[130]

The return of the conservative party in 2004 led to numerous legislative developments that focused on administering health service delivery and did not address other major issues, including fragmentation in funding. However, in 2005 the private finance initiative (PFI) was introduced in order to increase private support for construction and maintenance of the health sector infrastructure.[133]

Overall, the Greek health system has in place the necessary reforms to create a viable national health service along with a single-payer financing system, but only if the public funding and political will to implement existing policies is sufficient. Significantly, the consolidation of the 30 social insurance funds via the proposed ODIPY is one means to ensure sufficient revenue for the expansion of the ESY and to establish a single-payer system. Such consolidation, in combination with the ESY, would establish a public sector monopsony. That purchasing structure, with sufficient oversight and regulation, could then set the conditions for efficient purchasing of health services from both public and private health providers.[132]

Alternatively, because of the differences in revenue and risk across the social health insurance plans and the ESY, Greece should consider establishing a risk equalization scheme similar to those schemes recently introduced in Germany and the Netherlands. Such a change would continue the multipayer system currently in place. However, by equalizing risk via reallocating funds across the social health insurance plans and the ESY, there would be further incentives from all purchasers to promote efficient and high-quality care.

The Indonesian Healthcare System

As a Dutch colony, Indonesia received little investment in health care prior to 1910, with the exception of smallpox vaccinations. Starting in the 1930s, the government devoted resources to health education and disease prevention and had developed a robust public health infrastructure prior to World War II. After the Japanese invaded in 1942, the public system collapsed and the general health of the country deteriorated. Following the postwar period and independence from the Netherlands in 1950, a network of maternal and child health centers was established, but with only one physician for every 100,000 people. These centers gradually were expanded into a network of community health centers that were heavily frequented by the 1980s. However, Western-style medicine was often used in conjunction with *dukun* (traditional healers) especially in rural areas. Indeed, the Department of Health estimated that dukun attended upwards of 90% of rural births in the early 1990s.[135]

Current System Structure and Financing

The Republic of Indonesia's health system is a complex mix of private expenditures; tax-funded, direct provision of services; compulsory social insurance; and voluntary private insurance. In 2006, public expenditure on health accounted for 50.4% of total health expenditures, of which 10.1% of expenditures were raised from social security payroll deductions and 2.3% from external sources. Out-of-pocket expenditures accounted for 32.9% of all healthcare expenditures, and private health insurance accounted for only 16.7% of total health expenditures.[14]

Government employees, the military, Indonesians employed in the formal sector, and the poor are covered under the Indonesian social insurance programs (PT Askes, Jamsostek). Private insurance covers a small but growing percentage of the population. Public hospitals and outpatient facilities provide services for those without social or private insurance, estimated at 70% of the population. Both public and private facilities provide primary through tertiary services. Those covered by PT Askes receive services mainly in public facilities. Preventive and primary care are emphasized in public services. Patients pay user charges in public facilities.

Civil servants, civil service pensioners, the armed forces, and their families and survivors receive services from PT Askes, which is funded through payroll contributions of 2% and an additional 0.5% from the government. PT Jamsostek is a semicompulsory system for employees of firms with more than 10 employees and is also financed through payroll deductions of 3% to 6% paid entirely by the employer. To address the substantial increase in the underserved and poor, the government instituted an additional program called the National Social Security System, or Sistem Jaminan Sosial Nasional. Launched in 2005, this program covers around 60 million people. It is administered following managed care principles and receives a monetary contribution from the government.[136]

Hospitals

In 2005, Indonesia had 1268 hospitals, with 642 government and 626 nongovernmental hospitals. Of these hospitals, 995 were general hospitals and 273 were specialty hospitals.[137] Policy analysts argue that the high level and unpredictability of user fees deters utilization of hospitals. Private hospitals (both for-profit and not-for-profit), which represent about half of all hospital facilities, are the dominant provider of inpatient care.[138]

Physicians

In 2006, there were 44,564 general practitioners and 12,374 physician specialists, supported by 308,306 nurses and 79,152 midwives. Because of the many rural villages throughout the nation's archipelago, Indonesia relies on 7669 health centers to provide primary and some secondary care. These include District Health Centers (2077 with beds) that provide a wide range of medical, preventive and obstetrical services. One or more physicians, with nurse support, staff these centers. Sub-District Health Centers (5592 without beds) provide limited medical services and are staffed by either a physician or nurse. Transportation vehicles (all-terrain vehicles and/or motor boats) are available in most rural subcenters. Preventive and primary care is provided by Integrated Health Centers; these are managed by the community, provide maternal and child health, diarrheal control, family planning, nutritional development, and immunization services at the village level.[137,138]

Present Problems and Initiatives

The health sector experienced significant changes between 2001 and 2005 as a result of the political and socioeconomic decentralization process initiated in 2000. District governments were given full discretion in prioritizing which sectors to develop and were provided the authority to develop and budget their own health plans with funds they generate themselves and those received from the central government. Unfortunately, decentralization reduced the emphasis on health sector development and adversely affected the provision of services.

In response, the Ministry of Health issued a new strategic plan for health in 2006. The government's new health plan focuses on increasing health financing, particularly public funding, and extending social health insurance beginning with the expansion of the Sistem Jaminan Sosial Nasional, the noncontributory managed care program providing government-subsidized insurance for the poor.[137]

Indonesia's mixture of tax-funded, direct provision of services, along with social health insurance and voluntary private insurance, has had many difficulties ensuring access to quality services, particularly for the poor and lower income population. A major reform toward a national health system would probably result in the most benefit for the poor and lower-middle-class, if it can garner sufficient political support. Alternatively, Indonesia should consider establishing a single-payer system with substitutive private health insurance. This latter approach might encounter less resistance and allow the national government to continue to expand services to the poor.

The Mexican Healthcare System

The Mexican constitution of 1917 established the government's responsibility for social welfare, including health care, but the Ley del Seguro Social (social security law) of 1943 paved the way for a system of social security. During the 1950s, the most politically powerful groups of employees were granted access to health care through the ISSSTE; these groups worked primarily within the military and public service. Although the percentage of Mexican workers covered by the social security system increased through 1970, this has included only those working within the formal labor market. Other Mexicans—for example, self-employed professionals, craftsmen, landowners, and agricultural workers—were covered by the Ministry of Health (IMSS).[139]

During the economic crisis in the 1980s, reform focused on a complete overhaul of the health system and the establishment of a decentralized, national health system (IMSS-Solidarity). Article 4 of the constitution guaranteed the right to health care for all Mexicans. However, of the 31 Mexican states, only the 14 most economically stable ones achieved decentralization. In the remaining poorer states, healthcare services deteriorated when federal subsidy was reduced. The private health sector grew during this time partly due to changes in insurance regulations under NAFTA. In addition, most reforms were suspended under new presidential leadership.[139]

Beginning in 1995, another wave of reforms attempted to diversify services and financing, allow users some choice in providers, and open up the medical services industry for those with private insurance or coverage within social security. In addition, the IMSS-Solidarity offered a basic package of low cost, high impact, and public health interventions, which were designed to meet the needs of the one third of the Mexican population with no regular source of medical services. Thus, a clearer division between private and public health subsystems was created.[140]

Until recently, Mexico relied on a threefold method of insuring and providing health services: (1) a national health subsystem (Ministry of Health and IMSS-Solidarity); (2) a set of compulsory employment-based social insurance subsystems (IMSS and ISSSTE), which covered approximately 50% of the population in 2000; and (3) a private health insurance market. While about 50% were covered by social health insurance in 2000,[141] estimates of those who had access to at least basic health services ranged between 70% and 90%.[142,143]

Current System Structure and Financing

To address the needs of the uninsured, the Mexican health system recently underwent a massive reform, which allowed for the formation of the System of Social Protection in Health (SSPH). The reform focuses on the 50 million uninsured Mexicans who have not been able to access healthcare services through the compulsory social health insurance programs that previously were in place. The SSPH program is funded largely by federal taxes, as well as contributions from municipal governments. Families also pay a small premium; however, the poorest 20% of families are exempt from the payment. The insurance component of the plan covers all individuals who are not covered by social security because they are self-employed, unemployed, or out of the workforce.[144,145] The System of Popular Social Security (SISSP), another form of social insurance, was implemented in 2006 to reduce the number of marginalized individuals in Mexico. In addition to providing housing and retirement benefits, the SISSP offers health services to the nation's poorest population.[146]

In 2006, out-of-pocket expenditures accounted for 52.4% and private insurance 4.3% of all healthcare expenditures. Taxes at the federal, provincial, and municipal levels accounted for 12.9% of healthcare expenditures. Depending upon employment, social health insurance is financed through either bipartite employer and employee contributions or tripartite contributions that include federal funds; social health insurance accounted for 30.4% of total health expenditures in 2006.[14]

Hospitals

In 2004, there was 1 hospital bed per 1000 people.[14] During this same period, Mexico had more than 4000 hospitals and 77,705 beds; however, only 1047 hospitals were in the public sector. Nonetheless, the public sector accounts for most hospitals beds. Also, whether privately or publicly owned, 86.8% are general hospitals, and most provide emergency and secondary care services.[146]

Physicians

Mexico had 195,897 physicians (2 per 1000 people) in 2000,[14] with most providing primary care. In 2002, 45% of all physicians were specialists. Around 27% of physicians work only in private practice where they are paid on a fee-for-service or per capita basis, while the remaining 73% are in public practice. Most physicians in public practice receive salaries, which they may supplement through private practice.[146]

Present Problems and Initiatives

Structurally, the Mexican health system has a fragmented funding scheme, has had low public health expenditures, lacks resources and infrastructure within the public sector, has geographic and regional misdistribution of facilities, and is unevenly regulated.[147] The fragmentation of the public sector is a result of specific laws that govern social security. Both private and public sector salaried workers have a right to social security with comprehensive benefits; this legislation divides the population. One section of the population has compulsory health insurance and the other section without is covered by the federal and state ministries of health. Further problems are evidenced in the social security subsystem, which encourages duplication of supply, resource waste, unfair costs to consumers, and serious coordination problems. In the IMSS-Solidarity public subsystem, there is little consumer choice and concern for quality of care. Budgets and salaries are not tied to productivity or efficiency. Moreover, there is no regular system of accreditation for either public or private healthcare facilities.[148] At the same time, the health system has produced highly inequitable health outcomes, with the working poor suffering the most.[141]

Initial reports on the impact of Popular Health Insurance (PHI), the operational program of the SSPH, show that overall federal health expenditures had been growing substantially up until the year 2004, but was level in 2005 because social security spending dropped off that year. Overall federal health spending decreased 2.1% in 2006, which resulted in an overall decline of resources in the public sector as well as a redistribution that favored PHI at the expense of the IMSS. The health impact of PHI has also been examined, and although it is unlikely that PHI has had a measurable effect on health in a few short years, mortality data for 1995, 2000, and 2005 show a moderate decrease.[147] Moreover, a rigorous study of the PHI between 2005 and 2006 shows that it has had a positive impact on the public sector by creating greater access to health services for the poorest segment of Mexicans.[24]

In summary, Mexico has made significant steps toward improving access to the poorest segment of its population. However, it faces the daunting challenge of improving the quality of health services while containing costs. Consolidating the public and social health insurance subsystems into one fund and under one authority would reduce fragmentation and lower administrative costs.[149] A single-payer system would enhance the Mexican government's expansion of health insurance and services to the poor.

The Turkish Healthcare System

During the first two decades following the establishment of the Republic of Turkey in 1923, the country focused on public health programs to control malaria, tuberculosis, and other infectious diseases and established educational programs for healthcare personnel. After World War II, the establishment of the Social Insurance Organization (SIO) helped to provide health, disability, and retirement benefits to workers. During the next decade, the SIO developed a network of hospitals and other facilities for employees to receive health services. A turning point in the provision of health services occurred with the enactment in 1961 of the "Basic Health Law." This act authorized the provision of health services free or partly free-of-charge at the point of delivery. Health service providers were to be paid from premiums and general taxation. The aim was to expand healthcare services—ranging from preventive to tertiary care—and to ensure access to the whole population. However, key aspects under the act, such as collection of premiums, were not implemented.[150] As a result, a large number of public and private agencies emerged to provide and finance health care.[151]

Until recently, Turkey's health system was a combination of tax-funded, direct provision and social insurance–funded indirect provision of care. This system provided financial coverage to about 85% of the population through some kind of public or private health insurance. In 2003, most people were covered through one of three forms of social health insurance: (1) the Social

Insurance Organization (SSK; 46.3% of the population); (2) the Social Insurance Agency of Merchants, Artisans, and Self-employed (Bağ-Kur; 22.3% of the population); or (3) the Government Employees Retirement Fund (GERF; 15.4% of the population). Less than 1% of the population was covered by private insurance. Those without formal social or private health insurance were issued a Green Card, providing them with access to preventive, primary care, and emergency care in the healthcare facilities managed by the Ministry of Health (MoH). However, as in Greece, informal cash payments also existed, with most of it going toward physician services. Since 2003, Turkey has been implementing a Health Transformation Program (HTP) with the goal of establishing a national health service. The HTP objectives include improving governance, efficiency, user and provider satisfaction, and long-term fiscal sustainability.[152]

Current System Structure and Financing

In 2005, all healthcare facilities that were part of the SSK were transferred to the Ministry of Health.[153] This change was one key element of the eight-part plan underlying the HTP.

> Key elements of the HTP include: i) establishing the MoH as a planning and supervising authority; ii) implementing Universal Health Insurance (UHI) uniting all citizens of Turkey under a single Social Security Institute (SSI); iii) expanding the delivery of health care and making it more easily accessible and friendly; iv) improving the motivation of health personnel and equipping them with enhanced knowledge and skills; v) setting up educational and scientific institutions to support the system; vi) securing quality and accreditation systems to encourage effective and quality health-care services; vii) implementing rational drug use and management of medical materials and devices; and viii) providing access to effective information for decision making, through the establishment of an effective Health Information System.[152]

Other significant changes to the health system have included: (1) The integration of the social security and health insurance institutions—SSK, Bağ-Kur, and GERF—under one institution, the SSI; (2) unification of benefits and management systems (e.g., databases, claims, utilization review) across the different social health insurance plans; (3) movement away from fee-for-service and toward prospective-payment systems that include pay-for-performance incentives; (4) deployment of an integrated primary care system in about a third of the provinces; (5) increased hospital autonomy over resource allocations, coupled with greater accountability to the Ministry of Health; and (6) establishment via the 2008 Social Security and Universal Health Insurance Act of a single-payer system for all public patients.[152]

Taxes paid for 34.5% of total health expenditures in 2006. Out-of-pocket payments, including user charges, accounted for 20% of total health expenditures. Social insurance funded by employer and employee contributions accounted for about 37% of all healthcare expenditures. Private insurance accounted for 8.5% of all health expenditures in 2006.[14]

Hospitals

There were about 1200 hospitals in 2007 (2.7 beds per 1000 people in 2006).[14] The Ministry of Health owns and operates 850 hospitals, while 350 are privately owned. Certificate of need legislation restricts the growth of the private sector and reduces duplication of services with publicly owned hospitals. Payment mechanisms for both public and private hospitals are in flux, and the Australian DRG prospective payment system has been piloted in 47 public hospitals. It is likely that a combination of prospective payments and global budgets will be used to control the costs of public hospitals.[152]

Physicians

Turkey had 116,014 physicians, or about 1.6 per 1000 people in 2006.[14] There is a relatively high proportion of specialists compared to general practitioners. Most physicians are paid salaries, and hospital-based specialists are eligible also for performance-based bonuses, which are adjusted to encourage full-time status. There is and has been concern about the current number of physicians being able to meet the demand in Turkey. To overcome this shortage, the Ministry of Health has opened new medical schools and implemented a family medicine–based integrated primary care initiative. Much of primary care has been the responsibility of midwives and nurses, but the integrated primary care initiative has increased the supply of family medicine physicians, both through a rigorous training and an innovative payment system. Family physicians in the integrated primary care initiative receive capitation payments, with incentive bonuses for preventive care services.[152]

Present Initiatives and Problems

Turkey has made good progress in establishing universal access to its national health service. One of the more successful developments has been the introduction of family medicine as a model for providing integrated primary healthcare services. A pilot project was started in 2005, and as of 2008, 23 of 81 provinces in Turkey had adopted the family medicine model.[152] This model calls for the provision of greater preventive and curative basic services to the population. The main providers in this model are state-owned health centers, staffed by a physician, nurses, midwives, health technicians, and medical secretaries. The principal goal is to provide health care to the population with an emphasis on individuals in rural areas where access continues to be a problem. Primary care is also provided by vertically arranged preventive care centers and other primary care clinics operated by the private sector. The main barriers of this new primary care model are the lack of sufficiently trained public health professionals and low enthusiasm of medical practitioners to fulfill duties of preventive and public health services within community health centers. These obstacles might be overcome by providing better working conditions, especially salary, recruiting appropriately trained staff, and collaborating with academic public health departments to determine community health needs.[154]

Other future challenges include completing the HTP initiatives previously outlined, especially improving the quantity and quality of health personnel, developing and implementing quality and accreditation systems for healthcare services, managing drug and medical technology costs, and establishing a nationwide health information system. Long-term challenges include improving the public health infrastructure, addressing geographical inequities in access to health services, containing costs, and improving provider performance and efficiency.[152]

In summary, Turkey has traveled much farther along the path toward a tax-funded, direct provision model than its neighbor, Greece. It has done so by embracing a single-payer system, with public and private health service providers. The 2003 through 2008 reforms have created direct and centralized control of publicly owned healthcare services and have emphasized the coordination of financial, informational, and regulatory activities. On one hand, Turkey is rapidly developing a public system with a healthcare purchaser–provider arrangement similar in many ways to the NHS in the United Kingdom. On the other hand, Turkey has developed the flexibility to purchase services from both public and private healthcare providers, echoing the flexibility recently introduced in Sweden's NHS.

The United States Healthcare System

Organized health care in the United States began with the almshouses and pest houses of the 1700s. Local governments established these facilities to feed and shelter the orphaned, homeless, elderly, disabled, and chronically or mentally ill, and they provided health care as a secondary function. During the industrial revolution in the United States, advances in science and medical technology all aided in the demand for, and the subsequent development of, nongovernmental for-profit and not-for-profit hospitals. Along with medical advancements came the need to standardize medical education and training. In 1910, Abraham Flexner led a study of medical education. The Flexner Report sparked systematic efforts to standardize medical education.[155] At this same time, concerns about workers' access to health insurance led progressive politicians such as Teddy Roosevelt and the Bull Moose Party to support compulsory, employer-based, social health insurance in the 1912 presidential election. Roosevelt's loss to Wilson, coupled with the United States's entry into World War I, signaled the death of this reform effort. As with other attempts to create a federally supported national health insurance during the 1920s and 1930s, the Progressives met stiff resistance from both physicians and small businesses.[156]

During World War II the federal government controlled prices and wages, and many US employers began paying for health insurance as a way to attract and retain employees. At the same time, nonprofit hospitals expanded their missions to care for mentally and physically wounded veterans.[157] After World War II, President Truman pressed Congress for several years to approve legislation establishing national health insurance, but again, reforms were resisted by businesses and physicians.[156] Nonetheless, direct federal involvement in hospitals began in 1947. The Hill-Burton Act was intended to fund the construction of hospitals in rural areas, but amendments extended it to provide grants that matched the funds generated by a community. The federal government's involvement continued to grow in the mid-1960s with the creation of Medicare (social health insurance for the elderly) and Medicaid (health welfare for the poor) under President Johnson. These programs, along with employer-sponsored health insurance, increased the demand for hospital-based health services. By 1970, hospitals were the center of healthcare services, and healthcare costs had risen dramatically, fueled by Medicare's "cost-plus" reimbursements.[157,158]

From 1980 through 1990, health care became less centered in hospitals and outpatient care grew, as both the government and insurers tried various cost containment efforts. The enactment of an inpatient prospective payment system (PPS) for Medicare in 1983 encouraged hospitals, physicians, and healthcare entrepreneurs to enter the ambulatory care arena through joint ventures. In addition, managed care organizations gained market share, and for-profit hospital chains emerged. Moreover, medical technology permitted sophisticated procedures to be delivered in ambulatory rather than inpatient facilities. During the 1990s, small and large employers engaged in managed care contracting in opposition to the national health insurance reforms proposed by President Clinton. At the same time, integrated delivery systems emerged through hospital consolidations and mergers, and through acquisitions of physician practices, long-term care facilities, ancillary services, and health plans. The increasing cost of delivering health care and patients' demands for convenient "one-stop shopping" were two drivers for integration; a third driver was the bargaining leverage gained through market dominance as health systems and networks responded to cost containment pressures from managed care organizations and employers.[159,160]

Current System Structure and Financing

The current US health system comprises a voluntary, employer-based private insurance subsystem, social health insurance for the elderly, and tax-funded, direct and indirect provision of care. Health expenditures in 2006 were funded through a combination of taxation (32.7%), social health insurance (13.1%), private health insurance (41.5%), and out-of-pocket payments (12.7%).[14] Together, public (27.1%; 80.3 million people) and private (68.0%; 201.7 million people) health insurance covered about 84.2% of the population in 2006, with 15.8% of the population uninsured. Note: 10.9% of the population were covered both by public and private insurance.[161] Benefit packages vary with the type of insurance, but typically include inpatient and outpatient hospital care and physician services. Many private plans also include preventive services, dental care, and prescription drug coverage. User charges vary by type of insurance, but typically include outpatient and prescription drug co-payments, as well as deductibles for hospitalization.

The federal government is the single largest healthcare insurer and purchaser. Medicare covers health services for the elderly, the disabled, and those with end-stage renal disease. Administered by the Centers for Medicare and Medicaid Services (CMS), Medicare covered 13.8% of the population in 2006.[162] The program is financed through a combination of payroll taxes, general federal revenues, and premiums. It accounted for 19.04% of total health expenditures in 2006.[163] Medicaid, a joint federal–state health benefit program, covers targeted groups of the poor (e.g., pregnant women, families with children, and the disabled). Medicaid is administered by the states, which operate within broad federal guidelines overseen by the CMS. It covered 12.9% of the population in 2006[161,164] and accounted for 14.65% of total health expenditures in 2006. The program is financed by federal tax revenues (8.65% of total health expenditures in 2006), which match tax revenues raised by each state (6.4% of total health expenditures in 2006).[163] The ratio of matching federal funds varies for each state depending upon its per capita income. The State Children's Health Insurance Program (SCHIP) is a state–federal health benefit program targeting poor children. SCHIP is jointly administered by the CMS and the states and is funded by federal and state taxes (0.4% of total health expenditures in 2006).[163]

Private insurance is provided by not-for-profit and for-profit health insurance companies and is regulated by state insurance commissioners. Individuals can purchase private health insurance, although most people receive employer-based insurance. Many large employers self-fund health benefits for their employees, using insurance companies as third-party administrators. Private insurance covered 68.8% of the total population, with 59.7% of the population receiving employment-based insurance in 2006.[162] Private insurance, including that provided by employers, accounted for 34.61% of total health expenditures in 2006.[163]

Hospitals

In 2005, there were about 3.2 hospital beds per 1000 people.[14] In 2007, the United States had 4897 community hospitals, of which 2913 were not-for-profit, 873 were for-profit, and 1111 were public (owned by state or local governments). In contrast, the federal government operated only 213 hospitals (serving veterans, active members of the armed services, and Native Americans) in 2007. Hospitals typically are parts of organized delivery systems, with most US community hospitals being either a member of an integrated delivery system (*n* = 2730) and/or network (*n* = 1472) in 2007.[165] For-profit, not-for-profit, and public hospitals are paid through a combination of methods: per diem charges, case rates, capitation, and prospective payments based on DRGs (diagnostic-related groups).

Physicians

In 2000, there were 730,801 physicians, or about 2.6 physicians per 1000 people.[14] General practitioners usually have no formal gatekeeper function, except within some managed care plans. While the majority of physicians are in private practice, increasingly physicians are being employed by medical group practices, hospitals, health maintenance organizations, or organized delivery systems.[77] They are paid through a combination of methods: charges, discounted fees paid by private health plans, capitation contracts with private plans or public programs, and direct patient fees.

Present Problems and Initiatives

The US health system presently faces concerns about the rising number of the uninsured, increases in insurance premiums, and ineffective and uncoordinated care. Past efforts to address cost and quality issues highlighting the complexity of problems facing the fragmented US system of health care will be discussed.

To control costs, the United States has deployed managed care within the employer-based insurance market and has mandated various cost containment measures in both Medicare and Medicaid. During the 1990s, third-party payers and private insurers attempted to control cost growth through a combination of selective provider contracting, discounted price negotiations, utilization control practices, risk-sharing payment methods, and other managed care techniques. Although managed care techniques contained the costs of care during most of the

1990s, premium costs have recently increased at a rate above inflation. Government efforts to curb costs have had mixed results. Following the Balanced Budget Act of 1997, the federal government introduced additional prospective payment systems and reduced reimbursements for hospitals, physicians, and others providing services to Medicare and Medicaid recipients.[166] While these efforts contained governmental costs, many of these costs have been passed on through providers to patients, increasing the burden of out-of-pocket expenses. This problem is most noticeable for Medicare beneficiaries who often face steep out-of-pocket costs for drugs and other noncovered services.

Ironically, quality of care did not become a public issue until managed care, with its explicit rationing, became dominant in the United States; as a managed care backlash emerged within the public during the late 1990s, so did concerns about medical errors and reduced services.[167] Nonetheless, practically all US hospitals have established continuous quality improvement programs in order to comply with voluntary standards imposed by accrediting bodies such as the Joint Commission (http://www.jointcommission.org). A voluntary private–public endeavor, the National Committee for Quality Assurance (NCQA) accredits private health plans and has been instrumental in developing the Healthcare Effectiveness Data and Information Set (HEDIS), which is used by more than 90% of US health plans. During the 1990s, the NCQA had a growing impact on improving the quality of patient care provided through managed care organizations; participating organizations voluntarily report patient satisfaction and other measures of quality as measured using HEDIS, and NCQA produces report cards on their performance.[168] Additionally, the federal government through the Agency for Healthcare Quality and Research funds numerous efforts to improve clinical and overall quality, including evidence-based medicine guidelines and protocols. Other notable initiatives include pay-for-performance, which has been championed and piloted by the Bridges to Excellence coalition (programs reward physicians for improving cardiac and diabetes outcomes and using health information technology), the Leapfrog Group (Hospital Rewards Program), and Medicare (multiple demonstration projects for both hospitals and medical group practices). Lastly, the Institute for Healthcare Improvement (IHI) has promoted quality improvement and patient safety around the world. Within the United States, the IHI has had remarkable impact through campaigns such as the 100,000 Lives Campaign (2004–2006) and the 5 Million Lives Campaign (2006–2008).

Nonetheless, healthcare costs, quality (continued problems with effective, coordinated, safe, and timely care), and financial access remain concerns to the US public and legislators. Numerous proposals for reforming the US health system were proposed in 2000–2001 when the US federal government had a significant budget surplus. Several of those proposals took into account the long history of opposition to a National Health Service in the United States,[169] and put forth plans to achieve universal insurance coverage within the health system.[170–172] A consistent focus in these proposals was that voluntary, employer-based health insurance should become compulsory.

Now, under President Obama's administration, and in the face of an international recession and a significant federal deficit, health reform has reemerged as a high priority. The fiscal year 2010 budget includes $630 billion over the next 10 years to help finance health reform. Both the Senate and the House of Representatives have debated multiple models for reforming US health care, ranging from single-payer models to multipayer models, with either individual- or employer-based mandates. However, as of August 2009, the key legislative proposals from both the House and the Senate are focused on multipayer models, with individual-based mandates for health insurance.[173]

Recall that making financial access to and provision of health care both equitable and cost-effective are the predominant values driving most ethical and political arguments for changing national healthcare systems. Each national health system discussed in this chapter has dealt with trade-offs among financial access, cost, and quality in order to provide both equitable and cost-effective health care. These trade-offs are, in turn, influenced by two key factors: (1) financing, that is, how monies are mobilized and allocated for the provision of health care; and (2) how health services are organized, that is, who provides services and the relative weights placed on the provision of primary and tertiary care. Both of these factors provide the basis of our recommendations for reforming US health care, which we articulate in the concluding section of this chapter.

Summary Lessons: Using Mixed Models for Funding and Providing Health Care

All of the countries using mixed models for funding and providing health care have problems ensuring that quality care is equitably accessible and is cost-effective. As a result, all of these countries have been reforming their health systems. On one hand, during the past decade, Turkey enacted a transformational health reform to achieve universal financial access to care; on the other hand, Greece enacted incremental health reforms primarily to contain costs. However, most of these countries—Argentina, Brazil, Indonesia, Mexico, and the United States—have or are attempting to incrementally improve access to care.

Turkey has avoided many of the problems Greece has faced by establishing a decentralized, publicly funded primary care network, consolidating its social health insurance into one fund, centralizing the management of its public hospitals, and providing universal access to health insurance. If it can continue to grow its economy and implement its reforms, Turkey will soon transform its mixed model system to a national health service with a substantial public–private provider partnership.

Shared Concerns and Learning Opportunities

The comparisons of the United States with the 11 countries in this chapter raise a number of issues. Do these countries face the same social, economic, and demographic problems as the United States? On the one hand, the industrialized countries that have been examined to this point share many similarities with the United States; on the other hand, many of the middle- and low-income countries face greater social, economic, and demographic problems.

As **Table 1.3** illustrates, one major demographic characteristic of the United States is its large population—ranging from 32.4 times the size of Sweden to 3.4 times the size of

Table 1.3   Demographic, Economic, and Social Comparisons among 12 Nations, Ordered by GDP per Capita

	GDP per Capita (PPP US dollars, 2007 est.)	Distribution of Family Income (Gini Index)	Surface Area (square kilometers)	Population (2008; in thousands)	Population Density (square kilometer)	Growth Rate (2008)	International Ranking by Population (2008)
Indonesia	$ 3,121	36.3	1,919,440	237,512	123.7	1.2	4
Brazil	$ 9,500	56.7	8,511,965	196,343	23.1	1.2	5
Turkey	$12,000	43.6	780,580	71,893	92.1	1.0	17
Mexico	$12,400	50.9	1,972,550	109,955	55.7	1.1	11
Argentina	$13,100	49.0	2,766,890	40,482	14.6	1.1	30
Greece	$30,600	33.0	131,940	10,723	81.3	0.1	74
Germany	$34,100	28.0	357,021	82,370	230.7	0.0	15
United Kingdom	$35,000	34.0	244,820	60,944	248.9	0.3	22
Sweden	$37,500	23.0	449,964	9,045	20.1	0.2	88
Canada	$38,600	32.1	9,984,670	33,213	3.3	0.8	37
Netherlands	$39,000	30.9	41,526	16,645	400.8	0.4	59
United States	$45,800	45.0	9,826,630	303,825	30.9	0.9	3

Sources: US Bureau of the Census. 2008. *International Data Base: Vital Rates* [Internet: http://www.census.gov/ipc/ www/idb/summaries.html], and Central Intelligence Agency. 2008. *The World Factbook* [Internet: https://www.cia .gov/library/publications/the-world-factbook/index.html].

Germany. Only Indonesia and Brazil have a population nearing the size of the United States. Another major characteristic of the United States is its per capita income; it is the highest in this comparison group, but is typically grouped with other high-income nations such as Canada, Germany, Greece, the Netherlands, Sweden, and the United Kingdom. Others in this comparison have moderate per capita incomes, except Indonesia. Both the United States and Canada have moderate growth rates, while all of the European countries have low, and the middle- and low-income countries high, growth rates. Importantly, the high growth rates in the middle- and low-income countries place special demands on their healthcare systems for prenatal, maternal, and childcare services, which are best met by primary care networks of providers.

Arguably, of the 11 other countries that have been reviewed, the German and Dutch healthcare systems are the most comparable to the US system.[174,175] However, lessons can also be drawn from the United Kingdom's and Sweden's National Health Service and Canada's single-payer models, albeit with careful attention to the fundamental differences with the US system.

Toward US Convergence with the Three Prototypical Healthcare Systems?

During the early 1990s, the changes in not only Germany and the Netherlands, but also in both the United Kingdom and Sweden created a mixture of regulation and market competition that seemed to converge with the government-driven reforms that President Clinton proposed in the United States.[176] That is, the vision of a US healthcare system of managed competition with a budgetary cap on total spending was similar to what was already occurring in Canada and several European countries, including the Netherlands, Sweden, and the United Kingdom.[177] With regard to financing health care, Canada, Sweden, and the United Kingdom rely primarily on income as well as other taxes to fund health care, and a single payer—the government—disburses these funds. In contrast, Germany and the Netherlands rely largely on payroll taxes for funding health care, disbursing these funds via a multipayer mixture of either public or private insurance. The problem facing each country, as Chris Ham notes, is that it must determine how to combine the control of expenditures at the macro level with real incentives for efficiency at the micro level. The country that is able to solve this puzzle will indeed be the envy of the world.[178, p. 1224]

Within this context, it is significant that Canada, Germany, the Netherlands, Sweden, and the United Kingdom have been implementing various elements of managed competition in order to address the problem Ham has underscored. In each of these countries, managed competition has been viewed as a way to increase providers' efficiency when delivering health care, thus balancing the macromanagement of financing health care practiced in each country with a quasi-market mechanism for micro-managing expenditures.[179]

Aided by the concern over the rising costs of health care, market-driven reforms—predominately managed care mechanisms for financing and integrating systems or networks for delivering health care—were rapidly adopted throughout many regions in the United States during the 1990s. These reforms had the most impact, respectively, on reducing the demand for health care and improving the effectiveness of medical interventions across the continuum of care. Although the benefits of managed care and the effectiveness of integrated delivery systems certainly can be questioned, together they can be credited with containing the aggregate costs of health care in the United States to 13.6% of the gross domestic product from 1992 through 1996.[180]

Currently, while elements of the United States's managed care practices—ranging from DRGs to disease management—are being implemented or considered by almost all of the national health systems we have reviewed, and the integration of care delivery is a concern for all of these health systems, the convergence between the United States and these systems is limited. Emphasizing this point, Saltman and Figueras argue that the United States needs to consider both supply-side controls on, and more extensive federal regulation of, health care in order to achieve the same degree of cost containment as has been achieved by these prototypical healthcare systems.[181]

Conclusions about Health Systems Prototypes

Healthcare systems like the United Kingdom's and Sweden's provide universal access to health care by relying primarily on taxes to fund the direct provision of care, but each country must ra-tion health services in order to control costs. On one hand, the United Kingdom's network of primary care providers serve as gatekeepers, implicitly rationing by limiting access to specialists and hospitals, thus controlling costs. On the other hand, the already decentralized Swedish NHS uses explicit rationing to maintain high-quality care, to contain costs, and to uphold universal access to basic health services. Rationing, however, shifts the costs of elective health services to consumers, increasing out-of-pocket expenses.

An alternative to this prototype is Canada's tax-funded, indirect provision of care. The decentralized Canadian healthcare system achieves universal access, high quality, and moderate costs through implicit (e.g., primary care gatekeeping) and explicit (e.g., technology assessment) rationing of services. Like Sweden, the Canadian system's rationing shifts elective service costs to consumers, increasing out-of-pocket and supplementary private insurance expenditures.

Both the German and Dutch models of compulsory health insurance provide universal access and achieve high quality, albeit through public (German) and private (Dutch) insurance. Both have adopted certain US managed care techniques and have introduced different forms of managed competition between insurers and providers to increase efficiency. To counter the risk avoidance and resulting inequitable financial access inherent within any system relying on multiple social health insurance funds, both the Dutch and the Germans have introduced risk equalization schemes.

Lessons for Reforming the US Health System

As the United States addresses concerns about financial access for its uninsured population while attempting to contain the costs of health care, five recommendations may be drawn from this review of these 11 healthcare systems. These recommendations focus on providing equitable access and creating healthcare value through (1) universal financial access, (2) integrated primary care, (3) evidence-based health improvement, (4) performance-based payment systems, and (5) integrated health information systems.

Adopt an Individual Compulsory Health Insurance Model

The US health system is unique in relying on voluntary, employer-based health insurance for most of its population. As with Mexico, the reform that would be the least disruptive and would generate the least amount of stakeholder resistance in the United States would be the Dutch (individual) compulsory health insurance model. The legislation being debated in Congress proposes various ways that such a compulsory insurance model could be enacted; what has been lacking has been the political will and coherent vision to enact such a reform in a meaningful way.

A compulsory individual insurance model has several prerequisites, including (1) a basic set of services that every insurer must cover, (2) guaranteed issue to anyone seeking coverage from an insurer, (3) a fixed premium from the insurer for all those insured under the basic coverage, and (4) a *post hoc* risk equalization scheme. This fourth element, especially, is necessary since it would deter health insurers from making premiums unaffordable to high-risk individuals. On the one hand, an insurer with sicker enrollees would have those costs offset by the risk equalization fund at the end of each year; on the other hand, an insurer with healthier enrollees would forgo a portion of the premium set aside in the risk equalization fund. The four elements, taken together, would allow private insurance companies to offer basic insurance packages to anyone, without assuming untoward risk. Lastly, if health insurers are to compete on a level playing field across the United States, regulation of health insurance should be at the federal level.

Adopt Integrated Preventive and Primary Care

Regardless of the health system prototype, countries that have established integrated primary care services have had remarkable improvements in their population's health status. Brazil, Indonesia, and Turkey are exemplars of this trend in moderate and low-income countries. Variations of this model are also deployed in Canada, Germany, the Netherlands, and the United Kingdom. Because the focus is on preventive and primary care services that enhance wellness within families and across generations, integrated primary care is more than a gate-keeping model for controlling access to high-cost, tertiary care. Within high-income countries with rapidly aging populations, various models of integrated primary care address the problems of chronic diseases and help to coordinate the continuum of care. The after-hours primary care collaboratives in the Netherlands, in conjunction with a national health information system, is one innovative way to address concerns about 24-hour access to care. The medical home model in the United States is another way to approach these concerns while reaping the benefits inherent in providing preventive and primary care to everyone.

In the medical home model, the primary care provider is responsible for three types of services: (1) preventive care, including patient education to improve self-care; (2) primary care; and (3) coordination of secondary and tertiary care. On the one hand, preventive and primary care services maintain wellness and cure or manage common ailments; on the other hand, coordinating secondary and tertiary care reduces hospitalization and rehospitalization, especially for those with chronic illnesses. To establish medical homes, the United States must address several shortcomings in its current system, including funding for such services and the maldistribution of primary care physicians relative to specialists. Recognizing and encouraging the use of mid-level providers in underserved areas throughout the United States is one way to address the supply issue; another is to provide more equitable funding for primary care physicians; and a third is to expand the training and incentives for medical students choosing primary care as a specialty.

Put into Practice Evidence-Based Health Improvements

Closely linked with the need to adopt an integrated preventive and primary care model is the need to improve health care by using evidence-based medicine and evidence-based management practices. Different countries are using different approaches, ranging from comparative effectiveness research for drugs (e.g., Germany and the United Kingdom) to establishing evidence-based guidelines for treating various diseases (e.g., the Netherlands and Canada) to safety registries for medical devices (e.g., Sweden).

Within the United States, evidence-based medicine is well recognized and many guidelines have been developed, but there remain significant delays in the adoption of best medical practices among physicians, hospitals, and other healthcare providers. Currently, Medicare has implemented a pay-for-reporting system for physicians, hospitals, and other providers, allowing it to track various quality indicators and aspects of best medical practices. Moreover, the American Recovery and Reinvestment Act of 2009 created the Federal Coordinating Council for Comparative Effectiveness Research, providing both funding and oversight for such research within the Agency for Healthcare Research and Quality, the National Institutes for Health, and the Offices of the Secretary of Health and Human Services. While these initiatives are a start, the United States needs to maintain this investment in research and implement best practices by incentivizing health providers.

Establish Performance-Based Payment Systems

Aligning the incentives for health providers with the desired outcomes for patients, for communities, and for regional and national populations is a major challenge, but one worth addressing. Not surprisingly, Canada, Germany, the Netherlands, Sweden, Turkey, the United Kingdom, and the United States have, and are experimenting with, various forms of performance-based payment systems for hospitals and physicians, as well as other healthcare providers.

Within the United States, Medicare should deploy various performance-based payment systems for hospitals, physicians, and other providers. Fortunately, Medicare is testing a pay-for-performance payment system through the Premier Hospital Quality Incentive Demonstration, and has developed a plan for deploying value-based purchasing within its fee-for-service program. However, a system is needed to pay for integrated preventive and primary care services that maintain the wellness, cure the non-acute illnesses, manage the chronic conditions, and coordinate the secondary and tertiary care for Medicare recipients. The United States could base a performance-based system for primary care on the United Kingdom's system of GP payments, which uses a mix of capitation fees, fixed allowances for practice costs, bonus payments linked to quality processes and outcomes, and specific fees for enhanced services (such as coordination of care).

Implement a National Health Information System

The United States should develop a system for sharing electronic health records among healthcare providers and with patients. National health information systems are being established in most high- and some moderate-income countries. Canada, Germany, the Netherlands, Sweden, Turkey, the United Kingdom, and the United States are all in different phases of development, with the systems in Sweden and the United Kingdom the most developed at this time. Both the Swedes and the English have devoted significant funding to these initiatives. Importantly for the United States, the success of both performance-based payment systems and evidence-based health improvement initiatives depend on the rapid collection and sharing of health data.

In the United States, two critical initiatives for establishing a national health information system are included in the American Recovery and Reinvestment Act of 2009. One is a four-year program for each state to develop a health information exchange; the other is a four-year program for establishing 70 regional extension centers to promote the adoption of electronic health records by primary care providers. While the two initiatives provide a welcome launching pad for the adoption and meaningful use of electronic health records for primary care providers within underserved areas of the United States, a funding model is needed to develop a sustainable health information system. Given our recommendation that the United States adopt an individual health insurance model, private insurers should also be required to support the national health information exchange. One method would be a per capita charge that is part of the premium for each individual. At the same time, both the Medicare and Medicaid programs should have a portion of program funding devoted to supporting the national health information exchange.

In closing, the US healthcare system can benefit from looking at the successes and failures within other systems. We believe that the insular focus of many of the healthcare reform discussions during the past decade miss the opportunity to gain perspective and insight from other healthcare systems. Certainly, it is hoped that makers and all healthcare stakeholders will begin to take a look around the world in order to improve the financing, organizing, and delivery of health care in the United States.

References

1. Frenk J, Gomez-Dantes O. Globalization and the challenges to health systems. *Health Affairs*. 2002;21(3):160–165.
2. Blendon RJ, Schoen C, DesRoches CM, et al. Inequities in health care: a five-country survey. *Health Affairs*. 2002;21(3):182–191.
3. Jacobs A. Seeing difference: market health reform in Europe. *Journal of Health Politics, Policy and Law*. 1998;23(1):1–33.
4. Kitchener M, Caronna CA, Shortell SM. From the doctor's workshop to the iron cage? Evolving modes of physician control in US health systems. *Soc Sci Med*. 2005;60(6):1311–1322.
5. Shortell SM, Gillies RR, Anderson DA, Erickson KM, Mitchell JB. *Remaking Health Care in America: Building Organized Delivery Systems*. San Francisco, CA: Jossey-Bass; 1996.
6. McKee M, Garner P, Stott R, eds. *International Co-operation in Health*. New York: Oxford University Press; 2001:217.
7. Begley CE, Aday LA, Lairson DR, Slater CH. Expanding the scope of health reform: application in the United States. *Social Science and Medicine*. 2002;55(7):1213–1229.
8. Barer ML, Evans RG. Interpreting Canada: models, mind-sets, and myths. *Health Affairs*. 1992;11(1):44–61.
9. Danzon, PM. Hidden overhead costs: is Canada's system less expensive? *Health Affairs*. 1992;11(1):21–43.
10. Naylor CD. A different view of queues in Ontario. *Health Affairs*. 1991;10(3):44–61.
11. Sheils JF, Young GJ, Rubin RJ. O Canada: do we expect too much from its health system? *Health Affairs*. 1992;11(1):7–20.
12. Hurst JW. Reform of health care in Germany. *Health Care Financing Review*. 1991;12(3):73–86.

13. ———. Reforming health care in seven European nations. *Health Affairs*. 1991;10(3): 7–21.

14. WHO. WHOSIS: WHO Statistical Information System. Geneva, Switzerland: WHO; 2008. http://www.who.int/whosis/en/. Updated February 6, 2009. Accessed November 24, 2008.

15. Abel-Smith B. Cost containment and new priorities in the European community. *The Milbank Quarterly*. 1992;70(3):393–416.

16. Williamson OE. *Markets and Hierarchies*. New York: Free Press; 1975.

17. Anderson GF, Reinhardt UE, Hussey PS, Petrosyan V. It's the prices, stupid: why the United States is so different from other countries. *Health Affairs*. 2003;22(3):89–105.

18. PAHO. *Health in the Americas*. Washington, DC: Pan American Health Organization; 2007.

19. CIA. *The World Factbook*. Washington, DC: Central Intelligence Agency; 2009.

20. McKee M, Figueras J. For debate: setting priorities: can Britain learn from Sweden? *British Medical Journal*. 1996;312(7032):691–694.

21. US Census Bureau, Housing and Household Economic Statistics Division. Historical Health Insurance Tables. Washington, DC: US Bureau of the Census. http://www.census .gov/hhes/www/hlthins/historic/index.html. Updated September 22, 2009. Accessed April 24, 2009.

22. Maurer J. Assessing horizontal equity in medication treatment among elderly Mexicans: which socioeconomic determinants matter most? *Health Economics*. 2008;17(10):1153–1169.

23. Valencia-Mendoza A, Bertozzi SM. A predictive model for the utilization of curative ambulatory health services in Mexico. *Salud Publica de Mexio*. 2008;50(5):397–407.

24. King G, Gakidou E, Imai K, et al. Public policy for the poor? a randomised assessment of the Mexican universal health insurance programme. *Lancet*. 2009;373(9673):1447–1454.

25. Sakala C. The development of national medical care programs in the United Kingdom and Canada: applicability to current conditions in the United States. *Journal of Health Politics, Policy and Law*. 1990;15(4):709–753.

26. Roemer MI. *National Strategies for Health Care Organization: A World Overview*. Ann Arbor, MI: Health Administration Press; 1985:426.

27. Madden TA. The reform of the British National Health Services. *Journal of Public Health Policy*. 1991;12(Autumn):378–379.

28. Iglehart JK. Conference report: health systems in three nations. *Health Affairs*. 1991;10(3): 255.

29. National Health Services. *The New NHS*. London: Department of Health; 1997.

30. Timmins NA. Time for change in the British NHS: an interview with Alan Milburn. *Health Affairs*. 2002;21(3):129–135.

31. Robinson R, Dixon A. *Health Care Systems in Transition: United Kingdom*. Copenhagen, Denmark: European Observatory on Health Care Systems; 1999:117.

32. Department of Health. *The NHS Plan: A Plan for Investment, A Plan for Reform*. London: Department of Health; 2000:144.

33. Healthcare Commission and Audit Commission. *Is the Treatment Working? Progress with the NHS System Reform Programme: Health National Report*. London: Audit Commission; 2008:96.

34. HSC. Health and social care in Northern Ireland Web site. http://www.n-i.nhs.uk/index .php. 2009.

35. NHS Scotland. About the NHS in Scotland Web site. http://www.show.scot.nhs.uk/ introduction.aspx. Accessed April 25, 2009.

36. NHS Wales. What is NHS Wales Web site. http://www.wales.nhs.uk/sites3/home.cfm?Org ID=452. Accessed April 25, 2009.

37. NHS Choices. About the NHS Web site. http://www.nhs.uk/NHSEngland/aboutnhs/ Pages/About.aspx. Updated October 29, 2009. Accessed March 23, 2009.

38. ———. NHS services Web site. http://www.nhs.uk/NHSEngland/AboutNHSservices/Pages/NHSServices.aspx. Updated October 29, 2009. Accessed March 23, 2009.

39. Monitor. Monitor: independent regulator of NHS Foundation Trusts Web site. http://www.monitor-nhsft.gov.uk/. Accessed April 25, 2009.

40. BMA. British Medical Association: The professional association for doctors Web site. http://www.bma.org.uk/. Accessed April 25, 2009.

41. Darzi A. *High Quality Care for All: NHS Next Stage Review Final Report*. London: Department of Health; 2008.

42. Saltman RB. Renovating the commons: Swedish health care reforms in perspective. http://www.lse.ac.uk/Depts/lsehsc/pdf_files/paper2oct01.pdf. Updated October 28, 2009. Accessed December 13, 2002.

43. Hessler RM, Twaddle AC. Sweden's crises in medical care: political and legal changes. *Journal of Health Politics, Policy and Law*. 1982;7(2):440–459.

44. Twaddle AC, Hessler RM.. Power and change: the case of the Swedish Commission of Inquiry on Health and Sickness Care. *Journal of Health Politics, Policy and Law*. 1986;11(1):19–40.

45. Bergman, SE. Swedish models of health care reform: a review and assessment. *International Journal of Health Planning and Management*. 1998;13(2):91–106.

46. Whitehead M, Gustafsson RA, Diderichsen F. Why is Sweden rethinking its NHS style reforms? *British Medical Journal*. 1997;315(7113):935–939.

47. Diderichsen F. Market reforms in health care and sustainability of the welfare state: lessons from Sweden. *Health Policy*. 1995;32(1–3):141–153.

48. ———. Devolution in Swedish health care: local government isn't powerful enough to control costs or stop privatisation. *British Medical Journal*. 1999;318(May 1):1157–1158.

49. ———. Sweden. *Journal of Health Politics, Policy and Law*. 2000;25(5):931–935.

50. Harrison MI, Calltorp J. The reorientation of market-oriented reforms in Swedish healthcare. *Health Policy*. 2000;50(3):219–240.

51. Quaye RK. Internal market systems in Sweden: seven years after the Stockholm model. *European Journal of Public Health*. 2001;11(4):380–385.

52. León S, Rico A. Sweden. In: Dixon A, Mossialos E, eds. *Health Care Systems in Eight Countries: Trends and Challenges*. Copenhagen, Denmark: European Observatory on Health Care Systems; 2002:91–102.

53. Jönsson B. Economic evaluation of medical technologies in Sweden. *Social Science and Medicine*. 1997;45(4):597–604.

54. Hjortsberg C, Chatnekar O. *Health Care Systems in Transition: Sweden 2001*. Copenhagen, Denmark: European Observatory on Health Care Systems; 2001.

55. WHO. *Health Care Systems in Transition: Sweden*. Copenhagen, Denmark: World Health Organization; 1996:64.

56. Palmberg M. Quality improvement in Swedish health care. *Joint Commission Journal on Quality Improvement*. 1997;23(1):47–54.

57. Swedish Institute. *The Health Care System in Sweden*. Stockholm, Sweden: Swedish Institute; 1999;14.

58. Swedish Association of Local Authorities, Swedish National Board of Health and Welfare. *Quality and Efficiency in Swedish Health Care—Regional Comparisons 2008*. Stockholm, Sweden: Swedish Association of Local Authorities and Regions; 2008.

59. Glenngård AH, Hjalte F, Svensson M, Anell A, Bankauskaite V. *Health Systems in Transition: Sweden*. Copenhagen, Denmark: WHO Regional Office for Europe, European Observatory on Health; 2005.

60. Swedish Institute. *Swedish Health Care*. Stockholm, Sweden: Swedish Institute; 2007.

61. Swedish Medical Association. The Swedish Medical Association Web site. http://www
.slf.se/templates/Page.aspx?id=2033. Updated June 1, 2009. Updated June 1, 2009. Accessed
February 26, 2009.

62. ———. *Physicians in Sweden 2005*. Stockholm, Sweden: Swedish Medical Association;
2005. http://www.slf.se/upload/Lakarforbundet/Trycksaker/PDFer/In%2520English/L%
25C3%25A4karfakta_2005_eng_webb.pdf.

63. ———. National Board of Health and Welfare. *Working in Sweden: Information for Doctors
from EU/EEA Countries*. Stockholm, Sweden: Swedish Medical Association; 2009:12.

64. Sweden Ministry of Health and Social Affairs, Swedish Association of Local Authorities
and Regions, Socialstyrelsen (National Board of Health and Welfare), Vardfretagarna
(Association of Private Care Providers). *Swedish Strategy for eHealth: Safe and accessible information in health and social care—Status Report 2009*. Stockholm, Sweden: Government
Offices of Sweden; 2009.

65. Naylor CD, Fooks C, Williams I. Canadian Medicare: prognosis guarded. *Canadian
Medical Association Journal*. 1995;153(3):285–289.

66. Taylor M. *Health Insurance and Canadian Public Policy: The Seven Decisions that Created the
Canadian Health Insurance System*. Montreal, QC: McGill-Queen's University Press; 1978.

67. Neuschler E. *Canadian Health Care: The Implications of Public Health Insurance*.
Washington, DC: Health Insurance Association of America; 1990.

68. Litman TJ, Robins LS. *Health Politics and Policy*. New York: John Wiley & Sons; 1984.

69. Scully HE. Medicare: The Canadian Experience. *Annals Thoracic Surgery*. 1984;52:
390–396.

70. Coburn D. State authority, medical dominance, and trends in the regulation of the health
professions: the Ontario case. *Social Science and Medicine*. 1993;37(2):129–138.

71. Department of Finance. Canada's economic action plan: budget 2009: chapter 3: partnership with provinces and territories Web site. http://www.budget.gc.ca/2009/plan/bpc3f-
eng.asp. Updated January 27, 2009. Accessed June 1, 2009.

72. OECD. *OECD Health at a Glance—How Canada Compares*. Paris, France: Organisation
for Economic Co-operation and Development; 2001:1–12.

73. CIHI. *Health Care in Canada 2002*. Ottawa, ON: Canadian Institute for Health Information;
2002: 97.

74. ———. Number of hosptials and number of hosptial beds, by province, territory and
canada, 1999–2000 to 2005–2006. Quick Stats. http://secure.cihi.ca/cihiweb/dispPage
.jsp?cw_page=statistics_a_z_e#N. Updated October 29, 2009.

75. ———. Health human resources—physicians. http://secure.cihi.ca/cihiweb/dispPage.jsp?
cw_page=statistics_results_topic_physicians_e&cw_topic=Health%20Human%20Resources
&cw_subtopic=Physicians. Updated October 29, 2009. Accessed August 23, 2009.

76. ———. Canada's health care providers, 2007. Ottawa, ON: Canadian Institute for Health
Information; 2007.

77. Fujisawa, R, Lafortune G. The remuneration of general practitioneers and specialists in 14
OECD countries: what are the factors influencing variations across countries? In: *Health
Working Papers*. Paris, France: Organisation for Economic Co-operation and Development;
2008.

78. MacAdam M. *Physician payment incentives*. Health Policy Monitor Web site. http://www
.hpm.org/survey/ca/a13/1.

79. CIHI. Health indicators. Canadian Institute for Health Information Web site. http://secure
.cihi.ca/cihiweb/dispPage.jsp?cw_page=AR_152_E.

80. Hurst JW, Jee-Hughes M. *Performance Measurement and Performance Management in
OECD Health Systems*. Paris, France: Organisation for Economic Co-operation and
Development; 2001:68.

81. Accreditation Canada. About us: history. Accreditation Canada Web site. http://www.accreditation.ca/about-us/history/.
82. Sepehri A, Chernomas R. Is the Canadian health care system fiscally sustainable? *Int J Health Serv*. 2004;34(2):229–243.
83. Knox RA. *Germany: One Nation with Health Care for All*. New York: Faulkner & Gray, Inc; 1993.
84. Carr W. *A History of Germany, 1815–1990*. London, England: Edward Arnold/Hodder & Stoughton; 1991.
85. Stone DA. *The Limits of Professional Power: National Health Care in the Federal Republic of Germany*. Cambridge, MA: The MIT Press; 1980.
86. Bundesministerium fur Gesundheit. Health care system and health care reform in Germany. Bundesministerium fur Gesundheit Web site. http://www.bmg.bund.de/nn_1169696/EN/Gesundheit/gesundheit__node.html?__nnn=true. Updated April 15, 2009.
87. Busse R, Riesberg A. *Health Care Systems in Transition: Germany*. Copenhagen, Denmark: European Observatory on Health Systems and Policies; 2004.
88. van Ginneken E, Busse R. (2009) Mandatory health insurance enacted. Health Policy Monitor Web site. http://www.hpm.org/en/Surveys/TU_Berlin_-_D/13/Mandatory_health_insurance_enacted.html.
89. Schang L. Morbidity-based risk structure compensation. Health Policy Monitor Web site.
90. Busse R. Germany. In: Dixon A, Mossialos E, eds. *Health Care Systems in Eight Countries: Trends and Challenges*. Copenhagen, Denmark: European Observatory on Health Care Systems; 2002:47–60.
91. Birkner BR. National quality of care activities in Germany. *International Journal of Quality Health Care*. 1998;10(5):451–454.
92. Sauerland D. The German strategy for quality improvement in health care: still to improve. *Health Policy*. 2002;56(2):127–147.
93. Stock S, Redaelli M, Lauterbach KW. The influence of the labor market on German health care reforms. *Health Affairs*. 2006;25(4):1143–1152.
94. OECD. Policy brief: economic survey of the United Kingdom. *OECD Observer*. 2009;11.
95. Nasser M, Sawicki P. *Institute for Quality and Efficiency in Health Care: Germany*. New York: The Commonwealth Fund; 2009:11.
96. van der Gaag J, Rutten FFH, van de Ven WPMM. The Netherlands. *Advances in Health Economics and Health Services Research*. 1990;11(Supplement 1: Comparative Health Systems):28–41.
97. Schut FT. Workable competition in health care: prospects for the Dutch design. *Social Science and Medicine*. 1992;35(12):1445–1455.
98. Rutten FFH. Market strategies for publicly financed health care systems. *Health Policy*. 1987;7:135–148.
99. Enthoven AC. What Can Europeans Learn from Americans. In: *Health Care Systems in Transition: The Search for Efficiency*. Paris, France: Organization for Economic Cooperation and Development: 1990:57–71.
100. Busse R. 2002, Netherlands. In: Dixon A, Mossialos E, eds. *Health Care Systems in Eight Countries: Trends and Challenges*. Copenhagen, Denmark: European Observatory on Health Care Systems; 2002:61–73.
101. Muiser J. *The New Dutch Health Insurance Scheme: Challenges and Opportunities for Better Performance in Health Financing*. Geneva, Switzerland: World Health Organization; 2007.
102. OECD. *OECD Health Data 2009—How Does the Netherlands Compare*. Paris, France: Organisation for Economic Co-operation and Development; 2009.
103. Maarse H. Health care reform—more evaluation results. Health Policy Monitor Web site.
104. Van de Ven WP, Schut FT. Managed competition in the Netherlands: still work-in-progress. *Health Econ*. 2009;18(3):253–255.

105. Tange H. Electronic patient records in the Netherlands. Health Policy Monitor Web site.
106. Grol R, Giesen P, Uden C. After-hours care in the United Kingdom, Denmark, and the Netherlands: new models. *Health Affairs.* 2006;25(6):1733–1737.
107. Huibers L, Giesen P, Wensing M, Grol R. Out-of-hours care in western countries: assessment of different organizational models. *BMC Health Services Research.* 2009;9(105):1–8.
108. Netherlands Ministry of Health Welfare and Sport. Diagnosis and treatment combination. Netherlands ministry of health welfare and sport Web site. http://www.dbc2003.nl/new2/getpage.php?page=97. Accessed November 1, 2002.
109. Wild C, Gibis B. Evaluations of health interventions in social insurance-based countries: Germany, the Netherlands, and Austria. *Health Policy.* 2003; In Press, Corrected Proof.
110. Klazinga N, Lombarts K, van Everdingen J. Quality management in medical specialties: the use of channels and dikes in improving health care in the Netherlands. *Joint Commission Journal on Quality Improvement.* 1998;24(5):240–250.
111. Crebolder HF, van der Horst FG. Anticipatory care and the role of Dutch general practice in health promotion—a critical reflection. *Patient Education and Counseling.* 1996;28(1):51–55.
112. Belmartino S. The context and process of health care reform in Argentina, In: Fleury S, Belmartino S, Baris E, eds. *Reshaping Health Care in Latin America: A Comparative Analysis of Health Care Reform in Argentina, Brazil, and Mexico.* Ottawa, ON: International Development Research Centre; 2000:27–46.
113. Lloyd-Sherlock P. When social health insurance goes wrong: lessons from Argentina and Mexico. *Social Policy & Administration.* 2006;40(4):353–368.
114. Bertranou FM. Are market-oriented health insurance reforms possible in Latin America? The cases of Argentina, Chile and Colombia. *Health Policy.* 1999;47(1):19–36.
115. Iglesias-Rogers G. Poor prognosis for Argentina's health system. *Lancet.* 2001;358:2059.
116. PAHO. Regional core health data system—country health profile 2001: Argentina. Pan American Health Organization Web site. http://www.paho.org/english/sha/prflarg.htm. Updated 2001. Accessed October 26, 2002.
117. Cavagnero E. Health sector reforms in Argentina and the performance of the health financing system. *Health Policy.* 2008;88(1):88–99.
118. PAHO. Argentina. In: *Health in the Americas.* Washington, DC: Pan American Health Organization; 1998:18–39.
119. Belmartino S. Reorganizing the health care system in Argentina. In: Fleury S, Belmartino S, Baris E, eds. *Reshaping Health Care in Latin America: A Comparative Analysis of Health Care Reform in Argentina, Brazil, and Mexico.* Ottawa, ON: International Development Research Centre; 2000:47–77.
120. PAHO. Argentina. In: *Health in the Americas.* Washington, DC: Pan American Health Organization; 2007:26–48.
121. Iriart C, Merhy EE, Waitzkin H. Managed care in Latin America: the new common sense in health policy reform. *Social Science and Medicine.* 2001;52(8):1243–1253.
122. Lobato L, Burlandy L. The context and process of health care reform in Brazil. In: Fleury S, Belmartino S, Baris E, eds. *Reshaping Health Care in Latin American: A Comparative Analysis of Health Care Reform in Argentina, Brazil, and Mexico.* Ottawa, ON: International Development Research Centre; 2000:79–102.
123. Lobato, L. Reorganizing the health care system in Brazil. In: Fleury S, Belmartino S, Baris E, eds. *Reshaping Health Care in Latin American: A Comparative Analysis of Health Care Reform in Argentina, Brazil, and Mexico.* Ottawa, ON: International Development Research Centre; 2000:103–131.
124. PAHO. Brazil. In: *Health in the Americas.* Washington, DC: Pan American Health Organization; 2007:130–153.
125. Almeida C, Travassos C, Porto S, Labra ME. Health sector reform in Brazil: a case study of inequity. *International Journal of Health Services.* 2000;30(1):129–162.

126. OECD. *Policy Brief: Economic Survey of Brazil, 2009*. Paris, France: Organisation for Economic Co-operation and Development; 2009:11.

127. Jurberg C. Flawed but fair: Brazil's health system reaches out to the poor. *Bulletin of the World Health Organization*. 2008;86(4):248–249.

128. Aquino R, Oliveira NFD, Barreto ML. Impact of the Family Health Program on infant mortality in Brazilian municipalities. *American Journal of Public Health*. 2009;99(1):87–94.

129. Tragakes E, Polyzos N. *Health Care Systems in Transition: Greece*. Copenhagen, Denmark: World Health Organization; 1996.

130. Tountas Y, Karnaki P, Pavi E. Reforming the reform: the Greek national health system in transition. *Health Policy*. 2002;62(1):15–29.

131. Yfantopoulos J. Pharmaceutical pricing and reimbursement reforms in Greece. *Eur J Health Econ*. 2008;9(1):87–97.

132. Mossialos E, Allin S, and Davaki K. Analysing the Greek health system: a tale of fragmentation and inertia. *Health Economics*. 2005;14(Suppl 1):S151–S168.

133. Petmesidou M, Guillen AM. 'Southern-style' national health services? recent reforms and trends in Spain and Greece. *Social Policy and Administration*. 2008;42(2):106–124.

134. Liaropoulos L. Health policy in Greece: a new (and promising) reform. *Euro Observer*. 2001;3(2):5–6.

135. Frederick WH, Worden RL, eds. *Indonesia: A Country Study*, 5th ed. Washington, DC: Department of Defense; 1993. *Area Handbook Series*.

136. Ramesh M, Wu X. Realigning public and private healthcare in Southeast Asia. *The Pacific Review*. 2008;21(2):171–187.

137. Indonesia Ministry of Health. *Indonesia Country Profile 2006: Make People Healthy*. Jakarta, Indonesia: Ministry of Health Republic of Indonesia; 2007:39.

138. ———. Health care system Website. http://www.depkes.go.id/ENGLISH/index.htm. Accessed August 28, 2009.

139. Tamez S, Molina N. The context and process of health care reform in Mexico. In: Fleury S, Belmartino S, Baris E, eds. *Reshaping Health Care in Latin America: A Comparative Analysis of Health Care Reform in Argentina, Brazil, and Mexico*, Ottawa, ON: International Development Research Centre; 2000:133–152.

140. PAHO. Mexico. In: *Health in the Americas*. Washington, DC: Pan American Health Organization; 1998;356–371.

141. Barraza-Llorens M, Bertozzi S, Gonzalez-Pier E, Gutierrez JP. Addressing inequity in health and health care in Mexico. *Health Affairs*. 2002;21(3):47–56.

142. Gómez-Dantés O. Prospects of the Mexican health care reform. http://www.insmx/ichsri/country/reforma_mex.pdf. Accessed October 26, 2002.

143. Gonzalez Block MA, Sandiford P, Ruiz JA, Rovira J. Beyond health gain: the range of health system benefits expressed by social groups in Mexico and Central America. *Social Science & Medicine*. 2001;52(10):1537–1550.

144. Frenk J. Bridging the divide: global lessons from evidence-based health policy in Mexico. *Lancet*. 2006;368(9539):954–961.

145. Frenk J, Gonzalez-Pier E, Gomez-Dantes O, Lezana MA, Knaul FM. Comprehensive reform to improve health system performance in Mexico. *Lancet*. 2006;368(9546):1524–1534.

146. PAHO. Mexico. In: *Health in the Americas*. Washington, DC: Pan American Health Organization; 2007:466–485.

147. Laurell AC. Health system reform in Mexico: a critical review. *International Journal of Health Services*. 2007;37(3):515–535.

148. Tamez S, Molina N. Reorganizing the health care system in Mexico. In: Fleury S, Belmartino S, Baris E, eds. *Reshaping Health Care in Latin America: A Comparative Analysis of Health Care Reform in Argentina, Brazil, and Mexico*. Ottawa, ON: International Development Research Centre; 2000:153–182.

149. OECD. *Policy Brief: Economic Survey of Mexico, 2009*. Paris, France: Organisation for Economic Co-operation and Development; 2009:11.

150. Aktulay G. *Health Care Systems in Transition: Turkey*. Copenhagen, Denmark: World Health Organization; 1996.

151. Kisa A, Kavuncubasi S, Ersoy K. Is the Turkish health care system ready to be a part of the European Union? *Journal of Medical Systems*. 2002;26(2):89–95.

152. Hurst J, Scherer P, Chakraborty S, Schieber G. OECD *Reviews of Health Systems—Turkey*. Paris, France: OECD Publishing; 2008.

153. Tatar M, Ozgen H, Sahin B, Belli P, Berman P. Informal payments in the health sector: A case study from Turkey. *Health Affairs*. 2007;26(4):1029–1039.

154. Güne ED, Yaman H. Transition to family practice in Turkey. *Journal of Continuing Education in the Health Professions*. 2008;28(2):106–112.

155. Haglund CL, Dowling WL. The hospital. In: Williams SJ, Torrens PR, eds. *Introduction to Health Services*. Albany, NY: Delmar Publishers, Inc; 1993:134–159.

156. Starr P. *The Social Transformation of American Medicine*. New York: HarperCollins; 1982.

157. Kovner AR, Neuhauser D. *Health Services Management: Readings and Commentary*. 7th ed. Chicago, IL: Health Administration Press; 2001:492.

158. Wolper LF, Pena JJ. History of hospitals. In: Wolper LF, ed. *Health Care Administration*, Gaithersburg, MD: Aspen Publishers; 1999:391–400.

159. Savage GT, Roboski AM. Integration as systems and networks: a strategic stakeholder analysis. In: Fottler MD, Savage GT, Blair JD, eds. *Advances in Health Care Management*. New York: JAI Press; 2001:37–62.

160. Savage GT, Robinson JW. Managing health care organizations. In: Rabin J, ed. *Encyclopedia for Public Administration and Public Policy*. New York: Marcel Dekker; 2003:580–586.

161. US Census Bureau. Health Insurance Coverage: 2006. Washington, DC: US Census Bureau; 2007.

162. ———. Historical Health Insurance Tables. Washington, DC: US Census Bureau; 2007. http://www.census.gov/hhes/www/hlthins/historic/index.html. Accessed April 24, 2009.

163. CMS. National health expenditures by type of service and source of funds, CY 1960–2007. Centers for Medicare & Medicaid Services Web site. http://www.cms.hhs.gov/National HealthExpendData/02_NationalHealthAccountsHistorical.asp#TopOfPage.

164. Mills RJ. Health Insurance Coverage: 2001. Washington DC: US Bureau of the Census; 2002:1–24.

165. Health Forum. *Fast Facts on US hospitals*. Chicago, IL: American Hospital Association; 2008.

166. Levit K, Cowan C, Lazenby H, et al. Health spending in 1998: signals of change. *Health Affairs*. 2000;19(1):124–132.

167. Mechanic D. The managed care backlash: perceptions and rhetoric in health care policy and the potential for health care reform. *Milbank Quarterly*. 2001;79(1):35–54, III–IV.

168. Gabel JR., Hunt KA, Hurst K. When employers choose health plans do NCQA accreditation and HEDIS data count? New York: The Commonwealth Fund; 1998.

169. Derickson A. "Health for three-thirds of the nation": public health advocacy of universal access to medical care in the United States. *American Journal of Public Health*. 2002; 92(2):180–190.

170. Bilheimer LT, Colby DC. Expanding coverage: reflections on recent efforts. *Health Affairs*. 2001;20(1):83–95.

171. Davis K., Schoen C, Schoenbaum SC. A 2020 vision for American health care. *Archives of Internal Medicine*. 2000;160(22):3357–3362.

172. Kahn III CN, Pollack RF. Building a consensus for expanding health coverage. *Health Affairs*. 2001;20(1):40–48.

173. Kaiser Family Foundation. Side-by-Side Comparison of Major Care Reform Proposals. Menlo Park, CA: The Henry J. Kaiser Family Foundation; 2009:1–44.

174. Blendon RJ, Donelan K, Leitman R, et al. Health reform lessons learned from physicians in three nations. *Health Affairs*. 1993;12(3):194–203.

175. Reinhardt UE. Reorganizing the financial flows in American health care. *Health Affairs*. 1993;12(Supplement):172–193.

176. Jönsson, B. What can Americans learn from Europeans? In: *Health Care Systems in Transition: The Search for Efficiency*. Paris, France: Organization for Economic Cooperation and Development; 1990:87–101.

177. Altman SH, Cohen AB. Commentary: the need for a national global budget. *Health Affairs*. 1993;12(Supplement):194–203.

178. Ham C. Health care reform. *British Medical Journal*. 1993: 306(6887):1223–1224.

179. Reinhardt, UE. Response: what can americans learn from Europeans. In: OECD, ed. *Health Care Systems in Transition: The Search for Efficiency*. Paris, France: Organisation for Economic Co-operation and Development; 1990:105–112.

180. Levit, KR, Lazenby, HC, Braden, BR, Team, NA. National health spending trends in 1996. *Health Affairs*. 1998;17(1):35–51.

181. Saltman, RB, Figueras, J. Analyzing the evidence on European health care reforms. *Health Affairs*. 1998;17(2):85–108.

Organized Delivery Systems

Myron D. Fottler, Donna Malvey, and Keila Rooney

Multihospital systems have been redefined as multiprovider healthcare systems to incorporate structural changes in organizational arrangements and to reflect the provision of a wide range of services beyond acute hospital care. The American Hospital Association (AHA) defines a multihospital healthcare system as "two or more hospitals owned, leased, sponsored, or contract managed by a central organization."[1] This chapter will include multihospital systems, as defined by AHA's criteria, but will also cover the broader consequences of system development, including horizontal, vertical, and virtual integration, and other diversification activities. The chapter ends with a case study that looks at a large multihospital/organized delivery system.

No healthcare system in the world has undergone as much structural change as has that of the United States over the past three decades. It has been suggested that the extent and the swiftness of structural change in US hospitals are unprecedented in postindustrial society.[2] Some have characterized this change as fundamental and perhaps revolutionary. Nowhere is this more evident than in the transition to multiprovider healthcare systems. The previous cottage industry of individual, freestanding hospitals has become a complex web of systems, alliances, and networks.

The development of hospital systems in the United States initially integrated facilities horizontally, resulting in the creation of multihospital systems that provided similar acute care services in multiple locations. Later, system capability expanded through vertical integration and diversification into activities that may or may not have been related to a hospital's inpatient acute care business. More recently, expansion has reflected "virtual" integration that involves relationships based on contracts.[3] This system development reflects the transformation of multiprovider systems from providers of acute care to providers that are capable of addressing a continuum of healthcare needs.

Given this evolution and their varied arrangements and structures, multihospital systems have been redefined as organized or integrated healthcare delivery systems, the theme of this book. Thus, the following questions and issues should be addressed:

- How and why have multiprovider healthcare systems evolved and changed over time, and how are they expected to change in the future?
- How does the performance of systems compare to the performance of nonsystem organizations?
- How does the performance of not-for-profit systems compare to the performance of investor-owned systems?
- What factors are expected to contribute to profitability and success?
- Do functions such as governance or organizational structure make a difference in performance?
- What has been the impact of horizontal, vertical, and virtual integration?
- What managerial recommendations can be made concerning systems?

Healthcare System Development

A diversity of arrangements characterizes the configuration of US hospitals, including alliances, joint ventures, federations, consortiums, networks, and systems. A variety of environmental forces have shaped the delivery of healthcare services and brought about variations in the development of hospital systems. Preeminent among these forces has been the shift in the industry from an emphasis on providing hospital services to an emphasis on providing healthcare services. An aging population, the increasing demand for chronic care, and new technologies that support alternative delivery systems have focused attention on a broader spectrum of healthcare services.[4,5] Subsequent to this shift has been the recognition that the market for healthcare services is local rather than national in nature.[6,7] Indeed, industry performance has indicated that patients tend to feel allegiance to local hospitals and not to national hospital chains.[8] Thus, consumer choice at the local and regional levels has emerged as a powerful influence in the delivery of healthcare services.

The expansion of system capacity through horizontal integration, in which hospitals acquire other hospitals, has been declining, and this decline primarily has been attributed to economic forces. Specifically, rising healthcare costs, the shift to a risk-based payment system such as the prospective payment system (PPS), and other cost containment efforts and regulations have negatively influenced the horizontal growth of hospital systems. Moreover, these forces have precipitated a trend toward economic concentration, consolidation, and vertical and virtual integration in which both the production and distribution stages of health care are included.[9]

Although the economic concentration of hospitals is not a new trend and has its origins in the 1970s with the growth of investor-owned hospital systems, the shift toward a local and regional orientation is relatively new. Risk-based payment has compelled systems to consolidate, downsize, and divest because a large inventory of hospitals is no longer profitable.[10] Furthermore, government policies that in the past essentially subsidized hospital acquisitions through reimbursement of much of the acquisition cost now discourage horizontal integration by limiting reimbursement of capital expenditures for investments in facilities.[11]

Shortell has argued that most systems have formed as a defense against an increasingly uncertain, complex, and hostile environment.[12] The primary motivations for system formation have been to maintain or gain market share by becoming more competitive, to increase access to needed capital, to gain exposure to new ideas, and to further career development opportunities for system personnel. Another motivation behind industry consolidation has been the search for economies of scale and economic gain.

To understand fully the evolution of healthcare systems, it is necessary to examine both the external and the internal environments of hospitals (**Figure 2.1**). In the mid-1960s, the number of systems began to increase dramatically in all ownership categories.[13] By 1980, the number had grown substantially to a total of 267 systems. By 2001, 311 health systems existed in the United States (see **Table 2.1**).

The success and rapid expansion of horizontally organized delivery systems originated in a cost-based payment system and a price-insensitive environment that encouraged and rewarded system growth. Medicare reimbursement essentially provided coverage of costs and a reasonable return on investments. Consequently, systems could purchase high-cost, inefficient hospitals in diverse locations with little risk of failure.[14,15] In addition, investor-owned systems gained access to capital markets by being able to issue stock, and they used this financial resource to underwrite their acquisitions.[16]

Although both investor-owned and not-for-profit systems pursued horizontal integration, their methods of integration differed. Not-for-profit systems accumulated fewer hospitals per system and were less geographically dispersed, whereas their investor-owned counterparts tended to be larger, more geographically dispersed, and dominated by a few large systems.[17]

After the advent of prospective payment in the mid-1980s, organizations began to restructure, vertical integration increased, and diversification efforts focused on developing a continuum of care at the local or regional level. The failure of healthcare reform at the national level and the growing impact of managed care characterized the decade of the 1990s. As competition accelerated, organizations responded by documenting the cost and quality of the care that they provided and by creating both parent corporation–owned and virtually integrated delivery systems.[18]

Figure 2.1 details the evolution of stages in the development of multiprovider systems. In the first stage, patient/outpatient care was the "core business," and typically, two or more hospitals affiliated, consolidated services, or merged within a given market to achieve economies of scale (i.e., horizontal integration). In the second stage, the core hospital activities branched off into both forward vertical integration activities, such as physician group practices, and backward vertical integration activities, such as ownership of pharmacies and medical equipment companies. In this stage, there was relatively little coordination of activities across the system. The first two stages occurred from the mid-1960s to the mid-1980s.

The third stage involved efforts to coordinate and optimize physician primary care networks, satellite clinics, home healthcare agencies, and components of the continuum of care. However, the core business remained acute inpatient care, and the other activities generally fed

FIGURE 2.1 Environmental Factors Affecting the Healthcare Industry and Strategic Responses

External Economic, Political, and Social Environment	Internal Environment of Healthcare Organizations	Resulting Strategic Responses
Stage 1—Pre-1965 (Charitable/Technological Era)		
• Favorable reimbursement • Lack of competition • Plentiful philanthropic support • Favorable political environment • Minimal government regulation • Public support • Increasing physician and personnel specialization	• Rapid growth • Expanding technology • Rising costs • Treatment of medical disease	• Expansion/growth of autonomous, freestanding hospitals • Emphasis on community welfare
Stage 2—1965-1983 (Fee-for-Service/Cost-Based Reimbursement)		
• Substantial increase in the number of physicians • Increased competition • Decline in philanthropic support • Less favorable political environment • Government reimbursement through Medicare and Medicaid	• Slowing of individual growth • Duplication of technology • Outdated facilities • Increase in debt financing • Decline of political influence • Excess capacity • Increased rate of rising costs	• Horizontal integration • Consolidation of autonomous hospital systems • Growth of systems for the sake of growth • Debt financing of acquisitions • Diversification
Stage 3—1984-1993 (Prospective Payment)		
• Continuous hostile political environment • Less favorable reimbursement environment • Increased business and consumer concern with healthcare costs • Increased price competition • Aging population	• Lower profits • Downsizing • Job redesign • Excess capacity • Shift from inpatient to outpatient care • Decentralized decision making • Growth of professional management	• Greater differentiation of system strategies • Organizational restructuring • Vertical integration • Local and regional system orientation • Divestiture of unwanted facilities • Development of continuum of care at regional/local level
Stage 4—1993-2000 (Healthcare Reform and Managed Care Initiatives)		
• Increased competition • Increased domination by managed care organizations and other purchasers • Failed federal healthcare reform • Increase in federal and state mandates • Incremental attempts at political reform • Conflicts of managed care organizations with patients and providers	• Reengineering • Downsizing • Continued quality improvement • Continued shift to outpatient care	• Continuing organizational restructuring • Creation of both owned and virtual delivery systems • Competition based on documented cost and quality
Stage 5—Post-2000 (Consumer Choice Reshapes Managed Care)		
• Extensive consolidation of hospitals • Increased competition • Continuing federal and state mandates • Incremental attempts at political reform • Managed care losing its power to control costs • Increased consumerism and provider choice • Accelerating healthcare costs • Shifting costs to consumers • Increased bioterrorism threats • Technology to expand care delivery	• Continued downsizing • Increased measurement of clinical outcomes • Increased emphasis on patient satisfaction • Increased emphasis on disaster management and bioterrorism	• Customer service (patient orientation) • Divestiture of unprofitable units/services • A return to basic "core" services • Strategic linkages with public health infrastructure to respond to bioterrorism

Table 2.1 Multihospital Healthcare Systems in 2001 and 2006, by Type of Organizational Control

Type of Control	2001		2006	
	Number of Systems	Percent of Systems	Number of Systems	Percent of Systems
Roman Catholic church-related	45	14.5%	41	11.0%
Other church-related	11	3.5%	12	3.0%
Other not-for-profit	195	62.7%	245	64.5%
Investor-owned	55	17.7%	78	20.5%
Federal government	5	1.6%	5	1.0%
Total	311	100.0%	381	100.0%

Source: AHA Guide® 2002–2003 edition, Health Forum LLC, An American Hospital Association Company, copyright 2002; AHA Hospital Statistics, 2008 edition, Health Forum LLC, An American Hospital Association Company, copyright 2008.

or supported the acute care business. In the fourth stage, it was expected that disease prevention and/or health promotion would replace acute inpatient care as the core business for primary care. The goal of the system was to accept the risk for the health status of populations served, with incentives to keep the population well. Shortell, Gillies, and Devers believed most systems were in stage two or three in 1995.[19]

As noted in Figure 2.1, Stage 1 (pre-1965) predated the development of systems. Stage 2 (1965–1983) was a period of development and unbridled expansion of systems. Hospitals began to integrate horizontally by consolidating into organized healthcare delivery systems. Stage 3 (1984–1993) began with the implementation of prospective payment, declining system profits, downsizing, and restructuring. Prospective payment essentially reshaped the healthcare landscape by introducing price competition to the healthcare equation. It transformed hospital reimbursement for services, thereby altering financial incentives. Stage 4 (1993–2000) heralded a period of reconfiguration, rebuilding, and redesigning of systems. During this time, healthcare reform and managed care initiatives were the driving forces behind broad and sweeping changes in the healthcare industry. Chaos and creativity were the norms, as traditional boundaries disappeared and competition gave way to collaboration. The focus was on the provision of comprehensive healthcare services at the regional and local levels.

In the new millennium (Stage 5), the environment has shifted again, as managed care has loosened its control over patient access to providers. This increased access comes at a cost, however, as employers have transferred the burden of increased premium costs to their employees. The issue of increasing costs permeates throughout the healthcare environment of this stage. With 70% of healthcare costs generated by 10% of patients, health insurance plans are beginning to recognize the potential savings of fully reimbursing services dealing with preventive care and disease management by including them in their plans.[20] Healthcare systems are seeking alternative service provision mechanisms as low-cost alternatives to traditional healthcare practice methods such as telemedicine and electronic home monitoring of patients. Increased uses for information technology and innovation are essential components to system survival as health care faces a gradual loss of its share of government spending.[21] As political forces continue their quest for increased healthcare affordability, the medical marketplace struggles to meet the current demands of an aging population coupled with increasing rates of chronic illness. The climbing rates of obesity will further strain the nation's resources and require hospitals to strategize increasing their physical capacity while balancing financial constraints. Bioterrorism threats also have emerged and require a coordinated response within systems and between systems and other healthcare providers. In response to this changing environment, healthcare organizations have placed increased emphasis on patient satisfaction, consumer choice, and a customer service orientation. Strategies increasingly reflect a return to basic "core" services in an attempt to attain or sustain profitability. Yet some hospitals remain progressive by seeking to specialize in elective procedures and endeavor on profitable niches like hospital-led employer-directed programs.[22]

System Characteristics

Between 1992 and 2001, overall growth of systems was modest. In 1992, 309 systems were reported, but this number increased by only 2 systems in 2001 for a total of 311 systems. By 2008, the total number of systems had swelled to 381. Table 2.1 identifies the number of systems in 2001 and 2006 by type of organizational control. Not-for-profits continue to predominate in terms of numbers, representing about 80% of systems in 2001, but observed a small drop to 78.5% in 2006. Although there were no real changes in the overall numbers, there was a dramatic decrease in Catholic systems, which declined by 8.5%, from a total of 71 systems in 1992 to 45 systems in 2001 and 41 systems in 2006. Although investor-owned systems reported few changes in terms of numbers, these systems moved ahead of Catholic systems as the second largest category type. In 2001, investor-owned systems represented 17.7% of all systems. By 2006, investor-owned systems had gained more momentum, jumping up to 78 systems.

Table 2.2 provides a breakdown of the number of systems that owned, leased, sponsored, or contract-managed hospitals or other providers in 1992, 2001, and 2006. Although there was approximately a 5% decrease in the number of systems that owned, leased, sponsored, and contract-managed healthcare facilities in 2001, there was also a 5% increase in systems that either owned, leased, or sponsored these facilities. As such, there appears to be a trend toward more flexibility, with systems increasingly opting for "either–or" type arrangements that reflect impermanent relationships with other healthcare facilities and providers. This notion is further supported by the data collected in 2006.

Table 2.3 shows one measure of financial performance (operating margin) for both investor-owned and not-for-profit systems between 1996–2001 and 2007. For all systems, the operating margins have fallen in more recent years (1998–2007) as compared to earlier years (1996–1997). This is undoubtedly due to both increased competition in local markets and the impact

Table 2.2   Multihospital healthcare systems in 1992, 2001, and 2006

	1992 number (%)	2001 number (%)	2006 number (%)
Systems that own, lease, or sponsor	238 (77.0%)	258 (82.9%)	331 87.0%
Systems that only contract-manage	9 (2.9%)	5 (1.6%)	2 0.5%
Systems that own, lease, sponsor, and contract-manage	62 (20.1%)	48 (15.4%)	48 12.5%
Total	309 (100.0%)	311 (100.0%)	381 100.0%

Source: American Hospital Association. 2002. *2001 AHA Guide Issue*. Chicago: AHA, p. B3; AHA Hospital Statistics, 2008 edition, Health Forum LLC, An American Hospital Association Company, copyright 2008.

of the Balanced Budget Act passed by Congress in 1997 which reduced reimbursement for healthcare providers.

Table 2.3 also shows that the operating margin of for-profit systems consistently exceeds the operating margin of not-for-profit systems, although the margin is narrowing. The explanation is that the primary goal of investor-owned systems is to maximize return to stockholders. By contrast, not-for-profit systems are responsible to many more key stakeholders, whose goals may conflict. For example, eliminating unprofitable services is undoubtedly easier in an investor-owned system with a focus on profitability than in a not-for-profit system.

It is also interesting to note that the low point for operating margins for all was 1998. Between 1998 and 2001, investor-owned margins climbed significantly whereas margins for not-for-profit systems rose modestly. The reimbursement relief from the federal government from 1999 to 2001 enhanced the profit margins in investor-owned systems to a much greater degree than in not-for-profit systems. This may reflect the greater focus of investor-owned

Table 2.3   Median Hospital Operating Margin by System Status 1996–2001, 2007

System Status	1996	1997	1998	1999	2000	2001	2007
Investor-owned	20.0	13.3	2.8	3.5	8.6	10.1	4.27
Not-for-profit	4.8	4.2	1.4	2.2	1.1	1.9	3.46
All systems	7.6	5.7	1.8	2.5	2.3	3.2	3.42

Source: Data from M. Evans and V. Galloro. 2008. "Clouds gathering?" *Modern Healthcare*, June 16; D. Bellandi, B. Kircheimer, and V. Galloro. 2001. "Overall, Not Too Bad: Survey Finds Hospital System Posted a Modest Operating Profit in 2000," *Modern Healthcare*, June 4, 36–58; D. Bellandi, B. Kircheimer, and A. Sephir. 2000. "Profitability a Matter of Ownership Status," *Modern Healthcare*, June 12, 24–43; D. Bellandi and B. Kircheimer. 1999. "For-Profits Report Decline in Acute-Care Hospitals," *Modern Healthcare*, May 24, 23–34; D. Bellandi and B. Japsen. 1998. "While You Weren't Sleeping," *Modern Healthcare*, May 25, 35–56; V. Galloro and J. Piotrowski. 2002. "A Successful Operation," *Modern Healthcare*, June 3, 28–34.

systems on profitability, which caused a greater responsiveness to changing reimbursement incentives. In addition to the resolution of Columbia/HCA's problems, greater access to equity capital, greater willingness to cut unprofitable services, location in areas of high income, renegotiation of managed care contracts, and a focus on the most profitable services also may have enhanced profitability of investor-owned systems.

With the majority of hospitals belonging to systems (defined as a common corporate ownership) and most of the remaining hospitals being members of alliances of one form or another, the question of the advantages and disadvantages of independent versus freestanding hospitals is no longer relevant.[23] The "market" has spoken and it seems to be saying that independent, freestanding institutions are not competitive with systems (either owned or "virtual"). This appears to be at odds with the existing literature, which provides little evidence on the relative performance of the different arrangements (e.g., system-affiliated or independent facility), or the types of systems (e.g., those organized by hospitals, insurance corporations, or physician groups). Furthermore, a recent study of Florida hospitals by Tennyson and Fottler indicates that system hospitals have no advantage over freestanding hospitals in terms of their financial returns.[24] However, according to a Healthcare Financial Management Association (HFMA 2004) survey on hospital capital investment, the industry is advised to allocate a greater level of expenditures on plant modernization and information technology.[25] This costly initiative puts even financially sound freestanding hospitals at a distinct disadvantage and forces them to seek affiliation with multihospital systems to gain access to large sources of funding.[26]

Multiprovider systems of the 1980s, which emphasized administrative economies of scale and engaged in a variety of diversification activities, seemed to add value on almost any dimension of performance.[27] They tended to represent loose collections of hospitals that engaged in relatively unrelated diversification of services. They lacked "systemness" in that they did not behave as a system in which each operating unit understood its strategic role relative to other units of the system. Possibly, environmental and market pressures were not severe enough to require more integrative behavior at the time.

As a result, many systems have come to the realization that a system is an integrated, clinical continuum of care for a defined population with an ability to provide cost, quality, and outcome data for purposes of accountability. Understanding what a system is and being able to implement that understanding are two different things, however.

The Impact of Managed Care

Managed care has increasingly driven providers toward integration. Healthcare executives who previously were marginally aware of market share have entered into a variety of organizational arrangements that promised continued growth and survival in highly competitive managed care markets. They instituted integrative strategies aimed at improving the market and organizational powers of their system relative to those of their competitors. Montague Brown, a leading healthcare industry expert, has explained that being positioned for survival in a managed care market may represent the crown jewel of purpose of major national alliances. Furthermore, he predicted that regional multiprovider systems would be the best positioned organizations to become providers of choice for managed care or other types of direct contracting arrangements.[28] Early evidence from healthcare studies confirmed that hospitals joined local systems primarily as a competitive response.[29]

In large part, much of the impact of managed care has resulted from expectations about how managed care would reshape the healthcare industry and how organizations would respond to these changes. For example, it has been reported that in markets dominated by managed care systems, providers have pursued complete vertical integration more rapidly than in other markets because they believed it would help them compete effectively—even though there was no compelling evidence that vertical integration provided a competitive advantage.[30] Similarly, academic medical centers increasingly entered into strategic alliances and other collaborative relationships because they anticipated that integration would make them more competitive in a managed care environment and would assist them in preserving the educational and research missions of their institutions.[31] Boston's Massachusetts General Hospital and Brigham and Women's Hospital, two leading academic medical centers and fierce competitors, merged with the expectation that the resulting partnership would enable them to be more competitive on cost and quality in managed care markets. A merger typically creates possibilities for efficiencies by making it possible to consolidate hospital services such as finance and human resources, as well as to downsize clinical staffs.[32]

Managed care organizations have continued to revise the mechanisms by which they actually manage costs. They initially relied on price discounts to achieve savings; however, because price discounts did not completely control costs, managed care organizations then moved to include utilization management and capitated payment methods to achieve substantial efficiencies.[33] As a result, systems have come to expect managed care organizations to select providers who promise the most efficient and cost-effective delivery of a comprehensive range of services. Thus, competing in managed care markets requires multiprovider organizations to gain control over such things as physician practice patterns and resource utilization, because these elements play an essential role in determining cost.[34,35]

Effect on Physicians and Hospitals

Managed care has eroded the patient care market for both physicians and hospitals. In addition, physicians view managed care's intervention into day-to-day medical treatment as a threat to their autonomy and incomes.[36] Many independent practitioners have approached hospitals and medical centers, asking to be acquired or to be given employment contracts, because they have recognized that the health services market is becoming increasingly oriented toward managed care.[37] Physicians believe that hospital ownership of medical practices is preferable to managed care because this arrangement can be organized under structures that allow physicians to retain some control over medical practice.[38] In many circumstances, managed care has driven physicians and hospitals to integrate fully into single structures such as physician–hospital organizations or foundations that can gain leverage in negotiating managed care contracts or can contract directly with employers to provide medical services.

Managed care also has influenced systems to acquire and/or manage group practices. Previously, physicians actively sought integration with hospitals, although most hospitals, with the exception of larger hospitals, did not aggressively attempt to acquire group practices. When hospitals did enter into formal affiliation arrangements with physician group practices, it typically was through an employment arrangement rather than a contractual one.[39]

Although many hospitals and physicians have sought more permanent and enduring vertically integrated structures to accommodate their relationships, needs, and joint activities, others expect less permanent and more flexible relationships in the form of virtual integration. In California, for example, where unmanaged indemnity insurance no longer exists, organizational change is proceeding at an accelerated rate. In this context, complex ownership and contractual relationships with hospitals and outside specialists make up the core of an emerging healthcare delivery system based on capitated care.[40]

Effect on Systems

Many hospital systems have accelerated the development of delivery systems that are capable of providing healthcare services to a large number of people on a capitated basis. They have purchased medical clinics, other hospitals, and even prepaid managed care organizations. Some systems have aligned themselves with insurers in order to expand their markets. However, many systems have had little experience in capitated contract arrangements.[41] In addition, investor-owned systems have attempted alliances with not-for-profit systems in order to respond to the trend toward managed care.

A 2001 *Modern Healthcare* survey revealed that greater numbers of investor-owned chains were profitable compared to prior years, although losses on investments may have obscured their improvement. Merging institutions of different ownership types is not common, but it has the advantage of increasing patient volume and providing leverage that enhances negotiation for managed care contracts.[42,43]

Clearly, managed care has had a tremendous impact on health care in the United States. It has introduced incentives that call for patients to receive the appropriate type and amount of healthcare service, which generally involves settings outside the hospital.[44] Healthcare executives subsequently have adopted a different perspective regarding their viewpoint of the healthcare delivery system. They have shifted their thinking and outlook toward organizing a delivery system around other facilities, such as outpatient offices and sub- and postacute care facilities.[45] Thus, managed care has created incentives for hospitals to look for the most cost-effective means of providing healthcare services. Systems that can provide comprehensive services and can demonstrate high quality and cost-effectiveness will be "winners" in the emerging healthcare environment. Systems or individual providers that are unable or unwilling to move in this direction may well be among the "losers" over the next decade.[46]

System Integration

As systems have developed, they have evolved from horizontal, to vertical, to virtual integration. Integration is horizontal when hospitals buy other hospitals to become multihospital systems. Integration is vertical when hospitals (or other institutions) purchase or sign contracts with other healthcare organizations that are "upstream" or "downstream" from the original institution. For example, a hospital may purchase physician group practices to increase referrals to their inpatient services. Finally, virtual integration refers to horizontally or vertically integrated systems that are based primarily on a series of contracts rather than common ownership.

Corporate Structure

The existence of a corporate structure may be the most obvious characteristic that distinguishes a system hospital from a freestanding institution. Systems have an organizational structure that consists of a corporate or systemwide component and a field component of facility managers. At the institutional level, system ownership determines reporting relationships. Within investor-owned systems, the facility's chief executive officer (CEO) usually reports to a corporate officer. In not-for-profit systems, the facility's CEO may report to a hospital board of trustees, a corporate board of directors, or, less typically, to a system corporate executive.[47] With the move toward vertical integration, system organizational structure becomes even more complicated, as the linkages become incorporated into that structure.

When systems began to form there were no textbook models to follow. The investor-owned systems had already developed a corporate structure, but it was based on ownership of the majority of hospitals in the system. The not-for-profit systems learned to create structures largely as they went along.[48] As systems grew, they experienced problems with expanding corporate staffs, bureaucracy, and conflicts of interest between the corporate and field components. The potential for conflict generated is not arithmetic, it is logarithmic.[49] One study of nursing home administrators indicated that those who were a part of a system and reported to corporate officers experienced more stress and role conflict than did their counterparts in freestanding facilities.[50] Systems require managers who have superior mediation skills in order to respond to these challenges.[51]

Governance

Despite the unprecedented, rapid, and dramatic upheaval in the healthcare industry, governance of hospitals remains basically unchanged. For systems, the lack of development in governance is particularly problematic because governance must occur at a variety of levels in order to meet both systemwide and institutional needs. The presence of multiple governing boards to address multiple needs at various levels often causes conflict, enlarges the bureaucracy, and leads to power struggles. It has been suggested that systems should recognize governance on two levels: (1) the organizational or strategic level of governance where systemwide decisions and policies are considered, and (2) the operational governance level that addresses local operations of institutions and should be advisory to institutional management. The work of system facilities depends on the degree of success achieved through operational governance, so this level should be subsumed under systemwide governance.[52]

Systems have tended to rely on three models of governance. The most popular model, the parent holding company model, is also the most decentralized. Although it has a systemwide governing board, it also has a separate governing board for each institution. The second model is a modified parent holding company model, in which there is one systemwide governing board with advisory boards at the institutional level. Systems that represent large numbers of hospitals tend to use these two models. Systems affiliated with religious organizations are more likely to adopt the parent holding company model, whereas the investor-owned systems tend to favor the modified parent holding company model. The third model is the corporate model, which consists of one systemwide board with no other boards at any other level. The major advantage of this governance structure is its simplicity and clear lines of authority. Systems that have small numbers of hospitals tend to use this model; often, they are not-for-profit or public systems.[53]

The type of governance model in use has not been found to influence the strategic decision making for which systemwide boards assume responsibility. In decision making at the institutional level, however, the type of governance model appears to be influential. The parent holding company model tends to leave hospital-level decisions to the hospital governing boards, whereas the modified parent holding company model seems to give all boards equal involvement in most hospital-level decisions. The corporate model demonstrates greater involvement by the systemwide board in hospital decisions.[54]

The Joint Commission on Accreditation of Healthcare Organizations (JCAHO) has recognized the complexity of system governance and has changed its standards for governing boards accordingly. In 1986, the standards were upgraded to reflect the complex responsibilities that result from an increase in the number of boards and the dynamic relationships that exist among these boards and all levels of the organization. Specifically, if there are multiple levels of governance, the Joint Commission requires mechanisms to ensure communication and participation at all levels. In particular, these mechanisms must ensure that medical staff have the ability to communicate and participate at all levels of governance in matters involving patient care.[55]

Recent political forces have pushed for even greater board accountability to the viability and quality of care delivered by their organizations. Over the past decade boards have been preoccupied with focusing on mergers and acquisitions and on the financial and economic aspects of strategic planning. However, the judicial system is further pressuring boards to centralize on quality agendas through verdicts delivered in malpractice cases that "confirm the medical staff is responsible to the governing board for medical care quality."[56] Despite the fact that regulation and accreditation standards have changed to reflect this emphasis, boards have struggled with the task by being largely uninformed and unprepared for the depth of their role. In response, many hospitals have instituted orientation and education programs for their trustees. In 2007, the state of New Jersey escalated the issue a step further; a law was enacted that required hospital trustees to receive at least one full day of formal leadership training. Participation in similar certified training programs is likely to be financially favored by payers like Blue Cross and Blue Shield that have already announced their support of educated boards.[57] Thus, this unorthodox precedent could conceivably redefine the expectations of boards nationwide in the coming years.

The transition from hospitals to multihospital systems, to organized delivery systems, and to community care networks will require profound changes in governance.[58] The structures and processes of governance suited to one type of organization probably will not work equally well in others. Although systems have been doing a great deal of experimentation in their approaches, there are as yet no definitive models to suggest what governance structures and processes are likely to work best under differing conditions.

It is clear, however, that all board members need to understand their vision for the system, plans for future structural change, and the interactions of other systems with their governance. It is also important to build trust among all the system components by changing their internal incentives to reflect concern for system performance and by promoting communication/information exchange across all system components and levels of governance. Finally, the system's multiple boards need a clear definition of governance roles, responsibilities, and authority.

Horizontal Integration

Most systems during the 1980s could be characterized as horizontally integrated. Such systems were expected to offer hospitals several advantages:

- Increased access to capital markets
- Reduction in duplication of services
- Economies of scale
- Improved productivity and operating efficiencies
- Access to management expertise
- Increased personnel benefits, including career mobility, recruitment, and retention
- Improved patient access through geographical integration of various levels of care
- Improvement in quality through increased volume of services for specialized personnel
- Increased political power to deal with planning, regulation, and reimbursement issues

The pursuit of horizontal integration by hospitals has been attributed in part to hospitals' attempts to deal with an increasingly complex and often hostile environment that created intense financial pressures and risks that threatened institutional survival.[59] System affiliation offered hospitals opportunities to reduce or diversify certain facility-specific risks. Hospitals could gain management expertise and access to capital and improve their overall performance.

Systems were able to enhance their performance by "using size and scale to drive certain economies or to respond to certain opportunities such as competitive contracting."[60] Many of the proposed benefits of economies of scale in systems may actually be limited, as certain diseconomies of scale have been associated with extremely high corporate overhead expenditures.[61–63] According to healthcare analysts, hospital systems generally have failed to integrate fully and have been unable to perform as systems rather than as collections of facilities.[64]

The absence of shared or common institutional interests and organizational culture may contribute to systems' inability to integrate completely. Although not-for-profit systems have been more likely to select members based on commonality of missions, investor-owned systems have tended to be more sensitive to existing market conditions, the local economy, and the payer mix.[65,66] Furthermore, many hospitals have formed or joined systems to obtain access to expertise on regulatory matters and to enjoy advantages in the political environment. Affiliated hospitals can establish a political presence through name recognition, a coordinated message, and the financial ability to retain political advisors.[67,68] However, systems affiliation cannot be expected to reduce risks related to general economic conditions or the overall health care industry.[69]

Most analyses provide little support for the cost-reducing promises of horizontal integration. In cases reviewed, integration was often incorporated at an administrative level as opposed to a clinical level that may have yielded greater cost savings.[70] After comparing the 1988 performance of independent and system hospitals in California, Dranove and Shanley found that systems are no more able to exploit economies of scale than are independent hospitals.[71] They found that the benefits of horizontally integrated hospital systems are more in their ability to market themselves than in the economies they achieve.

Horizontal integration strategies dominated system development during the late 1960s, continued through the mid-1980s, and diminished in significance with the implementation of PPS and the cost reduction programs of other payers. In addition, there may actually be a saturation point for system horizontal integration, and hospital acquisition should be selective. Selection factors have been shown to include market characteristics, mission compatibility, and facility management. Thus, the potential for horizontal integration as a strategy will be limited to financing mechanisms and selective acquisitions.[72]

Vertical Integration

Diversification through the integration of clinical services transforms a horizontally integrated system into a vertically integrated one. Vertical integration involves incorporating within the organization either stages of production (backward integration) or distribution channels (forward integration) that were formerly handled through arm's-length transactions with other organizations.[73]

A vertically integrated system is described as offering "a broad range of patient care and support services operated in a functionally unified manner. The range of services offered may include preacute, acute, and postacute care organized around an acute hospital. Alternatively, a delivery system might specialize in offering a range of services related solely to long-term care, mental health care, or some other specialized area."[74] The purpose of vertical integration is to increase the comprehensiveness and continuity of care, while simultaneously controlling the channels or demand for healthcare services. Thus, vertical integration emphasizes connecting patient services with different stages in the healthcare delivery process.[75]

Vertical integration can occur through a variety of arrangements:

- Internal development of new services
- Acquisitions of another organization or service
- Mergers
- Leases or sales
- Franchises
- Joint ventures
- Contractual agreements
- Informal agreements or affiliations
- Insurance programs[76]

The advantage of a vertically integrated delivery system or network (IDS/N) is that unified ownership allows for coordinated adaptations to changing environmental circumstances.[77] In principle, vertical integration provides a unity of control and direction that allows the IDS/N to focus all the energies of the subunits on the same goals and strategies. There is a single mission statement, hierarchy of authority, and "bottom line." The unity of purpose is essential to truly manage care (as it is currently structured) and underlies the drive toward vertically integrated delivery systems that incorporate primary care physicians, specialty panels, hospitals, and managed care organizations.

If vertical integration worked in practice the way it works in principle, then markets and contracts would be rare.[78] The healthcare system could be structured as one large administered bureaucracy with centralized planning, centralized resource allocation, a single purpose, and a single process. Vertically integrated systems suffer from two weaknesses, however; incentive attenuation and influence costs. Vertical integration replaces the entrepreneurship of the owner-managed medical practice with administrative hierarchies where managers and clinicians are paid largely by salary. It also greatly increases influence costs, defined as the effect of internal struggles for control over resources by various incumbent constituencies (e.g., primary care physicians, specialists, managed care organizations, hospitals, system managers). At the extreme, the vertically integrated system or network could resemble public bureaucracies with a civil service mentality.

A careful analysis of the effects of integration shows that big, vertically integrated, investor-owned healthcare organizations are often clumsy and slow to innovate.[79] They are difficult to manage, requiring significant cash infusions and massive managerial efforts to keep their components networked. They typically act to suppress competition and are unresponsive to local communities. Consequently, the results of vertically integrated healthcare organizations have been disappointing. According to one survey, only 17% of hospitals that purchased physician practices achieved a positive return.[80] Conrad and Dowling explained the failure of vertical integration as follows: "Because many of the organizations considering vertical integration are acute hospital systems, expertise may be lacking at both the corporate and institutional levels. Yet expertise—in evaluating and negotiating . . . and in managing new services—is often the single most important ingredient in success."[81]

Diversification

Diversification strategies in the healthcare industry have mirrored the turbulence and uncertainty in the environment; they have involved introducing new services and deleting others on a trial-and-error basis. Some efforts have been more successful than others.[82] It has become apparent that diversification activities related to the hospital's core business, such as ambulatory care and physician joint ventures, tend to be more profitable than those that are only partially or totally unrelated to acute care.[83]

Regionalization

Vertical integration is consistent with the trend toward regionalization because it concentrates resources in local markets. The trend toward regionalization reflected that 99% of healthcare services delivered in the United States take place within the region in which the patient resides. Thus, systems are shifted in their focus to establish predominance in local and regional markets rather than national ones.[84]

Virtual Integration

It is difficult to manage a system that provides many different products or services in many different markets. It is impossible for managers of fully integrated systems to understand all the different products and services in their markets. For this reason, tight coupling and high degrees of vertical integration are not increasing in other parts of US industry. In fact, "decoupling" is occurring as corporations struggle to focus on their "core competencies."

It is true that healthcare providers will need to be part of a larger organization that provides a wide range of consumer and employer choices, economies of scale, cost-effectiveness, clinical quality, and service quality. It is not true that the only way to achieve these goals is through participation in a fully integrated system.

The advantages of virtual integration, that is, integration through contractual relations (more loosely coupled systems) lie in its potential for autonomous adaptation to changing environmental circumstances.[85] Organizational independence preserves the risks and rewards for efficient performance. Although coordination may result from negotiated authority, it must involve collaboration (i.e., creating new value), a dense web of interpersonal connections based on trust, and partners willing to nurture the collaborative relationship rather than simply trying to control it.

Because there is practically no hard evidence of the superiority of any one approach to structuring, it is prudent to proceed with caution. Much of the activity seen in the industry today is an imitation of the actions or presumed actions of others. The downside of all of the emphasis on new acquisitions, new enrollment, and restructuring has been that the consumer has been "lost in the shuffle." In the future, consumer choice of providers should increase rather than decrease.[86] Therefore, systems that do not provide open access to plans and broad networks of providers are at a competitive disadvantage.

In the future, it is likely to be risky for providers to rely on exclusive partnerships because the winners and losers are unknown. Rather, the emphasis should be on patient satisfaction, patient retention, flexibility, the availability of options for consumers, minimal paperwork, and multiple capitated contracts/partnerships for providers.

No one structure is necessarily the final answer. There are multiple possible paths to achieve increased integration and coordination of clinical services under managed care, and individual market dynamics will determine the appropriate level and structure of integration. Multiprovider systems face a trade-off between the advantages of coordinated adaptation through vertical integration and the advantages of autonomous adaptation through contractual networks. The current hyperturbulence and lack of definitive evidence makes it difficult to predict eventual outcomes. It also indicates the potential downside of giving up autonomy and/or making large capital investments in a vertically integrated (owned) system. The trend today, both within and outside of health care, is toward more contractual relationships and less vertical integration.

System Performance

Fear of managed care has been identified as a motivating force behind improvements in system performance. *Modern Healthcare* conducts annual surveys of multiprovider systems that provide a comprehensive view of system performance. In 1997 nonprofit systems outpaced investor-owned systems in terms of growth and profitability; by 2001 investor-owned systems were the clear winners. In 2001, investor-owned systems attributed outperforming their nonprofit counterparts primarily to downsizing and consolidation, as well as to returning to their core missions and services.[87]

From 1997 to 2001, investor-owned systems routinely reported increased profitability, whereas nonprofit systems consistently showed losses. However, the picture is more complicated than this statistic shows. For example, in 1999, despite their losses, nonprofit systems also reported increases in revenues. This meant that their labor and other operational expenses were increasing at a faster rate than revenues. Investor-owned systems, on the other hand, actually experienced a decline in their revenues, most of which resulted from selling off facilities. In addition, because investor-owned systems are responsible to their shareholders, they can be expected to shift quickly out of money-losing ventures. For example, when Medicare cuts in home healthcare payments were fully implemented in 1999, investor-owned systems divested themselves of home health services.[88]

In 2001, the negative stock market and economic problems led to modest increases for investor-owned systems and small gains for nonprofit systems, primarily because systems were unable to use their investments to cover losses. In past years, investment portfolios had provided a necessary cushion for both types of systems, which faced financial pressures from managed care and federal cutbacks. However, financial pressures are expected to continue, along with rising medical liability costs and increasing requirements for investment in information systems, technology, and plant replacement. Which type of system will fare best in the coming years? Investor-owned systems are expected to respond successfully to such challenges because of their greater access to capital and their ability to quickly divest themselves of unprofitable services and service areas. Meanwhile, nonprofit systems will most likely continue to struggle for survival because they are not able to eliminate costly services and because they often furnish the safety net for their communities.[89]

Healthcare analysts believe that, other than efficiencies in labor productivity related primarily to having fewer full-time equivalent employees and lower turnover, system hospitals have not demonstrated comparative advantages over nonsystem hospitals.[90–92] Furthermore, although system hospitals have greater opportunities to reduce their costs by sharing administrative services such as legal, data processing, and accounting services, the overhead costs involved in managing these and other activities have been extremely high. Even so, the sharing of services among system member institutions situated near each other may reduce costs by avoiding or eliminating the duplication of necessary, but marginally profitable (or unprofitable), services.[93]

Despite certain potential cost-saving benefits, primarily in the areas of purchasing and reduction of duplicate services, the creation and expansion of a system can also increase costs. As a system increases or anticipates increasing in size, its executives spend a significant amount of time on planning, policy enforcement, and related activities. They have less time available to devote to the day-to-day conduct of the system's business affairs or the delivery of healthcare services. Then the executives either overextend themselves trying to accomplish both present activities and future planning, or they hire new administrators to whom they delegate day-to-day operations. The quality of management may suffer and/or costs may rise. The better performing systems keep a very tight rein on corporate staff costs.[94]

Managed care increased administrative responsibilities, because it requires monitoring and evaluating patient satisfaction, documenting a variety of aspects of quality of care, keeping track of a variety of contractual obligations and their subsequent transaction costs, and managing the use of both clinical and administrative resources.[95] These new responsibilities called for sophisticated information systems, which were expensive. In addition, high costs may have been caused by additional administrative controls needed to manage medical resources across institutions.[96–98]

Arista Associates of Fairfax, Virginia, and Modern Healthcare magazine surveyed 141 system CEOs and examined the 17% who reported operating margins of 4% or more.[99] The survey found that these best-performing systems:

- Focus on core competencies
- Focus on quality of clinical outcomes and service, not size
- Have not become complacent in their success
- Focus on execution of details
- Focus on quality, not quantity, of physician integration
- Reduce duplication of services
- Control future growth

Another study conducted by Arthur Andersen and the National Chronic Care Consortium, based on interviews with executives from seven systems, concluded that (1) communications are vital to the success of integration; (2) a system hoping to succeed must devote sufficient staff, dollars, time, and energy to planning, preparation, and training for integration; and (3) systems must research and understand community needs, not make assumptions about their needs.[100]

A View from the Real World

Over the past two decades, hospitals, physicians, and nursing homes have rushed to merge or partner with one another, cheered on by consultants, academics, and experts who claimed that such networking was imperative for these organizations to survive in a highly competitive environment. Although each system should be considered in its unique market and contextual situation, the enormous financial, human, and clinical resources devoted to integration have not borne much fruit. Evidence of quantifiable sustained financial or clinical value is scant.[101]

Hospitals were reacting to dramatic changes in their environments by linking together into first horizontal and then vertical systems in the 1980s and 1990s. These systems took a variety of forms, from fragile and temporary alliances to full-blown mergers. During the same time period, other industries were abandoning the strategy of building large, complex, vertically integrated organizations. Major American corporations such as IBM, General Motors, and General Electric were downsizing, reducing layers, breaking up complex structures, spinning off marginally related businesses, outsourcing necessary but marginal functions, and refocusing on their "core competencies."

Healthcare organizations have now followed suit in order to keep up with increased competition. The horizontal and vertical shrinkage trend that now defines the healthcare culture has been coined as "flattening," indicative of eliminating levels of management and increasing the span of control up to threefold with an extended degree of autonomy as a result.[102] The leaner organizational charts allow for more efficient communication and faster decision making, as well as more responsive dispersement of company resources.[103]

Integration Successes

Ten years ago hospitals were acquiring physician practices as fast as they could. Then, one after another, they started losing money on them. Many have now decided to dump the groups, forget integration, and just run the hospitals.

Others, like Advocate Healthcare, have stayed the course.[104] Advocate made a financial turnaround because it did not treat physician groups like hospital departments. Instead, the system brought in people to run them who are dedicated to the building of physician group practices and know how to run that business. They focus on the operations of the office where health services are delivered rather than how many patients are referred to other parts of the system. Advocate, and other systems that have been successful with integrating physician practices, have gone back to basics: billing, training employees appropriately, writing clear policies and procedures, and maintaining basic management systems. The common themes among those who are performing better than average with integration are setting realistic goals, obtaining physician comments to the system, and managing according to a formal plan.

The creation and maintenance of a strong physician culture through adherence to a clear mission, vision, values, physician involvement, and service was another key to Advocate's success.[105] It runs the group of physician practices like a group practice, as if the physicians are private practitioners. The physicians' income is in proportion to how much revenue they bring in. Advocate now has three separate and distinct group practices, each with separate management teams and physician governance. They have tried to create a culture in which the needs of the group practice are more important than the needs of individual physicians. Although the three have somewhat different cultures, the common elements are standardized billing methodologies, one single information system, and one management system consisting of financial reporting, risk management, purchasing, and human resources.

Wisconsin's two-hospital ThedaCare health system also views its 100 physician primary care practices as an essential part of the organization's fabric.[106] Decentralized management empowers physicians to make their own business decisions, which has resulted in a fiscally strong physician practice. Physicians are provided with incentives to meet goals for outcomes as well as financial performance, because compensation is based on productivity.

Integration Failures

Most of the practitioner literature talks about system successes, but the reality is that there have been many failures. Recent research, in fact, has suggested that hospitals and hospital systems are perilously close to bankruptcy in the not-too-distant future. Market competition and managed care pressures combined with misguided strategies have contributed to the potential for financial disasters. There is some evidence that hospitals systems, in particular, may do better at the local market level where they can acquire the necessary leverage for successful negotiations with managed care plans.[107]

However, it is probably more realistic to assume that these failures derive from a variety of problems and factors that have led to failures in nonhealthcare organizations as well. For example, Enron, which in 2002 exploded into the pages of history by almost causing the collapse of the stock market, illustrated the moral and financial failings of a weak and corrupted corporate governance structure. In the healthcare industry, there is also evidence that organization and governance may have contributed to failures, or at least declining performance of systems.

The push toward integration of healthcare facilities has resulted in the adoption of more corporate forms of governance and management. As with business corporations, corporate governance structures create complexity associated with large bureaucracies. The result is often organizational ambiguity, whereby roles and responsibilities are not clearly specified and due diligence and monitoring go by the wayside. Two real-world healthcare failures provide interesting examples. Allegheny Health Education and Research Foundation (AHERF) is an example of a failure of a nonprofit system that suffered from severe governance and organizational problems. Allina Health System in Minneapolis presents an example of an investor-owned system that experienced similar problems, but appears to be on the road to recovery thanks to reorganization and the establishment of new governance structures.

The most conspicuous example of system failure is the collapse of AHERF. AHERF was established in 1983 and subsequently became one of the nation's largest nonprofit multiprovider systems. In 1998 AHERF also became the nation's largest nonprofit healthcare bankruptcy. Although AHERF's failure has been attributed to a variety of factors, clearly the organization and reorganization that occurred as the system evolved created bureaucratic layers of diffused responsibility and accountability. The end result was minimal financial oversight throughout the system.[108,109]

Allina Health System, similar to AHERF, experienced tremendous success initially as it forged a system that included integrated hospital systems and a health plan under one corporate umbrella. But an 18-month federal investigation found Allina to be out of control, with excessive spending on such things as corporate travel and entertainment, overpayments to consultants, minimal oversight activities, and conflicts of interest between the system hospitals and the health plan divisions. Allina has subsequently reorganized, spinning off its health plan, and now each organization has a separate governing board.[110]

Catholic Healthcare West, a San Francisco–based system, which is also the nation's third largest Roman Catholic healthcare provider, is implementing an ambitious reorganization plan in an effort to restore profitability, having lost almost $900 million since 1997. The reorganization focuses on streamlined governance systems and centralized management, and is expected to save approximately $100 million annually. For example, the reorganization removes middle layers of governance and management and restores control to a system that has experienced many strategic missteps such as acquiring physician groups. It also restores the focus of the organization to its mission and core services.[111]

Human Resources Management

Because healthcare systems are exceedingly complex and diverse organizational arrangements, human resources management may be among their greatest challenges. These systems require significant numbers of highly skilled and specialized personnel at a variety of levels. However, systems also offer opportunities not found in nonsystem hospitals. They can develop staff-sharing programs between hospitals that not only reduce personnel expenses, but also provide the potential for quality improvements. In addition, systems may have name recognition that facilitates recruitment of personnel. A comprehensive personnel data bank can provide system members with a pool of qualified applicants. Systems also represent variety, mobility, and job security for employees who can move to different jobs within the system.

The development of career ladders within a system can enhance the system's ability to attract and retain personnel. Promotions and transfers can occur without the employee exiting the system. A corporate office can also provide individual facilities with human resources expertise that they would not be able to afford otherwise. Finally, representing large numbers of employees can facilitate the development of more comprehensive and less expensive benefits packages that are attractive both to employees and to the system's budget.[112]

During 1992, system downsizing contributed to the increased profitability of both investor-owned and not-for-profit systems. Downsizing may be easier to manage in a system hospital than in a freestanding facility, because systems have more opportunities to move staff around within the system and, thus, are better able to protect employees' economic security. The stability of employment at one facility within the system can provide job openings for employees displaced by staff reductions at another system facility.[113]

Employees in systems, however, do face the stress of being exposed to the effects of vertical and horizontal integration. Almost no research has investigated the effect of mergers, acquisitions, and other strategies on employees, nor is there a human resources model to deal with the effects of system development on employees. Human resources managers must deal with system changes and ensure that employees are recognized as assets within the system.[114]

Compensation for system executives reflects the complexity and responsibility of system management. Multihospital system executives earn more than their counterparts in freestanding hospitals and have continued to earn more rapid salary increases along with cash incentives and other perks.[115] Systems also find advantages in reduced CEO turnover. CEOs have high-risk relationships with medical staff and boards, and they often lose their jobs because of failing relationships. In a system, the CEO can move to another facility, and the system does not lose an important management resource.[116]

One of the major challenges for a system is to align the interests of physicians with those of the system and promote physician participation.[117] Physicians may have the greatest opportunities to influence standards of care in systems. Investor-owned systems, in particular, have promoted physician participation in governance.[118] Yet, physician loyalties often are associated with the individual facility rather than with the larger system. Increasing the numbers of physician administrators within the system, increasing the numbers of physicians on corporate boards, and improving communication with physicians may improve physician loyalty.[119]

The most profitable and efficient systems appear to operate with fewer people on their management staffs and pay higher than average salaries to their employees. Financially successful systems have reported spending about one third more on human resources, planning, marketing, and public relations than do their lower performing counterparts.[120] In theory, these advantages should exist for all systems. In practice, many systems restrict themselves to only certain subcategories of personnel. For example, some religious organization–associated systems require or prefer their executives to be practicing members of the religious organization. This obviously restricts the talent pool, as does the practice of paying "below the market" in systems affiliated with religious organizations.

In addition, the development and enforcement of appropriate standards of professional qualifications and job performance are crucial to the success of systems. The development and operation of a system are complex and require significant numbers of highly skilled and specialized personnel. The system needs to set and enforce appropriate standards of qualification and performance and then recruit individuals who can meet these standards. If this is not done, the anticipated advantages will not be achieved.

Financial Management

Finances have to be centralized in a system. When seeking long-term debt or equity funds, investors are likely to insist on involving all of the related organization's assets. The system needs to approve budget, capital expenditures beyond a given amount, sale or purchase of property, and changes in rate structures.

System hospitals vary in the financial responsibilities of CEOs for capital management. Typically, CEOs of individual institutions in investor-owned systems have a reduced role in creating capital; that function normally resides with corporate officers. In both investor-owned and not-for-profit systems, expenditures that extend beyond yearly budgets routinely require corporate approval. Furthermore, the capital approval process may differ according to system ownership. Investor-owned hospitals tend to rely on authorization from the corporate office, and not-for-profit systems usually require approval from both the hospital-level and systemwide governing boards.[121] The success of capital management influences the cost and pricing structure and ultimately the ability of the facility to be competitive within its own defined market segment;[122] therefore, capital allocation has a prominent position in system management.

Allocating Capital

The traditional capital allocation approaches, which focus on discounted cash flow, net present value, and internal rate of return, may be inappropriate for multihospital healthcare systems. For systems, shaping capital structure involves a systemwide vision and the integration of local and corporate needs in a way that extends beyond the normal capital budget process.[123] The system includes different facilities that have different needs and face different risks. Several facilities can be located in markets with different financial performance trends and different future potentials, as well as widely diverse facility, management, and medical staff characteristics.[124] A multifactored model that incorporates varying needs and risks, and originates in the capital asset pricing model, can be derived to allocate capital among a variety of member institutions.[125]

Of particular importance to systems is the concept of a system-level mission fund. A member institution whose survival was in jeopardy could receive a significant subsidy from the system to continue its mission. As in a single institution, systems can establish allocations to mission activities based on either an ongoing cash flow subsidy or an endowment model. Often, a combination approach can be employed.[126]

Perhaps the most distinctive and important economic advantage of a system in terms of its capital allocation strategy is the system's ability to minimize the amount of aggregate safety stock that is required to protect the system. Safety stock represents a powerful advantage that reflects a system's ability to reduce or even eliminate specific risks to individual facilities through diversification of risk across multiple facilities. Thus, as the number of facilities in the system increases, the importance of a single facility's performance declines, and the contribution to safety stock can also be reduced. For systems, this reduction in safety stock requirements frees capital for allocation at other levels within the system and represents a substantial economic benefit.[127]

Systems should also focus on hospital growth pools that are similar in conceptualization to growth pools at the individual level, but include both system-level and hospital-level risk pools. After making all allocations, systems should assign the remaining capital to this pool in order to provide funding for system-level initiatives such as vertical integration and other diversification activities.[128]

Because the capital allocation process in a system involves both corporate and facility participation, it requires the support of a strong system culture; communication among all participants in the process; an incentive system that associates hospital management's compensation with the overall performance of the system, as well as the individual performance of the facility; appropriate management and financial systems; an effective budgeting process; and an implementation plan.[129]

Financial Difficulties within a System

Bankruptcy presents special problems for systems and their members. "When dealing with a financially troubled hospital that is part of a multihospital system, the problems seem to multiply geometrically."[130] Legal and practical problems arise from the existence of multiple boards and overlapping memberships on these boards. Fiduciary obligations of board members can conflict, especially when an action appropriate for one institution may not be beneficial to the system. Board members with multiple loyalties can be disruptive. Furthermore, statutes and case law of a particular state may support the community or individual hospital interests over the system interests.[131]

Systems have earned higher bond ratings than freestanding institutions and have shown stability in ratings over time, both important considerations for systems. This performance has been attributed to a system's ability to diversify risk and size. Rating agencies tend to measure successful system performance by centralized operations and mechanisms for monitoring planning, budgeting, and capital expenditures of system members.[132]

Systems have the potential to increase interest earnings through a cash sweep, a technique designed to eliminate the time lag between receiving and investing funds. It involves a daily electronic withdrawal of funds from all hospital operating accounts and the placement of these funds in one central account where the interest begins accruing immediately. This technique allows the system to eliminate the problem of idle cash in local banks.[133]

Systems also have access to pooled financing that permits a member institution to use financial resources that would be otherwise unavailable. The financial markets have appeared to favor systems as sounder credit risks than independent freestanding facilities. Empirical evidence indicates that systems have generally received higher credit ratings than most independent hospitals.[134] There can be disadvantages to this type of financing, however. Member institutions may have to submit their assets as collateral, and the system, overall, may find that it is subordinating its long-term financial goals and depleting its assets in its efforts to strengthen the financial position of weaker, less responsible member institutions.[135] The stronger facilities may be forced to pledge or otherwise encumber their assets to support the debt-financed operations and activities of the system. The separate long-range plans and goals of stronger member institutions may be subordinated and harmed to shore up other system institutions and to honor pledges and guarantees.[136]

Financially weaker institutions within the system may incur even greater costs if the system functions inefficiently or becomes overleveraged. High interest, debt service costs, and fees for system corporate services may negatively affect the survival prospects of weaker institutions to a greater degree than the more stable units.

Management Innovation

The upheaval in the healthcare environment has created a variety of pressures for managers, who are now expected to contain costs without jeopardizing quality of care, downsize while simultaneously increasing productivity, and maintain good relationships with medical staffs that have grown increasingly wary of management interference in patient care issues. As expectations for what managers can accomplish increase, so does the demand for managerial innovation. Given the growth of systems and the complexity of these organizations, it is important that these systems promote managerial innovation.

Systems have the organizational resources to encourage managerial innovation. Whereas freestanding hospitals are connected only through ad hoc relationships, systems have the benefit of group norms and more formal relationships that can be helpful in implementing innovation. Moreover, systems have standardized communication channels that promote the diffusion of innovation. Mature systems, in particular, are likely to foster managerial innovation. As a system matures, it recognizes the importance and value of communication and works to build channels and mechanisms that encourage the sharing of information. Mature systems also usually have a larger resource base from which to implement new programs.[137]

Technology Assessment

With the rapid increase in technology development and pressures to contain costs without decreasing the quality of healthcare services, institutions are focusing attention on evaluating new technologies. Unlike single facilities, systems must address the needs of multiple facilities that are frequently in multiple locations. Thus, decisions on technologies can occur at the interregional level and involve broader standards of assessment. When the organization extends beyond the local community, community standards may not be appropriate.[138]

The dilemma for systems depends on the extent of decentralization within the organization. A highly centralized system can assist individual hospitals in technology assessment, but the resulting guidelines for adopting or implementing the new technology may be inconsistent with community standards. A decentralized system, on the other hand, can allow local facilities to assess technology within the context of the facility's environment. This approach, however, can lead to expensive duplication.

Risk Management

Systems are positioned to take advantage of legislation that regulates financing mechanisms for insurance. Increasingly, systems are obtaining liability and other insurance coverages through alternative methods of financing. In particular, risk retention groups, a financing mechanism authorized by the Federal Risk Retention Act of 1986, offer systems unique opportunities for a reliable and stable source of liability protection. These groups are essentially insurance companies formed by institutions with similar interests, such as hospitals, to provide any casualty coverage, except workers' compensation. All policyholders must also be stockholders. Unlike traditional insurance companies, which must conform to the regulations of each state in which they operate, risk retention groups are able to operate nationwide once licensed in one state.

Captive insurance companies, another alternative to traditional insurance companies, write coverage for only one employer or one group of employers. Seven states have created tax laws that allow systems to take advantage of this arrangement.[139]

Marketing

Although little is known about the practice of marketing in systems, a study of marketing in multihospital systems revealed minimal differences between investor-owned systems and not-for-profit systems.[140] Marketing staffs were larger in investor-owned systems, however, where marketing responsibilities are more likely to be formally specified within the organization chart. The larger staffs tended to be associated with a decentralized approach to marketing. In contrast, not-for-profit systems reported smaller marketing staffs and employed a more centralized reporting structure for the marketing function. Overall, investor-owned and not-for-profit systems demonstrated remarkable similarities in patterns of influence over marketing mix, the status of marketing information systems, and attitudes toward marketing. The move by not-for-profit systems to a more aggressive and bottom-line orientation may have made marketing differences of the two systems less distinctive.

It has become evident in marketing that most hospital markets remain local or regional in nature. Local and regional systems have higher levels of market control in distinct areas than do larger, more geographically dispersed investor-owned systems.[141] The trend toward system strategies that focus on regional and vertical integration is likely to influence marketing efforts in systems.

Information Systems

Increasingly, systems are facing new information requirements to accommodate strategies that involve downsizing, reorganization, restructuring, and divestitures, as well as demands by payers for information on the costs of healthcare services. The management of information within systems must facilitate communication between a diversity of operations and across a variety of facilities.[142] In systems, the trend is toward centralizing information systems, with information systems managers reporting either to the CEO or to executive officers in charge of operations or finance. These managers typically face expanded responsibilities that include telephone systems, management engineering, and data communications. In addition, they have increasingly become involved in the implementation of alternative delivery systems through the development of systemwide clinical and managerial information systems. The growth of information systems management within hospital systems reflects the growing requirements and information needs of diversification and integration strategies.[143]

Healthcare systems linking hospitals, physicians, insurers, employers, and others form the foundation of most healthcare reform proposals. Shared information on health outcomes and costs of care will help identify and encourage the most efficient forms of care. This requires the development of a health information network.[144] Such an information network would help to direct patients to the most appropriate settings and reduce redundancies.

In-Depth Case Study: Southeast Medical Center

The following case study involving a large organized delivery system exemplifies many of the issues described earlier in this chapter.

History and Evolution

Southeast Medical Center (SMC; a pseudonym) was established as a public hospital in the 1920s, just before the Depression. Located in the Southeast, a $1 million bond financed the 250-bed facility. Major expansion projects in the 1950s increased the hospital's size to 600 beds. Formal affiliation with the local university's College of Medicine residency program in the 1970s further expanded capacity. Thus, SMC became a public academic health center and subsequently assumed multiple missions of patient care, teaching, and research. Capital improvement programs were conducted during the 1970s, and in 1982, a massive renovation and construction project ($160 million) added 550 beds to the facility. In the 1980s, a 59-bed freestanding rehabilitation center was opened adjacent to the hospital, and a physicians' office building was constructed next to the hospital. Medical helicopters were also acquired in 1989, expanding SMC's trauma services. In addition to serving as a regional provider for trauma, SMC also furnishes burn, neonatal, and transplant care for the region.

Responsibility for governance of SMC has shifted over the years. In the early years of operation, a hospital board ran SMC. In the 1940s, the city was given direct control over the hospital. In the 1980s, the state legislature created a public hospital authority (to be appointed by the county commission) to govern the hospital. In the 1990s, the hospital's board of trustees voted to turn operations of the hospital over to a private, not-for-profit corporation (501c-3), the SMC Corporation. However, oversight for charity care remained with the county's hospital authority. The SMC Corporation is directed by a 15-member board of directors and essentially manages the organized delivery system through a lease arrangement with the county hospital authority.

Today, SMC is a private, not-for-profit academic health center that is accredited by JCAHO. It also serves as the primary teaching hospital for the local university. Approximately 1100 private and university-affiliated attending physicians and more than 400 resident physicians in the university's College of Medicine residency program serve the community's medical needs. SMC also serves as the clinical site for associate, baccalaureate, and graduate nursing programs for the university and community colleges.

SMC serves as a regional and international referral service with more than 800 acute care beds. SMC has established community centers in a variety of locations, which has created increased access. In addition to specialized medical services, SMC is committed to providing community resources for education, information, and programs aimed at helping residents stay fit and healthy. Four out of ten patients that passed through the SMC's door came from outside the county.

SMC also operates an HMO health plan for charity care patients. In 1991, the County Commission established the SMC Health Plan to operate as a Medicaid HMO or insurance healthcare plan for the poor. The plan reimburses SMC on a case-by-case basis for medical services, but it also negotiates discounted rates and costs with the hospital. During the early 1990s SMC's payment from the health plan dropped substantially. In 1996, the program was under a freeze by the state and could not enroll participants for more than a year.

Thus, SMC is not just the hospital—it is a comprehensive organized delivery system that also includes facilities distinct from the hospital (i.e., SMC Health Plan). In addition, SMC ambulatory care centers are located throughout the county. SMC was the only public hospital in a metropolitan area with a population of one million or more that received no public subsidy. Most citizens believe that SMC was subsidized by their taxes. In 1971, the County Commission agreed to supplement hospital revenues with property taxes. In 1985, the county commissioners passed a quarter-percent sales tax to fund indigent care. The tax was repealed in 1987. In 1991, the county instituted a one-half percent sales tax to fund indigent care at all hospitals in the county, including SMC.

In sum, while SMC receives no public subsidy, it does receive a portion of the half-cent sales tax which depends on the preferences of the county commissioners each year. Unlike a direct subsidy, no public money is ever guaranteed.

As an academic health center (AHC) SMC has multiple, conjoined missions of teaching, research, and patient care. While providing patient care for approximately 40% of the nation's poor, AHCs are struggling to find a competitive position in today's rapidly changing healthcare environment. Until recently, they have enjoyed a privileged position atop the healthcare pyramid as a niche provider of tertiary services. With the growth of managed care and reductions in government funding, the ability of AHCs to compete is being drastically undercut.

It is widely recognized that multiple missions of teaching, research, and patient care contribute to the production of costly clinical services that are inconsistent with the demand for less expensive services in today's healthcare environment. The majority of the services that AHCs provide are now available elsewhere, such as local community hospitals and specialty private medical practices. Furthermore, it is estimated that roughly 70% of their clinical services can be provided elsewhere at a lower cost. It is believed, for example, that AHCs are approximately 30% more expensive, on a case-mix-adjusted basis, than their nonteaching competitors.

As a result, AHCs are losing ground to other hospitals and medical practices. They have become providers of a small number of expensive high-tech services involving unique and complex care. However, they continue to be the predominant providers of the nation's charitable care. As an AHC, SMC reflects these trends. For example, SMC's organ transplant center and burn unit are unique high-cost services that account for fewer than 2% of the patients treated at SMC each year.

SMC Leadership

In October 1994, the CEO of SMC abruptly resigned. A former county administrator assumed management of SMC on an interim basis. In 1996, SMC selected a new CEO and president. The new CEO left his current job as director of one of the largest public hospital systems in the United States because he had opposed privatization of that city's hospitals. Nonetheless, shortly after coming to SMC, the new CEO began laying out plans for privatization, and at a forum on the future of public hospitals, he publicly announced that privatization was the best path for many public hospitals, including his own, SMC.

Public hospitals deliver a disproportionate share of charity care compared with their private counterparts. Because the number of public hospitals is decreasing, either by conversion or closure, there is concern about where care to the poor will be provided. From 1985 to 1995, the number of public hospitals in SMC's state dropped from 57 to 29. Eight of these hospitals closed and 20 converted to private institutions.

In 1997, the new CEO explained that SMC could only decide its ownership status after it decided who its partners would be and whether it wanted primarily to be a community hospital, a teaching hospital, or a county charity hospital, and "we don't know that yet." One month later, he would become an advocate for privatization without identifying partners or articulating what it was SMC primarily wanted to be.

The following potential benefits of privatization were identified prior to conversion:

- Economic freedom—Private, not-for-profit hospitals can borrow and spend money more easily than public ones, which need government approval. Conversion could make SMC more competitive in the local market.
- Reduced tax burden—In theory, a more competitive hospital would require less help from state and local taxpayers to stay in the black.
- Reduced regulatory burden—Freedom from state public record laws would assist in strategic planning.

- Less political turmoil—Public hospital boards often get bogged down in politics. Private boards, which operate out of the limelight, generally can make decisions without such intense political pressure.
- Enhanced ability to enter into joint ventures—Essentially, it will become legal for the private institution, SMC, to partner with others, such as a group of doctors, to jointly develop and own ambulatory clinics and other outpatient facilities.
- Economic benefits—SMC could receive much lower interest rates from the bond market.
- Enhanced ability to raise private funds—SMC would be more appealing to potential donors as a private, not-for-profit hospital than as an arm of local government.

Potential disadvantages included the following:

- Change in mission—A private SMC might not meet the community's needs the same way a public one must. The hospital could reduce its commitment to needed services such as its burn center and trauma unit, which lose money.
- Reduced charity care—SMC provides millions of dollars in free care to poor and uninsured residents. Some indigent patients might find medical care tougher to get if the hospital went private.
- Less public scrutiny—Private hospitals do not necessarily have to comply with the state's open government laws, making it tougher for the community to keep tabs on their successes and failures.

Table 2.4 contains the results of a public opinion poll regarding the privatization of SMC. Respondents favored keeping the hospital publicly owned by a 3 to 1 ratio. However, the poll did not attempt to learn whether respondents understood the differences between public and private ownership.

The Strategic Plan: Move and Rebuild, 1997–2002

The strategic plan for SMC centered on privatization; that is, converting SMC to a private, not-for-profit corporation, Newco Health Sciences Center, Inc. All other strategic initiatives were based on SMC's conversion to private ownership. The strategic initiatives of the plan were:

- The 1.5 million square foot facility downtown will be demolished.
- A new 450-bed hospital and research complex will be built near the university.

Approximately $100 million will be raised from private donations to fund the new construction. This would address problems of SMC's aging physical plant. Also, the location near the university is preferable because downtown is vulnerable to severe weather disasters such as storms and hurricanes.

- The move near the university will require an estimated $100 million in private funds as well as approval from state healthcare officials to transfer the Certificate of Need (CON) to the new facility. It should be noted that other growing academic health centers (Portland, Oregon; Birmingham, Alabama; and University of Florida) were unable to raise this much money in private funds.

Table 2.4 Results of a Local Newspaper Poll, conducted March 23, 1997

Opinion on Going Private	
Should remain public	74%
Favor privatization	13%
Don't know	13%
Support for Remaining Public	
Non-white	88%
White	74%
African American	96%
Concern about Privatization	
Somewhat concerned	34%
Very concerned	28%
A little concerned	18%
Not concerned	17%

- Profits from the sale of the current SMC site downtown will be used to create and/or expand satellite clinics around the county.

The new CEO predicted that SMC would go out of business by the year 2005 unless this plan was adopted. Furthermore, he projected a $14.3 million profit by 2005 if the plan were implemented. The former SMC president asked the new CEO to explain what would be a fallback plan in the event things didn't go as planned. The new CEO responded that none existed. Alternatives to privatization had been considered, but none were acceptable.

The unacceptable alternatives to privatization included:

- selling the hospital to a private for-profit corporation
- closing the hospital
- asking for a public bailout in the form of a tax subsidy

In addition, the "Shands Model" was held out as a possible future for SMC as a private hospital. The Shands Model refers to Florida's Shands Hospital, which hit bottom in the late 1970s. As a public academic health center, Shands couldn't afford to make needed safety improvements or hire enough talented workers. Because lawmakers never provided the money executives believed was needed to run a top health center, Shands Hospital converted to a private, not-for-profit corporation in 1980. Shands ran a budget surplus that year and experienced 17 consecutive years of "record-breaking" financial performance. Privatization was credited with turning things around because it freed the hospital from political and financial constraints. SMC officials and board members who supported converting SMC to private status used the Shands Model as a reference. However, Shands, unlike SMC, receives a substantial state subsidy of approximately $10 million annually.

Financial Pressures and Charity Care

Much of the impetus for SMC's conversion was financial. According to the new CEO, SMC was not likely to survive financially as a public institution. He predicted a $31 million loss by 2001 if the hospital's governing board failed to make the hospital private. The auditors, who were retained to verify accuracy of these figures, put the number closer to $44 million. Under a worst-case scenario, the auditors said losses could reach $70 million. Clearly, the new CEO was not exaggerating the precarious financial future facing SMC.

SMC lost market share in the county every year since 1992 (dropping from 23.4% to 15.7%). More than half of SMC's beds were empty each night, and SMC continued to see fewer indigent, Medicare, and Medicaid patients than its competitors. Although SMC's revenues grew by $7 million between 1992 and 1996, expenses increased by $31 million, and annual net income dropped from $14 million to a loss of $46 million. Cash reserves also dropped substantially.

One of the most contentious issues that surfaced in the debate over privatization was the impact on the indigent care mission. Many worried that SMC, as a private entity, would not retain the same commitment to care for the poor and uninsured. Similar fears had sunk previous attempts to privatize SMC in 1990. This time, assurances were made by SMC's president, officials, and others that the hospital's mission would not change because of ownership. SMC's commitment to indigent care would remain a core mission and top priority. Furthermore, the County Hospital Authority would legally retain oversight authority for charitable care. Yet questions were raised about the public hospital authority's ability to carry out the state-mandated mission to serve the poor if SMC went bankrupt. The lease arrangement was also questioned because it did not specify how good, accessible, or extensive the charity care must be.

Despite these unanswered questions, the county officials approved SMC's request to become a private, not-for-profit corporation on the strength of the argument of SMC's CEO that such a move would preserve the hospital's commitment to charity care.

Less than two years after the vote to privatize SMC, the new CEO testified under oath that caring for the poor was no longer SMC's top priority. County officials now admit that they should have done more than rely on his promise—they should have (1) created an effective method for overseeing the hospital's contractual obligation to treat the poor, and (2) determined what sanctions or punishment would be used if SMC violated the lease agreement. A private SMC, without a commitment to serving the indigent, would place an additional burden on the county, which is required by state law to provide health care for poor people.

The Aftermath of Privatization

Ironically, in its final year as a public institution, SMC showed a profit of more than $4 million. As a private hospital, its losses have increased dramatically from 1997 to 2000. Unexpected losses were not part of the strategic plan to "move and rebuild." The CEO predicted a $7.2 million profit for SMC in its first year as a private hospital, but the hospital lost nearly $6 million in the first two months. SMC and its parent company lost $12.7 million that first year—$11.5 million on the hospital and $1.2 million on the health plan. Confronted with these losses, the

CEO continued to argue that SMC was on the right course. In addition, he and his staff attributed the losses to forces outside the hospital's control, including the Federal Balanced Budget Act, which reduced hospital funding, and an increase in the number of patients served by managed care in the region.

However, it turns out that the hospital's most significant losses were the result of the hospital's inability as a private corporation to retain "lien authority" and essentially be first in line to collect money from the accident victims it treated. Lien authority did not automatically transfer to the hospital when it converted to a private corporation. The county attorney, who now represents the public hospital authority, warned that the loss of lien authority could significantly cost SMC in incollectable revenue—as much as $20 million annually. The lien authority matter was raised prior to conversion, but had been dismissed by the new CEO, his staff, and consultants as not being a potential problem.

SMC was now mired in financial, political, and legal problems. Employee layoffs were anticipated, but multimillion-dollar losses were not. Many critical issues remain unresolved following SMC's conversion. For example, in order to sell the land on which the current hospital stands, the county would have to pay for demolition as well as removal of asbestos and hazardous waste cleanup. In addition, it has become clear that many important issues had been overlooked in estimating the impact of privatization. The hospital's loss of lien authority as a collection tool has led to unexpected poor financial performance and projections of major future losses (i.e., $20 million annually) for SMC. In addition, because the hospital had used lien money to help cover the cost of emergency care for trauma victims, some worried that SMC would be forced to reduce its trauma services. SMC officials now say the lien authority is crucial to fiscal turnaround.

In addition, when SMC went private it lost the financial protection that government agencies enjoy from lawsuits (litigation damage cap). Although legislative remedies are being pursued in an attempt to restore lien authority for SMC, the resolution of this issue appears elusive for the time being. The County Commission appears unlikely to grant SMC lien authority.

Indigent care clearly slipped as a top priority for SMC and became merely one of many priorities. In addition, the move near the university is on hold. SMC also explored buying other hospitals, the price of which could reach $200 million. How the purchase of these hospitals fit with the strategic plan was never explained.

Finally, SMC was not able to keep its meetings secret despite conversion. There has been intense media scrutiny, and local newspapers are suing SMC in order to open the hospital's records. Furthermore, the State Supreme Court recently ruled that (1) privately leased hospitals cannot meet in secret and cannot keep records from the public, and (2) it is illegal to transfer authority from a public to a private board in an effort to avoid the sunshine laws—essentially what SMC did.

The College of Medicine began to be concerned about how it would train medical students and resident physicians if its main teaching hospital could not survive. The patient census was dropping, employees were being laid off, and morale was deteriorating. The hospital began to look like a dinosaur on the brink of extinction in a hostile healthcare environment. Could a multiprovider teaching hospital and trauma center survive in this region?

The New Plan and New Leadership

In 1999, the physician leadership met to lay out a plan to show the community why the hospital was so essential. Local political leaders and members of the media were invited to view the hospital and its various programs one at a time. These individuals came, listened, wrote, and called their colleagues. The community became aware of the value of a robust and healthy multiprovider system. The Chamber of Commerce, the County Commission, and the County Legislative Delegation worked together to save SMC.

After a consultant's review, these groups spearheaded legislation that ultimately improved reimbursement for indigent care for hospitals across the state, including SMC. During that time, the SMC governing board selected another CEO with a mandate to turn the hospital around. This "turnaround" CEO went to work repairing morale, bringing in a new administration team, and assigning a broad range of tasks to existing and talented administrators. He met with employees on all three shifts, listened, and dealt with issues. Business practices improved dramatically. Managed care contracts were renegotiated. Patient- and physician-friendly operations became the mantra.

As operations improved, more physicians and patients came and the census increased. Admissions, ER visits, and surgeries all increased dramatically. Most of the increased occupancy has been in tertiary care. The improved fiscal viability allowed for the development of new programs (i.e., lung transplants and liver transplants). New state-of-the-art equipment was installed and the physical plant repaired. Finally, the hospital has not diminished its safety net healthcare services for the medically indigent.

Lessons Learned

This organized delivery system has experienced many ups and downs over the years as SMC's priorities have shifted. The leadership team in the mid-1990s tried to totally privatize the system and focused on legal and organizational restructuring rather than the core mission of patient care. This restructuring was in response to pressure from politically oriented board members who brought in a CEO specifically to privatize the hospital. The privatization has been a mixed blessing, with many unanticipated negative consequences. One of the major consequences of privatization, which negatively impacted revenue, was SMC's inability (as a private corporation) to retain lien authority to collect money from accident victims.

When the new leadership team arrived in 1999, it began to focus on meeting the needs of both physicians and patients. The physicians became integral members of the leadership team. The focus shifted to providing high-quality clinical care with high-quality service rather than handling legal and organizational structure issues. The new CEO had been given the authority by the board to focus on the core mission and has done so successfully.

A second major factor in the turnaround was the successful political efforts of the new administration to generate additional state revenue for indigent care, which benefited all hospitals in the state. This was accomplished through a political coalition spearheaded by SMC with support from many political and community groups.

The following lessons can be derived from this case study:

- The organizational structure, legal structure, and size of an organized delivery system may be less important in determining organizational performance than previously thought.

- The quality of the leadership team and its ability to communicate a common mission and vision to key stakeholders may be far more important than organizational structure in enhancing organizational performance.
- Political decision making to benefit a small group is antithetical to organizational performance.
- A focus on internal operations to serve physicians and customers is a fundamental necessity for achieving high levels of organizational performance.

Managerial Implications and Recommendations

The jury is still out on the future of organized delivery systems. It is unclear whether the many problems and issues identified here and elsewhere are due to a flawed strategy, flawed implementation (leadership), or both. Clearly, multiprovider integration has not worked well either in American industry or in health care. The point is not to lay blame when systems struggle or collapse. Rather, we need to identify managerial processes or methods that will enhance the probability that systems will survive and prosper. The overriding goal of systems should be to provide maximum value to the healthcare customer.[145]

The fundamental question is, What types of systems, networks, and alliances are best able to compete effectively and deliver cost-effective care? At this time, however, there is no definitive answer to this question, because there is almost no evidence associating different types of organized arrangements with successful performance or failure.

The future of healthcare systems is highly speculative, given the volatility of markets and future initiatives for healthcare reform. As the government's role in health care expands, these systems become more vulnerable to shifts in government policy.

It seems likely that most multiprovider healthcare systems will emerge successfully from their "growing pains" and continue to solidify their position in the healthcare market as long as they are virtually integrated rather than vertically integrated.

Health care will be purchased primarily on a local or regional basis. Quality and value will be increasingly important to patients who once again have a choice of provider. Fewer resources will be available to deliver care, and the delivery of health care will continue to shift from acute care to ambulatory settings. Barry noted the importance of a system CEO being a "change agent" in this future environment:

> Those who can understand and embrace change; those who can transform traditional but key values to tomorrow's environment; those who can educate their boards of trustees, medical communities, and the community at large; and those who can "right size" the production activities of their organizations, and provide both high quality and cost-effective services will be the winners of tomorrow.[146]

Recommendations

- Healthcare executives in multiprovider healthcare systems need to allow flexibility for member institutions to respond to specific local markets while providing a clearly articulated and well-understood vision for the system.

- Each system should develop a detailed mission statement and set of behavioral norms (i.e., culture) shared by each facility within the system in order to enhance cohesiveness.
- Each system should develop a formal strategic plan for the system with input and a high degree of interaction among the corporate office and institutions in all geographic regions.
- Each system should develop and implement explicit measures for quality of care, patient satisfaction, efficiency, and community benefit, and then provide these data to purchasers and other key stakeholders.
- Each system should develop an organizational structure that is simple, lean, flat, responsive, customer-driven, risk-taking, and focused.
- Governance at the corporate level should be strategic in nature, whereas governance at the institutional level should be operational in nature and focused on local community/region needs and concerns.
- Systems should provide formal and informal education for those responsible for governance at all levels in the system.
- Systems should provide a clear definition of governance roles, responsibilities, and authority among the system and institutional boards of its component parts.
- Systems should provide the leadership required for the individual units of a system to think in terms of overall system performance rather than just in terms of the particular unit's performance.
- Only institutions that fit a particular culture and strategy should be invited to join or remain a member of the system.
- Systems should align physician incentives and achieve clinical integration.
- Systems should develop information systems to support the integration of clinical and managerial information.
- Systems should use their mission and values as a guide in making difficult trade-off decisions.
- Systems should change their incentive structures to reflect concern for performance of the system as a whole, not just the individual components.
- Systems should own fewer facilities and contract for most services so that they are virtually integrated rather than vertically integrated.
- Systems should buy or contract for services only if the additions will add value to the systems' customers and are compatible with the existing mission, values, goals, and culture.
- Systems should allow the individual operating units within the system to have sufficient autonomy to be responsive to the needs of their local customers.
- Systems should focus on core competencies rather than trying to be all things to all system components.
- Systems should not allow success to breed complacency. Each integrative step must be evaluated for systemwide effects.
- Systems should focus on quality rather than the size of the program or system being integrated.
- Systems should focus on quality rather than quantity of physician integration.
- Systems should place high-performing executives in key positions to implement their integration plan.
- Systems should target selected patient populations and payers.

References

1. American Hospital Association. *Guide to the Health Care Field*. Chicago, IL: American Hospital Association Press; 1992:B2.
2. Shortell, SM. The evolution of multihospital systems: unfulfilled promises and self-fulfilling prophesies. *Medical Care Review*. 1988;45(2):177–214.
3. Robinson JC, Casalino L. Vertical integration and organizational networks in health care. *Health Affairs*. 1996;15(1):7–22.
4. Smith SD, Virgil PM. Multihospital systems: applying corporate structures and strategies. In: Filerman GL, ed. *A Future of Consequence: The Manager's Role in Health Services*. Princeton, NJ: Princeton University Press; 1996:54–75.
5. Conrad DA, Dowling WL. Vertical integration in health services: theory and managerial implications. *Health Care Management Review*. 1990;15(4):9–22.
6. Kaiser LR. The future of multihospital systems. *Topics in Health Care Financing*. 1992;18(4):32–45.
7. Risk RR. Multihospital systems: the turning point. *Topics in Health Care Financing*. 1992;18(3):46–53.
8. Kinzer DM. Twelve laws of hospital interaction. *Health Care Management Review*. 1990;15(2):15–19.
9. White WD. The "corporatization" of US hospitals: what we can learn from the nineteenth century industrial experience. *International Journal of Health Services*. 1990;20(1):85–113.
10. Nemes J. For-profit chains look beyond the bottom line. *Modern Healthcare*. 1990;20(10):27–36.
11. McCue MJ, et al.. An assessment of hospital acquisition prices. *Inquiry*. 1988;25:290–296.
12. Shortell. The evolution of multihospital systems. 177–214.
13. White. The "corporatization" of US hospitals. 102.
14. Risk. Multihospital systems: the turning point. 46–47.
15. Kaiser. The future of multihospital systems. 35.
16. Smith,Virgil. Multihospital systems. 54–55.
17. White. The "corporatization" of US hospitals. 102.
18. Shortell SM, Gillies, Devers. 1995. Reinventing the American hospital. *The Milbank Quarterly*. 1995;73(2):131–160.
19. Ibid.
20. Mongan JJ, Ferris TG, Lee TH. Options for slowing the growth of health care costs. *The New England Journal of Medicine*. 2008;358(14):1509–1514.
21. Bauer JC. Health reform and payment trends: Don't wait for politicians. *Business Trends*. 2008;62(4):40–42.
22. Ross H. Work of Heart. In employer-directed marketing, finding the right niche brings hospitals bottom-line profitability. *Marketing Health Services*. 2007;27(3):31–36.
23. Shortell et al. Reinventing the American hospital.
24. Tennyson DL, Fottler MD. Does system membership enhance financial returns in hospitals? *Medical Care Research and Review*. 2000;57(1):29–50.
25. McCue MJ, Diana ML. Assessing the performance of freestanding hospitals. *Journal of Healthcare Management*. 2007;52(5):299–308.
26. Fitch Rating Agency. *Non-Profit Hospitals and Health Care Systems Outlook*. New York: Author; 2006.
27. Shortell et al. Reinventing the American hospital.
28. Brown M. Mergers, networking, and vertical integration: Managed care and investor owned hospitals. *Health Care Management Review*. 1996;21(1):29–37.
29. Luke, et al. Local markets and systems. 571.

30. Borzo G. Closer ties with physicians skirt safe harbor fears. *Health Care Strategic Management.* 1992;10(11):19–22.
31. Andreopoulos S. The folly of teaching hospital mergers. *New England Journal of Medicine.* 1997;336(1):61–64.
32. Barnett A. The partners merger. *Hospitals & Health Networks.* 1995;69(11):46–50.
33. Shortell, et al. Reinventing the American hospital. 133.
34. Brown. Mergers, not working, and vertical integration.
35. Shortell, et al. Reinventing the American hospital.
36. Jacobson GK. A conceptual framework for evaluating venture opportunities between hospitals and physicians. *Health Services Management Research.* 1989;(2):202–212.
37. Montague J. Straight talk: doctor-driven systems tell how they've gained physician allies. *Hospitals & Health Networks.* 1993;67(13):22–27.
38. Unland J. Group practices and hospital affiliation of medical practices. *Health Care Strategic Management.* 1993;11(3):15–19.
39. Burda D. Most hospitals slow to join with group practices. *Modern Healthcare.* 23(34):33.
40. Robinson, Casalino. Vertical integration. 8.
41. Kenkel, PJ. Filling up beds no longer the name of the system game. *Modern Healthcare.* 1993;23(37):39–48.
42. Greene J, Lutz, S.. A down year at not-for-profits; for-profits soar. *Modern Healthcare.* 1995;25(25):43–63.
43. Nemes J. For-profit hospitals waving goodbye to era of high prices. *Modern Healthcare.* 1993;23(12):33–34, 37.
44. Shortell, et al. Reinventing the American hospital. 133.
45. Robinson, Casalino. Vertical integration.
46. Brown. Mergers, not working, and vertical integration.
47. Smith,Virgil. Multihospital systems. 59–61.
48. Kaiser LR. The future of multihospital systems. *Topics in Health Care Financing.* 1992;18(4):36.
49. Ibid.
50. McGee GM, et al. The impact of corporatization on administrator stress in nursing homes. *Health Services Management Research.* 1992;5(1):54–65.
51. Kaiser. The future of multihospital systems. 43.
52. Toomey RE, Toomey RK. The role of governing boards in multihospital systems. *Health Care Management Review.* 1993;18(1):21–30.
53. Morlock LL, Alexander JA. Models of governance in multihospital systems: implications for hospitals and system-level decision-making. *Medical Care.* 1986;24(12):1118–1135.
54. Morlock, Alexander. Models of governance. 1122–1123, 1125–1129.
55. Ibid, 1134.
56. Gautam KS. A call for board leadership on quality in hospitals. *Q Manage Health Care.* 2005;14(1):18–30.
57. Becker C. Getting schooled in governance. *Modern Healthcare.* 2007;37(22):6–7.
58. Alexander JA, et al. The challenge of governing integrated delivery systems. *Health Care Management Review.* 1995;20(4):69–81.
59. Shortell. The evolution of multihospital systems. 180.
60. Risk. Multihospital systems: the turning point. 47.
61. Cleverly WO. Financial and operating performance of systems: voluntary versus investor-owned. *Topics in Health Care Financing.* 1992;18(4):63–73.
62. Ramirez TL. Introduction to multihospital systems. *Topics in Health Care Financing.* 1992;18(4):9–10.
63. Shortell. The evolution of multihospital systems. 181.

64. Friedman L, Goes, J. Why integrated health networks have failed. *Frontiers of Health Services Management.* 2001;17(4):3–28.

65. McCue, et al. An assessment of hospital acquisition prices. 294–295.

66. Shortell. The evolution of multihospital systems. 178.

67. White. The "corporatization" of US hospitals. 105.

68. Ramirez. Introduction to multihospital systems. 7.

69. Federa RD, Miller TR. Capital allocation techniques. *Topics in Health Care Financing.* 1992;19(1):68–78.

70. Thaldorf C, Liberman A. 2007. *Integration of Health Care Organizations: Using the Power Strategies of Horizontal and Vertical Integration in Public and Private Health Systems.* 2007; 26(2):116–127.

71. Dranove D, Shanley M. Cost reduction or reputational enhancement as motive for mergers: The logic of multihospital systems. *Strategic Management Journal.* 1995;16(1):72.

72. Alexander JA, Morrisey MA. Hospital selection into multihospital systems: the effect of market, management, and mission. *Medical Care.* 1988;26(2):159–176.

73. Shortell. The evolution of multihospital systems. 207.

74. Conrad, Dowling. Vertical integration in health services. 10.

75. Ibid.

76. Ibid, 11.

77. Robinson, Casalino. Vertical integration.

78. Ibid.

79. Herzlinger R. *Market Driven Health Care.* Boston, MA: Addison-Wesley Publishing Co; 1997.

80. Jaklevic MC. Buying doctor's practices often leads to red ink. *Modern Healthcare.* 1996;26(25):39.

81. Conrad, Dowling. Vertical integration in health services. 21.

82. Alexander JA. Diversification behavior of multihospital systems: patterns of change, 1983–1985. *Hospital and Health Services Administration.* 1990;35(1):83–102.

83. Shortell SM. Diversification strategy benefits innovative leader. *Modern Healthcare.* 1990;20(10):38.

84. Brown M, McCool B. Health Care Systems: Predictions for the Future. *Health Care Management Review.* 1990;15(3):87–94.

85. Robinson, Casalino. Vertical integration.

86. Health Care Advisory Board. *Emerging from Shadows: Resurgence to Prosperity.* Washington, DC: Health Care Advisory Board; 1995.

87. Galloro V, Piotrowski, J. A Successful Operation. *Modern Healthcare.* 2002;22(21):28–34.

88. Bellandi D, Kirchheimer B, Saphir A. Profitability a matter of ownership status. *Modern Healthcare.* 2000;20(22):24–43.

89. Galloro and Piotrowski, "A Successful Operation."

90. Tucker LR, Zaremba RA. Organizational control and the status of marketing in multihospital systems. *Health Care Management Review.* 1991;16(1):41–56.

91. Shortell. The evolution of multihospital systems. 183.

92. Dranove D, et al. Are multihospital systems more efficient? *Health Affairs.* 1996;15(1): 100–104.

93. Ramirez. Introduction to multihospital systems. 1–23.

94. Greene J. 1992. Healthcare systems' newest balancing act: "doing more with less." *Modern Healthcare.* 1992;22(39):52, 54, 56–58.

95. Robinson, Casalino. Vertical integration.

96. Ramirez. Introduction to multihospital systems. 5.

97. Cleverly. Financial and operating performance of systems. 68.

98. Dranove, et al. Are multihospital systems more efficient? 102.

99. Bilynsky U. Integrated best performers: seven habits of successful healthcare systems. *Health Care Strategic Management.* 2002;20(1):12–14.

100. Egger E. Integration the right strategy despite health executives' increasing apprehension. *Health Care Strategic Management.* 1999;17(6):10–11.

101. Friedman L, Goes J. Why integrated health networks have failed. *Frontiers of Health Services Management.* 2001;17(4):3–28.

102. McConnell CR. *Larger, Smaller, Flatter: The Evolution of the Modern Health Care Organization.* 2005;24(2):177–188.

103. Galloro V. Reorganized, re-energized: Some for-profit chains are shaking up their organization charts as well as their strategic plans to better cope with competition. *Modern Healthcare.* 2006;36(22):6–7.

104. Lauer CS. Physician practice turnaround in an integrated system. *Modern Healthcare.* 2000; 32(12):39–42.

105. Ibid.

106. Tierman J. A profitable practice. *Modern Healthcare.* 2001;31(38):46–48.

107. Burns LR, Cacciamani J, Clement J, Aquino W. The fall of the house of AHERF: the Allegheny bankruptcy. *Health Affairs.* 2000;19(1):7–41.

108. Ibid.

109. Topping S, Malvey D. Management of academic health centers: the past, present, and future. In: Savage GT, Blair JD, Fottler MD, eds. *Advances in Health Care Management,* Vol. 3. Amsterdam: JAI/Elsevier Science; 2002:265–295.

110. Galloro V. Report grounds Allina. *Modern Healthcare.* 2001;31(40):14–16.

111. Bellandi D. CHW pulls in the reins. *Modern Healthcare.* 2001;31(7):4–8.

112. Ramirez. Introduction to multihospital systems. 5–6, 11.

113. McLaughlin T. Finding jobs for 1200 laid-off employees: Health One's goal. *Hospitals.* 1992;66(1):43–44.

114. Kaye GH. Multis, mergers, acquisitions, and the healthcare provider. *Nursing Management.* 1989;20(4):54–62.

115. Evans M. Competition still driving compensation. *Modern Healthcare.* 2007;37(30):S1–5.

116. Smith, Virgil. Multihospital systems. 66–69.

117. Gregory D. Strategic alliances between physicians and hospitals in multihospital systems. *Hospital and Health Services Administration.* 1992;37(2):247–258.

118. Burns L, et al. The impact of corporate structures on physician inclusion and participation. *Medical Care.* 1989;27(10):967–982.

119. Koska MT. Systems fight uphill battle to gain physician loyalty. *Hospitals.* 1990;64(6):60, 62.

120. Greene. Healthcare systems' newest balancing act. 56, 58.

121. Smith, Virgil. Multihospital systems. 64.

122. Schwartz GF, Stone CT. Strategic acquisitions by academic medical centers: the Jefferson experience as operational paradigm. *Health Care Management Review.* 1991;16(2):39–47.

123. Albertina RM, Bakewell TF. Allocating capital systemwide. *Health Progress.* 1989;70(4):26–32.

124. Federa, Miller. Capital allocation techniques. 72.

125. Albertina, Bakewell. Allocating capital systemwide. 21, 26.

126. Federa, Miller. Capital allocation techniques. 68–69, 73–74.

127. Ibid, 74–75.

128. Ibid, 75.

129. Ibid, 77–78.

130. Gerber L, Feinstein FI. When the system can't save the hospital: a practical overview of workouts and bankruptcy alternatives. *Topics in Health Care Financing.* 1992;18(4):46–62.

131. Ibid, 50–51.

132. Anderson HJ. Sizing up systems: researchers to test performance measures. *Hospitals.* 1991;65(20):33–34.

133. Solovy AT. Multis sweep cash, boost investment income. *Hospitals*. 1988;62(5):74–75.
134. Ramirez. Introduction to multihospital systems. 6.
135. Ibid, 6–7.
136. Ibid, 12.
137. McKinney MM, et al. Paths and pacemakers: innovation diffusion networks in multihospital systems and alliances. *Health Care Management Review*. 1991;16(1):17–23.
138. McGuire P. Kaiser Permanente's New Technologies Committee: an approach to assessing technology. *Quality Review Bulletin*. 1990;16(6):240–242.
139. Taravella S. Risk management: frustrated healthcare systems seek alternatives to traditional insurance. *Modern Healthcare*. 1988;18(20):30–32, 36, 41.
140. Tucker, Zaremba. Organizational control and the status of marketing. 47, 53–54.
141. White. The "corporatization" of US hospitals. 103.
142. Werner TL. A new approach to decision support at Adventist Hospital System/Sunbelt. *Computers in Healthcare*. 1990;11(3):49–50.
143. Hurwitz M. Multis move to centralize IS decisions. *Hospitals*. 1988;62(5):75.
144. Lumsdon K. Holding networks together: shared information will be glue for reformed health system. *Hospitals*. 1993;7(4):26–27.
145. Fottler MD, Ford RC, Heaton CP. *Achieving Service Excellence: Strategies for Healthcare*. Chicago, IL: Health Administration Press; 2002.
146. Barry DR. Commentary: are hospitals and their boards up to these challenges? *Health Care Management Review*. 1995;20(1):40–92.

Biographical Information

Myron D. Fottler, PhD, is a Professor and Director of Programs in Health Services Administration at the University of Central Florida. He has authored or coauthored 14 books, 30 book chapters, and more than 100 journal articles in most of the major management and health service journals. His most recent book is *Achieving Service Excellence: Strategies for Healthcare* (Health Administration Press, 2002). He received his MBA from Boston University and his PhD in business from Columbia University. He serves on many editorial review boards and is coeditor of the JAI Press/Elsevier series *Advances on Health Care Management*.

Donna Malvey, PhD, is an Assistant Professor of Health Administration in the College of Public Health at the University of South Florida in Tampa. Her area of expertise is the strategic management of health services organizations. Past experience includes teaching courses in labor relations and healthcare organizations and management. In addition, she has served as the executive director of a national trade association representing health professionals and also as a congressional aide. She has coauthored articles on a variety of healthcare-related topics and is currently a visiting assistant professor of Health Administration at the University of Central Florida. Dr. Malvey received her PhD in health services administration at the University of Alabama at Birmingham and her master's degree in health services administration from George Washington University.

Legal Implications of Business Arrangements in the Healthcare Industry

Gabriel L. Imperato, Lester J. Perling, and Mike Segal

Healthcare reform, rising costs, and an increased number of health management organizations have led healthcare providers to seek new and more profitable business relationships. These relationships include, among others, hospital mergers, hospital–physician joint ventures, and other types of hospital-affiliated physician networks. These types of arrangements often raise legal issues surrounding possible kickbacks, self-referrals, false claims, and even antitrust violations. Therefore, it is important that all applicable legal issues be understood, and that potential business relations be analyzed, not only from a financial perspective, but also from a legal and regulatory perspective. Taking such matters into account during the planning stage will help businesses and individuals structure organizations in a manner that avoids potential civil and criminal consequences of violating the law.

Legal Structure of the Healthcare Delivery System

Historically, the legal structure of the healthcare delivery system in the United States consisted almost exclusively of personal interactions between patients and physicians. Today, the healthcare delivery system is almost completely composed of corporate entities, many of which are invester owned. As a result, the industry has evolved from one made up mostly of individual physicians to an industry dominated by medical groups such as physician-owned entities, independent practice associations (IPAs), hospitals, and ancillary providers.

The authors wish to thank Barbara Viota-Sawisch, Esq., for her invaluable assistance in the preparation of this chapter.

Physician-Owned Entities

Physician-owned entities that provide medical care range in nature from those entities that are owned solely by physicians to those owned partly, or wholly, by nonphysicians. Generally, these entities are formed as professional corporations, limited liability companies, or business corporations. When deciding on a legal structure for a given medical practice, it is important to keep in mind what is referred to as the Corporate Practice of Medicine Doctrine (CPMD). In general terms, the CPMD prohibits unlicensed individuals or entities from practicing medicine. The term "practicing medicine" can range from employing healthcare professionals to owning professional practices, providing medical diagnoses, or treating patients. As a result, the doctrine prohibits the ownership of diagnostic testing facilities by someone other than a licensed physician.

Historically, the CPMD arose from physicians' fear that corporations might unduly influence their decisions regarding level of care and amount of treatment, in an effort to increase corporate profits. Consequently, some jurisdictions prohibit physicians from splitting professional fees with unlicensed entities or individuals.

State corporate practice of medicine laws can potentially affect the ability of a risk-sharing organization to offer both facility and professional services, or to create a single provider risk-sharing organization. The scope and effects of the CPMD vary from state to state and must be analyzed on an individual state level. In certain states, such as Florida, any person or entity can employ or contract with a physician. However, Florida does apply the CPMD to dentistry. Other states have created narrow exceptions dealing with specific types of organizations, such as not-for-profit corporations or hospitals. Still others will allow certain entities to contract with physicians, but only under an independent contractor arrangement. Finally, some states allow only licensed entities composed of physicians to employ or even contract with other physicians. Any exceptions to the CPMD, and whether a CPMD exists in a particular state, are state-specific issues that require individualized analysis.

Independent Practice Associations

In the late 1980s and early 1990s managed care contracts were very complex. It was no longer a situation in which physicians simply offered discounts to particular insurance carriers. In an effort to better control costs and help increase profits, insurance carriers began to take a greater role in the supervision of patient treatment. Soon, insurance carriers became so involved in the supervision of patient care that physicians began to feel that their physician–patient relationships were being adversely affected. Consequently, physicians approached insurance carriers in an attempt to find a way to regain the authority to independently manage their patients' care. The effect was the creation of what is known as an independent practice association (IPA).

IPAs are a form of business organization (generally formed as a limited liability company, professional corporation, business corporation, or partnership) that provides a very limited degree of integration between medical practices. They were created by physicians primarily to obtain capitated or other risk-sharing payer contracts. They are also often used to obtain pricing benefits for insurance and other items. All medical practices contained within a particular IPA continue to operate as independent business enterprises. In fact, many physicians within an IPA continue to compete among themselves. Thus, an IPA is simply a means of supplementing a physician's existing private patient base, not a vehicle to completely integrate their practices.

Nevertheless, each IPA is different and can choose to implement its own level of operational integration. Consequently, there are many "types" of IPAs, depending on the individual level of integration. IPAs do not actually provide medical care to patients; they simply arrange for the provision of healthcare services by independent physicians or small group practices. Some mature IPAs have created complex rules to govern clinical procedures provided under its contracts, called "clinical integration."

Generally, ownership interests in an IPA are sold to physicians in exchange for start-up working capital. The IPA then enters into payer contracts and collects fees related to professional services. Thereafter, the IPA enters into professional service agreements with its owners (physicians), who in return employ the majority of personnel that they need in order to operate their private practice. To the extent that an IPA takes over individual physicians' billing and collection activities and becomes clinically integrated, the IPA moves closer to becoming an integrated group practice.

The utilization of an IPA has both advantages and disadvantages. Some physicians prefer the IPA over a large medical practice because there is no need to transfer their existing practice to a new organization, and it allows them to retain a significant amount of control over their practice. Unfortunately, many IPAs have failed or have been disappointments. The reasons for this include undercapitalization, absence of management or administrative experience, an overemphasis on specialists in markets that need more primary care doctors, lack of effective cost controls, the inability of physicians to agree on an acceptable compensation plan that also is consistent with the goals of the IPA, and the inability of the IPA to be able to be effectively used to contract in a fee-for-service environment.

The main problem with IPAs is that they represent a group of physicians that are neither truly integrated nor completely independent. In fact, the competition among owners remains high. The result is a group of individual practitioners with competing interests and a lack of motivation to completely integrate their practices. With integration could come greater economies of scale, which could mean greater profits for the owners. Without greater integration the IPA owner will continue to work for the best interests of his or her independent practice rather than the best interests of the IPA as a whole.

Hospitals continue to develop new strategies to remain competitive in the rapidly expanding healthcare industry. This has resulted in hospitals utilizing a variety of legal and business structures. These structures include profit hospitals, not-for-profit hospitals, the acquisition and/or management of medical practices, and greater emphasis on freestanding outpatient facilities, often in competition with those created by the medical community, but sometimes as joint ventures with physicians.

A for-profit hospital is a hospital that is incorporated and run like any other for-profit organization. It has shareholders who demand a return on their investment, and is thus profit oriented. A portion of those profits eventually make their way down to shareholders in the form of dividends. A for-profit hospital must also pay taxes on its profits and dividend payouts.

The most significant distinction between a for-profit and a not-for-profit hospital is the not-for-profit hospital's tax-exempt status. Typically, healthcare organizations (e.g., hospitals) organize themselves and operate for "charitable" purposes in order to qualify for tax-exempt status. According to the Internal Revenue Service (IRS), a charitable purpose includes the provision of healthcare services, even if the class of beneficiaries receiving benefits from the hospital does not include the entire community, provided that the class of individuals is not so small as to be determined not to be of benefit to the community in which it operates. Generally, the IRS requires something more than simply the provision of healthcare services in order to qualify for tax-exempt status. As it concerns hospitals, the IRS used to require that hospitals provide charity health care in order to qualify for tax-exempt status. Since the late 1960s and early 1970s, the IRS has granted exempt status to hospitals that meet the "community benefit" or "public benefit" standard.

According to this standard, a hospital must show that it provides an overall benefit to the community in which it operates. This standard requires a facts and circumstances examination of, among other things, whether the hospital has a board of directors that is representative of the community, refrains from engaging in the practice of patient dumping, has an inclusive medical staff, provides community education programs, and provides health services to a broad class of individuals, regardless of ability to pay.

Apart from being required to provide a charitable or public purpose, in order to qualify for tax-exempt status a hospital is prohibited from providing a private benefit to those who operate it. In other words, no part of the net profits of a tax-exempt organization may inure to the benefit of a private individual. If any tax-exempt organization (including tax-exempt hospitals) violates the prohibition on private benefit or private inurement then that organization will be at risk of losing its status as a tax-exempt organization.

It is important to note that in 1991 the IRS released a general counsel memorandum in which it addressed issues related to fraud and kickback schemes in the context of tax-exempt organizations. It stated that tax-exempt organizations taking part in fraud and abuse or kickback schemes are at risk of losing their tax-exempt status because they may also be violating the IRS prohibition on private inurement and private benefit within tax-exempt organizations.[1] Therefore, it is very important that tax-exempt hospitals consider fraud and abuse and kickback regulations when evaluating their relationships with healthcare providers.

More recently, there has been considerable pressure, on both the federal and state level, for not-for-profit hospitals to adequately demonstrate that they actually benefit the community and deserve tax-exempt status. Not-for-profit entities must file an annual public IRS report, called a Form 990. The 990 has been expanded significantly, much more than not-for-profit entities would prefer.

Not-for-profit entities should also be aware of Section 4958 of the Internal Revenue Code. Section 4958 basically allows for the imposition of an excise "tax" as a penalty on "insiders" (i.e., those in a position to exercise substantial influence over the organization) and those connected to them, known as "disqualified persons," who receive an "excess benefit" from transactions with a tax-exempt organization. "Excess benefit" occurs whenever "the value of the economic benefit provided exceeds the value of the consideration received for providing the benefit," without regard to motive or intent.[2] This provision was intended to give the IRS additional means by which to fight corruption in the charitable sector.

Yet another way for hospitals to become involved in the delivery of health care is through the use of hospital-owned or hospital-controlled medical practices. Although hospitals that own medical practices often find them difficult to manage and difficult to operate profitably, these structures are effective ways of creating a fully integrated healthcare delivery system. They allow a hospital and medical group to be combined within a single organization.

The hospital, or a subsidiary or affiliate, directly employs the physicians, or an entirely new entity can be created by the hospital to serve as the hospital's medical services component. A number of business entities may be used to achieve such goals, including limited liability companies, limited partnerships, standard business corporations, professional associations, professional corporations, nonprofit corporations, trusts, foundations, and standard business corporations. Generally, the most important factor in choosing an appropriate entity is the applicable state law concerning an entity's ability to employ physicians. As previously discussed, corporate practice of medicine prohibitions may eliminate the ability to use separate entities, prohibit the direct employment of physicians by hospitals, or even limit the types of entities from which to choose. Because the corporate practice of medicine is a state law issue, it is important that individuals contemplating this option first research the law of their particular state. If state law does prohibit a hospital from owning a medical practice, a hospital may be able to circumvent the prohibition by utilizing a management services organization (MSO).

An MSO is an entity set up to provide assets and services to a medical practice. In most cases, the MSO purchases all the tangible assets of a medical practice and thereafter leases them back to a medical practice as part of a management services agreement. Other times, an MSO purchases new equipment and leases it to the practice. There are a variety of MSO types, but the overall concept remains the same. The distinction between the various types of MSOs is based on the MSO's specific combination of purpose (e.g., who will it serve, financial goals), function (e.g., degree of services offered), and ownership structure (e.g., subsidiary, joint venture).

Whenever hospitals have an ownership interest in medical practices, it is important to consider possible kickback and self-referral implications (both anti-kickback and self-referral laws are discussed later in this chapter). If a hospital (or any other entity that receives patient referrals) subsidizes an MSO (and by implication the medical group) and the medical group thereafter refers patients to the hospital, then the MSO arrangement could be considered indirect payment by the hospital to the MSO in an effort to obtain patient referrals, resulting in a possible violation of the anti-kickback statute.

Alternatively, if the MSO is owned by the hospital, then the physicians' patient referrals from the MSO for designated health services to the hospital could raise possible Stark Law violations. Even if the MSO is established as a separate and distinct entity from the hospital, the activities of the MSO may be attributed to the hospital for purposes of analyzing anti-kickback and self-referral laws if it is capitalized or controlled by the hospital. These are very complicated issues that need to be addressed prior to forming an MSO. Most importantly, attorneys should be strict in cautioning their clients with respect to MSO arrangements, especially if the MSO operates at a financial loss.

To minimize the risks of violating these federal laws, it is important to be aware of, and comply with, all "safe harbors" applicable to each component of the MSO arrangement. These safe harbors are discussed in more detail later in this chapter.

Ancillary Providers

Spurred by reimbursement incentives during the 1980s and rapidly growing levels of technological innovation, health care is being transformed from a hospital-based system to a less expensive outpatient-based system. This trend has been encouraging to health management organizations, corporations, and even the federal government, who have been working hard to find new ways of controlling the rising cost of health care in this country. This development has resulted in exponential growth in the number of ancillary healthcare providers.

Ancillary delivery systems can be divided into two major groups—outpatient delivery systems (e.g., surgical centers) and all other ancillary delivery systems (e.g., diagnostic centers, cardiac catheterization centers, and radiation therapy centers). Outpatient delivery systems typically are owned by physicians or hospitals or as a joint venture between physicians and hospitals.

Generally, all other ancillary delivery systems are organized and funded through outside business entities. Often the ancillary opportunities are structured as joint ventures with physicians. Some of these ventures have been very successful. However, today the trend in regulation is to make these joint ventures more difficult, often impossible, to pursue.

Because of the ownership structure of these ancillary systems, fraud, abuse, and self-referral issues are common. It is important to fully analyze all payments to be sure that none conflict with the anti-kickback statute or the patient self-referral statute. These issues are discussed in more detail later in this chapter. It is also helpful to seek guidance from previously released advisory opinions issued by the Health and Human Services Office of Inspector General (OIG). Even though OIG advisory opinions specifically state that they may not be relied upon by anyone other than the requester, it is nonetheless a way to obtain an indicator of how the OIG would view certain types of business arrangements.[3]

Legal Entities

Physicians and medical groups forming and operating under legal entities must be aware of the tax and personal liability consequences that the various entity structures entail. Generally, the two broad categories of entity structures available, incorporated and unincorporated entities, will afford the physician different levels of protections in those crucial areas. Although no business structure will protect or afford the physician immunity from liability stemming from his own professional actions, some entities provide better personal protection than others in the event the actions of a partner, colleague, or employee of a physician were the cause of a suit. A closer examination of the advantages and drawbacks of each entity is required to provide physicians and medical groups with a better idea of how to structure their business. However, one should not solely rely on the following brief overview regarding the choice of optimal physician entity. Laws and tax regulations concerning the various entities can vary from state to state and it is therefore crucial that a physician consult a legal expert from his or her own state before making the ultimate decision of which entity to operate.

Sole Proprietorship

For physicians who do not plan to work in a group or form a practice entity with other physicians, the sole proprietorship presents itself as a convenient choice of entity. Setting up a sole proprietorship involves minimal effort and expenses and provides the advantage that entity and physician are treated as one and the same for tax purposes. However, the sole proprietorship has the considerable drawback that it offers no form of personal liability protection whatsoever, and a physician's personal assets are subject to exposure to satisfy judgments against the business. For those reasons, a sole proprietorship is rare.

General Partnership (GP)

Physicians who plan on working together and forming small medical groups may be tempted to form a general partnership since they are uncomplicated and inexpensive to create and are not subject to federal income taxations. However, the general partnership presents the same considerable drawback of the sole proprietorship; personal assets are subject to company judgments. In addition to that downside, each physician is also personally liable for claims rendered against his or her partner. Due to the negative liability characteristics of a general partnership, general partnerships of individuals are not popular. However, often the structure of a general partnership of entities (such as professional corporations) owned by individual physicians is utilized to shield physicians from liability.

Limited Liability Company (LLC) and Limited Liability Partnership (LLP)

Limited liability companies and limited liability partnerships are relatively new forms of incorporated entity that did not emerge until the 1990s. They have attributes of both a partnership and corporation, offering limited liability to their members, flow-through of taxation on profits and losses, and, like the C corporation (see below), flexibility on the amount and nature of their owners. Additionally, profit distributions are not as rigid as with an S corporation (see below) since they may be distributed disproportionately to membership in the entity. Likewise, the limited liability company and limited liability partnership do not require the observation of corporate formalities like minutes or annual shareholder meetings. Due to the novelty of these structures, their liability protection has not faced the extensive court challenges and scrutiny that corporations have, and therefore their protection is not as judicially recognized.

Unlike the established corporate structure, some states might not recognize all rights and privileges afforded to the LLC or LLP by other states. There is a perception that upon receipt of considerable revenue, the risk of an IRS audit is higher with a limited liability company than it would be with a corporation. Moreover, if the members of a limited liability company wish to maintain earnings within the company rather than distributing them, a corporation might be a more suitable choice of entity to retain savings since, depending on the amount of income, the corporate tax rates could be lower than the individual income tax rates incurred upon distribution.

Like other forms of unincorporated entities, the limited liability partnership has the distinct advantage of not being subject to federal taxation. That is, all income flows directly to the partners and must only be reported by them as income. The limited liability partnership is unique, however, in the respect that it shields the physician's assets from liability caused by partners' malpractice. Nevertheless, a physician partner must be aware that the LLP's assets could still be lost to an unfavorable malpractice judgment, if such a judgment exceeds the amount guaranteed by the insurance policy. Limited liability partnerships also offer the advantage of flexible structuring by limiting a partner's decision-making rights, regardless of his or her individual income or status within the partnership.

Incorporated Entities

Despite the increased cost and the more formal structure of incorporated entities, to most physicians they represent favorable alternatives to unincorporated entities for the simple reason that a physician's personal assets are secure and will not be subject to any judgments against the business resulting from colleagues' malpractice. The most a physician could lose is his or her investment in the business. However, a physician must be aware that his or her own personal assets are not secure if judgment has been rendered against the practice as a result of the physician's own negligence.

C Corporation

The C corporation is a fairly flexible entity structure that may issue stock. Different forms of stock are allowed. Depending on the type of stock, different voting and distribution rights are assigned, allowing greater consideration for shareholder seniority. Since stock ownership represents one's interest in the entity, physicians may easily buy in or buy out of the entity by acquiring or selling stock. The C corporation is often a choice entity for large medical groups since the law imposes no limit on the amount and nature of the corporation's shareholders. The major drawback of the C corporation concerns its tax liability. Any income the corporation receives is taxed twice, first to the corporation and then to the shareholders receiving dividends on their shares. C corporations may seek to avoid the taxation to shareholders by distributing all of its profits to its physicians as "bonuses." However, if such bonuses are disproportionately large, the physician receiving the bonus may come under IRS scrutiny.

S Corporation

The S corporation has become a favorable alternative to the C corporation since it limits personal liability to the corporate investment and all profits flow through the corporation directly to the shareholders and, as such, are subject to only one layer of taxation. Election of an S corporation physician entity or group practice is often limited to smaller local physician entities as the corporation may not have more than 100 shareholders or have any nonresident aliens or (with very limited exceptions) entities as its shareholders. Another drawback concerns the limitation that an S corporation may only issue one class of stock (other than with respect to voting rights, which inhibits flexibility). However, the S corporation has the advantage that any losses incurred during the start-up of the entity are passed directly to the shareholder and therefore can be set off from taxable income derived from other sources. In a C corporation, such losses remain within the corporation and cannot be used to the benefit of its shareholders.

Federal Anti-Kickback Statute

The federal anti-kickback statute states in part:

1. whoever knowingly and willfully solicits or receives any remuneration (including any kickback, bribe, or rebate) directly or indirectly, overtly or covertly, in cash or in kind:
   a. in return for referring an individual to a person for the furnishing or arranging for the furnishing of any item or service for which payment may be made in whole or in part under a federal healthcare program, or
   b. in return for purchasing, leasing, ordering, or arranging for or recommending purchasing, leasing, or ordering any good, facility, service, or item for which payment may be made in whole or in part under a federal healthcare program, shall be guilty of a felony and upon conviction thereof, shall be fined not more than $25,000 or imprisoned for not more than 5 years, or both.
2. whoever knowingly and willfully offers or pays any remuneration (including any kickback, bribe, or rebate) directly or indirectly, overtly or covertly, in cash or in kind to any person to induce such person:
   a. to refer an individual to a person for the furnishing or arranging for the furnishing of any item or service for which payment may be made in whole or in part under a federal healthcare program, or
   b. to purchase, lease, order, or arrange for or recommend purchasing, leasing, or ordering any good, facility, service, or item for which payment may be made in whole or in part under a federal healthcare program, shall be guilty of a felony and upon conviction thereof, shall be fined not more than $25,000 or imprisoned for not more than 5 years, or both.[4]

Additionally, if the person submitted claims to the Medicare program because of an unlawful referral, he or she may be found to have violated the federal Civil False Claims Act (FCA).[5] A person found to have submitted false Medicare claims may be subject to civil monetary penalties for each item or service for which a fraudulent claim was submitted, and an assessment in lieu of damages of up to triple the amount of the claim submitted (see **Table 3.1**).

The anti-kickback statute also sets forth certain statutory exemptions (e.g., discounts, payments to employees, payments to group purchasing organizations), and authorizes the secretary of the Department of Health and Human Services to exempt specified transactions by safe harbor regulations.[6] It is very important to note that the anti-kickback safe harbors are extremely narrow in scope. Transactions that do not fit squarely within the regulatory safe harbors are not illegal per se, but must be analyzed according to the particular facts and circumstances of each transaction.[7]

Table 3.1 Comparison of Anti-Kickback Safe Harbors and Stark Law Exceptions

Anti-Kickback Safe Harbors	Stark Law Exceptions	Comments
Investment Interests[91]	*Ownership or Investment Interests*[92]	Note that the Stark Law exception does not have an equivalent to what is commonly called the "small entity" safe harbor, which allows investment in unlisted investments. This difference leads to a prohibition against joint ventures under the Stark Law.
1. For entities that possess more than $50 million in undepreciated net tangible assets, this safe harbor requires that:	Ownership of the following is not a prohibited ownership or investment interest:	
a. The entity must be registered with the SEC.	1. Ownership of investment securities (including shares or bonds, debentures, notes, or other debt instruments) that may be purchased on terms generally available to the public and which are	
b. The investment interest must be obtained on terms equally available to the public through trading on a registered national securities exchange.	a. Securities listed on the New York Stock Exchange, the American Stock Exchange, or any regional exchange in which quotations are published on a daily basis, or foreign securities listed on a recognized foreign, national, or regional exchange in which quotations are published on a daily basis, or	
c. The entity's services or items must be furnished or marketed the same to passive investors as noninvestors.	b. Traded under an automated interdealer quotation system operated by the National Association of Securities Dealers, and	
d. The entity must not loan or guarantee funds to an investor in a position to make referrals if used to obtain the investment interest.	c. In a corporation that had, at the end of the corporation's most recent fiscal year, or on average during the previous 3 fiscal years, stockholder equity exceeding $75 million.	
e. The amount of return to the investor must be directly proportional to the amount of capital investment.		
2. For entities that possess interests held by passive or active investors, this safe harbor requires that:		
a. No more than 40% of the value of the investment interests of each class of investors may be held by investors in a position to make referrals.		
i. The OIG has stated that those investors who promise in writing not to make referrals to the entity will not be considered as being in a position to make referrals.		

(continues)

Anti-Kickback Safe Harbors	Stark Law Exceptions	Comments
b. The terms of an investment interest offered to a passive investor in a position to make referrals must be no different than those offered to other passive investors.		
c. The terms of an investment interest offered to an investor in a position to make referrals or generate business must not be based on the volume or value generated from the investor to the entity.		
d. There is no requirement that a passive investor make referrals or generate business for the entity as a condition to remaining as an investor.		
e. The entity's services or items must not be marketed to passive investors differently than noninvestors.		
f. No more than 40% of the entity's gross revenue may come from referrals or business generated by an investor.		
g. The entity must not loan or guarantee funds to an investor in a position to make referrals if used to obtain the investment interest.		
h. The amount to the investor must be directly proportional to the amount of capital investment.		

Table 3.1 (*continued*)

Anti-Kickback Safe Harbors	Stark Law Exceptions	Comments
Space or Equipment Rental[93]	*Space or Equipment Rental*[94]	One of the key differences is that under the safe harbor, the *aggregate* payment for the term of the lease must be set in advance. The Stark Law exception does not require this. In fact, per use payments are permitted under Phase I of the Final Stark II regulations.
Space or equipment rental requires:	Payments made by a lessee to a lessor for the use of space or equipment are excluded if:	
1. Lease is in writing.	1. The lease is set out in writing, signed by the parties, and specifies the space/equipment covered by the lease.	
2. Lease specifies premises covered.	2. The space/equipment rented or leased does not exceed that which is reasonable and necessary for the legitimate business purposes of the lease or rental and is used exclusively by the lessee when being used by the lessee,	
3. If lease allows access/use for only periodic intervals rather than on a full-time basis, it must specify the schedule with the precise length and rent for such interval.	a. Except that for the rental or lease of space the lessee may make payments for the use of space consisting of common areas if such payments do not exceed the lessee's pro rata share of expenses for such space based on the ratio of the space used exclusively by the lessee to the total amount of space (other than common areas) occupied by all persons using such common areas.	
4. Term of lease is for at least 1 year.	3. The lease provides for a term of rental or lease for at least 1 year.	
5. Aggregate rent is set in advance, consistent with the fair market value, and is not based on volume or value of referrals or business generated between the parties.	4. The rental charges over the term of the lease are set in advance, are consistent with fair market value, and are not determined in a manner that takes into account the volume or value of any referrals or other business generated between the parties, the lease would be commercially reasonable even if no referrals were made between the parties, and the lease meets such other requirements as the Secretary may impose by regulation as needed to protect against program or patient abuse.	

Anti-Kickback Safe Harbors

Personal Services and Management Contracts[95]

Personal services and management contracts require:

1. Agreement in writing and signed by the parties.

2. Agreement specifies the services to be provided.

3. If the agreement for services is for only periodic or part-time intervals rather than on a full-time basis, it must specify the schedule with the precise length and charge for such interval.

4. Term of agreement must not be less than 1 year.

5. The aggregate compensation paid to the agent is set in advance, consistent with fair market value, and does not take into account referrals or business generated between the parties.

6. The services under the agreement do not involve the counseling or promotion of a business arrangement or activity that violates federal or state law.

Stark Law Exceptions

Personal Service Arrangements[96]

Remuneration from an entity under an arrangement (including remuneration for specific physicians' services furnished to a nonprofit blood center) is excluded if:

1. The arrangement is set out in writing, signed by the parties, and specifies the services covered by the arrangement.

2. The arrangement covers all of the services to be provided by the physician (or an immediate family of such physician) to the entity.

3. The aggregate services contracted for do not exceed those that are reasonable and necessary for the legitimate business purposes of the arrangement.

4. The term of the arrangement is for at least 1 year.

5. The compensation to be paid over the term of the arrangement is set in advance, does not exceed fair market value, and except in the case of a physician incentive plan described in subparagraph (B) (see Physician Incentive Plans below), is not determined in a manner that takes into account the volume or value of any referrals or other business generated between the parties.

6. The services to be performed under the arrangement do not involve the counseling or promotion of a business arrangement or other activity that violates any state or federal law.

7. The arrangement meets such other requirements as the Secretary may impose by regulation as needed to protect against program or patient abuse.

Comments

The key difference is that the safe harbor protects not only personal services (i.e., those provided pursuant to a contract with an individual), but also management services that could be provided by an entity. The Stark Law exception protects only personal services. Also note that the safe harbor requires that the aggregate compensation be set in advance, unlike the Stark Law exception.

(continues)

Table 3.1 *(continued)*

Anti-Kickback Safe Harbors	Stark Law Exceptions	Comments
Sale of Practice[97]	*Sale of Practice or Property*[98]	The safe harbor is much narrower, applying only to a hospital's acquisition of a practice. The Stark Law exception is not limited in this manner. Another key difference is that the safe harbor requires that the practice must be in a health professional shortage area and does not apply to any property other than the physician's practice.
This safe harbor allows a hospital or other entity to buy the practice of a practitioner so long as the following four standards are met:	An isolated financial transaction, such as a one-time sale of property or practice, is excluded if:	
1. The sale is completed within not more than 3 years.	1. The requirements described in subparagraphs (B) and (C) of paragraph (2) are met with respect to the entity in the same manner as they apply to an employer (see 2 and 3 of Bona Fide Employment Relationships below).	
2. The selling practitioner will not be in a professional position to make referrals to, or otherwise generate business for, the purchasing hospital or entity.	2. The transaction meets such other requirements as the Secretary may impose by regulation as needed to protect against program or patient abuse.	
3. The practice being acquired is in an HPSA for the practitioner's specialty.		
4. Commencing at the time of the first agreement pertaining to the sale, the hospital or entity must diligently and in good faith begin commercially reasonable recruitment efforts to obtain a new practitioner to take over the acquired practice within 1 year, pursuant to a recruitment arrangement that meets the recruitment safe harbor.		

Anti-Kickback Safe Harbors

Bona Fide Employment Relationships[99]

This safe harbor applies to employer payments to employees for covered services rendered in a bona fide employment relationship.

Stark Law Exceptions

Bona Fide Employment Relationships[100]

Any amount paid by an employer to a physician (or an immediate family member of such physician) who has a bona fide employment relationship with the employer for the provision of services is excluded if:

1. The employment is for identifiable services.

2. The amount of the remuneration under the employment

    a. is consistent with the fair market value of the services, and

    b. is not determined in a manner that takes into account (directly or indirectly) the volume or value of any referrals by the referring physician.

3. The remuneration is provided pursuant to an agreement that would be commercially reasonable even if no referrals were made to the employer.

4. The employment meets such other requirements as the Secretary may impose by regulation as needed to protect against program or patient abuse.

Subparagraph (B) shall not prohibit the payment of remuneration in the form of a productivity bonus based on services performed personally by the physician (or an immediate family member of the physician).

Comments

The safe harbor is far less restrictive than the Stark Law exception. Note, however, that the safe harbor only applies to payments related to "covered services."

(continues)

Table 3.1 *(continued)*

Anti-Kickback Safe Harbors	Stark Law Exceptions	Comments
Underserved Areas[101]	*Rural Provider*[102]	The Stark Law exception is far broader than the safe harbor, potentially applying to any area outside the Metropolitan Statistical Area, whether underserved or not, with very few specific requirements.
Investment interests in entities in underserved areas require that the entity be located in an underserved area (rural or urban) and that the following eight standards be met:	Designated health services furnished in a rural area (an area outside a Metropolitan Statistical Area as defined by the Office of Management and Budget) by an entity are not a prohibited ownership or investment interest, if substantially all of the designated health services furnished by such entity are furnished to individuals residing in such a rural area.	
1. No more than 50% of the investment interests of each class of investors may be held in the past fiscal year or 12-month period by "interested" investors (i.e., investors who are in a position to make or influence referrals to, furnish items or services to, or otherwise generate business for, the entity). In determining whether this requirement is met, equivalent classes of equity investments may be combined and equivalent classes of debt instruments may be combined.		
2. The terms on which a passive investment interest is offered to an "interested" investor must be no different than the terms on which passive investment interests are offered to other investors.		
3. The terms on which an investment interest is offered to an "interested" investor cannot be related to the volume or value of past or expected referrals, services, or business generated by the investor to the entity.		
4. Passive investors cannot be required to make referrals to, or be in a position to make or influence referrals to, furnish items or services to, or otherwise generate business for, the entity as a condition for remaining an investor.		

Anti-Kickback Safe Harbors	Stark Law Exceptions	Comments
5. The entity or any investor must not market or furnish the entity's items or services (or those of another entity as part of a cross-referral agreement) to passive investors differently than to noninvestors.		
6. At least 75% of the dollar volume of the entity's business in the past fiscal year or 12-month period must come from providing services to patients residing in a medically underserved area (MUA) or who are members of a medically underserved population (MUP).		
7. The entity or any other investor (or anyone acting on behalf of the entity or other investor) must not loan funds to or guarantee a loan for an investor if the investor uses any part of such loan to obtain the investment interest.		
8. The amount of return on the investment must be directly proportional to the amount of capital investment by the investor.		

123

Table 3.1 *(continued)*

Anti-Kickback Safe Harbors	Stark Law Exceptions	Comments
Physician Recruitment[103]	*Physician Recruitment*[104]	The Stark Law exception is broader than the safe harbor in that it does not apply only to underserved areas, although its use is limited to hospitals.
Practitioners recruited in underserved (rural or urban) areas must either have been practicing in their specialty for less than 1 year or be relocating their primary place of practice to the underserved areas, and the arrangement must comply with all of the following nine standards:	Remuneration that is provided by a hospital to a physician to induce the physician to relocate to the geographic area served by the hospital in order to be a member of the medical staff of the hospital is excluded if:	
1. The arrangement is in writing, signed by the parties, and specifies the benefits provided by the recruiting party, the terms under which the benefits are provided, and the obligations of each party.	1. The physician is not required to refer patients to the hospital.	
2. If the practitioner is leaving an established practice, at least 75% of the practitioner's revenues must come from treating new patients not previously seen by the practitioner at the previous practice.	2. The amount of the remuneration under the arrangement is not determined in a manner that takes into account (directly or indirectly) the volume or value of any referrals by the referring physician.	
3. The benefits cannot be provided for more than 3 years, and during this period the terms cannot be renegotiated in any substantial respect.	3. The arrangement meets such other requirements as the Secretary may impose by regulation as needed to protect against program or patient abuse.	
4. The practitioner is not required to refer, be in a position to refer or to influence referrals, or otherwise generate business for the recruiting entity, except that the entity may require the practitioner to maintain staff privileges.		
5. The practitioner is not restricted from establishing staff privileges or referring patients to other entities.		

Anti-Kickback Safe Harbors

7. The practitioner must agree to treat patients covered by any federal healthcare program in a nondiscriminatory manner.

8. At least 75% of the revenues of the practice come from treating patients residing in a health professional shortage area (HPSA) or MUA.

9. The payments may not directly or indirectly benefit any person or entity, other than the recruited practitioner, who is in a position to make or influence referrals covered by a federal healthcare program.

Stark Law Exceptions

Comments

(continues)

Table 3.1 *(continued)*

Anti-Kickback Safe Harbors	Stark Law Exceptions	Comments
Group Practice[105]	*In-Office Ancillary Services*[106]	Note that the safe harbor provision requires compliance with the Stark Law exception in terms of the definition of a "group practice" and in how ancillary revenues are distributed.
Protects ownership interests in the group itself. A physician may receive payment from investing in his or her own group practice as long as the following four standards are met:	Physician referrals are not prohibited for services that are furnished:	
1. The equity interests in the group practice are all held by licensed healthcare professionals who practice in the practice or group.	1. Personally by the referring physician, personally by a physician who is a member of the same group practice as the referring physician, or personally by individuals who are directly supervised by the physician or by another physician in the group practice, and	
2. The equity interests must be in the practice or group itself, and not in some subdivision of the practice or group.	a. In a building in which the referring physician (or another physician who is a member of the same group practice) furnishes physicians services unrelated to the furnishing of designated health services, or	
3. In the case of a group practice, the practice must meet the definition of group practice in the Stark Law, and must be a unified business with centralized decision making, pooling of expenses and revenues, and a compensation distribution system that is not based on satellite offices operating substantially as if they were separate enterprises or profit centers.	b. In the case of a referring physician who is a member of a group practice in another building that is used by the group	
4. Revenues from ancillary services, if any, must be derived from "in-office ancillary services" that meet the definition in the Stark Law and implementing regulations.	i. for the provision of some or all of the group's clinical laboratory services, or	
	ii. for the centralized provision of the group's designated health services (other than clinical laboratory services).	

Anti-Kickback Safe Harbors

Price Reductions Offered by Contractors with Substantial Financial Risk to Managed Care Organizations[107]

Remuneration does not include any payment made between a qualified managed care plan (MCP) and a first-tier contractor for providing or arranging for items or services where the following are met:

1. The agreement between the qualified MCP and the first-tier contractor must

   a. Be in writing and signed by the parties.

   b. Specify the items and services covered by the agreement.

   c. Be for a period of at least 1 year.

   d. Require participation in a quality assurance program.

   e. Specify a methodology for determining payment that is commercially reasonable and consistent with fair market value and includes the intervals at which payment will be made.

2. If a first-tier contractor has an investment interest in a qualified MCP, the investment interest must meet the criteria of "Investment Interests" above.

3. The first-tier contractor must have substantial financial risk for the cost or utilization of services it is obligated to provide through one of the following payment methodologies:

   a. A periodic fixed payment per patient that does not take into account the date, frequency, extent, or kind of service provided.

   b. Percentage of premium.

Stark Law Exceptions

Physician Incentive Plans and Risk-Sharing Arrangements[108]

In the case of a physician incentive plan that takes into account directly or indirectly the volume or value of any referrals or other business generated between the parties, the plan must meet the following requirements:

1. No specific payment is made directly or indirectly under the plan to a physician or a physician group as an inducement to reduce or limit medically necessary services provided with respect to a specific individual enrolled with the entity.

2. In the case of a plan that places a physician or a physician group at substantial financial risk as determined by the Secretary pursuant to § 1876(i)(8)(A)(ii), the plan complies with any requirements the Secretary may impose pursuant to such section.

3. Upon request by the Secretary, the entity provides the Secretary with access to descriptive information regarding the plan, in order to permit the Secretary to determine whether the plan is in compliance with the requirements of this clause.

Compensation pursuant to a risk-sharing arrangement between a managed care organization or an independent physician association and a physician (either directly or indirectly through a subcontractor) for services provided to enrollees of a health plan, provided that the arrangement does not violate the federal anti-kickback statute, § 1128B(b) of the Act, or any law or regulation governing billing or claims submission.

Comments

The Stark Law exception is again broader and less restrictive, but specifically requires compliance with the anti-kickback statute.

(continues)

Table 3.1 *(continued)*

Anti-Kickback Safe Harbors	Stark Law Exceptions	Comments

Anti-Kickback Safe Harbors

Price Reductions Offered by Contractors with Substantial Financial Risk to Managed Care Organizations continued

c. Inpatient federal healthcare program diagnosis-related groups (DRGs).

d. Bonus and withhold arrangements (see regulation for conditions).

4. Payments for items and services reimbursable by federal healthcare program must comply with the following standards:

a. The qualified MCP must submit the claims directly to the federal healthcare program in accordance with a valid reassignment agreement for items or services reimbursed by the federal healthcare program.

b. Payments to first-tier contractors and any downstream contractors for providing or arranging for items or services reimbursed by a federal healthcare program must be identical to payment arrangements to or between the parties for the same items or services provided to other beneficiaries with similar health status, provided that such payments may be adjusted where the adjustments are related to utilization patterns or costs of providing items or services to the relevant population.

Anti-Kickback Safe Harbors	Stark Law Exceptions	Comments
5. In establishing the terms of an arrangement		
a. Neither party gives or receives remuneration in return for or to induce the provision or acceptance of business (other than business covered by the arrangement) for which payment may be made in whole or in part by a federal healthcare program on a fee-for-service basis.		
b. Neither party to the arrangement shifts the financial burden of such arrangement to the extent that increased payments are claimed from a federal healthcare program.		
Remuneration does not include any payment made between a first-tier contractor or between downstream contractors to provide or arrange for items or services, as long as the three standards listed in 3, 4, and 5 are met.		

The 1996 amendments under the Health Insurance Portability and Accountability Act (HIPAA) extended the anti-kickback statute to all "federal healthcare programs," added a statutory exception for certain risk-sharing arrangements, and established several methods designed to increase the flow of information between the OIG and the public about the application of the statute to various transactions. Included among these methods was the requirement that the OIG establish a procedure whereby providers could apply for advisory opinions pertaining to the applicability of the anti-kickback statute or a particular safe harbor to a particular transaction.[8] Such a procedure has been established and a number of advisory opinions have been issued.[9]

All requests for OIG advisory opinions must be submitted in writing, the requestor must be a party to the existing or proposed arrangement, and an initial filing fee must be enclosed.[10] It is important to note that no individual other than the requestor(s) may rely on any advisory opinion issued by the OIG.[11] The OIG has developed a list of those subject matters appropriate for advisory opinions and those that are not. The OIG will issue advisory opinions regarding what constitutes prohibited remuneration; whether an existing or proposed arrangement satisfies the criteria under HIPAA and safe harbor regulations as an activity that does not result in prohibited remuneration; what constitutes inducement to reduce or limit services to Medicare beneficiaries or Medicaid recipients; and whether existing or proposed activity qualifies for imposition of civil or criminal sanction.[12] On the other hand, the OIG will not issue advisory opinions regarding questions related to fair market value of goods, services, or property; whether an individual is a bona fide employee under the Internal Revenue Code; or whether a course of action is the same or substantially the same as a matter under investigation or that has been the subject of a proceeding involving Health and Human Services (HHS) or another government agency.[13]

Tests and Requirements Under the Federal Anti-Kickback Statute
The One Purpose Test

As demonstrated by its plain language, the anti-kickback statute is extremely broad. In *United States v. Greber*,[14] the United States Court of Appeals for the Third Circuit announced the "one purpose test." The court addressed whether payments made to a physician for professional services related to tests performed by a laboratory could be the basis for Medicare fraud. A laboratory providing physicians with diagnostic services billed the Medicare program for the services. When the laboratory received payment, the laboratory forwarded a portion of the payment to the referring physician. The defendant (an osteopathic physician who owned the diagnostic laboratory) contended that the laboratory was merely paying the referring physicians "interpretation fees" for their initial consultation services, as well as for explaining the test results to patients. However, the amount paid to the referring physician was more than Medicare allowed for such services. The court stressed that the anti-kickback statute "is aimed at the inducement factor" and held that "if one purpose of the payment was to induce the physician to use [the laboratory's] services, the statute was violated, even if the payments were also intended to compensate for professional services."[15]

The OIG has since adopted the *Greber* "one purpose" standard as the test in its advisory opinions.[16] If any purpose of the transaction is to induce Medicare or Medicaid referrals, the position of the OIG is that the anti-kickback statute is violated.[17] Similarly, in its 1999 "General Comments" to the 1999 Final Safe Harbor Regulations, the OIG states, "Payment practices that do not fully comply with a safe harbor may still be lawful if no purpose of the payment practice is to induce referrals of federal health care program business."[18]

The *Greber* one purpose test also has been adopted by the Ninth Circuit in *United States v. Kats* and by the Fifth Circuit in *United States v. Davis*.[19] In *United States v. Kats*, the court concluded that when a payment is not incidental to the delivery of healthcare services or goods, the anti-kickback statute is violated.[20] In that case, the owner of a diagnostic laboratory "agreed to 'kick back' 50 percent of Medicare payments received by the laboratory as a result of referrals" from a medical services company. The appellate court held that the trial court's instruction that the "jury could convict [the defendant] unless it found the payment 'wholly, and not incidentally attributable to the delivery of goods or services' accurately stated the law."[21] The court quoted with favor the *Greber* one purpose test, opining that the *Greber* interpretation "is consistent with the legislative history."[22]

In *United States v. Lahue*,[23] the Tenth Circuit also adopted the one purpose test. *Greber* was applied and relied on in a series of related anti-kickback cases closely followed by healthcare lawyers and practitioners. In that case, the court upheld the convictions of two physicians after they entered into a contract to provide consulting services to a hospital in return for a significant yearly financial payment per physician per year, for which they provided little to no services. As long as one purpose of payments from the hospital to the La Hues was to induce referrals back to Baptist Medical, according to the court, the convictions would stand. The US Supreme Court ended the saga in 2002 when it denied certiorari on the issue of whether the defendants could be convicted of violating anti-kickback laws and the application of the one purpose test.

In *United States v. Anderson*,[24] the US District Court in Kansas also adopted *Greber*. In a companion case, *United States v. McClatchey*,[25] the Tenth Circuit officially adopted *Greber*, but with a caveat. A jury instruction in *McClatchey* provided that the defendant "cannot be convicted merely because [he] hoped or expected, or believed that referrals may ensue from remuneration that was designed wholly for other purposes."[26] In a somewhat analogous holding, the US District Court for the Middle District of Florida, in *United States v. Siegel*, held that if "one material purpose" of the payment was for illegal remuneration, the anti-kickback statute was violated.[27]

The Primary Purpose Test

The case of *United States v. Bay State Ambulance and Hosp. Rental Serv., Inc.* looked at the primary purpose, rather than any or one purpose, of a payment to determine its illegality.[28] *Bay State* contained a complicated set of facts, which involved a series of gifts and payments made by an ambulance company to a well-placed employee of a city hospital. The apparent purpose of the gifts was to influence the hospital's decision concerning its choice of ambulance services.

One issue under consideration concerned the correctness of the following jury instructions given by the trial court judge:

> [T]he government has to prove that the payments were made with a corrupt intent, that they were made for an improper purpose. If you find that payments were made for two or more purposes, then the Government has to prove that the improper purpose is the primary purpose or was the primary purpose in making and receiving the payments. It need not be the only purpose, but it must be the primary purpose for making the payments and for receiving them. You cannot convict if you find that the improper purpose was an incidental or minor one in making the payments.[29]

The appellate court agreed that the defendant's payments were made primarily for inducing referrals; therefore, it upheld the trial court's jury instructions, recognizing that the test applied by the trial court was less expansive than the *Greber* one purpose rule. The *Bay State* appellate court, citing Greber with favor, stated "the gravamen of Medicare fraud is inducement," and that the "key to a Medicare fraud case is the reason for the payment—was the purpose of the payments primarily for inducement."[30] However, the court chose not to adopt the *Greber* test.

Scienter Requirement

The anti-kickback statute also requires that the government establish scienter (i.e., criminal intent) under a "knowingly and willfully" standard.[31] The circuits are split as to the proper interpretation of these words. In *Hanlester Network v. Shalala*, a clinical laboratory established joint ventures with physician partners who made nominal investments.[32] Substantially all of the financial risk was borne by SmithKline Beecham Clinical Laboratories, the organizer and manager of the joint ventures. The joint venture agreements required the physicians to resell their interests at nominal prices if they moved out of the trade area, retired, or lost their licenses. As the joint venture manager, SmithKline took a management fee equal to 76% of revenues. The joint venture had no employees, and the laboratory work was done at SmithKline. The OIG alleged that the physicians were paid a disproportionate return (more than 50% annually) for their investment, which was financed by the manager, and that the physician investors were selected from among physicians expected to make referrals to the laboratories. There was, however, no requirement that physician investors make referrals to the labs.

The fundamental issue before the court was whether the "inducement" prohibition of the anti-kickback statute was met on the basis that the structure and operations of the joint venture laboratories "merely encouraged" the physician partners to refer patients to the laboratory, which may not violate the law (as opposed to "induced" the referral of business, which clearly would violate the statute). The Ninth Circuit Court of Appeal held that, in order for an individual to violate the Medicare anti-kickback statute, there must be a "knowing and willful" intention to violate a law.[33] In this case, the court found proof lacking that the defendant physicians knew that it was illegal to be paid for referrals or that they engaged in conduct with the specific intent to violate the law.

All courts that subsequently considered the issue have rejected the *Hanlester Network* holding. These courts have held that the defendant need not have intended to violate or known that he or she was violating the Medicare anti-kickback statute in particular. Rather, he or she needs only to have intended to engage in conduct that was unlawful.

In a typical case, the Florida Fourth District Court of Appeal easily set aside *Hanlester* when determining that a percentage commission paid to a marketing company by a durable medical equipment supplier was an illegal kickback:

> The Anti-Kickback Statute is directed at punishment of those who perform specific acts and does not require that one engage in the prohibited conduct with the specific intent to violate the statute. We therefore decline to follow the Hanlester interpretation of the Anti-Kickback Statute.[34]

Also in contrast to *Hanlester*, the court in *United States v. Jain* supported the position that the government must prove only that the defendant knew his conduct was wrong.[35] However, the court noted that the defendant's good faith belief that he was being paid for services rather than patient promotion would be a defense.[36]

In *United States v. Starks*, the Eleventh Circuit confirmed that payments of $250 for each referral from Future Steps to Project Support employees violated the anti-kickback statute.[37] Future Steps treated drug addicts. Two Project Support employees were paid for referrals that cost the Medicaid program $323,000. The Eleventh Circuit rejected the argument that the anti-kickback statute was technically complex and ruled that the defendant's specific knowledge of the statute did not have to be proved, especially in view of the fact that the payments for the referral were made to the employees in a clandestine fashion (cash under the table).[38]

In *United States v. Anderson*, hospital officials and doctors were convicted under the anti-kickback statute for fees paid by a hospital under consulting agreements to physicians.[39] The fees were excessive for the services rendered and the court therefore concluded that the consulting agreements were shams to disguise payments for patient referrals. The court found that although the anti-kickback statute was not a simple statute, it was not highly technical. It therefore adopted the general knowledge standard.

Although the Supreme Court has not interpreted the words knowingly and willfully in the context of the anti-kickback statute, it has done so in connection with another criminal statute. In the case of *Bryan v. United States*, the Supreme Court concluded that an individual acts willfully when he or she acts with knowledge that his or her conduct is unlawful.[40]

The question raised in the *Bryan* case was whether the defendant had to know that he was violating a specific statute prohibiting the unlicensed sale of firearms. The Court distinguished complex statutes that are highly technical and capable of entrapping people engaged in conduct they believed to be innocent from other statutes. When the law is complex and capable of trapping people, the Court concluded that a defendant had to have specific knowledge of the law being violated. The Court stated that when it came to the statute before it, the government had only to prove that the defendant acted with the knowledge that his conduct was unlawful. The Court held that as "a general matter, when used in the criminal context, a 'willful' act is one undertaken for a 'bad purpose.'"[41] The *Bryan* case lends support to the majority view that specific intent to violate the anti-kickback statute is not necessary for conviction.

Penalties for Violation of the Anti-Kickback Statute

The stakes in running afoul of the anti-kickback statute are high. Section 4304 (b) of the Balanced Budget Act of 1997 (BBA) granted HHS the authority to impose civil money penalties of (1) up to $50,000, and (2) three times the amount of remuneration in question, for each violation of the statute.[42]

In addition to the criminal and civil penalties under the anti-kickback statute, violations of the statute can lead to exclusion from participation in federal healthcare programs.[43] In 1998, the OIG issued a final rule extending its exclusion authority to "indirect providers" such as drug and device manufacturers.[44] The effect of such exclusion would be to eliminate coverage for any products of the excluded manufacturer. However, significant questions remain regarding the OIG's legal and practical authority to exclude manufacturers involved in the distribution of, or billing for, covered drugs.

Enforcement Action

An increase in criminal enforcement of the healthcare fraud and abuse laws has, not surprisingly, resulted in a greater number of successful enforcement actions under the anti-kickback statute. However, the increasing number of successful prosecutions is due not only to the greater number of enforcement actions initiated by the OIG and United States Attorneys, but also the government's increasingly creative application of the broadly worded statute. The anti-kickback statute establishes criminal penalties for anyone offering, soliciting, receiving, or paying remuneration, directly or indirectly, in cash or in kind, in return for the referral of a patient for whom healthcare services are paid by a federal healthcare program.

Since its inception, many legal practitioners predicted that this statute could be applied in a manner unforeseen by its original authors. This is because the statute's broad language allows it to be interpreted to prohibit not only egregious kickback schemes, but also seemingly innocuous transactions.

Joint venture transactions and compensation arrangements that implicate the anti-kickback statute may be viewed on a continuum ranging from blatant violations of the law to financial arrangements that implicate the law in less obvious ways. The recent enforcement efforts by the United States Attorneys and the OIG throughout the country evidence a trend to apply the anti-kickback statute not only to the most egregious forms of abuse, but also in those instances where its application may not be directly supported by prior case law and do not involve an obvious threat to patient and program abuse. Furthermore, perhaps due to the significant criminal and civil money penalties available to the federal agencies, enforcement actions have been aimed at small and large, as well as simple and sophisticated, transactions. In short, the recent enforcement actions of the United States Attorneys' office and the OIG signify an expansion of the applicability of the anti-kickback statute in as broad a fashion as its language permits and in a manner probably unforeseen by the original authors of the law.

Perhaps the most aggressive enforcement actions involving the anti-kickback statute have been undertaken in the Middle District of Florida, focusing on the mental health and substance abuse sector of the healthcare industry, and more recently including payments for referrals between physicians and ancillary service providers such as clinical laboratory, durable medical equipment, and mobile diagnostic providers.[45] These cases all involved alleged violations of the federal anti-kickback statute involving payment for remuneration in various forms in return for the referral of patients under the Medicare and Medicaid programs. The following are the alleged types of illegal payment for referrals that have been reflected in the indictments and plea agreements in these cases:

1. The solicitation and receipt of payment from hospitals providing inpatient care to psychiatric and substance abuse patients in return for the referral of those patients to the hospitals.

2. These payments were allegedly made by disguising their illegal nature in the form of fraudulent contracts and agreements falsely characterizing the payments made for the referral of patients as payment for management services, marketing services, initial psychiatric clinical assessments, aftercare treatment, and other purported services.

3. The hospitals that were paying remuneration in return for the referral of psychiatric and substance abuse patients would also request fraudulent claims for reimbursement on their cost reports for the salaries of persons who had entered into fictitious employment contracts with the hospitals.

4. There were also alleged payments for referrals in the form of the routine waiver of co-payments for patients and payments for their transportation, often involving air travel, from their cities of residence (which were often in the northern part of the United States) to the facilities (which were in Florida).

5. The payments for referrals of patients for clinical lab and other ancillary services were often purported to be for equipment and space rentals, phlebotomists and other employee salaries, and compensation for professional services, such as doctors acting as "testing review officers" or "medical review officers" for clinical lab work.

These cases represent the enforcement of the anti-kickback statute against arrangements that may appear on their face to be arrangements for legitimate services or for equipment or space and may also appear to fit into federal "safe harbors" under the anti-kickback statute. Nevertheless, these arrangements have formed the basis for indictments and successful prosecutions involving plea agreements based on the theory that they were "sham" arrangements that were designed to mask the intent to make payment for referrals. These enforcement actions underscore the idea that facial compliance with safe harbor criteria, such as personal services arrangements, equipment and space leases, and even employment agreements must be necessary, commercially reasonable, and bona fide in all respects; otherwise, they could be as vulnerable to attack as if payments were made in cash for the referral of patients.

Perhaps the most dramatic example of the use of criminal sanctions under the federal anti-kickback statute was the criminal plea agreements in *United States of Am. v. Kimberly Home Health Care, Inc. d/b/a/ Olsten Kimberly Quality Care*, a wholly owned subsidiary of The Olsten

Corp. (Olsten) (SD of FL and MD of FL 1999). In *Olsten*, the company agreed to the sale of home health agencies to a large unnamed hospital company in return for a management agreement to manage those same home health agencies and others, which the hospital would purchase in the future. The government alleged that the transaction violated the federal anti-kickback statute because the sale of the home health agencies was for a price below fair market value, which was in return for an agreement to enter into a lucrative management contract under which Olsten would be paid on a per-visit basis for serving the patients of the hospital-owned home health agencies. The cost of acquisition of the home health agencies is not reimbursable by the Medicare program, but the costs of management services are reimbursable. In plea agreements executed to resolve two separate proceedings in the Middle District of Florida and the Southern District of Florida, Olsten pled guilty to mail fraud and several violations of the anti-kickback statute. Olsten agreed to pay $61 million in criminal restitution and fines and civil penalties. Olsten further agreed to implement a corporate integrity agreement that was separately negotiated with the Office of Inspector General of the Department of Health and Human Services.

The anti-kickback statute remains actively enforced, routinely resulting in the imposition of criminal, administrative, and civil sanctions. These enforcement actions represent an effort by government agencies to expand the reach of the anti-kickback statute to be as broad as its language permits. The government's increasingly aggressive use of criminal penalties demonstrates its willingness to use all the tools at its disposal to eliminate healthcare fraud. Because seemingly small or simple transactions may later become the subject of a government investigation, it is imperative that healthcare providers have qualified counsel review all of their proposed transactions for compliance with applicable federal and state fraud and abuse laws.

Physician Self-Referral—Stark Law

The Stark Law generally prohibits a physician's referral of Medicare patients to an entity for the furnishing of designated health services (DHS) if there is a financial relationship between the referring physician or an immediate family member and the entity, unless an enumerated exception applies.[46]

Unlike other statutes and regulations that are applicable to the healthcare industry as a whole, Stark Laws apply only to physicians (which also includes dentists, podiatrists, and chiropractors).[47] The underlying purpose behind the Stark Laws was to deter physicians from referring patients only to facilities in which they had an ownership interest, rather than to a facility that could provide the patient with the best medical care. It was also believed that self-referrals could, and would, lead to physicians ordering unnecessary services/procedures based on the physician's financial interest in a given facility. By establishing the Stark Law, Congress was attempting to create a "bright line" rule whereby physicians would know, in advance, which types of business arrangements were illegal.

On January 4, 2001, the Centers for Medicare and Medicaid Services (CMS) issued Phase I of the final Stark II regulations (Phase I Final Rule).[48] The Phase I Final Rule, which became effective March 4, 2002, relates to the Ethics in Patient Referral Act of 1989 (Stark I) as amended by the Omnibus Budget and Reconciliation Act of 1993 (Stark II) (these are collectively known as the "Stark Law"). Phase I of the Final Rule concerns the Stark Law's prohibition and exceptions to the ownership and investment interests, compensation arrangements, and statutory definitions. Phase II of the final Stark II regulations (Phase II Final Rule) became effective on July 24, 2004, and addressed additional ownership interest and compensation arrangement exceptions, reporting requirements, sanctions, and the Stark Law's application to Medicaid.[49] In it, CMS clarifies and modifies the definition of several statutory terms in the Final Rule and creates a new exception for entities that submit claims for DHS where the entities could not have been aware of the physician who made the referral.[50] Phase III of the final Stark regulations (Phase III Final Rule) was published on September 5, 2007, and became effective on December 4, 2007.[51]

The most significant change in the Phase III Final Rule was CMS's broadening of the types of arrangements that fall within the scope of prohibited direct compensation arrangements by way of the physician "stand in the shoes" provisions. As a result of these provisions, arrangements that were previously not subject to the regulations, or subject to the less stringent rules for indirect compensation arrangements, became prohibited unless they met one of the exceptions to direct compensation arrangements.

Most recently, on August 19, 2008, CMS published its final rule regarding the Hospital Inpatient Prospective Payment System (IPPS Rule), which contained a lengthy section finalizing proposed revisions to the Stark regulations.[52] In it, CMS finalized revisions to the physician "stand in the shoes" provisions and its proposals to restrict certain "under arrangements" transactions and percentage-based compensation arrangements. Certain provisions in the Phase III Final Rule were not effective until October 1, 2009, to give the parties to newly prohibited arrangements time to restructure. The remaining provisions were effective October 1, 2008.

Sanctions for violating the Stark Law include the denial of payment, requiring refunds of claims that were billed in violation of the statute, civil monetary penalties of not more than $15,000 for services billed pursuant to a prohibited patient referral, and civil monetary penalties of not more than $100,000 for each unlawful arrangement or scheme that the physician or entity knows or should know has a principal purpose of ensuring referrals by the physician to a particular entity which, if the physician directly made referrals to such entity, would be a violation of the Stark Law.[53] Additionally, any person who fails to meet the reporting requirements under the act may be assessed a civil monetary penalty in the amount of not more than $10,000 for each day for which reporting is required to have been made.

Definitions

Statutes and regulations define DHS to include clinical laboratory services; physical therapy; occupational therapy; speech-language pathology services; radiology and certain other imaging services; radiation therapy services and supplies; durable medical equipment and supplies; parenteral and enteral nutrients, equipment, and supplies; prosthetics, orthotics, and prosthetic devices and supplies; home health services; outpatient prescription drugs; and inpatient and outpatient hospital services.[54]

The definition of referral does not include services performed personally by the referring physician.[55] This allows a physician to initiate and personally perform services without these services being deemed "referrals to an entity." However, all other Medicare-covered DHS performed at the request of a physician are still considered physician referrals. For example, services performed by a physician's employees and "incident to" services are still considered performed as a result of the physician's referrals.[56] CMS has taken the position that a referral is imputed to a physician if the physician directs or controls the referral. The regulations contain an exception to the referral definition for pathologists, radiologists, and radiation oncologists. The request for consultation may be made to a party with which the specialist is affiliated.[57]

Under the regulations, the definition of "entity" does not include referring physicians, but does include their medical practices. The regulations define entity to include any person or entity receiving payment for DHS.[58] Specifically, the Phase I Final Rule reasoned that the "payee" is the entity for purposes of determining to whom the beneficiary was referred. Additionally, the entity to which the patient has reassigned his or her Medicare benefits will be considered the entity furnishing the DHS service. Managed care organizations (MCOs), health plans, and IPAs are deemed entities if they employ a supplier or operate a facility that could accept reassignment from a physician or supplier.[59] The IPPS Rule further expands the definition of entity to include an entity that performs services that are billed as DHS by another entity.[60]

The Stark Law only addresses situations in which the referring physician has a financial relationship with the DHS entity. The two types of financial arrangements that the statute focuses on are (1) compensation arrangements and (2) an ownership or investment interest in the entity.[61] The Phase I Final Rule expanded the definition of "financial relationship," and made a distinction between a "direct" and an "indirect" financial relationship.[62] A direct ownership or investment interest exists if remuneration passes directly from the physician (or immediate family member of the physician) and the DHS entity without any intervening person or entity. An indirect ownership interest exists if there is (1) an unbroken chain of any number of persons or entities between the referring physician and the DHS entity with linked ownership or investment interests between them and (2) the entity furnishing DHS has actual knowledge of, or acts in reckless disregard or deliberate ignorance of, the fact that the referring physician has some direct or indirect ownership interest in the DHS entity. Ownership interest includes ownership or investment through equity, debt, or other means, including ownership in an entity that holds an ownership interest in another entity that provides DHS.[63] However, ownership in a subsidiary entity does not constitute ownership in a parent entity unless the subsidiary owns an interest in the parent.[64]

The definition of indirect ownership interest includes a knowledge requirement, which must be met before a DHS provider may be held liable for receiving a tainted referral. As a result, under the regulations, a physician must have had knowledge (or acted in reckless disregard or deliberate ignorance of) the existence of such an ownership interest in order to be held liable for receiving a tainted referral. Thus, a DHS provider without "knowledge" will not be liable for providing services originated by an impermissible referral.[65]

An ownership or investment interest is defined to include stock, partnership shares, limited liability company memberships, loans, bonds, or other instruments secured by an entity's property or revenues.[66] An unsecured loan, however, is not an ownership interest under the regulations.[67] Accordingly, if a physician provides secured financing to an entity, the physician possesses an ownership interest in the entity, and not a compensation arrangement.[68] Further, the Phase I Final Rule specified that interest in a retirement plan, stock options and convertible securities (until exercised), unsecured loans, and "under arrangements" between a hospital and an entity owned by a physician or physician group are not ownership or investment interests.[69]

The Phase I Final Rule added an exception that allows an entity lacking the requisite culpable mental state to submit a claim for DHS even when the services originate from an impermissible referral. The exception provides:

> Payment may be made to an entity that submits a claim for designated health services if—(a) the entity did not have actual knowledge of, and did not act in reckless disregard or deliberate ignorance of, the identity of the physician who made the referral of the designated health service to the entity; and (b) the claim otherwise complies with all applicable Federal laws, rules and regulations.[70]

This rule protects a DHS provider who is unaware or does not have reason to know that an oral or indirect referral originated from a party with a financial relationship with the DHS provider. CMS has stated that the new "knowledge exception" applies to indirect and oral referral where there is no written documentation of the referral. The Phase I Final Rule's language, however, does not specifically limit the knowledge exception to oral and indirect referrals. The DHS provider is not under an affirmative duty to investigate the origination of a referral unless the DHS provider has reason to suspect that such a financial relationship exists with the referring physician. It must be noted that although this exception allows the DHS provider to bill for the services, arguably, the physician remains liable for his or her prohibited referral.

The Stark Law broadly defines compensation arrangements to include any arrangement involving remuneration, direct or indirect, between a physician and an entity.[71] Remuneration can consist of (1) the forgiveness of amounts owed for inaccurate tests or procedures, mistakenly performed tests or procedures, or the correction of minor billing errors; (2) the provision of items or supplies used to collect or transport specimens for the entity, or orders to communicate the results of tests and procedures to the entity; and (3) a payment made by an insurer to a physician to satisfy a claim, submitted on a fee-for-service basis, for the furnishing of health services by that physician to an individual who is covered by a policy with the insurer if (a) the health services and the payment therefore are not furnished pursuant to a contract arrangements, (b) the payment which otherwise would be made to the individual was made to the physician on his behalf, and (c) the payment amount was set in advance and did not exceed market value.[72] The definition of the term "set in advance" was modified in the Phase II Final Rule to permit percentage compensation arrangements if the methodology for calculating the compensation is set in advance and does not change over the course of the arrangement in any manner that reflects the volume or value of referrals.[73]

Under the Stark regulations, a direct compensation arrangement exists if remuneration passes between the referring physician (or a member of his or her immediate family) and the entity furnishing DHS without any intervening persons or entities.[74] The Phase I Final Rule also sets forth three requirements that must be present in order for an "indirect compensation arrangement" to exist. The elements are: (1) the unbroken chain requirement, (2) the volume or value requirement, and (3) the knowledge requirement.[75] The unbroken chain test requires "an unbroken chain of any number (but not fewer than one) of persons or entities that have financial relationships between them." The second requirement is that:

> The referring physician . . . receive aggregate compensation from the person or entity in the chain with which the physician has a direct financial relationship that varies with, or otherwise reflects the volume or value of referrals or other business generated by the referring physician for the entity furnishing the DHS.[76]

If total payments to the physician rise or fall based on the volume or value of referrals, it is an "indirect compensation arrangement" that triggers the referral prohibition unless it complies with an exception. This requirement examines the entity's direct financial relationship with the referring physician. Once a direct financial relationship is found, it must be determined whether the compensation arrangement varies with the volume or value of referrals or "business otherwise generated." If the arrangement varies in the aforementioned manner, then an indirect compensation agreement exists. Almost all contracts between physician groups—in which the physicians have an ownership interest—and hospitals will be subject to the volume or value test. However, if the physicians do not have an ownership interest, the volume or value test will be applied to the compensation physicians receive to determine whether their compensation is based on the physicians' referrals to the hospital.

The regulations also provide that, for an indirect compensation arrangement to exist, the DHS provider must have "knowledge" that the referring physician's compensation is based on the physician's volume or value referrals or "other business generated by the referring physician" to the DHS provider.[77]

In the Phase III Final Rule, CMS introduced the "stand in the shoes" provisions for purposes of determining whether a physician has a direct or indirect compensation arrangement with an entity to which the physician refers.[78] A physician who has an ownership or investment interest in a physician organization will be viewed as "standing in the shoes" of his or her physician organization. In other words, the referring physician is considered to have the same compensation arrangements as the physician organization in whose shoes the referring physician stands. On the other hand, if the entity interposed between the physician and the entity to which the physician refers is not a "physician organization," then the indirect compensation arrangement rules still apply. The rules define a "physician organization" to mean a physician, including a professional corporation of which the physician is the sole owner, a physician practice, or a group practice. In the IPPS Rule, CMS scaled back on the "stand in the shoes" concept by limiting it to physician owners of a physician organization.[79] Physicians with only a titular ownership interest (physicians without the ability or right to receive the financial benefits of ownership or investment, including, but not limited to, the distribution of profits, dividends, proceeds of sale, or similar returns on investment) are not required to stand in the shoes of their physician organizations. Note that where a physician is viewed as standing in the shoes of a physician organization, arrangements must meet a direct compensation exception in order not to violate the Stark Law.

Where an indirect compensation arrangement exists, DHS referrals are prohibited unless the arrangement fits within the indirect compensation exception. The indirect compensation exception requires that:

1. The compensation received by the referring physician (or immediate family member) is fair market value for services and items actually provided, not taking into account the value or volume of referrals or other business generated by the referring physician for the entity furnishing DHS.
2. The compensation arrangement is set out in writing, signed by the parties, and specifies the services covered by the arrangement, except in the case of a bona fide employment relationship between an employer and an employee, in which case the arrangement need not be set out in a written contract, but must be for identifiable services and be commercially reasonable even if no referrals are made to the employer.
3. The compensation arrangement does not violate the anti-kickback statute or any laws or regulations governing billing or claims submission.[80]

The Stark Law also provides for various compensation arrangement exceptions which require that the arrangements set compensation in advance and not take into account the volume or value of referrals, other business generated between the parties, or condition compensation on referrals to a particular provider.

Exceptions[81]

The Stark Law provides for various enumerated exceptions to the general prohibition on financial relationships between the referring physician and DHS entity. General exceptions to both ownership interest and compensation arrangements apply to physician services in which the services are provided by a physician in the same group practice as the referring physician.[82]

A group practice is a group of two or more physicians legally organized as a partnership, professional corporation, foundation, not-for-profit corporation, faculty practice plan, or similar association.[83] A physician's referrals are excepted from the Stark Law's referral prohibition as long as the service is performed in the same building in which the nondesignated health services are performed, or in the case of a group practice, in a building used by the group exclusively for the provision of the group's designated health services. The services must be billed by the physician performing or supervising the services, the practice group, or the entity that is owned by the physician or the physician practice group.[84] The final overall exception concerns prepaid plans. Referrals for DHS services made by certain managed care organizations (health maintenance organization, Medicare + Choice organization) to individuals enrolled within the organization will not constitute a financial relationship under the Stark Law.[85]

The law further provides that the referring physician's ownership of publicly traded investment securities and mutual funds will not constitute ownership or investment interest if the securities are traded on a public market and the corporation that issued the securities has stockholder equity exceeding $75 million for the past three years.[86] Shares issued by a regulated investment company are also excluded if the company has total assets exceeding $75 million for the past year, or on average during the previous three years.[87] Ownership or investment interest in hospitals will not constitute ownership interest under the Stark Law if the referring physician is authorized to perform services at the hospital and the interest the physician owns is interest in the hospital itself, and not a hospital subdivision.[88] Furthermore, if any referrals for designated health services are made to hospitals in Puerto Rico or to rural providers, any investment or ownership interest the referring physician may have in such entities will not constitute a violation of the Stark Law.[89]

The Stark Law also lists various types of compensation arrangement exceptions that are permitted. Compensation arrangements between the referring physician and the entity providing the designated health services are allowed if the compensation is for the rental of office space or the rental of equipment.[90] Both rental exceptions require that there be an agreement in writing, that space or equipment rented does not exceed what is necessary for legitimate business purposes, and that the duration of the lease be for at least one year.[91] Compensation arrangements involving bona fide employment arrangements and personal service arrangements are also permitted. Amounts paid by an employer to a physician under a bona fide employment relationship do not constitute compensation arrangements under the statute as long as the employment is for identifiable services, the amount of remuneration is consistent with the fair market value, and the remuneration is provided pursuant to an agreement.[92] Amounts compensated under a personal service arrangement qualify as an exception if the arrangement is in writing, covers the services to be furnished by the physician, the services are reasonable and necessary for the legitimate business purposes of the arrangement, the duration of the arrangement is at least one year, the compensation to be paid is set in advance and does not exceed the fair market value, and the services performed under the arrangement do not involve counseling or promotion of a business arrangement or other illegal activity.[93]

Additional remuneration that does not qualify as compensation is remuneration received that is unrelated to the provision of designated health services, remuneration provided for physician recruitment by a hospital as long as the recruited physician is not required to provide the hospital with referrals, and isolated transactions between a hospital and physician, such as a one-time sale of practice if the remuneration is consistent with fair market value and is provided pursuant to an agreement.[94] The statute further provides that compensation received in certain practice arrangements between a group performing designated health services and a hospital billing for them is exempt if such an arrangement had been entered into and has been uninterrupted since December 19, 1989.[95] For such an arrangement to meet the exception, the arrangement has to be in writing, the group must substantially furnish all designated health services covered by the arrangement, and the amount of compensation must be consistent with fair market value.[96] Finally, any payments made by a physician to a laboratory in exchange for the provision of clinical laboratory services or payments made to an entity as compensation for other services or items furnished at a price consistent with the fair market value is exempted from a compensation arrangement.[97]

It is important to note that any remuneration received for the rental of office space exception, the rental of equipment exception, the bona fide employment relationship exception, the personal service arrangement exception, the exception concerning physician recruitment, and the certain practice arrangements with hospitals exception may not take into account the volume or value of referrals between the parties in determining the amount of remuneration.[98] An exception exists, however, for personal service arrangements that qualify as physician incentive plans. There, the compensation between physician and entity may consider the volume and value of referrals in establishing the amount of remuneration. However, no specific payment may be made that serves as an inducement to reduce or limit the medically necessary services provided by the physician enrolled in the entity.[99]

In addition to the above-mentioned exceptions that do not violate the Stark Law's general prohibition regarding financial relationships, Congress included in the Stark Law a provision giving the secretary of Health and Human Services authority to issue regulations creating additional exceptions to the general prohibition against physician referrals to entities with which the physician has a financial relationship if the secretary determines that the financial relationship "does not pose a risk of program or patient abuse." Accordingly, the Phase I and Phase II Final Rules contained several additional exceptions.

Under the Stark Law, physicians practicing in academic medical centers would have to conform to the personal service arrangement or employment exceptions, or the group practice definition. The Phase I Final Rule recognized that these exceptions and definitions do not fit the multiple relationships and monetary transfers inherent in most academic medical centers and has issued a new exception protecting those relationships if certain conditions are met. An academic medical center, for these purposes, consists of an accredited medical school, an affiliated tax-exempt faculty practice plan, and one or more affiliated hospitals in which the majority of medical staff members are faculty members and in which a majority of admissions are made by faculty members. The Phase I Final Rule included a fair market value exception, which requires:

1. The agreement must be in writing, must be signed by the parties, and must cover only identifiable items and services, all of which are specified in the agreement.
2. The agreement must specify the timeframe, which can be for any period of time and which may include a termination provision, but the parties may enter into only one arrangement for the same items or services during the course of a year. If the term is for less than one year, the parties may renew it any number of times if the terms and compensation do not change.
3. The agreement must specify the compensation, which must be set in advance, must be consistent with fair market value, and must not be determined in a manner that takes into account the volume or value of any referrals or any other business generated by the referring physician.
4. The arrangement must be commercially reasonable, taking into account the nature and scope of the transaction, and must further the legitimate business purposes of the parties.

5. The arrangement must meet an anti-kickback safe harbor, or must not otherwise violate the anti-kickback statute, or the parties must have received a favorable advisory opinion (note that only the parties requesting an advisory opinion may rely on it for these purposes).

6. The services must not involve the counseling or promotion of a business arrangement or other activity that violates a state or federal law.[100]

Yet another exception to the Stark Law pertains to nonmonetary compensation up to $300. This exception protects compensation from an entity in the form of items or services (not cash or cash equivalents) that do not exceed $300 per year, if certain conditions are met. In other words, the $50 limit has been dropped, and a physician may receive a single gift valued at $300, or several gifts totaling no more than $300, in a single year. The Phase II Final Rule added that the $300 will be adjusted annually for inflation to the nearest whole dollar effective January 1 of each year.[101] The other conditions of this exception are: (1) the compensation may not be determined in any manner that takes into account the volume or value of referrals or other business generated by the referring physician, (2) the compensation may not be solicited by the physician or the physician's practice, and (3) the compensation arrangement must not violate the anti-kickback statute.[102]

This exception applies only to gifts to individual physicians, not to group practices. All physicians in a group practice could receive gifts up to the $300 per year maximum, so long as the group did not solicit the gifts (i.e., make them a condition of the group doing business with the entity), and so long as they did not violate the anti-kickback statute.

The Phase I Final Rule recognized that it is common in the industry for hospitals to provide certain benefits to its medical staff members and that such benefits largely serve to benefit the patients and the hospital. Examples are free parking spaces for medical staff members while they are seeing patients in the hospital, free computer and Internet access on the hospital campus to enhance record keeping, and occasional meals for medical staff members while on hospital or patient business. Accordingly, CMS created an exception for such benefits, if all of the following conditions are met:

1. the compensation is offered to all members of the medical staff without regard to the volume or value of referrals or other business generated between the parties.

2. the compensation is offered only during periods when the medical staff members are making rounds or performing other duties that benefit the hospital or its patients.

3. the compensation is provided by the hospital and used by the medical staff members only on the hospital's campus.

4. the compensation is reasonably related to the provision of, or designed to facilitate directly or indirectly the delivery of medical services at the hospital.

5. the compensation is consistent with the types of benefits offered to medical staff members by other hospitals within the same local region, or by comparable hospitals in comparable regions.

6. the compensation is of low value—less than $25 (adjusted each calendar year for inflation to the nearest whole dollar effective January 1 of each year)—with respect to each

occurrence of the benefit (i.e., each meal given to a physician while he or she is serving hospital patients).

7. the compensation is not determined in any manner that takes into account the volume or value of referrals or other business generated between the parties.

8. the compensation arrangement does not violate the anti-kickback statute.[71]

The Phase II Final Rule added the additional condition that the compensation be offered to all members of the medical staff practicing in the same specialty, even if some members do not accept it.[103]

This exception protects many medical staff benefits that could not be covered under the fair market value exception (because there is often no written agreement), and which may, in the aggregate, constitute a value greater than $300 per year, taking it out of the *de minimis* exception. Note, however, that CMS explicitly states that medical transcription services are not considered to be of incidental benefit or nominal value and would not be covered under this exception. In the Phase I Final Rule, CMS recognized that many hospitals are offering compliance training to their medical staffs. The secretary believes that such training programs are beneficial and pose no risk of fraud or abuse. Therefore, the Phase I Final Rule contained an exception for compliance training provided by a hospital to a physician that practices in the hospital's local community or service area, provided the training is held in the local area or service area. Compliance training is defined as training regarding the basic elements of a compliance program (not setting up a compliance program for the physician), or specific training regarding Medicare or Medicaid requirements (such as billing or coding).[104] In the Phase II Final Rule, CMS also added a number of new exceptions. Among them, CMS created a specific exception for the provision of valuable information technology items and services, such as computer hardware or software, by a DHS entity to a physician to participate in a community-wide health information system designed to enhance the overall health of the community. The healthcare system must be one that allows community providers and practitioners to access and share electronic healthcare records. In addition to healthcare records, the system may permit access to, and sharing of, complementary drug information systems, general health information, medical alerts, and related information for patients served by community providers and practitioners.[105]

Another important exception included for the first time in the Phase II Final Rule is the professional courtesy exception.[106] Professional courtesy is defined as the provision of free or discounted healthcare items or services to a physician or his or her immediate family members or staff. To qualify for the exception, the arrangement must meet the following conditions: (1) The professional courtesy is offered to all physicians on the entity's bona fide medical staff or in the entity's local community without regard to the volume or value of referrals or other business generated between the parties; (2) the healthcare items and services provided are of a type routinely provided by the entity; (3) the entity's professional courtesy policy is set out in writing and approved in advance by the governing body of the healthcare provider; (4) the professional courtesy is not offered to any physician (or immediate family member) who is a federal healthcare program beneficiary, unless there has been a good faith showing of financial need; (5) if the professional courtesy involves any whole or partial waiver of any coinsurance obligation, the insurer is informed in writing of that reduction so that the insurer is aware of the arrangement; (6) the professional courtesy arrangement does not violate the anti-kickback statute or any billing or claims submission laws or regulations.[107]

The Phase II Final Rule also included a new exception for charitable donations by a physician. Under this exception, bona fide charitable donations made by a physician to a DHS entity will not constitute a financial relationship if the donation is made to a tax-exempt organization, does not take into account the volume or value of referrals, and does not violate the anti-kickback statute.[108]

Finally, in the Phase I Final Rule, CMS stated that it would consider an exception for relationships that fit "squarely into an anti-kickback safe harbor." In the Phase II Final Rule, however, CMS asserted that it had decided against it, and was opting instead to consider whether any safe harbored arrangements should be incorporated as exceptions to the Stark regulations from time to time as the anti-kickback safe harbors are amended. Moreover, after a review of the existing safe harbors for which there were no analogous exceptions under the Stark regulations, CMS concluded it would incorporate by reference the safe harbors for referral services and obstetrical malpractice insurance subsidies, thereby adding two new exceptions to the Stark regulations.[109]

Comparison of the Federal Anti-Kickback Statute to the Physician Self-Referral Act

The anti-kickback statute and the Physician Self-Referral Act (Stark Law) are two different statutes passed by Congress at different times that, nevertheless, target the same problem in our healthcare delivery system. The goal behind each statute is to eliminate the prospect of financial inducements as a factor in the referral of patients and the ordering of goods or services paid for, in whole or in part, by federal health programs. An ancillary purpose behind both laws is to eliminate financial considerations in the making of clinical and medical judgments involving patient care, which Congress has concluded lead to overutilization of services and potential overcharges, in addition to undermining the quality of care, all of which increase the costs to federal health programs. The goal of both statutes is to eliminate the financial inducement factor from clinical decision making in the care and treatment of patients so there is a positive effect on the escalating costs to federal healthcare programs. This section will examine these two statutes in detail to highlight their similarities, but even more importantly, their differences, in attempting to address the similar problems under federal healthcare programs. The anti-kickback statute prohibits the following:

- Soliciting or receiving remuneration for referrals of Medicare or Medicaid patients, or for referrals for services or items that are paid for, in whole or in part, by Medicare or Medicaid.[110]
- Soliciting or receiving remuneration in return for purchasing, leasing, ordering, or arranging for or recommending purchasing, leasing, or ordering any goods, facility, service, or item for which payment may be made, in whole or in part, by Medicare or Medicaid.[111]

- Offering or paying remuneration for referrals of Medicare or Medicaid patients, or for referrals for services or items that are paid for, in whole or in part, by Medicare or Medicaid.[112]
- Offering or paying remuneration in return for purchasing, leasing, ordering, arranging for, or recommending purchasing, leasing, or ordering any goods, facility, service, or item for which payment may be made, in whole or in part, by Medicare or Medicaid.[113]

The basic prohibition under the anti-kickback statute is against remuneration in return for the referral of patients or the ordering of goods or services paid for, in whole or in part, by federal health programs, whether it be direct or indirect, overt or covert, or cash or in-kind.[114]

In comparison, the Stark Law prohibits a physician or his or her immediate family member from having a financial relationship with an entity to which he or she may refer Medicare and Medicaid patients to receive any one of the statutorily defined designated health services.[115] A financial relationship can exist as an ownership or investment interest or as a compensation arrangement with such an entity.[116] An entity may not present a claim for payment for services provided to a patient as a result of a prohibited referral under the law.[117]

The anti-kickback statute is first and foremost a criminal statute that, upon conviction, may result in a penalty of up to $25,000, imprisonment of up to five years, or both.[118] The anti-kickback statute also has civil remedies, including the imposition of civil money penalties of up to three times the amount of remuneration paid for referrals, plus up to a $50,000 penalty for each kickback payment.[119] Additionally, the anti-kickback statute allows for discretionary exclusion from federal healthcare programs.[120] A conviction under the anti-kickback statute could, conceivably, include a felony with fine and imprisonment, a civil money penalty amount, and exclusion from federal healthcare programs, all for the same underlying offense.

In contrast, the Stark Law is a civil statute only, which carries with it a civil money penalty of a maximum of $15,000 for each service billed or furnished as a result of a prohibited referral.[121] Additionally, because the Stark Law's terms explicitly preclude an entity from presenting a claim for payment for services provided to a prohibited referral, it raises the specter of liability under the United States Civil False Claims Act and the Civil Money Penalty law for submission of an improper claim.

The anti-kickback statute is a broad-based statute which, potentially, could encompass conduct involving anyone arranging for, offering, or receiving remuneration in return for referrals.[122] Because the anti-kickback statute is primarily a criminal statute with criminal penalties, it is necessary for the government to prove that a party intended to violate the anti-kickback statute's prohibition with evidence beyond a reasonable doubt (the "intent standard"). This standard of proof would require proof beyond a reasonable doubt in a criminal prosecution, although in an action to impose civil money penalties or an exclusion from federal healthcare programs, the intent to pay remuneration in return for referrals may only be required to be established by a preponderance of the evidence.[123]

The Stark Law, on the other hand, is a "strict liability" statute, which does not require proof of intent to offer or receive remuneration in return for a referral.[124] The law merely requires proof that a physician referred a federal healthcare program patient to an entity that provides any one of a number of designated health services.[125] If the physician or an immediate family member has a financial relationship with this entity, then the law is violated, unless an exception in the Stark Law would apply. This is an important distinction between the anti-kickback statute and the Stark Law, which fundamentally affects the scope of either law's application and the ability of the government to impose liability through either of these statutes.

Finally, the anti-kickback statute prohibits certain activity and relationships between two or more parties, whereas the Stark Law, in addition to addressing relationships between physicians and another party, also focuses on what is commonly referred to as "physician self-referral," in that it addresses referrals for designated health services within a physician's own practice.[126] The Stark Law prohibits physicians from being compensated for services in their own practice, or as a member of a group practice, where such compensation is related, directly or indirectly, to the volume or value of referrals for designated health services, even if those ancillary services are performed within the medical practice.[127]

The following chart sets out the anti-kickback statute's safe harbor regulations and the Stark Law's exceptions, which address similar financial relationships, highlighting the similarities and differences between the two.

There are several safe harbors to the anti-kickback statute that do not have corresponding exceptions to the Stark Law. These exceptions are as follows:

- Warranties—Buyers must report any price reduction on the cost report or claim and must provide the secretary, upon request, the warranty information provided by the manufacturer or supplier. Manufacturers and suppliers must report the price reduction of the item on the invoice or statement submitted to the buyer and must not pay any remuneration to any individual or entity for any medical, surgical, or hospital expense incurred by a beneficiary other than for the cost of the item itself.[146]

- Discounts—If the entity reports the costs on a required cost report, discounts are not prohibited if the discount is earned based on goods and services bought within a single year; the buyer claims the discount in the year earned or the following year; the buyer reports the discount; and the buyer provides, upon request, information provided by the seller. If the buyer is an HMO or CMP, then there is no need to report the discount except as provided under the risk contract. For all other entities, discounts are not prohibited if they are made at the time of the sale or service; the buyer reports the discount when the item is separately reimbursed; and the buyer provides, upon request, any information provided by the seller.[147]

- Payments to Group Purchasing Organizations (GPOs)—These payments are not prohibited if there is a written agreement for which items and services are furnished and the agreement contains certain specifications. Where the entity receiving the goods or services is a healthcare provider, the GPO must disclose in writing the amount received from each vendor with respect to purchases made by or on behalf of the entity.[148]

- Waiver of Beneficiary Deductible and Co-Insurance Payments for Inpatient Hospital Services Under the Prospective Payment Plan—The hospital must not claim the amount reduced or waived as a bad debt for payment purposes, and it must offer the waiver without regard to the length of stay or diagnosis-related group for which the claim is filed. The waiver must not be made as part of a price reduction agreement between the hospital and third-party payer, unless the agreement is part of a contract for items or services under a Medicare supplemental policy.[149]

- Increased Coverage, Reduced Cost-Sharing Amounts, or Reduced Premium Amounts Offered by Health Plans—Risk-based HMOs, CMPs, and prepaid plans must offer the same increased coverage, reduced cost-sharing, or premium to all enrollees. If the health plan is not risk-based then the plan must not claim the cost as a bad debt for payment purposes.[150]

- Price Reductions Offered by a Contract Healthcare Provider to Health Plans in a Written Agreement for the Sole Purpose of Furnishing Covered Items or Services—The contract healthcare provider must not claim payment in any form from the department or the state agency for items or services furnished in accordance with the agreement except as approved by CMS or the state healthcare program, or otherwise shift the burden of such an agreement to the extent that increased payments are claimed from Medicare or a state healthcare program.[151]

- Arrangements for Ambulatory Surgical Centers (ASCs) to Cover Payments Received from Investments in Medicare-Certified ASCs—Certain joint ventures and the ownership of ASCs are permitted between various physicians as well as certain physicians and hospitals. Certain other requirements must be met in order to fit with the safe harbor.[152]

- Referral Agreements for Specialty Services—Referral agreements for specialty services allow physicians to agree to refer a patient to the other party for the provision of specialty services covered by a Medicare or a state healthcare program in return for an agreement by the other party to refer that patient back at a mutually agreed-upon time or circumstance as long as the four standards listed are met.[153]

- Cooperative Hospital Service Organizations (CHSOs)—Cooperative hospital service organizations (CHSOs) protect payments made between a tax-exempt CHSO and its tax-exempt patron hospital, where the CHSO is wholly owned by two or more patron hospitals, as long as payments from the patron hospital are for the purpose of paying for the bona fide operating expenses of the CHSO; or if the CHSO makes a payment to the patron hospital, the payments are for the purpose of paying a distribution of net earnings as required by the IRS.[154]

Similarly, there are several exceptions to the Stark Law that do not have corresponding anti-kickback statute safe harbors. These exceptions are as follows:

- Physicians' Services—Ownership and compensation arrangement prohibitions do not apply to physicians' services provided personally by another physician in the same group practice as the referring physician.[155]

- Prepaid Plans—Ownership and compensation arrangement prohibitions do not apply to services furnished to an individual enrolled in the organization if the services are furnished by an organization with a contract under § 1876 and described in § 1833(a)(1)(A). The prohibitions do not apply to services furnished to an individual enrolled in the organization if the organization is receiving payments on a prepaid basis.[156]

● Hospital Ownership—A prohibited ownership or investment interest does not include designated health services provided by a hospital if the referring physician is authorized to perform services at the hospital and the ownership or investment interest is in the hospital itself (and not merely in a subdivision of the hospital).[122]

● Hospitals in Puerto Rico—A prohibited ownership or investment interest does not include designated health services provided by a hospital located in Puerto Rico.[157]

● Remuneration Unrelated to the Provision of Designated Health Services—A prohibited compensation arrangement does not include remuneration that is provided by a hospital to a physician if such remuneration does not relate to the provision of designated health services.[158]

● Certain Group Practice Arrangements with a Hospital—A prohibited compensation arrangement does not include an arrangement between a hospital and a group under which designated health services are provided by the group but are billed by the hospital if the requirements listed in the statute are met.[159]

● Payments by a Physician for Items and Services—A prohibited compensation arrangement does not include payments made by a physician to a laboratory in exchange for the provision of clinical laboratory services, or to an entity as compensation for other items or services if the items or services are furnished at a price that is consistent with fair market value.[160]

● Academic Medical Centers—A prohibited compensation arrangement does not include payments to faculty of academic medical centers that meet certain conditions. These conditions, listed in the rule, ensure that the arrangement poses essentially no risk of fraud or abuse.[161]

● Fair Market Value—Certain compensation relationships that are based on fair market value are not prohibited. This exception is available for compensation arrangements between an entity and either a physician or any group of physicians as long as the compensation arrangement meets the requirements set out in the rule.[162]

● Nonmonetary Compensation up to $300—A prohibited compensation arrangement does not include noncash items or services that have a relatively low value and are not part of a formal written agreement, as long as the items or services do not exceed $50 per gift and an aggregate of $300 per year. The compensation must also be made available to all similarly situated individuals, regardless of whether these individuals refer patients to the entity for services. The compensation must not be determined in any way that would take into account the volume or value of the physician's referrals to the entity.[163]

Healthcare attorneys have debated whether it would be enough to meet an exception to the Stark Law to be protected from prosecution under the anti-kickback statute, even if the relationship at issue did not meet one of the safe harbors. In the preamble to Phase I of the final regulations governing the Stark Law (the Final Rule), the Center for Medicare and Medicaid Services (CMS) makes fairly clear that it believes that compliance with a Stark Law exception is not enough to protect a relationship under the anti-kickback statute. It repeatedly states that relationships that are permitted under the Stark Law could still be a violation of the anti-kickback statute and "may merit prosecution," although it points out that the conduct prohibited by the Stark Law may not violate the anti-kickback statute.[164] CMS goes on to state that the Stark Law "provides only a threshold check against fraud and abuse," but relationships still may involve an impermissible kickback.[165]

Several of the Stark Law exceptions require compliance specifically with the anti-kickback statute or compliance with one of its safe harbors. The following are some of the Stark Law's exceptions that CMS discusses in the Phase I and Phase II Final Rules in relation to the anti-kickback statute:

- Indirect Compensation Exception—This exception to the Stark Law, created in the Phase I Final Rule, protects compensation arrangements in which there is at least one entity between the referring physician and the entity providing the designated health service. One of the elements of this exception is that the arrangement cannot violate the anti-kickback statute.[166]

- Employment Exception—One of the requirements for the employment exception is that employees' compensation not vary with the volume or value of referrals made to the employer. CMS states that if the relationship otherwise complies with the requirement of the exception, the fact that the employer requires referrals to certain providers will not vitiate the exception, so long as certain other requirements are made. CMS goes on to specifically "caution that these mandatory arrangements could still implicate the anti-kickback statute, depending on the facts and circumstances."[167]

- Lease and Personal Services Exceptions—In the Phase I Final Rule, CMS states its approval of lease and personal services arrangements in which the payment to or by the physician is on a per-use basis, rather than a fixed monthly, annual, or similar fee. CMS states that its opinion would not change even if the physician is generating referrals. CMS points out, however, that these arrangements may violate the anti-kickback statute. Obviously, this would be particularly true if per-use payments vary with the volume or value of the physician's referrals.[168]

- Professional Courtesy Exception—CMS permits the provision of free or discounted healthcare items or services to a physician or his or her immediate family members or staff. Among the several conditions discussed in the Phase II Final Rule applicable to this exception is the requirement that the professional courtesy arrangement not violate the anti-kickback statute.[169]

- Durable Medical Equipment Exception—As part of the in-office ancillary services exception, CMS permits the dispensing of certain durable medical equipment (DME) by physicians in their offices for patients to use in their homes. CMS specifically points out that the arrangement may not violate the anti-kickback statute. CMS discusses specifically the issue of the DME company using consignment closets in the physician's office. This is a situation in which the DME company provides the physician with the DME at no cost. The physician does not pay for the DME until she dispenses it. CMS states, with regard to consignment closets, that the DME "raise significant questions" under the anti-kickback statute.[170]

- Fair Market Value Exception—CMS created an exception in the Phase I Final Rule for compensation arrangements between an entity and a physician for services provided by the physician to the entity. This is one of the exceptions that specifically requires, among other things, that the relationship either (1) meet a safe harbor to the anti-kickback statute, (2) not violate the anti-kickback statute, or (3) be "approved by the OIG pursuant to a favorable advisory opinion."[171]

- Charitable Donations Exception—The Phase II Final Rule created an exception for charitable donations made by a physician to a DHS entity. In order to qualify for the exception, donations must be made to a tax-exempt organization, may not take into account the volume or value of referrals, and cannot violate the anti-kickback statute.[172]

- Medical Staff Incidental Benefits—Another exception created by the Phase I Final Rule pertains to incidental benefits provided by a hospital to its medical staff members. These incidental benefits must be of low value. Once again, CMS points out that any such relationship also should be reviewed to ensure compliance with the anti-kickback statute. This includes professional courtesy discounts.[173]

- Services Provided to Hospitals "Under Arrangement"—In the Phase I Final Rule, CMS discusses a comment that suggested a special exception be created for compensation related to services provided to a hospital "under arrangement." CMS declines to create such a special exception because of significant issues under the anti-kickback statute associated with services rendered to a hospital under arrangement. CMS states that it will monitor such relationships for abuse and that they remain subject to the anti-kickback statute.[174]

Based on the above, it is clear that CMS does not believe that compliance with the Stark Law would necessarily mean compliance with the anti-kickback statute or protect parties from prosecution under the anti-kickback statute. Although CMS does not enforce the anti-kickback statute directly, the Final Rule was approved by the OIG prior to publication and, therefore, undoubtedly reflects the OIG's opinion on this issue as well. Consequently, this counsels healthcare providers in financial relationships with referral sources or providers to whom they refer to carefully review the implications for the relationships under both the Stark Law and the anti-kickback statute.

False Claims Act

The Civil False Claims Act (FCA) was originally enacted in 1863 and amended significantly in 1986. Liability under the FCA is statutory and requires showing that one of the relevant statutory provisions has been violated. In recent years, the FCA increasingly has been employed in matters of healthcare fraud. This is due, in part, to the greater awareness and publicity of fraud and abuse in the healthcare system, which brings forth individuals who serve as *qui tam* relators (whistle-blowers). The penalty structure of the FCA provides penalties for each claim.[175] This makes the FCA especially favorable in healthcare cases where providers typically submit thousands of claims, accruing high FCA penalties. The federal government, previously hostile to *qui tam* actions, has become more solicitous of such cases. This change is likely due to a recognition that detection and investigation of complex frauds, such as healthcare fraud, requires "insiders" who can provide detailed information about the facts and participants. *Qui tam* relators are a good source of insiders. Additionally, it makes sense for prosecutors to use the FCA instead of criminal prosecution because it is more difficult to prove intentional commission of healthcare fraud. Not only is the burden of proof less in an FCA case (preponderance, rather than beyond a reasonable doubt), but the *mens rea* requirement (knowing, reckless disregard for the truth, deliberate disregard of the truth) is less than "willfulness," which must be proven for many criminal causes of action.

In 2007, a bipartisan bill entitled the False Claims Correction Act that would make sweeping changes to the FCA was proposed to Congress. That legislation is the result of concern among legislators that court decisions in recent years, many of which are discussed in the following sections, have weakened the FCA and impaired its usefulness in fighting fraud. The False Claims Correction Act would expand liability under the FCA by broadening the pool of potential whistle-blowers, increasing the statute of limitations, reducing the pleading requirements under the FCA, and expanding the money sources subject to the FCA, among other things. Though the bill has not yet passed in either house, its existence is representative of the tension between Congress, who would like to see a broadening of liability under the FCA, and the courts, who have demonstrated in recent decisions a general trend toward limiting the FCA's reach.

Liability under the FCA arises under one or more of seven subsections of 31 U.S.C. § 3729(a), although not all are applicable to most medical practices.[176]

Section 3729(a)(1)

Section 3729(a)(1) is one of the most commonly cited sources of liability under the FCA, and provides that "[a]ny person who knowingly presents, or causes to be presented, to an officer or employee of the United States Government or a member of the Armed Forces of the United States a false or fraudulent claim for payment or approval . . . is liable to the United States Government." Most courts have ruled that the essential elements to a cause of action under § 3729(a)(1) include the presentation of a claim for payment or approval to the United States government, falsity or fraudulence of the claim, and knowing presentation of the claim.

Courts are split over whether an additional element, damages, is required to prove liability under § 3729(a)(1). The majority of courts have held that the plaintiff need not prove damages under this section of the FCA. However, many of these courts, finding no need for specific proof of damages, apparently do consider the fact that indirect costs are imposed on the US Treasury by false or fraudulent claims. Although some argue that the plain language of the FCA supports those courts finding that damages are a required element (e.g., in setting out the burden of proof, § 3731(c) refers to damages as a required element), a number of courts have ruled otherwise. The Supreme Court has yet to decide this issue. As a matter of policy, the imposition of significant penalties in cases for which no economic damages were suffered by the federal government raises serious questions about whether the nature of the statute is transformed into a punitive, rather than remedial, law.

Section 3729(a)(2)

Section 3729(a)(2) provides that any person who "knowingly makes, uses or causes to be made or used, a false record or statement to get a false or fraudulent claim paid or approved by the Government; is liable to the United States Government." For liability to be imposed under § 3729(a)(2), each of the elements of § 3729(a)(1) must also be proven. The relator or government must also demonstrate that a false claim was knowingly presented to the government for payment. The overlap between §§ 3729(a)(1) and (2) is significant. Section 3729(a)(2) may theoretically give rise to greater liability if, for example, numerous false records are made to support a single false invoice to the government. Only the single invoice is subject to liability under § 3729(a)(1), but the underlying records supporting the false claim are arguably individual sources of liability under § 3729(a)(2). In practice, however, courts have almost universally found that penalties are imposed only for each payment demand, rather than for each false document supporting the false claim.

Section 3729(a)(3)

Section 3729(a)(3) imposes liability on any person who conspires to defraud the government by obtaining approval or payment for a false or fraudulent claim. To prove a violation of § 3729(a)(3), the government or relator must demonstrate a false or fraudulent claim to the United States, payment or approval by the government, an agreement to submit the false claim, an act in furtherance of the agreement, and intent to defraud. Unlike §§ 3729(a)(1), and (2), § 3729(a)(3) requires specific intent to defraud the government. The clear language of the statute provides that the claim must be "allowed or paid." Most courts have noted correctly that damages are a required element of liability under § 3729(a)(3). Proof of all the elements necessary to impose liability under this provision must be proven by a preponderance of the evidence.

Section 3729(a)(7)

Section 3729(a)(7), referred to as the "reverse false claim" provision of the FCA, provides liability for any person who "knowingly makes, uses, or causes to be made or used, a false record or statement to conceal, avoid or decrease an obligation to pay or transmit money or property to the Government." The reverse false claim provision is the newest basis for liability under the FCA, adopted in 1986 because of a conflict in the case law as to whether false statements that resulted in loss to the government were actionable under the pre-1986 FCA in the absence of an affirmative claim for payment. To recover under subsection (a)(7), the government or relator must prove that: (1) an obligation exists to pay money to the United States; (2) a false statement was made; (3) the defendant "knew" (under Section 3729[c]) that the statement was false; (4) the statement was intended to, and did, avoid, conceal, or decrease the obligation; and (5) this caused some direct financial impact on the federal treasury. Alleged reverse false claims violations have been the source of significant litigation since the 1986 amendments to the FCA.

Standards for Liability

To successfully make out a claim under the FCA, the following elements must be alleged in the complaint: (1) the defendant submitted or caused another person to submit a claim for payment to the federal government; (2) the claim was false or fraudulent and/or the defendant made or used a false or fraudulent record or statement to obtain payment or approval of the false or fraudulent claim; and (3) the person submitting the claim had actual knowledge of its falsity, or acted in reckless disregard of its falsity.[177] The two most hotly debated elements of the FCA claim are in the areas that deal with the "falsity" of the claim and "knowledge" requirements.

"Knowingly," for purposes of the FCA, means that a person, with respect to information, either "has actual knowledge of the information," "acts in deliberate ignorance of the truth or falsity of the information," or "acts in reckless disregard of the truth or falsity of the information."[178] No proof of specific intent to defraud is required to make out a case.

A 1998 Justice Department memorandum concerning the handling of healthcare false claims cases listed a series of factors that should be evaluated in determining whether a claim was made "knowingly." The memorandum included the following factors:

- Notice to the provider—Was the provider on actual or constructive notice, as appropriate, of the rule or policy upon which a potential case would be based?
- The clarity of the rule or policy—Under the circumstances, is it reasonable to conclude that the provider understood the rule or policy?
- The pervasiveness and magnitude of the false claims—Is the pervasiveness or magnitude of the false claims sufficient to support an inference that they resulted from deliberate ignorance or intentional or reckless conduct rather than mere mistakes?
- Compliance plans and other steps to comply with billing rules—Does the healthcare provider have a compliance plan in place? Is the provider adhering to the compliance plan? What relationship exists between the compliance plan and the conduct at issue? What other steps, if any, has the provider taken to comply with billing rules in general, or the billing rule at issue in particular?
- Past remedial efforts—Has the provider previously on its own identified the wrongful conduct currently under examination and taken steps to remedy the problem? Did the provider report the wrongful conduct to a government agency?
- Guidance by the program agency or its agents—Did the provider directly contact either the program agency (e.g., CMS) or its agents regarding the billing rule at issue? If so, was the provider forthcoming and accurate, and did the provider disclose all material facts regarding the billing issue for which the provider sought guidance? Did the program agency or its agents, with disclosure of all relevant, material facts, provide clear guidance? Did the provider reasonably rely on such guidance in submitting the false claims?
- Prior audits—Have there been prior audits or other notice to the provider of the same or similar billing practices?
- Other information—Is there any other information that bears on the provider's state of mind in submitting the false claims?[179]

As discussed above, recent court decisions interpreting the FCA have demonstrated a general-ized trend toward narrowing the scope of liability under the act. One of the cases in which this trend is apparent is *Rockwell International Corp. v. United States ex rel. Stone*,[180] which involved the FCA's mandate that a relator be the "original source of the information."[181] The relator's knowledge, according to the FCA, cannot come from public sources such as criminal, civil, or administrative hearings, audits, investigations, or the news media. Rather, the FCA requires that the original source have "direct and independent knowledge of the information on which the allegations are based."

In its lengthy opinion in *Rockwell*, the Supreme Court defined the "direct and independ-ent knowledge" requirement. Prior to the *Rockwell* decision, the circuit courts were split as to whether the FCA required knowledge of actual facts about the fraud, or merely knowl-edge of the fraud alleged in the original complaint, whether or not those allegations ulti-mately prevailed. The Supreme Court held that the "direct and independent knowledge" requirement applies at every stage of the case and is not limited to the allegations in the original complaint. Therefore, according to the Court, the relator must have independent knowledge of the allegations in each amended complaint, including those in the pretrial or-der. The practical effects of Supreme Court's decision in *Rockwell* are significant, and restrict not only whistle-blower candidates under the FCA, but also the scope of recovery which a whistle-blower may be entitled to.[182]

In a unanimous decision, the Supreme Court in *Allison Engine Co. v. United States ex rel. Sanders*,[182] issued another major opinion significantly limiting liability under the FCA. That case involved an FCA claim in which the relators did not introduce any evidence that Allison Engine's claims were ever submitted to the federal government for payment. Instead, the rela-tors argued that Allison Engine violated the False Claims Act because the shipyard used govern-ment funds to pay the invoices. The district court concluded that the relator's evidence was legally insufficient because false claims were never presented to the government.

The Sixth Circuit reversed the district court and held that Allison Engine violated the False Claims Act because the use of government funds to pay the invoices was sufficient to establish liability under the FCA. This holding conflicted with the decision in *United States ex rel. Totten v. Bombardier Corp.*[183] The Supreme Court granted *certiorari* to resolve the conflict and decide what a plaintiff must prove regarding the relationship between the making of a "false record or statement" and the payment or approval of a "false or fraudulent claim . . . by the Government."[184] The United States participated in the Supreme Court appeal as *amicus*.[185] In *Allison Engine*, the Supreme Court held that a plaintiff suing under the False Claims Act must prove that the defendant intended that the false statement be material to the government's deci-sion to pay or approve the false claim. Thus, in order to successfully establish False Claims Act liability, a plaintiff cannot merely show (as had been allowed in several circuits) that a false claim was ultimately paid with government funds or that the false statement's use resulted in obtaining or getting payment or approval of the claim. This change in the requisite burden of proof represents a significant departure from past precedent and will make False Claims Act cases much harder for plaintiffs to successfully prosecute.

Finally, in *K & R Partnership v. Massachusetts Financing Agency*,[186] the United States Circuit Court for the District of Columbia further narrowed the scope of FCA liability. In that case, the court relied on the Supreme Court's decision in *Safeco Insurance Co. v. Burr*,[187] a non-FCA case, to define "reckless disregard" under the FCA. In *Safeco*, a case involving the Fair Credit Reporting Act, the Supreme Court held that "reckless disregard" was an objective standard, and could not be met in cases where the text of a statute is ambiguous, no authoritative guidance has been given on it, and the defendant's interpretation was reasonable.[188]

In *K & R*, the relator alleged that MassHousing, an organization that assists low-income families in obtaining housing, overbilled the Department of Housing and Urban Development in the amount of $28 million by certifying in its claims that interest reduction payments were calculated in accordance with interest rates established in mortgage notes. The court concluded that the mortgage notes were ambiguous because changes in its debt service varied the interest rates therein. The court, applying the Supreme Court's analysis in *Safeco*, concluded that MassHousing's interpretation of an ambiguous requirement was reasonable, and as such, the reckless disregard requirement had not been met.[189] More summary dispositions in FCA cases involving ambiguous requirements and (unless the proposed amendments to the FCA discussed above are successfully adopted) further limitations on liability under the FCA is expected as a result of these and other important decisions interpreting the act.

Three Major Categories of FCA Cases

FCA cases fall into one of three major categories—"classic" false claims, "standard of care" false claims, and "tainted" claims.

Classic FCA Cases

Classic false claims occur when reimbursement is being requested for services that either were never provided, were not provided as claimed, were not provided by the individual whose provider number appears on the reimbursement form, or were duplicate claims for the same service. Under these circumstances, "[n]o certification, implied or otherwise, is necessary when the liability stems from the [d]efendants' activities of billing for procedures which they did not perform. This would plainly constitute fraud."[190] These "classic" false claims are reflected in the following cases.

In *United States v. Krizek*, the United States filed suit against George Krizek, a psychiatrist, and his wife, Blanka Krizek, for violations of the civil FCA. The government alleged that between 1986 and 1992, Dr. Krizek submitted 8,002 false or unlawful requests for reimbursement in an amount exceeding $245,392. The government alleged that the Krizeks "upcoded" the reimbursement requests; that is, they billed the government for more extensive services than were, in fact, rendered.[191]

The court found that because of a "seriously deficient" system of record keeping, the Krizeks "submitted bills for 45–50 minute psychotherapy sessions . . . when Dr. Krizek could not have spent the requisite time providing services, face-to-face, or otherwise."[192] For instance, on some occasions within the seven-patient sample, Dr. Krizek submitted claims for more than

21 hours of patient treatment within a 24-hour period.[193] The court stated, "While Dr. Krizek may have been a tireless worker, it is difficult for the Court to comprehend how he could have spent more than even ten hours in a single day serving patients."[194] The court stated that these false statements were not "mistakes" nor merely negligent conduct. Under the statutory definition of "knowing" conduct the Court is compelled to conclude that the defendants acted with reckless disregard as to the truth or falsity of the submissions. As such, they [were] deemed to have violated the False Claims Act.[195]

Accordingly, both Dr. Krizek and his wife, Blanka Krizek, were found to have violated the FCA. The court remanded the case back to the circuit court for a recalculation of damages consistent with its written decision.[196]

In *United States v. Cabrera-Diaz*, Dr. Cabrera, a physician, provided anesthesia services to patients. Anesthesia services are covered services under Medicare Part B. As Dr. Cabrera's Part B carrier, Triple S, Inc. conducted a postpayment audit of the claims for anesthesia service provided by Dr. Cabrera to Medicare patients between 1994 and 1995. For statistical purposes, Triple S selected a random sample of 230 claims filed by Dr. Cabrera for the year 1994 and 231 claims for the year 1995.[197]

Once a valid random sample was chosen, Triple S requested the hospital medical records associated with those patients in the sample. The medical records of 73 of the patients included in the sample were unable to be produced. Therefore, the entire amount paid to Dr. Cabrera for those 73 claims was considered as an overpayment.[198]

Next, the remaining claim forms were compared to the time reported in the records obtained from the hospital. This audit revealed that Dr. Cabrera had overstated, falsely reported, unsupported, or undocumented the anesthesia time in all but 6 of the 461 sampled claims. In 1994, looking only at the sample data, Dr. Cabrera billed for 99,270 minutes of anesthesia time, when the evidence provided to Triple S supported only 21,371 minutes, for a difference of 77,899 minutes. In 1995, again using only the sample data, Dr. Cabrera billed for 90,930 minutes of anesthesia time, when the evidence provided to Triple S supported only 20,987 minutes, for a difference of 69,943 minutes.[199]

The amount overpaid to Dr. Cabrera based on the overstated, falsely reported, undocumented, or unsupported anesthesia time was $75,338.75 in 1994 and $56,448.99 in 1995, on the sampled claims only.[200] The results of the audit were then extrapolated to the universe of claims paid to Dr. Cabrera for the years 1994 and 1995. The result was an estimated overpayment to Dr. Cabrera of $237,600.39 for the year 1994 and $211,773.89 for 1995.[201]

Equally important, the audit revealed that in all but six (455 of the 461) of the sampled claims the anesthesia time had been overstated, falsely reported, unsupported, or undocumented. The court found that these results were enough to demonstrate that Dr. Cabrera had either actual knowledge or constructive knowledge of the falsity, in that he acted in reckless disregard of the truth.[202]

Dr. Cabrera failed to appear, answer, plead, or otherwise defend this case more than 120 days after receiving personal notice. As a result, the court entered a default judgment against Dr. Cabrera for treble damages in the amount of $1,348,122.80.[203]

In *United States v. Mackby*, Peter Mackby was the owner and managing director of a physical therapy clinic called Asher Clinic. Asher Clinic's operations included treatment of Medicare Part B beneficiaries. After a 3-day bench trial, the district court found that Mackby knowingly caused false claims to be submitted to Medicare between 1992 and 1996 in violation of the FCA.[204]

Medicare pays for physical therapy services under Part B "when rendered by a physician, by a qualified employee of a physician or physician-directed clinic, or by a qualified physical therapist in independent practice."[205] A physical therapist in independent practice (PTIP) is defined in relevant part as one who "renders services free from the administrative and professional control of an employer such as a physician, institution, agency, etc."[206] Medicare caps the amount it will pay a PTIP on behalf of any one Medicare beneficiary in any calendar year. From 1992 through 1993, the limit was $750 per year. From 1994 through 1996, the limit was $900 per year.[207] There is no payment limit on physical therapy services furnished by or under the supervision of a physician or incident to a physician's services.

In 1982, defendant Peter Mackby formed a partnership with Michael Leary, a licensed physical therapist, for the purposes of owning and operating Asher Clinic. Subsequent to the formation of the partnership, Asher Clinic billed Medicare Part B for services provided to Medicare patients by various physical therapists employed by Asher Clinic, using Leary's provider identification number (PIN). Consequently, Medicare checks were sent to Asher Clinic made payable to Michael Leary, RPT.[208]

In June 1988, Mackby purchased Leary's interest in the clinic. He incorporated the clinic under the name M1 Enterprises, and became its sole officer and shareholder. Mackby, a nonprofessional, did not provide any physical therapy or other services to patients.[209] After taking complete control of the clinic, Mackby directed Medicom, the clinic's billing service, to substitute the PIN of his father, Dr. Judson Mackby, for Leary's PIN on the clinic's Medicare Part B claims. Mackby also told Maridy Barnett, the clinic's office manager, to use his father's PIN in billing third-party payers, including Medicare.[210] The court found that Dr. Mackby did not know that his PIN was being used by Asher Clinic to bill Medicare for physical therapy services. It is undisputed that Dr. Mackby never provided medical services at or for Asher Clinic, never referred any patients to the clinic, and was never involved with the care or treatment of its patients.[211] For approximately eight years, Asher Clinic submitted claims to Medicare for physical therapy services using Dr. Mackby's PIN. Medicare reimbursement checks were made payable to "M. Judson Mackby, MD" and sent to the Asher Clinic address. Asher Clinic used a rubber endorsement stamp containing Dr. Mackby's name to endorse and deposit Medicare payments to its bank account.[212]

Dr. Mackby's PIN was inserted in boxes 24k and 33 on the Asher Clinic forms. Although the purpose of box 24k is not specified on the form itself, Medicare bulletins sent to Asher Clinic state that the box is to be used for the PIN of the performing physician or supplier. Placing Dr. Mackby's PIN in box 24k indicated that Dr. Mackby was the performing physician or supplier and therefore constituted a false statement. Box 33 is clearly labeled as requiring the PIN or group number of the physician or supplier providing the treatment, and Dr. Mackby was neither of these. Therefore, placing his PIN number in this box was a false statement as well.[213]

The court found that by instructing Medicom, Asher Clinic's Medicare billing service, and Ms. Barnett, Asher Clinic's office manager, to use Dr. Mackby's PIN, Peter Mackby "caused" the claims to be submitted to Medicare. In doing so, he caused the claims to be submitted with false information.[214]

Finally, the court found an obligation on the part of Mackby to be familiar with the legal requirements for obtaining reimbursement from Medicare for physical therapy services, and to ensure that the clinic was run in accordance with all laws. By breaching this obligation, he acted in reckless disregard or in deliberate ignorance of those requirements, either of which was sufficient to charge him with knowledge of the falsity of the claims in question. (See *Krizek* earlier in this section, where failing "utterly" to review false submissions prepared by his wife, the doctor acted with reckless disregard.[215])

There have certainly been additional "classic" FCA cases since the decisions discussed above. However, these remain representative of the typical "classic" false claim and how cases involving such claims are resolved in the courts.

Standard of Care FCA Cases

The second major category of cases includes those where the Medicare Part B services were in fact provided, but the quality of care involved in the procedure is alleged to fall below that required by the Medicare program. These claims are premised on implied false certification of compliance with applicable standards of care, and are therefore called "standard of care" false claims. They are displayed in the following cases:

In *United States ex rel. Aranda v. Cmty. Psychiatric Ctrs. of Okla., Inc.*,[216] the government brought an FCA action on behalf of a psychiatric patient who was under the care of the defendant. The government alleged that the defendant knowingly failed to provide a reasonably safe, secure, and quality environment for its residents and yet impliedly certified that it did by way of submitting bills to Medicare when it had previously agreed to abide by all statutes, rules, and regulations required under the Medicare programs.[217] The hospital submitted a motion to dismiss, which was denied by the court, stating that the failure of the hospital to meet recognized professional standards could conceivably constitute an FCA violation.[218] Thereafter, the case was settled and the government's theory was never challenged on a fully developed set of facts.

In *United States ex. rel Luckey v. Baxter Healthcare Corp.*, a *qui tam* action was brought by the plaintiff, a former laboratory technician, against her former employer (Baxter).[219] The plaintiff alleged that she had communicated to Baxter that its failure to test colorless blood plasma samples for saline contamination created a risk of inaccurate results that were later transmitted to the Food and Drug Administration (FDA). Raising an implied certification theory, the plaintiff argued that Baxter's noncompliance with the regulatory standard of care put the defendant in violation of federal statutes and regulations.[220] In effect, the plaintiff argued that every time the defendant submitted a claim to the federal government, it impliedly claimed adherence to those regulations, and therefore, its claims were necessarily fraudulent.

The court declined to accept this argument stating that "[e]quating 'imperfect tests' with 'no tests' would strain language past the breaking point."[221] In addition, according to the record, there was no indication that the government was anything less than 100% satisfied with the product or the representations made in relation to the sale.[222] Moreover, there is nothing in the record to even suggest that Baxter had the required intent to deceive the government.[223] The record simply indicates that there is a dispute as to "whether Baxter's testing protocols could be improved."[224] Accordingly, the court granted Baxter's motion for summary judgment.

In *United States ex rel. Mikes v. Straus*, a *qui tam* action was brought by a former physician employee (the relator) of defendant Straus' medical group practice. The relator alleged that Straus violated the FCA by submitting Medicare payments for spirometry tests, which did not meet the standard of care. It was alleged that the defendant knew the machinery was not calibrated correctly and yet nonetheless conducted and billed the federal healthcare program for the tests. Therefore, the relator alleged that all Medicare claims amounted to false claims under the FCA.[225] The district court, on the defendant's motion, entered summary judgment for the defense stating that FCA liability pertaining to certification of compliance with regulatory and industry standards could only exist, as a matter of law, where "the claimant's adherence to the relevant statutory or regulatory mandates lies at the core of its agreement with the Government. . . ."[226]

The district court determined that the relator failed to establish that Medicare reimbursement was in any way tied to compliance with § 1320c-5(a) of the Social Security Act (SSA). Essentially, the court adopted the Luckey analysis and declined to follow the Aranda court's rationale.

The district court's decision to grant summary judgment was affirmed on appeal.[227] In evaluating the relator's claim of implied false certification, the circuit court construed § 1395y(a)(1)(A) together with § 1320c-5(a). Section 1395y(a)(1)(A) of the Medicare statute states that "no payment may be made under [the Medicare statute] for items or services which . . . are not reasonable and necessary. . . ." Because there is an express condition of payment—that is, "no payment may be made"—it explicitly links Medicare payments to the requirement that the particular item or service be "reasonable and necessary."[228] Accordingly, defendants' submission of the claim forms implicitly certified the procedure as "reasonable and necessary."

On the other hand, § 1320c-5(a) contains no such express condition of payment. Instead, § 1320c-5(a) simply states that "it shall be the obligation" of a practitioner who provides a medical service "for which payment may be made . . . to assure" compliance with the section. Therefore, § 1320c-5(a) appears to act prospectively, setting forth obligations for a provider to be eligible to participate in the Medicare program.[229]

Accordingly, the court reasoned that § 1320c-5(a) is a condition of participation in the Medicare program. Because § 1320c-5(a) does not expressly condition payment on compliance with its terms, defendants' certifications on the CMS-1500 forms are not legally false. Consequently, defendants did not submit impliedly false claims by requesting reimbursement for tests that allegedly were not performed according to the recognized standards.[230]

Alternatively, the relator alleged that the defendant violated the FCA by submitting claims for worthless services. A worthless services claim is a distinct claim that alleges that the services provided were so lacking that, for all practical purposes, they are equivalent to no performance at all.[231]

The court stated that the "requisite intent is the knowing presentation of what is known to be false," not simply the result of negligence or an innocent mistake.[232] Mere allegations that the defendant submitted Medicare claims knowing they did not conform to the ATS guidelines were alone insufficient to satisfy the standard for a worthless services claim. The idea of presenting a claim known to be false does not mean the claim is incorrect as a matter of accounting, but rather that it is a lie.[233]

Overwhelming evidence of the defendant's genuine belief that its services had real medical value caused the court to conclude, as a matter of law, that it did not submit its claims with the requisite *scienter*. Therefore, the court concluded, there was no triable issue of fact sufficient to bar summary judgment.[234]

In *United States ex rel. Swafford v. Borgess Med. Ctr.*,[235] Swafford was a registered vascular technologist employed by the defendants. Accordingly, plaintiff participated in venous ultrasound studies ordered by defendant physicians and observed defendants' practices regarding the submission of Medicare/Medicaid reimbursement forms for ultrasounds performed on defendant physicians' patients.

For patients suspected of suffering from risk factors for blood clots, defendant physicians would order a venous ultrasound study. Using ultrasound, the patient's venous system would be examined to determine the presence or absence of certain "normal" characteristics for five blood clot risk factors. Typically, the procedure would be performed by either a technician or a technologist, who would then indicate the presence or absence of the five factors on a worksheet. The technician/technologist was assigned to determine either the presence or absence of the characteristics, and to indicate either "positive" or "negative" for each factor.[236]

Defendant physicians would review the technician/technologists' worksheet and then prepare a final report setting forth their findings and conclusions. Afterward, defendant physicians signed the following statement prior to submitting the results for reimbursement: "I certify that the services listed above were medically indicated and necessary to the health of this patient and were personally furnished by me or my employee under my personal direction."[237]

The plaintiff alleged defendant physicians did not review any hard copy data (videotape results) generated by the studies. Instead, the plaintiff contends the physicians merely reworded the technician's or technologist's "worksheet" to prepare a physician's ultrasound report. Defendant physicians then billed the government for these "interpretations" that, according to the plaintiff, constituted mere plagiarism of the worksheet prepared by the technician/technologist.[238]

The defendants sought summary judgment from the district court claiming that there was no issue of material fact, and that they should prevail as a matter of law. To succeed under an FCA theory, a plaintiff must establish at least three elements: first, that the defendant knowingly presented or caused to be presented a claim to the United States for payment or approval; second, that the claim was false or fraudulent; and third, that the defendant knew the claim was false or fraudulent.[239]

The parties did not dispute that the defendants presented "claims" as defined under the FCA by submitting CMS-1500 forms seeking reimbursement from Medicare. Therefore, there is no genuine issue of material fact as to the first element of the FCA claim.[240]

As to the second element of the FCA claim, the plaintiff argued that the defendants' practices fell short of the standard of care by (1) failing to review the underlying data of the ultrasound studies—the photographs, prints, or videotape of the ultrasounds taken by the technologist/technician; (2) assuming the accuracy of the worksheet information provided by the technician/technologist, a number of whom lack working knowledge of physics; and (3) failing to perform an independent review of the hard copy data, thus increasing the risk of unnoticed interpretative error. Therefore, by submitting claims for reimbursement that represent substandard care, plaintiff argued defendants impliedly presented false claims under the FCA.[241]

The court concluded that the plaintiff could not demonstrate a genuine issue of material fact with respect to false claims under the FCA, even if he could demonstrate the defendants' practice failed to conform to the applicable standard of care.[242] The court agreed with the Seventh Circuit decision in *Luckey v. Baxter Healthcare Corp.*[243] when it stated that "[e]quating 'imperfect tests' with 'no tests' would strain language past the breaking point." Consequently, the court found no genuine issue of material fact regarding the falsity of the claim.[244]

The court next considered the issue of *scienter*. To succeed under the FCA, a relator need not demonstrate specific intent to defraud the government. The FCA's *scienter* requirement, set forth in § 3729(b), requires either " 'actual knowledge' that one is submitting a false or fraudulent claim for payment or approval, acts in deliberate ignorance of the truth or falsity of one's false claim, or acts in reckless disregard of the truth or falsity of the claim."[245]

Accordingly, the plaintiff must demonstrate more than mere innocent mistakes or negligence on the part of defendants. Furthermore, "what constitutes the offense is not intent to deceive but knowing presentation of a claim that is either fraudulent or simply false. The requisite intent is the knowing presentation of what is known to be false."[246]

The plaintiff conceded that on at least three occasions the defendant contacted CMS seeking any "published guidelines" specific to the procedures in dispute. The answer from CMS was that no such published guidelines existed. The court concluded that this evidence demonstrated that defendants evinced concern and investigated the question of what procedures were required to submit a proper claim for reimbursement. Consequently, the court ruled that there was no genuine issue of material fact as to scienter.[247]

Finding no genuine issues of material fact at issue in the case, the court ruled in favor of the defendant's motion for summary judgment. On appeal, the Court of Appeal for the Sixth Circuit affirmed the lower court decision, finding no error in the granting of summary judgment.[248]

There have been a number of filings since these decisions, most of which have resulted in settlements or remain under seal, but the decisions discussed above are illustrative of typical "standard of care" false claims cases.

Tainted Claim FCA Cases

The third major category of FCA-based improper Medicare Part B reimbursement claims involves patients obtained, and services provided, that result from violations of the federal anti-kickback statute or the federal Stark Law.[249] These cases involve procedures that are billed to

Medicare Part B that are entirely proper except for the fact that the services, and therefore the subsequent claim, was a result of an illegal kickback, remuneration, or self-referral arrangement. These are the so-called "tainted" claims.

In *United States ex rel. Pogue v. Am. Healthcorp, Inc.*,[250] the plaintiff, Pogue, filed a *qui tam* action under the FCA, naming as defendants his former employer, Diabetes Treatment Centers of America (DTCA); American Healthcorp, Inc. (AHC), parent company of DTCA; West Paces Medical Center; five individual physicians; and a number of John Doe defendant hospitals and physicians.

The plaintiff alleged that the defendants were involved in a scheme by which individual physicians would refer their Medicare and Medicaid patients to West Paces for treatment in violation of federal anti-kickback and self-referral statutes. As a consequence of these referrals, the plaintiff alleged that defendants caused to be submitted to the government false and fraudulent claims. The plaintiff alleged that these claims are false and fraudulent because, had the government been aware of these violations, defendants would not have been able to participate in the Medicare and Medicaid programs.[251]

The defendants filed a motion to dismiss for failure to state a claim upon which relief can be granted. The court ruled that Pogue failed in his complaint to allege either actual damages or that defendants' conduct was fraudulent with the purpose of inducing payment from the government. Consequently, the district court granted the defendants' motion to dismiss.[252]

Upon the plaintiff's motion for reconsideration, the court vacated its earlier order to dismiss the complaint, holding that the plaintiff need not allege actual damages in order to recover under the FCA and that the plaintiff need not show false claims, but only that the defendants' conduct was fraudulent with the purpose of inducing payment from the government.[253]

The plaintiff, in *Pogue*, relied on the decision in *Ab-Tech Constr., Inc. v. United States*,[254] wherein the government brought a counterclaim under the FCA against a company that had been awarded a government contract for construction of a building pursuant to the Small Business Administration's (SBA) program for minority-owned businesses. The purpose of the SBA program was to assist minority-owned businesses in gaining the skill and experience necessary to be competitive in the marketplace. Consequently, the SBA required approval of any management agreement, joint venture, or other agreement relevant to the performance of a subcontract formed under the SBA program. The government alleged that the plaintiff had entered into a financial arrangement with a nonminority-owned enterprise without getting SBA approval, and thereby submitted false claims in the form of payment vouchers for services performed. The court agreed, finding that "the payment vouchers represented an implied certification by [the plaintiff] of its continuing adherence to the requirements for participation in the [SBA] program."[255] Stating that the FCA reaches beyond monetary claims that fraudulently overstate the amount due, the court reiterated that the FCA extends "to all fraudulent attempts to cause the Government to pay out sums of money."[256]

"By deliberately withholding from the SBA knowledge of the prohibited contract arrangement with [the nonminority-owned enterprise], [the plaintiff] not only dishonored the terms of its agreement with that agency but, more importantly, caused the Government to pay out funds in the mistaken belief that it was furthering the aims of the [SBA] program." In effect, "the Government was duped" by (the plaintiff's) active concealment of a fact vital to the integrity of that program. The withholding of such information—information critical to the decision to pay—is the essence of a false claim.[257]

Pogue argued that *Ab-Tech* governed in his case as well. The payment vouchers at issue in *Ab-Tech* were not themselves false in that the work was performed according to specifications and the government was properly charged. Rather, the court found that the plaintiff's assertion that he had complied with the regulations governing the SBA program, when in reality he had not, rendered the payment vouchers false. Similarly, Pogue argued that although there is no allegation that defendants overcharged Medicare, or charged it for services not rendered, defendants' failure to comply with Medicare laws prohibiting kickbacks and self-referrals rendered the Medicare claims submitted by defendants false or fraudulent. The court agreed.

Secondly, Pogue had not alleged that the government suffered any loss due to the defendants' alleged illegal activities. He had not asserted that the alleged kickbacks or self-referral profits were improperly included in the claims submitted by defendants to the government, nor any other facts that would suggest that the claims were somehow tainted. Apparently, the government would have paid these healthcare charges regardless of who performed the services and regardless of the reason the patients chose the provider.

Nonetheless, the court in *Ab-Tech*, and in the related case of *United States v. Inc. Vill. of Island Park*,[258] found that the defendants had violated the FCA despite a lack of risk to government funds. In *Ab-Tech*, the court noted that the government had suffered no loss because it still received a building built to its specifications.[259] In Island Park, the government would have paid the same amount for subsidized housing regardless of who eventually occupied those homes. In its ruling, the court said that the FCA "is violated not only by a person who makes a false statement or a false record to get the government to pay a claim, but also by one who engages in a fraudulent course of conduct that causes the government to pay a claim for money."[260] Therefore, Pogue alleged, the FCA clearly prohibits fraudulent acts even if they do not cause a loss to the government.

The court concluded that the FCA was intended to govern not only fraudulent acts that create a loss to the government, but also those fraudulent acts that cause the government to pay out sums of money to claimants it did not intend to benefit.[261]

Consequently, in order to bring his claim under the FCA, Pogue had to show that defendants engaged in the fraudulent conduct with the purpose of inducing payment from the government. If defendants' fraudulent conduct was not committed with the purpose of inducing payment from the government, that conduct does not operate to taint their Medicare claims and render the claims false or fraudulent under the FCA.[262]

In the present case, Pogue sufficiently alleged that the government would not have paid the claims submitted by defendants if it had been aware of the alleged kickback and self-referral violations. Thus, Pogue alleged that defendants concealed their illegal activities from the government in an effort to defraud the government into paying Medicare claims it would not have otherwise paid.[263] Thereafter, the court granted Pogue's motion to reconsider and vacated its earlier decision dismissing the case.[264]

The *Pogue* case was later transferred to the United States District Court for the District of Columbia pursuant to 28 U.S.C. § 1407(a), which provides for transfer of the actions pending in different courts to a single district to permit coordinated or consolidated pretrial proceedings. The defendant in *Pogue* again raised defenses similar to the ones raised earlier before the United States District Court for the Middle District of Tennessee. The District of Columbia court rejected these defenses and made it clear in its decision that the violation of the Medicare anti-kickback and self-referral laws can form the basis for a violation of the FCA.[265] The court's opinion went to great lengths to demonstrate that the "implied certification" theory of liability under the FCA has not been rejected by the other courts. The court concluded that this theory of liability was viable where compliance with laws such as the anti-kickback statute and the Stark Law would affect the government's decision to pay on claims to the Medicare and Medicaid programs.

In *United States ex rel. Scott Barrett v. Columbia/HCA Healthcare Corp.*,[266] the United States District Court for the District of Columbia followed in the footsteps of the *Pogue* court ruling that violations of the anti-kickback statute can form the basis of an FCA violation, and reaffirming its view that implied certification is a viable FCA theory in the DC Circuit.[267] In so ruling, the court stated that the "implied certification of compliance with the statute or regulation alleged to be violated must be so important to the contract that the government would not have honored the claim presented to it if it were aware of the violation."[268]

In *United States ex rel. Thompson v. Columbia/HCA Healthcare Corp.*,[269] James M. Thompson, MD, alleged that defendants submitted false or fraudulent claims under the FCA by submitting Medicare claims for services rendered in violation of the Medicare anti-kickback statute, and two versions of a self-referral statute. He further alleged that defendants made false statements to obtain payment of false or fraudulent claims in violation of the FCA by falsely certifying in annual cost reports that the Medicare services identified therein were provided in compliance with the laws and regulations regarding the provision of healthcare services.[270] Specifically, Thompson alleged that defendants violated the Medicare anti-kickback statute by inducing physicians to refer Medicare patients to Columbia/HCA hospitals.

On remand from the Fifth Circuit Court of Appeal, the district court denied the defendants' motion to dismiss and motion for summary judgment. First, the court concluded that the plaintiffs had stated a claim for violation of the FCA by the defendants' alleged false certification that the Medicare services identified in the annual hospital cost reports complied with the laws and regulations dealing with the provision of healthcare services. The alleged prohibited financial relationships among defendants and referring physicians made the certifications false statements. In addition to highlighting express statements in the relevant statutes and CMS form 2552, the plaintiffs provided evidence that CMS relied on the certifications in determining the issues of payment and retention of payment as well as continued eligibility for participation in the Medicare program. The evidence established a clear nexus between the certifications and the injury to the government.[271]

The second issue is whether the Stark Law's express prohibition on payment for services rendered in violation of its own terms makes such alleged violations actionable under the FCA. The court concluded that it does. The court ruled that Thompson had successfully stated a claim under the FCA for violation of the express terms of § 1395nn of the Stark Laws in alleging that the government was injured by the Columbia defendants' submissions for Medicare payments that they knew they were statutorily prohibited from receiving, because the claims came out of an alleged scheme of illegal self-referrals among the Columbia entities and physicians linked by illicit financial relationships. The court agreed with the plaintiffs that a pecuniary injury to the public is not required for an actionable claim under the FCA. In addition, the court found additional monetary losses to the government in investigative and administrative costs requiring expenditure of government funds.[272]

The court further found that Thompson had also stated a claim for a violation of the FCA based on the alleged scheme of self-remuneration in violation of the anti-kickback statute, which prohibits the making of any false statements, failing to disclose material information, or making false statements or representations to qualify as a certified Medicare provider in applying for Medicare payments.[273]

Thompson alleged that the explicit certifications of compliance with relevant healthcare laws and regulations were false and fraudulent, and provided evidence that the government conditioned its approval, payment, and defendants' retention of payment funds on those certifications. The court agreed that Thompson presented evidence of injury to the government and alleged that the government would not have paid the claims submitted by these defendants, in knowing violation of the statutory provisions, had it known of the alleged self-referral and kickback violations, which defendants allegedly concealed from the government.

The Thompson court cited *Pogue*, concluding that the FCA "was intended to include not only situations in which a claimant makes a false statement or submits a false record in order to receive payment but also those situations in which the claimant engaged in fraudulent conduct in order to receive payment."[274] Thus, it concluded "that the False Claims Act was intended to govern not only fraudulent acts that create a loss to the government[,] but also those fraudulent acts that cause the government to pay out sums of money to claimants it did not intend to benefit."[275] Consequently, the court denied the defendant's motion to dismiss.

In *United States ex rel. Barmak v. Sutter Corp.*, David Barmak brought an FCA claim against defendants alleging that the defendants fraudulently obtained Medicare overpayments by waiving co-payments for sales of continuous passive motion exercisers and related equipment, by forging certificates of medical need, and by paying kickbacks to hospitals and doctors for patient referrals.[276] As a result of a six-year investigation by the United States Attorney's Office, the government decided to intervene only on the claims regarding waiver of co-payments.

On the defendant's motion to dismiss, the court ruled that the complaint was so vague and overbroad that it failed to meet the specificity requirements of Federal Rules of Civil Procedure 9(b), which state that "[i]n all averments of fraud or mistake, the circumstances constituting fraud or mistake shall be stated with particularity."

In addressing the plaintiff's attempt to claim violations of the anti-kickback statute as a basis for an FCA claim, the court stated that it was "not convinced that a *qui tam* Plaintiff can use the FCA as a vehicle for pursuing a violation of the anti-kickback statute in this Circuit."[277] The court went on to state that it was "aware that some courts have permitted it, but that it remains a hotly disputed and controversial area of the law."[278]

First and foremost, the court pointed out that the anti-kickback statute is a criminal felony statute. As such, the court claimed that there is absolutely no private right of action provided, and the statute is to be enforced by the Department of Justice (DOJ). Furthermore, the court stated that it has "no reason to believe, nor have the parties provided any, that Congress intended to subvert the DOJ's exclusive jurisdiction over the anti-kickback statute by grafting the FCA's *qui tam* provisions onto it." This is a strong departure from the earlier decisions in Pogue and Thompson. Most importantly, the court indicated that it was "unwilling to presume . . . that a violation of the anti-kickback statute is ipso facto a violation of the FCA."[279]

In this particular case, assuming a right of action, the plaintiff failed to plead a causal relation between the violation of the anti-kickback statute and violation of the FCA. As stated by the court, the plaintiffs "have not alleged any certification of compliance with the anti-kickback statute, or that the Government relied on such certification in making payments to Defendants."[280] Consequently, the court dismissed plaintiff's claims for illegal kickbacks in violation of the anti-kickback statute.

More recently, in *United States ex rel. McNutt v. Haleyville Medical Supplies, Inc.*,[281] the Eleventh Circuit held that a violation of the anti-kickback statute can serve as the basis for an FCA claim. In that case, the relator, a former employee, filed a *qui tam* against a medical services company alleging that it had submitted to Medicare requests for reimbursement even though it knew it was not eligible for payment. Specifically, the relator alleged that the defendant had paid kickbacks camouflaged as rental payments in order to attract referrals from pharmacists and others. The government intervened and argued that the defendants' anti-kickback violations were actionable as false claims because the defendants had certified in their Medicare enrollment agreements that they would comply with the anti-kickback statute and that compliance was a prerequisite to payment. The district court denied the defendants' motion to dismiss and certified for interlocutory appeal the issue of whether a violation of the anti-kickback statute could serve as the predicate for an FCA action.

With little discussion, the Eleventh Circuit accepted the government's argument and concluded that it had alleged sufficiently that compliance with the anti-kickback statute is a condition of payment, that the defendants were aware of this condition, and had submitted claims "knowing that they were ineligible for the payments demanded."[282] The court focused not on the certification and its alleged falsehood, but rather the simple fact of submission of a claim by the defendants as forming the basis of an FCA violation. The Eleventh Circuit's holding in *McNutt* is significant because it suggests that once a provider signs the enrollment certification, it opens itself up to be sued under the False Claims Act for a violation of any Medicare law, regulation, or program instruction at any time. The decision further solidifies the idea that violations of the anti-kickback statute or the Stark Law can support claims against providers under the FCA.

Restitution Regarding FCA and Receipt of Referral Fees

In 2001, the Eleventh Circuit reviewed a criminal conviction regarding the district court's decision ordering a physician to pay restitution to Medicare for monies received in exchange for patient referrals in violation of the federal anti-kickback statute. The issue on appeal was whether a physician receiving remuneration for making patient referrals should be ordered to pay restitution in the amount of the illegal remuneration.

In *United States v. Liss*, a Florida laboratory (CCL) and its employees developed a scheme to defraud Medicare by paying doctors to refer their Medicare patients in return for kickbacks. CCL created a scheme of consulting agreements with doctors acting as testing review officers (TROs). The agreements allowed the doctors to authorize lab work for an individual without having to seek authorization from the individual's own physician. As such, the TRO agreements disguised the kickbacks that were given in return for the patient referrals.[283]

In August 1996, CCL signed a TRO agreement with a codefendant physician named Michael Spuza, in which Spuza was paid $600 a month. Between August 1996 and April 1998, CCL paid $12,000 to Spuza under the TRO agreement. In addition, CCL made 28 equipment sublease and office rental payments on behalf of Spuza totaling $55,371.36. Medicare reimbursed CCL $269,004.73 as a result of the referrals made by Spuza for clinical laboratory work. The court found that all the associated referrals were made for legitimate medical reasons.[284]

The government claimed that according to the anti-kickback statute, Spuza was required to pay the full amount of remuneration he had been paid by CCL for the referrals. The court agreed with the government's argument, but failed to make any findings of fact on the issue. Accordingly, Spuza was ordered to pay $55,371.36 in restitution.[285]

On appeal, Spuza contended that the district court erred in ordering him to pay restitution because the government offered no evidence to suggest that the Medicare program suffered any loss attributable to the illegal remuneration from CCL. Spuza argued that because the referrals made to CCL were medically necessary and because he was not involved in fraudulent billing, it was an error for the court to assume that Medicare suffered a loss that was attributable to his receipt of remuneration.[286]

According to *United States v. Martin*[287] an award of restitution must be based on the amount of loss actually caused by the defendant's conduct. The government bears the burden of proving the amount of the loss.[288] In Spuza's case, the government offered no evidence to prove that the Medicare program suffered any loss attributable to Spuza's receipt of remuneration. The amount paid by Medicare to CCL was not affected by what CCL did with the money it received. Although CCL may owe restitution if it fraudulently billed for the services allegedly referred by Spuza, billing fraud is not a part of Spuza's offense conduct.[289]

The court found there was no basis for such an assumption of loss to Medicare because the medical necessity of the referrals was unquestioned. Accordingly, the court vacated the district court's restitution order.[290]

In *United States v. Rogan*, the Seventh Circuit reached the opposite conclusion.[291] The defendant in that case, Peter Rogan, at one time owned Edgewater Hospital and later sold it, but continued to control the hospital and medical center through various management companies he owned. The hospital entered bankruptcy when four doctors, a vice president, and the management company pled guilty to federal criminal healthcare fraud charges involving the payment of kickbacks for patient referrals and medically unnecessary hospital admissions, tests, and services. Rogan was not charged criminally at that time, but in 2002, the United States filed a civil lawsuit against him alleging that he was responsible for Edgewater's submission of millions of dollars of false claims for reimbursement under the Medicare and Medicaid programs. The theory of the government's case was that Rogan conspired with the six indicted persons to defraud the United States by concealing the fact that many patients came to Edgewater only because of referrals that violated the Stark Law and the anti-kickback statute. The physicians' improper financial interests were created through a variety of contracts, such as medical director agreements, physician recruiting contracts, teaching contracts, EKG-reading contracts, and physician loan agreements, which provided the doctors with compensation that the court found was "grossly" above fair market value for services never substantially performed.

Rogan lost the civil FCA action after a bench trial. The district court concluded that the measure of damages under the FCA is three times the amount of money the government paid out by reason of the false claims over and above what it would have paid out if the claims had not been false or fraudulent, plus a per-claim penalty. It noted that the government did not need to prove actual damages in order to recover, but needed to show only that the claims were false. After calculating that Edgewater received approximately $17 million on its false claims and subtracting the amount of restitution paid by one of the defendants, the district court assessed damages at $64 million.[292]

At the appellate court level, Rogan did not deny that illegal referrals occurred, that kickbacks were paid, that the bills sent to the United States omitted this information, and that he knew what was going on. Instead he argued that the omissions were not "material" because prosecutors failed to offer testimony that a federal employee in a position to make a decision on behalf of the government was sure to enforce the statute.[293]

The appeals court rejected that argument, clarifying that such testimony was unnecessary because the proper inquiry is not whether Edgewater was sure to be caught, but whether the omission could have influenced the agency's decision, an objective standard. And in response to Rogan's argument that the damages assessed were excessive because most of the patients for which claims were submitted received some (and perhaps all) the medical care reflected in the claim forms, the district court observed that federal healthcare programs offer payment based upon a series of conditions. "When the conditions are not satisfied, nothing is due."[294]

Antitrust Laws and the Healthcare Industry

Antitrust laws were established to promote and protect competition, thereby ensuring lower consumer prices and new and better products available at market. In a freely competitive market, businesses tend to lower prices and create better quality products in an effort to attract a greater number of consumers. The idea is that greater competition and an increased potential for profits will stimulate product innovation and more efficient methods of production, both of which benefit the ultimate consumer.

While operating within a competitive market, there is no need for government intervention. On the other hand, when competitors collude to fix prices, limit output, divide business between or among themselves, or make other anticompetitive arrangements that provide no benefits to consumers, the government has the power to act to protect the interests of consumers and taxpayers.

In response to changes in the healthcare industry, many healthcare providers are merging or consolidating their practices. These mergers potentially can have a negative effect on competition among providers within the healthcare industry, and thereby run the risk of violating antitrust laws.[295] In recent years, at least two physician group practices have been attacked by the FTC based on alleged antitrust violations, and more are likely to come. The antitrust laws under which mergers in the healthcare industry are most likely to be challenged are Section 1 of the Sherman Act and Section 7 of the Clayton Act.

The Sherman Act

Enacted in 1890 and named after the late US Senator John Sherman, the Sherman Act[296] was designed to curb the public's concerns about the dangers of concentrating economic power in the hands of a limited number of individuals, predatory practices used by companies to restrain rivals, and extreme methods used by companies to achieve unjust ends or eliminate competitors.

Section 1 of the Sherman Act provides the following: Every contract, combination in the form of a trust or otherwise, or conspiracy, in restraint of trade or commerce among the several states, or with foreign nations, is declared to be illegal. Every person who shall make any contract or engages in any combination or conspiracy hereby declared to be illegal shall be deemed guilty of a felony, and, on conviction thereof, shall be punished by a fine not exceeding $10,000,000 if a corporation, or, if any other person, $350,000, or by imprisonment not exceeding three years, or by both said punishments, in the discretion of the court.[297]

Examples of such activities include horizontal price fixing, competitively motivated group boycotts, tying agreements, and other broadly interpreted activities unreasonably affecting commerce. By its very definition, Section 1 does not reach those actions that are unilateral in nature.

A preliminary question for analyzing a particular practice under Section 1 of the Sherman Act is whether the practice in question requires the concerted effort of two or more parties. In horizontal markets, courts generally consider conduct between competitors a *per se* violation when that conduct includes price fixing, market division, group boycotts, and coerced tie-in agreements.

On the other hand, if it is determined that the conduct in question is not a *per se* violation, then the court will apply the "rule of reason" analysis. This means that the court will balance the harmful conduct against pro-competitive activity such as the activity's effect on lowering costs. In applying this analysis, the court will consider the following factors: market share, ease of market entry, competitive effects, and efficiencies achieved by the questioned activity.

An example of an illegal combination would be an explicit agreement between producers to limit their output in such a way as to artificially "fix" the price of their product above the market-clearing price found in a truly competitive market. This is not to say that the Sherman Act cannot be violated without an explicit agreement between competitors. Implicit collusion can be construed as violating the law. Two companies need not have direct communication to violate the Sherman Act; the publication of pricing information in an effort to establish an implied understanding to "fix" prices can be sufficient.

The Clayton Act

Enacted in 1914, the Clayton Act[298] outlawed price discrimination, tying and exclusive dealing contracts, mergers of competing companies, and interlocking directorates. Section 7 of the Clayton Act deals with mergers of two or more entities. It prohibits mergers and acquisitions where the effect "may be substantially to lessen competition" or tends to create a monopolistic environment in the market.[299] According to the Hart-Scott-Rodino Act, parties to certain mergers and acquisitions must notify the federal government in advance if the parties and the transaction are of a sufficient size, as defined by the statute.[300]

In 1950, Congress modified Section 7 of the Clayton Act to prohibit one company from acquiring part or all of the assets of a competitor if it could result in substantially lessening competition or creating a monopolistic market. Prior to the 1950 amendment, the Clayton Act only prevented a corporation acquiring stock of a competitor, not other assets. In 1980, Congress further amended Section 7 of the Clayton Act, extending its reach to any person subject to Federal Trade Commission (FTC) jurisdiction, thus adding partnerships and sole proprietorships.

Unlike the Sherman Act, acts prohibited by the Clayton Act were not subject to criminal penalties, but rather only civil remedies. Whereas the DOJ directly enforces actions of the Sherman Act, both the DOJ and the FTC have the authority to enforce the Clayton Act. In addition, private parties may seek treble damages for injuries resulting from Section 7 violations.

Hart-Scott-Rodino Act

The Hart-Scott-Rodino Antitrust Improvements Act of 1976 modified the Clayton Act to require parties to a merger to notify the FTC and the DOJ prior to entering into certain transactions. A premerger notification must be filed if two parties merge, one party acquires the stock or assets of another party, or a new entity is set up to operate an enterprise, and all of the following three conditions are met: (1) at least one participant in the transaction is engaged in or affects commerce; (2) the transaction involves the acquisition of assets or voting securities and either (a) the acquired form is engaged in manufacturing and has total assets or annual net sales of $10 million or more, and the acquiring firm has annual net sales or total assets of $100 million or more; or (b) the acquired firm has total assets or annual net sales of $100 million or more, and the acquiring firm has total assets or annual net sales of $10 million; and (3) as a result of the transaction, the acquiring firm obtains 15% or more of the voting securities or assets of the acquired firm, or obtains voting securities or assets of the acquired party that in the aggregate exceed $15 million.

Notwithstanding the reporting requirements mentioned above, there are a number of transactions that may be exempt from such requirements, including transactions between related entities for investment purposes, by creditors and insurers involving nonvoting and convertible securities, and those involving acquisitions made in the ordinary course of business. It is also important to be aware of the existence of regulations that explicitly prohibit structuring a transaction to avoid the Hart-Scott-Rodino reporting requirements.[301] The DOJ and the FTC keep a sharp lookout for noncompliance with this regulation and are vigilant to prosecute such behavior.

In addition to the notice requirement, for transactions other than cash tender offers, the agencies implemented a 30-day waiting period before a merger could be finalized, or a 15-day waiting period for cash tender offers. The agencies are not prohibited from bringing actions subsequent to the applicable review period, but they generally do not intervene to undo a merger after the expiration of the review period.

Antitrust Safety Zones

In August 1996, the FTC and the DOJ issued a joint statement discussing six newly implemented antitrust enforcement policies regarding mergers and consolidations in the healthcare industry. The six policies discussed in the joint statement include safety zones related to hospital mergers, hospital joint ventures involving high technology or other expensive medical equipment, physicians' provision of information to purchasers of healthcare services, hospital participation in exchanges of price and cost information, healthcare providers' joint purchasing arrangements, and physician network joint ventures. Safety zones are to antitrust as safe harbor exceptions are to the federal anti-kickback statute. Similar to the anti-kickback statute, any arrangements that fall outside of a safety zone do not necessarily violate antitrust laws, but unless a situation fits squarely within the safety zone, the parties involved can never be sure that they will not be investigated and possibly prosecuted.

The safety zone dealing with hospital mergers is perhaps the most important. With respect to hospital merger safety zones, the DOJ and the FTC will not challenge any merger between two general acute-care hospitals if one of the hospitals (1) has an average of fewer than 100 licensed beds over the 3 most recent years, and (2) has an average daily inpatient census of fewer than 40 patients over the 3 most recent years, absent extraordinary circumstances. This particular antitrust safety zone will not apply if that hospital is less than 5 years old.

Historically, antitrust challenges to hospital mergers have been uncommon. That being said, procedures have been established by the FTC and the DOJ in which hospitals that are considering a merger can seek an advisory opinion (FTC) or a business review (DOJ) to verify whether they fit within an enumerated safety zone.[302] Responses to such requests are issued within 90 days of submission.

In reaction to changes in the healthcare industry, many providers and hospitals are responding by merging or consolidating their operations. This being the case, it is important for physicians and hospitals alike to be aware of potential antitrust implications involved in their decisions.

Other Considerations

The legal issues discussed herein have focused almost entirely on federal laws and regulations. This is not to imply that states do not have their own laws pertaining to kickbacks, physician self-referrals, and patient brokering. It is important to be aware that state laws also must be considered when evaluating certain types of business arrangements, such as those described herein.

References

1. Gen Couns Mem 39,862 (November 21, 1991).
2. IRC § 4958.
3. OIG advisory opinions can be obtained on the Internet at http://www.oig.hhs.gov/fraud/advisoryopinions.html.
4. 42 USC § 1320a-7b(b).
5. 31 USC §§ 3729-3733; see also 45 CFR § 79.
6. Id; 42 CFR § 1001.952.
7. See 56 Fed Reg 35952, 35954 (July 29, 1991).
8. 62 Fed Reg 7,350 (February 19, 1977).
9. Pursuant to authority under Section 205 of HIPAA and regulations under 42 CFR Part 1008.
10. 42 CFR § 1008.36; 42 CFR § 1008.11; 42 CFR § 1008.31.
11. 42 CFR § 1008.53.
12. 42 CFR § 1008.5(a).
13. 42 CFR § 1008.5(b).
14. *United States v Greber*, 760 F.2d 68 (3d Cir 1985).
15. Id at 71-72.
16. OIG advisory opinions available at http://www.oig.hhs.gov/fraud/advisoryopinions.html.
17. See Carrie Valiant and David Matyas, *Legal Issues in Health Care Fraud and Abuse: Navigating the Uncertainties* 30 (1997).
18. 64 Fed Reg 63518, 63519 (November 19, 1999) (emphasis added).
19. *United States v Kats*, 871 F.2d 105 (9th Cir 1989); *United States v Davis*, 132 F.3d 1092 (5th Cir 1998).
20. *Kats*, 871 F.2d 105 (9th Cir 1989).
21. Id at 108.
22. Id.
23. *United States v Lahue*, 261 F.3d 993 (10th Cir Kan 2001).
24. *United States v Anderson*, 85 F Supp 2d 1047 (D Kan 1999).
25. *United States v McClatchey*, 217 F.3d 823 (10th Cir 2000).
26. Id at 834 (citing the district court's Jury Instruction 32).
27. *United States v Siegel*, No. 94-156-CR-T-23C (MD FL 1996) (emphasis added).
28. *United States v Bay State Ambulance and Hosp. Rental Serv, Inc.*, 874 F.2d 20 (1st Cir 1989).
29. Id at 29 (citing the district court's jury instruction)
30. Id at 32-33.
31. 42 USC § 1320a-7b.
32. *Hanlester Network v Shalala*, 51 F.3d 1390 (9th Cir 1995).
33. Id at 1399.
34. *Med Dev Network, Inc, v Prof'l Respiratory Care/Home Med. Equip Serv, Inc* 673 So. 2d 565, 567 (FL App 4th Dist1996); see also *United States v Jain*, 93 F.3d 436 (8th Cir 1996), *cert denied*, 520 US 1273 (1997); *United States v Neufield*, 908 F Supp 491 (SD Ohio 1995).
35. *Jain*, 93 F.3d at 436.
36. Id.
37. *United States v Starks*, 157 F.3d 833 (11th Cir 1998).
38. Id at 838.
39. *Anderson*, 85 F Supp 2d at 1047.
40. *Bryan v United States*, 524 US 184 (1998).
41. Id at 191.
42. 42 USC § 1320a-7a(a)(7).
43. See 42 USC § 1320a-7; 42 USC § 1320a-7a.

44. See 63 Fed Reg 46,676 (Sept. 2, 1998).
45. See *United States v David Hutto* (MD FL 1998); *United States v Lindsey Huttleston* (MD FL 1998); *United States v Clearwater Clinical Lab, Inc.*, et al. (MD FL); and *United States v Jackie Krome* (MD FL 1998).
46. 42 CFR § 411.350.
47. 42 CFR § 411.351.
48. 66 Fed Reg 856 (Jan. 4, 2001).
49. 69 Fed Reg 16054.
50. 73 Fed Reg 48434.
51. 72 Fed Reg 51012.
52. 73 Fed Reg 48434.
53. 42 USC § 1395nn(g).
54. 42 USC § 1395nn(a); 42 CFR § 411.351.
55. See 42 CFR § 411.351.
56. See 42 CFR § 411.355(a).
57. See 42 CFR § 411.351.
58. Id.
59. Id.
60. 73 Fed Reg 48721.
61. See generally 42 USC §1395nn.
62. 42 CFR § 411.354(a).
63. 42 CFR § 411.354(b).
64. 42 CFR § 411.354(b)(2).
65. 42 CFR § 411.353(e).
66. 42 CFR § 411.354(b)(1).
67. 42 CFR § 411.354(b)(3)(iii).
68. 42 CFR § 411.354(b)(4).
69. See 42 CFR § 411.354(b)(3).
70. 42 CFR § 411.354(b)(5).
71. 42 CFR § 411.354(c).
72. 42 CFR § 411.351.
73. 69 Fed Reg 16066.
74. 42 CFR § 411.354.
75. 66 Fed Reg 865.
76. 42 CFR § 411.354(c)(2)(ii).
77. 42 CFR § 411.354(c)(2)(iii).
78. 72 Fed Reg 51026.
79. 73 Fed Reg 48693
80. 42 CFR § 411.357(p).
81. See next section for a more complete list of exceptions and comparison to the anti-kickback statute safe harbors.
82. 42 USC § 1395nn(b)(1).
83. 42 USC § 1395nn(h(4)(a).
84. 42 USC § 1395nn(b)(2).
85. 42 USC § 1395nn(b)(3).
86. 42 USC § 1395nn(c).
87. Id.
88. 42 USC § 1395nn(d)(3).
89. 42 USC § 1395nn(d)(1), (2).
90. 42 USC § 1395nn(e)(1).
91. Id.

92. 42 USC § 1395nn(e)(2).
93. 42 USC § 1395nn(e)(3).
94. 42 USC § 1395nn(e)(4), (5), (6).
95. 42 USC § 1395nn(e)(7).
96. Id.
97. 42 USC § 1395nn(e)(8).
98. 42 USC § 1395nn(e)(1), (2), (3), (5), (7).
99. 42 USC § 1395nn(3)(B).
100. 42 CFR § 411.357(d).
101. 69 Fed Reg 16112.
102. 42 CFR § 411.357(k).
103. 42 CFR § 411.357(m); see also 69 Fed Reg 16112.
104. 69 Fed Reg 16112.
105. 42 CFR § 411.357(o).
106. 69 Fed Reg 16113.
107. 69 Fed Reg 16116.
108. Id.
109. 69 Fed Reg 16115.
110. 42 USC § 1320a-7b(b)(1)(A).
111. 42 USC § 1320a-7b(b)(1)(B).
112. 42 USC § 1320a-7b(b)(2)(A).
113. 42 USC § 1320a-7b(b)(2)(B).
114. See 42 USC § 1320a-7b(b).
115. 42 USC § 1395nn(a)(1); 42 CFR § 411.350.
116. 42 USC § 1395nn(a)(2); 42 CFR § 411.354(a)(1).
117. 42 USC § 1395nn(a)(1)(B); 42 CFR § 411.353(b).
118. 42 USC § 1320a-7b(b).
119. 42 USC § 1320a-7a(a).
120. Id.
121. 42 USC § 1395nn(g)(3).
122. See 42 USC § 1320a-7b(b).
123. See 42 CFR § 1005.15(d).
124. See 42 USC § 1395nn(g).
125. Id.
126. See 42 USC § 1320a-7b; 42 USC § 1395nn.
127. See 42 USC § 1395nn(e)(3).
128. 42 CFR § 1001.952(a).
129. 42 USC § 1395nn(c); 42 CFR § 411.356.
130. 42 CFR §§ 1001.952(b)-(c).
131. 42 USC § 1395nn(e)(1); 42 CFR §§ 411.357(a)-(b).
132. 42 CFR § 1001.952(d).
133. 42 USC § 1395nn(e)(3); 42 CFR § 411.357(d).
134. 42 CFR § 1001.952(e).
135. 42 USC § 1395nn(e)(6); 42 CFR § 411.357(f).
136. 42 CFR § 1001.952(i).
137. 42 USC § 1395nn(e)(2); 42 CFR § 411.357(c).
138. 42 CFR § 1001.952(a)(3)(i).
139. 42 USC § 1395nn(d)(2); 42 CFR § 411.356(c).
140. 42 CFR § 1001.952(n).
141. 42 USC § 1395nn(e)(5); 42 CFR § 411.357(e).
142. 42 CFR § 1001.952(p).

143. 42 USC § 1395nn(b)(2); 42 CFR § 411.355(b).
144. 42 CFR § 1001.952(u).
145. 42 USC § 1395nn(e)(3)(B); 42 CFR § 411.357(n); 42 CFR § 411.356(d)(2).
146. 42 CFR § 1001.952(g).
147. 42 CFR § 1001.952(h).
148. 42 CFR § 1001.952(j).
149. 42 CFR § 1001.952(k).
150. 42 CFR § 1001.952(l).
151. 42 CFR § 1001.952(m).
152. 42 CFR § 1001.952(r).
153. 42 CFR § 1001.952(s).
154. 42 CFR § 1001.952(q).
155. 42 USC § 1395nn(b)(1).
156. 42 USC § 1395nn(b)(3).
157. 42 USC § 1395nn(d)(3).
158. 42 USC § 1395nn(d)(1).
159. 42 USC § 1395nn(e)(4).
160. 42 USC § 1395nn(e)(7).
161. 42 USC § 1395nn(e)(8).
162. 42 CFR § 411.355(e).
163. 42 CFR § 411.357(l).
164. 42 CFR § 411.357(k).
165. 66 Fed Reg 856, 860 (January 4, 2001).
166. Id at 861.
167. Id at 879.
168. Id at 877.
169. Id at 875-76.
170. 69 Fed Reg 16116.
171. 66 Fed. Reg 884-885.
172. 66 Fed Reg 856, 917-18 (January 4, 2001).
173. 69 Fed Reg 16116.
174. 66 Fed Reg 962.
175. Id at 941-942.
176. See generally 31 USC §§ 3729-3733.
177. *Blusal Meats, Inc. v United States*, 638 F Supp 824, 827 (SDN.Y. 1986).
178. 31 USC § 3729(b).
179. Eric J. Holder, Jr., Deputy Attorney General, Guidance on the Use of the False Claims Act in Civil Health Care Matters (June 3, 1998).
180. *Rockwell International Corp v United States ex rel Stone*, 127 S Ct 1397 (2007).
181. 31 USC § 3730(e)(4)(A).
182. *Rockwell*, 127 S Ct at 1397.
183. *Allison Engine Co v United States ex rel Sanders*, No. 07-214 slip op (US June 9, 2008).
184. *United States ex rel Totten v Bombardier Corp*, 380 F.3d 488 (DC Cir 2004).
185. Id.
186. *K & R Partnership v Massachusetts Financing Agency*, No. 07-7014, 2008 WL 2651008 (DC Cir July 8, 2008).
187. *Safeco Ins. Co. v Burr*, 127 S Ct 2201 (2007).
188. Id.
189. Id.
190. *United States v NCH Health Care Corp*, 163 F Supp 2d 1051 (W.D. Mo. 2001).
191. *United States v Krizek*, 111 F.3d 934, 936 (DC Cir 1997).

192. Id.

193. Id.

194. Id at 936-37.

195. Id at 937.

196. Id at 943.

197. *United States v Cabrera-Diaz*, 106 F Supp 2d 234, 237 (DPR 2000).

198. Id.

199. *Cabrera-Diaz*, 106 F Supp 2d at 237.

200. Id.

201. Id.

202. Id at 238.

203. Id at 243.

204. *United States v Mackby*, 261 F.3d 821, 824 (9th Cir 2001).

205. Id at 824 (citing Medicare Bulletin [Chico, CA], Mar 1993, at 22).

206. 42 CFR § 410.60(c)(1).

207. 42 CFR § 410.60(c)(2).

208. *Mackby*, 261 F.3d at 825.

209. Id.

210. Id.

211. Id.

212. Id.

213. Id.

214. *Mackby*, 261 F.3d at 828.

215. Id (quoting *Krizek*, 111 F.3d at 942).

216. *United States ex rel Aranda v Cmt. Psychiatric Ctrs of Okl., Inc*, 945 F Supp 1485 (WD Okla 1996).

217. Id.

218. Id at 1488.

219. *United States ex rel Luckey v Baxter Healthcare Corp*, 183 F.3d 730 (7th Cir 1999).

220. Id at 731.

221. Id at 732.

222. Id at 733.

223. *Luckey*, 183 F.3d at 733.

224. Id.

225. *United States v ex rel Mikes v Straus*, 84 F Supp 2d 427 (SDN.Y. 1999), aff'd, 274 F.3d 687 (2d Cir 2001).

226. Id at 435.

227. *United States v ex rel Mikes v Straus*, 274 F.3d 687 (2d Cir 2001).

228. Id at 700.

229. Id at 701.

230. Id.

231. Id at 702.

232. *Mikes*, 274 F.3d at 703.

233. Id.

234. Id at 704.

235. *United States ex rel Swafford v Borgess Med Ctr*, 98 F Supp 2d 822 (WD Mich. 2000), aff'd, 24 Fed. Appx. 491 (6th Cir 2001), *cert denied*, 535 US 1096 (2002).

236. Id at 824-25.

237. Id at 825.

238. Id at 826.

239. Id at 827.

240. Id.
241. *Swafford*, 98 F Supp 2d at 829.
242. Id at 828.
243. *United States ex rel Luckey v Baxter Healthcare Corp*, 183 F.3d 730 (7th Cir 1999).
244. *Swafford*, 98 F Supp 2d at 831.
245. Id at 832.
246. Id.
247. Id at 833.
248. See 24 Fed. Appx. 491 (6th Cir 2001), *cert denied*, 535 US 1096 (2002).
249. See 42 USC § 1395nn.
250. *US ex rel Pogue v Am Healthcorp, Inc.*, 914 F Supp 1507 (MD Tenn. 1996).
251. *US ex rel Pogue v Am Healthcorp, Inc.*, 1995 US Dist. LEXIS 16710, 3-4 (MD Tenn 1995), *vacated*, 914 F Supp 1507 (MD Tenn. 1996).
252. Id at *16-7.
253. *Pogue*, 914 F Supp at 1513.
254. *Ab-Tech Constr, Inc. v United States*, 31 Fed. Cl. 429 (1994), *aff'd*, 57 F.3d 1084 (Fed Cir 1995).
255. Id at 434.
256. Id at 433.
257. Id at 434.
258. *United States v Inc Vill of Island Park*, 888 F Supp 419, 439 (EDNY 1995).
259. *Ab-Tech*, 31 Fed Cl at 434.
260. *Inc Village of Island Park*, 888 F Supp at 439.
261. *Pogue*, 914 F Supp at 1513.
262. Id.
263. Id.
264. Id.
265. See *United States ex rel Pogue v Diabetes Treatment Ctrs of Am*, 238 F Supp 2d 258 (DDC 2002).
266. *United States ex rel Scott Barrett v Columbia/HCA Healthcare Corp*, 251 F Supp 2d 28 (DDC 2003).
267. Id at *4-7.
268. Id at *5.
269. *United States ex rel Thompson v Columbia/HCA Healthcare Corp*, 125 F.3d 899 (SD Tex 1997).
270. Id at 900-01.
271. *United States ex rel Thompson v Columbia/HCA Healthcare Corp*, 20 F Supp 2d 1017, 1046 (SD Tex 1998.)
272. Id at 1047.
273. Id.
274. Id at 1048 (citing *Pogue*, 914 F Supp 1507, 1511 [MD Tenn 1996]).
275. Id at 1048-49.
276. *United States ex rel Barmak v Sutter Corp*, 2002 US Dist LEXIS 8509, *1 (SD NY 2002).
277. Id at *17.
278. Id at *17-18.
279. Id.
280. Id.
281. *United States ex rel McNutt v Haleyville Medical Supplies, Inc.*, 423 F. 3d 1256 (11th Cir 2005).
282. Id at 1260.
283. *United States v Liss*, 265 F.3d 1220, 1224 (11th Cir 2001).

284. Id at 1224-25.
285. Id at 1231.
286. Id.
287. *United States v Martin*, 195 F.3d 961, 968 (7th Cir 1999).
288. 18 USC § 3664(e); *United States v McIntosh*, 198 F.3d 995, 1003 (7th Cir 2000).
289. *Liss*, 265 F.3d at 1232.
290. Id.
291. *United States v Rogan*, 517 F. 3d 449 (7th Cir 2008).
292. *United States v Rogan*, 459 F Supp 2d 692 (N.D. Ill. 2006).
293. *Rogan*, 517 F. 3d at 449.
294. Id at 453.
295. See *United States v Rockford Mem'l Corp*, 898 F.2d 1278 (7th Cir 1990), *cert denied*, 498 US 920 (1990).
296. 15 USC §§ 1-7.
297. 15 USC § 1.
298. 15 USC §§ 12-27.
299. 15 USC § 18.
300. 15 USC § 18a.
301. See 16 CFR § 801.90.
302. See 28 CFR § 50.6; 16 CFR §§ 1.1-1.4.

Biographical Information

Gabriel L. Imperato, JD, has practiced healthcare law in both the public and private sectors for more than 20 years and is board certified as a specialist in health law by the Florida Bar. Mr. Imperato presently represents individuals and organizations accused of criminal and civil health care fraud in jurisdictions throughout the United States. Prior to joining Broad and Cassel, Mr. Imperato was the Deputy Chief Counsel, Office of the General Counsel, United States Department of Health and Human Services, where he advised and represented various agencies of the Department of Health and Human Services, including the Health Care Financing Administration (Medicare and Medicaid), the Public Health Service, the Social Security Administration, and the Office of the Inspector General. Mr. Imperato has extensive criminal and civil trial and appellate experience in administrative, state, and federal courts, and has personally handled leading national cases concerning criminal and civil healthcare fraud and abuse and healthcare law and policy. He also has handled numerous matters involving the formation of integrated delivery systems and managed care organizations. He is considered a national expert on fraud and abuse, reimbursement, and antitrust matters in the healthcare field. He is a frequent lecturer and has published numerous articles on such issues as medical staff proceedings, antitrust in the healthcare field, handling a healthcare fraud investigation and administrative and judicial procedural rights and the fraud and abuse laws under Medicare, Medicaid, and private health insurance programs. He is a member of the Illinois, Florida, and District of Columbia Bars, the American Health Lawyers Association, the Health Law Section of the Florida Bar, the American Bar Association Antitrust Health Care Committee, the White Collar Crime Committee, and the Subcommittee on Health Care Fraud, where he has been a member of the Planning Committee of the American Bar Association Health Care Fraud Institution. Mr. Imperato was a long-time member of the now dissolved American Academy of Hospital Attorneys, where he was Chairman of the Reimbursement and Payment Committee and the Health Care Reform Task Force.

Mike Segal, JD, LLM, is a Florida native, born in Jacksonville and raised in Orlando. He attended the University of Florida, receiving his Bachelor of Arts in political science in 1967 and his Juris Doctorate in law in 1969. In 1971, he received an LLM in taxation from New York University. Thereafter, he was an attorney advisor for the US Tax Court in Washington, DC. He has been associated with Broad and Cassel for 25 years and has been a partner of the firm for more than 20 years. Mr. Segal is the managing partner of the Miami office of Broad and Cassel, serves on the firm's executive committee, and is cochairman of the firm's healthcare practice group. Mr. Segal's practice is primarily devoted to healthcare transactional matters, including structuring medical group practices throughout the United States, forming integrated delivery systems between physicians and hospitals, and representing buyers and sellers in complex purchases and sales of healthcare-related businesses. He is a member of AHLA, the healthcare sections of the American and Florida Bar Associations, and MGMA.

Matthew T. Staab, MA, JD, was born and raised in Montpelier, Vermont. He attended Saint Michael's College, where he received a Bachelor of Science degree in business administration in 1993. Mr. Staab later attended Florida International University where, in 1999, he received his Master of Arts degree in economics. In 2002, he attained his Juris Doctorate, with honors, from Nova Southeastern University. Mr. Staab is currently of counsel in the Ft. Lauderdale office of Broad and Cassel.

Financial Management of Organized Healthcare Delivery Systems

Leslie G. Eldenburg, Eldon L. Schafer, and Dwight J. Zulauf

Managing the financial viability of a healthcare organization involves a collection of processes or subsystems to obtain funds for the organization and to make optimal use of those funds once obtained. Financial management includes the following functions: design and operation of the financial information system; financial planning, reporting, and control; and providing information for decision making.

Financial Information Needs

Financial information must be generated for several purposes, some for external needs and some for internal needs.

- Entity financial statements prepared in accordance with generally accepted accounting principles (GAAP) are required for external reporting to stockholders and creditors; although not required, they generally are prepared for the board of directors as well.
- The financial information required for state and federal regulatory agencies generally focuses on cost data.
- Management needs information to plan the resources and to evaluate performance. Information is needed for segments or responsibility centers as well as for the entity as a whole.
- Management needs information for short-run decisions, such as determining prices, volume, and mix of services to be offered.
- Management also needs information to make long-range investment decisions involving large expenditures that have long lives; however, the financial information system generally provides very little information relevant to specific long-range decisions.

Accounting information generally falls into two broad classifications: financial accounting and management accounting. Financial accounting is concerned with the preparation and content of the conventional financial statements. The Financial Accounting Standards Board issues GAAP, which prescribe the form, content, and measurements of the financial statements for external reporting. There are no similar principles for internal reporting, but most healthcare organizations follow the same accounting standards for both external and internal reporting. The major exception is in ambulatory care organizations, particularly physician groups where emphasis is on cash flows rather than accounting income.

Conventional financial statements include the following:

- The financial position statement (also called the balance sheet) shows what the organization owns (assets), what the organization owes to outsiders (liabilities), and the resulting owners' equity (net assets).
- The operating statement (income statement) shows the revenues and expenses of the organization and the resulting net income or loss for a period of time. This statement is sometimes called by its older title, the profit and loss statement.
- The cash flow statement shows the cash flows from operating activities, investing activities, and financing activities for a period of time and the resulting change in cash balance.

Management accounting addresses the internal information needs for financial planning, control, and decision making. Healthcare executives are responsible for planning, implementing, and reporting the use of their organization's resources consistent with an established mission and the resulting strategic plan. Owners or governing boards review both plans and reported results to be certain that the mission of their healthcare organization is being fulfilled.

A decision is efficient if its benefits exceed its costs. Healthcare organizations must be able to identify, measure, and compare the benefits and costs attributable to particular kinds of decisions. Decisions fall into two general types: long-range decisions, which involve the addition or replacement of long-term capacity, and short-range decisions, which involve the use of existing capacity over a short period of time, usually a year or less. The information needs and decision criteria for long-range and short-range decisions are very different.

This chapter is presented in three major sections. The first discusses the four conventional financial statements; financial statements for an integrated healthcare organization are presented and analyzed. The second section discusses long-range decisions that involve the acquisition or replacement of resources that have long lives. The most common example is the acquisition of equipment or buildings. The third section deals with decisions involving the use of existing capacity over a short period of time. The most common short-range decisions involve what fees to charge and what volume and mix of services to offer. Most decisions take place within some segment of the healthcare organization, such as a hospital, an ambulatory center, or a physician group. It is important to ensure that decisions are consistent with the strategy or mission of the organized healthcare delivery organization, as well as its individual segments.

Understanding Financial Statements

Financial statements work from a basic accounting model or equation:

$$\text{Assets} = \text{Liabilities} + \text{Owners' Equity}$$

This is the framework of the statement of financial position, and other financial statements show changes to this model. For example, the income statement shows changes in owners' equity due to operations, and the statement of cash flows explains changes in cash. This basic model and the financial statements have evolved over centuries of use.

Financial statements prepared in conformity with GAAP follow a generally uniform format. GAAP require the use of accrual accounting and prescribe the type, format, measurements, and disclosures in general purpose financial statements. In accrual basis financial statements, as required by GAAP, revenue is recognized when service is performed, regardless of when cash is collected, and expenses are recognized when resources are consumed in providing that service, regardless of when cash is paid. Hospitals and many other healthcare organizations long have used accrual accounting. Until recently, however, physician and other ambulatory care groups generally have used cash basis accounting. In cash basis accounting, revenues are recognized when cash is collected, and expenses are recognized when cash is paid. As organized healthcare delivery systems acquire them, these physician groups generally change from cash to accrual basis accounting to be consistent with the rest of the system's accounting policies. A significant segment of the healthcare industry still uses cash basis accounting, however, and the management of an organized healthcare delivery system should understand both types of statements.

Types of Financial Statements

The following financial statements are adapted from a large, organized healthcare delivery system that includes hospitals, acute care centers, outpatient care centers, physician practices, and a foundation. The amounts are adjusted to maintain anonymity, but all financial relationships remain intact.

Statement of Financial Position

The combined statement of financial position or balance sheet for the sample health system combines the balance sheets of all the entities in the system (**Exhibit 4.1**). Intercompany transactions, such as an amount payable in the balance sheet of a hospital and a receivable in the balance sheet of a physician group, have been eliminated. Assets and liabilities are classified into types to provide a better understanding of the organization's financial position and to allow computation of ratios and other comparisons in analyzing the financial statements. Four types of assets are included in the statement of financial position:

1. Current assets (i.e., cash and those assets expected to be converted into cash or consumed in the normal course of operations within a year)—These assets are expected to be used to pay current liabilities and operating costs of the organization.

Exhibit 4.1   Sample Health System: Combined Statement of Financial Position
(December 31, 2002 and 2003)

Assets	2002 ($000)	2003 ($000)
Current Assets		
Cash and cash equivalents	3,371	4,891
Investments	59,671	112,833
Accounts receivable (less allowance for doubtful accounts of $6,673)	44,026	47,508
Inventories	3,805	3,962
Limited use assets—required for current liabilities	3,312	3,310
Prepaid expenses and other current assets	3,973	1,902
Total current assets	118,158	174,406
Limited Use Assets, net of current portion:		
By board for future use	50,571	43,672
Under bond indenture agreement	13,419	13,328
Under self-insurance arrangement	9,904	2,710
Donor-restricted	19,892	21,705
Total limited use assets	93,786	81,415
Property, Plant, and Equipment		
Land and improvements	17,300	18,018
Buildings	158,121	162,365
Equipment	126,318	140,196
Total	301,739	320,579
Less accumulated depreciation	(118,211)	(138,050)
Net	183,528	182,529
Construction in progress	6,701	6,489
Net property, plant, and equipment	190,229	189,018
Other Assets		
Unamortized bond issue cost	4,988	4,735
Other	9,983	8,364
Total other assets	14,971	13,099
Total Assets	417,142	457,936
Liabilities and Net Assets		
Current Liabilities		
Accounts payable and accrued expenses	$34,844	$45,343
Accrued interest payable	3,909	3,475
Estimated third-party payer settlements	4,700	8,754
Current portion of long-term debt	4,985	4,664
Total current liabilities	48,438	62,236
Accrued Pension and Medical Malpractice Liabilities	18,836	16,121
Long-Term Debt, net of current portion	145,693	141,104
Total Liabilities	212,967	219,461
Net Assets		
Unrestricted	184,490	216,948
Temporarily restricted	6,510	6,617
Permanently restricted	13,177	14,913
Total net assets	204,177	238,477
Total Liabilities and Net Assets	$417,144	$457,938

Source: Anonymous. (Note: Data may not add to totals due to rounding.)

2. Limited use assets (i.e., cash and other assets held for specified purposes in the future)—The use of these assets is restricted by the board, by donors, or by some other agreement. Restricted assets are common in not-for-profit organizations.

3. Property, plant, and equipment (i.e., tangible, long-lived assets used in the operations of the organization)—Any assets held for future use are classified as limited use assets. These assets are depreciated over their useful life.

4. Other assets (i.e., expenditures that will be amortized [expensed] over some future period of time, such as bond issue costs)—Intangible assets such as goodwill, patents, and copyrights are included in other assets.

Liabilities are present obligations to parties outside the entity that arose from past events and are payable in the future.

The statement of financial position for this health system includes three types of liabilities:

1. Current liabilities (i.e., liabilities due within 1 year, the same period used to measure current assets)—Current liabilities are used in several analytical ratios.

2. Accrued pension and medical malpractice liabilities—GAAP require the recognition of the costs and liabilities from postretirement benefits. This system also has recognized a possible liability arising from self-insuring for medical malpractice.

3. Long-term liabilities—(i.e., liabilities that are due beyond the time period used for current liabilities)—All long-term liabilities are measured as the present value of future cash flows to retire the obligation. This system has long-term accruals and long-term debt.

The form of owners' equity depends on the nature of the corporation. In a for-profit corporation, the owners' equity includes contributed capital, representing the par or stated value of the stock issued and the additional amounts paid by the stockholder investors, and earned capital, the earnings less distribution to stockholders since the corporation was formed. Because there are no "investors" in a not-for-profit corporation, the difference between assets and liabilities in this type of corporation is described as net assets. These net assets must be classified to reflect certain restrictions on the assets of the organization, however.

Statement of Operations

The sample system's statement of operations or income statement combines the operating statements of the various organizations included in this system (**Exhibit 4.2**). Intercompany transactions, such as the sale of goods or services between organizations, have been eliminated. The statement includes the following:

1. Revenue (i.e., the value of services provided and goods sold to patients, whether or not cash has been collected)—An estimate of bad debts to reflect patient billings that will not be collected is included in expenses.

2. Expenses (i.e., the consumption of resources in providing services and goods to patients, regardless of when cash is paid)—Some expenses, such as depreciation, involve estimates of the cost of long-lived assets amortized during this period. Others, such as pension expenses, represent an estimate of payments to be made in the future.

Exhibit 4.2   Sample Health System Combined Statement of Operations (for the Year Ended December 31, 2003)

	($000)
Revenue	
Net patient service revenue	288,322
Other	6,612
Total revenue	294,934
Expenses	
Salaries and wages	130,619
Employee benefits	27,546
Supplies	36,365
Depreciation and amortization	20,853
Interest	9,678
Provision for bad debts	9,608
Other	57,636
Total expenses	292,305
Income from Operations	2,629
Nonoperating Gains (Losses)	
Unrestricted contributions and fund raising activities	3,564
Income on investments	16,037
Other	(3,746)
Total nonoperating gains, net	15,855
Net Income	18,484

Source: Anonymous.

3. Income from operations—Operating income is a key measure of the performance of the healthcare organization; it is the excess (deficiency) of revenues over expenses. Unless there are significant nonoperating gains or donations, income from operations must be positive over time to provide the funds to replace assets and grow.
4. Nonoperating gains (losses) (i.e., the gains and losses from donations or other activities, such as income from investments and gain or loss from sale of assets, that do not involve the delivery of health care to patients)—These gains and losses are excluded in the analysis of current operating performance.

Statement of Cash Flows

The changes in cash during the accounting period are shown in the statement of cash flows. Three types of cash flows are identified: operating, investing, and financing.

Cash flows from operating activities include cash collected from providing healthcare services, cash paid for expenses, and cash paid for interest and taxes. Cash flows from investing activities include cash flows from buying and selling assets, including plant, property, equipment, and investments. Cash flows from financing activities include borrowings, repayment of debt, cash from equity investors, and dividends.

In practice, an organization may use either of two forms to present cash flows from operations. The direct method is a straightforward presentation of the amount of cash collected from patients and the amount paid for expenses, interest, and taxes. The indirect method—used by this system and most other organizations with external reporting requirements—begins with net income or loss from the operating statement (or change in net assets in a not-for-profit organization) and removes any transactions that do not involve cash such as billings not collected, expenses on account, and depreciation. The indirect method can be very complex and difficult to understand for those who are not accountants. Not-for-profit organizations, such as the sample health system illustrated in this chapter, present further complexities.

A detailed explanation of the statement of cash flow in **Exhibit 4.3** is beyond the scope of this chapter. Instead, the simple example that follows develops a cash flow statement for a small for-profit company. This should provide a general understanding of this important statement.

Assume the beginning and ending balance sheets are for a small for-profit service company.

	Beginning balance sheet	Ending balance sheet
Assets:		
Cash	$10,000	$ 4,000
Accounts receivable	$50,000	$ 57,000
Equipment	$40,000	$ 60,000
Less depreciation on equipment	($10,000)	($ 15,000)
Total	$90,000	$106,000
Liabilities:		
Accounts payable	$40,000	$ 36,000
Bank loan	$20,000	$ 30,000
Owner's equity:		
Capital stock	$20,000	$ 20,000
Retained earnings	$10,000	$ 20,000
	$90,000	$106,000

Assume the following operating statement:

Sales	$80,000
Less expenses:	
Operating expenses	($65,000)
Depreciation of equipment	($ 5,000)
Net income	$10,000

Exhibit 4.3   Sample Health System: Combined Statements of Cash Flows (for the Year Ended December 31, 2003)

	($000)
Operating Activities	
Change in net assets	34,300
Adjustments to reconcile change in net assets to net cash provided by operations:	
Depreciation and amortization	20,905
Other	2,918
Realized and unrealized losses on investments	(13,191)
Cumulative effect of accounting change	(10,356)
Restricted contributions	(4,300)
Cash provided (used) by changes in operating assets and liabilities:	
Accounts receivable	(3,483)
Inventories, prepaid expenses, and other assets	1,901
Accounts payable and accrued expenses	8,977
Estimated third-party payer settlements	4,054
Accrued pension and medical malpractice liabilities	(2,715)
Net cash provided by operating activities	39,010
Inventing Activities	
Purchase of property, plant, and equipment, net	(19,058)
Purchase of other long-term productive assets	(581)
Change in investments and limited use assets	(17,241)
Net cash used by investing activities	(36,880)
Financing Activities	
Repayment of long-term debt	(4,910)
Restricted contributions	4,300
Net cash used by financing activities	(610)
Net Increase in Cash and Cash Equivalents	1,520
Cash and Cash Equivalents	
Beginning of year	3,371
End of year	4,891

Source: Anonymous.

The direct method of presenting cash flow from operations deducts the $7,000 increase in accounts receivable from sales of $80,000 to determine the $73,000 of cash actually collected from customers. Payment of operating expenses was $69,000 (operating expenses of $65,000 plus the $4,000 paid to decrease accounts payable). Cash from investing involved the purchase of $20,000 of new equipment. Cash from financing involved the additional bank loan of $10,000.

The cash flow statement using the direct method is as follows:

Cash from operations:	
Cash collected from customers	$73,000
Cash paid for expenses	($69,000)
Total	$ 4,000
Cash from investing:	
Cash paid to purchase equipment	($20,000)
Cash from financing:	
Cash from bank loan	$10,000
Change in cash	($ 6,000)
Beginning cash	$10,000
Ending cash	$ 4,000

The indirect method of determining cash from operating activities begins with net income of $10,000, then deducts the increase of $7,000 in accounts receivable that did not bring in cash, deducts the decrease of $4,000 in accounts payable that did take in cash, and adds back the $5,000 of depreciation that did not take in cash. The cash flow statement for the indirect method is as follows:

Cash from operations:	
Net income	$10,000
Deduct the increase in accounts receivable	($ 7,000)
Deduct the decrease in accounts payable	($ 4,000)
Add back depreciation	$ 5,000
Total	$ 4,000
Cash from investing:	
Cash paid to purchase equipment	($20,000)
Cash from financing:	
Cash from bank loan	$10,000
Change in cash	($ 6,000)
Beginning cash	$10,000
Ending cash	$ 4,000

Statement of Changes in Net Assets

For external reporting, GAAP require an explanation of the changes in owners' equity (net assets in not-for-profit organizations). The reconciliation may be in the form of a statement or in a footnote (**Exhibit 4.4**). This system has three classes of net assets, based on whether there are any restrictions on the assets and, if so, the type of restrictions. Some of the assets have temporary restrictions, usually imposed by the board of directors, and some assets have permanent restrictions imposed by the donor of the assets.

Exhibit 4.4   Sample Health System: Combined Statement of Changes in Net Assets
(for the Year Ended December 31, 2003)

	($000)
Unrestricted Net Assets	
Balance, beginning of year	184,490
Net income	18,484
Increase in net unrealized gains on investments	2,986
Net assets released from restrictions—capital acquisitions	789
Cumulative effect of accounting change	10,199
Increase in unrestricted net assets	32,458
Balance, end of year	216,948
Temporarily Restricted Net Assets	
Balance, beginning of year	6,510
Contributions	3,741
Income on investments	274
Increase in net unrealized gains on investments	46
Net assets released from restrictions—capital acquisitions	(789)
Net assets released from restrictions	(3,324)
Cumulative effect of accounting change	159
Increase in temporarily restricted assets	107
Balance, end of year	6,617
Permanently Restricted Net Assets	
Balance, beginning of year	13,177
Contributions	559
Income on investments	1,101
Increase in net unrealized gains on investments	76
Increase in permanently restricted net assets	1,736
Balance, end of year	14,913
Total Net Assets	238,478

Source: Anonymous.

Cash and Accrual Accounting

The acquisition of physician groups presents a unique set of problems for an organized health-care delivery system. Because they often use cash basis accounting, the financial statements do not always provide all relevant financial information about the groups. Often, the commitments made by the organized delivery system to the acquired physician group result in financial surprises. The cash basis financial statements of the physician groups sometimes do not provide a basis for reliable projections on the accrual basis of accounting.

Exhibits 4.5 and **4.6** illustrate the differences in accounting methods that lead to problems. They record 11 transactions in a worksheet with columns representing balance sheet accounts

Exhibit 4.5 Accrual Basis Financial Statements

Transactions for Accrual Basis Financial Statements ($000)

Tran	Explanation	Cash Flow Statement	Assets				=	Liabilities		+	Owners' Equity		
			Cash	Patient Receivable	Prepayment	Equipment		Accounts Payable	Note Payable		Capital Stock	Revenue	Expense
1	Investment by owners	F	250								250		
2	Supplies and insurance	O	(50)		50								
3	Purchase equipment	I	(50)			1,000			950				
4	Billings to patients			1,000								1,000	
5	Expenses on account							50					(50)
6	Collect on account	O	800	(800)									
7	Pay expenses	O	(500)										(500)
8	Pay on account	O	(30)					(30)					
9	Pay on note	F	(100)						(100)				
10	Equipment depreciation	O				(100)							(100)
11	Distribution to physicians	O	(300)										(300)
			20	200	50	900		20	850		250	1,000	(950)

INCOME STATEMENT

Revenue from patients	$1,000
Operating expenses	(950)
Net income (loss)	$ 50

CHANGES IN OWNERS' EQUITY

Contributed capital:	
Beginning balance	$ 0
Issued capital stock	$250
Ending balance	$250
Retained earnings:	
Beginning balance	$ 0
Net income	50
Ending balance	$ 50
Total owners' equity	$300

BALANCE SHEET

ASSETS	
Cash	$ 20
Patient receivables	200
Prepayments	50
Equipment	900
Total	$1,170
LIABILITIES AND OWNERS' EQUITY	
Accounts payable	$ 20
Note payable	850
Total liabilities	870
Capital stock	250
Retained earnings	50
Total owners' equity	300
Total	$1,170

CASH FLOW STATEMENT

Cash from operations:	
Collections from patients	$ 800
Payment of expenses	(580)
Distributions to physicians	(300)
Total	(80)
Cash from investing	(50)
Cash from financing:	
Investment by owners	250
Payment on note	(100)
Total	150
Change in cash	20
Beginning cash balance	0
Ending cash balance	$ 20

Exhibit 4.6 Cash Basis Financial Statements

TRANSACTIONS FOR CASH BASIS FINANCIAL STATEMENTS ($000)

Tran	Explanation	Cash Flow Statements	Assets: Cash	Assets: Equipment	=	Liabilities: Note Payable	+	Owners' Equity: Capital Stock	Owners' Equity: Revenue	Owners' Equity: Expense
1	Investment by owners	F	250					250		
2	Supplies and insurance	O	(50)							(50)
3	Purchase equipment	I	(50)	1,000		950				
4	No entry									
5	No entry									
6	Collect on account	O	800						800	
7	Pay expenses	O	(500)							(500)
8	Pay on account	O	(30)							(30)
9	Payment on note	F	(100)			(100)				
10	Equipment depreciation			(100)						(100)
11	Distribution to physicians	O	(300)							(300)
			20	900		850		250	800	(980)

INCOME STATEMENT

Revenue from patients	$ 800
Operating expenses	(980)
Net income (loss)	$ (180)

CASH FLOW STATEMENT

Cash from operations:	
Collections from patients	$ 800
Payment of expenses	(580)
Distributions to physicians	(300)
Total	(80)
Cash from investing	(50)
Cash from financing:	
Investment by owners	250
Payment on note	(100)
Total	150
Change in cash	20
Beginning cash balance	0
Ending cash balance	$ 20

CHANGES IN OWNERS' EQUITY

Contributed capital:	
Beginning balance	$ 0
Issued capital stock	250
Ending balance	$ 250
Retained earnings:	
Beginning balance	$ 0
Net income	(180)
Ending balance	$ (180)
Total owners' equity	$ 70

BALANCE SHEET

ASSETS	
Cash	$ 20
Equipment	900
	$ 920
LIABILITIES AND OWNERS' EQUITY	
Note payable	850
Total liabilities	850
Capital stock	250
Retained earnings	(180)
Total owners' equity	70
Total	$ 920

and rows representing transactions. The balance sheet and income statement are generated from the column totals, which show ending balances for each account. The statement of cash flows is generated from an analysis of the cash column. The set of transactions used for both the accrual and cash basis examples follow:

1. The physicians invest $250,000 in the medical practice.
2. Supplies and insurance are prepaid at $50,000.
3. Equipment at $1 million is purchased with $50,000 as the down payment and the balance on a note payable. (It is assumed that the facilities are rented, and rent is included among operating expenses.)
4. Patients are billed for $1 million during the accounting period.
5. Expenses are incurred on accounts payable of $50,000.
6. Cash is collected from patients in the amount of $800,000.
7. Expenses are paid in cash for $500,000.
8. Payments are made on accounts payable in the amount of $30,000.
9. A principal payment is made on the note payable in the amount of $100,000.
10. Depreciation on equipment for the period is $100,000.
11. Distributions to physicians for the period are $300,000.

In Exhibit 4.5, all 11 transactions are recorded on an accrual basis. In the column next to cash, the cash flow transactions used to prepare the cash flow statement are identified as operating activities (cash flows related to providing service to patients); financing activities (cash flows related to investment by owners and borrowing and repayment of debt); or investing activities (cash flows involving purchase and sale of assets and investments).

In Exhibit 4.6, the transactions are recorded on the cash basis. Only cash collections are recognized as revenue. Receivables are not recorded in the accounts. Only cash payments for operations are recognized as expenses. Accounts payable are not recorded in the accounts. Depreciation is recognized in both systems, however.

Transactions 4 and 5, relating to billings to patients and expenses on account, are not recorded on the cash basis. The payments for supplies (transaction 2) and payments on account (transaction 8) are recorded as expenses in the cash basis, but involve asset or liability accounts on the accrual basis.

There are significant differences in the balance sheets and income statements. On the accrual basis, revenues are $1,000,000; expenses are $950,000; and net income is $50,000. On the cash basis, revenues are $800,000 and expenses are $980,000, resulting in a loss of $180,000. On the accrual basis balance sheet, assets are $1,170,000 and liabilities are $870,000, leaving net assets of $300,000. On the cash basis balance sheet, however, the patient receivables, prepayments, and accounts payable are omitted, leaving assets of $920,000 and liabilities of $850,000. The difference in income is exaggerated because there are no beginning balances of receivables or payables in the first period of a new business. In subsequent years, this difference will be smaller. On a monthly basis, wide differences will occur if billings fluctuate during the year. Because of the lag in collections, the month of highest collections often occurs in the month of lowest billings, and there is often a shortage of cash in the month of highest billings.

The statement of cash flows is the same for both bases of accounting because only cash is involved. In the cash basis statements, the net loss in the income statements ($180,000) is larger than the cash used by operations in the cash flow statement ($80,000) only because depreciation ($100,000) is included in the income statement, but does not involve cash. Because of receivables, payables, and other accrual accounts, there always will be differences between net income and cash flow from operations on the accrual basis. In the cash flow statement for the sample health system discussed earlier (see Exhibit 4.3), these accrual measurements were identified when cash flow from operations was computed by the indirect method.

Patient receivables, generally the major asset in physician group practices, are omitted from the balance sheet on the cash basis, requiring physician groups to provide supplemental information for creditors in a loan transaction, for buyers in the sale of the practice, and for physicians involved in the admission or withdrawal of a physician. This particularly is true when dealing with a party that has no experience with cash basis accounting.

These accrual and cash basis examples represent the extremes in the accounting measurements. In practice, few organizations use a full cash basis. Instead, most use a modified cash basis system that recognizes some accrual basis measurements (e.g., vacation pay) and some cash basis measurements. The modified cash basis reduces the differences between accrual and cash measurements, and it provides more consistent financial results.

Segment or Responsibility Center Reporting

Financial statements for external reporting are prepared for the organized healthcare delivery system as a whole. Although these statements may provide creditors, other external users, and the board of directors with an overall picture of the healthcare system, they are not useful to operating management for evaluating financial performance. Operating management needs statements for each responsibility center in the organization, that is, for any organizational segment for which financial data are accumulated and reported. For example, the sample health system shows a net income of about $18 million for the entity as a whole. A study of the income statements of the various responsibility centers shows wide differences in the incomes of individual centers, however, ranging from a net income of about $18 million for the hospital to a net loss of about $17 million for the physician network (**Exhibit 4.7**).

Types of Responsibility Centers

The identification of responsibility centers is the first step in determining the full cost of services to patients. There are three types of responsibility centers for the purposes of reporting financial information (**Table 4.1**):

1. Cost centers are responsibility centers that do not serve patients directly and, therefore, have no revenue. Only costs may be traced to cost centers, which then must be allocated to profit centers to generate the full cost of services to patients. Cost centers are evaluated based on their ability to minimize costs. Examples of cost centers include administration, occupancy, medical records, food service, and laundry.

Exhibit 4.7 Sample Health System: Responsibility Center Operating Report ($000) (for the Year Ended December 31, 2003)

	Metrocare Medical Center				Metrocare Health Services	Metrocare Physician Network	Urgent Care Centers	Other Medical Services	Metrocare Foundation
	Metro General Hospital	Metro Children's Hospital	Support Services	Metro Hospital					
PATIENT SERVICES REVENUE									
Daily patient services—inpatient	$ 63,625	$ 6,545	$—	$5,069	$—	$—	$—	$—	$—
Professional services—inpatient	81,709	10,956	—	19,282	—	1,020	—	—	—
Daily patient services—outpatient	1,456	628	—	332	—	—	—	—	—
Professional services—outpatient	75,896	20,844	—	41,191	—	64,355	3,209	—	—
Capitation	891	124	—	—	33,851	827	—	—	—
TOTAL	223,577	39,097	—	65,874	33,851	66,202	3,209	—	—
DEDUCTIONS FROM REVENUE									
Contractual adjustments	72,573	8,983	—	25,932	—	18,334	636	—	—
Charity care	2,889	836	—	520	—	104	—	—	—
TOTAL	75,462	9,819	—	26,452	—	18,438	636	—	—
NET PATIENT SERVICE REVENUE	148,115	29,278	—	39,422	33,851	47,764	2,573	—	—
OTHER OPERATING REVENUE									
Hospital services	688	168	1,446	937	785	2,114	—	—	—
Other	—	55	47	—	137	—	—	867	—
TOTAL	688	223	1,493	937	922	2,114	—	867	—
TOTAL OPERATING REVENUE	148,803	29,501	1,493	40,359	34,773	49,878	2,573	867	—
OPERATING EXPENSES									
Salaries and wages	48,065	12,693	9,420	13,480	11,408	33,711	1,804	37	—
Employee benefits	3,905	992	7,970	2,596	4,541	7,294	245	3	—
Supplies	20,901	1,538	2,248	5,846	735	4,936	149	10	—
Depreciation	10,541	817	782	2,217	3,422	2,543	191	340	—
Interest	8,085	—	—	1,075	—	126	—	392	—
Provision for bad debts	4,942	1,002	—	1,226	23	2,275	138	—	—
Corporate office services	32,620	6,838	(22,365)	3,177	(25,645)	4,934	210	45	—
Other expenses	2,735	4,277	3,564	3,825	44,843	10,734	870	290	—
TOTAL	131,794	28,157	1,619	33,442	39,327	66,553	3,607	1,117	—
INCOME (LOSS) FROM OPERATIONS	17,009	1,344	(126)	6,917	(4,554)	(16,675)	(1,034)	(250)	—
NONOPERATING REVENUE									
Unrestricted gifts	571	3,109	134	18	3	—	—	—	(510)
Income on investments	746	—	—	130	12,679	—	—	—	2,429
Other income (loss)	88	(17)	(11)	(1)	(3,873)	—	—	67	2
TOTAL	1,405	3,092	123	147	8,809	—	—	67	1,921
EXCESS OF REVENUES	$18,414	$4,436	$(3)	$7,064	$4,255	$(16,675)	$(1,034)	$(183)	$1,921
Assets Employed	306,305	41,142	—	34,330	226,963	66,043	2,455	3,047	36,697

Source: Anonymous.

Table 4.1   Types of Responsibility Centers

Type	Examples	Nonfinancial Measures of Performance	Traceability of Financial Information	Financial Measures of Performance	Evaluation Criterion
Cost center	Corporate supports, administration, occupancy, medical records, laundry, food service	Time spent, resources used, units of output	Total costs, costs per unit of output	Amount of costs: actual vs. budget, actual vs. previous period	Minimize costs; minimize dollars of cost per unit of activity
Profit or contribution center	Laboratory, radiology, pharmacy, surgery, patient rooms, medical specialties	Number of patients served, time spent, resources used, units of output	Total revenue, total costs, profit or contribution	Amount contributed by responsibility center to cover common costs and provide a profit	Maximize profit or contribution, maximize profit per unit of activity, control costs
Investment center	Entire system, hospital, ambulatory surgery center, medical group	Number of patients served, time spent, resources used, units of output	Total revenue, total costs, profit or contribution, assets employed	Return on assets employed, also measures cited above	Maximize return on assets employed

2. Profit or contribution centers are responsibility centers that perform a service directly to patients. Both revenues and costs directly related to the service provided to patients can be traced to profit centers. Costs of cost centers may be allocated to profit centers to generate a full cost for setting fees. Profit centers are evaluated on their ability to control costs and to generate a satisfactory income. Examples of profit centers are laboratory, radiology, pharmacy, surgery, patient rooms, and medical specialties.

3. Investment centers have responsibility for costs, revenues, and assets employed. The identification of investment centers generally is limited to an entire entity, such as the entire healthcare system, or a major segment such as a hospital, an ambulatory care center, or a physician group. In addition to evaluation based on cost containment or profitability, the investment center may be evaluated by the global measure of return on investment.

An organized healthcare delivery system has a variety of responsibility centers. The entire system entity is an investment center that may be evaluated by return on investment, as well as by profitability and cost containment measures. The nine major responsibility centers of this example system are all investment centers with responsibility for revenues, costs, and assets employed, except the corporate support center, which is a cost center that provides services to other entities in the system (see Exhibit 4.7). The physician network involves a number of physician group practices, each of which could be identified as an investment center.

For planning, control, and evaluation of their operations, each of the nine responsibility centers has identified a number of profit and cost centers. For example, one of the hospitals has identified 78 responsibility centers. Of those, 43 are cost centers that provide services to the 35 profit centers. In each profit center, the full cost of the various services provided to patients includes the direct costs traceable to the profit center, as well as the indirect costs of the other cost centers that support the profit center. The costs allocated from supporting cost centers to a profit center should be based on the quantity of resources used, rather than on an arbitrary allocation process. Much of the regulatory reporting involves the identification and management of costs in responsibility centers.

Evaluation of Responsibility Centers

A comprehensive budget provides the framework for setting priorities, allocating resources, and monitoring financial performance. It includes an operating budget (also called profit plan), a cash budget, a projected balance sheet, and a capital budget (**Figure 4.1**). The comprehensive budget for the entire healthcare organization originates in the budgets of the various segments or responsibility centers. Its development is an iterative process, in which the results of the combining process repeatedly are compared with the goals and objectives of the entire healthcare organization.

The heart of any financial planning and control system is the operating budget, because it reflects the planned activity levels, the pricing or fee structure, and the cost structure of a responsibility center of the healthcare entity. The operating budget may be considered a static budget, in that it establishes only one level of activity at the beginning of the budget year. The activity level in the operating budget drives the rest of the comprehensive budget, however.

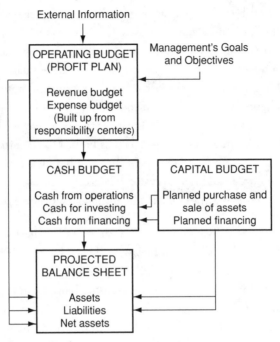

FIGURE 4.1   A Comprehensive Budget

Although the operating budget may serve as a valuable planning tool, it may be misleading as a performance evaluation tool if the actual activity has varied significantly from the planned level of activity. In a very simple example, a hospital projected 1000 patient days with average daily fees of $1,000. The fixed expenses were projected to be $700,000 for the year, and variable expenses were estimated to be $250 per patient day. (Variable expenses change in direct proportion to changes in activity, but fixed expenses do not change as activity changes.) Actual revenue during the year was $1,090,000, as the hospital incurred 1100 patient days; fixed expenses were $720,000, and variable expenses were $300,000.

In **Exhibit 4.8**, the actual operating results are compared with two budgets: the operating budget at the level projected at the beginning of the year and a performance budget based on the actual level of operations. The operating budget projected an income of $50,000, whereas the income statement showed an actual income of $70,000, a favorable variance of $20,000. This is misleading, because the variances represent an increase in volume, which was favorable, and changes in price and spending, which were unfavorable. The income should be higher than $50,000 when there are 10% more patient days than planned, but it is not possible to determine how much higher it should be with only a static budget. A comparison of actual results to the static operating budget does not make it possible to separate the effect of increased volume from the effect of price and spending variances.

A performance budget, prepared after the period, shows what revenues, expenses, and income should be for this hospital at 1100 patient days (see Exhibit 4.8). With many fixed expenses, a small change in volume results in a large change in income. The performance budget indicates that income should have been $125,000 if the hospital had maintained its fee structure and its

Exhibit 4.8   Comparison of Actual to Budget

Comparison of Actual to Operating Budget

	Operating Budget	Actual	Variances
Patient days	1,000	1,100	100
Patient revenue	$1,000,000	$1,090,000	$90,000
Operating expenses:			
Variable expenses	250,000	300,000	(50,000)
Fixed expenses	700,000	720,000	(20,000)
Total	950,000	1,020,000	(70,000)
Operating income	$50,000	$70,000	$20,000

Comparison of Actual to Performance Budget

	Operating Budget	Performance Budget	Actual	Variances
Patient days	1,000	1,100	1,100	0
Patient revenue	$1,000,000	$1,100,000	$1,090,000	$(10,000)
Operating expenses:				
Variable expenses	250,000	275,000	300,000	(25,000)
Fixed expenses	700,000	700,000	720,000	(20,000)
Total	950,000	975,000	1,020,000	(45,000)
Operating income	$50,000	$125,000	$70,000	$(55,000)

cost structure. Revenue should have increased by $100,000 (100 days × $1,000); the variable expenses should have increased by $25,000 (100 days × $250), but fixed expenses should have remained unchanged. According to a comparison of the actual results to the performance budget, the differences now reflect only price and spending variances. Apparently, fees were reduced, and both variable and fixed expenses were higher than they should have been. A summary of the difference between income in the operating budget and actual income follows:

Budgeted income in operating budget	$50,000
Variance due to volume ($125,000 – $50,000)	$75,000
Variance due to fee	
reduction ($1,100,000 – $1,090,000)	($10,000)
Variance due to spending in both fixed and variable expenses	
($1,020,000 – $975,000)	($45,000)
Actual income	$70,000

This very simple example shows that the operating budget may be misleading in an attempt to evaluate actual performance when there has been a significant change in volume. When there is a large change in volume, a difference in income will depend upon the cost structure—how much is fixed and how much is variable. This is referred to as operating leverage.

Exhibit 4.9 presents the operating report for one of the sample system's hospitals. The operating budget reflects management's estimates of activity, the pricing structure, and the cost structure planned for 2008. Patient service revenue was projected to be about $216 million; deductions from revenue, $79 million; other operating revenue, $2 million; operating expenses, $98 million; allocated corporate services, $34 million; and nonoperating revenue, $800,000; resulting in an excess of revenue over expenses of about $6 million.

The performance budget reflects the pricing structure and cost structure for the actual activity levels. It appears that total patient revenue increased by about 3%. Expenses with some variable component increased by about 3%, labor-related cost increased by about 4%, and allocated corporate services increased by only 1%. Expenses that were only fixed remained unchanged. The excess of revenue over expenses in the performance budget is about the same as that in the operating budget.

Except for small items (e.g., lease and rental fees), the variances from the performance budget are nearly all favorable and not very large. The combination of a 6% favorable variance in total operating revenue, a 2% favorable variance in operating expenses, and a favorable variance in allocated corporate costs led to an actual net income that was nearly three times the net income in the performance budget. Because the budgeted net income was very low—about $6 million—the small variances in revenues and costs resulted in a net income of about $18 million.

A performance budget, also called a flexible budget, is necessary when activity varies significantly from that estimated for the operating budget. In this situation, the operating budget is not a relevant basis on which to evaluate performance.

Analysis of Financial Statements

Creditors, long-term lenders, governing boards, regulators, donors, and investors are vitally concerned with changes in the financial status of the healthcare organizations with which they are associated. This is true whether the organization is not-for-profit or investor-owned. Estaugh noted the convergence of fiscal focus of both not-for-profit and for-profit hospitals: "Managers in both sectors are equally anxious about generating capital to secure a better future for their institutions."[1] To do this, they must not only achieve continued profitability, but also maintain short-term liquidity and long-term solvency.

Among the important tools used to evaluate an organization's financial health are financial ratios. Although the ratios themselves do not provide answers, they alert their user to areas that require deeper analysis. A single ratio for a single period gathers meaning when a comparison with the same measures for previous years reveals a trend or indicates compliance with an industry standard, for example.

Exhibit 4.9 Sample Health System: Hospital Operating Report ($000) (for the Year Ended December 31, 2003)

	Operating Budget	Performance Budget	Actual	% Change Due to Activity	Variance from Performance Budget	
					Amount (unf)	Percent – = unf
Patient service revenue	$215,624	$221,107	$223,577	3%	$2,470	1%
Deductions from revenue	79,269	81,280	75,462	3%	5,818	7%
Net patient service revenue	136,355	139,827	148,115	3%	8,288	6%
Other operating revenue	1,795	1,795	1,646	0%	(149)	-8%
Total operating revenue	138,150	141,622	149,761	3%	8,139	6%
Operating expenses						
Salaries and wages	46,351	48,207	48,065	4%	142	0%
Supplies	19,261	19,764	20,901	3%	(1,137)	-6%
Professional fees	3,129	3,198	2,807	2%	391	12%
Employee benefits	3,859	4,001	3,905	4%	96	2%
Lease and rental fees	386	386	519	0%	(133)	-35%
Interest	8,653	8,653	8,085	0%	568	7%
Depreciation and amortization	10,689	10,689	10,541	0%	148	1%
Provision for bad debts	4,977	5,104	4,942	3%	162	3%
Other operating costs	1,192	1,191	(591)	0%	1,782	150%
TOTAL	98,497	101,193	99,174	3%	2,019	2%
Income (loss) from operations	39,653	40,429	50,587	2%	10,158	25%
Allocated corporate services	34,140	34,397	32,620	1%	1,777	5%
Net income	5,513	6,032	17,967	9%	11,935	198%
Nonoperating revenue	837	837	834	0%	(3)	-0%
Excess of revenues over expenses	$ 6,350	$ 6,869	$18,801	8%	$11,932	174%

Source: Anonymous.

Measures of Profitability

Maintaining profitability in a healthcare organization is important for a number of reasons:

- If operations are to provide funding for the expansion of patient service capacity, those operations must be profitable. Even at the break-even point, a healthcare organization will not be able to maintain current capacity because inflation has resulted in higher replacement costs.
- Other than donations or subsidies, profits are the only way to build up owners' equity (net assets). Increased owners' equity (net assets) will lead to a better bond or mortgage rating when it is necessary to finance expansion with long-term debt. This will decrease future interest charges and, hence, overall debt service costs.
- A for-profit organization must achieve profitability to pay dividends and to provide growth for stockholders.

The following three profitability ratios—profit margin, return on assets employed, and return on equity—are computed from the sample health system's financial statements.

The profit margin indicates how much of each revenue dollar is net income. To understand changes in this ratio over time, it is necessary to examine changes in revenues and expenses. Profit margin is computed as follows (see Exhibit 4.2):

$$\text{Profit Margin} = \text{Net Income} / \text{Total Revenue} = \$18,484 / \$294,934 = 6.27\%$$

The return on assets provides an indication of how much each dollar of assets earns on an after-tax income basis during a given period of time. A global measurement, return on assets encompasses all financial factors of an organization: revenues, expenses, and assets. It is the basic measure of an investment center. Obviously, not-for-profit organizations that own no for-profit affiliates need not deduct income taxes to arrive at net income. For either for-profit or not-for-profit healthcare organizations, if the "bottom line" is negative, assets and owners' equity are declining. (See Exhibits 4.1 and 4.2.)

$$\text{Return on Assets} = \text{Net Income} / \text{Average Total Assets} =$$
$$\$18,484 / ((\$417,144 + \$457,938) / 2) = 4.22\%$$

Overemphasis on this ratio may cause managers to postpone investments in new assets and other important, but discretionary, expenditures, such as maintenance or training. Return on assets may be broken into a profitability component (profit margin) and an asset management component (asset turnover) that will provide management with a better insight into the causes of changes in this ratio. Return on assets may be computed as follows (see Exhibits 4.1 and 4.2):

$$\text{Return on Assets} = \text{Profit Margin} \times \text{Asset Turnover}$$
$$\text{Return on Assets} = (\text{Net Income} / \text{Revenue}) \times (\text{Revenue} / \text{Average Total Assets}) =$$
$$(\$18,484 / \$294,934) \times ((\$294,934 / ((\$417,144 + \$457,938) / 2)) =$$
$$6.27\% \times .674 = 4.22\%$$

Given the components of profit margin and asset turnover that make up return on assets, there are four major ways to improve profitability: (1) Increase revenues by more than expenses; (2) decrease expenses by more than the decrease in revenue; (3) generate more dollars of revenue while maintaining or increasing the net margin; and (4) decrease assets employed.

Traditionally, investors have placed more emphasis on return on equity than on return on assets, as owners' equity represents the owners' interest in the organization. Return on equity is computed as follows (see Exhibits 4.1 and 4.2):

$$\text{Return on Equity} = \text{Net Income} / \text{Owners' Equity or Net Assets} =$$
$$\$18,484 / ((\$204,177 + \$238,477) / 2) = 8.35\%$$

In summary, profitability ratios attempt to measure an organization's ability to generate sufficient funds from operations to provide an acceptable return to owners. Although a not-for-profit organization does not have owners in the sense of for-profit organizations, it must maintain itself. It must replace assets as they wear out, replace old technology with new, and sustain some rate of growth.

Measures of Short-Term Liquidity Risks

External parties who are concerned with the financial health of an organization usually compute financial ratios based on the historical data in the financial statements to determine the organization's debt-paying ability. Long-term lenders may require that the healthcare organization maintain minimum ratios as an assurance that the organization can meet current interest and principal payments. Bankers and other short-term creditors also look to a number of financial ratios to make decisions about granting credit. There are several useful short-term liquidity risk ratios: the current ratio, the average days receivables outstanding, and the cash flow from operations compared with the average current liabilities.

The current ratio is computed by dividing current assets by current liabilities. Although this ratio may be "improved" on the date of the balance sheet by a number of ingenious window dressing techniques, empirical studies have found it to have strong predictive power in bond issue defaults and bankruptcy.[2] (See Exhibit 4.1.)

$$\text{Current Ratio} = \text{Current Assets} / \text{Current Liabilities} =$$
$$\$174,406 / \$62,236 = 2.80 \text{ to } 1.00$$

The system's current ratio appears to be very satisfactory as of the balance sheet date. It indicates that the system has $2.80 of current assets for each $1.00 of current liabilities. Comparisons should be made with past years and with standard ratios for the healthcare industry.

One of the current assets that is a step away from being converted to cash is the amount of patient receivables. On the balance sheet date this amount is divided by the average amount of patient revenue per day over the period. The result is the estimate of time to convert receivables into cash. (See Exhibits 4.1 and 4.2.)

$$\text{Days Receivable Outstanding} = \text{Patient Receivables} / \text{Patient Revenue} / 365 \text{ days} =$$
$$\$47,508 / (\$288,322 / 365) = 60 \text{ days}$$

The system's days in receivables averaged 60 days in 2003. Because several different entities are involved (e.g., hospitals, physician groups), this aggregate number may be difficult to interpret. It should be compared with the patient payment policies established by the system.

The ratio of operating cash flows to current liabilities in financially healthy organizations tends to be 0.4 or more in financially healthy organizations.[3] (See Exhibits 4.1 and 4.3.)

$$\text{Operating Cash Flows to Current Liabilities} =$$
$$\text{Operating Cash Flow / Average Current Liabilities} =$$
$$\$39,010 / ((\$48,438 + \$62,236) / 2) = .70$$

In summary, the system's current financial position appears to be very strong. A current ratio of 2.80 to 1.00, 60 days of patient receivables outstanding, and an operating cash flow to current liabilities of 0.7 all indicate financial strength.

Measures of Long-Term Liquidity Risks

As indicated earlier, financial ratios based on the financial statements are very important to both external creditors and investors of healthcare organizations or any other firm using the capital markets. Four ratios are of particular importance to long-term creditors and owners: the financial leverage ratio, the debt/equity ratio, the debt/plant ratio, and the debt service ratio.

The financial leverage ratio is a comparison of the total assets employed in relation to the total capital provided by owners' equity. The point of financial leverage is that the system is using long-term debt to finance $219 million of assets. Interest payments on this debt already have been deducted in arriving at the $18 million in net income, leaving the entire $18 million of net income as a return on owners' equity, which represents the nondebt portion of the capital. (See Exhibit 4.1.)

$$\text{Financial Leverage Ratio} = \text{Total Assets / Total Owners' Equity (Net Assets)} =$$
$$\$457,938 / \$238,477 = 1.92$$

A simple explanation of the difference between return on assets and return on equity is that the total asset amount is used to compute the return on assets, and the owners' equity amount is used to compute the return on owners' equity. The return on equity is higher than the return on assets (8.35% as compared to 4.22%) because this system is using financial leverage. It is using debt to finance $219 million of its assets. Return on equity may be reconciled with return on assets as follows:

$$\text{Return on Equity} = \text{Return on Assets} \times \text{Financial Leverage} =$$
$$4.22\% \times 1.92 \text{ times} = 8.10\%$$

(Note: The difference between 8.35% and 8.10% is because of rounding errors.)

The good news about using financial leverage is that the return on equity is magnified when debt-financed assets are earning more than the after-tax cost of interest expense. If debt-financed assets are earning less than their fixed interest charges, however, decreases in return on equity also are magnified. This is bad news for the owners' profitability and risk position.

The debt/equity and the debt/plant ratios are of particular interest to present and potential long-term lenders. In their debt covenants, lenders often insist that the ratio of long-term debt to owner's equity be maintained at less than 1 to 1; that is, debt must be less than equity. A higher ratio indicates that the long-term creditors have provided more money than the owners to finance the organization and that the cushion for owners to absorb losses before they affect lenders is less than 50%. Lenders also are focused on a financial safety cushion when they ask for a limit on the amount of long-term debt as a percentage of property, plant, and equipment (see Exhibit 4.1).

$$\text{Long-Term Debt / Owners' Equity Ratio =}$$
$$\text{Long-Term Debt / Owners' Equity (Net Assets) =}$$
$$\$141,104 / \$238,477 = 0.59 \text{ to } 1.00$$
$$\text{Long-Term Debt / Plant Ratio =}$$
$$\text{Long-Term Debt / Property, Plant, and Equipment = } \$141,104 / \$189,018 = 74.7\%$$

This system's debt/equity ratio is much less than 1 to 1, but its debt/plant ratio appears a bit high. If these ratios were close to the critical limit in the lending agencies, they could deter growth of both plant and debt. In the balance sheet, however, this system is carrying investments in an amount more than $50 million larger than the previous year and a limited use asset available to the board for future use of more than $43 million. If these funds are held for future plant or equipment acquisition, both amounts may be used in interpreting the plant ratio.

The debt service ratio is important for both short-term risk evaluation and long-term solvency. Current interest and principal installments require immediate cash payments when they fall due. The ratio divides cash flow available to pay interest and principal during the period by the required interest and principal payment amounts. (See Exhibit 4.3.)

$$\text{Debt Service Ratio = (Cash Flow from Operations + Interest Payments +}$$
$$\text{Payments on Long-Term Debt Principal) / (Interest Payments +}$$
$$\text{Payments on Long-Term Debt Principal) =}$$
$$(\$39,010 + \$10,112 + \$4,910) / (\$10,112 + \$4,910) = 3.60 \text{ to } 1.00$$

The debt service ratio appears very satisfactory for this system, as the cash flow available to service the long-term debt is 3.60 times the amount required.

Profitability of Segments of the Organized Delivery System

The ratios computed to this point have concerned the overall system from an external vantage point. Operating management must evaluate individual segments or responsibility centers, however. Because the segments identified in Exhibit 4.7 are investment centers (with one exception), both profit margin and return on assets may be used as evaluation measures.

For the business segments in Exhibit 4.7, the profit margins are computed as follows:

$$\text{General Hospital} = \$18{,}414 / \$148{,}803 = 12.37\%$$
$$\text{Children's Hospital} = \$4{,}436 / \$29{,}501 = 15.04\%$$
$$\text{Metro Hospital} = \$7{,}064 / \$40{,}359 = 17.50\%$$
$$\text{Health Services} = \$4{,}255 / \$34{,}773 = 12.24\%$$
$$\text{Physician Network} = \$(16{,}675) / \$49{,}878 = (33.43\%)$$
$$\text{Urgent Care Centers} = \$(1{,}034) / \$2{,}573 = (40.19\%)$$
$$\text{Other Medical Services} = \$(183) / \$867 = (21.11\%)$$

The wide range of profit margins for the individual segments explains the low overall profit margin of 6.27% for this system.

Return on assets employed for the profitable segments is as follows:

$$\text{Return on Assets} = \text{Profit Margin} \times \text{Asset Turnover}$$
$$\text{General Hospital} = (\$18{,}414 / \$148{,}803) \times (\$148{,}803 / \$306{,}305) =$$
$$12.37\% \times 0.49 \text{ times} = 6.06\%$$
$$\text{Children's Hospital} = (\$4{,}436 / \$29{,}501) \times (\$29{,}501 / \$41{,}142) =$$
$$15.04\% \times 0.72 \text{ times} = 10.83\%$$
$$\text{Metro Hospital} = (\$7{,}064 / \$40{,}359) \times (\$40{,}359 / \$34{,}330) = 17.50\% \times 1.18 \text{ times} = 20.65\%$$
$$\text{Health Services} = (\$4{,}255 / \$34{,}773) \times (\$34{,}773 / \$226{,}963) =$$
$$12.24\% \times 0.15 \text{ times} = 1.84\%$$

Acquisition of new assets will cause the return on assets to drop; however, tracking margin and asset turnover separately should show that the asset turnover falls, but the profit margin remains the same. Over time, the separation will provide the manager with a better explanation for increases or decreases in the return on assets.

In summary, a healthcare organization can evaluate how well it has carried out its financial management strategies by computing and evaluating a number of financial ratios. The principal purpose of a financial ratio is to facilitate comparisons of relationships over time in the same entity, or with other healthcare entities or norms. Although there are many possible ratios, they tend to fall into three critical areas of analysis: profitability, liquidity, and solvency. The next section incorporates both financial and nonfinancial data in performance analysis.

Employing Benchmarking and Balanced Scorecards in Financial Analysis

The term benchmarking is often used to refer to the continuous process of measuring products, services, and activities against the best levels of performance. To determine these best levels of performance, an organization may use internal benchmarking information or external benchmarking information gathered from similar organizations or from consulting firms that offer benchmarking services. Benchmarking involves both financial and nonfinancial data. Financial information, such as the ratios computed earlier, are more important at the level of the entity or major responsibility center. At lower levels in the organization, nonfinancial information becomes more useful.

The hospital industry has a number of firms that specialize in producing benchmark information for departments, services, products, and activities undertaken by hospitals. Using cost information submitted by hospitals to various US regulatory bodies, these consultants generate reports that compare a hospital with numerous other US hospitals. Hospital administrators use these reports to direct attention to areas with above-average costs. The reliability of individual hospital cost data used in these benchmark reports varies widely, because many hospitals have not refined their cost accounting systems. In addition, the cost allocation process that a hospital uses greatly affects benchmarking information. Nonfinancial factors that need to be analyzed include perceived quality of service to patients, success rate of procedures and operations, and satisfaction of employees and physicians. Benchmarking information is a valuable source for developing best practices within individual organizations. Healthcare organizations that have no counterparts with which to share information can develop internal benchmarks and identify practices that facilitate services in the most cost-effective manner.

Another tool available to hospital administrators for measuring the total business unit performance is a balanced scorecard—a set of performance measures and targets that reflect an organization's performance with respect to its various stakeholders (e.g., customers, employees, business partners, community members). The word "balanced" is used because for many years performance was measured primarily from a financial or cost containment perspective. During the late 1980s and early 1990s, however, the focus of many organizations shifted from only the financial perspective to include quality and customer concerns. The balanced scorecard concept is an attempt to balance the focus of an organization between financial and other relevant performance measures. Healthcare organizations typically have multiple objectives, so balanced scorecards that incorporate both financial and nonfinancial performance measurements are especially useful.

The balanced scorecard translates mission and strategy into objectives and performance measures from four perspectives:[4]

1. The financial perspective, as discussed, continues with emphasis on operating margin and return on assets employed.
2. In the customer perspective, organizations identify the customer and market segments in which they expect to compete and devise measures of performance for these targeted segments. The performance measures emphasize customer satisfaction, customer retention, new customer acquisition, and market share in the targeted segments.
3. The internal business perspective focuses on the processes within the organization that will have the greatest impact on delivering value to the customer.

4. The learning and growth perspective targets the development of people, information technology, and systems necessary for delivering value to the customers and other stakeholders in the organization.

Financial Statements in Review

This section discussed the preparation, content, and evaluation of conventional financial statements. The balance sheet presents the financial position of an entity at a given point of time. It presents the assets, liabilities, and owners' equity of the entity. The operating statement measures the revenues and expenses and resulting income in providing services to patients. The cash flow statement identifies changes in cash due to operating, investing, and financing activities. The statement of changes in owners' equity (not assets) shows transactions with owners (donors) as well as the cumulative results of operation. Cash and accrual bases of measurements for physician groups were demonstrated and discussed. Financial statements of an actual integrated healthcare organization were presented.

It is necessary for operating management to evaluate financial performance for the various responsibility centers in the organization. Responsibility centers may be classified as cost centers that are evaluated on how well costs were contained, as profit centers that are evaluated on the amount of profit earned, or as investment centers that are evaluated on the return on assets employed. The concept of a performance or flexible budget was used to evaluate performance when actual activity differs significantly from planned activity.

Analysis of financial statements was examined from the perspective of ratio analysis. Ratios analyzing profitability, liquidity, and solvency were computed and discussed. Ratios gain more meaning when they are compared with data from past periods and with data from similar organizations. Benchmarking and the use of a balanced scorecard were introduced as management tools that employ both financial and nonfinancial data.

In an organized healthcare delivery system, the board of directors and senior management determine the corporate strategy and set the goals and objectives to be followed by the organization and its various entities. In a decentralized organization, decisions consistent with the corporate strategies, goals, and objectives are made at the segment or responsibility center level.

Decisions fall into two general classifications. Long-range decisions involve the addition or replacement of capacity with long lives, whereas short-range decisions involve the use of existing capacity. The information needs and decision criteria for long-range and short-range decisions are very different.

Long-Range Decisions

One of the most common examples of a long-range decision for a healthcare organization is the acquisition of equipment or buildings. Because of this investment, the capacity of the organization changes, and the delivery of health care is more comprehensive. The healthcare organization is able to provide a greater range of services or, in some ways, has the capacity to do something that was not previously possible.

Most of the information needed to measure the benefits and costs attributable to long-range decisions cannot be generated from the accounting system for two reasons. First, the decision relates to the future and often involves the acquisition of unique assets. Unless the new activity resembles an activity in the past, information about the past obtained from the accounting system will not be relevant to the decision. Second, because of the long periods of time affected by the decision, the healthcare organization should be concerned with cash flows—not accounting measurements of income. It is important to know when cash is invested and consequently unavailable for other purposes and when cash will be recovered and therefore available for other purposes. Both the amount and timing of cash flows are important in measuring the benefits and costs of a long-range decision. The length of time involved in long-range decisions makes it essential to take the time value of money into account.

Concept of Time Value of Money

The time value of money is the difference in value between having a dollar in hand today and receiving a dollar at some future time. As a result of the long period of time involved in most long-range decisions, it may take several years to realize fully the benefits of most long-range decisions. **Table 4.2** illustrates the time value of money by showing the growth of $1,000 invested at the beginning of year 1 and earning interest at the rate of 10% compounded annually.

Two concepts are important in explaining the time value of money: future value and present value. Future value is the amount to which a given amount of cash invested now will grow at the end of a given period of time when compounded at a given rate of interest. In Table 4.2, for example, the future value of $1,000, compounded at 10%, is $1,100 at the end of 1 year, $1,210 at the end of 2 years, and $1,331 at the end of 3 years.

A second concept involving the time value of money is to value all cash flows in terms of the present time. Present value is the amount of money that must be invested now to accumulate to a given amount of money at some future date when compounded at some given rate of interest. In the example, $1,000 is the present value of $1,100 to be received at the end of 1 year, compounded at 10%.

Table 4.2 Compounding Interest to Determine Present Value

	Investment at Beginning of Period	Interest (10%)	Investment at End of Period
Year 1	$1,000	$100	$1,100
Year 2	$1,100	$110	$1,210
Year 3	$1,210	$121	$1,331

Future and present values allow the comparison of any two or more dollar amounts of cash paid or received at different points of time. The two amounts can be measured in terms of future value (i.e., what they are worth at some future time), or they can be measured in terms of present value (i.e., what they are worth today). Because an investment is being made today, however, it is much easier to understand and to work with present values than to deal in future values.

Present Value Tables

For the concept of present value to be useful, it is necessary to have a way of computing the present value of any amount of cash at any future point. The present value of $1.00 may be computed by dividing each present value by its future value. For example, the present value of $1.00 to be received at the end of Year 1 is $0.909 ($1,000 / $1,100). This present value factor may then be multiplied by any amount to be received 1 year from now. In **Table 4.3**, the present value of $1.00 compounded at 10% is computed for each of 3 years. These present value factors are used for single payments or receipts of cash.

Application of Present Values in Decision Making

If it is necessary to earn 10% on an investment, which of the following investments is acceptable?

  A. Invest $2,000 now and receive $2,400 at the end of 2 years.
  B. Invest $2,000 now and receive $1,200 at the end of Year 1, $800 at the end of Year 2, and $400 at the end of Year 3.
  C. Invest $2,000 now and receive $400 at the end of Year 1, $800 at the end of Year 2, and $1,200 at the end of Year 3.
  D. Invest $2,000 now and receive $800 at the end of each of the next 3 years.

All four investments involve $2,000 of cash outflows and $2,400 of cash inflows. Timing of the inflows, however, is different in each case (**Exhibit 4.10**).

To earn exactly a 10% return, the present value of cash inflows and cash outflows must be equal. For Investment A, the present value of cash inflows is only $1,982, whereas the present value of cash outflows is $2,000. Therefore, Investment A earns less than 10% and should be rejected. For Investment B, the present value of cash inflows is $2,052, whereas the present value of cash outflows is only $2,000. Therefore, Investment B earns more than 10% and should be accepted. Like Investment A, the cash inflows of Investments C and D are less than

Table 4.3   Development of Present Value Factors

Period of Time	Present Value/ Future Value	Present Value of $1	Present Value of an Annuity of $1
One year	$1,000/$1,100	.909	.909
Two years	$1,000/$1,210	.826	1.735 (.909 + .826)
Three years	$1,000/$1,331	.751	2.486 (1.735 + .751)

Exhibit 4.10   Present Value of Investments

INVESTMENT A		
Present value of cash outflows	$(2,000)	
Present value of cash inflows		
Year 1—$0 × .909 =	$ —	
Year 2—$2,400 × .826 =	$ 1,982	
Year 3—$0 × .751 =	$ —	$ 1,982
Net Present Value of Investment A		$ (18)
INVESTMENT B		
Present value of cash outflows	$(2,000)	
Present value of cash inflows		
Year 1—$1,200 × .909 =	$ 1,091	
Year 2—$800 × .826 =	$ 661	
Year 3—$400 × .751 =	$ 300	$ 2,052
Net Present Value of Investment B		$ 52
INVESTMENT C		
Present value of cash outflows	$(2,000)	
Present value of cash inflows		
Year 1—$400 × .909 =	$ 364	
Year 2—$800 × .826 =	$ 661	
Year 3—$1,200 × .751 =	$ 901	$ 1,926
Net Present Value of Investment C		$ (74)
INVESTMENT D		
Present value of cash outflows	$(2,000)	
Present value of cash inflows		
Year 1—$800 × .909 =	$ 727	
Year 2—$800 × .826 =	$ 661	
Year 3—$800 × .751 =	$ 601	$ 1,989
Net Present Value of Investment D		$ (11)

the cash outflows, and both should be rejected. In each case, the cash flow for each year was multiplied by the appropriate present value factor.

An easier calculation is possible for an annuity, when the stream of future cash flows is equal and occurs at equal intervals of time. The present value of an annuity may be computed in either of two ways. First, with the present value factors for $1.00, the cash flow for each year may be multiplied by its appropriate cash flow factor. Second, with the present value factor for an annuity of $1.00 (see right-hand column in Table 4.3), the present value factor for Year 3 may be multiplied by one periodic amount in the annuity ($800 × 2.486 = $1,989). The present value factors for an annuity are determined by cumulating the present value factors for single amounts.

The process of computing the present value of future cash flows is called discounting. Amounts to be received or paid in the future are discounted to their present values. This process is often called discounted cash flow analysis. All discounted cash flow techniques use the same basic approach in identifying cash flows and computing present values; they differ only in the way that the results are presented.

Long-Range Decision Rule

A long-range decision rule may now be formulated. A long-range decision is favorable if the incremental discounted cash inflows attributable to the investment proposal are equal to or greater than the incremental discounted cash outflows attributable to the investment.[5]

Techniques That Satisfy the Long-Range Decision Rule

Three techniques satisfy the long-range decision rule. They use the same data and tools of analysis, but they vary in the way that the decision criteria are stated. In the first technique, discounted cash outflows are deducted from discounted cash inflows; the difference is called net present value. If the net present value is zero, the project has earned exactly the predefined rate of return used as the discount rate and should be accepted. A positive net present value shows that the project earned more than the predetermined rate of return and should be accepted; a negative net present value shows that the project earned less than the predetermined rate of return and should be rejected. The net present values of the investments in Exhibit 4.10 are Investment A, ($18) ($1,982–$2,000); Investment B, ($52) ($2,052–$2,000); Investment C, ($74) ($1,926–$2,000); and Investment D, ($11) ($1,989–$2,000). Only Investment B has a positive net present value and should be accepted.

When the second method, the profitability index or discounted benefit cost ratio, is used, the discounted cash inflows are divided by the discounted cash outflows to show the dollars of discounted benefits for each dollar of discounted cost. The profitability indexes for each of the investments in Exhibit 4.10 are Investment A, $0.991 ($1,982 / $2,000); Investment B, $1.026 ($2,052 / $2,000); Investment C, $0.963 ($1,926 / $2,000); and Investment D, $0.994 ($1,989 / $2,000). Only Investment B will return more than $1 of discounted benefits for each $1.00 of discounted costs.

The third method, the internal rate of return method, involves computing the actual rate of return by the investment instead of using a predefined rate of return. A minimum acceptable rate of return, the cutoff rate, must be set. Any investment project earning less than the cutoff rate should be rejected; any investment project earning at or above the cutoff rate should be accepted. The internal rate of return may be computed in one of two ways, depending on the nature of the cash flows. For example, what is the internal rate of return for a piece of equipment with an initial cost of $31,270 and annual cash inflows of $10,000 for 5 years? This approach involves two steps. First, determine the present value factor that equates the initial cash inflow and the stream of cash outflows ($31,270 = $10,000 × 3.127). Second, find the present value factor computed in the first step in Appendix 4.A, the present value of an annuity of $1.00 in the 5-year row. The present value factor of 3.127 is found in the 18% column and the 5-year row, indicating an internal rate of return of 18%. If the computed present value factor falls between two values in the table, it will be necessary to estimate the actual rate of return by interpolating between the two columns in the table. If the future cash inflows are not in a single amount (as in Investment A) or in an annuity (as in Investment D), a trial-and-error method must be used. When the net present value is zero, the internal rate of return is exactly equal to the predefined discount rate. To determine the internal rate of return, it is necessary to compute this at different rates until a net present value of zero is achieved. This can be a very tedious process. An easier approach is to use the internal rate of return function on a computer spreadsheet. **Exhibit 4.11** uses Microsoft Excel to illustrate the three methods on the basis of an investment of $31,270 and annual cash inflows of $10,000 for 5 years.

Information Relevant to Long-Range Decisions

Data needed to apply the long-range decision rule are the amount and timing of cash outflows, the amount and timing of cash inflows, and a discount rate to measure the time value of money.

Relevant cash outflows are incremental cash outflows over the life of the project that are directly traceable to the investment, regardless of what they are called. Cash outflows generally involve a large initial cash outflow for the acquisition of the asset and include maintenance, income taxes, and other cash outflows traceable to the project. Additional working capital to support the increased activity must be included as cash outflows as they occur and treated as cash inflows as they are recovered. When an investment decision involves any noncash resources, such as present equipment, presently owned by the organization, the relevant "cost" is the cash value of the asset, not the book value or the balance of undepreciated cost carried in the accounting records.

Relevant cash inflows are the incremental cash inflows over the life of the investment, regardless of what the particular cash inflow is called. All cash inflows, including cash from service to patients, annual cost savings from new equipment, and estimated salvage value from the disposal of the asset at the end of its estimated useful life are treated as cash inflows.

In not-for-profit healthcare organizations or in physician practices whose goal is to pay no income taxes, taxes are not relevant to any decision. For-profit organizations must be concerned with income taxes, however. Any income taxes paid as a result of a long-range decision must be considered a cash outflow. The amount of taxes to be paid in a given year will be affected by depreciation of the assets acquired, as well as cash inflows and cash outflows from the operation of the asset.

Exhibit 4.11   Discounted Cash Flow Analysis Using a Spreadsheet

	A	B	C	D
1				
2				
3				
4	Period	Cash Flows		NET PRESENT VALUE
5				Net present value of future cash flows less investment
6	0 (now)	$(31,270)		=NPV(Discount rate, Range of future cash flows) / Investment
7	1	$10,000		=NPV(.10,B7:B11)+B6
8	2	$10,000		=37,908 - 31,270 = $6,638
9	3	$10,000		
10	4	$10,000		PROFITABILITY INDEX
11	5	$10,000		Net present value of future cash flows divided by investment
12				=NPV(Discount rate, Range of future cash flows) / Investment
13				=NPV(.10,B7:B11) / B6
14				=37,908 / 31,270 = $1.21 per dollar of discounted investment
15				
16				INTERNAL RATE OF RETURN
17				Rate of return that produces a zero net present value
18				=IRR(Range of all cash flows, Guess rate)
19				=IRR(B6:B11,.10)=18%
20				
21	Note: The NPV function computes the net present value of future cash flows. It assumes			
22	the first flow is at the end of Period 1. Therefore, it is necessary to deduct the investment			
23	from the present value of the future cash flows.			
24	The IRR function assumes that the first cash flow is at the beginning of the first period (or			
25	the end of period zero). It is necessary to provide a guess rate as a starting point in			
26	computing net present value. The function performs several iterations to reach net present			
27	value of zero. The actual rate return is reached when the net present value is zero.			
28				

The tax code is very complex. The amount of depreciation allowed for recovery of an expenditure for long-lived assets depends on three factors:

1. Depreciation method—The tax code provides a specified schedule based on the declining balance method or allows the straight-line method.
2. Recovery period—The tax code identifies a number of property classes with a specified cost recovery schedule.

3. First-year convention—The tax code allows a choice between treating the asset as having been placed in service mid-year (half-year convention) or as having been placed in service in the middle of the quarter in which the asset was acquired.

Table 4.4 presents the depreciation percentages allowed for a piece of equipment with an asset class of 5 years that was purchased the first day of the year. The 5-year property class applies to assets with a life of more than 4 years, but less than 10 years, including automobiles, trucks, property used in research or experimentation, computers and peripheral equipment, and office equipment. Actually, the 5-year class extends over 6 years. If the asset is held less than 6 years, the schedule will be followed to the point of disposal with the balance of the undepreciated cost (less salvage) expensed in the year of disposal. An organization may expense up to $18,500 of the cost of tangible property in the year an asset is acquired if the total qualifying asset purchases in the year are less than $200,000.

Exhibit 4.12 shows the tax impact on the acquisition of a piece of equipment costing $50,000, with a 5-year life and no salvage value. The new equipment will reduce annual operating expenses by $8,000 and will generate additional patient billings of $16,000 per year. The before-tax cash flows for this asset are the investment of $50,000 now and cash inflows of $24,000 each year. The after-tax cash flows change by the tax reduction (cash inflow) in Year 1 of $1,934 as well as the tax payments in years 2 through 5. The example (i.e., Exhibit 4.12) expenses $18,500 of the equipment in the first year and uses the 5-year cost recovery schedule. The use of the cost recovery schedule results in a postponement of the taxes when compared with using the straight-line method. Any postponement of cash outflows or advancement of cash inflows increases the present value of the project and makes it more favorable. Clearly, the determination of the tax effect of an investment project is very complex, and tax provisions must be considered.

The discount rate is the rate of return desired by the particular healthcare organization. It is composed of three elements: a risk-free rate of return, expected inflation, and the degree of risk. The appropriate discount rate in determining the present value of an investment is the weighted average cost of capital, that is, the weighted average of the expected returns to be provided on

Table 4.4 Asset Recovery Allowances for Taxes: 5-Year Asset Class

Year	Half-Year Convention	Quarterly Convention (1st qtr.)	Straight-Line
1	20.00%	35.00%	20.00%
2	32.00%	26.00%	20.00%
3	19.20%	15.60%	20.00%
4	11.52%	11.01%	20.00%
5	11.52%	11.01%	20.00%
6	5.76%	1.38%	

Source: Reprinted from Internal Revenue Service.

Exhibit 4.12   Impact of Taxes on Long-Range Decision

			Years			
	0 (Now)	1	2	3	4	5
Before-tax cash flows:						
Cash outflows						
1. Purchase of equipment	$(50,000)					
Cash inflows:						
1. Annual cost savings		$8,000	$8,000	$8,000	$8,000	$8,000
2. Additional patient billings		16,000	16,000	16,000	16,000	16,000
Total annual cash flows	$(50,000)	$24,000	$24,000	$24,000	$24,000	$24,000
Present value factor 10%	1.000	0.909	0.825	0.751	0.683	0.621
Present value of cash flows	$(50,000)	$21,816	$19,800	$18,024	$16,392	$14,904
Net present value	$40,936					
After-tax cash flows:						
Cash outflows:						
1. Purchase of equipment	$(50,000)					
2. Payment of taxes		$1,934	$(5,534)	$(6,680)	$(7,186)	$(7,034)
Cash inflows:						
1. Annual cost savings		8,000	8,000	8,000	8,000	8,000
2. Additional patient billings		16,000	16,000	16,000	16,000	16,000
Total annual cash flows	$(50,000)	$25,934	$18,466	$17,320	$16,814	$16,966
Present value factor 10%	1.000	0.909	0.825	0.751	0.683	0.621
Present value of cash flows	$(50,000)	$23,574	$15,234	$13,007	$11,484	$10,536
Net present value	$23,836					
Computation of income taxes:						
Annual cost saving		$8,000	$8,000	$8,000	$8,000	$8,000
Additional patient billings		16,000	16,000	16,000	16,000	16,000
Total		$24,000	$24,000	$24,000	$24,000	$24,000
Depreciation:						
First-year expensing	18,500					
Year 1—$31,500 × 35.00%	11,025					
Year 2—$31,500 × 26.00%			8,190			
Year 3—$31,500 × 15.60%				4,914		
Year 4—$31,500 × 11.01%					3,468	
Year 5—Balance of cost						3,903
Taxable income (loss)		$(5,525)	$15,810	$19,086	$20,532	$20,097
Income tax, payment (refund)						
35% rate		$(1,934)	$5,534	$6,680	$7,186	$7,034

equity capital and long-term debt capital. The weights are determined by the percentages of debt capital and equity capital. The weighted average cost of capital is computed as follows:

$$
\begin{aligned}
&\text{Weighted Average Cost of Capital} = \\
&\text{After-Tax Cost of Debt Capital} \times \\
&(\text{Proportion of Debt Capital / Total Capital}) + \\
&\text{Cost of Equity Capital} \times (\text{Proportion of Equity Capital / Total Capital})
\end{aligned}
$$

When prices are increasing at a 2% or lower annual rate, it is safe to ignore the impact of inflation on most long-range decisions. It is necessary to consider the impact of a high rate of inflation in projecting cash flows over the life of a project, however, and to adjust these estimates for the impact of anticipated price changes. There are several cash flows involved (e.g., salaries, supplies, maintenance, fees charged to patients), and the appropriate rate of price changes should be applied to each cash flow. The discount rate, if properly determined, already has taken inflation into account, because investors' required rate of return includes their expectation of inflation.

Techniques That Do Not Satisfy the Long-Range Decision Rule

Two investment techniques that do not involve the time value of money and therefore do not satisfy the long-range decision rule are in widespread use. These methods are the payback period and the accounting rate of return. They are simple, easy to use, and easily understood. However, because they do not consider the time value of money, they do not always identify the best choice.

Of the techniques of investment analysis examined in this chapter, the payback period method is the simplest; it has been widely used in ambulatory healthcare organizations. With this method, the question is simple: How soon will the initial investment be recovered? The payback period method calculates the amount of time in which the projected cash inflows will recover the initial investment. All cash inflows after the recovery of the initial investment are ignored. Calculation of the payback period in **Table 4.5** for the four investment projects examined earlier (see Exhibit 4.10) shows a range from $1\frac{5}{6}$ years to $2\frac{2}{3}$ years. If this organization requires a cutoff time period of less than 2 years, only Investment A is acceptable. Investment B

Table 4.5 Illustration of Payback Period

Investment	Investment Amount	Period 1	2	3	Payback Period
A	$2,000	—	2,400	—	$1\frac{5}{6}$ years
B	$2,000	1,200	800	400	2 years
C	$2,000	400	800	1,200	$2\frac{2}{3}$ years
D	$2,000	800	800	800	$2\frac{1}{2}$ years

would probably be accepted, but Investments C and D would be rejected. In this illustration, Investment A was found unacceptable by the net present value method, but evaluated as the best project under the payback period method.

The major deficiency in the payback period method is that it does not take into account the profitability or the life of the investment beyond the payback period. For example, the following two investments have the same payback period, but substantially different net present values:

	Investment S	Investment T
Initial investment	$100,000	$50,000
Annual cash inflow	$ 50,000	$25,000
Estimated useful life	2 years	5 years
Payback period	2 years	2 years
Net present value at 10%	$(13,223)	$44,770

When there is a high degree of risk associated with the investment, or when the rate of obsolescence is high, the payback method provides an excellent supplement to the discounted cash flow methods. When two or more projects meet the rate of return criterion, the better investment is the one with the shortest payback period.

In the accounting rate of return method, accounting income rather than cash flows is used to compute a rate of return for a particular investment. It is computed as follows:

Accounting Rate of Return = Average Annual Accounting Income / Initial Investment

Because average income is used, all investments with equal lives, equal total income, and equal initial investments are evaluated the same, regardless of when the cash is recovered. The accounting rate of return is computed in **Table 4.6** for the four investments examined earlier. As in the payback method, the accounting rate of return method shows the highest value for Investment A because of its shorter life. Investments B, C, and D have identical accounting rates of return because average cash revenues and average costs for the 3-year period are the same. Their net present values are different, however.

Table 4.6   Illustration of Accounting Rate of Return

Investment	Average Inflows	Straight-Line Depreciation	Annual Income	Initial Investment	Accounting Rate of Return
A	$1,200	$1,000	$200	$2,000	10.0%
B	$800	$667	$133	$2,000	6.7%
C	$800	$667	$133	$2,000	6.7%
D	$800	$667	$133	$2,000	6.7%

The accounting rate of return uses accounting measurements and, therefore, is consistent with the accounting records. Most healthcare organizations that use this method do so because it is easily understood, but it is not a good long-range decision-making technique.

Long-Range Decision Illustration

The following example comes from an actual organized healthcare delivery system. The names, location, and some key amounts are disguised to maintain the anonymity of the organizations involved.

As a part of its newly developed strategic plan, the sample health system proposes to acquire ownership of the resources that it uses to provide services to its patients. For some time, the system has had a joint venture and partnership with Radiology Unlimited, a radiology group adjacent to the system's hospitals. Radiology Unlimited operates three businesses in a building that it owns. These businesses share common areas and personnel, and the radiology group provides professional radiology services for each business.

A joint venture of Radiology Unlimited and the health system, called MRI, provides magnetic resonance imaging and stereotactic breast biopsy service; the health system owns one third and Radiology Unlimited owns two thirds of MRI. The system and Radiology Unlimited are partners in the third business, called CT, which provides computed tomography scanning services; the system owns two thirds, and Radiology Unlimited owns one third of CT.

The health system has offered to purchase the technical component of Radiology Unlimited's practice and Radiology Unlimited's equity in MRI and CT. The radiologists are to form a hospital-based radiology group, performing its own billing. Long-term agreements with the system will ensure continuing patient referrals to the group, and a management contract will be obtained to control the hospital-owned imaging center. The system has agreed to pay the fair market value of the three businesses. The fair market value will be determined as the replacement cost of the assets for the technical component of Radiology Unlimited, and the present value of future cash flows for Radiology Unlimited's equity in MRI and CT.

The system contracted with the healthcare consultant from a major accounting firm to perform the present value analysis for MRI and CT. They also contracted with a certified appraiser to determine the replacement cost of the technical component of Radiology Unlimited. Both the system and Radiology Unlimited agreed to provide all information requested by the consultants.

Cash flows were projected from 1998 through 2002, at which time operations were expected to reach a level of normal long-term growth. **Tables 4.7** and **4.8** show the determination of the present value of MRI and CT, respectively. The projections in these tables use a time horizon of 20 years. The certified appraiser set the appraisal of the technical assets at approximately $1 million, an amount agreed to by both sides. The offering price by the system was set as follows:

Replacement cost of assets of Radiology Unlimited	$1,000,000
Present value of MRI (2/3 of $3,375,318)	2,250,212
Present value of CT (1/3 of $6,194,158)	2,064,719
Total purchase price	$5,314,931

Table 4.7 Determination of Present Value of MRI

	Cash Inflows		Cash Outflows			
Year	Operating Revenues	Operating Expenses*	Estimated Taxes	Working Capital Additions	Capital Expend.	Net Cash Flows
1998	$1,381,700	$600,865	$271,367	$1,255	$5,000	$503,213
1999	1,425,720	617,640	280,903	7,483	5,000	514,694
2000	1,464,540	633,967	288,776	6,599	5,000	530,198
2001	1,503,040	650,237	296,556	6,545	5,000	544,702
2002	1,531,720	666,050	301,060	4,876	5,000	554,734
2003	1,531,720	666,050	301,060	4,876	5,000	554,734
2004	1,531,720	666,050	301,060	4,876	5,000	554,734
2005	1,531,720	666,050	301,060	4,876	5,000	554,734
2006	1,531,720	666,050	301,060	4,876	5,000	554,734
2007	1,531,720	666,050	301,060	4,876	5,000	554,734
2008	1,531,720	666,050	301,060	4,876	5,000	554,734
2009	1,531,720	666,050	301,060	4,876	5,000	554,734
2010	1,531,720	666,050	301,060	4,876	5,000	554,734
2011	1,531,720	666,050	301,060	4,876	5,000	554,734
2012	1,531,720	666,050	301,060	4,876	5,000	554,734
2013	1,531,720	666,050	301,060	4,876	5,000	554,734
2014	1,531,720	666,050	301,060	4,876	5,000	554,734
2015	1,531,720	666,050	301,060	4,876	5,000	554,734
2016	1,531,720	666,050	301,060	4,876	5,000	554,734
2017	1,531,720	666,050	301,060	4,876	5,000	554,734

*Excluding depreciation.
Present value of net cash flows = NPV(.15, range of net cash flows) = $3,375,318
Present value of net cash flows = NPV(.12, range of net cash flows) = $4,041,794
Source: Anonymous.

The radiologists analyzed the assumptions of the valuation performed by the accounting firm and took exception to the 15% discount rate. The exceptions involved the consultant's assumptions about the capital structure and risk adjustments. The consultant had used an average of the capital structures of comparable healthcare organizations to develop a 1 to 3 debt-to-equity ratio for weights in computing the cost of capital, but the radiologists argued that the capital structure should reflect the industry average or cost of capital for the buyer. As to risk adjustment, the radiologists argued that the projections of future cash flows already reflect probable reimbursement under managed care. In doing the buildup method of determining a discount rate, the consultant included an additional factor for reimbursement risks. Thus, the radiologists argued that this risk was included twice in the valuation. Under these circumstances, they suggested a discount rate of 10 to 12%. The entities to be acquired are well-established ventures with little competition and, therefore, low risk. In an

Table 4.8 Determination of Present Value of CT

	Cash Inflows		Cash Outflows			
Year	Operating Revenues	Operating Expenses*	Estimated Taxes	Working Capital Additions	Capital Expend.	Net Cash Flows
1998	$2,441,400	$933,936	$398,112	$(9,655)	$5,000	$1,114,007
1999	2,447,170	946,780	411,387	961	5,000	1,083,042
2000	2,452,200	959,523	424,437	855	5,000	1,062,385
2001	2,452,550	973,842	435,298	60	5,000	1,038,350
2002	2,452,440	988,160	442,498	(19)	107,000	914,801
2003	2,452,440	988,160	442,498	(19)	107,000	914,801
2004	2,452,440	988,160	442,498	(19)	107,000	914,801
2005	2,452,440	988,160	442,498	(19)	107,000	914,801
2006	2,452,440	988,160	442,498	(19)	107,000	914,801
2007	2,452,440	988,160	442,498	(19)	107,000	914,801
2008	2,452,440	988,160	442,498	(19)	107,000	914,801
2009	2,452,440	988,160	442,498	(19)	107,000	914,801
2010	2,452,440	988,160	442,498	(19)	107,000	914,801
2011	2,452,440	988,160	442,498	(19)	107,000	914,801
2012	2,452,440	988,160	442,498	(19)	107,000	914,801
2013	2,452,440	988,160	442,498	(19)	107,000	914,801
2014	2,452,440	988,160	442,498	(19)	107,000	914,801
2015	2,452,440	988,160	442,498	(19)	107,000	914,801
2016	2,452,440	988,160	442,498	(19)	107,000	914,801
2017	2,452,440	988,160	442,498	(19)	107,000	914,801

*Excluding depreciation.
Present value of net cash flows = NPV(.15, range of net cash flows) = $6,194,158
Present value of net cash flows = NPV(.12, range of net cash flows) = $7,328,603
Source: Anonymous.

economic environment of low inflation (2%) and low business risk, the radiologists argued that a lower discount rate was appropriate.

The use of a 12% discount rate would have produced a purchase price of $6,137,397, a figure $819,466 above the consultant's price of $5,314,931 using a 15% discount rate. Clearly, it is very important to select a proper discount rate. There are two general ways of determining the appropriate discount rate for measuring the present value of future cash flows. The first approach, used by the consultant for the health system, involves the weighted average cost of capital. The second approach involves the opportunity cost of the funds to be invested. As a general rule, the minimum rate of return on a particular investment should not be less than the cost of acquiring and maintaining the entity's capital resources.

The consultant for the system and Radiology Unlimited felt that the appropriate discount rate in valuing an investment is the weighted average cost of capital. This rate is the weighted average of the expected returns on equity capital and long-term debt capital. The weights are determined by the projected long-term debt/equity position. The weighted average cost of capital has three components:

1. Capital structure (the proportion of debt and equity)—The consultant used a capital structure of 33% debt and 67% equity, basing this decision on an average capital structure of seven large diversified healthcare companies.
2. Cost of debt capital—The average rate on borrowed funds was set at 7.3%, based on "yield in percent per annum" for corporate Baa bonds, published by the Federal Reserve Statistical Release on December 31, 1997. This yields an after-tax cost of debt of 4.7% calculated as follows:

$$7.3\% \times (1-35.0\%) = 4.7\% \text{ (assuming a tax rate of 35\%)}$$

3. Cost of equity capital—The consultant estimated the cost of equity capital by using the capital asset pricing model (CAPM), which is measured as follows:

$$\text{Equity Rate of Return} = Rf + (ERP \times B) + SSRP + CR$$

where Rf = risk-free rate (i.e., the 20-year Treasury bond yield at 6.02%).

ERP = equity risk premium (i.e., the large company stock total returns minus long-term government bond income returns as reported in Ibbotson Associates 1997 yearbook). ERP equaled 7.5% in the 1997 yearbook.

B = beta (i.e., a coefficient that relates a specific company's risk to the average risk of a group of stocks, such as the Standard & Poor's 500). The overall market is equal to a beta of 1. The consultant computed the beta for MRI and CT at 1.05, approximately equal to the average in the market.

SSRP = small stock risk premium. Investors in small capitalization stocks have historically earned a premium over large capitalization stocks. A small size premium was added to the cost of equity to reflect the investment characteristics of the imaging businesses relative to selected comparable companies. The premium of 5.78% was drawn from Ibbotson Associates 1996 yearbook.

CR = company-specific risk premium. A specific risk premium of 0.5% was developed from the consultant's evaluation of management depth, market position, access to capital markets, public versus private ownership, and management projections.

Equity Rate of Return for MRI and CT = 6.02% + (7.5% × 1.05) + 5.78% + 0.5% = 20.02%

Exhibit 4.13 presents the calculation of the weighted average cost of capital for the investment project. Clearly, for long-range decisions, this example demonstrates the importance of accuracy in estimating cash flows, the timing of these cash flows, and the key role of the discount rate employed. Lack of reasonably correct information for any of these variables may produce a poor long-range decision.

Exhibit 4.13 Computation of Weighted Average Cost of Capital

	Cost of Capital		Capital Structure	Total
Cost of Debt	4.70%	×	33%	1.55%
Cost of Equity	20.20%	×	67%	13.53%
Total Weighted Average Cost of Capital				15.08%
Concluded Weighted Average Cost of Capital			15.00%	

Source: Anonymous.

Long-Range Decisions in Review

The long-range decision-making process is not well developed in many healthcare organizations. This chapter advances a long-range decision criterion that incorporates theoretically superior decision criteria. This methodology is appropriate for all levels in the healthcare organization. It states that an investment is economically sound if the discounted incremental cash inflows equal or exceed the discounted incremental cash outflows attributable to the investment. The information needed to apply the long-range decision criterion is the incremental cash inflows and outflows projected for each investment alternative and a discount rate that reflects the cost of capital of the healthcare organization. All cash flows directly traced to the investment proposal are relevant.

Three techniques satisfy the long-range decision criterion: the net present value method, the profitability index, and the internal rate of return. They differ only in the way the decision criterion is applied.

Determination of the proper discount rate is critical for the use of discounted cash flow techniques. The illustration in this chapter shows the effect of using a high discount rate. As the discount rate is increased, the present value of future cash flows is decreased. The appropriate discount rate in valuing an investment is the weighted average cost of capital.

Two techniques that do not satisfy the long-range decision criterion are in widespread use. They are the payback method and the accounting rate of return. Both are simple, easily understood, and easily computed. The payback method is an excellent supplement to the net present value method if the project involves a significant degree of risk, or if there is a high rate of obsolescence.

Short-Range Decisions

Short-range decisions involve the use of existing capacity in accomplishing the goals, strategic plans, and objectives of the healthcare organizations. These decisions involve volume and mix of services to be offered and the prices to be charged. Although a clear understanding of costs is critical, recently healthcare organizations have achieved dramatic returns by increasing their emphasis on the management of the revenue cycle.

Fixed and Variable Costs

Costs change for a variety of reasons: people simply spend more, inflation occurs, or quality or volumes of service vary. Changes in quality must be dealt with on a case-by-case basis. Changes in cost due to changes in inflation and volume are easiest to accommodate. The behavior of costs as volume changes involves the determination of fixed and variable costs. The most basic information for planning, decision making, and evaluation of performance in the short run is an understanding of the underlying behavior of costs as activity changes for an organization, a department, or a service.

Economists model cost behavior as shown in **Figure 4.2**. In this model, fixed costs are the intercept, and variable costs are the change in slope. Economists' cost curves are idealizations. The organization gains increasing returns to scale at low levels of activity, then goes through a range of stable operations, and finally incurs decreasing returns to scale as capacity is approached. In actuality, cost curves are likely to be jagged rather than smooth. Many costs come in "lumps." For example, to go from serving 2000 patients to 2001 patients may mean that another healthcare provider will go on the payroll.

Accountants use an approximation of the real cost curve. Because most operations are in the stable portion of the economist's cost curve, accountants assume that cost is a linear function of volume (**Figure 4.3**). The cost function that accountants use is $C = a + b(q)$, where C is total cost, a represents total fixed cost, b represents the variable cost per unit of service, and q represents units of service. In using this cost function, accountants make several assumptions. Fixed costs are assumed to remain fixed within a relevant range, reflecting the past experience of the organization. Both variable costs per unit of service and the service mix are assumed to remain constant within the relevant range. To the extent that a variable cost (e.g., supplies) decreases with volume discounts, or other fixed or variable costs change due to forces other than volume, these cost behavior assumptions may not reflect actual operations. Accountants assume that the linear function represents cost accurately enough to permit appropriate short-term decisions, however.

Very seldom is the accounting system designed to provide fixed and variable costs. Therefore, total cost must be separated into its fixed and variable portions to use the linear cost function. Accountants have developed two practical means for determining cost behavior patterns: inspection of accounts and study of past cost behavior patterns. The methods differ with the sources of data used.

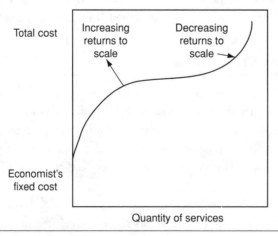

FIGURE 4.2   An Economist's Cost Curve

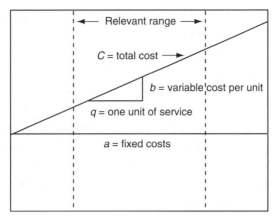

FIGURE 4.3 An Accountant's Cost Curve

Inspection of Accounts

The most intuitive method of determining whether a cost is fixed or variable is to examine the nature of each cost in the chart of accounts. Many costs are fixed or variable by their very nature. Because inspection is both intuitive and arbitrary, it is subject to some degree of error. For those situations in which analysis is not very sensitive to error in classification of fixed and variable costs, however, this method may provide a quick and inexpensive measure of cost behavior.

Even if data for only one period are available, a cost function can be developed by using the inspection of accounts method. For example, an analysis of the accounts for the Community Health Center in **Exhibit 4.14** would probably identify salaries and administrative costs as fixed, and drugs and contributed services costs as variable. With 10,000 patient visits, the aver-

Exhibit 4.14   Community Health Center Operating Statement for 1997

		Fixed Expenses	Variable Expenses
Patient visits	10,000		
Revenue:			
Patient fees	$750,000		
Donations and grants	950,000		
Total revenue	1,700,000		
Expenses:			
Salaries	900,000	$ 900,000	
Drugs	400,000		$400,000
Administration	350,000	350,000	
Contributed services	150,000		150,000
Total expenses	1,800,000	$1,250,000	$550,000
Excess of expenses over revenue	$(100,000)		

age variable cost per patient visit is $55 ($550,000 / 10,000). The cost function is $C = $1,250,000 + $55q$. This cost function can be used to estimate costs at any level of activity. If the number of patient visits is expected to be 10,500 in 2003, the total cost is estimated to be $1,250,000 + ($55 × 10,500) = $1,827,500.

Study of Past Data

Analysis of past experience assumes that past data are accurate and that future cost behavior patterns will be like past cost behavior patterns. Several methods can be used to determine cost behavior patterns. Among them are the scattergraph approach, in which data points are plotted on a graph across time; regression analysis, which fits a line to several observations statistically; and the high–low point method, which fits a line to two data points.

To illustrate the separation of past cost data into fixed and variable costs, **Table 4.9** presents cost and volume relationships for supplies and patient visits within a clinic setting. When these data points are plotted across time, as in **Figure 4.4**, there appears to be a linear relationship between the cost of supplies and the number of patient visits. A line may be fit to the scattergraph by visual inspection so that approximately half the data points lie above the line and approximately half lie below the line. The point where the line crosses the vertical axis is the estimate of fixed costs, and the slope of the line is the estimate of variable cost per patient visit. A scattergraph should be used to determine whether a linear relationship exists or whether unusual observations exist. If a linear relationship exists, regression analysis is an appropriate tool for determining cost behavior. Abnormal observations identified by examining the scattergraph may be dropped from the data to allow a better fit when regression analysis is used.

Table 4.9   Cost and Volume Data for Cost-Behavior Analysis

Month	Cost of Supplies	Patient Visits
January	$1,120	500
February	$1,310	660
March	$1,380	1,040
April	$1,100	850
May	$1,610	1,240
June	$1,700	940
July	$1,770	1,560
August	$1,500	1,440
September	$1,970	1,710
October	$2,100	1,950
November	$1,660	1,840
December	$1,500	1,650
January	$1,400	1,340
February	$1,760	1,380
March	$1,420	1,170

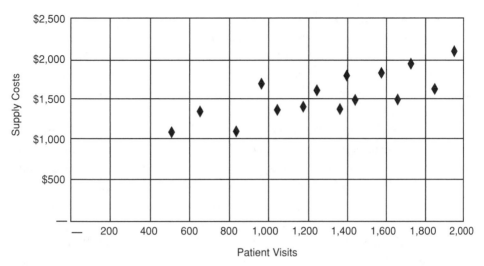

FIGURE 4.4   Plot of Supply Cost Against Number of Patient Visits

The most accurate method for determining fixed and variable costs is regression analysis. Least squares regression selects the single straight line that minimizes the sum of the squared deviations from the line. Regression analysis may be performed with any current spreadsheet package, such as Excel or Lotus. Although it may be performed with a small number of observations, statisticians caution that if the number of observations drops below 15, regression analysis is not an appropriate tool to use.

Exhibit 4.15 presents the regression summary output from the data for supplies and patient visits (see Table 4.9). The key regression output data are shaded. The intercept coefficient in

Exhibit 4.15   Regression Analysis for Supplies in Relation to Patient Visits

SUMMARY OUTPUT
Regression Statistics

Multiple R	0.78591283
R-Square	0.61765897
Adjusted R-Square	0.58824812
Standard Error	182.119724
Observations	15

ANOVA

	df	SS	MS	F	Significance F
Regression	1	696554.611	696554.611	21.0010594	0.00051362
Residual	13	431178.722	33167.594		
Total	14	1127733.33			

	Coefficients	Standard Error	t Statistic	P-value
Intercept	884.026826	153.434217	5.76160159	6.5815E-05
X Variable 1	0.52099624	0.11368783	4.58269128	0.00051362

this regression is $884, reflecting the fixed portion of total supplies cost. The X variable 1 coefficient is $0.52, reflecting the slope of the regression line and representing the variable supplies cost per patient visit. Therefore, the cost function for supplies is $C = \$884 + \$0.52q$. This cost function may be used to estimate total supplies costs at any level of activity within the relevant range. For example, the estimate of total supplies costs at 1500 patient visits is $C = \$884 + (0.52 \times 1500) = \$1,664$.

The regression analysis output gives an adjusted R-square statistic that indicates the percentage of the change in supplies that is explained by changes in the number of patient visits. In this example, the figure is 58%. An R-square of less than 50% indicates one of two things: either the cost is primarily fixed and changes in a stepwise fashion, or the choice of the volume measure is not strongly related to cost. Plotting the data helps to identify scatter patterns for which regression results will produce misleading cost functions. Ideally, the plots fall in a perfectly straight line, and the R-square is 1.00, indicating that changes in the number of patient visits explain 100% of the variation in supplies costs. This does not happen in practice, however. An examination of the plot for supplies costs and the R-square of 0.58 shows a great deal of variation in the cost behavior pattern, and any cost estimates may be subject to considerable error.

Some potential problems arise when managers attempt to use regression analysis to develop a cost function. If the accounting system records the costs of supplies as expenses when purchased rather than when used, for example, regression analysis will not provide an accurate representation of the relationship between costs and changes in volumes. A regression analysis of supplies costs in an intensive care unit at one of the sample health system's hospitals resulted in an R-square of only 5%. During the year, the hospital was expensing intensive care supplies when purchased. Therefore, the resulting monthly supplies cost was not useful in planning or evaluating operations. Moreover, total costs in many healthcare organizations are mostly fixed costs. If the variable costs are a very small proportion of total cost, regression analysis will not reflect the large jumps in fixed costs as capacity limits are reached.

When there are too few data points to perform regression analysis, the high–low method can be used. A representative high point and a representative low point are used in the calculations. From the data in Table 4.9, for example, the highest activity (1950 patient visits with $2,100 of cost) and the lowest activity (500 patient visits with $1,120 of cost) are selected. Variable cost is calculated as the change in cost over the change in volume:

Variable Cost = ($2,100 − $1,120) / (1950 − 500) = $0.68 per Patient Visit

To determine fixed cost, the high total cost is used with $0.68 substituted for variable cost and 1950 for quantity. Substitute these values into the equation

Total Cost = Fixed Cost + (Variable Cost per Visit × Patient Visits)

and solve for fixed costs

$2,100 = Fixed Cost + ($0.68 × 1,950) Fixed Cost = $774

Using the high-low method, the cost equation is

$$C = \$774 + (\$0.68q)$$

When the results from the high–low method are compared to the results of the regression analysis, fixed costs are higher for regression (\$884) and the variable cost is lower for regression (\$0.52) than for the high–low method (\$774 and \$0.68, respectively). Regression is a more accurate analytical tool because it uses all of the data points, whereas the high–low method uses only two points; furthermore, these may not reflect normal levels of operations. Also, unfortunately, there is no measure like the R-square to show how well the cost equation fits.

Cost-Volume-Profit Analysis

Underlying most short-range decisions, cost-volume-profit analysis provides a framework for evaluation of performance when the organization faces significant changes in volume. It involves the impact of a change in activity on costs and profit.

The total cost function developed for the Community Health Center can be considered a flexible budget or performance budget for determining whether the health center is operating in an efficient manner. If 10,500 patients were served in 2003 and the actual costs were \$1,900,000 (variable costs \$625,000 and fixed costs \$1,275,000), then the Community Health Center overspent by \$72,500.

Using a flexible budget in which costs are divided into fixed and variable is the most accurate method of measuring performance. It is preferable to the comparison of a static budget set at a particular level of operation that is compared to the actual costs at a different level of operation.

Cost-Volume-Profit Analysis Through Graphs

The easiest way to visualize and understand cost-volume-profit analysis is through a break-even chart. Such a chart shows much more than the point at which an organization will break even. It provides a picture of the profit or loss at all levels of activity within the relevant range of activity.

For example, a hospital has a small laboratory that has shown a loss for some time. The October operating statement is presented in **Exhibit 4.16**. Fixed costs total \$14,000 per month, and variable costs are \$5,700 (\$3 × 1,900 tests). Management is looking for ways to eliminate the loss, so they construct a break-even chart (**Figure 4.5**). The break-even point, where the total revenue line crosses the total cost line, is 2000 tests. The laboratory is currently operating at the level of 1900 tests per month, showing a loss of \$700. From the break-even chart, it is possible to estimate the profit or loss at any level of activity within the relevant range.

In a fee-for-service setting, there is a strong motivation to increase patient visits to show a profit or reduce a loss. The break-even chart for a mature health maintenance organization (HMO) shows just the opposite (**Figure 4.6**). With a constant membership in a mature HMO and no co-payments, the revenue line on a capitation basis is flat. The total cost line is similar to the total cost line in a fee-for-service setting, however. The HMO will show a profit if it keeps its members healthy, thereby reducing patient visits. In this case, a low level of patient visits will produce a profit and a high level of activity will result in a lower profit or a loss.

Exhibit 4.16   Laboratory Operating Statement for October

		Variable Costs	Fixed Costs
Number of tests	1,900		
Gross charges	$19,000		
Operating expenses:			
Wages and benefits	5,760		$5,760
Supplies	3,800	$3,800	
Other variable costs	1,900	1,900	
Depreciation	500		500
Allocated costs	7,740		7,740
Total	19,700	$5,700	$14,000
Operating income (loss)	$(700)		

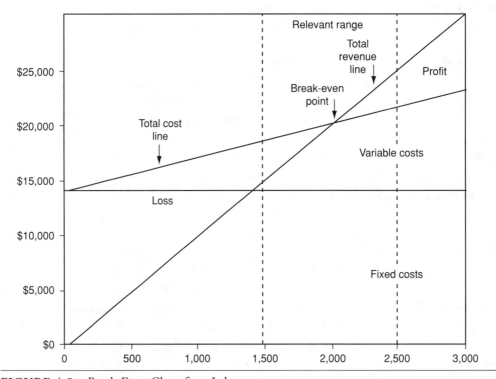

FIGURE 4.5   Break-Even Chart for a Laboratory

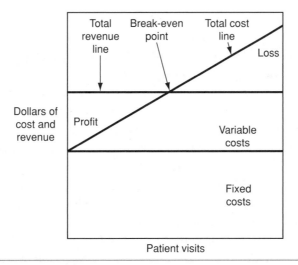

FIGURE 4.6   Break-Even Chart for a Mature HMO

Cost-Volume-Profit Analysis Through Equations

The break-even point may be determined by an equation dividing the total fixed costs by the contribution margin per unit. The contribution margin is the difference between revenue and variable costs. In the laboratory example, the fee is $10 per test ($19,000 / 1900). The variable cost per test is $3 ($5,700 / 1900). Each test thus generates a contribution margin of $7 ($10 − $3) toward covering fixed costs and providing a profit. The break-even point is 2000 tests ($14,000 / $7). Each test beyond 2000 will generate $7 of income because fixed costs are covered at 2000 tests. Each test below 2000 will result in an additional loss of $7.

The number of tests to generate a desired profit can be determined by dividing the contribution margin per unit into the sum of fixed costs and desired profit. If the management wants to show a profit of $700, the laboratory must perform 2100 tests ([$14,000 + $700] / $7).

This equation may be adapted to determine the dollar amount of revenue needed to break even or to generate a given amount of income, even when a single measure of volume is not available. In the laboratory example, the number of tests was used as the measure of volume. If the laboratory conducts a variety of tests that consume different amounts of variable costs, it is possible to determine the overall break-even point in dollars of revenue by using the contribution margin ratio. The contribution margin ratio is the ratio of contribution margin to revenue. In this case, the contribution margin ratio is 70% ($7 / $10). The break-even point in dollars of revenue is $20,000 ($14,000 / 70%).

Identifying the fixed and variable costs and computing the average contribution margin ratio make it possible to perform a cost-volume-profit analysis for the overall healthcare system. Although the contribution margin ratio may vary greatly among the various segments of an organized healthcare delivery system, it is still a useful tool of analysis. For example, if the contribution margin ratio of each segment is known, the analyst at the organization level may determine the impact of a change in activity in any segment on the overall organization profit. If a hospital has a contribution margin ratio of 20%, an increase of $100,000 in revenue should increase profit by $20,000. If a laboratory has a contribution margin ratio of 40%, an increase of $100,000 in revenue should increase profit by $40,000.

Contribution margin is a very useful concept in short-range decisions. Fixed costs are constant in the short term within the relevant range, so analysts can ignore fixed costs and focus on contribution margin in many short-range decisions. For example, what would be the impact on the laboratory's loss in Exhibit 4.16 if the hospital contracted with another healthcare organization to perform 300 tests per month at $6 per test? The contribution margin per unit on these tests would be $3 per test ($6 – $3), and the contract would add $900 to income, or change the $700 loss to a $200 profit. Any price above variable cost per unit of service will generate a positive contribution margin and, therefore, increase profits.

At some point capacity constraints must be considered. If the special contract pushes the laboratory's level of services over current capacity, we may have to add personnel to relax the capacity constraint. Another important factor to consider is whether these special contract patients are part of the laboratory's current business. If they are, the relevant costs must include the portion of fixed costs that will be lost because regular business will decrease. Sometimes, other opportunities may arise, and the cost of these opportunities also warrants consideration.

Relaxing a constrained resource is another short-term decision that managers often face. If the firm is operating beyond the break-even point, regular operations are covering all the fixed costs. Therefore, all the contribution margin that occurs when the constraint is relaxed is available to pay for the resources needed to relax the constraint. Often, the contribution margin is unexpectedly large. For example, if the laboratory is operating at 2000 tests per month and facing a labor constraint, the laboratory could afford to pay up to $1,400 ($7 contribution margin × 200 tests) to hire additional personnel and serve an additional 200 patients. In the short run, managers often underestimate the amount of money available to relax a constrained resource.

Establishment of Fees

In the short term, managers may set the price for a special order to generate some contribution margin. On this type of contract, they should seek to maximize total dollars of contribution margin. Over time, however, they cannot ignore fixed costs; they must cover all costs of providing a service and generating a desired income. Most reimbursement mechanisms are based on covering the full cost of providing a service. To determine cost-based fees, the healthcare organization must be able to establish the full cost for each procedure or class of procedures, including the direct cost of providing the service and a fair share of other indirect costs.

Pricing for the Community Health Center can be analyzed with this flexible budget (see Exhibit 4.14). Fees this period were $750,000 for 10,000 patient visits, for an average fee of $75. The contribution margin per patient visit is $20 ($75 – $55). For every patient visit, $20 is available to cover fixed cost and then add to "income." The flexible budget can be written as

$$I = G + (p - v)q - F$$

where *I* is income, *G* represents grants and donations, and *p* reflects price. This type of flexible budget is used in cost-volume-profit analysis by forecasting the variables included in the analysis. For example, if grants and donations are expected to decrease in the next period, the price of services may be raised to compensate. Thus, if donations and grants are expected to drop to $850,000 and patient visits increase to 12,000, the estimated income is:

$$I = \$850,000 + [(\$75 - \$55) \times 12,000] - \$1,250,000 = (\$160,000)$$

The loss (excess of expenses over revenues) is expected to increase to $160,000. To cover all costs, the Community Health Center must increase fees by $13.33 per visit ($160,000 / 12,000), arriving at a new fee of $88.33 ($75.00 + $13.33).

This flexible budget does not incorporate the effect of price changes on demand. If the new price is not competitive, volumes may decrease and the anticipated revenue from patient fees will be less than expected. In the prediction of future volumes, the sensitivity of demand to price must also be predicted and incorporated explicitly.

Activity-Based Costing to Measure the Full Cost of Services

Organizations in the manufacturing sector developed activity-based costing to provide the full cost of products and services in a complex setting. Historically, manufacturers have used a single overhead rate to allocate indirect costs to products and services, usually on the basis of direct labor. A single plantwide overhead rate cannot reflect the complexities of automation and other modern manufacturing techniques, however, and products with a high labor content were over-costed while products in complex manufacturing processes with automation were undercosted.

When firms use activity-based costing, they must first analyze production processes to determine the many activities that drive production costs. Once a set of cost pools and drivers has been determined, standards can be set and costs allocated to products and services using the activity as an allocation base. The resulting full cost of a product or service then reflects the level of complexity involved. For example, after tracking the cost of purchasing all of its materials and supplies, a firm can designate the number of purchase invoices as the activity that drives these costs. This results in a cost per unit for the activity of purchasing. Those products and services requiring many purchases will bear the additional costs.

Activity-based costing treats all costs as variable costs in the long run, although fixed costs remain fixed in short-term decision making (such as pricing and product emphasis). The fully allocated cost under activity-based costing does not reflect the large changes in fixed costs needed to expand capacity, and it overestimates (sometimes substantially) the marginal cost of providing additional service when there is excess capacity. Hence, activity-based costing can lead to suboptimal decisions in any service organization characterized by a large proportion of fixed cost.

Healthcare organizations are characterized by large fixed costs, regardless of the activities undertaken. When Noreen and Soderstrom examined a sample of hospital overhead costs for an average of 108 hospitals over a 15-year period, they found, on average, that 80% of costs were fixed and that an activity-based costing model overstated their marginal costs by more than 40%.[6] Because of the preponderance of fixed costs in healthcare organizations, activity-based costing is appropriate for setting and monitoring efficiency variances (i.e., analyzing time and procedures used in an activity) and determining full cost for fee setting when the organization is at capacity, but its poor estimates of marginal cost make it inappropriate for decision making involving changes in activity. In healthcare organizations, marginal cost may be very small until capacity becomes an issue. As volumes of service increase, fixed costs will increase in large increments at some point (e.g., the cost of hiring another full-time service provider).

Decision to Drop an Activity

When an activity or service has been showing a loss and there is no way to reduce the loss, the healthcare organization may face the decision of whether to drop the activity or service. In the earlier laboratory example (see Exhibit 4.16), hospital management may try to determine how much the hospital can save by eliminating the unprofitable laboratory. Although fixed costs are generally irrelevant in short-term decisions, the hospital must know which costs will be avoided by dropping the laboratory service and which costs will continue. The hospital administrator then approaches a pathologist with an offer to sell the laboratory. The pathologist agrees to purchase the equipment at its undepreciated cost and pay the hospital a monthly rental of $3,000. An examination of the avoidable and unavoidable costs of dropping the laboratory indicates that the hospital will not incur $2,000 of the costs allocated to the laboratory (e.g., occupancy, administration) if it drops the laboratory service (**Exhibit 4.17**). However, $5,740 of allocated fixed costs are unavoidable and will continue if the laboratory is sold. The rental income of $3,000 will not fully offset the $5,740 of unavoidable allocated fixed costs; thus, the effect of selling the laboratory is to lose $2,740 per month.

Dealing with Constraints

At some point in time, all organizations experience resource shortages, that is, constraints or bottlenecks in services upon which patients, physicians, or others rely. These constraints limit an organization's ability to increase operating income. The constraint may be a piece of equipment producing at capacity, limited labor or professional hours, or limited physical space, such

---

Exhibit 4.17   Illustration of Decision to Drop a Service

Type of Expense	Cost Behavior	Amount	Avoidable	Unavoidable
Wages and benefits	Fixed	$5,760	$5,760	
Supplies	Variable	3,800	3,800	
Other variable costs	Variable	1,900	1,900	
Depreciation	Fixed	500	500	
Allocated costs	Fixed	7,740	2,000	$5,740
Total		$19,700	$13,960	$5,740

as the number of exam rooms. To manage constraints, each resource that is a primary constraint must be identified and its capacity increased.

Following is an example of a constraint that involves one medical office within a health network. The physicians' office support staff is overextended and doctors are spending some of their valuable time performing support tasks. The front office employees complain that they must use some of their lunch time for office-related work and the medical assistants have to work overtime to complete their duties. Medical assistants accompany patients to exam rooms, take patients' vitals, update their medical records, and perform other tasks requested by physicians. If the medical assistants are not available in a timely manner, physicians again use their valuable time to complete some of these duties.

Increasing overtime led to the identification of the bottleneck: medical assistant hours. In general, a constraint can be relieved in two ways (**Table 4.10**):

1. Increase the supply of the constraining resource.
2. Reduce the demand on the constraining resource by changing the process.

Adding the full-time medical assistant had many benefits. Revenue increased because an additional eight patients could be served, overtime was eliminated, and the flow of patients and general operation of the office improved.

Operating Leverage

Many healthcare organizations are characterized by a large percentage of fixed costs, which leads to a high degree of operating leverage. Operating leverage reflects the proportion of costs that are fixed and is an important concept for healthcare service managers and accountants to understand. When operating leverage is high, profits will vary a great deal as volume varies. Operating leverage is unimportant if revenues are based on cost, because payment will always exceed cost. When revenues are based on volume rather than cost, however, profits become highly variable when operating leverage is high.

A simple example can illustrate how changes in the proportion of fixed costs affect earnings variability under a flat-fee per-patient reimbursement scheme. A hospital has two departments, Department A and Department B. Fixed costs in Department A are $100, and variable costs

Table 4.10

	No change	Option 1 Adding a half-time MA	Option 2 Adding a full-time MA
Weekly cost and revenue:			
Revenue	$36,270	$36,270	$39,990
Total employment costs	(5,756)	(5,980)	(6,240)
Employee benefits	(1,899)	(1,973)	(2,047)
Overtime	(370)	(34)	—
Operating income	$28,245	$28,283	$31,703

per patient are $5. If 25 patients receive services during a particular period, the cost per patient is $9 ($100 / 25 patients + $5). If reimbursement is on a flat-fee basis at $10 per patient, the income will be $25. If the patient volume drops to 20 patients during the next period, the cost per patient becomes $10 ($100 / 20 patients + $5). If reimbursement is still $10 per patient, the department just breaks even.

Department B has total costs similar to those of Department A, but Department B has lower fixed costs, $75 per period, and higher variable costs, $6 per patient. The total cost for the treatment of 25 patients is $225 ($75 + [$6 × 25 patients]). With a reimbursement of $10 per patient, the total reimbursement is $250 and earnings are $25, the same as for Department A. When volume drops to 20 patients, however, the total cost in Department B is only $195 ($75 + [$6 × 20 patients]). Reimbursement is $200 ($10 × $20), and the department has earnings of $5 rather than just breaking even as in Department A. Thus, lower operating leverage (the fixed portion of costs) reduces earnings variability.

Use of Information from Regulatory Reports for Decisions

Healthcare organizations must gather information for regulatory reports. Consequently, they often design their internal accounting systems to produce the required information. Unfortunately, these reporting systems are not designed to provide relevant information for the wide variety of decisions that managers must make. Managers need to consider carefully the types of decisions that they make and develop appropriate accounting techniques and systems to support their decision-making process fully.

Target Costing

The Japanese developed target costing for the manufacturing sector. Although target costing is used primarily in manufacturing, the principles are certainly applicable to the healthcare and service sectors. Target costing is a cost-control method that takes place at the design phase of new product development. After a market survey, a target price is set and a target cost calculated. The decision to produce that product is based on whether it is possible to meet the target cost. Thus, cost control is built into the production process at the outset. As the design team develops a new product, they consider trade-offs in price, functionality, and quality to meet a product's target cost.

As healthcare and not-for-profit organizations focus on cost containment, they can develop new services or product lines at a price that will maximize volumes. Using techniques that analyze the relevant time and costs to provide a particular service, healthcare organizations can develop a production plan to provide the service at a specified target cost. Because a large proportion of cost is fixed in many healthcare and service organizations, capacity levels have a greater impact on the variability of costs in any service product. If a firm has ample capacity, fixed cost will not be part of the target cost. If there are capacity limits, however, the costs of increasing capacity or using capacity more efficiently enter into the target cost.

Revenue Cycle Management

Revenue cycle management is important in every business. However, because revenues are so complex in health care, efficient management of the revenue cycle is much more difficult.

Other industries may have complex revenue cycles, but they are usually consistent over time and lack the dynamics of health care where frequent changes occur in contracts with payers, legislative mandates, and managed care, all of which increase the complexity of the revenue cycle. The business office of a healthcare center is no longer just a cost center—today it is a profit center with opportunities to maximize revenue.

Good revenue cycle management has a significant impact on operating profit, cash flows, and patient receivable balances. From interviews with hospital and medical group CFOs, controllable write-offs were estimated to be 2% or more of gross revenues. Two examples of controllable write-offs include denials for inadequate documentation and late billings. One small hospital lost approximately $300,000 of revenue in 1 year because of missed billing deadlines. Applying a 2% controllable write-off to the statement of operations for the Sample Health System in Exhibit 4.2, the potential increase in operating profit and cash flows would be approximately $5.77 million. This represents an increase of 219% in income from operations and an increase in cash flow from operations of 15%. The return on investment for additional funds to improve revenue cycle management can be quite high. Every analytical ratio discussed in the "Analysis of Financial Statements" section presented earlier in this chapter could be improved.

The Revenue Cycle

The revenue cycle involves a series of steps with potential problems and opportunities for revenue enhancement. The steps include:

1. Front-end processes including admitting, precertification, insurance verification, and managing medical necessity
2. Charge description through coding
3. Billing and follow-up of denials and potential bad debts
4. Receipt of payer remittance

Revenue cycle management must start with front-end processes and continue through the receipt of the entire amount of cash owed. The processes are complex and interconnected. Focus on an individual part may produce higher collections, but it will be of limited effectiveness.

Problem Areas

Although problems arise in specific areas of the revenue cycle, they are interrelated. The most significant problem areas identified through interviews with healthcare CFOs include:

- Patient complaints and a backlog of correspondence with patients
- Poorly trained personnel managing the revenue cycle
- Inadequate information systems that track documentation and billing
- Denials for medical necessity and sequence of care
- Denials for incorrect coding
- Delays in billing
- Excessive days in receivables

- Excessive bad debts
- Lack of prospective cost data for negotiating managed care contracts

Approaches to Solving Revenue-Cycle Problems

Solutions must combine management of the revenue cycle, technology, hiring and continued training of capable people, establishing accountability, effective contract administration, and benchmarking.

- Management of the revenue cycle—Creation of a revenue cycle management team provides an integrated approach. The team must have representation from the business office and major patient care departments. Revenue cycle management must span the entire cycle from front-end reception to final collection of cash.
- Integrated information technology system—Technology solutions are difficult and costly to implement. Ideally, the revenue management system integrates patient accounting, contract management including revenue and cost by contract, and revenue and cost by type of service. Accuracy of eligibility and precertification information is greatly improved with an online information system connected to payers. Claims editing, denials tracking, and tracking of claims held for further information help solve revenue cycle problems.[7]
- Managing denials—Denials represent a major problem. One hospital CFO indicated that some payer organizations budget for the denial of a portion of claims. This CFO believes that many first-time claim denials are merely an attempt by the payer to slow cash flows to the provider. Two denial recovery processes are: (1) a preventative process whereby accurate claims are filed to avoid denials, and (2) a claims recovery process whereby denied claims are corrected and refiled. When the provider has a good working relationship with major payers, improvements are more likely to occur.[8]
- Accountability—Accountability for accurate claims information begins at the site of service delivery. Medical necessity is documented and procedures are coded. The business office staff filing claims may not understand or have information to correct inaccurate claims.
- Contract management—Revenue cycle management in managed health care begins with the knowledge of two key variables: (1) the medical demographics of the patients to be served, and (2) the cost of serving those patients, including the direct patient-related costs and allocated support costs. Without this knowledge the provider cannot negotiate prices that will cover costs and generate a reasonable target net income. Part of the negotiation process involves carve-outs and stop losses when the risk to the provider is greatest. In many cases, the managed care payer understands the impact of specific contract terms better than the provider, giving the payer an advantage in the negotiations. Knowledge of patient demographics and cost structure are critical to more accurate contract analysis.
- Benchmarking—To achieve good performance, key measures need to be tracked, benchmarked, and published on a regular basis. Suggested key variables that should be tracked include:
  - Days in receivables
  - Bad debts as a percent of gross revenue

- ° Denials as a percent of net revenue
- ° Dollar amount of denials
- ° Dollar amount of recovered denials
- ° Average number of unbilled days
- ° Average number of days claims were held for further information
- ° Profitability by major managed care contract

Short-Range Decisions in Review

Different information needs must be considered in the design of accounting and information technology systems. This includes cost behavior (fixed and variable costs) and traceability of costs (direct and indirect support costs). When an activity or service is added or dropped, cost and revenue information unique to that decision must be generated. A system designed to provide information for regulatory and other reports for outsiders seldom provides the relevant information for most short-range decisions.

Although a clear understanding of costs is critical, healthcare organizations have dramatically increased income and cash flow from operations by increasing emphasis on pricing and management of the revenue cycle.

Conclusion

Accounting information falls into two broad classifications: financial accounting and management accounting. GAAP require the presentation of four financial statements—the financial position statement (balance sheet), the operating statement (income statement), the cash flow statement, and the statement of change in owners' equity (not assets). All these statements are presented to stockholders and creditors and to the healthcare organization's board of directors. Management within healthcare organizations needs financial statements for responsibility centers. Evaluation of operations for responsibility centers requires the development of a performance or flexible budget if actual volume varies significantly from planned volume.

The discounted cash flow approach is appropriate for long-range decisions at any level in the healthcare organization. The superior method for evaluating the decision to acquire long-term assets considers the time value of money. A long-range decision is favorable if the incremental discounted cash inflows attributable to the investment proposal are equal to or greater than the incremental discounted cash outflows attributable to the investment. In practice, the payback method and accounting rate of return method are used because they are simple and easy to apply, but they may lead to less desirable decisions.

Short-range decisions involve what fees to charge, and the volume and mix of services to provide with existing capacity. The most basic information for short-range decisions is the behavior of costs as activity changes. Variable costs change in proportion to changes in volume, and fixed costs remain unchanged with changes in volume. Because fixed costs do not change with changes in activity, the concept of contribution margin (the difference between price and variable costs) is useful in many short-range decisions.

In most healthcare organizations, a very large percentage of total costs are fixed in nature, causing wide swings in income as volume changes. The concept of operating leverage (the extent of fixed costs in the organization) must be understood by management at all levels of the organization.

References

1. Estaugh SR. *Health Care Finance*. New York: Auburn House; 1992:416–417.
2. Stickney CP. *Financial Reporting and Statement Analysis*. New York: Dryden Press; 1996:119.
3. ———. *Financial Reporting and Statement Analysis*. New York: Dryden Press; 1996:120.
4. Kaplan RS, Atkinson AA. *Advanced Management Accounting*. Englewood Cliffs, NJ: Prentice Hall; 1998:367–380.
5. DeCoster DT, et al. *Management Accounting*, 4th ed. New York: John Wiley & Sons; 1988.
6. Noreen E, Soderstrom N. The accuracy of proportional cost models: evidence from hospital service departments. *Review of Accounting Studies*. 1997;2(1):89–114.
7. Burckhart K. Integrated, automated revenue management for managed care contracts. *Healthcare Financial Management*. April 2002:40–43.
8. Hodges J. Effective claims denial management enhances revenue. *Healthcare Financial Management*. August 2002:40–50.

Biographical Information

Leslie G. Eldenburg, CPA, PhD, has been a Professor of Accounting at the University of Arizona since 1993. Her research areas are healthcare accounting and managerial accounting issues in an international setting. Her research papers have been published in academic accounting journals, as well as in *Healthcare Financial Management*, *Medical Decision Making*, and *Controllers Quarterly*. Before she began her academic career, she worked in the finance department at Virginia Mason Hospital in Seattle. She received her doctorate in accounting from the University of Washington.

Eldon L. Schafer, CPA, PhD, is Professor Emeritus at Pacific Lutheran University. With teaching interests in management accounting systems, he has been a faculty member or visiting faculty member at the University of Nebraska, California State University–San Jose, Syracuse University, University of Washington, Massey University in New Zealand, University of Southeast Asia in Macao, Riga Technical University in Latvia, and most recently at the University of Arizona. He has also served as a consultant to the Washington State Hospital Commission and on the board of an HMO. Dr. Schafer has coauthored a number of books in management accounting and healthcare administration. He holds a master's degree and a doctorate from the University of Nebraska.

Dwight J. Zulauf, CPA, PhD, is Professor Emeritus and the founding dean of the School of Business Administration at Pacific Lutheran University. His teaching has focused primarily on undergraduate and graduate accounting courses. He has been a Visiting Professor at Riga Technical University, Massey University in New Zealand, University of Minnesota, University of Washington, and California State University–Long Beach, and he is Professor Emeritus at Humboldt State University. Over the years, he has served on the boards of a number of organizations providing health care in the state of Washington, including the Good Samaritan Hospital, the Pierce County Health Council, Lutheran Social Services of Southwest Washington, and the Health Systems Agency. He has also been a consultant to the Washington State Hospital Commission. Dr. Zulauf has coauthored three books in accounting systems for medical groups. He holds a master's degree from Columbia University and a doctorate from the University of Minnesota.

$$PV = \frac{1}{(1+\gamma)n}$$

PRESENT VALUE OF $1

Period	2%	4%	6%	8%	10%	12%	14%	16%	18%	20%	22%	24%	26%	28%	30%	35%	40%	45%	50%
1	0.980	0.962	0.943	0.926	0.909	0.893	0.877	0.862	0.847	0.833	0.820	0.806	0.794	0.781	0.769	0.741	0.714	0.690	0.667
2	0.961	0.925	0.890	0.857	0.826	0.797	0.769	0.743	0.718	0.694	0.672	0.650	0.630	0.610	0.592	0.549	0.510	0.476	0.444
3	0.942	0.889	0.840	0.794	0.751	0.712	0.675	0.641	0.609	0.579	0.551	0.524	0.500	0.477	0.455	0.406	0.364	0.328	0.296
4	0.924	0.855	0.792	0.735	0.683	0.636	0.592	0.552	0.516	0.482	0.451	0.423	0.397	0.373	0.350	0.301	0.260	0.226	0.198
5	0.906	0.822	0.747	0.681	0.621	0.567	0.519	0.476	0.437	0.402	0.370	0.341	0.315	0.291	0.269	0.223	0.186	0.156	0.132
6	0.888	0.790	0.705	0.630	0.564	0.507	0.456	0.410	0.370	0.335	0.303	0.275	0.250	0.227	0.207	0.165	0.133	0.108	0.088
7	0.871	0.760	0.665	0.583	0.513	0.452	0.400	0.354	0.314	0.279	0.249	0.222	0.198	0.178	0.159	0.122	0.095	0.074	0.059
8	0.853	0.731	0.627	0.540	0.467	0.404	0.351	0.305	0.266	0.233	0.204	0.179	0.157	0.139	0.123	0.091	0.068	0.051	0.039
9	0.837	0.703	0.592	0.500	0.424	0.361	0.308	0.263	0.225	0.194	0.167	0.144	0.125	0.108	0.094	0.067	0.048	0.035	0.026
10	0.820	0.676	0.558	0.463	0.386	0.322	0.270	0.227	0.191	0.162	0.137	0.116	0.099	0.085	0.073	0.050	0.035	0.024	0.017
11	0.804	0.650	0.527	0.429	0.350	0.287	0.237	0.195	0.162	0.135	0.112	0.094	0.079	0.066	0.056	0.037	0.025	0.017	0.012
12	0.788	0.625	0.497	0.397	0.319	0.257	0.208	0.168	0.137	0.112	0.092	0.076	0.062	0.052	0.043	0.027	0.018	0.012	0.008
13	0.773	0.601	0.469	0.368	0.290	0.229	0.182	0.145	0.116	0.093	0.075	0.061	0.050	0.040	0.033	0.020	0.013	0.008	0.005
14	0.758	0.577	0.442	0.340	0.263	0.205	0.160	0.125	0.099	0.079	0.062	0.049	0.039	0.032	0.025	0.015	0.009	0.006	0.003
15	0.743	0.555	0.417	0.315	0.239	0.183	0.140	0.108	0.084	0.065	0.051	0.040	0.031	0.025	0.020	0.011	0.006	0.004	0.002
16	0.728	0.534	0.394	0.292	0.218	0.163	0.123	0.093	0.071	0.054	0.042	0.032	0.025	0.019	0.015	0.008	0.005	0.003	0.002
17	0.714	0.513	0.371	0.270	0.198	0.146	0.108	0.080	0.060	0.045	0.034	0.026	0.020	0.015	0.012	0.006	0.003	0.002	0.002
18	0.700	0.494	0.350	0.250	0.180	0.130	0.095	0.069	0.051	0.038	0.028	0.021	0.016	0.012	0.009	0.005	0.002	0.001	0.001
19	0.686	0.475	0.331	0.232	0.164	0.116	0.083	0.060	0.043	0.031	0.023	0.017	0.012	0.009	0.007	0.003	0.002	0.001	0.001
20	0.673	0.456	0.312	0.215	0.149	0.104	0.073	0.051	0.037	0.026	0.019	0.014	0.010	0.007	0.005	0.002	0.001	0.001	
21	0.660	0.439	0.294	0.199	0.135	0.093	0.064	0.044	0.031	0.022	0.015	0.011	0.008	0.006	0.004	0.002	0.001		
22	0.647	0.422	0.278	0.184	0.123	0.083	0.056	0.038	0.026	0.018	0.013	0.009	0.006	0.004	0.003	0.001	0.001		
23	0.634	0.406	0.262	0.170	0.112	0.074	0.049	0.033	0.022	0.015	0.010	0.007	0.005	0.003	0.002	0.001			
24	0.622	0.390	0.247	0.158	0.102	0.066	0.043	0.028	0.019	0.013	0.008	0.006	0.004	0.003	0.002	0.001			
25	0.610	0.375	0.233	0.146	0.092	0.059	0.038	0.024	0.016	0.010	0.007	0.005	0.003	0.002	0.001	0.001			
30	0.552	0.308	0.174	0.099	0.057	0.033	0.020	0.012	0.007	0.004	0.003	0.002	0.001	0.001	0.001				
35	0.500	0.253	0.130	0.068	0.036	0.019	0.010	0.006	0.003	0.002	0.001	0.001							
40	0.453	0.208	0.097	0.046	0.022	0.011	0.005	0.003	0.002	0.001									
45	0.410	0.171	0.073	0.031	0.014	0.006	0.003	0.001	0.001										
50	0.372	0.141	0.054	0.021	0.009	0.003	0.001	0.001	0.001										

PRESENT VALUE OF $1

$$PV = \frac{1+(1+\gamma)^n}{\gamma}$$

Period	2%	4%	6%	8%	10%	12%	14%	16%	18%	20%	22%	24%	26%	28%	30%	35%	40%	45%	50%
1	0.980	0.962	0.943	0.926	0.909	0.893	0.877	0.682	0.847	0.833	0.820	0.806	0.794	0.781	0.769	0.741	0.714	0.690	0.667
2	1.942	1.886	1.833	1.783	1.736	1.690	1.647	1.605	1.566	1.528	1.492	1.457	1.424	1.392	1.361	1.289	1.224	1.165	1.111
3	2.884	2.775	2.673	2.577	2.486	2.402	2.322	2.246	2.174	2.106	2.042	1.981	1.923	1.868	1.816	1.696	1.589	1.493	1.407
4	3.808	3.630	3.465	3.312	3.170	3.037	2.914	2.798	2.690	2.589	2.494	2.404	2.320	2.241	2.166	1.997	1.849	1.720	1.605
5	4.713	4.452	4.212	3.993	3.791	3.605	3.433	3.274	3.127	2.991	2.864	2.745	2.635	2.532	2.436	2.220	2.035	1.876	1.737
6	5.601	5.242	4.917	4.623	4.355	4.111	3.889	3.685	3.498	3.326	3.167	3.020	2.885	2.759	2.643	2.385	2.168	1.983	1.824
7	6.472	6.002	5.582	5.206	4.868	4.564	4.288	4.039	3.812	3.605	3.416	3.242	3.083	2.937	2.802	2.508	2.263	2.057	1.883
8	7.325	6.733	6.210	5.747	5.335	4.968	4.639	4.344	4.078	3.837	3.619	3.421	3.241	3.076	2.925	2.598	2.331	2.109	1.922
9	8.162	7.435	6.802	6.247	5.759	5.328	4.946	4.607	4.303	4.031	3.786	3.566	3.366	3.184	3.019	2.665	2.379	2.144	1.948
10	8.983	8.111	7.360	6.710	6.145	5.650	5.216	4.833	4.494	4.192	3.923	3.682	3.465	3.269	3.092	2.715	2.414	2.168	1.965
11	9.787	8.760	7.887	7.139	6.495	5.938	5.453	5.029	4.656	4.327	4.035	3.776	3.543	3.335	3.147	2.752	2.438	2.185	1.977
12	10.575	9.385	8.384	7.536	6.814	6.194	5.660	5.197	4.793	4.439	4.127	3.851	3.606	3.387	3.190	2.779	2.456	2.196	1.985
13	11.348	9.986	8.853	7.904	7.103	6.424	5.842	5.342	4.910	4.533	4.203	3.912	3.656	3.427	3.223	2.799	2.469	2.204	1.990
14	12.106	10.563	9.295	8.244	7.367	6.628	6.002	5.468	5.008	4.611	4.265	3.962	3.695	3.459	3.249	2.814	2.478	2.210	1.993
15	12.849	11.118	9.712	8.559	7.606	6.811	6.142	5.575	5.092	4.675	4.315	4.001	3.726	3.483	3.268	2.825	2.484	2.214	1.995
16	13.578	11.652	10.106	8.851	7.824	6.974	6.265	5.668	5.162	4.730	4.357	4.033	3.751	3.503	3.283	2.834	2.489	2.216	1.997
17	14.292	12.166	10.477	9.122	8.022	7.120	6.373	5.749	5.222	4.775	4.391	4.059	3.771	3.518	3.295	2.840	2.492	2.218	1.998
18	14.992	12.659	10.828	9.372	8.201	7.250	6.467	5.818	5.273	4.812	4.419	4.080	3.786	3.529	3.304	2.844	2.494	2.219	1.999
19	15.678	13.134	11.158	9.604	8.365	7.366	6.550	5.877	5.316	4.843	4.442	4.097	3.799	3.539	3.311	2.848	2.496	2.220	1.999
20	16.351	13.590	11.470	9.818	8.514	7.469	6.623	5.929	5.353	4.870	4.460	4.110	3.808	3.546	3.316	2.850	2.497	2.221	1.999
21	17.011	14.029	11.764	10.017	8.649	7.562	6.687	5.973	5.384	4.891	4.476	4.121	3.816	3.551	3.320	2.852	2.498	2.221	1.999
22	17.658	14.451	12.042	10.201	8.772	7.645	6.743	6.011	5.410	4.909	4.488	4.130	3.822	3.556	3.323	2.853	2.498	2.222	2.000
23	18.292	14.857	12.303	10.371	8.883	7.718	6.792	6.044	5.432	4.925	4.499	4.137	3.827	3.559	3.325	2.854	2.499	2.222	2.000
24	18.914	15.247	12.550	10.529	8.985	7.784	6.835	6.073	5.451	4.937	4.507	4.143	3.831	3.562	3.327	2.855	2.499	2.222	2.000
25	19.523	15.622	12.783	10.675	9.077	7.843	6.873	6.097	5.467	4.948	4.514	4.147	3.834	3.564	3.329	2.856	2.499	2.222	2.000
30	22.396	17.292	13.765	11.258	9.427	8.055	7.003	6.177	5.517	4.979	4.534	4.160	3.842	3.569	3.332	2.857	2.500	2.222	2.000
35	24.999	18.665	14.498	11.655	9.644	8.176	7.070	6.215	5.539	4.992	4.541	4.164	3.845	3.571	3.333	2.857	2.500	2.222	2.000
40	27.355	19.793	15.046	11.925	9.779	8.244	7.105	6.233	5.548	4.997	4.544	4.166	3.846	3.571	3.333	2.857	2.500	2.222	2.000
45	29.490	20.720	15.456	12.108	9.863	8.283	7.123	6.244	5.552	4.999	4.545	4.166	3.846	3.571	3.333	2.857	2.500	2.222	2.000
50	31.424	21.482	15.762	12.233	9.915	8.304	7.133	6.246	5.554	4.999	4.545	4.167	3.846	3.571	3.333	2.857	2.500	2.222	2.000

Labor and Employment Laws Applicable to Organized Delivery Systems

John D. Blair, Peter D. Stergios,
Patrick M. Collins, and Aimee Sato

Introduction

The healthcare industry has been characterized by significant technological and scientific changes during the past century. Continuing technological and scientific breakthroughs are becoming almost a routine part of medical practice. By understanding this evolution one can better appreciate how far the industry has advanced and, in certain situations, predict future technological and scientific changes. The labor and employment laws that regulate the healthcare field have also evolved because of legislative enactments and judicial rulings over the same period. Organized labor and unions in the industry evolved out of the early guild system. Understanding the labor and employment laws applicable to the industry is therefore necessary. Despite dependence on technology and science, the healthcare industry remains labor intensive.

Initially, the healthcare industry was controlled by a conservative medical profession, along with related healthcare institutions, which were entrepreneurial. They were not, and did not desire to be, "governmentally controlled." They did not regard themselves as related to, or as having an affinity with, labor organizations. Approximately 50 years ago, the president of the American Medical Association debated Senator Hubert Humphrey's Medicare proposals and attacked "socialized medicine," emphasizing the fact that the medical profession in the United States provided a better level of health care than in those countries that had "socialized medicine."

In contrast, doctors are now (along with the American Medical Association) contemplating unionization as a means of dealing with large healthcare organizations, the related insurance companies, and complex governmental regulations. Doctors may be acting in restraint of trade in violation of federal antitrust laws if they combine to set prices, so they have contemplated utilizing unions and the labor laws to bargain with healthcare corporations as a means of obtaining a lawful exemption from coverage under the antitrust laws. In many cases, doctors, as well as others in the medical profession, assert a variety of individual rights—relating to their civil rights, sex, age, disability, or other protected status—if they disagree with the way they are treated in the workplace.

It is important to understand the labor and employment laws that affect the industry. The labor laws, which cover healthcare professionals and employees (in not only the private sector, but also the public sector), have evolved from federal laws that were passed over the decades leading up to, and through, the New Deal, which ultimately resulted in (and also evolved from) the National Labor Relations Act (NLRA). The NLRA became the template for most of the labor laws that relate to collective bargaining rights and enforcement of those rights for the healthcare industry in the public and private sectors. Unions fought for legislation that enabled them to have the right to organize, to participate in recognition elections, to determine whether they could be certified as the exclusive bargaining representatives of employees, and then to establish agency and judicial mechanisms for collective bargaining negotiations, enforcement of agreements through arbitration, and judicial review. Initially, the employees eligible for unionization were regarded as nonsupervisory and nonmanagement (physicians and staff in the medical professions were excluded from membership and representation by unions); however, there has been an evolution. Today, many doctors and nurses, who are regarded as professionals, are actively litigating their ability to be eligible for inclusion in labor organizations.

The success of labor organizations in obtaining status, recognition, the ability to enforce agreements, and the ability to utilize administrative agencies and the courts under the NLRA was observed and emulated by other interest groups, which has had an impact on the healthcare workforce. Initially, civil rights groups sought legislative recognition, status, and agencies to enforce their rights, which resulted in employment protection under laws such as Title VII of the Civil Rights Act. Their success was followed by similar activities among environmental groups to achieve workplace protection and safety laws as well as other environmental laws. These successes, in turn, were followed by the efforts of those who wanted similar legislation to protect individuals who were over 40 and individuals who were disabled. Current efforts are pending to seek use of the same legislative protection to protect individuals who are gay and lesbian.

Many other laws affect the rights of individuals in the healthcare workplace. There is every reason to believe that there will be new laws that not only protect individuals by giving them the right to complain of retaliation or to utilize "whistle-blowing" provisions, but also additional rights that may result in expanded family medical leave, greater freedom from certain practices such as polygraphing, additional privacy rights, and more workplace safety regulations. As a result of these numerous rights, however, conflicts can exist between those healthcare workers under collective bargaining agreements (seeking the use of seniority) and those individuals within protected classifications who may oppose utilization of seniority because it blocks them from obtaining redress from perceived or actual discrimination, such as protection that they feel they are entitled to because of a disability.

Today, federal, state, and local legislation has given individual rights cases similar prominence. Cases are proliferating involving assertions of individual rights such as payment of minimum wages and overtime, civil rights, freedom from age discrimination, and other protected categories.

The courts have recognized that to resolve case overload, they need to be proactive in channeling litigation through other, "alternative dispute resolution" systems. The Supreme Court of the United States has expanded the ability of parties to use final and binding arbitration of statutory rights as a substitute for federal or state court litigation, subject to procedural safeguards that provide due process and other protections. These principles continue to evolve nationally in both federal and state jurisdictions.[1] The courts have borrowed from the traditional concept of arbitration under collective bargaining agreements and applied the arbitration process to enable resolution of even statutory disputes, subject to certain judicial guidelines. The courts have also sanctioned the use of informal complaint processes, such as mediation, enabling employers to create individual complaint systems that do not rely on binding arbitration, but rather allow for an informal review process. If established correctly, such informal review processes must be used by employees. If employees do not use such review processes by filing a complaint and allowing the employer to correct certain types of conduct alleged to have occurred, the employer may have an affirmative defense against litigation filed by the employees. The Supreme Court also has utilized the concept of seniority, even in the absence of a collective bargaining agreement, as a potential defense against a claim of disability discrimination. Thus an employee may not automatically claim that a disability entitled the employee to work in a position awarded under a seniority arrangement to another employee with greater tenure or seniority.

The one constant in the healthcare workplace is change, in terms of not only technology and science, but also the law and the nature of workforce rights and remedies. The traditional law that involved, first, collective bargaining, and then individual rights, follows a certain pattern, however. To understand whether doctors are able to join or create unions, or whether some of the traditional professional nursing jobs will be eligible for unionization, one must understand labor laws. To understand whether healthcare workers have rights, and the scope of such rights, even if they are not in traditional unions, one must understand employment laws.

Although the statutes reviewed in this chapter generally apply to organized delivery systems, a careful analysis should always be undertaken to determine whether an employer–employee relationship exists, whether there are jurisdictional prerequisites to the application of a statute or a state's common law, and whether a claim might be precluded by a statute of limitations. Often, in an organized delivery system, an engagement between an individual and an entity, such as a hospital or physician practice group, is not an employer–employee relationship but something else entirely—most commonly, an independent contractor relationship. Many of the statutes discussed here do not extend protections to persons engaged as independent contractors (see, for example, the sections below on "Wage and Hour Laws" and "Employment Eligibility Verification"). Therefore, before deciding on a course of action regarding a particular individual who provides services to the organization, a careful chief executive must first consider the character of the relationship between the organization and the individual—whether he or she is an employee or an independent contractor.

This chapter is not by any means exhaustive, but instead provides an overview and an analysis of the basic substantive provisions of labor and employment laws regulating the healthcare industry.

Federal and State Civil Rights Laws

Federal Protections

Various federal, state, and local laws prohibit discrimination in the workplace on the basis of race, color, national origin, sex, disability, religion, veteran status, and age. Additionally, some states and municipalities have enacted laws protecting an individual from discrimination on account of sexual orientation, marital status, criminal record, and recreational activities. The unifying theme behind these laws is that an employer should not treat individuals differently because of personal characteristics unrelated to job performance (i.e., race, sex, disability, age, etc.). In general, an employer should hire, promote, advance, discipline, or discharge an individual on the basis of that individual's job skills and work performance. Moreover, an employer should treat employees with similar job skills and performance records similarly.

Race, Color, National Origin

Federal law, as embodied in Title VII of the Civil Rights Act of 1964,[2] and similar state and local laws make it unlawful for an employer to discriminate against an employee on the basis of race, color, or national origin (as well as sex and religion as discussed later in the chapter) by (1) failing to hire, discharging, or otherwise discriminating with respect to an employee's terms and conditions of employment; (2) depriving an individual of employment opportunities; or (3) retaliating against an employee who opposed discrimination.

Under Title VII, an individual may prove discrimination under one of two theories. First, an individual may show that he or she suffered disparate treatment discrimination, which consists of intentional discrimination directed at the individual specifically. In a disparate treatment case, the focus is on whether the individual (or group of individuals referred to as a "class") suffered intentional discrimination. The pertinent question is whether the employer treated the individual differently or less favorably than another similarly situated individual because of the individual's personal characteristics. Disparate treatment claims also encompass complaints asserting a hostile work environment or harassment.

Another method by which an individual may prove discrimination is by demonstrating a disparate impact (or adverse impact), which refers to facially neutral practices that affect members of a protected group more severely than others. In a disparate impact claim, the individual does not need to demonstrate an intent to discriminate, as that is inferred. In either a disparate treatment or a disparate impact case, the employee bears the burden of proof to establish discrimination.

An employer may defend against discrimination charges by demonstrating that it engaged in nondiscriminatory practices or that its actions were justified. General defenses include a legitimate, nondiscriminatory business reason, a bona fide seniority or merit system, a professionally developed test that is job-related and consistent with business necessity, or a bona fide occupational qualification (not applicable with respect to race and has limited applicability with respect to sex).

An individual claiming discrimination may initiate a formal complaint in one of several ways depending on the locality in which the individual lives. An individual may initiate a discrimination claim by filing a charge of discrimination with the federal Equal Employment Opportunity Commission (EEOC), or by filing a discrimination complaint with a state or local fair employment practice agency. Additionally, in some jurisdictions an individual may file a complaint directly in state court. No litigant may file a complaint directly in federal court without first having instituted a proceeding before a fair employment practice agency and allowing that agency to handle the charge. If the fair employment practices agency declines to handle the charge, then an individual may file a complaint in federal court, but only after the individual receives what is known as a "right to sue" letter from the EEOC.

A successful claimant may be entitled to one or more remedies: instatement to the position sought, backpay, front pay, emotional distress damages, punitive damages, attorney's fees, or other relief that a court deems appropriate.[3]

Sex, Sexual Harassment, Pregnancy

Under federal law and various state and local laws, discrimination against an employee on the basis of sex is prohibited. Like claims for race, color, and national origin discrimination, sex or gender discrimination claims can arise in several different ways. A litigant may file for disparate treatment, including hostile work environment or harassment, or may file a claim for disparate impact. Employers also must take care not to discriminate on the basis of sex with respect to compensation.[4]

Sexual harassment can manifest itself in two ways. First, in so-called "quid pro quo" harassment, an employee may claim that she or he was pressured to provide sexual favors to someone in authority to obtain an employment-related benefit in return. Second, in a "hostile work environment" claim, the employee asserts that the employer has created a work atmosphere so offensive or unpleasant that it amounts to an adverse work condition. In a hostile work environment claim, the harassment may involve verbal, physical, or visual conduct, and the harassing conduct may be committed by a supervisor, coworker, or even a nonemployee.

Under certain circumstances, even if the victim employee was subjected to harassment, an employer may be able to defend against the charge. First, however, employers automatically will be liable for sexual harassment by supervisors that culminates in a tangible employment action against the employee, such as discharge, demotion, failure to promote, or significant loss of benefits. On the other hand, an employer may escape liability for alleged discrimination by a supervisor if no tangible job action was taken against the employee who was the subject of the alleged discrimination, so long as the employer provided a means of redress and the employee failed to take advantage of the opportunities the employer provided.[5] If the harassing behavior was not committed by a supervisor but by a coworker, then the employer may defend itself by showing that the employee failed to demonstrate that it knew or should have known of the harassment or, if it had notice, that it took immediate and corrective action.

Furthermore, for purposes of employment, discrimination on the basis of pregnancy is considered discrimination on the basis of sex. It is a violation of Title VII to deny a woman employment because she is currently pregnant or might become pregnant, or to terminate her employment because she is pregnant.[6] Moreover, if an employee requests leave because of pregnancy or childbirth, employers are urged to check whether the request falls within the Family and Medical Leave Act, which allows up to 12 weeks of unpaid leave for the birth of a child, or other applicable law. Employers should also consult the laws in their states or municipalities for other laws covering sex discrimination and pregnancy.

Disability

Title I of the Americans with Disabilities Act[7] (ADA) prohibits discrimination[8] against qualified individuals with disabilities.[9] On September 25, 2008, President George W. Bush signed into law the ADA Amendments Act of 2008 (ADAAA).[10] The ADAAA took effect on January 1, 2009.[11] The definition of a disability under the ADA, although seemingly simple, was the subject of extensive discussion by courts and fair employment agencies. In brief, the ADA defines a person with a disability as an individual who has a physical or mental impairment that substantially limits a major life activity (or has a record of an impairment or is regarded as having an impairment). The ADAAA expands the scope of individuals covered by the ADA by providing that an "episodic" impairment or impairment "in remission" will constitute a disability if the impairment, when active, would substantially limit a major life activity.[12] The ADAAA sets forth a nonexclusive list of "major life activities," including "caring for oneself, performing manual tasks, seeing, hearing, eating, sleeping, walking, standing, lifting, bending, speaking, breathing, learning, reading, concentrating, thinking, communicating, and working."[13]

The ADAAA further expands the definition of "major life activities" to include "the operation of a major bodily function," including, but not limited to, "functions of the immune system, normal cell growth, digestive, bowel, bladder, neurological, brain, respiratory, circulatory, endocrine, and reproductive functions."[14]

Often, an employer will be asked to make a reasonable accommodation for an individual with a disability. A reasonable accommodation is a change in the work environment or in the way things are customarily done that enables an individual with a disability to enjoy equal employment opportunities. Employers must be aware that the ADA prohibits discrimination against qualified individuals with a disability who can perform the essential functions of the position with or without a reasonable accommodation.

Generally, accommodations are made on a case-by-case basis, because the nature and extent of a disabling condition and the requirements of the job will vary. The principal test in selecting a particular type of accommodation is that of effectiveness (i.e., whether the accommodation will enable the person with a disability to perform the essential functions of the position). A reasonable accommodation may include job restructuring, part-time or modified work schedules, or reassignment to a vacant position. An employer should keep in mind, however, that it does not have to provide an accommodation that causes an "undue hardship" (i.e., significant difficulty and expense in providing the accommodation).

If the employee makes a request for a reasonable accommodation, the employer should initiate the "interactive process" in which the employer meets with the employee to discuss the employee's request and available alternatives if the request is too burdensome. Generally, the employer may ask for certain limited information about the disability, such as the nature, severity, and duration of the impairment; the activity that the impairment limits; and the extent to which the impairment limits the employee's ability to perform the activity or activities. In considering a reasonable accommodation, the company does not have to eliminate or reassign an essential function of the position, lower production standards, or create a new job as a reasonable accommodation.

The ADA also prohibits employers from requesting a medical examination of a prospective employee prior to extending an offer of employment. However, an employer may require that an individual submit to a medical examination after the job offer has been extended as a condition of employment, as long as the employer requires all new employees to the position to submit to an examination, keeps the results confidential, and does not use the results to discriminate on the basis of a disability.

As with other fair employment laws, several states and localities have disability laws, many of which may be different in their scope and coverage than the ADA.[15]

According to the Equal Employment Opportunity Commission (EEOC), healthcare is the largest industry in the United States economy.[16] The EEOC further notes that while healthcare workers are "committed to promoting health through treatment and care for the sick and injured, healthcare workers, ironically, confront perhaps a greater range of significant workplace hazards than workers in any other sector."[17] Such workplace hazards include airborne and bloodborne infectious diseases, sharps injuries, back injuries, and latex injuries. In addition, the work may be physically demanding and mentally stressful.[18]

Due to the many workplace hazards in this industry, the ADA is especially pertinent for healthcare workers and employees.[19] Moreover, due to the fact that facilities that offer healthcare services often operate 24 hours a day, seven days a week, shift work is common among healthcare workers, many of whom may work part-time or hold more than one job. Thus, despite the fact the ADA is the same for all industries, the healthcare industry often presents unique challenges for employers and employees in connection with the ADA.[20]

For example, the ADA's protections cover applicants and employees but not independent contractors. Oftentimes, healthcare workers are referred to as independent contractors when placed through temporary or staffing agencies. However, healthcare employers should be mindful that designating a worker as an "independent contractor" or by some other title is not determinative of that individual's status as an employee or nonemployee for purposes of the ADA.[21]

Another example of an issue often encountered in the healthcare field is under what circumstances may an employer bar a healthcare worker from employment for safety reasons. The EEOC has observed,

> healthcare employers oversee workplaces that raise unique safety questions and concerns. Various care settings may involve invasive procedures, exposure to body fluids or bio-hazardous materials, car-

ing for immune-compromised patients, and making specific assessments and determinations according to medical protocols, sometimes in a fast-paced setting. Errors may result in health or safety consequences for the patient, while at the same time demanding duties or exposure to illness may pose health or safety consequences for the healthcare worker. For these reasons, health or safety risks posed by the disability of an applicant or employee may be of particular concern to healthcare employers.[22]

An employer may exclude an applicant or an employee from the workplace due to a disability under the ADA if that individual is a direct threat to health or safety. "Direct threat" is defined as a significant risk or substantial harm to the individual or others in the workplace that cannot be reduced or eliminated through reasonable accommodation."[23] An individualized determination, taking several factors into account, must be made prior to rejecting an applicant or removing an employee on the basis of being a direct threat.[24]

Religion

Federal law under Title VII prohibits discrimination based on religion, and it also imposes an affirmative duty upon an employer to reasonably accommodate an applicant's and employee's religious beliefs, observances, and practices, unless the requested accommodation would cause an undue hardship to the employer's business. Additionally, many states and municipalities have laws containing provisions that address religious accommodation in the workplace.

Although, in general, an employer does not have to bear more than a minimal cost to accommodate an employee's religious need, in practice, responding to requests for religious accommodation can often be difficult. For instance, if an employee requests time off for a religious reason and this request creates a scheduling conflict, the employer should attempt to accommodate the request by finding a voluntary substitute or arranging a flexible work schedule, although an employer may not discriminate against one employee to satisfy the religious accommodation request of another. Similarly, if an employee requests a religious accommodation from performing a certain task, the employer generally should attempt to accommodate the request, unless the request consists of a major portion of the employee's work. Employers often face difficult questions about accommodating an employee's request to engage in religious practices during the workday. Again, the question is whether the request infringes upon the workplace and the rights of other employees or whether the request may be accommodated with little or no cost.

Age

The Age Discrimination in Employment Act[25] (ADEA) prohibits employers from discriminating against persons age 40 years or older because of their age. The ADEA protects employees in all aspects of employment, including hiring, promotion, and discharge. The general question in an age discrimination case is whether age was a "determining factor" in the employment decision. At issue is how the complaining party's performance and treatment compared to younger, similarly situated employees and the reasons offered by the employer for the challenged action.

Additionally, employers should take care to avoid making comments that indicate a bias against older workers as such "anecdotal" evidence can form the basis for an actionable complaint. As with all fair employment practices laws, employers should check their state and local laws, which may also prohibit discrimination on the basis of age.

State and Local Protections

Although federal law prohibiting discrimination is quite extensive, federal law does not ban certain forms of workplace behavior, such as discrimination based on sexual orientation or marital status. However, several states and municipalities have enacted laws banning discriminatory conduct in these areas. Similarly, many states and localities have enacted laws prohibiting discrimination because of a criminal record or recreational activities. In general, an employer is advised to check the laws in the employer's state and municipality regarding questions in these areas.

Sexual Orientation

Title VII's prohibition against discrimination because of sex prohibits employment discrimination on the basis of gender, but it does not cover claims on the basis of sexual orientation (e.g., homosexuality). However, at least 17 states (California, Connecticut, Hawaii, Illinois, Maine, Maryland, Massachusetts, Minnesota, Nevada, New Hampshire, New Jersey, New Mexico, New York, Rhode Island, Vermont, Washington, and Wisconsin) and the District of Columbia[26] have laws prohibiting discrimination based upon sexual orientation, as do several municipalities, including New York City[27] and San Francisco.[28]

Marital Status

Federal law does not prohibit an employer from using marital status as a factor in making employment decisions, as long as the employer applies this factor in the same fashion to all employees, whether male or female. Again, though, several states and localities have passed fair employment laws prohibiting an employer from using an employee's marital status as a factor in employment. Similarly, federal law does not prohibit nepotism laws, which are laws that either favor or disfavor the hiring of family members of current employees. These policies must be scrutinized, however, to ensure that they are not proxies to exclude women or members of minority groups.

Criminal Record

Several, if not most, states have enacted laws prohibiting an employer from discriminating against an employee on the basis of an arrest or conviction. These laws restrict an employer's ability to request and use an individual's arrest or conviction record as a condition of employment particularly where the basis for conviction does not reasonably relate to the job sought. In general, employers may not inquire about prior arrests, but under certain circumstances may inquire about prior convictions when they are job-related. In the healthcare context, laws governing prior arrests and convictions can vary, but in almost all cases the laws governing this area are more relaxed to permit healthcare institutions flexibility to avoid having employees with certain types of convictions (e.g., violent crimes) working with certain patient populations (e.g., children). Indeed, some jurisdictions have background check procedures that must be followed prior to hiring a new employee who will work in the healthcare field.

Recreational Activities

Several states have enacted statutes prohibiting discrimination against employees for off-duty conduct. The general thrust of the statutes is to prohibit employers from discriminating against an employee for engaging in certain types of lawful conduct outside of the workplace and during nonworking hours. Conduct covered by these statutes may include political activities, use of consumable products (such as alcohol and tobacco), recreational and leisure activities, and membership in a union.

Affirmative Action/Federal Contractor Requirements

Federal affirmative action requirements are based on Executive Order 11246, issued by President Johnson in 1965, which requires all businesses with substantial federal government contracts to take affirmative action to ensure that all individuals have an equal opportunity for employment, without regard to race, color, religion, sex, national origin, disability, or status as a Vietnam-era or special disabled veteran.[29] Many hospitals and health systems are considered federal contractors based on their receipt of federal monies, usually in the form of research grants.

The US Department of Labor's Office of Federal Contract Compliance Programs (OFCCP) is responsible for enforcement of federal affirmative action requirements. In this regard, the OFCCP has the authority to conduct evaluations to determine whether a contractor is in compliance with such requirements by monitoring nondiscriminatory hiring and employment practices and taking affirmative steps to ensure that such hiring and employment practices are maintained without regard to race, color, religion, sex, or national origin.[30] The OFCCP has taken the position that healthcare organizations that provide services to federal employees will be subject to its jurisdiction. The OFCCP requires a contractor, as a condition of having a federal contract, to engage in a self-analysis to discern the existence of any barriers to equal employment opportunity. A contractor in violation of affirmative action mandates may have its contracts canceled, terminated, or suspended in whole or in part, and the contractor may be declared ineligible for future government contracts.[31]

In December 2000, the US Department of Labor issued new regulations that changed the format and content of affirmative action plans and altered the manner in which federal contractors must provide information.[32] Nonconstruction contractors with 50 or more employees and government contracts of $50,000 or more are required, under Executive Order 11246, to develop and implement a written affirmative action plan for each establishment. The plan must identify those areas, if any, in the contractor's workforce that reflect utilization of women and minorities.[33] The regulations define "underutilization" as having fewer minorities or women in a particular job group than would reasonably be expected by their availability. When determining availability of women and minorities, contractors consider, among other factors, the presence of minorities and women having requisite skills in an area in which the contractor can reasonably recruit.[34] Based on this analysis and the availability of qualified individuals, the contractor must then establish goals to reduce or overcome the underutilization, which may include expanded efforts in outreach, recruitment, training, and other activities to increase the pool of qualified minorities and females.[35]

Individual Employment Rights

Whistle-Blowers

Whistle-blowing is a term often used to describe an employee's dissemination of information critical of, or reflecting adversely on, an employer, typically for the purpose of correcting or preventing some violation of the law or other harm.[36] Over a dozen federal laws attempt to protect whistle-blowing employees from retaliation in many areas of private sector activity where public health and safety are at stake.[37]

Of particular importance for healthcare facilities are the antiretaliation provisions of the False Claims Act (FCA),[38] which prohibits any person or company from filing a false claim against the federal government. The FCA is intended to deter companies from fraudulently procuring federal funds.[39] Under the FCA, a private citizen may file suit against an alleged violator on behalf of the US government. This is referred to as a "qui tam" action, and the private citizen is the "qui tam relator" or "whistle-blower."[40] Under the FCA, any employee who is discharged, demoted, suspended, or otherwise adversely affected in the terms and conditions of employment by his or her employer because of lawful acts done by the employee in furtherance of an action under FCA, including investigation or initiation of, testimony for, or assistance in an action, is entitled to appropriate relief to make that employee whole, including backpay and other damages.

The FCA has been referred to as the "centerpiece of the healthcare antifraud effort."[41] Its provisions have been applied not only to situations involving misrepresentations of the facts surrounding the services for which federal payment is requested, but also to alleged violations of Medicare and Medicaid quality of care requirements.[42]

Additionally, many states have enacted whistle-blower protection legislation in recent years, often specifically addressed to the healthcare industry. For example, the New York State legislature recently expanded the scope of its general whistle-blower protection law to specifically prohibit a healthcare employer from taking retaliatory action against an employee because of that employee's threat to disclose, or actual disclosure of, a practice of the employer that the employee reasonably believes constitutes improper quality of patient care, or because of an employee's refusal to participate in any activity, policy, or practice that the employee in good faith reasonably believes constitutes improper quality of patient care.[43]

In order to offer employees an outlet for internal whistle-blowing activities, an effective compliance and reporting program should be instituted. Such a program can help identify weaknesses in internal systems and management, demonstrate to employees and the community the employer's commitment to obeying the law, create a centralized source for the distribution of information on fraud and false claims, develop better communications between management and employees, and enhance the ability to initiate immediate and appropriate corrective action.[44]

Fair Credit Reporting Act

Employee background checks should be considered an essential element in the hiring process of all healthcare employees. A thorough background check can reveal instances of dishonesty, incompetence, and unreliability, and under certain circumstances limit an employer's liability from negligent hiring lawsuits.[45] However, in certain situations an employer's background check may subject it to burdensome federal and state regulations. The employer must take special care to either comply with applicable requirements or take actions to ensure that the requirements are not applicable.

The Fair Credit Reporting Act (FCRA)[46] governs the collection, dissemination, and use of an individual's credit information. The statute has specific provisions in regard to the furnishing and use of consumer reports for employment purposes.[47] Its main impact on hospitals and healthcare employers governs the acquisition of background checks on current and potential employees. In most cases, for a covered employer legally to receive background information on an employee or applicant from a third party, such as a credit reporting agency, that employer must comply with the comprehensive regulations set forth under the FCRA.

Generally, in order to acquire reports on employees, the employer must meet special eligibility, disclosure, and use requirements. This includes certifying to the credit reporting agency that it is eligible to receive such reports, making a disclosure of the background check to employees and applicants, and following specific procedures before taking adverse actions against employees. If an adverse action, such as firing or refusing to hire an employee, is based in whole or in part on a consumer credit report, the employer must provide the individual a copy of the report and a statement of one's rights under the FCRA.

If an employer wishes to avoid the onerous requirements imposed under the FCRA, it may limit its background checks to information that it obtains directly from public entities, without the assistance of a third party. In general, information that is obtained by an employer directly from a federal, state, or local record repository is not a "consumer report" subject to FCRA regulations, because the repository (such as a courthouse or a state law enforcement agency) is not normally a "consumer reporting agency." Similarly, if an employer desires to use its own personnel to check an applicant's references or past job performance, the provisions of the FCRA may not apply.[48]

Healthcare employers also should be aware of a recent interpretation of the FCRA which may affect an employer's obligation to investigate claims of sexual harassment and discrimination.[49] In a series of staff opinion letters, the Federal Trade Commission has interpreted the FCRA to apply to an employer's use of a third party to investigate employee sexual harassment and discrimination claims.[50] This interpretation, although not binding on the courts, would make the use of a human resource consultant or law firm to investigate such claims subject to the FCRA's notice and compliance procedures.[51] This obligation would create an obvious tension between an employer's duty to fully investigate and keep confidential workplace discrimination claims, and employee rights under the FCRA. Although amendments limiting the scope of this legislation may be forthcoming, the simplest way to avoid these potential requirements may be to investigate claims internally.

Failure to comply with the FCRA may result in state or federal enforcement actions, as well as private litigation. In addition, any person who knowingly and willfully obtains a consumer report under false pretenses may face criminal prosecution. In order to help safeguard against liability under the FCRA, an employer should either avoid adopting practices that would trigger the requirements of the FCRA or institute reasonable procedures in order to ensure compliance. Generally, if a company can establish that it has maintained reasonable procedures to ensure compliance, it can set forth an affirmative defense to liability.

Employee Polygraph Protection Act

The Employee Polygraph Protection Act of 1988 generally makes it unlawful for an employer to directly or indirectly require, request, suggest, or cause any employee or prospective employee to take or submit to any lie detector test.[52] Violators of the act can be assessed civil penalties of up to $10,000 and incur civil damages in suits brought by affected employees. However, for a healthcare employer, numerous exceptions may apply.

The act does not apply with respect to any state or local government, or any political subdivision of a state or local governmental employer.[53] This exemption has been successfully used by a hospital whose administration was appointed by public officials, its board of trustees.[54] Additionally, a limited exemption exists for polygraph tests administered in connection with an ongoing investigation involving economic loss or injury to an employer's business (such as theft, embezzlement, or misappropriation), provided that the employee had access to the property that is the subject of the investigation, that there is a reasonable suspicion that the employee was involved in the incident, and that certain pretest notifications are provided to the employee.[55] The economic loss must relate to the business of the employer; therefore, a theft committed by one employee against another employee of the same employer would not satisfy the requirement.[56]

Another exemption exists in regard to drug security, drug theft, or drug diversion investigations.[57] Employers authorized to manufacture, distribute, or dispense certain controlled substances can administer polygraph tests if the test is administered to a prospective employee who would have direct access to the controlled substances, or if the test is administered in connection with an ongoing investigation of misconduct involving the controlled substances and the employee had access to the property that is the subject of the investigation.

WARN Act

The Worker Adjustment and Retraining Notification Act (WARN) was passed by Congress in 1988.[58] WARN requires certain employers to provide notice to affected employees, their union (if any), and state and local officials, 60 calendar days in advance of a plant closing or mass layoff.[59] Advance notice is required to provide workers and their families with time to adjust to the prospective loss of employment, to seek and obtain alternative jobs, and, if necessary, to enter skill training or retraining that will allow these workers to successfully compete in the job market. WARN also provides for notice to state dislocated worker units, so that dislocated worker assistance can be provided.[60] In addition to WARN, state and local laws may place additional notice requirements upon employers planning a mass layoff or plant closing. The penalties for failing to comply with WARN's notice requirements include up to 60 days' backpay and civil penalties of up to $500 for each day of the violation.

An employer with more than 100 employees may be subject to WARN's requirements. WARN can be triggered when there is either a permanent or temporary closing of a single site of employment or at one or more facilities or operating units that affect 50 or more employees during any 30-day period. A mass layoff is one that results in an employment loss at a single site of employment during any 30-day period for (a) at least 33% of the employees and at least 50 employees, or (b) at least 500 employees.

WARN does contain exemptions from the notice requirements and, in some cases, provisions that allow for reduction in the amount of notice required.[61] The Act provides for a shortened notice period under a faltering company exception when the employer was actively seeking capital, and that capital, if obtained, would have enabled it to avoid or postpone a closing, and the employer reasonably believed that giving the 60-day notice would have jeopardized its opportunity to obtain the capital. Other justifications for providing shortened notice may arise when unforeseeable business circumstances preclude such notice,[62] or when a natural disaster is the cause of the shortened notice. A complete exemption from the notice requirement is provided when the closing or layoff constitutes a strike or lockout not intended to evade the requirements of the act, or when the closing or layoff is the result of the completion of a particular project or undertaking, and the affected employees were hired with the understanding that their employment was limited to the duration of that project or undertaking.[63]

Wage and Hour Laws

The Fair Labor Standards Act (FLSA) establishes minimum wage, overtime, and record-keeping requirements for most public and private employers. However, many employees are exempted from the FLSA's requirements. Difficult issues often arise in determining whether an employee qualifies as exempt under the FLSA. This chapter addresses some common issues that arise under the FLSA, particularly in the healthcare setting.

The FLSA's requirements apply only to employees, not to independent contractors. It is therefore very important to understand whether a worker is an independent contractor or an employee. Courts generally conduct a very fact-specific inquiry on this issue and consider five factors to determine whether an independent contractor is in reality an employee: (1) the degree of control exerted by the alleged employer over the worker (e.g., who sets the worker's hours, provides tools and working materials, uniforms, transportation, expenses, etc.); (2) the worker's opportunity and risk for profit and loss; (3) the worker's investment in the business; (4) the permanence of the working relationship; and (5) the degree of skill required to perform the work.[64] Although a written consulting agreement may constitute evidence of contractor status, it is not determinative.

Many healthcare institutions rely on the services of volunteers. Under some circumstances, however, a hospital could incur liability under the FLSA for failing to compensate volunteers at least the minimum wage. Courts typically employ an "economic reality" test and consider a "true" volunteer to be one who donates his or her services to a charitable, educational, or religious organization and performs a service normally thought of as voluntary or charitable.[65] A volunteer ordinarily must not be displacing an employee or performing services that are customarily performed by an employee. Thus, although a traditional "candy striper" would meet the test of a volunteer, a person who works in a hospital's gift shop may not be a true volunteer.

Minimum Wages and Overtime

Generally, under the FLSA, employers must pay not less than the federal minimum wage for each hour worked by an employee.[66] (Note, however, that state law may set a higher minimum wage rate than that established under the FLSA. Employees in such states must receive the higher rate established by applicable state law.) Under the FLSA, an employee's workweek spans seven consecutive 24-hour periods. Under certain circumstances, an employer may average an employee's earnings over the workweek, and if the average hourly earnings for nonovertime hours equal at least the minimum wage, the minimum wage requirement is considered satisfied for that week. Of course, hourly wages below the minimum in one workweek may not be offset by wages above the minimum in another.

Under the FLSA, a nonexempt employee also must be paid one and one-half times the employee's regular hourly rate for hours worked over the maximum hour standard.[67] The maximum hour standard, and in turn an employee's overtime compensation, is generally figured on a weekly basis. For most employees, the maximum number of hours an employee may work in one week without being paid overtime is 40 hours.[68] At least one court has found a hospital jointly liable for overtime worked by a temporary nurse's assistant, even though the nurse's assistant surpassed the 40-hour work overtime threshold by working at one hospital through three different employment agencies.[69]

For certain hospital and healthcare workers, overtime pay may be calculated on either a 7-day, 40-hour workweek, or on a 14-day, 80-hour basis. Specifically, hospitals or institutions primarily engaged in the care of resident patients may use the 14-day work period to calculate overtime compensation if an agreement or understanding exists between the employer and employee prior to performance of the work. Overtime compensation is paid for hours worked in excess of 80 hours during the 14-day period and in excess of 8 hours in any work day.[70]

White-Collar Exemptions

There are many statutory exemptions under the FLSA, the most common of which are those that apply to certain executive, administrative, and professional employees, and certain outside sales employees, among others (the so-called "white-collar" exemptions). The executive, administrative, professional, and computer professional exemptions are discussed here.

An exemption allows an employer to avoid the FLSA's overtime pay requirements with respect to the exempt employee. For any of the white-collar exemptions to apply (with the exception of computer professionals), the employee in question must satisfy various "tests" under the FLSA. First, the employee must be paid a predetermined weekly salary that does not vary based on the quantity or quality of the employee's work (the "salary basis" test). Deductions or docking of pay for disciplinary reasons, for poor performance, for partial day absences, and for other reasons may jeopardize an employee's exempt status because such deductions are inconsistent with the salary basis test.[71]

An employee's duties also must be considered to ensure that they are in accord with one or more of the white-collar exemptions. For example, to satisfy the exemption for executive employees, the employee generally must manage an enterprise or department, regularly direct two or more employees, and his or her primary duties must relate directly to management policies or general business aspects, such as interviewing, selecting, training, directing, recommending employees for promotions, hiring, firing, disciplining, or delegating work, among others.[72] Officers and high-ranking employees of a hospital or health system ordinarily will meet the requirements of an exempt executive employee.

To satisfy the requirements for the administrative employee exemption, an employee generally must, in addition to the salary basis test, primarily perform work related to management policies or general business operations, and exercise discretion and independent judgment in the performance of his or her duties. In addition, an exempt administrative employee must have the authority to make independent choices without immediate supervision.[73] Examples of employees who generally qualify as administrative employees are executive assistants, department heads, and managers.

Employees who satisfy the FLSA's white-collar exemption for professionals generally include doctors, registered nurses, certain registered (or certified) medical technologists,[74] and other highly skilled employees who spend most of their time doing work requiring advanced knowledge that is acquired by a specialized course of study. An exempt professional generally must, in addition to being paid on a salary basis, perform original and creative duties in work requiring scientific or specialized study and the exercise of independent judgment.[75] One court of appeals has ruled that home care nurses are exempt from the FLSA's overtime provisions as professionals,[76] while another has ruled that physician assistants and nurse practitioners are not.[77] The latter decision deferred to an informal interpretive statement by the Department of Labor that the positions of "physician assistant" and "nurse practitioner" were not exempt, "despite higher barriers to entry and the increasing sophistication of their practice, [both physician assistants and nurse practitioners] are nascent professions in need of the FLSA's protection against the threat of the evil of overwork as well as underpay."[78]

The computer professional exemption applies to highly skilled employees, generally not computer technicians or operators. Although computer professionals usually have a bachelor's degree or higher, no specific degree is required. To qualify for the computer professional exemption, an employee must be highly skilled in computer systems analysis, programming, or related software functions, and must primarily plan, schedule, and coordinate activities "required to develop systems to solve complex business, scientific or engineering problems of the employer or the employer's customers" in order to qualify for the exemption.[79] In addition, a senior or lead computer programmer may qualify as an exempt employee if that programmer manages the work of two or more other programmers and that the programmer's recommendations as to hiring, firing, promotion, or other employment status decisions as to other programmers is given "particular weight."[80]

Whether an employee is exempt from the requirements of the FLSA is not always easy to determine. An employee's job title alone does not make the employee exempt. Rather, an employer must examine the employee's actual job duties and individual circumstances. The FLSA's exemptions are narrowly construed, and the employer bears the burden of proving that its employees are exempt. Should the determination that an employee is exempt be made erroneously, backpay and penalties could be assessed by the Department of Labor.

Joint Employment Under the FLSA

An important consideration in an organized delivery system is the effect of a finding of "joint employment" under the FLSA. Two or more employers may be considered "joint employers" under the FLSA, which would require aggregating all hours worked for the two employers for purposes of the act's overtime pay requirements. Aggregation of all hours worked for two employers may dramatically increase the joint employers' liability for overtime pay for affected employees.[81]

The determination of whether an individual's employment by two or more employers constitutes joint employment for purposes of the FLSA depends on all the facts of a particular case. If two or more employers are acting "entirely independently of each other and are completely disassociated" with respect to an individual's employment, each employer may disregard all work performed for the other in considering its obligations under the FLSA.[82] However, if the facts establish that the employee is employed jointly by two or more employers, that is, that employment by one employer is not completely disassociated from employment by the other employer(s), all of the employee's work for all of the joint employers during the workweek is considered as one employment for purposes of the Act.[83]

The effect of a finding of joint employment of an individual is that all such joint employers are responsible, both individually and jointly, for compliance with all applicable provisions of the FLSA, including overtime, with respect to the individual's entire employment for the particular workweek.[84]

A joint employer relationship generally will be considered to exist (1) where there is an arrangement between the employers to share the employee's services, as, for example, to interchange employees; (2) where one employer is acting directly or indirectly in the interest of another employer in relation to the employee; or (3) where the employers are not "completely disassociated" with respect to the employment of a particular individual and may be deemed to share control of the employee, directly or indirectly, by reason of the fact that one employer controls, is controlled by, or is under common control with the other employer.[85]

For example, assume that an acute care hospital was in negotiations to form a system which would include a not-for-profit parent organization, three acute care facilities, a nursing home, and a for-profit home healthcare organization. The parent corporation would be a separate organization providing administrative services to the hospital and the other facilities. It would own all the shares of stock of the for-profit home healthcare organization; be the sole corporate member of all the not-for-profit organizations, except for the nursing home; appoint the entire boards of directors of the acute care facilities and the home healthcare organization; and have reserve powers for planning, budget approval, capital expenditure approval, and appointment of the CEOs of the affiliated corporations. The system would not plan to interchange employees among the entities. One of the acute care facilities would also have its own executive offices and human resources department and make its own decisions regarding hiring and terms of employment. It would also share a campus with the home healthcare organization, but they would have different CEOs. The home healthcare organization would also make its own hiring decisions regarding hiring and terms of employment, and its employees would not participate in the same pension plan as would employees of the other facilities.

Considering such an example, the Department of Labor opined that certain joint employer relationships existed under the FLSA. "[I]t is our opinion that the parent organization, acute care facility A, acute care facility B, acute care facility C, nursing home and home health care organization must aggregate all hours worked by an individual who worked for more than one unit, since the units are under common control."[86]

Family and Medical Leave Act

The Family and Medical Leave Act of 1993 (FMLA) generally requires private sector employers of 50 or more employees to provide up to 12 workweeks of unpaid, job-protected leave, within any 12-month period, to eligible employees for certain family and medical reasons.[87] Covered employers are also required to maintain eligible employees' preexisting group health insurance coverage during the leave and to restore eligible employees to the same or an equivalent position at the conclusion of the FMLA leave.[88]

To be eligible for FMLA benefits, an employee must:

1. Work for a covered employer
2. Have worked for the employer for at least 12 months
3. Have worked at least 1250 hours for the employer over the previous 12 months
4. Work at a location in the United States or in any territory or possession of the United States where at least 50 employees are employed by the employer at a single worksite, or at multiple worksites within a range of 75 miles.[89]

Eligible employees may be entitled to take FMLA leave for any of the following reasons: the birth and care of a newborn child of the employee; the placement with the employee of a child for adoption or foster care; to care for an immediate family member (spouse, child, or parent) with a serious health condition; or when the employee is unable to work because of his or her own serious health condition.[90]

FMLA Notice Requirements

Both the employer and the employee have notice requirements under the FMLA. Specifically, employees seeking to use FMLA leave are required to provide 30-day advance notice of the need to take FMLA leave when the need is foreseeable and such notice is practicable. The notice from the employee can be verbal. However, the employer may request that employees comply with its customary and usual notice and procedural requirements for requesting leave.[91]

Employers also may require employees to provide medical certification supporting the need for leave because of a serious health condition; second or third medical opinions (at the employer's expense) and periodic recertification; and periodic reports during FMLA leave regarding the employee's status and intent to return to work.[92] Employers also must provide notice to the employee as to whether he or she is eligible for FMLA leave within 2 days of making the eligibility determination and prior to the date the requested leave is to begin.[93]

Other Notable FMLA Provisions

Spouses employed by the same employer are jointly entitled to a combined total of 12 workweeks of family leave for the birth and care of a newborn child, for placement with the employees of a child for adoption or foster care, and to care for a parent who has a serious health condition.[94]

Under some circumstances, employees may take FMLA leave intermittently—which means taking leave in separate blocks of time, or by reducing their normal weekly or daily work schedule.[95]

Although most employees are entitled to be returned to the same or an equivalent position at the conclusion of their FMLA leave, employers can deny job restoration to a salaried employee who is among the highest paid 10% of the employer's workforce, if that person is considered a "key employee." However, this designation must occur at the time the leave is designated.[96]

State Wage and Hour Laws

Although the FLSA imposes no limit on the number of hours an employee may work per day or week, so long as he or she is appropriately compensated for hours worked on a minimum wage and overtime basis, certain states' laws do restrict the number of hours an employee may work per day and per week.[97] Similarly, although the FLSA does not require that an employer provide meal periods for employees, some states' laws do.[98]

Many states have enacted laws dictating when an employer is allowed to withhold or make deductions from an employee's wages. Some typical state laws restrict an employer from withholding or diverting any portion of an employee's wages unless (1) the employer is required to do so under state or federal law (e.g., Social Security or income tax deductions); (2) the employee has given the employer written authorization for the withholding; or (3) there is a reasonable good faith doubt as to the amount of wages set off or amount owed by the employee to the employer.[99]

Other states have enactments that are more strict, prohibiting an employer from making deductions from wages unless it has obtained prior written authorization from the employee, and such deductions are for specific items, as defined by the law.[100] Other states are stricter still, permitting an employer to make only those deductions as are required by law, or expressly authorized in writing by the employee, so long as such deductions are "for the benefit of the employee," such as for group health or life insurance, 401(k) contributions, and union dues.[101] In such states, an employer is prohibited from making wage deductions for spoilage or breakage, cash shortages or losses, or fines or penalties for lateness, misconduct, or quitting without notice.

Some states may also permit an employer to withhold wages from a terminated employee's final paycheck for the value of any property belonging to the employer that is not returned by the employee.[102] However, under no circumstances should any such withholding cause a nonexempt employee's wages to be reduced below the applicable minimum wage for that pay period.

Employers must also consider whether state law requires any particular time for and/or method of payment of wages. For example, some states require wages to be paid no less frequently than monthly, semimonthly, or weekly.[103] Many states also require that terminated employees receive all wages due within a certain number of days following termination of employment.[104]

Many states also regulate the method of payment of employees' wages, such as requiring payments in cash or check, with appropriate time off for employees to cash paychecks. With the increasing popularity of direct deposit of wages by electronic funds transfer, some states also have enacted laws restricting employers from directly depositing the wages of nonexempt employees without the employee's advance written consent.[105]

Employee Benefits in the Healthcare Industry

The range and variety of benefits available to employees of healthcare entities are similar to those available for employees in other industries. For those entities that are tax-exempt organizations,[106] however, special rules and exceptions may apply. Generally, these benefits are principally subject to two comprehensive federal laws: the Employee Retirement Income Security Act of 1974 (ERISA)[107] and the Internal Revenue Code (Code). In recent years, through piecemeal legislation, Congress has added a number of additional requirements for group health plans.[108] Moreover, significant amendments to the Code and ERISA were made by the Consolidated Omnibus Budget Reconciliation Act of 1985 (COBRA), which also has had an impact on group health plans.

Deferred Compensation

Many employees are attracted by the potential retirement benefits offered in the healthcare industry. Those benefits fall into three categories: (1) qualified retirement plans under Section 401(a) of the Code; (2) tax-deferred annuities under Section 403(b) of the Code; and (3) unfunded deferred compensation plans under Section 457 of the Code. The sections contain numerous requirements for participation, vesting, funding, and distributions.

Qualified Retirement Plans

These plans must satisfy specific statutory and extensive regulatory requirements.[109] The two types of plans most often utilized are pension and profit-sharing plans.

A defined benefit pension plan provides participants with a fixed or determinable retirement benefit at normal retirement age, based on a formula set forth in the plan.[110] The formula may provide for a monthly or yearly benefit, which often is based on the participant's length of service and compensation. Employers sponsoring such plans must make minimum and maximum contributions each year in accordance with an actuarial determination.

A money purchase pension plan provides the participant with a fixed contribution each year. The contribution is based on a fixed percentage of annual compensation or a fixed amount per hour, week, or other unit of work, and the employer is obligated to make that contribution regardless of profits. These plans have been less popular in recent years because they guarantee a retirement benefit, or at least a fixed level of contributions.

A defined contribution pension plan, often some form of profit-sharing plan, has become more popular for tax-exempt organizations since 1980, when the Internal Revenue Service determined that they could maintain such plans.[111] Such a plan has individual accounts, and the number of retirement benefits will depend on the value of the account investments upon retirement or termination of employment.

A recently popular variation to this type of plan is the cash or deferred arrangement (CODA) plan, also known as the 401(k) plan, which permits employee salary deferrals on a pretax basis and employer matching contributions, which are usually limited to a percentage of salary reduction. Salary deferrals are capped on an annual basis and are adjusted for cost of living increases on an annual basis. These types of plans usually are designed as participant-directed accounts under ERISA Section 404(c), thereby removing fiduciary liability from employers or their designated fiduciaries who administer the plans. Tax-exempt employer sponsors have only been permitted to offer CODAs since 1997.[112]

The benefits under 401(k) plans for highly compensated employees (HCEs) also are limited by nondiscrimination requirements, which limit HCEs from contributing or matching contributions in excess of a certain percentage of the contributions for nonhighly compensated employees (NHCEs).[113]

Tax Deferred Annuities Under Section 403(b)

Prior to 1997, an alternative similar to the 401(k) plan was the 403(b) plan, which could be adopted by tax-exempt organizations only.[114] These types of retirement plans contain similar participation, vesting, distribution, and other requirements as for qualification under Section 401(a) of the Code.

The Economic Growth and Tax Relief Reconciliation Act of 2001 (EGTRRA)[115] contains a number of reforms that enhance the benefits provided under all types of plans. These include increases in the annual deferred contribution and defined benefit contribution and compensation limits, elective deferral limits, and a new provision for catch-up contributions for individuals over age 50.

Unfunded Deferred Compensation Plans

Unfunded deferred compensation plans (or Section 457 plans) are permitted by the Revenue Act of 1978, which was codified as Section 457 of the Code. In 1986, Congress extended to private tax-exempt organizations the ability to maintain Section 457 plans.[116] There are two types of plans—eligible[117] and ineligible.[118] Although an eligible Section 457 plan can offer immediate 100% vesting, the unfunded status of the plan makes its benefits susceptible to economic downturns, which could result in nonpayment of benefits.

Welfare Benefits

The term welfare benefit plan generally refers to any employee benefit plan that does not provide for deferral of contributions.[119] These plans are heavily regulated by the Code and ERISA.

In recent years, other laws, especially the Health Insurance Portability and Accountability Act (HIPAA), have had serious impact on the administration of these plans by, among other things, implementing privacy and related requirements with respect to personal health information of plan participants.[120]

Favorable tax treatment for employees (e.g., nonincludible income) under the Code and avoiding incurring excise taxes are of primary importance to the tax-exempt organization. Accordingly, a welfare benefit plan must abide by various rules under the Code.[121] Additionally, ERISA imposes reporting and disclosure requirements, fiduciary duties, and claims administration procedures on employers sponsoring such plans.[122] Most welfare benefit plans are subject to ERISA because of the broad definition of the term "welfare benefit plan,"[123] but certain benefits are excepted.[124] A group health plan subject to ERISA also must comply with ERISA Parts 6 (COBRA) and 7 (portability, access, and renewability requirements under HIPAA).

The specific types of welfare benefit plans subject to ERISA's requirements that most often are adopted by employers are as follows:

- Group term life insurance (Section 79 of the Code)
- Health and disability benefit plans (Sections 105 and 106 of the Code, and for group health plans, COBRA, HIPAA, Medical Secondary Payor Requirements, and related laws cited in footnote 88 above)
- Disability income plans (Section 105 of the Code)
- Educational assistance benefits (Section 117 of the Code for tuition reimbursement programs and Section 127 for educational assistance plans)
- Group legal services plans (Section 120 of the Code)
- Cafeteria plans (Section 125 of the Code)
- Dependent care assistance programs (Section 129 of the Code)
- Fringe benefits (Section 132 of the Code)
- Adoption assistance programs (Section 137 of the Code)
- Long-term care insurance (Sections 7702B and 106 of the Code)

Funding arrangements similar to those utilized for non-tax-exempt organizations include the following:

- Voluntary employee benefit association (VEBA) (Section 501(a)(9) of the Code)
- Supplemental unemployment compensation benefits trust (Section 501(a)(17) of the Code)
- Section 501(c)(3) supporting organizations for charities
- Grant or trusts (Sections 671–677 of the Code)

Related Significant Legal Requirements

In order to qualify or couple with various sections of the Code and/or ERISA, health industry employers must be aggregated under Section 414(b) and (c) (parent–subsidiary group and brother–sister group of employers) of the Code (incorporating Code Section 1563 with respect to "controlled groups"). The Internal Revenue Service has taken the position that nonstock corporations are subject to Sections 414(b) and (c).[125] Similar aggregation rules apply under Section 414(m) of the Code (service organizations), Section 414(n) (leased employees), and Section 414(o) (all other potential employee benefit requirements). Aggregation would result in treating employers of the aggregated employees as if they were a single employer for (1) nondiscrimination requirements and (2) funding requirements.

The administration of employee benefit plans is also subject to civil rights in employment laws, including the Age Discrimination in Employment Act, Title VI and VII of the Civil Rights Act of 1964, the Americans with Disabilities Act, the Family and Medical Leave Act, the Rehabilitation Act of 1973, and the Equal Pay Act.

Privacy Issues in the Workplace

Few areas of the law have undergone such significant change in recent years as the area of workplace privacy. This change has been driven in large part by the technological advances that have taken place in our day-to-day society. Previous generations simply were not faced with questions relating to the privacy of computer use, electronic mail, telephone and voice mail, the Internet, and the like. At the same time, it has become increasingly important for employers, including organized delivery systems, to know as much as possible about their employees and prospective employees in light of reports of increasing workplace violence and widening avenues of employer liability. Employers must seek to balance their legitimate business interest in obtaining sufficient information about an employee or applicant against an employee's right to privacy. In an organized delivery system, the significant responsible entities, such as hospitals and nursing homes, owe their patients the balancing of these competing interests.

The issue of employee privacy arises in a variety of contexts within the employment relationship, from background checks of applicants to employee surveillance and monitoring of employee communications. The legal standards employers must follow depend on a number of factors, including the nature of the activity at issue and the work environment. Employee privacy rights may arise from a number of sources: federal and/or state constitutions, federal and/or state statutes, and the common law. For example, the Fourth Amendment to the US Constitution extends certain privacy rights to government employees in the public workplace, but not to employees of the private sector. Some state constitutions also provide additional privacy protections.[126]

In addition, federal and state statutes give certain privacy protections to employees. For example, the Omnibus Control and Safe Streets Act, as amended by the Electronic Communications Privacy Act (ECPA),[127] restricts such conduct as employer monitoring of employee telephone calls. Finally, a number of common-law torts that address violations of employee privacy, including intrusion upon seclusion and public disclosure of private facts, are recognized in some states. All of these different protections combine and overlap to provide varying degrees of employee protection depending on the nature of the employer, the state in which the workplace is located, and the kind of conduct at issue.

Privacy in the Hiring Process

Privacy issues may arise even before the commencement of the employment relationship. Employers have an obvious need to investigate the qualifications and trustworthiness of potential employees for a number of reasons, not the least of which is the need to avoid potential liability to third parties for the tort of negligent hiring or retention. At the same time, however, this need for information is tempered by the danger of potential liability for claims of invasion of privacy or violation of other federal or state protections.

As part of the hiring process, employers should require all applicants to complete an application form. The application should elicit information relating to past employment, references, education, licenses, and criminal convictions (being mindful that some state laws may restrict this line of questioning and may limit an employer's ability to use a criminal conviction as an absolute bar to employment). The application materials also should include a written consent and release of liability allowing an employer to contact former employers and references and to conduct a background check. Inclusion of a statement regarding the consequences of the falsification of an application and the failure to provide complete responses, as well as an affirmation of the truthfulness of the application, will leave little doubt in the applicant's mind that the employer will conduct a thorough background check. Employers should verify the information provided and create a written record that demonstrates verification and details the results of any investigation.

Generally, in order for an employer to legally receive background information from a third party, the employer must comply with the provisions of the Fair Credit Reporting Act (FCRA).[128] The FCRA has specific provisions with regard to the use of consumer reports for employment purposes. A consumer report includes any written, oral, or other communication of information by a consumer reporting agency bearing on a consumer's creditworthiness, credit standing, character, general reputation, personal characteristics, or mode of living that is used for employment purposes. In order to acquire a consumer report an employer must meet certain eligibility, disclosure, and use requirements. It must certify to the reporting agency that it is eligible to receive such reports, must make a clear and conspicuous disclosure to the employee or applicant, and receive written authorization from the employee or applicant. In addition, before taking adverse action, the employer must follow specific procedures such as the provision of a copy of the report and additional disclosure of rights to the employee. Additional notice requirements must be followed when an employer procures an "investigative consumer report," which the FCRA defines as a consumer report in which the information is obtained through personal interviews with neighbors, friends, associates, or other acquaintances of the consumer. As a result of the complex requirements of the FCRA, employers should consult with counsel to ensure compliance.[129]

Electronic Surveillance and Monitoring of Employees

Privacy issues continue after the employment relationship begins. Advancements in technology provide both increased opportunity and added responsibility for employers to monitor the activities of their employees. One avenue for employee monitoring is video surveillance. Silent video surveillance (recorded audio on a videotape may run afoul of the federal and state wiretap laws, as detailed below) usually is considered lawful when the employees or others under surveillance have no reasonable expectation of privacy, such as when cameras are placed in hallways, lunchrooms, and other public areas. However, employers are well advised to take care in conducting this type of monitoring, because it may raise constitutional issues for public employers and invasion of privacy issues for private employers. Monitoring restrooms or locker rooms, for example, absent extremely unusual circumstances and specific warnings that the areas are under video surveillance, likely will lead to claims of invasion of privacy or intentional infliction of emotional distress. Unionized employers may be obligated to bargain over the issue of employee surveillance.[130]

In addition to video surveillance, employers increasingly monitor the electronic communications of their employees. Although a number of states have laws that limit monitoring of employee communications, including criminal statutes, electronic and telephone surveillance also are governed by the Federal Omnibus Crime Control and Safe Streets Act, as amended by the ECPA. The ECPA prohibits the intentional interception, use, and disclosure of oral, electronic, and wire communications, which includes communication via telephone, voice mail, and electronic mail.

There are a number of exceptions to the ECPA. For example, the "consent" exception allows monitoring when at least one party to the communication consents, either expressly or implicitly (note, however, that some state laws require two-party consent). Because the issue of implied consent is very fact-specific, it is safest to obtain written consent from the employee prior to monitoring. The "service provider" exception allows an employee of the owner of a communication system to monitor communications if it is done within the normal course of his employment and the interception occurs as a result of necessary activity or in order to maintain and protect the rights and property of the service provider. The "business extension" excludes monitoring with telephone equipment or components furnished to the user by a provider in the ordinary course of business and which are being used by the subscriber in the ordinary course of business. This exception potentially allows an employer to monitor an employee's telephone calls through the use of a standard telephone extension provided in the ordinary course of business.

The ECPA also protects "stored" communications (as opposed to communications in transit, as discussed above). However, the ECPA provides a broad exception that allows employers access to stored communications if accessed pursuant to authorization by the entity providing the service. This exception should allow employers to access e-mail on computer systems provided by the employer.

Although monitoring of an employee's Internet use or computer files does not necessarily fall within the protective scope of the ECPA, there may be restrictions based on state laws and common-law privacy claims. To minimize claims, employers should reduce employees' expectation of privacy through a clear and well-publicized Internet and e-mail policy, and be consistent in exercising their right to manage the workplace in a legitimate, business-related manner.

Searches in the Workplace

On occasion, a healthcare employer may wish to search employer-provided lockers, desks, offices, or even personal items brought into the workplace. Because the Fourth Amendment's prohibition on unreasonable searches and seizures applies to government agencies and officers, public entities face some restrictions on their right to conduct workplace searches. Private employers, however, may conduct searches (if not acting in conjunction with police or government agents) without violating the US Constitution. However, employers still must be careful, because state constitutions, statutes, and common law may limit the nature and scope of permissible searches.

Liability for employer searches turns in large part on the reasonableness of the employee's expectation of privacy and the reasonableness of the search. To minimize liability, employers should post notices and otherwise make clear to employees that they and the employer's property may be subject to searches and that the employer's request that they submit to a search is not an accusation of wrongdoing. In addition, employers should make efforts to limit the intrusiveness and potential for embarrassment of the search. The search should be kept confidential to the extent possible. Employers should notify employees that assigned offices or lockers may be searched, that the employer will keep an extra key, and that refusing to consent to a search may result in discipline. Persons who conduct the search should never physically touch the employee.

Safety in the Workplace

The Occupational Safety and Health Act (OSHA) is the primary workplace safety statute.[131] Under OSHA employers have two primary duties: compliance with the health and safety standards promulgated by the Occupational Safety and Health Administration and compliance with the "general duty clause," which requires employers to provide a place of employment free from recognized hazards that are likely to cause death or serious physical harm. OSHA mandates additional record-keeping and reporting requirements as well.

There are a number of health and safety issues specific to the healthcare industry, including blood-borne pathogens and biological hazards, potential chemical and drug exposures, waste anesthetic gas exposures, ergonomic hazards, laser hazards, hazards associated with laboratories, needle stick hazards, latex allergy, and radioactive materials and X-ray hazards, just to name a few. In addition to the medical staff, most large healthcare facilities maintain a wide variety of nonmedical functions that have health and safety hazards associated with them, such as mechanical maintenance, housekeeping, laundry, and food services. OSHA specifically addresses many of the hazards in the healthcare workplace. Because of the broad spectrum of potential risks to employee health and safety and the numerous regulations managing those risks, employers are advised to seek counsel's assistance in maintaining compliance.

Drug and Alcohol Testing

Drug and alcohol testing is an area full of potential legal pitfalls and may involve a number of legal issues, including the Americans with Disabilities Act, common-law privacy protections, and, for public employers, state and federal constitutional issues. Even so, due in large part to the costs of substance abuse in the workplace, including lost productivity, absenteeism, and workplace accidents, employers are increasingly testing their employees and applicants. Moreover, failure to test, considering the safety-sensitive nature of healthcare jobs and the general acceptance of drug testing by employers, may increase the possibility of liability for those employers who choose not to test. In addition, many federal contractors and grant recipients must take specific measures to ensure a drug-free workplace under the Drug-Free Workplace Act of 1988, although drug testing may not be required.[132]

Privacy claims likely are limited in many cases, considering that so many workers in the healthcare industry provide direct patient care and are thereby involved in safety-sensitive work. As such, the duty of care and responsibility owed a patient will invariably outweigh the privacy interests of a healthcare worker when the healthcare worker's responsibilities relate to the patient's welfare.[133]

There are many different aspects of a testing program to consider. For example, drug and alcohol testing programs may provide that tests be conducted preemployment, on reasonable suspicion, post-accident, and/or on a random basis. Substance abuse policies should address such issues as who will be tested, what tests will be used, when testing will take place, the decision maker and the basis for the decision when reasonable suspicion testing is involved, notification of employees and applicants, the consequences of a positive test, and safeguards for maintaining the confidentiality of testing information. As a result of the number and complexity of issues, employers are advised to obtain assistance of counsel when seeking to design and implement a substance abuse policy.

Environmental Issues

Materials handling practices at healthcare facilities can have an impact on patients, healthcare workers, and the surrounding community. Healthcare facilities face a number of environmental issues on a day-to-day basis, including medical waste, hazardous waste, and wastewater discharge. A hospital may generate solid, chemical, infectious, hazardous, and radioactive waste streams, which are all governed by a variety of state and federal regulations. As with health and safety issues, involvement of counsel will assist in achieving and maintaining compliance.

Collective Bargaining and Protected Concerted Activities

Under the National Labor Relations Act of 1935 (NLRA), nonsupervisory private sector employees have the right to form, join, or assist labor organizations to bargain collectively and to engage in other protected, concerted activities.[134] This congressional affirmation of rights ushered in a new era of union organizing. From the mid-1930s to 1958, the percentage of the private sector workforce represented by unions increased from approximately 14% to nearly 40%. Today, however, only about 7.5% of all employees in the private sector are represented by unions.[135] A variety of factors—the change from a manufacturing to a service-oriented economy, union corruption, increased efforts by management to oppose organizing, and the proliferation of laws designed to protect employees—contributed to this decline. Despite the relatively low levels of representation in the broader workplace, in recent years unions have dedicated significant resources to organizing employees in the healthcare industry.

The NLRA applies to nearly all private sector workplaces. Even though a hospital may not have a union representing its employees, hospital management should still be mindful of the

NLRA. In addition to protecting employees' right to organize, the NLRA protects employees' rights to engage in "concerted activities" for mutual aid or protection. Protected concerted activities are not limited to union organizing and strikes. Employee petitions, letter-writing campaigns, or organized protests, if undertaken with a view to discussing and/or improving the terms or conditions of employment, are activities protected by the NLRA. Consequently, an employer that disciplines an employee for engaging in this type of conduct violates federal labor law. Such a violation is deemed an unfair labor practice.[136]

Unfair Labor Practices

It is beyond the scope of this chapter to discuss all conduct that constitutes an unfair labor practice. Although unions also can commit unfair labor practices, this chapter focuses on the general prohibitions that apply to employers. An employer commits an unfair labor practice by doing any of the following:

- Interfering with, restraining, or coercing employees in their efforts to organize a union or to engage in other protected concerted activity
- Dominating or interfering with the formation or administration of a labor organization or contributing or supporting a labor organization[137]
- Refusing to hire applicants, or terminating or otherwise discriminating against an employee because of the individual's support for or membership in a union
- Discharging or discriminating against an employee because he or she filed charges or provided testimony under the procedures of the NLRA
- Refusing to bargain collectively with a representative of its employees

Some general rules of conduct are obvious under these rules; for example, an employer cannot refuse to hire an applicant or cannot terminate an employee for being a union member or trying to organize a union in the workplace. Other rules are less intuitive. For example, the National Labor Relations Board (NLRB), with the approval of federal courts, has consistently held that an employer may not prohibit its employees from discussing their wages in the workplace.[138]

Although it has been subject to much criticism and many past reversals, the current interpretation of the NLRA requires an employer to allow an employee to request and have a representative of his or her own choosing present during any interview or investigation that may lead to the employee's discipline or termination.[139] The representative must be a co-worker, and contrary to prior interpretations of the NLRA, this right exists even if the employees do not have a union representing them in the workplace.

Employees' rights to engage in protected, concerted activity are not unchecked. Generally, employees cannot disparage an employer's product or services.[140] In the healthcare setting, at least one federal court found that two nurses engaged in protected, concerted activity when they were interviewed on television about their wages and staffing conditions at the hospital.[141]

In the context of labor organizing campaigns, an employer should anticipate that its conduct is likely to be scrutinized at a later date by the NLRB. Many labor law practitioners have reduced the NLRA's basic prohibitions in organizing campaigns to the helpful acronym, TIPS.

An employer cannot *Threaten* or *Interrogate* its employees about union organizing or other protected concerted activity. An employer cannot *Promise* its employees any inducements (e.g., increased pay) to discourage interest in a union organizing effort. Nor can an employer *Spy* or otherwise engage in any surveillance of its employees' efforts to organize employees. Notwithstanding these rules, an employer has the right, as do its employees, to communicate its position on unions and union organizing and any facts relevant to that effort to its employees in a noncoercive, truthful manner.

Solicitation and Distribution

A common issue for employers, particularly in the context of an organizing campaign, is to what extent an employer may limit or govern employees' rights to solicit support for the union or other protected, concerted activity or to distribute literature in the workplace. For most workplaces, the rules are fairly well settled. Lawful prohibitions for an employer include:

- Nonemployees generally can be prohibited from soliciting or distributing literature on the employer's property.[142]
- Employees can be prohibited from soliciting other employees on employer property when the person soliciting or being solicited is on working time. Working time does not include rest, meal, or other authorized breaks.
- Employees can be prohibited from distributing literature on employer property in non-working areas during working time.
- Employees can be prohibited from distributing literature on employer property in working areas.

Many healthcare institutions, however, have facilities that are open to the public, and with their missions to care for sick or injured patients, special rules have emerged to govern solicitation and distribution issues in that setting. A hospital or healthcare institution may prohibit solicitation or distribution of materials by any employee of the hospital at any time in immediate patient care areas of the hospital. Immediate patient care areas include patient rooms, operating rooms, patient treatment areas, and corridors adjacent to those areas as well as elevators or stairways that are used substantially to transport patients.[143]

On the other hand, a healthcare institution generally may ban distributions and solicitations in nonpatient care areas only if necessary to avoid interference with the hospital's operations or disturbance to patients.[144] For example, in a ruling upheld by a federal appellate court, the NLRB ruled that a hospital committed an unfair labor practice when it banned off-duty employees from distributing, at the hospital's front entrance, literature that addressed the alleged adverse impact on patient care resulting from the hospital's downsizing and restructuring of nursing staff.[145] The NLRB rejected the hospital's argument that the distribution of the literature, which allegedly contained "shocking and sensational headlines" and "horror stories" of patient injuries due to allegedly unsafe care at other hospitals, constituted interference with the hospital's operations and disturbance to its patients.[146]

For any solicitation and distribution policy to be valid, an employer must uniformly enforce the policy against all solicitation and distribution conduct, regardless of whether it is related to union activity. Courts have recognized, however, that permitting employee solicitations for charities such as the United Way or the Girl Scouts will not invalidate an otherwise broadly enforced nonsolicitation policy. Finally, a hospital may have trouble enforcing bans on solicitation and distribution outside the hospital building, particularly if the conduct is scheduled at times to coincide with shift changes.[147]

Electronic media have blurred the distinction between solicitation and distribution, and the law governing the use of such media is still emerging. The NLRB recently ruled regarding employee usage of employer-provided e-mail in connection with union affairs in *The Register-Guard*, 351 NLRB No. 70 (2007). Specifically, the NLRB held that an employer may bar its employees from nonwork-related use of its e-mail system, including use for union-related purposes, as long as the employer's e-mail policy or its enforcement of such policy does not discriminate against section 7 activity.[148] In *The Register-Guard*, the employer had an e-mail policy prohibiting the use of its communication systems to "solicit or proselytize for commercial ventures, religious or political causes, outside organizations, or other non-job-related solicitations."[149] The NLRB examined three e-mails sent by an employee, Suzi Prozanski, who was a union member and the union president, and the disciplinary measures the employer took as a results of her sending the e-mails. The first e-mail Prozanski sent was to *The Register-Guard* employees and it sought to correct misinformation provided by the employer to its employees regarding a union rally. The e-mail contained a statement that the union "would like to set the record straight," and was signed, "Yours, in solidarity, Suzi Prozanski."[150] The employer issued Prozanski a written warning for violating its e-mail policy by using company e-mail for union business.[151]

Prozanski sent a second and third e-mail to *The Register-Guard* employees at their company addresses shortly thereafter. One asked union employees to wear green to support the union's position during negotiations with the company. The other sought employee participation in the union's entry at an upcoming local parade. The company issued Prozanski one combined written warning for these two e-mails.[152]

The NLRB found the employer's enforcement and resulting discipline of Prozanski for the first e-mail providing information only to be discriminatory and a violation of the NLRA because Prozanski's first e-mail only provided nonwork-related information, which the employer permitted in contexts other than union activities, such as baby announcements, party invitations and offers of tickets to sporting events, despite the company's e-mail policy to the contrary.[153]

On the other hand, the NLRB found that the company's enforcement of the e-mail policy with respect to Prozanski's second and third e-mails to be nondiscriminatory because there was no evidence the company permitted its employees "to use e-mail to solicit other employees to support any group or organization."[154] Therefore, the company's discipline of Prozanski for soliciting her fellow employees to support the union by wearing a certain color and for participation in a local parade was not discriminatory.

Other NLRB cases regarding electronic communications include one where an employee who sent an e-mail to all employees critical of a new vacation policy was found to have engaged in protected, concerted activity.[155] Similarly, an employer violated the NLRA by prohibiting an employee from displaying a union-related screen saver message on her computer that was seen by her coworkers.[156]

Organizing Rights

Until the 1970s, union organizing in the healthcare industry under the NLRA was not particularly widespread. Federal, state, and municipal hospitals are exempt from the NLRA's coverage, and until 1974 private nonprofit hospitals were not covered by the NLRA.[157] In 1974, however, Congress amended the NLRA to delete the exemption for nonprofit hospitals and to clarify the bargaining and strike obligations of employers in the healthcare industry.

As a result, nonsupervisory employees of a healthcare institution may organize a union to represent them to bargain with their employer over the terms and conditions of their employment.[158] Under the NLRA, there are two ways for a union to gain the right to represent employees. First, an employer may voluntarily recognize a union as the majority representative of its employees. Second, if a union petitions the NLRB and can show support for the union among at least 30% of the employees in an appropriate unit, the NLRB will schedule an election among all the eligible employees in that unit to determine whether the union will represent those employees. If a majority of the employees voting in that election request that the union represent the employees for purposes of collective bargaining, then, absent any findings of election irregularities, the NLRB will certify the election results in favor of the union. Within certain parameters, an employer and its employees have the right to oppose the union's efforts to organize the employees.

Before the 1970s, a nettlesome issue in organizing hospital employees was what constituted an appropriate unit (for purposes of holding elections, and if the election was successful, for purposes of bargaining) among hospital employees. One of the touchstones of the NLRA is that the NLRB will only certify a union as the representative of an appropriate unit for bargaining; that is, a group of employees with occupationally similar interests and concerns. For example, the NLRA provides that professional employees and nonprofessional employees may not be members of the same unit.[159]

Since 1935, the NLRB, through its quasi-judicial decision-making process, has developed general principles for units in a wide variety of industries. But in its 1974 amendments to the NLRA, Congress signaled to the NLRB that it should avoid the proliferation of bargaining units in the healthcare industry. In 1989, the NLRB responded by formally adopting a rule that established eight specific appropriate units for bargaining in acute care hospitals.[160] The eight units are:

1. Registered nurses
2. Physicians
3. All other professionals
4. Technical employees
5. Skilled maintenance employees
6. Business office clericals
7. Guards
8. All other nonprofessionals

Thus, in private acute care hospitals, the NLRB will conduct elections among employees seeking to be represented by a union petition only within one of these units. Narrow exceptions to the unit rules may apply in certain situations where (1) the eight-unit rule would result in units of less than five employees; (2) nonconforming units already exist; or (3) unions seek two or more of the eight specified units. The US Supreme Court approved of the NLRB's rule making to define appropriate units for acute care hospitals.[161]

Definition of "Healthcare Institution" Under the NLRA

An organized delivery system consists of many components, not every one of which is considered a "healthcare institution" under the NLRA, which defines the term as including "any hospital, convalescent hospital, health maintenance organization, health clinic, nursing home, extended care facility, or other institution devoted to the care of sick, infirm, or aged persons."[162] The legislative history of the 1974 amendments to the NLRA links the definition of the term "healthcare institution" to the concept of "ongoing patient care."

> The scope of the application of the amendment is meant to include patient care situations and is not meant to include purely administrative health connected facilities. As an example, an insurance company specializing in medical coverage would not fall under the scope of these amendments, but would remain under general coverage of the act. An administrative facility or operation within a hospital, however, would be within the scope of the amendments as there would be a connection directly and indirectly with ongoing patient care. The crucial connection is the welfare of the patients and such connection would in certain cases be mere geographical proximity to ongoing patient care.[163]

Therefore, in its application of the healthcare amendments, the NLRB has distinguished between institutions directly involved in ongoing patient care and those it deems not directly involved. For example, in an early case applying the 1974 amendments to bargaining unit determinations, the NLRB determined that an independent, nonprofit blood bank, which served the needs of a number of area hospitals by recruiting blood donors and testing, processing, and distributing blood, was not a healthcare institution.[164] The NLRB relied on the legislative history quoted above to distinguish between patient care situations and purely administrative health-connected facilities. "Since supplying blood to hospitals obviously does not involve patient care, blood banks are not healthcare institutions within the meaning of the amendments."[165]

The NLRB relied on its blood bank decisions in determining the applicability of the 1974 amendments to medical laboratories. In another early case, the NLRB found that an employer that operated a diagnostic medical laboratory service that tested human blood, body fluid, and tissue for hospitals, clinics, nursing homes, and individual doctors was not a healthcare institution within the meaning of the NLRA.[166] The NLRB determined that "the Employer's operations is [sic] analogous to that of blood banks which the Board has found not to be involved in patient care."[167]

More recently, the NLRB again considered whether a blood bank constitutes a healthcare institution for unit determination purposes. In *Syracuse Region Blood Center*,[168] the blood center at issue was the sole source of blood-related services for 38 hospitals in a 15-county area in central

New York state, operating at a central facility, three fixed satellite sites, various mobile sites, and, to a limited degree, at hospitals. The blood center primarily performed homologous blood collections (i.e., from healthy donors), as well as autologous collections, donor pheresis (in which platelets or other components of the blood are retained by the bank for future use), patient pheresis (in which diseased or unwanted components of the blood are removed and the rest returned to the patient), and therapeutic phlebotomies (drawing blood for therapeutic purposes). The center's laboratories tested blood samples for blood type, antibodies, and diseases; performed laboratory work related to pheresis procedures; and performed 25 to 30 immunohematology consultations per month with hospitals or physicians seeking medical advice. The blood center's operations also included a bone marrow donor program and a tissue bank program.

The NLRB found that only two of the blood center's activities, patient pheresis and therapeutic phlebotomies, "indisputably involve patient care."[169] Although such activities made up only a small fraction of SRBC's overall operations (a combined total of 400 to 600 per year, in contrast with about 94,000 donor blood collections per year), the Board found it sufficient to accord SRBC healthcare institution status, stating that "we find that [patient pheresis and therapeutic phlebotomies] are performed with sufficient regularity and in a sufficiently large number . . . that the Employer is properly viewed to be devoted to the care of sick . . . persons" within the meaning of the NLRA.[170]

The Board in *Syracuse Region Blood Center* summarily discounted the center's performance of laboratory services and its consultations with hospitals and physicians as "[n]either of those functions is an indicator of healthcare institution status."[171] The center's participation in bone marrow and tissue donor programs likewise provided no basis for the NLRB's decision, which rested solely on the activities that it deemed "indisputably" to involve the care of patients.[172]

Special Issues in Organizing Campaigns

Supervisors have no authority to organize a union in the workplace because they are not covered by the NLRA. Among healthcare employers, the question of whether a particular group of employees are supervisors within the meaning of the NLRA has been a difficult issue. Employees with advanced education or training are not necessarily supervisors. Indeed, the NLRA provides for organizing among professional employees. Under the NLRA, a supervisor is any individual having authority, in the interest of the employer, to hire, transfer, suspend, lay off, recall, promote, discharge, assign, reward, or discipline other employees, or responsibly to direct them, or to adjust their grievances or effectively to recommend such action, if in connection with the foregoing the exercise of such authority is not of a merely routine or clerical nature, but requires the use of independent judgment.[173]

Defining whether a registered nurse is a supervisor is a fact-intensive issue, and litigation over that issue, particularly in the long-term healthcare industry, has been widespread.[174] In acute care hospitals, registered nurses are often found not to be supervisors, but this generalization has exceptions, particularly for those nurses, such as charge nurses, who are involved in assigning work and managing other registered nurses. The NLRB recently attempted to clarify when nurses are included in the bargaining unit or excluded as supervisors under the NLRA.[175] In *Oakwood Healthcare*, the NLRB examined the terms "assign" and "responsibly direct others" contained in the NLRA in conjunction with the requirement of the use of independent judgment to determine whether charge nurses were unit member employees or supervisors.

After defining the aforementioned terms ("assign," "responsibly direct others," and "independent judgment"), the NLRB determined that charge nurses who worked in areas of the hospital where they made staffing "assignments that are both tailored to patient conditions and needs and particular nursing skill sets, and [attempted to execute] a fair distribution based upon an assessment of the probable amount of nursing time each assigned patient will require on a given shift" exercised a "substantial degree of discretion" to constitute independent judgment and therefore made the charge nurses "supervisors" within the meaning of the NLRA.[176]

The NLRB contrasted the aforementioned charge nurses who exercised independent judgment from the charge nurses who worked in the hospital's emergency room. These charge nurses assigned employees to areas within the emergency room without taking an employee's level of experience or skill or the nature or severity of a patient's condition into account and therefore did not exercise "independent judgment" and were therefore not "supervisors" within the meaning of the NLRA.[177] Therefore, the NLRB included the emergency room charge nurses in the bargaining unit.

Building upon the definitions it established in *Oakwood Healthcare*, the NLRB decided another charge nurse case in which the NLRB refused to exclude from the bargaining unit charge nurses who did not have the authority to "*require* that a certain action be taken; supervisory authority is not established where the putative supervisor has the authority merely to *request* that a certain action be taken."[178] In addition, while the NLRB found that the charge nurses at issue in this case had the authority to direct other employees in that they oversaw and corrected where necessary the job performance of other employees, they were not held responsible ("responsibly direct") or accountable for their performance in this "directing" role,[179] that is, the employer presented no evidence that "any charge nurse has experienced any material consequences to her terms and conditions of employment, either positive or negative, as a result of her performance in directing [certified nursing assistants]."[180]

Another issue of special interest to hospitals is whether interns and residents are "employees" under the NLRA. If so, then interns and residents have the right to organize unions and have the other protections afforded them under the federal labor law. The NLRB recently overturned 20 years of precedent by concluding that interns and residents—who are usually students as well—are covered by the NLRA.[181] This decision will likely generate new efforts at union organizing among hospital interns and residents.

The applicability of the NLRA to employees of a contractor, such as a temporary services agency, may also prove nettlesome for employers in the healthcare industry, where the use of temporary workers is commonplace. In 2000, the NLRB, overturning its own precedent, determined that temporary workers may be included in the same bargaining unit with an employer's regular employees, even if the temporary agency and the employer do not consent to bargain as joint employers.[182] In *MB Sturgis Inc.*, the temporary workers performed the same work as the employer's employees, were subject to the same supervision, and were disciplined by the employer's supervisors (as opposed to the temporary agency's supervisors). The employer and the temporary agency were found to be joint employers of the temporary workers. The NLRB ruled, contrary to its prior decisional law, that where such a joint employer relationship exists between a temporary agency and a contracting employer, the NLRB may apply its established standards for determining whether all the relevant workers, irrespective of their particular employer, may be included in a single bargaining unit, notwithstanding that the employers may not consent to bargaining jointly with a union over terms and conditions of employment.[183]

Unless and until the courts have had an opportunity to review the NLRB's new interpretation of the NLRA in *MB Sturgis Inc.*, or the NLRB revisits its determination, the case will pose new and complicated challenges to healthcare employers. The decision will complicate the collective bargaining process for agencies and employers alike and may subject them to bargaining obligations and collective bargaining agreements covering employees over which they may actually exercise very little control on a daily basis.

Private Recognition Agreements

Aside from NLRB-governed elections, there are other ways for employees and unions to persuade employees to select a union to represent them for purposes of collective bargaining. Over the last few years, unions have increasingly requested employers to agree to use private recognition agreements allowing employees to decide whether a union should represent their workforce. Private recognition agreements are being used with more frequency when a union already represents some portion of the employer's employees. In the healthcare industry, particularly in California, these agreements have become a more commonly used means of resolving issues of employee representation.

Private recognition agreements come in a wide variety; they are purely contractual arrangements between an employer and a union that govern the process by which employees decide whether a union should represent them. The hallmark of a private recognition agreement is that the parties decide not to use the NLRB election process. Some agreements are purely "card-check" agreements, whereby if a union presents signed authorization cards from a majority of the employees within a particular unit, the employer voluntarily agrees to recognize the union as the exclusive bargaining agent for the employees in that unit. Alternatively, the parties may agree to have an election that requires the employer to remain neutral in the campaign or grants the union certain access rights to share information with the employees.

Another common feature is an agreement that the parties will rely on arbitration to resolve disputes over unit definitions, voter eligibility, or conduct in violation of the parties' agreement. If a majority of the employees in an appropriate unit select a union to represent them, the employer agrees to recognize and begin bargaining in good faith with the union over terms and conditions of employment. Management and labor often disagree on the wisdom or fairness of private recognition agreements, but their increased use means employers must be prepared to deal with requests to use them.

Strikes and Picketing at Healthcare Institutions

A major purpose of Congress's 1974 amendments to the NLRA was "to minimize the potential for increased disruption of health care delivery resulting from increased labor activity by employees of health care institutions now that their activities were protected by the Act."[184]

Congress recognized that the traditional legal means employed by unions to bring pressure upon employers could cause disruptions and threats to health and safety in the healthcare industry if unchecked. Therefore, in addition to expanding the NLRA's coverage in the healthcare industry, the 1974 amendments also added Section 8(g) of the NLRA, which requires that a labor organization give 10 days' written notice "before engaging in any strike, picketing, or other concerted refusal to work at any health care institution. . . ."[185] Note, however, that only "health care institutions" are entitled to such notice. In an organized delivery system, therefore, some, but not all, component entities may enjoy the protection of this provision.[186]

Section 8(g)'s mandate applies to all picketing, regardless of the nature, character, or objectives of the picketing or the type of economic pressures generated.[187] Determining what activities require advance notice under Section 8(g) is a very fact-specific inquiry, but the NLRB has found it to extend beyond traditional ambulatory picketing and to include a union's mass demonstration[188] and a press conference conducted by a union outside a hospital entrance, accompanied by persons "milling around" the hospital and holding signs regarding hospital staffing levels.[189] On the other hand, in an advice memorandum, the general counsel of the NLRB opined that a large number of union supporters' confrontational disruption and demonstration at a health fair held by a hospital on hospital grounds was not "picketing" within the meaning of Section 8(g).[190]

Mergers and Effects Bargaining

Given the proliferation of mergers and alliances in the healthcare industry, it is important for unionized institutions to be cognizant of their potential bargaining obligations with respect to mergers. The duty to bargain under the NLRA is limited to matters of "wages, hours, and other terms and conditions of employment. . . ."[191] There is no duty to bargain over management decisions that have an indirect and attenuated impact on the employment relationship and that are at the "core of entrepreneurial control."[192] Some management decisions involving the scope and direction of an enterprise are not primarily about conditions of employment, although the effect of the decisions necessarily may be to terminate employment. In such cases, although there may be no duty to bargain over a managerial decision, there is a duty to bargain about the results or effects of that decision.[193] Bargaining over the effects of a decision must be conducted in a meaningful manner and at a meaningful time.[194]

A decision to merge two unrelated corporate entities is not subject to a duty to bargain, but an employer may or may not have an obligation to bargain about the effects of a decision to merge.[195] Although there may be no duty to bargain about effects of a merger, there may still be a duty to provide information relevant to "effects bargaining." In general, an employer has "a duty to provide relevant information needed by a labor union for the proper performance of its duties as the employees' bargaining representative."[196] In one case, the NLRB found that two hospitals had breached their duty to bargain in good faith by withholding information that a union had requested in connection with a planned merger. The union sought copies of documents explicating the merger's terms, plans for, or information about proposed staffing changes at one hospital in consequence of the merger, and all documents pertaining to the hospitals' proposed corporate status within the merged group of facilities. The NLRB found the information to be relevant to the union's obligations, even though not directly linked to terms and conditions of employment. The Court of Appeals upheld the Board's determination, stating that "as long as a pending merger is sufficiently advanced, a union is entitled to request information shown by the totality of the circumstances to be relevant in order to prepare for effects bargaining."[197]

Employment Eligibility Verification

Form I-9 Requirements

The primary immigration-related issue for all employers involves the verification of employees', including US citizens', authorization to work in the United States. The Immigration Reform and Control Act of 1986 (IRCA), and its various amendments in 1990 and 1996, subject all employers and recruiters to civil and criminal penalties for knowingly hiring, recruiting or referring for a fee, or continuing to employ an unauthorized worker. IRCA attempts to balance the interests of prohibiting unauthorized employment of aliens and preventing discrimination against aliens and citizens alike. Performing their responsibilities under IRCA can be complicated and confusing for employers. Healthcare employers, which are often dependent on transient or less-skilled workers for a variety of tasks, receive and review more than their share of confusing documents, made all the more difficult by the often ready availability of fraudulent work-authorization and identity papers. The next few pages will touch on most of the important issues with regard to verification, especially in regard to the healthcare industry.

Employers and employees alike have responsibilities under IRCA, which prohibits an employer from knowingly hiring or continuing to employ an alien who does not have authorization for employment in the United States.[198] An employer must screen each employee for identity and employment authorization. Every individual hired after November 6, 1986, must present evidence of employment authorization and identity to his or her employer. Every employer must examine and record this evidence on a Form I-9, which must be retained and made available upon request to US Citizenship and Immigration Services (USCIS, formerly the Bureau of Citizenship and Immigration Services [BCIS], formerly the Immigration and Naturalization Service) and other government agencies.

The first step in ensuring employment verification compliance is understanding who is and is not an "employee" who is subject to IRCA. Relevant exceptions for the healthcare industry include independent contractors. The regulations promulgated pursuant to IRCA define independent contractors as "individuals or entities who carry on independent business, contract to do a piece of work according to their own means and methods, and are subject to control only as to results."[199] Thus, for example, individuals who provide services to a hospital, but who are employed by an agency contracted to provide such services to the hospital (such as a temp or employee leasing agency), are not considered employees of the hospital under IRCA.

Nevertheless, it should be noted that any person who enters into a contract, subcontract, or exchange to obtain the services of an alien, knowing that the alien does not have authorization to perform the services, is considered to have violated the employer sanctions provisions of IRCA.[200] For example, a hospital that contracts with a physical therapist as an independent contractor, knowing that he or she has an H-1B work authorization for another unrelated hospital, could be found to have violated IRCA.

Another class of individuals not considered to be employees are volunteers. Volunteers are individuals who provide their services without any compensation, including room and board, gifts, or other benefits.[201] A volunteer may receive certain benefits from the "employer," but the work arrangement must have been entered into without the expectation of compensation, and the benefit must not have been offered in exchange for the work.[202] Thus, a resident physician "moonlighting" in an ER is likely not a "volunteer" for I-9 purposes, and if that resident is a foreign national and does not have valid work authorization for the hospital, the hospital faces violations of both the verification and sanctions provisions of IRCA.

Employees have the affirmative duty under IRCA of proving both their identity and work eligibility.[203] At their time of hire, employees are required to complete the first section of the I-9 employment eligibility verification form. In addition, the employee must verify, under penalty of perjury, his or her status as a citizen or national of the United States, a lawful permanent resident, or an alien authorized to work in the United States. Failure to sign or date Section 1 of the I-9 is one of the most frequent mistakes made in completing the form. Ultimately, ensuring that the employee completes Section 1 fully is the employer's responsibility.

Section 1 of the I-9 form must be completed "at the time of hire," which is defined by the regulations as "the actual commencement of employment of an employee for wages or other remuneration."[204] The employee has 3 business days from the date of hire in which to present the documentation supporting the assertions in Section 1.[205] Upon reviewing these documents, the employer must immediately complete Section 2 of the I-9. If the employee cannot produce the actual documents within 3 days, then he may present a receipt showing application for a replacement document or a Form I-94 indicating either temporary evidence of permanent resident status or refugee status.[206] These are the only three situations in which a receipt can be accepted; a receipt is otherwise unacceptable.

In Section 2 of the I-9, the employer or its agent must attest under penalty of perjury that it has reviewed Section 1 and the documents required to attest to the accuracy of the responses. The I-9 form contains a list of the acceptable documents that an employee may present to the employer for inspection within 3 days of hire. If the individual is employed for less than 3 days, the documentation must be presented the day of hire. The employer is also required to note on the I-9 form the information disclosed in the documents and to sign and date the form.

Form I-9 contains three lists of documents from which the employee may choose to show identity and/or employment authorization in order for the employer to complete Section 2. It is the employee's choice; the employer may not request or suggest any particular document. The employee may produce one document from list A that shows both identity and authorization to work in the United States or he or she may present one document from list B, establishing identity, and one from list C, showing employment authorization. The employee must produce originals, not copies, for the employer to review.[207]

Although verification is very important, the employer always must be careful not to demand more or different documents than those necessary to comply with the verification requirements. An employer who demands more or different documents can be guilty of discrimination if it is proven that the demands were made with discriminatory intent. An employer cannot refuse to honor documents that on their face reasonably appear to be genuine and relate to the person presenting them. The employer may, but is not required to, photocopy and attach to the I-9 form the documentation presented by the employee.[208] Photocopies do not excuse failure to complete the form, however. If the employer decides to make copies, he should do so for all employees so as to avoid a charge of discrimination.

An employer of an individual who is a member of a collective bargaining unit and who is employed under a collective bargaining agreement between one or more unions and a multi-employer association may use an I-9 form completed within the past 3 years by a prior employer who is a member of the same association. This applies to persons hired 60 days or more after September 30, 1996, the effective date of the Illegal Immigration Reform and Immigrant Responsibility Act (IIRAIRA).

An employer is not required to verify eligibility for employment if the employee is not a new hire but is "continuing" his or her employment.[209] An employee is continuing his employment if at all times he has a "reasonable expectation of employment."[210] The USCIS regulations set out a number of situations in which employment is deemed to be continuing, such as during paid or unpaid leaves, strikes or labor disputes, and corporate reorganizations.[211]

Section 3 of the I-9 form is used when appropriate to update and reverify employment information. Employers are required to reverify employment eligibility when an employee's work authorization expires, and it is the employer's responsibility to maintain a system to prompt him to reverify employee information by the correct deadline.[212] The same rules regarding documents apply for reverification as for verification. If, at the time of updating and/or reverification, the employee's name has changed, then the employer must complete Section 3, block A, of Form I-9. If an employee is rehired within 3 years of the date the I-9 was originally completed, and the employee is still eligible for employment on the same basis as indicated on the form, the employer would complete Section 3, block B, and the signature block.[213]

If the employer needs to correct the I-9 form, the new information should be inserted, signed, and dated as of the time of the insertion. If the omission or mistake was in Section 1, the employee should also sign and date the correction. The form should never be backdated.

The employer must retain all I-9 forms, which are actually the property of the US government. The employer is required to retain the I-9 forms for at least 3 years, or for 1 year after the employee's termination date, whichever is later.[214] I-9 forms should not be destroyed if the USCIS is in the process of investigating the employer. The employer must produce the forms at the request of the USCIS or other selected government entities; failure to do so is considered a violation of the Immigration and Naturalization Act (INA).[215]

Failure to complete, correct, update, reverify, retain, or produce the I-9 form may result in a finding of a violation of the verification requirements. Employers may also face liability for failure to comply with the timeliness requirements (e.g., completion of the I-9 form within 3 days of starting employment).[216] Fines for paperwork violations occurring before September 29, 1999, are between $100 and $1,000 for each individual for which a mistake or omission was made; fines for violations occurring on or after September 29, 1999, are between $110 and $1,100.[217] In addition to imposing fines, the USCIS has the authority to require employers to take corrective action, such as education and posting notices.[218] Five factors are to be considered when setting the penalty: (1) the size of the employer's business, (2) the employer's good faith, (3) the seriousness of the violation, (4) whether the individual involved was an unauthorized alien, and (5) whether the employer has a history of previous violations.[219] Additional factors may be considered, such as the ability of the employer to pay the proposed penalty.[220]

The IIRAIRA added an exemption for employers who have technical or procedural violations of the regulations. For technical or procedural failures to complete the form properly, if the employer made a good faith attempt to comply, the USCIS must explain the problem to the employer and allow 10 days for correction. If the failures are not corrected, penalties are imposed. The exemption does not relieve an employer who has engaged in a "pattern and practice" of violations. This provision, added by the IIRAIRA, applies to failures occurring on or after September 30, 1996. Some examples of technical errors include failing to include an address or date on the form, accepting a list B document with a missing expiration date, or failing to date Section 2 of the form.

Substantive Violations of IRCA

Employers and recruiters are prohibited from knowingly hiring, recruiting or referring for a fee, or continuing to employ an unauthorized alien.[221] If the employer has attempted in good faith to comply with the employment verification requirements of IRCA, it has an affirmative defense against a violation finding, but that presumption can be rebutted if the USCIS can establish that the documents relied upon did not reasonably appear to be genuine. Employers are also prohibited from continuing to employ an unauthorized alien once his or her status is known.[222]

An employer's knowledge of the status of the unauthorized worker may be actual (evidenced by other employees or admissions of the employer's agents) or constructive. The regulations define constructive knowledge as "knowledge that may fairly be inferred through notice of certain facts and circumstances that would lead a person, through the exercise of reasonable care, to know about a certain condition."[223]

Individuals or entities who knowingly employ unauthorized workers are subject to civil fines.[224] First-time violators for offenses that occurred prior to March 27, 2008, can be fined $275 to $2,200 for each alien. First-time violators for offenses that occur on or after March 27, 2008, can be fined $375 to $3,200 for each unauthorized alien. Second-time violators for offenses that occurred prior to March 27, 2008, can be fined between $2,200 and $5,500 for each unauthorized alien. Second-time violators of offenses that occur on or after March 27, 2008, can be fined between $3,200 and $6,500 for each unauthorized alien. After that, repeat offenders (who have committed two or more such offenses) can be fined in the range of $3,300 to $11,000 per alien for offenses occurring before March 27, 2008. For offenses committed on or after March 27, 2008, the offender may be fined in the range of $4,300 and $16,000 for each unauthorized alien.

In addition to its regulations, the USCIS has set out guidelines for determining penalties within these ranges.[225] These guidelines provide for leniency for first-time violators and calculate fines starting at the statutory minimum with adjustments upward depending on aggravating factors.

Fines for repeat violators start at the statutory maximum and work down accounting for mitigating factors. Criminal penalties (up to a $3,000 fine for each unauthorized alien and 6 months imprisonment) may be imposed for pattern or practice violations.[226] The term pattern or practice covers "regular, repeated, and intentional activities" but does not include "isolated, sporadic, or accidental acts."[227]

In addition, it is a criminal violation for any person to knowingly or in reckless disregard of the fact that the alien has come to, has entered, or remains in the United States in violation of the law to conceal, harbor, or shield from detection such alien in any such place, including any buildings or any means of transportation.[228] An employer may face criminal fines and/or imprisonment for up to 5 years for hiring 10 or more aliens that the employer knows were brought into the United States illegally in violation of the alien smuggling/criminal harboring provision.

Discrimination

The INA also contains antidiscrimination provisions that make it unlawful for persons or other entities (employers with four or more employees) from discriminating against an individual in hiring, discharging, recruiting, or referring for a fee because of national origin or citizenship status.[229] An employer cannot set different employment verification standards or require different groups of employees to present additional documentation, nor can it request that an employee present more or different documents than are required or refuse to accept a document that on its face appears genuine and related to the individual presenting it, if done for the purpose of discriminating against the individual.[230] An employer cannot retaliate against an individual because he or she intends to file a charge or complaint, testify, or participate in any way in a proceeding under IRCA.[231] Moreover, an employer cannot refuse to accept a document or to hire an individual on the basis of a future expiration date on the document.

There are exceptions to the antidiscrimination provisions. For example, the provisions do not apply to employers with three or fewer employees.[232] In addition, the citizenship discrimination provisions do not apply to actions that are required in order to comply with any law, regulation, or executive order; required by any federal, state, or local government contract; or determined by the attorney general to be essential for an employer to do business with the federal, state, or local government.[233] The antidiscrimination provisions do not apply to national origin discrimination if the individual is covered by Section 703 of the Civil Rights Act of 1964.[234] On an individual basis, an employer may legally prefer a US citizen or national over an alien with equal qualifications,[235] but the qualifications of each must be equal.

The antidiscrimination provisions are controversial because of their inherent conflict with the sanctions imposed against employers who hire unauthorized aliens. Balancing these two obligations can be burdensome to employers, who are prohibited from asking for different documents or more information, but are nevertheless subject to civil or criminal liability if they hire an unauthorized alien.[236]

The civil penalties for violations of the antidiscrimination provisions range from $250 to $2,000 per person for a first offense; $2,000 to $5,000 for a second offense; and $3,000 to $10,000 for violations occurring prior to September 29, 1999. For offenses on or after September 29, 1999, the penalties increase by 10%: $275 to $2,200 per person for the first violation; $2,200 to $5,500 for the second violation; and $3,300 to $11,000 for the third violation. There are no criminal penalties for violations of the antidiscrimination provisions.

Conducting an Effective Internal Investigation

Employers in the healthcare industry, like those in virtually every other industry, face a burgeoning number of employee complaints and lawsuits alleging discrimination, harassment, financial improprieties, and other forms of alleged unlawful conduct in the workplace. In response—and as part of their continuous efforts to comply with increased federal and state regulation of workplace conduct—employers in the last decade drafted and disseminated to their workforce policies regarding equal employment opportunity, antidiscrimination, and workplace conduct. By the latter half of the decade, employers were, as never before, enforcing these policies by conducting internal investigations into employee complaints of misconduct.

For every action there is a reaction, and as employers increased their use of investigations, employees' lawyers responded by challenging the manner in which employers conducted their investigations. Employers began to see a new kind of legal claim—that they failed to conduct a proper investigation into the alleged misconduct. The difficult irony of this type of claim is that it has been made by the employee who raised the issue that resulted in the investigation and/or by the employee who was the subject of the investigation, depending on whichever individual was dissatisfied with the outcome.

Internal investigations have become an integral part of today's workplace. Effective investigations will often provide an employer with a successful defense to employment-related lawsuits. Conversely, an inadequate investigation may expose an employer to additional legal liability. For these reasons, it is critical that employers understand how to conduct effective internal investigations.

The Employer's Burden of Proof: What You Need and Do Not Need to Establish

Many employers fail to understand their "burden of proof" in conducting internal investigations, incorrectly fearing they have to prove "beyond a reasonable doubt" that the alleged misconduct occurred or did not occur. The real world does not work that way. Most employers lack the time and resources necessary to conduct the type of protracted and exhaustive fact-finding process that one associates with our judicial system. Fortunately, when reviewing employers' internal investigations in employment-related lawsuits, most courts do not impose on employers the same jurisprudential burdens of proof required in a court of law.

The standard of proof adopted by most courts can be paraphrased as follows: When reaching a decision in response to a workplace complaint of misconduct, the employer must make a good faith determination based on reasonable grounds that sufficient cause existed for its decision. The bottom line is that in order to take action against an employee for suspected misconduct, the employer need not be absolutely certain that the misconduct actually occurred; the employer need only have acted in good faith and based on reasonable grounds.

What an Employer Must Do Before Conducting Any Investigation

The first step in conducting any investigation is to determine the most appropriate and effective method.[237] It generally is advisable to contact competent legal counsel for assistance on this important threshold determination. It is important to make sure that the investigation is overseen and controlled by one person with competence, training, experience, and impartiality. Although it is sometimes necessary to have more than one person involved in the investigation (where, for instance, numerous interviews need to be conducted in a very short period of time), it is important to keep the investigation in as few hands as possible. This approach reduces the risk of inadvertent disclosure and aids in the ability to make consistent credibility assessments and factual findings.

Typically, the company's human resources department should be responsible for ensuring the integrity of the investigation process. A well-trained HR representative should conduct the investigation, collect the facts, draw conclusions, document the results, and make a recommendation to management. Management typically should be responsible for reviewing the recommendations of HR and making the decision to implement some or all of HR's recommendations. The investigation, when done properly, is an interactive, collaborative process between HR and management.

Initial Meeting with the Complaining Employee

The second step in the investigation generally is to meet with the complaining employee to determine whether an investigation is even necessary and, if so, to determine the nature and scope of that investigation. As with all investigative interviews, it is extremely important that the investigator take accurate and thorough notes during the initial meeting.

In addition to identifying all of the relevant issues and assembling all of the relevant facts, the initial meeting should accomplish the following: give the complaining employee confidence in the investigation process; emphasize the company's commitment to resolving the issues promptly and effectively; reassure the employee that the company does not tolerate retaliation against an employee who comes forward with a legitimate complaint, and invite him or her to let you know if he or she subsequently feels that he or she has been subjected to any retaliation; tell the employee that the company will limit the disclosure of information to those persons who have a legitimate business need-to-know (but do not promise confidentiality); instruct the employee that he or she has a duty to keep the investigation and underlying issues confidential, and that the failure to do so may unduly affect the outcome of the investigation and result in discipline; and make sure the employee understands that his or her continuing cooperation is necessary for a complete investigation and an effective resolution.

If, after the initial meeting, the investigator determines that an investigation is warranted, the investigator should encourage (but not require) the complaining employee to provide a written summary of the issues and facts, and to identify all relevant documentation and witnesses. That will ensure that the investigator correctly understands all of the facts and issues raised and will avoid any misunderstandings later on. Regardless of whether the complaining employee provides a written summary, the investigator generally should give the employee a memo confirming the substance of the issues raised. Confirming the issues in writing will give the investigator and the complaining employee an opportunity to make sure all of the issues are clearly understood before starting the investigation.

Planning the Investigation

It is critical that the investigator organize and plan the nature and scope of the investigation before beginning to interview witnesses. Before interviewing anyone, therefore, consider whether there are any company policies or practices that apply to the situation. Identify and review all documents that may assist in conducting the investigation. If the company has a unionized workforce, consider whether the complaint implicates the collective bargaining agreement.

The investigator must give careful thought as to which employees should be interviewed. Cast too broad a net, and the investigator risks interviewing individuals to whom the existence and facts of the investigation should not be disclosed; cast too narrow a net, and he or she risks not interviewing individuals who may have valuable information. The obvious individuals include the complaining employee, the employee who is the subject of the investigation, percipient witnesses, and persons with relevant information and/or documents.

Give some thought to the order of the interviews. Sometimes there are strategic benefits to be gained by speaking with certain individuals before or after others. It is usually better to hold off on interviewing the peripheral players until after interviewing the key individuals, because it may be possible to conclude the investigation without even interviewing the peripheral players. A thoughtful ordering of witnesses may prevent unnecessary disclosure of information and lead to a more effective use of the company's resources.

Conducting the Investigation—Interviewing Witnesses

The effectiveness of an investigation will depend on how adept the investigator is at gathering the facts and then sifting through the facts to determine which ones are relevant and which ones are not. In most investigations the fact-gathering process is composed largely of interviewing witnesses, and it is critical that the investigator be well trained in the art of the interview. Preparation is the key.

Prepare a standard opening statement to use for each interview. The statement should address the concerns that the interviewee typically might have, such as the general subject of the investigation, what role the interviewee is playing in the investigation, how the information you receive from the interviewee will be used, whether the information will be kept confidential, and the possibility that the interviewee could be disciplined as a result of the investigation.

Outline the issues to be covered for each interview. Under each issue, list every fact that pertains to that issue. Under each fact leave room to write down the interviewee's response. Careful note taking is critical. Get down as many of the facts as possible during the interview, and complete the interview notes immediately after the conclusion of the interview.

Knowing how to ask a question is just as important as knowing what questions to ask. It is beyond the scope of this chapter to provide detailed pointers on effective interview questioning. However, the following are some issues that should be covered:

- Anticipate the questions likely to be asked by the interviewees and be ready with logical, reasonable responses.
- Be sensitive to the fact that being interviewed as part of an investigation can be stressful (putting the interviewee at ease also helps elicit information).
- Stress that no conclusions will be reached until all of the facts are gathered and analyzed.
- Stress that information will be disseminated on a need-to-know basis only (again, do not promise confidentiality).
- Stress that the interviewee has a strict duty to keep the investigation information confidential.
- Inform the interviewee that the company will not tolerate retaliation against employees who participate in an investigation.
- Explain that any employee who intentionally misdirects or interferes with an investigation will be subject to discipline.

Develop a standard closing:

- Ask the interviewee if there is anyone else he or she thinks should be interviewed.
- Review the interviewee's answers.
- Instruct the interviewee to contact you if he or she remembers or learns of additional information.
- Reemphasize the interviewee's obligation to maintain the confidentiality of the investigation.
- Answer any questions the person may have.
- Explain in general terms what will happen with the investigation from that point forward and when you expect to reach a determination.

When an Employee Asks to Have a Representative Attend the Interview—Weingarten Rights

Regardless of whether you have a unionized or union-free workforce, you need to be aware of your employees' Weingarten rights. First recognized by the US Supreme Court in 1975 with respect to unionized employees only,[238] Weingarten rights entitle an employee under the NLRA to have a coworker present during an investigative interview that the employee reasonably believes may result in his or her being disciplined.[239] In 2001, a federal court of appeals for the first time extended these Weingarten rights to nonunionized employees.[240] Although it remains unclear whether other federal courts of appeal or the US Supreme Court will adopt that extension of the law, nonunionized employers need to be aware of the possibility that Weingarten rights may apply to their workforce.

If an employee who reasonably believes that he or she may be disciplined in connection with an investigative interview requests the presence of a coworker in the interview, you must comply with that request in order to avoid the risk of having an unfair labor practices charge filed against you under the NLRA. If you are presented with a request to have a coworker present, you should decide among the following three options: (1) decline to proceed with the interview entirely; (2) proceed with the interview with the requested coworker present; or (3) represent to the employee that he or she will not be subjected to any discipline in connection with the investigation, thereby allowing you to proceed with the interview without the coworker being present.

Reaching a Conclusion and Making a Recommendation

After the investigator has conducted all of the necessary interviews and assembled all of the relevant facts, the investigator must analyze those facts and reach a conclusion as to what actually took place. Basic life experiences, common sense, and logic skills are required to do so. In determining what actually took place, examine the objective facts in order to reach a logical conclusion. Remember, it is permissible to be wrong in your conclusion—so long as you acted in good faith based on reasonable grounds.

After analyzing the facts and reaching a conclusion as to what happened, the investigator makes a recommendation to the appropriate member(s) of management regarding what, if any, action(s) should be taken. In formulating a recommendation, consider the following factors:

- Were any of the company's policies violated, and if so, was it a serious offense?
- What has the company done in the past in response to similar violations?
- How long has the employee who violated the policy been with the company, has he or she violated any other policies in the past, and what is his or her performance history?
- Are there any other circumstances that could affect your recommendation?
- What is your goal, and will the proposed course of action achieve that goal?

The investigator generally should conclude his investigation by memorializing his or her findings, conclusions, and recommendations in an investigative report.

Implementing the Results of the Investigation

Management depends on the investigator to assist it in reaching an appropriate resolution of the issue. However, it ultimately must be a member of management who makes the decision as to what action to take and who will implement that action.

Management must make sure that the appropriate person follows up with the complaining employee to make sure he or she is properly informed of the investigation results. Management also must make sure that the appropriate person follows up with the accused employee and describes the course and results of the investigation. The person who meets with the accused must be prepared to explain why the company reached the results it did. Anticipate the employee's questions and be prepared to answer them. Typically the accused should be notified in writing of the results of the investigation. The memo is important, so it must be drafted carefully. Explain the issues that were raised, the steps that were taken, the conclusions that were drawn, the information on which those conclusions were based, and the actions being taken as a result. Encourage the employee to provide any additional information, and conclude by informing the employee whom to contact if he or she has any questions or additional information.

In most cases it is inappropriate to inform other employees about the results of the investigation. If you should be asked about the results by an employee who was interviewed in connection with the investigation, simply explain that the information is confidential and thank him or her for the assistance.

The Final Investigation File

At the conclusion of the investigation, a final investigation file should be assembled. The file should consist of whatever information needs to be kept for the company record. The file generally should show the key steps that were taken to investigate and respond to the issues raised, including the following:

- Written communications from the complaining employee and other witnesses/interviewees
- Issue confirmation memo to complaining employee
- Any interim action notifications
- Investigation report
- Results and notifications
- Notes and supporting documentation necessary to support key facts and conclusions in the investigation summary
- Communications with others that may be important to demonstrate the steps taken in the investigation.

Only final copies of documents should be placed in the final investigation file. Drafts of the documentation listed should not be included in the file and should be destroyed if not inconsistent with the company's document retention policy. No other files containing investigation information should be kept. HR and management working files and notes should be reviewed to determine what is to be kept in the final investigation file and what is to be destroyed. Eliminate information stored on computers or disks.

The final investigation file should be marked as "need-to-know, confidential," and access to the file should be limited accordingly.

Conclusion

The foregoing is a general outline of how to conduct an effective internal investigation. Obviously, the specific mechanics of any investigation will differ, depending on such variables as the nature of the issues raised, the person(s) raising them, and the size and structure of your organization. It is important, therefore, that you contact your employment counsel as soon as you receive an employee complaint of misconduct so that you will be sure you conduct the investigation in a manner well-suited to the particular needs of your organization.

Employment Records and Record Keeping

In general, the goals of a records management system are to create and preserve records in compliance with the requirements of state, local, and federal law; preserve records in the event of litigation; create records to support personnel decisions; create and preserve records that will document rights that may be enforced at a later time (e.g., confidentiality and noncompete agreements); maintain a system that allows for efficient retrieval; and in general assist in effectively managing the workforce. Compliance always requires periodic follow-up to make sure that all staff handling employment records understand their responsibilities.

Human resources should have a records retention policy that deals with all records created and maintained by the department.

Limiting Access

Personnel records should be available only on a need-to-know basis. Paper records should be kept in a limited number of locations in cabinets that can be locked and in offices that are locked at the end of the day. Computer records should be protected through limited access via password. When an employee who works with those records leaves the company, the ex-employee's password should be disabled immediately.

Segregating Records

To protect the privacy of employees, and to comply with statutory requirements, certain records must be kept separate from the employee's regular personnel file. In general, records relating to medical treatment and the employee's medical condition, as well as drug test results, must be segregated from other records. Additionally, attorney–client and work-product materials should be kept separate from the personnel file, such as attorney–client correspondence, notes of conversations with the company's attorney, and notes of internal conversations with respect to pending or threatened litigation. At times it may be necessary to produce the file to third persons, such as a government agency, in response to a subpoena or in connection with ongoing litigation involving the institution. Segregating records in advance will prevent the harm that may occur in the too-often-seen scenario where the entire file is copied and produced to a third party without a careful review of its contents.

It is important to note that there are varying state laws relating to whether an employee may obtain access to his or her personnel file. Some states vest the employee with specific rights to inspect and copy the contents of the personnel file and may even provide deadlines as to when those tasks need to be accomplished. In those states, it is of particular importance that no privileged documents be included in the file.

Periodic Review of Forms and Records

The human resources department should conduct a periodic review of all forms to ensure compliance with state, federal, and local requirements, such as employment applications, FMLA forms, and I-9 forms. Not only should the form itself be reviewed, but also the manner in which staff are completing the forms should be scrutinized. For example, an audit should check to ensure that forms are signed when and where required, and that narratives such as employee reviews are grammatically correct and do not contain statements that are improper or that may give rise to liability.

Records Retention

A records retention program should balance the requirement to ensure compliance with all relevant laws with the business needs of the entity. The program contains two main components: a retention schedule, which specifies the length of time that records are to be kept, and procedures by which the program is implemented. The retention schedule should list every type of record maintained by human resources and the retention period for each record. In general, records must be maintained for at least the minimum period of time as set forth by statute, regulation, or general law.

Any destruction of records should follow a standard policy. Most importantly, as soon as the institution is made aware of pending or threatened litigation, there must be a mechanism in place to stop destruction of records that may relate to the litigation. If a court finds that an employer has adopted a destruction policy in bad faith for purposes of eliminating documents that may be used in anticipated litigation, that employer is subject to being sanctioned, and defense objectives seriously may be compromised. Even if documents routinely are destroyed pursuant to a record retention policy, and even if there is no pending litigation, the employer still may be required to maintain certain records if it knows that it will regularly be involved in a particular type of litigation, or if it knows that it has in the past and will in the future receive requests for certain documents on a routine basis through subpoena or otherwise, such as an audit by one or more governmental agencies.

The retention schedule and procedures should be reviewed annually so that the program can be revised to take into account changes in the records that the institution maintains, the changing needs of the institution, and any changes in the law. Further, vital records must be appropriately safeguarded, and provisions made for protection of records in case of a disaster. In many cases, the law may permit, and the entity may prefer, to store records electronically or on microfilm.

Special Issues Involving Electronic Mail

Electronic mail presents its own set of issues in creating and implementing a records retention policy. An e-mail is not simply the equivalent of a business record; rather, in practice it substitutes for hallway conversations, Post-it Notes, and informal memos, as well as being the repository of more formal documents. E-mail raises issues of particular concern in the area of employment law. Since e-mail is treated as an informal means of communication, and encourages informality and imprecision, it often results in the use of language that otherwise might not be expressed in the workplace.

Most e-mail messages are not of any long-term importance, and they should be deleted within a short period of time, preferably through an automatic system that deletes all messages that are more than a certain number of days old. Any messages that need to be retained can be transferred to a saved box or printed out and placed in a file.

Not only is e-mail discoverable in litigation and not protected from governmental agency investigations, but failure to preserve evidence, including such electronic data, may harm a party's case. "[W]hen the party has notice that the evidence is relevant—most commonly when suit has already been filed, providing the party responsible for the destruction [of evidence] with express notice, but also on occasion in other circumstances, as for example when a party *should have known* that the evidence may be relevant to future litigation," it may render that party's summary judgment motion vulnerable to denial[241] or otherwise subject that party to sanctions[242] if such evidence is not preserved. It is particularly important, therefore, to devise and carefully monitor a policy that is sensitive to these potential concerns.

Particular Record-Keeping Requirements Under Federal Law

The following sections are a summary of some of the record-keeping requirements under various federal regulations dealing with labor and employment laws. In preparing a records retention schedule, each statute and regulation should be consulted and periodically reviewed for changes in the law.

Title VII, Civil Rights Act of 1964[243]

Employers must maintain employment records dealing with hiring, promotion, demotion, transfer, layoff or termination, rates of pay or other terms of compensation, and selection for training or apprenticeship. Records must be retained for 1 year from the date the record was created or the personnel action taken, whichever is later. If the employee is terminated involuntarily, the records must be kept for 1 year from the date of termination.

If a charge of discrimination is filed, all relevant personnel records must be preserved until final disposition of the charge. This obligation extends to preserving records not only relating to the charging party, but also of others holding similar positions and, in the case of a failure to hire charge, applications and tests of other applicants who applied for the same position.

Fair Labor Standards Act[244]

Employers are required to keep for 3 years all payroll records, collective bargaining agreements, trusts, and employment contracts and to keep for 2 years all basic time and earnings cards showing daily starting and stopping times and wage rate tables.

Americans with Disabilities Act[245]

Medical records relating to disabilities must be maintained as confidential and kept separate from the main personnel file.

Family and Medical Leave Act[246]

In general, the record-keeping requirements for the FLSA apply. All records must be kept for 3 years and should include basic payroll and identifying employee data, dates of leave taken, hours of leave if taken in increments, and employee and employer notices of leave.

Records or documents relating to medical certifications, recertifications, or medical histories must be maintained as confidential medical records in separate files from the usual personal files, and if the ADA is applicable, in conformance with ADA confidentiality requirements.

Age Discrimination in Employment Act[247]

The employer must maintain the following records for a period of 3 years: employee's name, address, date of birth, occupation, rate of pay, compensation earned each week; job applications, resumes, other forms of employment inquiry, including records relating to failure or refusal to hire, promotion, demotion, transfer, selection for training, layoff, recall, or discharge; job orders submitted to any employment agency or labor organization for recruitment of personnel; and test papers disclosing the results of any employer-administered aptitude test considered by the employer in connection with any personnel action.

Equal Pay Act[248]

The employer must keep records that relate to payment of wages, wage rates, job evaluations, merit and incentive systems, and seniority systems, including records of any practices that explain the basis for payment of wage differential, such as collective bargaining agreements. Records must be kept for at least 2 years.

Occupational Safety and Health Act[249]

The Occupational Safety and Health Administration has established a hazard communication rule. The purpose of the rule is to provide workers with information on hazardous chemicals that they may be exposed to in the workplace, so they can take steps to protect themselves. Under this rule, chemical manufacturers are required to review scientific information regarding chemicals produced or imported to determine if they are hazardous. For each such hazardous chemical, the manufacturer or importer must develop a material safety data sheet and appropriate warning labels. Finally, employers are required to develop a written hazard communication program and provide information and training to employees regarding the hazardous chemicals in the workplace.

Employers must prepare and retain records containing an analysis of the manufacturer's or importer's hazard determination procedures, a written hazard communication program, and material safety data sheets pertaining to each chemical found at the employer's premises.

Immigration Reform and Control Act of 1986[250]

The employer must keep the completed Form I-9 for the longer of 3 years from the date of hire or 1 year after the date that the individual's employment is terminated. The employer is not required to make or keep copies of the supporting documentation, but may do so. USCIS investigators may inspect an employer's I-9 forms at any time. Department of Labor officials may also inspect I-9 forms; this usually arises in the course of a wage and hour audit.

Other Federal Laws

There are specific record-keeping requirements under a number of other labor and employment statutes, including requirements for federal affirmative action programs, the Employee Retirement Income and Security Act (ERISA), the Vietnam-Era Veterans Readjustment Assistance Act, the Rehabilitation Act of 1973, and Executive Order 11246.

Other Record-Keeping Requirements—State Laws

State laws often dictate record-keeping requirements for documents relating to workers' compensation, unemployment insurance, state wage and hour laws, employment contracts, other employment agreements and policies, and similar documents.

Disclaimer

This publication is designed to provide accurate and authoritative information in regard to the subject matter covered. It is sold with the understanding that the publisher is not engaged in rendering legal, accounting, or other professional service. If legal advice or other expert assistance is required, the service of a competent professional person should be sought. (From a Declaration of Principles jointly adopted by a committee of the American Bar Association and a committee of publishers and associations.)

References

1. See *Circuit City Stores, Inc v Adams*, 532 US 105, 121 S Ct 1302 (2001).
2. 42 USC §§2000e, *et seq.*
3. Individuals subject to race discrimination also may bring a lawsuit under the Civil Rights Acts of 1866 and 1871, which gives all persons the same right "to make and enforce contracts, to sue, be parties, give evidence, and to the full and equal benefit of all laws and proceedings." Procedurally, courts treat lawsuits under these statutes similar to lawsuits brought under Title VII, although there is no requirement that an individual file an administrative charge with a fair employment practices agency.
4. See Equal Pay Act of 1963, 29 USC §§206–209.
5. *Faragher v City of Boca Raton*, 118 S Ct 2275 (1998); *Burlington Indus v Ellerth*, 118 S Ct 225 (1998).
6. See also Pregnancy Discrimination Act of 1978, 42 USC §2000e(k).
7. 42 USC §§12111–12117.
8. The Rehabilitation Act of 1973, 29 USC §§701, *et seq*, enacted prior to the enactment of the ADA, prohibits disability discrimination with respect to government contractors or federal grant recipients.
9. The ADA also prohibits discrimination with respect to public accommodations or commercial facilities (i.e., structural issues such as access ramps).
10. Pub L No 110-325, 122 Stat 3553 (Sept 25, 2008).
11. Id.
12. Id at §4(4)(D) (to be codified at 42 USC §12102[4][D]).
13. Id at §3(2)(A) (to be codified at 42 USC §12102[2][A]).
14. Id at §3(2)(B) (to be codified at 42 USC §12102[2][B]).
15. Employers are advised to be aware that the ADA and the Family and Medical Leave Act often address similar issues, such as medical leaves of absence, medical certifications, and a return to work from a medical leave. Accordingly, it is strongly suggested that employers review both laws before making certain employment decisions.
16. See *Questions and Answers About Health Care Workers and the Americans with Disabilities Act*, http://eeoc.gov/facts/health_care_workers.html.
17. Id (citation omitted).
18. Id.
19. Id.
20. Id.
21. Id (citing *Clackamas Gastroenterology Assocs, PC v Wells*, 538 US 440, 123 S Ct 1673 [2003]).
22. *Questions and Answers About Health Care Workers and the Americans with Disabilities Act*, http://eeoc.gov/facts/health_care_workers.html.
23. Id.
24. Id.
25. 29 USC §§621, *et seq.*
26. See Cal Govt Code §12940 (West 2008); Conn Gen Stat §46a-81c (2008); Haw Rev Stat §378-2 (2008); 775 Ill Comp Stat Ann 5/1-102/103; ME Rev Stat Ann Title 5, §4572 (2008); Md Code Ann, Art 49B, §16 (West 2008); Mass Gen Laws Ann Ch 151B, §4 (West

2008); Minn Stat Ann §363A.08 (West 2008); Nev Rev Stat §613.330 (2008); NH Rev Stat Ann §354-A:7 (2008); NJ Stat Ann §10:5-12 (West 2008); NM Stat Ann §28-1-7 (West 2008); NY Exec Law §296 (McKinney 2008); RI Gen Laws §28-5-7 (2008); Vt Stat Ann Title 21, §495 (2008); Wash Rev Code Ann §49.60.180 (West 2008); Wis Stat Ann §111.36 (West 2008); and DC Code §2-1402.11 (2008).

27. NYC Admin Code §§8-107, *et seq.*

28. Ordinance No 433-94.

29. See Facts on Executive Order 11246—Affirmative Action, www.dol.gov/esa/regs/compliance/ofccp/aa.htm (Rev Jan 4, 2002) (The OFCCP is responsible for the enforcement of Executive Order 11246, as amended, Section 503 of the Rehabilitation Act of 1973, as amended, and the affirmative action provisions [Sec. 4212] of the Vietnam Era Veterans' Readjustment Assistance Act, as amended).

30. See 41 CFR §60-1.20; In order to prevent systemic compensation discrimination in particular by contractors, the Department of Labor has promulgated final interpretive standards to govern OFCCP's determination of whether a contractor has engaged in such a discriminatory practice. Interpreting Nondiscrimination Requirements of Executive Order 11246 with Respect to Systemic Compensation Discrimination; Notice, 71 Fed Reg 35,137-38 (Jun 12, 2006). These standards have two major characteristics: (1) an analysis as to whether the employees whose compensation is being compared are "similarly situated" and (2) utilization of a statistical technique known as multiple regression.

31. Id.

32. Id; see also 41 CFR §§60-1 and 60-2, revising the OFCCP regulations originally issued in 1978.

33. See Facts on Executive Order 11246, *supra*.

34. Id.

35. Id.

36. Fidell ER. Federal protection of private sector health and safety whistleblowers. *Administrative Law Journal*. 1988; 2.

37. Id.

38. 31 USC §§3729–3733.

39. See John Kruchko, The Whistle Blower Protection Provision of the False Claims Act: Advising Government Contractor Clients and Minimizing Liability, 2001 ABA Crim Just, Health L, Lab & Empl L, and Pub. Cont L Secs, and Nat. Assoc. Med. Fraud Contrl. Units, 7, 8.

40. Id.

41. Krause JH. Medical error as false claim. *American Journal of Law & Medicine*. 2001;27: 181–182.

42. Id. at 182–84. For example, in *United States ex rel Aranda v Comm'y Psychiatric Centers*, 945 F Supp 1485 (WD Okl 1996), a psychiatric hospital was accused of failing to provide Medicaid patients with the "reasonably safe environment" required by federal law. In that case, the government argued an implied certification theory, that is, that by billing Medicaid for its services, the hospital had implicitly certified that it was in compliance with the program's quality requirements.

43. See NY Labor Law §741. See also Ohio Rev Code Ann §4723.33 (prohibiting retaliation against nurses and dialysis technicians who report health care violations); 2002 Cal Stat §2056 (prohibiting retaliation against physicians who advocate for medically appropriate health care for patients); 2002 Ill. Comp. Stat Ann 45/3-608 (same re: Nursing Home Care Act).

44. Kruchko, *supra*, section V.B.

45. See, eg, Fla Stat Ann §768.096.

46. 15 USC §§1681, *et seq.*

47. See 15 USC §1681b(b).

48. See Meisinger Letter, n.1 (Aug 31, 1999), at FTC Web site, www.ftc.gov/os/statutes/fcra/index.htm.

49. See *Faragher v City of Boca Raton*, 118 S Ct 2275 (1998).

50. See, eg, Meisinger Letter, *supra*, and Vail Letter (Apr 5, 1999), at FTC Web site, *supra*.

51. But see *Hartman v Lisle Park District*, 158 F Supp 2d 869, 876 (ND Ill 2001) (rejecting argument that FCRA abrogated the attorney-client or work-product privileges in regard to workplace misconduct investigation, and finding that a report prepared by an attorney about an employee's transactions or experiences with the attorney's client [the employer] qualified as a report containing information solely as to transactions or experiences between the consumer and the person making the report within the meaning of the FCRA, even through the report was prepared by an entity other than the employer).

52. See 29 USC §§2001–2009.

53. See 29 USC §2006.

54. See *Hossaini v Western Missouri Medical Center*, 140 F.3d 1140 (8th Cir 1998).

55. See 29 USC §2006(d).

56. See *Lyle v Mercy Hospital Anderson*, 876 F Supp 157 (SD Ohio 1995).

57. 29 USC §2006(f).

58. 29 USC §§2101–2109.

59. 20 CFR §639.1.

60. Id.

61. See 29 USC §§2102, 2103.

62. In regard to the healthcare industry, a hospital's reliance upon the unforeseen business exception was upheld under circumstances where the hospital foundation's decision to discontinue making subventions to the hospital caused it to close and employees were not given 60 days advance notice of the closing. See *Jurcev v Central Comm'y Hospital*, 7 F.3d 618 (7th Cir 1993).

63. See 29 USC §2103.

64. See, eg, *Doty v Elias*, 733 F.2d 720, 722 (10th Cir 1984).

65. See *Tony and Susan Alamo Found'n v Sec'y of Labor*, 471 US 290 (1985).

66. See 29 USC §206(a)(1).

67. See 29 USC §207.

68. Id. Note, however, that the FLSA's regulations contain many exceptions to this rule, such as for employees with irregular hours of work ("Belo" plans), fluctuating workweeks, union contracts with guaranteed hours, etc.

69. *Barfield v New York Health and Hospitals Corp*, 537 F.3d 132 (2d Cir Aug 8, 2008). See also *Chao v Gotham Registry, Inc*, 514 F.3d 280 (2d Cir 2008) (finding nursing agency liable under the FLSA for overtime pay to nurses despite the agency having no control over whether its nurses were offered overtime by its hospital clients or whether its nurses had accepted such offers).

70. See generally 29 CFR §778.601.

71. See 29 CFR §541.602. Note, however, that a disciplinary deduction from an exempt employee's pay is permissible if it is for the infraction of a "safety rule of major significance." 29 CFR §541.602(b)(4). Although the issue has not been squarely addressed by the courts, the Wage and Hour Administrator of the US Department of Labor has taken the position that a registered nurse's violations of hospital rules "relating to patient well-being and job performance are not the type of deductions that would be permitted by . . . the regulations." See Wage & Hour Admin Op Ltr No 90-42NR (Mar 29, 1991). See also *Klein v Rush-Presbyterian-St. Luke's Medical Center*, 990 F.2d 279 (7th Cir 1993).

72. See 29 CFR §§541.101, *et seq*.

73. See 29 CFR §§541.201, *et seq*.

74. A registered or certified medical technologist is considered an exempt professional if he or she has successfully completed "3 academic years of preprofessional study in an accredited college or university plus a fourth year of professional course work in a school of medical technology approved by the Council of Medical Education of the American Medical Association . . . ." 29 CFR §541.301(e)(1).
75. See 29 CFR §§541.301, *et seq.*
76. *Fazekas v Cleveland Clinic Found'n Health Care Ventures, Inc*, 204 F.3d 673 (6th Cir 2000).
77. *Belt v EmCare, Inc*, 444 F.3d 403 (5th Cir 2006), *cert. denied*, 127 S Ct 349 (2006).
78. Id at 417 (citation and quotation marks omitted).
79. 29 CFR §541.402
80. Id.
81. See *supra* _____ [Barfield endnote, *supra*].
82. 29 CFR §791.2 (a).
83. Id.
84. Id.
85. 29 CFR §791.2(b).
86. W&H Div Op Ltr. (July 13, 1998). See also W&H Div Op. Ltr. (January 7, 1999) (opining that certified nurses assistants were jointly employed by group of affiliated nursing homes); W&H Div Op. Ltr. (May 20, 1999) (opining that large acute care hospital facility and small hospital, each of which had its own administrator, personnel policies, and separate management of day-to-day labor relations policies, including separate human resources departments, but which were both owned by nonprofit hospital parent corporation, were joint employers).
87. See 29 USC §2612; 29 CFR §§825, *et seq.*
88. See 29 USC §2601; 29 CFR §§825.100, *et seq.*
89. See 29 USC §2611(2); 29 CFR §§825.110, *et seq.*
90. See 29 USC §2612(a)(1); 29 CFR §§825.112, *et seq.*
91. See 29 CFR §2612(e); 29 CFR §§825.208, 825.302, *et seq.*
92. See 29 CFR §2613; 29 CFR §§825.305, *et seq.*
93. 29 CFR §825.301(c). The US Supreme Court rejected the DOL's position that an employee, whose employer had failed to give the employee timely notice of designation of FMLA leave, was entitled greater than the 12 weeks of leave mandated by the FMLA. See *Ragsdale v Wolverine Worldwide, Inc*, 122 S Ct 1155 (2002).
94. See 29 CFR §2612(f); 29 CFR §825.202.
95. See 29 CFR §2612(b); 29 CFR §§825.203, *et seq.*
96. See 29 CFR §2614(b); 29 CFR §§825.217, *et seq.*
97. See, eg, Cal Lab Code §§1810, *et seq.*; Nev Rev Stat §608.18.
98. See, eg, NY Labor Law §162.
99. See, eg, Ariz Rev Stat §23-352.
100. See, eg, Cal Lab Code §§200, *et seq.*
101. See, eg, NY Labor Law §193.
102. See, eg, Ariz Rev Stat §23-352 (3).
103. See, eg, NY Labor Law §191; Ariz Rev Stat §23-351.
104. See, eg, NY Labor Law §191; Cal Lab Code §201; Ariz Rev Stat §23-353.
105. See, eg, NY Labor Law §192.
106. See §501(c)(3) of the Internal Revenue Code (IRC).
107. Pub L 93-406, 88 Stat 829 (1974).
108. See, eg, Health Insurance Portability and Accountability Act of 1996 (HIPAA), Pub L No 104-191; Mental Health Parity Act of 1996 (MHPA), ERISA §712, IRC §9812, 4980D; Newborns and Mothers' Health Protection Act of 1996 (NMHPA), ERISA §711, IRC §9811; and Women's Health and Cancer Rights Act of 1998 (WHCA), ERISA §713.

109. See Treas Regs §§1.401(a), *et seq.*

110. Treas Regs §1.401-1(b)(1)(i); see also Rev Rul 79-90, 1979-1 CB 155.

111. IRS GCM 38283. The recently enacted Pension Protection Act of 2006 was a reaction to a rash of corporate bankruptcies which occurred in the early to mid-2000s, which caused workers to bear the brunt of corporate mismanagement. Pension Protection Act of 2006, Pub L No 109-280, 120 Stat 780 (codified as amended in scattered sections of 26 USC and 29 USC). See also Daniel B. Klaff, The Pension Protection Act of 2006: Reforming the Defined Benefit Pension System, 44 HVLJ 553, 553 (2007). The Pension Protection Act's goal is to promote the "long-term solvency of the system and therefore the protection of workers' deferred benefit pensions." Id.

112. IRC §401(k)(4)(B).

113. See IRC §414(q) and the regulations promulgated thereunder.

114. See IRC §403(b)(1)(A)(i); Treas Regs §1.403(b)-1(b)(1)(i).

115. Pub L No 107-16.

116. Tax Reform Act of 1986, Pub L No 99-514.

117. IRC §457(a)–(e).

118. IRC §457(f).

119. ERISA §3(1).

120. For a discussion of HIPAA, see Chapter 3.

121. See, eg, IRC §§79, 105, 106, 127, 129, 419, 419A & 4980B.

122. ERISA §§101–111, 401–414 & 503.

123. See ERISA §3(1).

124. See DOL Regs §2510.3-1(b)(1a).

125. See IRS GCM 39616; PLRs 702063, 9442031, 9629033, & 9722039.

126. See, eg, Cal Const, Art I, §1; Fla Const, Art I, §23; Ill. Const, Art I, §6.

127. 18 USC §§2510, *et seq.*

128. 15 USC §§1681, *et seq.*

129. For a more detailed discussion of the FCRA, see pp. 9–10, *supra.*

130. *Colgate Palmolive Co*, 323 NLRB No 82 (1997).

131. 29 USC §§651, *et seq.*

132. 41 USC §§701, *et seq.*

133. See, eg, *Amer Fed'n of Gov't Employees, Local 2110 v Derwinski*, 777 F Supp 1493 (ND Cal 1991).

134. 29 USC §157.

135. US Bureau of Labor Statistics, Union Membership by Industry, 2007 (Feb 11, 2008) http://www.bls.gov/cgi-bin/print.pl/opub/ted/2008/feb/wk2/art01.htm.

136. The National Labor Relations Board, a five-member federal administrative agency, enforces and resolves disputes under the NLRA.

137. The NLRA defines the term labor organization broadly and includes, but is not limited to, a formally constituted union. An employer may commit an unfair labor practice by dominating or assisting any employee committee that exists for the purpose, in whole or in part, of dealing with employers concerning grievances, labor disputes, wages, rates of pay, hours of employment or conditions of work. Employers have violated this provision by financing or forming employee committees. See *Grouse Mountain Assoc. II*, 333 NLRB No 157 (2001). Recent Congressional efforts to amend this portion of the statute have been unsuccessful.

138. See, eg, *Brockton Hosp v NLRB*, 294 F.3d 100 (D.C. Cir 2002).

139. *Epilepsy Found'n of Northeast Ohio v NLRB*, 268 F.3d 1095 (D.C. Cir 2001), *cert. denied*, 122 S. Ct. 2356 (2002).

140. *NLRB v IBEW Local 1229 (Jefferson Stan. Broadcasting)*, 346 US 464, 74 S Ct 172 (1953).

141. *Comm'y Hosp of Roanoke Valley v NLRB*, 538 F.2d 607 (4th Cir 1976).

142. If a hospital has a cafeteria, restaurant, or other place generally open to the public, then nonemployees can solicit or distribute literature so long as the activity does not disrupt or interfere with the hospital's administrative or treatment activities.

143. See *Beth Israel Hosp v NLRB*, 437 US 483, 98 S. Ct. 2463 (1978); see also *NLRB v Baptist Hosp*, 442 US 773, 99 S Ct 2598 (1979).

144. *Brockton Hosp v NLRB, supra.*

145. Id.

146. Id.

147. See *Medical Center Hosp*, 244 NLRB 742 (1979); see also *NLRB v Presbyterian Medical Center*, 586 F.2d 165 (10th Cir 1978).

148. Id at 7.

149. Id at 2.

150. Id.

151. Id.

152. Id. at 3.

153. Id at 10–11.

154. Id at 10.

155. See *Timekeeping Systems*, 323 NLRB 244 (1997).

156. See *St Joseph's Hosp*, 337 NLRB No 12 (2001).

157. See *Damon Medical Lab*, 234 NLRB 333 (1978).

158. The NLRA defines health care institutions, as including "any hospital, convalescent hospital, health maintenance organization, health clinic, nursing home, extended care facility, or other institution devoted to the care of sick, infirm, or aged persons." 29 USC §152 (14).

159. 29 USC §159(b).

160. Acute care hospitals are defined as those in which (1) the average length of patient stay is less than 30 days; or (2) over 50% of all patients are admitted to units in which the average length of stay is less than 30 days.

161. *American Hosp Ass'n v NLRB*, 111 S Ct 1539 (1991).

162. 29 USC §152(14).

163. 120 Cong Rec 13,559 (1974) (remarks of Sen Taft).

164. *San Diego Blood Bank*, 219 NLRB 116 (1975).

165. Id at 116, n.17. See also *Sacramento Med Found'n Blood Bank*, 220 NLRB 904 (1975); *Greene Cty Chap Amer Red Cross*, 221 NLRB 776 (1975).

166. *Damon Medical Laboratory, Inc*, 234 NLRB 333 (1978).

167. Id at n.1. See also *Boston Medical Laboratory, Inc*, 235 NLRB 1271, n.2 (1978) (concluding that "testing human medical specimens does not involve patient care"); *Center for Laboratory Medicine, Inc*, 234 NLRB 387 (1978).

168. 302 NLRB 72 (1991).

169. Id.

170. Id.

171. Id at n.8.

172. Cf *North Suburban Blood Center v NLRB*, 661 F.2d 632, 635 (7th Cir 1981) (stating that "the crucial factor in the definition of health care institution is patient welfare" and rejecting the NLRB's view that patient care must physically occur at the facility to qualify it as a health care institution).

173. 29 USC §152(11).

174. See generally *NLRB v Kentucky River Comm'y Care*, 121 S. Ct. 1861 (2001).

175. *Oakwood Healthcare, Inc* 348 NLRB No 37 (2006).

176. Id at 12.

177. Id at 13–14.

178. *Golden Crest Healthcare Center*, 348 NLRB No 39, 3 (2006).

179. Id at 5.
180. Id.
181. *Boston Medical Center*, 330 NLRB No 30 (1999).
182. *M.B. Sturgis Inc*, 331 NLRB No 173 (2000).
183. Id.
184. *North Suburban Blood Center v NLRB*, 661 F.2d 632, 635 (7th Cir 1981) (citations omitted).
185. 29 USC §158(g).
186. See pp 28–30, *supra*.
187. *District 1199 and Parkway Pavilion Healthcare*, 222 NLRB 212, *enforc den'd without opin.*, 556 F.2d 558 (2d Cir 1976).
188. *District 1199 and United Hospitals of Newark*, 232 NLRB 443 (1977).
189. *Amer Fed'n of Nurses, Local 535, SEIU and Kaiser Found'n Hospitals*, 313 NLRB 1201 (1994).
190. 1992 NLRB GCM LEXIS 91 (*Western Medical Ctr*, Dec 21, 1992).
191. 29 USCA. §158(d).
192. See *First National Maintenance Corp v NLRB*, 452 US 666, 101 S. Ct. 2573 (1981); *Fibreboard Paper Products Corp v NLRB*, 379 US 203, 85 S Ct 398 (1964).
193. *First National Maintenance*, 452 US at 677.
194. Id at 681–82.
195. See *Providence Hosp and Mercy Hosp v NLRB*, 93 F.3d 1012, 1018 (1st Cir 1996).
196. *Detroit Edison Co v NLRB*, 440 US 301 (1979).
197. *Providence Hosp and Mercy Hosp v NLRB*, 93 F.3d at 1019.
198. Employment is defined as "any service or labor performed by an employee for an employer within the United States." 8 CFR §274a.1(h).
199. 8 CFR §274a.1(j).
200. 8 CFR §274a.5.
201. See CFR §274a1(c) & (f).
202. See 66 Interpreter Releases 1173-74, 1188-89 (Oct 23, 1989).
203. See INA §274A(b)(2).
204. 8 CFR §274a.1(c).
205. 8 CFR §274a.2(b)(1)(ii).
206. 8 CFR §274a.2(b)(1)(vi).
207. The actual document list is set out in the Handbook for Employers M-274 (available from the USCIS Web site: www.uscis.gov), which was recently revised and released on November 1, 2007.
208. 8 CFR §274a.2(b)(3).
209. 8 CFR §274a.2(b)(1)(viii).
210. Id.
211. 8 CFR §274a.2(b)(1)(viii)(A).
212. 8 CFR §274a.2(b)(1)(vii).
213. See *Handbook for Employers*.
214. INA §274A(b)(3)(B).
215. INA §274A(b)(3).
216. See *US v Peking Inc*, 2 OCAHO 329 (June 18, 1991) (holding that employer may not have individual commence work prior to inspection of documents).
217. INA §274A(e)(5); 8 CFR §274a.10(b)(2).
218. INA §274B(g)(2)(B)(v)-(vi).
219. 8 CFR §274a.10(b)(2); see also 69 Interpreter Releases 253, 255-256 (Mar 2, 1992).
220. *US v Morgan's Mexican & Lebanese Foods*, 8 OCAHO 1013 (1998).
221. INA §274A(a)(1).

222. INA §274A(a)(2).
223. 8 CFR §274a.1(l)(1).
224. INA §274A(e)(4); 8 CFR §274a.10(b)(1); 28 CFR §68.52(c).
225. See 69 Interpreter Releases 253, 255, App. II (Mar 2, 1992).
226. INA §274A(f)(1).
227. 8 CFR §274a.1(k).
228. INA §274.
229. INA §274B.
230. INA §274B(a)(6). The IIRAIRA added the requirement that the request for more or different documents or refusal to accept proffered documents had to be done with the intent to discriminate.
231. INA §274B(a)(5).
232. INA §274B(a)(2)(A).
233. Id (citing INA §274B[a][2][C]).
234. INA §274B(a)(2)(B).
235. INA §274B(a)(4).
236. INA §274B(a)(6).
237. In some cases, and for some employers, the investigation should be conducted by an outside counsel or other qualified professional. It is beyond the scope of this chapter to discuss investigations conducted by outside experts; suffice it to say that such investigations merit additional considerations, including (1) the possibility that federal and state law may afford certain employee notification rights not implicated by an investigation conducted strictly by the employer itself and (2) the possibility that an investigation conducted by outside counsel may protect certain information under the attorney-client privilege and attorney work product doctrine.
238. *NLRB v Weingarten*, 420 US 251 (1975).
239. There may be state law exceptions to Weingarten rights. For example, the New York State Court of Appeals recently held that New York State public employees do not have a Weingarten right under the New York's Taylor law, which is a state equivalent of the NLRA for New York State government employees. Matter of *New York City Transit Authority v New York State Public Relations Board, 8 NY3d 226, slip op (2007)*
240. *Epilepsy Found'n of Northeast Ohio v NLRB, supra.*
241. *Kronisch v US*, 150 F.3d 112, 126 (2d Cir 1998) (citations omitted), *overruled on other grounds, Rotella v Wood*, 528 US 549, 120 S Ct 1075 (2000).
242. See, eg, *Zubulake v UBS Warburg LLC*, 229 FRD 422 (SD NY 2004).
243. 29 CFR §1602.14.
244. 29 CFR Part 516.
245. 29 CFR §1630.14.
246. 29 CFR §825.500.
247. 29 CFR §1627.2.
248. 29 CFR §1620.32.
249. 29 CFR §1910.1200.
250. 8 CFR §274a.

Biographical Information

John D. Blair, PhD, is the Trinity Company Professor in Management and Health Care Strategy at the Rawls College of Business Administration (and the School of Medicine) at Texas Tech University. He is the founding director of the Center for Healthcare Leadership and Strategy and serves as the Center's Chief of Bioterrorism Studies. He is also a founding coeditor of *Advances in Health Care Management*, a JAI/Elsevier research series. He has also served as chair of the Health Care Management Division of the National Academy of Management. His forthcoming book with Myron Fottler and Albert Zapanta is *Bioterrorism Preparedness, Attack and Response: Advancing Theory and Practice* (2003). His other recent books include *Strategic Leadership for Medical Groups: Navigating Your Strategic Web* (1998); *Challenges in Military Health Care* (1993); and *Challenges in Health Care Management: Strategic Perspectives for Managing Key Stakeholders* (1990). He received his PhD from the University of Michigan in 1975.

Peter D. Stergios is a partner in the law firm of McCarter & English, LLP's Labor and Employment Practice Group. His work includes all aspects of healthcare organization representation, such as hospital merger and acquisition, system reorganization and development, labor contract negotiation, arbitration, mediation, defending against strikes and boycotts and illegal picketing activity, and advising employers in union representation campaigns. He obtained his juris doctor degree from Harvard Law School in 1972 after returning from military service. He is rated AV by Martindale-Hubbell, the national directory and rating service for law practitioners.

Patrick M. Collins is a partner in the law firm of McCarter & English, LLP's Labor and Employment Practice Group. He represents management clients in a variety of industries, including health care, energy, retail, construction, and high-tech. Mr. Collins graduated cum laude from the Boston University School of Law in 1990 and earned a bachelor of arts degree from Fordham University in 1984.

Aimee Sato is an associate in the law firm of McCarter & English, LLP's Labor and Employment Practice Group, where she specializes in employment counseling and litigation. She is a graduate of Haverford College and St. John's University School of Law.

The contributions of Joseph Z. Fleming, Ronald M. Rosengarten, John F. Scalia, Elissa McGovern, David B. Spanier, Leigh Anne Ciccarelli, Alan Jockers, Scott Johnson, John F. Lomax Jr., and Eric Sigda are acknowledged.

The Management of Nursing Services

Wilhelmina M. Manzano and Gina M. Bufe

Nursing services are typically the largest service in a healthcare organization and require executive leadership that has the competencies necessary to manage, advocate for resources, and create an environment that provides quality compassionate nursing care. The practice of nursing is defined by state laws and supported by American Nurses' Association (ANA) standards to support the provision of safe, quality, and ethical nursing practice across the continuum of services across an organization. The organization's structure for a department of nursing is determined by various factors such as size and complexity of the organization and may include both centralized and decentralized functions. The functions for an organization's department of nursing continuously evolve to meet daily operational needs.

Nursing Services Structure

The first step in establishing an optimally functioning department of nursing is to ensure that the structure of the department is well defined. With the ever-changing nature of health care in the 21st century, it is not uncommon that the structure of nursing services has evolved over the last several decades. Traditional models—with a single-leader hierarchy and pyramid-type organizational structure, as described by Westphal (2005), where members of the organization report to one supervisor and decisions flow typically from the leader down to members of the team—are no longer seen in the complex healthcare organizations and healthcare systems of the 21st century. Traditional models have been replaced with matrix models and service line models and often a combination of the two models.

Matrix models, as described by Westphal, are based on having two supervisors, one being a functional supervisor of the specialty area in which the individual works; the other is the supervisor of the current work initiative. Though this model is frequently seen in engineering, the model is also seen in health care where care is structured to meet the needs of a particular population such as orthopedic, cardiovascular, or psychiatric services. Service line models have demonstrated increase in volume and market share and decreased costs in healthcare organizations (Tesch & Levy, 2008).

Service line models are helpful in managing nursing services in an organization as financial indicators such as volume, market share, and costs are routinely a part of the nurse executive's financial dashboard and are reviewed routinely and acted upon as indicated to ensure appropriate levels of nursing services. Successful service lines have a clear definition of what comprises the service line so that the organization is able to stay focused on outcomes and benchmarks. Tesch & Levy (2008) describe five characteristics of service line definitions that lead to successful outcomes: (1) the service lines are patient centered to where patients would be receiving services for treatment of a particular issue, (2) the patient population identifies with the service line, (3) the service line improves quality as well as efficiency through the coordination of services, (4) the services cross multiple sites, and (5) there are clear benchmarks to measure the service line's performance. Litch (2007) also declares that there are short-term as well as long-term benefits to service line structure such as improving access to quality care to the community, creating branding for an organization in caring for a particular population, and creating continuums of care with well-defined outcomes.

The development of service lines fall into four phases: (1) service line marketing, which focuses only on marketing services to a particular population; (2) service line leadership, which focuses on leaders being the champion for care of a particular population; (3) service line management, where managers have operational responsibility for the care of a particular population; (4) service line organization, where there is organizational redesign and support services report to the core structure that provides care to a particular population (Litch, 2007). Service line organizations have senior leadership, and often, the nurse executive takes on the roles of both site administrator and service line leader. Patterson (2008) indicates that organizations over the last 25 years have gone through several phases of service line development and that in many organizations where development was halted and the service line did not evolve, service lines in these organizations began to disappear. Westphal (2005) concurs that successful organizations are those that are resilient and whose service lines have responded to changes in the market, which is imperative in today's tough economic environment.

Frequently, the nurse executive is the individual in the organization that provides the leadership in this type of matrix service line structure. Another example of a matrix reporting structure is a model of the functional reporting structure of a nursing department combined with a patient care services model, whereby other services that support patient care such as social work or respiratory therapy matrix report through nursing and patient care services. A premise behind the patient care services model is to ensure that care is delivered in a patient-centered manner and all services that support patient-centered care are managed at the unit level. The structure adopted by a healthcare organization will set the stage for the nurse executive to create the environment and secure the resources necessary to provide quality patient care at the bedside.

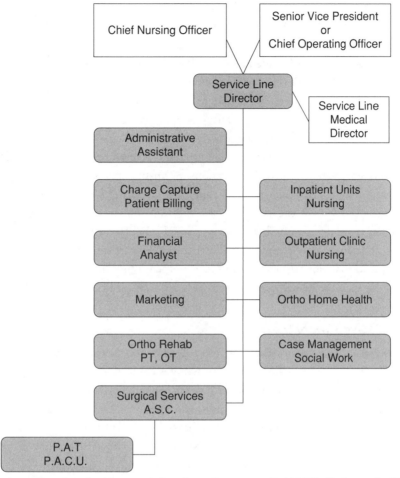

FIGURE 6.1 Reprinted with permission from Patterson, C. (2008) *Orthopaedic Nursing*, *27* (1) p14.

Role of the Nurse Executive

The role of the nurse executive has evolved over the last several decades and is reflected in the title of nurse executives at various levels as well as in reporting structure. The senior nurse executive in an organization is typically titled Chief Nursing Executive or Chief Nursing Officer and is usually a senior member of the executive team who reports to the Chief Executive Officer of the organization. The Chief Nursing Officer (CNO) may lead a single organization or lead a multisite system (**Figure 6.1**). CNOs with multisite span of control must possess leadership skills that foster a shared vision across the various sites. The role of the healthcare system CNO is challenging and complex with numerous opportunities (Caroselli, 2008). The increasing demands and complexity of the CNO role frequently leads to increased turnover in this population. Rollins (2008) reports that a 2007 AONE (American Organization of Nurse Executives) survey showed 62% of CNOs expect to change jobs in five years.

The CNO may have Vice Presidents of Nursing and Patient Care Services reporting to the CNO who are accountable for the oversight of patient care, planning, and daily nursing operations. The responsibilities of the Vice President of Nursing and Patient Care Services include fiscal planning and resource allocation, staffing, employee relations, and strategic planning, as well as the quality of all nursing practice at their respective areas.

Reporting to the Vice President of Nursing and Patient Care Services is a Director of Nursing who has oversight of the daily operations for nursing in a particular service line such as pediatrics, cardiovascular, psychiatry, or rehabilitative medicine. Reporting to the director are the frontline leaders, who are called patient care directors in many organizations. The front-line leader's title has evolved from nurse manager to patient care director to be more reflective of the organization and provision of patient care. The title patient care director is also reflective of the resources required to be managed at the unit level in today's healthcare environment, which encompasses more than the management of nursing staff only. (See **Figure 6.2.**)

Nurse Executive Competencies

The increased span of control for the nurse executive has necessitated the development of both clinical and business acumen. Clinical acumen requires competency related to nursing practice in various settings. Business acumen requires skill sets which include business planning, budgeting, conflict resolution, and management of human resources. The nurse executive is required to have keen communication and negotiating skills, especially when dealing with labor management issues. The American Organization of Nurse Executives (AONE) has recognized the evolving role of the nurse leader and the need for additional competencies. AONE states that core competencies for nurse executives include communication and relationship building; knowledge of the healthcare environment; professionalism; business skills; and at the center, leadership (**Figure 6.3**).

The landmark publication by the Institute of Medicine in 2004, *Keeping Patients Safe: Transforming the Quality of the Work Environment*, identified that more than 98,000 individuals die per year as a result of medical errors. The Institute of Medicine (National Academy of Sciences, 2004) identified key strategies to potentially prevent medical errors related to nursing services which included focus on management, work processes, workforce, and organizational culture. The strategy of management focuses on developing effective leaders in the organization. Nurse leaders, to be effective, create an environment that engages trust from employees. Employees are actively engaged in redesign initiatives, and decisions are collaborative in nature. The environment is also one that promotes ongoing learning in the organization. Another strategy to potentially prevent medical errors related to nursing services is to strengthen work processes in the organization. Work processes are strengthened by addressing work environment issues related to streamlining work flow and using technology enablers such as computerized

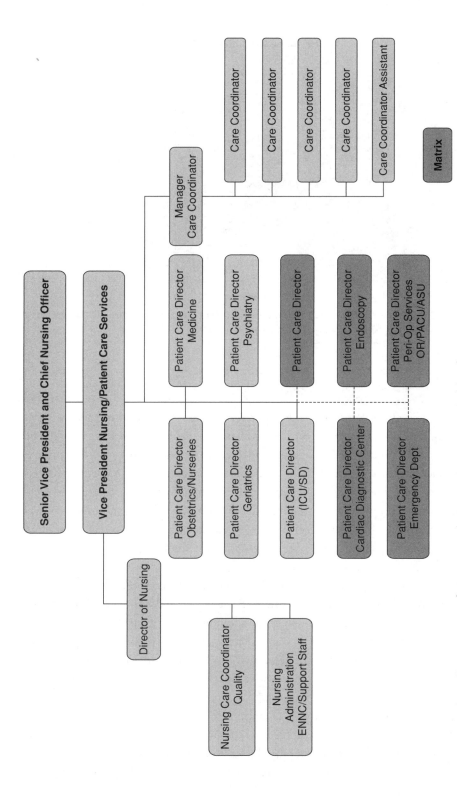

FIGURE 6.2 Department of Nursing and Patient Care Services Table of Organization

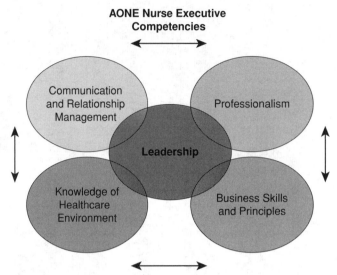

FIGURE 6.3   AONE Nurse Executive Competencies. Reprinted with permission from the American Organization of Nurse Executives. All rights reserved.

medical records. The effective nurse leader also addresses environmental factors that contribute to work fatigue, such as limits on the number of hours a nurse works in a day and ensuring that ancillary support staff are trained adequately to support the role of the nurse. Effective nurse leaders also ensure that the workforce is developed and functioning effectively through fostering interdisciplinary communication, relationships, and enhanced technical and clinical skills through mentoring. Finally, the culture of the organization is one in which there is effective conflict resolution and the culture is one that is "just" and not punitive in nature. These four key strategies are congruent with the five core competencies defined by AONE.

The first AONE core competency on communication and relationship building focuses on nurse executives' ability to effectively communicate through oral and written media to diverse groups within nursing and to other disciplines. In addition, effective communication should also encompass resolving conflicts when they arise. The nurse executive should also possess the skill of building trust in relationships with peers, staff, physicians, community leaders, legislators, and others. The nurse executive asserts viewpoints in nonthreatening, nonjudgmental ways and influences others through creating a shared vision. The nurse executive promotes diversity through establishing an environment of cultural competency and includes cultural beliefs in patient care. Effective communication is established through shared decision making with staff and involvement in the community. Effective communication is also essential in managing relationships with medical staff as well as academic relationships with partnering schools and colleges of nursing.

The core competency related to the knowledge of the healthcare environment includes maintaining clinical knowledge of current nursing practice as well as standards established by regulatory agencies such as the Joint Commission. As the senior nurse leader in the organization, the nurse executive also must ensure current knowledge of state nurse practice acts and key legislation that affects nursing practice at all levels. Part of ensuring knowledge of the healthcare environment is to also ensure current evidence-based policies and standards to support nursing practice in the organization. This knowledge of the healthcare environment is also demonstrated through assessment of care delivery models and leadership in work redesign initiatives. Knowledge of healthcare economics is essential, including knowledge of the organization's case mix index (CMI) and current trends in reimbursement such as no payment for specific hospital-acquired conditions, which became effective October 1, 2008 (CMS, 2008; National Conference of State Legislatures, 2008).

It is imperative that the nurse executive understand the implications and history behind no payment for specific hospital-acquired conditions. In April 2007, "preventable errors" and "never events" were proposed and implemented as a provision of the Deficit Reduction Act of 2005 (DRA). The Centers for Medicare & Medicaid Services (CMS) then identified at least two hospital-acquired conditions that may have caused cases to be grouped into a higher-weighted DRG. These conditions were also identified as being potentially high-cost and high-volume conditions.

On August 1, 2007, CMS issued the final Inpatient Prospective Payment System (IPPS) rule for hospitals. It had three components:

1. Expansion of hospital quality measurement and reporting obligations
2 Penalties for failures to meet obligations
3. Elimination of additional reimbursement for selected conditions and complications acquired in the hospital

The IPPS rule became effective October 1, 2008, eliminating payment for the following hospital-acquired conditions:

1. Objects left in surgery
2. Air embolism
3. Blood incompatibility
4. Catheter-associated UTIs
5. Decubitus ulcers, stage III and IV
6. Vascular catheter-associated infection
7. SSI—mediastinitis after CABG
8. Falls with specific trauma codes
9. Manifestations of poor glycemic control
10. Deep vein thrombosis (DVT)/pulmonary embolism

These conditions must be coded as present on admission (POA) or they will not be considered for reimbursement purposes. POA is defined as being present at the time the order for inpatient admission occurs. Therefore, conditions that develop during outpatient services, which include ED, observation, or outpatient surgery, are considered as present on admission. Hospitals began using the POA flag in October 1, 2007, and on October 1, 2008, CMS suppressed hospital-acquired conditions for coding purposes. Public reporting is also under consideration for hospital-acquired conditions. The reporting would be similar to the public reporting currently done for the Joint Commission core measures, but instead for several nursing-sensitive indicators such as pressure ulcer prevalence, falls, falls with injury, urinary catheter-associated UTIs, and failure to rescue. Implications for nursing practice and reimbursements include the elimination of higher payment for nursing-related preventable complications, continued investment in nursing quality, and strategies to avoid adverse events. Nurse executives should be involved in the identification of financial impact of CMS changes and ongoing education to staff on the prevention of the hospital-acquired conditions.

The core competency related to leading the environment for nursing services also requires that the nurse executive possesses knowledge of outcome measurement, case management, risk management, patient safety, and performance improvement. The healthcare environment competencies include knowledge of healthcare policy and organizational governance. The nurse executive needs to demonstrate fiscal responsibility and understanding of current credentialing processes for all nurses in the organization.

The core competency of professionalism is defined by AONE (2005) as taking personal and professional accountability in creating an environment that is conducive to change and producing results, and also by holding others accountable as appropriate. The nurse executive demonstrates professionalism by also developing others through career planning and coaching. The nurse executive exemplifies professionalism through membership in professional organizations and also through incorporating ethical principles into practice. The nurse executive is also the primary advocate of the patient by ensuring nursing practice is patient-centered.

The core competency of business acumen is one competency that many nursing administration programs at the graduate level have developed further over the last decade. Nurse executives are expected in today's complex organizations to be able to identify and develop business plans and models of care. AONE (2005) defines this competency further by breaking down the business skill sets into analysis of financial statements, development of business plans, and education of the healthcare team on the financial implications of healthcare delivery plans. Business acumen is also exemplified through management of human resources through workforce planning, assessment of workforce satisfaction, shared decision making, reward and recognition programs, selecting top talent, and succession planning. A component of business acumen is competencies in strategic planning, implementation, and marketing.

The fifth and center core competency of nurse executives as identified by AONE (2005) is the leadership competency. In order for the nurse executive to be proficient in the other four aforementioned competencies, basic leadership competency must be attained. Leadership competency includes identification of decision-making skills and visionary leadership. Competent nurse executives also demonstrate leadership skills that value feedback and seek mentorship from colleagues. The nurse executive that excels in leadership acumen is noted to be an effective change agent and also exemplifies knowledge of systems.

ANA Scope and Standards for Nurse Administrators

The ANA Scope and Standards for Nurse Administrators are currently under review (Scott & Craig, 2008). Currently there are 14 standards that guide nursing services in organizations (ANA, 2004). The Magnet Recognition Program is a recognition program by the American Nurses' Credentialing Center that acknowledges excellence in nursing services based on the ANA Scope and Standards (Morgan, Lahman, & Hagstrom, 2006). Morgan, Lahman, and Hagstrom (2006) indicate that fewer than 200 healthcare organizations currently hold magnet status. Whether or not an organization decides to pursue magnet status, nurse executives should be familiar with the ANA Scope and Standards for Nurse Administrators (2004) and use these standards to assess nursing services in his/her organization. These 14 standards are noted in the following sections.

Assessment

Nurse executives are charged with ensuring that all consumers of health care receive nursing assessments for the consumers' presenting issue. Nurse executives ensure that policies and procedures are evidence-based and current to ensure appropriate nursing assessments are conducted in the organization. Nurse executives ensure that nurses are trained in appropriate assessment techniques through orientation and precepting programs. Ongoing assessments are validated through competency assessment programs. Many organizations use nurses in advanced roles such as clinical nurse specialists (a nurse with a master's degree in a clinical specialty and successful American Nurses Credentialing Center certification) as expert resources for the frontline nurse. Nurse executives also support the structure of ongoing training in assessment through nursing education functions such as unit-based education, nursing grand rounds, and case studies.

In addition to the oversight of assessment of care, the nurse executive also requires the skill set to make organizational assessments and changes. This is illustrated by Mustain, Lowry, and Wilhoit (2008) through an organizational assessment to facilitate the implementation of an electronic medical record system in a healthcare organization. These authors emphasize that nurse executives are crucial in the planning, vision, and implementation of system changes that affect an organization. The nurse executive also uses assessment skills in addressing work environment issues, which have been identified as a critical factor regarding nurse turnover, satisfaction, and retention (Lacey et al., 2008).

Problem/Diagnosis

Nurse executives ensure that nursing staff have the skills necessary to use assessment information and identify nursing diagnoses to address actual or potential health problems of the clients they serve. This has been accomplished in many organizations through support of electronic medical records and structured notes. The nurse executive supports the frontline staff in attaining the skills to identify issues, problems, or trends based on their nursing assessment. The nurse executive also uses data available from quality monitoring, LOS, and CMI to assess global trends regarding a specific patient population. For example, the identification of an increase in patient falls on a specific unit may be an issue where the frontline manager identifies a root cause for the increase in falls on a particular unit and then identifies the appropriate fall reduction strategies to implement. Clancy (2003) illustrates the importance of effective identification of organizational issues by the nurse executive in order to make sound decisions. He emphasizes that many executives have a tendency to skip the process of analysis of a problem, which leads to ineffective decisions and poor resolutions to problems, which then leads to ineffective use of human, financial, and material resources.

Identification of Outcomes

Nurse executives ensure that outcomes of nursing care are identified for any problems/diagnoses. On a global/system level, the nurse executive identifies targets for reduction of trends through national benchmarks or established thresholds. For example, a service that had an increase in falls that were above the national benchmark may establish a target reduction of 5% in the next quarter. Furthermore, the nurse executive provides the leadership to drive outcomes and establish priorities for the department of nursing.

Staffing and work environment are factors that are overseen by the nurse executive and have been linked to nursing-sensitive quality outcomes (Kane et al., 2007; Aiken et al., 2008) and should be considered when establishing priorities. In order to drive the identification of priority outcomes, the nurse executive must ensure that a clear vision is established through thoroughly considering national priorities along with organizational priorities that drive patient care and ensure that the strategic plan reflects this (Young, 2008).

Planning

The planning process is usually led by the nurse on the interdisciplinary team based on assessment data, problems identified, and outcomes. Many organizations use case management to look at the continuum of care options for consumers of health care. Care is coordinated by nurse case managers who look at anticipated services needed based on treatment plans and established clinical guidelines. Case managers begin to anticipate discharge needs, begin to plan for services anticipated at discharge, and look at care options for managing throughput (AONE, 2005). The planning for nursing services is done by the nurse executive to plan for resources needed throughout the department of nursing to provide quality patient care. The nurse executive also allocates nursing resources based on patient acuity as needed. The strategic planning process by nurse leaders enables the vision of the chief nurse executive to be executed across the organization in order to meet identified needs of the organization and produce desired outcomes (Young, 2008).

Implementation

The nurse monitors clinical care that is implemented according to the plan established and ensures that all resources have been gathered that are indicated. The frontline manager ensures that care is provided, as planned, for the population that is served on the unit through coordination of care, patient education, and consultation. The nurse executive ensures that the strategic plan for nursing services is implemented and congruent with the mission and vision of the organization, while being responsible for human, material, and fiscal resources.

Evaluation

The nurse evaluates the plan of care and services provided to the patient. The frontline manager evaluates unit performance through analysis of financial reports, staff performance, and nursing-sensitive indicators for the patient population that is served. The nurse executive evaluates nursing services for the organization to ensure that staffing needs are adequate across the organization and that budget and financial resources are secure and meet the needs of the organization. The nurse executive assesses supply and demand and identifies future trends and skill sets needed of professional staff to effectively address trends that are identified.

Quality of Care/Administrative Practice

Nurse executives are charged with closing the quality gap with regard to nursing sensitive indicators in organizations. Donald Berwick (2003) states: "The U.S. healthcare system is simply not performing at acceptable levels. . . . There's no question at all that quality can be improved, not just a little, but dramatically. Unfortunately, we in the United States are so used to thinking that our healthcare system is first-rate that our eyes are closed to the truth." Nurse Executives are positioned to set the stage in the organization to create a culture of safety and ensure systems are in place to prevent healthcare errors from occurring. One method in preventing healthcare errors is to ensure that the processes related to providing care minimize the risk of error through quality and performance improvement activities. A challenge to frontline nursing staff and frontline leadership is the amount of monitoring of processes that is required to address regulatory requirements from organizations such as the Joint Commission, the National Quality Forum, and CMS. The goal of quality initiatives is to improve the quality of care for the consumer (patients, families) and the provider (hospital, nursing services). Quality initiatives evaluate the environment of care, the provision of care, and outcomes, that are typically based on regulatory requirements and hospital standards. Successful healthcare organizations have quality programs that are consensus driven and evidence-based, well-defined processes for implementation, community programs for disease prevention and health promotion, and a system to review performance and recommend process improvements (Griffith & White, 2007). Key management factors to support quality improvement include creation of a safety culture, personal engagement of leaders, leaders' relationship with clinical staff, support of quality assurance activities with organizational structures, and procurement of organizational resources (Bradley et al., 2003). The nurse executive must also be familiar with quality tools used to monitor progress with quality initiatives such as fishbone diagrams, FMEA (failure mode and effects analysis), process maps, histograms, pareto charts, scatter diagrams, run charts, and control charts. It is active engagement of nursing leaders and frontline staff in quality initiatives that will ultimately demonstrate strong performance and begin to close the quality gap.

Performance Appraisal

Nurse executives must ensure that on a regular basis staff performance and competencies are assessed. Ongoing competencies are established through the use of existing data of low-volume, high-risk, and problematic areas. Ongoing competencies are assessed along with core competencies to ensure that staff possess the necessary skills to carry out duties and responsibilities in a safe and efficient manner. The appraisal process ensures that an organization also identifies top talent. Regular appraisals also identify opportunities for further development of staff though mentoring and additional educational offerings. Succession planning is a key component of the appraisal process through reviewing progress toward goals and identifying opportunities to enhance skill sets of employees (Cadmus, 2006). By linking succession planning and organizational talent reviews to the appraisal process, employees are developed through opportunities that maximize current strengths, and action plans are identified to further develop skill sets that would be required for future promotional opportunities. When assessing competencies it is important to distinguish between a staff member that is having true competency difficulties versus staff members that have the necessary knowledge acquisition but instead are demonstrating a compliance issue (Wright, 2005).

Professional Knowledge

Skill acquisition is obtained through various forums. The nurse executive must ensure that resources are available for orientation to the organization and mentoring/precepting with experienced clinicians. Many organizations have adopted professional practice models, such as Benner (2001), to address the variations in skill acquisition, from the novice clinician to the expert nurse. A primary goal of nursing services is to reduce nursing (RN) turnover and vacancy rates despite the national nursing shortage. Ensuring that staff have the appropriate skill sets is a factor in preventing nurse turnover and vacancies. Nursing services are concerned about the effects that a nursing shortage has on the quality of nursing care and quality of patient care outcomes, along with the costs incurred by turnover among personnel. Replacement costs associated with RN turnover are estimated to be 100% of a nurse's annual salary; direct and indirect recruiting costs; and productivity, training, and termination costs (Golden, 2008; Halfer & Graf, 2006). In addition, uncontrolled staff turnover creates identified gaps in the areas of teamwork, talent, or the availability of "in-house experts." One vulnerable group that nationally is at high risk of turnover is the new graduate RN population. Casey et al. (2004) states that the median turnover rates for graduate nurses during their first year of employment range from 35 to 61%. Many organizations have instituted nurse residency programs to assist the transition of the new graduate RNs to professional nursing practice. New graduate RNs frequently lack the skills needed to transition to the inpatient medical–surgical, pediatric, and critical care setting, creating a gap that increases the risk for turnover. The success of such programs is well documented in the literature (Beecroft et al., 2001; Casey et al., 2004; Goode & Williams, 2004; Halfer, 2007; Pine & Tart, 2007).

Professional Environment

Work environment has long been identified as a reason for retention of experienced staff. Lake (2002) has noted that some factors that are attributed to work environment include peer support, physician and nurse relationships, relationships with frontline managers, and workload. One method of promoting a positive work environment is through securing organizational commitment. To secure organizational commitment one needs to understand that an organizational culture is made up of a system of symbols and interactions unique to each organization that includes ways of thinking, behaving, and believing that members of a unit have in common (Marquis & Huston, 2009). Factors that influence organizational culture include leadership that is viewed as having integrity, consistency, clearly communicated goals, and a commitment to the promotion of learning. The leader should have influence of the members of the organization and be aware of external variables, including industry and governmental systems (Marquis & Huston, 2009). Empowered organizations include those that are low-hierarchy organizations whose working practices orient toward teamwork, coherent values and strategies, and personnel management that creates opportunities and has influence over issues concerning practice and work environment (Kuokkanen, Leino-Kilpi, & Katajisto, 2003). Empowered organizational cultures support the development of organizational commitment. The extent of an individual's commitment to an organization includes an attachment to the organization, including its goals and values. There are three types of organizational commitment:

- Affective—identifies with the goals of the organization and desires to remain a part of the organization ("happy or ideal state")
- Continuance—remains in the organization because the individual believes he has invested a great deal of time and effort and has to remain
- Normative—remains in the organization because of feelings of obligation (Meyer & Allen, 1997)

Through development of organizational commitment, the nurse executive fosters retention of experienced nurses and prevents turnover in this population.

Ethics

Nursing practices conducted according to the ANA code of ethics and nurse executives ensure that ethical principles are applied to daily operations of healthcare organizations. The nurse executive fosters an environment where ethics are a core principle in daily activities and ensures that forums are available to discuss and resolve ethical issues as they arise and can be easily accessed by all levels of nursing staff.

Collaboration

Collaboration among members of the healthcare team is essential for the provision of quality care at the bedside. The nurse executive is poised to take the leadership role in interdisciplinary collaboration as the essence of a nursing paradigm that is holistic in nature. Collaborative work environments lead to increased productivity and job satisfaction. Navigating relationships in the healthcare setting is crucial to collaboration and is highlighted in the AONE core competency of communication and relationship building (AONE, 2005). Service recovery, to both internal customers (physicians, peers, support staff) and external customers (patients, families), is accomplished through effective communication that is empathic, trusting, assertive, nonaggressive, and demonstrates follow-through and follow-up. In addition, accomplishments are celebrated in forums that are interdisciplinary. For example, many organizations have instituted physician-of-the-year awards whereby interdisciplinary relationships are built and honored via nurse nominations of physicians that exemplify collegiality. Furthermore, Lake and Friese (2006) state that collegial nurse/physician relations is a factor that characterizes the nursing practice in the original study on magnet hospitals that were identified as exemplary organizations.

Research

Evidence-based practice is the cornerstone of professional nursing practice in the 21st century. Nurse executives today support backing nursing practice with evidence through having divisions of nursing research. Evidence-based practice empirically answers the question of "Why do we practice nursing the way that we do?" Evidence-based practice can be defined as "a problem-solving approach to clinical decision making within a healthcare organization that integrates the best available scientific evidence with the best available experiential (patient and practitioner) evidence, considers internal and external influences on practice, and encourages critical thinking in the judicious application of such evidence to care of the individual patient, patient population, or system" (Newhouse et al., 2005). Evidence-based practice includes research activities such as research utilization and the conducting of nursing research studies. Evidence-based practice includes identification of research questions in the clinical setting and, in a systematic and scientific manner, finding the answers to those questions. Evidence-based practice skills are incorporated into many nursing orientation programs and provide the foundation for the development of nursing practice policies and standards. In today's age, with the explosion of information and literature, evidence-based practice skills are essential in managing the information and crucial for nurses at all skill levels from bedside frontline nurses to chief nursing officers.

Resource Utilization

A nurse executive's business acumen is essential in the management of resources for nursing services. The nurse executive must possess knowledge of business planning and financial modeling when discussions regarding new services are held in order to advocate for staffing (human resources) for new services. In addition to advocating for capital expenditures, the nurse executive must possess keen negotiating skills for resources to support the ongoing training, development, and competencies of staff at all levels. Nurse leaders must receive ongoing training on fiscal responsibility and project management, besides traditional frontline nurse manager functions on staffing a unit. The nurse executive must demonstrate knowledge in managing finances, human resources, strategic planning, marketing, and use of information and technology. The nurse executive is the voice of nursing services in the boardroom and must illustrate business acumen in advocating for resources.

Challenges for Nurses in Executive Practice

The key to a nurse executive's development of successful and effective nursing services is to have a clear mission and vision and to develop an effective leadership team. The nursing leadership team is empowered regarding collaborative decision making and innovation in work design and service delivery. The nurse executive establishes recognition and reward systems and provides opportunities for professional growth and accountability (McManis & Monsalve Associates, 2003). Nurse executives must develop effective nurse leaders through investment in nursing management leadership capacity, organizational commitment to skills training, succession planning, and ongoing feedback and evaluation. Empowered collaborative decision making is established through both shared governance and service line models. In addition, job satisfaction, productivity, and retention are related to professional recognition. Innovation in work design and service delivery is accomplished through ensuring capacity for continuous organizational learning and process improvement, involving the frontline staff and emphasizing the importance of leadership in defining organizational initiatives. The successful nurse executive communicates a clear mission and vision of the organization and nurtures and reinforces the culture of the organization in an ongoing manner. The successful nurse executive also fosters an environment where professional growth and accountability of staff are established through career development opportunities, coaching and mentoring, constructive feedback, and accountability for practice.

The nurse executive must invest in building a strong workforce and retaining that workforce once developed. Gelinas and Loh (2004) state: "To build a strong workforce and a culture of consistently high quality care, healthcare organizations need to focus on and devote resources to strengthen leadership at all levels, develop a healthy culture, assure optimal work design, implement benchmark human resource processes, and grow the next generation of workers." In order to develop a strong workforce, the chief nursing officer needs to have a strong skill set that matches his/her increased span of control. Successful chief nursing officers develop and articulate vision, are engaged in strategic planning, build relationships and connect with others, facilitate transitions, are strong negotiators that successfully manage increased financial responsibilities and accountability, foster stewardship, have knowledge of integrating systems, mentor and role model, and use data to demonstrate ability to achieve results. The aforementioned skill set is congruent with AONE (2005) Core Competencies and ANA Scope and Standards for Nurse Administrators (2004).

The nurse executive transforms the culture in the organization by utilizing these core competencies and creating a culture of retention. The nurse executive creates an environment whereby people want to stay through putting the staff first, forging authentic connections, providing coaching, expecting competence, focusing on results, and partnering with staff (Manion, 2004). Boyle (2004) and Force (2005) add that the influential and effective nurse executives are those that seek out and value contributions of staff, share information in a team-building environment, and exemplify group cohesion with their leadership teams.

Summary

Nurse executives are faced with many challenges in today's healthcare settings. They are asked to be fiscally responsible in an era of federal and state budget cuts in health care. They are asked to recruit and retain nurses in the longest-running nursing shortage in history. They are asked to build leadership teams in an environment where, in the past, business acumen was not a required competency for a nurse leader. In order to thrive in this setting, the nurse executive must possess the competencies necessary to manage, advocate for resources, and create an environment that provides quality compassionate nursing care. By having a clear vision, solid structure, and the five core competencies of communication and relationship management, professionalism, knowledge of healthcare environment, business skills, and leadership, the nurse executive is poised to assist the organization to thrive in today's complex environment.

References

1. Aiken LH, Clarke SP, Sloane DM, Lake ET, Cheney T. Effects of hospital care environment on patient mortality and nurse outcomes. *Journal of Nursing Administration.* 2008;38(5):223–229.

2. American Nurses Association. *Scope and Standards for Nurse Administrators.* 2nd ed. Washington, DC: ANA.

3. American Organization of Nurse Executives. AONE nurse executive competencies. *Nurse Leader.* February 2005:50–56.

4. Beecroft PC, Kunzman L, Krozek C. RN internship: outcomes of a one-year pilot program. *Journal of Nursing Administration.* 2001;31(12):575–582.

5. Benner P. *From Novice to Expert: Excellence and Power in Clinical Nursing Practice.* Upper Saddle River, NJ: Prentice Hall Health; 2001.

6. Bold response is needed to new RAND health study [news release]. Cambridge, MA: Institute for Healthcare Improvement; June 25, 2003. http://www.ihi.org/ihi.

7. Bowles C, Candela L. First job experiences of recent RN graduates: improving the work environment. *Journal of Nursing Administration.* 2005;35(3):130–137.

8. Boyle SM. Nursing unit characteristics and patient outcomes. *Nursing Economics.* 2004; 22(3):111–119.

9. Bradley EH, Holmboe ES, Mattera JA, et al. The roles of senior management in quality improvement efforts: what are the key components? *Journal of Healthcare Management.* 2003; 48(1);15–28.

10. Cadmus E. Succession planning. Multilevel organizational strategies for the new workforce. *Journal of Nursing Administration.* 2006;36(6):298–303.

11. Caroselli C. The system chief nurse executive: more than the sum of the parts. *Nursing Administration Quarterly.* 2008;32(3):247–252.

12. Casey K, Fink R, Krugman M, Propst J. The graduate nurse experience. *Journal of Nursing Administration.* 2004;34(6):303–311.

13. Centers for Medicare and Medicaid Services. Hospital acquired conditions. CMS Web site. http://www.cms.hhs.gov/HospitalAcqCond/06_Hospital-Acquired_Conditions.asp#Top OfPage Updated July 20, 2009. Accessed October 13, 2008.

14. Clancy T. The art of decision-making. *Journal of Nursing Administration.* 2003;33(6):343–349.

15. Force MV. The relationship between effective nurse managers and nursing retention. *Journal of Nursing Administration.* 2005;35(7/8):336–341.

16. Gelinas LS, Loh DY. The effect of workforce issues on patient safety. *Nursing Economics.* 2004;22(5):266–272, 279.

17. Golden TW. An outcomes-based approach to improve registered nurse retention. *Journal for Nurses in Staff Development.* 2008;24(3):E6–E11.

18. Goode CJ, Williams CA. Post-baccalaureate nurse residency program. *Journal of Nursing Administration.* 2004;34(2):71–77.

19. Griffith JR, White KR. Clinical performance. In: *The Well-Managed Healthcare Organization.* 6th ed. Chicago, IL: Health Administration Press; 2006:155–202.

20. Halfer D. A magnetic strategy for new graduate nurses. *Nursing Economics.* 2007;21(1):6–11.

21. Halfer D, Graf E. Graduate nurse perceptions of the work experience. *Nursing Economics.* 2006;24(3):150–155.

22. Kane RL, Shamliyan T, Mueller C, Duval S, Witt T. *Nursing Staffing and Quality of Patient Care.* Rockville, MD: Agency for Healthcare Quality and Research; 2007.

23. Kramer M. *Reality Shock: Why Nurses Leave Nursing.* St Louis, MO: CV Mosby Co; 1974.

24. Kuokkanen L, Leino-Kilpi H, Katajisto J. Nurse empowerment, job-related satisfaction, and organizational commitment. *Journal of Nursing Care Quarterly.* 2003;18(3):184–192.

25. Lacey SR, Teasley SL, Henion JS, et al. Enhancing the work environment of staff nurses using targeted interventions of support. *Journal of Nursing Administration.* 2008;38(7/8): 336–340.

26. Lake ET. Development of the practice environment scale of the nursing work index. *Research in Nursing & Health.* 2002;25(3):176–188.

27. Lake ET, Friese CR. Variations in nursing practice environments: relation to staffing and hospital characteristics. *Nursing Research.* 2006;55(1):1–9.

28. Litch BK. The RE-EMERGENCE of clinical service line management. *Healthcare Executive.* 2007;22(4):14–18.

29. Manion J. Strengthening organizational commitment. Understanding the concept as a basis for creating effective workforce retention strategies. *The Health Care Manager.* 2004;23 (2):167–176.

30. Marquis BL, Huston CJ. *Leadership Roles and Management Functions in Nursing (Theory and Application).* 6th ed. Philadelphia, PA: Wolters Kluwer Health/Lippincott Williams & Wilkins; 2009.

31. McManis & Monsalve Associates, American Organization of Nurse Executives. (2003). *Healthy work environments: striving for excellence volume II. Insights from a key informant survey on nursing work environment improvement and innovation.* Published May 2003. http://www.mcmanis-monsalve.com/assets/publications/healthy_work_environments_full.pdf

32. Meyer JP, Allen NJ. *Commitment in the Workplace: Theory, Research and Application. Advanced Topics in Organizational Behavior.* Thousand Oaks, CA: SAGE; 1997.

33. Morgan SH, Lahman E, Hagstrom C. The Magnet Recognition Program transforming healthcare through excellence in nursing services. *Journal of Nursing Care Quarterly.* 2006;21 (2):199–120.

34. Mustain JM, Lowry LW, Wilhoit KW. Change readiness assessment for conversion to electronic medical records. *Journal of Nursing Administration.* 2008;38(9):379–385.

35. The National Academy of Sciences. *Executive summary: keeping patients safe: transforming the work environment of nurses.* http://nap.edu/openbook.php?record_id=10851&page=1.

36. National Conference of State Legislatures. Medicare nonpayment for hospital acquired conditions. National Conference of State Legislatures Web site. http://www.ncsl.org/statefed/health/HAC.htm Accessed October 14, 2008.

37. Newhouse R, Dearholt S, Poe S, Pugh LC, White K. *The Johns Hopkins Nursing Evidence-based Practice Model.* Baltimore, MD: The Johns Hopkins Hospital & Johns Hopkins University School of Nursing; 2005.

38. Patterson C. Orthopaedic service lines-revisited. *Orthopaedic Nursing.* 2008;27(1):12–20.

39. Pine R, Tart K. Return on investment: benefits and challenges of a baccalaureate nursing residency program. *Nursing Economics.* 2007;21(5):13–18.

40. Rollins, G. CNO burnout. *Hospital and Health Networks.* 2008;82(4):30–34.

41. Scott ES, Craig JB. Analysis of ANA's draft scope and standards of practice for nurse administrators. *Journal of Nursing Administration.* 2008;38(9):361–365.

42. Tesch T, Levy A. Measuring service line success: the new model for benchmarking. *Healthcare Financial Management.* 2008;62(7):68–74.

43. Westphal JA. Resilient organizations: matrix model and service line management. *Journal of Nursing Administration.* 2005;35(9):414–419.

44. Wright D. *The Ultimate Guide to Competency Assessment in Health Care.* 3rd ed. Minneapolis, MN: Creative Health Care Management, Inc; 2005.
45. Young C. Establishing a nursing strategic agenda. The whys and wherefores. *Nursing Administration Quarterly.* 2008;32(3):200–205.

Biographical Information

Wilhelmina M. Manzano, MA, RN, NEA, BC, is Senior Vice President and Chief Nursing Officer for New York Presbyterian Hospital and New York Presbyterian Healthcare System, and Chief Operating Officer for the Allen Hospital at New York Presbyterian Hospital. Her responsibilities include ensuring the implementation of initiatives that promote innovation and excellence in nursing practice, and to work with the hospital's senior management team, physicians and leaders to enhance patient care and service delivery outcomes. Ms. Manzano also has responsibility for nursing education, quality, and research. As Chief Operating Officer for the Allen Pavilion, she is responsible for hospital operations. Prior to joining the hospital in 1998, Ms. Manzano held leadership positions at Mount Sinai Medical Center, Lawrence Hospital, and Beth Israel Medical Center. She is a fellow of the New York Academy of Medicine and has presented nationally on a variety of nursing leadership topics.

Ms. Manzano obtained her undergraduate degree in nursing and her master's degree from New York University and attended the Johnson & Johnson–Wharton Fellows Program for Nurse Executives at the Wharton School, University of Pennsylvania. She is Assistant Dean for Clinical Affairs at Columbia University School of Nursing and an Adjunct Assistant Professor at the NYU Wagner Graduate School of Public Service.

Gina M. Bufe, PhD, RN, is the Director of Nursing for Education, Quality, and Research at New York Presbyterian Hospital and Assistant Professor of Clinical Public Health at Weill Cornell Medical College. Her responsibilities include directing and coordinating educational initiatives for nursing across the five campuses at New York Presbyterian. She also is responsible for the budget and operations of the Division of Nursing Education. Dr. Bufe oversees nursing quality assurance and performance improvement initiatives across the five campuses with a matrix relationship to hospital quality programs. She coordinates the Department of Nursing's Joint Commission and regulatory activities. Dr. Bufe is also responsible for the development and implementation of the Nursing Research Program at NYP, which includes generation of nursing-related research activities and nursing grant acquisition. Dr. Bufe received her BSN from Southeast Missouri State University and a MSN(R) and PhD in nursing from St. Louis University. Dr. Bufe completed the Georgetown University Healthcare Leadership Institute in 2007.

Marketing Healthcare Services

Roberta N. Clarke

A slow-moving flood of changes in the healthcare field has had a growing impact on the practice of marketing. The prospect of empowered consumers who more actively select their physicians, hospitals, and insurers than in the past suggests that marketers will have to provide the necessary information to empower them. The growth of retail health clinics, due in part to the impending shortage of primary care physicians, offers new channels by which to access care—a necessity as hospital emergency departments become ever more overcrowded. Providing care through various telemedicine technologies also promises to change both the nature of the services provided as well as the location at which the services are available. The envisioned personalized medicine of the future would imply a whole new way of segmenting healthcare markets, as would the currently fuzzily defined medical home concept. However, the ability to attract and market to a significant portion of the US population continues to be threatened by a lack of insurance coverage sufficient to meet the public's medical needs. Healthcare commercial interests have seen fit to provide coverage, albeit incomplete coverage, for those already ill, while sidestepping programs and tactics that would prevent sickness; that is, they have generally failed to invest in health-related social marketing that could potentially have high levels of ROI in the long term. All of these trends are modifying the practice of healthcare marketing.

The Obama administration's plans for the US healthcare system may offer opportunites for an alternative scenario. While maintaining the prospect of more empowered consumers, greater investments in healthcare information technology which are planned in the coming years, coupled with clearer performance standards for both hospitals and physicians, should allow for widespread implementation of pay for performance programs. Although consumers have historically paid little attention to provider report cards and presumably will treat performance reports similarly, insurers are likely to attend to this information. Providers that meet performance standards are likely to either provide better medical care, provide care more cost-effectively, or both; insurers are obviously interested in both and will reward those providers that can meet the performance standards that promise these results. In this scenario, marketing efforts will focus more on producing healthcare services that meet or exceed performance standards (i.e., on product and service attributes) than on the advertising, communication, and promotional efforts, which have generally been where providers have put the majority of their marketing efforts in the past.

Marketing continues to evolve into a more sophisticated management function in healthcare organizations when those organizations allocate sufficient funds to the marketing function. When the economics in the healthcare industry are solid, the marketing function expands; when healthcare organizations see their bottom lines in the red, marketing is often the first management function to be sculpted or discounted. This reflects a lack of understanding of marketing, because this is commonly the time when the marketing effort should be expanded rather than deleted. However, with healthcare costs continuing to rise to unprecedented levels, organizations are being forced to cut costs; marketing under these conditions incorrectly tends to be viewed as expendable.

Historically (which, for healthcare marketing means 30 or fewer years ago), marketing erroneously had been introduced into healthcare organizations as a "quick fix"—a speedy, simple way to address an increasingly competitive healthcare environment. Some, unfortunately, still perceive it as a little Internet presence, a few radio ads, an occasional piece of market research, and glorified public relations (which overlaps the promotional aspects of marketing), a very important tactical tool and often an undervalued function itself, but not in any way the equivalent of marketing. Others, particularly managed care organizations, initially defined it largely in terms of sales and promotional activities, and then more recently incorporating more of the customer/member service experience into their marketing thinking.

Far too often healthcare organizations have created their own definitions of healthcare marketing without taking into account the data collection and analytical components of marketing. As a result, they either have developed marketing strategy in a vacuum or, possibly worse, have failed to develop a cohesive marketing strategy at all. They may have a Web site, an annual patient survey, a couple of full-time positions dedicated to physician outreach or contact, and an advertising agency relied upon for the occasional advertisement. However, a grocery list of poorly related marketing tactics do not add up to a comprehensive marketing strategy. Even though the marketing function entered the healthcare world more than two decades ago, it is still not uncommon to find healthcare organizations that, when asked, cannot produce their marketing plan; they have none.

To appropriately use marketing, it is first necessary to have a clear understanding of what it is. One of the leading experts in the field defines marketing in the following way: "We can summarize the customer-focused marketing philosophy with the acronym CCDV; the aim of marketing is to *create, communicate, and deliver value*. Value is the fundamental concept underlying modern marketing. It is not value just because the supplier believes he or she is giving value; it must be perceived by the customer."[1] In order to carry out this process, marketers rely on the tools called the marketing mix: product and/or service, price, promotion, and place (also thought of as distribution and access).

Often, the promotional component of marketing, which includes (but is not limited to) advertising, sales promotion, collateral materials, direct mail, telemarketing, Web 2.0 and Internet capabilities, events, selling, and price promotion, has been mistaken for the equivalent of marketing. All the tools in the marketing mix must be considered together in developing a marketing strategy, however, because they are closely interrelated. To rely on one or two marketing tools to the exclusion of the others is to invite disaster. The marketing mix can be viewed as a jigsaw puzzle; unless all the pieces of the puzzle are in place, the puzzle is not complete. It takes only one tool in the marketing mix, one piece of the puzzle, to be out of place for the marketing strategy to fail.

As marketing sophistication in health care has increased, resulting in greater recognition of the analytical component of the marketing function, the use of marketing intelligence, the performance of market research, and the consistent collection of internal operational data that reflect the nature of the customer experience have become more common. Healthcare organizations can, as a result, better understand their market, their competition, the operational performance of their own organization and the impact of that performance on their customers, and the regulatory, technological, legal, and healthcare environments within which they must function. Furthermore, their increasing use of marketing performance benchmarks allows them to evaluate the effectiveness of their marketing efforts.

Marketing is a process that involves the performance of market research, assessment of internal performance, an environmental market scan, the collection of marketing intelligence and other relevant data, careful analysis of all available data, coupled with consideration of the organization's strategic plan, and finally, the development of marketing strategy and tactical marketing plans. Ultimately, there must be an evaluation of the results of marketing efforts in order to improve future investment in the marketing function. There is a tendency to confuse marketing with strategic planning. A strategic plan relies heavily on market planning, which may explain the confusion. Strategic planning is the effort to align the organization's mission, resources, and capabilities with its external environment, its current and potential markets, and its competition. It not only must extend beyond market planning to include financial, human resource, technological, regulatory, operational, and information system considerations, but also must build on the values and mission of the organization.

There is consensus among marketers that data collection and analysis should precede marketing strategy, which should then be followed by marketing plan development (to include marketing tactics), implementation, and control. Healthcare marketers are not in agreement, however, about whether marketing should have a heavy consumer focus or instead emphasize business-to-business marketing. Nor do they agree on the value of, and relationship between, customer satisfaction and customer loyalty, nor on the appropriate allocation of resources between customer attraction and customer retention. These are key issues for any organization. If the mission statement and strategic plan of the healthcare organization do not address these considerations—and many of them do not—then the marketing efforts may be focused on goals that do not reflect the values of the organization.

Marketing Mission and Objectives

The function of healthcare marketing is difficult to define. The movement a decade ago toward a predominantly managed care and capitated environment turned the traditional mission and objectives for marketing upside down. Healthcare marketing efforts historically attempted to increase the volume and usage of hospitals, medical practices, nursing homes, and other medical care providers. The introduction of managed care and capitation modified the objectives of most healthcare providers to aim to minimize volume or use and, as a result, cost. Success no longer was defined in terms of high occupancy rates and a high volume of patients or procedures, but in terms of the ability to keep the cost of "covered lives" low. As managed care organizations and employers continued to transfer the capitated risk for patients onto the providers with whom they contracted, these providers found themselves forced to assume a "womb to tomb" approach to caring for patients. Some responded by then applying marketing to a variety of tasks, from promoting patient compliance (i.e., encouraging patients to follow through with all their physicians' instructions with regard to medications, exercise, lifestyle, and so on) to educating patients about the appropriate time to see the physician.

This movement was followed by the attempts to move consumers into consumer-directed health plans and into high-deductible health plans coupled with health savings accounts. These placed the consumer more at risk for their own healthcare expenditures. Employers who encourage their employees to adopt consumer-directed health plans are hoping that the financial incentives built into these plans will enhance the likelihood that consumers will lessen unnecessary care and will seek lower-cost providers and options. However, as will be later discussed, the assumption that these plans will work is predicated upon the consumer having adequate decision-making tools available to them. Further, even if the tools and necessary information is available, critics of these health plan options fear that consumers will skimp on nonacute and preventive care since the cost of care comes from the consumer's pocket. The questions this raises for marketing then include how to develop and share information with the consumer such that they can make intelligent and informed choices and how to provide incentives to the consumer to seek preventive care and nonurgent care which, if provided early, might prevent higher health cost needs from arising in the future.

Recent business and industry attempts to measure medical care quality; to decrease medical errors, which carry both a human and a financial cost; and to reintroduce greater consumer choice are reforming mission and objectives. These efforts hold the promise of raising quality and performance above cost in their mission priorities. Under the Obama presidency, there is a further expansion of the US healthcare mission to provide healthcare coverage for the 47 million people who lacked insurance in the eight years into the new millennium and to make health insurance more affordable for employed individuals and families. This would allow providers to focus more simply on volume without having to dice and slice the market into financially reimbursable and nonreimbursable segments. The additional intent of the Obama administration to invest heavily in the prevention and management of chronic medical conditions may result in whole new service lines offered by traditional providers.

For example, obesity, which affects one out of three US adults and 15% of US children, has been poorly reimbursed—or not reimbursed at all in the case of obese children—by health insurers. Although the long-term effects of obesity (certain types of cancer, heart disease, the rising prevalence of diabetes, and so on) are quite costly to the US healthcare system, insurance companies have a short-term view and see that their customers turn over every three years; if the insurance company invests in a customer's obesity treatment today, that person might no longer be a customer in one, two, or three years, having switched to a different insurer. If the Obama administration is able to implement its promise to provide better integrated preventive care and management of chronic diseases, either through the regulation of insurance coverage in these areas or through other forms of funding, the mission of healthcare providers will have to expand to include these types of services.

Volume will continue, nonetheless, to be an objective for healthcare marketers. Managed care organizations will aim to increase the size of their memberships, and hospitals, some after downsizing, others after adding new "centers of excellence," will aim to maintain a high occupancy level in order to cover their fixed costs. Similarly, providers will seek to attract a sufficient quantity of patients to maintain an acceptable level of quality in performing certain surgical and other procedures. Volume management also manifests itself in the form of demarketing, that is, attempting to lower volume, as many hospitals with overcrowded emergency rooms have done. Managed care organizations often try to demarket medical services to the "worried well," that component of members who perceive themselves to suffer from various ills when there is no apparent medical problem. One alternative used to address these medical-visit overutilizers is to schedule their requested return appointments further and further apart, thereby lowering the volume of appointments for these individuals over the long term. The danger here, of course, is that the member may have a legitimate medical problem which simply has not yet been correctly diagnosed; demarketing to this member (lessening the volume of visits) could conceivably result in less than adequate care.

Anyone who defines the marketing objectives of a healthcare organization as simply seeking to increase volume has underestimated the complexity of the new healthcare marketplace. The necessity of conceptualizing organizations as parts of larger systems requires a recognition of multiple and sometimes conflicting marketing objectives.

One of the tasks, then, of the marketing function is to define carefully the full range of its objectives. A health maintenance organization (HMO) must simultaneously seek a high volume of membership and foster a low volume of usage. Even this is simplistic, however. It is necessary to encourage visits for preventive care and early diagnosis of disease, but to discourage visits for certain nonacute symptoms, such as sore throats that are likely to disappear by themselves with no treatment within a week. Each of these objectives, even if directed at the same market or individual customer, may require a different marketing strategy.

The Competition Defined

The same complexity in the healthcare environment that leads to multiple marketing missions and objectives also requires a more systematic and skilled approach to defining the competition. A competitor often is defined as any organization that lessens the likelihood of another organization achieving its desired marketing exchange. Previously, hospitals competed with other hospitals, and nursing homes competed with other nursing homes, for example. Even so, however, there was some overlap between types of providers. An inpatient psychiatric unit of an acute care hospital might have competed with a freestanding psychiatric hospital; physical therapists, chiropractors, and orthopedic surgeons might all have competed for the same patient with chronic acute lower back pain. Cardiac surgeons on a community hospital's medical staff who set up a cardiac specialty hospital within a short distance of the community hospital, while historically providing a high volume of surgical patients to the community hospital now become that hospital's competitors as they redirect cardiac surgery patients away from the community hospital to their own hospital.

The formation of systems expands those included in the definition of competitors. Moreover, the uncertainty of future organized healthcare delivery membership in these systems makes it unclear who may be a current competitor, a future collaborator or, as some combined health systems have begun to disband, which current joint partner may soon be vying to take away one's business. This makes it more difficult to invest in competitive positioning strategies or to develop strengths and competencies based on a competitor's strengths and weaknesses (see Chapter 4, "Financial Management of Organized Healthcare Delivery Systems").

The Changing Competitive Environment

The current healthcare environment promises confusion in identifying the competition. Not only do organizations have to ask themselves, "What business are we in?" but they also have to ask about the competition: "What businesses are they in? What businesses will they be adding tomorrow? Which providers and organizations that contract with us now will choose to contract with our competitors tomorrow?" This difficulty in defining long-term competitors arises even when managed care does not play a significant role in the competitive environment. Orthopedic surgeons and podiatrists compete for patients needing foot surgery, while neurologists and interventional radiologists compete for spinal surgery patients. The Society of Interventional Radiology encouraged its members to set up clinics that would provide coronary angiograms and balloon angioplasties, procedures which they are well able to perform but which would place them in direct competition with cardiologists.[2]

The vertical integration of a variety of healthcare organizations into systems can make competition out of customers. For example, an HMO with which one hospital used to contract may now contract in the same service area with a competing hospital, making the two former allies competitors. Yet, it may not be wise for the hospital to launch a marketing offensive against that HMO, because it might once again contract with the hospital in the future. Few healthcare vertical integration relationships specify exclusivity; the relationship of the HMO with the competing hospital does not prevent it from once again developing a relationship with the first hospital as well.

Alternatively, organizations that were once ardent competitors may become part of the same system. Sometimes, they continue to offer the same services that they provided before becoming part of a system; other times, the system expects them to complement each other rather than compete. The former instance is an example of a federation, the latter of a partnership. An even more extreme competitive change is the merger of two or more former competitors. Such mergers abounded in the late 1990s as healthcare providers and managed care organizations concluded, at least at that time, that the greater size, geographic coverage, and service coverage produced by a merger made them more marketable. Some merged entities appear to demonstrate that this is true. In California, six entities, formed from combining a number of smaller healthcare provider organizations, controlled roughly one third of all California hospitals. The ability to compete in the California market depends in part on whether one is part of one of these large entities.

On the other hand, some well-known mergers did not do well at all. Many well-known mergers formed in the mid- and late 1990s have since either fallen apart or are performing badly from a financial perspective. The Allegheny Health, Education, and Research Foundation in Pittsburgh, a well-publicized $1.3 billion entity encompassing teaching hospitals, community hospitals, and a medical school, went bankrupt in July 1998. CareGroup, a combined group of Harvard teaching hospitals and smaller community hospitals in Massachusetts, had shown deficits for a number of years and had to divest itself of some of its constituent parts in order to stay afloat financially. Gabel noted that the mergers and acquisitions in managed care, the shift from vertically integrated staff models to virtually integrated network models, and the increased patient cost sharing (including capitating primary care physicians) did not improve patient satisfaction or quality of care.[3]

In the long term, the widely held belief that the larger merged entities function more effectively and are more marketable may not hold true, particularly if several network members provide poor-quality services and, thus, potential customers elect to use other networks. Many networks may be trading away long-term marketability for short-term assumed economies of scale and presumed competitive advantage. The economies of scale that a number of merged healthcare organizations have expected have not always materialized in the basic services that they provide. As Sidorov points out: "If the leadership of the new organization fails to deal effectively with the inevitable winners and losers, underestimates the role of cultural differences, does not have the management skills necessary to achieve cost savings and address the operational inefficiencies resulting from a larger clinical enterprise, does not anticipate the distrust of other local healthcare providers, and fails to anticipate the market forces that determine the success or failure of a managed healthcare system, mergers can fail."[4]

Smaller merged entities may not offer marketing advantages either. The heavy cross-functional dependence of many medical specialties and services, for example, prevented two hospitals that had formally merged from eliminating certain specialties from one hospital and placing them solely in the other, originally a goal of the merger in order to cut costs. Both hospitals needed infectious disease, cardiology, nephrology, endocrinology, psychiatry, otolaryngology, and other diagnostic and treatment capabilities in-house for their inpatients. The inconvenience, cost, and possible clinical repercussions of having to move a patient from one hospital to the other because the necessary diagnostic equipment was not available in the first prevented the hospitals from eliminating the services as they had initially planned. This scenario has been repeated around the United States.

The more common result of hospital mergers essentially has been to eliminate one of the hospitals as an acute care hospital. The eliminated hospital may become a psychiatric facility, substance abuse center, rehabilitation provider, walk-in facility, chronic care center, congregate living quarters for the elderly, or a housing center for needy women and infants, for example. These are valuable services for which there may be more demand than for the acute care services that the hospital facility used to provide. This process is not one of merging with the competition, however, as much as it is a process of eliminating the competition. The weakest hospitals begin to provide nonacute care services or acute psychiatric services, whereas the stronger hospitals with which they merged remain in the general acute care business. The merger of hospitals with more equal status is less likely to result in the closure of one of them, but it is not yet proved that there are significant economies of scale to be achieved when these hospitals both continue to operate as acute care facilities.

There is an argument to be made that healthcare entities that do not truly merge, but that sit down together at the negotiating table, may gain market power. Massachusetts General Hospital (MGH) and Brigham & Women's Hospital formed a corporate entity, Partners Healthcare. The two hospitals did not merge their services, however. To the contrary, once Partners was created, MGH added a maternity unit to its long list of service units, in spite of the fact that the Brigham & Women's Hospital already had the largest maternity service in New England. The true advantage of creating Partners was not to prevent the two hospitals from competing with each other, but rather to give the two hospitals more negotiating power when they met with insurers and managed care organizations to agree upon reimbursement rates and terms.

Mergers outside the healthcare industry may provide a glimpse of the future and, in fact, have already been replicated in many instances in the healthcare world. The period of high-flying mergers and acquisitions that characterized the 1980s in the general commercial sector within a decade led to a less than exciting and sometimes traumatic period of divestitures and fraudulent conveyances.[5] Businesses that had merged later discovered that the gains expected from the mergers were not to be found. Idiosyncratically, parts of the healthcare industry have exhibited the same cycle of merger followed by divestiture; it is already clear that these arrangements do not necessarily guarantee an increased flow of patients and/or members. Organizations still must compete for patients and members. Until provider networks become more stable, the naming of competitors may be possible only on a short-term basis.

Analysis of Competitive Position

The development of a good marketing strategy requires an analysis of the organization's competitive position. Customer-oriented analysis is one possibility; this approach involves determining who the customers are, what benefits and values they seek, and how well the organization is providing those benefits and values to the customers compared to how well the competition is doing so. Then, if one or more of the competitors are doing a better job of delivering the desired benefits to the customer, the organization investigates further to determine which of the competitors' activities it needs to emulate or, if possible, surpass in order to equal or exceed the competition.

Competitor-oriented analysis, a second form of competitive analysis, involves benchmarking. With this technique, the organization regularly compares its performance on key performance attributes and benefits desired by the customer against the "best in class." Benchmarking allows the organization to get a sense of context; it provides the organization with answers to questions such as: Where do we stand in the marketplace? How far behind the strongest or best competitors are we? What will it take for us to draw ourselves up to an equal level of performance with our best competitors?

Another useful tool is a perceptual map. An organization positions itself and its competitors along a two-axis grid according to the variables that the two axes represent (**Figure 7.1**). For example, consumers often compare hospitals on the basis of whether they are teaching hospitals (or whether they provide tertiary care) or community hospitals (which provide non-tertiary basic acute care). They also often compare hospitals on the basis of their nursing and support staff care being friendly, warm, and responsive, and on the nurse-to-patient ratio. Through the use of market research, a hospital can ask a sample of consumers in its service area to rate it and its competing hospitals on these two attributes. Then, using these research findings, the hospital can position all the hospitals that the consumers rated along these two axes (see Figure 7.1). In addition, the hospital can, with further research, determine where the consumer segments in the market are positioned. For example, the people inside the oval marked (1) care primarily about being in a tertiary care or teaching hospital, even if that means not receiving the friendliest or warmest care. For them, a community hospital, such as hospitals E, F, or G, would not be satisfactory. Those who fall inside the oval marked (3) prefer to go to the local community hospital. They obviously trust the community hospital to provide adequate acute care, and they want the friendliness and warmth that they feel a community hospital is more likely to provide. Clearly, this would be the segment to which hospital E would appeal. Those in the oval marked (2) are not willing to sacrifice either friendly, warm care, nor do they want to forgo the capacity for tertiary care. Hospital B best meets their needs, followed by hospital D. In comparing the position of the consumer segments with the position of the various hospitals on the perceptual map, it becomes apparent that hospitals C, F, and G may want to modify their positioning in the marketplace to attract a larger portion of the existing market segments.

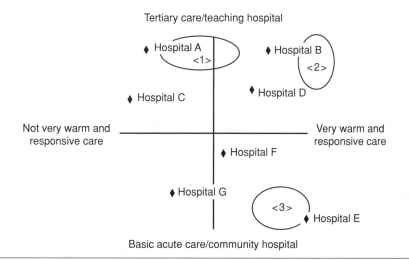

FIGURE 7.1   Perceptual Map

The Changing Economic and Commercial Environment

Economic recessions, such as the one that began in 2008, have an impact on capital expenditures undertaken by companies and organizations, including those in the health sector. Hospitals, for example, borrow on a regular basis, not only for capital expenditures, but also sometimes for ongoing operational costs; they need to continually upgrade their technology and deal with a replacement schedule for existing equipment and supplies. When a downturn in the economy causes the cost of capital to rise, willingness to borrow declines. Advertising and promotion have often been characterized as capital expenditures. When one adds this to what was noted in the second paragraph of this chapter, that when healthcare organizations see their bottom lines in the red, marketing is often the first management function to be sculpted or discounted, and one can predict that many healthcare organizations will deep-six all marketing activities. However, this is the time when organizations that readjust their marketing strategies wisely are able to position themselves to retain their current customers and capture business they might otherwise not have had.

Economic downturns do herald in cuts in advertising and expenditures in traditional media. Advertising and marketing firms had already announced only two weeks after the dramatic economic announcements in early October 2008 that they would be issuing pink slips to many of their own employees as they anticipated the loss of clients and the appearance of little new business.[6] Similarly, healthcare firms would be expected to pare their expenditures in these areas. However, this does not mean that most or all marketing efforts cease. Rather, it should call for a reformulation of marketing activities that either cost less or have the promise of cementing customer loyalty at a time when customer defection may be more likely, as it is in difficult economic times.

In the category of lower cost, the use of digital media, which has been vastly underutilized in the health sector, could be looked to as an alternative to more costly broadcast and print advertising. In the past, because digital ROI had been difficult to demonstrate, many healthcare marketers were hesitant to sink significant resources or time into developing digital media strategies. This might be particularly true for marketing efforts that target small business-to-business markets; how does one measure the cost per thousand reached when your target market is only the 45 pediatric endocrinologists practicing in your large metropolitan area? Many marketers are also still unfamiliar with emerging digital promotional channels such as blogs, mobile networks, and social media; their confidence thus limited their willingness to experiment with these new avenues to reach their customers. However, these promotional channels are only going to become more dominant in the media mix and their increased efficiency in targeting markets suggests the need to develop competency in their use.

An example of the wise use of a digital medium is the blog written by Paul Levy, CEO of Beth Israel Deaconess Medical Center in Boston, Massachusetts. He has been sharing his vision of his hospital network and of the healthcare field since August 2, 2006, shortly after the time that he became CEO through his blog, Running a Hospital (http://runningahospital.blogspot.com). In it, he discusses everything from the hospital's financial condition to employee-driven process improvement to citations of books that certain segments of patients might find to read to the recipe for Beth Israel Deaconess' "Best of Boston" chocolate chip cookies. The blog also has links to the blogs of other physicians and managers in the hospital staff, to relevant healthcare Web sites such as Diabetes Mine (www.diabetesmine.com) and Look Me in the Eye (http://jerobison .blogspot.com), a blog about "Asperger's, autism, and life." By engaging a wide variety of communities (clinical communities, patient communities, insurers and managed care provider communities, and so on) through his blog, this CEO has built a loyal following, not only online but for the services, medical staff, and employees of his hospital.

In a similar vein, Scripps Hospital has a number of videos such as its *Your Family Health Series* as well as an employee recruitment video online on YouTube. These videos allow the hospital to promote its physicians, their specialties, the hospital's services, and the benefits of employment at the hospital to distinct market segments. St. Jude Children's Research Hospital has an official Facebook page with 9700 "fans" (as of 10.20.08) and a listing of "latest news" such as a donation from Chili's (the restaurant chain) to the hospital, a St. Jude's research finding, and a prospective St. Jude's event. As consumers increasingly go online in search of health information—and health is one of the top three online search focuses already—it will become both imperative as well as more efficient for healthcare organizations to present and promote themselves in the digital media.

Another change in the economic environment is the recent rollover of certain healthcare organizations from nonprofit to for-profit. The American Hospital Association noted that, from 1990 to 2003, the number of physician-owned, for-profit specialty (i.e., limited service) hospitals had tripled.[7] As healthcare organizations seek to protect their bottom line in a difficult economic period, there may be more exploration of conversion to for-profit status (which places no expectation upon the healthcare entity of providing service to the uninsured or underinsured). It is already known that there are a number of variables that contribute to the prevalence of larger for-profit healthcare entities:

- the market strength of the local Blue Cross plans
- the relative market strength of local for-profit versus nonprofit hospitals and insurers
- the presence or absence of certificate of need laws
- the prevailing local attitudes with regard to the appropriateness of for-profit healthcare provision.[8]

In states where for-profit providers are more prevalent, for-profit insurers generally have a larger market share and the Blue Cross plans have a smaller share of market than in states where for-profit providers have a smaller share of market; stated another way, on a geographic basis, there appears to be a correlation between the market share of for-profit providers and for-profit insurers, with Texas, Florida, California, and Tennessee having the highest concentration of for-profit healthcare entities. The location of for-profit hospitals is also tied to high levels of Medicare spending and to the lessened likelihood of there being certificate of need laws.

Because for-profit entities are not expected to accept nonpaying patients as part of the exchange for not paying taxes as non-profit entities are, there have been horror stories of for-profit hospitals turning away women in labor or unstable patients because their insurance or lack of insurance characterized them as not being "good business," even though this may have increased the medical risk for the patient. For-profit health insurers that, like nonprofit insurers, seek to control expenditures by rejecting risky—meaning potentially expensive-to-cover—customers, may be quicker to cancel the policies of sicker insurees. With more consumers losing their insurance in a difficult economy, it may be that more nonprofits will feel the lure of converting to for-profit status rather than try to determine how to cross-subsidize the uninsured and underinsured in an economy where government subsidization of this segment is likely to decline. This becomes a de facto exercise in market segmentation along economic lines.

There may be reason to believe that a significant economic slowdown may finally cause all the entities involved in the healthcare system to evaluate and adopt new models for care and coverage. The hundreds of millions (if not trillions, in the long run) of dollars dedicated lifting the US economy out of recession translates into dollars that might instead have been funding Medicaid, Medicare, and other forms of healthcare subsidies. Healthcare organizations that had increased their debt over the past decade and had invested their funds in the stock market were exposed to the same risks as the home owners whose mortgages subsequently became worth more than their homes and property. In a similar vein, healthcare consumers were equally affected. The Kaiser Health Tracking Poll: Election 2008 found that the economic downturn resulted in a dramatic increase in the number of Americans who felt that "it is more important than ever to take on health care reform." One in three noted that their family had had difficulty paying their medical bills in the previous year and nearly two out of ten people reported that they had to pay almost $1000 out of pocket in the previous 12 months. This then explains why 47% of those polled reported that someone in the family had cut their consumption of medical products (largely medications) or of medical services.[9] Marketing's ability to affect levels of demand becomes far more constrained in times of severe economic downturns. It also alerts both businesses and consumers that they may want to reevaluate "business as usual."

The discomfort that caused new models of care to be rejected in the past is now overwhelmed by the need to try new ways to keep patients healthier at a lower cost and to provide care with the provision of fewer resources.

In this vein, the adoption of electronic medical records, the implementation of medical homes that offer the potential of better managing chronically ill patients, a more patient-centered system providing better face-to-face and electronic access with one's physician or primary care provider, and the use of personalized medicine and genetic information to better diagnose and treat patients are among the new models we can expect to be embraced. With each of them are changes in the way that health care will be marketed; we can only begin to envision what these changes will be.

Business-to-Business Marketing

The need to market to businesses and organizations, referred to as industrial or business-to-business (B2B) marketing, remains as strong as ever. Whether the target market consists of employers, the government, insurers, physician groups, healthcare oversight groups like the

Leapfrog Group, hospitals, or managed care organizations, the nature of business-to-business marketing remains the same. Marketers must be skilled in organizational analysis in order to understand to whom and what to sell. Failure to identify the decision-making unit or buying center, as it is called in a business-to-business marketing setting, is likely to result in unsuccessful marketing efforts. Thus, marketers must know who within the organization plays the roles of initiator, influencer, decider, purchaser, gatekeeper, and user.

Historically, for example, pharmaceutical companies hired salespeople to sell existing and new drugs to physicians, who then prescribed or recommended them to their patients. In this scenario, the physician was the decider and the patient was the user (and often the purchaser as well). Increasingly, however, organizational healthcare providers such as hospitals and managed care organizations are examining the cost and efficacy of the various drugs available and using their findings to create formularies that specify the drugs that their physicians may prescribe. The individuals who select drugs for the formularies (e.g., infectious disease physicians, pharmacists, quality assurance nurses) are now the initial deciders. The practicing physician can decide on a drug only within the limited set of formulary drugs. A pharmaceutical company that continued to sell its drugs only to physicians and did not attempt to address the formularies might unnecessarily lose significant business. Pharmacy benefit managers, who are often employed by pharmaceutical companies charged with containing pharmaceutical costs for a managed care or insurance entity, continue to sell to physicians; in recognition of the influence and decision-making power of hospital and managed care organizations in the purchase of pharmaceuticals, their marketing efforts remain within the limits of the drugs approved for the formulary.

A buyflow map permits a more systematic analysis of a buying center. It traces the buying process through the customer's recognition of need that presumably must be met through the purchase of a good or service, specification of a technical product or service, potential supplier identification, solicitation of proposals, selection of a supplier, negotiation of the final contract, and performance evaluation. The map identifies who, within the customer's organization, participates in each step of the process, in what order each person affects the process, and where the process slows and may need the further attention of the supplier (marketer).

Organizational buyers are fewer in number than are consumers (individual buyers), but they represent larger overall volumes of purchases. For example, a physician can sell more streptococcus test services to an HMO than to an individual consumer or family within 1 year. Because of the smaller number of business buyers, the investment in analyzing their buying center behavior may be less, even though the potential purchase volumes are greater. The analysis of an organization's buying centers may take at least two forms. "Snowball" research within the target organization entails asking the individuals within the organization thought to be involved in the purchase to identify all others within the organization who might also influence the particular purchase. The analysis proceeds by determining the role that each named individual plays, soliciting from those individuals more names, identifying the roles of those newly named, and continuing until no new names are given. The sum of this type of information usually allows the marketer to detect who plays what role in the decision-making unit/buying center.

Focus group research is another common source of information in organizational analysis. This approach generally involves a number of similar organizations rather than just one. For example, a medical software company that had traditionally sold products to the hospital market was planning to enter the managed care market with a new type of software. Within the hospital market, the company knew that the decider was most often the planner. The title "planner" was not a common one in most managed care and preferred provider organizations, however, and the company was uncertain who should be the target of its promotion and personal selling. Therefore, the company held six focus groups with a variety of people in different jobs at a number of managed care organizations in order to assess who would be the likeliest deciders and influencers in the purchase of this new product.

The expansion of the marketing of certain healthcare products is going beyond traditional organizational buyers to include consumers. The reclassification of certain previously ethical drugs (those that consumers could buy only with a prescription from a physician) to over-the-counter (OTC) drugs, and the decreasing influence of physicians over which drugs may be prescribed for a patient (because of managed care plans and hospital formularies) have resulted in a dramatic explosion in pharmaceutical and medical device advertising directed to consumers. This direct-to-consumer advertising boon for prescription as well as over-the-counter pharmaceutical products has caused such pressures on physicians to prescribe according to the patient's wishes that physicians have at times become incensed at their loss of power and insurers have, not very successfully to date, supported political efforts to limit the extent of this advertising, given that the most heavily advertised products are also usually among the most expensive in their product categories. Mail order catalogues sent to consumers now carry products, such as special chairs for arthritic patients and self-monitoring products for diabetics, that used to be available only through specialty retailers or other organizational sellers. Marketers whose expertise had in the past been limited only to business-to-business selling must now learn how to market directly to consumers.

Derived Demand

Some marketers believe that consumer marketing should not require as much attention as does business-to-business marketing in the healthcare marketplace. They rationalize that employers make the first choice of health plans, before the individual employees are given any purchase choices, and that health plan members must choose their physicians or hospitals from panels approved by their health plan. Therefore, they conclude that the individual plays a less significant role in healthcare purchase decisions.

This set of beliefs does not take into account derived demand. For example, a hospital is trying to convince the management of an HMO new to the area that it should be the HMO's primary hospital. Although factors such as the hospital's willingness to negotiate on price and the extent to which it can provide the full range of medical care will influence the HMO, the desirability of the hospital to potential HMO members is a key consideration. If the potential HMO members consider the hospital unacceptable as the HMO's primary hospital, then the HMO itself will be a less attractive health plan and will have difficulty enrolling members. The HMO derives its demand in part from the attractiveness of the hospital(s) to which it sends patients, as well as from the physicians who are on its panel.

In essence, derived demand requires a two-stage marketing process. The marketer must develop a set of products and services to appeal not only to the immediate customer, but also to the customer of the immediate customer. A large medical group practice can make itself attractive to a managed care organization by agreeing to significant discounts. To reduce costs sufficiently to permit these discounts, however, the medical group may understaff and, as a result, deny quick access to all but the sickest patients. Although the discounts initially may be appealing to the managed care organization, the lack of access would soon become apparent to the patients, would make the medical practice unattractive to them, and would cause them to steer away from this practice in future enrollment periods. Thus, the managed care organization would derive little long-term demand from consumers through contracting with this practice. Ultimately, with little derived demand, this practice would become unattractive to the managed care organization.

With the right information available, derived demand offers marketers an opportunity to influence business-to-business buyer behavior. Any healthcare provider (of significant size) that can produce credible market research to establish consumer preference for its services within its target market area is in a good position to negotiate with managed care organizations, with other organizational buyers, and with potential contract partners; the stated consumer preference indicates that the provider can bring to the organization derived demand for its services. Similarly, managed care organizations do their own consumer preference research to identify the providers that are so attractive to consumers that their presence on the managed care provider list overwhelms the need for a significant discount from them. For example, the two top-rated independent children's hospitals in the country, Children's Hospital Boston and the Children's Hospital of Philadelphia, have such far-reaching and loyal demand from families in the larger metropolitan areas of the two cities that no insurer in either of these markets can attract significant enrollment among families with children unless they include the relevant hospital in the list of covered providers.

The key to using derived demand is information—market research data on consumer preferences and on consumers' intended use or purchase behavior. The relatively unsophisticated research that characterizes some healthcare marketing efforts does not uncover derived demand very well. Asking consumers if they prefer hospital A to hospital B may establish a preference for one over the other, but it does not assess any trade-off that consumers may be willing to make, such as accepting the less preferred provider for a specified lower premium, quicker access, or more convenient location. To capture this level of information, it is probably necessary to do a trade-off analysis, commonly called conjoint measurement. This market research methodology requires the identification of those variables that appear most likely to affect a buyer's purchase decision (in a specific, not generic, type of purchase situation). These variables include those that make it possible to measure the attractiveness to the consumer at different levels, such as a $5 vs. $10 vs. $20 co-pay per visit. Each of the variables, at different levels, are combined with other variables and presented as a package to the consumer interviewee, who is asked to assess the attractiveness of the overall package. For example, a shortened version of two packages for an HMO might be:

Option A
- $5 co-pay
- Primary care visits with nurse practitioner

- Acute illness appointments available within 48 hours
- Admits to most preferred hospital in the area

Option B

- $20 co-pay
- Primary care visits with a physician
- Acute illness appointments available within 24 hours
- Admits to moderately preferred hospital in the area

The consumer is asked to rate the preferability of several of these packages. Using an algorithm, conjoint analysis can determine which variables at which levels prove to be most attractive to the consumer, and when to trade one variable for another. Most healthcare organizations do not have the capability to carry out this type of market research in-house, but market research firms should be qualified to do so. Over time, healthcare marketers may add this type of research to their expected set of skills. Other research approaches include surveys focusing on customers' most recent service experiences with the organization; focus group interviews; service review interviews (a formal process of periodic visits with customers to discuss the service relationship); customer complaint and inquiry systems; employee field reporting and surveys; and a system to track and analyze operating data, such as service response times and waiting times. A very useful but sometimes controversial option is mystery shopping, where hired researchers acting as patients, members, or other forms of customers "shop" and take notes on both one's own and competing services to evaluate the quality of services delivered. Some marketers find that they can capture information through mystery shoppers that doesn't appear through the use of other types of market research. However, others believe that mystery shoppers waste the time and resources of an already overburdened healthcare system.[10]

Some network managers have failed to take derived demand into account. For some, the natural tendency has been to put together the lowest cost hospitals and practices. As a result, their provider list may not have tertiary care facilities, a local women's health center, or a specialty children's hospital, for example. The network managers' assumption underlying this choice of providers is that low cost will outweigh all other considerations. For many potential members, however, cost is secondary to access to preferred high-quality providers. Moreover, if those for whom cost is the primary concern find, once in the network, that they are unhappy with the quality of the services, they are likely at the next enrollment period to search out another network or managed care organization, even at a slightly greater cost. Failure to consider derived demand may be effective in the short run, but it is likely to create a higher turnover of customers in the long run.

Consumer Behavior: Information Search and Use

The overwhelming availability of healthcare information is changing, or at least has the potential to change, the way that consumers make their healthcare choices. In 2008, the federal government spent $1.9 billion advertising its newly revised Web site, www.hospitalcompare.hhs.gov, which would reputedly allow patients to assess their local hospitals on more than 30 measures regarding hospital quality and access.[11] The National Committee on Quality Assurance (NCQA) has been producing report cards on managed care and health plans since the mid-1990s, reporting on rates of cesarean section, rates of mammography in women over the age of 50, rates of use of other early disease detection methodologies, and member satisfaction. By 2002, it was also offering report cards on managed behavioral healthcare organizations and on health plans that were less than 3 years old. Local magazines in cities such as Philadelphia, New York, and Boston provide an annual list of the best regional physicians and hospitals. The Massachusetts Department of Public Health offers ratings of all the state's skilled nursing facilities on its Web site and updates them every 6 months, based on semiannual surveys of the facilities. Insurers sometimes provide online ratings of their physicians to their members. Zagat (the restaurant rating organization) and Angie's List (which allows members to rate local neighborhood services) are now offering online ratings of physicians, based on member input. "Report cards" on healthcare providers and managed care organizations presumably allow consumers to compare these healthcare providers and insurers intelligently and make informed choices.

From a marketing and consumer behavior perspective, the implications are enormous. Historically, the dissonance reduction model of consumer behavior, under which consumers make a high-involvement (i.e., very important) decision with very little information, has characterized most annual healthcare enrollment or purchase behavior. To assure themselves that they are not making the wrong decision, consumers often choose what they perceive to be the safe choice: the most well-known organization, the organization recommended by the benefits clerk (the most immediately available expert to someone who is enrolling in a healthcare plan at work), a trusted friend, or the organization in which they already have been enrolled, where the feeling of safety is based on personal experience. As the *McKinsey Quarterly* noted with regard to health insurance, "confusion and unpreparedness characterize the way consumers buy health insurance: rather than shop, they stick with familiar products."[12] Rarely, in the recent past, have consumers incorporated valid, objective, and comprehensive provider and insurance carrier information into their decision-making process,[13] in no small part because the information had not been available.

Availability of Information

The growing availability of new information on healthcare providers and carriers as well as on specific medical problems and disease processes suggests that a far larger portion of the population in the future will behave, or at least try to behave, according to the complex buying behavior model. The basic assumption of the model is that all purchase behavior is information based; consumers compare and contrast purchase alternatives, form intelligent opinions regarding the alternatives, and purchase based on these informed opinions. For those able to analyze the somewhat complex information related to healthcare plans, the option to behave according to the complex buying behavior model may now be available. For example, the nonprofit organization Consumers Union has recently launched a hospital rating service with information on 3000 hospitals. Consumers can look up, for each hospital, based on the time spent in the hospital and on the number of physician visits to the patient while in the hospital, how aggressively that hospital treats patients. Marketers should be sensitive to consumers' desire for data and should constantly be attuned to what the data say about the quality of the organization's healthcare services. For the marketer, this database should be a welcome addition (if it does not already exist) to the tools used for continuous quality improvement.

Unfortunately, it is clear that consumers are not receiving all the information they want. Some of the information that is available is not viewed by consumers as being significant in their decision making. For example, the Consumers Union hospital rating data may not prove itself valuable to consumers as they may not be able to translate intensity or aggressiveness of care into outcomes or results. In fact, the data could confuse the consumer as a higher level of intensity of treatment is not necessarily correlated with better outcomes. Further, some of the attributes important to the consumer, such as the denial of access to a specialist when it is necessary, are difficult to measure. Consumer self-reports of needing to see a specialist may be inflated; patients may think they need a specialist when, in fact, they do not. The reporting organization, on the other hand, has an incentive to downplay the number of reports of denied access to specialists. Because the task of measuring a void—of measuring what did not happen—is usually more difficult than measuring what did happen, this information is generally not reported.

Other types of consumer-desired data are not only not measured, but also represent the type of data that the provider may not wish to have measured. Most people, for example, before selecting a health plan or primary care physician (PCP), would want to know the average amount of time one must wait to make a nonurgent appointment with the PCP. Many components of service quality, such as waiting time, physician's acceptance and knowledge of alternative medicine, and willingness to take on managed care protocols when he or she does not think that the protocol is in the best interest of the patient, are difficult to measure, sensitive in an organizational political sense, and therefore not reported.

It also appears that consumers are not seeing or using many of the data provided to them. The *2008 Update on Consumers' Views of Patient Safety and Quality Information* reports that only 30% of the US population say that they saw comparative healthcare quality data on either health insurance plans, hospitals, or physicians, which is less than reported in 2006 (36%) and 2004 (35%). Further, only 14% said that they used any of this comparison data, down from 20% in 2006 and 19% in 2004.[14] Although consumers may consider specific plan benefits, premium costs, and out-of-pocket costs essential information when choosing a healthcare plan, they seldom use such information as the ratings of plans by independent experts, the percentage of members who are satisfied with the overall plan, and comparisons in the convenience of the administrative paperwork. Other research has shown that consumers do not use much of the information provided, particularly if it cannot be easily and readily understood.[15, 16] Scanlon et al found that, when presented with seven health plan report cards, only 34% of consumers used them at all in making their health plan selection.[17] The elderly, in particular, have difficulty in utilizing the information presented to them in health report cards.[18] Hibbard and associates discovered that even employers (that is, the managers within companies who were responsible for selecting healthcare plans for the company's employees and who should have been knowledgeable about healthcare plan data) did not use much of the information made available to them, nor did they seek out other information that could have allowed for a more informed purchase choice.[19] Therefore, it appears that even if far more data were available, many healthcare purchasers may continue to act according to the dissonance reduction model.

Consumers do appear to make better use of disease-related information as opposed to service provider (health insurer, hospital, physician) information. Estimates, while varied, suggest that roughly 10 to 15% of the US population goes online every day seeking some non-provider-specific health information; for those with chronic diseases, this can rise to 75% or higher. The sources of this type of information are numerous, including general medical sites such as WebMD and mayoclinic.com, as well as medical research sites (e.g., clinicaltrials.gov, PubMed, MedlinePlus), disease-specific sites (e.g., cancer.org, diabetes.org.), and medical management sites (e.g., Destination Rx, www.drx.com, which is used to compare drug prices, and sugarstats.com, which allows the patient to track, monitor, and manage blood sugar levels and other diabetes-related statistics). Patient disease community sites have proven particularly useful for some patient groups where patients are able to share their combined knowledge of disease processes and treatments and provide each other with emotional support. The result of all this information now available to consumers is that they are more likely to make demands of and to challenge their physicians, potentially changing the decision-making dynamic within the physician–patient relationship.[20]

Integrity and Validity of Information

Much depends not only on the availability of the data, but also on the integrity and validity of the information. There is a great deal of generic healthcare and medical data on the Internet that can empower patients and give them a great deal of information about their diagnoses and potential treatments, but it can also mislead them. No one is charged with reviewing studies or data cited on the Internet, as there is in the case of medical journals; yet, one of the two most common reasons for logging on to the Internet is to obtain health information. Currently, there is no way to judge how much of this information is correct and how much may do harm.

Another problem arises if the aggregation of healthcare data changes its meaning. For example, healthcare services within healthcare organizations are of variable quality. An aggregation, averaging, or collapsing of the data makes them easier for everyone to use; some of the consumers report excellent experiences, whereas others report terrible experiences, which could average out simply to mediocre experiences. Failure to note the extremes could easily mislead those who wish to use and are capable of using the full range of data. A healthcare organization with a bimodal distribution of satisfaction ratings could hide the high level of dissatisfaction on the low end by reporting only means or medians. Moreover, Nuovo et al. reported that medical researchers generally report their findings in a way that makes the results seem better than they are. Of 359 studies in leading medical journals, only 18 reported absolute risk reduction; the rest reported only relative risk reduction, which magnifies the reduction of risk and the benefit provided from the intervention or treatment.[21]

It may be difficult to promulgate objective information. One method of reporting aggregated information that can help to overcome this problem is to provide not only the means and medians, but also more complete information on the unaggregated data: How many answer categories were there? What percentage of the respondents fell into the lowest category? What percentage fell into the highest category? A survey of customer satisfaction ratings with answers ranging from 1 to 5 (where 1 is extremely satisfied and 5 is extremely dissatisfied) may show a mean rating of 3 for both HMO A and HMO B. This may suggest that the HMOs are performing similarly in terms of satisfying the customer. If only 2% of those rating HMO A responded by rating it a 5, but 14% of those rating HMO B gave it a rating of 5, the potential customer may be far more likely to experience extreme dissatisfaction in HMO B than in HMO A.

Some marketers may find themselves under pressure to use the data to portray their healthcare organization in the best possible light, even if that portrayal is misleading or incomplete. In this scenario, a marketer takes the single best rating or set of ratings and positions the organization on that one rating or set while ignoring the other ratings. For example, a hospital may receive very high ratings on nursing care while receiving average or below-average ratings on maintaining its physical plant, having up-to-date diagnostic equipment, having a wide array of specialists, and providing coordinated care. The hospital management, in the interests of best representing the hospital, may then advertise that the hospital provides some of the best nursing care in the area, failing to mention the remaining data.

From a policy perspective, the danger is that many consumers will rely on the advertisements, which may represent predigested information, rather than on the full body of information available. Few advertisements are likely to provide information that portrays the organization negatively; after all, the job of advertising is generally to sell the organization, not to demarket it. (Demarketing is the act of making a product, service, or organization less marketable.) The subjugation of available and/or required data from informing the consumer to selling the consumer has been a common practice in other industries and can be expected in the healthcare industry as the government, employers, or other outside bodies require the collection of outcome, medical error, and satisfaction databases. Although the consumer and employer may wish to use the collected data and act by the complex buying behavior model, the act of analyzing large amounts of data is foreign to most people.[22] The natural tendency is to substitute the predigested data, as presented in an advertising form or in a format that is oversimplified by the data collectors.

It is not yet reasonable to assume that the relevant data will be available. One of the major problems in reporting customer quality perceptions and satisfaction data is the failure of senior management in many healthcare organizations to budget for the measurement of the data.[23] Requirements by the government, by accrediting organizations, or by employers may force healthcare organizations to budget for the collection of such data, but the data measures may not be standardized from organization to organization. What one hospital or HMO labels as a condition leading to high consumer satisfaction (e.g., a 30-minute wait for urgent care) may be labeled as unacceptable by another hospital or HMO. These differences make it even more difficult for consumers to compare and contrast healthcare organizations intelligently.

As a result, the dissonance reduction model is likely to remain the predominant model of consumer behavior in the healthcare field as it is in many other industries. Most people do not have the capacity or the desire to wade through the data and turn it into usable information, or they do not trust the integrity of the data. The healthcare industry does not yet have an independent, unbiased agency that can collect information agreed upon as the most relevant, objectively analyze it, and present it in a trustworthy predigested format.

Consumer Behavior: Differentiation

Marketers look to three variables that matter to consumers and, therefore, could act as differentiators: cost, quality, and access. Definitions of quality are anything but consistent across healthcare studies and healthcare consumers. The way in which the NCQA measures quality includes a number of early disease detection tests that many consumers perceive as largely irrelevant, for example. The measures of service quality that are now standard in the service marketing literature do not apply particularly well to healthcare settings. The focus on medical errors as a significant indicator of quality resulted in two reports from the Institute of Medicine, the more recent of which, *Crossing the Quality Chasm*, cites six dimensions of quality: timeliness, safety, effectiveness, efficiency, equity, and patient-centeredness, although one of the authors of the report, diverging somewhat from the report itself, states that "patients' experiences should be the fundamental source of the definition of quality."[24]

Even the definition of access may mean different things to different people. One person may speak of access as the ability to get an appointment with the physician on the same day, someone else may mean the ability to see a specialist at will, and a third may define access as the ability to find a physician who is willing to take new patients and whose office is closer than 30 minutes away.

Clearly, these and other factors can differentiate one provider or insurer from another. For a healthcare plan, the composition of benefit packages is one source of differentiation. Does it include drug coverage? Does it allow self-referral to an obstetrician-gynecologist? To what hospitals can plan members be admitted? Many of these provisions can allow for differentiation between plans and can give the consumer (and employer) a real choice. In geographic areas where the benefit packages of the different healthcare plans are quite similar and the panel of physicians and hospitals offered are nearly the same, consumers seeking points of differentiation between plans will have to rely more heavily on satisfaction and service attributes, on location of physicians and facilities, and on other factors that the plan chooses to use for differentiation purposes, such as free membership in a health club. The implications for marketers are that they must attend to those areas where they can effectively differentiate themselves.

Price as a Differentiator

One of the easiest areas of differentiation conceptually involves pricing. In straightforward marketing situations, it does not require extensive advertising, promotion, and education to demonstrate a lower price. The ability to maintain a competitively low price is dependent on having a low cost structure, however. If a low cost structure does not result from significant reengineering of the service process so as to continue to deliver a consumer-perceived high quality of service, but rather results from limited coverage, denial of access to services, long waits, and so on, differentiation on the basis of pricing will be advantageous only in the short run. Members dissatisfied with the level and quality of service will opt to join competing plans (even though they may be higher priced) in the next reenrollment period. From a marketing standpoint, the ability to differentiate on price means that price-sensitive consumers are given the choice of buying less service or lower quality (at least lower perceived quality) for less money;

conversely, price-insensitive consumers are given the choice of buying more and paying more for the choice. Also, true innovation, which may entail vastly different prices (both higher and lower) is possible. The result should heighten the ability of organizations to differentiate themselves and should enhance consumer choice.

A differentiated approach supports the concept of customer-responsive marketing. It allows the organization to segment the market; develop a product, package, or set of services that meets particularly well the needs and wants of that specific segment; and differentiate itself from its competitors. Unfortunately, the marketplace has not yet focused on quality or access as much as it has focused on price in the past. Therefore, price competition has been fierce, and differentiation on the basis of factors other than price has been limited. One of the few well-known healthcare organizations that did differentiate in other ways was the former Oxford Health (now part of UnitedHealthcare). Oxford Health gained a significantly differentiated reputation, in part due to the broad access to alternative medicine providers allowed to its members at a time when few other managed care plans covered alternative providers in any meaningful way.

In reality, pricing decisions are not nearly as straightforward in the healthcare industry as in most other industries. Regulations often dictate prices for healthcare services, for example, and retroactive denials of payment after the delivery of services are common. Normally, organizations set a price floor (below which the price does not fall) at the cost of producing the service. As in most service environments, fixed costs are high for health care, whereas variable costs are low. Determining the full cost of a service can be quite difficult because it involves a somewhat arbitrary distribution of fixed costs among the various services that share the fixed costs of overhead. Because each organization can allocate overhead in a different way and competitors have different overhead structures, different providers of service have different costs for any specific service. In business-to-business relationships, healthcare providers may face fierce price competition as they negotiate payment structures and often feel compelled to try to match the low price of their competitors. If they are unsure of the full cost of the service in question, they may price the service below its true fixed cost in order to match competing prices. Furthermore, if regulated prices are based on the market's low prices, which arose from a mix of fierce price competition and uncertainty about services' full costs, then these low prices can be regulated into long-term existence.

The decreasing amount of cross-subsidization in the healthcare market exacerbates the problem. Historically, those who had "good" insurance (usually fee-for-service or, until diagnosis-related groups [DRGs], Medicare) cross-subsidized those with "poor" insurance (e.g., Medicaid) and those without insurance. Those with "good" insurance paid a higher price for the same procedure, room, or diagnostic test, thus compensating for those with "poor" insurance. This cross-subsidization was viewed as serving the public good, ensuring that all who needed healthcare would receive it. As more healthcare providers came to see themselves as businesses and as price competition intensified, healthcare organizations sought increasingly to price their services as low as possible in order to make themselves as marketable as possible. This left little room for cross-subsidization. With fee-for-service now all but erased from the health sector, such cross-subsidization is increasingly difficult to identify.

Yet another way in which pricing decisions are not straightforward in healthcare is evident in the way in which healthcare organizations try to raise their prices by segmenting patients according to their insurance coverage. For example, Wildwood Health Care Center, an Indianapolis nursing home owned by Vencor, Inc., the fourth largest nursing home in the United States, had a significant number of nursing home patients who were covered by Medicaid. Wildwood indicated that it was losing money on these patients, however, because Medicaid was willing to pay only $82 per day. Because Wildwood could not persuade Medicaid to raise the reimbursement to be closer to the $125 per day that private pay patients paid, Wildwood sought to raise the aggregate price mix of its patients by forcing out its Medicaid residents. It then planned to admit only private pay patients in the future so that all its patients would then be paying $125 per day.[25] Their inability to change regulated prices may cause healthcare organizations to aim their marketing strategies at those segments of the market whose prices or reimbursement rates are already the most favorable. In this way, some healthcare providers differentiate themselves on price indirectly by directly targeting well-reimbursed market segments.

Access as a Differentiator

Healthcare organizations can differentiate themselves on the basis of access in a number of ways. For example, some physician practices have begun to provide greater patient access to the physician by allowing the patient to have e-mail conversations with the physician about nonacute nonurgent matters (as patient safety considerations require face-to-face contact if the patient could be at greater risk). A smaller (estimates vary from 1.5 to 2 million visits a year) but notable number have started to provide home visits, particularly to the elderly and to the homebound for whom a visit to the physician's office requires an ambulance or other expensive form of transportation. Physicians who have incorporated this into their practices say that it allows them to have a better understanding of the environmental forces affecting the patient's health and therefore to provide better quality care for these patients. The difficulty with home visits is, of course, that traditional reimbursement does not cover transportation costs nor the unreimbursed time of physician travel. Therefore, many home visits by physicians are often associated with nonprofit organizations who subsidize the cost of the visits. Group medical practices that provide easy access to primary care physicians (PCPs) also differentiate themselves, as a growing shortage of PCPs makes it increasingly difficult for consumers to locate a new PCP or to get a timely appointment with their own PCP.

Hospitals have increasingly been exposing patients to problems of access in both their emergency departments as well as on their inpatient floors. Many hospitals, particularly academic medical centers and those in large cities, have been running at or close to 100% occupancy, making it difficult for new patients to be admitted. As a result, patients waiting to be admitted from the emergency department may be backed up, placed in exam rooms or corridors while waiting to be moved to an inpatient floor. According to the American College of Emergency Physicians, 96% of emergency department physicians surveyed stated that inpatient boarding (for patients admitted through the emergency department) was their top safety concern.[26] Even those patients who do not need to be admitted as an inpatient are likely to wait, many for hours, before they are seen by the physician. This is a nationwide problem and is not limited to the uninsured. Emergency department visits increased by 26% from 1996 to 2004; many of these visits were made by people whose incomes exceeded the federal poverty level by 400%. During that same period, the percentage of emergency department visits by the uninsured declined by 1%.[27] That this problem is not limited to one market segment or income group led one article in the *Journal of the American Medical Association* to declare, "Emergency departments (EDs) today are in crisis, facing significant overcrowding, unreimbursed care, and long waiting times."[28]

The concept of waiting can be characterized as an operational problem: too little capacity, both physical capacity and throughput capacity. The end result of extended waiting times in medical settings is in part a quality issue; patient safety can be compromised. It is also, however, a marketing problem. Customers who are forced to wait may soon become dissatisfied customers and, if other options are available, they may become customers who defect to other healthcare providers who can decrease the waiting time needed to receive service. Some hospitals that could not decrease the actual waiting time in the emergency department recognized that dissatisfaction could at least be lessened by keeping the patients informed about wait times. The Mountain States Alliance, a system of 14 hospitals, posts the wait times at each of the hospitals' emergency departments online so that patients know in advance how long the wait is likely to be and so that they might also choose to visit the emergency department at the nearest hospital with the shortest posted wait time.

The difficulty in accessing timely care from both primary care physicians (PCPs) and emergency departments has resulted in the growth of a new distribution channel—the retail medical clinic. These clinics provide a limited menu of primary care services on a walk-in basis (i.e., no or very short waits); are located in convenient locations, often in high-traffic retail locations; are usually staffed by a nurse practitioner or physician's assistant; and may be covered by some insurers or otherwise charge on a fee-for-service basis; the fee-for-service charge is usually well under what a primary care physician in private practice would charge and significantly less than an emergency room would charge. The market positioning of retail clinics can best be captured as affordable and convenient service in comparison to PCPs and emergency rooms. Retail clinics have experienced high growth between 2006 and 2008, due in part to the high levels of customer satisfaction due to the short waits and easy access.[29] While critics correctly point out that retail clinics can cause disruptions in the patient's continuity of care, the same can be said for visits to the emergency departments. Further, with other channels of access being overburdened by demand that exceeds capacity, the use of retail clinics to lessen low acuity demand on PCPs and emergency departments would seem wise. It also fits very well with the movement toward consumer-directed health plans which incorporate high deductibles and HSAs where the patient pays out of pocket for noncatastrophic medical expenses; under these conditions, the customer appreciates knowing in advance what the cost of the visit will be and what will be provided.[30]

Other and Combined Sources of Differentiation

Healthcare plans also compete on the basis of location, customer service, and distribution/access issues. Location is the most obvious issue; physician practices, hospitals, outpatient facilities, and other healthcare providers make choices relative to the areas in which the served market works and lives. Acquisition of other providers and plans has become a fast-growing mode of expanding geographically within the healthcare market. Convenience of location clearly is one of the key decision factors that people use in selecting their healthcare providers and in deciding to stay with those providers.

Implicitly, many healthcare plans now are differentiating themselves by serving certain market segments particularly well. Disease management programs single out those with a specific condition (e.g., asthma or diabetes) and provide specialized services related to that condition. This is intended to be an application of one-to-one marketing and is dependent on information systems that can collect member information to identify those in need of specific services. For example, a program that focused on asthmatic patients would keep track of such occurrences as how many times an asthmatic patient needed to go to hospital emergency departments within a 6-month period and how many times the patient had filled a daily medication (to help determine if the patient was using the medication as often as prescribed) and tailor its services to that patient. Someone who had paid multiple visits to emergency departments in a short period of time probably would need more training in how to use the small diagnostic peak flow meter instrument that allows the patient to assess his or her air intake and how to use the inhaler medications that can arrest the development of the asthma incident before it requires an emergency department visit.

Healthcare providers who contract with managed care plans seek to differentiate themselves to employers, to managed care plans, and to consumers. The ways in which they differentiate their services should vary according to the audience. Although a hospital's ability to capture data on resources used in serving its employees may impress an employer, the employees may see little value in this data and want information instead on the postsurgical therapies offered by the hospital. Again, using the power of technology, a hospital can engage in one-to-one segmentation to differentiate itself. It can, for example, identify all patients coming for breast cancer surgery and arrange for all those patients to talk to a volunteer from Reach for Recovery, to receive literature on breast reconstruction if they have had a mastectomy, and to consult a representative from the local store that specializes in clothing for patients who have undergone breast surgery. Insurers, hospitals, and clinicians can differentiate themselves in markets where many of the population come from different ethnic, cultural, and linguistic backgrounds by hiring a diverse workforce to reflect the populations served. Hospitals also are differentiated in some cases on the basis of characteristics inherent in their incorporation, such as Catholic, Jewish, Adventist, public, city, private psychiatric, or specialty children's hospitals.

Medical tourism combines a number of forms of differentiation. The most obvious, price differentiation, is dramatic. A heart bypass in the United States, which would likely cost around $130,000, costs only $10,000 in Thailand; an angioplasty costing $57,000 in the United States can be done for only $13,000 in India.[31] It is not only the uninsured and the poorly insured who are seeking less expensive care outside the United States. With consumer-directed health plans causing the insured to dig deeper into their own pockets to pay part of the cost of care, the lower costs of medical care abroad can become more attractive to all but the very wealthy. Even health insurance companies have begun to provide incentives to their customers to get their medical care abroad, with some of them waiving co-pays and deductibles, providing a monetary incentive to become medical tourists, and paying for family members to travel with the patient to induce the insured customer to travel for care. If the heart bypass can be done at $10,000 outside of the United States (as noted above) rather than $130,000, then it pays the insurer to cover all these additional costs for the insured because the total cost to the insurer will still be lower than the total domestic price for care. It is estimated that the global market for medical tourism is between 60,000 and 85,000 patients a year, with the potential to save $20 billion in US healthcare costs.

However, there are other sources of differentiation that may make medical tourism attractive. These include easier access to procedures for which there may be longer waits at home (this is particularly true of organ transplants but with the complicating factor of dubious organ sources outside of the United States, especially when the organ is "donated" by someone in a developing economy) and sometimes equal or even better technology and quality care. As noted in *Business Week*, "Foreign hospitals in such arrangements are typically approved by Joint Commission International, part of the same nonprofit organization that accredits American hospitals."[33] Then there is the location, which could be viewed as both a positive source of differentiation ("ooh, a chance to travel and have someone else pay for it") or a negative source ("I don't feel comfortable having surgery so far away from home"). Negative sources of differentiation exist as well. Patients who feel that they have received less than adequate care and have been damaged by the care that they have received abroad will find it difficult to pursue malpractice claims as no other country provides the same extent of malpractice protection as the United States does. Further, some medical tourists, upon returning home after receiving care abroad, find that it is difficult to find a physician who will provide the follow-up care for a procedure in which they had no earlier involvement. Once again, as in the use of other new channels, the issue of continuity of care becomes a challenge. Still, the differentiable benefits of medical tourism offered by price and channel access variables make this service a potential growth market.

Customer Retention

Many consumers feel they must remain with their current health insurance or managed care organization in the belief that a preexisting condition precludes them from switching to a different provider organization. The promise of the Health Insurance Portability and Accountability Act, a law that was intended to guarantee consumers continued healthcare insurance when they changed jobs, has not been fulfilled because the premiums have been exorbitant and some insurance companies have discouraged their agents from writing these policies. As a result, many consumers who appear to be highly loyal to a healthcare provider or plan may simply fear losing their coverage. If the healthcare system ever develops in a way that allows these captive consumers to switch from one plan to another without penalty, healthcare plans would have a greater incentive to keep their members satisfied and their marketers would have to work harder at maintaining a high enrollment level.

The belief that consumers have few options because many employers have in the past limited the number of options available to their employees is not fully correct. According to *Business &*

Health, "Managed care has not put an end to choice. . . . Nationwide, nearly two out of three workers whose employers provide health coverage had a choice of plans. Even many employees whose firms offered only one health plan had options. According to the AAHP (American Association of Health Plans), 90 percent had coverage with a non-network component."[34] Consumers who have more choices switch plans more often. Because the choice of healthcare plan is a high-involvement decision, however, consumers must be convinced through advertising, personal selling, word of mouth, or some other form of promotion that their new choice of healthcare plan is a safe choice.

Historically, the marketing efforts of healthcare providers, health insurers, and health maintenance plans have appeared to focus more intently on attracting patients, customers, and members than on retaining them. Hospitals and medical group practices that have formally engaged in marketing have relied heavily on tactics such as promotion and advertising to the detriment of the more strategic functions of marketing. Insurers and health maintenance plans have done the same, with an additionally heavy use of sales personnel to market the product. Managed care penetration has now reached such a high level, however, that it no longer draws its new members from the indemnity sector, but rather draws them from other managed care plans during reenrollment periods. Taken together, these events challenge healthcare organizations to find new ways to retain patients and members. No amount of advertising, promotion, and selling can retain a customer who is unhappy with a service, unless that customer has no choice; promoting great nursing care or short waits will not counteract a patient's own experience of nonempathic and abrupt delivery of care. The focus of marketing efforts, if retention is the goal, shifts away from advertising, promotion, and selling to the provision of visibly good service quality.

Service marketers and academics in the last 10 years have been trying to measure and quantify service quality. Parasuraman and associates devised a now-well-accepted model of service quality that has been applied to healthcare settings with mixed results.[35–37] Although this model, called the SERVQUAL instrument, may not apply fully to healthcare settings as it was developed, it is likely to fit healthcare consumer behavior better with modification over time. It measures constructs such as reliability, responsibility, tangibles, assurance, and empathy. Once its measures are better related to healthcare consumers' satisfaction, marketers will be able to rely on it and on other validated measures of customer-defined quality in their search for ways to retain customers.

Those in healthcare marketing often fail to examine the consumer decision to stay with a provider. Even though it costs five times as much to capture a new customer as to keep an existing one,[38] most healthcare organizations continue to define marketing as encouraging trial (capturing new patients or members) rather than retaining members. This is not a wise choice fiscally, given the higher cost of attracting new customers. Greater effort should be directed toward retaining existing customers.

One reason for the failure of healthcare organizations to address customer retention is that most do not have information systems designed to identify retention variables.[39] It is the rare hospital, group medical practice, or outpatient rehabilitation facility, for example, that can easily produce a list of patients who have been using its services for more than 2 years and those who have used them for less than 1 year. Even more difficult is the task of identifying patient or member defectors. Few physician practices are aware of when patients leave their practices. Those who request their medical records are only a small subset (estimated to be approximately 13%) of the total number who defect.[40] The number of defectors from health plans is estimated to be 20%, meaning that the average health plan would have to replace the equivalent of its whole membership every five years.

Further, physician practices do not collect or input their patient data in a way that would allow them to retrieve information on lost patients. The most likely method that could be used to identify defected patients would be through the billing records. However, the billing system was developed to capture dollars, not patient defection information. As a result, most systems cannot pull up this information when asked to do so.[41] Even managed care plans, which have annual enrollment periods that make it easier to distinguish years of use, cannot generally identify those who have voluntarily disenrolled. If an organization cannot identify those who have chosen to go elsewhere (presumably to a competitor), then the organization cannot learn from them what it can do better in the future so as to keep its members (or patients).

Customer service and a variety of service marketing issues, such as managing the service process experience so that the customer can project a positive outcome based on a positive process experience, have become a major focus of continuous quality improvement efforts. Most larger healthcare organizations have instituted total quality management, continuous quality improvement, or some other form of patient- or member-based reengineering process management that is designed to deliver a seamless service and, if introduced to the organization correctly, to build long-term relationships with its customers rather than a series of one-time transactions. Very often, only those with authority over the operations of the organization can solve what marketing research identifies as dissatisfaction caused by poor service. If patients are kept waiting for an average of 2 hours to get a laboratory test, the marketing resolution of the dissatisfaction requires modifying the operational component by expanding the capacity of the laboratory (e.g., adding technicians, space, equipment, information systems, or some combination of these).

The area of distribution and access is only one of the battlefields where the fight to retain customers will be fought. The concept of access always has been a sensitive one to consumers of health care. Time access is a constant and consistent source of irritation, if not anger, in healthcare market research; waiting for an appointment, waiting for a procedure or test, and waiting for the results of tests all have caused great customer dissatisfaction and have conveyed a sense of poor service.

The continuing movement of most of the marketplace into managed or capitated care, where one of the primary cost-saving measures is based on denial of access (presumably in the positive sense of forgoing unnecessary care or substituting equally adequate, but less expensive care), expands the sensitivity of the issue of threatened access. Denial of access is most often seen as negative, such as denial of access to choice of provider, denial of access to any specialist without the gatekeeper's approval, or denial of tests deemed to be too expensive for 98% of cases. Healthcare organizations have seen and can expect to see much higher levels of dissatisfaction stemming from perceived (or real) access problems. Some managed care organizations already have sensed this and have removed the barriers that prevent members from seeking medical specialist care on their own, without having first to seek the permission and referral of their primary care physicians.

Physicians, too, have become highly sensitive and vocal about denial of access. In great numbers, they have described to their patients and the press the barriers presented by the managed care gatekeepers whose job it is to assess the need for tests, procedures, and care, supposedly in the interests of the patients. The physicians often view the gatekeepers as those who deny patients needed care in the fiscal interests of the organization. In fact, the denial of access may be based on a legitimate recognition that unnecessary tests and care are driving up healthcare costs. Anecdotally, consumer dissatisfaction stems from real fears of improper denial of access. In market research, consumers say things such as "What if an X-ray can't show the problem, and I really do need an MRI?" "What if my physician is right, and I really do need this surgery?" "What if my physician gives up too easily and doesn't fight for the surgery I need?" When gatekeepers are young, inexperienced, or possibly not well trained in specialty areas, denial of access becomes not only a marketing and retention problem, but also an ethical and clinical problem that cuts to the very heart of the healthcare business and the practice of good medicine. If a patient seeks alternative opinions from non-network physicians who disagree with the initial conclusions of the patient's plan physician, the result may be conflict and potential liability. Some primary care physicians have addressed this in part by setting up concierge or boutique medical practices; they dramatically decrease the size of their practices and charge the patient a significant fee for increased service, which can be categorized largely as increased access to the physician.[42]

The marketing task in addressing retention is to explain denials of access to consumers and physicians in such a way that they can appreciate and agree with the decision, assuming that the rationale to deny is wise. Alternatively, the task is to examine the denial process to ascertain that denials are not, in fact, inappropriate. Unless this is done, dissatisfaction may be manifested not only through increasing retention problems, but also through medical malpractice suits and angry verbal assaults in the press. Either way, the healthcare organization places itself in long-term fiscal jeopardy if its retention rates drop dramatically.

Customer Satisfaction

Many of the regional and national healthcare accrediting organizations require the healthcare organizations that they accredit to collect and share customer satisfaction information. The obvious assumption is that organizations want to satisfy their customers and should do so. It is not yet clear, however, whether customer satisfaction correlates with customer retention; that is, are satisfied customers loyal customers? There is anecdotal information to suggest that the correlation might not be as high as one would expect.

Service Recovery

Dissatisfied customers have the potential not only to go to a competitor, but also to spread negative word-of-mouth about the organization's services. Instead of being a missionary (one who speaks enthusiastically in favor of the organization and recommends it to others), a dissatisfied customer is more likely to be a market terrorist (one who says negative things about the organization and tries to dissuade people from using its services). The cost of counteracting the efforts of a market terrorist can be quite high. The advertising and promotion undertaken by the organization do not have near the credibility of a former or current customer who can cite specific instances of bad service. Therefore, it is in the organization's best interests to keep its customers happy.

Keeping customers happy is not merely a matter of providing the routinely good service that customers expect. The real test of a service organization's ability to satisfy its customers is its ability to solve problems. No organization is perfect; all organizations sooner or later make a mistake or inadvertently provide poor service. The true test of an organization's service competence is its ability to recover after a service problem occurs.[43] It is essential to anticipate service problems rather than simply to respond to them. Management must decide in advance the amount of flexibility that employees should have to solve customer problems on the spot and the amount of resources that should be available to employees for the purposes of service recovery.

Some organizations do not believe that their employees are capable of responding to service problems appropriately. In these organizations, a customer who feels that a service has been of poor quality must tell not only the frontline employee of the problem, but also the employee's immediate superior and anyone else in the chain of command who must be part of the problem-resolution effort. This repeated explanation of the source of dissatisfaction, often two or more times, runs contrary to good problem resolution or service recovery, which dictates that the customer should have the problem resolved as quickly as possible. Each time the customer has to "tell the story" about the problem without obtaining resolution of the problem, the customer becomes increasingly uncertain that the problem will be resolved; customers frequently will resort to magnifying the problem in telling it to the next level in the organization in the hope that maybe this time it will be resolved. Any person who has suffered through this process is ripe to become a market terrorist in communicating about this organization.

In contrast, good service recovery organizations provide both flexibility and resources at the front line so that problems can be solved or addressed in a fashion that satisfies the customer immediately. In order for this approach to work effectively, the organization must inculcate its employees with an understanding that an important part of their job is to recognize and solve customer problems—whatever it takes. Educating employees to the concept of the lifetime value of a customer supports this outlook. If an HMO member stays with that HMO for an average of 10 years, bringing in an average of $1,200 a year, then the lifetime value of the member is $12,000. If a member of the HMO becomes upset because she spent $15 ($30 round trip) for taxi fare to be on time for her doctor's appointment, only to find that the physician was not in that day and no one thought to call her, it makes sense, given her long-term value to the HMO of $12,000, to reimburse her for the $30 taxi fare. The trade-off of $30 in order not to risk $12,000 seems more than reasonable for the service recovery.

Measurement of Customer Satisfaction

Ways of measuring customer satisfaction vary, as do the reasons for measuring satisfaction. First, many healthcare providers have been trying to measure customer satisfaction more aggressively in the past decade because of the requirements of accrediting organizations and employers. Often, these accrediting organizations require the use of standardized measures to allow comparisons across healthcare facilities. Although this requirement has obvious value, it also has draw-backs. Standardized measures usually are generic in nature so that they apply equally well to all the healthcare organizations using them; however, generic measures are generally so broad and nonspecific that they do not give the healthcare organization enough information to identify and correct problems revealed in the customer satisfaction research. For example, a poor rating on a patient survey for the Joint Commission on Accreditation of Healthcare Organizations may alert a hospital to the fact that there was a problem, but may not indicate what the specific problem was, thereby limiting the hospital's ability to correct the problem. Thus, although standardized customer satisfaction studies are valuable for the purposes of providing industry report cards with needed information, they are not generally managerially useful.

Second, satisfaction is known to be in part a function of the amount of choice the customer had in the purchase decision.[44] Thus, satisfaction ratings are likely to be lower among healthcare plan members whose employers gave them no choice of healthcare plan than among members who had at least some choice of plan, even if only one other choice. This then raises the question, exactly what is being measured in customer satisfaction research? Choice at the time of purchase becomes one of the key items reflected in customer satisfaction studies rather than customer satisfaction with the organization's performance after purchase.

Third, the interpretation of customer satisfaction research often focuses on the nature of the customers. Medicare managed care plans, for example, have recently been prone to explain their low patient satisfaction ratings as a function of the age of the people who are the subjects of the research. Their assumption is that older people are, by definition, more dissatisfied. Studies have shown, however, that patient or member characteristics account for only 9% of the variation in customer service research; the rest is due to the performance characteristics of the organization itself.[45]

Fourth, some satisfaction studies in the healthcare industry have biased the response categories by loading them too heavily in the positive direction. For questions such as "How satisfied are you with your care?" for example, they have provided the answer categories: highly satisfied, somewhat satisfied, satisfied, not satisfied. Because the respondent has three positive (satisfied) categories from which to choose and only one negative category, there is a bias toward a positive response. The willingness of many in the industry to interpret any of the top three categories as satisfied exacerbates the problem. The public has become cynical about the multitude of managed care plan advertisements claiming 94%, 95%, 98% (and so on) customer satisfaction levels. In reality, only those who answer in the most positive response category are truly satisfied and likely to return to the organization for services. More than half of those in the second highest category can be expected to defect to a competitor. Obviously, customer satisfaction studies are neither simple to devise nor simple to interpret; when performed correctly with the appropriate expertise, however, they can be quite valuable.

Data-Driven Marketing

Correctly performed marketing always has been data driven. A marketing function that is fully supported will be given the tools with which to do its job. Insufficient data support, whether for internal data capture and analysis; for market research; or for market, competitive, and other external data analysis, cuts at the very heart of the marketing function. Healthcare organizations that hope to thrive in the future must expect to position marketing not only as a creative function, but also as a data-driven, analytical, and strategic function.

References

1. Kotler P, Shalowitz J, Stevens RJ. *Strategic Marketing for Health Care Organizations*. San Francisco, CA: Jossey-Bass; 2008.
2. Shepard S. Interventional radiology clinic opens amid physician "turf wars." *Memphis Business Journal*. April 9, 2004:1.
3. Gabel J. Ten ways HMOs have changed during the 1990s. *Health Affairs*. 1997;16(3):134–145.
4. Sidorov J. Case study of a failed merger of hospital systems. *Managed Care*. 2003; 12(11):56–60.
5. Michel A, Shaked I. *Takeover Madness: Corporate America Fights Back*. New York, NY: John Wiley & Sons; 1986.
6. Vranica S. Ad firms, already lean, are cutting their payrolls: economic turmoil prompts layoffs. *The Wall Street Journal*. October 13, 2008:B1.
7. Avalere Health. *Physician ownership and self-referral in hospitals: research on negative effects grows*. April 2008.
8. Dietrich M. Healthcare market structure and its implication for valuation of privately held provider entities: an empirical analysis. *Business Valuation Review*. 2008; 27(2):90–106.
9. The Henry J. Kaiser Family Foundation. Election 2008. *Kaiser Health Tracking Poll*. October 2008;(11):1–4.
10. Aiello M. Behind waiting room lines: why mystery patients are turning marketers and practitioners into enemies. *Healthcare Marketing Advisor*. September 2008;(9).
11. Appleby J. US ads push patients to shop for hospitals. *USA Today*. May 20, 2008:10.
12. Cordina J, Shubham S. What consumers want in health care. *The McKinsey Quarterly*. 2008;(4):81.
13. Kotler P, Shalowitz J, Stevens RJ. *Strategic Marketing for Health Care Organizations*. San Francisco, CA: Jossey-Bass; 2008.
14. Kaiser Family Foundation. *2008 Update on Consumers' Views of Patient Safety and Quality Information*. Menlo Park, CA: KFF/Agency for Healthcare Research and Quality; 2008.
15. Hibbard J, Jewett J. What type of quality information do consumers want in a health care report card? *Medical Care Research and Review*. 1996;53(1):28–47.
16. Hibbard J, Jewett J. Will quality report cards help consumers? *Health Affairs*. May/June 1997;218–228.
17. Scanlon D, Chernew M, Sheffler S, Fendrick AM. Health plan report cards: exploring differences in plan ratings. *Journal on Quality Improvement*. January 1998;5–20.
18. Hibbard J, Slovic P, Peters E, Finucane M, Tusler M. Is the informed-choice policy approach appropriate for Medicare beneficiaries? *Health Affairs*. May/June 2001:199–203.
19. Hibbard J, Jewett JJ, Legnini MW, Tusler M. Choosing a health plan: do large employers use the data? *Health Affairs*. December 1997:47–63.
20. Chiaramonte D. Who's afraid of the empowered patient? *Journal of the American Medical Association*. 2008;300(12):1393–1394.
21. Nuovo J, Melnikow J, Chang D. Reporting number needed to treat and absolute risk reduction in randomized clinical trials. *Journal of the American Medical Association*. 2002;287(21):2813–2814.
22. Hibbard J, Harris-Kojetin L, Mullin P, Lubalin J, Garfinkel S. Increasing the impact of health plan report cards by addressing consumers' concerns. *Health Affairs*. October 2000:138–143.

23. Woodside A. What is quality and how much does it really matter? *Journal of Health Care Marketing*. 1991;11(4):61–67.

24. Berwick D. A user's manual for the IOM's 'Quality Chasm' report. *Health Affairs*. May/June 2002:80–90.

25. Moss M, Adams C. Evictees relish nursing homes' reversal. *Wall Street Journal*. February 1998:Bl, B12.

26. Cole B. The politics of healthcare. *HealthLeaders*. July 2008:15.

27. Ibid, 14.

28. Newton M, Keirns C, Cuningham R, Hayward R, Stanley R. Uninsured adults presenting to US emergency departments. *The Journal of the American Medical Association*. 2008;300(16):1914–1924.

29. Laws M, Scott KS. The emergence of retail-based clinics in the United States: early observations. *Health Affairs*. 2008;27(5):1293–1298.

30. Christianson JB, Ginsburg PB, Draper DA. The transition from managed care to consumerism: a community-level status report. *Health Affairs*. 2008;27(5):1362–1371.

31. Medical tourism soars as Americans seek major savings on health care. *Chicago Tribune*. April 1, 2008.

32. Ehrbeck T, Guevara C, Mango PD. Health care and the consumer. *The McKinsey Quarterly*. 2008;(4):80.

33. Outsourcing the patients. *Business Week*. March 13, 2008.

34. Data watch—employee choice: alive and well. *Business & Health*. February 1998;58.

35. Parasuraman A, Zeithaml VA, Berry LL. A conceptual model of service quality and its implications for future research. *Journal of Marketing*. 1985;49(2):41–50.

36. Shewchuk R, O'Connor SJ, White JB. In search of service quality measures: some questions regarding psychometric properties. *Health Services Management Research*. 1991;4(1):65–75.

37. Headley D, Miller S. Measuring service quality and its relationship to future consumer behavior. *Journal of Health Care Marketing*. 1993;13(4):32–41.

38. Kotler P, Shalowitz J, Stevens, RJ. *Strategic Marketing for Health Care Organizations*. San Francisco, CA: Jossey-Bass; 2008.

39. Clarke R. The first step in addressing voluntary disenrollment. *The Health Care Strategist*. December 1997;7–9.

40. ———. Costs and prevention of patient defection. *Journal of Medical Practice Management*. July/August 2001;11–14.

41. ———. Measuring patient loss. *Journal of Medical Practice Management*. January/February 2002;2–5.

42. Brennan TA. Luxury primary care—market innovation or threat to access? *New England Journal of Medicine*. 2002;346(15):1165–1168.

43. Spreng R, Harrell GD, Mackoy RD. Service recovery: impact on satisfaction and intentions. *Journal of Services Marketing*. 1995;9(1):49–58.

44. Ullman R, Hill JW, Scheye EC, Spoeri RK. Satisfaction and choice: a view from the plans. *Health Affairs*.1997;16(3):209–217.

45. Clarke R. *Measuring consumer satisfaction*. Paper presented at the Health Care Policy and Regulation Workshop; December 9, 1994; New Brunswick, NJ.

Biographical Information

Roberta N. Clarke, DBA, is an Associate Professor in Boston University's Health Care Management Program. She is Vice-Chairman of the Board of the Academy for Educational Development, the world's largest human development agency, and also a member of the

Board of Trustees of the New England Organ Bank. Professor Clarke is the 1995 recipient of the American Marketing Association's prestigious Philip Kotler Award for Excellence in Healthcare Marketing. She is former President of the Society for Healthcare Planning and Marketing, a national professional society of 3500 members affiliated with the American Hospital Association. Dr. Clarke won the Healthcare Marketer of the Year Award from the American College of Healthcare marketing in 1985, the first year it was awarded. She has been teaching healthcare marketing courses at Boston University's Health Care Management Program since January 1974, and her executive and graduate student audiences range from health care and nonprofit to high technology, communications, and service industries. Professor Clarke has served on the editorial review board of the *Journal of Healthcare Marketing* since its inception and is on the editorial boards of many other healthcare publications. With Philip Kotler, she coauthored *Marketing for Healthcare Organizations*, considered to be the first and leading text in the field of healthcare marketing. Professor Clarke received her master's and doctorate from the Harvard Graduate School of Business Administration.

Healthcare Information Technologies in an Era of Healthcare Reform: A Complex Adaptive System Perspective

Joseph Tan and Joshia Tan

Introduction

Fueled by increasing trade deficits, implied signs of impending cuts in US federal agencies' funding of Medicare–Medicaid payments,[1] and the annual growth in healthcare expenditures, healthcare reform in the United States has now become one of the most hotly debated topics. Multiple stakeholders, including health economists and policymakers, institutional lobbyists, various sociopolitical and advocacy groups, the media, healthcare administrators and professionals, health researchers, and private citizens, have been giving this subject increasing and intensifying attention.

More recently, in response to the growing number of uninsured Americans under 65, as well as emerging signs of wear and age in the US healthcare system, the Obama administration has decided to further highlight the subject as an area requiring urgent dialogue and resolution. Today, the United States is spending well over 16% of its gross domestic product (GDP) on health care annually, a percentage that far surpasses the amount spent by many other countries; this is clearly illustrated in **Figure 8.1**, sourced from newly released 2007 OECD data. On the basis of this trend, Keehan et al.[2] have observed that by 2017, the total US healthcare expenditures will likely top 20% of the projected GDP, or $4.3 trillion.

The burden of rising healthcare costs, on both current and future generations of taxpayers, is rather disconcerting when coupled with new indications that the "well-being" of the average American citizen is still below that of those living in several other G8 countries. "Well-being," in this discussion, refers to a standard measure of the human development

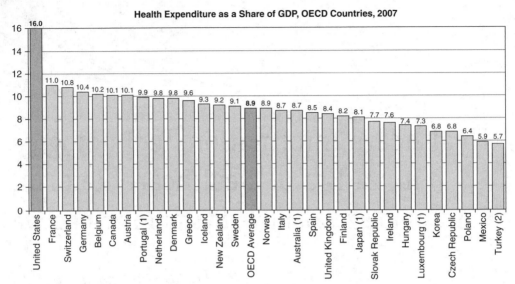

FIGURE 8.1 OECD Comparative 2007 Data for Healthcare Expenditure Among Various Countries in Terms of Percentage of Gross Domestic Product. OECD (2009), OECD Health Data 2009: Statistics and Indicators for 30 Countries, www.oecd.org/health/healthdata

index (HDI),[3] a comparative gauge of life expectancy, literacy, education, and standards of living. A disturbing trend, then, arises in the fact that although G8 countries such as Canada, Japan, and various nations in the European Union (EU) have spent considerably less on health care compared to the United States, survey results and census data, drawn from as recent as 2006, provide somewhat consistent evidence that the majority of citizens from these industrialized nations have, and still are, enjoying longer life expectancy and much more affordable healthcare services delivery than many Americans. Equally unsettling is the rising trend of American businesses and families trying to reduce their healthcare insurance coverage. However, with inflationary pressures, rising unemployment rates, a prolonged economic crisis, and further anticipated hikes in annual healthcare insurance premiums, many Americans have few alternatives.[4] Thus, the United States faces the unfortunate scenario where, in a country that has outspent almost every other country on healthcare expenditures in terms of GDP percentage, almost five million are still denied access to the care they need in times of illness. Until significant changes are made by the current administration, one out of every three Americans under 65 may still have to live, at one point in time or another, without health insurance coverage. This statistic is based on a recent press release about findings abstracted from the data of a 2007–2008 study sponsored by the consumer health advocacy group Families USA.[5] Nonetheless, to the credit of the Obama administration, many of these issues have been acknowledged, and various solutions have now been proposed—chief among them, improving the use and adoption of healthcare information technology (HCIT). Indeed, one strategy that has already been acted upon is the call for formation of "regional centers" that will shepherd care providers in their quest to become proficient HCIT users, as required under section 3012(c) of the Public Health Service Act, an addition in the American Recovery and Reinvestment Act of 2009 (ARRA 2009).[6]

Indeed, the Obama strategy is not without merit, because various forms of healthcare technologies have, over the years, risen to similar challenges—for example, particular technologies such as online claims processing, electronic prescription (e-prescription) systems, and teleradiology, all of which have been successfully leveraged by different parties, at one time or another, to serve as tools for combating rapidly escalating healthcare administrative costs while simultaneously increasing efficiencies, eliminating redundancies, and improving the quality of healthcare services. Raghupathi and Tan,[7–8] for instance, reported on various strategic applications of health IT that would easily add significant value to existing, legacy-based healthcare services delivery systems, and further alluded to the importance of charting a strategic path for HCIT applications and innovations in integrating fragmentary and isolated healthcare services. Their arguments not only cited the power of such technologies to streamline increasingly complex routine health information management processes—some of which require multiprovider, cross-organizational collaboration—but also the ability for interoperable HCITs to augment enterprisewide efficiencies and care provider network connectivity.

As this new age of healthcare reform materializes, health policymakers and administrators are faced with a series of critical questions, decisions, and actions regarding the appropriation of HCITs as a strategy and stimulus for healthcare reform. These questions, decisions, and actions will not be of special interest just to students and practitioners in healthcare administration, but will likely appeal to many clinical specialists, health professionals, and business managers as well. Although there are numerous needs that must be fulfilled before health IT can be leveraged for American healthcare reform, the most pressing among them would be, first, an understanding of the priorities, policies, and issues that members of Congress and the current administration must take into consideration and then act upon accordingly (and swiftly), so that health IT can be channeled as an effective stimulus in bringing about progressive healthcare reform; second, a recognition for the need to institute a national HCIT strategy, specifically for US healthcare reform, that would be championed by the highest office in the nation in order to lead and steer both the public and private healthcare sectors through such a strategy; and finally, in contrast to the somewhat entrenched "fragmentary" view of the US healthcare system, Americans need a new systems-theoretical understanding and perspective—only through such an education can health IT be leveraged to allow for adaptive, flexible changes and conscious actions, which will, in turn, guide, redirect, and improve existing healthcare systems performance. This would then dramatically reduce health disparities while improving healthcare equities, especially for the underserved, the underinsured, and the uninsured.

All of these aforementioned steps are imperative to the realization of a strategic national vision for the future of HCIT development in America and any subsequent desired healthcare reform. Hence, in the next section, the focus will be to highlight key recommendations recently articulated by the Healthcare Information and Management Systems Society

(HIMSS)[9] in an attempt to provide insight into the immediate critical issues—problems that must soon be addressed by the 111th US Congress and the Obama administration in their oversight of healthcare reform. Following is an overview of a promising national HCIT strategy currently championed by the Department of Health and Human Services (HHS)[10] through the Office of the National Coordinator (ONC) for Health IT, in which a strategic framework will be laid out for guiding the role health IT can play in America's healthcare reform. Following this, the next section of this chapter will shift focus to discuss why it is important to reconceptualize the evolving US healthcare system as a complex adaptive system (CAS)[11]—such a conceptual paradigm shift from the traditional "fragmentary" view of the US healthcare system promises to restore the totality of the current, disintegrated US healthcare system. Simply stated, the CAS theoretic perspective will engender a change in thinking designed to reshape the US healthcare system by leveraging the rapidly changing landscape of the HCIT future.

Aside from becoming aware of the need for a national, strategic HCIT vision in bringing about healthy and holistic healthcare reform, it is important that students and practitioners of healthcare administration also be familiar with the e-healthcare movement, which is also gaining rapid attention among global healthcare researchers.[12] The expansion of this movement in health care is particularly distinguished in the growing efforts to replace archaic clinical files and legacy administrative systems with advancing and innovative HCITs, including but not limited to:

1. Patient-centric data management systems, such as electronic medical records (EMRs), electronic health records (EHRs), personal health records (PHRs), payer-based health records (PBHRs), computerized physician order entry (CPOE), and e-prescription systems (EPS)
2. A new generation of administrative HCITs, such as supply chain management (SCM), customer relationship management (CRM), and enterprise resource planning (ERP)
3. Virtual communities and Internet-based social networks, such as community health information networks (CHINs) and regional health information networks (RHINOs)
4. Interoperating Web services, mobile health, telehealth, and remote sensor–based devices

Accordingly, part of the chapter has been designed to review and illustrate the many HCIT applications that will be important in the coming age of healthcare reform. Owing to space limitation, however, a selection of the key HCITs will be surveyed to highlight their distinguishing features and functions in summary tables; interested readers may refer to the latest edition of Tan[13] for additional details. Indeed, becoming aware of and being familiar with the use of these various HCITs will prepare students, as well as today's practitioners of healthcare administration, for the rapidly changing HCIT field in the near future. It is clear that the intelligent use of these emerging HCITs will inevitably lead to the transformation of health care in America, and subsequently benefit Americans with a more accountable, available, accessible, and affordable healthcare services industry.

Finally, two additional themes should also be included in the discussion of this chapter. These include:

(1) Major challenges for managing HCITs in the context of healthcare reform, such as how existing and future HCITs should be managed

(2) The prospects for HCIT futures in term of software development, education, research, and practices

Following, the challenges in managing HCITs, including governance, policy and legal issues, standardization issues, systems interoperability issues, confidentiality and security issues, and intellectual property issues will be discussed. This chapter concludes with a look at how open-source software may change the face of software development for future HCITs and returns to emphasize the significance of understanding "systems interoperability" by highlighting its potential impacts on the future of the US healthcare system. Specifically, additional insights and comments will be provided on what achieving a state of systems interoperability means, and how achieving systems interoperability in HCIT implementation can ultimately lead to US healthcare reform.

Critical Health IT Issues for Healthcare Reform: The HIMSS Recommendations

Today, advocates of HCIT point to its use and diffusion as a competitive weapon for achieving higher quality in, and greater quantities of, healthcare services. History has shown that even traditionally-oriented tactical and operational applications of health IT, and not just strategic HCIT use, can bring about improved administrative and clinical efficiencies as well as managerial and clinical decisional effectiveness, thereby achieving greater affordability, accessibility, and availability of health care.[14-16] Hence, it is not surprising to find that the HIMSS has recently championed a call endorsing widespread HCIT adoption as the primary strategy for achieving healthcare reform, aside from limiting the growth on the number of uninsured Americans under 65. More recently, HIMSS has further updated its recommendations in line with the newly enacted health IT provisions included in the ARRA 2009.

Accordingly, the updated HIMSS report argues that health IT "holds great promise for healthcare throughout the US" and that significant benefits will result when policymakers aptly address several key issues.[17] Among the more prominent issues identified by the HIMSS report are: (a) codifying a senior HCIT leadership within Congress and the current administration; (b) resolving standardization challenges, as well as commonly encountered systems interoperability issues, so that the use of e-payments and e-prescription systems will be realized throughout the current US healthcare delivery system; (c) providing adequate and substantial funding to support the design, implementation, management, adoption, use, and diffusion of time-tested, certified, and highly promising HCIT products across various members and sectors of the US healthcare system; (d) empowering and elevating the education of health consumers through HCIT adoption and use; and (e) overcoming concerns about confidentiality, privacy, and security challenges in applying HCITs.

More specifically, the HIMSS report to the 111th Congress and the Obama administration states:[18]

> Health IT, such as electronic medical records (EMRs), electronic
> health records (EHRs), personal health records (PHRs), payor-based

health records (PBHRs), and electronic prescribing (e-prescribing), shows promise for transforming the delivery and payment of healthcare in the US, and improving population health and the overall efficiency and effectiveness of healthcare.

Briefly, the HIMSS proposal[19] recommends the following:

(1) A funding level of no less than $25 billion for the purpose of aligning HCIT investments with the ARRA 2009 legislation. Here, the request is for the government to assist privately funded hospitals and physician practices in adopting EMRs, and to provide incentives throughout the Medicare–Medicaid reimbursement systems in rewarding "eligible providers for demonstrating a meaningful use of certified EHRs."

(2) The promotion of standards and certified HCIT products for all federally funded health programs. This requires federal funding to support those providers and/or payers who adopt recognized standards and HCIT products that have been certified by the Certification Commission for Health Information Technology (CCHIT) or have followed Healthcare Information Technology Standards Panel (HITSP) interoperability specifications.

(3) An initiative that respects anti-kickback safe harbors for EMRs and promotes the Stark exemptions expansion. This initiative is to enhance use of healthcare software and appropriately certified devices for information sharing and care coordination among caregivers and patients.

(4) A series of codifications, including (a) codifying HITSP as the national standards harmonization body to encourage public–private sector collaboration on standardization, thereby achieving widespread interoperability among healthcare software applications; (b) codifying HCIT leadership within the current administration at the most senior level so as to promote a national HCIT strategy; and (c) codifying and/or authorizing a federal advisory and coordinating body for current and future HCIT development.

(5) Organization of a summit, backed by the White House, to bring together innovative and unique solutions on applying HCITs for healthcare reform. Here, it is envisioned that a public forum will evolve to address critical, national health IT issues within the context of US healthcare reform.

Readers interested in the full report can easily download its details from the HIMSS Web site referenced earlier. Essentially, HIMSS has placed HCIT as the key strategy for healthcare reform by focusing on relevant key policy, administrative, and technological issues. Addressing these issues intelligently will bring about a more transparent, secure, and safe environment for interoperable HCITs. In turn, this will efficiently and cost-productively link the sensitive and needed patient data, currently stored securely in electronic databases, from across the myriad of US healthcare institutions and agencies.

Among the many recommendations offered by the HIMSS report, one of the most critical elements is that of the need for a senior HCIT leadership within the current administration to bring about the realization of a national HCIT strategy. Therefore this national HCIT strategy is highlighted in the next section.

Leading a National Health IT Strategy: The HHS's Strategic Framework for US Healthcare Reform via HCIT Applications

In May 2005, the US Government Accountability Office (GAO) published and released a report entitled, *Health Information Technology—HHS Is Taking Steps to Develop a National Strategy.*[20] In this report, the GAO reviewed the national efforts of the Department of Health and Human Services (HHS) in championing a health IT strategy to guide nationwide HCIT implementation efforts throughout both public and private healthcare sectors. The HHS strategic initiative was clearly an undertaking to help fulfill part of former President George W. Bush's vision of achieving "greater value for healthcare expenditures" or, more specifically, addressing the growing concerns and major challenges surrounding US healthcare services delivery system as identified by the Institute of Medicine (IOM) report.[21] Such challenges included an urgent need to curb escalating US healthcare costs, increase care provider accountability, eliminate unjustified and preventable medical errors, and, by setting a high-quality standard for US healthcare services delivery, fuel a call for improved provider performance accountability.

Essentially, the HHS framework—depicted in **Table 8.1**, sourced from HHS—calls for a nationwide strategy that will uphold systems interoperability standards, deploy interoperable HCITs through a sustained set of actions to be implemented over several years, and encourage collaborative efforts among federal, state, and local governments as well as the private healthcare sector. Three major phases, four main goals, and 12 essential strategies are envisioned for the national HCIT strategy. *Phase I* aims at stabilizing the market for HCIT products via the creation of a more business-friendly environment; this will not only lower the risk of HCIT procurement, but will also, eventually, support HCIT investment and acceptance. *Phase II* purports to encourage greater investment, use, and diffusion of clinical management and support tools and enhanced health informatics capabilities such as EMRs, EHRs, PHRs, PBHRs, e-health care methods and strategies, telehealth, health information exchanges (HIEs), virtual community networks, and other electronic-based vehicles to produce high-performance healthcare services delivery. Finally, *Phase III* attempts to steer the HCIT market toward achieving a benchmark for high-quality healthcare services and imposing greater health provider and health organizational performance accountability. With each of these phases moving toward completion, it is envisioned that, ultimately, US caregivers will be empowered to work collaboratively; they will have the needed health informatics capabilities on hand to not only offer reliably high-quality care, but also to manage patients and populations in a productive, efficient, and cost-effective manner.

Nevertheless, the GAO report also indicates that the major drivers in moving the HHS-proposed national HCIT strategy forward would require the following key conditions to be in place: a sustained senior HCIT leadership, greater and continuing clarity of the HHS framework's vision and directions, and a detailing of specific milestones to gauge progress for the completion of the different phases. These milestones should specify and define robust mechanisms for provider performance accountability, such as measurable goals.[22] Although the HHS's framework was previously built upon established federal health IT work that was, in turn, championed through the

Table 8.1   The National Health IT Strategy

Goals and Strategies of HHS's Framework for Strategic Action

Goals	Strategies[a]
Goal 1: Inform clinical practice with the use of electronic health records (EHRs)	1. Incentivize EHR adoption 2. **Reduce risk of EHR investment** 3. Promote EHR diffusion in rural and underserved areas
Goal 2: Interconnect clinicians so that they can exchange health information using advanced and secure electronic communication	1. **Foster regional collaboration** 2. **Develop a national health information network** 3. **Coordinate federal health information systems**
Goal 3: Personalize care with consumer-based health records and better information for consumers	1. **Encourage use of personal health records** 2. Enhance information consumer choice 3. Promote use of telehealth systems
Goal 4: Improve public health through advanced biosurveillance methods and streamlined collection of data for quality measurement and research	1. Unify public health surveillance architectures 2. Streamline quality and health status monitoring 3. Accelerate research and dissemination of evidence

[a]Phase I strategies are shown in bold type.
Source: HHS.

ONC, there are still, embedded within its specifications, explicit plans for reaching out to private industry. Indeed, the success of executing the HHS national strategy is dependent upon actions taken not only by the public healthcare sector, but also by the private healthcare sector.

As early as November 2004, for instance, the HHS department had propagated a request for information, seeking wide representation of public input and ideas for building a national health information network. More than 500 responses to this request were subsequently received from both the public and private sectors, and a task force of federal agencies was then set up to evaluate these responses.

More recently, in view of the agenda for healthcare reform under ARRA 2009, the ONC has again issued a call for responses and reactions to the idea of funding and setting up "regional centers," which would aid interoperable HCIT implementation efforts for healthcare providers across the nation.[23] Simply stated, in hope of achieving nationwide HCIT interoperability, HHS is clearly aware that it must work actively and collaboratively with the private sector to develop standards and certification procedures for HCIT interoperability.

Another important contribution from the GAO report is a number of key lessons that were uncovered from past experiences in implementing HCITs at the Department of Defense (DOD) and Veterans Affairs (VA)—two of the largest healthcare delivery networks in the nation. Some of the lessons shared in the report included the necessity of recognizing and addressing the needs of the varied stakeholder communities, the need to obtain complete support from senior management leading the HCIT efforts, the significance of defining and adopting common standards and terminology, and the importance of patience in executing HCIT strategies so that past successes can be built upon in small but sturdy incremental steps. Experiences in reforming healthcare services delivery via the administration of HCIT implementations in countries such as Canada, Denmark, and New Zealand have also provided insight into the critical success factors underlying HCIT implementation. Readers who are interested in more details about these important lessons on the establishment of a national health IT strategy should consult the relevant Web sites as referenced.

Basically, these lessons corroborated with the evidence gained from the DOD and VA studies in that not only is high-level government support critical to the success of HCIT implementations, but nationwide implementation of HCIT solutions should also follow a three-step process. First, there should be a focus on standards creation before shifting to the second step of establishing clear health IT leadership; this leadership should be in the form of a central organization that would lead efforts on progressing a national health IT strategy agenda. Finally, there should be a development of milestones to mark incremental success in the deployment of appropriate HCIT solutions.

This leads us to a discussion of why, if the vision of a national health IT strategy is to be realized, it is important for Americans to adopt a new systems-theoretical perspective on the US healthcare system—the complex adaptive system (CAS) perspective.

Rethinking the US Healthcare System: A Complex Adaptive System (CAS) View

Today, we are at the crossroads of a paradigm shift in our conceptualization of the US healthcare system. In order to set the national healthcare reform agenda into momentum, many Americans will need to make a conscious and very powerful shift in perspective on healthcare to a complex systems-theoretical level. The intent of such a shift in thinking is to detach the general population from the widespread, strongly held belief that the increasingly "fragmentary" American healthcare system has only led to, on the one hand, massive administrative and clinical inefficiencies for the care providers, and, on the other hand, appalling health inequities and disparities for the care receivers. Embedded somewhere within this thinking is often the vision of an impending global e-healthcare revolution. At a more technical level, this revolution would embrace the adoption, use, and diffusion of advancing, interoperable HCITs at a pace that most healthcare administrators and clinical professionals have yet to experience. We now know that such a revolution in health care is inevitable in the near future, when many Americans, healthcare professionals or otherwise, realize that HCITs must indeed play a major role in the "prescription for change" defining future health care.[24,25]

Recently, a growing number of researchers have been observing how the fragmentary nature of the US healthcare system is making it very difficult for Americans to be served with accessible, affordable, and high-quality care.[26–28] Paul Krugman and Robin Wells, for example, noted in their article, *The Health Care Crisis and What to Do About It*:[29]

> ... the evidence clearly shows that the key problem with the US healthcare system is its fragmentation. A history of failed attempts to introduce universal health insurance has left us with a system in which

the government pays directly or indirectly for more than half of the nation's health care, but the actual delivery both of insurance and of care is undertaken by a crazy quilt of private insurers, for-profit hospitals, and other players who add cost without adding value. A Canadian-style single-payer system, in which the government directly provides insurance, would almost surely be both cheaper and more effective than what we now have. And we could do even better if we learned from "integrated" systems, like the Veterans Administration, that directly provide some health care as well as medical insurance.

Regardless of whether there is agreement with the arguments advanced by these authors on the benefits of a single-payer model or even that of an integrated system, it is clear that the US healthcare system is much too convoluted and the myriad uncoordinated care providers, insurers, payers, and clinical specialists and/or nonspecialists in patient care assessments and treatments will only tend to compromise the integrity of the entire system. As a result, enforcing or realizing some measures of objective assessments, comparative evaluations, and/or performance accountability among care providers will be even more difficult. In a humorous 2009 editorial commentary, Martin Sipkoff[30] lamented:

> Our healthcare system is huge and cumbersome as an elephant, and all the players—like the blind men in the story—see the elephant differently. Doctors holding the tail perceive the system as constraining as a rope, purchasers touching the leg find it as immovable as a tree, and plans holding the trunk see it as devious and unmanageable as a snake. We are blind to the system's true shape. . . . The system is opaque, abstruse, variable, incredibly complex, and weirdly fragmented. Its very nature makes vision of the whole impossible.

Martin then went on to quote Donald Berwick, the president and CEO of the Institute of Healthcare Improvement, as saying: "Healthcare is a fragmented system. It has many defects and broken parts, so it's impossible to isolate one element of it and say that's what's wrong. Most of us don't think in system terms, so it's very difficult to gain momentum for change across the whole enterprise."

Herein lies the crux of the argument, calling attention to a new perspective on the US healthcare system—one that is grounded in chaos theory and the complex adaptive system (CAS) perspective. Essentially, in a landmark article published in *Communications of the ACM*, Tan et al. noted that a CAS may be conceived as one that typically harbors a large number of interacting parts, is interactively complex, and is also self-organizing.[31] This phenomenon of system complexity aptly captures the statement that the whole (system) is greater than the sum of its parts.

Healthcare services delivery in the United States comprises multiple providers and, in most cases, electronic and mechanical components and coordinated networks as well. Even simple outpatient care has to be serviced by a small network of clinicians, administrators, and mechanical and/or electronic devices. Critically ill inpatients are cared for in unusually complex systems with a broad range of human and nonhuman elements. In this sense, many of the characteristics of CASs may be found in describing the nature of the US healthcare system: (a) it is influenced by a great number of interacting components; (b) it is interactively complex, and the causes and effects are distant in time and space, making it difficult to predict the future; and (c) its complex nature often requires a flexible strategy and self-organization capability to handle medical emergencies and unknown situations.

More importantly, CASs may be perceived as evolving into one of the following three different stages on a continuum at any one time: (a) static stage, (b) edge of chaos stage, and (c) chaos stage. At the static stage, the system goes through a period of order, and subsequently, if it fails to respond to changes in its environment, it is likely to self-destruct. In contrast, when systems are at the chaos stage, these systems become unmanageable, and their "ability to find a niche in the fitness landscape disappears in a flurry of uncontrollable, dizzying oscillations."[32] The current view of fragmentation in the US healthcare system is often described, from limited viewpoints, as a system in the chaos stage within the *chaos theory*—how would one expect administrators and clinicians to behave when all they know, imagine, and believe is that the current "diversely fragmented" structure, "multistakeholder" organization, and "isolated third-parties" payment systems of the "longstanding, seemingly broken" US healthcare system is "chaotic," "massive," and "somewhat irreparable?" Most of them would be happy if they managed to avoid lengthy litigations, and furthermore, many Americans have to confess that they simply lack the substantial managerial expertise and skills to manage "chaos." Between the static and chaos stage, however, is the "edge of chaos." Here, systems are thrust into a perpetual fluctuation between static and chaos, as feedback loops in these systems assign them, in a seemingly random fashion, to one stage or the other. Yet, this is the one state where CASs can be spontaneous, adaptive, and alive; most apparently, the desired US healthcare system may actually be more accurately described and characterized as a system largely in such a stage! Tan with Payton[33(p329)] argued:

> At the edge of chaos, increased operational efficiencies and reduced clinical errors will result if appropriate HMIS [in the context of this chapter discussion, we could use HCIT as a substitute acronym here] technologies are readily accessible, and relevant and high quality health information can be made available more promptly. Shortened response time here will improve the ability for the system to self-organize. As well, some form of redundancy can only curtail the failure rate given that human errors are inevitable. A small failure rate may, in fact, be preferable to the administrative burden associated with reducing it to zero. Thus, most high-performing systems are designed to "absorb" errors, and/or mitigate their consequences, rather than eliminating all errors.

Although viewing hospitals, multiprovider health maintenance organizations (HMOs), and integrated delivery systems (IDS) as CASs would prevent them from being entirely controlled, understanding a few principles within the HCIT context, especially for healthcare organizations alternating between the different CAS stages, can help guide the administrators in ensuring the survival, growth, and progress of such systems. These observations, which are detailed in Tan et al.[34] include: (a) important CAS changes may be accomplished through small-scale initial perturbation;

(b) CAS performance may also be improved with timely, relevant, and appropriate feedback; (c) when leaning toward a more static stage, standardization with managerial judgment and flexibility will help to maintain care quality; (d) when leaning toward chaos, it is essential that HCIT leadership be capable of intensive motivation, effective communications, and trustworthiness; and (e) at the edge of chaos, shortened response time with backup redundancy will improve both administrative and clinical effectiveness. Based on our discussion regarding the current, essentially fragmented (chaos) view of the US healthcare system, impeccable HCIT leadership from the highest level of this nation will be needed to usher in US healthcare reform.

While many see healthcare services organizations today as being too disjointed and difficult to control, the CAS perspective summarized above unveils the strategies that would be most effective for the different stages that these organizations undergo. More importantly, we have seen that HCIT innovations, adoption, and diffusion can provide an effective solution to the challenge. Of course, with relentless management-driven changes, it is possible that erratic consequences could result. Hence, our analysis, along with the lessons distilled from the GAO report, recommends incremental structural and process changes, particularly as starting conditions. The purpose of such an approach would be to test the intended effects on a small scale whenever possible. As these newer technologies are being introduced into the system, senior management should then be ready to take further actions depending on how the system behaves at various levels and with different HCIT interventions. Feedback loops, therefore, must be operating at all times, so that all progress with these changes is properly gauged. Indeed, experience has shown that direct, specific, intelligent, constructive, and appropriate feedback would be more effective in guiding system performance improvement than inconsistent feedback; this is especially true for feedback from a third party, either after a long period of inactivity, or after unannounced changes are pushed through without early warning signs or meaningful explanations. With more input and perspectives from participating stakeholders, the stage will be set, with respect to the specific role of HCITs and their anticipated impact on healthcare reform, for even more exciting debates and exchanges of views.

For example, the development of nanosensor-based chips—which may prove invaluable and useful for unobtrusive remote tracking and monitoring of diverse healthcare-related information pieces, such as blood pressure and heartbeat rate, which are essential for maintaining the "well-being" of aging citizens from their homes—may easily become a battlefield for human rights, religious communities, and privacy advocacy groups. They may challenge such uses by HCIT vendors as an insensitive violation of personal rights and/or certain religious beliefs, and may even assail the occasional failure to obtain, in transmitting personal health records, specific written patient consents as evidence of such violations. In contrast, advocates of the technology may argue that this will not only be a potential area of enhancement in quality of life for the senior population but, by reducing unnecessary and unacceptable wait times found in many emergency rooms across the nation, will also be a means of saving lives. Hence, there exists no easy HCIT solution for an increasingly competitive system set within a sensitive environment, where many medical errors have already occurred. Yet, incremental changes that are clearly supported by the masses will gradually diffuse to replace worn out technologies and poor-quality healthcare services.

Consequently, the chaos theory underlying the CAS theoretical thinking becomes of central importance when attempting to understand the changing behavioral characteristics of adaptive complex systems, such as the US healthcare system. Here, it should also be noted that CASs are, in fact, not best understood as "the sum of parts," but rather as a large evolving entity, where the starting conditions as well as the evolution of the entity's elements are important. The US healthcare system is an area filled with opportunities and great potential for the execution of timely and significant improvements, whether these improvements will aid how physicians treat patients, how insurance providers serve clients (which could be patients or clinicians), or how health institutions share information with other health institutions—from physician referrals to patient histories to interpretations of stored patient radiological images. Multiprovider HMOs and today's IDS may be viewed as instances of CASs that are nested within the larger US healthcare system, while in actuality the entire system involves an intricate network of subCASs that are nested within the larger CAS. On a deeper level, these subsystems exert complex relationships with one another, just like the "organic" structures that make up the backbones of most social systems. Therefore, if the HHS succeeds in implementing a national health IT strategy, this will also likely lead to eventual successes in the use, adoption, and diffusion of HCITs among the HMOs and IDS, as aided by the HHS-funded "regional centers."

When such a perspective is adopted, stakeholders from different sides of the healthcare fence will find their roles gradually evolving from that of worrying about "turf-protection"—that is, the safekeeping of isolated pieces of healthcare information—to that of ambassadors of change, and can thus begin to put aside many of their differences. In this manner, the entire healthcare community will soon be ready to share key and relevant information, easing the process of improving healthcare services provision, delivery, and distribution at a higher system level.

Reform in the healthcare industry, just like revolutions in other information-intensive industries, is likely to advance the adoption of systems interoperability standards, leading to shareable interoperable HCITs and speeding up the e-healthcare movement. Indeed, many healthcare practitioners and informaticians are now predicting that this trend is likely to see a considerable increase, mostly because of new initiatives proposed by the Obama administration to reduce healthcare costs while simultaneously improving the quality of healthcare services. The next section explores the wide-ranging scope of existing and emerging HCITs that promise to bring about US healthcare reform.

The E-Healthcare Movement: Virtual Communities, Web Services, and Other Enterprisewide, Interoperable HCITs for US Healthcare Reform

E-health care is a relatively new umbrella term, defining a large scope of healthcare practices that are powered by electronic processes; these include interoperable middleware, the Internet, World Wide Web (WWW), and other related technologies. Broadly speaking, e-health epitomizes not just a technical development, but also a state of mind, a way of thinking, an attitude, and a commitment toward networked, global healthcare services via the use of the Internet, intranets, extranets, community networks, and virtual private networks (VPNs). Its overarching goal is to improve health care locally, regionally, nationally, and worldwide by advancing information and telecommunication technology for health care. Essential to the emerging e-health concept is the incorporation of many recent technological advances in HCIT devices. Such advances have primarily occurred in network and telecommunication technologies (interoperable HCITs), telematics, public health informatics, community health informatics, health management information systems, Web portals, and Web services, and in the tools, methodologies, and strategies of health and medical informatics.

Today, e-health covers a wide range of evolving HCIT services and devices, as well as new forms of electronically delivered health and information services—some of which may truly be valuable for spearheading US healthcare reform. Because of space limitation, however, we can only highlight particular HCITs that have previously been mentioned in preceding sections of this chapter. In any case, readers of the HCIT field will find that many of the terminologies used in a young, cross-disciplinary field, such as that of e-health/HCIT, are still rapidly evolving and, in some instances, are therefore inconsistently or somewhat interchangeably used. For example, some would argue that expressions such as e-health, health IT, HCIT, telehealth, and health management information systems (HMIS) can be considered broadly interchangeable terms. In contrast, some would strictly prefer to use the term "telehealth" to cover important aspects of, and functional features employed in, healthcare informatics, medical informatics and telematics, and telemedicine, while reserving the term "e-health" for referring to healthcare practices via Internet-based technologies. Another term, "m-health," would then refer more specifically to the deployment of wireless and mobile technologies in administrative and clinical healthcare services.

For the purpose of this discussion, where the focus is on the more popular HCITs that may be valuable for healthcare reform, the reader must be familiar with a wide selection of commonly used acronyms in the e-health/HCIT field. These include EMRs, EHRs, PHRs, PBHRs, CPOE, CHINs, RHINOs, SCM, CRM, ERP, e-prescribing, telehealth, Web portals, Web services, mobile health (m-health), and radio frequency identification (RFID) microchips. To ease the process, the presentation is divided into four related technology groups.

The first group of HCITs will primarily consist of interoperable systems that are essentially patient-centric data management systems. These include:

1. EMRs (electronic medical records)
2. EHRs (electronic health records)
3. PHRs (personal health records)
4. PBHRs (payer-based health records)
5. CPOE (computerized physician order entry)

According to Tan,[35(p94)] EMRs are restrictively institution-based and capture patient medical histories within a single data repository, whereas EHRs "are the records of longitudinal patient experiences from birth to death," including all encounters between patients and their healthcare providers across institutions. PHRs are emerging systems that source and link patient information from various care providers, so that patients and those to whom the patients would authorize access can easily access their information. Meanwhile, PBHRs, by and large, provide insurers and authorized third parties a cross-referencing of all patient encounters across the spectrum of the US healthcare system, based on available claims data from respective payers. A case study on

EMR implementation at Dryden Family Medicine is given in O'Neill and Klepack,[36] and an illustrative discussion of Google Health as a PHR portal may be found in Tan.[37(p118–119)]

Finally, CPOE refers to unique software technology that captures the physician's orders in order to improve the efficiencies and effectiveness in managing a patient's care plan. Fourth-generation EHRs typically incorporate CPOE capabilities. Essentially, CPOE promotes administrative efficiencies and clinical effectiveness by making a physician's orders available electronically. With this technology, various staff and clinical departments throughout a healthcare facility will be able to accurately carry out orders at any time of day.

All of these interoperable HCITs have been ordered alphabetically and further elaborated in **Table 8.2.**

As the group name suggests, most of these systems are intended to aid the process of patient care by capturing the histories of patient encounters throughout the US healthcare system. Key concerns about these systems that have been expressed repeatedly involve the confidentiality, privacy, and security of electronically stored patient records, which are discussed later.

The next group of HCITs encompass, primarily, interoperable systems that support health information exchanges (HIEs) in virtual communities and social networks. Two major developments of such interoperable HCITs include:

1. CHINs (community health information networks)
2. RHINOs (regional health information networks)

Both CHINs and RHINOs are examples of virtual community networks. One very specific illustration is the Mayo Clinic setup as depicted functionally in **Figure 8.2**, sourced from Doswell et al.[38(p104–107)] The primary difference between the two is that a CHIN focuses more on networking within a single community, whereas a RHINO would be more regional in scope with respect to its social network connectivity. The underlying motivation for promoting these technologies is the integration of community organizations as partners in achieving a more accountable, available, accessible, and affordable healthcare delivery system.

In brief, constructing virtual community networks involves the use of both the Internet and a combination of the following: Internet-associated technologies, hardware, software, and computer-user interface design, as well as telecommunications and network technologies. Further details on these technologies have been presented in **Table 8.3**.

The third group of HCITs focuses on the next-generation, enterprisewide administrative technologies that will soon replace existing legacy health information systems, the likes of which are still being used in physician practices, hospitals, health provider organizations, and community healthcare facilities. Major developments in these administrative HCITs include:

1. SCM (supply chain management)
2. CRM (customer relationship management)
3. ERP (enterprise resource planning)

ERP, or conceptually linked enterprisewide software, aims to connect the various data elements and processes found within the enterprise. ERP combines these into a single system to improve costs, efficiencies, and business data flow, as well as managerial policy and decision

Table 8.2   Evolving and Emerging Healthcare Information Technologies for US Healthcare Reform (Patient-Centric Data Management Systems)

Acronym	Expanded Name	Brief Description and Summary Discussion
CPOE	*Computerized Physician Order Entry*	A technology that promotes administrative and clinical efficiencies by allowing a physician's orders to be entered and transmitted electronically to various staff and clinical departments such as pharmacy, laboratory, and radiology throughout a healthcare facility.
		In order to better manage and execute a patient's care plan, CPOE effectively increases order processing efficiencies and accuracy, permits orders to be entered at the point-of-care or off-site, and decreases errors by allowing cross-checking on duplicate orders, incorrect prescribing, and/or illegible handwriting.
EHRs	*Electronic Health Records*	A powerful automated system that is often accessible on a virtual private network (VPN) and is capable of storing most, if not all, historical encounters. It would also streamline the clinical workflow for a patient securely. It may also be able to source data from disparate systems and pull them together in a centrally controlled depository that is accessible to all caregivers who are authorized to access it. The patient health information and data is thus maintained by a central authority, and the system provides for electronic order entry of processes, authorizes updates and changes, and allows for the electronic view/review of different parts of the patient information. In addition, it typically provides needed information management and decision support to the clinical care teams that have authorized access to the system.
EMRs	*Electronic Medical Records*	In general, EMRs are restrictively institution-based systems, capturing patient medical histories within a single, access-restricted data repository that is often not connected to other systems outside the enterprise. Therefore, patient information about treatments outside the institution is not typically included and patients do not have access to these systems. EMRs evolved from the earlier conceptualization of computerized patient records (CPRs). An institutional EMR will enable easy communication of patient data between different healthcare professionals (GPs, specialists, care team, pharmacy) associated with, or employed in, the institution.
PBHRs	*Payer-Based Health Records*	PBHRs transform claims data submitted by the providers into clinically relevant information that is conveniently accessible to caregivers and care managers. It is therefore a technology that provides a cross-provider snapshot of all patient encounters across the spectrum of the US healthcare system, including patient histories of drug prescription, laboratory testing, radiological images, doctor visits, hospitalization, and immunizations, as well as diagnostic details.
PHRs	*Personal Health Records*	A Web-based PHR system will empower patients with access to their own health records that are often kept separately from the different healthcare institutions where they have been treated and assigned to a third party (e.g., Google Health) for safekeeping privately and securely. PHR is also a convenient technology that is powerful enough and sometimes capable of sourcing directly stored records from different healthcare institutions and agencies

Table 8.2   *(Continued)*

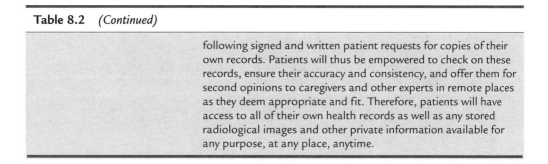

following signed and written patient requests for copies of their own records. Patients will thus be empowered to check on these records, ensure their accuracy and consistency, and offer them for second opinions to caregivers and other experts in remote places as they deem appropriate and fit. Therefore, patients will have access to all of their own health records as well as any stored radiological images and other private information available for any purpose, at any place, anytime.

making. **Figure 8.3** highlights the linkages of major stakeholders and various support services that should be integrated within ERP, while a diagrammatic rendering of the ERP conceptualization is given in **Figure 8.4**.

CRM is also an enterprisewide technology that, by combining software and methodologies, supports and sustains a relationship between an institution and its customers. SCM, meanwhile, is an enterprisewide technology that essentially manages the relationships between suppliers and customers; this is achieved by focusing on controlling associated business processes with the primary aim of achieving systemwide supplier-purchaser information exchange efficiencies. Specific illustrative examples of these enterprisewide technological applications, such as CRM with Blue Cross Blue Shield of Minnesota, may be found in Tan with Payton.[39(p69–85)] It is believed that CRM, ERP, and SCM are the next-generation, enterprisewide HCIT administrative applications that will significantly affect the future quality of healthcare services delivery.

Table 8.4 orders these different enterprisewide technologies alphabetically and further elaborates on their descriptions, functionalities, and differences. Isolated legacy systems—such as hospital financial and payroll systems, nurse scheduling systems, drug inventory tracking and purchasing systems, admission-discharge-transfer systems, hospital accounting and billing systems, facility planning systems, and the like—have been used for decades in healthcare facilities and will soon give way to business-oriented systems such as SCM, CRM, and ERP.

The last group of HCITs to be discussed is comprised of various other e-health and associated technologies that, together, form an important part of the larger movement toward a global e-healthcare revolution. These emerging and innovative HCITs include:

1. E-prescribing
2. Telehealth
3. Web portals and Web services
4. Mobile health (m-health)
5. Radio frequency identification (RFID) microchips

E-prescribing is a technology that aids in the ordering of prescriptions via electronic systems. Telehealth is the application of information and communications technology to medical information transfer for the purposes of clinical, administrative, and education services delivery; this includes all types of physical and psychological measurements that do not require a personal visit to the specialist by the patient. Web portals, or gateways, are Web sites that link users to relevant

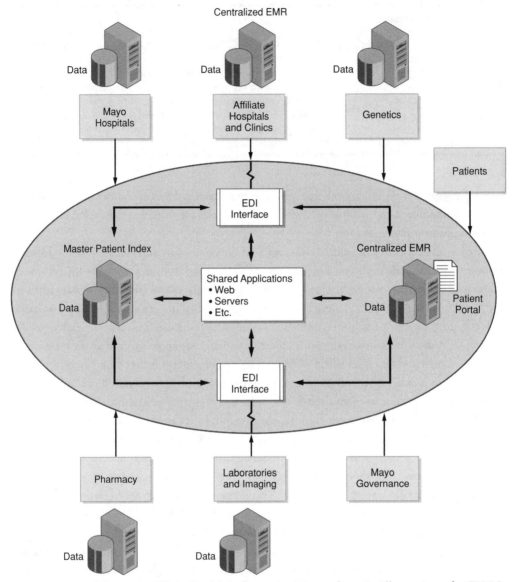

FIGURE 8.2 The Mayo Clinic Health Information Networks – An Illustration of a CHIN-RHINO Setup (A Virtual Community and Social Network).

Web information on particular topics, whereas Web services are interoperable software that interface with other systems via specialized middleware technology, standards, and a common technological platform.

Essentially an extension of the e-health concept, mobile health (m-health) involves pervasive computing that, through the use of satellite-based and other forms of wireless information transfer technologies, encompasses remotely accessible healthcare services. This is accomplished through the use of satellite-based and other wireless forms of information transfer technologies,

Table 8.3 Evolving and Emerging Healthcare Information Technologies for US Healthcare Reform (Virtual Communities and Social Networks)

Acronyms	Expanded Name	Brief Description and Summary Discussion
CHINs	*Community Health Information Networks*	A technology structure supporting the sharing of financial and clinical information via networking capabilities. It is typically set up to link information electronically from various "smart zones" or "smart spaces" within a community. The scope of these "smart zones" could include parks, fitness centers, homes, and restaurants connected to available health provider networks and other community services such as police, fire, ambulance, and ambulatory care. Access to the network connection is frequently via the high-speed or wireless Internet that is often supported by a team of vendors in the community to aid the exchange of information services.
RHINOs	*Regional Health Information Organizations*	RHINOs are multistakeholder organizations that act like "regional centers" sponsored primarily by the Office for the National Coordinator (ONC) of Health IT, appointed under the secretary of the Department of Health and Human Services. The role that these regional centers play will be chiefly to solicit public input within a defined geographic area. More recently, these regional centers are called upon to aid the implementation of health IT among care providers and to promote health information exchange (HIE) among the different community stakeholders with the aim of improving health care and care services in that community.
		Basically, HIE is the exchange of health-related information electronically among organizations following some form of well-recognized national standards. Often, HIE also has the capability of sourcing clinical information from disparate legacy systems without altering the accuracy and/or quality of the information being exchanged. In this sense, the data mining and data integration capabilities of HIEs will also contribute to higher quality research in many areas, including public and community health, nursing, biomedical, pharmaceutical, and clinical informatics, as well as consumer health informatics. Ultimately, with continuing improvements in the availability and accessibility of clinical data because of HIEs, the outcome to be expected will be less health disparities in the system. This, then, will result in more cost-effective and higher quality patient-centered care. A RHINO may therefore be viewed as a specialized mobilization of HIE.
		RHINOs are therefore generally responsible to encourage, motivate, and promote collaboration and integration of regional health information among community and regional stakeholders. Today, HIE is to occur within RHINOs for the purpose of progressing US healthcare reform. Hence, community stakeholders are expected to collaborate with each other to create a RHINO that will improve accessibility, availability, and affordability of health care via the use and adoption of health IT. In the longer term, all HCIT use and adoption propagated within RHINOs are expected to significantly impact on the resulting safety, efficiency, and quality of regional healthcare services. For example, Table 8.3 presents the Mayo Clinic RHINO as discussed in Doswell et al (in Tan, 2009, pp. 104–107) to illustrate a RHINO setup. Other RHINOs could comprise of multiple hospitals or organizations that include corporate employers, third-party payers, and medical associations.

FIGURE 8.3   The Enterprise Resource Planning (ERP) Conceptualization – An Illustration of the ERP Infrastructure for US Healthcare Reform.

including wearable medical devices and chips with remote health information monitoring and sensing, such as radio-frequency identification (RFID) microchips.

Further details on these various e-health and associated technologies are summarized in **Table 8.5.**

As noted, illustrative examples and detailed elaboration on most, if not all, of the aforementioned HCITs may be found in the most recent edition of *Adaptive Health Management Information Systems* (3rd edition) edited by Tan with Payton,[40] published by Jones and Bartlett (2009).

In a previous version of this chapter, Tan[41] wrote:

> In an increasingly competitive healthcare environment, the healthcare organization's efficient and effective management of data, information, and knowledge to support strategic planning, control costs, improve the quality and relevance of information for health

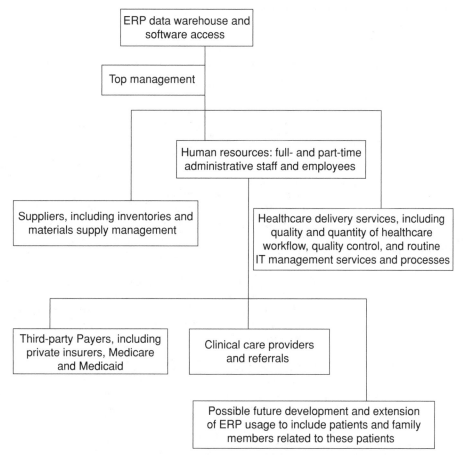

FIGURE 8.4   The Enterprise Resource Planning (ERP) Linkages among Major Stakeholders to Support Health Care Services Delivery

managerial and clinical decision making, improve the quality of healthcare services, enhance productivity, and generate more user-friendly designs of healthcare products and services will become critical. . . . In this context, the significance of computer-based patient records in supporting the management of care is well known. Equally significant, however, are HCITs such as expert systems and decision support systems technologies, electronic claim processing, and remote computing capabilities. These technologies will enable the multiprovider organization not only to improve communications, but also to extend its cognitive understanding and organizational learning across geographic, time, social, and cultural boundaries, thus achieving the characteristics of an intelligent healthcare organization.

Table 8.4   Evolving and Emerging Healthcare Information Technologies for US Healthcare Reform (Enterprisewide Administrative Technologies)

Acronyms	Expanded Name	Brief Description and Summary Discussion
CRM	*Customer Relationship Management*	An enterprisewide technology combining software and methodologies to support and sustain a relationship between an institution and its customers. Often Internet-accessible by employees within the enterprise, CRM is also typically enhanced with an organized database of customer information in terms of knowing detailed demographics about the customer; the type of customer interactions that have transpired with the institutions such as customer purchasing habits, noted telephone conversations, comments, and complaints; special notes about customers such as allergies or medical conditions; and customer needs for specific product or service specification.
ERP	*Enterprise Resource Planning*	ERP is essentially a linked enterprisewide software that connects the various data elements and processes found within the enterprise and combines them into a single system to improve costs, efficiencies, business data flow, and decision making. With its ability to integrate intraorganizational processes, it is a powerful tool for executing strategic management throughout the enterprise. However, to successfully implement ERP systems, the enterprise must also be sold on the philosophy of holistic change on information-sharing habits that would result from ERP implementation. For example, an information-functional culture that tends to limit the flow of information among users within different functional departments of an enterprise will not be ready to easily adopt a changed ERP philosophy.
SCM	*Supply Chain Management*	A technology employed in executing and managing the relationships between supplier and customer by focusing on controlling associated business processes. The SCM philosophy entails the planning and management of all activities involved in sourcing, procurement, conversion, and logistics management activities. It also includes the crucial components of coordination and collaboration with channel partners, which can be suppliers, intermediaries, third-party service providers, and customers. In essence, supply chain management integrates supply and demand management within and across companies.

It is apparent that there are more HCITs than can ever hope to be covered in a single chapter. However, the comments regarding the extension of the "cognitive understanding" and "organizational learning" hold true even today. In the case of US healthcare reform, the promotion of interoperable HCITs throughout the national healthcare system will, hopefully, provide the needed change stimulus for creating dialogues among the different stakeholders; this, in turn, will further encourage them to set aside their differences in order to agree on the specific systems interoperability standards that are essential for secure health information exchanges. Moreover, organizational learning gathered from implementing HCITs will serve to augment the cognitive understanding of knowledge workers, who will, in turn, help to move a CAS back to an edge-of-chaos state from a

Table 8.5 Evolving and Emerging Healthcare Information Technologies for US Healthcare Reform (E-Health and Other Emerging Technologies)

Acronyms	Expanded Name	Brief Description and Summary Discussion
E-Prescribing	*Supply Electronic Prescribing*	E-prescribing is a technology that employs electronic systems to aid in the ordering of a prescription. Such enhanced communications tend to avoid unnecessary order filling, help prevent unacceptable medication errors due to illegible writing, and speed up medication refills. It is also useful as a tool to guide medication inventory control and to assist clinical decision making on the administration, choice, and/or supply of a medicine, with the advantage of having a thorough audit trail of the entire medication process.
M-Health	*Mobile Health*	Mobile health (m-health), essentially an extension of the e-health concept, entails pervasive computing that encompasses remotely accessible healthcare services delivered through the use of satellite-based and other forms of wireless information transfer technologies such as wearable medical devices and RFID microchips.
RFID Microchips	*Microchips Frequency Identification Microchips*	Using radio waves, RFID microchips essentially tag objects wirelessly by tracking their identities (via unique serial numbers). In this sense, RFID data can be transmitted through any object, including clothing, the human body, and other nonmetallic materials. For security applications, this technology can be combined with biometric technology. Examples include SpeedPass and EZPass.
Telehealth	*Telehealth*	Telehealth is the application of information and communications technology to medical information transfer for clinical, administrative, and education services delivery, including all types of physical and psychological measurements that do not require a patient to travel to a specialist. Conceptually, telehealth is wide-ranging in its scope of applications. Examples of such applications would include teleprocessing, telemedicine, teleconsultation, telemonitoring, teleradiology, tele-education, telesurgery, telepathology, and other telespecialties as well as telecare or telehome care. When this service works, patients will need to travel less to a specialist or, conversely, the specialist has a larger catchments area.
Web Portals and Web Services	*Web Portals and Web Services*	Web portals, or gateways, are Web sites that offer users links to access related Web information on particular topics. In this sense, general portals such as Google, Yahoo!, and MSN provide Web information searches via keywords, whereas specialized or niche portals such as Apple.com provide information regarding Macintosh and Apple products. Web services are interoperable software that interface with other systems via specialized middleware technology, standards, and a common platform.

state of chaos. Such a change will, over time, promote lifelong learning activities through the constantly operating feedback loops, so as to improve healthcare services within the United States. Ultimately, all of these activities will only lead to improving the well-being of Americans.

Interestingly, the "e" in e-health does not stand only for "electronic," even though that was the sole intention when this term was first coined. There are indeed many other important aspects of the "e" that apply suitably in the characterization of strategic HCIT applications for CASs. These characteristics, over time, should energize the global "e-health" movement, resulting in a speedier and better US healthcare reformation in terms of "efficiency," "effectiveness," "empowerment," "equity," "evidence-based," and "excellence." Such improvements are no simple feats and, as such, must be examined at a more detailed level.

First, e-health promises to increase healthcare efficiencies and effectiveness, leading to lower cost and, perhaps, better quality of health care. By using rapid electronic transfer of patient data, administrative costs and potential medical errors may now be largely eliminated. For example, Tan with Payton[42(p123)] noted that we are currently entering the fourth generation of EHRs and that these systems are expected "to reduce preventable errors by up to a 90% level." In other words, e-health technology such as EMRs, EHRs, PHRs, and PBHRs would not only lower costs by improving administrative efficiencies and clinical effectiveness, but would also eventually help progress the needed healthcare reform. Based on current EHR and associated electronic patient data management systems development, one can imagine how it may be possible to eliminate almost 100% of medical errors found within the current healthcare system if we were to move into fifth-generation technology—this would eventually lead to comprehensive and high-quality health care, a hallmark of the US healthcare reform that has been envisioned within the HHS national health IT strategy framework.

Second, e-health systems and interoperable HCITs are expected to empower both clinicians and health consumers by widening access to the growing knowledge bases of medicine and patient information. Greater accessibility of these records, together with new knowledge in science and medicine, will better prepare the caregivers to provide the appropriate and necessary care for their respective patients, who rightfully deserve to have their health and well-being restored as quickly as possible. For the health consumers, the ease of access to their own personal health records (PHRs), coupled with the diffusion of medical knowledge via the Internet and/or other associated technologies, will also yield greater confidence and assurance in the belief that proper care is being administered to them, whether it is by others or even themselves. Indeed, greater transparency in the healthcare system can be expected to open up new avenues for self-care, alternative care services, and delivery modes. Perhaps this may also be the path toward achieving more equitable, patient-centric health care—thereby enabling cross-examination of relevant medical claims, peer reviews, and second opinions on questionable treatment protocols.

Third, e-health systems and interoperable HCITs conveniently extend the scope and boundaries of traditional health care in both time and space. These newer forms of e-technology permit care services to be practiced anywhere and at any time; for example, e-technology offers the possibility of having virtual physician visits, as opposed to waiting in line at physician offices.

This further implies that, in the near future, health consumers will be empowered to have tele-consultations from the comfort of their home with care providers of their choice, as long as they have basic computing equipment and Internet access. Such services can range from simple advice to more complex interventions and may even involve asking physicians and other reputable experts interactively about specific health product purchases, such as over-the-counter pharmaceuticals. As always, there are potential risks and challenges involved in using e-technology, which will be covered later in the chapter. Here, the emphasis is that efforts to diffuse and popularize these newer e-technologies will eventually lead to "a leveling of the playing fields," greater transparency in health services delivery, and, perhaps, more affordable health care—in effect, greater health equity for the underserved, the underinsured, and the uninsured.

Finally, e-health systems and interoperable HCITs can also support convenient online clinician and patient education. Specifically, these e-technologies provide a format for evidence-based medicine by allowing data to be conveniently gathered, stored, and mined so that medical knowledge discoveries may guide current practices. Imagine a caregiver who has access to all of the relevant information on the effects of different pharmaceutical products simply by making an educated series of clicks. Then, he or she can informatively decide which specific drug type may be best to dispense for a patient, leaving behind other clinicians who rely heavily on memory. Therefore, powerful electronic drug-referencing capabilities and having an electronic audit trail of one's treatment protocols will improve convenience for both the care providers and patients, especially if questions should arise about a particular physician–patient interaction or care episode.

To this end, e-technologies and interoperable HCITs promote service excellence. Today, whenever the term "e-health" is mentioned, most of what comes to mind are in things like Web portals, electronic databases, and health-related communications. Many traditional healthcare providers remain wary about providing medical information via the Web, and, for one reason or another, many physicians have hesitated in, or are even opposed to, encouraging patients to seek health information on their own via the Internet. This will soon change, as e-technologies continue to mature with advancing secured networking and telecommunication capabilities, as well as tighter privacy and human rights legislations. Indeed, expansion and diffusion in e-health systems and interoperable HCITs among healthcare providers is projected to grow at a rapid pace in the coming years—just as how, in the last two decades, as many readers may remember, personal computers (PCs), laptops, cell phones, and mobile computing quickly became household items only shortly after coming into existence. As increasing numbers of stakeholders play a role in e-technology innovations and healthcare reform, there will be continual evolutions, developments, and maturations of the HCIT and e-health movements. Perhaps there may be a groundbreaking shift in the US health reform agenda as new generations of happy computer users replace old, defiant ones. Not only will our healthcare system be filled with just e-consumers, but it will soon be populated by e-physicians, e-suppliers, e-vendors, and e-payers as well.

Nonetheless, as is expected with any innovation, significant resistance and new challenges from many sides have risen to challenge the e-health and HCIT movement. The following section focuses on managing e-health barriers and mitigating HCIT risks and challenges.

Managing E-Health Barriers: Risks and Challenges for HCIT Implementation and Innovation

In this section, focus is placed on the barriers that, for years, have plagued the US healthcare system by impeding the implementation of e-health and HCIT innovation. As they encapsulate most, if not all, of the contributing factors to HCIT project failures, such barriers have contributed to the underlying causes of why the American healthcare system exists as an unorganized stack of fragmented puzzle pieces today. Practitioners and students of healthcare administration who are aware and knowledgeable about these barriers can, and should, be trained to better manage our current transitional stage. This is made possible through recent efforts to propagate health IT initiatives by the HHS, as well as the ARRA 2009 legislation passed by members of Congress under the leadership of the Obama administration for the purpose of establishing interoperable HCITs that will drive American healthcare reform in the coming years.

We will highlight the key barriers here that individuals in the field of healthcare administration should be aware of, including technological issues, financing issues, sociopolitical and cultural issues, and legal issues.

Technological Barriers

Chief among the technological barriers in championing a national e-health and health IT strategy are issues relating to HCIT leadership, systems interoperability and compatibility challenges, and standardization. Commonly encountered HCIT service quality issues, such as HCIT service availability and access to technical assistance, service reliability and capacity, overall quality of IT services that can be expected, and planning of new HCIT projects, add to the barriers.

E-health, telemedicine, and interoperable HCITs cannot be successfully adopted, used, and diffused until a national vision of health IT strategy can be clearly articulated and funded. As noted, senior HCIT leadership is essential for the direction and progression of such a vision. Such leadership is needed to bring about active collaboration among the growing number of key stakeholders, both in the US public and private healthcare sectors. A critical, albeit very difficult, question here is, How would this leadership ensure that each and every stakeholder group is equally represented? In addition, if systems interoperability is to be achieved, do people have a network of large-scale support systems infrastructure and architecture in place, and if so, is this infrastructure sufficient for securely handling the massive transmission and exchange of private patient information and sensitive payment information among e-payers, e-vendors, e-providers, e-clinicians, and e-patients?

In light of these challenges, one significant breakthrough technological step would be to arrive at a systemwide standardization for systems interoperability and compatibility among caregivers. Such broad standards, if cleverly and appropriately established, would allow data to be shared conveniently among care providers serving across the spectrum of the US healthcare service delivery system. **Figure 8.5**, sourced from the GAO report[43] on HHS efforts regarding US health IT reform, provides an overview of how the standardization process, to be set in place, will bring different stakeholders together for US healthcare data exchange.

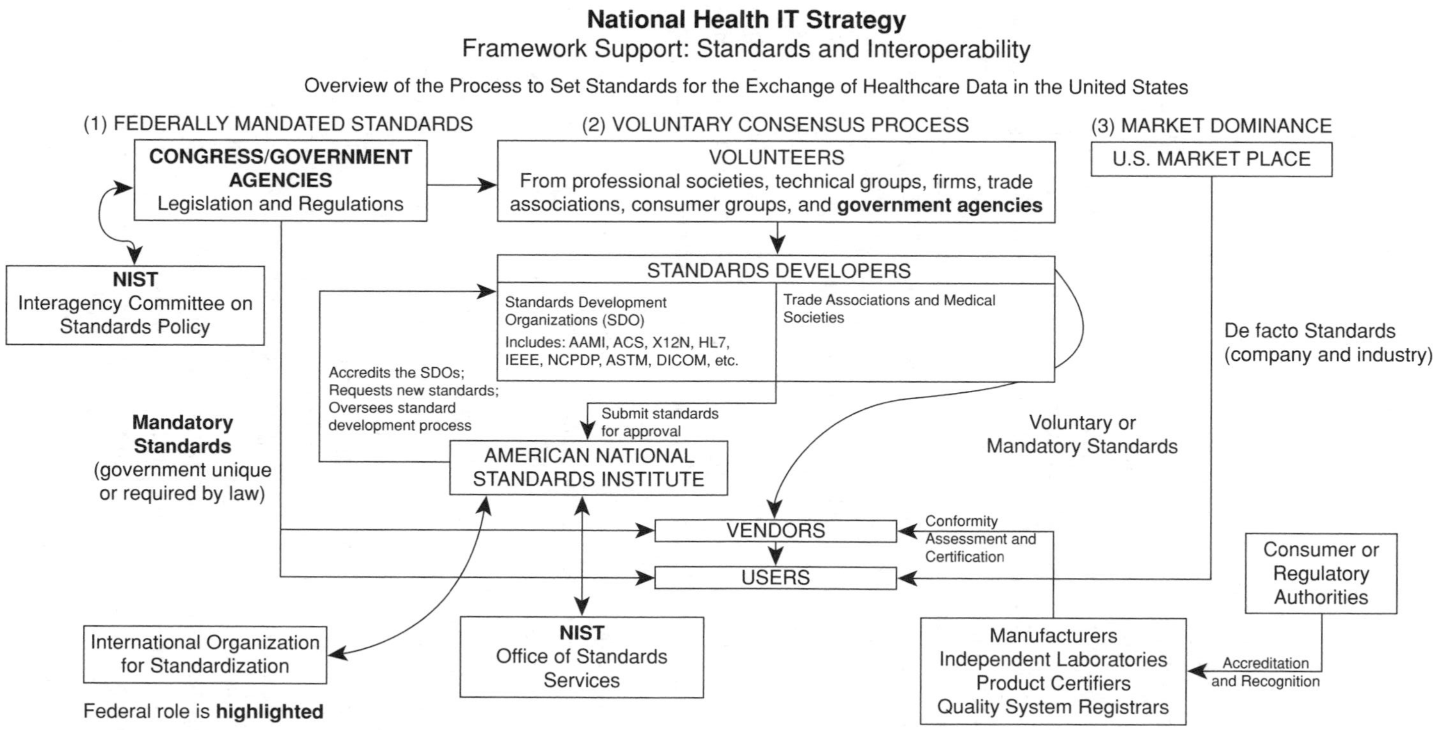

National Health IT Strategy

Framework Support: Standards and Interoperability

Overview of the Process to Set Standards for the Exchange of Healthcare Data in the United States

(1) FEDERALLY MANDATED STANDARDS | (2) VOLUNTARY CONSENSUS PROCESS | (3) U.S. MARKET DOMINANCE / MARKET PLACE

CONGRESS/GOVERNMENT AGENCIES
Legislation and Regulations

NIST
Interagency Committee on Standards Policy

Mandatory Standards
(government unique or required by law)

International Organization for Standardization

Federal role is **highlighted**

VOLUNTEERS
From professional societies, technical groups, firms, trade associations, consumer groups, and **government agencies**

STANDARDS DEVELOPERS

Trade Associations and Medical Societies

Standards Development Organizations (SDO)
Includes: AAMI, ACS, X12N, HL7, IEEE, NCPDP, ASTM, DICOM, etc.

Accredits the SDOs; Requests new standards; Oversees standard development process

Submit standards for approval

AMERICAN NATIONAL STANDARDS INSTITUTE

NIST
Office of Standards Services

Voluntary or Mandatory Standards

De facto Standards (company and industry)

VENDORS

USERS

Conformity Assessment and Certification

Manufacturers
Independent Laboratories
Product Certifiers
Quality System Registrars

Consumer or Regulatory Authorities

Accreditation and Recognition

AAMI = American Association of Medical Instrumentation
ASC = Accredited Standards Committee
ASTM = American Society for Testing and Materials
DICOM = Digital Imaging and Communication in Medicine
HL7 = Health Level Seven
IEEE = Institute for Electrical and Electronics Engineers
NCPDP = National Council for Prescription Drug Programs
NIST = National Institute of Standards and Technology (part of the Commerce Department)

FIGURE 8.5 Coordinating Standardization Process Among Public and Private Healthcare Sectors. Institute of Medicine, *Patient Safety: Achieving a New Standard for Care* (Washington, DC, 2004) and GAO-05-628 Report, p. 42. www.gao.gov/cgi-bin/getrpt?GAO-05-628

385

It is apparent that the standardization process requires massive collaboration among the major stakeholders that currently populate the US healthcare system. While the standardization process is never an easy goal to accomplish, as stakeholders from both public and private healthcare sectors have to be coordinated efficiently and effectively in order to achieve any form of consensus, one common problem that is often encountered when attempting to achieve a consensus on standards is the challenge of being all-inclusive—how can the HHS ensure that all members of the stakeholder communities, independent of the vendors, will be satisfied with the final decisions on the adoption of particular standards?

Closely related to standardization, systems interoperability, and compatibility issues are barriers arising from lack of hardware–software compatibility. Because of their complexity, these issues are more difficult to resolve across multiple organizations than within a single organization. Fortunately, for interorganizational processes, many new forms of middleware technologies have evolved and are now available to circumvent such compatibility problems; for example, Web services, which were discussed in previously, is one solution. With intraorganization processes, however, the approach is slightly different: If a large installed base of equipment has already been established, management should direct the organization toward an "open systems" platform using a careful planning of the system transition, such as via an evolutionary approach. Alternatively, management may decide to acquire an entirely new system that conforms to "open systems" architecture and standards. By applying emerging HCITs to link users' hardware and software, the organization enables its employees to share information-processing capabilities and consciously encourages them to work collaboratively rather than individually.

Even after issues related to standardization, systems interoperability, and compatibility are resolved, there are still those posed by organization and IT services management barriers. As they relate specifically to routine HCIT service quality issues, these barriers may be considered a subset of the technological challenges. Some of the more commonly encountered complaints in this area have been the availability and accessibility of technical assistance whenever systems appear to "break down." For example, there is a lack of attention paid to the regular maintenance of quality IT services, including IT service reliability, capacity, and planning for new HCIT projects. In this situation, CASs should attempt to educate employees at all levels about two main topics that will allow their organizations to efficiently and effectively perform and operate within the American healthcare system: changing trends, and why HCIT services must assume the highest priority for healthcare organizations in order to achieve US healthcare reform. HHS is conceivably taking some form of leadership in this area by funding and attempting to set up "regional centers." The supposed purpose of these centers is to engage in helping care providers to implement interoperable HCITs or, if necessary, offer private consultation on the unique IT challenges that the care provider organizations may face.

We strongly believe that the best business model for these HHS-funded "regional centers"—that is, one that will allow them to thrive in providing organization and IT services management consultation to care providers—would be to follow that of the IT services management concepts business model, which is rooted in the United Kingdom (UK) ITIL standards and guidelines as recommended and discussed in Tan with Payton.[44] In this regard, Tan[45(p253)] noted that many nonprofit organizations around the world, including a growing number of UK governmental bodies, have already "been formed to assist in the establishment of best practices in IT services management based on core principles of ITIL standards and guidelines." ITIL, an acronym for "IT Infrastructure Library" and a registered community trademark of the Office of Government Commerce, essentially covers a set of "best practices" publications that, together, offers a framework of management guidance for all aspects of IT services. In other words, ITIL offers concisely written guidance on IT from a business perspective: IT infrastructure management, IT service management, IT application management, IT service delivery, IT service support, and IT security management. Interested readers may consult the ITIL Web sites[46] to gain further insight into ITIL standards and guidelines.

Financial Barriers

Even though HCIT hardware and software development costs have somewhat declined over the decades, the cost of engaging qualified technicians with HCIT expertise has risen significantly. This makes it very difficult for healthcare organizations and agencies to fund ambitious interoperable HCIT projects, as such projects would require expert human resources in a cross-disciplinary area that already has a very limited supply of students and professionals. Thus, it should come as no surprise that many care provider organizations are still hesitant to invest in building the enterprisewide network and infrastructural support that is needed for major HCIT implementation and expansion activities. Additionally, most private clinics and physician practices in the United States are also not yet ready to give up their paper-based records and, because of the lack of technological expertise among employees, argue against an investment in HCITs. The necessity of training new employees in the use of e-technology and interoperable health IT, the inconvenience of changing the way business has always been conducted, and the added costs of running parallel systems during a major HCIT development and implementation have scared many potential HCIT adopters.

Even large-scale provider organizations that may have the means to fully fund and implement e-health systems and interoperable HCITs may hesitate due to another factor—the rapidly changing HCIT marketplace. Indeed, past experiences with newly installed HCITs suggest that such systems can easily become obsolete within a few years—sometimes even before employees are fully trained on the use of these systems or before the systems can be properly evaluated. Stories about the high rate of past HCIT implementation failures abound as well.[47] While learning from the mistakes of other forerunners can truly be an illuminating exercise, top management often fluctuates on their support of HCIT implementation efforts for fear of losing their own jobs should these implementations fail.

Fortunately, with new governmental initiatives and legislation (ARRA 2009) to help fund and protect HCIT investments while simultaneously encouraging rapid and massive interoperable HCIT implementations, the uncertainty of financial risks for such ventures can now be better mitigated. For instance, researchers have found that widespread utilization of one of the more popular e-health and innovative HCIT solutions—implementing a teleradiological program to electronically exchange digital patient radiological images—can contribute to a significant cost reduction. Teleradiology, the most commonly used type of teleconsultation, has also been shown as an area in which financial risks could be lessened. Empirical evidence has shown that, with 200 teleconsultations performed in a wide-area shared network, a teleconsultation session might cost less than $150 as opposed to costing $7,328 if only a single session had been conducted.[48] In short, when there is a critical mass in the participation rate, the true cost-effectiveness benefits of programs such as teleconsultation or similar HCIT-related projects may be rather inexpensive due, primarily, to economies of scale. Hence, wide-area e-health networks and/or innovative HCIT investments will be truly beneficial if they can be simultaneously adopted, used, and diffused among a large number of public sector health agencies and privately funded practices. The situation is not unlike any new invention or innovation; take, for example, the design, production, and sales of hybrid cars—cars that run on both batteries and gasoline—the more interested purchasers are in the technology, the cheaper these hybrids can be produced and priced.

Sociopolitical and Cultural Barriers

Even so, for e-health technologies and interoperable health IT initiatives, the lack of a strong "political will" to drive collaboration—especially at the most senior management level—may explain why there are still so many stand-alone, fragmented legacy health information systems functioning within the US healthcare system today. Not only do these fragmented systems prevent better healthcare services from being delivered, but their widespread use also obstructs the growth and successful deployment of interoperable HCITs. With the push for healthcare reform, it is critical that top management at all levels of the US healthcare system display direct interest and a strong political will to replacing legacy systems with enterprisewide, interoperable HCITs. Hence, whether the US healthcare reform will be successful depends on the commitment from various sociopolitical groups, especially the senior management of these health provider groups, the members of the US Congress, and the HCIT leadership in the White House.

Because different health administrators tend to take dissimilar approaches in healthcare policymaking and planning, not only at strategic, but also at tactical and operational levels, it can be expected that no two HCIT implementations will have the same impact on how the organizational business processes and culture will be affected. Similarly, it will not be known what the impact that HCITs bear on the relationships between various employee groups within an organization and their reporting habits until we also understand the sociopolitical and cultural changes that may result from such implementations.

In fact, a primary characteristic of CASs is that these systems will continually promote a culture of learning and knowledge empowerment among the organizational knowledge workers.[49] In the context of the current US healthcare system, these knowledge workers can range from senior executives to various professional clinical members, administrative and managerial personnel, and even the clerical and operational staff members of various organizational units. Ultimately, an intelligent organization is one that focuses on the development of a supportive organizational culture that also promotes effective management. In the HCIT context, a learning culture that is anxious to acquire HCIT knowledge and expertise is a critical component of HCIT implementation success.

The management of HCITs within a learning organization also has to be organic, adaptive, and changing, rather than mechanistic.[50] Accordingly, HCIT management in this "edge of chaos" environment would emphasize systems flexibility: a systemwide focus on IT strategic vision, planning, and management and the nurturing of technological expertise among staff members. At the same time, management should also be completely familiar with the details of the technological processes, as they may need to be continuously revised and improved. Culturally speaking, an intelligent CAS is one that can continually assess, improve, and replace old technologies with new and emerging ones, since these technologies serve as building blocks for change and organizational evolution.[51]

From another perspective, one cannot expect to successfully implement HCITs without giving due consideration to the sociopolitical factors and cultural environments surrounding the application of HCITs, including the health organizational information management culture, the differences in the employees' attitudes toward learning about computing and knowledge sharing, and concerns about how HCITs may impact the lifestyles and habits of the organization's knowledge workers. Thus, it is almost impossible to ensure that a specific HCIT application will be adopted and diffused similarly across different organizations, societies, and/or cultures. In short, successful HCIT implementation typically requires flexibility in order to conform to the CAS's sociopolitical and cultural environment.

Legal Barriers

The confidentiality, privacy, and security of computerized (and paper-based) clinical and administrative health data are of major concern to healthcare administrators. At present, these important issues are, perhaps, the greatest legal barriers to HCIT adoption, use, and diffusion. No care provider wants to be responsible for identity theft or the leakage of stored patient information. As such, the management, use, and retention of patient records, as well as the security of health networks, are particularly critical. As HCIT usage increases, IT managers must also consider the potential, significant threats posed by unauthorized access to electronically stored sensitive health information.

The Fourth Amendment to the US Constitution basically guarantees American residents fundamental rights to their freedom and privacy of information. One critical step toward maintaining health information confidentiality, privacy, and security, then, is simply to educate those who routinely use and handle HCITs. Health employees, especially those who are asked to manage such sensitive data as patient records, must have the ethical responsibility and wisdom to uphold the laws that protect the appropriate and authorized usage, access, and exchange of patient information within our dynamic, innovative technological environment.

In 1996, Congress passed the Health Insurance Portability and Accountability Act (HIPAA), Public Law 104-191.[52] HIPAA required HHS to establish—with far-reaching implications and consequences—new guidelines, key principles, and national standards for the handling of electronic healthcare transactions, applicable to everyone working within the US healthcare system. Covered entities include, but are not limited to, individuals such as doctors, nurses, and pharmacists; groups and organizations such as hospitals, clinics, nursing homes, private physician organizations (PPOs), private health insurance companies, and HMOs; and even government programs such as Medicaid and Medicare. HIPAA not only established national standards and guidelines to protect access to, and use of, patients' health information, but also bestowed specific rights on the patients. Under this legislation, individual patients reserve the right to review the content of stored records and to request a copy of their medical records for their own safekeeping. Patients also have the right to request corrections and/or have notes appended to these records if any errors are found, as well as the right to file a complaint with the healthcare provider organization and, at an even higher level, the US government.

Indeed, following the US Congress's passing of HIPAA, the HHS introduced the "Privacy Rule" to further refine and clarify HIPAA's articulated view of privacy. Between 2001 and 2002, HHS released a series of guidelines to clarify questions pertaining to the original privacy rule, which eventually led to the Final Rule.[53] In general, the Privacy Rule comprises five key principles: (1) consumer control, (2) the setting of boundaries, (3) accountability, (4) public responsibility, and (5) security. Interested readers who want elaboration and illustration for each of these principles may consult Tan with Payton.[54(p280–290)]

Also, given the relatively poor control over information posted and exchanged on the Internet, initiatives have been taken to improve the quality of Internet-based health information. As an example, Web sites that adhere to agreed quality principles can now be stamped with the Health on the Net (HON) code. Also, the "e-Health Code of Ethics" has been proposed by the Health Internet Ethics (Hi-Ethics) community to address concerns surrounding the reliability of electronic health information, privacy, and confidentiality.[55,56]

Admittedly, the security, privacy, and confidentiality of data stored in EMRs, EHRs, PHRs, and PBHRs require greater attention. On one hand, concerns about the confidentiality of patient records typically underlie the positive attitude that many patients maintain toward these electronic data management systems. Ornstein and Bearden[57] interviewed 16 patients of eight different physicians from a medical university and found that a common strategy for easing patient concern is to keep them informed about their personal records and uses. Borst[58] noted that most patients thought computer-based medical records were unsafe, especially due to their vulnerability to blackmail. However, it is inevitable that insurance companies and future employers will want, and are able, to use information from these records to determine who to insure or hire. Thus, the potential does exist for possible discrimination against cases of individuals with mental illness, HIV infection, or other problems.

But on the contrary, technologies have been developed and are available to ensure the security of these modern data management systems. Examples of security measures include firewalls, intrusion-detection programs, digital certificates, RFID biometric, and other authentication and authorization software. Andreae,[59] for instance, discussed how public key cryptography could be used to reliably enhance authentication and authorization of data transfers, thereby eliminating unauthorized access to confidential information on networks. Unfortunately, as much as 60% of all cybercrime goes undetected or unreported, and no one really knows the extent of cyber attacks today. However, the same legal requirements that apply to paper records will still apply to computer-based records. Waller and Fulton[60] argued that "insiders" (i.e., employees who use the computers on a daily basis) pose the greatest threat to security, given that they are "closest" to the data.

The last point to consider is the emergence, in recent years, of wireless Internet services and mobile wearable devices, and the resulting introduction of a new dimension of safeguarding and protection for individuals' private healthcare information. In August 2007, the standards for electronic transactions, which cover the rules and regulations for sending and receiving an individual's private health and medical records, were released.[61] Previous legacy systems made interoperability among systems a challenging issue, but the lack of such data-sharing capabilities also provided an easier and better privacy control environment. The implementation of Web services, as well as other advancing data interchange technologies today, will raise further concerns over the privacy and security of personal health data, since data is being shared among automated intelligence and applications.

HIPAA addresses what strategies are appropriate for staying in compliance with the federal law. To ensure HIPAA compliance, HHS issued seven regulatory steps that healthcare services organizations must follow, which are listed here in no particular order. These steps are: (1) access control, to minimize the inappropriate retrieval of critical, electronically stored information; (2) encryption of private health data, to prevent intruders from locating transmissions across cyberspace, and to make recoding the transmission more difficult; (3) integrity control, to protect the validity and reliability of HCIT-accessible data; (4) authentication, to help the organization identify who is authorized and therefore allowed to access specific documents and records; (5) audit control, to allow for meaningful tracing of inappropriate information access and retrieval; (6) alarms, to provide warnings and alerts about attempted or intended intrusions into stored private data; and (7) event reporting, to ensure that any breach of HIPAA standards and regulations is swiftly reported and the resulting damages controlled quickly and effectively.

Together, the barriers that have been highlighted imply that strong HCIT leadership is critical for the progression of the US healthcare reform agenda. As an example, planning EHRs for a CAS entails more challenges than just deciding what platform is preferred, which software tools to build or buy, whether to construct a firewall (for security) or to use some form of encryption, and how many workstations to purchase and install. Challenges are also posed by the HCIT-corporate alignment of the strategic mission, goals, and objectives, and the identification of barriers to system integration. Additionally, barriers also arise from employee training and education, including human–computer interface design and changes in reporting relationships among workers in an evolving, technologically complex healthcare services delivery system environment.

Championing an EHR project for success means building the right team, capturing the right data content for the system, detailing the site management process, putting the pre- and post-launch measurements in place to gauge effectiveness and user satisfaction, developing a system promotional plan, conducting training on the uses and abuses of the organization's electronic space, and making a host of other diverse procedural and policy-related decisions.

HCIT software development approaches have not been discussed. An aspect of this topic will be highlighted in the beginning of the conclusion as the focus is shifted back to the significance of understanding "systems interoperability" and highlight its potential impacts on the future of the US healthcare system.

Conclusion

New forms of HCIT applications will have to evolve in order to assist healthcare providers and managers in meeting new challenges. In this section, we highlight the significant role of interoperable HCITs and how having such systems implemented throughout US healthcare organizations will free HCIT analysts, programmers, and systems engineers from the chores of maintaining isolated information and systems, thereby allowing them to focus on integrating HCIT solutions that will improve data quality, eliminate medical errors, and shrink large-scale software development cycles. Ultimately, these new technological solutions will be the driving force in altering the traditional static, hierarchical organizational structures into team-based, highly productive, learning, and intelligent organizations—in essence, the manifestation of the evolving CAS concept in today's complex multiprovider health organization services environment.

Nonetheless, the current lack of standards and absence of systems interoperability continue to challenge the successful deployment and adoption of innovative health IT applications; however, a large part of HCIT implementation success oftentimes hinges on what happens during its software design and development stage. Indeed, just like any new construction project, the failure of an HCIT software development project may simply be the result of dwindling commitment from the project sponsor(s) and the associated consequences: poor HCIT vision and leadership, inadequate project management expertise, ambiguities with respect to user needs and requirements, unsettled conflicts between HCIT project team members, unanticipated budget cuts, and/or other possibilities such as mishandlings in the complexities of the HCIT software development process. This, then, warrants a discussion of open source software (OSS)—an emerging trend in HCIT software development that has recently gained considerable attention among healthcare practitioners, health systems analysts, and researchers.

With OSS, rich libraries of source codes previously used in well-tested products, such as Massachusetts General's COSTAR and the VA's VISTA, can be conveniently adopted, reused, and modified without incurring licensing fees—so long as the derivative products will also be made freely available to other interested HCIT analysts and programmers. Hence, unlike the more established systems development approaches such as structured methodologies,[62] prototyping,[63] and multiview,[64] OSS will give HCIT designers greater opportunities for innovation. This will help proliferate, with very limited resources, a wide range of key products that can resolve many of the major challenges facing the healthcare system—especially those posed by the constraints of growing interoperable HCIT software project backlogs. The primary advantages of OSS adoption include promoting systems interoperability, increasing the diffusion of OSS products, and supporting efficiencies of the software development process—all of which will reduce overall HCIT development costs and decrease backlogs associated with complex HCIT product design and development. An additional advantage for programmers adopting the OSS approach is that, frequently, the OSS community will provide, at a virtually negligible cost, needed consultation to challenges posted online during the course of HCIT software development. In addition, with the advancing of software security technologies and the diffusion of more OSS products, these products will gradually become more mainstream, reliable, and secure, thereby not only enabling standards and scalability but also minimizing vendor lock-in.[65]

Paradoxically, some researchers have noted that it is the vendors who have played the primary role in fueling OSS adoption in hospitals, and that it is actually the lack of in-house development and/or the "perceived lack of security, quality, and accountability of OSS products" that is slowing down OSS adoption.[66(p16)] Furthermore, given that these OSS applications are more likely to be developed under budget constraints, they are frequently subject to the perception that they can better serve the general-purpose software market than the domain-specific software market. Despite these arguments, the rapidity of which many useful HCIT products can be generated, whether it is through collaborative exchanges or reuse of software codes, is undeniable; the same applies for the broad applicability of the OSS methodology—it can be used among governmental agencies, publicly funded and private university researchers, nonprofit care provider organizations, and even for-profit healthcare institutions. Because of this, it is believed that the OSS trend is here to stay.

Interoperability, in essence, links diverse systems infrastructure with multiple platforms and software languages to enable the convenient and secure sharing of electronically captured and stored information. It can open up new avenues for secure and meaningful data transmittals from one health institution to another, resulting in a breakthrough of the "fragmentation" that has, thus far, characterized the history of the US healthcare information services that support the care provider organizational delivery system. In the current US healthcare software development environment, where rapid progress in the US healthcare reform agenda is a critical step for most healthcare services delivery organizations, taking the OSS approach of infusing interoperable HCITs across CASs provides a strategic position for the eventual fulfillment of the HHS health IT agenda. Evidently, the urgent call for "systems interoperability," which encourages the sharing of HCIT expertise and data throughout the US healthcare system, is crucial to healthcare reform. A nationwide response to such a call would not only enable a flexible adaptation of already implemented, large-scale legacy systems, but would, effectively, also act as a driving force for OSS adoption.

An interesting demonstration of "interoperability" as applied to health data and systems integration and sharing is the SAPHIRE project,[67] an initiative championed within the European medical community. In brief, the SAPHIRE project aims to address the challenges posed by the growing medical workload intensity; this is accomplished by implementing an interoperable, intelligent healthcare monitoring and health decision management and support system across diverse healthcare institutions in Europe. Using the SAPHIRE platform, the interoperability problem is resolved by capturing and integrating data sourced from monitoring sensors and elsewhere. These data are then intelligently combined, via standard-based ontologies, with data previously stored in existing medical information systems. The result is a set of semantically enriched Web services that provide care providers with alerts, meaningful insights to a well of questions regarding medical treatment protocols, and diverse options in clinical care delivery services.

In the coming years, health information technology interoperability will alter the ways in which medicine is practiced. The diffusion of knowledge on how different medical tools, new techniques, clinical protocols, and health informatic methodologies can be effectively applied to help patients depends on a means through which these knowledge elements can be shared in a convenient fashion among care provider institutions. One of the chief contributions of interoperability, therefore, lies in its role of aiding the decision makers, whether they are clinicians, administrators, or even patients, in intelligently capturing, integrating, and processing the most relevant and critical data, information, and knowledge from scattered sources. Moreover, not only will these interoperable HCITs help care providers and their affiliated healthcare institutions in responding quickly and flexibly to patients' changing needs, but the synergistic effect of the medical knowledge diffusion will also lead to new discoveries in science and medicine. As a result, interoperable systems will impact the future practice of medicine in America, leading to more abundant, accessible, affordable, and accountable health care.

In the next few years, there will certainly be even more HCIT innovations, especially considering the learning and experience we would have gained with the implementation, use, and adoption of interoperable HCITs. With increased knowledge, there will be an evolution of new HCIT applications such as Internet-based HCIT systems, which can be used to educate different groups of the US population on preventive and self-care, new scientific discoveries about aging and health, and warnings about unhealthy lifestyle practices such as drug abuse and addiction, smoking and excessive drinking habits, and work stress and overeating—ultimately leading to more healthy Americans. New advances in client-server technology, AI-based decision support systems, hyperlink processing and computer networking, computer animation and multimedia technology, robotics, and other areas will also drive new research and practices in HCIT informatics and telematics.

Health IT, including interoperable EMRs, EHRs, PHRs, PBHRs, CPOE, CHINs, RHINOs, SCM, CRM, ERP, e-prescribing, telehealth, Web portals, Web services, m-health, and RFID microchips can reduce medical errors, improve coordination among care providers, and diminish administrative and clinical inefficiencies. According to the RAND Corporation, an annual savings of $77 billion or more can be achieved from the widespread implementation and adoption of interoperable HCITs and its resulting increased clinical and administrative efficiencies alone. In this sense, interoperable HCITs would not only save significant amounts of money and improve the quality healthcare services delivery but, as added health and safety benefits, would also reduce illness and prolong life expectancy. Just as the industrial revolution and its social implications have changed the way of life for not only workers, but also for families and communities in general, so would interoperable HCITs and the global e-health revolution in the coming years. E-technology, representing interoperable HCITs and other emerging technologies, will infuse every imaginable component of the US healthcare system—from software development to medical education to clinical research and practices—and, as a result, will significantly impact healthcare services delivery at large institutional healthcare facilities and privately funded physician clinics alike, both at home and abroad. With all of the potential benefits that e-technology promises, however, there also arise many inevitable challenges with its diffusion. Fortunately, there are ways of overcoming such challenges, and our new administration seems optimistic that it can overcome the barriers while helping improve health care for all. What must be done, then, is put resources and energy behind the new initiatives put forth by the new administration, and help usher in a new era of healthcare reform.

References

1. White J. Obama calls for cuts in Medicare and Medicaid. World Socialist Web site. http://www.wsws.org/articles/2009/jun2009/pers-j16.shtml. Published June 16, 2009. Accessed July 19, 2009.
2. Keehan S, Sisko A, Truffer C, Smith S, Cowan C, Poisal J, et al. Health spending projections through 2017. *Health Affairs Web Exclusive*. February 2008;W146.
3. UNDP. Understanding human development, American human development report, 2008–2009. Available at: http://measureofamerica.org/wp-content/uploads/2008/07/ahdr-under standing.pdf. Accessed July 12, 2009.
4. The Henry J. Kaiser Family Foundation. *Employee health benefits: 2008 annual survey.* The Henry J. Kaiser Family Foundation; September 2008.
5. Families USA. Too great a burden: Americans face rising health care costs. Available at: http://money.cnn.com/2009/03/05/news/economy/health_uninsured/index.htm. Accessed June 30, 2009.
6. Public Health Service Act, The American Recovery and Reinvestment Act (ARRA), 2009 Pub L No. 111–115.
7. Raghupathi W, Tan J. Strategic IT applications in health care. *Communications of the ACM.* 2002;45(12):56–61.
8. Raguphati W, Tan J. Information systems and healthcare XXX: charting a strategic path for health information technology. *The Communications of the Association for Information Systems.* 2008;23(1):500–525.
9. HIMSS. A call for action: economic stimulus for the healthcare IT industry, HIMSS report. Available at: www.himss.org/2009CalltoAction. Accessed July 3, 2009.
10. National Committee on Vital and Health Statistics. Information for health: a strategy for building the national health information infrastructure. Report and recommendations from the National Committee on Vital and Health Statistics. Available at: http://ncvhs.hhs.gov/nhiilayo.pdf. Published November 15, 2001. Accessed July 3, 2009.
11. Tan J, Wen HJ, Awad N. Health care and services delivery systems as complex adaptive systems health care applications. *Communications of the ACM.* 2005;48(5):36–44.
12. Tan J. *e-Health Care Information Systems: Introduction to Students and Professionals.* San Francisco, CA: Jossey-Bass Inc; 2005.
13. Tan J, Cobb Payton F, eds. *Adaptive Health Management Information Systems: Concepts, Cases and Practical Applications.* 3rd ed. Sudbury, MA: Jones and Bartlett Publishers; 2009.
14. Tan J. *Health Management Information Systems: Theories, Methods, and Applications.* Gaithersburg, MD: Aspen Publishers; 1995.
15. Iecovich E, Carmel S. Differences in accessibility, affordability, and availability (AAA) of medical specialists among three age-groups of elderly people in Israel. *J Aging Health.* 2009; 21:776–797.
16. Tan J, Cobb Payton F, eds. *Adaptive Health Management Information Systems: Concepts, Cases and Practical Applications.* 3rd ed. Sudbury, MA: Jones and Bartlett Publishers; 2009.
17. HIMSS. A call for action: economic stimulus for the healthcare IT industry, HIMSS report. Available at: www.himss.org/2009CalltoAction. Accessed July 3, 2009.
18. Ibid.
19. Ibid.

20. US Government Accountability Office. Health information technology: HHS is taking steps to develop a national strategy. GAO-05-628. Available at: http://www.gao.gov/cgi-bin/getrpt?GAO-05-628. Published May 2005. Accessed July 2, 2009.

21. Institute of Medicine. Preventing medication errors: quality chasm series. Available at: http://www.iom.edu/CMS/3809/22526/35939.aspx. Published July 20, 2006. Accessed June 30, 2009.

22. US Government Accountability Office. Health information technology: HHS is taking steps to develop a national strategy. GAO-05-628. Available at: http://www.gao.gov/cgi-bin/getrpt?GAO-05-628. Published May 2005. Accessed July 2, 2009.

23. Office of National Coordinator for Health IT. Call for Regional Centers. Notices 25551: [FR Doc. E9–12419 Filed 5–27–09]. *Federal Register.* 2009;74(101). May 28, 2009.

24. Gupta A. Prescription for change: Health care has managed to avoid the information-technology revolution. But it won't for much longer [Information Technology section]. *The Wall Street Journal.* October 20, 2008.

25. Tan J. *e-Health Care Information Systems: Introduction to Students and Professionals.* San Francisco, CA: Jossey-Bass Inc; 2005.

26. Ginzberg E. Ten encounters with the US health sector. 1930–1999. *JAMA.* 1999;282: 1665–1668.

27. Nichols LM, Ginsburg PB, Berenson RA, Christianson J, Hurley RE. Are market forces strong enough to deliver efficient health care systems? Confidence is waning. *Health Affairs.* 2004;23(2):25–27.

28. Sultz HA, Young KM. *Health Care USA: Understanding Its Organization and Delivery.* Sudbury, MA: Jones and Bartlett Publishers; 2009.

29. Krugman P, Wells R. The health care crisis and what to do about it. *New York Review of Books.* 2006;53(5).

30. Sipkoff M. Can transparency save health care? *Managed Care Magazine.* Available at: http://www.managedcaremag.com/archives/0403/0403.transparency.html. Published March 2004. Accessed July 14, 2009.

31. Tan J, Wen HJ, Awad N. Health care and services delivery systems as complex adaptive systems health care applications. *Communications of the ACM.* 2005;48(5):36–44.

32. Ibid.

33. Tan J, Cobb Payton F, eds. *Adaptive Health Management Information Systems: Concepts, Cases and Practical Applications.* 3rd ed. Sudbury, MA: Jones and Bartlett Publishers; 2009.

34. Tan J, Wen HJ, Awad N. Health care and services delivery systems as complex adaptive systems health care applications. *Communications of the ACM.* 2005;48(5):36–44.

35. Tan J. *e-Health Care Information Systems: Introduction to Students and Professionals.* San Francisco, CA: Jossey-Bass Inc; 2005.

36. O'Neill L, Klepack W. Integrating electronic medical records and disease management at Dryden Family Medicine. In: Tan J, Cobb Payton F, eds. *Adaptive Health Management Information Systems: Concepts, Cases and Practical Applications.* 3rd ed. Sudbury, MA: Jones and Bartlett Publishers; 2009:359–372.

37. Tan J, Cobb Payton F, eds. *Adaptive Health Management Information Systems: Concepts, Cases and Practical Applications.* 3rd ed. Sudbury, MA: Jones and Bartlett Publishers; 2009.

38. Doswell et al. Community health information networks: building virtual communities and networking health provider organizations. In: Tan J, Cobb Payton F, eds. *Adaptive Health Management Information Systems: Concepts, Cases and Practical Applications.* 3rd ed. Sudbury, MA: Jones and Bartlett Publishers, 2009;95–108.

39. Tan J, Cobb Payton F, eds. *Adaptive Health Management Information Systems: Concepts, Cases and Practical Applications.* 3rd ed. Sudbury, MA: Jones and Bartlett Publishers; 2009.

40. Tan J, Cobb Payton F, eds. *Adaptive Health Management Information Systems: Concepts, Cases and Practical Applications.* 3rd ed. Sudbury, MA: Jones and Bartlett Publishers; 2009.

41. Tan J. Health care information systems: an organized delivery system perspective. In: Wolper LF, ed. *Health Care Administration: Planning, Implementing, and Managing Organized Delivery Systems.* 4th ed. Sudbury, MA: Jones and Bartlett Publishers; 2004.

42. Tan J, Cobb Payton F, eds. *Adaptive Health Management Information Systems: Concepts, Cases and Practical Applications.* 3rd ed. Sudbury, MA: Jones and Bartlett Publishers; 2009.

43. GAO Report, ibid.

44. Tan J, Cobb Payton F, eds. *Adaptive Health Management Information Systems: Concepts, Cases and Practical Applications.* 3rd ed. Sudbury, MA: Jones and Bartlett Publishers; 2009.

45. Tan J. Managing health management information system projects: system implementation and information technology services management. In: Tan J, Cobb Payton F, eds. *Adaptive Health Management Information Systems: Concepts, Cases and Practical Applications.* 3rd ed, Sudbury, MA: Jones and Bartlett Publishers; 2009:191–216.

46. ITIL. ITIL (IT Infrastructure Library) and ITSM Directory. ITIL Web site. Available at: http://www.itil-officialsite.com/home/home.asp, Accessed July 14, 2009.

47. Berg M. Implementing information systems in health care organizations: myths and challenges. *International Journal of Medical Informatics.* 2001:64(2):143–156.

48. Panjamapirom A, Musa PF. Citation of the work reported by Spaulding RJ et al, 2007. In: Tan J, Cobb Payton F, eds. *Adaptive Health Management Information Systems: Concepts, Cases and Practical Applications.* 3rd ed, Sudbury, MA: Jones and Bartlett Publishers; 2009:304–305.

49. Burn J, Caldwell L. *Management of Information Systems Technology.* Hong Kong, China: Alfred Waller Ltd; 1990.

50. Boynton AC, Zmud RW, Jacobs GC. The influence of IT management practice on IT use in large organizations. *MIS Quarterly.* 1994;18(3):115.

51. Burn J, Caldwell L. *Management of Information Systems Technology.* Hong Kong, China: Alfred Waller Ltd; 1990.

52. Department of the Army. Status of HIPAA. Available at: http://www.drum.amedd.army.mil/HIPAA/FD%20MEDDAC%20REG%2040-45.doc. Accessed July 2, 2009.

53. United States Department of Human and Health Services. Medical privacy—national standards to protect the privacy of personal health information. United States Department of Human and Health Services Web site. Available at: http://www.hhs.gov/ocr/hipaa/. April 2007. Accessed July 2, 2009.

54. Tan J, Cobb Payton F, eds. *Adaptive Health Management Information Systems: Concepts, Cases and Practical Applications.* 3rd ed. Sudbury, MA: Jones and Bartlett Publishers; 2009.

55. Kind T, Silber TJ. Ethical issues in pediatric e-health. *Clin Pediatr (Phila).* 2004;43:593–599.

56. Maloney R, Clay DL, Robinson J. Sociocultural issues in pediatric transplantation: a conceptual model. *Journal of Pediatric Psychology.* 2005;30(3):235–246.

57. Ornstein S, Bearden A. Patient perspectives on computer-based medical records. *Yearbook of Medical Informatics.* 1995;247–251.

58. Borst F. Synopsis: computer-based patient records. *Yearbook of Medical Informatics.* 1995.

59. Andreae M. Confidentiality in medical telecommunication. *Lancet.* 1996;347:487–488.

60. Waller A, Fulton D. The electronic chart: keeping it confidential and secure. *Journal of Health and Hospital Law.* 1993;26(4):104.

61. Department of Health and Human Services. Standards for electronic transactions and code sets. HIPAAdvisory Web site. Available at: http://www.hipaadvisory.com/regs/finaltrans/summary.htm. Published August 17, 2000. Accessed July 2, 2009.

62. DeMarco T. *Structured Analysis and System Specification.* Englewood Cliffs, NJ: Prentice-Hall; 1979.

63. Avison D, Wood-Harper A. Information systems development research: an exploration of ideas in practice. *Computer Journal.* 1991;34(2):98–112.

64. Wood-Harper A, et al. *Information Systems Definition: The Multiview Approach.* Oxford, UK: Blackwell Scientific Publications;1985.

65. Raguphati W, Gao W. An eclipse-based development approach to health information technology. *International Journal of Electronic Healthcare*.

66. Munoz-Carnejo G, Seaman CB, Koru AG. An empirical investigation into the adoption of open source software in hospitals. *International Journal of Healthcare Information Systems & Informatics*. 2008;3(3):16–37.

67. Zhang JK, Tan J. Health management information system integration: achieving systems interoperability with web services. In: Tan J, Cobb Payton F, eds. *Adaptive Health Management Information Systems: Concepts, Cases and Practical Applications*. 3rd ed. Sudbury, MA: Jones and Bartlett Publishers, 2009;143–162.

Biographical Information

Joseph K. H. Tan, PhD, is the Wayne C. Fox Professor of E-Business Innovation and E-Health at McMaster University, Hamilton, Ontario, Canada. Previously, Dr. Tan had served as Professor and Head of the Information System and Manufacturing (ISM) Department at Wayne State University, and as Acting Chair of the Masters in Health Administration (MHA) Program in the Department of Healthcare and Epidemiology, Faculty of Medicine, at the University of British Columbia. Currently, as the Editor-in-Chief of the *International Journal of Healthcare Information Systems & Informatics* (IJHISI), Professor Tan sits on various journal advisory and editorial boards as well as on numerous organizing committees for local, national, and international meetings and conferences. Professor Tan is well published, and his research, which has enjoyed significant support in the last 21 years from local, national, and international funding agencies and other sources, has also been widely cited and applied across a number of major disciplines, including healthcare informatics and clinical decision support, health technology management research, human processing of graphical representations, ergonomics, health administration education, telehealth, mobile health, and e-health promotion programming. His hobbies include writing and editing books, book chapters, and journal articles; working on collaborative grant projects; engaging in philosophical discussions with colleagues and peers; and reading his son's work.

Joshia Tan is a junior and on the dean's list at the Olin Business School, Washington University in St. Louis. Even at an early age, Joshia displayed affection for, and an interest in, a vast range of pursuits. So it comes as no surprise that, years later, he is involved in an incredible variety of activities.

Recently, Joshia has expanded his knowledge of the healthcare industry by interning at Blue Cross Blue Shield of Michigan. At school, Joshia has served as a college council representative, a columnist and director for *Eleven Music Magazine*, and a public relations specialist for the Hong Kong Student Association and has worked at the Washington University Law School. A National Merit Finalist Scholar and Washington University in St. Louis Book Award recipient, Joshia has also received numerous other awards, including cum laude, AP Scholar with Distinction award, the John M. Olin scholarship, Cranbrook Prize Papers, Michigan Math Prize Competition Finalist, and Brook Film Festival's third place as lead actor and codirector of *The Broken Silence*. In addition, one of Joshia's most recognized film productions, *Tao Te*

Cranbrook, has been presented at a number of classes and seminars in the Business Department, School of Business Administration, at Wayne State University, Michigan.

He has also brought his activities to new levels by sharing them with others; for example, for two years he volunteered as a snowboarding counselor for Bloomfield Hills Ski & Snowboard Club in Michigan. Joshia also played violin with various schools orchestras and served as assembly pianist for one of his schools.

The literary world plays a large role in Joshia's life, as he has coauthored "The Oliver Home Case" (with J. Tan/G. Demiris) and "CyberAngel: The Robin Hood Case" (with J. Tan), both appearing in J. Tan (ed.) *E-Healthcare Information Systems: An Introduction for Students & Professionals* (Jossey-Bass: A Wiley Imprint), April 2005: 52–55 and 290–294, respectively. In 2008, Joshia self-published *The Apprentice Bistro: A Feast for Amateur Writers*, an adaptation of his 2007 Davidson Fellows entry, for which he received an honorable mention. More recently, he has completed another major work, *Concord in Calamity: Taming the Awakening Armageddon*.

Joshia is also an avid traveler with numerous countries under his belt; however, he keeps a steadfast hold on his life dream of seeing the world—and changing it for the better. True to this vision, he has studied various languages, including English, French, and two different dialects of Chinese, and has plans to study Arabic. Moreover, to better appreciate the Chinese language and culture, Joshia spent an entire semester fulfilling the challenge of his dream by accepting an invitation to intern in Shanghai, China, and will spend another semester at the Hong Kong University of Science and Technology. Furthermore, he incorporates this dream into his hobbies—such as drawing from international influences for his foray into fiction authorship. Ultimately, it is this vision that continues to drive him, it is this dream that he works toward, and it is this dream that may, years later, very well become reality.

Management Engineering

Karl Bartscht

Management engineering is the practice of industrial engineering in the healthcare field. The name of the discipline has been changed, not only to encourage acceptance by healthcare professionals, but also to indicate its application to management. The healthcare delivery system will continue to undergo significant changes in the next decade because of consolidations and continued pressures for reduction in healthcare expenditures. Changes are driven by increased managed care, competition among the large healthcare systems, structural change related to new federal initiatives, and the attendant requirement that healthcare providers ensure high-value (and in some cases, low-cost) services. This already is being achieved through the consolidation of healthcare providers into organized delivery systems. Management engineering tools and techniques, with particular emphasis on increased productivity, will be invaluable in achieving high-value, low-cost services. Hospital mergers and contraction resulting in downsizing and reengineering needs will require the management engineer to apply long-standing, cost control, and productivity measures. These long-standing measures will be planned from the corporate levels of emerging organized delivery systems and will be implemented at all other levels. This chapter concentrates on cost control, productivity, and quality control.

The discipline of engineering is defined by the Accreditation Board for Engineering and Technology (ABET), formerly the Engineers Council for Professional Development (ECPD), as the "profession in which a knowledge of the mathematical and natural sciences gained by study, experience, and practice is applied with judgment to develop ways to economically utilize the materials and forces of nature for the benefit of mankind."[1] The key words in this definition are:

- Mathematical and natural sciences—particularly with emphasis on a quantitative approach
- Applied with judgment—implying that not everything can be quantified
- Economically—implying a concern with costs

According to the American Institute of Industrial Engineers (AIIE), the special field of industrial engineering is concerned with:

> the design, improvement, and installation of integrated systems of 360 health care administration people, materials, equipment and energy. It draws upon specialized knowledge and skill in the mathematical, physical, and social sciences together with the principles and methods of engineering analysis and design to specify, predict, and evaluate the results to be obtained from such systems. The element that is unique to industrial engineering . . . is the explicit reference to people and to the social sciences in addition to the natural sciences.[2]

The key words in this definition are:

- Design, improvement, and installation—implying that whether one starts from scratch or with an existing system, installation is also a part of the job
- Systems of people, materials, equipment, and energy—hereafter referred to as a resource system or systems
- Specify, predict, and evaluate—implying that not only is the system defined, but also its expected outcomes or performance are defined, and evaluation of systems operations is a part of the process

The *Handbook of Industrial Engineering*[3] has defined the following 12 areas of industrial engineering specialization:

1. Organization and job design
2. Methods engineering
3. Performance measurement and control of operations
4. Evaluation, appraisal, and management of human resources
5. Ergonomics/human factors
6. Manufacturing engineering
7. Quality assurance
8. Engineering economy
9. Facilities design
10. Planning and control
11. Computers and information systems
12. Quantitative methods and optimization

With the exception of manufacturing engineering, all of these areas of specialization are applicable to healthcare systems and hospital operations. Several of them are covered in other chapters of this book, including human resource management, management information systems, quality assurance, strategic planning, materials management, and facilities planning. Quantitative management engineering methodologies and techniques are used in each of those areas.

Quality assurance, as expanded by Deming to include total quality management (TQM) and subsequently continuous quality improvement (CQI), as well as current case management and disease management efforts, is the basic application of management engineering, which has been described as the design, improvement, and installation of integrated systems of people, materials, equipment, and energy.

After briefly describing the history of the application of management engineering to the healthcare field, this chapter focuses on cost containment and productivity management, and then briefly describes some other areas of management engineering specialization.

History

In their book, *Hospital Management Engineering: A Guide to the Improvement of Hospital Management Systems,*[4] Smalley and Freeman provide a complete history of the use of management engineering in hospitals. They trace the history from the motion study of a surgical procedure by Frank B. Gilbreth at the turn of the century, through the dearth of hospital activity in the 1920s and 1930s, and the post–World War II period to the present. Some events of interest are the employment of the first (recorded) full-time hospital management engineer in 1952, the development of university programs for education and service in the 1950s and 1960s, and the founding of the Hospital Management Systems Society (HMSS) in 1961.

HMSS's membership first expanded from the original group of management engineers, who were primarily hospital-based or university faculty, to include administrators and consultants. Subsequently, HMSS has evolved into the Healthcare Information and Management Systems Society (HIMSS), which includes thousands of information system specialists.

More than 700 hospitals have organized management engineering departments, and an equal number secure management engineering services from either multihospital system programs or consulting firms.

The 1960s and 1970s

In simplest terms, management engineering is directed at increasing the utilization of system resources, either through reducing costs or by increasing productivity, including throughput. As the healthcare environment has changed, so has the utilization of management engineering.

The first significant use and expansion of management engineering services occurred during the 1960s and 1970s. However, because hospitals generally were reimbursed on a cost basis, there was little incentive to reduce costs. Hospital management engineering efforts were directed at improving operations in problem departments utilizing engineering techniques. Examples of such efforts were improving the patient admission process and supply systems and developing employee-scheduling systems. It was rare that real economies were achieved, except in cases where accounts receivable or inventory holding costs were reduced.

As hospitals initiated more sophisticated budgeting processes, it became clear that a more objective system for determining personnel requirements than the one of "needing more personnel than we have now" was necessary. Early work at the University of Michigan in the 1960s resulted in the development of staffing methodologies[5]: quantitative, detailed, step-by-step procedures for determining personnel requirements. They were subsequently refined and modified by hospital association–sponsored efforts in order to make them easier to apply. These staffing methodologies were then applied through educational programs, booklet format, and shared data collection systems. However, the need for quantitative methodologies still was not appreciated. In general, the incentive to reduce costs was not there, except where hospital management recognized the need to contain costs by managing more effectively.

During the 1960s and 1970s, the other use of management engineering that evolved was its application in planning new facilities. In particular, as hospitals increasingly utilized debt financing for replacement and expansion of facilities, ways to reduce operating costs were sought in order to pay debt service. Berg[6] reports on one such analysis that projected an annual operating savings of $4.5 million generated by the operation of more efficiently designed facilities.

The 1980s

The advent of the federal prospective payment system (PPS), combined with state Medicare and statewide/regional Blue Cross plans, changed the incentive system for hospital payment in the 1980s. The emphasis was on reducing acute hospitalization, particularly lengths of stay. Not only did lengths of stay drop during the decade, but admissions also fell. Admissions dropped because of several outside influences, including physician peer review organizations and the shift of care to other settings, such as outpatient and nursing homes, and through technological advances and the increased availability of alternative settings. The result was a drop in occupancy, which resulted in excess personnel (the nursing shortage of the 1970s became a surplus in the late 1980s and early 1990s). Management engineering provides an objective approach to staffing issues that ensures that reductions occur where the change in workload is actually warranted and in a way that is sensitive to the disposition of employees.

However, hospitals were able to work the system to maximize reimbursement, with minor personnel reductions. Once personnel costs and other costs such as drugs, supplies, and food were reduced, then shifts to outpatient services resulted in increased revenues and cost shifting to the fee-for-service payers. This resulted in financial health for hospitals at the end of the 1980s.

The 1990s

Maximizing the PPS system was short-lived, when pressures to reduce healthcare costs became a primary issue with employers (particularly as they incurred the cost shifting arising from the perceived federal and state underpayments). In the late 1980s and the early 1990s, this resulted in the development of the new reimbursement system of managed care.

Early managed care insurers sought pure discounts in exchange for guaranteed volumes and rapid payment, but the real objective was the reduction in utilization. Although PPS primarily influenced length of stay reductions, the managed care insurer has prompted further length of stay reductions, plus it has forced inpatient services to the outpatient setting and to the physician's office. This has been enhanced by technological advances that facilitate relocation of important services to facilities specializing in skilled nursing, home care, subacute care, and rehabilitation—all of which provide alternatives to long inpatient stays.

These changes in service settings have resulted in resource and information management problems. Resources of people, equipment, and facilities are particularly underutilized in the inpatient setting. However, they are in short supply in the ambulatory and postacute settings. Information systems that provide effective resource management are still insufficient in the inpatient setting, as well as for alternative settings. The full application of management engineering tools and techniques will be needed to solve these resource problems in the coming years.

The Future

In many ways, the real benefits of management engineering are yet to be achieved in healthcare operations, particularly organized delivery systems. Benefits will be achieved through realistic pricing strategies, effective information systems, and efficient facility design, with the ultimate goal of ensuring the health of constituents through aggressive disease management. The major objective of the PPS is to create a price-competitive healthcare environment by enabling purchasers of health care to solicit bids from healthcare providers to provide specific disease category services or total hospital care for specific population groups. Management engineering can be used to do the following:

- Reduce costs of present operations, be it for a department, a disease entity, or a total organized delivery system
- Provide a resource standard as a basis for a cost-accounting system to facilitate effective pricing
- Provide a productivity management system to monitor and control utilization of resources
- Develop care "maps" and disease management protocols

Management engineering can increase the effectiveness of information systems by applying systems design and analysis techniques for analyzing manual systems being replaced by the computer. Such techniques include:

- Measure the existing systems: labor, costs, response times, storage space, and so on
- Identify improvements in the manual system that could be achieved without computerization
- Provide design criteria that ensure that all necessary procedures are provided and all unnecessary procedures are deleted
- Monitor implementation to ensure that replaced functions are eliminated
- Monitor operations to ensure that goals are met

The use of management engineering in the planning of new facilities is directed at ensuring that:

- The space plan reflects the actual amount of space required based on projected workloads and systems
- Workstations and departments are located to minimize travel
- Movement, communication, and information systems satisfy current requirements and have the ability to expand to meet future needs

The application of management engineering to healthcare operations is a necessity for survival.

Cost Containment

The change in reimbursement systems from a cost base to a PPS, the decrease in inpatient occupancy, and the emergence of price competition make cost containment a top priority for all healthcare provider managers. Cost containment implies that (1) total operating costs are reduced; (2) labor costs, the largest cost item, are reduced; (3) costs per unit produced are reduced or at least maintained; or (4) more service is provided for the same cost—all while maintaining acceptable quality.

As defined earlier, management engineering is primarily concerned with containing or reducing operating costs. And, in the author's opinion, the cost of providing management engineering services has to be justified by a reduction in operating costs.

Labor Cost Containment Has the Largest Payoff *

Labor costs are only one part of the cost containment equation. What is important is the output that results from a labor expenditure. The ratio between output and resources expended to obtain a desired output is also called productivity. Therefore, one approach to labor cost containment is to increase productivity. Productivity always implies a given level of quality for any output. Increased quality for the same amount of input (labor) may result in cost containment. Low quality may result in the reprocessing or redoing of the work. Further, cost containment can be achieved only if one takes the broad view or total systems approach to the organized healthcare delivery system under study. One may be able to maximize productivity of one department, but if doing so has adverse effects on other departments, its benefits may be outweighed by the disadvantages to the total delivery system.

Another method of labor cost containment is to replace labor with either personnel with lesser skills or nonlabor expenditures. For example, a practical nurse may replace a registered nurse. This question—can someone at less cost do the same job?—is asked too infrequently. Automated systems (i.e., utensil washers, floor-cleaning machines) and monitoring devices can also reduce labor costs. The computer to date has not yet fulfilled its labor-reduction potential. However, an effective case management information system can reduce length of stays and utilization of ancillary services and supplies. Computerization seems to reduce costs in the accounting/patient billing area, but when looking at the total systems cost (the fixed cost of computer programming, operating, and leasing equipment), it is not clear that there has been cost containment, particularly labor savings. However, outsourcing of information services may stabilize labor costs and reduce capital requirements. Labor costs also have been reduced through other types of expenditures, such as use of disposable products. Many disposable products have not only reduced labor due to the elimination of reprocessing, but also have enabled the use of better healthcare techniques. Again, one must look at the total delivery cost. Disposables increase storage and disposal requirements, and, in some cases, environmental pollution.

---

*The remainder of this chapter is adapted from Bartscht K and Coffey R. Management engineering—a method to improve productivity. *Topics in Health Care Financing.* 1977;3(3):39–62.

A more significant goal in the containment of labor costs is to reduce the demand for service and, in turn, labor. Is it feasible? Yes! Outpatients can be scheduled for more efficient service, pre-admission procedures and outpatient surgery can eliminate certain inpatient care tasks, and proper inventory levels can eliminate handling requests. In fact, rather than a last step, the first step in any cost containment effort should be answering the question: Do we have to do this job at all?

Finally, effective cost containment must have a long-term effect. Two key ingredients—the involvement and commitment of management, and a monitoring system to provide management with continuing, updated reports on productivity and quality—are required to sustain cost savings.

Deterrents to Labor Cost Containment

The cost-based reimbursement system has been a deterrent to labor cost containment. Current and continuing limitations on reimbursement conflict with the continuous demand for new and additional services by patients and physicians. When they are sick, patients feel that care at any cost is not too much, yet upon recovery and receipt of the bill, they may feel that the price is rarely worth the care. The physician, as manager of the care required and delivered, often ignores economic factors in pursuit of this care by misusing inpatient facilities or demanding exotic equipment and services that are provided elsewhere.

In the middle stands the healthcare and organized delivery system executive. In the past, as long as a hospital's cost increases were equal to those of its neighbors, there was no problem and the hospital manager could keep the physicians happy and stay financially viable. However, with PPS managed care and more competition, the executive of an organized health delivery system is feeling the pressure of holding costs on a daily basis. But what can be done?

Direction for Achievement

Clearly, equipment purchases can be delayed, and nonessential outside services dropped—but for how long? Greater numbers of healthcare providers are faced with fixed debt service requirements and other new expenses, such as increasing malpractice insurance premiums. There are three possible directions for containing costs:

1. Increase total revenue without raising rates; do more business with the same resources
2. Decrease supply costs through more effective purchasing
3. Increase labor productivity

The first direction is achieved through decreasing length of stay and increasing the throughput of outpatients: more outpatients treated per hour, extended outpatient hours, and Saturday and Sunday utilization, among other things. As a result, fixed assets (plant and equipment) are maximized, but this direction still requires some labor. The second direction (decreased supply costs) can be achieved through group purchasing and application of value analysis techniques. The key is to ensure that supplies do not result in increased labor costs due to greater processing or handling requirements.

The third direction is through increasing labor productivity. Although much effort has been expended in this direction, the net effect unfortunately has not always been significant, primarily because of the limited applications in restricted areas. For example, a study of the housekeeping department may achieve significant reductions in its labor costs, but these improvements may be small relative to overall staffing. Gray and Steffy, in their book *Hospital Cost Containment Through Productivity Management*,[7] describe a series of cost containment systems that show how to:

- Measure, analyze, and monitor productivity
- Conduct a value analysis
- Organize hospital functions into a top-efficiency operation
- Improve and evaluate worker performance
- Institute a quality control system
- Use space as efficiently as possible
- Share services
- Manage equipment
- Audit all hospital operations
- Schedule patients
- Plan and control budgets
- Determine the benefits of capital investments

Productivity Management

Productivity management provides the techniques that can make the greatest contribution to cost containment. Unfortunately, even with the pressures for cost containment, it is not obvious at this time that such techniques are considered standard management tools by today's healthcare manager, as opposed to marketing, strategic, or planning techniques. The lack of importance placed on productivity management is a major problem. Some healthcare providers have a policy that any expenditure over $1,000 (or $10,000) must be approved by the board. However, no approval is necessary to hire one new employee, who may cost $20,000 to $50,000 per year and may be there for 10 years. This is actually a $200,000 to $500,000 decision. The expenditure for labor must be placed in the proper perspective.

As the American Hospital Association stated in 1973, which is still true today:

> Many hospital administrative personnel have been reluctant to attack the task of managing their employees' productivity. They often are unaware of (1) the approaches and tools available to them in the trade literature, and (2) the basic techniques and steps that provide the needed foundation for effective use of the more sophisticated techniques.[8]

This reluctance was further substantiated in an Arthur Andersen study.[9] Not only are many managers not trained in productivity concepts, but also they perceive their employees as loyal and hardworking. Until recently, employee salaries have been low, and their hours were long. This is no longer the case. In fact, in many areas of the country, the hospital pays the highest wages of any employer. There also are certain human characteristics that contribute to this reluctance to explore productivity management. It is always difficult to suspend or lay off employees, and there is always fear of upsetting the employees. Concerns of union activities are always present. Besides, whenever management is observing, all employees are busy. The real question is: Is this always the case, and what are they busy doing? We have reached a point in hospital productivity management at which we can no longer live with the status quo.

Cost containment achieved through improvement of productivity of ongoing operations should strive for a minimal goal of savings of 5%, an expected goal of 10%, and in many instances, a realizable goal of 15% in any year. This is not a one-time cost or savings, but an annual savings.

The approach for improving productivity has seven steps (**Figure 9.1**).

1. Management orientation
2. Overview studies
3. Productivity reporting
4. Quality control
5. In-depth studies
6. Performance/reward systems
7. Monitoring, review, and change

Management Orientation

First, a philosophical framework must be established, which in turn should establish why productivity improvements are necessary and what benefits are expected. As Figure 9.1 suggests, the management orientation includes at least two levels—the individual department manager or supervisor, and the manager's superior (and top management).

A set of objectives must be stated next. These objectives should be related to expected benefits within a certain period of time. For example:

- Objective 1—All departments will be analyzed as to existing manpower productivity levels within an 18-month period.
- Objective 2—Changes resulting in a $400,000 annual savings should be initiated within 12 months.
- Objective 3—Productivity for all departments will be reported on a monthly basis.

The objectives also must state the responsibility of top and middle management and detail the commitment and support they will contribute. Finally, the costs of increasing productivity must be a consideration, so return on investment should therefore be included in the objectives. One would not want to expend more dollars on a cost containment program than it could return in additional service and in reduced costs.

Top management's major input focuses on four areas:

1. Establishment of objectives
2. Creation of an environment that allows managers to effect change, and the provision of technical assistance where needed
3. Control of individual productivity increases so that changes are not made at the expense of the overall organization or the quality of service
4. Utilization of productivity measures to assess personnel performance evaluation and long-range planning of facilities and labor

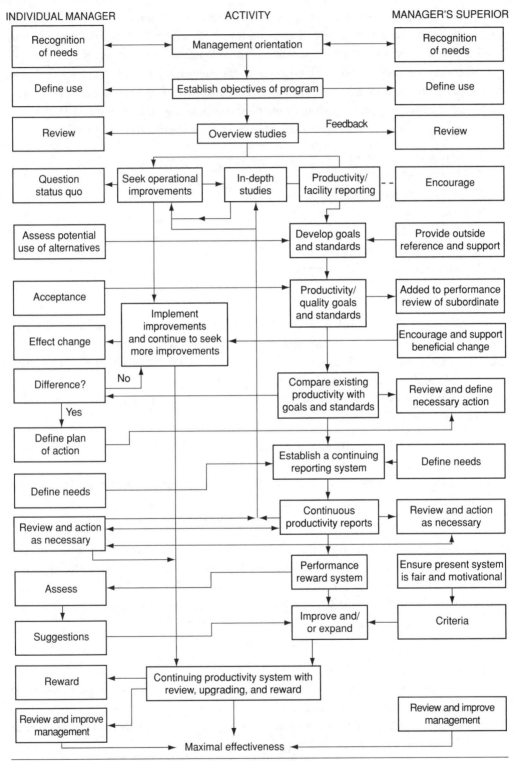

FIGURE 9.1 Productivity Improvement Steps. *Source:* Courtesy of Superior Consultant Company, Inc.'s Chi Systems Practice, Ann Arbor, Michigan.

The achievement and maintenance of cost containment goals only can take place if the department manager or supervisor is committed and involved. They can make improvements work or make sure they do not. The first step in obtaining their involvement and commitment is to explain why cost containment is necessary. The second step is to review goals and secure agreement on (or negotiate) specific goals for each department. The usual problem is that the establishment of a cost containment program in a department implies that department members are not performing as expected. It therefore is important to emphasize that cost containment is a new management direction in which all managers are to be involved. Likewise, it should be emphasized that the agreed-upon cost containment goals will be added to their performance measures as part of their periodic evaluation by top management. The establishment of departmental cost containment goals must be accompanied by provision of adequate staff support to achieve these goals.

Overview Studies

An overview study has two purposes. First, at a relatively low cost, it provides data that enables management to decide whether an in-depth analysis will prove economically justifiable. Second, it enables the engineer or analyst to direct his or her efforts to specific problem areas during an in-depth analysis, thus minimizing the cost of the more detailed study.[10] In addition, the overview provides a profile of labor productivity and the initial baseline for a productivity reporting system.

An overview study should be directed by a person trained in the use of such a technique. If a staff person with these qualifications is not available, consultants from shared management engineering programs[11] or management consulting firms should be retained. This initial study can then be the basis for future work by existing staff (if available).

The overview study should provide three outputs: staffing analysis, quality survey, and systems and management review. The staffing analysis utilizes gross workload data and predetermined productivity standards to determine total staffing needs in comparison with existing staff. The quality survey measures performance relative to quality. This is particularly crucial to ensure that increased productivity does not have a negative impact on quality. Quality surveys are conducted by random sampling, involving observations and work counts. The systems and management review identifies and analyzes problems involving the management structure of the department and the systems, methods, and procedures for performing work. The management structure analysis looks at organization, skills, and work assignments. Systems analysis looks for duplication of effort, unnecessary steps, and imbalance of workstations.

As a result of the overview study, four directions can be pursued.

Productivity and Quality Reporting

A productivity reporting system is one part of a resource utilization management information system that measures labor productivity. The other part is the quality control system, which measures the quality of services. An effective productivity reporting system should generate a continuous—at least monthly—timely report on productivity of each department and a comparison of productivity over time to show trends; for example, this month compared to last month, this month compared to the same month last year, or year-to-date compared to last year-to-date. In addition, this system should provide the following information.

Measurement of Actual Productivity in Person-Hours per Output

Actual productivity can be measured in person-hours per output or output per person-hour; these outputs are specific for each department. See the radiology example in **Table 9.1**. Increased labor productivity may result from:

- A decrease in person-hours invested with no change in output; staffing is reduced, decreasing both direct and indirect salary costs for the hospital
- An increase in output with no change in staff; additional services are provided with increased efficiency, avoiding additional salary costs by not having to hire more staff

Actual Productivity Compared to a Performance Goal

Actual productivity (person-hours per output) can be compared to a performance goal of person-hours per actual output.

The reason for analyzing productivity is to determine if the existing productivity level is acceptable. One of several methods to establish a comparative value must be selected to make this judgment. A comparison of current productivity to historical performance, comparison to other institutions or groups of institutions, guidelines developed by professional societies, and measured (engineered) time standards are used most frequently.

Most comparatives provide meaningful information, which can be translated into improvement objectives. Comparisons with predetermined measured, or engineered, standards appear to be the most meaningful form of evaluation. The standards assumedly represent an objective, unbiased, per-occurrence representation of labor requirements necessary to produce a single unit of output. They are unadulterated by any existing nonproductive labor practices or inefficient work methods.

Measured productivity time standards can be viewed in a number of different ways. Several elemental work tasks must be performed in a department regardless of the workload unit volumes produced. Conversely, other tasks will be performed in direct proportion to the workload unit volume. Consider that the activities of a department manager require one full-time position, and staffing will not vary according to the number of procedures, tests, and so on performed. On the other hand, the number of person-hours necessary to perform procedures will depend upon the number of procedures performed. The position-hours associated with managing the department become a fixed task, and the processing of procedures a variable task.

Fixed tasks can be viewed as components of the cost of doing business. In addition to routine department management supervision, other fixed tasks include preparation of departmental statistics, administrative clerical services, daily activation and quality control of diagnostic devices, routine supplies inventory and replenishment, departmental/hospital meetings, and giving or receiving in-service educational sessions. Similarly, variable work tasks, such as scheduling appointments, prepping patients, and filing new reports, contribute directly to the production of each

Table 9.1 Workload Unit Recording Systems: Productivity Measurement Results for Radiology (Input = Person-Hours)

Method/Component	Person-Hours Invested (Input)	Workload Units Produced (Output)	Person-Hours per Unit
Aggregate:			
Total procedures	930	1,820	0.51
Totals	930	1,820	0.51
Service specific:			
Radiography	600	1,400	0.43
Fluoroscopy	250	400	0.63
Specials	80	20	4.00
Totals	930	1,820	0.51
Procedure specific:			
Radiography			
Chest—PA & lat.	50	250	0.20
Chest—PA	30	180	0.17
⋮	⋮	⋮	⋮
Subtotal for radiography	600	1,400	0.43
Fluoroscopy			
Barium enema	20	20	1.00
Gallbladder	10	20	0.50
⋮	⋮	⋮	⋮
Subtotal for fluoroscopy	250	400	0.63
Specials			
Head angiography	30	10	3.00
⋮	⋮	⋮	⋮
Subtotals for specials	80	20	4.00
Totals	930	1,820	0.51

processed workload unit. The time required to perform each variable task may be either the same or different for each specific procedure.

Engineered productivity time standards frequently are established by developing a fixed component and a variable component. The fixed component represents the labor requirements necessary to perform all fixed work tasks; the variable component represents the additional resources required for each processed workload unit. All departments will have at least one fixed component. The number of variable components will relate to the level of detail reflected in the workload unit recording system. Mathematically, this relationship is expressed as follows:

$$\text{Standard time} = \text{fixed component} +$$
$$(\text{variable standard component workload} \times \text{unit volume})$$

These time standards can be used to determine the required person-hours for processing the observed workload unit volumes over a specified period of time. The predetermined time interval between reporting cycles—the reporting period—typically is defined to coincide with the availability of data concerning inputs or outputs.

In the radiology example, if an aggregate measure of workload (total procedures) is used, one variable component appears in the equation. If the workload unit recording system uses service-specific information (radiography, fluoroscopy, and special procedures), three variable components are required. If the workload unit recording system is procedure specific, the productivity standard equation will include as many variable components as there are specific procedures. The required person-hours for the three alternative workload unit recording systems for a four-week period are illustrated in **Table 9.2**.

To determine how effectively departmental labor resources were utilized during the reporting period, required person-hours determined by using the productivity standards can be compared to the actual person-hours used. This measure of labor utilization—the department's productivity index—is expressed as a percentage of required person-hours divided by actual person-hours.

If 4200 person-hours were utilized, the productivity index for the radiology department example presented in Table 9.2 would be calculated as:

$$\text{Productivity Index} = 3500 \ / \ 4200 \times 100 = 83.3\%$$

At this point, the value of a service- or procedure-specific workload unit recording system becomes apparent. The detailed information produced can be compared to existing staffing patterns for each major facet of departmental operations. Often, such comparisons provide the basis for staff reallocation or schedule adjustments.

The key to the development and utilization of time standards is their acceptance by department managers. Because the measurement of work is, in most instances, a new concept to department managers, gaining this acceptance is not always an easy task. In particular, managers have realistic concerns such as the difference in patients served (age, diagnosis, cooperativeness) and the random demands for services placed on most departments. To overcome these concerns,

Table 9.2 Workload Unit Recording Systems: Total Required Person-Hours for Radiology Procedures (Period = 4 Weeks)

Method/Component	Volume (Procedures)	(Hours/ Procedure)	Required Person-Hours
Aggregate:			
Total procedures	7,640	0.41	3,122.00
Totals			3,500.00*
Service specific:			
Radiography	5,200	0.33	1,716.00
Fluoroscopy	2,378	0.50	1,189.00
Specials	62	3.50	217.00
Total required person-hours			3,500.00*
Procedure specific:			
Radiography			
Chest—PA and lateral	600	0.16	96.00
Chest—PA	520	0.13	67.60
.	.	.	.
.	.	.	.
.	.	.	.
Subtotal for radiography	5,200	0.33	1,716.00
Fluoroscopy			
Barium enema	65	0.83	53.95
Gallbladder	60	0.35	21.00
.	.	.	.
.	.	.	.
.	.	.	.
Subtotal for fluoroscopy	2,378	0.50	1,189.00
Specials			
Head angiography	22	2.60	57.20
.	.	.	.
.	.	.	.
.	.	.	.
Subtotals for specials	62	3.50	217.00
Total required person-hours			3,500.00*

*Totals include a standard time of 378 hours for fixed work tasks over a 4-week period.

it must be recognized that, in reality, all department managers actually are measuring work when they establish labor budgets and work schedules. From there, one proceeds to define major work activities. Time standards are applied to these major work activities. These then are modified to take into account fluctuations in workloads as caused by patients with different degrees of illness, peak and valley demands, delays, and approved time off for staff members.

In some cases, the department managers may not accept the predetermined time standards. Because the first objective is to establish a productivity reporting system, an interim time standard may be established as an initial goal. This "negotiated" time standard would then be used at the initial reporting phase.

It has been the experience of the author, as well as colleagues in the field, that the establishment of a system to report productivity is beneficial in itself. It provides a regular vehicle by which the department manager can review the performance of his or her department. As a result of this report, the department manager may initiate further studies and changes to increase productivity. Most good managers want to do a better job, and the report provides them a way of measuring improvement.

Written Reports to All Management Levels

The productivity report should be shared with all management levels: hospital, divisions within the hospital, departments within each division, and sections within each department. The report should cover the level of detail necessary at each level for effective management control.

Exhibits 9.1 and **9.2** illustrate monthly reports produced under the CHIMIS productivity reporting system for two different levels within the sample organization.

Productivity continuously must be updated because the procedures being performed (the output) change over time, new ones are added, and others are deleted. Second, as more data are developed for each department, more refined time standards can be derived by dividing certain comprehensive procedures into more specific procedures. In addition, negotiated time standards, set as initial goals, should be reviewed and revised as necessary.

Quality Control Program

The myth that increasing productivity reduces the quality of care has limited efforts to increase productivity. Not only is this generally not true, but there also is significant evidence that increased quality can be consistent with increased productivity. Common sense tells us that, if something is done correctly the first time, there is no need to repeat the effort.

The primary objectives of a quality control program are to provide:

- A quantitative measure that indicates the level of quality on a continuing basis
- Positive feedback that allows corrective action to be taken
- Quality assurance upon implementation of new systems, equipment, or workload revisions

Quality

The ultimate measure of the quality of the healthcare system is the health status of the community. Determination of quality of health in an area can be derived from indices of unnecessary disease, unnecessary disability, and unnecessary untimely death.[12] However, the relationships of

Exhibit 9.1   Sample of Hospital Report

CHI SYSTEMS	22:35	REPHOS.L38	PAGE 1
HOSPITAL		******CHIMIS******	
		******HOSPITAL REPORT******	

DIVISION	EARNED MAN-HOURS	PAID MAN-HOURS	% PROD
HOSP ADMINISTRATION	519.000	528.000	98.3
EMPLOYEE SERVICES	14746.417	13528.000	109.0
ALLIED SERVICES	21135.314	21784.000	97.0
FISCAL SERVICES	21410.943	21834.000	98.1
SUPPORTIVE SERVICES	35482.832	32818.000	108.1
NURSING SERVICES	66734.731	68158.000	97.9
DEVELOPMENT	173.000	177.000	97.7
PLANNING	519.000	531.000	97.7
TOTALS	160721.238	159358.000	100.9

---HISTORICAL---   *INDICATES CURRENT MONTH

JAN	FEB	MAR	APR	MAY	JUN	JUL	AUG	SEP	OCT	NOV	DEC
PERCENT PRODUCTIVITY											
90.5	102.7	100.9*	0.0	0.0	0.0	86.2	86.0	91.9	92.0	92.3	85.6

THIS MONTH EARNED FTE   929.0
THIS MONTH PAID FTE   921.1

PAST 12 MONTHS PRODUCTIVITY   91.9

Source: Courtesy of Superior Consultant Company, Inc.'s Chi Systems Practice, Ann Arbor, Michigan.

such measures of quality to the services provided by specific physicians or hospital departments are undefined. Therefore, one should use measures that are more specific to the services being provided by the respective physicians or departments.

A comprehensive definition of quality is difficult to develop because of its many components and the need to determine the relative values of "good" and "bad" qualities. Rather than attempt a synthesized definition of quality, existing definitions and concepts are examined to specify the dimensions of quality relevant to a quality productivity program.

Random House Dictionary defines quality as "character with respect to fineness or grade of excellence."[13] Gavett's definition of quality related to production is that "the quality of a product or service is expressed in terms of a given set of attributes that are required to meet the . . . needs for which the product or service is created."[14]

Many definitions of quality refer to quality control, which can be defined as "the sending of messages which effectively change the behavior of the recipient."[15] A more useful definition of control is "that function of the system which provides direction in conformance to plan, or in

Exhibit 9.2   Sample of Section Report

CHI SYSTEMS   22:34   REPSEC.L38   PAGE 7

HOSPITAL	—	*****CHIMIS *****
DIVISION	—ALLIED SERVICES	*****SECTION REPORT*****
DEPARTMENT	—P.M. & R.	

SECTION   —PHYSICAL THERAPY

WORKLOAD UNIT	VOLUME	M-H/PROC STANDARD	EARNED MAN-HOURS	PAID MAN-HOURS	%PROD
THERAPEUTIC EXERCISE	780	0.601	468.780		
GAIT TRAINING	569	0.694	394.886		
HOT PACKS	340	0.432	146.880		
ULTRASOUND	281	0.555	155.955		
ROOM VISIT	503	0.324	162.972		
TRACTION	128	0.447	57.216		
HUBBARD-UNASSISTED	4	0.863	3.452		
HUBBARD-W/THERAPIST	7	1.202	8.414		
WHIRLPOOL-ALL	76	0.478	36.328		
EXERCISE-OTHERS	267	0.554	147.918		
MASSAGE-ALL	314	0.516	162.024		
DIATHERMY-ALL	119	0.468	55.692		
P.T. LEVELS-ALL	11	0.678	7.458		
OTHER MODALITIES	66	0.615	40.590		
FIXED			221.000		
EPI			0.000		
SECTION TOTALS			2,069.565	1,799.000	115.0

---HISTORICAL---   *INDICATES CURRENT MONTH

JAN	FEB	MAR	APR	MAY	JUN	JUL	AUG	SEP	OCT	NOV	DEC
PERCENT PRODUCTIVITY											
95.5	116.8	115.0*	0.0	0.0	0.0	95.6	95.5	106.1	153.3	112.8	94.8

THIS MONTH EARNED FTE   12.0

THIS MONTH PAID FTE   10.4

PAST 12 MONTHS PRODUCTIVITY 108.7

Source: Courtesy of Superior Consultants Company, Inc.'s Chi Systems Practice, Ann Arbor, Michigan.

other words, the maintenance of variations from system objectives within allowable limits."[16] Components of a control system include:

- A monitored characteristic or operational variable
- A monitoring device or method
- A standard of performance for each monitored characteristic

- A comparison of actual to predetermined standard performance
- An activator that can effect change

In a quality control system, therefore, the rating of operational variables is done by comparison to standards or, at least, predetermined values of quality. The purpose of a quality control system is to give some assurance that the standards of services are maintained.

Quality control systems exist, and can be developed, for both medical care provided by physicians and services provided by hospital departments. Some departments, such as nuclear medicine and tissue pathology, have strong medical components. Quality of medical care is monitored by the hospital's utilization review and medical audit programs. Medical record abstracting services provide information for use by the medical review committees of the hospital.

Quality of services can be measured from three perspectives: input, process, and output. A comprehensive system measures quality from all three perspectives, with an emphasis on output measures.

Input measurement involves the quality of inputs (labor, facilities, equipment, and supplies) used to provide departmental services. Input quality measurements include staff educational requirements, types of linen purchased, type of lighting installed in the operating room, and the physical characteristics of the building.

Process measurement involves the quality of the organization and the methods it uses to provide services. Assessment of process answers the question: Is the process proper or performed correctly? Methods are compared with standard procedures, and when standards do not exist or are not applicable, relative values are determined. Examples of process quality measurements include written procedures for the care of isolation patients, identification procedures for patients going to surgery, staffing schedules, sterile technique maintained in the operating room, and appropriate tagging of contaminated linen.

Output measurement involves the quality of the services provided by a department. Examples include timely delivery of drugs by the pharmacy, cleanliness of a patient's room after discharge cleaning, timely and courteous answering of telephones, and achievement of nursing care objectives.

A distinction between absolute and relative measures of quality should be made. An absolute quality measure requires no interpretation, whereas relative quality measures require interpretation and rating. The question "Does the surgical light work?" is an absolute quality measure; the light either works or doesn't work. However, the question "Is the ambient room temperature sufficient?" is relative to the activity being done and the judgment of the observer.

Measurement Variables and Standards

Measurement variables are activities on which judgments or decisions can be based. Both qualitative and quantitative measurement variables can be used, but quantitative variables are less subjective. Examples of measurement variables are sterility of instrument trays, accuracy of accounting records, cleanliness of patient rooms, and person-minutes per pack.

Standards are specific values of measurement variables. Each quality and productivity measurement variable can have specific levels or standards established as acceptable or unacceptable. Examples of standards are 95% acceptably cleaned rooms or five instrument trays packed per hour.

Measurements to Develop Standards

Continuous measurement of quality often is prohibitively expensive. Therefore, quality and productivity are usually measured by sampling the measurement variable.[17] Problems to be avoided in sampling include concentrating on only one of the many quality and productivity variables, sampling only problem situations, and taking nonrepresentative samples. Three methods of avoiding these problems are to randomize the samples, take a large enough sample to be representative, and include all relevant variables in the sample.

In measuring quality and productivity, the concepts of reliability, validity, and bias must be considered. Reliability refers to the ability of two or more persons to make similar judgments on the measurement variables or for the data to be judged similarly on multiple occasions. Validity refers to the ability of the observation to measure what it is supposed to measure. Bias occurs when one judge or observer of the data systematically rates the variable differently than others.

In addition, quality and productivity measurement needs to be applicable to repetitive measurement over time, as opposed to a one-time evaluation. Measurements should also be responsive to changes in input or process during the sample interval (commonly one month). The quality question for a maintenance department "Does the department have a preventive maintenance program?" would always be answered "yes" if such a program existed, regardless of the performance of the program. The question "Has a minimum acceptable number of items been preventively maintained during the sampling period?" would measure departmental performance during the period.

Interaction among Departments

In the development of measures of quality and productivity for the services provided by the various functional units or departments within the hospital, the point is eventually reached where the performance of a given element of service is dependent upon some other element previously performed by another department or functional unit. Before the laboratory can be expected to run a battery of tests on a sample of blood, it must first receive a requisition for this service from nursing or from a physician. Most of the time, responsibilities for required prior services can be assigned to either of the two units directly involved. However, there are some instances in which a third party or element enters the picture. These are the "network" systems. Consider the situation in which an X-ray examination is requested for an inpatient. All forms have been properly processed. Before the examination can occur, however, the patient must be transported from his or her bed to the X-ray department, a function that belongs neither to nursing, the X-ray department, nor the physician. The network system is patient transportation, which is likely handled by a patient transport or messenger service, and its own quality of performance can be measured as an individual functioning unit. Other network systems include communications (verbal and physical, hard copy, electronic, or recorded), material supply (procurement, reprocessing, storage, distribution), education, and equipment and facility maintenance. The responsibility for the operation of each network system can, in fact, be assigned to some functioning unit or individual, and the performance of that responsibility can be measured.

When interaction among departments does not involve a third party, the concern becomes the accurate definition of the department's interface with another department and the determination of where one department's responsibility ends and that of the other begins. The quality and productivity measurement variables must be defined consistently with the interface definition so that monitoring and reporting will be appropriate.

Relationship of Quality and Productivity

The relationship of quality and productivity is neither easily determined nor consistent; it varies with the levels of quality and productivity and the procedures used by the hospital.

Beginning with the current quality level and current productivity, both usually can be increased to some point. At that point, they cannot be simultaneously increased, but other alternatives are (1) increasing quality at the same productivity level, (2) increasing productivity at the same quality level, (3) increasing productivity while decreasing quality, and (4) decreasing both quality and productivity. The difficulty is knowing at what quality and productivity levels the hospital is currently functioning and monitoring where it is on future dates.

Providing this information is a major reason for a quality–productivity program that simultaneously measures and integrates quality and productivity. Then, as changes in either level are planned, the impact on the other can be determined.

The following examples demonstrate increases in both productivity (decreasing cost) and quality. Most of these involve several departments, emphasizing the importance of interdepartmental effects on quality and productivity.

Pharmacy Ordering

In some hospitals, physicians write pharmacy orders on the patients' charts. These orders then are transcribed by a ward clerk, checked by the head nurse, and sent to the pharmacy to be filled. Changing the system so that a computerized copy of the physician's order is sent directly to the pharmacy decreases errors of interpretation of the physician's order, thereby increasing quality, and reduces staff time needed to transcribe and verify the physician's order, which can increase productivity or decrease cost.

Early Admission Testing

Traditionally, after hospitals have admitted patients to their rooms, orders for admission tests are written by the physicians, and then the patient receives the admission tests. Earlier admission testing both reduces cost and improves quality. Earlier testing is done one of two ways: on the day of admission before the patient reaches his or her bed (early testing—ET) or before the day of admission (preadmission testing—PAT). ET and PAT often improve quality because physicians receive test results earlier, reducing the probability of surgery or other action being taken before test results are available. Costs are also decreased by reducing the length of stay of patients[18,19] and reducing the amount of time needed to escort patients from patient floors to testing areas.

Paging System

Many institutions take advantage of paging systems for their communication needs. Quality is improved by reducing response time of services required by patients. Physicians, nurses, and others can be reached in emergencies or other situations. Productivity is improved by reducing walking time and delays.

Coordinated Admission and Surgery Scheduling

Close coordination of admission scheduling and surgery scheduling is very important for surgery patients. This can be done several different ways, but the advantages are similar. Quality is improved when fewer schedule changes and cancellations result in less patient and physician disruption. Productivity is improved by reducing the personnel time needed to schedule and reschedule both admissions and surgery. The probability of unused surgical time due to last-minute cancellations is also reduced. The shift to outpatient surgical sites has further influenced productivity.

In-Depth Studies

The in-depth study is a detailed study of a function or department directed at either the entire operation or a specific problem identified by the overview study or the productivity–quality reporting system. An in-depth study is warranted in the case of significant differences between existing and required staffing levels; significant quality control problems creating safety, health, or public relations problems; or ineffective interaction with other departments and functions that creates problems for those other departments.

In-depth studies are far more expensive than the overview study, often costing between 10 and 15 times more. Therefore, the expected benefits must at least exceed this amount by a minimum of two or three times. One must be cautioned that some difference in staffing levels could be due to the scope of work and activities in the department, not improper staffing. The in-depth study accounts for these activities and establishes time standards for the work required to perform them.

The in-depth study usually is directed at a specific problem, such as organization, scheduling, employees, patients, information flow and handling, methods improvement, patient/materials movement, and layout and equipment. Many references are available on identification of problems and problem-solving approaches.[20,21] A few comments on each of these problems follow.

Organization

Organization studies are directed at achieving the correct balance between span of control and delegation of responsibility with related authority. Too large a span of control may result in poor supervision and, in turn, low productivity. Determining the appropriate number of persons to be supervised by each supervisor is further complicated by their location of work. In a hospital, staff members may work on different floors and in different departments, for example, housekeeping personnel. Conversely, too small a span of control may result in additional levels of hierarchy. Such levels may be established to provide opportunities for promotions within departments. In a nursing department, there may be several levels of supervision before one finds a nurse totally committed to patient care; these levels may include a nursing director, associate nursing director, assistant nursing director, nursing supervisor, head nurse, assistant head nurse, team leader, or nurse. Are they all necessary?

Scheduling

The installation of effective scheduling systems can yield a big payoff in terms of achieving cost containment and improvement in productivity. This very broad area involves patients, employees, and available facilities. Facilities is a limiting factor (that is, not enough rooms available), although it is an artificial one in many ways, if one thinks of 24-hour-a-day, 7-day-a-week operations.

Scheduling of patients may be difficult because of the random arrival of certain types of patients. Statistically, however, arrivals do follow certain patterns, and upon further analysis, one finds that a majority of inpatients and outpatients can be scheduled. The biggest fault in scheduling is the peak load syndrome. In too many cases, patients are scheduled "en masse" for a block of time. Examples are 8:00 A.M. surgery, admissions from 1:00 P.M. to 3:00 P.M., and the noon meal from 11:00 A.M. to 12:00 P.M. When one realizes that the processing of 10 patients in 1 hour takes twice as many personnel as 5 patients per hour for 2 hours, the peak load scheduling problem should be obvious. The usual case is that the number of required employees is determined by the peak load, with the rest of their 8 hours being used with fill-in operations. Usually, reduction of the peak load requirements—spreading out the patient schedule—results in reduction of staff.

A larger inefficiency in scheduling employees is in the 7-day operations (nursing, dietary, housekeeping) that involve the majority of employees. Because most employees work only 5 days, coverage is required for the other 2. The actual requirement for a 7-day position is 1.4 full-time equivalents (FTEs). It is not uncommon to see scheduling of 3 employees for every 2 positions, which results in an excess of 0.2 FTEs for every 3.0 FTEs. In a 300-bed hospital with 450 nursing, 90 housekeeping, and 75 dietary personnel, this coverage represents more than 40 extra personnel.

Scheduling work for hospital personnel is made difficult by the lack of repetition of tasks during an 8-hour shift. The key to effective scheduling of tasks is to ensure that personnel understand all tasks that must be performed, why they are necessary, when they must be done (not necessarily at which time, but by what time they must be completed), and what the priorities are. Peak load requirements must be smoothed as much as possible, and traditional hours (that is, 7:00 A.M. to 3:30 P.M., 8:00 A.M. to 5:00 P.M.) must be examined to determine whether they are the times appropriate to the necessary tasks. In past studies, the author has found that a midnight nursing shift (11:00 P.M. to 7:30 A.M.) primarily was staffed to provide personnel for the early morning activities for patients (6:00 A.M. to 7:30 A.M.).[22] A change in the daily shift hours resulted in reducing the midnight shift requirements by almost 50%. Scheduling studies and analyses really are just the application of common sense. Why must a task be performed, for whom, by what skill, by what time?

Information Flow

Information technology systems have profoundly influenced hospital information storage, retrieval, and flow. Information flow is not only concerned with how effectively information flows from one organization level to another and from department to department, but also, just as importantly, what information does not flow.

Management cannot function without a proper flow of information, both historical reporting and projecting for the future. Departments cannot effectively interact with and serve other departments without the timely receipt of adequate information indicating the others' needs. Some studies have suggested that up to 25% of all activities in a hospital involve information handling. Therefore, a reduction in this activity must lead to improved productivity. The major problem in achieving real cost containment is that most of the information handling effort is spread over all employees. Therefore, an improvement in information handling may decrease an employee's workload by 30 minutes, but he or she still has 7.5 hours of work to do. To realize this 30-minute savings may require extensive reorganization of tasks.

Several improvements in information flow and handling result in cost containment benefits. Improvement in record keeping in many hospitals has resulted in increased revenue and greater knowledge of resources expended. Planning ahead can enable services and supplies to be requested on a scheduled "batched" basis, eliminating "stat" requests and processing of single requests. However, a deterrent to achieving cost containment through the substitution of automated information processing equipment may be the increased cost of hardware and skilled computer programming staff.

Case management is yet another organizational development that utilizes information systems. With integrated health delivery systems, case management must coordinate an episode of illness in multiple settings with varied resource use. Both case management and disease management make economic and organizational sense.

Disease management spans the entire continuum of care from prevention to diagnosis and treatment including follow-up and ongoing maintenance. Informational flow allows both management techniques greater efficiency.

Methods Improvement

Methods improvement is the study of how work is performed, and its objective is to reduce human motion (walking, handling, reaching). In the global sense, everything mentioned in this section is methods improvement. There always is a better way to perform a task, and there is never a "best" way, only a "least worst" way. Improvement is always possible.

Patients and Materials Movement

Patients and materials movement studies apply methods improvement and information handling analysis. This is the key to effective interaction among departments. Too often one hears from a department manager that department members are doing the best they can but that they never have the patients or materials on time. It is rare to find a hospital staff that does not complain about its messenger service or its patient escort system; they are easy scapegoats for all problems. The important step in this analysis is the recognition that movement problems cannot be solved by individual departments because they involve all those departments that must interact with each other. It is difficult to project the potential cost savings from an effective patient and material movement system because there are usually new costs associated with the system. System benefits come from smoothing the workload in the individual departments.

A related activity is material management studies: the analysis of the purchase, storage, handling, movement, and use of supplies and other purchased materials. Greater benefits are being derived from these studies because of both the increased use of such items and the inflationary price spiral. Labor considerations become important when one analyzes handling and movement requirements.

Layout and Equipment

Layout and equipment studies should be geared toward the reduction of walking distances and total labor input. For existing operations, layout of equipment and workstations is usually limited by the space within existing walls and the cost of moving permanent fixtures. The management engineer usually is frustrated by this analysis because many mistakes could have been avoided by more effective facility planning. It is rare that significant labor savings can be achieved through layout changes. The major benefit is usually a more effective use of space that results in the availability of more space, which in most hospitals is a real benefit. One must recognize that this benefit is still limited by total existing space.

Labor savings are being achieved through automation, such as in the dietary department (automated dishwashing and tray preparation) and in housekeeping (floor washers). The clinical laboratory also benefits from highly automated processing of procedures, as does the radiology department. A major question is whether the labor replacement results in real cost reduction. In the clinical laboratory, if one is seeing an increased volume and number of procedures, is it clear that productivity is increasing? Is this increase proportionate to the capital investment in equipment? Even more serious is the question that medical professionals are asking: Is this increase in laboratory procedures really necessary?

When an analysis of the cost benefits of an equipment investment is made, the objectives of using the new equipment must be clearly understood. For example, is the objective of the investment to increase service, reduce labor, or both? If the objective is labor reduction, a labor savings must be realized; saving one hour per day for each of eight persons is not a cost reduction unless work can be reassigned to achieve a reduction in one staff position. Another weakness in equipment studies lies in the basis for comparison. Most comparisons are with the existing operations. Despite the many reports that have justified a large investment in automated material handling systems, one is hard pressed to justify such systems when looking at how the existing system can be improved without (or with very little) capital investment. In other words, justification for equipment should be made based on comparison with the most effective manual system.

Implementation of Productivity and Quality Control Programs

The development of recommendations and new systems is academic if it is not followed by implementation.

A variety of quality and productivity systems have been developed over the last 20 years and are in use today in various institutions. Key problems encountered with the implementation and use of these productivity and quality control programs have been:

- Complexity and subsequent difficulty in implementation that have resulted in only partial use

- Reports produced that are neither used at all nor integrated into the management process or review of managers' performance
- Systems that have not been comprehensive or specific enough, resulting in the common and easy practice of blaming lack of productivity or quality on another department
- Lack of attention paid to interactive effects among departments

The process of implementation requires that the responsible operating manager fully understand and concur with it. The manager must understand the basis for the recommendations, how the new systems and procedures are to work, and what the expected benefits are. Many times, all of the recommendations may not be acceptable to the manager. This situation may result in partial implementation, with further development by the analyst and the manager of the remaining recommendations.

The next step in implementation is to establish with the manager a timetable of activities and expected results. This should then be followed by an orientation of all employees involved in any changes. They in turn must be informed of the desired goals and the timetable of the implementation. If a change in procedures, methods, or use of equipment is proposed, instructions must be formalized and training must take place. If new schedules are developed, then assignment of tasks must be developed to be consistent with new schedules.

The actual change to new schedules and procedures necessitates close monitoring and continuous support in the form of directions and encouragement. As the new recommendations become more and more routine, this monitoring and support can be decreased. Included in the implementation plan must be a periodic review, such as monthly, to ensure that everything is going as expected.

In implementing changes, people are being asked to change their routine way of doing things. This is never easy!

Performance Reward Systems

Underlying the entire process of managing productivity gains is the realization that some reward should ultimately result from the improved performance. The nature and extent of the reward mechanism are certainly dependent upon the level of employee considered. The range, however, should encompass cost-reduction cash bonuses, incentives, perquisites, improved reimbursement formulas with third-party payers, alternative uses of funds, and compensatory time off. In no case can it be expected or warranted that improved results will be obtained without some form of recognition of an individual's contribution to these results.

Monitoring, Review, and Change

Cost containment for ongoing operations must be a continuous activity. Productivity and quality control reporting systems provide regular feedback that must be monitored on an exception basis; that is, to detect when productivity and quality deviate from an expected range, including both high and low deviations. When productivity or quality is below performance expectations, it should be investigated. Above-expected performance, which should be examined as well, may be due to the use of new procedures, services, or equipment. This would then require updating the productivity and quality control program.

This continuous reporting system has several by-products. Evaluation of new equipment purchases may be based on their effect on productivity. Personnel budgets can be developed based on existing utilization of personnel. The justification for new positions should have a very reliable basis. Performance objectives for management can target increased productivity- or quality-level goals that can be quantified. Performance reward systems also must be reviewed and updated. When a hospital has gone through these cost containment steps, it should be able to compare itself favorably with any well-managed business.

Management Engineering for Future Operations

Management engineering should be as useful in long-range planning as it is in ongoing operations. Many planning decisions have major effects on the cost of operating any facility. Initial decisions establishing demand projections are used to establish staffing budgets. Facility layout and design affect movement distances, and equipment decisions influence labor utilization.

The first step in long-range planning is to determine who the institution is serving with what services. Next, projected changes in service areas and services to be provided are made. Management engineering can provide mathematical forecasting models. Too often the effects of these changes are assumed without question. For example, if the projected service area is doubling in size, the planner assumes that a proportionate change will take place in the institution. Likewise, the planner assumes that all new technology must be provided by the institution. It is rare to have the planner say, "Wait a minute, we can't be all things to all people!" This happens only after some sort of financial study is performed and infeasibility is indicated, which occurs usually after large amounts of time, dollars, and effort have already been expended.

Early in the planning stages, the resource implications of programmatic decisions must be assessed. The two major resources of a hospital are facilities and labor. The early question to be answered is: Who is going to pay for the new service? A part of any early long-range planning efforts must be a preliminary financial feasibility or debt load study to determine how much money is required. Another realistic concern is the availability of sophisticated skills to operate new services.

The technology of the management engineer must be utilized in the planning effort. Labor forecasting, itself a skill, should not be based on what is now done, but on what should be done and what can be done if the constraints of existing sites, buildings, and equipment are removed.

The projected volume of service workload will dictate the amount of space required. There is a direct relationship between workload, labor, and space. Most space programmers now determine space based on workstations, the major centers of activity within a department. These workstations either are a function of labor or dictate labor. Inaccurate or nonprecise projections of workload may have a negative effect on the utilization of manpower.

Facility design can affect labor utilization in at least two ways. Layouts of departments and workstations would be based on the function that is to be performed and should incorporate ways in which labor utilization can be reduced, such as reductions of walking distances, elimination of reaching at workstations, or provision of sufficient and easily accessible storage. It is rare that the management engineer and users are brought into the facility design process.

The other effect on labor utilization is lack of sufficient facilities. Seldom does a health facilities planner consider life cycle costs, the total costs of acquiring and operating a facility over the life of the facility. Ongoing operating costs and initial capital costs are equated utilizing present value or present worth techniques.[23] Too often, the capital budget is exceeded and must be reduced, resulting in smaller spaces, less elevators, and less automation, all of which increase labor requirements. Because the operating costs of any health institution exceed the initial capital costs in 2 to 4 years, they should be the deciding factor in the establishment of the initial capital budget.

Most Certificate of Need regulations and investment bankers require financial feasibility studies and labor budgets. These studies establish a base for developing a productivity reporting system and illustrate the relationship between operating costs and capital investment costs. The author recently has been involved in two building programs ($20 million-plus and $60 million-plus) in which projected labor savings due to increased productivity provided the basis for pursuing the project. In one case, a one-year cost containment program reduced the payroll in excess of $4 million. The effect on the profit and loss and balance sheets was sufficient to handle the additional debt financing required for the project. In the second case, projected labor savings due to more efficient facility organization, layout, and equipment was accepted by planning authorities for the issuance of a Certificate of Need.

New facilities can be designed, planned, and operated in many ways to increase productivity and achieve cost containment goals. One such way is to eliminate a centralized nursing station in nursing unit design. The "no-nursing station" concept decentralizes many nursing duties, transfers non-nursing administrative duties to non-nursing personnel, provides sophisticated communication and message handling systems, and enables storage of all supplies in the patient room. A study in one hospital, which was subsequently confirmed in several others, showed that although the number of non-nursing personnel increased, the same quality of patient care had been provided with a 14% reduction in total labor.[24]

Management Engineering in the Organized Delivery System

The tools of the management engineer are applicable to a department or a multiunit organized healthcare delivery system. The major differences are in one's perspective. The major need for an organized delivery system is to be price competitive in a highly competitive healthcare delivery environment. Price competitive implies that the organized delivery system can satisfy all the healthcare needs of its customers (constituents, covered lives) at a price that is equal to (with service differentiation) or less than a competitor. The major elements are keeping your customers healthy, identifying and containing costs, using pricing strategies that differentiate both customer needs and services provided, and monitoring and reporting on the quality/service levels of its customers.

Keeping Your Customers Healthy

Disease management is the current term used to produce "healthy" customers. The development of a disease management program for any "at-risk" population is the basic application of management engineering tools:

- Measure existing system (how large is the population group, what are the outcome measures)

- Identify improvements (decreased mortality, reduced hospitalization)
- Provide design criteria (monitoring behavioral changes, therapeutic interventions)
- Monitor implementation (compliance of constituents to plan)
- Monitor output (goal achievement)

Identifying and Containing Costs

Most, if not all, organized delivery systems result from the consolidation of healthcare providers and in some cases payers. This consolidation, with the decrease in inpatient utilization of inpatient healthcare services, has resulted in significant excess capacity. Many authors have suggested that consolidation of healthcare providers has not resulted in decreased healthcare delivery costs. Some even imply increased costs. The author's perspective is that in most cases, this is true. However, this is not because the opportunity for reduced costs does not exist, but because the management engineering tools are not applied.

The key word in consolidation is "resize." Resize to recognize the change in market demand (decreased inpatient, increased outpatient) and the duplication of services, be it diagnostic and treatment or administrative.

This resizing can be facilitated by management by:

- Identifying the market demands
- Allocating these to locations (both current and new)
- Translating these workloads into manpower and space requirements
- Resizing the existing facilities to accommodate the projections and/or sizing new locations
- Establishing a resized management organization to implement and manage the resizing
- Identifying the cost of the resized delivery system
- Establishing management controls to contain the resized costs

Pricing Strategies

The resizing provides the first step in developing pricing strategies. The potential that costs are too high to be competitive still exists. The resizing step identifies costs of all programs. The next step will require the reduction, elimination, or outsourcing of certain services. The management engineer's analysis provides the basis for these decisions. The analysis also should provide a basis for "loss leader" pricing.

Quality and Service

The final application is to engineer a monitoring and reporting system that can be utilized to demonstrate to the customers/payers how the organized delivery system works. This requires a systemwide quality and productivity reporting system.

References

1. Salvendy G. *Handbook of Industrial Engineering*. New York, NY: John Wiley & Sons, Inc; 1982.
2. Ibid.

3. Ibid.
4. Smalley HE, Freeman JR. *Hospital Management Engineering: A Guide to the Improvement of Hospital Management Systems.* Englewood Cliffs, NJ: Prentice-Hall; 1982.
5. Bartscht KG, et al. 1968. *Hospital Staffing Methodology Manuals.* Ann Arbor, MI: Community Systems Foundation; 1968.
6. Berg NH. Medical center applies financial strategies to renovation project. *Hospitals.* February 1970;53.
7. Gray, SP, Steffy W. *Hospital Cost Containment Through Productivity Management.* New York, NY: Van Nostrand Reinhold Co; 1983.
8. American Hospital Association. *Management of Hospital Employee Productivity: An Introductory Handbook.* Chicago, IL: American Hospital Association; 1973:1.
9. Arthur Andersen & Co, American College of Hospital Administrators. *Health Care in the 1990s: Trends and Strategies.* Alexandria, VA: ACHA; 1984.
10. Bartscht KG. Productivity management: integral element in the management process. *Health Care Systems.* 1976;15(3).
11. American Hospital Association. *Management Engineering for Hospitals.* Chicago, IL: American Hospital Association; 1970:13.
12. Rutstein DD. *Blueprint for Medical Care.* Cambridge, MA: MIT Press; 1974.
13. Urdang L, ed. *Random House Dictionary of the English Language, College Edition.* New York, NY: Random House; 1968:1080.
14. Gavett WJ. *Production and Operations Management.* New York, NY: Harcourt, Brace & World, Inc., 1968.
15. Weiner H. *The Human Use of Human Beings.* Boston, MA: Houghton Mifflin Co; 1950.
16. Johnson RA, Kast FE, Rosenzweig JE. *Theory and Management of Systems.* New York, NY: McGraw-Hill; 1963.
17. Chi Systems, Inc. *A Proposal to Develop and Implement an Innovative Quality-Productivity Management Program to Blue Cross of Greater Philadelphia, Pennsylvania for Graduate Hospital of The University of Pennsylvania, Philadelphia, Pennsylvania.* Ann Arbor, MI: Chi Systems, Inc. 11.
18. Coffey RJ. *Preadmission Testing of Hospitalized Patients and Its Relationship to Length of Stay* [dissertation]. University of Michigan; 1975.
19. Warner DM. *Preliminary Analysis of Benefits of Preadmission Tested (PAT) Patients* [unpublished paper]. University of Michigan.
20. Grant EL, Ireson GW. *Principles of Engineering Economy.* 5th ed. New York, NY: The Ronald Press Co; 1970.
21. Comptroller General of the United States. *Study of Health Facilities Construction Cost, Report to Congress.* Washington, DC: US Government Printing Office; 1972.
22. Bartscht KG. September 1963. *An Analytic Approach to Nursing Scheduling.* Hospital Topics.
23. Rutstein DD. *Blueprint for Medical Care.* Cambridge, MA: MIT Press; 1974.
24. Comptroller General of the United States. *Study of Health Facilities Construction Cost, Report to Congress.* Washington, DC: US Government Printing Office; 1972.

Biographical Information

Karl Bartscht, MSE, FAAHC, has planned, designed, and managed health systems since 1961. He was the CEO of The Chi Group, Inc., and its affiliated companies: Chi Systems, Inc., Michigan Health Systems, and International Health Care Management, Inc.

Mr. Bartscht has directed the development of long-range strategic plans and implementation strategies for numerous healthcare institutions. His expertise includes strategies for minimizing institutional life cycle costs through evaluation of the trade-offs between capital investment and reduced operating costs.

Consulting assistance has been provided by Mr. Bartscht for some of the nation's largest healthcare organizations, as well as for the US and Canadian governments. In addition, Mr. Bartscht has been extremely active in research and development efforts, including the development of computerized financial planning models; the design of planning/marketing databases; development, design, construction, and operation of a prototype nursing station; design of burn care units; design of patient scheduling systems; development of hospital staffing methodologies; and development of methodologies for planning and evaluating departmental space requirements.

Mr. Bartscht is publisher of two monthly professional journals: *Health Care Strategic Management*, which deals with the full range of strategic planning issues facing today's healthcare organizations, and *Hospital Materials Management*, a journal of healthcare materials management.

Ambulatory Care

Kevin W. Barr and Charles L. Breindel

Prompted by the managed care reimbursement incentives of the 1980s, and facilitated by continued advances in medical technology, surgery, and anesthesia throughout thereafter, the delivery of health care continues to shift from the traditional hospital-based platform to ambulatory and nonhospital-based settings. The traditional hospital has experienced an erosion of its share of the ambulatory care market as physician, independent, corporate, and payer-sponsored facilities entered the marketplace in the 1990s in search of revenue diversification and/or cost management benefits. During the mid-1990s to current times, the migration from inpatient-based care to ambulatory care has been further fueled by increasing pressure from managed care organizations, national corporations, local businesses, and the federal government to curb the unbridled growth of healthcare expenditures. During the 2000s, new microsurgical technology and other technologies have helped to streamline hospital efficiency for ambulatory services. The general downturn of the economy beginning in 2007 has affected the number of patient visits and staff, and many infrastructure building projects have slowed or been placed on hold indefinitely.

Simply defined, ambulatory care includes those diagnostic and therapeutic procedures and treatments provided to patients in a setting that does not require an extended overnight stay or overnight recovery in a hospital. Ambulatory care service settings include medical groups and group practice plans, home health programs, community health clinics, industrial clinics, ambulatory surgery centers, outpatient diagnostic centers, urgent care facilities, oncology centers, rehabilitation centers, and hospital-based ambulatory care facilities. Most HMOs, managed care organizations, and payers routinely define outpatient or ambulatory care as any treatment episode that does not exceed 24 hours in length, regardless of whether the protocol includes an overnight stay in an inpatient or recovery care bed.

The most common hospital-based and nonhospital-based ambulatory care services include:

- Urgent care or emergency care
- Outpatient diagnostics (including diagnostic radiology, ultrasound, CT, mammography, electrocardiograms, endoscopy/colonoscopy/arthroscopy, and MRI)
- Home care
- Outpatient surgery
- Physician care
- Outpatient radiation therapy treatment
- Outpatient infusion therapy

Many of these services fall into the category of high-volume procedures that industry experts believe are appropriate and will continue to be performed predominantly outside the traditional hospital facility setting. These services represent the core of most hospital-based outpatient revenues today. They also represent the core of services provided by organized delivery systems and the growing number of nonhospital competitors. These competitors include a variety of niche service players organized as proprietary and publicly held corporations, and single and multispecialty physician entities.

The range of ambulatory care services and providers in today's healthcare marketplace is large; entire texts have been dedicated to this topic. Accordingly, this chapter focuses on that portion of the service spectrum most closely aligned with traditional organized delivery systems and emerging freestanding ambulatory care services. This includes those outpatient treatments and/or procedures that do not require an overnight stay or recovery in an inpatient facility, as well as care provided by organized delivery systems and nonhospital-sponsored facilities. The chapter also includes a discussion on home care and the routine cognitive and diagnostic ambulatory care services provided by physicians in a traditional medical office setting.

Ambulatory Care Services: Past and Present

Providers in the 1980s and 1990s

The provision of ambulatory care services evolved dramatically during the 1980s and mid-to-late 1990s. Traditionally, the vast majority of outpatient care (excluding cognitive and basic diagnostic care provided in physicians' offices) has been provided in hospital-based facilities and, in most cases, on the campuses of such hospitals. However, during the 1980s and 1990s, the healthcare industry experienced explosive growth in the type and ownership of facilities in which ambulatory care was offered, blurring the definitions of what historically has been defined as hospital-based outpatient care and other ambulatory care services (**Exhibit 10.1**).

Until the late 1980s, competition for ambulatory care services was limited to a few traditional healthcare providers, including hospitals, independent physician groups, and other community health providers. Hospitals, once the dominant players in the outpatient market, now face aggressive competitors with significant capital resources, including organized delivery systems, IPOs, and private venture capital funding. In some markets, the traditional hospital represents the

Exhibit 10.1   Ambulatory Care Service Settings

Past	Present
• Hospital outpatient departments	• Radiation therapy centers
• Physician offices	• Dialysis centers
• Home health agencies	• Diagnostic imaging centers
• Outpatient surgery centers	• Mobile imaging centers
• Hospital emergency rooms	• Occupational health clinics
	• Rehabilitation centers
	• Freestanding ambulatory surgery centers
	• Urgent care centers
	• Women's imaging centers
	• Wound care centers
	• Sleep study labs
	• Infusion/chemotherapy centers
	• CT/whole-body screening clinics
	• Endoscopy centers

minority player. The competition for ambulatory care has evolved to include a range of traditional and nontraditional providers and owners, including corporate employers, managed care organizations (e.g., health maintenance organizations [HMOs] and other insurers), corporate physician organization chains, and national and regional specialty niche corporations (see **Exhibit 10.2**). Such competition has largely occurred in areas of abundance where financial access to care, a population base, and a supply of clinical subspecialists facilitate provider entrance. Geographically, these areas of abundance have translated into urban–suburban markets populated by employer-insured residents, Medicare recipients, and affluent self-pay populations. Conversely, in other areas of limited abundance (e.g., rural and inner-city markets) and for certain populations (e.g., the poor, uninsured, and elderly), access to ambulatory care and breadth of provider types are still limited, and in many markets, particularly urban ones, access

Exhibit 10.2   Ambulatory Care Providers/Owners

Past	Present
• Hospitals (community based and proprietary)	• Corporate employers
• Independent physician practitioners	• Insurance companies/managed care companies
• Community health providers/agencies	• Hospitals/hospital chains
• Home health agencies	• Independent physician practitioners
	• Independent corporate chains
	• Community health providers/agencies
	• Home health companies
	• National/regional specialty niche firms

may have degraded. Hospitals and organized delivery systems, once the dominant outpatient providers in areas of abundance, now face aggressive competitors with significant capital resources and agility.

In rural areas, often hospitals are still the dominant providers of ambulatory care. Independent physicians, national ambulatory care corporations, and HMOs represent a source of continued competition for the traditional hospital organization. This is particularly true in those markets that may be characterized as areas of abundance. The ambulatory care market of the 1990s has evolved to include numerous owner organizations, for example:

- Outpatient chains
- Imaging companies
- Managed care organizations (declining ownership in the late 1990s)
- Healthcare systems
- Physician chains/franchises
- Large dominant single-specialty physician groups

Changing Clinical Technology and Reimbursement

The rapid growth of ambulatory services and the movement to freestanding and independently owned facilities primarily has been driven by the following five factors:

1. Payer pressure to check rising healthcare costs associated with inpatient care
2. Increased availability of reimbursement for ambulatory care procedures and providers
3. Technological advances in ambulatory care occurring at an unprecedented pace
4. Increasing acceptance of outpatient surgical interventions and endoscopic surgical techniques
5. Decreasing professional fee payment rates to physicians for traditional cognitive and evaluative services, particularly Medicare program fees under RBRVS (resource-based relative value scale)

An additional factor contributing to the rapid growth of ambulatory services (in many states) is the deregulation of certificate of need (CON) legislation. CON laws traditionally have restricted the expansion of new health services and providers. This trend reached a plateau due to scrutiny in the aftermath of deregulation in other industry sectors (e.g., the deregulation of the electric industry in west coast US states), decline in the housing market, and substantial state budget deficits in the first decade of the 2000s. Many states have amended or repealed these laws in light of more recent studies showing little or no cost savings. The economic slowdown and stock/equity market declines coupled with the growing uninsured population and overstressed emergency centers in our nation's hospitals have slowed CON deregulation initiatives in various states.

Dramatic breakthroughs in diagnostic imaging, pharmaceuticals, therapeutics, biotherapeutics, anesthesia, analgesics, and optical and laser surgical instrumentation have resulted in significant reductions in inpatient stays and sharp growth in same-day surgical procedures. The development of new and advanced technologies and instrumentation, such as endoscopic surgery, occurring at this historically unprecedented rate, will continue to affect the growth of ambulatory care through the first decade of the 21st century.

Technological advances and reimbursement pressures have had a dramatic impact on hospital-based surgery. In 2000, slightly more than 63% of total community hospital surgical procedures were performed on an outpatient basis. Between 1996 and 2006, the rate of visits to freestanding ambulatory surgery centers increased to nearly 300%, while there was no change in that rate for hospital surgery centers.

Such changes accent a range of management and medical staff challenges for healthcare executives, including careful selection and acquisition of new technologies, physician privileging criteria for new procedures, training of surgical support staff, and continuing medical education for medical staff. Operational costs must balance hands-on delivery of care with rising administrative costs, which include complying with ever-changing federal and state regulations, insurance billing and processing claims, data analysis and reporting, maintaining accurate records guided by HIPAA regulations, admissions/discharge records, safety regulations, analyses of utilization of services, and assessment of quality.

Hospital-Based Services

In the past decade or two, hospital administrators have realized that establishing a firm position in the ambulatory care market is critical to the continued survival of their organizations. The Health Care Advisory Board (a national healthcare research and advisory group based in Washington, DC) has emphasized that "the shift to ambulatory care is not simply another trend in healthcare; it is the future of the hospital. Outpatient [care] is . . . the only part of the hospital business that is booming."

As the percentage of community hospital gross revenue generated by ambulatory care services increases, hospitals are expected to evolve into high-acuity service sites with significant ambulatory care components, rather than the full-continuum inpatient facilities of the late 1980s and late 1990s. This transformation will produce new challenges for healthcare executives in the way they structure, organize, manage, staff, and market their organizations. It is important that organized delivery system executives view ambulatory care as an essential portion of their overall healthcare business rather than a supplemental product line of an inpatient facility. This change in the culture of management thinking comes at a time when the hospital industry's share of the ambulatory care market is declining.

Prior to 1990, outpatient care constituted less than 20% of total gross patient revenue for all community hospitals in the United States. The shift in treatments and procedures to the outpatient setting has been dramatic, with a typical community hospital capturing 30% or more of its total gross patient revenue from outpatient care by 2000. Many hospitals obtain a majority of the revenues from outpatient care systems (**Figure 10.1**).

Hospital-Based Medicare Payments

Medicare payments for hospital-based outpatient services have grown dramatically. Medicare payments for hospital-based outpatient services include diagnostic tests and therapeutic treatments (e.g., laboratory, radiology, and physical therapy), renal dialysis, and ambulatory surgery.

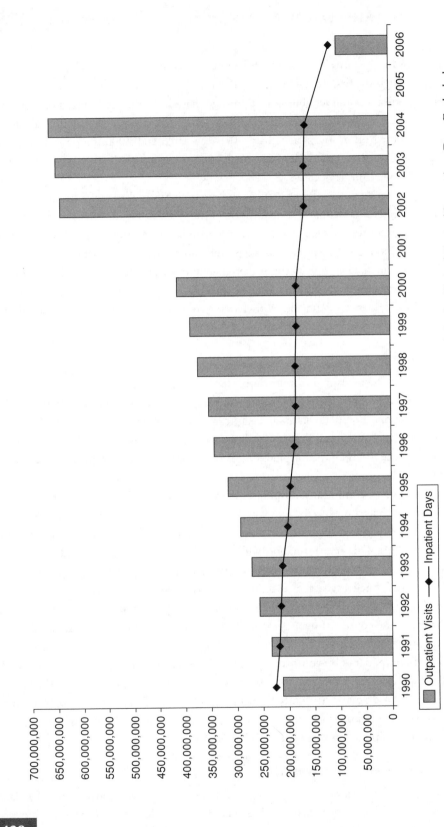

FIGURE 10.1 Shifting Trends in Hospital Utilization, All Community Hospitals in the United States (Outpatient Data Excluded Emergency Department Visits). *Source:* Data from AHA Hospital Statistics 1992, 1993, 1994, 1995, 1996, 1997, 1998, 1999, 2000, 2001 and 2002, Health Forum LLC, an affiliate of the American Hospital Association and www.cdc.gov.nchs/faststats/docvisist.htm

The growth of outpatient payments for services provided to Medicare beneficiaries has been influenced by several significant developments (see **Table 10.1**):

- Introduction of Medicare's inpatient prospective payment system (PPS)
- Growth of managed care plan enrollment and market penetration
- Technological innovations in outpatient surgery and diagnostic testing

The introduction of diagnosis-related groups (DRGs) encouraged hospitals to find lower-cost treatment options, leading to the transfer of diagnostic testing and therapeutic treatments from the inpatient environment to outpatient service departments and freestanding outpatient facilities. This result was further enhanced by similar reimbursement control incentives introduced by commercial managed care organizations focused on physician behavior. As managed care organizations worked to influence physician behavior, favoring more aggressive referral to outpatient care environments, Medicare utilization of outpatient services has been likewise affected.

The rapid growth in Medicare outpatient service payments to hospitals has proven to be a significant force in regulatory mandates to develop prospectively based reimbursement methodologies for ambulatory surgery, home care, and general outpatient service areas. Such prospectively based payment methodologies are examined later in this chapter.

Freestanding Ambulatory Care Services

Freestanding ambulatory care centers can provide a variety of diagnostic and therapeutic services, including rehabilitation, diagnostic radiology, mammography, radiation therapy, chemotherapy, urgent care, and outpatient surgery. The most common types of freestanding centers are:

- Diagnostic imaging centers
- Urgent-care centers
- Outpatient surgery centers

Diagnostic imaging centers typically have capabilities such as basic radiographic and fluoroscopic radiology, ultrasound, mammography, and often computed tomography (CT) and magnetic resonance imaging (MRI). Highly competitive and mature markets tend to have other types of freestanding ambulatory care services complementary to these conventional facilities, including women's imaging centers, women's health centers, mobile imaging units, rehabilitation centers, and sports medicine centers. Similar services often are available in independent physician and medical group practices as well, particularly obstetric/gynecologic physician groups likely to offer mammography, ultrasound, and osteoporosis testing.

Forces influencing the evolution of ambulatory care services from traditional hospital-based settings to freestanding facilities include:

- Tightened reimbursement, particularly for high-volume Medicare procedures (e.g., cataracts and cardiac catheterization)
- Emerging technology supportive of freestanding facilities

Table 10.1 Growth in Total Medicare Payments, Hospital Payments, and Home Health Agency Payments (Most Current Data Available)

Calendar Year	Total Payments Medicare Services	Medicare Payments for Hospital-Based Services				Medicare Payments for Home Health Agency Services	
		Outpatient Services Only				Home Health Agency Payments	% Total Medicare Payments
		All Hospital Payments	Outpatient Payments	% Total Medicare Payments	% Total Hospital Payments		
1984	$59,146	$41,887	$3,387	5.7	8.1	$1,666	2.8
1985	$63,694	$44,282	$4,082	6.4	9.2	$1,773	2.8
1986	$88,883	NA	NA	NA	NA	$1,796	2.0
1987	$75,816	$49,688	$5,600	7.4	11.3	$1,792	2.4
1988	$81,403	$53,251	$6,372	7.8	12.0	$1,948	2.4
1989	$93,844	$59,783	$7,161	7.6	12.0	$2,432	2.6
1990	$101,419	$64,888	$8,172	8.1	12.6	$3,714	3.7
1991	$110,887	NA	NA	NA	NA	$5,389	4.8
1992	$120,710	$74,917	$9,941	8.2	13.3	$7,397	6.1
1993	$129,388	$78,378	$10,939	8.5	14.0	$9,726	7.5
1994	$146,549	$82,437	$11,814	8.1	14.3	$12,661	8.6
Change 1984–1994							
>$ Amount (Millions)	$87,403	$40,550	$8,427	—	—	$10,995	—
> Average Annual Growth	9.5%	7.0%	13.3%	—	—	22.5%	—

Note: All $ amounts shown in millions.
Source: Reprinted from *Health Care Financing Review: Medicare and Medicaid Statistical Supplement*, 1996, Office of Research and Demonstration, Health Care Financing Administration.

- Dramatic growth of proceduralists and the lucrative reimbursement thereof for outpatient procedures
- Easing of CON laws
- Physician interest in increasing efficiency resulting from a one-stop location

The growth of independently owned and freestanding ambulatory care centers is forcing hospitals to become more responsive to customers' needs and preferences, including factors such as convenience, easy access, and limited waiting time. Freestanding ambulatory care centers are consuming an ever-larger portion of the market for outpatient procedures. In the 1980s, hospital emergency departments were challenged competitively by a significant growth in minor emergency and urgent care centers, which focused on the minor injury and simple urgent care needs of the population. These facilities successfully skimmed off higher margin business from the traditional hospital emergency department and filled a void for consumers without an established family physician relationship.

Another example, the freestanding ambulatory surgery center (ASC) market, is heavily dominated by independents and physicians. The most active specialty group to enter the freestanding ASC market was ophthalmology. As Medicare pushed for more cataract operations to be performed on an outpatient basis, and implemented its ASC payment groups, physician interest and ownership of freestanding surgical facilities increased dramatically. Other specialties that became involved in building independent surgery centers include orthopedics, gastroenterology, and urology. The list of procedures routinely performed on an outpatient basis has grown steadily to include cataract surgery, breast biopsies, arthroscopic knee surgery, hernia repair, upper gastroenterological endoscopies, colonoscopies, removal of lesions, and gynecological procedures such as dilation and curettage. The number of freestanding surgery centers increased in excess of 138%, from 239 in 1983 to more than 3300 facilities in 2006.

Four factors account for the rapid success of freestanding surgery centers:

1. Rising consumer demand for same-day surgery
2. Market penetration of managed-care plans and pressure from third-party payers to control costs
3. Additions to the Medicare-approved list of ambulatory procedures covered for outpatient reimbursement
4. Technological advances in surgical techniques

In 2008, the Centers for Medicare and Medicaid Services (CMS) imposed tighter regulations on Conditions for Coverage (CfCs) for ambulatory care facilities and reimbursement schedules for 2009, a departure from a decade-long period of expanding approval. Some adjustments include: facilities will be surveyed to ensure they adhere to operational and environmental regulations; radiologic services must meet hospital conditions for personnel certification and supervision as well as required documentation (§482.26); duration of patient care is limited to less than 24 hours before discharge; a physician or other qualified practitioner conducts a postsurgical review before the patient is discharged; and every patient is discharged in the company of an adult unless exempted by the attending physician. For the same service, Medicare reimbursement to ambulatory care facilities are discounted at approximately 60% of hospital outpatient prospective pay system (OPPS) rates. Managed care plans are expected to follow suit and should continue to be an important ingredient in the growth of freestanding surgery centers, particularly as their market penetration increases.

Although the transition of inpatient procedures to the outpatient setting is certain to continue as medical technology advances, certain new technologies will be dependent on access to advanced hospital-based services in cases where inpatient backup or conversion may be required. This will somewhat buffer the erosion of the hospital industry's share of the ambulatory surgery market. However, innovative freestanding center executives already are beginning to adjust by establishing accommodations for overnight or extended stays. This is taking the form of extended recovery capabilities, including 23-hour recovery care and nurse-attended overnight stay facilities.[3]

Home Care Services

Broadly defined, home care service providers include certified and noncertified skilled nursing agencies, private duty nursing agencies, home infusion therapy companies, home respiratory therapy providers, and durable medical equipment (DME) suppliers. Most providers have a dominant core service complemented by ancillary service offerings, rather than a full spectrum of home care services/products. Consequently, home care providers generally have followed a market niche strategy, with many agencies maintaining a very narrow service offering (**Exhibit 10.3**).

The market opportunities for niche players is changing, however, as more hospitals develop integrated full-service home care organizations and home care reimbursement tightens.

Exhibit 10.3   Typical Home Care Providers and Services Offered

Provider Types	Core Services
• Skilled nursing (certified and noncertified)	• RN/LPN nursing care
• Private duty nursing	• Physical/occupational/speech therapies
• Home infusion therapy	• Personal care (homemakers/aides)
• Home respiratory therapy	• Assisted living activities (housekeeping/shopping/transportation)
• Durable medical equipment	• Intravenous pharmaceuticals/antibiotics
	• Home chemotherapy
	• Respiratory treatments/education
	• Oxygen
	• Rental/sale of respiratory equipment
	• Sale of medical supplies
	• Rental/sale of medical equipment (e.g., hospital beds, wheelchairs, IV pumps)

Proprietary home care agencies dominate the industry, accounting for 40% of the Medicare-certified home care providers in the United States; payments in 2009 will increase to about $30 million. Hospital-based organizations follow, claiming 30% of the industry. Visiting nurse associations (VNAs), which used to hold 20 to 35% of the home care industry in the 1970s and early 1980s, represent only 7% of all Medicare-certified providers. Between 1990 and 1995, the total number of Medicare-certified providers increased approximately 60% from 5695 certified agencies to 9120 agencies. This number has remained relatively flat in 2007 at 9284 certified agencies, probably because of the introduction of Medicare's prospective payment system for home health services (**Figure 10.2**).

The most common home care service is skilled nursing care. Historically, hospital-based agencies have focused primarily on skilled nursing care whereas proprietary agencies have been more aggressive in developing home infusion, chemotherapy, assisted living services, and DME products. Home infusion and nutrition therapies are becoming more prevalent offerings as a result of pharmacological breakthroughs, home chemotherapy treatment, and a growing trend for home-based rather than institutional treatment approaches for these care needs. Skilled nursing care and physical therapy services continue to grow, fulfilling a critical role in the postsurgical care of ambulatory and inpatient surgical patients.

Home care services have been one of the fastest growing segments of the ambulatory care marketplace for the past decade due to clinical and treatment advances, emphasis on noninstitutional approaches to care, aging of the population, and advanced life span for Americans. Accordingly, home care agencies continue to see increases in the number of patients suffering from Alzheimer's disease, other forms of dementia, AIDS, and other types of chronic illnesses.

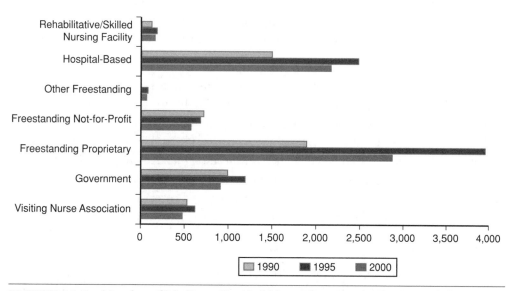

FIGURE 10.2 Number of Medicare-Certified Home Care Agencies by Type of Ownership. Data from Basic Statistics About Home Care, Updated November 2001, National Association for Home Care & Hospice, http://www.nahc.org/Consumer/hcstats.html, Chicago, Illinois.

Formation of hospital-based organized delivery systems in the late 1990s prompted hospital systems to develop large home care organizations with full-service offerings from skilled nursing care, DME, and infusion therapy to hourly home health aide and homemaker services. With pressure to reduce inpatient lengths of stay, many patients are discharged to home care for continued rehabilitative care, including chronic medical and postsurgical care needs. The growth of Medicare patients discharged to home care is expected to increase further as Medicare HMOs successfully penetrate the population.

Medicare Payments for Home Care Services

Medicare payments for home health agency services have increased even more dramatically than hospital-based outpatient services, growing to approximately 8.7% ($12.6 billion) of total Medicare service payments in 1994. Prior to 1984, home health agency payments were less than one-half of Medicare expenditures for hospital-based outpatient services. By 1994, however, home health agency payments had grown so dramatically that Medicare expenditures for home health services exceeded the aggregate dollar amount and percentage of total Medicare program payments made for hospital-based outpatient services. In 2009, payments to these agencies will rise by $300 million because of a 2.9% market basket increase from 2008.

Growth in Medicare home health agency expenditures were influenced by several significant developments beginning in 1989. These developments include:

- Revision of Medicare coverage guidelines in the Medicare Health Insurance Manual (HIM-11)
- Rapid growth of Medicare-certified home health agencies
- Increased home health agency utilization in terms of visits per member served
- Introduction of Medicare's inpatient prospective payment system
- Growth in the over-65 population (the largest single consumer group of home care services)

Home health coverage for Medicare eligibles was significantly affected by revision of the HIM-11, effective July 1, 1989. A key objective of the revised HIM-11 was to clarify coverage policies governing Medicare home health benefits. HIM-11 specified that certain services requiring skilled nursing judgment and technical skill should be considered skilled services (for Medicare eligibility and coverage purposes), and that beneficiaries who require such skilled services should be eligible for all Medicare-covered home health benefits (e.g., home health aide service visits). As a result, Medicare home health aide eligibility and coverage provisions were significantly expanded and skilled nursing and home health aide visits increased (**Figure 10.3**).

Hospice

Hospices offer a special approach for delivering care to individuals who are terminally ill. This care is organized around a core interdisciplinary team of skilled professionals—physicians, nurses, medical social workers, therapists, counselors, and volunteers. Unlike the traditional medical model of health care, hospices provide palliative care, as opposed to curative care (the

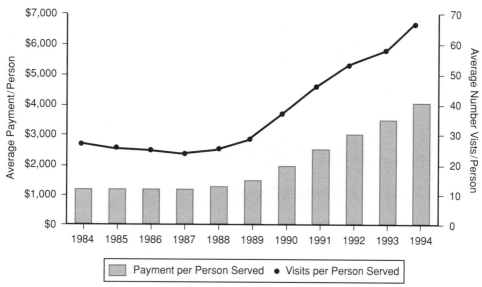

FIGURE 10.3   Medical Program Utilization of Home Health Agency Services.
Source: Reprinted from *Health Care Financing Review: Medicare and Medicaid Statistical Supplement*, 1996, Office of Research and Demonstration, Health Care Financing Administration.

custom in acute care settings), emphasizing pain and symptom control measures. Hospices may be freestanding, home health agency based, skilled nursing facility based, or hospital based (**Figure 10.4**).

Freestanding hospices are independent, mostly nonprofit organizations. Home health agency–based hospices are owned by nonprofit and proprietary home care agencies, typically as an ancillary service offering to a Medicare-certified home health agency. Hospital-based hospices are operating units or departments of nonprofit or proprietary hospitals. Skilled nursing facility–based hospices are operating units or departments of skilled nursing home facilities. Since 1984, the number of Medicare-certified hospices has grown rapidly, with an average annual growth rate of approximately 105-fold in January 2008. Freestanding hospices represent the fastest growing type of hospice provider (**Figure 10.5**).[4] Between 1990 and 2000, Medicare-certified hospices had an average annual growth rate of approximately 18%, increasing from 806 to 2273 Medicare-certified hospices. This significant rate of increase in Medicare hospice participation is largely the result of a 1989 congressional mandate that increased rates by 20%.

Care primarily is provided in the patient's home in order to maintain the peace, comfort, and dignity of the patient and to support family participation. The underlying principle of hospice care is to afford terminally ill patients and their families the right to participate fully in the end-of-life (or as many hospices prefer calling it, "preparing for the next life") experience. Although the US hospice movement, as defined formally, began in the 1960s, some religiously

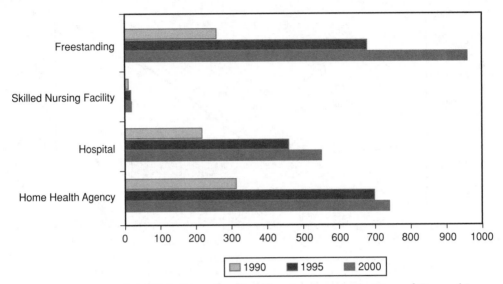

FIGURE 10.4 Number of Medicare-Certified Hospice Agencies by Type of Ownership. Data from Basic Statistics About Hospice, Updated July 2001, National Association for Home Care & Hospice, http://www.nach.org/Consumer/hpcstats.html, Chicago, Illinois.

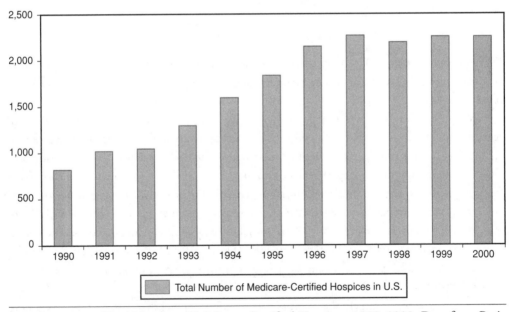

FIGURE 10.5 Total Number of Medicare-Certified Hospices: 1990–2000. Data from Basic Statistics About Hospice, Updated July 2001, National Association for Home Care & Hospice, http://www.nahc.org/Consumer/hpcstats.html, Chicago, Illinois.

sponsored groups serving the poor and dying began providing hospice services in the United States decades earlier.

Nursing care is provided by a registered nurse or by a licensed practical nurse under the supervision of a licensed registered nurse. Medical social services are provided by social workers, typically with a bachelor's degree. Hospice programs are required to have a hospice medical director who is a licensed doctor of medicine or osteopathy. The medical director assumes the overall responsibility for the medical component of the patient care program.

Counseling services (including caregiver support, dietary services, and bereavement counseling) are provided to the patient and family or other caregivers in the home. Typically, bereavement counseling is provided to the family for up to one year after the patient's death.

Short-term inpatient care may be provided in a participating hospice inpatient unit, hospital, or skilled nursing facility. Inpatient care is provided for the administration of advanced pain control or acute and chronic symptom management not readily available in the home setting. A short-term inpatient stay (respite care) also may be provided to support the family or primary caregiver. DME (including "self-help" appliances), medical supplies, and personal comfort items for palliation or management of the patient's terminal illness typically are offered to hospice patients. Drugs and biologicals for the relief of pain and symptom control are keys to the overall quality of hospice service. Home health aides and homemakers may provide personal care services or perform household services to maintain a safe and sanitary environment. Services include bed changes, light cleaning, and laundering essential to the comfort and cleanliness of the patient, and they are provided under the general supervision of a registered nurse. Rehabilitation services (e.g., physical and occupational therapies and speech language pathology) are used for symptom control or to enable the patient to maintain basic activities of daily living and functional skills.

Volunteers fulfill a significant role for most hospices and are trained to perform specific patient support functions. Volunteers provide patients and their families an extra measure of support that is not often available from salaried staff. Typically, volunteers participate in administrative (e.g., correspondence with families, particularly after death), patient visitation, and community awareness/education activities.

For acute care and home care organizations, a quality assessment committee oversees the quality of care delivery, staff skills, program policies, and patient treatment considerations. The committee includes the medical director, the chief administrative officer (e.g., vice president or director), and representatives from each professional and support service area. Committee responsibilities can include:

- A review of hospice program performance and quality indicators
- An evaluation of the appropriateness of the scope of services offered
- An evaluation of staffing policies, including personnel qualifications, position descriptions, and education policies
- An evaluation of admission, discharge, and complaint handling policies
- A review and evaluation of the medical record and treatment plans for a sample of active and discharged patients

Physician-Based Services

Independent and group medical practices account for a significant portion of ambulatory care treatment activity in the United States. Per capita physician office utilization has remained relatively steady over the last decade. The National Ambulatory Medical Care Survey reported an average of 4.0 physician visits per person per year in the United States in 2006, as shown in **Table 10.2**.

Faced with a trend toward tightened hospital and physician reimbursement throughout the 1980s and 1990s and beyond, and growth of outpatient care alternatives, a significant number of entrepreneurial physicians and for-profit corporate chains have evolved within the ambulatory care market. These new entrants have focused on the more profitable business segments within this market. Physicians represent perhaps the most aggressive source of competition, one that essentially controls all outpatient referrals. In many communities, physicians represent a significant challenge to hospital executives because they have established independent outpatient service capabilities.

In the face of declining reimbursement, physicians have found diversification into conventional hospital-based outpatient service areas to be an enticing and lucrative source of additional revenue. Factors accelerating this progression and its financial attractiveness include:

- Introduction of Medicare's Physician Payment Reform and payer conversion to resource-based relative value scale (RBRVS) payment methodologies, causing compression of physician revenues
- Inflation of medical practice overhead expenses, resulting in increased attention to future practice profitability
- Growth of large group practices creating sizable patient bases, an immediate source of referrals for outpatient services
- Growth of national clinical niche franchises (organizations with significant capital and management resources) making physician-owned ventures increasingly feasible
- Decreasing price of technologies, making equipment more affordable

Table 10.2 Physician Office Visits* in the United States, 1990 and 1995–2000

	1990	1995	1996	1997	1998	1999	2000
Number of Office Visits (in Thousands)	704,604	697,082	737,493	787,372	829,280	756,734	823,542
Visits per 100 Persons per Year	286.3	266.2	277.8	295.2	307.8	278.5	300.4
Visits per Capita per Year	2.9	2.7	2.8	3.0	3.1	2.8	3.0

*Represents office visits made to nonfederally employed, office-based physicians in the United States.
Source: Data from National Ambulatory Medical Care Survey: 1990 Summary (No. 213), 1995 Summary (No. 286), 1996 Summary (No. 295), 1997 Summary (No. 305), 1998 Summary (No. 315), 1999 Summary (No. 322), 2000 Summary (No. 328), U.S. Department of Health and Human Services, Centers for Disease Control and Prevention, National Center for Health Statistics.

Nontraditional Ambulatory Care Services

During the late 1980s and currently, some hospitals follow a path of diversification into nontraditional ambulatory care services as a means to expand beyond traditional hospital-based services and augment current sources of revenue. Hospitals following this strategy largely were in pursuit of new sources of revenue to offset declining inpatient volume and income. They also sought new geographic markets to create additional community loyalties. Examples of some of the more frequently developed programs and services include:

- Medical malls
- Wellness and fitness centers
- Weight management programs
- Urgent care centers
- Occupational health and industrial medicine programs

Such service diversifications were successful for some hospitals, but others did not capture the financial returns sought. In retrospect, some of these "early adopters" recognized the shifting delivery of health care from traditional inpatient settings to new and ambulatory service settings.

Organization and Management of Ambulatory Care Services

Types of Ownership

Before discussing the various organizational and management structures for ambulatory care service providers, it is useful to briefly define several common classifications of ambulatory facility ownership, specifically, hospital-based, hospital-owned, joint venture, and freestanding. Hospital-based ambulatory care facilities are solely owned by and are a central part of the physical plant of a hospital organization, whether the hospital organization is a taxable or not-for-profit corporation. Hospital-owned ambulatory care facilities are owned (in full or jointly) by the hospital organization, but usually are not part of the core physical plant of the hospital. A hospital-owned facility may be located on the hospital's campus or off-campus, whether wholly or jointly owned. Joint venture ownership is defined as a legal entity controlled by two or more parties organized under a contract or lease agreement, corporation, general partnership, or limited partnership. Freestanding ambulatory care facilities are not owned by a hospital. Common freestanding facility owners include independent physicians, physician partnerships, for-profit corporations, and insurance companies.

Organization and Management

Various organizational and management structures are found within the ownership arrangements identified in the previous section. Hospital-based ambulatory care services are usually organized under a traditional pyramid-style management design with various portions of the overall ambulatory care services reporting to multiple managers or administrators on the hospital's management team. The distinguishing characteristics of this form of organizational structure are the lack of a separate manager with distinct line authority for all outpatient services and the resulting hierarchical process for decision-making (**Figure 10.6**). Under the hospital-based organizational structure, the provision of ambulatory services typically is fragmented and viewed as an ancillary component to the more dominant inpatient service lines. Some hospital systems have established more progressive management structures for ambulatory care, organizing all outpatient functions (including patient registration) into an integrated business line under a single member of the hospital's senior management team.

Joint venture and freestanding ambulatory care facilities frequently have more streamlined organizational and management structures. These facilities commonly are organized under the direction of a policy board or management committee with a senior manager or administrator responsible for day-to-day operations and management. Representation on the policy board or management committee is determined by the degree of ownership and status of the shareholder corporation(s), or the general and/or limited partners.

The large majority of hospital-based ambulatory services are located on campus and thereby are affected by the constraints of the site, inpatient-oriented units, and other physical limitations of the hospital plant. Typically, this contributes to a lack of convenience and accessibility to routine, frequently performed outpatient procedures such as radiology, ultrasound, rehabilitation, and oncology. Frequently performed low-end procedures are those for which convenience and accessibility are critical to customer satisfaction. Such attributes of service quality are less serious, yet not inconsequential, to the more intermittent ambulatory procedures and tests, such as MRI, ambulatory surgery, and cardiac catheterization.

Physician Practice Structures

Physician practices can be organized using various designs and structures, including independent practice, group practice (single specialty and multispecialty), hospital-based, hospital-affiliated, faculty practice plan, or group and staff model HMO practices. Common physician ownership configurations include sole proprietor, professional corporation, and partnership arrangements.

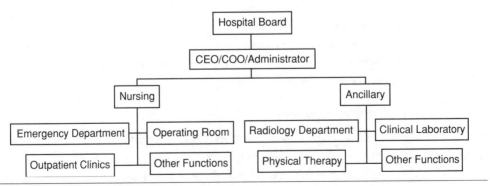

FIGURE 10.6   Typical Hospital-Based Structures

Hospital-affiliated physician practices include solo and group medical practices linked to a hospital (or hospital system) contractually through a management services organization (MSO) or employment by the hospital or a subsidiary hospital corporation or physician organization. A faculty practice plan is a multispecialty physician group practice based at a medical teaching university. This type of physician practice, although typically independent of university or medical school ownership, is an integral part of the school's medical education and residency programs. Group model HMO practices are prepaid group practices, commonly multispecialty groups, under contract to provide health care to members enrolled in the HMO plan. Group model physicians are not employees of the HMO. Staff model physician groups fulfill a similar function but are employed by the HMO plan.

There is a distinct trend for physicians to seek out group practice opportunities as they face growing economic and efficiency challenges. The growth of managed care and flattening reimbursement are the two largest forces prompting physicians to seek out group practice opportunities. Many physicians have found the group practice setting to be a more secure environment, providing additional leverage in negotiating with managed care plans as well as an alluring method for controlling practice overhead expenses and realizing economies of scale benefits.

The consolidation of physicians into group practice organizations is taking shape under several approaches, including:

- Mergers of individual physicians and groups into single-specialty and multispecialty groups
- Formation of group practices without walls (a hybrid group practice model whereby independent office locations and some autonomy are maintained)
- Growth of national medical practice franchises
- Formation of hospital-affiliated group practices

Other less formal group networking initiatives include physician contracting networks and physician–hospital organizations (PHOs). These initiatives typically take the form of an alliance or coalition of independent practitioners joined with a hospital for direct contracting with self-insured employers and other payer groups.

Evolution of Hospital-Affiliated Medical Groups

The benefits driving physicians and hospitals to physician–hospital networks include the opportunity to:

- Facilitate managed care and self-insured employer contracts
- Enhance contract negotiating leverage
- Offset increased administrative overhead
- Share skilled expertise and staff required to handle the increased business complexity of medical practice
- Improve recruitment and retention of physicians

A definite trend for hospital organizations to acquire physicians' practices has emerged or re-emerged since the late 1990s. This has been motivated by hospital executives' desire to protect market share, preserve historical referral sources, enhance payer contract negotiating leverage, and support the formation of vertically integrated delivery systems. The most popular acquisition target is primary care. Specialty practice acquisitions are occurring at a relatively infrequent pace. Instead, hospital-based and specialty physician relationships are forming around affiliations and alliances. Many practice acquisitions have met with failure, increased practice costs, and diminished practice revenues.

The growth of hospital-affiliated and hospital-owned medical practices is demonstrative of a transformation in the way many healthcare executives are thinking about and approaching the marketing strategies for their organizations. In the 1980s, promotional-based marketing (specifically, consumer-focused advertising) dominated the marketing strategies of most hospitals. This approach, although still effective for very focused objectives and target audiences, is now outdated. A new direction, marketing distribution channel strategies, began to emerge as the dominant strategy for the 1990s and is the foundation of many of today's organized healthcare systems.

The development of hospital-affiliated group practices—whether they be through ownership, organizational affiliation, merger, or new corporate entities like a PHO—is representative of this shift, and a means for hospitals to protect their position in the ambulatory care market. Ironically, most hospitals may have introduced hospital-owned and affiliated medical group actions as an inpatient strategy rather than an outpatient approach. Two other compelling, yet often less recognized, factors driving the formation of hospital-affiliated medical groups are the need to improve efficiency in the delivery of care and to support the transition to bundled and capitated payment methodologies, a near-future reality for hospitals nationwide.

Future Considerations

The future prospects for ambulatory care are limitless. Some elements of the future are clear; others are less clear; and some have yet to be imagined. What is clear is that the future of ambulatory care will be significantly affected by clinical trends, regulation, and reimbursement.

Clinical Trends

Advances in technology will continue to affect ambulatory care throughout the 21st century and beyond. Industry experts predict that genetic medicine and drug therapy may eradicate various major diseases over the next 20 to 40 years, the result of emerging technologies such as gene transplants, antisense viruses and vaccines, advanced drug therapy, and genetically engineered vaccines tailor-made for the patient requiring the treatment.

Continued advances in diagnostic and surgical instrumentation and treatment techniques will provide opportunities to increase the range of treatments furnished on an outpatient basis. These advances will include improved laser technology, bloodless surgery, programmable home infusion pumps, equipment miniaturization, advanced computerization of test results and transmission via ISDN telephone networks, and advances in fiber optics. These new technologies and treatment approaches will shift the focus of hospital-based ambulatory providers off-campus and into the home. As patients are discharged from inpatient treatment settings earlier and more are directed to ambulatory surgery, managers and clinicians will need to enhance their educational programming and home care services to ensure that patients get proper, thorough, and timely education and follow-up.

Regulation

Many physicians fear that the enactment of stricter restrictions on physician ownership in ambulatory centers is inevitable. Countless new regulations already have been considered and proposed. Passage of safe harbor legislation will have a significant impact on physician ownership of ASCs because most prevailing ASCs employ some form of physician ownership. There is a shifting mindset among physicians about the long-term viability of ambulatory facility ownership. Physician actions to divest or alter existing ownership positions in ambulatory care centers will affect hospital strategies and relations with medical staffs. This already is seen in mature markets where physician ownership has been transferred to national nonhospital ambulatory care chains. Additionally, many physicians (primarily subspecialty physician groups of moderate to large size) will pursue development of and ownership in freestanding diagnostic care services as a means to offset declining Medicare and commercial insurance reimbursement for professional cognitive-based services. These initiatives will include such ventures as endoscopy, general screening CT, specialty screening CT (electro-beam CT), MRI, and infusion/chemotherapy centers.

Reimbursement

Hospital-based and freestanding ambulatory care providers will face challenges associated with changing reimbursement, including Medicare's APG methodology. The introduction of APGs will create significant management and information systems challenges for hospital-based providers, because hospital outpatient statistics have not evolved to the extent that their inpatient counterparts have, and are often fragmented through individual department collection efforts. Further, the volume of data transactions is significantly greater.

Medicare program expenditures outstripped workers' earnings in 2007. Very serious concerns remain as to how long the program can be funded in light of the decreasing number of US workers and increasingly aging population. The alarming growth of Medicare and Medicaid in the 2000–2010 decade in comparison with the shrinking GDP places an enormous financial burden on future Medicare beneficiaries, workers, and the national budget. While the HR 1 American Recovery and Reinvestment Act did pass in Congress in February 2009, the adjustments on fiscal caps and moratoriums on Medicare rules are temporary. Everyone in the healthcare industry will continue to balance cost-cutting measures with provision of high-quality care.

Management Considerations

Future prospects for ambulatory care raise numerous management and medical staff challenges for healthcare executives, including careful selection and acquisition of new technologies, physician privileging criteria for new procedures, training of surgical support staff, and continuing medical education for medical staff. A thorough understanding of ambulatory care trends is critical to maintaining a strong position in this segment of the healthcare market. For many hospitals, developing a focused approach to ambulatory services has been handicapped by:

- Fragmented measures of volume and costs
- A long-standing perspective of such services as supplementary to their inpatient counterpart
- An inability to focus planning efforts due to the diverse nature of outpatient care

In developing strategies for ambulatory care, healthcare executives must pursue new relationships with physicians, nontraditional management structures, and heightened attention to standards for and measurement of service quality. Many healthcare organizations are applying continuous quality improvement (CQI) principles to outpatient service areas with the goal of improving customer satisfaction and service quality. As a result, some organizations have seen dramatic results in improving key process variables such as patient registration time, reducing the overall patient waiting and registration time from 25 or more minutes to less than 10 minutes.

Organizing outpatient service areas as a separate operational division, or developing discrete ambulatory care centers, is another example of a fundamental change in the management culture. The characteristics of the effective ambulatory care manager will include superior service and customer-oriented qualities with solid marketing skills, an acute attention to customer satisfaction, and a passion for superior service quality.

Reimbursement and healthcare reform changes visible on the horizon are prompting hospitals to develop new relationships with physicians and other institutional providers in order to expand care delivery vehicles and develop a comprehensive ambulatory care network. Greater integration in the provision of care will require new treatment and service protocols, systems to measure outcomes, quality report cards, and investment in hospital information systems.

Service Excellence

With outpatient services making up an increasingly more significant portion of the healthcare industry, providing quality, customer-oriented service is a paramount concern. Most healthcare managers have tested the total quality management (TQM) waters of the 1980s; some presumably found TQM to be useful, whereas others found it faddish. TQM essentially involves attention to process, commitment to customer, involvement of employees, and benchmarking of best practices.

The two primary customer groups for outpatient services are the referring physician and the patient. Key service quality indicators important to the physician as customer include:

- Convenient location
- Timeliness of service, specifically the speed in processing tests and/or treatments and reporting results
- Rapid scheduling, specifically the ability to schedule a procedure or test within days (versus weeks) of identifying a need

Speed and timeliness of service are the most important criteria to this customer group. Universally, physicians characterize a superior outpatient provider as one with early appointment dates, coordinated registration of multiple tests, and minimal turnaround time for results reporting.

Key service quality indicators important to patients as customers include:

- Convenient location and easy access
- Speedy service, specifically registration and waiting time
- Low-anxiety atmosphere

As with physicians, patients rate outpatient service providers according to the speed and timeliness of service, characterizing a superior provider as one with minimal waiting time, smooth registration procedures, and limited interdepartment transfers. Nearby parking and a pleasant atmosphere where outpatients are not comingled with sicker inpatients are also important attributes.

With the exception of ambulatory surgery, service sites should be located such that patient convenience and access are maximized. Ambulatory surgery facilities should be placed in a location that surgeons find convenient and easy to use. For the hospital-based provider, this may mean the provision of services proximal to each other yet separate from inpatient areas that an outpatient may find unpleasant.

For many hospital-based providers, a focus on outpatient customer preferences and satisfaction has not been an acute priority. Until recent years, outpatients typically have been treated as second-class citizens in a setting dominated by inpatients, which favors the more acutely ill patient who receives more immediate attention and treatment. In short, the "well" outpatient with lower acuity received lower priority. Further, most inpatient service facilities and support systems (modified to handle outpatients) were not designed to meet the specific service needs of the ambulatory patient. As a result, many hospital-based providers have aggressively worked to improve service quality for outpatients through implementation of numerous customer-friendly programs, such as valet parking, controlled-access outpatient parking, escort service, rapid results, express testing protocols, and electronic transmission of results reporting to physician offices. The overriding goal of these efforts has been to win customers by providing unparalleled convenience.

Conclusion

The framework a healthcare organization uses to define itself in the future will depend on how it envisions its role in the provision of ambulatory care. Many industry experts have argued that hospital-based providers have been slow to respond to the changing consumer and payer demands for different care delivery options. Furthermore, these experts argue that the very foundation of a hospital-based provider—the way it operates, manages itself, and is embodied through its physical plant—are barriers to superior success in the ambulatory care market. All of these premises are true to some degree. More important, however, to the future of healthcare providers in the ambulatory care market is the organization's ability to recognize the changes in the industry and conceive the possibilities (i.e., vision) of providing health care outside of the typical inpatient setting and treatment protocols.

References

Note: CMS, the agency responsible for administering Medicare, was known as the Health Care Financing Administration (HCFA) until July 1, 2001. This chapter refers to the agency as HCFA when referring to actions before the name change and as CMS when referring to actions taken since the name change.

American Hospital Association. *Trendwatch*. July 2008. Available at: http://www.aha.org/aha/trend watch/2008/twjuly2008admburden.pdf.

Americans make nearly four medical visits a year on average [news release]. Centers for Disease Control and Prevention; August 6, 2008. Available at: http://www.cdc.gov/nchs/pressroom/08news releases/visitstodoctor.htm.

Becker's ASC REVIEW. Rate of visits to freestanding surgery centers increased about 300 percent from 1996–2006. Becker's ASC REVIEW Web site. January 29, 2009. Available at: http://www.beckersasc.com/news-analysis-asc/business-financial-benchmarking/rate-of-visits-to-freestanding-surgery-centers-increased-about-300-percent-from-1996-2006.html.

The Boards of Trustees, Federal Hospital Insurance and Federal Supplementary Medical Insurance Trust Funds. 2008 Annual Report of the Boards of Trustees of the Federal Hospital Insurance and Federal Supplementary Medical Insurance Trust Funds.

Centers for Medicare & Medicaid Services. Home Health Agency (HHA) Center. Centers for Medicare & Medicaid Services Web site. Available at: http://www.cms.hhs.gov/center/hha.asp.

Centers of Medicare & Medicaid Services. OSCAR data. February 2008.

CEOs outline outpatient management strategies. *Hospitals*. 1992:1.

Cherry, DK, Burt, CW, Woodwell, DA. National ambulatory medical care survey: 2001 summary. *Adv Data*. August 11, 2003; (337):1–44. Available at: http://www.ncbi.nlm.nih.gov/pubmed/12924075.

Henderson J. Hospitals seek bigger cut of outpatient surgeries. *Modern Healthcare*. June 28, 1993: 82–85.

Hospice Association of America, Hospice Facts & Statistics.

Maximizing Outpatient Revenues—Existing Hospital Strategies and Tactics. Washington, DC: The Advisory Board Company; 1991:xv.

McDermott Will & Emery. Ambulatory surgery center conditions for coverage and 2009 payment update finalized. McDermott Will & Emery Web site. November 5, 2008. Available at: http://www.mwe.com/index.cfm/fuseaction/publications.nldetail/object_id/317a6dd0-41a9-4177-a97a-e849bc232ea2.cfm.

Medicare changes lead to rise in outpatient surgeries. Healthcare Finance News. http://www.health carefinancenews.com/news/medicare-changes-lead-rise-outpatient-surgeries. Published January 29, 2009.

Medicare program—changes to the hospital outpatient prospective payment system and calendar year 2003 payment rates and changes to payment suspension for unfiled cost reports. *Federal Register*. 2002;67(212):66718–67406.

National Association of Home Care. Basic statistics about hospice. National Association of Home Care Web site. July 2001. Available at: http://www.nahc.org/Consumer/hpcstats.html.

National Center for Health Statistics 2006 survey. *National Health Statistics Reports.* January 28, 2009; (11). Available at: http://www.cdc.gov/nchs/data/nhsr/nhsr011.pdf.

Outpatient-care providers notch another year of robust growth: rehab, dialysis among top gainers. *Modern Healthcare.* May 24, 1993:76, 78, 80.

TQM–more than a dying fad? *Fortune.* October 18, 1993:66–72.

United States General Accounting Office. *Medicare Home Health Care—Payments to Home Health Agencies Are Considerably Higher than Costs.* GAO-02-663. May 6, 2002.

Biographical Information

Kevin W. Barr, MBA, is a member of the senior management team of Bon Secours Richmond Health System located in Richmond, Virginia, where he serves as the executive vice president of Bon Secours-Virginia HealthSource, Inc., the corporation's subsidiary organization for hospital-affiliated physician activities, home care and hospice services, managed care contracting, and various community and diagnostic service centers. Prior to joining Bon Secours Richmond Health System in July 1991, Mr. Barr worked with the Northeast Healthcare Consulting Practice of Ernst & Young serving hospital and physician clients.

His career experience includes financial feasibility studies, strategic planning, certificate of need, assessment of healthcare service needs, valuation of medical practices, medical practice management, physician–hospital networks, managed care, and integrated delivery systems. He has contributed various articles to healthcare management literature and is a senior lecturer to the faculty for the Department of Health Services Administration at the Medical College of Virginia.

Mr. Barr holds a BS in healthcare management/administration from the Medical College of Virginia and an MBA from Virginia Commonwealth University. In addition, he has an AAS degree in radiologic technology and worked in hospitals in a clinical capacity for several years.

Charles L. Breindel, PhD, is pastor of Sacred Heart Catholic Church, Danville, Virginia. Previously Dr. Breindel was professor and director of the graduate program in health services administration at the Medical College of Virginia campus of Virginia Commonwealth University, Richmond, Virginia, and director of International Development at Virginia Commonwealth University. Prior to joining the university, he was a senior manager in the Mid-Atlantic Healthcare Consulting Practice of Arthur Young & Company (later Ernst & Young), where he directed strategic planning services.

Dr. Breindel has extensive experience in assisting public and private organizations in strategic, program, and marketing planning for health and hospital services. He has published more than 60 articles, book chapters, and monographs, and has done consulting in the United States and internationally for hospitals, governments, and private organizations with healthcare interests.

In addition to his doctorate from Pennsylvania State University in health planning and administration, he holds three degrees in areas of mathematics and one in sacred theology. He has been a professor of health planning and marketing and has held executive positions in hospital, nursing home, and health systems management.

Bioterrorism Preparedness

John D. Blair, Ephraim Perez, Cynthia A. Holubik,
Robert K. Keel, Angela M. Roberson, and Steven R. Tomlinson

Shafal grew up in a small village near San'a, Yemen, the poorest country of the Arabian Peninsula. He came from a devout Muslim family and attended a madrassa (Islamic school) whose curriculum was based entirely on teachings from the Q'uran. When he was six, his parents were killed while visiting San'a's marketplace in a shootout between armed tribesmen heading to a wedding and Yemeni guards at the British Embassy, who were trying to prevent the tribesmen from crossing the roadblock in front of the embassy. Shafal never forgave the arrogant British for the personal loss he felt he suffered at their hands. An uncle's family stepped in to raise Shafal and his six orphaned siblings. As one of the brightest and most talented students in his village, Shafal was able to continue his education in the Yemeni capital, San'a. While a student, he was recruited by the outlawed Yemeni militant group the Aden-Abyan Islamic Army. This militant group was affiliated with al-Qa'ida, known as "the base" of a widespread network of militant Islamic organizations active in 40 countries.

Shortly thereafter, Shafal received operational training in urban warfare and sabotage, first by the group that recruited him, and then in an al-Qa'ida training camp in Afghanistan. His keen tactical sense made him valuable to al-Qa'ida's military operations in support of the Afghan Taliban against the Soviets. The Taliban's eventual success ensured al-Qa'ida's ability to operate openly and expand its training facilities within Afghanistan, where Shafal was asked to head one of the largest of these training camps. His charismatic leadership, technical proficiency, and innovativeness resulted in his elevation to a key lieutenant to Osama bin Laden.

In 1998 he was tasked with a new mission. With the aid of falsified documentation, Shafal slipped into the United States across the border it shares with Canada as a temporary legal worker. At the same time, a small but important package was making its way across the southern border.

Within the small package were several small vials containing a white powderlike substance. These vials contained anthrax, a biological weapon of choice for terrorists. This supply was sold to al-Qa'ida by scientists from the former Soviet Union's (FSU) extensive biowarfare (BW) effort. After the end of the Cold War, Russia could no longer afford to maintain its BW programs, its facilities, or the personnel at these sites, which suffered from lax security and fell into terrible disrepair. Al-Qa'ida identified five disaffected former scientists of a BW research facility in Kazakhstan susceptible to bribery and offered to pay them US$5m each for a stock of weaponized anthrax and detailed plans and procedures for culturing and weaponizing their own.

The scientists produced a seed stock of 22 kg of anthrax spores, which had been milled and coated to Soviet biowarfare standards. Rich patrons of al-Qa'ida in Saudi Arabia provided the money for the facilities, the equipment, and the scientific personnel.

After production, 45 kgs of anthrax spores were shipped across the US–Mexican border, hidden as pesticide for crop dusting. It had been shipped by a well-known American chemical subsidiary whose financial backing included wealthy patrons from the Arabian Peninsula. The shipments ultimately reached the Sacramento cell that is described later in the chapter.

Starting in 1997, a select group of al-Qa'ida members were grouped into four cells that were tasked with conducting a series of attacks in the United States. Unfortunately for them, counterterrorism agents of the United States discovered the cell in Buffalo, New York. In November of 2002, Kamal, a Yemeni-American and leader of the Buffalo cell, was killed by a Hellfire missile from a CIA Predator drone in Yemen's Empty Quarter. Also killed was the senior al-Qa'ida leader responsible for the attack on the *USS Cole*.[1] The three undiscovered cells were in Sacramento, California; Chicago, Illinois; and Birmingham, Alabama. The Buffalo cell members did not know of the existence of the other cells and had never met any cell members besides their own.

Shafal, as the leader of these sets of cells, forwards the information to each cell leader. He leads this set of cells as a member of the Majli-al-shura, al-Qa'ida's consultation council, which reports directly to Osama bin Laden. As the intermediary between the operation and the Majli-al-shura, Shafal recruited the four cell leaders, but does not know their members, who have been recruited by the cell leader. The cell leaders do not know Shafal's actual name or location and contact him only through the methods discussed later in the chapter.

Each cell has gone through a 4-year recruiting and planning phase and is now ready for the execution phase. Cell members do not know the identities of the people they are communicating with from the other cells. The different cells communicate by mail drops where possible, and by posting preplanned code words on certain Web sites. In an emergency, encrypted e-mail, prepaid calling cards, and disposable cell phones can be used.

The seven-person cell in Chicago consists of Yemeni immigrants and graduate students, all attending universities in the Chicago area and specializing in computer engineering, computer science, and information technology. Three have PhDs, and the rest have worked for a number of years in computer programming and network security. Several are already American citizens. The cell leader is Mukhtar, who is 42 years old and a second-generation American. All cell members are active in the Yemeni community and its related mosques in Chicago.

The cell in Sacramento is made up of four Yemeni immigrants and current American citizens. They were recruited while students at California public and private universities. All members of the Sacramento cell work in the airline industry. Two are pilots for small commuter airlines. One owns a crop duster company with two non-Arab pilots and two planes. Al-Qa'ida funneled the capital from rich jihadist supporters in Sudan through the Bank of Almusia to Chase Manhattan Bank. The fourth airline industry specialist is a radar technician for the Federal Aviation Administration office at the Sacramento airport. The cell leader is Sahim, who is 29, has been in the United States for 10 years, and has a Green Card.

The four members of the Birmingham cell are healthcare professionals. They are all associated with the University of Alabama at Birmingham's renowned medical center; one is an emergency room physician, another has a PhD in infectious diseases, one is a medical technologist and laboratory manager, and the last is a male nurse. The nurse is the cell leader named Faysal. He is 37 years old, has been in the United States for 15 years, and is an American citizen. Faysal's immigration was easy, because nurses have been and remain in short supply in the United States.

The Majlii Shafal's overarching strategic aims are:

- To create maximum fear and panic (i.e., terror) throughout California and the United States
- To bring the jihad home to Americans by denying them physically and psychologically key family entertainment outlets, which are a source of escape from stress
- To make the United States seem to be a dangerous place for foreign visitors and create tensions with American allies in order to create both political and economic problems for Americans

All cell members are tasked to research and plan in their areas of expertise: computer security, health care, and aviation. The cell members and their leaders are unaware of what other cells exist and what they have been tasked to do.

The planned terrorist attack uses two lethal components—a weaponized biological agent attack and a sophisticated cyber attack. Shafal carefully coordinates use of the two different weapons.

Shafal assigns the Birmingham cell the following three specific objectives:

- To research the healthcare preparedness and response literature from the Centers for Disease Control (CDC), the American Hospital Association (AHA), the Association for Professionals in Infection Control and Epidemiology (APIC), the Medical Group Management Association, and other federal, state, and local templates and suggested plans.
- To assume that Houston, Texas, with its widely dispersed population connected by freeways, is the target. (This includes looking closely at all major hospitals, medical groups, and public health systems.)
- To identify key weaknesses and vulnerabilities in preparedness and response—both within the public health system and within healthcare provider organizations.

This information is forwarded to Shafal.

The Sacramento cell's assigned operational goal is to launch a bioterrorist attack on Disneyland and its visitors from throughout the United States and the world. Shafal gives the cell members four specific objectives:

- To disguise the actual nature of the attack, because people will be dispersed by the time the first symptoms will have occurred; it will initially be unclear where they were exposed
- To undermine the response capability of the United States and the National Pharmaceutical Stockpile by the appearance of many cases throughout multiple areas, thus hindering the capacity of many shipments to reach exposed destinations, with the exception of the Los Angeles area
- To create fear of exposure on the American West Coast initially, and throughout many other areas of the United States
- To create tension between the United States and many other countries, generally allies, because their citizens were not protected

The bioterrorist attack itself will use crop dusting airplanes for dissemination as instructed by Shafal. The owner of the crop dusting service makes arrangements for the planes' spraying systems to be upgraded in San Diego first thing on a Friday morning. The non-Arab employees are given vacation while the planes are being fixed. The cell's two pilot members fly the planes, which leave during the night from Sacramento. Each plane's transponder has been modified to show intermittent displays. This allows the pilots to drop below radar coverage and then divert to Anaheim and fly over Disneyland before the sun comes up.

Twenty-two kilograms of anthrax spores will be put into a solution to be sprayed through special nozzles with which the cropduster is equipped. The aerosolized solution will drop to the ground and cover all the Disneyland park and its accompanying hotels. Each plane will approach the park from a different direction and spray only once each way to reduce the noise. They then will intersect their original flight plan and continue to San Diego. If anyone contacts the police, they will contact local crop spraying services and no one will be aware of any flights.

When the sun rises, the anthrax spores will begin to dry out as the last of the liquid solution evaporates. Dried anthrax spores will float nearly indefinitely in a contained space or, in high winds, the anthrax will be dispersed and ineffective. However, when made into a liquid suspension and then aerosolized, the droplets will fall to the ground and, after drying, will be stirred up by the movements of people or animals. Visitors at Disneyland unknowingly will carry the spores on their clothes from outside the park area into covered rides, such as Indiana Jones or the Haunted House.

The Chicago cell's operational goal is to destroy, for as long a period of time as possible, the availability of all information about what is happening related to a bioterrorist attack in the Anaheim area. They have three specific objectives:

- To paralyze the local, state, and national public health system warning and response capability, including their ability to provide information describing the nature and size of the attack or how to best respond

- To create chaos in the healthcare organizations trying to treat the exposed patients by ensuring that no information will be available for either the bioterrorism patients or the patients already there for other reasons
- To undermine as much of the first response and law enforcement capability as possible in the Anaheim and Los Angeles areas

The second weapon is to be used four days later—just as the first clear anthrax symptoms are about to appear. The Chicago cell has been researching the levels and types of computer security for healthcare information systems. Specifically, they have examined the hospitals, managed care organizations, and medical groups in the Anaheim area. They also have become familiar in great detail with all emergency communication systems, the emergency response plans, and the capability of local and state governments. They have also probed the security of the California Department of Health's computer and communication systems.

Most importantly, they have spent two years focused on the network security and cataloguing vulnerabilities of the Centers for Disease Control's (CDC) epidemiological surveillance system that was designed by the CDC to coordinate symptom information from emergency rooms, hospitals, and physician offices to the CDC facility. The failure of this surveillance system will hinder the US government's ability to identify the beginnings of an attack, to search out the likely biological agent involved as the source of unusual symptoms, and to locate others who have been exposed to the agent used.

The cell has formulated detailed plans to launch a sophisticated and coordinated cyberattack on each of the systems they have researched. They have acquired the needed hardware and off-the-shelf software through normal sources. They have devoted the past year to developing the computer code needed to introduce viruses and worms into each system, as needed.

Panic and chaos will inevitably result from the restrictions of information and communication. The only source of information will be through the mass media, whose systems will be deliberately left intact. The extent of casualties and the nature of the attack will appear on the 24-hour cable channels as well as the local news outlets. That information will not come from any organized data but from large numbers of interviews with very distraught hospital administrators, physicians, and other healthcare professionals; patient families; and local, state, and national emergency response officials. None of them will have any clear information on what has happened.

Worried people from the Los Angeles area and throughout the country will be rushing for treatment. Those who live in the region where the attack occurred, and who have—or believe they have—a cold, the flu, a cough, or a fever will be rushing to emergency rooms or their own doctors to find out if they have been exposed to anthrax. The same will be true of all those who visited Disneyland during the past several weeks, including several whom have since flown back to their home countries outside of the United States, where they will cause other outbreaks to occur. Confusion will be capitalized because information about exactly when the attack occurred and how long the park grounds were contaminated with anthrax spores will arrive in an intermittent, jumbled manner.

There will be long lines and waiting times in emergency rooms and in public health clinics, in many cases overwhelming the healthcare capacity of these localized institutions. Since the media will have facilitated the terrorists' goal of spreading fear and panic, private physicians' office staff, who are generally not trained or prepared for bioterrorism, may be reluctant to allow patients in for fear of exposure to the clinging anthrax spores. Initially there will be considerable confusion about what the agent may be and whether it is also infectious. Some of this confusion will continue because of the public's lack of confidence in "official" pronouncements, which will have been highly contradictory and confusing because of information and communication disruptions by the Los Angeles computer security and cyberterrorism cell.

Public health, hospital, medical group, and reference laboratories will be overwhelmed. Local pharmacies will be unsure what pharmaceuticals and in what quantities to stock. Pharmacists will also be struggling with physicians over whether the drugs they have prescribed are appropriate or safe for whatever the medical emergency is. Medical supplies airlifted and trucked from the National Pharmaceutical Stockpile will not be distributed according to plan because of communication and information system problems.

To expand the terror, the Chicago cell also attacks—one month later—healthcare information systems throughout Florida, especially in the Orlando area. One member of the Birmingham cell has driven to Orlando and spread 2 kg of anthrax 4 days before throughout Disney World by having a Sacramento cell member release it through a container hidden in his pant leg as he walks throughout the park. He releases most of it within confined areas, such as the most popular rides, like Space Mountain and in a 3-D auditorium. Based on a tip (from the Birmingham cell, using careful communication security), spores are found by local authorities, and all Orlando entertainment parks are closed, just in case. Eighteen kgs of highly weaponized anthrax remain in Shafal's control. This is just the beginning . . . welcome to the "new reality."

The Broader Context of Bioterrorism

This chapter's objectives are to facilitate the reader's (1) understanding of bioterrorism, (2) appreciation for how it operates, (3) recognition and acknowledgement of homeland vulnerabilities, and (4) ability to transition their organization into being prepared to react to, and care for, patients exposed to bioterrorism. The purpose of the chapter is to enlighten decision makers about this "new reality." This detailed discussion of preparedness will be followed with potential resources for healthcare leaders to ensure appropriate preparation and response.

This chapter began with a complex hypothetical scenario and some observations about bioterrorist attacks, including the nature of the agents that could be used by terrorists and the exposure of wide-ranging vulnerabilities in healthcare organizations during a response to such an attack. It is also necessary to understand the larger picture or context of warfare in general and bioterrorism in particular. Several key factors are displayed in **Figure 11.1**.

There are a number of domestic and/or international social conditions that can impact the development of a perceived need for change and, potentially, lead to war and terrorism. These conditions may be ideological, political, economic, religious, or ethnic; and often, terrorist

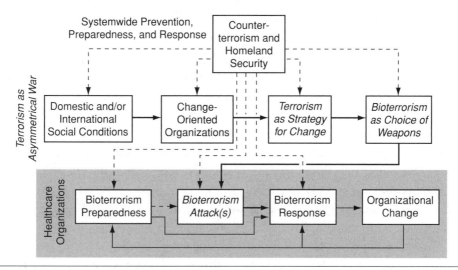

FIGURE 11.1   Bioterrorism Preparedness, Attack, and Response: The Terrorism and Counterterrorism Context for Healthcare Organizations

groups in the Middle East are reacting to a combination of these social conditions. The conditions can be within a country or may cross international borders.[2–3]

Because of social conditions that often create poverty, lack justice, or are inconsistent with the beliefs of many people, it is likely that change-oriented organizations will emerge. These may be "traditional" political parties or interest groups. They may be either nonviolent or violent in their ideology and philosophy. They may operate overtly or covertly and may be found in the military or among civilians. When a desired change is frustrated, sometimes change-oriented organizations become terrorist-like.[4–5]

Many strategies to change the political status quo may also emerge. Conventional strategies use elections, political influence, or even legal action. Sometimes conventional war is used by organizations in power, or guerrilla war by those who are not. Terrorism always remains an alternative to coerce change when the aforementioned fails.[6]

Terrorism is, in fact, the first of three stages of violent change by an organization not in political power. As strength grows, guerrilla war is waged against the ruling government's military. Potentially, the strength of the challenging organization grows so that its army can fight and defeat the ruling group's military forces. Such was the strategy pursued by Mao Tse Tung in China and Ho Chi Minh in Vietnam,[7] in their respective "wars of national liberation." Closer to home are the patriots of the American Revolution, who utilized a similar strategy to win freedom from the British colonies in America. The British considered them terrorists by today's definition, complaining that the Americans didn't abide by the current rules of war of the day which called for fighting as organized divisions on the battlefield.

Terrorism actually is a reflection of weakness, not strength. A more recent concept to clarify this is called asymmetrical war, in which the weak attack the strong and use their strength against them.[8] For example, on September 11th, the terrorists used American transportation infrastructure against the United States. Commercial jets were turned into very powerful bombs by a handful of men armed only with box cutters—and the desire of the leaders to die for what they believed to be their religious cause.

The anthrax attack in the fall of 2001 relied on the logistical infrastructure of a government service to distribute a biological agent. The US Postal Service provided the delivery mechanisms to attack US leaders and citizens. Both the September 11th and the anthrax attacks illustrate innovation in using the target's own infrastructure to carry out asymmetric warfare.

Terrorists have considerable choice in conventional and unconventional weaponry.[9] Some time-tested methods include intimidation, gunfire (including assassination), and explosives of all kinds (including fully fueled airplanes). The more recent concern is the potential growing availability to terrorists of what are called weapons of mass destruction (WMD). These include chemical, radiological, and nuclear weapons in addition to biological agents. Alone, or coupled with other weapons that are designed to injure or kill people directly, cyberterrorism makes use of computer-based subroutines designed to attack hardware, software, and data plugged into national infrastructure, by means of electronic codes commonly referred to as trojans, worms, and viruses. Cybersecurity has become a growing concern to the federal government, and in late 2002, the Cyber Security Research and Development Act was passed, providing more than $900 million for network security research grants over the next 5 years.

At least 17 nations are known to have offensive biological weapons programs. The former Soviet Union weaponized many agents, and some may have fallen into terrorists' hands since the collapse of the Soviet Union. These may include anthrax or smallpox. Large amounts of resources are not always required to produce large numbers of casualties. The September 11th attacks show that large numbers of casualties can be inflicted if terrorists are skillful and imaginative. Asymmetrical weapons of mass destruction can inflict a great amount of damage, and an attack could take place anywhere, especially against vulnerable civilian targets.

Although counterterrorism and homeland security have not traditionally been thought of as the responsibilities of healthcare leaders, the emergence of mass casualty terrorism in the United States is changing that perception. The primary responsibility of healthcare workers is to participate in securing the homeland by mitigating the damage that terrorists can do (i.e., the casualties that they can create—including the healthcare providers themselves).

Counterterrorism (CT) and homeland security (HLS) efforts are increasing dramatically and are designed to impact both rows in Figure 11.1. CT and HLS efforts want to impact terrorism's asymmetric war as well as improve the resources available for preparedness and response. CT and HLS involve the "hardening" of targets, where possible and appropriate, but also preventing and going after terrorists and those who support them through improved intelligence, covert operations, psychological and other kinds of special operations, and the use of military force where effective.

Terrorists also enjoy a favorable "force ratio" in that large numbers of people, resources, and money are required to combat them, whereas the terrorists themselves need use only small amounts of resources in their attacks. Consider that the forecasted 2003 Homeland Security budget of almost $5 billion was in response to a terrorist attack that cost approximately $500,000 to fund.

Homeland security is defined as: A concerted national effort to prevent terrorist attacks within the United States, reduce America's vulnerability to terrorism, and minimize the damage and recover from attacks that do occur. The 2002 strategy statement from the Office of Homeland Security attaches special emphasis to preventing, protecting against, and preparing for catastrophic events. The "National Strategy for Homeland Security" aligns and focuses homeland security functions into six critical mission areas: intelligence and warning, border and transportation security, domestic counter terrorism, protecting key infrastructure and assets, defending against catastrophic terrorism, and emergency preparedness and response.[10]

Key initiatives of the "National Strategy for Homeland Security" will include support of research and development that prevents terrorist use of nuclear weapons, detects chemical and biological materials and attacks, develops high-efficacy vaccines and antivirals against biological agents, and tracks laboratory use of biological agents.[11] The objective of terrorism is to have the entirety of the target audience feel threatened.

The Specific Context of Terrorism

The hypothetical scenario at the beginning of this chapter illustrates a number of key dimensions that set the threat of bioterrorism above that of other unconventional disasters. It also points to a complex context with which to understand terrorism, as well as the role of counterterrorism and homeland security as they impact healthcare organizations. In order to interrelate these concepts, there is a need to have a working definition of terrorism.

Terrorism is officially defined as any premeditated, unlawful act (threatened or actualized) dangerous to human life or public welfare that is intended to intimidate or coerce civilian populations or governments. This description covers kidnappings, hijackings, shootings, and conventional bombings. It also includes attacks involving chemical, biological, radiological, or nuclear weapons. Terrorists can be US citizens or foreigners, acting in concert with others, on their own, or on behalf of a hostile state.[12]

Terrorists attempt to destabilize targeted societies and to cause such fear that the citizens of the targeted countries demand that their government accommodate the terrorists' demands.

Terror organizations are becoming less state controlled and more self-oriented. They have the ability to act without direction from above and have become even less centralized as US counterterrorism efforts have become more effective. Eventually the lack of outside support will make them less effective but also harder to track down. A goal of terrorists is to increase their power and freedom of action while they minimize the capabilities of, and increase the constraints on, targeted governments. They are able to tie down large amounts of government resources while expending little relative effort. Terrorists have the initiative and can strike when and where they want.

Terrorism inflicts a psychological attack on society. Terrorists want to take away people's expectations for the satisfaction of basic needs such as health, food, and security, and want to overwhelm the public services system, including those that provide medical services. Terrorism is an attempt to discredit the established order and to cause people to lose faith in their government. Governments validate their existence only if people are able to go on with their normal lives and continue to have faith in their society.[13]

Bioterrorism has been defined as the unlawful use or threatened use of microorganisms or toxins derived from living organisms to produce death or disease in humans, animals, or plants over short or extended periods of time. The act is intended to create fear and/or intimidate governments or societies in the pursuit of political, religious, or ideological goals.[14]

Due to terrorist goals, biological weapons are appealing to terrorists because of the silence of their attack and the sizable number of potential victims.

It is critical to recognize that a bioterrorism attack is not comparable to a natural disaster like a tornado or a large accident like a plane crash at the airport or in a country field. Unlike conventional, nuclear, or chemical terrorism, a bioterrorism incident does not have concrete boundaries that delineate the extent of the damage because the contagion involved, in many instances, can spread far beyond the point of origin. Bioterrorist attacks create an ongoing fear and danger not only to those initially under direct attack, but also to their families and friends. Bioterrorism is especially alarming given that patients may very likely be potentially dangerous to the healthcare professionals who will take care of them.

During the next segment of this chapter, biological agents will be described, with a focus on anthrax, the agent used in the scenario. Key steps that can be followed by healthcare managers in preparing their organizations for such types of biological attacks will then be examined. The chapter will end with our conclusions and ongoing concerns.

Biological Agents

Recent events have raised concern regarding the potential of a biological attack on the citizens of the United States. In 2000, a list of biological "agents of concern" was published.[15] This list included: *variola virus* (smallpox), *Bacillus anthracis* (anthrax), *Yersinia pestis*, *botulinum toxin*, *Francisella tularensis*, *filoviruses*, and *arenaviruses*. This discussion will be limited to anthrax, smallpox, and the botulinum toxin. Anthrax will be analyzed more closely in light of the scenario presented earlier; the chapter will discuss complications that arise from an attack of this nature, public concerns, and availability. In addition, sarin gas has been included due to its past use as an effectively dispersed chemical agent. An overview of these agents is presented in **Table 11.1**.

Anthrax

Anthrax is an infectious disease that is not contagious. Anthrax is caused by the bacterium *Bacillus anthracis*. Many different "types" (strains) of *B anthracis* are known to exist naturally, the earliest recorded outbreak where *B anthracis* is thought to have occurred killed large herds of cattle in Egypt around 1200 BC. However, not all strains of the bacterium are a significant threat to humans.[16] Under a depleted nutrient supply, *B anthracis* has the ability to form environmentally resistant spores that can be viable for decades. The spores can then later germinate when they enter an environment that is rich in amino acids, nucleosides, and glucose, an environment that is similar to that of an animal or human host.[17]

Table 11.1 Biological and Chemical Agents

Agent	Incubation	Symptoms	Dissemination	Contagiousness	Mortality (untreated)
Bacteria					
Anthrax (Inhalational)	Early—FLS* 1–6 days	Late—severe respiratory distress, shock, papule, fluid-filled vesicle, black eschar	Aerosol	Very low	95–100%
Anthrax (Cutaneous)	Early—FLS* 1–12 days	Late—severe respiratory distress, shock, papule, fluid-filled vesicle, black eschar	Direct contact	Very low	95–100%
Virus					
Smallpox	3–19 days	FLS* with backache, possible delirium, chickenpox-like rash on extremities	Aerosol	Very high (airborne precautions)	70%
Biological Toxin					
Botulinum toxin (Inhalational)	Symptoms evident within 12–72 hours	Early—ptosis, progressive descending bulbar, muscular, and respiratory weakness Late—respiratory failure	Aerosol, ingested	None	None reported
Chemical Agent					
Sarin (GB)	Symptoms evident within seconds (vapor) or minutes to hours (liquid)	SLUDGE—Salivation, Lacrimation, Urination, Defecation, Gastric disturbances, Emesis (vomiting)	Vapor, liquid	None	None reported

*FLS (flu-like sickness): fever, chills, cough, malaise, headache, myalgias

Three types of anthrax infection can occur in humans:

1. Cutaneous
2. Gastrointestinal
3. Inhalation

Cutaneous anthrax (skin anthrax) is the most naturally occurring form of the infection, with 224 cases having been reported between 1944 and 1994. It is usually contracted following exposure to anthrax-infected animals.[18]

Gastrointestinal anthrax is fairly uncommon, as the acid present in the stomach usually consumes the spores. Onset occurs after the ingestion of insufficiently cooked meat that is contaminated with a large number of anthrax spores. However, limited information exists concerning the deliberate contamination of food or water using *B anthracis*.

Though inhalation anthrax is considered rare and does not occur frequently on a natural basis, this form of anthrax exposure has nearly perfect mortality rates and has generated the largest mortality figures following a deliberate biological attack using aerosolized *B anthracis* spores. In 1970, the World Health Organization predicted that 50 kgs of dried anthrax spores disseminated along a 2-km line upwind of a population center of 500,000 would result in the death of 95,000 people. These figures have changed as weaponization techniques have been perfected.

In September 2001, envelopes containing *B anthracis* spores were sent through the US Postal Service to the *New York Post*, NBC anchor Tom Brokaw, Senator Tom Daschle, Senator Patrick Leahy, and American Media, Inc., located in Boca Raton, Florida. Though this particular bioterrorist attack utilized the crudest of dissemination techniques and resulted in comparatively few deaths (principally due to the dissemination technique), the spores themselves were of a very high grade of processing. Aside from the relatively small number of human fatalities, the Hart Senate Office Building was closed for 3 months for thorough decontamination. After 1 year, the Brentwood mail processing facility in Washington and the Hamilton post office near Trenton, New Jersey (both sorted anthrax-contaminated mail), were still undergoing decontamination. The decontamination of the American Media, Inc., building in Boca Raton, Florida, is estimated to cost between $7 million and $9 million. This relatively small attack resulted in 22 cases of anthrax infection, leaving five people dead. One victim, a 94-year-old retiree, died from inhalation anthrax because her mail was sorted at one of the post offices contaminated with anthrax spores.

Prior to this attack no one imagined the degree of contamination that would result, much less the difficulties related to the decontamination process. Who would have thought that an elderly woman would contract and die from inhalation anthrax months after the initial attack simply because her mail was sorted by an anthrax-contaminated machine. These anthrax attacks sparked an enormous amount of attention in areas ranging from biological attack preparedness to more effective vaccine research.

Smallpox

Smallpox is a disease that is caused by a virus and can be easily transmitted from person to person.[19] Transmission of the virus usually occurs by close interaction with an infected person, contaminated clothing, or bedding. Two primary forms of the disease existed before its eradication in 1977, *variola major* and a much milder *variola minor*.[20] Stockpiles of the smallpox virus have been maintained at the CDC in Atlanta and at a laboratory in Moscow (well secured) for research purposes. Recently, the CDC released a plan that will allow for the vaccination of every US citizen if an outbreak of smallpox is detected.

Most national offensive bioweapons research programs were terminated in the early 1970s with the signing of the Biological Weapons Convention (BWC).[21] Ken Alibek, a former deputy director of the Soviet Union's civilian bioweapons program, reported that the Soviet Union embarked on an offensive bioweapons research program beginning in 1980.[22] This program was successful in producing large quantities of the virus for use in bombs and intercontinental ballistic missiles, and sought to produce more virulent and contagious recombinant strains. If genetic engineering programs were successful and recombinant strains of the smallpox virus were developed, the current vaccine program in the United States would have little to no effect. The decline in financial support for Russian laboratories increases the concerns that the expertise and equipment required might have fallen or may yet fall into the wrong hands.

Botulinum Toxin

Botulism is a rare noncontagious neuromuscular disease usually contracted from the presence of a biological toxin in uncooked or inappropriately cooked food. First used militarily in World War I, the *Clostridium botulinum* bacterium produces the most acute paralytic toxin known to mankind. Exposure to the botulinum toxin will immobilize voluntary and involuntary muscle alike, including the respiratory system. This bacterium, like anthrax, has the ability to form spores and occurs naturally in soil. The botulinum toxin is only produced when the bacteria are actively growing.

Three types of botulism occur naturally in humans: food borne, intestinal, and wound. However, the present concern involves the use of the botulinum toxin as a biological weapon on a civilian population. Possible targets that have been identified include food sources and water supplies; aerosolized dissemination of the toxin also is possible.

Heating contaminated materials to temperatures above 185°F for a period of at least 5 minutes can effectively neutralize the botulinum toxin. Therefore, food sources that are not cooked (e.g., salad bars, condiments, bottled beverages, etc.) are considered vulnerable to toxin contamination. The contamination of water supplies with the botulinum toxin is not considered possible because of water treatment procedures and dilution factors.

Sarin Gas

Even though sarin gas is not a biological weapon, its availability and past use make it an important agent for discussion here. Sarin is classified as a nerve agent, which work rapidly by disrupting nerve impulses and causing muscles to be stimulated uncontrollably. In March 1995, a then-obscure apocalyptic Japanese cult named Aum Shinrikiyo used sarin gas in a series of coordinated attacks on Tokyo's subway system. This attack killed 12, seriously injured 54, and made 980 individuals seriously ill. Some estimates project that the attack injured a total of 5000 people. Even though 12 lives were lost, many view this particular attack as a failure because of the amount of sarin gas used and the crude dissemination techniques.

Additional information can be found in *Germs* by Judith Miller, Stephen Engelberg, and William Broad; *Biohazard* by Ken Alibek; *Living Terrors* by Michael T. Osterholm and John Schwartz; and *When Every Moment Counts* by Senator Bill Frist.

Bioterrorism Preparedness by Healthcare Organizations

Visions of the bombing, casualties, and heroism of September 11, 2001, still linger in the minds of all American citizens. However, what has changed since that detrimental event are the preparation techniques that the US government is using to prevent the magnitude of destruction that another terrorist attack could bring to the trust of the American people in their land of liberty. Steps have been taken to form the Department of Homeland Security, and virtually every healthcare institution nationwide must have bioterrorism plans. The Office of Public Health Preparedness in the US Department of Health and Human Services was created in November 2001. Although this department did not exist a year before this chapter was written, its charge is to address some of the most critical challenges that the United States has ever experienced in terrorism.[23]

Not only is the US government becoming more agile in its manners of preparedness against bioagent-bearing terrorists, but the terrorists are also swiftly updating their preparation methods. From statements made by the Office of Public Health Preparedness and the Department of Homeland Security, biological agents can be developed "in relatively small places, with dual-use equipment, and at a relatively low cost."[24] Their means of dissemination vary in extremes from air to blood. As a result of the extensive media coverage on these agents in the past year, one could not help but ask, "Why wasn't the United States preparing for these possibilities before the anthrax attacks of 2001? Was the federal government aware of these threats? Why wasn't the American public ready for a potential bioagent terrorist attack before 2001?"

Steps to Bioterrorism Preparedness

Without argument, preparation of healthcare facilities in the United States is a daunting, overwhelming task. The following are four basic preparation steps that may be implemented by healthcare managers and facilities to prepare for a bioterrorism event. These steps, as well as discussion on confounding challenges and tasks, are based on a template released by the Department of Defense in August 2000. They have been included in this chapter, unaltered, as a means of structuring and summarizing the significant amount of literature available on the subjects of preparation and response.

These four steps are:

1. Prepare for public health issues.
2. Prepare for healthcare delivery issues.
3. Prepare for support issues.
4. Prepare for security and hazard issues.

These steps are explicitly devoted to the preparedness of a community in terms of a bioterrorist event. They are divided into roles taken by local community authorities. The first step is directed toward public health authorities and their preparedness actions. The second step is inherent to healthcare managers and clinicians, followed by the third step of support issues handled by both the public health and private healthcare sectors. The fourth step is directed toward security and policing efforts. They are specifically ordered in this manner in recognition that this may be the order in which they would become relevant to healthcare facility managers.

Another hypothetical scenario: Imagine receiving a postcard from a sister who chaperoned the high school band to Disney World during a holiday break. As this section is read, ponder how this preparedness issue for bioterrorism is going to affect you, the reader. Your sister just called—they took a side trip in the Midwest on the spur of the moment, just for fun. She hurriedly announces that they have been "out of touch for awhile, quite rushed, and were so relieved to have left Disney World just moments before its mysterious and chaotic shutdown." You then hear your nieces in the background as they interrupt your conversation to share vague complaints of feeling "weird."

Step One: Preparing for Key Public Health Issues

There are five key challenges in preparing for public health issues, as follows:

1. Medical surveillance
2. Medical diagnosis
3. Epidemiological investigation
4. Mass prophylaxis
5. Coordination of preparation efforts[25]

The first three issues will initially occur locally during a bioterrorist event and will require intricate communication networks between community healthcare facilities and personnel. After notification of local healthcare personnel and verification of a bioterrorist agent attack, local community representatives, the public health departments, and infectious disease physicians should notify representatives at the state level who, in turn, will notify federal-level offices. Because these issues will be addressed in such a consistent stepwise fashion, they are grouped and explained together.

Medical surveillance of disease, the first challenge of step one, is conducted in the United States via the CDC; however, the CDC has not been consistently supported by every practicing clinician in the United States. Because a bioterrorist attack is ultimately a local response, this chapter advises that every community should take action to make agent and disease surveillance a priority throughout their local healthcare industry. The specific tasks for medical surveillance are:

- Identify departments responsible for medical surveillance and reporting.
- Develop a surveillance plan for detecting unusual medical events.
- Establish medical baselines.

The public health sector, if efficient, must provide effective medical diagnosis of infection by a possible bioterrorism agent. The specific tasks for medical diagnosis, the second challenge to public health officials, are:

- Identify the department responsible for contacting and coordinating sample submission policies and procedures with the CDC and United States Army Medical Research Institute of Infectious Diseases (USAMRIID).
- Identify the process by which the public health department will provide support to the criminal investigation.

Early detection of the released organism is vital to an efficient and effective healthcare preparation and response plan. Physicians suspecting the release of a bioagent should notify public health authorities and ask for aid in defining the suspected problem. However, D.A. Henderson, director of the US Office of Public Health Preparedness from November 2001 to April 2002, remains somewhat skeptical of this process. He notes that reporting

> . . . must take place in a public health infrastructure, which is virtually nonexistent in many, many municipalities, and very weak at the state level. To investigate, we need laboratories to identify what the organisms are. But these organisms are not usually looked at by laboratories, so we began with virtually no capability to diagnose.[26]

Thus, detection of these organisms requires an intricate level of stakeholder management between local community authorities and federal authorities such as the CDC and USAMRIID. A task beyond a mere diagnosis will be the notification of the proper authorities (local, state, and federal) that a terrorist crime may have been committed with proof of symptomatic patients.

In the case of a bioterrorist attack, local healthcare personnel also must oversee the unfolding of an epidemiological investigation. The specific tasks in this, the third challenge to public health preparedness, are:

- Identify departmental responsibility for epidemiological investigation.
- Determine the method of reporting.
- Identify processes and procedures for reporting suspicious disease patterns or bioterrorist health problems to law enforcement officials.

The epidemiological investigation should take the medical surveillance and medical diagnosis measures one step further in terms of reporting and aiding investigation. The epidemiological investigation should be used to determine when and where the agent was initiated and with whom the patient has come in contact prior to their arrival at the healthcare facility.

The fourth challenge in public health preparation is to prepare a plan for the mass prophylaxis of a community and its surrounding areas. For example, the National Pharmaceutical Stockpile has been implemented by the US federal government and requires efficient communication and channeling before a community may access it. The process of mass prophylaxis includes agent identification, delivery and training of protective equipment, dissemination plans for prophylaxis of the community, and, again, establishing lines of communication that will facilitate these actions. The specific tasks for this, the fourth challenge, are:

- Devise a plan to access the National Pharmaceutical Stockpile created by the US federal government.
- Equipment:
  ° Acquire needed equipment to implement a bioterrorism disaster plan (i.e., masks, gowns, filters, biohazard waste disposal systems).
  ° Train personnel on equipment use.
- Determine departmental responsibility and plan for supply and dissemination of prophylaxis.
- Develop policies and procedures for sharing information among the criminal investigation team, the public health department, and those responsible for mass prophylaxis.
- Identify points of contact for each area of support and establish lines of communication.

The last challenge for the public health system is for community leaders to address the structure of coordinating preparation efforts in their community in terms of both the infrastructure and communication networks. According to Janet Heinrich, Director of Health Care and Public Health Issues, in her testimony before the US Senate Subcommittee on Public Health, Committee on Health, Education, Labor, and Pensions, on October 9, 2001, the coordination of departmental infrastructure for bioterrorism preparation remains too fragmented:

> For example, several different agencies are responsible for various co-ordination functions, which limits accountability and hinders unity of effort; several key agencies have not been included in bioterrorism-related policy and response planning; and the programs that agencies have developed to provide assistance to state and local governments are similar and potentially duplicative.[27]

Communication plans also have the potential to be duplicative, or worse, lacking in the case of a bioterrorist attack. For example, when the West Nile virus began plaguing New York City, lines of communication were unclear and confused. Conference calls endured for hours and involved countless numbers of professionals in their efforts to stay informed on the latest developments.[28]

To minimize this confusion, which would be greatly magnified in the event of a bioterrorist attack, coordination procedures and communication links should be identified for the following key stakeholders. Accordingly, the fifth challenge is the development of intra-agency communication methods to unite:

- Local public health agencies
- Local institutional providers
- Local health professional providers
- Centers for Disease Control and Prevention (CDC)
- Department of Health and Human Services Office of Emergency Planning (HHS-OEP)

- Federal Emergency Management Agency (FEMA)
- Federal Bureau of Investigation (FBI) for criminal investigation
- Department of Defense (DOD)
- Department of Justice (DOJ)

The critical ability for networking to occur among these agencies can increase or decrease the level of response taken by a healthcare organization. Thus, preparedness and communication among the local, state, and federal public health representatives is essential in a bioterrorist event.

Step Two: Preparing for Healthcare Delivery Issues

These issues become more important as the reader hypothetically deals with the update on his sister and nieces. They subsequently reported to a primary care clinic where they were treated as "walk-in" patients. Not realizing the significance of their visit to Disney World, they failed to mention it to the practitioner. They were sent home with the diagnosis of flu, only to return a few days later with major complaints of breathing difficulties. Upon further exam, inhalation anthrax was diagnosed. As a result of the earlier misdiagnosis and the disease progression, the usual recommended protocol with Cipro was ineffective.

Step two consists of two key preparation challenges separate from those of the public health systems:

1. Care of presented casualties and the worried well
2. Emergency management operations

Care of presented casualties and the worried well is defined as the actual steps and procedures necessary for healthcare facilities to prepare emergency medical systems that are fully integrated with aspects of bioterrorism, their agents, and terrorism tactics. Bioterrorism items that should be addressed and answered in this stage include the provider's liability, worker's compensation for healthcare facilities' employees, obtaining state and federal aid for bioterrorism plan development and implementation, and patient symptom assessment questionnaires specifically addressing the agent(s) in question.

The "worried well" aspect of this step implies that when a publicized bioterrorist event occurs with a biological, chemical, or radiological agent, many patients, anxious about symptoms of the publicized agent, will flock to and overwhelm acute care facilities even when they have not been credibly exposed. How a healthcare facility handles, separates, and treats the presented casualties and "worried well" patients can strengthen or prohibit the spread of hysteria and true symptomatic identification.

Along with the problem of hysteria among the uninfected is the issue of how a healthcare facility will handle the surge of truly afflicted patients into their facility. Henderson again remains skeptical:

> At the present time hospitals are running very near to capacity. They are financially strapped and short of personnel. Many of the hospitals in major metropolitan health settings could not accommodate a sudden surge of 50 acutely ill new patients.[29]

Thus, issues of personnel and finance must be addressed in terms of the "worried well" and the possibility of a surge of patients, both infected and uninfected, to healthcare facilities across the nation in the event of a bioterrorist attack. The first challenges in providing health care for presented casualties and the worried well are:

- Creating a modular emergency medical system (MEMS) or similar plan
- Coordinating MEMS with all hospital emergency preparedness plans (EPPs)
- Preparing plans for legal issues such as liability of providers and worker's compensation
- Formulating plans to integrate mutual aid and state and federal assistance
- Developing a detailed questionnaire for rapidly collecting victim identification and background information (such as where the patients were in the previous few days, etc.)
- Performing exercises of MEMS and/or EPPs

The Citizens are likely to believe they will receive the best care possible by EMS and hospital personnel; thus, the public believes that hospitals "have an inherent obligation to the community for disaster preparedness."[30] The question is, will hospitals actually be getting it done? Or will hospitals provide incomplete, misleading information to the public in order to ease public opinion?

Coupled with addressing presented casualties and worried well patients is the preparation of an actionable emergency management plan and definition of continuing operations. The most vital piece of this plan is the recognition and report of key signs to the emergency operations center (EOC). The specific emergency management operations tasks to achieve this second challenge of healthcare delivery are:

- Review local plans that call for activation of an EOC and make sure an "unusual medical event" triggers activation.
- Identify key stakeholders (i.e., FBI local agent, CDC) and develop training exercises to forge relationships in advance.

Possible key signs and symptoms should be outlined in the written plan to notify the proper personnel in healthcare facilities that an "unusual medical event" may be occurring. If these are not built into a facility's EOC, the preparation technique of an EOC could be useless; if unusual signs and symptoms are not reported early, continuing infection may occur. As in the previous steps mentioned, proactive communication with personnel is vital to an efficient and useful EOC.

Step Three: Preparing for Support Issues

Step three consists of four support issues for which the healthcare facility and its community must be prepared:

1. Fatality management
2. Resource and logistic support
3. Continuity of infrastructure
4. Family support services

Fatality management, the first challenge of support issues, comprises the creation of a fatality management plan and includes tasks such as:

- Creating a fatality management plan that deals with the potential for overwhelmed city morgues and the religious concerns of relatives
- Establishing safe handling procedures for criminal investigators and other personnel who analyze bioterrorist fatalities or are involved in identification of the dead (fingerprinting, etc.)

This plan is different from the EOC in that it must include how the facility and/or community will deal with overwhelming surges at city morgues, funeral homes, and family counseling services. Another aspect to be considered, based on the mission of the healthcare facility, is religious counseling and religious services provided for the dying and their families. While caring for the fatally sick, healthcare facilities must develop plans for positive identification of the dead, as well as handling and tracking procedures as the deceased are moved from facility to facility.

The resource and logistic support aspect of this step includes the development of plans to organize and statistically quantify the resources used and on which patients they are used. This second support issue includes these tasks:

- Creating and assigning responsibility for a resource support plan
- Creating and assigning responsibility for a logistic support plan

Resource and logistic plans should include recommendations for supply continuation in case a facility's primary supply source is terminated or difficult to use during the bioterrorist event. Barbera, Macintyre, and DeAtley acknowledge the shortage of supplies and the confusion of resource logistics in their paper titled, "Ambulances to Nowhere: America's Critical Shortfall in Medical Preparedness for Catastrophic Terrorism:"

> Due to the current financial crisis of the United States health care system, hospitals that use "just-in-time" inventory, for example, will have minimum on-site storage of sterile supplies, vital equipment, and pharmaceuticals. "Re-supply" and "back-up" mechanisms are often shared by all local and regional medical institutions: a community's hospitals all count the same capability as their individual surge capacity.[31]

Thus, there is a fear among healthcare personnel and physicians that the tracking of resources may not be efficient enough to enable facilities to access needed resources and/or that resources will be easily depleted in particular communities. Devising resource and logistic communication networks prior to a bioterrorist event is vital in ensuring that healthcare facilities have the ability to respond with necessary equipment. Confusion will ultimately reign in a bioagent event of large magnitude, and the ability to obtain resources effectively will aid in lessening this inevitable confusion and enhance a healthcare facility's ability to respond.

Continuity of infrastructure refers to plans made in order to continue providing services (health care, water, sewage, electricity, foodstuffs, etc.) once a bioterrorist event has occurred. To help ensure the continuity of infrastructure, the third challenge of support issues, it is important to assign responsibility for completion of a local infrastructure plan.

"Few hospitals now have comfortable operating margins" due to the restrictions of government support, a number of expensive or underfunded regulatory mandates, high expectations that hospitals maintain increasing levels of charity medical care, and the national shortage of nurses and personnel, and many are without the provisions for extraordinary surge capacity or disaster casualty of care. Accordingly, it is unlikely that hospitals can meet surges of capacity during a mass casualty event and expect to immediately continue their normal care after the surge capacity of patients has been treated.[32] Although many of the primary services in this plan must be operated by the local city government, it is vital that hospitals, emergency clinics, and physician offices prepare plans on how they will provide professionally trained personnel administering to the community during a time of bioterrorist crisis.

Family support services must be involved with the previously mentioned plans. The key task in supporting family services is ensuring that hospital emergency preparedness plans reference local emergency response plans for family support services.

Not only should healthcare-related facilities be prepared to continue their services, but they also may wish to plan for additional family support services such as religious services, counseling, social services, financial services, and guidance to find missing loved ones. Some of these concerns will be covered in the fatality management aspect of support issues, but the ideas for family support that are neglected should be added in this step.

Step Four: Preparing for Security and Hazard Issues

Least likely to be handled by an individual healthcare facility, but still pertinent to the preparation for a bioterrorism event, are the challenges regarding security and hazard issues. Tasks to be accomplished by authorized personnel in the community are:

1. Control of affected area/population
2. Criminal investigation
3. Residual hazard assessment and mitigation

Controlling the affected area/population is a security issue that is primarily the responsibility of the local and state police departments during the event of a bioterrorist attack. Police departments must have physical security plans for the affected buildings, crop land, streets, subway and transportation systems, and so on. Police departments should also set up proper communication channels enabling the local public health department, police departments, fire departments, and EMS respondents to communicate with one another. The key tasks in controlling the affected area and population, the first challenge of security and hazard issues, include:

- The local police department should establish physical security plans that address the potential areas affected by a bioterrorist event.
- Consider establishing and promulgating a policy that only public affairs officials talk to the press.
- Establish points of contact for a local public affairs office with the police/fire departments.

The creation of policies indicating that only public affairs officials should talk to the press is extremely critical to maintaining the credibility of healthcare facilities. This will also limit the communication of inaccurate information, control hysteria among the population, and control the response of the "worried well" and community individuals worried about their loved ones.

The second aspect of security issue preparedness is the handling of a criminal investigation, if pertinent to the bioterrorism attack. Preparation for an effective criminal investigation should include being ready to:

- Identify key agencies with which law enforcement officials should coordinate unified command activities
- Develop protocols for the following situations to facilitate response to a bioterrorist threat:
  - Credibility threat assessment process (in coordination with the FBI)
  - Recognition of warning signs and indicators of bioterrorist incidents
  - Detection and handling of secondary devices
  - Interviewing potentially contaminated or infectious victims
  - Methods for collecting, handling, decontaminating, transporting, preserving, and storing biological evidence, including maintaining the chain of custody
- Coordinate criminal investigation with epidemiological investigation
- Determine how and when results are reported to the emergency operations center

Again, this step will be most pertinent to local police officials and possibly state and federal investigation teams. Although healthcare facilities most likely will not be handling the criminal investigation, it is important for their administrations to work closely with investigators with regard to epidemiology and infectious disease questions. The criminal investigators and public health advisors should also be held responsible for determining how and when results of the investigation are reported to the emergency operations center.

The last aspect in preparing for security and hazard issues is residual hazard assessment and mitigation. To be efficient and effective in this area requires plans that will:

- Divide federal funds provided to local governments for bioterrorism preparedness[33]
- Determine departmental responsibility for hazard assessment and decontamination
- Determine departmental responsibility for vector and animal control
- Establish protocols for timely communications and sharing of information among the key agencies involved and the criminal investigation team

Preparing for a bioterrorist attack, as outlined in this chapter, will be efficient and effective only if state and local government plans for division of funding and responsibilities for control, reporting, and communications have been made. Without prior planning, all of these momentous issues can be professionally and emotionally overwhelming, and will be difficult to assign appropriately to prevent chaos.

Conclusion Regarding Preparedness

The readers of this chapter are likely to be managers of healthcare organizations that will encounter bioterrorism in the future. For such organizations, there are three related issues: bioterrorism preparedness, response, and change in response to a direct attack or based on experience from other attacks.

Multiple biological agents were examined in this chapter with a focus on anthrax as the weapon of choice for our hypothetical attack. Bioterrorism attacks can vary dramatically based on type of agent used, the availability of the agent, how it is disseminated, the target selected, its vulnerability to biological attack, and the likely success of the attack. Although no one can foretell the specifics of these, the healthcare systems must have response plans in place for any number of biological, chemical, and radiological events, because each type of WMD has a set of characteristics and dangers, and needs specialized equipment and very specialized treatment means and procedures. Bioterrorism preparedness should be bioagent-specific and involve significant levels of planning.

The preparation by a healthcare facility for a bioterrorist attack is by no means simple or inexpensive. Outlined and practiced procedures, instructional manuals, the development of communication networks, and the training of personnel on bioagents and terrorist tactics are absolutely vital to any facility, healthcare or not, to be ready for a potential attack. This chapter serves only as an introduction to how intricate and, at times, extremely difficult preparing for an event of such magnitude can be for the administrators of a healthcare facility.

Extensive training and retraining is needed so that the plans are not sitting on shelves and pulled out for review only for Joint Commission for Accreditation of Healthcare Organizations (JCAHO) visits. Perhaps most important, healthcare leaders and professionals must participate in realistic exercises to practice skills developed in training and to identify areas that need improvement. All too often the healthcare members who believe they are prepared come to discover gross inadequacies during simulation exercises. Until practice and drill exercises can be performed to perfect emergency terrorism reaction plans, it is probably safe to say that healthcare facilities are unprepared and there is reason to have serious concern about their preparedness.

Epilogue

Since September 11, 2001, the United States has made enormous efforts to assess its national, state, and local vulnerabilities as well as the capabilities agencies have to respond to and counter bioterrorism attacks. Significantly, these actions have led to the creation of emergency operations plans by many healthcare facilities, but it is questionable whether all of our healthcare facilities can respond effectively to bioterrorist attacks. Healthcare leaders and professionals must be involved in several profound organizational changes to improve effectiveness and to save lives. Problems should be identified, resources changed, plans revised, and new exercises planned and implemented. Perhaps the most difficult problem will be to accept an organizational culture that now requires preparation and response in the first place. Our professional response cannot be a cry that all the problems came from "them"—it must be that we are now becoming prepared to manage and provide care for extraordinary events.

In April 2002, the Department of Justice (DOJ) noted in its national health assessment that less than 40% of the public health workforce was cross-trained with emergency response personnel. According to the assessment, virtually all of the states reported a "poor" performance in the following categories:

- Health outcome monitoring
- Emergency telecommunications service
- Resources to reduce barriers to health services
- Assessed ability to increase health care fivefold
- Assessed pharmaceutical inventories
- Medical triage procedures
- Emergency protective equipment in hospitals
- Assessed emergency response of public health workforce
- Education of healthcare providers/lab workers
- Training on decontamination procedures
- Public health workforce cross-trained with emergency response system
- Training on emotional/mental health aspects
- Dissemination of research information by local public health system

The DOJ report clearly showed that public health, healthcare facilities, police and fire departments, and local and state governments are not ready for a bioterrorist event. With the dissemination of information, incomplete communication structures, and inefficient emergency operation plans, the US government is also not prepared. Although these stakeholders are taking active roles in trying to adequately prepare for any new bioterrorist event, the DOJ assessment demonstrates that we have a long road to travel yet.

Because an emergency preparedness plan can never plan for all possibilities of mass casualty, responding to a bioterrorism event is extremely difficult to plan for in its entirety. The current financial crisis of the US healthcare system directly affects preparedness and response for mass casualty incidents in a number of ways. It is argued that the lack of proper funding to hospitals and response facilities causes an inadequate response to lack of equipment, personnel, and training; even if a preparation plan is devised by the facility, a plan cannot be implemented if the financial institutions do not exist to implement the plan.[34] The lack of financial infrastructure in current healthcare facilities is only one hindrance to an adequate response to a bioterrorist event.

Therefore, should the US population still worry about adequate preparedness? Most definitely, but it should not stop there. The public should help prepare local organizations, but also should work with others in the community. Everyone needs to be ready to "defend in depth" patients, coworkers, and loved ones. The truth of the new reality of bioterrorism in the United States is not that it can kill, but that it has the potential to kill alarming numbers of people in a cost-effective manner for the instigator.

To keep up-to-date on the changing bioterrorism context, a variety of sources should be monitored—not only the news, but also specific Web sites. These sites will enable the reader to access a wide range of insights into terrorism, bioterrorism, counterterrorism, and homeland security as those realities continue to change.

References

1. Moaveni A. They didn't know what hit them: how the US killed a senior al-Qa'ida leader without putting a pilot's life at risk. *Time.* November 18, 2002.
2. Laquer W. *A History of Terrorism.* New Brunswick, NJ: Transaction Publishers; 2001.
3. Pillar PR. *Terrorism and US Foreign Policy.* Washington, DC: Brookings Institution Press; 2001.
4. Laquer W. *A History of Terrorism.* New Brunswick, NJ: Transaction Publishers; 2001.
5. Pillar PR. *Terrorism and US Foreign Policy.* Washington, DC: Brookings Institution Press; 2001.
6. Hoge, JF Jr, Rose G. 2001. *How Did This Happen?* New York, NY: Public Affairs; 2001.
7. Pike D. *Viet Cong: The Organization and Techniques of the National Liberation Front of South Vietnam.* Cambridge, MA: The MIT Press; 1966.
8. McKenzie KF. *The Revenge of the Melians: Asymmetric Threats and the Next QDR.* Washington, DC: Institute for National Strategic Studies, National Defense University; 2000.
9. Rappaport DC. Theories of terrorism: instrumental and organizational approaches. In: *Inside Terrorist Organizations.* New York, NY: Columbia University Press; 1988:13–31.
10. Office of Homeland Security. *National Strategy for Homeland Security.* 2002.
11. Office of Homeland Security. *National Strategy for Homeland Security.* 2002.
12. Office of Homeland Security. *National Strategy for Homeland Security.* 2002.
13. Lenaghan P, LTC (Special Forces) Retired, personal communication.
14. Center for the Study of Bioterrorism and Emerging Infections. Slides presented at Saint Louis University School of Public Health; May 2001: St. Louis, MO.
15. Cieslak TJ, Eitzen EM. Bioterrorism: agents of concern. *Journal of Public Health Management Practice.* 2000;6(4):19–29.
16. Keim P, Smith K, Keys C, Takahashi H, Kurata T, Kaufmann A. Molecular investigation of the Aum Shinrikyo anthrax release in Kameido, Japan. *Journal of Clinical Microbiology.* 2001;39:4566–4567.
17. Williams R. Bacillus anthracis and other spore forming bacilli. In: *Infectious Disease and Medical Microbiology.* Philadelphia, PA: WB Saunders Co; 1986.
18. Summary of notifiable diseases, 1945–1994. *Morbidity and Mortality Weekly Report.* 1994;43:70–78.
19. Fenner F, Henderson DA, Arita I, Jezek Z, Ladnyi ID. *Smallpox and Its Eradication.* Geneva, Switzerland: World Health Organization; 1988:1460.
20. Inglesby TV, Henderson DA, Barlett JG, et al. Anthrax as a biological weapon: medical and public health management. *Journal of the American Medical Association.* 1999; 281:1735–1745.
21. Monterey Institute for International Studies. Chemical and biological weapons. Monterey Institute for International Studies Chemical and Biological Weapons Resource Page Web site. Available at: http://cns.miis.edu/research/cbw/index.htm.

22. Alibek K. *Biohazard*. New York, NY: Random House Inc; 1999.

23. Henderson DA. *Public Health Preparedness. Science and Technology in a Vulnerable World*. Washington, DC: American Association for the Advancement of Science; 2002:33–40.

24. Henderson DA. Public health preparedness. In: *Science and Technology in a Vulnerable World*. Washington, DC: American Association for the Advancement of Science; 2002:33–40.

25. Bardi J. Aftermath of a hypothetical smallpox disaster. *Journal of Emerging Infectious Diseases*. 1999;5(4).

26. Henderson DA. *Public Health Preparedness. Science and Technology in a Vulnerable World*. Washington, DC: American Association for the Advancement of Science; 2002:33–40.

27. Heinrich J. *Bioterrorism: Public Health and Medical Preparedness*. GAO-02-141T, October 9, 2001.

28. Heinrich J. *Bioterrorism: Public health and medical preparedness*. GAO-02-141T, October 9, 2001.

29. Henderson DA. *Public Health Preparedness. Science and Technology in a Vulnerable World*. Washington, DC: American Association for the Advancement of Science; 2002:33–40.

30. Barbera J, Macintyre A, DeAtley C. Ambulances to nowhere: America's critical shortfall in medical preparedness for catastrophic terrorism. BCSIA Discussion Paper 2001-15, ESDP Discussion Paper ESDP-2001-07; John F. Kennedy School of Government, Harvard University. October 2001; Cambridge, MA.

31. Barbera J, Macintyre A, DeAtley C. Ambulances to nowhere: America's critical shortfall in medical preparedness for catastrophic terrorism. BCSIA Discussion Paper 2001-15, ESDP Discussion Paper ESDP-2001-07; John F. Kennedy School of Government, Harvard University. October 2001; Cambridge, MA.

32. Barbera J, Macintyre A, DeAtley C. Ambulances to nowhere: America's critical shortfall in medical preparedness for catastrophic terrorism. BCSIA Discussion Paper 2001-15, ESDP Discussion Paper ESDP-2001-07; John F. Kennedy School of Government, Harvard University. October 2001; Cambridge, MA.

33. Heinrich J. *Bioterrorism: Public health and medical preparedness*. GAO-02-141T, October 9, 2001.

34. Barbera J, Macintyre A, DeAtley C. Ambulances to nowhere: America's critical shortfall in medical preparedness for catastrophic terrorism. BCSIA Discussion Paper 2001-15, ESDP Discussion Paper ESDP-2001-07; John F. Kennedy School of Government, Harvard University. October 2001; Cambridge, MA.

The Hospital in an Organized Delivery System

The History of Hospitals

Lawrence F. Wolper and Jesus J. Peña

Medicine and Hospitals as Political Factors

Traditionally, medical historians and educators often have overlooked the relationship of medicine, in general, and hospitals, in particular, to political and economic affairs, prevailing social attitudes, and discoveries related to medicine. Medicine and surgery date back to the beginning of civilization. Early medical treatment was always identified with religious services and ceremonies. Priests were also physicians or medicine men, ministering to spirit, mind, and body. Priests/doctors were part of the ruling class, with great political influence, and the temple/hospital was also a meeting place.

The role of the priest/doctor, and later the role of the temples as houses of refuge for the sick and infirm and as training schools for doctors, are closely associated with a civilization's level of political development. The sophistication of the healthcare system has often been used for political propaganda to demonstrate the superiority of civilization. The pagan Greek temples served a political role, as was evidenced when the Christian Emperor Constantine closed the Aesculapia. The same political motivation can be seen in the spread of Muslim hospitals under Islamic rule in the seventh century and the efforts of the Soviet bloc healthcare system to manipulate health statistics to prove its claims of success in Cuba. For example, in a careful analysis of Cuban demographic data, Kenneth Hill of the National Academy of Sciences found that "the consistency between the indirect and official incidence of infant mortality disappears. The indirect estimates indicate constant, or even rising child mortality, while the official figures show a continuous rapid decline."[1] This is a classic example of the use of the healthcare system for political purposes.

The current movements toward healthcare reform in the United States, as well as in many European countries and the former Soviet Union, are current examples of the interrelationships among politics, economics, and societal values.

Other chapters in this text will explore a range of topical areas that relate to the current healthcare system and organized delivery systems. The remainder of this chapter explores the historical origins of hospitals.

Mesopotamia

Medicine as an organized entity first appeared 4000 years ago in the ancient region of southwest Asia known as Mesopotamia. Between the Tigris and Euphrates rivers, which have their origin in Asia Minor and merge to flow into the Persian Gulf, this fertile land has been called the cradle of civilization. The first recorded doctor's prescription came from Sumer in ancient Babylon under the rule of the dynasty of Hammurabi (1728–1686 BC). Hammurabi's code of laws provides the first record of the regulation of doctors' practices, as well as the regulation of their fees. The Mesopotamian civilization made political, educational, and medical contributions to the later development of the Egyptian, Hebrew, Persian, and even Indian cultures.

Greek Hospitals

For hundreds of years, the Greeks enjoyed the benefits of contact and cross-fertilization of ideas with numerous other ancient peoples, especially the Egyptians. Although patients were treated by magic rituals and cures that were often related to miracles and divine intervention, the Greeks recognized the natural causes of disease, and rational methods of healing were important to them. In addition, what was known of human anatomy and physiology was more of a rational than a superstitious or religious nature.

Hippocrates usually is considered the personification of the rational nonreligious approach to medicine, and in 480 BC, he started to use auscultation, perform surgical operations, and provide historians with detailed records of his patients and descriptions of diseases ranging from tuberculosis to ulcers. His work greatly enhanced the knowledge of anatomy. The temples of Saturn, Hygeia, and Aesculapius, the Greek god of medicine, all served as both medical schools for practitioners and resting places for patients under observation or treatment.

Indian Hospitals

Historical records show that efficient hospitals were constructed in India by 600 BC. During the splendid reign of King Asoka (273–232 BC), Indian hospitals started to look like modern hospitals: They followed principles of sanitation, and cesarean sections were performed with close attention to technique in order to save both mother and infant. Physicians were appointed—one for every ten villages—to serve the healthcare needs of the population, with regional hospitals for the infirm and destitute.

Roman Hospitals

The Roman talent for organization did not extend as readily to institutional care of the sick and injured. Although infirmaries for sick slaves were established, it was only among the military legions that a system for hospitalization was developed. After the injured were cared for in field tents, the soldiers were moved to valetudinaries, a form of hospital erected in the garrisons along the frontier. Apparently, those stone and wooden structures were carefully planned and were stocked with instruments, supplies, and medications.

The decree of Emperor Constantine in AD 335 closed the Aesculapia and stimulated the building of Christian hospitals. However, it was not until AD 369 that wealthy Romans, converted to Christianity, started to build hospitals. Benefactors included Justinian and Fabiola, who built a hospital in AD 394.

Islamic Hospitals

During the seventh century, the new evangelical religion of Islam began to preserve the classical learning still extant, which it later yielded to the European world. The development of efficient hospitals was an outstanding contribution of Islamic civilization. The Roman military hospitals and the few Christian hospitals were no match for the number, organization, and excellence of the Arabic hospitals.

The Arabs' medical inspiration came largely from the Persian hospital in Djoundisabour (sixth century, Turkey), at which many physicians studied. Returning to their homes, they founded institutions that were remarkably well organized for the times. During the time of Mohammed, a real system of hospitals was developed. Asylums for the insane were founded 10 centuries before they first appeared in Europe. In addition, Islamic physicians were responsible for the establishment of pharmacy and chemistry as sciences. Some of the best known of the great hospitals in the Middle Ages were in Baghdad, Damascus, and Cairo. In particular, the hospital and medical school of Damascus had elegant rooms, an extensive library, and a great reputation for its cuisine.

In the Arabic hospitals, separate wards were set aside for different diseases, such as fever, eye conditions, diarrhea, wounds, and gynecological disorders. Convalescing patients were separated from sicker patients, and provisions were made for ambulatory patients. Clinical reports of cases were collected and used for teaching.

The Middle Ages

From the early Middle Ages in the fourth century to the late Middle Ages in the fifteenth century, trade was almost totally suppressed, and many city dwellers returned to the land. Religious communities assumed responsibility for care of the sick. The rational nonreligious approach that characterized Greek medicine during the era of Hippocrates was lost, as hospitals became ecclesiastical, not medical, institutions. Only the hopeless and homeless found their way to these hospitals, in which the system of separation of patients by diseases was eliminated, three to five patients were accommodated in each bed, and principles of sanitation were ignored. Surgery was avoided, with the exception of amputation, in order not to "disturb the body" and to avoid the shedding of blood per the Church edict of 1163 that, in effect, forbade the clergy from performing operations. Religious orders emphasized nursing care; the first religious order devoted solely to nursing is considered to be the St. Augustine nuns, organized in approximately 1155.

Yet, hospital construction increased in Europe during the Middle Ages for two reasons. First, Pope Innocent III in 1198 urged wealthy Christians to build hospitals in every town, and second, increased revenues were available from the commerce with the Crusaders. The oldest hospitals still in existence are the Hotels Dieu in Lyons and Paris, France. The term Hotel Dieu indicates that it is a public hospital. The earliest mention of the Hotel Dieu in Lyons is found in a manuscript of AD 580, in which its establishment by Childebert is recorded. The Hotel Dieu of Paris was founded by Bishop Landry in 660, on the Ile de la Cite. In 1300, the hospital had an attending staff of physicians and surgeons caring for 800 to 900 patients, and its capacity was doubled in the fifteenth century. By the seventeenth century, it had been enlarged to two buildings, linked by the Pont au Double. In about 1880, these buildings were replaced on the island by the present Hotel Dieu.

St. Bartholomew's Hospital, which was established in London in 1123, was attached to the Augustinian Priory of (Great) St. Bartholomew. Both church and hospital still exist, but the hospital was rebuilt between 1730 and 1759. The Hospital of Santo Spirito was built in Rome in 1204 by Pope Innocent III. By 1447, it housed 360 beds and utilized a system of stretcher-ambulances. The hospital survived on the same location until 1922, when it was destroyed by fire, but it was later rebuilt.

The development of hospitals in Germany occurred largely in the thirteenth and fourteenth centuries through the activities of the Order of the Holy Ghost and the Order of the Lazarites. In Belgium, the still-active hospital of St. John in Bruges was established in the twelfth century.

In contrast, in Asia and Africa during the same period, construction of effective and efficient hospitals was spurred by Islamic rule and the Crusades. The two hospital systems enforced sanitary measures, performed surgery, and separated patients according to diseases—the Islamic hospitals because they were still following the Greek and early Roman traditions, and the hospitals created by the Crusaders because injuries sustained in combat necessitated surgery and the presence of pests and contagious diseases necessitated sanitary conditions and the strict separation of patients.

During the period of the Crusades (1096–1270), religious orders, which had as their chief duty the care of the sick, built a number of hospitals in the Mediterranean area. The most famous of these orders was the Knights of Saint John of Jerusalem. Because of the need to treat the casualties of combat, large hospitals with up to 2000 beds were built. For years, those hospitals were the only active institutions following advanced hospital practices, other than the Islamic hospitals. For the first time, medical systems of the East and West vied for the supremacy of medical care.

Hospitals During the Renaissance

The Renaissance period lasted from the fourteenth to the sixteenth centuries. It received its name from the Italian *rinascita*, meaning rebirth, because of a common belief that it embodied a return to the cultural priorities of ancient Rome and Greece. The healing arts were again characterized by a scientific, rational approach. The academic world of northern Italy was tolerant of new cosmopolitan ideas. By the mid-fifteenth century, all major courts and cities of Europe sent their finest physicians to Italy for advanced training.

If the Middle Ages can be seen as the period of the great hospitals, the Renaissance was the period of the great schools of medicine. Schools of medicine flourished in Germany and in Central and Eastern Europe. The study of human anatomy as a science was facilitated by dissections of animals. In 1506, the Royal College of Surgeons was organized in England, followed by the organization of the Royal College of Physicians in 1528.

The major contribution of the Renaissance to the development of hospitals was in improved management of the hospital, the return to the segregation of patients by diseases, and the higher quality of medicine provided within the hospital. Clinical surgery took great strides during this period, not only in Italy, but also in France, especially under Ambrose Pare, who reintroduced the ancient methods of stopping hemorrhage by using ligatures, and abandoned the barbaric system of cauterizing irons. Epidemic chorea, sweating sickness, and leprosy had almost ceased to exist, although syphilis continued to be common.

In the English Reformation from 1536 to 1539, hospitals affiliated with the Catholic Church were plundered by King Henry VIII and were ordered to convert to secular uses or be destroyed. Many hospitals in the countryside of England were forced to close their doors and remained closed for two centuries. Only the powerful hospitals in London survived when the citizens petitioned the king to endow St. Bartholomew, St. Thomas, and St. Mary of Bethlehem hospitals. This was the first instance of secular support of hospitals.

Hospitals on the American Continent

The first hospitals of the New World were built in the colonies of Spain, France, and England. Those built under the flags of Catholic Spain and France retained the ideals of the Jesuits, the Sisters of Charity, and the Augustinian Sisters, with their hundreds of years of hospital knowledge. Hospitals built in the English colonies, however, reacted against English traditions.

The first hospital in the New World was constructed as part of a system for the occupation of overseas territories. Bartolome de las Casas, one of the priests who accompanied Columbus on his first voyage and a well-known historian, referred to the founding of the village of La Isabella in Hispaniola (today, Santo Domingo) in January of 1494: "Columbus made haste in constructing a house to keep supplies and the ammunition for the soldiers, a church and a hospital."[2]

No further information survives to indicate whether the hospital was actually built. However, extant documents show that a hospital was built in St. Nicholas of Bari by mid-1494 and that, during the same year, it housed 40 Spaniards who were injured during an Indian revolt. Unfortunately, most of the hospital records were destroyed during the pillage of the city by Sir Francis Drake in 1586. The same hospital, in a different location, provided health care until 1883.

In Mexico, Hernan Cortes erected the Immaculate Conception Hospital in Mexico City in 1524, which is still an active hospital. In 1541, the Spanish crown passed a decree that required construction of a hospital in all Spanish and Indian towns of the New World. In Quebec, Canada, in 1639, the French constructed the first hospital, the Hotel Dieu du Precieux Sanz, which was founded by the Duchess d'Aquilon. The Hotel Dieu de St. Joseph was founded in Montreal in 1644. In the English colonies, the oldest hospital was a small almshouse for the poor that was supported by a church in the city of New Amsterdam. This house and a tiny hospital established by the West Indian Company in 1658 eventually were combined and grew into the City Hospital of Bellevue in New York City.

The eighteenth-century American hospitals, except for the New Amsterdam Hospital and one constructed in New Orleans by the Catholic Church in 1720, departed from the charitable and religious spirit of the Old World hospitals. American institutions followed the model of the Pennsylvania Hospital, which was founded in 1751. According to an inscription on its wall, the institution intended to foster patients' self-respect and remove any stigma from a hospital visit by charging fees. Benjamin Franklin helped to design the hospital, which was built to provide a place for Philadelphia physicians to hospitalize their private patients. Franklin served as president from 1755 to 1757.

In another break with tradition, the New York Hospital was founded in 1771 by private citizens who formed the Society of the New York Hospital and obtained a grant to build it. The hospital was characterized by a spirit of learning and research. As with other hospitals founded before the era of large fortunes, the New York Hospital was built on the contributions of small merchants and farmers. Another innovation was the first hospital conducted only by women. The New York Infirmary for Women and Children was opened in 1853 by the first woman to earn a medical degree in the United States, Elizabeth Blackwell, and her sister. Again, this is another example of a privately owned hospital that was founded to accommodate physicians' needs.

The earliest federal involvement in hospital care was mandated by the 1798 United States Marine Hospital Service Act, which provided hospital care for disabled seamen. This act was, in reality, a compulsory insurance plan, because wages were deducted for healthcare coverage. As a result of the act, the first Marine hospital was built in Norfolk, Virginia, in 1802, and in the same year, another was built in Boston, Massachusetts. In the following year, another Marine hospital was built in Newport, Rhode Island, and by 1861 there were 30 Marine hospitals. After the Civil War, the Marine hospitals admitted Army and Navy personnel and became the forerunner of the Veterans Affairs Hospitals. At the beginning of the twentieth century, nearly all US hospitals were independent, either under voluntary or private auspices. However, after 1926, the number of tax-supported hospitals increased dramatically, and tax refunds were used to pay for many poor patients in voluntary hospitals.

The European and Latin American tradition of charity hospitals, based on love of God and neighbors and the conviction that the government owed a responsibility to helpless citizens, was never part of US hospital traditions. As a result, a more competitive system of hospitals developed, with fewer subsidies and less involvement of religious organizations in total health care. Massive government involvements in health care began in 1926 with the return of veterans from World War I. The possible bias in the system is indicated best by the fee schedule of 1870, in which delirium tremens cases were charged twice the normal fee. Yet, the positive element of the early system was that those who paid and those who did not slept side by side, but nonpaying patients were assigned housekeeping or simple nursing duties.

Hospitals in the Seventeenth, Eighteenth, and Nineteenth Centuries

The seventeenth century was the age of the scientific revolution, a major turning point in the history of hospitals and medicine. The mood of the century was not to find out why things happened, but how they happened.

No longer was speculation accepted, but experimentation was the common denominator of scientific work. William Harvey's (1578–1657) proof of the continuous circulation of the blood within a contained system was the seventeenth century's most significant achievement in physiology and medicine. Experimentation led to the wide use of thermometry in clinical practice. One of the most important inventions in the development of medicine and general science was the microscope. The two giants of seventeenth-century microscopy were Marcello Malpighi (1628–1694) and Anthony van Leeuwenhoek (1632–1723).

In 1661, a book published in England, *Natural and Political Observations . . . Made Upon the Bills of Mortality*, by John Gaunt, for the first time presented the idea that a large population was an asset to a country and that public health measures were a necessity. The book advocated measures to preserve and restore health, such as separate hospitals for plague victims, specialized maternity institutions, government concern for the health of occupational groups, and the establishment of a central health council to organize public health. However, these measures were too far advanced for seventeenth-century thinking and were ignored.

In the seventeenth century, new hospitals were constructed in the new lands colonized in the Americas. The old hospitals in Europe were either slumbering under the maternal care of the Church, as in Italy, or passing into the control of national or municipal governments, as in France and Germany, or new hospitals were being founded by an enlightened crown, as in Denmark, Germany, and Austria.

During the eighteenth century, there was a partial revival in the construction of hospitals in England. A movement was started to build a hospital in every parish by 1732. A total of 115 hospitals were already built by the parishioners, with the best known of them being St. Peter's of Bristol. At the same time, philanthropists, such as Thomas Guy, founded hospitals for both charity and paying patients, including the Guy's Hospital in 1724, St. George's Hospital in 1733, and the Great London Hospital in 1740. The Quakers were very active in hospital construction as well, with William Tuke (1732–1822) founding the York Retreat for the Humane Care of the Mentally Ill.

The discovery of vaccination was the key medical achievement of the eighteenth century. Lady Mary Wortley Montagu (1689–1762) brought back to England the Asian technique of variolation, which she had observed in Turkey. In this procedure, serum extracted from the sore of a person with smallpox was injected into another person's skin to produce a resistance resulting from a mild case of the illness.

The eighteenth century was not merely a period of mass construction of new hospitals, but a period of consolidation and systematization. Physicians and hospitals, overwhelmed by the revolutionary discoveries of the previous century, struggled bravely to absorb and utilize the mass of new technology.

The nineteenth century is the keystone in the history of hospitals and is considered to be the beginning of modern medicine. Several events combined to produce the framework for the modern hospital. During the Industrial Revolution (1790–1825), the building of factories and the expansion of cities led to the overcrowding of urban areas. The health of workers in the factories was important to their efficient functioning, and because the spread of epidemic disease was a danger to all segments of the population, the need for remedial measures was obvious. As a result, in every major city the construction of hospitals accelerated.

The assembling of large numbers of troops for the American Civil War (1861–1865) was accompanied by the inevitable outbreaks of communicable diseases. In the armies of both the North and South, little attention was paid to camp sanitation, and no provision was made for decent housing or food. Because of the lack of planning, the enormous numbers of casualties from the first few battles lay abandoned in the field for as long as 2 or 3 days.

Gradually, both armies evolved effective ambulance and hospital systems, procured adequate medical supplies, and developed well-trained surgeons. Yet, it was not until the battle of Gettysburg (July 1863) that the Union forces were able to remove their wounded from the field at the end of each day's fighting. It took two years of bloodshed to develop a good medical corps and an effective system of field hospitals. These advances in hospital management became part of the increasing development of the American hospital system and led to the creation of the Veterans Affairs hospitals.

The legacy of Florence Nightingale may be the greatest contribution of the nineteenth century to the evolution of hospitals. The introduction of professional nursing services, which provided kindly treatment and emphasized a clean environment, was a giant step forward in institutional treatment. Miss Nightingale began nursing training in Germany in 1836 and almost immediately wrote about the lack of hygiene in the German hospitals. Upon returning to England, she started implementing her ideas and acquired a reputation as an innovator. In 1854, the English government asked her to improve the conditions of the sick and wounded soldiers during the Crimean War. She organized laundry services, kitchens, and a central supply department, and in 10 days reduced the death rate from 38% to an acceptable 2%.

Her capacity for organization and administration was endless. After returning to England, Nightingale founded the first school of nursing in 1860. In 1863, the school graduated the first group of 15 nurses, who later devoted their efforts to the promotion of nursing schools. Nightingale's writings were largely responsible for the transformation of nursing from a low, unpopular, and almost casual endeavor into a highly respected, essential part of the healing art.

Another important event in the history of hospitals was the discovery of bacteria as a cause of disease. Before that discovery, the principal focus of preventive medicine and elimination of infections in hospitals was sanitation: The provision of potable water and the dispersal of foul odors remedied problems that were considered to be the important factors in causing epidemics.

It was Ignaz Semmelweis (1818–1865) who, in keeping with the new statistical spirit of the nineteenth century, assembled and analyzed the clinical care data in the obstetrical wards of the Allgemines Krankenhaus Hospital in Vienna to prove the contagious nature of postpartum infections. The next step for Semmelweis was clear: to require physicians and students under his charge to scrub their hands with soap and water and soak them in a chlorinated lime solution before entering the clinic or ward and to repeat this after each examination. In 3 months, the obstetrical death rate declined from 18% to 1$\frac{1}{2}$%.

A few years later, Louis Pasteur (1822–1895) proved that bacteria were produced by reproduction and were not spontaneous, as previously believed. He is considered the father of bacteriology. Joseph Lister (1827–1912) continued Pasteur's work. Lister noticed that broken bones over which the skin was intact usually healed without complication; when they were exposed, however, fractures developed the same type of infection that grew in amputations and other operations. He suggested that this finding provided additional evidence that some element circulating in the body was responsible for the infections. By 1870, the hospitals in Germany were paying strong attention to Lister's theories and sprayed carbolic solution in the operating room, drenching both surgeons and patients. As a result, it was possible to perform major surgery without fear of infection.

The discovery of anesthesia and steam sterilization modernized the practice of surgery and enabled it to be performed frequently. By 1831, all three basic anesthetic agents—ether, nitrous oxide gas, and chloroform—had been discovered, but no medical applications of their pain-relieving properties had been performed. It is believed that Dr. Clariford W. Long (1815–1878) of Georgia was the first to perform minor operations using sulfuric ether in 1842. The introduction of steam sterilization in 1886 was the beginning of surgical asepsis, in contrast with earlier, less effective antisepsis measures.

The three discoveries—bacteria as the cause of diseases, anesthesia, and steam sterilization—enabled the development of the modern hospital. By 1895, the foundation of the modern hospital was completed with the discovery of the X-ray by Wilhelm Konrad Roentgen (1845–1923). Hospitals were no longer a place where the sick and homeless found refuge and care, but rather a special place where treatment and more exact diagnosis were aided by technology. At the same time, the cost of hospital care increased dramatically, and hospitals were placed in direct competition with the private practitioner, who usually was unable to afford the costly equipment.

The American Medical Association was founded in 1847 under the leadership of Dr. Nathan Smith Davis (1817–1907). In 1864, 16 nations signed a treaty establishing the International Red Cross and specifying regulations for the treatment of wounded soldiers, including the provision that all hospitals—military and civilian—were to be neutral territory. Another landmark in the history of hospitals occurred in the nineteenth century when women were finally accepted as full-fledged medical practitioners, after a long struggle. The next logical step in the development of medicine was specialization. By the end of the nineteenth and the beginning of the twentieth centuries, specialties and subspecialties developed to the extent that no general branch of medicine or surgery was without its subdivision of specialization.

As a result of all the above-mentioned discoveries and events, a great number of hospitals were constructed in the United States in a short period of time; for example, in Chicago: Mercy Hospital, 1852, Cook County, 1863, St. Luke, 1864, Chicago Hospital for Women, 1865, and the Jewish Hospital, 1868; in New York City: Roosevelt Hospital, 1871, Presbyterian Hospital, 1872, Polyclinic, 1881, and Cancer Hospital, 1886; and in Baltimore: Johns Hopkins Hospital, 1889. By the end of the nineteenth century, there were 149 hospitals in the United States with a bed capacity of 35,500. Less than 10% of all these hospitals were under government control of any kind.

The Modern Hospital and Health Systems

The ideal modern hospital is a place both where ailing people seek and receive care and where clinical education is provided to medical students, nurses, and virtually the whole spectrum of health professionals. It provides continuing education for practicing physicians and increasingly serves the function of an institution of higher learning for entire neighborhoods, communities, and regions. In addition to its educational role, the modern hospital conducts investigation studies and research in medical sciences both from clinical records and from its patients, as well as basic research in science, physics, and chemistry.

The construction of the modern hospital is regulated or influenced by federal laws, state health department regulations, city ordinances, the standards of the Joint Commission on Accreditation of Healthcare Organizations, and national and local codes (building, fire protection, sanitation, etc.). These requirements safeguard patients' privacy and the safety and well-being of patients and staff, and control cross-infections. The popular ward concept of the mid-nineteenth century is no longer permissible, and today hospitals have mainly semiprivate and private rooms. Although permissible in most states, four-bed rooms are seldom used.

The changing emphasis from inpatient to outpatient service and rapid advances in medical technology have focused recent facility planning activities on medical ancillary expansion and freestanding outpatient centers. Developing separate or freestanding buildings has allowed hospitals to minimize the financial impact of restrictive hospital building codes and regulations.

However, the rapid expansion of nonhospital-based and independent ambulatory care facilities slowed substantially beginning in the late 1980s as a result of changes in reimbursement rules, deteriorating rates of reimbursement, and an overall decline in the economy. Hospital failures increased, as did bed closings. In addition, there was an increase in federal and state anti-kickback and safe harbor regulations that dampened the enthusiasm for joint ventures for nonhospital-based facilities.

The early 1990s and beyond place the hospital in the position of being only one component in the evolution toward organized delivery systems and other provider networks. This trend, and particularly the emphasis on ambulatory care, continues in the twenty-first century and is likely to continue for decades. In fact, hospitals in the future may be the subordinate organization within the emerging organized delivery system, replaced by a corporate enterprise with responsibility for operating a large system. In the future, and as a new generation of healthcare system executives replace the hospital executive, the role of the hospital may be narrowed to serve patients with complex problems, or those with no financial or insurance capability to be cared for at home or at nonhospital provider organizations.

Inpatient care will diminish with continued advances in medicine, and hospitals are likely to downsize. Simultaneously, ambulatory and doctors' office care will increase. The hospital, particularly compared with its earliest days, will play a very different role in the future as part of an integrated collection of providers and sites of care.

References

1. Hill K. *Wall Street Journal.* December 10, 1984.
2. de las Casas B. *History of Hispaniola.* 1945.

Biographical Information

Jesus J. Peña, MPA, JD, was a senior Vice President at Saint Michael's Medical Center, Newark, New Jersey. In this capacity, he was responsible for day-to-day operations and marketing. A member of the American Arbitration Association, he has studied hospital settlements that have affected the health industry and has served as a consultant to the World Health Organization in several Latin American countries. Mr. Peña worked with the Office of Technical Assistance of the United Nations to improve the healthcare system in Latin America through the application of new managerial techniques by those committed to serving large numbers of indigent patients.

Note: Please find Lawrence Wolper's biographical information on page ix.

Laboratories

Paul J. Brzozowski and Paul D. Camara

Clinical laboratories are one of the most dynamic environments in health care today. The medical community is exerting pressure on laboratories to expand their scope of service and improve quality at a time when changes in reimbursement regulations, the advent of organized delivery systems, and competition are forcing laboratories to become even more efficient and operate under increasing fiscal constraints. Those responsible for laboratories need to look beyond traditional management styles and marketing strategies to keep their laboratories viable, while at the same time remaining technologically up-to-date.

Patient testing has expanded well beyond the traditional acute care and reference testing settings. Today's laboratory environment ranges from reference laboratories where low-volume esoteric testing takes place to physician offices where phlebotomy and basic laboratory analyses are routine. Quality and cost-effective laboratory services have become a major requirement of integrated networks that cover the continuum of care and whose sites include wellness centers, home care, physician's offices, acute care settings, and long-term care operations. The testing requirements at each of these sites vary significantly.

No single laboratory can provide all the testing services required in today's healthcare delivery system. Therefore, efforts to integrate testing from all provider sites in a well-designed, organized system are important. Because the laboratory's product is information, much of the change in technology is related to the information systems needed to register patients, track specimens, and report patient results for testing performed in a variety of settings across the continuum of care. This includes more timely management of clinical data. Integration of laboratory results from various locations (testing sites) is only one part of this clinical data management. Combining clinical information from other disciplines and sources, such as diagnostic imaging and medication profiles, with laboratory findings is also part of the laboratory's challenge. This is changing both how the information system is used and the role of laboratory professionals.

Change related to analytical equipment is twofold. First, the development of point-of-care testing (POCT) equipment enables providers of varying skills and training to perform basic laboratory analyses in the same location and at the same time that other services are provided. This reduces the amount of testing that needs to be referred to larger regional centers, improving services and decreasing their cost. This type of testing continues to grow in importance and scope as the demand for service increases and the technology improves. Second, the development of robotics to process specimens, combined with the expansion of test menus and throughput on larger analytical systems, has allowed for the growth of large, low-cost regional centers that serve many providers in today's integrated networks.

In response to these changes in technology and service demands, laboratory professionals are redefining their roles to serve patients effectively in all types of settings. This redefinition of roles is a major issue as health care continues to evolve beyond traditional boundaries with new tools and technology. Managed care initiatives for increased efficiency, reduced utilization, and expansion of test menus have accelerated the process of change in a manner that will make it impossible for laboratories to remain in existence if they do not remain flexible in their approach to staffing, skill mix, and technology.

To provide a better understanding of the laboratory operation and the changes in organization, roles, and technology necessary to manage the limited resources available to clinical laboratories, the following characteristics of clinical laboratories are discussed:

- Service levels
- Organization
- Staffing
- Information systems
- Physical plant, instrumentation, and equipment
- Emerging technologies
- Laboratory outreach services
- Laboratory regulation and compliance
- Strategic planning

Issues such as skill mix, workstation configuration, workload, workflow, and customer service are examined in the context of these operational characteristics.

Service Levels

The variety of tests offered; the turnaround time associated with that testing; and other services, such as technical and clinical consultation, access to information systems, and/or phlebotomy and courier services, determine a laboratory's service level. Properly defined service levels provide the basis for effective laboratory management because they drive decisions on staffing, skill mix, information systems design, equipment configuration, facility design, and strategic planning. Factors to consider in developing the range of testing performed by a laboratory fall into one of these four categories:

1. Medical needs
2. Legal or professional requirements
3. Technical and personnel capabilities
4. Administrative/financial considerations

Questions pertaining to the factors in each category were incorporated into a questionnaire/worksheet format that has been used as a formal decision-making tool to help answer two questions: Should we offer this service? What is the appropriate site? Originally developed by Boutweil and Stewart at the Centers for Disease Control,[1] the criteria have been updated and the format modified by Hager and Brzozowski.[2]

Defining 75% of a laboratory's on-site test menu is not difficult. It is the remaining 25% that presents a significant challenge. Condensing information into a well-defined, easy-to-use, structured format enables a laboratory to use a multidisciplinary approach to define the remaining 25% of its services. Administrative, fiscal, clinical, and laboratory professionals are all encouraged to offer input into a final decision on whether a procedure will be performed in the laboratory, sent elsewhere in the network, or not performed at all. Once the service level has been determined, a laboratory can evaluate the other operational characteristics necessary to support the organization's mission.

With more of the laboratory business coming from the outpatient population, laboratories have had to adjust their service-level definition in order to remain competitive. Service-level changes include more frequent courier pickups, on-site phlebotomy and POCT services and drawing stations, expanded POCT, longer hours of operation, access to the laboratory information system, and use of telecommunication technology for technical and clinical consultation.

Organization

Laboratories usually are divided into two major divisions: anatomic pathology and clinical pathology. Anatomic pathology relates to the processing of surgical and gynecological specimens (e.g., Pap smears). Its subsections usually include surgical pathology, histology, and cytology. Occasionally, in reference laboratories or teaching centers, other specialties may be assigned to the anatomic division.

Clinical pathology is the division that processes the test requests more familiar to the general public, such as blood cell counts, coagulation studies, urinalyses, blood glucose levels, and throat cultures. Its subsections include chemistry, hematology, microbiology, urinalysis (microscopy), and blood bank. Laboratories have begun to combine some of these sections into more efficient larger units, such as an automation section that incorporates many aspects of hematology and chemistry. Other subsections may include flow cytometry, endocrinology, toxicology, serology, tissue typing, molecular diagnostics, and cytogenetics. The number of formally designated subsections reflects the previously defined service levels. **Appendix 13.A** contains a representative list of tests performed in these sections.

Laboratory Configuration

In order to deliver these services in a high-quality, cost-effective manner, an organized delivery system needs several types of laboratory configurations.

- A large regional laboratory
- Rapid response laboratories located at acute care facilities, ambulatory surgery centers, and large clinics
- Drawing stations at various locations throughout the network
- POCT capabilities

Figure 13.1 illustrates the organized delivery system structure and the flow of specimens throughout the system.

A variety of relationships may exist throughout the network. These may include but are not limited to:

- Direct ownership of additional entities or subsidiaries
- Contractual agreements with other individuals or organizations
- Joint ventures

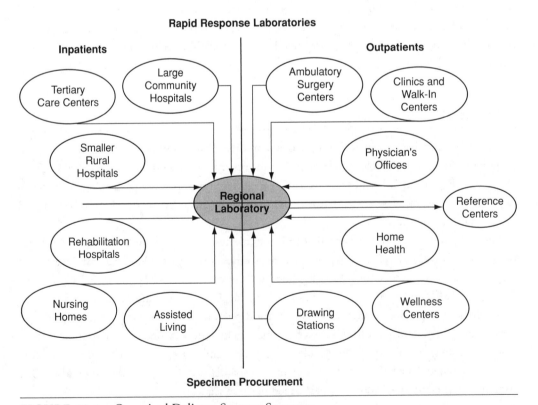

FIGURE 13.1   Organized Delivery Systems Structure

The overriding objective of providing the highest quality care that is also the most cost-effective is usually comprised of a blend of the relationships described above.

Large regional laboratories function as hubs for the organized healthcare delivery system's laboratory service. Technology at this site includes the central information system, robotics for pre-analytical specimen processing, and highly automated large-capacity testing equipment. The regional laboratory is likely to operate 24 hours per day, with the busiest times and bulk of the testing performed during the early evening and late night hours to accommodate the testing needs of the physicians' offices, late admissions into hospitals, and home healthcare providers. Other services often located at this site include marketing, client support, and courier functions.

The services offered at regional laboratories include the full range of clinical laboratory testing, with the exception of transfusion services and the anatomic pathology services that require the presence of a physician. It is becoming more common for the regional laboratory to process surgical specimens, however. A regional center may be one of a system's larger laboratories located at a large teaching center, an acute care hospital, a commercial reference laboratory, or a separate freestanding operation centrally located within the network's service area. Location is a key operational characteristic of the regional laboratory.

There are two major types of rapid response laboratory: one in the acute care setting and another in the outpatient clinic or physician's office. The rapid response laboratory in the acute care setting has a broader test menu than that in the outpatient settings, and it provides transfusion and anatomic pathology services. Furthermore, it remains open 24 hours per day. In the outpatient setting, the rapid response laboratory's hours of operation reflect the hours that the clinic or office is open for patient appointments. In both settings, the goal is to refer as much testing as possible to the regional laboratory, where the technology available and the economies of scale make the cost of performing laboratory analyses significantly less.

Drawing stations fill an important role in the organized healthcare delivery system. They can be located almost anywhere, but are most frequently found in clinics, physicians' offices, and locations convenient to patients (e.g., drugstores, major shopping areas). They allow patients to have their laboratory work drawn with minimal interruption in their daily routines. In today's competitive marketplace, customer service must be a goal of any organization. Drawing stations also provide a drop-off point for home care professionals, enabling them to initiate their patient testing in a timely and efficient manner.

POCT is one of the most controversial topics in laboratory medicine. The controversy is principally due to the cost of the testing, the competency of individuals who perform the testing, the need for aggressive quality management of the data, and correlation of results with similar testing performed at the main hospital laboratory and other sites in the system. POCT is most often performed by clinical personnel whose primary training is not in the clinical laboratory sciences (e.g., nurses, medical assistants, physicians, respiratory therapists), or by patients themselves. Testing may be performed at the bedside, within an emergency department (ED), critical care unit, operating room or cardiac catheterization laboratory, in physicians' offices, at home, or in other venues. This approach is very convenient for all concerned and, in some cases, very important clinically, with results available almost immediately, thus increasing the speed of therapeutic intervention. This approach becomes essential for glucose testing on the brittle diabetic and coagulation testing in the cardiac cath lab, and is increasingly used for cardiac marker testing in the ED for patients presenting with acute chest pain. The cost of POCT may be several times higher than the cost of the same test in a rapid response or regional laboratory, however. Therefore, it should be used only when indicated.

Given the number of individuals, devices, and locations involved in POCT, it is difficult to control quality and ensure proper documentation of results and billing. Laboratory professionals should have overall responsibility for the management of the POCT program and for monitoring compliance through rigorous training, proficiency testing, and quality control programs. A direct computerized interface between POCT instruments on the hospital units and the laboratory information system (LIS) is now a fundamental component of POCT management. This connectivity allows immediate downloading of patient results and quality control data to the LIS and facilitates uploading of new quality control ranges and user identification information to POCT instruments. With this technology, laboratory personnel responsible for hospital-wide POCT can manage the program in real time, correlating POCT results with core lab data and proactively managing the quality aspects of the testing.

Reengineering efforts in many organizations have significantly affected laboratories. One of the major changes is the consolidation of services along functional rather than clinical characteristics. For example, many laboratories now have a section referred to as the automation laboratory that contains high-throughput analyzers used for both chemistry and hematology tests, eliminating the need for separate chemistry and hematology sections. This type of change has a significant impact on physical plant layout, staffing, skill mix, and cross-training. Less space is required, and the layout is more open—in the past, there were walls between the various sections, even though an open design is more conducive to an efficient workflow. Now there are fewer workstations, requiring less staff. In larger laboratories a more cost-effective skill mix with an increased use of technicians and support staff is possible because they are easier to supervise in an open laboratory with well-defined workstations and more pre- and post-analytical activity.

Entire functions have also been reengineered out of the laboratory. Some examples include phlebotomy and POCT. Staff in hospitals, walk-in centers, home health agencies, and long-term care facilities perform these functions.

The goal of any system should be to minimize the bureaucracy and to have clearly defined reporting relationships. Although reengineering has had a positive impact on this issue, problems may arise in the laboratory manager role. Many times, this person's loyalty is split between the medical director and a hospital administrator, such as the chief operating officer or vice president. Divided loyalties particularly are common when an individual is managing several sites or departments, usually in an acute care setting or large regional center. Ideally, the medical director should assume overall responsibility for the medical direction of the laboratory, and the laboratory manager should be the key administrative and operational person. Access to senior management and a high degree of autonomy are crucial to the success of both the laboratory manager and the medical director.

Through formal and informal feedback from the medical staff and other providers, the medical director determines the appropriate service levels, including the variety of testing to be available at each site, the turnaround times associated with that testing, and the tolerance limits (e.g., quality control, utilization) for services rendered. On receiving this information, the laboratory manager can identify the resources necessary to carry out these services. Issues such as the physical plant, staffing/skill mix, information systems, and equipment needs must be resolved within the financial and administrative constraints placed on the operation by the board and senior management and must reflect the hospital mission statement.

The medical director also provides feedback to direct care providers. He or she must take an active role in effecting changes in physician practice patterns (e.g., ordering of microscopic urines, routine differentials, and general utilization of laboratory services). To be successful, the medical director needs a reliable database of physician utilization of laboratory services and a thorough understanding of viable alternatives and constraints that the laboratory operation presents. These factors have caused clinical laboratories to pay more attention to administrative duties, expectations, and compensation for these services in their contractual arrangements. **Appendix 13.B** contains a sample job description of a clinical laboratory medical director.

As a result of the time required to prepare for and perform these duties, the medical director needs a strong laboratory management team to keep him or her informed and to deal with the day-to-day operation.

In addition to the operational issues mentioned, the responsibilities of the management team include:

- Development of strategies that improve staff productivity
- Cost reduction
- Development and interpretation of management reports—Today, management reports also include the tools necessary to monitor utilization of laboratory services and the impact of laboratory data on clinical outcomes. This approach has the most significant impact on quality and cost.

The laboratory management team must be responsive to budget performance, maintenance of service levels, and personnel administration—recruitment, retention, and individual performance—and should have direct access to the people and information necessary to carry out this role. The medical director and the management team need a strong clinical and supervisory team, not only to address the day-to-day technical issues, but also to support them in the financial performance of the laboratory operation.

Bureaucracy grows when an organization tries to reward employees with new, impressive titles and roles in lieu of proper recognition through promotions, pay raises, or similar incentives. In the long run, an organization will suffer if reporting relationships become confused and territorial issues arise and cause deterioration in the quality of relationships. A key lesson learned from reengineering is that appropriate incentives must be in place both to motivate staff and to support the mission of the organization.

In summary, organizational structures should be as flat as possible, with a minimal number of titles; they should be based on the size and scope of the operation and the number of people employed.

Staffing

Proper laboratory staffing is possibly one of the greatest challenges facing laboratory management today. To staff their operations, laboratories employ a blend of medical, technical, and support staff. The number, titles, and job descriptions vary according to the size of the organization and the scope of services provided.

Personnel Requirements

Most hospital-based clinical laboratories employ personnel in the following positions:

- Pathologists
- Administrative director (laboratory manager)
- Section supervisors
- Medical technologists (MTs) and medical laboratory technicians (MLTs)
- Phlebotomists and specimen processors
- Clerks, medical secretaries, and transcriptionists
- Laboratory information system (LIS) manager
- Outreach support staff (e.g., manager, sales and marketing representatives, client service staff, couriers)

With the exception of the physician's office laboratory, all laboratories, from large regional centers and reference laboratories to small rural hospital laboratories and drawing stations, have pathologists associated with them. Usually, one pathologist serves as the laboratory medical director. Large teaching and research facilities may appoint one pathologist the director of anatomic pathology and another pathologist the director of clinical pathology. The medical director is assisted by other pathologists in their group who take responsibility for directing subsections of the laboratory (chemistry, hematology, microbiology, blood bank/transfusion medicine, histology, and cytology). The pathologists are physicians who are generally board-certified in anatomic and/or clinical pathology. In some cases, pathologists are employees of the laboratory (e.g., in some large tertiary care centers, academic medical centers, and commercial laboratories), but this is not usually the case in community hospitals. The medical director and other pathologists are most often members of a private physician practice group and not hospital employees. The group is typically contracted by the hospital to provide medical direction, and professional services (medical diagnoses) in surgical pathology, cytopathology, and other pathology subdisciplines.

Contractual arrangements and negotiations with pathologists are important issues for laboratories. It is important, therefore, to have well-written contracts with pathologists that clearly specify all responsibilities and expectations. For example, pathologists should have agreements with all third-party payers (for professional billings) with which the hospital or laboratory has agreements. This will eliminate confusion on the part of patients when they receive bills for laboratory services. The contract should also include performance standards for pathology report turnaround time and should clearly state the administrative and medical director responsibilities of the pathologists.

In larger academic laboratories, doctoral-level laboratory scientists in biochemistry, microbiology, virology, and other disciplines may be employed to assist pathologists in directing the laboratories. These individuals may also serve as laboratory medical directors, depending on the scope of services provided in the laboratories where they work.

The laboratory administrative director (called a laboratory manager in smaller facilities) serves as the day-to-day operational director of the laboratory service. The responsibilities of this individual extend to all budget and expense issues, human resources management, scheduling, contract negotiations, labor productivity, outreach growth and development, and strategic planning. The laboratory supervisors report directly to the administrative director. The administrative director and supervisors are usually medical technologists with administrative skills acquired through experience and formal graduate education (e.g., master's degree in business administration). In the uncommon instance that the administrative director does not have a laboratory background, it is necessary that an additional laboratory-trained leader be employed (as associate administrative director, operations director, or another appropriate title) to handle the day-to-day technical aspects of the department. It is also essential that, for the sake of the successful operation and development of the laboratory, the medical director, administrative director, and supervisors develop and maintain collegial and supportive working relationships.

Section and site supervisors usually are assigned to one section of a large laboratory operation, such as the chemistry or hematology sections. Their time is usually split between bench work (performing test analyses) and supervision. In small laboratories, such as a rapid response laboratory, one supervisor may oversee work in several disciplines. In larger laboratories, where one section may employ from 30 to 40 staff technologists, section supervisors do very little, if any, bench work. The size and scope of the operation determine their roles. Senior technologists may assist supervisors in major subsections of a department. For example, in the chemistry department of a large laboratory, senior technologists may be assigned to subsections, such as those that deal with immunoassays, toxicology, or automation. Senior technologists also may have functional rather than line management roles, such as responsibility for POCT, quality control, preventive maintenance or lab safety. Medical technologists usually possess a bachelor of science degree in medical technology and have passed a registry examination given by one of several accrediting bodies, such as the American Society of Clinical Pathologists (ASCP) or the National Accrediting Agency for Laboratory Personnel (NCA). These individuals perform all types of laboratory analyses and function independently. Additionally, there are now 11 states that require medical technologists and other laboratory testing personnel to be licensed.[3] Medical laboratory technicians possess less formal education, usually an associate of science degree. They require more supervision and function less independently. In some facilities, they make up a major portion of the technical staffing at laboratories. Along with technologists, they provide the core of the laboratory staffing.

The primary job of phlebotomists is to procure blood specimens. Many hospitals now require that phlebotomists receive certification (e.g., through the National Phlebotomy Association, Landover, Maryland) to maintain employment. Training is usually received on the job. Specimen processors, clerks, and secretaries process the information in the laboratory, receive and accession specimens, register outpatients, send out specimens to reference laboratories, sort patient reports, do general typing, and handle departmental mail. With more formal training, secretaries transcribe pathology reports and perform duties such as cross-indexing reports and slides, and assisting with tumor registry. Often, smaller laboratories combine clerk and phlebotomist duties, and secretary/receptionist functions.

The LIS manager is a laboratory-based employee responsible for the implementation and maintenance of the LIS and management of all laboratory databases. Oversight extends to the clinical and anatomic pathology software, applications, modifications and upgrades, instrument interfaces, connectivity to disparate hospital information systems and electronic medical records (EMRs), interface to external client EMRs, and training of all users, in addition to daily operation, monitoring, and troubleshooting of the LIS. Hardware responsibilities often fall under the hospital information systems department.

Outreach programs (described later in this chapter) require several key positions for successful operation. They include an outreach manager (for oversight of the program, strategic planning, and supervision of all staff); sales and marketing staff (to develop new business, and maintain existing client relationships); client services (to handle all incoming client calls, troubleshoot problems, and call clients with stat results); and couriers (for retrieving specimens from client sites and patient service centers, and delivering reports). Larger laboratories may also employ in-house billing staff to check and improve claims prior to billing and/or to bill claims.

Laboratories with formal medical technology training programs and complex service levels may also employ full-time education coordinators, quality control supervisors, quality assurance/improvement coordinators, and stand-alone POCT coordinators.

Workload and Staff Utilization

The workload in a clinical laboratory can be divided into two major categories: technical and nontechnical. The technical workload can be defined as the number of analyses (tests) performed by the laboratory. The hours needed to complete these analyses are linked primarily to the methodology employed and secondarily to the turnaround time required and the staff proficiency. In the past, the College of American Pathologists (CAP) used time and motion studies to determine the amount of labor necessary to perform individual analyses,[4] and the results have provided the basis for many staff measurement tools. Standards were expressed in terms of CAP units, with one CAP unit equal to one minute of supervisory, technical, clerical, and aide time necessary to perform an analysis. These time studies paid particular attention to the degree of automation, often establishing unique labor standards for different manufacturers' analyzers. Applying these standards to both patient and nonpatient (i.e., quality control, calibration, repeat) test volumes determines the number of minutes required to perform the technical portion of the workload. The technical workload usually consumes 60 to 70% of paid hours.

The nontechnical workload consists of activities such as regulatory tasks, inventory and ordering of supplies, continuing education, human resource functions, and equipment evaluations, among others. The time required for these activities is more difficult to assess. Laboratory organization, mission statement, size, support systems, and physical facilities vary too much from institution to institution to permit industry-wide standards for nontechnical laboratory activities. Allowances are also necessary for downtime, personal time, fatigue, delay, and standby, such as on the night shift in acute care settings. Together, nontechnical workload and downtime consume 15 to 25% of paid hours. The remaining 10 to 15% of paid hours are consumed by benefit hours (i.e., vacation, sick, holiday). Actual labor distribution/payroll reports can be used to determine benefit hours.

These ratios vary, depending on the type of laboratory and support services offered. A rapid response laboratory will have a larger percentage of downtime and nontechnical work than a regional laboratory. The provision of a great many support services, such as specimen pickup, report delivery (by couriers), and blood collection (by phlebotomists), will add significantly to the nontechnical workload.

To properly assess the time requirements associated with workload, some basic quantitative analyses are needed. Work sampling, frequency distributions, or time ladders (self-logging techniques) can all be useful. An organization's management engineering department, consultant, or professional society can be used to assist laboratory personnel in completing these studies. Not only should the studies be comprehensive, but they should also include technical activities. Much of the information in the literature, as well as that available for purchase, is based on averages. Thus, test batch size and skill mix have influenced the data, and they may not be applicable in a laboratory with operational characteristics that do not reflect industry averages (usually the case with both very large and very small laboratories). A detailed quantitative analysis will determine if the staffing ratios or relative value units (RVUs) assigned to various laboratory activities are appropriate for a particular laboratory; at the same time, it will appropriately identify the technical activities, nontechnical activities, and downtime characteristics. Often, this complete approach results in work simplification and streamlining of the operation through better integration of all activities and skills. Internal studies should be combined with labor productivity benchmarking, available through various third parties (e.g., professional societies and consulting firms) and can be conducted as part of other studies.

Cost accounting is one approach to quantifying billable tests and associating them with a cost. The cost of laboratory testing varies dramatically, based on the size, type, and location of the laboratory. Total direct costs generally range from $7.50 to $9.50 for well-performing laboratories. **Table 13.1** shows how labor and supply costs contribute to overall expense.

In smaller laboratories and specialty laboratories, costs may run higher; in larger regional laboratories, lower. Although labor remains the largest single cost (approximately 50% in most

Table 13.1   Laboratory Expense Benchmarks by Test Volume

| | Billable Test Volume (Annual) | |
	< 600,000	600,000–1 million
Total cost per test	$8.50–9.50	$7.50–8.50
Non-salary cost per test	$3.50–4.25	$3.00–3.75
Salary cost per test	$4.25–5.50	$4.00–4.75

Data represents 2008 industry benchmarks for hospital-based clinical laboratories, including histology and cytology.

laboratories), costs associated with the blood bank and the cost of blood products are significant in laboratories that are in acute care settings. (Blood product cost is typically > $1M in most laboratories.) Because of automation and large test volumes, chemistry and hematology are the least expensive lab sections (incrementally) at approximately $3 to $4 per billable test. Blood bank, microbiology, and histology have higher costs per test because they involve less automation, the volumes of billable tests are lower, and they are labor intensive.

In June 1993, the CAP ceased using its workload recording method. Instead, it is supporting the Laboratory Management Index Program (LMIP), a series of productivity modules that use specific input data to allow the assessment of individual laboratory sections. The input data provide a central core of information to calculate productivity, utilization, and cost-effectiveness ratios. Peer group analyses are structured into billable groups and complexity groups, and take into account the variability between sections in laboratories.

Once these analyses are completed, workload can be compared to staffing levels to determine staff productivity. Staff utilization should not be confused with productivity. Someone can be busy without being productive (e.g., turn out one test result per hour in a very inefficient laboratory). In the laboratory, productivity is measured as the number of patient test results reported per unit of time.

Monitoring two ratios—paid hours per billable test and billable tests per patient encounter—helps avoid the confusion between staff utilization and productivity. These ratios are also useful in assessing batch size, number of urgent requests, single test draws, number of nonpatient tests, and impact of equipment in terms of degree of automation. For example, a small laboratory with minimal automation and small batches will require more time per billable test than a large operation with large batches and a high degree of process and analytical automation. An institution with a low number of urgent requests and few single test draws (e.g., as seen in many lab outreach programs) will have a higher number of billable tests per encounter, a desirable trait.

The manner in which tests are counted will affect these ratios. Basically, if a laboratory counts groups of tests as outlined in the American Medical Association's Current Procedural Terminology (CPT) coding guidelines—a complete blood cell count (CBC) or a basic metabolic profile (BMP) as one billable test each—a traditional hospital laboratory with volumes of 300,000 to 600,000 billable tests per year can expect to see 0.20 to 0.25 paid hours per billable test and two to four billable tests per venipuncture. If that hospital has a significant number of tests from the outreach market and annual volumes of 600,000 to 1 million, the labor requirements will drop to 0.18 to 0.22 paid hours per test. Large regional laboratories and reference centers will have even lower labor requirements. Regional laboratories can process tests with 25 to 50% less labor and lower supply costs than even the best traditional laboratories. This is one of the driving forces behind regional networks. **Table 13.2** shows how labor productivity improves with increasing test volume.

Workstation Configuration

The basic functional unit in the laboratory is the workstation. Tests performed at a particular workstation usually require the same skill level, the same equipment, and the same general re-

Table 13.2 Laboratory Labor Productivity Benchmarks by Test Volume

Total Billable Tests per Year	Labor Productivity (paid hours/billable test)
< 300,000	0.28–0.35
300,000–600,000	0.20–0.25
600,000–1 million	0.18–0.22
> 1 million	0.14–0.17

Data represents 2008 industry benchmarks for hospital-based clinical laboratories, including histology and cytology.

sources; often, they provide the same type of clinical information. For example, most laboratories have a coagulation workstation. Two common procedures performed at this workstation are the determinations of prothrombin time and activated partial thromboplastin time, which aid the physician in assessing the ability of a patient's blood to clot. These procedures are usually highly automated.

A workstation may not be staffed for an entire shift. Properly configured workstations offer the manager the most flexibility in moving people from workstation to workstation as the day progresses to obtain maximum staff utilization and peak productivity. For example, after completing the morning batch of testing at the coagulation workstation, the person assigned to that workstation often assumes responsibility for other workstations in the laboratory (e.g., urinalysis or white blood cell differentials). This flexibility leads to the best possible service at the lowest possible cost. Large laboratories may have more than one technologist assigned to one workstation, each managing separate instruments, or performing a limited number of similar procedures. Smaller laboratories may assign one individual to several workstations throughout the shift. Such work assignments present challenges to managers and strategic planners because they affect skill mix and cross-training, two operational characteristics linked directly to cost.

Skill Mix and Cross-Training

To understand skill mix, three ratios should be studied:

1. Percentage of staff made up of support personnel (clerical/aide)
2. Percentage of medical technologists that are registered
3. Full-time to part-time staff ratio

A low percentage of support staff in a laboratory usually indicates that technicians are performing clerical functions, certain clerical activities are automated, or some clerical activities are going undone. A high percentage of registered medical technologists usually increases labor costs. Having too few part-time staff members reduces flexibility in terms of staff scheduling and can lead to increased downtime by having personnel on the premises when they are not needed.

Small laboratories tend to have a higher percentage of registered medical technologists and a lower percentage of support staff or medical technicians than do large laboratories.

The technologists in small laboratories function more independently, exercise more judgment, do more of their own troubleshooting, are more extensively cross-trained, and may use less automation. These individuals may also function as phlebotomists, clerks, and technicians when necessary to meet the workload fluctuations of the department. Although a clerk cannot perform testing, a technologist can fill downtime with clerical activities. The skill level of a technologist makes his or her time more expensive, however, and is one major reason why smaller laboratories have higher unit costs.

Skill mix and cross-training are closely related, particularly in the technical areas. A great opportunity exists for cross-training among phlebotomy and clerical personnel. Staff who are cross-trained in these areas could support a central specimen-processing area. To facilitate this, many laboratories have introduced a laboratory assistant job classification. Employees in this category would have four levels through which they could be trained: clerical, phlebotomy, specimen processing, and basic testing, such as planting of cultures. This strategy would have several benefits:

- Increased staffing flexibility
- Provision of relief to the technical staff
- Reduced turnover
- Combined clerk and phlebotomist positions
- Opportunity for promotion

Cross-training of medical technologists and technicians across clinical laboratory specialties has become essential as the shortage of available personnel has worsened. Current estimates predict a need to fill 10,000 MT and MLT vacancies each year with only 4500 graduates. During the next 10 years, the Baby Boom generation will retire with increasing frequency, exacerbating the shortage. Laboratories must implement cross-training in chemistry, hematology, microbiology, and blood bank and improve labor productivity through increased process and analytical automation, result autoverification, and other means to help ameliorate this significant threat to successful laboratory operations.

Information Systems

The laboratory's product is information. The primary objective of any laboratory information system is to present data in the most orderly, legible, and timely manner possible. Clinical laboratory information systems have become highly automated and sophisticated in data-handling systems. A well-designed network laboratory information system has the benefit of integrating inpatient and outpatient laboratory data. In an organized healthcare delivery system, all testing centers—reference laboratories, regional laboratories, rapid response laboratories, and POCT facilities—should be encompassed by this information system.

In the late 1960s and early 1970s, when most laboratory services were provided at a hospital site, and only a limited number of software systems were available in the marketplace, the in-house development of information systems was a popular decision. In the mid-1970s and mid-1980s, stand-alone turnkey systems became popular because of problems in the integration of the laboratory information system with the hospital's main clinical and financial information systems. The more recent trends have used the integrated system approach. There have been major improvements in the ease and cost of interfacing stand-alone systems with network system mainframes and file servers. Also, several major laboratory vendors have developed systemwide clinical information systems. This integration provides many benefits from both a system administration and cost perspective. The level of integration includes off-site locations such as satellite laboratories, drawing stations, nursing homes, physicians' offices, and bidirectional interfacing between the network laboratories and those not part of the system, such as commercial reference laboratories. These interfaces eliminate time-consuming manual entry of requisitions and automate the result entry process for tests performed out of the network.

Vendor-supplied clinical information systems have become well established as a regular part of the laboratory and are critical to its mission and management. Not only do these systems organize the work, accumulate data on specimens, generate clinical reports, maintain a longitudinal patient record, and post bills, but they also keep audit trails, monitor quality, log workload, and keep department policies and procedures online. Laboratory clients, such as physicians' offices, nursing homes, and home healthcare agencies, can have access to patient results via their personal computers (PCs), terminals, and scheduled reports to printers. Most laboratory information systems use PCs that are part of the network's information system. Improved communications and easy access to databases have been the key factors behind the numerous gains in productivity.[5] Properly designed clinical information systems also integrate the laboratory data into a single database with other clinical data from diagnostic imaging, pharmacy, and other departments. This allows all parties to provide valuable input into the design of treatment protocols, monitor outcomes, and determine the best course of treatments and safeguards for the healthcare delivery system in which they provide care.

The benefits of information technology to the laboratory are in the more orderly and timely presentation of laboratory data and the utilization of these data beyond traditional uses, such as effecting changes in physicians' ordering patterns, performing laboratory–pharmacy reviews, monitoring changes in antibiotic susceptibility patterns more completely, and conducting product line and diagnosis-related group (DRG) costing studies. **Exhibit 13.1** shows the benefits of automation.

Among the leading information systems, the key features include:

- Bar coding
- Handheld devices (particularly useful for the phlebotomy team or POCT)
- Image scanning and storage (e.g., of outpatient requisitions and insurance cards)
- Voice recognition for dictation
- Improvements in remote communication
- Improvements in graphics
- Electronic medical record (EMRs)

Bar coding is standard at most institutions, and most laboratory analyzers have the capability to interpret bar code labels on the primary sampling tubes. Bar coding provides several advantages, including improved turnaround time, better specimen tracking and accountability, and fewer specimen identification errors.

Exhibit 13.1   System Improvement Because of Automation of Laboratory Information Systems

Benefits	Reason
Reduced errors in reporting results	• Online delta checks and autoverification
	• Bidirectional instrument interfaces
	• Better presentation of data for supervisory review
Shorter turnaround time of patient results	• LIS inquiry versus manual file searches
	• LIS/instrument interfaces with autoverification and autorelease features
	• More organized cumulative report format
Increased productivity	• Less transcription
	• Reduced filing
	• Less time spent charting, with telephone inquiries, and finding results
	• Automated statistics gathering
New features available with no increase in personnel	• Ability to update procedure manuals online
	• DRG/case mix analysis
Reduced paper costs	• Use of stock computer paper rather than expensive multipart forms
Improved legibility	• Reports printed, not handwritten, and prepared in more orderly fashion
Automated statistics gathering	• Statistics computerized

The improvements in remote communication have allowed laboratories to market their services to physicians' offices, with one of the key components being access to a patient's test results throughout the continuum of care by means of terminals, handheld devices, or printers located in the physician's office or home. Many physicians have access to both the laboratory test results and to other pertinent clinical information through their personal PCs.

In response to what was perceived as neglect (i.e., improper monitoring, maintenance, and repair protocols), inspection has become part of the laboratory information system operation. Voluntary accrediting agencies (e.g., College of American Pathologists [CAP], American Association of Blood Banks [AABB]), and federal regulatory agencies, like the Food and Drug Administration (FDA), and others have begun focusing attention on laboratory information systems to ensure that they are properly tested and monitored.

The CAP has included questions about laboratory information systems on its accreditation checklist for many years. In 1989, the AABB updated its guidelines to include more stringent documentation, testing, and standard operating procedures for blood bank computer systems. Since 1987, the FDA has made the inspection of the computer system a routine part of every blood bank inspection. Through the Clinical Laboratory Improvement Act (CLIA) regulations, laboratory information systems are part of regular laboratory inspections.[6] Clearly, these agencies are requiring proof of validation of information systems used in clinical laboratories.

The administrative laboratory director oversees both bench technologists and the computer support group as they generate, process, store, and transmit information. In the past, these supervisory responsibilities consisted primarily of selecting, purchasing, and deploying laboratory information systems, analytical instruments, and test methods. In the future, the administrative laboratory director will work more closely with the daily information management component of the laboratory and the healthcare delivery system. Some of the elements of this collaboration are the following:[7]

- As major capital expenditures, the laboratory information system and other components of the information architecture are carefully scrutinized at higher organizational levels in hospitals for gains in quality and efficiency.
- The success of the laboratory increasingly will be measured in terms of the value added to the laboratory database.
- Competition is increasing within hospitals for control of the laboratory and other clinical databases, adding a political dimension to information management that requires the close attention of laboratory managers.
- Decisions involving information management tend to have a horizontal effect on all laboratories and are frequently mission critical, thus requiring macromanagement expertise.
- Information systems increasingly generate so-called information by-products, such as test turnaround times, that enhance the efficiency and quality of all laboratory operations.
- Patient confidentiality has become a major issue for laboratory personnel.

Physical Plant, Instrumentation, and Equipment

After human resources, the physical facility, instrumentation, and equipment are the most important elements in providing laboratory services. Service levels and workload dictate staffing and equipment configuration, which, in turn, dictate the amount of space required. Workflow influences layout, and the size and type of institution determine the location(s) of the laboratory within the facility. In general, laboratory equipment is becoming smaller, more self-contained, and more efficient to operate. As a result, less space is necessary for both equipment and staff, and fewer safety issues, such as toxic waste and noxious fumes, arise. More tests are being performed in the patient care areas, and this trend is likely to continue. These features make design of the laboratory easier.

Very good sources of specific guidelines for determining actual space requirements include the Laboratory Design Approved Guideline from the Clinical and Laboratory Standards Institute,[8] and the CAP Manual for Laboratory Planning and Design.[9] The CAP manual's appendix lists such indicators as net square feet or linear feet of bench space per bed, test, or full-time employee (FTE), which can be used to calculate the size of a laboratory. All of these figures and ratios are meant to be used as guidelines and starting points, not absolute standards. In general, wide-open rooms with movable cabinetry are preferable to small sectioned areas. Open space allows flexibility in altering the layout in this dynamic environment and enhances productivity and staff utilization through improved workflow and people movement.

An open floor plan for the laboratory provides the greatest opportunity for staff and operational efficiencies and effectiveness. Most laboratories have broken down the walls that traditionally separated the clinical areas into chemistry, hematology, microbiology, and blood bank sections. Laboratories are establishing workstations by arranging equipment according to function rather than clinical definition. For example, a workstation may include coagulation, drug testing, fertility, and endocrine testing. Traditionally, these workstations would have been separated between the hematology and chemistry sections. With an open floor plan, workstations, and cross-trained technologists, a laboratory is able to configure itself based on its customers' needs and maximize the efficiency and productivity of its staff.

Work areas such as virology, histology, or microbiology laboratories that perform testing for tuberculosis and other contagious diseases should be excluded from the open-space approach. Because these sections handle virulent pathogens and toxic chemicals, they should be in more isolated areas. When possible, these areas should be located near outside walls to facilitate installation of exhaust hoods and to meet more stringently controlled HVAC requirements.

The functional relationship between the laboratory and direct care providers also influences the appropriate location for the laboratory. In acute care settings, the rapid response laboratories should be near the intensive care unit, emergency department, operating rooms, and clinic areas. This approach minimizes the need for satellite laboratories and thus avoids any inefficiencies and expense that they may bring to an operation through smaller batch sizes, minimal staffing levels and corresponding downtime, and duplication of equipment. For some acute care settings, usually larger tertiary care facilities and healthcare networks, satellite laboratories may be necessary to reduce test turnaround time for patients in critical care and outpatient areas located great distances from the rapid response laboratory. The use of pneumatic tube systems has made the location of the laboratory a less critical issue, as they allow the movement of laboratory specimens between locations in a fast and efficient manner. Many of these systems have carriers large enough to transport blood products. This eliminates trips to the blood bank.

The use of satellite ancillary services is a major concern in today's reimbursement environment. Decentralization makes monitoring and controlling utilization more difficult. Not only are systems and equipment duplicated, but also the output itself may be different. Requisitions, reporting procedures, and charting policies may vary significantly from those in the central laboratory, causing confusion for clinicians.

Instrumentation and Techniques

Analytical instrumentation and other laboratory devices play a major role in the organization, staffing, physical layout, budgeting, finance, and clinical success of the laboratory. Early laboratory techniques and instruments relied on manual methods that lacked nearly all the operational qualities considered indispensable today. These include accuracy, precision, specificity, short turnaround time, and financial economy. The characteristics of today's instrumental systems and methods contrast sharply with their predecessors in all respects. Two significant design achievements that are now well entrenched in laboratory instrumentation are automated task performance (robotics) and miniaturization of technology (viz, electronic components, analytical electrodes, signal detectors, cuvettes, etc). Instruments incorporating these analytic and operational characteristics have allowed dramatic changes in how laboratories are configured and staffed, and how quickly physicians and other caregivers have access to laboratory results.

Nonanalytical Automation

Laboratory instrumentation and equipment is divided logically into those devices that prepare specimens or automate manual processes (nonanalytical) and those that produce test results (analytical). Some current systems incorporate features of both types onto one platform. **Table 13.3** shows a list of nonanalytical equipment common to most clinical laboratories, in addition to the more recently introduced and less common "sample processing automation."

Centrifuges, incubators, water baths, stainers, and tissue processors are indispensable components of all clinical and anatomic pathology laboratories. Combined slidemaker/stainers are offered routinely by several vendors in clinical hematology (e.g., Abbott Diagnostics, Sysmex Corporation, Beckman-Coulter). Automated slidemaking has also found an important niche in cytology to aid in the diagnosis of cervical cancer as well as cancers of the lung, bladder, and gastrointestinal tract and in the preparation of fine needle aspiration of thyroid and breast (e.g., the Hologic/Cytyc Thin-Prep Processor and the BD SurePath PrepStain Slide Processor). Automated sample processing in clinical pathology, however (also referred to as "front-end"

Table 13.3 Nonanalytical Laboratory Equipment for Specimen Preparation and Process Automation

Device/System	Type	Function
Centrifuge	Specimen preparation	Separate cells from serum or plasma and other components based on differential density.
Incubator/water bath	Specimen prep, often a component of the analytical process	Creates a temperature-controlled environment for specimen incubation.
Tissue processor	Specimen prep and process automation	Exposes tissue samples to chemical treatment in various solvents in a carefully timed sequence in order to stabilize (fix) the tissue prior to histologic sectioning.
Slidemaker/stainer	Process automation	The slidemaker creates a thin film of blood or other body fluid on a glass slide. The stainer prepares it for examination by selectively coloring cellular components. Often used to differentiate white blood cell components, to count cells in body fluids, or to prepare slides for cervical cancer screening. The slidemaker and stainer components may be combined or separate modules.
Sample processing automation	Process automation	Automates pre- and post-analytical laboratory processes including computerized specimen receipt, sorting, transport, centrifugation, decapping, aliquotting, transport of specimens to analyzers and to online refrigerated storage.

automation or "total laboratory" automation), is still finding its way into routine use due to the major capital investment ($250,000 to greater than $1 million), space requirements, and the need for high annual test volumes to justify implementation. In the correct environment (e.g., in laboratories with > 1 million billable tests per year), process automation can provide high cost savings, can improve service levels and quality in the clinical laboratory, and can impact every phase of analysis from specimen processing and analysis to online refrigerated archival storage of patient samples. This technology integrates robotics and information system features such as bar coding with the actual technical analysis. Systems often include specimen processing (e.g., specimen receipt into the LIS, centrifugation, sorting, decapping, aliquotting, and sampling) followed by transport of the specimen to the correct analyzer for testing. Several analyzers (e.g., chemistry, immunoassay, urinalysis, cell counting, and coagulation) can be linked on a single automated track using these systems.

This level of automation is already paying big dividends in larger laboratories and will continue to evolve so as to become a routine addition to most laboratory operations. Within the past two years, all major instrument vendors have introduced versions of front-end automation created to connect to their analyzers, with some systems also accommodating analyzers from other vendors. Significantly, all companies offering process automation systems either currently offer modules for high-volume, online, refrigerated archival specimen storage or will soon introduce them.

Automated Analytical Instrumentation

Automated instruments began taking prominent hold in the clinical laboratory in the late 1950s with the introduction of the Skeggs Autoanalyzer.[10] Working as a hospital chemist faced with an increasing workload and a paucity of trained technical staff, Skeggs endeavored to build an instrument that would perform blood analysis from start to finish with no operator intervention. The Autoanalyzer system was finally introduced in 1957 and became a standard for analytical automation in the clinical chemistry laboratory for the next 15 years. These early systems produced 20 to 40 results per hour. The development and miniaturization of electronic components during the 1970s and the rapid development of advanced information processing technology in the 1970s and 1980s led to the introduction of superior laboratory automation with each passing year. In the twenty-first century, an escalating staffing shortage and persistent cuts in reimbursement from the federal government and other third-party payers are driving developments in automation.

Using current automated systems, laboratories can process large volumes of tests and specimens without a concomitant increase in technical personnel. These automated analyzers also are self-regulating. Software-driven protocols operate continually to monitor operational characteristics (e.g., water bath temperature, light source intensity, sample and reagent carousel position) as well as analytical performance (e.g., acceptability of quality control results, need for calibration, when to run an automated dilution, when to run an additional test based on other results [reflex testing]). The principal advantages of these systems include error reduction, improved analytical precision, decreased labor costs due to increased productivity, and significant potential for revenue enhancement (ability to add testing with little or no additional technical personnel and at very low incremental supply cost per test).

In the modern clinical laboratory, the number of tests performed by automated instruments far surpasses those performed manually, and at a considerably lower cost per test. This is seen most dramatically in the chemistry, hematology, and coagulation sections of the laboratory. Automated instruments in these areas routinely process several hundred to several thousand tests per hour using a single analyst per instrument per shift. In many cases, one analyst can successfully operate multiple analyzers simultaneously. Automation has led not only to significant improvements in labor productivity, but also to much improved result turnaround times. For example, expected analyzer turnaround times for a complete blood count* or a basic metabolic panel† range from 4 to 10 minutes, depending on the analyzer used. This allows most laboratories to publish results for these assays within 25 to 35 minutes from time of receipt in the laboratory.

Historically, the blood bank, microbiology, and histology laboratories have relied heavily on manual techniques (very low specimen-to-analyst ratio), but some opportunity for automation exists in these areas as well.

- Gel-based technology in the blood bank (e.g., the ID-Micro Typing System Gel Test, Ortho Clinical Diagnostics) can be used for antibody screening and identification, ABO blood grouping and Rh phenotyping, compatibility testing, reverse serum grouping, and antigen typing. Although this system is still inherently manual, it is amenable to automation for specimen and reagent identification and pipetting, centrifugation of the analytical device, and interpretation of results. Additionally, both Ortho Clinical Diagnostics and Immucor Gamma have introduced analyzers to automate this testing for high test volume laboratories (viz, the Ortho ProVue and the Immucor Galileo and Echo).
- In microbiology, high-volume testing, such as blood culture incubation with preliminary interpretation, and antimicrobial susceptibility testing are usually automated. Highly automated systems for *C trachomatis* (CT), *N gonorrhea* (NG), and human papillomavirus (HPV) are also in routine use.
- Certain aspects of histologic specimen preparation have been successfully automated including tissue processing and routine staining and coverslipping of microscopic slides.

When highly automated instrumentation and technology is introduced into clinical and anatomic pathology laboratories, potential exists for dramatic change in how these laboratories are staffed and managed. Among the possible service and management improvements are:

- Decreased turnaround time due to significantly reduced manual specimen handling requirements, shorter incubation times, bidirectional interfaces to the laboratory information system (LIS), and automated result autoverification.

---

*Complete blood count (CBC) includes white blood cell count, red blood cell count, hemoglobin, hematocrit, platelet count, and automated white blood cell differential.
†Basic metabolic panel (BMP) includes glucose, urea, creatinine, calcium, sodium, potassium, chloride, and carbon dioxide.

- Reduced frequency of errors in specimen identification due to computerized bar code labeling and reading, and direct download of test results from analyzers to the LIS (reduction in clerical errors).
- Workstation consolidation as a direct result of increased specimen throughout and larger test volume on a single instrument.
- Improved utilization of scarce technical staff due to workstation configuration along functional (operational) rather than clinical lines. Historically, staff have been trained and assigned based on scientific specialty. In highly automated laboratories, technical staff utilization improves when core automated laboratories are established that cross technical disciplines and focus on the operating characteristics of instruments.

Emerging Technologies

In addition to the developments in laboratory technology mentioned above, scientific progress in the application of molecular diagnostics to clinical laboratory medicine and the continued refinement, reduction in cost, and subsequent acceptance of process automation will have major impacts on how laboratories are managed in the years to come.

Molecular Diagnostics

Since 2004, the volume of molecular diagnostic tests ordered annually in the United States has grown by more than 30% and net revenue has grown from $2.6 billion to a projected $4.9 billion in 2008. It is the fastest growing and most profitable sector of clinical laboratory testing. Broadly defined, molecular diagnostic testing refers to the use of specialized reagents, analytical methods, techniques, and instrumentation, which employ cellular nucleic acids (DNA and RNA[‡]) as analytical targets to gain information that aids in the diagnosis of disease. Clinical laboratory methods range from the commonly used and highly automated direct probe assays for infectious diseases such as *C trachomatis* and *N gonorrhea*, as well as HPV and the hepatitis B and C antigens, to much more esoteric and labor-intensive tests for genetic mutations including Fragile-X Syndrome, Niemann-Pick Disease, and many others. Test complexity, expense, and the need for greater clinical and scientific expertise in performing and interpreting the tests increases across this range of assays.

It is easy to predict that continued advancements in nucleic-acid-based detection of microorganisms will have a significant effect on how microbiology laboratories will function in the future. The historic approach to identifying microorganisms in the laboratory has been to plant blood and body fluid specimens on appropriate growth media, incubate the planted specimen, watch for growth of the organism, and then identify the organism through biochemical and other tests. This process typically takes 1 to 5 days and requires large amounts of hands-on time by highly trained microbiology technologists. Using molecular diagnostic techniques, it is possible to construct probes, with or without signal amplification, that are specific for the nucleic acids inherent in the microorganisms of interest. When increased sensitivity is required, poly-

---

[‡]DNA—deoxyribonucleic acid; RNA—ribonucleic acid

merase chain reaction (PCR) and similar methodologies may be used. Significantly, these techniques do not require a growth period for the microorganisms to be detected. Introduction of molecular diagnostic methods decreases the turnaround time for microbiology results from days to hours. It also decreases the number of hands-on steps involved and has given rise to automated systems for testing. As the cost of these techniques decreases and the number of applications increases, molecular diagnostics will become the *sine qua non* in clinical microbiology, dramatically shortening result turnaround time and significantly improving the labor productivity of the microbiology laboratory. The relative benefits and risks of molecular testing are shown in **Table 13.4**.

Historically, the adoption of molecular diagnostic techniques in hospital-based clinical laboratories has been slow due to lack of local expertise, cost of reagents and instrumentation, and lack of billable test volume needed to make in-house performance cost-effective, with the possible exception of direct nucleic acid probe assays. Additionally, prior to the introduction of highly automated systems for performing this testing, space planning was difficult due to the need to separate certain components of the testing process to avoid specimen contamination. This is considerably less of a problem today with many vendors of molecular diagnostic reagents, methods, and instrument systems developing automated devices to perform all aspects of specimen preparation, nucleic acid extraction, amplification, and detection, within a closed system on a single platform. Another impediment to early adoption has been third-party reimbursement lagging behind expenses. Reimbursement is still a challenge but, for several molecular methods and analytes, significant clarification and improvement in reimbursement has occurred in recent years.

Laboratory Outreach Services

Prior to the phase-in of prospective reimbursement for Medicare inpatient services (diagnosis-related groups; DRGs) in the early 1980s by the former Health Care Financing Administration (HCFA; now CMS), much of a laboratory's test volume was performed for hospital inpatients. After DRGs were introduced and the era of cost-based reimbursement came to an abrupt end,

Table 13.4 Benefits and Risks of Molecular Testing

Benefits/Advantages	Risks/Disadvantages
• Remarkably shortened turnaround time for many infectious disease tests (vs. culture)	• More expensive than other esoteric testing (e.g., immunoassays)
• Increased sensitivity and specificity	• Intellectual property royalty issues
• Ability to determine drug resistance and/or drug sensitivity	• Dedicated space required (less of an issue for highly automated testing)
• Identification of genetic risk	• Reimbursement can be problematic for certain tests (although much improved for many analytes and methods)
• Identification of nonviable, unculturable, or slow-growing organisms	
• Gold standard for certain tests (viral load, pharmacogenetics, others)	• Genetic counseling required for some testing

hospital-based laboratories lost their status as major revenue providers; in the space of a few years they became an enormous budget-draining expense for hospitals. Entrepreneurial laboratorians, medical directors, and hospital administrators were forced to look for ways to leverage their costly fixed assets in high-tech analytical instrumentation, information systems, and physical plants, while decreasing their incremental costs. Since laboratory testing for Medicare outpatients would still be paid using the Medicare clinical laboratory fee schedule rather than DRGs, shifting laboratory testing from inpatient to outpatient venues became a prime hospital and laboratory focus. Laboratory outreach programs were born as a result of these dramatic changes.

During the ensuing 25 years, the growing of laboratory outreach services has become the principal way hospital laboratories have ensured a positive contribution margin for their departments. Outreach is defined as providing laboratory testing services to patients who do not present to the hospital for testing but rather have their blood collected at physician offices, or in community-based patient service centers (blood drawing stations), long-term care facilities, stand-alone emergency walk-in centers, dialysis clinics, or at home. These specimens are then transported to the hospital laboratory for testing. These patients are classified "nonpatients" and are not considered hospital outpatients. Because this work is defined as outside the primary mission of not-for-profit hospitals, associated revenue is considered unrelated business income and is taxable under federal guidelines.

Most hospital laboratories engage in some type of outreach testing regardless of laboratory size. Industry data shows that hospital laboratories typically collect $15.00 to $18.00 per billable test for outreach work, and well-run programs can expect contribution margins of 20 to 40%.[§] It is not uncommon that an average-sized laboratory (e.g., 650,000 billable tests per year) with a well-developed outreach program comprising 20 to 30% of its total volume (130,000 to 195,000 billable tests per year), would collect $2.2 to $3.3 million per year in net revenue, contributing $750,000 to $1 million to the hospital's bottom line annually. This type of program brings significant value to the hospital.

Essential characteristics of profitable outreach programs include:

- Strong laboratory leadership.
- Demonstrated support from hospital senior administration.
- Excellence in laboratory testing and client services; the laboratory should be highly regarded in the community, and the medical and administrative directors must be well respected.
- Interfaces between the LIS and physician office electronic medical records (EMRs) must be readily available for immediate reporting of test results and for test ordering.
- Result turnaround time must be aggressive: 1 hour for stat requests, and routine results returned within 4 hours of specimen receipt in the laboratory.

[§]Reimbursement and profitability will vary with payer mix and with types of outreach patients served. For example, physician offices and public patient service centers are typically much more profitable than testing performed for long-term care facilities. Collecting blood in patients' homes is the least profitable segment of laboratory outreach.

- The laboratory must be a low-cost, high-quality provider of lab services.
- Sales, marketing, and client services staff should be in place and well trained to provide immediate solutions to problems or referral to knowledgeable staff, to maintain existing client relationships and to develop new ones.
- Billing for testing should be accurate, timely, and aggressively managed to eliminate billing errors for patients and denied claims for the laboratory.

Developing a hospital laboratory–based outreach program should be seriously considered in order to significantly increase net revenue, improve laboratory and hospital profitability, decrease incremental cost, improve service to patients of all types, support existing relationships with medical staff and community physicians, and create new revenue streams that currently do not exist for the hospital.

Laboratory Regulation and Compliance

At one time, federal regulations for clinical laboratories applied only to those that participated in the Medicare and Medicaid programs or engaged in interstate commerce. All of this changed significantly in October 1988. After conducting extensive hearings on the quality of laboratories in the United States, Congress passed the Clinical Laboratories Improvement Act (CLIA) of 1988. This act superseded other regulations and brought under its regulation all US laboratories that conduct testing on human specimens for health assessment or for the diagnosis, prevention, or treatment of disease. Only three types of testing are excluded from regulation by CLIA:

1. Testing for forensic purposes
2. Research testing for which patient-specific results are not reported
3. Drug testing performed by laboratories certified by the Substance Abuse and Mental Health Services Administration (SAMHSA)

Published on February 28, 1992**, the final regulations set minimum standards for laboratory practice and quality, and specify requirements for proficiency testing, quality control, patient test management, personnel, quality assurance, certification, and inspections to ensure accuracy, reliability, and timeliness of patient test results regardless of where the test was performed. The same regulations apply to all testing sites, including physicians' office laboratories. The regulations are based on technical complexity in the testing process and risk of harm in reporting erroneous results.

CLIA has established four categories of testing based on the complexity of the test methodology:

1. Waived tests
2. Physician-performed microscopy (PPM)
3. Tests of moderate complexity
4. Tests of high complexity

**A final rule was published on January 24, 2003, and was effective April 24, 2003; CMS-2226-F: 42 CFR 493.

For waived tests, the regulations do not specify quality control, quality assurance, personnel, or proficiency testing. Laboratories that have a certificate of waiver and carry out PPM are not subject to routine inspections. Laboratories that perform moderate- or high-complexity testing, or both, must meet requirements for proficiency testing, patient test management, quality control, quality assurance, and personnel. The regulations for moderate- and high-complexity testing differ mainly in the standards for quality control and personnel.

All laboratories that are subject to regulations under CLIA must obtain appropriate certification documents. Initially, laboratories must obtain either a certificate of waiver or, if performing nonwaived testing, a registration certificate from the Centers for Medicare and Medicaid Services (CMS). A certificate of waiver is valid for a maximum of two years. A registration certificate is valid for two years or until an inspection to determine compliance can be conducted, whichever is shorter. A laboratory that meets the requirements of inspection receives either a certificate (for laboratories complying with the Department of Health and Human Services [DHHS] program) or a certificate of accreditation (for laboratories complying with DHHS-approved private, nonprofit accreditation programs). A laboratory may acquire a state license in lieu of either certificate if it is a state with a federally approved licensure program. Laboratories that obtain state licenses must comply with state rules and are exempt from the CLIA program.

With these regulations comes additional cost. There is cost associated with participation in a proficiency testing program and with the implementation of a system to ensure the integrity and identification of patient specimens throughout the testing process, as well as the accuracy of results. For some laboratories, particularly in remote areas, there is cost associated with the personnel standards. For all laboratories, there is the cost of inspections in order to maintain certification. Laboratories that perform unsatisfactorily on two consecutive or two of three proficiency testing events risk sanctions for that specialty, subspecialty, or test. Sanctions may include suspension of the laboratory's certificate or cancellation of its Medicare approval.

Concern about the quality of cytology testing services, particularly Pap smears, was one of the issues that prompted Congress to pass CLIA. Although the act does not contain standards for the other laboratory subspecialties, the law contains specific requirements for cytology proficiency testing, quality control, and personnel. The cytology standards became effective in March 1990, in advance of the other components of CLIA. One of the most significant requirements for the cytology section is that the technical supervisor must establish and monitor the workload of each person who evaluates slides by a nonautomated microscopic technique. Personnel can examine no more than 100 slides in no less than 8 hours, but no more than 24 hours, regardless of location. Personnel who have other duties or who work part-time must have their workload limit prorated by the number of hours spent examining slides. There also are specific requirements for the review of slides and the correlation with histopathology results. These regulations make an information system with these tracking abilities almost a necessity.

In addition to CLIA, laboratory management must deal with other regulatory agencies (e.g., CAP, the Joint Commission, the American Association of Blood Banks, etc.) and their requirements. Many states also have enacted regulations for clinical laboratories. The Food and Drug Administration (FDA) regulates and inspects (unannounced) several thousand blood banks and facilities that manufacture or produce blood products. SAMHSA operates an inspection and approval program for laboratories that test blood and urine specimens obtained from federal employees for the presence of drugs of abuse. SAMHSA has comprehensive standards for its inspection program, which is separate from those under the direction of CMS.

Laboratories are subject to regulation regarding safety and infection control, and they need stringent hazardous chemicals and universal precautions programs in order to meet the regulations and ensure a safe working environment for their employees. The major agency involved in this area is the Occupational Safety and Health Administration (OSHA). For occupational exposure to hazardous chemicals in laboratories, OSHA's final rule outlines specific requirements for:

- Written hazard communication programs
- Labels and other forms of warning
- Material safety data sheets (MSDSs)
- Employee information and training
- Exposure monitoring

OSHA published its final rule for occupational exposure to bloodborne pathogens on December 6, 1991 (revised in 2001 in response to the Needlestick Safety and Prevention Act). The regulation requires an exposure control program with the following components:

- Exposure determination for employee infection control
- Control methods including:
  ° Universal precautions
  ° Engineering controls
  ° Work practices controls
  ° Personal protective equipment
- Hepatitis B virus vaccination
- Postexposure evaluation and follow-up
- Regulated waste disposal
- Labels and bags
- Housekeeping practices
- Laundry practices
- Training and education of employees
- Record keeping

Additional requirements of the Nuclear Regulatory Commission and the Department of Transportation may also apply, depending on the scope of services offered or the need to transport specimens across state lines.

In recent years, the Office of the Inspector General (OIG) of the DHHS has established a zero-tolerance policy for fraud and abuse of federally funded healthcare programs and has created anti-abuse programs directed at investigating fraudulent activities associated with laboratory testing. In 1997, the OIG published a model compliance plan for clinical laboratories. This was revised in August 1998. The model is a guide to help laboratories establish a compliance program that will identify, minimize, and/or eliminate fraudulent actions associated with federally funded healthcare programs. The government is recommending that laboratories voluntarily establish such programs, although those laboratories previously found in violation of Medicare's rules have been required to implement such programs as part of their penalty negotiations. Elements of a true program include the following:

- Documented standards of conduct for employees
- Development and distribution of policies that promote the laboratory's commitment to compliance and address specific areas of potential fraud (e.g., billing, marketing, claims processing)
- Designation of a chief compliance officer
- Compliance education and training programs that are offered to employees
- Use of audits to demonstrate compliance
- Policies that specify the disciplinary action to be taken against employees who violate the compliance plan
- Investigation and remediation of identified systemic and/or personnel problems
- Evidence in the performance evaluations of supervisors and managers that adherence to compliance plan is a performance criterion for them
- Policy to address the dismissal or retention of sanctioned individuals
- Hotline mechanisms to receive complaints anonymously
- Policies regarding record creation and retention

Laboratory regulation will continue to be an increasingly important area that requires laboratory management and staff time as well as coordination with other hospital departments.

Strategic Planning

Extensive regulation and competition among clinical laboratories have forced them to expand their service areas and develop networks in order to remain viable. These changes began with the design and implementation of ventures that allowed hospital laboratories to enter new markets. Often, they used a two-tiered approach. Hospitals initially marketed their services within the hospital community and then transferred the benefit of their efforts to external users. The traditional issues of price and service gain importance in this phase of marketing. Entering new markets resulted in volume increases that reduced unit costs and enabled the expansion of service levels in-house to include procedures that were not economically viable without this additional volume.

Current government cost containment efforts include experimentation with managed care, risk sharing, and regional bidding. This type of pressure is not new in laboratories. In the late 1970s, the lowest charge reimbursement regulations had a similar cost containment objective; in the early 1990s it was regional competitive billing. Some specific alternatives that hospital laboratories are considering to respond to these pressures include the following:

- Entering into joint ventures with other hospitals to form regional laboratories
- Sharing resources with other hospitals through cooperative ventures in which certain nonemergent procedures are performed in only one of the participating hospitals (e.g., microbiology studies at Hospital A and chemistry profiling at Hospital B)

- Marketing excess capacity to both traditional users, such as physicians' offices and group practices, and nontraditional users, such as other hospitals, industry, and veterinarians

The major goal of any of these ventures is to reduce unit costs, increase profitability, and generate additional revenue while improving or, at a minimum, maintaining quality and service. In the recent past, marketing the excess capacity was deemed the most desirable method for achieving these goals. Findings reported in the literature, however, indicate that joint ventures consisting of four hospitals in a geographic area with a total of 750 beds could reduce their workforce by 25 to 33% while reducing overhead and equipment needs and gaining more sophisticated data processing systems.[11]

A critical mass of 1.5 to 2 million tests is necessary to make such a joint venture feasible. It appears that 40 to 60% of hospital laboratory chemistry and hematology testing can be sent off-site to a regional or reference center. Nearly all the microbiology, histology, and cytology testing can go off-site. Significant political issues (involving medical staff, particularly pathologists, infectious disease physicians, hematology/oncology physicians, and collective bargaining units) and operational issues (involving information systems, equipment configuration, and test menus) must be resolved prior to implementing such a venture.

The pressure to reduce costs remains intense. In six years, from 1992 through 1997, the hospital share of the laboratory marketplace decreased from 50 to 35%.[12] Therefore, finding new ways to remain competitive will continue to be high on the agenda of clinical laboratories. Other alternatives have some savings associated with their strategies but are less attractive than a joint venture regional laboratory.

In evaluating these alternatives, laboratories have developed more sophisticated management information systems than have other clinical services. The previously mentioned CAP workload reporting system was one of the first attempts to apply management engineering concepts in the laboratory workplace in order to identify various components of cost, specifically labor, the largest component. The incorporation of these concepts into costing systems makes it possible to determine unit costs. Costing systems are crucial in determining if an institution is competitive and what the parameters should be in developing fee schedules and managed care contracts.

Product line costing has become an important topic in health care. Many laboratories have been developing costing systems to determine marginal and incremental costs as a way to evaluate a variety of issues, ranging from equipment purchases to joint ventures. Those hospital laboratories that have not kept pace are finding that their laboratory services may be in jeopardy. Commercial laboratories and other hospitals are taking over in-house operations with the support of government regulations and policies that seem to foster this type of marketplace behavior.

Conclusion

The location and type of laboratory (i.e., regional, rapid response, or reference) in an organized healthcare delivery system will determine the service levels that a clinical laboratory will provide. The operational characteristics of a well-designed laboratory will reflect these service levels. Furthermore, they provide the basis for determining what goals and objectives the planning process must develop and implement to keep a laboratory system viable in today's healthcare environment.

References

1. Boutweil JH, Stewart CE Jr. Service levels in a hospital laboratory. *Laboratory Management*. November 1971.
2. Hager RE, Brzozowski PJ. Determination of service level feasibility: should we buy and staff this new gizmo? Paper presented at: Center for Hospital Management Engineering Forum; June 13–14, 1983; Boston, MA.
3. States that currently require licensure for laboratory professionals are California, Hawaii, Florida, North Dakota, Rhode Island, Tennessee, Louisiana, Nevada, West Virginia, Montana, Georgia. Puerto Rico also requires licensure.
4. College of American Pathologists. *Manual for Laboratory Workload Recording*. Skokie, IL: CAP Workload Recording Committee; 1984.
5. Lincoln TL, Essin D. Information technology, health care, and the future: what are the implications for the clinical laboratory? *Clinical Laboratory Management Review*. 1992;6(1):95.
6. Aller RD. The laboratory information system as a medical device: inspection and accreditation issues. *Clinical Laboratory Management Review*. 1992;6(1):59.
7. Friedman BA, Dito WR. Managing the information product of clinical laboratories. *Clinical Laboratory Management Review*. 1992;6(1):6.
8. Clinical and Laboratory Standards Institute. Laboratory design—approved guideline GP18-A. 1998;18(3).
9. College of American Pathologists. *Manual for Laboratory Planning and Design*. Danville, IL: CAP Subcommittee on Laboratory Resources; 1977.
10. Skeggs, LT Jr. An automatic method for colorimetric analysis. *American Journal of Clinical Pathology*. 1957;28:311–322.
11. Fattal GA, et al. Operational and financial outcomes of shared laboratory services in a consolidated hospital system. *Journal of the American Medical Association*. 1985; 253(14): 2076–2079.
12. Steiner JW. The virtual laboratory: regional clinical diagnostics for integrated delivery systems. *Healthcare Financial Management*. 1997.

Additional Readings

Hawker CD, Garr SB, Hamilton LT, et al. Automated transport and sorting system in a large reference laboratory: part 1. Evaluation of needs and alternatives and development of a plan. *Clinical Chemistry*. 2002;48:1751–1760.

Hawker, CD, Roberts WL, Garr SB, et al. 2002. Automated transport and sorting system in a large reference laboratory: part 2. Implementation of the system and performance measures over three years. *Clinical Chemistry*. 2002;48:1761–1767.

Uettwiller-Geiger D. Implementation of laboratory robotics in a community hospital. *Journal of Clinical Ligand Assay*. 2001;24:245–247.

Appendix 13.A

Sample of Test Type by Section

Anatomic pathology

- Gross and microscopic examination of surgical specimens
- Special stains including immunohistochemistry
- Cell blocks
- Decalcification

Cytology

- Papanicolaou smears
- Fine needle aspirates
- Body fluid (e.g., bronchial washings, pleural fluids) examinations
- Human papilloma virus (HPV)

Chemistry

- Electrolytes (e.g., sodium, potassium chloride, CO_2)
- Blood glucose levels
- Renal function (BUN, creatinine)
- Therapeutic drug monitoring, drug screening
- Cardiac markers (troponin-I, CK-MB, BNP, myoglobin)
- Enzymes (ALT, AST, amylase, lipase)
- Thyroid testing (TSH, T4, T-uptake)
- Electrophoresis studies (serum protein, immunofixation, hemoglobin)

Hematology

- Complete blood cell count (CBC)
- White blood cell differential
- Coagulation studies (e.g., prothrombin time, activated partial thromboplastin time, factor assays)

Microbiology

- Cultures (throat, sputum, wound—from any body source)
- Gram stains
- Sensitivities (studies used to determine the most effective antibiotic therapy)
- Influenza, herpes simplex, respiratory syncytial virus, cytomegalovirus, toxoplasmosis, varicella zoster

Microscopy

- Urinalysis
- Examination of other body fluids (e.g., synovial or joint fluid; spinal fluid) for cells, crystals, etc.
- Semen analysis

Blood bank

- Crossmatch (compatibility) testing
- ABO and Rh typing
- Antibody identification

Appendix 13.B

Job Analysis Checklist: Medical Director

1. Clinical service
   a. The medical director must review annually, or as changes occur, procedure manuals (or their equivalent) for requesting laboratory services, specimen collection, patient preparation, reference values, and other pertinent information for utilizing laboratory services. This is to ensure that the manuals are available, that they are up-to-date, and that their testing parameters are acceptable to users.
   b. * Test methodologies and procedure manuals must meet the approval of accrediting agencies.
   c. * The quality control program must be directed so that it is acceptable to accrediting agencies and the medical staff.
   d. A pathologist, qualified physician, or, when appropriate, a qualified doctoral scientist must be available to provide consulting services that include
      i.   Frozen section diagnosis in the surgical suite on both an emergency and scheduled basis.
      ii. Requests by staff physicians for help in selecting and interpreting laboratory tests.
   e. Frozen section diagnosis must be ready in a timely fashion and recorded on the patient's chart while the patient is in the operating room.
   f. Reports of laboratory findings and analyses must be completed and in the patient's chart in a timely fashion.
   g. * Appropriate outcome criteria must be established, monitored, and reported to the hospital quality improvement committee.
   h. Slides, reports, and other appropriate materials must be sent to pathology specialists when so requested by the attending physician, or when deemed necessary by the medical director.
   i. Work with the medical and surgical staff and transfusion committee to determine the adequacy of the inventory and utilization of blood products.
   j. * All departments must meet the standards of the College of American Pathologists, the Joint Commission, Food and Drug Administration, and other agencies (e.g., American Association of Blood Banks) when accreditation is requested by the hospital.
   k. * The laboratory must conform to hospital standards for data and systems control, forms control, computer applications, and results delivery.
   l. Records must be maintained in accordance with hospital, government, and accrediting agency requirements.
   m. * New procedures must be introduced as appropriate for physicians, nursing service, laboratory staff, and patient needs.
   n. * Assistance must be provided to other clinicians when necessary to obtain specimens for analysis. Such assistance includes bone marrow aspirates and fine needle biopsies.
2. Human resources management
   a. * The continuing education program must meet standards of accrediting agencies and the organization. A minimum continuing education requirement must be established for each category of employees.
   b. Appropriate meetings of the laboratory department must be held for announcements and education. A record of such meetings will be included in monthly and annual laboratory reports.
   c. * Input must be provided as to the type of reference material to be maintained so as to meet standards of the hospital medical library. Appropriate technical books and manuals must be available at the workbenches.

Job Analysis Checklist: Medical Director *(continued)*

d. * There must be participation in clinical department meetings.

e. The continuing education requirements of the American Medical Association, College of American Pathologists, or equivalent must be met.

f. * Appropriate CEU credits must be maintained.

g. * There must be participation in the development of staff performance criteria and staff performance evaluations when appropriate. The medical director should provide input into the administrative laboratory director evaluation, and sectional medical directors should review the section supervisor evaluations regarding technical ability.

3. Administrative responsibilities

a. Goals and objectives put forth by laboratory management and approved by the medical director must be compatible with those of the hospital, as judged by the senior management of the organization.

b. Policies, rules, and regulations must be appropriate, understandable, and complete, as judged by the senior management of the hospital. They must conform to those of the organization and not violate those of any government, accrediting, or regulatory agency.

c. Physical plant and departments must be organized to provide maximum efficiency.

d. * Services must be scheduled with full consideration of need, cost, and regulatory priorities to the satisfaction of clinicians and administrators.

e. It is essential to determine feasibility and maintain fiscal responsibility in introducing changes; therefore, requests for space, equipment, services, and personnel must be reasonable and justified with data. Purchases should be evaluated in light of cost-effectiveness, quality, and service.

f. There must be participation in the strategic planning process.

g. Budgets (capital and operating) must be submitted on time and adhered to unless deviations are adequately justified and approved.

*Function often delegated to section medical directors.

Biographical Information

Paul J. Brzozowski, MT (ASCP), MPA, is a partner with Applied Management Systems, Inc. (AMS), a healthcare consulting firm in Burlington, Massachusetts. He is responsible for the clinical and general consulting services of AMS. He is also experienced in mergers and consolidations. Prior to joining AMS, Mr. Brzozowski was the Executive Vice President of Addison Gilbert Hospital in Gloucester, Massachusetts. As Chief Operating Officer, he was responsible for the daily operation of the hospital. Prior to joining Addison Gilbert Hospital, he was a healthcare consultant for Peat, Marwick, and Mitchell, and the Massachusetts Hospital Association, with a primary focus on clinical laboratory operation.

Mr. Brzozowski has participated in many seminars, client in-service programs, educational programs, and special lecture series, such as those sponsored by EI DuPont. He has more than 30 years of healthcare experience.

He received a BS in medical technology from SUNY Upstate Medical Center, Syracuse, New York, and an MPA from Pennsylvania State University. He is also a Fellow of the Healthcare Information and Management Systems Society (HIMSS).

Paul D. Camara, MS, is a vice president with Applied Management Systems, Inc. (AMS), a healthcare consulting firm in Burlington, Massachusetts. Mr. Camara is an expert in the clinical and administrative aspects of laboratory services. At AMS he manages detailed laboratory assessments, conducts hospital-wide productivity studies, and provides consultation for laboratory mergers, information system selection and implementation, and clinical diagnostic process improvement. Prior to joining AMS, Paul was the Director of Laboratories at South Shore Hospital, S. Weymouth, Massachusetts. Previously, he was the Director of Diagnostic Services at Roger Williams Medical Center, Providence, Rhode Island, with responsibility for the laboratories, diagnostic imaging, cardiology, radiation oncology, and the sleep laboratory.

Mr. Camara is an Adjunct Assistant Professor in the Department of Biochemistry, Microbiology & Molecular Genetics, University of Rhode Island, and is a frequent speaker on scientific and management topics in laboratory medicine.

He received a BS degree in clinical chemistry from Providence College, Providence, Rhode Island, and an MS from the University of Rhode Island, Kingston, Rhode Island.

Pharmacy

Andrew L. Wilson and Karol Wollenburg

Introduction

Pharmacy services in hospitals and organized delivery systems have continued to change. Changes in pharmacy practice reflect the transformation that is occurring in healthcare delivery, and the continuing emphasis on medication therapy. Growing interest in medication safety, by payers, regulators, and the public[1,2,3] has created a renewed interest in medication use systems and has fostered standards and quality efforts, and the development and implementation of new technology to support medication ordering, dispensing, administration, and monitoring. The continuing evolution of pharmacy services encompasses this renewed emphasis on safety, an increasing focus on patient care outcomes and treatment costs, and a renewed focus on formulary development and drug use policy.[4,5] Suboptimal therapy outcomes, serious medication errors, and a renewed appreciation for the complexity of the medication use process have broadened the pharmacy's focus to include the multidisciplinary nature of medication use, including acquisition, prescribing, preparation, drug administration, and monitoring, and to include collaborative efforts with physicians, nurses, and with information technology to meet these goals. The implementation of electronic health records in hospitals presents a unique opportunity to connect a broad range of information and promote more effective communication across the entire medication use continuum.

The professional practice mission of pharmacists focuses on direct patient care and interaction, the assessment and monitoring of medication effects, the management of medication therapy to meet treatment goals, and the development of systems and processes to support safe and effective medication delivery to all patients.[4,6,7] As a result, pharmacists continue to increase their involvement in team care provided at the inpatient bedside and in the ambulatory care clinic, and to focus on building systems to support effective management of medication information, individualization of therapy, and the safe and reliable delivery of medications.

The goal of pharmacy education is to give practitioners a well-rounded body of knowledge regarding the clinical use of drugs and the direct patient care delivery skills to support this patient care emphasis.[8] Individualization of complex medication therapy to achieve improved patient care outcomes is a key initiative.[9] As pharmacy practice acts, state regulations, and government and private payer programs have broadened to encompass pharmacist-managed medication therapy management (MTM) and independent prescribing, health systems have taken advantage of these skills to support enhanced patient care access and improved medication therapy outcomes.[10] This is particularly true in the management of anticoagulation, asthma, patients receiving large numbers of prescriptions, and other complex medication therapy.

Although pharmacies in health systems have continued to adjust to these changes, direct patient care activities are the core of pharmacy's mission in care delivery. Effective pharmacies in healthcare systems take responsibility for medication therapy through patient care activities that ensure appropriate and effective use of pharmacy resources. Particular emphasis and impact for pharmacists' medication management activities occur at care interfaces, particularly admission and discharge from the hospital and transition to other care locations and providers. Pharmacy departments in health systems where these changes in emphasis have not taken place are moving to develop the necessary human and information resources.

Serious medication errors reported widely in the lay press have renewed the focus of the public, government and other regulators, health system leadership, and pharmacists on systems, processes, and controls to improve the safety and reliability of the medication use system.[11–15] Lean and Six Sigma processes, a focus on staff competency, comprehensive reviews of process and policy, and technology, including bar coding, bedside scanning, provider order entry, and other strategies, are being brought to bear on a complex and multistep system in a broad effort to improve performance.

Pharmacy Practice

Contemporary pharmacy practice is based on the concept of pharmaceutical care. Hepler and Strand proposed the seminal definition of this concept in 1990. "Pharmaceutical care is the responsible provision of drug therapy for the purpose of achieving definite outcomes that improve a patient's quality of life. These outcomes are (1) cure of a disease, (2) elimination or reduction of a patient's symptomatology, (3) arresting or slowing of a disease process, or (4) preventing a disease or symptomatology."[16] The authors define pharmaceutical care as a core service, similar to medical care or dental care, and emphasize the responsibility of pharmacists in all care practice settings and delivery models.

Pharmacists delivering pharmaceutical care have the task of integrating multiple drug therapies to achieve the best outcome for each disease or condition. Pharmacists working in this practice model have an overview of all medication therapies and treatment goals and practice as generalists with specific expertise in, and attention to, drug therapy. They initiate or recommend treatment and order laboratory tests and other assessments. They consult with nurses, physicians, other caregivers, and the patient to direct drug therapy, set treatment goals, avoid or minimize side effects and adverse drug events, and optimize treatment outcomes. The basic model for pharmaceutical care was developed in the acute care setting, but it translates well to ambulatory care clinics, home care, and other ambulatory care settings.[4,17] The pharmaceutical care model is particularly suited to pharmacy practice in healthcare systems, as it focuses on continuity of care and supports the transitions between acute care, ambulatory care, and chronic care.

The total patient management focus of the pharmaceutical care model also makes it particularly effective in a healthcare system. Contracting, discounting, prospective payment, and capitation are used by payers to control treatment expense in today's competitive healthcare marketplace. A healthcare system can compete and be successful only if it controls costs, ensures the appropriate and effective utilization of resources, demonstrates optimal treatment outcomes, and delivers patient services and customer satisfaction. Control and management of pharmacy costs have generally focused on the minimization of drug costs. The pharmaceutical care model focuses on drug therapy decisions that are in accord with the overall goals of treatment and are carried out in a time frame that provides for effective management, evaluation, and assessment.

The broadest and most effective structure to manage and focus drug use is through the creation of a formulary and associated medication use policies and procedures. A health system formulary is a continually revised compilation of pharmaceuticals that reflects the current clinical judgment of the medical and pharmacy staff. The formulary reflects current clinical practice established through a thorough and systematic assessment of published medical literature and the specific needs of the patients served by the organization. The formulary is developed by the organization's pharmacy and therapeutics (P&T) committee, a committee composed of physicians, pharmacists, nurses, and administrators. The P&T committee's primary goal is to ensure the most safe, effective, and appropriate use of medication, supporting the highest quality care. A thoughtfully developed and well-managed formulary that incorporates a complete drug purchase contract portfolio has the opportunity to deliver the most cost-effective drug therapy outcomes. The selection of a drug for formulary inclusion is only a portion of the process necessary to facilitate appropriate and effective treatment outcomes. Systems and controls to manage and monitor utilization and to assess patient response are also required. A full assessment of medication therapy must take into account:

- Drug administration schedules and dosing frequency
- Complexity of dosing and the need to change dose as patient condition changes
- Potential effect on length of stay storage and preparation costs
- Cost of ancillary devices, such as infusion pumps, and monitoring devices, such as blood glucose monitors
- Nursing effort associated with drug administration and monitoring
- Costs and likelihood of side effects and adverse reactions
- Safety issues such as the likelihood of confusion with another product on the formulary
- Costs of medical monitoring, including clinic visits and laboratory tests
- Costs and likelihood of treatment failure
- Costs and likelihood of drug interactions

The task of selecting the most appropriate drug therapy can be complex, particularly in patients with multiple diseases or conditions. The consumption of resources, the effects of drug therapy on length of hospital stay, clinic visit frequency, and monitoring costs must be included in the assessment. Studies on the costs associated with a tightly controlled formulary have demonstrated that a narrow focus on drug costs can lead to cost growth in other areas, resulting from readmissions, emergency department visits, and outright treatment failures.[18] A focus on reducing the number of drugs, or aggressive restrictions placed on new drugs, may provide short-term cost reduction for an episode of care, but lead to greater overall costs over the course of the disease or the patient's lifetime.

The global assessment of treatment costs and outcomes ensures the optimal use of resources and focuses on a more robust model of cost-effectiveness. Older cost models were more concerned with drug acquisition costs and developed little information and limited assessment of results and outcomes based on the effectiveness of a treatment. Formularies, medication use review, technology assessment, the integration of new therapies, and the development of guidelines and support resources for drug use are appropriately evaluated under this model. A full spectrum of policies, procedures, and practices to support effective medication use includes:

- Methods and process for review of medications for addition to or deletion from the health system formulary, including who performs the reviews
- The process for developing, implementing, and monitoring medication use guidelines
- Methods for ensuring the safe prescribing, distribution, administration, and monitoring of medications, including their incorporation into information systems and computerized provider order entry (CPOE) systems
- Methods for selection of suitable sources (manufacturers, repackagers, and distributors) for specific medications
- The process for securing and using nonformulary drugs within the institution
- The process for managing drug product shortages
- Policies and processes for developing an organization-specific medication use evaluation (MUE) plan, and specific medication use, with a specific emphasis on high-risk medications
- Privileges and processes to support the medication supply chain (e.g., procurement, prescribing, distribution, administration, monitoring, diversion identification, and prevention)
- The process for disseminating medication use policies and how users will be educated regarding the process

Integrated pharmacy information systems support the rapid and accurate identification of treatment strategies and patient responses, ensuring both cost-effectiveness and optimal treatment outcomes. Increasingly these pharmacy systems are fully integrated into the larger information technology of the health system, and the resulting electronic health record. The medication use systems used in acute care arise at the development of the formulary and encompass the creation of treatment protocols and resources under the guidance of the P&T committee.

The pharmaceutical care practice model also uses data from the published medical and pharmaceutical literature, combined with internally generated patient care, operations, and cost data to determine appropriate medication therapy. This evidence-based approach ensures that treatment decisions are based on current empirical evidence, within the context of larger scale patient treatment issues specific to the organization. Selecting the therapy most likely to reliably produce the optimal treatment outcome at the lowest overall cost includes a critical assessment of the likelihood of treatment failure and the frequency and impact of adverse reactions, drug interactions, and side effects. Effective treatment selection and management also encompasses the assessment of individual patient characteristics, including compliance with treatment protocols. It further incorporates the cost of the medication itself and medication preparation, administration, and the costs of monitoring and managing patient response to treatment. Economic models that fail to include these aspects of pharmaceutical care often minimize drug acquisition costs at the expense of higher overall costs outside the traditional pharmacy budget.

Pharmacy Leadership and Management

An effective pharmacy service in a healthcare delivery system must be led by a trained pharmacist leader with high-level management experience. The pharmacy director must be able to synthesize the needs for clinical pharmacy services with drug distribution, information systems and automation technology, the demand for safety, and mitigation of risk with general management principles and leadership objectives under the pharmaceutical care model. He or she must create measures of the effectiveness of pharmaceutical care and department services and ensure that systems, drug products, and services meet the objectives of the healthcare organization, the objectives of the medical staff, and the care needs of patients. The pharmacy director must be able to effectively coordinate department efforts with those of medicine and nursing, and communicate effectively with senior leadership regarding medication use system and department management issues.

The pharmacy director must utilize an integrated information system that collects and organizes real-time patient care data to support drug therapy decision making in the clinic and at the bedside. The pharmacy information system must be developed to collect and categorize summary data about drug therapies for use in determining the global effectiveness and cost of each type of therapy and support management decisions. Examples of areas of management focus include nonformulary drugs used, drug costs and drug use by therapeutic category, and details about specific drugs used by each physician or medical service. Additionally, data describing drug costs and use by diagnosis and detailed drug utilization by disease state should be collated and collected to serve as the basis for determining trends in prescribing and planning strategic efforts to manage and direct medication use for enhanced efficiency and improved patient care outcomes. Summary statistics collected and assessed in a regular and timely manner offer rapid insight into prescribing trends and changes in patient mix and drug use. These data can be combined with demographic information, laboratory results, and other patient data to provide information about product selection, information about the success or failure of therapies, and information to support the assessment of operational effectiveness and efficiency. A competent pharmacy director uses this type of information to develop drug use policy and systems to manage drug utilization, thereby decreasing cost, minimizing risk, enhancing safety, and optimizing patient care outcomes. A well-run pharmacy also utilizes patient care automation and robotics to ensure timely, accurate, consistent, and cost-effective medication handling.

The pharmacy director leads a staff composed of trained specialist pharmacist clinicians who manage specific therapy programs and services; a larger number of generalist clinical pharmacist practitioners who are trained in patient care service delivery; and staff pharmacists and pharmacy technicians who are responsible for the logistics of drug procurement, preparation, delivery, and management. The pharmacy of today continues to deliver the right drug at the right time to the right patient, but it is further involved in the drug selection and prescribing process at the patient and prescriber level. It works effectively with systems that support physicians and nurses in their responsibilities for selection, administration, monitoring, and management of drug therapies. It develops and provides pharmacy-based medication monitoring and management and develops and implements policies to support the goals of the health system or network. These goals are based on continuing assessment of the effectiveness and outcomes of medication therapies. Control of drug costs is centered on the effective utilization of medications. It requires effective information systems and a sophisticated pharmacy leadership team that understands patient care and business and operational data and creates management systems to implement pharmaceutical care services based on them. Effective communication with senior leadership in medical, nursing, finance, and information technology and to the hospital's board or audit committee is critical to achieving these goals. As a result of the growing cost of pharmaceuticals and the rising profile of medications in patient care, pharmacy leaders are increasingly reporting to the COO or chief clinical officer and are being recognized as chief pharmacy officer.[19]

The health system's pharmacy service should be organized in a manner that ensures an integrated approach to patient care and promotes an integrated concept of pharmaceutical care. The structure of the pharmacy should mirror that of the overall healthcare organization, with specific pharmacists or pharmacy service teams assigned to each patient care service or unit. Each pharmacist should be responsible for determining the portion of the overall agenda that applies to his or her service or patient care unit. This ensures that overall medication management goals are achieved in a manner that maximizes synergy with the patient care goals set in each service area. Although it is tempting to create a centralized, functionally organized pharmacy, this approach can focus the pharmacy service agenda internally, creating conflict with larger organizational goals.

In larger integrated healthcare systems with multiple hospitals, specialty services in ambulatory care, retail pharmacies, home care, or those that include HMO or other insurance or health benefit programs, it is desirable to have senior corporate pharmacy leadership to identify and leverage internal pharmacy resources across the system, including manpower, information technology, medication use policies, and supply chain activities. However, it may be more effective to retain a degree of autonomy in each pharmacy business unit to ensure high performance in each sector. Although pharmacists and pharmaceuticals are common across all business types and care locations, business practices and resource needs may vary across each setting.

The pharmacy should be organized in a fashion that meets laws and regulations promulgated by the state and federal government, and by standard-setting agencies such as the Joint Commission and the American Society of Health-System Pharmacists (ASHP).[20,21] Pharmacy services and drug products are among the most regulated parts of the healthcare delivery system. Pharmacy directors should review compliance and changes in regulations on an annual basis to ensure continued compliance. Many standards and agencies overlap in jurisdiction, so a careful reading and thoughtful review are required. **Table 14.1** contains a partial list of agencies and jurisdictions that may review the pharmacy practice or drug use and records of a health system.

Table 14.1   Pharmacy Standard-Setting and Regulatory Agencies

Agency	Type	Review Functions	Frequency of Review
State board of pharmacy	Regulatory	Pharmacy Practice Act, pharmacy records, facilities, personnel, computer systems, automation, policies and procedures, licensing and credentialing	Annual site inspection and document review, at the time of physical changes, for example, renovation and upon complaint
State narcotic control board	Regulatory	State controlled substance act, narcotic dispensing records, practitioner records, facilities, security procedures	Annual site inspection and document review, or upon report of loss or complaint
State board of health	Regulatory	Pharmacy services, staffing, drug use, distribution, storage, pharmacy records, quality assurance	Unannounced inspections often relating to a complaint or sentinel event
US Drug Enforcement Administration (DEA)	Regulatory	Federal Controlled Substances Act, practitioner record review, records of dispensing	Upon report of loss or diversion, or based on complaint
US Food and Drug Administration (FDA)	Regulatory	Federal Food, Drug, and Cosmetic Act, drug recall records, drug storage	No scheduled visits to providers or pharmacies; random visit to assess drug recall compliance
State medical board	Regulatory	Practitioner records	Upon report of diversion or based on complaint
Joint Commission (TJC, JCAHO)	Professional standards, accreditation	Facilities, policies and procedures, training, competency, formulary	Every 3 to 5 years, random inspections, and upon complaint or sentinel event
National Committee on Quality Assurance (NCQA)	Professional standards, accreditation	Facilities, policies and procedures, training, competency, formulary, patient satisfaction	Every 3 to 5 years, random inspections, and on complaint
American Society of Health-System Pharmacists (ASHP)	Professional standards, accreditation	Facilities, policies and procedures, training, education, and competency	Inspect training sites every 6 years
American Council on Pharmaceutical Education (ACPE)	Professional standards, accreditation	Education and training	Inspect training sites as a part of college degree program accreditation
United States Pharmacopoeia (USP)	Professional standards	Facilities, policies and procedures, education, and training	No inspections
Centers for Medicare Services (CMS)	Regulatory	Pharmacy services, staffing, drug use and storage, pharmacy records, error reporting	No scheduled visits to providers or pharmacies; random visit to assess compliance, or upon complaint

The pharmacy should be organized to provide the full spectrum of clinical, patient care, drug information, drug preparation, storage and distribution, purchasing, quality review, and medication use evaluations. The exact characteristics of the pharmacy will depend upon the size of the health system and a number of other factors, including:

- The division of medication use responsibilities between pharmacists, physicians, and nurses (e.g., medication reconciliation)
- Patient care programs and services offered at each location
- Patient populations served (e.g., geriatric, pediatric, general, or specialty)
- Scope of services provided by the corporate pharmacy leadership
- Drug distribution system(s)
- Level of computerization and automation
- Participation in pharmaceutical research activities
- Clinical training and experience programs, including medical, pharmacy, and nursing student and resident programs
- Level of pharmacy staff experience, education, and training

The organization of the pharmacy should support the mission of the health system. Pharmacy departments generally report though the pharmacy administrator to an associate administrator for clinical services or to a chief operating officer. Because of the significant impact of drug therapies in the clinical environment, reporting relationships with the chief medical officer and the organization's pharmacy and therapeutics committee are also important. The pharmacy director and administrator should be comfortable addressing the competing business and clinical priorities in their reporting relationship. Contemporary human resources management techniques and philosophies are critical to ensuring that the pharmacy personnel work well together to meet their responsibility to the larger health system agenda. The pharmacy service team is usually composed of pharmacists, pharmacy technicians, and clerical support staff.

Patient Care Committees

Because the relationship between pharmacists and physicians is so close in setting and implementing drug policy, the pharmacy director and the representative clinical and management staff of the pharmacy should participate in hospital, ambulatory care, and medical staff committees at the local business unit and healthcare system level to ensure adequate policy development and implementation support. The quality of the medication use process is directly related to the sharing of information in the multidisciplinary review of medication use, medication misadventures, and pharmacy business information. Pharmacists typically participate in the pharmacy and therapeutics, quality improvement, infection control, safety, risk management, institutional review board (human subjects research), emergency preparedness, and intensive care committees. They may also serve on other continuing or ad hoc committees that address regulatory review, cost and revenue management, patient care, quality, efficiency, and cost issues.

The Pharmacy and Therapeutics Committee

The most important committee relationship for the pharmacy is the pharmacy and therapeutics (P&T) committee. The P&T committee is generally a standing committee of the organization's medical staff. It advises the medical staff on drug use through the development of a formulary and policies and procedures to support appropriate and optimal use of medications by physicians, nurses, pharmacists, and patients. The committee is the direct link between the medical staff and the pharmacy service. It also supports staff and patient education, reviews drug use, and investigates drug-related problems and issues. The composition of the committee varies between organizations. Membership typically includes several physicians representing the spectrum of medical and surgical specialties of the organization, one or more nurses, the director of pharmacy, clinical pharmacist(s), at least one administrator, and other practitioners who prescribe or administer medications.

Pharmacy and therapeutics committees and the formulary system date back a number of years.[22] Although the emphasis of formulary management has evolved, the primary goal of a formulary is to create a current, focused, usable listing of the most effective medications and to foster their proper and appropriate use through policies, procedures, and support systems. Due to the nature of medication use, pharmacy and therapeutics committees typically meet on a monthly or bimonthly basis.

Some healthcare systems delegate some or all P&T committee functions to local operating units. The distributed approach makes sense if geography or diversity of services or patients supports opportunities for closer monitoring of medication use, clinical practice, and prescriber activity locally. Most healthcare systems have centralized some P&T committee functions to achieve economies of scale and to ensure that decisions that affect the quality of care, patient outcomes, and the financial stability of the system are made at an appropriate level. These functions generally include the core formulary, medication use policies, drug quality and purchasing specifications, clinical pathways, service and pharmaceutical contracts, Joint Commission and regulatory compliance, and quality assurance. Where a systemwide approach to information technology is in place, P&T committees also support the associated functions. System pharmacy and therapeutics committees are generally composed of senior managers in nursing, pharmacy, and administration, and of medical directors or medical staff leaders within the system.

The functions of these committees have been described by ASHP as follows:[22]

1. Advising medical staff and administrators on all matters pertaining to the use of drugs (including investigational drug use)
2. Developing a formulary of drugs accepted for use in the health system and providing for its regular review and revision (selections should be based on objective evaluation of therapeutic merit and economic impact)
3. Establishing programs and procedures that ensure cost-effective, safe drug therapy
4. Establishing suitable educational programs for the system's professional staff on matters related to drug use
5. Participating in quality assurance activities related to prescribing, preparation, distribution, and use of medications

6. Reviewing adverse drug events, medication errors, and other medication misadventures occurring in the health system
7. Initiating and directing medication use evaluation activities
8. Advising the pharmacy service on the implementation of effective drug distribution and clinical pharmacy services

Managing the Formulary

The architecture of sound medication use is a well-designed and meticulously maintained formulary with supporting policy and quality management activities. A formulary is a continually updated list of medications and related information, representing the clinical judgment of physicians, pharmacists, and other experts in the diagnosis, prophylaxis, or treatment of disease and promotion of health. A formulary includes, but is not limited to, a list of medications and medication-associated products or devices, medication use policies, important ancillary drug information, decision-support tools, and organizational guidelines. A formulary system is the ongoing process through which a healthcare organization establishes policies regarding the use of drugs, therapies, and drug-related products and identifies those that are most medically appropriate and cost-effective.[5]

P&T committees and formularies have come under increasing pressure as the focus on medication use quality, medication errors, drug shortages, and high-cost medications has grown. To meet these challenges, the formulary system should include review and approval of all policies related to the medication-use process. Policy review and revision should occur as new information becomes available and at regularly established intervals. Medication use policies should address methods to add or delete drugs from the formulary; methods for ensuring the safe prescribing, distribution, administration, and monitoring of medications and monitoring medication use; and the process for using nonformulary drugs, managing drug product shortages and policies regarding procurement, prescribing, distribution, administration, and monitoring of medications.

Common strategies for managing medication use using a formulary include increasing the use of generic drugs, therapeutic interchange in key medication classes, policies directing use of specific drugs, clinical practice guidelines, and policies outlining acceptable off-label prescribing and the use of research pharmaceuticals. Medication use evaluation is also an important formulary-based strategy to evaluate and manage medication use.

Pharmacist Training and Education

At a minimum, all practicing pharmacists must have completed a five-year baccalaureate program in pharmacy accredited by the Accreditation Council for Pharmacy Education (ACPE)[23] and be licensed by the state in which they practice. Since 2000, all pharmacists have received the doctor of pharmacy, or PharmD, degree. The PharmD degree is conferred after six years of study and provides a more extensive clinical experience component than the BS degree. Clinical pharmacy programs in progressive pharmacy departments utilize PharmD-trained practitioners for clinical pharmacy service delivery. Some practice standards and programs require the PharmD credential, including education, residency training, and research programs.

A substantial number of pharmacists continue their education through general and specialty residencies, and fellowships in pharmacy practice and in clinical pharmacy specialties. A pharmacy residency is an organized postgraduate program that focuses on developing applied knowledge and skills in the practice environment, under the mentorship of an experienced practitioner. Specialty residencies provide training in a specific practice or clinical area such as oncology or pediatrics. Fellowships are directed individual programs designed to develop an independent researcher. Postgraduate pharmacy residency programs are accredited by ASHP. Pharmacists may also advance their knowledge through master of science in pharmacy, master of business administration, and master of public health programs.

Pharmacy has developed a number of board-level certifications to document the attainment of specific knowledge and clinical skill sets. Experienced PharmD-trained practitioners may sit for board examinations in pharmacotherapy, nutrition support, oncology, psychiatry, and nuclear pharmacy practice.[24] Specialty certified pharmacists generally practice in higher-level clinical practice environments with a greater degree of autonomy and also as researchers and teachers. They often support specialty clinical practice within a healthcare system. Pharmacist-run clinics in anticoagulation, psychopharmacy, home IV therapy, congestive heart failure, hypertension, and other specialties have achieved great success. Pharmacotherapy referral clinics run by pharmacists can be used to optimize medication use and decrease both drug cost and adverse drug events in healthcare systems. Clinical pharmacist services in these areas may be covered by medication therapy management (MTM) programs offered by insurers to optimize medication use by patients.[10]

Pharmacy practice education also continues after the receipt of a pharmacist license. Virtually all states require that 10 to 15 hours of approved continuing education be completed each year for license renewal. Much of this education is targeted toward the development of knowledge about new drugs and as a means to develop new practice skills.

Pharmacy Technician Training and Education

Many of the drug preparation and distribution tasks of pharmacists can be delegated to trained pharmacy technicians. Pharmacy technicians work under the direct supervision of a pharmacist. All pharmacy technicians have completed high school, and most have completed one or two years of college. In the past, technicians were trained in hospitals and health systems "on the job." As skill requirements and delegated tasks increased, pharmacy technician training programs were developed to provide basic skills and experience. Most such programs are found in local technical schools or community colleges.

Pharmacy technicians are trained to work in a variety of care delivery areas, including inpatient care, home care, and ambulatory care. Most states register or license pharmacy technicians and require applicants to pass an examination and complete continuing education to maintain registration. A growing number of pharmacy technicians seek certification on a national level to document skills and facilitate registration. The Pharmacy Technician Certification Board is a coalition of pharmacy organizations that supports testing of applicants for basic skills and pharmacy practice knowledge.[25] Applicants who pass the test are awarded the designation Certified Pharmacy Technician (CPhT).

Certified technicians are able to provide valuable support for the pharmacist and pharmacy service. While certification is not required to perform most technician duties, the education and experience allow CPhT holders to perform at a higher level than the typical on-the-job–trained technician. Certified technicians are also required to receive continuing education to retain certified status. A growing number of states are restricting specific pharmacy and medication-related duties to certified and/or licensed technicians in the interest of patient safety.

Pharmacy Information Systems and Automation

An effective pharmacy information system is necessary to support an integrated approach to delivering and managing pharmaceutical care in a healthcare system. It is vital in both the inpatient and outpatient pharmacy service areas. The pharmacy system should be part of the larger clinical and medical information management system of the healthcare system to ensure that pharmaceutical care and drug therapy are supported and evaluated with the same level of scrutiny as other treatments and services. Integration also provides a high level of coordination in care delivery by assembling information from all disciplines and ensuring consistency of patient care in all clinical practice areas. Integrated information technology is crucial to effective, real-time communication to support the medication use process.

Exhibit 14.1 lists the support functions provided by pharmacy information systems. These systems provide a means to support the operations of the inpatient and outpatient pharmacy services. They further enhance the ability of pharmacies to meet patient care needs and respond to growth in demand using only limited additional resources. They assist in identifying medication costs and in billing third parties or internal accounts for medications. Pharmacy information systems support clinical pathways and practice guidelines. They also ensure compliance with a formulary by providing cost and therapeutic information to prescribers and pharmacists for consideration in prescribing.

An integrated information system supports delivery and administration of medications to inpatients by nursing staff and ensures limited waits and complete prescription records for outpatient prescriptions. A well-run pharmacy information system can also provide cost data to prescribers and determine the clinical and financial status of patients at the time and point of service. Determinations of benefit eligibility for outpatients and of clinical need for inpatients can be made through an effective pharmacy information system. Interfaces with physician office–based systems can also support appropriate prescribing and allow remote entry of medication orders by physicians for more effective service.

The chief medical officer, chief financial officer, medical staff committees, and pharmacy directors can use retrospective data generated by pharmacy information systems to identify trends in drug use, support formulary and inventory management decisions, and determine

Exhibit 14.1   Pharmacy Information System Functions

Drug distribution
- Patient medication profiles
- Outpatient prescription records
- Drug/dosage form selection support
- Drug use data
- Point-of-care automation, including bedside bar code drug administration documentation
- Robotics
- Decrease in order entry errors
- Purchasing and inventory control
- Printing of labels, fill lists, reports
- Bar code drug administration support
- Work planning and staffing

Clinical pharmacy service
- Drug dosing support—overdose/underdose detection
- Drug–lab interaction detection
- Drug–drug interaction detection
- Drug allergy review
- Drug–nutrient interaction detection
- Drug treatment protocol support
- Clinical intervention tracking
- Medication use evaluation
- Drug use trend identification

Business support functions
- ADT
- Medication billing
- Cost review reports
- Outpatient Rx adjudication
- Decentralized services support
- Standardized data collection
- Workload and productivity analysis

Healthcare team
- Prescriber order entry (POE)
- Prescriber and treatment order sets
- Remote prescriber order entry
- Decrease in medication order errors
- Medication administration records (MAR)
- Prescriber profiling
- Patient medication profiles
- Point-of-care automation, including bedside bar code drug administration documentation

Clinical support and development
- Clinical guideline support
- Decision support protocols; "Clinical Rules"
- Drug therapy outcome review
- Clinical benchmarking
- Formulary decision support
- Medication error and adverse drug reaction (ADR) review
- Ad hoc query of clinical and financial data

compliance with guidelines or protocols. Medication use evaluation (MUE), adverse drug reaction (ADR) review, and other clinical and regulatory requirements can also be met through effective use of a pharmacy information system. These include the requirements of the state board of pharmacy, the Drug Enforcement Administration (DEA), the Joint Commission, the Centers for Medicare and Medicaid Services (CMS), and private and government payers. Pharmacy information systems can also help meet the research and patient care needs of medical and surgical specialties with high drug use profiles, such as oncology and anesthesiology. They can synthesize information to support development of treatment methods and guidelines that direct the appropriate selection of drug therapies and to determine algorithms and provide guidance for patient treatment.

Pharmacy information systems also provide data to support formulary decisions, select proper treatments, and improve financial results for a hospital, health system, or organized delivery network. Pharmacists and pharmacy technicians use these systems to manage and monitor the delivery and the results of care after treatment decisions have been made. Information systems can also support business decisions, including the decision to bid for managed care business, and can help ensure that medication budget projections are met.

Pharmacy information system development has recently focused on the entire medication use process, including prescriber order entry (POE) and related clinical decision support (CDS) functions through to drug administration, patient monitoring, and documentation at the bedside. Studies of medication errors have outlined the role of miscommunication and misinterpretation of orders related to poor handwriting, incomplete and ambiguous orders, and the use of abbreviations and other shortcuts used in traditional manual record systems. Several controlled studies and a number of surveys and anecdotal reports have highlighted the success of direct entry of medication orders into information systems by prescribers in decreasing certain types of medication errors.[26–29] The reluctance of physicians to accede to this clerical task has been overcome by the accumulating evidence of effectiveness, and the growing interest of health systems and the public in error prevention. Several notable business and payer groups and key standard-setting organizations have made prescriber order entry a criterion for evaluating quality efforts within a health system.[3,30]

CDS functions further enhance the utility of POE systems by providing feedback to prescribers at the time of ordering and by supporting rational and evidence-based prescribing. At the time of the publication, all major information systems vendors provide basic systems that support POE. The specifics of POE functions should be a portion of the decision regarding purchase and a key consideration in the development and maintenance of a pharmacy information system. CDS functions are more limited in scope as the information systems industry, health systems, and key involved professional groups define the scope and utility of CDS function. The development of CDS functions related to medication selection, use, and monitoring remain a key pharmacy obligation, with significant clinical and financial consequences for a health system. The integrated nature of vendor selection program development and CDS implementation raise the pharmacy information system selection, development, and management to a medical and administrative leadership level.

Bedside bar code drug administration (BCDA) software applications vary in their functionality but, in general, use bar code scanning technology to provide current information on medication orders, patient allergies, medication administration history, clinical observations, and other patient care information. A BCDA system uses a laptop or handheld bedside computer to communicate with other hospital information systems. The BCDA system communicates through interfaces constructed between other information systems (ADT, pharmacy, billing, POE, etc). The use of BCDA systems provides the nurse with current patient and medication information.

BCDA technology automates the nurse's bedside check by prompting the nurse to bar code scan his/her name badge, patient identification band, accessing the patient's medication profile, and actual medication to verify that the patient, drug, dose, route, and time are all correct. If there is any variance, or an error, the nurse is alerted prior to administering the drug. BCDA also supports the information system's electronic medication administration record (eMAR). Changes to the patient's medication orders are entered into the pharmacy system and sent "instantaneously" to the patient's bedside, updating clinicians on adjustments made to a patient's orders and preventing administration of doses after an order is modified or discontinued. The BCDA system also supports the medication administration record for inclusion in the patient medical record, and supports correct, complete, and accurate posting of charges for medications.

Inpatient Pharmacy Services

Inpatient pharmacy services focus on providing clinical and operational support for the correct utilization of drugs. Typically, clinical pharmacists assigned to a specific medical or surgical service provide pharmacy services supporting this objective in the patient care area. The pharmacist who works in each area is accountable for the level and quality of pharmaceutical care and should participate in the development of resources and plans to support improvements in care quality and the efficiency of care delivery. Patient care area pharmacists have responsibility for the full spectrum of pharmaceutical care, as described earlier. They organize other professionals who participate in drug therapy selection, administration, and monitoring and ensure that reliable, consistent, effective therapy is delivered. Following prescribing, they coordinate the delivery and monitoring of the medication therapy. Pharmacists assigned to patient care areas support the execution of the medication therapy by evaluating the therapy to maximize the efficacy of drug delivery and administration.

The pharmaceutical care practice model creates efficiency and positive outcomes by ensuring timely, correct decision making, by managing medication therapy to make certain that it achieves the desired goal, and by directing the medication selection process. Inefficiencies, therapeutic failures, and higher costs are associated with insufficient monitoring, selection of less than the optimal medication alternatives, and micromanagement of therapies (e.g., frequent changes based on individual clinical findings rather than on documented clinical evidence).

Support resources, particularly information systems, can be used to identify patients for whom targeted interventions by pharmacists can benefit both patient care outcome and the healthcare provider. The assignment of pharmacists to patient care teams also allows direct interaction with prescribers and the provision of feedback on the clinical and economic impact of drug therapy decisions. Pharmacists identify drug-related issues across the continuum of care, including drug therapy–related admissions and readmissions. They facilitate the pharmaceutical transition from acute inpatient care to skilled care, home care, or an ambulatory environment. Skilled pharmacists responsible for a program or service participate in reviewing physician practice patterns related to drug therapy and suggesting alternatives to achieve the clinical and financial goals of the organization.

Inpatient clinical pharmacy services should be developed and targeted to meet the needs of the patients, the medical staff, and the healthcare system or hospital. Hospital-specific plans should be made to ensure that necessary services are provided and that patient care quality and cost needs are met. Clinical pharmacy services vary with the nature of the patient care delivered by an organization, and are driven by patient acuity and length of stay. The pharmaceutical care needs of an acutely ill heart attack patient differ from those of a psychiatric patient or a geriatric patient admitted for a prosthetic hip replacement. Patients discharged to self-care require different types of support than those who move to skilled care facilities or to assisted living. Targeting pharmacy services to meet the needs of the patients treated in a given healthcare system ensures both positive outcomes and cost-effective service delivery.

Although clinical pharmacy services must be tailored to both the patient needs and organizational mission, there is a group of core services typically accepted as a component of appropriate pharmacy services. These services generally are required or encouraged by standard-setting agencies such as the Joint Commission or ASHP. They may also be addressed in state health department, hospital, or pharmacy practice regulations. Increasingly, they are among the baseline services expected by payers. Basic inpatient clinical pharmacy services provided by a health system pharmacy should include:

- ADR review
- Antibiotic use review
- Serum drug concentration (SDC) review
- Renal and pharmacokinetic dosing of drugs
- Management of drug therapies under approved protocols
- Medication profile review
- General dosing review and support
- Drug interaction screening
- Assessment of medication allergy and pregnancy status
- Medication histories and patient discharge teaching
- Discharge planning and patient teaching
- Medication use evaluation
- Clinical practice guideline support and development

- Drug information services
- Management of parenteral nutrition support (TPN)
- IV to oral medication therapy conversion

The effectiveness of clinical pharmacy programs is best evaluated with a system that tracks the patient-specific clinical interventions of pharmacists assigned to each team or patient care area.[31] A number of manual and automated methods for tracking interventions have been developed. An intervention-tracking program should identify every direct patient care activity of pharmacists. Several authors and ASHP have developed methods to categorize and assess the impact and desirable outcomes of interventions.[32–35] A well-run intervention program identifies the nature of the clinical activities of pharmacists and ascribes them to specific pharmacists, patients, patient care programs, and physicians. It further develops an index of the costs and benefits associated with each intervention and the total for all interventions. Outcomes for an organization can be determined based on the quality and impact of patient care and on the avoidance of drug and other treatment costs, such as those associated with laboratory tests or increased length of inpatient stay. Pharmacy clinical intervention tracking programs should also develop methods to pass detailed intervention information to other providers. They can be of further use in the evaluation of pharmacist work performance and physician practice patterns.

The clinical activities of pharmacists should be recorded in the paper or electronic medical record. Recommendations and outcomes should be visible to all patient care disciplines to ensure the inclusion of drug therapy recommendations in care planning and monitoring. Electronic recording of interventions allows routine tracking and analysis. Most current pharmacy information systems support recording, tracking, and communication of pharmacist clinical interventions. Several stand-alone computer programs have been developed to facilitate recording and analysis of pharmacist interventions when these are not supported by the pharmacy information system.[36,37]

Inpatient Drug Distribution and Management

The primary method for drug distribution in the inpatient setting is the unit dose method. The unit dose medication distribution system was developed more than 40 years ago to provide a safe and effective means to distribute medications.[38] It has been endorsed by a number of standard-setting and accrediting organizations, including the Joint Commission and ASHP. Pharmacy regulations and rules in most states now require some variation of the unit dose system for drug delivery. The unit dose system allows detailed tracking of medication use, and it avoids many opportunities for medication error by ensuring that a limited number of medications are available for administration. Further, the medications are sorted and organized to facilitate correct administration. The unit dose system minimizes drug costs by limiting waste, loss, spoilage, and diversion of medications in patient care areas. The unit dose system also supports the use of unit-based medication cabinets and bar code drug administration documentation, and facilitates correct posting of medication charges.

The unit dose system is defined as a system in which medications are dispensed in labeled, single-unit packages in ready-to-administer form. In most acute care settings, a 24-hour supply or less is available for use in the patient care area.[39–41] On-site packaging requirements in acute care pharmacies are a significant cost and a necessary part of the medication distribution process. Appropriate packaging to support automation, meet medication safety requirements, and provide doses not readily available commercially is necessary. The effort, packaging materials, equipment, and staff costs are not inconsequential, particularly in pediatric hospitals. Packaging to meet regulatory and compendial requirements also requires record keeping, quality control, and the ability to perform recalls as in the commercial sector.

Pharmacists review electronic medication orders from a POE system for appropriateness, dose, allergies, drug interactions, or direct copies of the prescriber's orders prior to medication being dispensed or made available from a point of care (POC) device (a bedside handheld device for scanning medications, patient identification, vital signs, and other patient care data). Where POE has not been implemented, pharmacists enter medication orders into the pharmacy information system, where the checks of appropriateness, dose, allergies, drug interactions, and appropriate inventory quantities and items to dispense are identified. In health systems where physicians enter medications directly into a computer, a pharmacist reviews orders before they are made fully active for medication dispensing and administration.

The core of the drug distribution system is the complete pharmacy information system. Pharmacy information systems are designed to support numerous functions, but a primary purpose is to support accurate, safe, timely, cost-effective medication distribution. In the acute care environment, patient conditions, therapeutic needs, and medication orders change rapidly. A computerized information system provides the most accurate current description of each patient's medication needs. It also supports correct entry of medication orders and checking for errors in prescribing and dosing, and for drug allergies and interactions. Pharmacy information systems support both manual and automated unit dose distribution systems.

In a unit dose system, active current medications are available on the patient care unit in sufficient quantities at all times. However, when a new order is placed, a supply of medication must be sent to cover the period until the next regular supply is delivered. The "first-dose turnaround time" can be a significant issue if transportation systems and pharmacy location preclude rapid delivery of newly ordered medications to the patient care area.

In a manual unit dose system, a medication supply for each patient is prepared by the pharmacy for each 24-hour period. The specific medications and quantities are based on the current medication order profile maintained in the information system for each patient. A sufficient quantity of each medication is placed in a bin specifically designated for that patient. Individual bins are combined in cassettes and delivered to each patient care area. Medication cassettes are placed in a secure area or in a locked cart on each unit. A duplicate set of patient medication bins and cassettes is kept in the pharmacy, where it is refilled for daily exchange. Most pharmacies using this system exchange medication cassettes once daily at a predetermined time.

Although the unit dose system confers many safeguards and advantages in delivering medications, as a manual system it is highly labor intensive, so automation has been developed to support the patient care advantages of the system at a decreased labor cost and with enhanced security and tracking. Two methods are used to improve unit dose drug distribution. The first method automates the bin-filling process in the pharmacy using robotics. The second places automated medication dispensing units on the patient care unit at the point of care (POC).

Direct automation of the manual processes described above using a pharmacy information system, bar codes, and a robot is the most straightforward approach. Vendors have developed robots that fill unit dose bins for the next 24-hour period based on the patient's computerized medication profiles. When an order is entered in the pharmacy information system, it is translated into information that directs the robot to select an appropriate number of the correct unit dose medication and place it in the patient's medication bin as it moves along a conveyor. The use of bar codes ensures accuracy and allows detailed information, including lot numbers, expiration dates, and even unique dose identifiers, to be retained. Pharmacies using this type of automation generally continue to use a single daily cart exchange and operate the robot to fill the unit dose bins and cassette once each day.

First doses of drugs resulting from new medication orders can also be selected and prepared for delivery by the robot, ensuring the accuracy and consistency that automation confers. However, each new medication still must be delivered from the robot's location to the patient care area. Advantages of the robotic cart-filling method include improved accuracy in medication dispensing and accounting. Disadvantages include high start-up costs (partly resulting from needed facility renovations), high continuing support costs, significant pharmacy space requirements, the need to purchase equipment and hire staff to package most doses in a form usable by the robot, and limited robot capacity. Transportation from the robot's location, typically the main pharmacy, also means that delays in delivering first doses for new medication orders also remain, as in the manual unit dose system. Most general hospitals have 2500 to 3500 medications on their formulary; robots capable of handling so many medications are costly. Many medications require special storage and handling precluding their being dispensed by a robot. These medications must continue to be dispensed manually. Some state pharmacy regulations limit multisite robot use and decrease the financial benefits by requiring manual checks of robot-dispensed doses by pharmacists.

Capital expense or lease costs for robotic technology are high, limiting use to larger hospitals. The decision to purchase and implement an automated bin fill system should be based on a complete analysis of the financial benefit, return on investment, and potential for demonstrated improvements in service quality and patient care. Although the cost of a cart-filling robot continues to decrease, information systems and other continuing support costs will remain high enough to make the decision to purchase or lease a robot hard to justify in many cases.

The second strategy for automating unit dose distribution is POC automation. POC automation places supplies of medications on the patient care unit in computer-controlled dispensing cabinets that function in a manner similar to the familiar automated teller machines used by the banking industry. Nurses or other authorized patient care staff are provided with personal identification codes and passwords that confer access to medications. Users, by responding to prompts given on a screen, select the appropriate medications for particular patients. Although a bin and cassette system is not used, dispensing cabinets are stocked with individually packaged and labeled drugs, a key component of the unit dose method. The available medication supplies are specific to each patient and are controlled by the pharmacy information system. Users can only access those medications that are currently ordered for a specific patient. A current medication order, reviewed and approved by a pharmacist, enables access to a specific drug for that patient. Although a 24-hour supply is not dispensed for each patient, access is directed by the electronic medication profile in the POC unit. This ensures tracking of drug use and also provides support to ensure that ordered medications are given in a timely fashion. Emergency medications are available through an override function that allows specific medications to be accessed without pharmacist review of a medication order.

Patient data are transferred to the POC system through the admissions (ADT) module of the information system. Patient census, transfers, billing, and pharmacy medication profile data must be supplied to the unit on a real-time basis. Pharmacy data, including medication orders and substantial drug product details, must pass to the POC system instantaneously. Billing data, drug withdrawal, and medication administration information must be passed from the unit to the pharmacy and patient care information system. POC device users, including nurses, physicians, and pharmacy staff, must be credentialed and maintain access privileges to ensure both the security of medication supplies and the effective use of the POC system. A complete record of medication-related information for each transaction must move between the pharmacy, patient billing, and other information systems and the POC device or its computer server.

POC devices can eliminate a high percentage of the manual bin fill process if properly sized and configured. Substantial customization of the hardware devices and the software that drives each device is possible at each site. Medication inventories can be managed to follow trends in utilization to minimize cost and maximize resource use.

POC systems eliminate delays in medication delivery to the unit for the approximately 90% of medications supplied on the unit. POC systems suffer from several of the same shortcomings mentioned for robotics above. For example, medications that require special storage and handling cannot be delivered through POC automation and must be dispensed manually. Although 90% of medications are available on the patient care unit in a well-run POC system, the 10% that are unavailable can consume substantial staff time and cause considerable delays in therapy due to delivery logistics and system reconfiguration and loading. Pharmacy regulations in some states limit POC functions and decrease the realizable cost benefits by requiring pharmacist checks.

Advantages of POC devices include the increased accuracy and accountability for dispensing of medications seen with manual and robotic systems. POC systems extend the accountability to medication administration and other medication-related functions occurring in the patient care area. Nurses or other authorized staff are given access to necessary and appropriate medications based on current real-time medication profiles. Medications that are discontinued are immediately removed from access and cannot be administered. Unauthorized access to medications is prohibited, and controlled substance accountability is high. Bar code–supported filling and refilling of POC cabinets also provides enhanced accuracy and safety and the ability to manage drug recalls and expiration dating effectively. Disadvantages of POC systems include significant support costs, space needs on patient care units, and a requirement for a high level of accuracy in order review.

POC devices have an advantage over both robotic and manual systems in anesthesia care, operating rooms, postanesthesia recovery areas, and emergency departments. In these areas POC devices use ADT information and user data to support a very high level of accountability for stock medications and improved charge capture. Although the system is not strictly "unit dose" in nature, the detailed accountability and rich transaction data allow for ready access to drugs in emergent situations with a high level of accountability for drug use and inventory. The POC supports similar stock medication procedures on the patient care unit. POC devices allow emergency access to selected medications that are not part of the patient's current medication profile. This access is generally limited to defined patient care needs and is supported by policies developed by the pharmacy and therapeutics committee of the hospital or healthcare system.

The task of selecting a manual, robotic, or POC system is not simple. Substantial resources are consumed in setting up any of these systems. Vendor and pharmacy department expertise are required to accomplish the projected efficiencies and cost decreases. **Table 14.2** compares features of the three methods and their advantages and disadvantages. Some general principles do apply when trying to determine the best method, but all three systems have been successfully used in all sizes and types of healthcare systems. Some healthcare systems have implemented combinations of robotics and POC devices to gain the advantages of each across diverse sites and care needs.

Patient care bedside devices can be used to support further automation of pharmaceutical care delivery. These "handheld" devices can accomplish more than medication administration documentation, and they interface with both robotic and POC pharmacy systems. Advantages of bedside charting devices include enhanced accountability and medication safety, plus data management for medications, along with convenience and accuracy in charting medications and other aspects of care.

Sterile Products Preparation

In the acute care and home IV therapy environment, substantial pharmacy effort is devoted to the preparation of sterile products for intravenous and other parenteral administration. Intravenous admixtures consist of drugs added to IV solutions. These encompass antibiotics,

Table 14.2 Comparison of Unit Dose Distribution Systems

	Manual Unit Dose System	Robotic Unit Dose System	Point-of-Care Drug Delivery System
Capital cost or lease cost	Low	High	High
Personnel cost	High; high pharmacist time requirements	Lowest; limits both pharmacist and pharmacy technician time	Low; limits pharmacist time, shifts work functions to pharmacy technicians
Computer support required	Basic	Substantial	Highest
Dispensing and billing accuracy	Low	High	Highest
Drug administration accountability	Limited	Medium	Very high
Stock medication capability	Open stock on patient care unit; manual accountability	Open stock on patient care unit; manual accountability	Limited user-specific access; high accountability
First dose delivery delays	Substantial and frequent	Substantial, but less frequent	Lowest; none for 90% of medications
Medication error prevention	Lowest	Intermediate	Highest
Medication capacity	95–100% of all medications	75–80% of all medications	90% of all medications
Medication packaging requirements	Modest	Highest; limited commercial production of "robot-specific" packaged doses	Intermediate
Refill frequency	Daily 24-hour supply	Daily 24-hour supply	Daily restock of about 10% of items in POC device
Controlled substance applications	Limited; locked stock on patient care unit; manual accountability	Best; locked, with patient- and user-specific controlled access	Limited; locked stock on patient care unit; manual accountability
"Best fit" application type	Small hospitals with lower "medication intensity" and hospitals that include long-term and skilled care	Large hospitals with high "medication intensity"	Medium to large hospitals at all medication use levels

cytotoxic cancer chemotherapy agents, vasoactive and critical care IV drips, and total parenteral nutrition (TPN) solutions.

Drugs added to IV solutions may undergo degradation caused by the diluting solution and the effects of light, heat, and the storage environment. Drugs mixed in an IV solution also can interact with each other, leading to decreased effectiveness or to toxicity. The IV admixture itself may be contaminated through manipulation, leading to bacterial growth and transmission of bacteria to the patient. Some new biotechnology-derived drugs have very short periods of stability and may require special techniques to achieve dilution and dispersion. Accuracy in preparation supports delivery of the labeled amount and ensures consistency from dose to dose and from patient to patient. For these reasons as well as technique and quality assurance issues, Joint Commission and ASHP standards, and most state pharmacy regulations, require pharmacy preparation of IV solutions. In the past, IVs were prepared by nurses on the patient care units, but this is no longer recommended.

ASHP provides a number of standards and recommendations for facilities, procedures, training, and qualifications for sterile products preparation.[41,42] An appropriate dedicated space for IV preparation, with written policies and procedures that meet practice standards, is also required. Pharmacies should meet these standards and institute process controls and staff training to foster appropriate preparation of parenteral medications. ASHP documents offer sound recommendations on quality assurance, staff education and evaluation, policies and procedures, facilities and equipment, and quality improvement.

USP 797 is a far-reaching regulation issued by US Pharmacopoeia (USP) that governs a wide range of pharmacy practices.[43] It is designed both to cut down on infections transmitted to patients through pharmaceutical products and to better protect staff working in pharmacies in the course of their exposure to pharmaceuticals. USP 797 sets standards for pharmacies that prepare "compounded sterile preparations" (CSPs). The intent of USP 797 is "to prevent harm and fatality to patients that could result from microbial contamination (nonsterility), excessive bacterial endotoxins, large content errors in strength of correct ingredients, and incorrect ingredients in CSPs." USP 797 also addresses:

- Responsibility of compounding personnel
- Microbial contamination risk levels
- Verification of compounding accuracy and sterilization
- Personnel training and evaluation in aseptic technique
- Manipulation skills, environmental quality and control
- Processing
- Verification of automated compounding devices (ACDs) for parenteral nutrition
- Compounding
- Finished preparation release checks and tests
- Storage and beyond-use dating
- Maintaining product quality and control after the CSP leaves the pharmacy
- Patient or caregiver training
- Patient monitoring and adverse events reporting
- Quality assurance program

The availability of suitable facilities is of paramount importance for ensuring the integrity of the final CSP.

Practice standards include the maintenance of process records for both products and staff performance. Practice standards are particularly important in the home care environment, where caregiver training and storage conditions typically fall below the high standards associated with inpatient care. An annual assessment of compliance with USP 797 standards and state regulations should be performed. A sterile products preparation system utilizing trained pharmacy technician staff under the supervision of pharmacists has been demonstrated to provide appropriate, cost-effective service.

Cytotoxic agents used in the treatment of cancer create specific preparation challenges.[42] Safe handling procedures should be a part of the training of all pharmacy staff who handle these agents. The pharmacy staff should participate in an active, vigorous program to train others who work with these agents, including nurses, physicians, and housekeeping personnel who handle waste, trash, and spills. Similar, even more stringent procedures are required for gene therapy agents.

Improved methods and equipment are available for IV preparation. Computer-controlled compounding pumps are available to prepare intravenous nutrition (TPN) solutions. Software programs exist that perform calculations for preparations, provide product preparation worksheets, and support label preparation and quality assurance efforts. Pumps and devices that provide controlled delivery of drugs for treatment of pain, such as patient-controlled analgesia (PCA), and for epidural administration of drugs offer therapeutic benefits. Syringe pumps can provide medications in higher concentrations or with lower fluid volumes. A pharmacy with a well-run sterile products program can adapt to these changes easily, as the same techniques and procedures are used for calculations and preparation.

Automation has also become available to support the aseptic preparation of IV solutions and syringes in the pharmacy. Robots that reliably and consistently prepare medications offer significant advantages, including labeling and bar coding of individual doses, product scanning and verification, and decreased preparation errors. Initial and ongoing costs are substantial; however, the mitigation of risk in this critical part of the medication use system has seen strong acceptance of the technology.

Outsourcing of the preparation of intravenous medications is also an available option. Home infusion providers and some specialty pharmacies provide services to hospitals, from preparing specialty medications, such as parenteral nutrition and patient controlled analgesia (PCA) pump solutions, up through outsourcing the entire IV preparation process. Outsourcing offers the opportunity to meet regulatory or other requirements without capital outlay, streamlines workflow, and reduces preparation errors and waste. Disadvantages may include higher costs, fixed processes and ordering and delivery schedules, and limited flexibility. The decision to outsource this critical and risk-laden pharmacy service should be made thoughtfully.

Pharmacy Service Location

Pharmacy services such as drug preparation, sterile products compounding, and unit dose distribution are typically housed in a main pharmacy area. This area may be far removed from the patient care areas, limiting interactions between physicians, nurses, and pharmacists regarding drug therapy. Of necessity, a number of pharmacy staff must work in the main drug preparation area to perform activities that require special facilities or conditions. This is also true of outpatient pharmacy services, where preparation, compounding, and distribution continue to occur in a pharmacy behind a counter or closed doors.

To achieve the goals of pharmaceutical care described above, pharmacists must be housed and work in areas where patients and professionals meet to assess, plan, and deliver care. Achieving this goal can be complicated by the distance, physical layout, and transportation systems available in a given facility. Several alternatives have been developed to accomplish the goal of clinical pharmacy service delivery in harmony with the pharmacy's traditional distribution and medication control functions. Many hospitals and healthcare systems utilize substantial information systems development and either type of automation described above to support these alternatives. The models described below are not mutually exclusive, and most healthcare systems use a combination of systems to achieve patient care quality and efficiency goals.

Creating satellite pharmacies in patient care areas and remote clinics is one method used for placing pharmacists closer to patient care. Immediate medication needs, drug information, patient monitoring, and consultation services are delivered from the satellite pharmacies. The central pharmacy continues to be responsible for daily unit dose bin fill, sterile products preparation, maintenance of POC dispensing inventory, and other support services. In an inpatient decentralized system that uses satellite pharmacies, the bulk of pharmacy staff practice in the satellite pharmacy locations, while a core group remains in the main pharmacy. Advantages of this method include rapid delivery of first doses and ready availability of pharmacy staff for consultation and care planning. Disadvantages include space requirements in patient care areas, inventory growth, and staffing requirements to keep the satellites open.

A second approach involves placing pharmacy staff in patient care areas without creating satellites to provide distribution services. The pharmacists provide information and participate in care planning, patient education, and other services, but do not use a satellite location to dispense. This practice model can be supported by distribution and drug preparation services located in a central pharmacy. Automated POC devices can also deliver doses. In ambulatory care environments, mail order and remote site filling of prescriptions also utilize this model.

This second alternative allows for the pharmacy services to be delivered in patient care areas and ensures a high level of support for appropriate prescribing and correct medication administration. Decentralized pharmacists located in patient care areas can identify and resolve medication problems and misadventures, including drug interactions, adverse drug reactions, and medication errors. This model is most frequently supported by POC device–based drug distribution. Information systems must support access to the pharmacy profile and pharmacy clinical and order management systems throughout the patient care areas. Advantages of this model include the high level of participation of pharmacists in patient care, staffing flexibility, and the absence of space needs. Disadvantages are few, but the requirement for access to pharmacy information systems in the care area is nearly absolute.

Table 14.3 compares the three types of pharmacy service delivery systems. No particular system is best across all organization types. In many hospitals and healthcare systems, a combination

Table 14.3   Comparison of Pharmacy Staffing Models

	Centralized Pharmacy Services	Satellite-Based Pharmacy Services	Decentralized Pharmacy Services
Space requirements	Main pharmacy only	High; in proximity to patient care units and main pharmacy	Main pharmacy only
Capital issues	None	Inventory growth; drug preparation equipment duplicated in satellite(s)	None
Computer support required	Basic to advanced	Basic to advanced; satellites must have access	Advanced; pharmacy information system must be accessible on care units
"Best fit" unit dose model(s) supported	Manual, robotic, and point-of-care	Manual, robotic	Point-of-care
Sterile products preparation model	Centralized preparation and distribution	First dose from satellite, then centralized	Centralized preparation and distribution
First dose delivery delays	Longest	Minimal	Intermediate
Medication transportation needs	Highest	Lowest	Intermediate
"Best fit" application type	Smaller hospitals; hospitals with good transportation systems; hospitals with homogeneous patient population	Hospitals with large physical plants or distant patient care areas; hospitals with diverse or dissimilar patient populations (e.g., pediatric unit in general hospital), hospitals with large numbers of specialty care units (e.g., ICUs)	All hospital types with advanced information systems; POC devices add significant value

of two or all three of the service models may be used. Some regional systems have accomplished centralization of portions of the pharmacy service model across a city or service area. Major changes in the application and effectiveness of both centralized and decentralized models are generally driven by automation and information system capabilities.

Ambulatory Care and Outpatient Pharmacy Systems

Healthcare systems have expanded their scope far beyond the traditional inpatient stay. Many systems include physician practices, short-stay surgery centers, urgent care centers, hospices, home care agencies, skilled nursing and long-term care facilities, rehabilitation centers, and retail pharmacies. In some larger systems, mail order prescriptions and pharmacy benefits management also have become included in the services provided. These two functions are generally added by systems when they move into providing and managing health maintenance organization (HMO) and insurance products. Many systems have created executive-level pharmacy director positions to tie these services together and to ensure regulatory compliance and consistency across organizational components. If the scope and size of ambulatory services warrant it, they may report to a pharmacy manager whose sole responsibility is to manage an ambulatory care pharmacy.

In many cases, some or all of these pharmacy services may be contracted to outside vendors under the oversight of a system or corporate pharmacy director. Services should be contracted outside the system whenever the pharmacy is too small to possess the necessary professional and management staff expertise. It may also be advisable when the unique drugs purchased to support a program do not allow contracts for the lowest available cost. "Alternate site delivery program" contracts are a part of most group purchasing portfolios. However, because of the diversity of "alternate site" definitions by groups, healthcare systems, and vendors, these contracts are generally not as advantageous as inpatient contracts, where class of trade definitions are more uniform. In the case of larger functions, such as mail order prescriptions and pharmacy benefit management services, the size of the patient population required for development of a viable program may be beyond the scope of most systems.

Principles for managing the daily operation of pharmacy services for each of these units are generally similar to those described for an inpatient pharmacy. However, the application can vary greatly based on the population served and the pharmaceutical care needs of the patients. Physician office practices, urgent care centers, and short-stay surgery centers generally do not require daily on-site pharmacist staff, unless they are quite large. Pharmaceutical purchasing and drug policy can be coordinated from a central pharmacy and global pharmacy, and therapeutics and other policies can be modified to apply to each of these areas. Purchasing and inventory control generally are held separate from a system's hospitals, both because products used are somewhat dissimilar and to prevent contract problems. A business manager, nurse, or other technician in the practice or surgery center can order drug supplies and manage inventory under the supervision of a central pharmacy buyer or manager. This ensures that drug purchasing and disposition meet appropriate regulations and that storage, record keeping, and other regulatory and practice standards are met. In some states, specific regulations apply to pharmacy practice in surgery centers. Particular attention should be paid to controlled substance regulations in all areas.

Hospice and home care pharmacies bridge the gap between traditional inpatient care and ambulatory care. They typically draw on the expertise of inpatient-trained staff for the knowledge and mechanics of clinical care. They do, however, place a high premium on customer service, as in the ambulatory care model, so they also capitalize on the patient care skills of outpatient pharmacy. Home care and hospice pharmacies may be combined, particularly in a system that emphasizes oncology, where the patient populations served and the physicians involved in care management may overlap significantly. An emphasis on collaborative efforts and dedicated staff in these areas ensures that pharmacy service agendas are consistent with global system agendas. Home care and hospice pharmacies can operate independently, but many make use of the system's hospital pharmacy professional staff to cover emergencies and nights or other off-hours. Patient access problems and delivery requirements generally make home care pharmacies that are separate from inpatient facilities more advantageous. Because of limited downtime for equipment, and the amount of time staff spent in inpatient sterile products labs, there is little opportunity to capture unused hospital facility and staff time to deliver home care services.

Skilled nursing facilities (SNFs) and long-term care facilities have long been served by centralized pharmacies. These services typically grew out of retail pharmacies in the private sector, and this model continues to work well in this sector in a healthcare system. SNF drug use and patient acuity levels match those of an outpatient pharmacy most closely. Specific, detailed regulations exist for SNF and nursing home pharmacies. There are requirements for independent professional review of the need for continuing medication and for drug use evaluation. Communication with physicians regarding these requirements must be documented, and routine scheduled reviews must be performed to ensure both regulatory compliance and payment. System pharmacy directors should have methods to ensure that continuing compliance is kept in place.

Retail pharmacy services constitute a growth area for health systems. Opportunities generally start with medical office building patients, discharged hospital patients, and health system employee prescription benefits coverage, and then expand as systems develop insurance and HMO products. Retail pharmacies must purchase independently of other parts of a system by law and regulation. In many cases, the ability to capture prescriptions from discharged patients and their families, along with support for physician practices, makes retail pharmacies an excellent supplement to ambulatory care services. Each retail pharmacy can operate autonomously, but all pharmacies should fall under the oversight of the system's pharmacy and therapeutics committee, general pharmacy policies, and a system pharmacy executive.

Many specialized pharmacy systems and applications have been developed in ambulatory care environments. Outpatient pharmacy services also have become a growth area for healthcare systems, particularly where sophisticated or unique drug therapies are delivered, such as in home intravenous therapy or where the continuation of inpatient care provides efficiencies and better treatment outcomes. Centralization of resources, drug inventories, and distribution services works well when decentralized pharmacy staff are placed in clinics and in the field. Business plans and customer service issues drive ambulatory care pharmacy service planning. An effective information system and automation can support high-level, cost-effective services in the outpatient environment as well. Physician office and patient usable automation devices are available to support the same sophistication in delivery as on the inpatient care side of pharmaceutical care.

Financial Management

Expenditures for drugs vary widely in healthcare systems. Most systems devote less than 20% of their total expenditures to drug therapies, but many organizations with large specialty treatment populations, such as AIDS or oncology patients, may experience higher expenses. All organizations are experiencing growth in expenditures related to new drugs and therapies and, to a lesser extent, increased patient demand.

The annual budget is an important part of the pharmacy manager's financial responsibility. ASHP practice standards and guidelines refer to the budget and financial leadership responsibilities of pharmacists and identify key roles and responsibilities related to financial management of a pharmacy service.[44,45]

The pharmacy executive manages the health system pharmacy's financial performance within the context of the broader health system. He or she develops budgets aligned with organizational and departmental objectives and monitors financial performance appropriately, performing financial audits and analysis as needed to ensure accurate, appropriate, and timely recording and classification of actual revenue capture and expenses.

The overwhelming majority of pharmacy supply expense is drugs. A well-documented drug budget is critical for the pharmacy's and the hospital's success and has a material impact on the hospital's finances. Forecasting drug and other supply expenses is a combination of price inflation, drug utilization, drug product mix, and a blend of utilization and mix representing expensive, innovative medications. The authors of a continuing series of articles examining trends in drug cost recommend a nine-step process to ensure success in forecasting this expense:[46]

1. Collect historical purchase data from distributor data systems and utilization data from hospital and pharmacy information systems. Consider how new medical and surgical services or changes in service and patient volume will affect the application of this information to the coming fiscal year.
2. Review financial history; evaluate the pharmacy's performance against budget for the most current fiscal year.
3. Build a high-priority drug budget. A relatively small number of drugs (50–60 products) represents 80 to 90% of total drug purchases and utilization in most health systems.
4. Build a new-product budget. Consider new drugs expected to be approved during the period covered by the budget.
5. Build a nonformulary drug budget.
6. Build a low-priority drug budget. The low-priority drug budget represents a small portion of the total drug budget and can be safely budgeted as a lump sum.
7. Establish a drug cost containment plan. Include drug use evaluation results indicating inappropriate prescribing, drug classes with multiple competing agents, and reports of successful cost containment efforts published by other institutions.
8. Finalize and present the total drug budget. The total drug budget is the sum of expected expenditures on the high-priority list, new products, nonformulary agents, and low-priority products, minus the total cost impact expected from the cost containment plan.
9. Vigilance. Monitor actual performance and variance throughout the year.

In all cases, the director of the pharmacy and key members of the pharmacy staff, including clinical staff and business and purchasing managers, should collaborate with the pharmacy and therapeutics committee and other stakeholders to develop the most thoughtful and accurate forecasts for this part of the budget. Because of the magnitude of the cost of drug therapy, hospital administration and boards rely on pharmacists to contribute to the understanding of the impact of medication costs, and to develop a plan for this expense. Increasingly, a key role of pharmacy leadership is to articulate a coherent plan for clinical pharmacists and other pharmacy staff to understand the balance of cost, benefit, and outcome in their daily professional decision making.[46]

Reimbursement for inpatient drug expenses is bundled with overall patient costs and contracts. In this area, minimizing drug supply costs is the most effective financial strategy. In some cases, reimbursement for cost outliers may offer an opportunity to capture some additional revenue when high-cost drugs are used.

Healthcare systems are often "at risk" for outpatient drug expenses in newer delivery models. In general, selection of the most effective and least costly alternative is the prudent course of action. Involvement of the P&T committee and frontline clinical pharmacists will lead to better patient care and financial outcomes. Balancing effectiveness and cost is perhaps the most challenging part of pharmaceutical care today.

Pharmacy revenue should also be carefully considered in the budget process. Although case-based reimbursement remains the most widely used model for inpatient care reimbursement, outpatient and ambulatory care prescriptions, and inpatient care for key specialty areas, particularly oncology, make the appropriate setting of revenue targets and the development of systems to capture charges and revenue crucial. Pharmacy charges are generally based on the cost of the drug ingredient and are multiplied by factor(s) that add the handling and other costs based on relative value units (RVU) consumed to deliver the medication to the patient. Because the formulary and the cost of medications purchased by the health system change frequently, systems and controls to manage this information should also be developed.[47]

Cost and Productivity Management

Pharmacy departments are most often charged with the responsibility for managing drug and delivery system costs. Systems should be developed to utilize drug and delivery resources in a cost-effective fashion. Daily, weekly, monthly, and quarterly assessments of drug costs and salary costs should be completed and reviewed. Performance targets for both categories can be developed based on activity levels such as admissions, outpatient visits, or prescriptions filled. Financial management systems in contemporary pharmacies should provide methods to quantify costs, monitor financial performance, and relate clinical information and service data to costs. Drug budgeting by therapeutic category and routine reporting of cost by service and by therapeutic category can support continued success in meeting financial targets. Adding detail to general reports also allows rapid evaluation of trends and changes in drug purchasing and utilization.

The pharmacy management team should focus on developing effective strategies to maximize leverage of drug and human resource costs. These include automation of distribution tasks and the use of technicians and other support personnel when warranted. Attention should also be paid to the level of experience and qualification of the pharmacist engaged in a particular activity. A mix of specialists, generalists, and support system pharmacists should be developed to meet the organization's needs. Specialist-trained clinical pharmacists are paid premium wages, so their use in drug distribution should be limited. Staff pharmacists can be appropriately deployed to maximize the productivity of professional resources.[48]

To achieve the highest degree of effectiveness, the pharmacy management team can utilize a number of tools to assist in analyzing labor and supply parameters. The traditional comparison of total actual and budgeted expenses does not give the pharmacy manager enough information to promote the most cost-effective use of supplies and services throughout the institution.

In a cost-critical environment, staff utilization requires ongoing weekly and, if supported by information systems, daily monitoring. Staffing depends on the mix of clinical pharmacists, pharmacists, technicians, and other support staff, and on the ability of each team to meet its care responsibilities effectively. A premium should be placed on the interaction between the pharmacy service and the other members of the care delivery team. Staffing ratios and the functions of each staff type should be evaluated at least yearly. Staffing systems should be reviewed and revised with an eye toward promoting productivity and staff morale as well as creating savings. Program changes, market competition, and therapy changes can dramatically affect the volume and distribution of the pharmacy workload within a healthcare system.

Productivity measures should be established through a work measurement system, using standards established for different product and service categories (e.g., drug doses dispensed per adjusted discharge or clinical pharmacy service units per discharge). There are a number of benchmarks for staffing, drug cost, and worked hours. Systems can create internal systems for benchmarking, but most subscribe to services such as ACTION O-I (Solucient Inc., Evanston, IL) that provide a range of benchmarks, including indicators for pharmacy expense and drug use. Published data sources include pharmaceutical industry–sponsored digests, such as the *Managed Care Digest* (published by Sanofi Aventis) and the *Prescription Drug Benefit Cost and Plan Design Report* published by the Pharmacy Benefit Management Institute; both available online.[48]

Comparisons to published benchmarks generally work when considering an individual hospital and somewhat less well, but effectively, when comparing pharmacies within a larger health system where costs and definitions of service volume and patient type are consistent. Comparisons between systems may be problematic, as definitions for work are not standard and patient and drug product mix can vary. In addition, key labor-intensive programs in the medication use process may be assigned to other professionals (e.g., medication reconciliation may be performed by physicians, nurses, pharmacists, or a combination of all three, leading to variation in labor activity and cost between hospitals with differing systems). Global comparisons should serve as a starting point, but most benchmarks, even in the case of similar systems, bear substantial scrutiny before serious use, particularly as one drills down into detailed benchmarks.

By comparing a hospital pharmacy department to those in other systems, areas of opportunity can be identified. Comparisons often relate a specific indicator or ratio that applies to both organizations; the indicator or ratio is then compared to industry-wide ratios (e.g., supply costs, hours worked, and prescription volumes divided by patient days, discharges, or ambulatory care visits for some predetermined period). Common indicators are doses dispensed, patient care work units (PCU) earned (earned hours), full-time equivalents, IV doses prepared, prescriptions filled, drug costs, total supply costs, salary costs, and total costs. The functional strengths and weaknesses among the comparison organizations can be evaluated. It is important not to focus on a single indicator of cost or quality, as it may reflect differences in measurement or underlying differences outside the pharmacy. A constellation of indicators that map a function or service allows a more accurate and critical analysis of services. The areas that provide the highest value to the pharmacy manager can be explored further. The best practice or system in an area can be ascertained. By networking with other institutions, it is possible to identify excellent practices and low-cost providers.

Because labor input does not always conform to volume changes, productivity should be monitored frequently. Significant volume increases may signal the need for additional staffing in a given area. On the other hand, volume decreases may lead the pharmacy manager to consider not replacing employees who resign or replacing pharmacists with technicians for the more traditional distributive functions. The use of overtime may be appropriate instead of hiring additional staff. However, overtime expenses can be limited by the use of part-time employees and per diem staff. Automation can also smooth productivity variances between high- and low-volume periods.

Understanding the impact of changes in the type of services performed (e.g., pharmacokinetic dosing versus order clarification) and in the products dispensed (e.g., oral dosage forms prepared versus parenteral chemotherapy doses prepared) will also help to determine staffing requirements. Productivity variances are related to volume shifts and to the use of products that are more labor intensive versus ingredient cost intensive. The type of patients being treated may be the source of a variance, although the cause may not always be readily apparent. Analyses of cost per patient unit and changes in the drug volume per patient day on different units may help to assess the impact throughout the healthcare system. Similar variances may be seen in outpatient prescription drug costs and drug utilization. These can also be related to patient characteristics such as age and chronic disease prevalence, and to benefit design and the structure of physician incentives and risk in drug prescribing. Careful data analysis should be performed prior to taking action, particularly in the case of outpatient drug use, where patient choice and physician behavior play a greater role.

Managing Drug Costs

Two types of strategies can be applied to manage drug costs: administrative control and clinical review. Administrative control is implemented through reductions in drug acquisition costs, inventory management, use of appropriate drug distribution systems, and computerization.

The goal of reducing drug acquisition costs is to provide quality drugs at the lowest possible price. There are many chemically identical drug entities, known as generic equivalents, manufactured and distributed by many drug companies. The Food and Drug Administration requires that generic equivalents all act the same in the human body. Therefore, pharmacies can control drug acquisition costs by selecting the least expensive equivalent, whether through internal bidding, group purchasing, or negotiation with acceptable vendors. When a drug goes "off patent," equivalent versions appear in the marketplace and the cost per unit decreases. Pharmacy managers should stay abreast of patent changes. Group purchasing organizations generally focus on this aspect of the marketplace and provide a reliable source for current cost-effective contracts.

Newer brand name drugs that are patented generally consume the largest portion of the drug budget. These agents are least amenable to switching, as many are unique or possess properties that make changing therapies less desirable. Pharmacies and pharmacy and therapeutics committees should not avoid the therapeutic controversies that can arise from evaluating these agents. Much of the theoretical difference between these agents does not stand up to objective scrutiny. Although there may be limited opportunities for savings, they should be pursued, as the cost impact of ignoring them may be substantial. Pharmaceutical companies have engaged in serious direct-to-consumer marketing to involve the patient in drug selection decisions, in some cases, to great effect. A sound basic formulary strategy provides the best opportunity to manage costs and achieve the best outcome in this portion of the drug marketplace.

A more critical emerging category of drugs that permit the pharmacist and the physician to select cheaper alternatives consists of "therapeutic equivalents." While not chemically identical, these drugs have similar therapeutic outcomes. Examples include two or more antibiotics that are effective in treating an infection or several drugs that reduce the action of stomach acid. Because this type of interchange is more advanced, implementation of a therapeutic interchange program requires medical staff commitment. The pharmacy and therapeutics committee should develop the programs, set policies and procedures, and manage and monitor the program. Therapeutic equivalents can also be candidates for group purchasing, internal bidding, or negotiation, but only after the pharmacy and therapeutics committee has approved the drug candidates as therapeutic equivalents.

Bidding and contracting for pharmaceuticals have become more complex because healthcare systems have blurred the differences between inpatient acute care and outpatient or ambulatory care. The pharmaceutical industry has traditionally provided "own use" contracts to hospitals under a clause in the Robinson-Patman Act. This clause offers very favorable pricing for inpatients and the employees of a health system. The prices are not available for use in traditional retail or nonacute areas. This restriction may even apply to "non-inpatient" programs owned by healthcare systems. Contracts for these classes of trade are generally less favorable, and many drugs are substantially more expensive. These classes include home care, ambulatory care, mail order, and retail pharmacy services. Healthcare systems are moving into these areas of pharmacy practice and must adjust accordingly.

Administrators and pharmacy managers must make certain that contracts are correctly applied to ensure legality. In some cases it may be desirable or necessary to completely separate drugs purchased under different contracts to prevent the mixing of drugs purchased for a specific use with those for another use. Drug cost projections should only be made using a contract portfolio that applies to the patient types being served. Healthcare systems can and should apply pressure on purchasing groups and pharmaceutical manufacturers to provide favorable pricing for alternative sites and services to protect their cost positions.

Inventory management is another important management tool that can be used by the pharmacist to control costs. Avoiding redundant inventory increases working capital that can be used more productively in other areas of the system. Improving inventory turnover can be partially achieved by implementation of both generic and therapeutic equivalence policies. Numerous other inventory control techniques, such as ABC and economic order quantity

(EOQ) analysis, should be incorporated into the management system. Most drug wholesale vendors supply computer programs and services that allow for the detailed accounting of drug purchases using these techniques. These products and services are generally included in an overall agreement negotiated by a purchasing group or health system.

ABC analysis is a method for ascertaining the volume of products by expense (i.e., dollars) and by utilization (i.e., units). Whether sorting by a single criterion or by multiple criteria, the manager is able to analyze product use for various scenarios. This type of analysis can be useful as a snapshot of product movement for a given period of time as well as for identifying product shifts and utilization.

EOQ analysis is a mathematical method for determining the optimum product quantity to order. Its objective is to minimize the inventory costs associated with the product. The basic EOQ model takes into account the total costs associated with inventory (e.g., carrying costs and ordering costs). Carrying costs increase and ordering costs decline with higher inventories. The EOQ is defined as the level at which the total inventory cost is the lowest. This is at the point on an EOQ model line graph where the carrying cost and ordering lines intersect—the point where carrying costs and ordering costs are equal. Pharmacy directors should strive to meet a calculated EOQ and inventory level to minimize costs and ensure the reliable availability of drugs.

Clinical strategies for reducing drug costs offer opportunities for affecting patient outcome positively while reducing institutional costs. Some of these strategies include formulary management, medication use review, and clinical (or therapeutic) intervention by pharmacists at the time the physician is writing the drug order. Other clinical strategies to manage drug costs include:

- Developing guidelines for prescribing agents or classes of drugs
- Converting intravenous medication use to oral route
- Creating educational programs for prescribers
- "Academic detailing" by clinical pharmacists representing the health system
- Setting selective restrictions on specific drug use
- Requiring specialist approval for specific drugs
- Using stop orders and expiration dates for medications

A formulary is a list of drugs approved by the pharmacy and therapeutics committee that the pharmacy will routinely stock and always have available for patient care. Although the formulary is primarily a clinically oriented tool, it will also have a major impact on costs by reducing the number of drug entities that the pharmacy carries in its inventory. This reduction is achieved by continually reviewing opportunities to reduce the number of therapeutic and generic equivalents and dosage forms.

Drug use can be measured against treatment guidelines developed by standard-setting organizations and government regulators, including the FDA. Basic criteria for drug use originate with package insert recommendations and develop further as medical practice and published research move forward. Prescription records provide data on aspects of the prescribing process, patient compliance, and therapeutic outcomes. The P&T committee of the health system most often supports and directs a treatment guideline strategy. Prescriber order entry programs offer increased utility and effectiveness for the treatment guideline strategy. The development of evidence-based guidelines is the core of a clinical decision support strategy; POE provides the engine to ensure a high level of compliance.[49]

The ready availability of prescribing and utilization data has provided an opportunity to manage drug costs and has led to the creation of a new entity in the healthcare industry, the pharmacy benefits management (PBM) company. PBMs offer opportunities to control the costs of drug therapy based on collection and analysis of clinical and financial information from a healthcare system or payer database. PBMs typically focus on ambulatory drug use and work on behalf of insurers or payers.

PBMs use demographic and patient care data to direct drug use. They typically develop a drug formulary and use prescription data to profile patients, physicians, and the use of specific drugs and treatment modalities, and to identify disease outcomes. In turn, they use these data to determine changes that would foster the prescription of more effective or less costly agents. Networks, hospitals, and healthcare systems can use similar data generated by their own pharmacy information systems to understand current practice and allocate resources to direct both pharmacy services and pharmaceutical care.

PBMs also develop provider networks that offer outpatient prescription services, typically a mix of retail and chain drugstores. These networks often extend beyond traditional service boundaries. PBMs adjudicate drug claims and ensure that providers meet the cost and service requirements of the healthcare system.

PBMs have also utilized outcomes management and disease management. Service quality is measured not only by service consumption but also by substituted services, including emergency department visits and other nonpharmacy costs. Disease management strategies apply to medication-intensive diseases such as diabetes or congestive heart failure, where effective medical management can prevent both long-term complications and decrease the cost and utilization of specific services. Disease management programs generally focus on the selection of appropriate therapies, aggressive monitoring of drug efficacy and side effects, and improving patient compliance. These programs have achieved impressive clinical and financial success in the case of patients with diabetes mellitus, asthma, congestive heart failure, and other diseases. Healthcare systems with comprehensive pharmacy information systems can develop the data and methods to support this type of program through their pharmacy and therapeutics committee and pharmacy department.

Conclusion

An effective pharmacy service has become more important than ever for healthcare system success in the changing healthcare environment. Biotechnology is providing expensive new agents that can achieve improved patient care outcomes—but at a high cost. Well-managed pharmacy services can ensure the appropriate, cost-effective delivery of care and maximize patient benefits while minimizing costs. Drug purchase costs are only one component of a healthcare system's overall costs. The implementation of a pharmaceutical care practice model can ensure the appropriate deployment of professional resources to manage the costs and benefits of medication therapy. Pharmacy should be viewed as a clinical department with substantial business interests and high impact in the health system. A well-run pharmacy can effectively balance the clinical and financial aspects of drug therapy.

References

1. The Leapfrog Group for Patient Safety. The Leapfrog Group fact sheet. Available at: http://www.leapfroggroup.org/about_us/leapfrog-factsheet. Accessed March 28, 2009.
2. The Joint Commission. 2008 national patient safety goals. Available at: http://www.joint commission.org/NR/rdonlyres/82B717D8-B16A-4442-AD00-CE3188C2F00A/0/08_HAP_NPSGs_Master.pdf. Accessed March 27, 2009.
3. Kohn LT, Corrigan JM, Donaldson MS, eds. *To Err Is Human: Building a Safer Health System*. Washington, DC: National Academy Press; 1999.
4. American Society of Hospital Pharmacists. ASHP statement on pharmaceutical care. *Am J Hosp Pharm*. 1993;50:1720–1723.
5. Knapp KK, Ray MD. A pharmacy response to the Institute of Medicine's 2001 initiative on quality in health care. *Am J Health Syst Pharm*. 2002;59:2443–2450.
6. Hepler CD, Strand LM. Opportunities and responsibilities in pharmaceutical care. *Am J Health Syst Pharm*. 1990;47:533–543.
7. Zellmer WA. Expressing the mission of pharmacy practice. *Am J Health Syst Pharm*. 1991; 48:1195.
8. American Association of Colleges of Pharmacy. AACP Commission to Implement Change in Pharmaceutical Education—What is the mission of pharmaceutical education. Available at: http://www.aacp.org/resources/historicaldocuments/Documents/BackgroundPaper1.pdf. Accessed March 28, 2009.
9. American Society of Health-System Pharmacists. Health-system pharmacy 2015 initiative. Available at: http://www.ashp.org/s_ashp/docs/files/2015_Goals_Objectives_0508.pdf. Accessed September 28, 2008.
10. Tracy SA, Clegg CA. *Collaborative Drug Therapy Management Handbook*. Bethesda, MD: American Society of Health-System Pharmacists; 2007.
11. The Leapfrog Group for Patient Safety. The Leapfrog safety practices. Available at: http://www.leapfroggroup.org/for_hospitals/leapfrog_hospital_survey_copy/leapfrog_safety_practices. Accessed March 28, 2009.
12. The Institute for Safe Medication Practices. ISMP mission and vision statement. Available at: http://www.ismp.org/about/mission.asp. Accessed March 28, 2009.
13. Re-engineering the medication-use system. Proceedings of a national interdisciplinary conference conducted by the Joint Commission of Pharmacy Practitioners. *Am J Health Sys Pharm*. 2000;57:537.
14. Pharmacy-nursing shared vision for safe medication use in hospitals: executive summary session. *Am J Health Sys Pharm*. 2003;60:1046–1052.
15. Proceedings of a summit on preventing patient harm and death from IV medication errors. *Am J Health Sys Pharm*. 2008;65:2367–2379.
16. Hepler CD, Strand LM. Opportunities and responsibilities in pharmaceutical care. *American Journal of Hospital Pharmacy*. 1990;47:533–543.
17. American Society of Health-System Pharmacists. ASHP guidelines: minimum standard for pharmaceutical services in ambulatory care. *Am J Health-Syst Pharm*. 1999;56: 1744–1753.

18. Horn SD, et al. Intended and unintended consequences of HMO cost containment strategies: results from the managed care outcomes project. *American Journal of Managed Care.* 1996;2:253–264.

19. Ivey M. Rationale for having a chief pharmacy officer in a health care organization. *American Journal of Health System Pharmacy.* 2005;62:975–978.

20. The Joint Commission. *2009 Comprehensive Accreditation Manual for Hospitals (CAMH): The Official Handbook.* Oakbrook Terrace, IL: The Joint Commission; 2008.

21. American Society of Health-System Pharmacists. *Best Practices for Hospitals and Health-System Pharmacy: Position and Guidance Documents of ASHP.* Bethesda, MD: American Society of Health-System Pharmacists; 2008.

22. Tyler LS, Cole SW, May JR, et al. ASHP guidelines on the pharmacy and therapeutics committee and the formulary system. *American Journal of Health System Pharmacy.* 2008;65:1272–1283.

23. Accreditation Council for Pharmacy Education. Accreditation standards and guidelines for the professional program in pharmacy leading to the doctor of pharmacy degree. Available at: http://www.acpeaccredit.org/pdf/ACPE_Revised_PharmD_Standards_Adopted_Jan152006.pdf. Accessed March 30, 2009.

24. Board of Pharmaceutical Specialties. Establishment of pharmaceutical specialties. Available at: http://www.bpsweb.org/01_About_History.html. Accessed March 30, 2009.

25. Pharmacy Technician Certification Board. About the exam. Available at: https://www.ptcb.org/AM/Template.cfm?Section=About_the_Exam1&Template=/CM/ContentCombo.cfm&NavMenuID=805&ContentID=3122. Accessed March 30, 2009.

26. Bates DW, Teich JM, Lee J, et al. The impact of computerized physician order entry on medication error prevention. *J Am Med Inform Assoc.* 1999;6:313–321.

27. King WJ, Paice N, Rangrej J, et al. The effect of computerized physician order entry on medication errors and adverse drug events in pediatric inpatients. *Pediatrics.* 2003;112:506–509.

28. Kaushal R, Shojania KG, Bates DW. Effects of computerized physician order entry and clinical decision support systems on medication safety: a systematic review. *Archives of Internal Medicine.* 2003;163:1409–1416.

29. First Consulting Group. Computerized physician order entry: costs, benefits, and challenges—A case study approach. Available at: http://www.leapfroggroup.org/media/file/Leapfrog-AHA_FAH_CPOE_Report.pdf. Accessed March 27, 2009.

30. The Leapfrog Group. Leapfrog Group fact sheet: computerized physician order entry. Available at: http://www.leapfroggroup.org/media/file/LeapfrogComputer_Physician_Order_Entry_Fact_Sheet.pdf. Last updated April 9, 2008. Accessed March 27, 2009.

31. Guerrero RM, et al. Documenting the provision of pharmaceutical care. *Topics in Hospital Pharmacy Management.* 1992;11(4):16–29.

32. McGhan WF, Rowland CR, Bootman JL. Cost-benefit and cost-effectiveness: methodologies for evaluating innovative pharmacy services. *Am J Hosp Pharm.* 1978;35:133–140.

33. Gibson FM, Hyneck ML, Scherrer JJ. Documented effectiveness of clinical pharmacy services. *Am J Hosp Pharm.* 1982;39:1902–1903.

34. Johnson ST, Brown GC, Shea KM. Reengineering a pharmacist intervention program. *Am J Health-Syst Pharm.* 2002;59:916–917.

35. Youngmee K, Schepers G. Pharmacist intervention documentation in US health care systems. *Hosp Pharm.* 2003;38:1141–1147

36. Fox BI, Felkey BG, Berger BA, et al. Use of personal digital assistants for documentation of pharmacists' interventions: a literature review. *Am J Health Syst Pharm.* 2007;64(14):1516–1525.

37. Simonian AI. Documenting pharmacists intervention on an intranet. *Am J Health Syst Pharm.* 2003;60:151–155.

38. Black HJ, Tester WW. Decentralized pharmacy operations utilizing the unit dose concept. *Am J Health Syst Pharm.* 1967;24:120–129.

39. American Society of Health-System Pharmacists. *ASHP Statement on Drug Unit Dose Distribution. Practice Standards of the American Society of Health-System Pharmacists 1997–1998.* Bethesda, MD: American Society of Health-System Pharmacists; 1998:10.

40. American Society of Health-System Pharmacists. *ASHP Technical Assistance Bulletin on Hospital Drug Distribution and Control. Practice Standards of the American Society of Health-System Pharmacists 1997–1998.* Bethesda, MD: American Society of Health-System Pharmacists. 1998;102–110.

41. American Society of Health-System Pharmacists. *ASHP Technical Assistance Bulletin on Quality Assurance for Pharmacy Prepared Sterile Products. Practice Standards of the American Society of Health-System Pharmacists 1997–1998.* Bethesda, MD: American Society of Health-System Pharmacists. 1998;171–181.

42. American Society of Health-System Pharmacists. ASHP guideline on handling hazardous drugs. Available at: http://www.ashp.org/DocLibrary/BestPractices/ASHPGuidelinesHandling HazardousDrugs.aspx.

43. The United States Pharmacopeia, 27th rev, National Formulary, 22nd ed. USP General Information Chapter. Pharmaceutical Compounding–Sterile Preparations. Rockville, MD: The United States Pharmacopeial Convention; 2003.

44. American Society of Health-System Pharmacists. *ASHP Statement on the Roles and Responsibilities of the Pharmacy Executive. Best Practices for Hospital & Health-System Pharmacy 2008–2009.* Bethesda, MD: American Society of Health-System Pharmacists; 2009;289–291.

45. American Society of Health-System Pharmacists. *ASHP Guidelines on Medication Cost Management Strategies for Hospitals and Health Systems. Best Practices for Hospital & Health-System Pharmacy 2008–2009.* Bethesda, MD: American Society of Health-System Pharmacists; 2009;294–308.

46. Hoffman JM, Shah ND, Vermeulen LC, et al. Projecting future drug expenditures—2009. *American Journal of Health System Pharmacy.* 2009;66:237–257.

47. Jorgenson JA, Fox-Smith K, Conlon PJ. Budgeting revenue. In: Wilson AL, ed. *Financial Management for Health-System Pharmacists.* Bethesda MD: American Society of Health-System Pharmacists; 2008.

48. Rough S, Stashek C. Benchmarking and productivity analysis. In: Wilson AL, ed. *Financial Management for Health-System Pharmacists.* Bethesda MD: American Society of Health-System Pharmacists; 2008.

49. Oinonen MJ. Understanding drug use ssing administrative data. In: Wilson AL, ed. *Financial Management for Health-System Pharmacists.* Bethesda MD: American Society of Health-System Pharmacists; 2008.

Biographical Information

Andrew L. Wilson, PharmD, FASHP, is the Director of Pharmacy and Educational Services for Safety Net Hospitals for Pharmaceutical Access, based in Washington, DC. He has worked as a hospital pharmacy director in academic health care and as a pharmacy consultant for more than 25 years. Dr. Wilson's areas of interest include health policy, formulary management, and pharmacoeconomics. He holds a bachelor of science in Pharmacy from the University of Connecticut and a doctor of pharmacy degree from Wayne State University. Dr. Wilson has made numerous invited presentations and has authored more than 60 articles in the pharmacy literature.

Karol Wollenburg, MS, RPh, currently serves as Vice President and Apothecary-in-Chief at New York Presbyterian Hospital (NYP). In this capacity, she is administratively responsible for pharmacy services at the five sites of NYP as well as contracted services to several other hospitals. Ms. Wollenburg received her bachelor of science degree from the University of Connecticut, completed a management-focused residency in hospital pharmacy from Lenox Hill Hospital, and earned her master's degree in clinical pharmacy from St. John's University. Active in professional organizations, Ms. Wollenburg has served on numerous state and national committees, most recently chairing ASHP's Council on Administrative Affairs. In 2003 she received the American Society of Health-System Pharmacists John W. Webb Lecture Award, which recognizes a hospital or health system pharmacy practitioner or educator who has distinguished themselves through extraordinary dedication to fostering excellence in pharmacy management. She is also the recipient of the 2004 Joel Yellin Award of Merit from the New York City Society of Health-System Pharmacists and was awarded the St. John's University, College of Pharmacy and Allied Health Care Professions Distinguished Alumna Award in 2005. The major focus of her publications and lectures in recent years has been leadership and medication safety.

Material and Resource Management

William L. Scheyer and Barbara B. Friedman

It is commonly estimated that 30 to 50% of a hospital or organized delivery system's budget is related to material, equipment, and purchased services. Approximately half of this amount derives from the direct cost of acquiring materials and services; the other half comes from the cost of managing them after acquisition. Labor expenses make up the largest portion of this second component.

Prior to 1970, the management of material was often haphazard, which was one of the contributing factors to the escalation of the cost of hospital care. In the 1970s, as these costs reached increasingly unacceptable levels, the concept of centralized materials management began to gain favor. As a result, methods of controlling expenses that had been used for many years in other industries began to be applied routinely in the healthcare industry. During the 1980s, greater emphasis was placed on group purchasing programs, centralized management of total inventories, and increased reliance on suppliers to provide additional services, such as consignment buying, supplier management of in-house inventories, and "just-in-time" shipments. In fact, this shift to the practice of using the supplier to provide hospital support services continued into the 1990s to such an extent that some people had difficulty defining the rightful place of a material/resource manager in the hospital.

As the national debate over healthcare cost control continues to intensify, so does the search for ways to reduce the total cost of acquiring and managing materials and services. Much progress has been made, but the pressures continue into the 21st century. The shift to organized healthcare delivery systems created an ideal opportunity to consolidate the function of material/resource management and to achieve exemplary economies of scale for all entities in a system.

The classic definition of materials management in hospitals is "the management and control of goods, services, and equipment from acquisition to disposition."[1] To accomplish this most effectively, there should be centralization of management responsibility for the purchasing, receiving, supply, storage, and distribution functions within the hospital. There also should be centralized control of the reprocessing of sterile, reusable supply items. The three most critical elements in a materials management program are (1) a corporate strategy for ensuring that materials (i.e., goods, services, and equipment) are purchased at the lowest total cost, (2) a related strategy to ensure that inventories and their associated carrying costs are aggressively monitored and controlled, and (3) a system for ensuring the ready availability of all required materials.

Supply Chain

The flow of materials can best be visualized as a closed loop. This supply chain is shown in **Figure 15.1**. Opportunities for significant cost reductions exist at each point along the chain.

Originating Department

The actual decision to acquire supplies and equipment almost always takes place in individual departments throughout the hospital or organized delivery system. The material/resource manager can assist the head of the originating department in a number of ways, however, such as helping forecast needs for the coming year, providing information on sources of supply and prevailing market conditions, conducting negotiations with suppliers, and designating effective systems for distributing, storing, and maintaining materials until they are consumed.

Generally, hospital managers have been trained either in specific clinical disciplines or in general administration, but rarely have they been trained in the techniques of material/resource management. As a result, the material/resource manager is a valuable source of expertise for ensuring that supplies, equipment, and purchased services are used in a cost-effective manner throughout the organization. The material/resource manager normally has direct responsibility for managing the functions of centralized purchasing, receiving, storage/distribution, and central sterile reprocessing. He or she normally has no direct relationship with the accounts payable department.

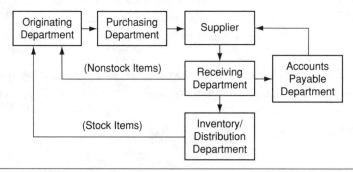

FIGURE 15.1 Supply Chain

It is vital that there be open lines of communication between the accounts payable, purchasing, and receiving departments, however. These departments should work together effectively to process the high volume of purchase/receipt/payment transactions that occur in healthcare organizations every day.

Because usually no direct relationship exists between the material/resource management department and other departments within the hospital, there should be a corporate-level statement of policy concerning the execution of material/resource management functions. The material/resource manager should establish a consultative relationship with all of the departments within the hospital in order to ensure that appropriate material/resource management practices are followed.

As hospitals utilize more special services from suppliers, the originating departments have come to play a more critical role in ensuring proper management of their supplies. For example, suppliers may deliver orders directly to the originating department (**Figure 15.2**). Another variation is for the supplier to conduct pre-authorized replenishment-level (PAR-level) inspections in the originating department and then deliver the needed materials directly to the department (**Figure 15.3**).

In both of these cases, the receiving department may not control the actual receipt of the materials. Therefore, the originating department head should make sure that the goods are actually received in the right quantities and reported correctly to the accounts payable department. There is a risk that the originating department personnel will not exercise sufficient care in accepting and documenting the delivery or, particularly in the PAR-level situation, that the supplier may overstock the department in order to increase sales. The material/resource manager also needs to be involved in setting up and monitoring these special supplier services so that the interests of the hospital or organized delivery system are protected.

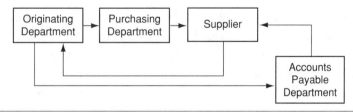

FIGURE 15.2   Supply Chain (Alternate 1)

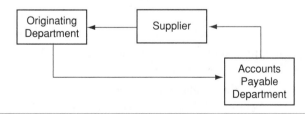

FIGURE 15.3   Supply Chain (Alternate 2)

Purchasing Department

The primary contribution of the purchasing department is to lower the price of goods and services. Two classic tools used in accomplishing this objective are competitive bidding and direct negotiation. By consolidating control of the purchasing function under the direction of the material/resource manager, the use of these tools can be made more consistent and effective throughout the organization. In addition to negotiating lower prices, the purchasing department can obtain favorable terms and conditions, which managers outside the purchasing department often neglect to request at the time the transaction is conducted. Payment of freight charges, extended warranties, and other special services frequently can be obtained.

Over the last few decades, material/resource managers have delegated much of the negotiation efforts to group purchasing organizations (GPOs). These groups have grown in size and effectiveness. By pooling the purchases of hundreds of hospitals, significant cost savings are available to their members. In addition to lower prices and better terms, some of the additional advantages are:

- Extensive legal review of contracts
- Purchasing staff freed from routine bidding of products
- Promotion of standardization
- Agreements with national product leaders

To ensure the effectiveness of the group, the material/resource manager must maintain a focus on contract compliance. Managers responsible for large healthcare systems should also continually evaluate the benefits of maintaining the GPO relationship as opposed to negotiating with suppliers on the strength of their own organization's committed volumes.

The Supplier

Although suppliers are not under the direct control of the material/resource manager, and their contributions to cost reduction are essentially extensions of the efforts of the purchasing agents, suppliers have the power to provide the hospital or organized delivery system with many cost reduction opportunities, such as lower prices, favorable payment terms, local warehousing, consulting assistance, special data reports, in-service training, and just-in-time deliveries. The material/resource manager should become skilled at establishing relationships with suppliers that result in the hospital's receiving as broad a range of benefits as possible. The hospital invests its business in the relationship with the supplier, and the supplier invests benefits and services that go beyond the normal selling price. It is important that both participants receive an adequate return on their investment.

In an effort to lower cost within the supply chain, many hospitals and organized delivery systems rely on a just-in-time approach to the delivery of supplies. Accurate forecasting of department needs is required, along with accurate interaction between the computer systems of both hospital and supplier. In essence, the supplier makes more frequent deliveries of smaller quantities in order to ensure that the hospital department has the needed items just in time for use.

This reduces on-hand inventories within the hospital, thus freeing the funds related to maintaining inventories.

Some professionals in the industry feel so strongly about this approach that they believe organized delivery systems and hospitals should not even be in the materials management business. Suppliers would not provide these services, however, if the services did not add to their own profits. Administrators and material/resource managers should keep in mind that the basic work must be done; the question is whether it is more efficient and less costly for the supplier or the hospital/organized delivery system to do the basic work. Issues such as cost of labor, economies of scale, and access to technology must be weighed. Another circumstance to be considered is that the organization that controls the details of the work usually controls the outcome of the process. Thus, if the hospital relinquishes too much control over the work to the supplier, it risks losing control over the final cost of the program.

Special supplier services definitely are of value, particularly when the supplier is willing to be creative and work with the hospital or organized delivery system to customize programs that meet the special needs of the organization. Such programs are an increasingly common component of the management armamentarium of the modern hospital or organized delivery system. As in any area of management, however, measurement and monitoring are the keys to success.

Receiving Department

It is the responsibility of the receiving department to ensure that the correct items, in proper condition, are officially received into the organization. Savings result from detection of supplier shipping errors, identification and correction of damaged goods, and timely notification of receipt to the accounting department in order to obtain all available discounts. This department's contribution to the hospital or organized delivery system's bottom line rests largely on two key functions: (1) matching invoices and (2) adjusting the timing of payments to suppliers. It is essential that the supplier's invoice be matched accurately to the documents verifying receipt of the goods in the hospital. If this is not done consistently and accurately, there is a high risk of paying for goods not actually received.

When goods bypass the receiving dock and go directly to the originating department, the challenge to the receiving supervisor is to make sure that the goods are properly inspected and recorded into the inventory and payment records of the hospital. In many hospitals, inspection of the inner contents of packages remains with the ordering department. Typically, they just have to communicate mistakes prior to the payment of the invoice.

In general, payments should be held for as long as possible—up to the point at which a discount will be lost. Excessive delays in making payments damage the business reputation of a hospital or organized delivery system and weaken its future negotiating power. Excessive speed in making payments unnecessarily gives away the use of the hospital's money, however. In fact, two principles are inherent in getting excellent prices: (1) provide a decent size order, usually a minimum of $100, and (2) pay on time, preferably within 30 days. Above all, in order to maintain an effective schedule of correct payments, there must be a smooth flow of communication and data between the purchasing, receiving, and accounts payable departments.

Inventory and Distribution Departments

In recent years, a great deal of attention has been paid to managing inventories within hospitals or organized delivery systems. Benefits that result from reducing inventory levels include the release of money to be used for other purposes; the release of space to be used for other purposes; avoidance of the need to construct new space; lower expense as a result of reduced obsolescence, damage, and theft; and somewhat less labor needed to handle the reduced level of supplies. In other words, the opportunity cost of utilizing monies for a more beneficial cause.

Most hospitals and organized delivery systems still spend the major part of their efforts on controlling official inventories, usually found in the central storeroom, but the more aggressive hospitals are starting to concentrate on the unofficial inventories. Some have adopted the special supplier-services approach to the extent that they have eliminated their central inventories. Unofficial inventories are stocks of supplies that already have been entered as an expense in the accounting records. They should be considered inventories, though, in that they are in storage and awaiting consumption. There is a particularly significant cost reduction potential in supply-intensive departments, such as operating rooms and catheter laboratories.

The selection of methods for distributing materials throughout the organization also can have an impact on the total cost of operations, particularly in organized healthcare delivery systems. In general, the most effective systems are those that replenish supplies to predetermined levels on a scheduled basis, without the end user having to initiate the request. Such automatic replenishment systems reduce the amount of time spent by relatively higher paid, clinically trained employees in ordering and handling supplies. In addition, such systems more accurately link the issuance of supplies to actual patterns of consumption, for example, through bar coding. As a result, they tend to reduce overall inventory levels, with associated savings. The maintenance of such systems provides another opportunity to monitor and promote product standardization, which further enhances the efficiency of the inventory system.

Technology Support

In the past, many materials management information systems were integrated with the organization's financial information systems. Enhancements to the materials management system sometimes received lower priority. It is now possible to acquire specialized hardware/software packages to support material/resource management functions at a more affordable cost. These programs increasingly are flexible and can be operated as stand-alone systems or can be linked in networks. In order to maximize the benefits of a material/resource management program, it is vital to have accurate and detailed information about the multitude of transactions that take place within the system every day. Larger hospitals and organized delivery systems almost have to computerize the material/resource management function in order to handle the large volume of transactional data generated each day. If the basic material/resource management functions are well designed, the advantages of computerized information support in any size hospital far outweigh the costs of the computer system.

The Internet has opened new doors for the material/resource management team. E-procurement, the act of ordering via the Internet, should grow rapidly over the next few years. The

Internet can assist the material/resource manager in reducing costs and streamlining operations through the use of online catalogs, product research, online ordering, order delivery status reviews, price confirmations, contract administration, and invoice payment.

Technology is also streamlining the distribution process. Point-of-use systems automate the distribution and replenishment process, while providing patient supply usage data and cost accounting information.

Managing the Core Functions

Purchasing

An effective purchasing department is the cornerstone of a successful material/resource management program. The keys to success in this area lie in (1) setting up well-designed systems for routinely processing large amounts of information both effectively and efficiently, and (2) establishing operational priorities that focus the most attention on those items that have the greatest impact on the organization. The three purposes of the purchasing department are to:

1. Assist all departments in obtaining products and services of appropriate quality from reputable and reliable suppliers at the lowest total cost to the organization
2. Ensure that appropriate and ethical business practices are applied throughout the organization
3. Serve as a source of information for the rest of the organization concerning available products, sources of supply, current and anticipated market conditions, and application of effective purchasing techniques

The first step in establishing a strong purchasing program is to obtain a written statement of support from the organization's chief executive officer (CEO). Circulating this statement to all entities and departments, along with a description of the way that the purchasing system will work, will make it clear to everyone that all purchasing transactions must be carried out by means of the centralized purchasing process. The best method for enforcing this requirement is to establish a numbered purchase order system and to refuse delivery of any item not covered by a hospital purchase order number. In the 1990s, some organizations began to use procurement cards.

The physical layout, procedures, and filing systems of the purchasing department can be organized in any number of ways as long as adequate provision is made for the following elements:

- Use of a legally acceptable purchase order form that ensures terms and conditions favorable to the organization
- A method for determining who is authorized to make purchases for the organization
- A file of approved signatures for use in ensuring that purchases are made only by authorized people
- A clearly defined requisitioning process
- A list of approved suppliers from whom purchases can be made
- Clearly defined procedures for obtaining competitive bids from suppliers

- A method for tracking and expediting open purchase orders
- A method for ensuring that proper credit is received for goods returned to the supplier
- A method for monitoring and documenting supplier performance
- A method for monitoring the timeliness and effectiveness of the performance of the purchasing department

The purchasing manager should develop and adhere to a strategic plan that focuses attention on primarily those items that have the greatest financial impact. Application of a technique known as ABC analysis is helpful in developing this strategic plan. This technique is most frequently used in the area of inventory control, but it can also be used in analyzing purchases. First, all expenditures are classified into major categories. Then, the individual items within each category are rank-ordered according to dollar value. Approximately 80% of the dollars expended will come from approximately 20% of the items acquired. Some items, such as X-ray film, certain classes of pharmaceuticals, and capital items, represent a major portion of the budget, and their purchases warrant particular attention. Specific strategies for handling capital acquisitions, supplies, and purchased services should be developed.

Competitive Bids

Ideally, competition for the hospital's or organized delivery system's business will be sought in every case. Competitive bids can be obtained by:

- Requesting formal, sealed bids to be opened publicly
- Requesting written quotations to be evaluated in the purchasing department
- Seeking comparative prices over the telephone
- Negotiating fixed contract prices for items or groups of items
- Joining a purchasing group that provides access to negotiated, competitive prices

The method used to obtain competitive prices depends on the nature of the items being purchased. Major capital items may require sealed public bids, whereas smaller routine items may require only telephone price checking. Items that are purchased repeatedly lend themselves to fixed contract pricing.

The Internet provides another innovative way to obtain competitive prices. In this system, called online bidding or reverse auction, the buyer announces the date, time, and Web site location of an online bidding event. Interested suppliers obtain bid specifications and notify the buyer of their intention to bid for the business. If the supplier wishes to vary from the base specifications, any variation must be approved by the buyer in advance in order for the supplier to be given online access to the event. At the date and time specified, the reverse auction begins. Suppliers can see what ranking their bid price has afforded them. If they wish to lower their bid, they do so online. All suppliers see the current status of their bids. The auction event is open for only a specified period of time. At the close of the event, the supplier whose price is lowest will be awarded the business, as long as its final product description, terms, and conditions are verified as acceptable. This process typically yields significant savings when compared to traditional sealed bid processes.

No matter what method is used, it is good practice to routinely document the percentage of purchases made using competitive bidding of any sort. Sample bidding instructions are shown in **Appendixes 15.A** and **15.B**.[2]

The first step in the competitive bidding process is to issue a request for proposal (RFP) or request for bid (RFB) to potential suppliers. The request should very clearly specify the goods or services sought and should have sufficient detail to ensure a fair evaluation of competing proposals or bids. If additional negotiation will take place after the bids have been received, the initial request should include a statement to this effect.[3]

All qualified suppliers should have the opportunity to compete, and the purchasing agent should not divulge the details of one supplier's proposal to another. After all bids have been received, the proposals should be evaluated not only on the basis of price, but also on total cost to the hospital. Such elements as price protection, warranties, freight charges, installation, operating costs, and repair costs should be considered part of the total cost. When the final selection has been made, sufficient time should be taken in preparing the purchase order so that all of the benefits obtained through the competitive process are protected in writing. Finally, all of the unsuccessful bidders should be notified of the selection. The hospital or organized delivery system should maintain a reputation for considerate and professional treatment of its suppliers in order to ensure active competition for future transactions.

Capital Equipment Purchasing

The process of acquiring capital equipment provides some of the greatest opportunities for cost savings. Whereas an entire supply inventory may account for $500,000, a single piece of high-technology clinical equipment can cost that much or more. As a result, reducing the cost of such items by even a few percentage points can lead to significant savings.

The initial step in managing capital acquisitions is the establishment of a program for financial justification. Ultimate approval of major requests must come from the CEO and the finance committee of the board of directors, but the process begins with the head of the originating department. In order to promote uniform practice throughout the hospital or organized delivery system, and to enable the final decision makers to rationally evaluate competing requests, a standard system for developing financial justifications should be used. A worksheet for this purpose is shown in **Exhibit 15.1**.

After a project has been approved, the purchasing manager should assist the requesting department head in the development of functional specifications. These should be written in terms of expected performance, and every effort should be made to make the specifications generic. Requesting department heads, as well as physicians involved in using the equipment, sometimes resist making the specifications generic. Traditionally, suppliers have focused their marketing efforts on the end users, who may be persuaded to write the requirements so that only one supplier's equipment is able to meet the specifications. Such specific requirements diminish, if not eliminate, the opportunity for competition, however, and the hospital pays a higher than necessary price for the item.

The standards of performance should be given to the competing suppliers so that all bids are submitted in an acceptable format for evaluation. In addition, once the equipment has been

Exhibit 15.1   Worksheet to Evaluate Purchasing Requests

I. Costs

A. Estimated cost of equipment $ _____   _____
(including shipping)   Dept. Manager
                                                        Purchasing

B. Estimated cost of installation, building $ _____   _____
modifications (please attach details)   Dept. Manager
                                                        Maintenance

C. Depreciable life of project   _____   _____
                                        Yrs.   Dept. Manager
                                                        Accounting

D. Equipment to be replaced:

1. Description _____

    _____

    _____

2. Fixed asset number   _____

3. Present age   _____

4. Assigned useful life   _____

5. Current book value $ _____   _____
                                                        Dept. Manager
                                                        Accounting

6. Current market value $ _____   _____
                                                        Dept. Manager
                                                        Purchasing

E. Associated increase in expenses

	Year 1	Year 2	Year 3	Year 4	Year 5	Year 6	Year 7	Year 8	Year 9	Year 10
Training										
Labor										
Utilities										
Supplies										
Other										
Total increase in expenses										

II. Revenue and Decrease of Expenses

	Year 1	Year 2	Year 3	Year 4	Year 5	Year 6	Year 7	Year 8	Year 9	Year 10
A. Increases in revenue										
1. Revenue increases from additional inpatients										
a. Medicare										
b. Medicaid										
c. Others										

Exhibit 15.1 *(Continued)*

2. Revenue increases from additional list of current inpatients										
a. Medicare										
b. Medicaid										
c. Others										
3. Revenue increases from additional outpatient testing										
a. Medicare										
b. Medicaid										
c. Others										
B. Decreases in revenue										
1. Revenue decrease from reduced length of stay										
a. Medicare										
b. Medicaid										
c. Others										
2. Revenue decrease from reduced number of inpatients										
a. Medicare										
b. Medicaid										
c. Others										
C. Net increase or decrease in revenue										
D. Decrease of expenses										
1. Reduction in expenses from reduced length of stay										
a. Labor										
b. Supplies										
c. Utilities										
d. Other										
2. Reduction in expenses from reduced number of inpatients										
a. Labor										
b. Supplies										
c. Utilities										
d. Other										
3. Reduction in expenses from new technology										
a. Labor										
b. Supplies										
c. Utilities										
d. Other										
4. Total reduction in expenses										

Source: Departmental document, reprinted with permission of St. Francis–St. George Hospital, Inc., Cincinnati, Ohio.

purchased and installed, these written standards should serve as the basis for ensuring that the equipment meets all safety and regulatory requirements. The assistance of in-house technical support staff or, if necessary, outside consultants should be obtained to verify that the equipment is fully acceptable. Any deviations or problems should be identified and resolved quickly in order to ensure that the hospital receives full value for its money.

As in all purchases, capital acquisitions require that:

- A clear set of generic specifications be developed to serve as the basis for decision making
- As many reputable and reliable suppliers as possible be allowed to submit bids for the order
- All quotations be fairly evaluated
- Negotiations be coordinated through the purchasing department
- Upon installation, all equipment be tested according to written standards and by qualified technical personnel to ensure that all requirements are satisfactorily met

Purchasing Techniques

Group Purchasing

As the healthcare industry has shifted toward larger hospitals and large multihospital networks, the question of participation in a particular GPO is often made at a higher corporate level. The focus of the material/resource manager may be concentrated on performance tracking and contract compliance. In smaller hospitals, and ones that are not affiliated with a network, it may still be important for the material/resource manager to be skilled in assessing and deciding upon what GPO relationships to undertake. The following elements should be assessed before committing to a particular group:

- How well do group goals and objectives correlate with those of the system or institution?
- Is the group program well focused and mature, or does the group still have to get its program fully organized?
- What are the administrative costs of the group? How efficiently does the group operate?
- How skilled is the group at negotiation? Is the group going to negotiate major contracts? Is the system or institution satisfied that the group can do that job well?
- How does the group handle product evaluation and standardization? Because product standardization is an essential element of group purchasing, is the system or institution sure it can participate effectively in that process?
- How does the group track record compare with that of other groups—or with what the system or institution can do on its own?
- As for the suppliers who hold agreements with the group, are the products, quality, and service they offer generally acceptable to the organization? As for the others in the group, are they larger or smaller than the system or hospital? Generally, smaller hospitals benefit most from being in groups with larger ones.
- What is the level of commitment of the member systems or hospitals? More committed groups generally produce lower prices.

- How well managed are the others in the group? Will the organization be able to work closely with the other institutions?
- Has thought been given to the competitive position of the organization vis-à-vis others in the group?

Other hospitals, including members, should be asked about the group. Those questioned should include other hospitals that might have belonged to the group, but do not (Why not?) and hospitals that once belonged to the group, but left (Why did they leave?).[4]

The keys to maximizing the benefits of group purchasing include:

- Carefully selecting strong and effective groups to join
- Establishing control over product standardization and support of the group within the system or hospital
- Establishing a leadership position or, at least, a position of strength within the group
- Consistently using the group contracts
- Continually monitoring the price performance of the group to ensure that the system or hospital is getting the best value
- Gaining hospital staff support at department head levels

Prime Suppliers

Another approach to obtaining lower prices and better service is to establish a relationship with a single supplier for a major portion of the system's purchases. In return, the supplier is expected to provide:

- Lower prices
- Extended price protection
- Minimal back orders
- Lower in-house inventory levels
- Simplified paperwork in purchasing, receiving, and paying for items
- Other special services

Potential disadvantages of using a prime supplier include the following:

- Economic competition may be reduced over a period of time
- Quality may be inconsistent across the supplier's complete line of products
- The hospital may become overly dependent on the supplier, so that the change in suppliers would be disruptive to hospital routines
- Prices may creep upward if inadequate controls are placed on the relationship

Overall, a prime supplier relationship can provide significant economic and operational advantages to the hospital if it is well thought out, effectively negotiated, designed with adequate controls to protect the hospital or organized delivery system, and carefully monitored. The absence of any of these elements can have a negative effect.

Buying on Consignment

In consignment buying, the hospital or organized delivery system takes physical possession of items, but does not pay for them until they are actually consumed. Obviously, this method provides a cash flow advantage to the hospital or organized delivery system. It also should cause the supplier to work more aggressively to reduce inventory levels, because higher inventories mean more supplies for which payment has not yet been received.

As in any special arrangement, however, there are potential disadvantages, including the following:

- Proper inventory control practices are necessary to avoid payment for lost or damaged goods
- Prices may rise more than a normal amount to cover the supplier's additional costs
- The supplier may place too little stock in inventory
- The supplier may place too much stock in inventory in order to obtain free warehouse space
- If the supplier "buys out" existing supplies, it becomes difficult to terminate the relationship because a major one-time expense will be required to re-establish the hospital's or organized delivery system's inventory.

Consignment buying traditionally has been used most often for expensive, specialized items that are not needed every day, but to which the user must have immediate access when they are needed. Examples include orthopedic hardware, intraocular lenses, and special types of sutures. However, a number of companies are now providing consignment programs for broad categories of medical/surgical supplies, including pacemakers and leads.

Stockless Purchasing

In some cases, certain categories of supplies are removed from the hospital's or organized delivery system's inventory and are kept in the supplier's warehouse. Departments send requisitions for supplies directly to the supplier instead of to the storeroom. The supplier then prepares the orders for shipment directly to the individual departments.

The purchasing staff does not review orders, nor does the receiving department staff check them in. Staff in the accounts payable department review consolidated invoices only to verify that they are generally reasonable in size. The risk, of course, is that payment will be made for items that were not actually received. The control on these purchases must reside in the ordering departments, because their staff both check in orders when they are received and reconcile charges against their department budgets at the end of the month.

This purchasing technique improves the cash flow of the hospital or organized delivery system because of reduced inventories and leads to operating savings because of the simplified paperwork and reduced workload in the purchasing, receiving, and, to some extent, accounts payable departments. It also allows the hospital or organized delivery system to make use of the large-volume buying power of the supplier. For example, items that may be important but of low volume to the hospital or organized delivery system would normally have a relatively high price. The supplier, because it buys for multiple accounts, usually can obtain a lower price. Part of this price reduction should be passed on to the hospital or organized delivery system as a benefit of the program.

One disadvantage is that there is no emergency stock in a central on-site inventory, which makes accurate forecasting and ordering by the individual departments even more important. Building a small reserve in the basic supply level of the ordering department can mitigate this problem, but this should be done carefully in order not to diminish the inventory reduction savings. As in consignment buying, the removal of supplies from the organization's inventory has the effect of tying the hospital or organized delivery system closely to the particular supplier. As a result, it can be difficult to terminate the relationship.

Stockless purchasing can afford the hospital or organized delivery system significant savings. It is vital, however, that the supplier be selected carefully, and that performance, in terms of prices, order fill rate, and stock picking/billing accuracy, be closely monitored. In addition, the hospital or system should identify a list of critical items that it must have available at all times. The contract should include this list and bind the supplier to always have these items on hand. Finally, the hospital or organized delivery system should always have final authority over product selection; this should never be relinquished to the supplier.

Receiving

As noted earlier, the goal of the receiving department is to make sure that all ordered items are correctly counted, received into the organization's accounting records, and then delivered to the ordering departments. Every effort should be made to have receiving documents or computer images awaiting the arrival of shipments. These should be a duplicate of the purchase order, but without the expected quantities listed. This serves as a control to ensure that the receiving clerks actually count the items when they are being received.

Once the initial counting and paperwork are completed, the receiving documents should be reviewed by a receiving control clerk. This person compares the receiving documents to the log of open purchase orders and reconciles any problems involving overshipments, undershipments, unit of measure errors, or counting errors.

Separate areas within the receiving department should be designated for counting and completion of paperwork, holding items that are awaiting delivery, and holding items that are awaiting return to the supplier. Physical separation of shipments so that they do not become intermingled is important.

Many of the special supplier programs involve shipments directly to the ordering departments. Whenever possible, it is still best to bring the shipments physically through the receiving department. A special challenge for the receiving supervisor will be to make sure these shipments are processed not only accurately, but also rapidly. When shipments must go directly to the ordering department, it is worthwhile to assign a receiving clerk to work with the ordering department personnel to verify accurate receipt and posting. Even under new programs it is worth the effort to follow tried-and-true material/resource management practices.

Inventory Control

The goal of inventory control is to have on hand the least possible number of supplies, while not running out of critical items. Usually, inventory has been considered to be only that material stored in the official storeroom and carried as an asset in the accounting records. It is more appropriate, however, also to classify as inventory those supplies stored in the various operating departments, even though they have been charged out as an expense to the department accounts. These so-called unofficial inventories can be worth up to three times the value of the official inventory.[5] Obviously, they provide a significant opportunity for total cost reduction.

The first step in reducing inventories is to conduct a physical count in each department. Most areas do not use a perpetual inventory system, that is, one that keeps a running record of the inventory's value as supplies are added to and deducted from storage. It is harder to determine the value of the inventory in these areas, because in addition to finding and counting each item, it is necessary to look up the most recent price of the items and calculate the total value for each storage location. Then the figures should be compared to the value of supplies charged to the departments during the past year. A turnover rate can then be determined using the following formula:[6]

$$\text{Turnover} = \frac{\text{Annual dollar value of issues}}{\text{Average inventory value}}$$

Some department inventories turn over slowly, whereas others turn over more quickly because of their special nature. On the average, the goal should be inventory turnover approximately 12 times per year.

After the initial inventory values and turnover rates have been determined, targets can be established for each department. The department head and the material/resource manager should work together to determine the goals and the strategies for achieving those goals. After the strategic plans have been established, periodic follow-up physical inventories should be taken to monitor progress.

The strategic plan should address (1) the identification of obsolete, expired, or slow-moving items and ways to dispose of them, and (2) the identification of excess supplies of normally moving items and ways to bring the inventory levels back into line and keep them there. Obsolete and slow-moving supplies may be disposed of through the following means:

- Returning to the supplier for credit (a restocking charge may be applied)
- Finding a user elsewhere in the organization
- Selling or trading to other organizations
- Selling to a salvage dealer
- Donating to charity

Normally moving items that have become grossly overstocked can be reduced by returning the excess to the central inventory, finding a user elsewhere in the organization, or returning the excess to the supplier for credit. The last option should be used only if there is a significant excess that will not be consumed for a long period of time and if there is little or no restocking charge.

Otherwise, these items can be brought into line simply by not reordering until a calculated re-order point has been reached. A formal reorder point (ROP) can be calculated using the follow-ing formula:[7]

$$ROP = \text{Usage per day} \times \text{Lead time (in days)} + \text{Safety factor}$$

After reorder points have been established for items, it is necessary to calculate how much to or-der. A standard method for determining order quantity in most other industries is to use the economic order quantity (EOQ) formula, which mathematically balances ordering cost and holding cost to determine the quantity that results in the lowest total cost.[8]

The key elements of this formula include:

- Ordering cost—Generally considered the cost to place an order, which includes labor, supplies, and overhead in the purchasing, receiving, and accounts payable departments
- Holding cost—Generally considered the cost to handle and maintain the items once they are in the system's possession, which includes opportunity cost, labor, supplies, and over-head in the inventory departments
- Unit cost—Generally considered the cost of a single unit of the item for which the EOQ is being calculated

The EOQ formula sometimes results in quantities that are impractical because the necessary storage space is unavailable; in those cases, the actual order quantity can be adjusted. Many hos-pitals do not use this formula, however, because the calculation is cumbersome unless it can be computer-generated. The EOQ formula is helpful, though, as a check system in setting final quantities.

In another approach, the inventory manager may determine order quantity by (1) deciding how many days of inventory to keep on hand or, alternatively, the turnover rate desired; (2) adding the required safety stock; and then (3) calculating the required order quantity based on the lead time of the particular supplier.

A sound strategy for reducing and effectively managing inventories, then, includes the fol-lowing steps:

1. Conduct physical inventories of each storage location
2. Calculate turnover rates for each location
3. Establish target turnover rates for each item and each location
4. Calculate reorder points and EOQs for each item
5. Conduct periodic follow-up physical inventories to assess progress toward the goals
6. Adjust goals, reorder points, and EOQs as appropriate, based on changes within the system

Distribution

The selection and design of systems for distributing materials throughout an organization and for replenishing stocks of supplies in user departments are key variables in the effective manage-ment of inventory levels.

Types of Distribution Systems

There are four basic options for distributing material: (1) requisitions, (2) exchange carts, (3) PAR-level systems, and (4) point-of-use systems. The application of computer software programs, which accurately and quickly handle the large volume of data generated by the multitude of daily transactions, can enhance any of these systems, but computerization does not change the basic systems themselves.

Requisitions

The most traditional distribution system, and generally the least effective, is requisitioning. In this system, the personnel of individual departments control the process of deciding when and how much to order. It is common to find this function either performed by highly paid, clinically trained employees or delegated to lower paid employees without an inventory control background. In either case, it is often a low priority and does not receive adequate attention. As a result, the quality of the ordering process is inconsistent and random, which can lead both to unnecessarily high inventory levels and, at other times, to unacceptably low inventory levels. This system also can have the effect of inflating the inventory in the central storeroom, as the storeroom supervisor builds an extra cushion to prepare for random large orders. A final result of this system is that it generates many extra requisitions and telephone requests for additional supplies; these are time-consuming and expensive for both the ordering department and the central storeroom. The only advantages to this system are that it is simple, easy to understand (if not to do well), and requires minimal capital investment.

Exchange Carts

In this system, all or most of the supplies for a department are placed on a movable cart. The standard quantities can be adjusted dynamically through the application of a computer program, if desired. A second, identical cart is also prepared. On a scheduled basis, the first cart, which has been depleted, is taken from the user department and the second cart, already filled to standard levels, is exchanged with it.

The primary advantage of this system lies in the greater control possible over the productivity and performance quality of the employees who fill the carts. By having all carts replenished in a central area, the storeroom supervisor is better able to monitor performance. In addition, compared to a PAR-level system, this system reduces travel time by replacing multiple trips between the ordering department and the storeroom with a single trip to exchange the carts. The disadvantages are that a large capital investment in carts is required, and that costly space is needed for holding carts in both the user department and the storeroom. In addition, inventory is duplicated, and the efficient use of staff time is reduced by having to move partially used carts back and forth.

A variation of this system for use in the surgery department is the surgical case cart system in which carts are not exchanged, but are set up especially for each surgical case and then delivered to the surgery department when needed. The disadvantages of high capital investment and space intensity are also present here. However, space formerly set aside in the surgery suite, a particularly expensive location, can be released for more productive purposes. The carts can be prepared and stored in a separate, less expensive location.

In addition, the cart can be used as a back table during the surgical procedure and can then be used to transport all used or soiled supplies and instruments back to the central processing area. This is helpful from an infection-control standpoint.

PAR-Level Systems

When an organization uses a PAR-level system, a person from the central storeroom visits each ordering department on a scheduled basis, counts the supplies, writes an order to bring quantities up to PAR levels, obtains the supplies, returns them to the department, and replenishes the supplies up to a standard or PAR level. In a variation of this system, personnel use computer support to analyze data about past consumption and calculate a predicted order, and the storeroom employee delivers this order to the unit. Additional supplies that may be required are delivered on a later trip. In either case, this is a relatively labor-intensive system, and it provides somewhat weaker control over the productivity of the employees who deliver the orders.

The advantages of this type of system are that it more effectively links the disbursement of supplies to actual usage. It places the distribution function in the hands of employees who are lower paid than clinical employees and for whom the function is a high priority. Finally, it requires a relatively low capital investment.

Point-of-Use Systems

The newest distribution system is known as the point-of-use inventory management system. It is a variation of the PAR-level system. PAR levels are established for each item maintained on the nursing unit. Whenever a nurse or caregiver utilizes an item, he or she performs some simple function to indicate that the item has been used. This action reduces the quantity on hand for the item and eventually triggers a replenishment order. The function that the nurse or caregiver performs is typically the touching of a button or the scanning of a bar code. The vast majority of point-of-use systems utilize computer support. Some require closed or restricted access cabinets, whereas others use open storage systems. Some systems provide both restricted and open storage options.

Point-of-use systems also can provide patient charging or cost accounting information if the user identifies the patient when the supply is distributed. When properly designed and managed, information on the total cost of supply usage for a patient with a particular diagnosis or for particular procedures can be obtained. This assists senior management in making strategic marketing and operational decisions.

Point-of-use systems can reduce material management labor expenses associated with the distribution process and the collection of patient charge or cost accounting information. Inventory information for each PAR location is available in a real-time mode, so inventory levels can be reduced and the quality of service to the nurses is typically improved. Critical alert notices, available with most systems, can assure both material/resource managers and nurses that supplies will be available for the patients as needed. Many organizations have seen reductions in supply usage as a result of the accountability required by these systems. In addition, improvements in patient charge accuracy usually result in increases in revenue capture.

These systems do require capital investment, which must be balanced against the benefits described. In addition, the system is effective only if the nurse or caregiver utilizes the system properly. Therefore, a commitment from the management team is necessary to ensure that the benefits are actually obtained.

Selection of a Distribution System

Several factors are important in the selection of a distribution system:

- Design of existing systems and how well they are working
- Number of individual departments and storage locations
- Quantity and mixture of supplies in each area
- Existing storage and handling equipment
- Available space
- Physical relationship between departments
- Traffic routes
- Labor costs for each area
- Cash flow considerations

JC Kowalski, a materials management consultant, has developed a 15-step planning model for selecting, designing, and implementing distribution systems.[9]

1. Determine on-hand inventory levels in each affected department. This calculation will become the basis for identifying appropriateness and costs of the current inventory level, as well as for establishing target inventory levels and turnover rates.

2. Identify supply/demand/usage for each user department for a 24-hour period. The need/demand can be determined by sampling actual consumption for a period of time; usually 31 days is an adequate time period. High, low, and average daily demand figures for that sample should be noted. Numerical averages create a smoothing effect so the peak demands should be planned for. Finally, input should be obtained from the users by having them evaluate the data gathered. They often can identify a peak period that is unrepresentative of routine activity and can help establish more appropriate levels of inventory.

3. Draft a list of all products to be used for each department. This list should include such information as item number, source, description, units of issue, unit cost, optimum inventory level, and charge versus noncharge status.

4. Determine the frequency of supply replacement, which depends on the type of system selected and the targets for on-hand inventory levels and turnover rates.

5. Identify the functional requirements and specifications required for all exchange carts, if that system is used. Different-sized carts may be required for different areas, depending on the volume of products being maintained on the cart, as well as the frequency of restocking.

6. Determine the appropriate location for supplies at the user area. This should include a configuration for those supplies to facilitate reordering and restocking, as well as on-demand item location. It is important to include user department input in this vital process. Standardization layouts should be established as much as possible in order to enhance the productivity in the ordering, restocking, and retrieval-for-use processes.

7. Determine the timing for inventory review, ordering, and restocking. Essential variables for making this decision include times of peak supply demand, corridor and elevator congestion, and staff availability.

8. Identify and determine the preferred methodology: individual order processing or batch or zone processing.

9. Establish the appropriate paperwork/record-keeping systems. This step includes designing forms, setting up automated data systems communications, and so on.

10. Adjust layout, configuration, and inventory levels at the supply source in order to accommodate the new system.

11. Conduct in-service education programs for all personnel involved and affected by the system.

12. Establish a mechanism for tracking nonroutine/random demand for supplies that occur outside the basic system to determine the continuing effectiveness of the system and the appropriateness of the product mix and inventory levels.

13. Establish a policy and procedure for making changes as appropriate. It is essential to ensure that inventory levels will be adjusted routinely to match changing demand.

14. Begin implementation on either a pilot project basis, batch or zone basis, or systemwide. Each way can be successful, depending on the degree of complexity and sophistication of the method selected and the extent of the impact of the change.

15. Schedule meetings for reviewing progress and making any necessary modifications.

Central Sterile Reprocessing

The essence of materials management is to be found in the processes of purchasing, receiving, storing, and distributing materials. However, a number of other functions that involve these processes have come to be associated with the materials management program. The most common of these is the central sterile reprocessing (CSR) department, which is responsible for the decontamination, inspection, packaging, and sterilization of reusable materials. In some hospitals and organized healthcare delivery systems, this department's responsibilities also include the collection and disposal of trash and the collection and decontamination of dishes and utensils for the food service department. In any case, the CSR department should be responsible for the reprocessing of all reusable materials for the medical and surgical departments.

This department has three primary objectives. The first is to ensure that a well-designed and documented program is in place to assess and adjust the quality of reprocessing functions throughout the organization. Such a program involves (1) establishing policies and procedures, (2) monitoring compliance with the policies and procedures, and (3) correcting deviations from the policies and improving inadequate performance of the procedures. The program should include elements such as the following:

- Assignment of responsibility for the collection of soiled items
- Definition of methods for containing soiled items during transport to the decontamination area
- Procedures for decontamination
- Procedures for inspecting items before repackaging
- Definition of what constitutes acceptable packaging material
- Procedures for properly setting up, packaging, and labeling reusable items
- Procedures for operating and ensuring proper performance of sterilization equipment
- Procedures for storing, distributing, and handling sterile items throughout the facility
- Procedures for operating and ensuring proper performance of equipment used in decontamination

The second major objective is to ensure that all items leaving the CSR department have undergone a properly defined and executed sterilization process. The majority of items are sterilized—that is, made free of all living microorganisms—in a large-volume steam sterilizer. These are simply pressure vessels into which items to be sterilized are placed. All air is removed from the chamber, and then it is filled with saturated steam. The removal of all air is critical, because air acts as a buffer between the surface to be sterilized and the steam, which is the sterilizing agent. The steam must be of a defined temperature, and the contact with the steam must be maintained for a defined period of time. In order to state with confidence that sterilization has been achieved, it must be shown that the following steps have been taken:

- Items were properly packaged
- Items were properly placed into the sterilizing chamber
- All air was evacuated from the sterilizing chamber
- The chamber was filled with saturated steam of the required temperature
- The temperature and contact with the steam were maintained for the required period of time

The only way to prove that an item is sterile is to open the package and perform a laboratory analysis of the item. Obviously, this is not feasible because it destroys the item before it can be used. The most rigorous method available for testing the efficacy of the sterilization procedures and equipment is the use of bacteriological monitors. In this method, a package of live spores—the most difficult microorganisms to kill—of known strength is placed into the sterilizer. Upon completion of the sterilization process, the spores are analyzed in the clinical laboratory. If the spores are shown to have been killed, the assumption is that all other microorganisms in the sterilizer were also killed.

Because bacteriological monitoring is relatively expensive, it is not commonly used in every sterilization cycle. At most, it is performed daily, and in many cases on a weekly basis. A program that includes (1) well-defined policies and procedures, (2) tests to ensure proper air evacuation, time, and temperature for every cycle, and (3) periodic use of bacteriological monitors should provide sufficient confidence that sterilization is being properly performed.

The third major objective of the CSR department is to perform the second most common type of sterilization in hospitals, which involves the use of ethylene oxide (EtO) as a sterilant. A toxic chemical, EtO can be hazardous to employee health, but it is an extremely effective agent for sterilizing items that cannot withstand the rigors of steam sterilization. As a result, it must be used, but in a carefully controlled manner.

The Occupational Safety and Health Administration has established strict rules for the use of EtO. The current standard sets a limit for personal exposure of one part EtO per one million parts of air.[10] In order to ensure that this standard is met, a clearly defined safety program must be established. It should include:

- Policies and procedures for the use of EtO equipment
- Proper design of the room containing EtO equipment
- Proper ventilation of the room
- Routine preventive maintenance and testing of the equipment and ventilation
- Routine scheduled exposure testing of the work environment and the individual employees who operate the EtO equipment

Documentation must be maintained to prove compliance with all of these elements.

Other Related Functions

The material/resource manager almost always has direct management responsibility for the purchasing, receiving, central inventory, distribution, and CSR departments. In addition, this person is often given responsibility for other departments that are involved with the production and distribution of material. The most common of these are transportation services, including patient escort services, mail services, print shop, and laundry. In some cases, the pharmacy also may be attached to the material management division.

No matter what organizational arrangement is used, the most important fact is that materials make up a major portion of the operating budget of the modern hospital and healthcare system. Effective management of these materials is crucial to the survival of any facility in the increasingly competitive environment of today's healthcare industry.

Materials Management in Alternate Site Locations

The healthcare industry continues to experience rapid change. More patient activity takes place in alternate settings outside a hospital, such as in physicians' offices and ambulatory care centers. In many cases, hospitals provide ownership and/or management support for these off-site locations. Because the need for cost reduction is intense throughout the industry, effective materials management practices are vital in these alternate locations as well.

Basic techniques are valid no matter where they are used. The challenge in offices, clinics, and outpatient centers is to apply the principles of materials management with smaller staff, smaller space arrangements, and usually, smaller volumes of material. The key is to stay focused on the basic principles and find ways to adapt them to the nonhospital settings. Hospital material/resource managers, as well as suppliers, can be used as a resource in developing the nonhospital materials management control system. Administrators should commit themselves to ensuring good materials management practice in all operating settings under their control.

Future Trends in Materials Management and Purchasing

A survey of group purchasing executives conducted in March 1998 indicated that the primary goal of purchasing organizations rests on the promise to deliver a specific purchasing volume to suppliers.[11] The group purchasing executives described their perception of success as contract compliance. The key observations were that group purchasing organizations are endeavoring to fulfill their promise to deliver market share to suppliers, that for-profit hospital chains will obtain lower pricing than group purchasing organizations, and that these chains will obtain lower pricing than the committed volume programs of group purchasing organizations. In addition, they noted that more manufacturers will sell directly to organized healthcare delivery systems.

In the future, the healthcare materials manufacturers and distributors will clearly distinguish themselves by the value that they bring to the supply process, rather than simply the products and services that they can provide. A value-oriented, rather than a supply-oriented, environment will be created for a seamless flow of products by integrated information and financial flows.

Now that we have entered the 21st century, the world's economy and sociopolitical landscape are more volatile than ever, and the financial pressures on all industries continue to be intense. As a result, it is clear that the healthcare industry will continue to be in transition. Some of the challenges ahead are mergers and acquisitions, managed care, vertical integration, competition (both in the United States and around the world), cost control, government regulation (local and national), an aging population with high expectations of quality and service, and inadequate systems integration, both within and between entities.

References

1. Housely CE. *Hospital Material Management*. Gaithersburg, MD: Aspen Publishers; 1978:2.
2. Dattilo JA, Meredith G. Capital equipment purchasing. In: Scheyer WL, ed. *Handbook of Health Care Material Management*. Gaithersburg, MD: Aspen Publishers; 1985:156–164.
3. Rourke RE. 1985. Streamlining the purchasing process. In: Scheyer WL, ed. *Handbook of Health Care Material Management*. Gaithersburg, MD: Aspen Publishers; 1985:73.
4. Ibid, 101.
5. Kowalski JC. Supply distribution options—A new perspective. In: Scheyer WL, ed. *Handbook of Health Care Material Management*. Gaithersburg, MD: Aspen Publishers; 1985.
6. Rayburn JW. Inventory control. In: Scheyer WL, ed. *Handbook of Health Care Material Management*. Gaithersburg, MD: Aspen Publishers; 1985:202.
7. Ibid, 190.
8. Ibid.
9. Kowalski JC. Supply distribution options. 229–230.
10. Corn RL. Designing a safety program for EtO. In: Scheyer WL, ed. *Handbook of Health Care Material Management*. Gaithersburg, MD: Aspen Publishers; 1985:260.

11. Survey of group purchasing executives. *Healthcare Purchasing News*. 1985; 22(3):11, 16.

Biographical Information

William L. Scheyer is President of Southbank Partners, an organization that works to promote development in Northern Kentucky's urban core. Prior to joining Southbank, Mr. Scheyer served for more than 18 years as the City Administrator for the City of Erlanger. He has served as President of both the Northern Kentucky City/County Management Association (NKC-CMA) and the Kentucky City/County Management Association (KCCMA). He was named Outstanding City/County Administrator in 1993 and again in 2007. Mr. Scheyer has been active in numerous regional projects. He served as Chairman of the NKCCMA's Greenspace Committee in 1996, which released the first unified 3-county analysis of public greenspace needs in Northern Kentucky. Mr. Scheyer has also served as President of the Board of Trustees for Green Umbrella, a greenspace alliance, which serves the Ohio-Kentucky-Indiana region.

In addition to his involvement in government and environmental areas, Mr. Scheyer is a former chairman of the board of Northern Kentucky Family Health, now known as Health Point Family Care, a healthcare organization that provides primary medical care for low to moderate income residents of Northern Kentucky. He is also a member of the Cincinnatus Association and currently serves as President.

In 1999, Mr. Scheyer was the recipient of the Intergovernmental Unity of Effort Award given by the Northern Kentucky Area Development District to a person who is particularly instrumental in fostering collaborative efforts between diverse groups and jurisdictions. In 2003, he received the Innovator Award presented by the Greater Cincinnati Chapter of the American Society for Public Administration. Most recently, he led the team that developed the Erlanger paramedic service that provides advanced life support to the residents of six neighboring cities. In 2006, this program was awarded a Gold Level Award of Excellence by the National League of Cities.

Prior to joining the City of Erlanger, Mr. Scheyer spent 20 years in the healthcare field. He concluded his healthcare career as an Assistant Vice-President for Materials Management at Bethesda Hospitals in Cincinnati, Ohio. He is the author of *The Handbook of Healthcare Materials Management* and was a contributing author for *The Handbook of Healthcare Administration*. Mr. Scheyer is a graduate of Northern Kentucky University and an alumnus of both Leadership Northern Kentucky and the Greater Cincinnati Regional Leadership Forum.

Barbara B. Friedman, MA, MPA, FASHMM, CPHM, is the Director of Material Management at Kingsbrook Jewish Medical Center in Brooklyn, New York. Her career spans more than 20 years as a healthcare administrator in both the public and private sectors, specializing in purchasing and material management. Ms. Friedman has been an instructor at two colleges, lectured at numerous national conferences, is the author of many articles, and has served as an active participant on national professional committees.

The authors thank Mr. Marty Edelman, Director of Material Management at New York University Medical Center, New York, for assistance in reviewing the material contained in this chapter.

Appendix 15.A   Bidding Instructions

(Simple Format)

ITEMS BELOW APPLY TO AND BECOME A PART OF TERMS AND CONDITIONS OF BID. ANY EXCEPTIONS THERETO MUST BE IN WRITING.

1. Bidding Requirements:

    a. Late bids properly identified will be returned to bidder unopened. Late bids will not be considered under any circumstances.

    b. Bid prices must be firm for acceptance for thirty (30) days from bid opening date. Cash discount will not be considered in determining the low bid. All cash discounts offered will be taken if earned.

    c. Bids must give full firm name and address of bidder. Failure to manually sign bid should show title or authority to bind his firm in a contract. Firm name should appear on each page of a bid, in the space provided in the upper right-hand corner.

    d. Bid cannot be altered or amended after opening time. Any alterations made before opening time must be initiated by bidder or authorized agent. No bid can be withdrawn after opening time without approval by the Hospital, based on an acceptable written reason.

    e. Telegraphic response to any bid invitation must show: price bid, requisition number, opening date, description (brand, model, etc.) of product offered, and delivery promise. Confirmation on bid form should be postmarked on or before opening day and/or received within forty-eight (48) hours after opening day. Show regular information on envelope and add the word: "Confirmation." Telephone bids are not acceptable when in response to this invitation to bid.

    f. Engineering checklist must be completed and returned with this bid.

2. Specifications:

    a. All items bid shall be new, in first-class condition, including containers suitable for shipment and storage, unless otherwise indicated in invitation. Verbal agreements to the contract will not be recognized.

    b. Samples, when requested, must be furnished free of expense. If not destroyed in examination, they will be returned to the bidder, on request, at his expense. Each sample should be marked with bidder's name, address, and requisition number. Do not enclose or attach bid to sample.

    c. All quotations must be accompanied by descriptive literature giving full description of details as to type of material and equipment that is to be furnished under this contract. Samples, where required, shall be delivered to the purchasing department before the opening of quotations, unless otherwise stated in the specifications; failure of the bidder to either submit literature or supply samples may be considered sufficient reason for rejection of the quote. All deliveries under the contract shall conform in all respects with samples, catalog cuts, etc., as submitted and accepted as the basis for the award.

    d. In addition to the requirements of paragraph c, all deviations from the specifications must be noted in detail by the bidder in writing at the time of submittal of the quote. The absence of a written list of specification deviations at the time of submittal of the quote will hold the bidders strictly accountable to the Hospital to the specifications as written. Any deviation from the specifications as written not previously submitted, as required by the above, will be grounds for rejection of the material and/or equipment when delivered.

3. Award:

    Award of bid will be based on the information provided by the bidder. The award will be made consistent with PRUDENT BUYER POLICY of the Hospital. Considerations to this award will be:

    *   Price
    *   Quality

Appendix 15.A   *(Continued)*

- Service
- Delivery
- Design

(Not necessarily listed according to priority)

a. Cash discounts will not be taken into consideration in determining an award.

b. With regard to differences between unit prices and extensions, unit prices will govern and extensions will be modified accordingly.

c. Freight charges may be a determining factor only when all price, quality, and service specifications are equal.

4. Delivery:

a. Failure to state delivery time obligates bidder to complete delivery in fourteen (14) calendar days. A five- (5-) day difference in delivery promise may break a tie bid. Unrealistically short or long delivery promises may cause bid to be disregarded. Consistent failure to meet delivery promises without valid reason may cause removal from bid list.

b. No substitutions or cancellations will be permitted without written approval of the Hospital.

c. Delivery shall be made during normal working hours only, 8:30 A.M. to 4 P.M., unless prior approval for late delivery has been obtained from Agency.

d. Any freight charges applicable to this quotation must appear on the quotation. All freight agreed to by the Hospital must be prepaid and added to the Hospital's invoice.

e. In all cases, seller will be responsible for filing damaged freight claims with the transporter of the merchandise.

5. Patents and Copyrights: The contractor agrees to protect the Hospital from claims involving infringement of patents or copyrights.

TEFRA STATEMENT

Section 1861(v)(1) of the Social Security Act (42 U.S.C. § 1395x) as amended, requires us, as Medicare providers, to obtain the agreement of persons who contract with us for services with a value or cost of $10,000 or more in any twelve- (12-) month period, that the books, documents, and records of such contractors must remain available for verification of cost by the Comptroller General for a period of four (4) years following completion of the contract. Seller acknowledges and expressly agrees to this requirement, on its behalf and on behalf of any subcontractor who shall perform any part or all of this contract for Seller having a value or cost of $10,000 or more.

OSHA STATEMENT

Seller represents and warrants that all articles and services covered by this purchase order meet or exceed the safety standards established and promulgated under the Federal Occupational Safety and Health Law (Public Law 91-596) and its regulations in effect or proposed as of the date of this order. Seller will submit OSHA Form 20, material safety data sheet, upon request.

SUBMITTAL OR QUOTE CONSTITUTES ACKNOWLEDGMENT AND ACCEPTANCE OF THE TERMS AND CONDITIONS AS OUTLINED ABOVE.

INQUIRIES PERTAINING TO BID INVITATIONS MUST BE DIRECTED TO DEPARTMENT MANAGER, PURCHASING.

Appendix 15.B Bidding Instructions

(Complex Format)

Authorized Signature

A. INSTRUCTIONS TO BIDDERS

In accordance with the contract documents set forth herein, proposals will be received by Hospital through _____, at the (describe location).

1. PROJECT SCHEDULE

    Schedule installation to be completed by _____.

2. PREPARATION OF PROPOSALS

    a. The bidder shall submit his/her proposal on the attached proposal forms and specification sheets. No other forms will be accepted. A unit price and extended price shall be stated on the specification sheets for each item either typed or written in ink.

    b. Each bidder is to bid on all items that he manufactures or supplies.

3. SUBMISSION OF PROPOSALS

    a. All bidders shall submit __ proposals enclosed in a sealed envelope marked "Bid Document Equipment" on or before _____.

    b. The proposals with all literature and the Bond shall be delivered to: (address and designate)

    c. Where proposals are sent by mail, the bidders shall be responsible for their delivery before the date set for the receipt of proposals. Late proposals will not be considered and will be returned unopened.

4. WITHDRAWAL OF BIDS

    a. Bids may be withdrawn on written request received from bidders prior to date fixed for opening bids.

    b. Negligence on the part of the bidder in preparing the bid confers no right for the withdrawal of the bid after it has been opened.

5. COMPETENCY OF BIDDER

    a. A contract will not be awarded to any person, firm, or corporation that has failed to perform faithfully any previous contract with the Hospital.

6. CONSIDERATION OF PROPOSALS

    a. The Hospital reserves the right to reject any or all quotations or to waive any informalities or technicalities in any quotations in the interest of the Hospital.

7. BID GUARANTEE

    a. Each proposal shall be accompanied by a bid guarantee for five percent (5%) of the amount of the total bid. Bid guarantees shall be a Bond made on the Proposal Bond Form or a cashier's check.

    b. The Proposal Bond shall guarantee that the bidder will not withdraw, cancel, or modify his bid for a period of sixty (60) days after the scheduled closing date for receipt of bids. The Proposal Bond shall further guarantee that, if his/her bid is accepted, the bidder will enter into a formal contract in accordance with the method of contracting hereinafter specified.

    c. In the event the bidder withdraws his bid within the sixty- (60-) day period or fails to enter into a contract if his bid is accepted, he shall be liable to the Hospital for the full amount of the bid guarantee.

    d. The Proposal Bond shall be returned to all unsuccessful bidders after the successful bidder has executed the Performance Bond and the bid has been accepted by the Hospital.

    e. The Proposal Bond must be endorsed by surety or sureties, and names of endorsers must be typed immediately below signature.

Appendix 15.B   *(Continued)*

8. METHOD OF CONTRACTING

    a. Award of contracts will be in the form of a Purchase Order made by the Hospital on the basis of the best bid from a qualified contractor.

    b. The successful bidder shall deliver to the Hospital a Performance Bond with sureties satisfactory to the Hospital in the amount of one hundred percent (100%) of the total accepted bid.

    c. The agent of the surety bonding company must be able to furnish on demand:

       (1) Credentials showing power of attorney.

       (2) Certificate showing the legal right of the company to do business in the state of the Hospital.

9. INTERPRETATION OF CONTRACT DOCUMENTS

    a. Discrepancies, omissions, or doubts as to the meaning of the specifications should be communicated in writing to the Hospital for interpretation. Bidders should act promptly and allow sufficient time for a reply to reach them before the submission of bids. Any interpretation made will be in the form of an addendum to the specifications, which will be forwarded to all bidders and its receipt by the bidder must be acknowledged on the Form of Proposal.

10. RESPONSIBILITY OF THE BIDDERS

    a. Bidders shall visit the site and note local pertinent field conditions such as availability of loading docks, elevators, and all other receiving and inspecting facilities.

    b. Bidders are responsible for the installation and start-up of their equipment including the following: _____

    c. Bidders are to include with this quotation complete information on the local service center including:

    d. Bidders are to include with this quotation all warranty information concerning the system components outlined in Bidder's Proposal.

    e. Bidders shall provide an annual price for manufacturer's recommended preventive maintenance program to be provided by factory-trained and qualified personnel, after the warranty period.

11. SALES TAX

    a. The Hospital is a tax-exempt institution.

    b. Copies of the exemption certificate will be furnished upon request.

12. METHOD OF PAYMENT

    a. Requests for payments (invoices) must include the following information for processing:

       (1) Purchase order number

       (2) Manufacturer name and catalog item number

       (3) Dollar amount

    b. Payment for equipment shall be made according to the following schedule:

       (1) Ten percent (10%) of contract price as down payment shall be made within ten (10) days of acknowledgment of order.

       (2) Eighty percent (80%) of contract price shall be due and payable within ten (10) days of delivery, installation (to include field assembly, interconnection, equipment calibration to manufacturer's specification, and checkout), and acceptance by the Hospital of all system components as outlined in Bidder's Proposal.

       (3) Ten percent (10%) shall be payable six (6) days after acceptance by the Hospital.

    c. The Hospital reserves the right to refuse payment on an invoice due to damaged item(s), quantity variance, model variance, or any failure to comply with the contract documents.

(continues)

Appendix 15.B *(Continued)*

B. FORM OF PROPOSAL

Submitted by: _____ Date: _____

TO: HOSPITAL

We, the undersigned, have familiarized ourselves with the local conditions affecting the cost of the work, and with all contract documents for this work, including:

INSTRUCTIONS TO BIDDERS   PROPOSAL BOND

PROPOSAL FORM   BID SPECIFICATIONS

And also have received and incorporated into the makeup of the specifications the following addenda:

Addendum No. _____ Dated _____ Addendum No. _____ Dated _____

Hereby propose to furnish all labor, equipment, and transportation to delivery and install all materials, and to perform and supervise all work as required.

TIME OF COMPLETION: Installation must be complete by _____.

EXECUTION OF CONTRACT: If written notice of acceptance of this bid is mailed, telegraphed, or delivered to the undersigned within sixty (60) days after date required for the receipt of the bid, or any time thereafter before this bid is withdrawn, the undersigned will, within ten (10) days after date of such notice, execute and deliver a Performance Bond.

NOTE A: Bids submitted by virtue of the proposal hereby acknowledged by the Hospital to be made under the assumption that the successful bidder will not be prevented, on account of strikes or other disruptions affecting sources of supply or affecting normal progress of the work, from obtaining the materials necessary to carry out this contract to complete the work covered thereby.

NOTE B: It is understood and agreed by the undersigned that the Hospital reserves the right to reject any or all bids, or to accept the bid that embraces such combination of proposal that will promote the best interest of the Hospital.

NOTE C: It is agreed that this proposal shall be irrevocable for a period of sixty (60) days after the date set for the receipt of proposals.

NOTE D: It is understood and agreed by the undersigned that they will cooperate and coordinate their work with the contractor who will be in the final stage of work at the Hospital.

The undersigned hereby designates the office to which such notice may be mailed, telegraphed, or delivered:

_____

_____

_____

Enter here the service information requested in 10-D of "INSTRUCTIONS TO BIDDERS":

_____

_____

Appendix 15.B *(Continued)*

SIGNATURE OF BIDDER

SEAL (if a corporation)   Date _____

    Name of Firm _____

    By   _____

    Title   _____

    Business Address _____

                       _____

                       _____

    Telephone Number _____

    State of Incorporation _____

NOTE 1: If bidder is a corporation, write state of incorporation, and if a partnership, give full name of all partners.

NOTE 2: Any deviation from the specifications must be specifically stated. Include also an explanation where the bidder's project exceeds the above specifications.

NOTE 3: Alternatives, where presented in addition to the base bid, will be considered but must follow the instructions above, listing deviations to the specifications, and include complete descriptions and literature.

C. PROPOSAL BOND

    KNOW ALL MEN/WOMEN BY THESE PRESENTS, THAT WE, _____,

_____ (hereinafter called the Principal), as Principal, and

_____ (hereinafter called the Surety), as Surety, are firmly bound unto the Hospital in the amount of _____ (amount not less than five percent (5%) of the accompanying bid plus the sum of all additive alternates) in lawful money of the United States for payment of which said Principal and Surety bind themselves, their heirs, executors, successors, administrators, and assigns, jointly and severally.

    WHEREAS, said Principal has submitted to the Hospital a written proposal for certain work in connection with the (describe project), a copy of which is hereto attached.

    NOW THEREFORE, the condition of this obligation is such that if said Proposal be accepted, the Principal shall, within ten (10) days of written notice thereof, enter into proper contract for the work covered by the Proposal, and shall furnish a Performance Bond satisfactory to said Hospital. If there is a difference between the amount of the Proposal and the amount accepted then, this obligation shall be reduced to five percent (5%) of the value of the Proposal accepted. This Proposal Bond shall be valid for a period of sixty (60) days from the date set for the receipt of the Proposal attached thereto.

Signed and sealed this _____ day of _____, _____

Witness: _____ (SEAL)

_____, _____

_____ Principal

Countersigned at _____(SEAL)

By _____

(continues)

Appendix 15.B   *(Continued)*

D. SPECIFICATIONS

PART 1—GENERAL

1. RELATED DOCUMENTS
   a. Contract Documents, including General and Supplementary conditions and General Requirement, and contract drawings for the Hospital, apply to the work specified in this section.

2. DESCRIPTION OF WORK
   a. Successful bidder shall furnish, delivery FOB jobsite, and install all equipment specified herein, including all necessary attachment devices and all incidentals and accessories required for a complete and operable installation. Any omissions of the details in specifications does not relieve the bidder from furnishing a complete functioning installation of highest quality for all purposes intended.
   b. The work shall be coordinated with the mechanical and electrical trades where services and connections are required for proper installation and operation of equipment.
   c. It shall be noted that all interconnecting cabling throughout the installation shall be furnished by the bidder at no additional cost to the Hospital.
   d. The Bidder is required to clean up, remove, and dispose of all debris resulting from work hereunder.

3. QUALITY ASSURANCE
   a. Manufacturer's Qualifications:
      (1) Only manufacturers having a minimum of five (5) years experience in the manufacture and installation of the quality and type of the respective items of equipment specified herein shall be considered qualified.
      (2) Manufacturer shall be able to demonstrate to the Hospital's satisfaction, proximity of spare parts and availability of experienced, competent maintenance service.
      (3) Should the manufacturer find at any time during the progress of the work that, in his opinion, existing design or conditions require a modification of any particular part or assembly, he shall promptly report in writing such matter to the Hospital.
   b. Substitutions:
      (1) The following specifications are to establish a standard of quality and performance and are not intended to exclude any manufacturer or company from bidding quality equipment that can be proven to meet functional standards as set forth. The equipment to be furnished must meet the highest standards of the profession.

4. CODE COMPLIANCE
   a. All equipment furnished and installed under this section shall comply with all requirements of local, state, and federal building, health, sanitary, and NFPA Codes.

5. STANDARDS
   a. In addition to the above, the following standards shall apply to the extent referenced herein:
      (1) Underwriters Laboratories, Incorporated (UL): Listings and approvals as required.
      (2) Electrical components and wiring: Furnish and wire electrical components of equipment in this section to conform to NFPA 70 (National Fire Protection Association).
      (3) All new equipment must be HHS certified.

6. SUBMITTALS
   a. Roughing-In Drawings:
      (1) The Bidder will provide roughing-in drawings and will coordinate and verify the dimensions and required service with the architect.

Appendix 15.B   *(Continued)*

  (2) Roughing-in drawings must be supplied within two (2) weeks after receiving notice of the award, to provide information to other contractors performing the roughing-in.

 b. Shop Drawings:

  (1) Submit shop drawings and catalog cuts of standard manufactured items. Indicate in detail the methods of installation, connections, and all pertinent data relating to each item of equipment.

  (2) Catalog cuts shall indicate the specified model and characteristics of the item being furnished.

 c. Operating and Maintenance Instructions:

  (1) The Bidder shall furnish the Hospital with four (4) bound copies of written instructions, giving detailed information as to how the equipment is to be operated and maintained. Maintenance manuals shall include appropriate parts list and the name of the service representative.

  (2) In addition, a representative from the equipment manufacturer shall visit the project and instruct the Hospital personnel on the proper operation and maintenance of the equipment. The instruction period consists of not less than two (2) separate sessions, to be scheduled by the Hospital after occupancy.

 d. Guarantee and Preventive Maintenance:

  (1) Upon completion, and as a condition for acceptance of the work, the Bidder shall submit written guarantee(s) covering each item included in this section for a period of one (1) year from date of beneficial use. The guarantee shall cover all workmanship and materials and the Bidder agrees to repair or replace all faulty work and defective materials and equipment, including labor.

  (2) The Bidder shall be responsible for maintenance of the equipment for the first six (6) months, with all costs for parts, labor, and trips to and from the hospital covered by the warranty.

Facility Design and Planning for Ambulatory Care Centers

Richard Sprow, Sonya Dufner, and Christian F. Bormann

Introduction

The intent of this chapter is to outline some of the key planning processes and steps in working with an architect and what is entailed in building new ambulatory care facilities as well as to provide a basic framework of information for making decisions about facilities that will directly impact operations and finances for the life of the organization. The goal is to better understand the design process and the guidelines for the design of efficient outpatient practice space in order to be a more informed buyer of these specialized consultant services whether it is to fit out a new space or construct a new building. These ambulatory care facilities may be hospital based, freestanding, jointly owned (hospital and doctors), surgery centers, imaging centers, health and wellness facilities, doctors' offices, and others.

Today's modern ambulatory care facilities have evolved from simple healthcare practice facilities that once offered basic healthcare services to patients on an outpatient basis similar to private physician or ambulatory care centers, to more sophisticated and comprehensive healthcare facilities that can offer nearly all the services of a hospital, except for admitting patients for an overnight stay. This is the essential criteria that separates hospitals from ambulatory care centers; otherwise, the two facility types can be quite similar. Before a discussion about the planning and design of ambulatory care facilities, it is first necessary to become familiar with how professional architectural services are obtained and delivered.

The Design Process

Basics of Architectural Design Services

The planning and construction decisions for a healthcare facility, whether it is an inpatient acute care facility or an outpatient ambulatory facility, are complex and the assistance of trained and licensed professionals to advise the owner or operator of the new facility is essential. An ambulatory care center facility project could include a new building, a renovation, or interior design of existing constructed space. Each of these options requires a slightly different planning approach. To begin the design process for a new healthcare facility, the owner needs to hire the services of a professional architect. The architect has the special skills and training to help the owner define and quantify their functional needs. Depending on the scale of the project, often a team of design consultants is needed.

Design Consultants

A new healthcare facility project almost always requires the additional design expertise of various engineering disciplines such as mechanical, electrical, plumbing, and fire protection engineers. If the project is a new building or addition to an existing building, it will also require structural engineers to design the structural system and civil engineers to design the site on which the building is situated. Some architectural firms include these engineering disciplines (referred to as architectural/engineering or "A/E" firms); others hire these additional design experts as subconsultants to their own firm.

Architects

In the United States, architects are professionals trained in building design and renovation, and are licensed by each state. The terms architect and registered architect are legally protected, because of their responsibility to protect public health and safety by creating code-compliant facilities. Some architects are general practitioners, while others specialize in certain facility types such as healthcare facilities. When a project involves significant construction, a building permit with an architect's seal is required on the drawings before construction can begin.

Interior Designers

Interior designers are professionals specifically trained to plan and design interior spaces, including space planning and renovations. Although some states license interior designers and their training is similar to that of architects, they are not generally able to be legally responsible for new buildings or major renovations that involve structural work. Although architects may also deliver interior design services, interior designers are trained more specifically in the creation of interior space and the use of furnishings, finishes, and lighting. A project is most successful when both architects and interior design skills collaborate.

Specifically trained in the planning and design of interior architectural space, the interior designer works closely with the architect and the design team, and for the renovation of interior space often completely leads the design effort. The interior designer may develop the program and may create the interior space design and concept, including the overall plan layout with partitions and all surfaces, ceilings, lighting, and furnishings. Part of this responsibility includes the selection and specification of all finish materials and built-in furnishings. Sometimes the scope of work for an interior designer includes furniture, accessories such as window treatments, signage, and artwork.

Consulting Engineers

Like architects, engineers are licensed professionals who have skill sets and capabilities unique to their specific discipline. Some architectural firms include licensed engineers and are referred to as architectural/engineering or "A/E" firms. Others do not have these additional disciplines in house and have to hire engineering consulting firms as subconsultants. Engineering firms can also be contracted directly to the owner in cases that do not involve architectural or interior design work. Typically the architect is contracted directly to the owner for the complete design of a facility, and contracts out whatever additional expertise is required. This way, the architect is contractually responsible for the total coordination of all the work of the various disciplines.

Mechanical/Electrical/Plumbing Engineers

In the simplest of terms, building systems engineers are responsible for the design and specification of the working parts of the facility and infrastructure: heating, air conditioning, lighting, electrical systems, plumbing, and fire protection. The engineer works closely with the architect and interior designer, coordinating system layout and design with the architectural layout. Depending on the size and scope of the project, they may be assisted by specialized subconsultants in areas such as information technology, data networks, audiovisual, vibration control, specialized lighting design, acoustic design, and communication systems.

Structural Engineers

Structural engineers are responsible for the design and calculation of the supporting structure and foundations for a building or for renovation, based on the architectural design. Critical design considerations such as seismic requirements are often a critical part of their work. The structural engineer also evaluates and designs how to support very heavy equipment or systems such as overhead surgical lights, MRIs, CTs, or high-density storage systems.

Site/Civil Engineers

Civil engineers design and plan all the work outside a building's walls, such as site grading, paving, drainage, underground site utilities, site lighting, and of course, parking and access roads. They may also handle special design elements such as flood hydrology or traffic studies. Depending on the project scope, they may also work with landscape architects to design exterior spaces and other specialized consultants such as traffic engineers or parking structure designers.

Medical Equipment Planners

Especially because few healthcare facilities have the staff to devote time to planning out the detailed equipment needs of a major facility project, a medical equipment planning consultant can help to select, specify, purchase, and install medical equipment. This can be especially critical in early design stages, when the design team needs equipment information for coordination before the owner has typically begun to consider these details.

Furniture Vendors Planners and Suppliers

Furniture dealers provide and install furnishings and furniture systems based on the interior designer's design and specifications. From detailed quotations through warehousing, delivery, and setup, they can be hired to relieve the owner of many of the details of furniture coordination.

Miscellaneous Specialty Consultants

Depending on the complexity of the project, the architect may need to bring in still additional specialized expertise to address more specific aspects of the design solution, including acoustics, building and systems vibrations, information technology, security systems, vertical circulation (elevators), signage, and even artwork.

Commissioning Agents

Specialized consultants can assist an owner with organizing moving and new facility start-up services. Such consultants are usually only included as part of very large projects. They are responsible for planning and purchasing moving services, coordinating with furniture dealers, and adjusting and testing building systems before occupancy.

Selecting an Architect/Interior Designer

The selection of the design team needs to be based on trust and comfort, because it will be a long-term relationship of months or years, with significant long-term financial implications. Achieving this relationship requires a clear two-way flow of information in terms of the owner's requirements, budget, and constraints for their new ambulatory care facility and the design team's knowledge and approach. The best relationships have at their core a trusted advisory role for the design consultant, rather than an artist dictating solutions or the owner issuing instructions but not involving the professionals in decision making. As a consultant acting for the owner, an architect can translate goals and needs into a specific design solution, but is not in a position to guarantee schedule, cost, or the final construction.

Like selecting any other service professional, referral sources are a starting point for an informed choice. For design services, professional organizations such as the American Institute of Architects (AIA), American Society of Healthcare Engineers (ASHE), American Society of Interior Designers (ASID), and the International Interior Design Association (IIDA) have both local and national databases of member firms organized by type of expertise. An Internet search using these and other directory sources can identify professionals with specific types of experience, rather than just a geographic listing. Firm information including previous project examples is often available on the Web to help identify firms with a style and approach that may align with the ambulatory care center's project needs.

Preparing a Request for Proposal

Selecting a design team for a major facility project, such as a hospital-based ambulatory care facility, is an important decision with long-term implications, and should be done in an informed businesslike way, not simply by reacting to recommendations or brochure presentations. The request for proposal (RFP) is the key to an organized selection of design professionals because it obtains parallel responses from potential architects to a set of critical questions. In order to determine which architecture/interior design firms have the best qualifications for the particular project before engaging in a proposal, the owner may opt to qualify firms by sending out request for qualifications (RFQ) to select firms prior to issuing an RFP. The RFQ typically asks for qualifications, background, and basic firm information, but not a formal proposal. The RFP is a very important document because the quality and thoroughness and accuracy of the architect's proposal depends in large part on the quality and content of the RFP.

The most basic requirement of the RFP is a clear project description, including anticipated size and cost, required scope of services, and key schedule milestone dates. Will the project be a new building or renovation? Will it include interior design services and selection of furnishings and equipment? How many square feet (or square meters) of space is involved? Does the owner have a master plan or a detailed program of space needs available for the ambulatory facility, or is that to be part of the consultant's work scope? Are there specific time or budget constraints that will impact services to be provided or limit potential design solutions? The information is specific. Sometimes it makes sense for the owners to hire an architect to help them write the RFP.

Besides outlining the extent of professional services needed, the RFP should include a clear statement of the expected selection process. In a typical approach, design firms are asked to first submit qualifications materials describing their experience on similar projects, resumes of specific staff that would work on the projects, and their general approach. After the owner reviews and evaluates these capabilities, only the best qualified firms (the "short list") are asked to make more detailed technical proposals, including work plan, schedule, and fee proposal. Some or all of these firms may then be interviewed. To get the clearest responses, it is useful to explain whether the final selection will be based on experience, owner–architect chemistry, approach, fee proposed, or some balance of these factors.

Interview Process

For the owner of the ambulatory care facility, the point of interviews with the prospective design team is to test the interpersonal chemistry and professional responsiveness of the short-listed design firms and to learn something about their approach to the specific assignment. There is little benefit in simply having a personal presentation of the firm's generic experience and background or asking for design solutions from the design team without the opportunity for them to really understand the needs of the project first. Successful design solutions require engagement and interaction with the owner and the owner's staff, not just a striking architectural image. An effective way to achieve this goal is with structured interviews with the design firm and an agenda of items to be discussed. Interviews can normally be accomplished in 45 to

60 minutes, including time for questions and discussion. Often members of the interview group will ask similar questions of each presenter, to gauge their relative strengths. The interview process is in and of itself an educational process for the owner, which enables them to see the differences between design teams and their approaches to the project.

Key Interview Questions

Firms invited for interviews should be given an agenda in advance, with a request to introduce the specific team members to carry out this assignment, a discussion of the key planning, design, budget, and schedule issues that the team thinks will drive the direction of the project, and a discussion of singular examples of the firm's previous work that best highlight these issues. The goal of the interview is to assess which design team would be the best one to work with, how knowledgeable they are about related project issues, and their level of interest and commitment to the project. Because the design team usually will not have had access to all of the ambulatory care center's information about the project or a chance to work with the ambulatory care center team to discuss issues and develop alternatives prior to the interview, the interview generally does not include a design solution. The goal is to select a professional advisor with confidence, not to choose the most attractive idea at such an early stage. Some sample interview questions should be focused on the projects goals but also more general to allow discussion.

- What is the experience of the proposed specific individuals with similar projects?
- Clarify the roles of the individuals on the team. For example:
  - Who will be the prime contact on a day-to-day basis?
  - Who is in charge from the consultant side?
  - What specialized consultants (such as engineers, lighting designers, and medical equipment planners) are proposed?
- How are the firm's financial resources, stability, staff resources, and facilities?
- Is the design firm's location convenient to the ambulatory care center team for frequent interaction?
- What is your approach to this project, including key ideas to be considered in design?
- Do you have an understanding of local codes and the construction market?
- What is your design philosophy, style, and approach?
- Do you have similar project experience, with references?
- Please describe the scope of services proposed, with work plan and design schedule.
- Please supply examples of the architectural design aesthetic of your other work.

Once the architect has determined the detailed scope of required services for the project, professional staff with appropriate skills are assigned to the project. This is done concurrently with preparation of the project schedule because experience relates directly to the time required to accomplish a task. The most experienced and senior staff are normally responsible for the overall leadership and management of a project as well as setting the overall design strategy that best aligns with the owner's goals and objectives. Their level of experience and expertise typically enables them to effectively address the specific needs of the client and arrive at successful solutions efficiently, quickly, and most economically.

Depending on the services available from the architect's firm, additional consultants may be needed to complete the design of the new facility. Although some architecture and design firms have in-house engineers on staff to provide these services, many do not, so these services must be obtained from separate consultants. It is typically the responsibility of the architect to obtain whatever additional services are required by subcontracting to these specialty consultants and including them on the design team. The subconsultants' fees are added to the architect's fees.

Architects' Design Fees

Negotiation of professional fees should be a separate process, after the interview to select the preferred firm, because fees are essentially dictated by staff time needed for the project. The discussion should focus on the right fee for the specific team, scope of services, and work plan discussed and needed by the health system related to ambulatory care. Professional firms in a given market region have generally similar labor and overhead cost and in general ought to be similar in their fees. A very low fee compared to the others might usually indicate the use of less staff time or of less experienced staff rather than the senior presenters who may have made such a good impression at the interview.

Architectural fees for professional planning and design services represent the amount of time and associated expense it requires the professional(s) to provide the contracted services, plus a reasonable margin for profit. In architectural design and planning, the physical "deliverable" is traditionally the articulation of design solutions in the form of drawings and specifications. In addition, depending on the level of contracted services, the ambulatory care center may have a need for design concepts to be developed and explained in a written narrative, diagrams, graphics, photographs, notes, material samples, and presentations. Depending on the unique needs of the ambulatory care center, together with the architect, they can determine what medium might be best to represent the ambulatory care center's goals for their particular needs.

There are several different methods by which the design professional may determine the fees required to design the project, and each of them requires several initial steps in order to determine the total cost for a professional team to provide the required services. The design professional assesses the complexity of the problem in terms of a design solution, and all these requirements are tallied, their value in terms of billable rates of professional staff is totaled, reimbursable expenses are estimated, a profit margin included, and the total is normally the fee for service.

Types of Fee Structures

The architect and the administration representing the ambulatory care center can engage in an agreement for services based on a variety of compensation structures. The following are a few of the more common fee structures:

- Fixed fees: This is perhaps the most common form of compensation agreement between the ambulatory care center and the architect. A fixed fee is a total compensation figure, often referred to as a lump sum, inclusive of all services the architect and all required consultants agree to provide the owner for the agreed-upon scope of services. Reimbursable expenses, discussed later, are usually in addition to this fixed fee.

- Hourly fees: As the name implies, an hourly fee arrangement means for each hour the architect works on the project, he or she is compensated within the limits of the agreed-on maximum fee limit. Sometimes this is referred to as working on a "time-and-materials" or a "timecard project" basis because it costs the ambulatory care center the direct expense of the professionals' time and expenses for producing the work. There is often a maximum limit, or "upset" to an hourly fee, thereby giving the architect some budgetary limits. Usually hourly fee arrangements are better suited for smaller consulting or limited planning services in which the architect or designer is kept on a retainer basis for services as they are needed.
- Other fee structures: There can be as many different types of fee structures as there are unique needs of clients. The exact structure depends on how the office suite will be constructed, furnished, leased, subleased, or what time constraints there are for the construction schedule. These agreements typically are used more by developers, design–build teams, and construction managers; they are not the typical fee-for-service arrangement that architects use.

Determining the Scope of Work

On the macro level, the overall project schedule summarizes the major steps to a project, starting with the initial response to a request for proposal, through design, construction, owner occupancy of the new space, and perhaps even a post-occupancy evaluation. On the micro level, a more detailed, well-constructed project schedule becomes a work plan for the project. It takes into account all individual and sequential tasks involved in producing a design, and scheduled duration for each task. The architect is usually responsible for establishing and maintaining the design portion of the project schedule and clearly communicating this timeline of events to the owner and the entire design team. The tasks on this master schedule are given time durations, for which hours and, subsequently, fees can be assigned. Of particular importance to the owner are the key decision milestones and the expected time commitment of the owner and the staff, so that the ambulatory care center can plan this into its work schedule.

Project-Related Expenses

In addition to the professional fees paid directly to professional staff, other expenses incurred in the process of delivering the design services usually include:

- Plotting, printing, and reproducing drawings and documents
- Overnight mail and courier services
- Travel costs for the design team in connection with the project (airfare, train fare, rental car, etc.)
- Subsistence allowance for the meals when traveling
- Photography/film development
- Three-dimensional models and materials required to build physical models
- Other miscellaneous items as negotiated between the architect and owner

The architect is typically entitled to be reimbursed for these expenses. Depending on the size of the project and the extent of the accounting paperwork required by the architect, sometimes the architect charges a nominal fee for accounting management of all of the expenses as well those of his design subconsultants, usually in the range of 5 to 10% of the expense total.

Understanding the many steps involved in determining a fee is important to an ambulatory care center because its members are often involved in the fee negotiations with the architect. Knowing some of the complexities of the architect's work, or at least the many considerations that go into a fee calculation, helps explain the rationale behind the fee, and therefore takes some of the mystery out of the fee negotiation. Once the overall project schedule is established, all the tasks have been identified, the design team has been selected, and the consultant team has been assembled, the architect can then calculate the required fee to deliver the project. A basic method by which the architect may begin to calculate the fee is to determine the hours required by each professional on his/her team to deliver the scope of work required of the project. Then the billable rates for each professional can be added up, an anticipated amount can be added for expenses, and an overhead factor for a reasonable profit can be added.

Architectural/design firms should provide a list of their hourly billable rates for each level of professional in their employ. Billable rates normally include the actual hourly rate the employee earns based on salary, plus the firm's overall overhead expenses, which include the employee's benefits, cost of their office, equipment, utilities, and the general costs of doing business. Once the hours have been determined, the total dollar value for each of these categories becomes the overall fee. If required, the architect will break down the fee into each of these categories to show how it was calculated. An example of a simple fee tabulation is summarized below. This calculation assumes a project team for a hypothetical, small project.

Sample Project Team with Billable Rates for Fee Determination

Staff	Hours	Billable Rate	Subtotal Fee
Principal in charge	40	$200	$ 8,000
Senior designer	60	$150	$ 9,000
Project architect	120	$110	$13,200
Junior staff	200	$ 75	$15,000
Subtotal			$41,700
Engineering consultant fees			$20,000
Direct expenses (estimate)			$ 5,000
Subtotal			$25,000
Total professional fees			$66,700
Anticipated reimbursable expenses			$12,000

The fee is calculated and negotiated based on as specific a scope of work as possible. If the scope of the work changes, which means work is either added or subtracted, there is normally an adjustment made to the professional fees. When the scope changes, the owner and architect should review the agreed-on fees and make adjustments as appropriate to fairly compensate the design team for the services they have or must yet provide.

Professional Service Fees

The conventional method of fee determination is a basic, direct, illustrative example of precisely where each required element falls into the overall fee. However, this is only one method. There are other methods for fee calculation used throughout the architectural industry, some of which are shorthand approaches for coming up with a fee that is generally in the same range as the analytical steps outlined above.

Cost of Construction Method

Another approach that architects sometimes use to determine fees, and for the ambulatory care center to compare fees, is to charge a fee that is based on a percentage of the anticipated cost of construction for the project. For example, if a project construction budget is $5 million, a design fee could potentially be 5 to 10% of the cost of construction, depending on regional economic factors that affect the cost of construction and the complexity of the project. For example, an administrative office suite or exam room suite is easier to design (i.e., might require less time and fees) than an endoscopy practice that requires a special ceiling structure for lights, high-output ventilation systems, medical gases, and more durable and expensive finish materials. This method of fee calculation is sometimes used to determine an order-of-magnitude fee for budgeting purposes, but in general, is less accurate than the analytical approach previously outlined.

Cost per Drawing Sheet Fee Calculation

It was once common practice to determine a fee for a project by determining the total number of drawing sheets required for the construction documents and assigning a set number of work hours per sheet. This number of hours was amalgamated from years of experience and would include a percentage of time for design, coordination, and actual drawing. This method was more effective when architectural drafting was all done by hand. Now that the architectural and design profession is predominantly computerized and drawings are mostly done electronically, the hours per sheet method is not an accurate assessment tool. Sharing and reusing electronic information leads to improved efficiencies and saved time; however, sometimes the time savings are offset by the additional time required to manage the computer drafting systems and vast libraries of electronic information.

Getting the Project Started

Once the owner or administration of the ambulatory care center hires a design firm, they need to understand the steps in the design process. With a planning and design team on board, the ambulatory care center's first need is to clearly define the mission and goals of the project: What are you trying to achieve? This needs to be discussed at the first working session. Budget limitations, approval processes, schedule constraints, functional needs, internal political issues, and broader issues such as brand identity are ideas to consider when defining goals for the project. A well-prepared RFP would include much of this project background information. The parameters of a successful project include a clear and agreed-upon direction from the start, and a sharing of that direction among the team that is comprised of ambulatory care center members and the design consultants. It is important to have shared goals and a common definition of a successful project, in terms of design, image, function, budget, schedule, and quality, before beginning a design solution.

There are traditional well-defined "phases" of architectural design that start with general design concepts and then gradually add layers of design specificity until the project is completely defined, described, and detailed in drawings and specifications. It is important to know what these phases are because designers use them frequently as a matter of shorthand, and each has fairly well-defined parameters and definitions.

Architectural Programming

The architectural program defines functional and space needs and ideally the quality and character of the space that will be accommodated in the project. At a minimum, it is a listing of required rooms and their sizes, but properly used, the program can be an important planning tool to explore organizational and operational assumptions. Wherever possible, it should be quantified in terms of function and clearly define such items as:

- How many patient records need to be stored in the file room?
- How many patient visits will each provider handle each day?
- How many clerical staff will work in the billing office?
- How many visitors will accompany each patient?
- What will be the hours of operation?

The discussions leading to answers for such questions can often be facilitated by the design professional, who specializes in the "what if" questions that can lead to design insights and creative solutions. Planning a space to accommodate several functions can potentially reduce total space needed and improve flexibility. For example, smaller private offices and more shared conference and consult spaces can reduce the amount of space that remains unused at any given time. It is unrealistic to expect every space to be used all the time. An efficiency factor of 80% use of typical exam rooms, for example, is a reasonable goal. The use of specialized procedure or diagnostic rooms will often be much lower, due to more complicated room cleaning, setup, and turnaround times.

Programs set out as a spreadsheet can also serve as a preliminary budgeting tool to track staff needs, equipment, and cost of space based on typical unit costs. The balance of space by type can be adjusted and the cost impact considered. In addition, the correlation between practice volume and space needs can be seen. For example, if each exam room can serve 10 to 12 daily patient visits, or 2500 to 3700 per year (depending on hours of operation, procedure time, and days worked), it is possible to see the point at which a six–exam room suite will become overtaxed, and eight rooms will be needed in order to handle the anticipated patient volume.

In order to understand space in buildings and how it is calculated, it is important to understand a few key definitions. Programming classifies space in three categories:

- *Net square footage*, or nsf, is the actual space within a specific room or work area. (A simple analogy to remember this is the net area of a room is the space that could get carpet.)
- *Departmental gross square footage*, or dgsf, includes the nsf plus the circulation space between rooms, such as corridors, stairs, housekeeping space, and building construction components like interior partitions and columns. The dgsf is measured from the exterior windows inward. The dgsf is calculated with a multiplier that ranges from 1.4 to 1.7 times the nsf.
- *Building gross square footage*, or bgsf, includes the dgsf plus the area occupied by the overall building construction, such as thickness of exterior walls, mechanical shafts, egress stairways, and elevator shafts.

The key point in the programming phase is to get the architect/planning and ambulatory care center team to be as analytical as possible and to avoid anecdotal statements of space needs such as the amount of space one has now or had in some previous practice, or simply a fixed number of rooms per provider. Testing and adapting the program is the point at which planning decisions have the greatest leverage in terms of cost savings for the life of the facility. The cost of a facility is primarily (80 to 90%) dependent on the size of the facility (which is defined by the program) and the resulting infrastructure required. This infrastructure would include the building structure and enclosure and its heating, air-conditioning, electrical, and plumbing requirements. Many requirements are dictated by local building codes or health department regulations based on the overall size and purpose of the facility. The spreadsheet in **Table 16.1** is an example of a program. The entire design is derived from the architectural program so it is a very important piece of the process. The architectural program should be finalized and correlated to a construction budget *before* design begins. Ideally, all key decision makers sign a final program as their approval to commence design since it is difficult to alter the program after design begins.

Schematic Design (SD) Phase

With agreement on program needs as defined in the architectural space program, schematic or preliminary concepts are developed to fit the program plans and the site. This early phase is the time to test the program fit by considering basic stacking of functions if a multifloor structure and horizontal adjacencies of the program elements, as well as to establish the basic design concept. Schematic drawings are normally made to scale, but sometimes show walls on drawings as only a single line, often without the detail of doors and other construction. The point of this step is to establish an understanding of the size, layout, design intent, and physical scope of the project. Conceptual interior or exterior designs are often discussed, but require considerable design development. See **Figure 16.1**.

If the project is a new building, then schematic design is more extensive because it involves development of the architectural concept for the building, as well as proposed engineering systems for infrastructure, structural framing, and site work. A preliminary order-of-magnitude cost

Table 16.1 Generic Program—Orthopedic Center

Area/Function	Qty	SF Each	Total	Comments
Entry	1	100	100	Vestibule
Waiting	1	300	300	For 10–15
Business office	1	180	180	2 workstations. Check-in/check-out
Nurse station	1	100	100	Counter. Medicine cabinet
Exam room	4	100	400	
Cast room	1	150	150	No plaster—storage along 1 wall
Radiology room	1	200	200	Use patient toilet
Processing	1	30	30	Rapid processor
Control	1	30	30	
Dressing	1	55	55	Size for handicapped
Patient toilet	2	55	110	Size for handicapped
Doctor office	2	125	250	Potential second doctor
Doctor view/chart	1	100	100	1 per doctor
Education/credit/counseling	1	100	100	
Staff lounge	1	100	100	
Staff toilet	1	55	55	Size for handicapped
Storage	1	50	50	
Soiled hold	1	50	50	
Wheelchair storage	1	40	40	
P. T. reception	1	150	150	2 people
P. T. waiting	1	250	250	For 10–12
P. T. toilet	2	55	110	Size for handicapped
P. T. office	2	80	160	
Exercise	1	1000	1000	Open area
Modality	1	300	300	4 stations—open area
P. T. equipment/wheelchair	1	60	60	
Janitor closet	1	30	30	
Mechanical	1	130	130	
Total Net Square Feet			4590	
Net-to-gross factor			1.4	
Total Gross Square Feet			6426	

Planning Assumptions
• Orthopedic Center including offices and Physical Therapy, Occupational Health, and Sports Medicine
• Parking: 10 spaces / doctor plus parking for Physical Therapy
• Needs to be handicapped accessible

estimate can be made based on the final program and the schematic design. The entire package should be presented to the ambulatory care center's decision-making group for approval before proceeding further. A physical sign-off on the documents by the various representatives of the practice is a useful technique to get everyone focused on the importance of this phase and ready

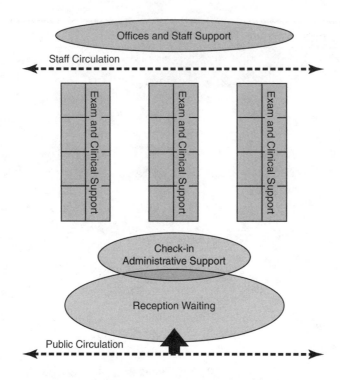

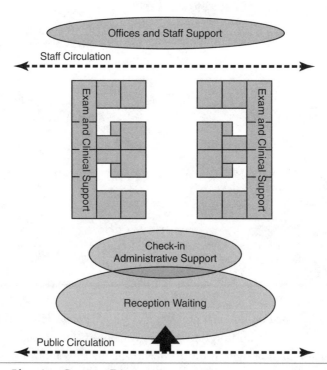

FIGURE 16.1   Planning Concept Diagrams

to commit to the approved design. Once the design has progressed, it is more difficult and expensive to go back to the issues of how many rooms, how much space, and what planning adjacencies are required.

Design Development (DD) Phase

With owner approval of the schematic design and the SD budget, the design team leads the process of making more detailed design decisions, room by room, system by system. Working closely with the ambulatory care center's team and facility users, the designers review the features and requirements for each element of the facility design in preparation for making detailed construction drawings. This is the point in the design process where furnishings, cabinetry, medical equipment, computer and communication systems, and interior finishes all need to be discussed in detail. Items that are not identified and recorded here, even including apparently minor items such as special electrical outlets, telephone and data locations, special hardware needs, or specific finishes, will not appear in the final construction documents and will thus not be included in contractor bids. Adding these items into the design later will be at a much higher cost. Room data sheets, such as the one in **Table 16.2**, are a method architects use to collect this important and detailed information from the owner to incorporate into the design.

This is also the stage where input from the ambulatory care center is essential, including such information as a highly detailed medical and office equipment list with catalog sheets, sizes, clearances, and utility requirements. For comparison, in the schematic design phase, a cardiology exam room might be identified as a stress test room and sized accordingly, but at the design development phase the actual make and model of the treadmill, its voltage requirements, and its computer system all need to be determined in order for the design to include the space and services required. Design development is the time to explore the detailed look of the facility too, with three-dimensional drawings, renderings, or physical or electronic models of key interior and exterior spaces, samples of proposed materials, and preliminary studies of construction details.

The product of the design development phase will be both drawings and a written outline specification that describes most of the products, fixtures, and materials to be used in the construction. In general, the overall project scope of work and definition of the major architectural and engineering systems must be clearly defined. From the DD package of drawings and written specifications, a detailed cost estimate should be prepared for approval. Although previous unit cost estimates may have been prepared by the design team or a contractor for the schematic design at little cost, the design development estimate should be a detailed professional estimate by an independent construction cost estimating consultant or a construction manager retained to provide what's called preconstruction services. Architects and engineers generally do not have the firsthand experience with construction costs that is required at this phase. The best interest of the ambulatory care center at this point is a realistic and conservative estimate by a qualified cost estimator, plus provision of both design and construction cost contingencies to allow for the unknown.

Ideally, after the design development estimate is completed, the ambulatory care center architect and estimator should meet to review cost and schedule assumptions and discuss alternatives

Table 16.2   Generic Room Data Sheet

Project Information	RDS	Approvals	√ Date
Project Name:	General Hospital Medical Office Building		☐ Initial
Project Number:			☐ Interim
Department:	Orthopedic Center		☐ Final
Room Name:	Staff Break Room		☐ Revisions
Room No.	1003		

√ Walls	√ Floor	√ Base	√ Ceilings
☐ GWB (painted)	☐ VCT	☐ Vinyl	☐ ACT 2x2
☐ Ceramic Tile (full ht.)	☐ Sheet Vinyl	☐ Rubber	☐ ACT 2x4
☐ Ceramic Tile (wainscoating)	☐ Carpet (broadloom)	☐ Ceramic Tile	☐ GWB
☐ Fabric	☐ Carpet (tiles)	☐ Carpet	☐ Mylar/Vinyl Clean Tile
☐ Vinyl	☐ Ceramic Tile	☐ Other (specify)	☐ GWB w/ACT adhered
☐ Other (specify)	☐ Epoxy Terrazzo	☐ Other (specify)	☐ Special
Notes:	☐ Wood	☐ Other (specify)	☐ Other (specify)
	☐ Wood Simulation	Notes:	☐ Other (specify)
	☐ Other (specify)		Notes:

√ Electrical Items	√ Power	√ Communications/Data	√ Lighting Fixtures
☐ Clock	☐ General	☐ Telephone	☐ Fluorescent 232
☑ E/T Clock	☐ Life Safety	☑ Intercom	☐ Fluorescent 234
☐ TV	☐ Emergency	☐ Nurse Call	☑ Pendant Fixtures
☐ CCTV	☐ Ground Jack	☐ Emergency Code	☐ Under Cabinet Task
Lights			
☐ Duplex	☐ GFI	☐ Dictation	☐ Reading Light
☐ Other	☐ Other	☐ Paging	☐ Over Bed Light
Notes:	Notes:	☐ Fax	☐ Exam (ceiling mtd)
		☑ Computer	☐ Night Light
		☐ Other	☐ Other (specify)
		Notes: Dishwasher and garbage disposal	Notes:

HVAC	Gases	√ Plumbing	Environment Conditions
☐ Air Change Requirements	☐ Comp Air QTY:	☐ Sink QTY: 1	☑ Acoustical Trtmt
☐ Exhaust	☐ Oxygen QTY:	☐ Toilet - HC QTY:	☐ Daylight Req.
☐ Temp. Range:	☐ Vacuum QTY:	☐ Shower QTY:	☐ Radiation Shldg.
☐ Humidity Range:	☐ Nitrogen QTY:	☐ Urinal QTY:	☐ RF Shielding
☐ Negative Pressure	☐ Nitrous Oxide QTY:	☐ Tub QTY:	☐ Leaded Glass
☐ Positive Pressure	☐ Evac. QTY:	☐ Flush Rim Sk QTY:	☐ Special:
☐ WAGE	☐ Natural Gas QTY:	☑ Floor Drain QTY:	Notes:
☐ Other:	Notes:	☐ Bed Pan Washer	
	☐	☐ Other	
	√	Notes: Dishwasher	

Fire Protection	√ Casework	Structural Issues	Special Requirements
☐ Alarm	☐ Base Cabinet	☐ Floor Loading	☐ Handrails
☑ Sprinkler Heads	☐ Wall Cabinet	☐ Floor Mtd Equip.	☐ Wall Protection
☐ Exiting Signage	☐ Desk	☐ Ceiling Mtd Equip.	☐ Corner Guards
☐ Smoke Detector	☐ Base Cb. w/Sink	☐ Vibration Isolation	☐ Bed Locator
☐ Heat Detector	☐ Pedestal	☐ Slab Depression	☐ Bumperguards
☐ Other	☐ Custom	☐ Add'l Ceiling Structure	☐ Combo Handrail/ Bumper
Notes:	☐ Metal	☐ Add'l Floor Structure	Notes:
	☐ P-lam	☐ Coordinate Ductwork	
	Notes:	Notes:	

and possible savings. Once again, at the end of the design development phase, a specific sign-off and approval from all members of the ambulatory care center team is highly recommended.

Construction Document (CD) Phase

Construction documents, sometimes called "working drawings," describe in detail the final project required by the ambulatory care center. The drawings and written specifications form the basis of the bid price by contractors. The specifications, or project manual, describe in writing the specific materials, workmanship, and systems to be used and how. This package of detailed drawings, specifications, and materials for bidding by contractors are the "blueprints" that are the basis for building the facility. New printing technology in fact makes them black and white, but the essential purpose remains. The importance of these documents is critical. If something is not included in the drawings, it will not be in the bid price and will not be included in the construction of the finished facility, except at extra cost. Design requirements and features that may have been discussed with the design team or thought to be promised at some point along the way need to be indicated explicitly in the construction documents, otherwise they will not be included. The design team often implements a series of checks and balances throughout the CD phase to ensure all the details have been thoroughly worked out and shown on the drawings.

Construction Administration (CA) Phase

Once a contractor or construction manager has been selected, either through low bid or by negotiation, the design team typically assists the ambulatory care center in working with the contractor. Early in the construction phase, they request and review for approval a detailed construction schedule and a detailed breakdown of construction cost. In addition, the contractor submits samples of the actual materials selected by the design team, catalog copies of products to be used, and shop drawings prepared by subcontractors for items they will fabricate such as cabinetry and windows.

During the construction process, representatives from the design team observe and advise the ambulatory care center on progress, usually attending periodic owner-architect-contractor meetings that are led by the contractor. The design team reviews all of these various submittals for compliance with the design drawings and specifications and provides comments back to the contractor. As an important protection, architects are often asked to sign off on contractor payment requests to confirm the extent of progress and the presence of construction materials on-site.

At substantial completion of the work, the architect will assist the ambulatory care center in final inspections and prepare a written "punch list" of deficiencies that the contractor needs to correct. Sometimes more extensive on-site services by the design team are available as an option, such as detailed inspections or full-time on-site representatives—all at additional cost. In any case, it is important to understand that the designer is legally prevented from directing the actual construction work itself and can act only as an agent reporting to and advising the ambulatory care center.

Sustainable Building and LEED

Sustainable building practices increase the efficiency by which building projects use resources while reducing impacts on the environment and human health. These so called "green practices" are achieved through efficient use of water, energy, and other natural resources, in addition to paying attention to reduced waste, pollution, and environmental degradation. The healthcare sector is the second most energy-intensive user in the United States, and with energy costs going up, it is worthwhile to aggressively consider reducing climate-changing impacts. In an era when energy costs are increasing dramatically and societal concerns turn toward global warming, conservation of resources, and recycling, having a facility that is responsive to those societal concerns may be in the best interests of the ambulatory care center and its employees. In addition to environmental concerns for energy and natural resource consumption and conservation, green design also takes into consideration construction materials that are harmful to the environment and directly to human health. Polyvinyl chloride, or PVC, found throughout healthcare facilities, exposes people to chemicals, and fumes from cleaning products are also harmful to human health. New, greener products are becoming available to replace these harmful materials.

The Leadership in Energy and Environmental Design (LEED) Green Building Rating System is a third-party certification program and a benchmark for the design and construction of sustainable buildings, communities, and developments created by the US Green Building Council (USGBC). LEED is a nationally recognized tool for measuring overall sustainable performance in five categories: sustainable site development, water savings, energy efficiency, materials selection, and indoor environmental quality. An integrated design process is essential to the successful development of a sustainable project. Sustainable design strategies should be linked to the specific client goals and values, leading to the broader pursuit of design excellence.

There is a growing awareness of these concerns among design professionals, and an accreditation program through LEED has emerged for those who demonstrate understanding of sustainable processes, systems, and design, as well as proficiency in applying sustainable design approaches. Many sustainable design strategies are just part of good, responsible design by well-trained architects, such as siting a building to maximize its solar orientation for optimum solar heat gain in the winter and minimized solar heat gain in the summer. This might also translate into treating the exterior elevations of the building differently to optimize the solar, heat, light, and wind conditions, such as low-emissivity glass on windows, or adding passive solar shades to exterior elevations. Sustainable design measures such as these are simple and add little or no cost to the construction, while they can have dramatic effects on the energy required to heat and cool the building.

Some sustainable strategies, such as incorporating a combined heating and power system or using captured rainwater from the site for sewage conveyance, for example, are more complicated and require specialized expertise to implement. Measures such as this, while adding construction-first costs to the building, eventually pay for themselves and yield savings over the life of the building. As owners increase their awareness of sustainable design practices, the construction industry will become more accustomed to building ecologically responsible designs. In turn, more recycled materials and sustainable products will emerge and reach the market, and it will be easier and more affordable to build sustainably designed buildings. Utility companies have become avid supporters of buildings that have reduced energy demands, and many of them offer grants and financial incentives to owners to implement energy-saving systems in their buildings.

As community-based businesses relying on serving the community, health facilities and physician practices may be expected to be part of a healthy, ecologically responsible facility. They will be expected, therefore, above all other facilities, to provide a healthy, nonharmful environment in which to provide medicine. Achievement of LEED certification can help demonstrate that the practice and business value these concerns and are responsible members of the community they serve.

Construction Services

Once the ambulatory care center has a design solution for its new facility(ies), it needs to hire a builder to construct the architect's design. A common misperception by those unfamiliar with the design and construction process is that the architect builds the project. The architect is trained to design the project, not actually construct it. There are different types of builders and approaches to building. Below are some of the more common builder types.

General Contractors

Typical contractors provide building services based on bids from detailed construction documents developed by the architect. Usually the general contractor will handle basic building shell work directly but will subcontract specialized trade construction, such as mechanical, plumbing, electrical services, or site work to other, more specialized tradesmen.

Construction Managers

More than a contractor, a construction manager (CM) is equipped to provide fee-based supervision, scheduling, and direction of the construction process. Depending on the ambulatory care center's needs, these services may include preconstruction cost estimating and construction planning services. The CM may provide some construction services directly or may subcontract some or all of the work. Through negotiation, the CM may be asked to provide a fixed price for the project at any stage of design, called a guaranteed maximum price (GMP) contract, which by definition include substantial design and construction contingencies.

Subcontractors

Trade contractors, usually working under the direction of a general contractor or CM, provide specific construction services, such as plumbing or electrical work, with bids based on detailed construction documents prepared by the architect. It is usually up to the general contractor or CM to schedule and coordinate their work, again prepared by the architect.

Design/Build Contractors

In order to meet some ambulatory care centers' needs for a simplified, single source of responsibility, design/build contractors provide construction management and design services as one package, usually through subcontractors. Architectural, interiors, and engineering services are provided and directed by the design/build (D/B) firm. The features of this approach are negotiated price and quality. When the D/B firm is responsible for a fixed price and content, it is also responsible for the design and quality decisions needed to meet that price.

Construction Delivery Methods

There are various approaches to how a business can elect to construct its clinical space. The best choice depends on how the ambulatory care center wants to finance construction.

Design/Bid/Build: The Traditional Approach

In the traditional model for building projects, the ambulatory care center selects all team members, including both the design and construction components. Architects, interior designers, and other consultants are selected and hired by the ambulatory care center. Once the ambulatory care center hires these consultants, it must manage all of them and the process. After a design and its construction documents have been developed by this team, and the design is complete, the final construction cost is fixed by multiple contractor bids on these specific design documents. The contractor bids are analyzed and generally the lowest bid that includes all of the specified scope of work is accepted. Because all of the team members work directly for the ambulatory care center, the project's design quality is determined by practice members, who approve the final design. Depending on the experience of the team and the clarity of the ambulatory care center's goals, the result can be a slower but more transparent process. In the end, all decisions are approved by the ambulatory care center, which also pays all of the costs of the project.

Design/Build Method

A contrasting approach is one in which a contractor assembles and controls all the members of a completely integrated team of designers and builders. The contractor offers to provide a facility to meet the ambulatory care center's stated needs, essentially as a "package deal," and to be the single point of contact to simplify the process. In this approach the ambulatory care center relinquishes some control of the design team, and to some extent the control over project quality, but has the benefit of having to deal with only one entity, the contractor. The package price is fixed by negotiation at any stage of design and can be a lump sum or "cost plus with savings returned" arrangement. To meet the agreed price, the contractor retains the design team, directs design choices, and sets the overall quality of the project. The design/build method is not as transparent to the ambulatory care center as the design/bid/build process because many of the design decisions are made internally between the contractor and the design team. If needs are clear and decisions can be made easily, this can be a faster process, but at the cost of reduced ambulatory care center input and control.

Programmatic Needs of an Ambulatory Care Center

Projecting Ambulatory Care Center Programming Needs

Facility planning for medical practices or clinics was once comparatively simple and formulaic. It was generally the rule that each physician would occupy a private office used for patient consultation and after-hours work, with one or more adjoining examination rooms. Highly productive physicians or nurse practitioners in certain specialties might have three or four exam rooms in their cluster of space. Office and exam space was often a function of rank or seniority and did not necessarily have any direct correlation to patient visit volume. The procedures that could be done in the office were comparatively minor, and it was impractical and too costly to have extensive diagnostic testing or imaging equipment beyond basic laboratory analyzers and X-ray capabilities.

The changing organization and economics of health care have made the highly efficient use of facilities much more critical, and accepted ambulatory care planning benchmark standards have evolved in the industry. These new standards reflect both a volume-driven programming method and the collective experience of major ambulatory care organizations. Instead of planning for the number of rooms based on old rules of thumb or anecdotal needs by individual practitioners, planning now starts with the idea that medical practice involves specific procedures that each have a well-defined space need and that when strategically grouped together in an ambulatory care center, a more comprehensive array of integrated services can be provided. Exam rooms, consulting rooms, testing, and procedure spaces each have specific equipment needs and minimum space requirements for their functions, often defined by regulation or clinical guidelines and protocols. Exam rooms, for example, are generally required to have a minimum clear floor area of 80 sq ft (7.43 square meters), including space for an exam table, hand-washing sink, and writing surface, at a minimum. As more equipment and technology is added to assist with care over time, the specialization and corresponding size of the common exam room has grown to 120 to 135 dgsf.

Physical Settings for Ambulatory Healthcare Services

The types and complexities of healthcare services that can be delivered outside a licensed hospital setting are regulated by building codes and the local state department of health. Basic medical services administered to patients in a typical business day, and thereby not requiring any kind of overnight hospitalization or accommodations, can normally be provided in a building type that is classified as, and designed as, office space. More complex outpatient treatments that might require sedation usually must be done in an ambulatory care center. The physical difference is subtle and pertains primarily to fire and life safety codes, travel distances, and whether patients are capable of self-preservation or are sedated or completely anesthetized for a procedure. By construction codes, ambulatory care centers allow for but limit the number of anesthetized patients in the facility at any one time. Ambulatory care centers can have extensive diagnostic and treatment services within them, much like hospitals; however, the specific services they provide are limited by their hours of operation and inability to accommodate overnight patients. For example, if the ambulatory care center includes an ambulatory surgery center, the surgical procedures provided will have to be limited to those where patients can recover without being admitted overnight.

Volume-Based Programming

Based on the organization and operational structure for the facility, the programming requirements can begin to be assessed. Programming is both an analytical and a conceptual process by which the functional and operational goals of the business are identified, defined, and quantified.

Some of the space requirements are derived from mathematical calculations using guidelines for utilization and volume projections, while others are based on the unique operational and staffing needs of the practice. This is one of the more important and complicated steps in the process because all design and budgeting parameters henceforth are derived from the program. Therefore, it is important to understand some of the key aspects of the complex process architects refer to as "programming."

Volume-based programming builds on these facts by taking into account the estimated practice volume and typical procedure times, which can vary substantially among different specialties. For example, to accommodate a projected 20,000 annual patient visits, key assumptions might be hours of operation (e.g., five days per week, 10 hours per day), typical visit time in the exam room (e.g., 30 minutes), and percentage of utilization for each room, to allow for patient turnover, cleaning, and staff downtime (e.g., 60%). With that set of beginning assumptions to test, the number of rooms needed would be:

- 5 days × 10 hours × 50 weeks/yr = 2500 hours available per room per year
- Utilization at 60% of available hours = 1500 utilized hours per year per room
- At 30 minutes per use, each room could accommodate 3000 annual visits
- 20,000 target annual visits/3000 = 6.66 rooms, or rounded, 7 exam rooms
- With 250 working days per year, each room would average 11, 30-minute visits per day if utilized at 60%

Although physicians may see 15 or 20 patients per session in bursts of activity, many academic medical centers find that actual visits average only six to eight per day, due to irregular patient scheduling, low utilization on certain afternoons, reduced operating hours, or use of exam rooms for nonessential purposes such as patient counseling or education, which could be done elsewhere in nonmedical spaces. Before creating more specialized and expensive space, attention to operational issues can help to ensure that the best use is made of capital investments.

Similar methods can be used to project space needs for other patient contact areas and for the support and staff work space required. Once the model is developed, different assumptions (Saturday hours, better utilization, faster visits, more volume) can be easily tested and their impact on space needs clearly seen. The basic model also assumes a fairly even flow of patients spread throughout the day. Block scheduling (having all patients report to the office at 9 A.M. or 1 P.M., for example) and allowable waiting time have a direct impact on the number of rooms needed to accommodate peaks of patient flow. So also does the decision to provide certain specialized services, such as EKG testing or nutrition counseling, only at certain times.

Programming Benchmark Standards

In its simplest and most logical terms, effective programming requires that you work through a projection of realistic space and facility needs based on the unique organization and operations of the practice. Some typical guidelines for very efficient primary care practices have been defined.

- 1.1 to 1.5 sq ft of gross practice space per HMO member served
- Three to four annual patient visits per gross square foot (33–44 visits per square meter)

- 2500 gross sq ft per full-time care provider or physician
- 4000 minimum annual visits per full-time provider (about 16 per day)
- Two to three exam spaces per full-time provider (usually for consultation also), depending on specialty
- Staff support of one RN per team and one medical assistant per two providers
- Six to eight exam room visits/day for academic medical centers

Modular Planning for Optimum Flexibility

Modular planning for flexibility is another key step in determining space needs. Because most ambulatory care centers or primary care centers have a number of individual providers or specialties who work at different times and may have very different patient volume, the most efficient facilities allow for flexible use of medical practice spaces at different times to optimize efficiency. If generic clinical spaces are provided and organized for varying uses, high-volume services such as internal medicine or cardiology might use four rooms for six half-day sessions per week, whereas a specialty such as dermatology might use one half-day session for a number of shorter patient visits.

To facilitate this kind of flexible use, exam/consult rooms are often organized in "pods," each with dedicated support spaces such as nurse work space, storage, and patient toilet. Each pod has a direct connection to the public zone (patient waiting and reception) and staff work areas (private offices, specialized procedure, and diagnostic testing areas), and clean and soiled work areas. Pods might range from four to eight exam rooms, so that a practice group could schedule, for example, 2.5 modules for five half-day sessions per week.

Efficient planning should also consider the need for basic small examination rooms, where most patient visits can be done, versus the need for a smaller number of larger procedure rooms to accommodate more specific treatments or equipment. Using procedure space for routine exam visits is both less intimate for patients and an inefficient use of space and equipment. Physician consult space needs to be provided, either as a defined area within the exam room or as a nearby shared space. The economic need for higher efficiency and physician productivity makes the more traditional use of a dedicated office consult before or after the exam visit a luxury of time and space.

Office Space Planning Trends

Office size standards in all industries have been trending toward smaller spaces, in response to cost pressures and also new uses of office areas. The traditional secretarial and private office spaces, furnished with large desks and credenzas with files, have given way to flexible modular clerical workstations, which provide more work surface and storage in a more ergonomically designed environment. Open or private offices with wall-mounted furniture systems and larger multifunction conference areas and spaces for collaboration are typical spaces needed to support the interactive and collaborative way some clinicians practice today. All work spaces are sized for computers and their accessories, such as printers and flat screens, with multiple data and telephone connections at each location for printers, scanners, etc.

Scheduled Use of Rooms

To make the most efficient use of valuable space, a trend is shared space for conference rooms, which can be scheduled by multiple users, and for shared support areas such as file rooms, work areas, and staff break rooms. "Hoteling" and shared-use offices are often provided for staff that may be at one location only part-time. Each generic work cubicle or private office has data and telephone connections to accommodate laptop computers, plus basic work and temporary file space. Typical net space allocations for office areas are:

Clerical workstation	48 sq ft (6 × 8)	workstation with computer and file storage
Clinical workstation	64 sq ft (8 × 8)	workstation with computer, storage, and guest chair
Private office	110 sq ft (10 × 11)	work space, files, guest chair
Senior staff office	150–180 sq ft (10 × 15+)	work and meeting areas
Executive office	180–240 sq ft (10 × 18+)	sofa, conference, work areas

Operational Considerations

Patient Flow and Program Spaces

While the inner operations of any ambulatory care center are unique to that business, there are typically strong similarities for how patients flow through and what clinical and support functions are required. Space planning or layout design for medical practice facilities starts with an analysis of patient circulation and work flow and its impact on adjacencies and design choices. A growing consideration is the marketing and brand identity of medical practice groups and the way that planning decisions can reinforce or subvert those marketing choices. Here are a number of typical room functions located in a typical ambulatory care center.

Patient/Public Entrance

The way that patients access and approach the practice should be visible, clear, and welcoming. Access should consider adequate parking and proximity to public transportation. The entrance space sets the image of the suite and is the first area the patient experiences. Clear signage, a convenient way of getting from the street to the front door, and a gracious entry are more welcoming and hospitable to patients and families and help provide a positive encounter. Simple architectural details such as a window or glass wall next to the entrance door, from the exterior, or from the corridor provides visibility and helps patients to confirm they are in the right place and that the practice is open.

Reception

From the moment the patient enters the practice, the receptionist should have clear visibility to the door, in order to visually acknowledge the patient's arrival. The functional goal should be a personal welcome from a caring member of the practice, not a window in a wall with a bell to call for assistance. Planners and designers need to consider this first encounter and design to make it a positive experience in a professional setting. Signage should be positive and friendly and kept to a minimum. Procedural rules and payment terms are not as welcoming and ideally should not be posted inside the initial encounter space. Reception work spaces say a lot about the practice, need to be low enough to accommodate a person in a wheelchair, and should be as open and welcoming as possible. The patient and family often enter with many questions and are looking for positive reinforcement, so the design emphasis should not be on shielding the staff from them and screening off working areas, but rather creating opportunities for them to engage the patients. Material quality conveys a visual sense of reassurance and professional quality as well.

Waiting Area

Once acknowledged, patients and their accompanying family members need a welcoming space, with comfortable and small-group seating. Because waiting time is typically limited, long-term comfort and a lounge feeling may not be appropriate. The seating itself needs to meet the needs of people who may be older, frail, and probably not feeling well and may need assistance in getting up or sitting down. For the elderly and infirm, seat height needs to be high, generally at least 18 inches, and seats need to be fairly firm, with fixed arms that can help someone settle into or rise out of a chair. Low, soft seating or chairs that can tip or tilt are very difficult for some people to use and can be uncomfortable. A mix of movable individual armchairs and small two-seat sofas offer a choice to the patient and their families as well as an inviting appearance. Two-seat sofas are ideal for two people or a parent and a child. Larger sofas tend to become the territory of only one or two persons and reduce the overall seating capacity of the room. Appropriate lighting levels and quality furniture that can be moved for small family groups make the space friendly, professional, and ultimately flexible.

Coat storage should be provided in the waiting room and should be both convenient and reasonably secure. For practices with business-oriented patients or long waiting times for accompanying family, such as in an oncology practice or a treatment facility, a commonly seen amenity is a work counter with electrical outlets for laptop computers, charging cell phones, Internet access, and often a small pantry or coffee hospitality bar. Computer access is ideal for a patient to fill out medical history online, to access patient educational materials, or to look at upcoming clinic-related activities and programs.

Whether to provide a television in the waiting area is a common question and depends on the image and character of the practice. Generally pediatric practices require several TVs and video game areas for different age groups, but adult practices may find TVs to be intrusive. The design question, as with the whole issue of waiting room style, is to match the expectations and comfort level of the target patient market, or provide a choice of smaller spaces in which to wait.

Appointments and Scheduling

Every practice needs an appointment desk, located conveniently to see patients on the way out of the office in a natural flow. This area should be distinct from the reception area, even if only at the other end of the same work counter and with acoustical separation. Departing patients need to be accommodated promptly, without waiting while new arrivals might have an extended conversation with the receptionist. Like the reception area, this function needs to accommodate wheelchair patients with a low counter area and convenient work space. Unlike the reception area, this function often requires some privacy to discuss billing instructions, insurance coverage, financial matters, and follow-up appointments.

Billing and Payments

Although routine payment arrangements can be processed at the appointment desk, more privacy is needed for payment arrangements. A small private office adjacent to the accounting area works well, with entrances from the patient corridor and from within the office suite. Acoustical privacy should be incorporated into the design of this area.

Medical Records

Although computerized record keeping is now part of almost every practice, the idea of paperless offices has proven to be a challenge. Patient records accumulate both paperwork from internal procedures and a variety of related records such as lab test results, images, and records from other providers outside the practice. Most large practices have found open-shelf filing to be the most flexible and efficient. Records storage space needs to be estimated based on average file size, volume of patients, and length of time records must be held in active storage before being archived elsewhere. Filing space is estimated based on typical folder thickness, which may be one inch for common practices or more for specialized, long-term care. Open shelf files more than seven shelves high can only be accessed with a step device or ladder, which creates a typical limit on shelf height. Open library-type shelving would require aisle space, but compacting shelving that rolls to create aisles only as needed would require less space. In addition to planning convenient file space adjacent to admitting and billing, the ambulatory care center administrator also needs to take note of the heavy weight of filing areas, especially if high-density files are stored in the upper floors of a building, because structural upgrades to the floor might be required

Staff Services

Staff Entrance

In even the smallest practice, if space allows, there should be a separate staff and physician entrance, not readily visible to patients. Patients who are waiting for their appointments are not likely to understand the normal comings and goings of staff during the day, especially if the physicians have to visit their patients in the hospital. Staff should have their own discreet entrance. Location and design of the staff entrance should consider a plan for security, both for the office and for staff entering and leaving. Good visibility, good lighting, and easy access to the street are all elements to consider.

Staff Break/Multipurpose Room

Because much of the staff may remain on-site all day, especially if the practice has evening hours with little opportunity to leave the office suite for breaks and usually no private work space for meals, a dedicated staff break room is a very useful space. The staff break room is a mixed-use space for people to take breaks and meals, and a common area to check e-mail and vendor presentations, all out of patient sight. With kitchen facilities and tables and chairs, the staff room can serve multiple purposes and may be the only area that can accommodate a large staff meeting. Consideration should also be given to lockers or other storage areas for personal items such as coats, uniforms, purses, and shoes for staff members who may have no other private storage areas or offices but need to secure their personal items.

Staff Work Areas

The staff members who support the clinical activities need individual work areas located close to patient care areas to minimize their own travel. Each location should provide needed supplies and computer work space, with the ability to sit down and record patient information. In most ambulatory care settings, what is needed are decentralized workstations in each pod or cluster, rather than a central nurse station or office arrangement typically seen in hospitals. Work spaces should be designed ergonomically for maximum comfort. Thoughtful planning of work spaces and their coverage of patient areas can help to minimize staffing needs by allowing staff in one location to supervise several patient areas.

Clinical Areas

Exam Rooms

The examination room is the most basic outpatient planning unit. Almost all primary care patient interactions occur within the exam room: interviews, consultations, examinations, minor treatments and procedures, follow-up, blood draw, and vitals. The overall throughput productivity and capacity of a practice comes down to how well the exam room is utilized; it's the basic building block of the business. The design of the exam room demands careful consideration and attention to detail. Well-designed exam rooms can pay dividends in both patient perceptions and operational efficiency.

Exam rooms, while typically modest in size, really have three discrete and overlapping zones: the family zone, the physician documentation/work zone, and the patient exam zone.

Patient and family space is the first requirement, with some privacy for changing clothes and provisions for accompanying family seating. The Mayo Clinic, for example, has developed a standard exam room that provides a built-in sofa for family seating, which can accommodate a varying number of people and provides a welcoming, noninstitutional look to the room. Clothing hooks, shelves for clean gowns, and privacy curtains are all useful, depending on patient type and the proposed use of the room.

A place for the physician to write or dictate notes should occur in a separate zone within this room, preferably arranged to allow the physician to be face to face with the patient as he or she charts. The charting area requires a computer workstation, probably with a printer, plus telephone, paper and supply storage, reference literature or pamphlets, chairs for the patient and a family member, and an office chair or stool for the physician.

Examination space should be arranged with recognition that many physicians are trained to work from the right-hand side of the patient, with the patient's head to their left. The physician should be able to stand at the table, out of the swing of the door. The patient's lower body should be oriented away from the door, to provide extra privacy, especially in rooms used for gynecological exams. Privacy issues, and especially the feeling of privacy, are very important in the patient's perception of the quality of the service provided. In some layouts, cubicle curtains can help define the patient territory, and an alternative in very small rooms is to reverse the door swing to shield views, by having the door open toward the table rather than back against the wall.

The exam table may be fixed or adjustable, powered or manual, but should be standardized throughout the practice as much as possible. Wall-mounted diagnostic instrument sets, with oto/ophthalmoscope and blood pressure cuff, if used, are often located on the wall behind the exam table, with a nearby electrical outlet for the rechargeable battery. Fluorescent room lighting is usually adequate, but some specialties may require portable or fixed procedure lights. Incandescent lighting can provide a less institutional feel, but is less efficient than fluorescent fixtures.

For maximum provider productivity and interchangeable use of rooms, highly efficient designs include one room type, with all exam rooms essentially the same, from general layout down to the location of supplies and details of the rooms. Having identical rooms may be more useful over the long term than the construction economy of having left- and right-handed rooms to allow sink plumbing to be shared, because standardization of physical components for frequent tasks helps to minimize operational variabilities which can result in increased efficiencies. In other words, if the alcohol and cotton swabs are in the same drawers in every exam room, then the staff will spend less time looking for these items over the course of the day. All of the rooms should have doors and exam tables in the same relationship, and all should have equal work spaces, storage areas, and similar finishes.

Designers should work closely with the physician group on the development of the design for this room, which is where they will spend most of their working hours over the years and generate most of the practice income. For larger projects, it is often helpful to construct one full-size room mock-up early in the process to fine-tune these issues.

Nurse Work Space

The nurse or assistant work area usually serves a group of exam/procedure rooms, and often a communication or visual signal system is used to keep the process moving. Some practices use systems of colored lights or signage flags outside exam rooms to indicate to nurses and physicians when patients are in the room or ready for a specific procedure. The work area needs a computer, telephone fax machine, and printer, because staff cannot easily leave to go to a central location for this equipment. Storage for medications and clean supplies should be provided very close to the work area.

Procedure Rooms

In addition to basic exam rooms, a practice often includes larger rooms for special purposes, such as minor surgery, endoscopy, or orthopedics. Determining space and planning needs for these rooms starts with considering what equipment will be used. Will procedures require a typical exam table, a procedure stretcher, or a special unit, such as an ENT/dental chair? Is specialized procedure lighting required, and if so, will it be portable, ceiling-, or wall-mounted? Is it a medical equipment item or part of the general lighting provided in the building? Sinks and cabinets may be needed, and for some rooms a specific location, type, and size of sink may be needed, with or without special hands-free controls. Special finishes, such as provisions for wet areas, seamless flooring, washable walls, or a cleanable ceiling may be needed. Some rooms, such as endoscopy suites, may require specific storage cabinets for items such as long scopes and carrying cases and may have very specific size and construction requirements and need adjoining utility and cleanup spaces, with specialized equipment.

Diagnostic Imaging Suites

Diagnostic imaging is part of many practices and has its own set of very specific space-planning considerations, starting with patient waiting and dressing areas and gowned waiting space.

X-Ray Rooms

Digital imaging has rapidly become the technology of choice for almost all types of imaging, because it offers greater flexibility, allows remote sharing of images, and eliminates darkrooms and reduces film or image file space. Typical modalities include radiography, fluoroscopy, chest X-ray, and mammography. Processing and reading areas are required, whether or not a digital system is used. This central technician work area includes digital film printers, X-ray processor for film, view boxes for films, and picture archiving and communication system (PACS) terminals for viewing digitized images.

For all of these imaging functions, radiation shielding design issues include lead-lined wall partitions, doors, and leaded glass view windows. The thickness and extent of shielding required is based on a calculation by a consulting radiation physicist, usually retained by the ambulatory care center. Detailed design of the imaging rooms relies on specific layouts provided by the equipment vendor for use by the design team; equipment is installed only after the general construction work is complete.

Computed Tomography (CT) Scan

Similar to other diagnostic imaging rooms, computerized tomography (CT) scanners have unique planning requirements. Space and planning issues include the large size of the gantry and table unit, its weight, and its orientation. As patients on the table are positioned in the doughnut-shaped gantry for an X-ray cross-section of their body, it is important for the technician in the adjoining control room to be able to look down the bore of the machine, to keep the patient in sight. Access to the unit for servicing requires space around it, and a separate adjoining room is usually required to house the electronics cabinets for the equipment. A dedicated refrigeration unit provides additional cooling for the gantry. Lead shielding is required because X-ray radiation is used. The lead shielding is based on specific radiation physicist calculations.

Magnetic Resonance Imaging (MRI)

Magnetic resonance imaging (MRI) machines combine radio waves in a strong magnetic field to produce cross-sectional images that can show more detail of soft tissue than other imaging methods. Although no X-rays are used, and lead shielding is not required, the special nature of these units requires both radio frequency (RF) shielding to screen out other signals and often magnetic shielding to contain the strong magnetic field. The heart of the system is a very large and heavy doughnut-shaped, superconductive electromagnet that is cooled internally with liquid helium.

The magnetic field, even while contained within the room, presents special dangers from loose ferrous metal objects. The strength of the magnetic field can erase magnetic media, such as credit cards and ID badges. Safety protocols impose specific space-planning requirements for safety zones around the unit, which are under the control of the technical staff and can exclude dangerous, noncompatible objects and equipment. Within the safety zone, all equipment and construction must be nonferrous, including items such as stretchers, tools, and oxygen tanks. If the MRI system is turned off ("quenched") suddenly, the helium can absorb the heat and boil off as a gas and must therefore be vented through a large vent pipe to a safe area outside the building. Because of the weight of the magnet, often about seven tons, and its sensitivity to vibration, it requires special structural engineering design and a structural analysis of how to move it into and out of the space. Exterior access must be considered for the future, when outdated equipment will need to be replaced, and many layouts provide removable wall or roof panels to accommodate this. Like the CT suite, the MRI requires an adjacent control room and electronic equipment room, plus its own patient holding and stretcher transfer spaces within the controlled zone.

Ultrasound

Unlike other common imaging modalities, ultrasound diagnostic or procedure/biopsy rooms use portable equipment and require no room shielding. The equipment itself is a large, bulky cart, which needs to be positioned alongside an exam table. A work space in the same room is needed for technician charting, and the room needs to be large enough to accommodate seated family members.

Special Testing Suites

DOPPLER ULTRASOUND FOR ECHOCARDIOLOGY

Similar to ultrasound technology often used for prenatal testing, Doppler ultrasound uses large but portable equipment for post-stroke testing. Results are monitored on video and often videotaped for review later.

STRESS TESTING/TREADMILLS

In addition to a treadmill, space is needed for the computer system and EKG that monitors the patient's response and charts the result. In the same room, a work counter and exam table are needed. The treadmill itself is a heavy-duty, commercial-grade type that may require special electrical service.

Nuclear Medicine

Nuclear studies use radioactive isotopes and monitor their absorption and distribution within the body by placing the patient in a large gamma camera, similar in size to an X-ray machine. Depending on the type and amount of isotope to be used, lead shielding of the room may be required. Nearby space is needed for a "hot lab," where isotopes are stored and prepared; a "hot injection" area, where isotopes are administered to patients; and a gowned waiting area for patients who have been injected. These areas may also need to be shielded, and the "hot lab" itself needs special finishes and equipment, such as stainless steel counters and lead-lined storage cabinets.

Laboratories

Advances in automated clinical laboratory equipment, such as chemistry analyzers, have allowed laboratories to be faster, more automated, and to employ fewer people and thus be less costly. Remote centralized laboratories are far more cost-efficient, because they can also be linked to the ambulatory care center and provide a digital medical record. Instead of the traditional chemistry lab look, the facility is now a flexible environment for larger electronic instruments, with flexible utilities and supply storage instead of lab workbenches and cabinets.

Planning Typologies and the Clinical Environment

The unique programmatic and operational needs will vary among clinical practices within an ambulatory care center. Here are just some sample questions that demonstrate some of the operational variability of any ambulatory care center:

- Will the ambulatory care center have a central patient reception/information desk in a main lobby for all patients as well as decentralized departmental-specific reception desks to receive patients at individual clinical departments? Will waiting, registration, and other administrative functions also be centralized or decentralized?
- Are any clinical services affiliated with functions at an acute care facility? If so, how might the functions provide coordinated and convenient service to the patient?
- What are the hours of operation? For the entire center? For specific clinical services? Will the clinical program require late evening hours? For example, if the ambulatory care center includes an ambulatory surgery program component, will two staff shifts be required in order to receive preoperative patients in the early morning, yet remain open so that afternoon surgical cases can recover without the patient needing to be admitted to an acute care facility for recovery?
- Logistically, will the ambulatory care center purchase and receive supplies centrally and then be distributed by a paid staff? Or will individual supplies be purchased, tracked, and received by individual practices within the ambulatory care center?
- How many access points to the facility are needed? Exit points? Will there be a dedicated patient discharge lobby for patients recovering from surgery and waiting for transportation home? What are the security implications from the access points?

- Are there any electronic systems that will help move patients through the facility? For example, electronic appointment making?
- Will there be any medical education or teaching components anticipated?
- Will the ambulatory care center be connected to an acute care hospital? If so, will there be dedicated connection corridors to allow for supplies and services to flow between the hospital and the ambulatory care center as well as corridors for patient flow? If not, will the ambulatory care center be near an acute care facility? How will patient transportation be handled between the two if the ambulatory care center requires acute care backup?

These are just a few samples of the in-depth questions that need to be asked when structuring the physical typology of an ambulatory care center. Questions such as these help determine how the overall ambulatory care center will operate and how the various clinical, administrative, and support functions will interact and coordinate.

Patient Registration—Centralized Versus Decentralized

Perhaps one of the more perplexing and challenging operational considerations to handle effectively in a large ambulatory care center is that of centralized or decentralized administrative functions. The ambulatory care center should function as a coordinated and integrated system of ambulatory clinical services, much like a hospital, but without the inpatient bed component. Ideally, the administrative systems are integrated and coordinated so that the patient experience is convenient, simple, well coordinated, compact, and efficient. The larger the ambulatory care center gets, the more challenging this becomes, especially if the ambulatory care center is on multiple floors of a building. One method to ensure complete coordination of the patient experience through the facility and, in fact, through the system, is to carefully construct the administrative interaction points in order to keep the flow of patients consistent, simple, and steady.

A centralized patient registration/check-in/check-out/payment/financial counseling/scheduling function for an ambulatory care center with diverse medical departments requires a large number of administrative staff to provide all of these services in a coordinated, efficient way. The check-in process normally requires patients to provide updated background information, medical history, verify their insurance coverage, pay co-pays, and more upon entering the ambulatory care center. If all patients must go though this process, either it results in a huge patient flow logjam or, to keep it flowing, it requires more staff to keep up with the flow. The best answer is usually a combination of the two, but either way, it can require substantial space.

If all the multiple services and clinical departments make use of the centralized administrative receiving and check-out points, instead of duplicating this function within their own departments, it can save space and overhead full-time employee positions and make the overall ambulatory care center more operationally efficient. An effective way to ensure all the miscellaneous administrative functions that a patient/visitor must experience during their visit to the ambulatory care center is with a traditional flow chart diagram. Each step and each potential procedural scenario for the patient must be anticipated in order to ensure that space and staff are planned to facilitate a smooth, uninterrupted, and linear flow. If the ambulatory care center is geared toward the patient as the customer, a more patient-focused approach will ensure maximum convenience for the patient through all these processes, meaning that whenever possible, the services are either brought to the patient or are at least collocated so the patient can get all these various administrative functions completed in one location without having to be sent to other locations, which is not a patient satisfier.

Clinical Planning Typologies

There are various methods for arranging clinical spaces in an outpatient setting, each in response to operational models, as well as personal preferences. The most common and basic planning unit for outpatient clinical services is the common exam room. Exam rooms range in size from a small code minimum of 80 net square feet up to 135 nsf; their size depends on the type of practice that will use it and the processes and equipment the room is to accommodate. Let's review a few ways to organize exam rooms and their support functions for comparative purposes.

Finger Corridors

A basic, flexible, and efficient layout of exam rooms is the finger corridor where parallel corridors of exam rooms are arranged next to each other. Generally the waiting and administrative functions are at the front of the department, and the finger corridors extend away from the administrative areas, which provides visibility down the corridors to see the exam room doors and the room status indicator lights projecting slightly from the walls, indicating whether the room is in use or not. Toward the far end of the exam room corridors is normally a band of support functions, the physician office or internal administrative functions. This "layering" of spaces allows for a transition of spaces from public to semipublic to private. Exterior windows at the end of the corridors is an effective way to allow natural daylight into the clinical corridor and a sense of daytime orientation. The real advantage of the exam room finger corridors is that it allows the exam rooms in adjacent corridors to be used for spillover if volumes require, without changing the staffing needs. In addition, the plan can be readily converted to other clinical departments or even office space with little remodeling required.

Exam Room Pods

Another arrangement of exam rooms is the cluster or "pod" whereby four to eight exam rooms are clustered around a dedicated subwaiting room and staff support functions. It is normally accessed by a single door, creating a suite. The pod concept lends itself to teams of clinicians who operate out of a pod or two and who have their own dedicated nursing or technician staff, as well as administrative staff, all working within the exam room pod. While this configuration may allow for a more intimate and private setting for patient care, it also tends to separate the clinical and administrative staff and can result in the duplication of services, thus creating some level of inefficiency. In addition, the exam room pod configuration prevents visibility from a central location of whether the exam rooms are occupied or need service. The pod configuration normally does not provide the needed flexibility to adjust to volume variations as well as finger corridors and sometimes requires the staffing of an adjacent pod of exam rooms even when there may be only one patient in there.

Ballroom

A variation on the exam room cluster or pod is the ballroom model, which can be used when all the exam rooms for a particular medical specialty are collocated and wrapped around the perimeter of a shared waiting room. This model is a self-contained ambulatory department and can include reception/registration, waiting seating, public toilets, and clinical support space, although support functions are usually not accessible from the waiting areas. While this model provides clinical autonomy for the specialty and allows visibility of the exam rooms for managing patient flow, it does not provide for privacy in and out of the exam rooms. This type of configuration is more commonly found in the planning of emergency departments, where the visibility and movement of patients of all types through the clinical space based on an unpredictable intake is the priority.

Shared Support Functions

Similar to the shared administrative functions of a centralized reception area, a well-planned and efficient ambulatory care center might want to consider having "institutional support functions" distributed throughout the building. Institutional support functions include staff lounge/break room, staff conference room, staff multipurpose room/library/education, staff locker rooms, showers, and toilets, as well as larger subdividable conference rooms with some amount of breakout space outside them for handling refreshments. Institutional spaces are meant to be shared, and conference/classroom functions are reserved via a scheduling mechanism. When these spaces are combined and shared, they can be larger and can offer more amenities for more people. This model is in contrast to having decentralized and dedicated staff break rooms and locker rooms closer to each department.

The Clinical Neighborhood Model

As ambulatory care centers become more sophisticated and provide more hospital-like services, they are increasingly as functional as full-service hospitals, minus the overnight patient capability, which is restricted by code. As these practice group types become more specialized, thus creating multiple patient access points throughout the facility, they are also starting to become increasingly more integrated in order to optimize clinical and operational efficiencies. Fewer access points for specialized care and one-stop health care are more patient-friendly and simple. The clinical neighborhood model emerged and grouped clinical services around diseases, with the simple objective of collocating all the related services a patient suffering from a particular illness or condition might need throughout their path to wellness. For example, instead of having separate clinical departments for orthopedics, physical and/or occupational therapy, spine and back care, hand surgery, and imaging, each with their own support functions and "front door," the clinical neighborhood model groups all these related and similar services into the "musculoskeletal neighborhood." Now a patient with any one of these ailments can go the musculoskeletal neighborhood and receive all the clinical consultation, treatment, and care they might need within the neighborhood.

The neighborhood model can incorporate the models of shared institutional support functions, as well as centralized or quasi-centralized reception/check-in functions. This model is particularly effective when the ambulatory care center is affiliated with an academic medical center because additional specialties can be incorporated into the continuum of care of the neighborhood, but also because clinical research can be conducted on a broader set of related disciplines.

Planning for Future Growth and Change

Ambulatory care center facilities, even more so than hospitals, are faced with a lack of data for reliable long-term planning. Although the aging of the population can be predicted to an extent, changing practice approaches, new technology, and new ways of paying for services make predicting the future difficult. Often the only safe assumption is that over the life of the facility the practice will evolve, but in ways that cannot be predicted with certainty. Changes in technology and reimbursement cause frequent changes in facilities, as services and specialty staff are added or discontinued, and as the patterns of patient flow change. Because the ambulatory care center administrator can never really know what lies ahead, the best planning response is to think in terms of maximum flexibility at reasonable cost, rather than a plan that exactly reflects the practice as it exists now. Assume that staff, operations, and equipment will change, and plan accordingly.

Flexible future planning starts with floor area size; larger, rectilinear floors are easier to configure in different ways than unusual shapes or narrow wings. Higher floor-to-floor heights offer more flexibility for changing building services such as air-conditioning. Lay-in acoustical tile ceilings are common, largely because they provide a high degree of future flexibility as compared to more architectural ceilings. Electrical and data/telecommunications services can be routed through the flexible ceiling, Multiple vertical risers are needed throughout the space to provide some level of flexibility in the location of plumbing fixtures.

Sometimes a flexible planning approach is to provide generically equipped rooms of similar sizes, so that exam rooms can serve different specialties as needed, and office, consult, exam, and procedure functions can be interchanged later. Designers work by looking for relationships and evolving models, so the challenge is to look beyond current practice because a new facility should offer more potential arrangements rather than reflect the old model.

The Quality of the Interior Environment

The ambulatory care center administrator needs to be aware of some of the more technical details that will be handled directly by the design team, but require input and decisions by the administrator and facility users, such as final materials and finish selections.

Interior Materials and Finishes

The selection of materials and visible finishes is an important part of reducing operating costs and representing the desired brand identity of the ambulatory care center. The look and feel of the built space should convey and reinforce the desired image or branding characteristics of the practice, whether the image wants to say traditional, conservative, modern, cutting edge, comforting, warm, reassuring, clearly organized, or technologically advanced. The choice of materials can also be a trade-off between durability and flexibility, and first cost versus life-cycle cost. Lighter materials, such as drywall construction and acoustical tile ceilings, offer a high degree of flexibility and are relatively easy to change or replace when needed—even if finish materials are more elaborate, such as wood paneling or special finishes. Heavier construction, such as masonry, plaster, and terrazzo, is considerably more durable but more difficult to change and sometimes impossible to reuse when functional needs change.

The choice of finish materials is a balance between the desired appearance and the realities of maintenance. Commercial facilities such as hotels and stores often plan for more extensive continued cleaning and maintenance and more frequent replacements of damaged material than is typical for medical practices. Delicate or easily soiled materials that are not well maintained are less attractive than simpler materials that can be kept clean and presentable. Designers generally are well aware of the limitations and maintenance needs of materials, but must be apprised of the anticipated cleaning and maintenance services in order to select the appropriate materials.

Maintenance Issues

Commercial-grade carpet and upholstery fabrics, for example, are designed to be durable even when subjected to heavy wear and are easier to maintain, but will still require prompt attention to spills and stains. If the facility operator or maintenance service contract is not able to provide this level of attention, more durable materials should be appropriate.

In areas subject to spills and liquids and bodily fluids, water-repellant and waterproof, resilient, and easily cleaned materials are recommended. In addition to a careful choice of materials, the space-planning process also needs to consider convenient space for housekeeping and maintenance equipment. Equipment such as vacuums and floor polishers should be stored near the point of use.

In addition to cleaning, consider the maintenance issues of items such as lamp replacements for light fixtures, design of ventilation and plumbing systems to minimize ongoing maintenance, and the durability of surfaces and their ease of repair. Painted walls and doors are easily damaged, but can be repainted with little effort and expense. Wall covering is more durable than paint, but when it gets damaged it costs more to repair or replace. Wood surfaces can be scratched and scarred, but also sanded and refinished. Plastic laminate, once chipped, cannot be fixed. Finishes and materials should be carefully selected to provide the desired high-quality appearance in select areas of the office suite, and more durable, lower maintenance materials in the more utilitarian, heavy work spaces. The challenge is when a space is both for patients and a work space such as an exam room. Here the choice of materials must be weighed against patient appeal and durability.

Millwork and Casework

A common feature of most medical space is the standard use of built-in cabinetry (architectural millwork or casework), which often becomes one of the larger cost items. Millwork is generally custom-made for a facility and might include special paneling, woodwork, reception desks, or custom doors. Casework, in comparison, is a system of cabinets and counters, which may be entirely custom-made or selected from a vendor's standard cabinet components and countertops. Millwork can be constructed of many materials, but most commonly of wood, particleboard, plastic laminate, glass, metal, stone, solid surface (such as Corian as a name brand), or other materials, depending on the design intent. Casework, by contrast, is most often made of plastic laminate on particleboard, but can also be made of wood or metal.

Because millwork and casework are both expensive and space-consuming, one approach for the ambulatory care center administrator is to start the plan with little or no casework and adding it only as needed for specific uses. Although many areas such as exam rooms do require work counters, sinks, and storage immediately, the amount of casework needed may be less than expected. Current standards, for example, require sinks accessible to the physically challenged with no storage below, so the traditional sink base cabinet has been replaced by an apron panel to conceal plumbing but allow maintenance or, alternatively, a wall-hung sink with no cabinet below. More wall space is needed above and around sinks for accessories such as soap and towel dispensers, sharps disposal containers, and glove dispensers.

Accommodating all these items results in less space and less need for wall-hung cabinets. Some practices may choose to use mobile carts for supply storage instead of built-in cabinets. The carts can be a flexible way to restock supplies and provide a mobile work surface in an exam or treatment space. Sometimes spaces are more flexible and optimized when less specificity is built in and more functions are accommodated on mobile carts. Often times, cabinetry storage is either overdesigned or underdesigned. For instance, below-counter storage is typically underutilized because it is not convenient or ergonomic to use for frequently needed items. It sometimes results in the unnecessary and expensive hoarding of supplies, simply because the space is available. Where substantial storage is needed, as in procedure rooms, clean supply rooms, or workrooms, more expensive but highly adaptable and mobile storage systems can be more effective than the usual casework or built-in shelves.

Lighting

Natural lighting is often preferred by patient and staff for all the positive physiologic effects it offers to one's psychological outlook and mood. Whenever natural light cannot be achieved, artificial lighting and how it is designed becomes an important factor in any well-designed space that affects both the function and the ambiance. Specialized lighting may be needed in certain procedure areas, but often portable lamps are as effective as more expensive built-in lights. Large-scale procedure or surgical lights require specific structural design to provide heavy-duty mountings above the ceiling. In exam and general areas, current designs often use inexpensive direct/indirect fluorescent lighting in lay-in acoustic tile ceilings, which creates attractive lighting while still providing a high level of light. Additional task lighting under upper storage cabinets or above a hand-washing sink may also be welcoming. In waiting and public areas, lower levels and indirect light may be more appropriate. Low-voltage halogen lighting is useful for accents, displays, or artwork.

Plumbing Fixtures

Some medical areas may have specific requirements for hands-free fixtures at hand-washing locations where invasive procedures are performed and sterile environments are required. These special fixtures can be either wrist blades or infrared electronic faucet controls. Foot or knee controls tend to have higher maintenance and cleaning issues and are usually avoided. Details such as faucet spout heights, size and depth of sinks, and special equipment requirements all need to be coordinated between users and designers. Sinks in specialized areas, such as plaster work and darkrooms, may need specific traps to screen out plaster or chemicals. Wall-mounted plumbing fixtures are typically easier to clean around but require provision of steel carrier frames inside the walls during construction. Floor-mounted fixtures are simpler but may be an effort to clean.

Codes and Standards

Healthcare facilities, more so than most buildings, need to meet very specific governmental or regulatory requirements in their facilities and their operations. One of the architect's or designer's important legal responsibilities is to understand these code requirements and create designs that will be code compliant, if properly constructed by the contractor and maintained by the ambulatory care center.

Guidelines for Health Care

One of the most comprehensive and easily accessible references for medical facility requirements is the publication *Guidelines for Design and Construction of Hospital and Health Care Facilities*, produced by the Facilities Guidelines Institute with assistance from the American Institute of Architects and the US Department of Health and Human Services (HHS). The HHS finances and regulates medical practice. As the latest edition of the general standards first published by the federal government in 1947, the *Guidelines* book has become the established minimum national standard for medical facilities. As a guideline, not a prescriptive code; it is one of the reference standards for organizations such as the Health Care Financing Authority (HCFA), which provides Medicare/Medicaid funding for services and the Joint Committee on Accreditation of Healthcare Organizations (JCAHO), which accredits hospital-based services. Many, but not all, states have adopted a specific edition of the *Guidelines* as their state code for health facilities. It is important to point out that the *Guidelines* outline minimal standards for safety and operations, not optimum planning parameters. In different sections, the *Guidelines* publication sets out requirements for primary care and ambulatory care services, as well as hospital, nursing home, rehabilitation, and mental health facilities.

Local Codes

Practice managers must be familiar with health codes in the city in which they are located, which may include city, county, and/or state codes. Some of these codes are oriented more to the operational requirements for medical practice, and some have specific physical requirements (such as minimum room sizes, locations for hand-washing sinks, or limitations on exiting and safety requirements). Often, local codes will cross-reference national standards such as the *Guidelines* or the Life Safety Code (NFPA 101), published by the National Fire Protection Association. The design team should be familiar with what the local codes are. Some states or jurisdictions also have their own codes for accessibility, which may exceed the requirements of the ADA.

Building Codes—Business Use

Each locality also has its own regulations for building construction and use, which must be met along with the health-related codes. Building functions are often designated by use groups, each with a range of permitted functions or services. In most areas, basic group medical practice functions fall under a "business" use, assuming no patients are kept overnight or are incapacitated by use of anesthetics or other means. More extensive services would fall under ambulatory care or outpatient hospital or institutional use, with more stringent standards for construction and fire protection. An important factor to analyze in this regard is the special requirements imposed if ambulatory care services are provided by a hospital or licensed entity at an off-site location. In some cases, to be reimbursed as hospital-provided services, the facilities need to meet the higher standard for hospital outpatient services, which may require more specialized air-conditioning, ventilation, fire protection, or emergency power requirements than are typically found in a business-use facility.

Health and Safety Issues

Medical facility space planning includes an awareness of health issues that could affect patients and staff. In addition to the basic safety regulations, most notably the Life Safety Code (National Fire Protection Agency, NFPA101), other environmental regulations include OSHA workplace requirements and the removal of hazardous material. Renovation of existing facilities may require a specialized hazardous materials consultant to survey and test for the presence of hazardous items such as lead paint or asbestos-containing materials that may not be visible or apparent. If found, these materials all require a specific treatment plan, which could range from permanent encapsulation in a covering material to removal under highly controlled conditions and disposal in a hazardous materials landfill. The removal process requires temporary enclosures, special air handling, and the use of licensed contractors to remove materials according to a plan approved by local authorities having jurisdiction.

When construction of an office suite takes place adjacent to other suites, or renovation is done inside an office suite, careful precautions must be taken to isolate and control construction dust, debris, and whenever possible, noise. Often a contractor will wall off a construction area with temporary partitions or wrap the area in heavy plastic to curtain dust and dirt. If there are no operable windows in the office suite, a mechanical system is moving and filtering all the interior air. Containing the dust is important so that it doesn't get caught up in the ventilation system and potentially recirculated throughout the suite.

Accommodating Disabilities

Access for disabled users is required by the Americans with Disabilities Act (ADA), which is a civil rights law rather than a code or regulation. ADA requires that facilities make provisions to accommodate both patients and staff who may be disabled and allows those users to sue the facility owner if access is not provided. Designers are generally familiar with the details required to comply with ADA. The effect of this set of regulations has been to require more space in healthcare facilities. Corridors are wider, there is more space around doors, accessible toilets and showers are more generous, and rooms become larger to allow for wheelchair access. Small, tight plans with narrow passages and sliding doors are no longer allowed. Simpler, smoother-flowing plans with more generous space are required. Changes in floor levels require more space for ramps or wheelchair lifts, and even a step or two up to a staff work area requires a ramp and railing; sections of counters and reception desks and windows are lower, whereas sinks and other items may be higher to allow for wheelchair access under the sink. Doors are wider and may require power operators. All of these changes are generally an improvement, but many require more space and additional cost to implement.

Cost and Quality

All facilities' design and construction decisions have an impact on time (to design and construct), cost (capital, operations, and maintenance), and quality (durability and image). The preferred solution is a balance of these issues, which lies somewhere in the middle. Shortening construction time limits material choices and leads to increased labor costs to meet deadlines; higher design quality and better materials often (but not always) tend to increase first costs and may or may not reduce future maintenance costs.

In considering the cost and quality issues of traditional methods versus a design/build arrangement, there is an important link between the decision-making role and the final cost and quality. One of the realities of the design and construction process is that in the end the facility owner is the only party who will pay for the result, in terms of both capital and maintenance, regardless of the form of contract used. Making a designer or builder responsible for meeting a set cost requires making them the final arbiters of overall quality; trying to enforce a promise of high quality in one area will lead to less visible cuts in others, if the overall cost is fixed. As the representative of the ambulatory care center, the administrator should be looking for a clearly articulated balance of cost and quality for decision making, not a reliance on assumptions, promises, and guarantees.

The two most immediate concerns for the practice manager undertaking a facility project are control of the cost and time for the project. Because design and construction time is largely a reflection of the complexity of the project and the clarity of the process, the budget is the key starting point to establish a plan and to use as a tool for maintaining control.

Budget

Casual discussion often involves the budget as a general statement, but it is critical for the ambulatory care center to define terms and be very specific, because the "construction budget" often referred to by team members is in fact only a small part of the total eventual cost of the facility project. Although the construction cost is clearly the cost of constructing the design, consider also the other elements required:

Overall Project Budget Items

- Land acquisition cost includes both the purchase price of the land for a new building or the purchase of an existing building for renovation and also all of the associated real estate transaction costs, such as broker fees, boundary survey, transfer taxes, closing costs, and the like.

- Soft costs are the costs incurred by the owner of the project, such as leasing costs, legal fees, local and state government application and approval fees, taxes, consultants, brokers, advisors, and the internal labor and overhead costs of the facility-planning effort itself. An important component of this item can be salary costs for the ambulatory care center staff who are spending time to organize and manage the project, which should properly be considered part of its cost.

- Fees include the design team (architect, interior designer, consulting engineers) and also other potential consultants: elevator design, signage, furniture, artwork, materials handling, data network, equipment planning, space programming, and many others.

- Equipment cost includes both the medical equipment needed to operate the facility (such as exam tables, X-ray equipment, instruments, and supplies) but also the general office equipment (copy machines, computer system, telephone system, maintenance equipment).

- Furnishings are the loose items that are not equipment—not only desks and chairs, but office accessories, plants, artwork, wastebaskets, and shelving. If not selected by the medical equipment consultant or interior designer, all of this will require the practice's staff time to select, specify, purchase, receive, assemble, and put in place.

- Ambulatory care center testing costs include information needed for the design team, such as site topographic survey, subsurface investigations and geotechnical consulting, hazardous material surveys (and remediation costs), air- and water-quality testing, hydrology studies in flood areas, and quality testing during construction for materials such as concrete and welded steel.

- Moving costs include not only packing, shipping, and unpacking but also consulting fees to help plan a complicated move. If phased occupancy is needed, moving costs might also include temporary swing space or temporary utility services.

Construction Cost Factors

When professional estimators or construction managers offer projected construction costs, they take into account a number of factors beyond simply the design shown in the documents provided to them:

- Size of the project can impact overall costs. A small project will still have contractor mobilization, overhead expenses, and site general conditions (such as protection, cleanup, and temporary office space) that must be applied to the project. These costs are not related to the area constructed but rather to the length of time the construction goes on. For a large project, these costs are a lower proportion of the total cost.

- Quality level of the project, besides being reflected in the cost of materials, also has other implications. The use of costly or unusual materials or systems requires more supervision time and probably more rework to correct errors in the field. Very high standards of workmanship, if required by the designer, can also increase overall costs for supervision and coordination. Are sprinkler heads required to be centered in ceiling tiles exactly, or not? These quality assumptions invite the contractor to budget more effort.

- Complexity of planning and design reflects in the contractor's assumptions about productivity and time to build the project. Relatively simple, independent, or repetitive identical components are easier to build than complex assemblies of many different items. A free-standing, easily accessible project site is easier and less costly to build than one with limited contractor access and restricted work hours.

- Phasing of the project can multiply cost assumptions, because each construction phase needs more supervision and requires trade contractors, such as electricians and plumbers, to return several times. Each distinct phase requires inspections and approvals before moving on to the next.

- Schedule flexibility also impacts on overall cost. Are there outside schedule constraints and specific dates at which things must be complete? Is timing of the work limited, for example, to only weekends or after hours?

- Access and staging also complicate the process. Work in existing buildings requires dust-control partitions, security, protection of elevators, and accommodating existing users' schedules. Difficult or complex access from truck-loading areas, or temporary staging of materials in some other area, adds to costs. Construction work in congested urban areas tends to be more expensive due to lack of space for receiving and staging construction materials.

Financing Ambulatory Care Center Facilities

Ambulatory care center facilities are usually financed under some form of developer model, with either an external developer providing some or all of the services or the group itself acting as developer. Even when the facility is associated with a larger healthcare provider, the provider will often look to a developer for the financing in order to preserve its own resources for other programs, typically in acute care.

When an external developer is involved, they can function either in a traditional developer role or in a build/operate role. In the former, the developer will secure project financing, develop the building, and then lease the facility to the group. In the build/operate model, the developer retains a more active long-term role, operating the facility on behalf of the group. This could be just operating the physical plant, but more often includes provision of some functional services, such as reception and the like. There are many developers who have established a specialism in the ambulatory care center and medical facility field for this very reason.

The advantage of having a developer in the project, whether traditional or build/operate, is that they can deal with many of the complexities around development and finance and free the group to focus on healthcare delivery. The main disadvantage is that the developer needs to be rewarded for its contribution, and the costs to the group, in the longer term, can be higher.

When a group acts as its own developer, it must bring the same level of expertise to the table as an independent developer. There is significantly more to developing an ambulatory care center facility than a conventional office development, and the practice has to be well versed in these issues if it is to act as its own developer. In order to secure financing, it will need access to both bank and private equity funds, since bank or conventional loan financing is usually not sufficient to cover all costs. Because of the risks associated with the income streams for medical providers, the lending institutions will typically require significant levels of equity, or at-risk, funds in the project. Private equity funds will often be available, quite possibly from group members, but establishing appropriate terms and rewards can be challenging, and having group members as investors in the property, often at different proportions to their membership in the group, can lead to long-term conflicts if the structures are not well defined.

In order to secure the funding, the group will need to have appropriate income models, both reflecting anticipated revenue and addressing income risks due to changing reimbursement patterns over time; competition from other providers, including major healthcare providers, who are increasingly using market dominance to develop satellite group facilities; changing patient demographics; etc. All of these are areas that require expertise that may not reside with the group members. If, however, the group can provide these, either internally or through the use of consultants, the risks and rewards can be higher.

For groups that act as their own developer, the sources of financing will vary greatly over time; bank or institutional loans will usually be a significant source, but not all banks or institutions will fund medical projects at any given time. Costs and levels of equity investment or risk coverage will vary between institutions, and there will be a large element of research required to find the best financing for a given project. Private equity investors are much more difficult to find without strong connections in the equity market. There is a danger that the group could make a poor selection, either in cost or relationship, in its eagerness to secure private equity funding. Typically, other financing is not available to ambulatory care centers. Major providers can be faced with antitrust or tax issues if they fund facilities, and bond financing is rarely open to such practices.

Planning Your New Facility

Before you begin to plan and design a new office space, an overall strategy is needed to serve as a roadmap for facility development. It is imperative for the architect to know the strategic plan and understand the vision of the organization in order to help guide the decision-making process with the best interest of the ambulatory care center in mind.

Ideally, a strategic plan exists and simply needs to be confirmed. The plan should define how the organization intends to function and grow, relative to both external and internal factors. External factors include demographics, patient types, competition, and reimbursement structures; internal factors are relative to an analysis of strengths and weaknesses in the services and operations.

The ambulatory care center should carefully consider how to improve and prepare the organization for the future. Due to rising demand and facility costs, operational efficiency is a key consideration. What can be done to improve client service? Are there gaps in clinic schedules, or can hours of operation be extended? A building program will not solve operational problems, but it can help serve as a catalyst for change, and it can be designed to support the organization's practice model.

It is important to carefully consider who will attend the design meetings and how these chosen few will communicate with the rest of the practice. It is impractical for all members of the practice to be involved directly with the design process, but everyone should feel they are participants. Those who attend design meetings need to be the voice of all staff, representing a cross-section of people who work in the practice. Who has the experience and skills to manage the design process and the trust of their counterparts in the practice? Those persons attending meetings should be consistent throughout the project and do their best to attend all of the design and planning meetings with the design team.

Commitment to a design project takes time but can be very rewarding for an ambulatory care center. As consumers of healthcare services become savvier, one of the ways an ambulatory care center can promote itself is through the design. The design of the facility can help to identify a feeling of professionalism; it can make staff feel supported and patients feel welcome and cared for. An excellent source of information on how built environments can support health care is the Center for Health Design (http://www.healthdesign.org), which is a nonprofit organization working to demonstrate that using evidence-based design in hospitals and healthcare facilities can improve the quality of health care.

Biographical Information

Christian F. Bormann, AIA, NCARB, LEED AP, is a principal with Perkins+Will architects in New York City. Chris's career has focused on the planning and design of healthcare facilities of all scales and complexities. He studied architecture at Princeton University, and afterwards was introduced to healthcare facility planning and design while an officer with the US Army Health Facility Planning Agency. Chris managed the design of some of the Army's largest state-of-the-art teaching medical centers. After the military, Chris obtained a master's degree in architecture from the Architecture and Health graduate program at Clemson University, which focuses specifically on healthcare facilities. At Clemson, Chris received an American Institute of Architects/American Hospital Association fellowship grant for graduate work. Since then, Chris has been planning, managing, and leading the development of complex healthcare facilities. He currently manages the healthcare practice in the New York office of Perkins+Will, where he has been since 2000. Chris resides in Hunterdon County, New Jersey, with his wife Holly and their three children.

Sonya Dufner, ASID, is an interior designer who has focused on the programming, planning, and design of healthcare facilities for the last 15 years. Her experience across the United States ranges from small clinics, cancer centers, and community hospitals to major university teaching hospitals. She has written articles, spoken at industry events, and been published in design and healthcare journals. She is an active member of both ASID and IIDA and currently holds a position on a national committee with ASID. Ms. Dufner holds a bachelor of arts degree in interior design from Michigan State University and is a senior designer with the New York office of Perkins+Will. Sonya most currently has led the interior design for the Yawkey Center for Outpatient Care at Massachusetts General Hospital and has worked for clients such as Barbara Ann Karmanos Cancer Institute, the Mayo Clinic, New York Presbyterian Hospital, and Memorial Sloan-Kettering Cancer Center, among others.

Richard Sprow, AIA, is an architect who has specialized in the planning and design of health-care and hospital facilities for 30 years. His experience includes more than 200 projects, ranging from small clinics and rural hospitals to major university teaching hospitals and medical schools. Mr. Sprow has written papers on healthcare planning topics and has led postgraduate seminars on planning issues at New York University and at Peking Union Medical College. He holds a bachelor of architecture degree from Pennsylvania State University and was a senior health planner with the New York office of Perkins+Will, where he directed programming, planning, and design projects for work in New York and China.

Quality and Patient Safety

Eliot J. Lazar, Anthony Dawson, Brian K. Regan,
Daniel Hyman, and Karen Scott Collins

Quality Metrics/Indicators

A fundamental assumption in the field of quality and patient safety is the ability to accurately and reliably measure relevant indicators. In 1966, Avedis Donabedian published his seminal article "Evaluating the Quality of Medical Care," published in the *Milbank Memorial Fund Quarterly*. His concept that quality indicators could be categorized into structure, process, and outcome measures has become the best known classification scheme in health services research and is the measurement framework for contemporary quality assessment in health care.[1,2] Of note, in the same 1966 issue of the *Milbank Quarterly*, Odin Anderson complained that all of the healthcare research until that time had negligible influence on public policy and that decisions about public health were not supported by scientific evidence.[3]

During the four decades since publication of the Donabedian framework there has been an abundance of indicators, and despite concerns about their validity, it is apparent that they are increasingly used to guide public policy as well as to populate hospital report cards, physician profiles, medical staff credentialing algorithms, consumer-directed marketing, pay-for-performance initiatives, tiered pricing of healthcare insurance products, and a range of other applications.

Defining the Metrics

Modifying Donabedian's original categorization schema,[1] healthcare quality metrics may be classified as measures of volume, structure, outcome, or process (VSOP), with each approach offering significant advantages and disadvantages.

Volume

Volume has become an important indicator of healthcare quality. In 1916, E.A. Codman suggested that experience was an important factor in outcomes. "A hospital which was organized to obtain the best results could not possibly allot such cases to its less experienced surgeons."[4] The basic premise, which on the surface may seem intuitive, is that the higher the volume, the better the quality. However, this simplistic view may significantly underestimate the complexity of the issues.

The following example may be illustrative. Over the past two years the authors have informally polled leaders in clinical medicine and healthcare quality as to the choice they would make in the following hypothetical situation:

> You need to have a surgical procedure and have your choice of two hospitals. Hospital A performs 750 procedures annually, divided equally between two surgeons. Hospital B performs 2000 procedures annually divided equally among 10 surgeons. You have no information about clinical outcomes at the two facilities. Which would you choose?

While not scientifically valid, the results have been striking. Respondents were almost equally split in their preferences. Clearly some respondents believe that individual operator volume is most important, while others feel that "team" or institutional volume is the more important driver of quality. Additionally, when respondents were queried as to whether an annual operator's volume could ever be too high, many concurred, although no specific thresholds were suggested. Most notable is the fact that there did not seem to be a predilection for once choice or another based on professional background. In one session in which several surgeons were in attendance, they remained equally split as to their preference.

Volume metrics are seductive because data is often readily available in administrative and financial data sets, and because the ratio scaling of volume data is easily analyzed with parametric approaches. However, while volume/outcomes relationships have been well established for some procedures, this has not been demonstrated for others.[5]

Structure

Structural metrics are for the most part binary. They represent features of an institution which either are, or are not, present. Structural metrics may pertain to the facility, equipment, or technology. Examples may include presence or absence of intensive care units, CT scanners, or computerized practitioner order entry systems. Structural metrics may also apply to programs or certification/accreditation, such as a cardiac center offering open heart surgery or designation as a "stroke center." Structural metrics may also describe individual clinicians, such as "board certified" or "licensed" or "registered." Structural metrics are generally easy to collect by simple survey or inventory, without need of clinically trained abstractors.

Outcomes

The concept of outcomes as an important quality metric in health care can be traced back to the beginning of the 20th century. In Codman's seminal work, the importance of an "end result system" to assess quality was described.[4] Although "outcomes" measures would seem to be the most important and straightforward, since patients and clinicians alike want to know which facility or practitioner will produce the best results, data of this type are often difficult both to obtain and to interpret.

One of the most difficult problems in comparing outcomes data is the frequently heard comment that patient populations are disparate and thus cannot be compared. Various approaches have been employed to address this issue, focusing on some type of risk or severity adjustment in order to "normalize" the populations. Unfortunately, there is no gold standard, and many of the methodologies are proprietary and thus difficult to analyze and compare, even for healthcare statisticians.

A second issue is that of ensuring that clear data definitions exist. The institution employs a data dictionary in which for every metric, inclusions, exclusions, sources of compliance, time periods, and sampling methodologies are enumerated. Statistical testing is also specified as well.

Finally, outcomes data are often harvested from administrative data sets, which are used for billing and regulatory submissions. While inexpensive and large in number, they are clinically barren, often depending on coders to abstract clinical information. In many instances, physician notes are the only permissible source, thereby excluding the notations of other clinicians such as nurses and therapists. Moreover, in order to ensure compliance with payment policies, coders will only abstract specific terminology. For example, in current coding practice in the United States, lab values alone may be insufficient for coding purposes. A specific notation of a clinical issue by a practitioner is required. Furthermore, specific notation is frequently required. Often shorthand notation or symbols and abbreviations are not sufficient documentation. While these issues may not alter the determination as to whether a patient survived or expired, it would likely affect the process of risk adjustment, thus skewing the results significantly.

Recently, attention has been given to the distinction of whether a comorbid condition was truly present on admission versus occurring at the hospital. Lack of attention to the notation of "present on admission" codes may have a similar effect on risk/severity adjustments.

Data definitions may also affect the apparent outcomes, particularly when benchmarking across widely disparate geographic regions. Mortality is variably defined as inpatient versus 7-day mortality versus 30-day mortality. In institutions in which inpatient length of stay is relatively high, the mortality rate will be worse when inpatient mortality is utilized as compared to 30-day mortality. Regional practice variations and availability of post acute discharge services may affect this as well. Various approaches are being employed to minimize the impact of these variations on outcome data. The Center for Medicare and Medicaid Services (CMS) has recently adopted a 30-day mortality definition that should minimize this regional variability.

Process Measures

In contrast to outcomes measures, process measures evaluate elements of care provided. Did the patient with an acute myocardial infarction receive aspirin or a beta blocker? Did the patient with pneumonia receive antibiotics in a timely manner? Process measures require the same attention to definitions as to outcomes measures. However, process measures must be abstracted from the clinical record as the desired information is not present in coding data. The original

CMS Core Measure set included process measures for acute myocardial infarction, congestive heart failure, and pneumonia. Historically, data of this type required manual abstraction, but with increasing deployment of electronic medical record systems, much of this data is available electronically. It is critically important to underscore the importance of involving quality and patient safety leaders in the design and implementation of these systems, as the focus is generally on input of data and preservation of the record rather than harvesting of specific metrics.

More May Not Be Better

The current proliferation of quality indicators and report cards may have untoward effects. First, organizations, as well as individuals, have a finite capability for collecting and processing information. Moreover, the institutional attention span may also be compromised as the "initiative du jour" competes for attention with ongoing organizational imperatives. Clearly, institutional resources must be conserved and appropriately focused in order to fulfill the goals of improved quality and patient safety. In this way, the quality infrastructure must protect the organization by serving a filtering function that analyzes the cost and benefit of each competing initiative along with the organizational resources (staff time, data cost, processing) before presenting it for consideration by the governance and management structure of the institution. All too often we find situations in which the same metrics are collected month after month, and sometime for years, with little variation in the results and no attempt at intervention. We advocate the concept of an "intervention quotient," which reflects the number of interventions/number of metrics collected. It is imperative for healthcare organizations to periodically inventory the metrics being collected and critically appraise the value of them. While it is important to follow some indicators even if no intervention is contemplated, there may be some of little significance that can be discontinued. At the very least, the sampling intervals and size may be adjusted in order to conserve resources.

From the perspective of information technology, Davenport and Beck[6] describe a three-dimensional space for measuring the value of information, with ratings along the continua of aversive–attractive, captive–voluntary, and forefront–background value. Such tools are needed to respond to the "explosion" of information and the demands for multitasking within the knowledge economy, while considering that all valuations are relative and must be tailored to the context of the user of the information.

However, examples from health care typically focus on the "value" of an indicator as judged by the strength of its "evidence base" or support in the medical and academic community, or merely the availability of the data (e.g., indicators that are easily abstracted from billing or administrative data sets).

What is needed is a systematic framework for considering the value of an initiative, indicator, or data set in the context of the individual healthcare provider. Consideration should be given to the science of quality metrics, but also to the external mandates and concerns of the market. Potential evaluation criteria, measuring along a continuum, might include the following:[7]

- Clinical value added—Indicator contributes to improved standards of care
- Best practice—Indicator assesses clinical care clearly identified as best practice

- Actionability—Indicator provides information that is actionable
- Regulatory importance—Indicator may be required by regulatory or accrediting bodies
- Financial importance—Indicator can impact P4P or reimbursement
- Organizational alignment—Indicator is aligned with institutional/system priorities
- Resource requirement—Indicator can be collected within organization's structural framework without undue requirement of incremental resources
- Benchmarkability—Indicator can be compared with benchmark data
- Reputational impact—Indicator may have an impact, either positive or negative, on institutional reputation
- Compatibility—Indicator overlaps with same or similar indicators already being collected

Conclusion

The number of quality and patient safety metrics employed in health care today has skyrocketed. The acronym VSOP provides a classification framework modeled after the seminal work of Donabedian and facilitates consideration of the advantages and disadvantages of each data type. These metrics have significant limitations and must be carefully delineated. Attention to data definitions, as well as the importance of a solid evidence base prior to dissemination, is critical to enhancing the value and utility of these indicators. Nonetheless healthcare organizations can suffer from indicator overload, and care must be taken to evaluate the utility of those indicators being measured.

Medical Error/Patient Safety

Over the last 10 years, the strong interest by healthcare systems, patients, and government in medical errors and patient safety has ushered in a new era of healthcare quality and patient safety. Much of the current level and type of activity in healthcare quality is directed to the goal of making health care safer, as well as effective and efficient. Increasingly sophisticated methods of identifying unsafe care, measuring and improving health care, and creating regulatory and payment policies that support safe care are being employed.

In 1999, the Institute of Medicine (IOM) published a groundbreaking report on medical errors.[8] This report, "To Err Is Human," catalyzed a sea change in the level of attention and understanding of harm that occurs in the course of receiving healthcare services. Based upon published studies at the time, the report concluded that medical errors were responsible for, at a minimum, 44,000 deaths in the United States per year, and possibly as many as 98,000 deaths.[8] These levels of mortality surpass mortality from breast cancer, traffic accidents, and AIDS. Annual total costs related to these errors were estimated to be in the range of between $17 billion and $29 billion across the nation's hospitals. In addition, these levels of medical errors lead to a significant burden on patients and families who are harmed and left disabled, stressful work environments for healthcare professionals, and overall loss of productivity and health status of the nation's population.

The IOM report defined an error as an event in which there is a failure for a process to lead to the intended outcome, or where the incorrect process of care was selected in the first place.[8] An adverse event is defined as an injury to a patient caused by medical management rather than the patient's medical condition. Preventable adverse events are injuries caused by errors. It is the category of preventable adverse events in which significant focus on measurement and prevention, with respect to both policy and practice, has focused over the past 10 years.

The IOM findings were based on studies conducted over the previous 20 years, though each was localized by geographic focus or topic. The most prominent and influential of these in the IOM report were the Harvard Medical Practice Study and the study of adverse events in Colorado and Utah. The Harvard Medical Practice Study was published in 1991 by Troy Brennan and Lucien Leape, MD. In a study of more than 30,000 medical records of patients discharged from 51 different hospitals in New York State, Brennan, Leape, and their collaborators found that adverse events occurred in 3.7% of hospitalizations.[9] In these adverse event cases, patients had prolonged hospitalizations, temporary or permanent disability, or died; in 13.6% of the cases, the patient died. They assessed that more than half of those adverse events (58%) were attributable to an error and thereby preventable.

The second large-scale study of general adverse events rates in the United States was published in 2000. Based upon a 1992 review of a random sample of 15,000 hospital discharges from a sample of hospitals in Colorado and Utah, Thomas et al. found an overall adverse event rate of 2.9%.[10] This study also found that more than 50% of the adverse events were preventable (53%) and assessed the proportion of deaths due to adverse events at 6.6%.[10]

International data has reinforced the IOM conclusions. The Quality in Australian Health Care Study, published in 1995, found rates of adverse events at more than 16%, with half preventable.[11] In 2004 the Canadian Adverse Events Study determined a rate of 7.5% across 20 hospitals in Canada, with nearly 40% assessed as preventable.[12]

A clear limitation of all the major studies on errors and safety has been the focus on hospital care. While hospitals were a reasonable place to examine first with respect to the intensity and complexity of care provided, the availability of more standardized documentation of care processes and outcomes for the majority of health care in the United States occurs outside the acute inpatient setting. The current wave of research on the epidemiology of adverse events includes attempts to assess nonhospital settings.

Improving Healthcare Quality and Patient Safety: Broad Principles

Systems Versus Individuals

The IOM report called attention to the need to focus attention on the highly complex systems in which health care is delivered—and which can lead to errors despite the best skills and efforts of the individual healthcare workers and professionals delivering care.[8] Systems are defined as many interdependent parts working together to achieve an outcome.[13] When systems fail (i.e., there is an error or preventable adverse event) both human and nonhuman factors may be involved.[13] The work on systems and human factors by J. Reason has been illustrated by the "Swiss cheese" model: Systems may have multiple components or layers that can help protect against an error reaching a patient—when an error does reach the patient, all those layers have lined up in a manner that allowed the protections to fail. To improve, the overall system must be assessed to understand the factors that led to the "holes" lining up; another possibility is the need for strengthened or additional layers.

As health care focused on improvement at a systems level, analogies and lessons from other high-risk, highly complex industries integrated. Aviation and nuclear industries in particular have been highlighted, with the focus on communication, team functioning, reliability, and error-reporting systems for learning. Some key examples of how these industry lessons have been translated into improving health care are described below.

Learning from Errors

Voluntary reporting systems for adverse events and "near misses" provide the content for learning from errors to improve and prevent repeated errors. Many hospitals have developed voluntary reporting systems as a component of their patient safety programs. The focus is on capturing as many examples as possible where an error occurred or nearly occurred, in an environment in which staff does not feel at risk for reporting. These reporting systems are recognized as an important component for assessing an organization's level of safety or harm.[14] The information collected through these systems can identify new problems or areas of risk, identify trends, and provide opportunities for systematic learning.

Communication

The development and testing of a checklist in the ICU by Peter Pronovost, MD, mirrored the aviation industry's approach to achieving standardized, reliable processes with every airline flight.[15] Pronovost applied the checklist to the task of preventing bloodstream infections related to central line catheters. The best chances at prevention require that multidisciplinary teams ensure a set of tasks are done in a standardized manner. The ICU central line checklist became the way of organizing and communicating the required tasks and served as a reminder for the correct ways to complete the task. As a component of a statewide intervention to reduce central line infections, Pronovost reported an overall reduction in infections of 66%.[15]

"To Err Is Human" initiated a series of national reports from the IOM on quality. In 2001, a second report, "Crossing the Quality Chasm," described six components of a quality healthcare system: effectiveness, efficiency, safety, patient-centeredness, equity, and timeliness.[16] As described in the balance of this chapter, performance metrics, analysis and improvement initiatives, and local and national policies are now shaped with consideration to these components.

Medical error is an ongoing problem for the healthcare industry and all people who come into contact with it as patients or as family members of patients. The changes seen over the last 10 years in how the healthcare industry thinks about, identifies, and evaluates error have been dramatic. Initiatives across the country to improve care and outcomes have been accelerating and in some cases have demonstrated large-scale benefit. The potential for computerized physician order entry and other information technology to further reduce risk and error in hospitals is significant, but has been only partially realized to date. It is critical that hospitals and health-care providers continue to develop and improve their ability to identify, evaluate, respond to, and plan for errors. This will require teamwork, attention, and partnership among care providers and with patients and families to realize the safest system of care possible in the coming years.

Performance Improvement Methodologies

For as long as there have been errors in health care, hospitals and individuals have worked to improve processes. From when Semmelweis discovered the connection between hand hygiene and mortality[17] to the invention of computerized physician order entry (CPOE) as a way to prevent medication errors, hospitals have struggled to reduce error and variation in health care. After the publication of the Institute of Medicine report "To Err Is Human,"[8] and as the public became more aware of the potential breakdowns in the healthcare process, hospitals looked to quality improvement to maintain their reputation as reliable providers of medical treatment. In this section, we will review several of the methodologies hospitals typically employ to reduce variation in the healthcare process, minimize the occurrence of medical errors, and reduce unnecessary costs.

Six Sigma

Six Sigma is a quality management methodology that uses statistical tools to measure operational processes and uses data to drive improvement and eliminate defects.[18] Six Sigma should be used when an organization looks to improve a complex process where performance data is readily available. Six Sigma helps organizations understand the causes of defects, or errors, and identify the most critical elements for improvement success.

Sigma is the measure of variation that reflects how well a process meets customer (patient, physician, staff) expectations. The Greek letter sigma–σ–is the symbol for standard deviation, a measure of how much variation exists in a data set or process. The higher the sigma value, the less variation or defect exists. Six Sigma is equal to 3.4 defects per million opportunities, while a value of three Sigma is equal to 66,807 defects per million opportunities. To illustrate the importance of low variation in a process, a typical hospital operating at 3.8 Sigma (99% perfect) would lose approximately 20,000 lab requisitions per year. A Six Sigma hospital operating at 99.9997% perfection would lose only seven requisitions per year. In most industries, defects lead to customer dissatisfaction and corporate waste. In health care, while defects also lead to customer (patient, physician, staff) dissatisfaction, they can also cause medical errors that threaten the health of customers.

DMAIC is an acronym for *Define, Measure, Analyze, Improve, Control*. Six Sigma uses the DMAIC tool to implement quality improvements.[18] DMAIC is the tool by which performance teams achieve their stated quality goal. The first step in DMAIC requires that the improvement team defines the process at hand by understanding and identifying factors that customers consider critical to quality. Teams can then develop their "charter." The charter serves as the project blueprint and typically includes the business case for improvement, statement of the problem, constraints or challenges to improvement, scope of project, players and responsibilities, and preliminary project plan.

Measure is the second step in the improvement process. By gathering data on a process, the team can first quantify the potential performance opportunity and define performance standards. Six Sigma teams focus their measurement on inputs—things coming into the process; outputs—end results; and process—actions that can be measured. Performance standards are the boundaries of acceptable values for the output of a process or product. In health care, performance standards may vary based on the particular process at hand, whether it is clinical, operational, or mechanical. The measurement step allows the team to validate data and set parameters for improvement before beginning a more thorough, structured analysis.

The goal of *Analysis* is to identify sources of process variation. An effective Six Sigma team will evaluate many potential causes of variation, preventing biases or past experience influence the team's thinking. Common areas for teams to investigate include *methods*—procedures or techniques; *machines*—technology and equipment; *materials*—data, instructions, forms; *measures*—data; *Mother Nature*—environmental elements; and *people*—how elements are processed together.[18] Teams may use standard graphic representation to analyze the data, or more advanced statistical analysis for complex processes.

Improve is the step in the process where teams identify the improvement strategy and pilot and implement solutions. The improvement strategy is dependent on the information gathered in the measure and analyze stages in the process, as well as the nature of the process inputs. Brainstorming is one tool used for developing improvement strategies. Brainstorming allows teams to generate a high volume of ideas quickly. Process mapping is another tool teams can use to produce improvement strategies. Process mapping helps teams identify redundancies and nonvalue-added steps in a process and create alternate work flows. An important benefit of process mapping is it helps teams visualize the differences between what people believe to be the current process and how the process actually performs.

The final step for a Six Sigma project is *Control*. *Control* prevents the process from returning to its original state once the team steps away from the active improvement process. The control plan is created to ensure that the process inputs are consistent and do not negatively impact the process outputs. The plan should include ongoing data monitoring and a detailed reporting process so that changes can be tracked.

While DMAIC is an important improvement methodology that can be employed in hospital quality improvement projects, both on a small and large scale, there are other tools that a Six Sigma team can use to advance change. A *Work-Out* is a structured, facilitated meeting designed to empower people to make decisions and drive change. Work-Outs can be used to implement a known solution, problem solve in a process without a lot of data, build consensus, and build team ownership of a solution. These sessions typically last four to eight hours and include 10 to 12 team members. The *Change Acceleration Process* (CAP) examines barriers to change and effectively works through those barriers to accomplish established goals.[19] CAP outlines the steps required to change a process: lead at the top, create a shared need, shape a vision, gain commitment, operationalize change, modify systems and structures, and monitor and control progress.

Lean

Lean management principles have been used in manufacturing companies for decades, particularly in Japan. Lean thinking has its roots in the work of W. Edwards Deming. Deming, a founder of the quality movement, was a statistician who worked with Japanese industrialists to change work processes in post–World War II Japan. Deming's guiding philosophy was known as the 14 points and stressed employee participation, reliance on data, and use of careful analysis to drive change.[20]

Lean thinking involved reducing waste so that only the work that adds value to a system or process is performed. Lean thinking is not a manufacturing tactic or a cost-reduction program, but a management strategy that is applicable to all organizations seeking to improve process.[20] Health care is an industry where the consumer (patient) pays a high price for both the value of the product (treatment) and the cost of waste (medical errors, delays).

Before implementing Lean, hospital leadership must carefully evaluate the major tenets of Lean thinking in their organization: leadership, culture, and process. Leadership must be willing to reevaluate their organizational structure, reducing hierarchical layers and reorganizing staff based on operational products or services.[20] A clear mission statement outlining the goals of the hospital's Lean strategy is often necessary. As medicine is traditionally a hierarchical system that can reward seniority over ingenuity, this can be a challenging first step for many organizations.

Lean culture is also very different from traditional medical culture. In traditional culture, work (treatment) is expert driven; in Lean culture, work is process driven. In traditional culture, benchmarks can be used to justify not improving. For example, when analyzing national Core Measure benchmarks, a top-performing hospital may not look further into improving certain operations; Lean thinking would seek the "ultimate" performance and absence of waste.[20] Leaders must drive the process by helping staff embrace the concept of Lean and the impact that value-based process can have on their environment.

Lean thinking pushes hospitals to create value for the customer and reduce waste in internal and primary processes. A process is a set of actions that must be accomplished in the correct sequence at the right time to create value. Primary processes serve the external customer (patient and family); internal processes serve employees and staff. Often in health care internal processes are given priority over primary processes; for example, the early morning schedule of rounds may accommodate the physician staff, but are not primary process focused. While serving internal purposes, we fail the customer by making it more difficult for the patient and family to be actively involved in care and able to communicate with physicians. The complexity of the healthcare system can make it easy to justify the focus on internal processes, but quality improvement necessitates creating value and making care "patient centered."

While Lean thinking is an overall strategy, there are several tools that make Lean an ideal quality improvement methodology for the healthcare setting. The Lean improvement process typically begins in a *kaizen*, a multiday session where key constituents focus solely on reviewing the current process and brainstorming improvements. In this way, staff members who are responsible for implementing change are total and active participants in the change process.

Often in healthcare, quality improvement initiatives are enforced in a "top-down" edict, without input or "buy-in" from frontline staff.

A kaizen begins with the team creating a value stream map. Value stream maps illustrate the current process, specifying value from the standpoint of the customer. After visualizing the current process, including waste, delays, and rework, the team brainstorms a process with less waste. This can be a valuable process for hospitals, as many processes go on "behind the scenes" in labs and offices. Having all team members understand the overall process and identifying opportunities for improvement can have a positive impact on staff culture as well as the overall success of the improvement process.

Plan, Do, Study, Act (PDSA)

The Plan, Do, Study, Act (PDSA) methodology is based on the scientific process. It is attributed to Walter Shewhart,[21] an early-20th-century engineer, and originally involved the cycle of Plan Do, Check, Act. W. Edwards Deming later modified the cycle replacing "check" with "study." PDSA is a method that can be incorporated into hospital quality improvement projects on both the micro and macro level. It can be used for a small, unit-based initiative or a major hospital-wide quality improvement effort. The benefit of PDSA is that it is both flexible, in that it can be applied to a variety of projects, and structured as a process.

The *Plan* stage requires an understanding of the process, proposal of an improvement, and a decision as to how the improvement will be tested. *Do* requires an implementation of the action or improvement strategy. *Study* requires that teams analyze the effect of their improvement strategy. *Study* is sometimes substituted by *Check* as the third step in the process. *Act* is full implementation of the action, or a reassessment of the proposed strategy.

PDSA is sometimes combined with FOCUS-PDSA, a method developed by the Hospital Corporation of America. FOCUS adds five steps at the beginning of the improvement process: Find a process to improve, Organize a team that knows the process, Clarify current knowledge of the process, Understand causes of process variation, and Select the process improvement.

The most common evaluation method in hospitals following a serious adverse event or medical error resulting in patient harm is the root cause analysis, or systems analysis. The RCA, as it is frequently called, is a linear evaluation of the event that occurred, wherein staff involved in the incident are interviewed and leadership assesses the event to understand the underlying causes and the human errors and systems failures that led to the adverse outcome. These analyses originate in high-risk industries, including aviation, nuclear power, and manufacturing where accidents and near-misses were investigated in order to reduce risks and costs of future events.

States have differing requirements for RCAs, but generally require that the hospital come to some conclusion as to the corrective actions that should be effected in order to reduce the risk of a similar event in the future. There are numerous benefits, but also numerous weaknesses to the RCA approach as conceived and as implemented in healthcare settings.

It is of course imperative to evaluate and understand the circumstances leading up to an event in a healthcare setting that causes or almost causes serious harm to a patient. Staff competency problems, training gaps, communication errors, supervision issues in teaching hospitals, staffing shortages, and equipment failures are among the almost limitless potential underlying factors that can singly or together combine in the development of any serious adverse event. Healthcare leaders must begin with a structured analysis to understand the root causes of each event and to identify the changes that should be implemented to prevent similar errors or adverse events in the future. Despite the self-evident nature of this approach, the impact of RCAs are frequently limited, in that incidents rarely have single root causes and can occur again due to other factors not occurring in the event under review. The primary purpose of the analysis should not be to understand the reasons for this event, but rather to identify existent gaps and ongoing risks in the relevant system(s) of care delivery relevant to the case under review. Of course one of the great limitations of this approach is that key findings and recommended changes do not naturally spread from one organization to another, or, too often, even to other units in the same organization. By identifying the root cause, hospitals can more readily identify fixes to prevent the error, or similar errors, from reoccurring.[22] Fixes can be system based, such as separating "look-alike/sound-alike" drugs in a medication storage area, or human, focusing on education or team training.

It has been almost 10 years since the Institute of Medicine released its landmark report "To Err Is Human."[8] During this time, hospitals and other healthcare providers have focused increasing attention on the nature of errors, the causes of adverse events, and potential strategies to reduce risk in the delivery of patient care. This internal activity is being driven by numerous external factors, including public reporting of clinical outcomes and trends toward nonpayment for adverse events.[23]

Failure Modes Effects Analysis

Unlike the standard root cause analysis that is conducted in the aftermath of a serious adverse event or near-miss, the failure modes effect analysis (FMEA) is conducted to identify potential risks that can cause accidents and adverse events. FMEAs have been used in industries for many years to help determine the potential ways that machines or processes can fail and destabilize a process. In industry, design FMEAs examine product components; process FMEAs analyze processes used in making those products. FMEAs can be easily adapted to healthcare environments. In fact, the Joint Commission now requires failure modes and effects analysis[24] as a systematic, proactive method for evaluating the ways a process or system may fail and to identify ways the process can be made safer and more reliable.[24] FMEA has historically been used in general manufacturing as an approach to risk management. FMEA is well suited for health care, an industry with high variation in practice and low tolerance for undesired outcomes.

The FMEA process involves several key steps: (1) Identifying steps in the process; (2) Identifying failure modes (What could go wrong?); (3) Identifying failure causes (How could it go wrong?); and (4) Failure effects (What would be the consequences of the failure?). FMEA methodology assigns risk to a system or process, not only based on the probability of failure, but also on the severity of the effect of failure and the ability to detect the possibility of failure.

Other tools associated with FMEA include "Five Whys," fishbone diagrams, and root cause analyses. The Five Whys is a method for identifying the "root" of a problem. By repeatedly asking "why" a variation or error occurred, you can retrace the steps in the process that led to the system failure.

A fishbone diagram, also known as a cause-and-effect diagram or Ishikawa diagram,[25] delineates and organizes the possible causes of an event. The event is placed at the end of an arrow; the possible causes, grouped by similarity, are spines coming out of the arrow. Fishbone diagrams are especially useful in healthcare quality improvement because they help teams understand that there is often more than one cause to an event, and they display the relationship of the causes to the effect.

Attempts to improve process after a medical error can often fail because of a culture of blaming and the inability of the players to see how their individual actions contributed to the event. The fishbone diagram graphically represents the many actions that contribute to a failure, and helps the team identify the best opportunity for process improvement. FMEA priorities may be set by hospitals based either on their own experience or as a response to Joint Commission sentinel alerts. The required components of the FMEA include:

- Identify potential failure mode
- Identify the effects for each failure mode
- Conduct a root cause analysis for the most critical effects
- Develop, test, and implement system changes to reduce risk
- Monitor the impact of changes

In order to conduct the FMEA, it is recommended that a team of people from various disciplines and levels of experience gather to study the process with access to relevant information so as to facilitate an effective analysis of the risks inherent in the existing care process. It may be worth having a team member be someone from outside the group of people usually involved in the process being studied. In the course of the FMEA, and particularly during the analysis of hazards, the team assesses the impact of various potential failures/errors, ranks the severity of these effects and the probability of the failure or error actually occurring. In doing so, it becomes possible to prioritize among the many potential system changes that may be recommended by the FMEA team.

The details of conducting the FMEA are beyond the scope of this summary but can be easily found in numerous sources in the public domain. Tools are available on the Web site of the Institute for Healthcare Improvement.[26]

Root Cause Analysis

While FMEA as a methodology is proactive, root cause analyses are a reactive tool to identify system, human, or combined failures that lead to an error. The National Quality Forum has identified 28 "Never Events" and stated that these should never occur in hospitals.[27] Numerous insurers and payers, including the Federal Center for Medicare Services, are now communicating their intent to stop reimbursing hospitals for the care of such events, and this is resulting in a number of responses from hospitals, hospital associations, and professional groups, all of whom will be impacted by this change in reimbursement.

The changes in payment are hardly the most critical aspect of the industry's focus on error and risk in healthcare settings. Physicians, nurses, hospital staff members, trustees, and healthcare executives share a common desire to provide safe, reliable, consistent, and excellent care to patients. In almost all situations where errors occur, it is due to systems failures in which care processes are not constructed and implemented in a way that anticipates and effectively mitigates the impact of the human errors that will occur at some small frequency over time. Health systems must now respond to errors and adverse events that occur for a number of reasons beyond their moral and ethical duties as caregivers to the public. They must do so under federal and/or state regulatory statute, to plan for potential litigation, and to understand the reasons for the adverse event so as to implement changes that will reduce the risk of a similar event in the future.

Risk Resiliency

Combining some of the strengths of root cause analyses with those of failure modes effect analyses is a new approach to addressing system failures called risk resilience. First presented in 2007 at the Annual Forum of the Institute for Healthcare Improvement, this method was being tested and developed by a number of healthcare organizations in 2008.

It entails conducting a linear analysis of the RCA, but then engaging with the participants in a forward-thinking conversation about the defenses and adaptive ability the system would require in order to effectively reduce future risk.[28] After describing and discussing the events leading up to an error or significant near-miss, the multidisciplinary group identifies the existing "predesigned systems" that are in place to prevent the error from occurring. These are frequently policies or other practices that are not uniformly followed for numerous reasons, from lack of supplies to lack of time resulting in "work-arounds" that often more accurately define actual practice than do an organization's policies.

It is frequently the case that root cause and failure modes effect analyses conclude that additional "predesigned defenses" should be implemented in the form of new rules, double-checks, and other additional steps that may alter the intended boundaries of practice, but in reality may not make the system any safer. This makes the second part of the risk resilience conversation about adaptability and escalation a critical piece of this approach. The teams are asked to consider how the system recognized the fact that an error was occurring or a patient was at risk, whether the problem was escalated to the most appropriate person, and what the environmental factors were that contributed to the event that if recognized in advance could have led to some adaptive response that would reduce the risk for the error or adverse event.

In this model there are endless potential threats that can lead to an adverse event. Policies of the organization and its behavioral norms, along with the expected training and competencies of the staff providing care, contribute to a "rigid boundary" that prevents most threats from occurring and causing harm. Actual practice, however, deviates from policies and norms and may not be consistent with the expected staff training. This "actual boundary" exists in an intermediate zone wherein many threats are still prevented from causing harm, but others are not. Sometimes the patient and the organization get lucky and these events and errors do not reach the patient because someone recognizes an error, or they may reach the patient but not cause harm. But sometimes resiliency is fully eroded; no one recognizes, adapts, or escalates a problem; and catastrophe occurs.

Special Populations

"Children are not little adults." It is practically a "Golden Rule" of pediatric training that children are different from adults, although they generally receive care in hospitals that are not primarily focused on providing care to children. Many children with severe illness are cared for in freestanding children's hospitals, but in other settings it is important that hospitals recognize the special risks of children when being cared for in settings that are primarily involved in caring for adult patients. Medication dosing in particular is a well-recognized special risk for children for whom weight-based dosing is critical, especially given their special susceptibility to overdoses and the risk of "tenfold" errors in ordering, dosing, and administering medications. Imaging studies are another special area of risk for children receiving care in nonpediatric facilities. Radiation dosing must be tailored to a child's weight and requires special settings or sophisticated decision support on scanners in order to ensure correct procedures.

Similarly, the evaluation of events related to children must consider the risks of care systems adapting to situations different from those routinely faced by the people working in that setting. Preparing for these potential risks through the use of FMEA and other planning tools can reduce risk to patients by preparing teams for the necessary steps they must follow when caring for a small child and by helping them recognize when a situation is progressing in a way that creates potential for harm.

Quality and Patient Safety (QPS): Key Participants and Stakeholders

The landscape for quality and patient safety is constantly changing as key participants and stakeholders refine their positions, introduce initiatives and indicators, and exert their influence on the national agenda. The interests of government and the various regulatory structures, as well as those of providers, payers, patients, and profit-oriented enterprises, are constantly competing with each other for dominance of the QPS agenda. This has resulted in a multitude of approaches, many of which fail to align and in some cases substantially conflict with each other. A further consequence has been what some have termed an "avalanche of indicators" with a lack of clear priority in the QPS agenda.

The practical impact of these developments has been a somewhat fragmented approach, with initiatives that compete for limited resources at the level of the provider, as well as conflicting and confusing information available to the consumer. Acknowledgement of these factors has led to a call for alignment of quality indicators and priority setting at the national level. In order to understand the complex organizations and relationships in the QPS arena, the following is a survey of the predominant entities.

Centers for Medicare and Medicaid Services (CMS)

The Centers for Medicare and Medicaid Services (CMS, formerly known as the Healthcare Financing Administration, or HCFA) is the federal agency responsible for Medicare, Medicaid, and several other programs related to health care.[29] As the dominant payer, the federal government, through CMS, has significant impact on the indicators and initiatives for QPS. The CMS focus on QPS followed directly from the 1999 Institute of Medicine report, "To Err Is Human," which concluded that medical errors may be responsible for as many as 98,000 deaths annually.[8] In 2001, Congress authorized CMS to initiate "pay-for-reporting" programs that required hospitals to report on a standard set of 10 quality indicators or lose increases in reimbursement. Since that time CMS has added new measures to the list. CMS also uses the data submitted through this process to assess QPS in hospitals and posts it for consumers to access on the CMS Hospital Compare Web site.

Evidence indicates that the very act of publicly reporting data in this way has led to improvement in QPS, especially when linked with payment incentives such as pay-for-performance (P4P) programs.[30]

In 2006,[31] Congress further authorized CMS to reduce payments for "hospital acquired conditions." Under the prospective payment system of diagnostic-related groups (DRGs), hospitals are generally paid an average rate for each illness, regardless of actual expense. Under the DRG system, however, a case with a complication or comorbidity, such as an infection, is paid at a slightly higher rate to cover the additional costs of care. Under new rules implemented by CMS in 2008, however, the incremental reimbursement would be prohibited if certain complications are not "present on admission" but develop in the hospital.

Peer Review Organizations (PRO)

Peer review organizations were established by Congress in 1984 to add accountability to Medicare and Medicaid programs. PROs are contracted by CMS to review medical services provided by hospitals and individual practitioners, including issues of reimbursement and quality. Each year the CMS contract defines specific areas of focus that are consistent across the country, but the review work is contracted to individual PROs in each geographic area. PROs have the power to request patient records and conduct on-site record reviews. When lapses are detected, PROs also have the power to invoke sanctions and require corrective action plans.

National Quality Forum (NQF)

Established in 1999, NQF is a "voluntary consensus standard setting body" as specified by the National Technology and Transfer Act of 1995. After the Institute of Medicine report cited high rates of medical errors in the US health system, AHRQ asked NQF to develop a list of best practices based on the consensus of experts in the field.[32] Currently CMS and other major purchasers use NQF metrics, including 400 indicators approved to date, as the "gold standard." (CMS will generally not adopt a measure for their own initiatives until endorsed by NQF.)

NQF is a not-for-profit membership organization with more than 375 members comprising eight councils: Providers, Purchasers, Health Plans, Consumers, Health Professions (AMA,

ANA, medical specialty societies), Public/Community Health Agencies, Supplier/Industry, and a Quality Measurement, Research, and Improvement Council (e.g., TJC, NCQA, NIH, NPSF). The NQF Governing Board includes permanent seats for AHRQ, NIH, and CMS. Consumers and purchasers hold a majority of seats on the board.[33]

NQF standards and indicators are typically developed by expert panels appointed by the NQF based on nominations from members. Measures proposed by the expert panels are subject to a comment period and voting by NQF members.

NQF has also acknowledged the need for "harmonizing" or aligning measures across settings and providers, recognizing that the current process for developing measures will lead to conflicting expectation for physicians and hospitals regarding the same conditions, conflicting incentives, and confusion among consumers.

Coordination of measure development for physicians and hospitals would include consistent definitions and calculation algorithms across provider types, consistent measures across settings, methodological consistency (e.g., consistent definitions of denominators across process and outcome domains) and consensus on composite or summary measures that are meaningful to users.

Of note, coordination of measures and standard definitions are also needed to support the next generation of electronic health records, which are expected to include embedded measures for QPS and public reporting on a broad, national scale.

Agency for Healthcare Research and Quality (AHRQ)

AHRQ is part of the US Department of Health and Human Services, funding health services research, including QPS, as well as studies of outcomes and effectiveness. Research aims to reduce medical errors and improve patient safety, as well as uncover effective methods to organize and deliver quality care. The focus includes efforts to strengthen quality measurement and improvement. AHRQ also maintains the National Guideline Clearinghouse, which is a free, Web-based compendium of objective, detailed information on specific illnesses and treatments. AHRQ oversees the Patient Safety Task Force and directly provides metrics and measurement tools to healthcare organizations to track changes in ambulatory care–sensitive conditions, inpatient quality (volume, mortality, and resource use), and patient safety.[34]

The Joint Commission

The Joint Commission is the primary accreditation body for hospitals and other institutional providers, deriving its authority from its status as the designee of CMS in determining that providers are meeting the "conditions of participation" for Medicare reimbursement.

Founded in 1951, the Joint Commission is an independent, not-for-profit organization that currently evaluates more than 15,000 provider institutions in the United States. Its corporate members are the American College of Physicians, the American College of Surgeons, the American Dental Association, the American Hospital Association, and the American Medical Association. The board of the Joint Commission includes providers, employers, consumers, and health plan representatives.

The Joint Commission provides accreditation of hospitals through on-site surveys in which a team of physicians, nurses, and administrators assesses each organization against a comprehensive list of standards. Standards are developed by experts in the field and include "functional" areas such as patient treatment, patient rights, and infection control, which are evaluated via "tracer" activity that actually traces the course of a patient or provider in the process of care.

Since 1997, participating providers are required to submit periodic data to the Joint Commission, including process and outcomes measures defined by the Joint Commission under their ORYX initiative. In 2001, they began requiring 10 Core Measures including process measures for acute myocardial infarction (AMI), heart failure (HF), pneumonia (PN), and subsequently, for the Surgical Care Improvement Project (SCIP). These measures were substantially similar to measures adopted by CMS, and in 2003 the Joint Commission and CMS were able to completely align these measures.

The Joint Commission also maintains a report-carding process of survey attainment and Core Measure rates on their Quality Check Web site, www.qualitycheck.org.

Recently, other organizations have expressed an interest in accrediting hospitals and healthcare organizations, and hospitals may be faced with an array of accreditation choices in the future.

State Health Departments

Although there are wide variations across states, regulatory and QPS initiatives are widespread. As public concern about errors and adverse events in health care has risen, state initiatives and report-carding processes continue to grow. One of the early efforts in this regard was the New York State Cardiac Surgery Reporting System, which has published cardiac outcome data since 1989 and has demonstrated a reduction in cardiac mortality in the state over that time.[35] States have also implemented various requirements for providers to report adverse events, and certain states have ruled that providers should lose reimbursement revenue for adverse events that occur in the hospital. Many states have implemented adverse event reporting systems such as the New York Patient Occurrence Report Tracking System. These systems provide benchmarking opportunities.

Healthcare Industry Groups (HQA, Premier, VHA, UHC)

Providers are increasingly interested in QPS data in order to measure their own progress over time as well as benchmark against other providers. For these reasons, providers are often most interested in the relatively small number of indicators that are well defined and readily available across the healthcare industry.[36]

Providers want to improve and to provide the best possible care in the most efficient way. Providers are also concerned with how others view them, in the sense that they will likely respond to report-carding efforts by external groups as well as regulatory and reimbursement-related initiatives. Negative information in the media or provided directly to the public can significantly undermine a provider or healthcare organization's reputation.

However, given the plethora of initiatives and indicators, providers are concerned about the best way to deploy the limited resources that are available for collecting, analyzing, and responding to QPS metrics. Further, once information is provided to publicly available sources, others are free to combine metrics from various sources to depict the provider in ways that may not be balanced or fair. Finally, a great concern of providers is the lag between data collection and public reporting, which may be several years. In a sense, public report cards are showing a picture of where the provider used to be, and this frequently does not reflect current performance or outcomes.

The Hospital Quality Alliance (HQA) is the major point of influence for providers at the national level. HQA is a voluntary alliance of the American Hospital Association, the Federation of American Hospitals, and the Association of American Medical Colleges. HQA works with NQF, CMS, and AHRQ on the development and promulgation of indicators and endorses those proposed by CMS and the Joint Commission. HQA encourages the voluntary public reporting of QPS data: 98% of the hospitals in the United States are voluntarily reporting data to CMS, which is made publicly available via the CMS Hospital Compare Web site.[37]

Other industry groups and provider collaboratives such as Premier, VHA, and UHC are also influencing the national quality agenda. Premier, with its alliances among academic medical centers, has developed an extensive databasing capability for QPS benchmarking and has participated in acclaimed demonstration projects that have shown the ability of P4P to influence the collective behavior of providers. VHA (Voluntary Hospitals of America) likewise provides data support and collaborative projects across more than 2500 hospitals. UHC, the University HealthSystem Consortium, encourages collaboration across more than 100 academic medical centers, with a substantial effort on internal report carding on dimensions of QPS as well as efficiency and patient perception.

Employers: The Leapfrog Group

Employers and employer groups are concerned with value: quality and efficient care will keep healthcare costs down and result in happier and healthier employees. By focusing on healthcare metrics, employers hope to steer their employees to "better" providers. Employers are also increasingly interested in partnerships with providers as well as pay-for-performance (P4P) initiatives that will reward preferred providers (or penalize those that fail to meet benchmarks).

One dominant player in this field is the Leapfrog Group, which began as a consortium of employers, the Business Roundtable, and is largely supported by major employers. Their stated purpose includes "mobilizing employer purchasing power" on QPS so that "quality and customer value will be recognized and rewarded."[38]

Three areas were initially identified by Leapfrog for improving quality and patient safety: computerized physician order entry, staffing of intensive care units with board-certified intensivists, and maintaining a baseline volume of procedures. Leapfrog has subsequently expanded this list and developed a quality report card that is available through its Web site.

The healthcare community in general has acknowledged that the areas surveyed by Leapfrog may help improve QPS, but has expressed concern as to the impact of these indicators on overall care. Moreover, Leapfrog data are collected through a voluntary, self-reported survey of providers, and are not generally validated. Finally, Leapfrog measures have not always been aligned with those used by the CMS, Joint Commission, and NQF.

Consumers

Consumer groups generally support the idea that consumers will make better-informed choices regarding healthcare providers and treatments if information about QPS is readily available in an easily digestible format. A report card of provider ratings is expected to guide patients when they choose a physician or hospital.

The general rise of consumerism as well as the trend toward more involvement in self-care and healthcare decision making is contributing to the rise of consumer groups in this area. For this reason, some consumer-oriented approaches are combining healthcare information, tools, and education with a provider rating format. Moreover, some feel that as consumers are asked to pay a larger portion of the healthcare dollar, through deductibles, co-pays, medical savings accounts, and other mechanisms, they will become more value-conscious when making healthcare choices.

These efforts by consumer groups may be hampered by the inherent difficulty in obtaining valid and reliable healthcare data, as well as the significant expense. For this reason consumer groups have tended to rely on the repackaging of data that is otherwise available through other public sources.

Finally, perhaps most daunting, is the conflicting information that is available from otherwise reputable sources. Conflicts may result from differences in definitions, sampling, risk adjustment, or methodological variation. However, it is difficult for consumers to reconcile report card information that may differ sharply between sources. There is also the risk that an attempt to clarify these differences will result in oversimplification to the point of misleading the consumer.

While indicators and initiatives have proliferated, a number of companies have developed products to provide information directly to consumers.

- HealthGrades provides profiles and report cards on hospitals and providers to consumers for a fee. Reports are accessed via their Web site[39] and are comprised of data from other publicly available sources.
- WebMD also provides procedure volume and a "complications index" for individual hospitals on their Web site, using data from state and federal agencies.[40]
- UCompareHealthCare,[41] a unit of About, Inc., a New York Times company, offers volume and mortality data as well as "quality" reports based on data from the CMS Hospital Compare Web site.

These and other efforts aim to address the need for consumers to conveniently access healthcare data when choosing a provider. However, these efforts vary considerably in their methodology and generally include publicly available data that may be several years old.[36]

Further, although there is some evidence that publicly reported data stimulates improvement efforts at the level of the hospital provider, to date there has been little evidence that public reporting has any impact on QPS or consumer choice.[42]

As these sites proliferate, however, providers must attend to the information about healthcare QPS that is publicly available and may be reformatted and spread through electronic means.

Conclusion

In summary, a successful quality and patient safety program for a healthcare organization must be supported by the twin pillars of a robust program of quality data reporting, as well as a series of strategically determined initiatives. The decision as to which metrics to collect and analyze should be a thoughtful one, based on numerous criteria, including actionability. These indicators should be reviewed on a regular basis and updated as appropriate. Retirement or modification of indicators that no longer provide value should be considered. Indicators should drive initiatives and must have a broad base of support, particularly from providers. These initiatives can be implemented using a variety of tools and techniques, though organizations should resist the concept of changing these tools too frequently, resulting in staff perception of the improvement methodology du jour. Adverse event reporting systems are an important adjunct to a good QPS program, with careful attention to the tracking and trending reports. Children represent an example of a special population for which traditional quality and safety programs must be tailored. Technology will be an important enabler, but must not be viewed as a cure for suboptimal process.

References

1. Donabedian A. Evaluating the Quality of Medical Care. *Milbank Memorial Fund Quarterly*. 1966;44:166–206.
2. Best M, Neuhauser D. Avedis Donabedian: father of quality assurance and poet. *Quality and Safety in Health Care*. 2004;13:472–473.
3. Anderson O. Influence of social and economic research on public policy in the health field. *Milbank Memorial Fund Quarterly*. 1966;44:11–48.
4. Codman EA. *A Study in Hospital Efficiency*. Classics of Medicine Press. 1992.
5. Helm E, Lee C, Chassin M. Is volume related to outcome in healthcare? *Annals of Internal Medicine*. 2002;137:511–520.
6. Davenport T, Beck J. *The Attention Economy: Understanding the New Currency of Business*. Cambridge, MA: Harvard Business School Press; 2002:95–104.
7. HANYS Quality Institute. Which quality improvement initiatives are right for your organization. Rensselaer, NY: HANYS Quality Institute; 2008.
8. Kohn LT, Corrigan JM, Donaldson MS, eds. *To Err Is Human: Building a Safer Health System*. Washington, DC: Institute of Medicine. National Academies Press; 2000:1–2.
9. Brennan TA, Leape LL, Laird NM, et al. Incidence and adverse events and negligence in hospitalized patients. Results from the Harvard Medical Practice Study I. *NEJM*. 1991;324(6):370–377.
10. Thomas EJ, Studdert DM, Burstin HR, et al. Incidence and types of adverse events and negligent care in Utah and Colorado. *Medical Care*. 2000;38(3):261–271.
11. Wilson RM, Runciman WB, Gibberd RW, Harrison BT, Newby L, Hamilton JD. *Med J Australia*. 1995;163:458–471.
12. Baker GR, Norton PG, Flintoft V, et al. The Canadian Adverse Events Study: the incidence of adverse events among hospital patients in Canada. *Canadian Medical Association Journal*. 2004;170(11):1678–1686.
13. Reason J. Human error: models and management. *BMJ*. 2000;320:768–770.
14. Cullen DJ, Bates DW, Small SD. Incident reporting system does not detect adverse drug events: a problem for quality improvement. *Jt. Comm J Qual Improv*. 1995;21:541–548.

15. Pronovost P, Needham D, Berenholtz S, et al. An intervention to decrease catheter-related bloodstream infections in the ICU. *N Engl J Med.* 2006;355:2725–2732.

16. Committee on Quality Health Care in America, Institute of Medicine. *Crossing the Quality Chasm: New Health System for the 21st Century.* 2001. Washington DC: National Academy Press.

17. Childbed Fever: A 19th Century Mystery. Available at: http://www.sciencecases.org/childbed_fever/childbed_fever.asp.

18. Pande P, Holpp L. *What Is Six Sigma?* New York: McGraw-Hill; 2002.

19. Smith, Ilese J, ed. *Using Performance Improvement Tools in Healthcare Settings.* Oakbrook Terrace, IL: Joint Commission Resources.

20. Institute for Healthcare Improvement. Going lean in health care. IHI Innovation Series white paper. Cambridge, MA: Institute for Healthcare Improvement; 2005.

21. Quest for Quality. Available at: http://processandqualityimprovement.blogspot.com/2007/07/waltershewhart.html.

22. Percapio KB, Watts BV, Weeks WB. The effectiveness of root cause analysis: what does the literature tell us? *The Joint Commission Journal on Quality and Patient Safety.* 2008;34:391–398.

23. Pronovost PJ, Goeshcel CA, Wachter RM. The wisdom and justice of not paying for preventable complications. *Journal of the American Medical Association.* 2008;299:2197–2199.

24. FMEA Info Centre. Available at: http://www.fmeainfocentre.com.

25. McLaughlin CP, Kaluzny AD. *Continuous Quality Improvement in Health Care.* 3rd ed. Sudbury, MA: Jones and Bartlett Publishers; 2006:115–120.

26. Institute for Healthcare Improvement. Available at: www.ihi.org.

27. Torrey T. What is a medical error. About.com: Patient Empowerment. Available at: http://patients.about.com/od/atthehospital/a/mederrorlist.htm.

28. Frey K, Hyman D, Resar R. Evaluation of the safety system surrounding adverse events. Available at: www.ihi.org. 2007.

29. Centers for Medicare & Medicaid Services. Available at: www.cms.hhs.gov.

30. Lindenauer PK, Remus D, Roman S, et al. Public reporting and pay for performance in hospital quality improvement. *N Engl J Med.* 2007;356:486–496.

31. Deficit Reduction Act of 2005. Public L No. 109-171. S 1932. § 5001 (2006).

32. Leape LL, Berwick DM, Bates DW. What practices will most improve safety? evidence-based medicine meets patient safety. *JAMA.* 2002;288(4):501–507.

33. National Quality Forum. Available at: www.qualityforum.org.

34. Agency for Healthcare Research and Quality. Available at: www.ahrq.gov.

35. Chassin MR. Achieving and sustaining improved quality: lessons from New York State and cardiac surgery. *Health Affairs.* 2002;21(4):40–51.

36. HANYS Quality Institute. Understanding publicly reported hospital quality measures. Rensselaer, NY: HANYS Quality Institute; December, 2007.

37. American Hospital Association. Hospital Quality Alliance. Available at: www.aha.org/aha_app/issues/HQA/.

38. The Leapfrog Group. Available at: www.leapfroggroup.org.

39. Health Grades. About us. Available at: www.healthgrades.com/about-us.

40. WebMD. Available at: www.webmd.com.

41. UCompareHealthCare. Available at: www.ucomparehealthcare.com.

42. Fung CH, Lim Y, Mattke S, Damberg C, Shekelle PG. Systematic review: the evidence that publishing patient care performance data improves quality of care. *Ann Intern Med.* 2008; 111–123.

Physician Practice:
Organization and Operation

Michael J. Kelley, Steven Falcone, and Stephen G. Schwartz

More than 20% of the national healthcare budget is spent on direct physicians' services. In 2007, expenditures for physician practice and clinical services accounted for $479 billion, out of total national health expenditures of $2.24 trillion (**Table 18.1**).[1A] Although significantly less than the expenditures for hospital care ($697 billion), the impact of physician practices on the healthcare industry is greater than the number would indicate. It is estimated that 50 to 60%

Table 18.1 2007 US National Health Expenditures	
All figures in billions of US dollars	
Physician and clinical services	$ 479
Hospital care	$ 697
Prescription drugs	$ 227
Nursing home care	$ 131
Dental services	$ 95
Other professional services	$ 62
Home health care	$ 59
Durable medical equipment	$ 24
Other non-durable medical products	$ 37
Other personal health care	$ 66
Personal health care expenditures	$1,877
Other health expenditures	$ 363
Total national health expenditures	$2,240

of healthcare costs are directed by physicians.[1] Physicians not only personally perform medical services, but also admit patients to the hospital, order hospital- and nonhospital-based services, prescribe drugs and therapeutic treatments, and order disposable and durable medical equipment and various ancillary and home healthcare services.

The physician and physician group sectors of the industry have traditionally been considered highly fragmented and vertically isolated. More recently, the physician sector has had to respond to radical changes in the medical environment, undergoing change consistent with, and often in conflict with, other sectors of the industry.

Forms of Physician Practice

There are four major forms of physician practice: individual or solo physician practice, single-specialty group practice consisting of two or more physicians, multispecialty group practice, and physician practice management companies (PPMCs). Any of the forms may be either hospital based or independent.

Solo Practice

Solo practice is the choice of fewer and fewer individuals currently embarking on a medical career. Only 5.5% of physicians under the age of 35 years are reported to be in solo or two-physician practices.[4] Physicians in solo practices often cite the freedom and self-determination made possible by independence as one of the major benefits. With no other physicians involved in the practice, a solo practitioner can make business decisions and develop a practice style and work ethic without the need to consult associates. The practice is able to directly meet the personal needs of the practitioner in terms of professional income, scheduling, and professional interests.

The autonomy and flexibility of solo practice is not without costs—financial, professional, and personal. Solo practitioners have lower average earnings than members of a group practice. It also can be difficult for a solo practitioner to develop areas of special interest or competence within the field of medicine due to the time constraints of constantly being available to patients and referring physicians. The lower overall revenue stream makes it difficult, if not impossible, to hire managers to run the practice, and those employed, including the physician-owner, must often perform multiple roles within the business. It is also fair to speculate that the lack of collegial exchange of opinion and information can lead to professional stagnation.

Of increasing importance, solo practitioners, particularly those who do not have a highly specialized area of practice, have difficulty obtaining and retaining managed care contracts. This lack of individual negotiating power tends to lead to lower contract rates for the physician, unless one becomes affiliated with an external contracting organization such as an independent practice association (IPA) or preferred provider organization (PPO).

The autonomy of solo practice also creates a corresponding responsibility for all aspects of the practice. Delegation of areas of responsibility among other physicians or specialized administrative business personnel is financially unaffordable, and decisions need to be made without the benefit of alternative opinions and group decision making. The time spent in decision making and business activities detracts from the time available for patient care activities.

A solo practitioner may function as a self-employed individual or as an employee of the corporation that the physician wholly owns, whether a subchapter S or subchapter C corporation. Selection of the specific form of practice is determined in conjunction with legal and financial planning experts. Each form has its own specific tax planning issues, including the deductibility of certain expenses, retirement plan options, and taxation of fringe benefits. In addition, there are legal consequences including, among other things, the degree to which the practitioner's estate is protected from ordinary business liabilities and uninsured professional liabilities.

Single-Specialty Group Practice

Single-specialty group practices are a common form of practice. In a single-specialty group practice, all the physicians practice within the same field of medicine. This does not mean, however, that the practices need to be identical. For example, an ophthalmic single-specialty group might incorporate subspecialties of the eye, such as retina, cornea, oculoplastic, and external disease subspecialists.

Physicians in group practice can enjoy a number of benefits. Historically, compensation for group practicing physicians, whether single or multispecialty, is higher than that of solo practitioners. Although often cited as a reason for group success, there is little evidence that economies of scale are created in a group. In fact, group physicians have a higher expense ratio than do nongroup-affiliated physicians. Group practices, however, often are able to make larger capital investments. Two factors lead to this increase in capital investment. First, group practices tend to have substantially larger financial resources and cash flow. There is a general tendency toward greater predictability of financial performance due to diversification of both providers and services, and a lessened reliance on the performance of any one individual physician. As an example, cross-coverage during times of vacation, illness, and disability do not shut down the income stream; frequently, another physician in the group has some excess capacity that will generate revenues from the absent physician's existing patient population.

Second, there are more viable capital investment opportunities. New equipment often can be profitably utilized in a group setting because higher aggregate numbers of patients with the appropriate diagnostic or treatment modality need are available to amortize the capital equipment cost. A new laser, for example, might not be a cost-effective investment for a solo practitioner because the physician's patient population does not generate enough utilization. When that same investment analysis occurs in a four-member group, the utilization increases an additional 300%, making resultant positive cash flow and profitability more likely.

Additionally, these practices are often able to employ more highly trained support staffs that are not required to multitask. Group practices often have specialized personnel devoted to diagnostic procedures requiring little direct physician involvement. The physician gains productivity by, essentially, outsourcing the technical component of the service and concentrating on the provision of professional services. In other words, those tasks that require skill, but do not require professional decision making (the art of medicine) can be performed by other employed nonphysicians who are compensated at a lower rate. A solo physician, by way of contrast, must personally perform all aspects of the service.

Group practice makes affordable specialized staff members who are able to concentrate their efforts and learned expertise on billing, insurance, finance, and operational matters. These nonphysician operational specialists are able to manage the increasingly complicated insurance-imposed precertification processes and utilization limits, and the group can successfully and profitably contract with managed care organizations. Solo physicians are often unable to support the costs associated with management of the processes and must outsource these services with the associated loss of control, or perform these services personally and often less effectively and efficiently than those with dedicated expertise. Or they may choose not to perform (or neglect) certain financial and regulatory activities with the attendant risk of legal and monetary costs.

The experience level and training of the nonphysician leadership also is different from in solo practices. In solo and small groups, the office manager frequently will not have earned a college degree, but will have many years of on-the-job experience in clinical or financial positions performing multiple functions within the practice. Group practices, by contrast, have increasingly sought managers with formal education, frequently requiring a master's degree or CPA certification. Many of these managers also will have achieved certification through professional associations, such as the American College of Group Practice Executives' Certified Medical Practice Executive (CMPE) and Fellow in the American College of Medical Practice Executive (FACMPE) programs.

This may help explain both the higher expense ratios and the higher incomes of physicians in group practice, a setting in which physicians generally see more patients per week while working a comparable number of hours.[7] The physician in a group practice also can achieve lifestyle benefits from delegated responsibility, reduced call schedules, and cross-coverage during times of vacation, illness, or disability.

Another possible explanation for the relative advantage enjoyed by multiphysician practices is that, in certain circumstances, groups may make better decisions than individuals. The "wisdom of the crowd" phenomenon has been noted in many areas and may play a role in group decision making.[7A]

Not all the attributes of group practice are necessarily positive. Offsetting the advantages of group practice is the need to develop consensus among physicians regarding practice philosophies and administrative policies. The difficulty of this task, combined with the inherent interpersonal relationships, causes a large number of group practices to end in either dissolution or the departure of individual physician members, reported at a rate of 6.1% annually.[7B] This often can be traced to failures in the recruiting process. During the recruiting process, physicians often spend insufficient time gaining an understanding of each other as individuals, determining the compatibility of personality traits, leadership styles, and expectations. More often, an inordinate amount of time is focused on the medical experiences and scholastic achievements of the candidate. The individual physicians who are part of the same group should ideally have the same vision, goals, and objectives. The costs, both personal and financial, associated with the need to disassociate can be extremely high.

When investigating group practice opportunities, physicians should not overlook the personal and business relationships that are characteristic of group practice. Group practices are, in a social and economic sense, group marriages. Individuals need to reconcile expectations about standards of care, professional competency, financial matters, social and personal behaviors, personality, and ethics. This is particularly true, and may be difficult to reconcile, when more experienced and seasoned physicians are hiring younger, less experienced physicians of an entirely different generation. Generational differences can result in a completely different concept of how many hours constitute a workweek, and the younger and older physicians can be at complete odds. To some older physicians, limits on residency program training time (80-hour workweek maximum) may be seen as a lack of commitment and a loss of work ethic in the new generation of doctors.

The recruitment or affiliation process should start with the basic requirements, including licensure and clinical competence acceptable to all parties. Thereafter, the process should be driven by the factors that will influence professional and group success. How will the candidate "fit in" in terms of life goals? Is there a compatibility of styles, approaches, and decision making? Are the expectations of the senior members achievable? Will the junior associate essentially act as an overflow for the other group members, or be expected to develop an individual practice through practice-building activities, such as seminars, physician entertainment, and civic involvement? The goal of all parties should be to achieve a viable, pleasant, and profitable long-term relationship, and the decision process needs to be handled with this in mind. The importance of taking a more behaviorally based approach to joining a group practice cannot be overstated.

Group practices can be formed under different legal entities. A partnership is an unincorporated form of practice that can be established as a vehicle for group practice. Group members own and distribute practice income based on their partnership agreement. Notably, there are clear disadvantages to partnerships with regard to liability issues. Each partner may be held individually responsible for the acts of any other partner related to the operation of the partnership. In some states, limited liability partnerships (LLPs) afford some protection from creditors that are unavailable to general partnerships.

Group practices are more often incorporated as either subchapter S or C corporations, with the same advantages and disadvantages as previously discussed with regard to solo practitioners. The group physicians act as employees of the corporation. The governance of the group is carried out under the articles of incorporation and bylaws of the corporation. Not all group physicians need to be shareholders and officers of the corporation. Indeed, it is common for physicians new to the group to work for some period of time before they are offered the opportunity to purchase stock in the corporation.

Increasingly, physicians are not being offered ownership in the group. Rather, they are compensated through incentives that recognize the role they play as individuals in the achievement of the corporate mission. This can include phantom stock plans, bonuses based on productivity, incentives for proper utilization, retention bonuses, and other rewards for tangible and intangible achievements. The lack of partnership or ownership opportunity, however, may be a factor that limits the group's ability to recruit if other practices in the same market space offer this opportunity.

Multispecialty Group Practice

A multispecialty group practice shares many of the characteristics of a single-specialty group practice, but will include a range of specialties. Such groups might include primary, secondary, and tertiary care. Often these types of groups exist in a managed care or academic organization. Many advantages can be cited for this model of practice. Multispecialty group practices tend to be, by their nature, larger than single-specialty groups. Many patients will have more than one significant medical problem, thereby creating opportunities for cross-referral to physicians within the group practice. A diabetic patient, for example, may require an endocrinologist to assist in the management of blood sugar levels, an ophthalmologist to treat diabetic retinopathy, a neurologist to treat diabetic neuropathy, and a wound specialist to care for slow-healing foot ulcers. The size of the enterprise can produce opportunities whereby each practitioner can benefit from the professionally developed corporate administrative systems and cross-marketing plans. Multispecialty group practices often can position themselves as regional centers, drawing both self- and physician-referred patients from a larger geographic area than they would otherwise enjoy.

Offsetting these cited advantages are a number of problems associated with operating a large enterprise. The number of physicians in a multispecialty group can make governance a difficult issue. In the typical single-specialty group practice, each physician may play a role in the governance of the enterprise. In the typical multispecialty environment, governance is accomplished through an executive committee with a chief medical and administrative officer. Income and resource allocation often is a rancorous subject. Primary care and surgical specialties are often at odds because of financial and professional conflicts. Primary care physicians frequently seek to be subsidized by the higher revenue-producing specialists and subspecialists for whom primary care generates referrals, patient volume, and surgical cases.

Notwithstanding the negative issues associated with group practice, many physicians believe the support services generated by the group and the presence of ancillary services, as well as the freedom from administrative and managerial tasks, can offset the disadvantages. Group practice, whether single-specialty or multispecialty, is a growing force in the healthcare industry. Mergers and affiliations are becoming more common given the changes in the healthcare marketplace. Many healthcare experts predict the trend toward group practice medicine will accelerate and become an increasingly attractive choice for physicians beginning medical careers, as well as an alternative to be considered by solo and small group members. The trend toward consolidation often is viewed as a natural economic result of increased competition within the larger healthcare market.

Physician Practice Management Companies (PPMCs)

PPMCs are organizations that exist primarily to perform nonclinical services that support the delivery of healthcare services. Several factors have led to their existence.[14A] Entrepreneurs, including hospital organizations, healthcare professionals, venture capitalists, and Wall Street, realized that health care represents a huge segment of the economy, and therefore, cash flow. Physicians also were increasingly aware of both their role in the delivery system and the threat posed by the evolution taking place in the nonphysician segments of the industry. The consolidation of hospital systems; the emergence of large, powerful, and restrictive health plans; and the diminishing role of indemnity insurance gave rise to new concerns, business imperatives, and strategic choices. Some large multispecialty groups are now positioned to negotiate for exclusive contracting relationships with large insurers. These new arrangements have the potential to affect revenue, not only to the physicians, but also to a web of interdependent organizations (**Figure 18.1**).

Another driving force that led to an expanded PPMC industry was the exponential growth in the complexity associated with operating the nonclinical activities of the physician practice. Authorization processing, contracting with managed care organizations (MCOs), and compliance with federal guidelines all created new administrative burdens that some physician practices were ill-prepared to perform. Theoretically, business practices used in other industries,

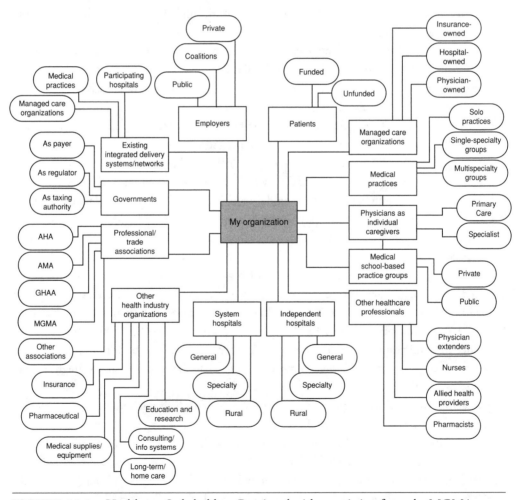

FIGURE 18.1   Healthcare Stakeholders. Reprinted with permission from the MGMA Center for Research, 104 Inverness Terrace East, Englewood, Colorado 80112-5306; 303-799-1111. www.mgma.com. Copyright 1995.

such as consolidation and specialization of activities, could significantly impact both the effectiveness and efficiency of the operation, leading to increased revenues and profits. Also significant was the need for capital to invest in data processing, to implement capitation systems, and to build new cost-effective business and administrative systems.

PPMCs also offered the potential, but not the certainty, of financial gain through stock appreciation. The overwhelming majority of PPMCs have significant equity positions held by affiliated physicians who hope to achieve not only business objectives, but also long-term equity appreciation.

PPMC Structure

There are a variety of PPMC structures. Equity model PPMCs purchase the assets of the physician practice and manage, through supervisory oversight, the nonclinical activities of the practice, including employment of all nonphysician personnel, supplies contracting, and, frequently, centralized accounts receivable and payable management. At the time the PPMC purchases the physician practice, an exchange of cash, notes, and equity in the PPMC occurs at a negotiated value. This value is derived from an estimate of the value of the cash flow that the PPMC will derive through a contract that entitles it to a percentage of profits, frequently between 10 and 30%. The management contract is typically for a period of 15 to 40 years and is noncancelable.

Service model PPMCs also emerged to provide management services to physicians without acquiring the practice. These often take the form of management service organizations (MSOs). MSOs provide, under a fee basis, selected management services, which could include managing contracting activity for the practice or a group of practices that are affiliated with an IPA or other network. The service model PPMC may provide centralized billing and collection activity, centralized group purchasing systems, and discounted consulting services. Frequently, these organizations are capitalized by the physicians themselves as a way to build aggregate negotiating power. The difference between the models is that the practice remains in the ownership of the physicians.

PPMCs may provide services to a variety of organizations. Single-specialty PPMCs have emerged in ophthalmology, oncology, neurology, pediatrics, and emergency care, to name a few. Some PPMCs concentrate only on larger multispecialty practices with significant market penetration. Large, multibillion-dollar PPMCs emerged in the mid to late 1990s, often with the assistance of public capital. Hundreds of other smaller organizations, both public and private, were formed to address this new market dynamic. A few have been successful, although some of the largest firms failed.

Concerns arose in the financial markets that the pace of acquisitions and the high prices paid for physician groups led to a lack of effective integration and poor financial performance of the PPMC. Additionally, many physicians did not achieve the income growth promised through the sale of their practices to PPMCs. Many saw their compensation drop because of high management fees that were not offset by revenue growth. Some PPMC executives reported that the physicians at the newly acquired practices were less productive after acquisition. At the same time, the financial markets devalued the PPMC stock values and physicians had large losses on the equity that they had acquired in the PPMC or related organizations. Over a relatively short period, many PPMCs either stopped expanding or were forced to sell the practices back to the original physician-owners.

The ultimate question is whether this new form of practice will create value for both physicians and investors. The potential for value exists. PPMCs may develop disease management and care pathways that are effective and more efficient. This will give their organizations pricing advantages in the pursuit of managed care contracts. Frequently cited contraindications to PPMC success include the high costs associated with the infrastructure necessary to accomplish their tasks, and the social, economic, and professional conflicts that exist between the service provider (PPMC), their employed physician providers, and the service purchaser (MCO), with all parties seeking to maximize profits at the expense of the others.

Managed Care Delivery Systems and Forms of Physician Organizations

Faced with the high cost of, or the inability to, obtain traditional medical insurance, organizations began to experiment with alternative delivery systems and insurance mechanisms in the 1920s and 1930s.[8,9] In 1965, a survey conducted by the Department of Health, Education, and Welfare identified 582 prepaid medical plans.[10] For the overwhelming majority of Americans, traditional fee-for-service medicine was the only available option. It wasn't until the 1970s and 1980s that managed care plans showed significant growth. Nearly half of all employees covered by employer-sponsored group health plans were enrolled in managed care plans by 1991. The report noted that 25% were enrolled in HMOs, 22% were in PPOs, and 5% were in point-of-service plans.[11] Managed care continued to expand its penetration as healthcare expenditures grew. By 2002, 26% were enrolled in HMOs, 52% in PPOs, and 18% in point-of-service plans.[12]

Recently, employees have had the option of enrolling in high-deductible health plans with a savings option (HOHP/SO) (Figure 18.2). HDHP/SOs are defined as (1) health plans with a deductible of at least $1,000 for single coverage and $2,000 for family coverage offered with an HRA (referred to as HDHP/HRAs) or (2) high-deductible health plans that meet the federal legal requirements to permit an enrollee to establish and contribute to an HSA (referred to as HSA-qualified HDHPs).

A health reimbursement arrangement (HRA) is a tax-qualified plan offered in conjunction with a high-deductible health plan, and is funded by the employer for each participating employee. It pays for eligible healthcare expenses typically covered under the medical plan. Employer contributed funds that were not used to pay claims can be carried over to the next year to cover future healthcare expenses, an incentive to employees to use their personal HRA wisely. If funds are exhausted, the employee is responsible for satisfying the remaining deductible before the plan begins to pay. If the employee changes jobs, the money stays with the employer.

A health savings account (HSA) is a tax-advantaged medical savings account available to employees enrolled in a HDHP. The funds are a pretax employee contribution to their account and are not subject to federal income tax at the time of deposit. HSAs are owned by the individual, which differentiates them from the company-retained funds in a health reimbursement arrangement (HRA). HSA funds may be used to pay for qualified medical expenses at any time without federal tax liability. Withdrawals for nonmedical expenses are treated very similarly to those in an IRA in that they may provide tax advantages if taken after retirement age, and they incur penalties if taken earlier.

Since 2002 there has been a reduction in the percentage of employees choosing HMO coverage from 27 to 30%, while HOHP/SO plans have grown to approximately 8% of the covered employee market. Similarly, PPO growth has continued, while POS and indemnity have weakened in the marketplace.[12A]

Although many physicians decry the complexity, utilization rules, and preapproval process that complicate managed care participation, net incomes of physicians that participate in managed care average more than $28,000 more than those who do not participate. Those physicians with managed care representing 25 to 50% of practice revenues had incomes greater than $44,000 higher than nonparticipants.[13]

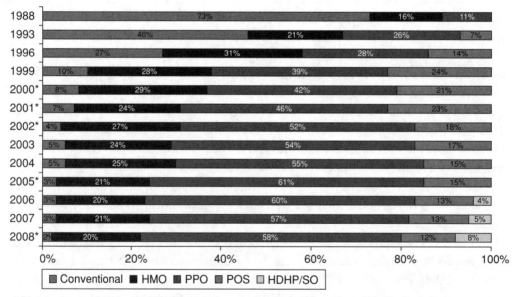

* Distribution is statistically different from the previous year shown ($p < .05$). No statistical tests were conducted for years prior to 1999. No statistical tests are conducted between 2005 and 2006 due to the addition of HDHP/SO as a new plan type in 2006.

Note: Information was not obtained for POS plans in 1988. A portion of the change in plan type enrollment for 2005 is likely attributable to incorporating more recent Census Bureau estimates of the number of state and local government workers and removing federal workers from the weights. See the Survey Design and Methods section from the 2005 Kaiser/HRET Survey of Employer-Sponsored Health Benefits for additional information.

FIGURE 18.2   Distribution of Health Plan Enrollment for Covered Workers, by Plan Type, 1988–2008. *Source*: "Distribution of Health Plan Enrollment for Covered Workers, by Plan Type, 1988–2009" Kaiser Fast Facts, The Henry J. Kaiser Family Foundation, September 2009.

Managed care is a widely used phrase, but one that is not necessarily easily defined. Strictly speaking, managed care could be defined as medical care being directed and paid for by a third party, generally an insurance company. Under strict interpretation, this would define virtually any insurance policy or government program as a managed care program. Few policies or programs contain no restrictions on the services an insured party can obtain. Virtually all have limits on overall spending, types of services covered, and frequency of services provided. Managed care plans can be sponsored by a profit or nonprofit organization and may reimburse physicians on a capitated or discounted fee-for-service basis. Services can be provided by salaried healthcare providers or by contract with independent physicians. They may have large open or closed panels of providers. They can function by directly providing medical services or through the indemnification or reimbursement of incurred costs. On the basis of just these five characteristics, 32 permutations are theoretically possible. On a more general basis, though, managed care is defined as care that offers comprehensive benefits delivered by selected providers and financial incentives for members to use providers who are members of the plan.

Health Maintenance Organizations (HMOs)

HMOs are medical care organizations that are responsible "for the provision and delivery of a predetermined set of comprehensive health maintenance and treatment services to a voluntarily enrolled group for prenegotiated and fixed periodic capitation payment."[14] Cowan defines five common characteristics shared by such plans:

1. A defined population of enrolled members
2. Payment by the members determined in advance for a specific period of time and made periodically
3. Medical services provided on a direct service basis rather than on an indemnity basis
4. Services provided to patients by HMO physicians for essentially all medical needs with referrals to outside physicians being controlled by HMO physicians
5. Voluntary enrollment by each family or member[15]

In an HMO, a primary care physician typically is responsible for determining what services are necessary and who will provide the services for enrolled patients. The physician becomes the "gatekeeper" for the patient's access to services. In the event the patient seeks care on a non-emergent basis from any healthcare provider not authorized by the HMO physician, payment is denied for the services. The effect of this healthcare delivery model is that it limits the services received by the patient to those deemed medically necessary by the primary care provider and attempts to eliminate duplicative or unnecessary costs. A frequently cited problem of traditional fee-for-service medicine is that the provider receives a direct financial benefit from ordering additional tests and procedures. Under the HMO model, the provider receives no financial benefit from the tests and referrals initiated. In fact, in the event that utilization targets are exceeded, the primary care physician may be penalized for excessive healthcare costs incurred by the patients for whom he has accepted medical and financial responsibility.

Patients have the least amount of choice about the medical care and provider selection in an HMO plan. Because all care is directed by the "gatekeeper," the gatekeeper may view the need for care as less urgent, or unnecessary, than the patient does. Further, patients may desire to obtain specialty care from well-known physicians and academic medical centers that are not part of the HMO's panel. Should they, nonetheless, want to obtain the care from non-HMO physicians, they will have to pay the cost of the care completely out of pocket, with no benefits coverage.

There are three models for organizing physicians in an HMO: the staff model, the group model, and the IPA model.

Staff Model HMO

In the staff model HMO, physicians are salaried employees of the HMO. They furnish care exclusively to members of the HMO, with the HMO responsible for all nonclinical management. In some cases, these physicians are given incentives to control costs through bonus mechanisms that reward the physician for controlling costs and lower utilization.

Group Model HMO

In a group model HMO, the physicians are organized as a multispecialty group. These groups often have their own separate legal entity and contract with the HMO to provide services to its members. The group receives a direct capitation payment from the HMO, which has been predetermined by negotiation, and may be entitled to supplemental payments based on the profitability of the HMO. The group then compensates individual physicians based on either a salary, productivity, or utilization basis, or a combination of all three methods.

The group model HMO can result in significant risk shifting to the group practice. Inasmuch as the physicians often are the owners of the group practice, their net income can be directly affected by services provided to HMO members. Incentives to hold down overall health costs can take two forms. First, there may be prenegotiated accruals, or withholds, payable in the event costs are under budget. Second, higher profits can be generated internally within the group through the lower costs associated with the provision of fewer services. The physician group often provides services to patients who are not members of the HMO, as well, and may operate that component of the group practice on a traditional fee-for-service basis.

IPA Model HMO

An IPA is a legal entity composed of physicians and physician groups, each of which functions as a separate and independent practice. Under an IPA model HMO, large panels of physicians contract with the HMO to provide health services within a defined geographic area. Traditionally, physicians have been paid on a fee-for-service basis, but at a rate that discounts their customary charges. In many cases, the fee schedule is set by a discount to or a multiple of the Medicare fee schedule. A portion of the discounts, referred to as withholds, may be paid to physicians if a surplus exists after payment of hospital, external, and administrative costs.

Faced with the desire of insurers to decrease their claims cost risk, some IPAs are developing capitated payment agreements. Under such an agreement, the IPA contracts to provide specified services at a fixed cost per beneficiary per month. The IPA then controls utilization issues within its organization and compensates individual practitioners for care on either a discounted fee-for-service or capitated basis. IPA physicians often derive a large percentage of their practice income from traditional fee-for-services patients. One of the cost control weaknesses of this model is that the overwhelming majority of the physician's income is still generated on a fee-for-service basis with the smaller remainder being dependent on the IPA's cost behavior. Physicians continue to receive the bulk of their income from the number of examinations, procedures, and tests they perform.

Preferred Provider Organizations

PPOs are similar to IPAs in that physicians function on a fee-for-service basis. Unlike the HMO model, in which there usually is a primary-care gatekeeper who controls the services provided to enrollees, PPO-enrolled patients are free to make their own choice of member providers. PPO physicians enter into an arrangement with the sponsoring organization, often an insurance company or hospital-affiliated organization, and agree to a discounted fee for service. By offering the discount and thereby maintaining access to patients converting from traditional indemnity plans, the physicians hope to stabilize or increase the size of the patient population they service.

Subscribers typically are free to seek the care of physicians outside of the PPO panel, but are penalized by receiving a lower rate of reimbursement, resulting in a higher out-of-pocket cost to the beneficiary. PPOs often incorporate low co-payments and limited or nonexistent in-network deductibles in order to create an incentive for patients to obtain discounted care and remain within the PPO panel. The patients may opt out of the panel and seek care elsewhere if they feel value is generated equal to the higher cost. Unlike HMO patients who have no coverage outside of the plan, PPO subscribers receive partial reimbursement of their out-of-network medical services, subject to co-pays and deductibles. PPO physicians typically do not share in any withhold pool and receive no direct incentive to hold costs down. The physician practices medicine on a discounted fee-for-service basis; income is directly related to the value and volume of services rendered.

System Comparison

All of these managed care models share a common goal: the reduction of healthcare costs. They vary substantially in the method and degree of control they exert on the individual practitioners. Not surprisingly, the lowest physician costs are typically found where control upon physician activity is highest (**Table 18.2**). Indemnity insurance, the traditional insurance program in which patients are free to choose any physician for any healthcare problem, has the highest

Table 18.2   Relative Costs of Managed Care Models

Model	Control on Physician Activity	Costs
Indemnity insurance	Low	High
Preferred provider organization (PPO)	Moderate	Moderate
Health maintenance organization (HMO)	High	Low

costs. PPOs, which are the least restrictive of the managed care models regarding physician selection, are also the most expensive managed care product. HMOs, with the highest levels of physician control, are generally the lowest cost model.

Operational Aspects of Physician Practice

The operations of a traditional physician practice can be divided into a few key functional areas.

Resource Management

Operations management in a physician setting is similar to that of any other organization. The goal is to maximize net revenue through the efficient utilization of resources. Resources include plant and equipment, physicians, ancillary staff, and time. A number of resource costs are fixed, including rent and many other occupancy expenses. Other expenses, such as supplies, are variable in that they rise and fall in direct relation to the volume of production. Some expenses, such as staffing costs, are semivariable in that they can be changed only in an incremental fashion, with a minimum level of cost that is essentially fixed within a specific range of activity. For example, a receptionist is necessary whether the physician sees one or six patients per hour. Hence, the cost is fixed if volumes stay in the range of one to six patients per hour, in this example. Once the capacity of the receptionist to adequately perform the duties is exceeded, even if only by one patient per hour, another receptionist needs to be hired.

Operations management seeks to provide services at the lowest possible cost. For most medical practices, the highest-cost resource is the physician staff. Effective utilization of this resource requires that the physician's activity be concentrated in areas where he or she is uniquely qualified: the practice of medicine.

Principles of Staffing

Physician activity can be optimized by delegating some aspects of patient care. For example, many scientific measurement aspects of medicine, such as vital signs, weight, and height, can generally be provided at a lower cost by well-trained clinical assistants or physician extenders. Measurement activities take time, and time is the limiting resource for many physicians. When an activity is performed by physician extenders, the physician may increase the number of patients served as a result of the time savings. The "art" of medicine, a function that can be performed only by a qualified provider, is the cognitive function, the evaluation of quantitative and subjective data, followed by the definition of a disease management plan. Practices that utilize staff for measurement activities and physicians for the cognitive functions tend to have higher revenues than models utilizing fewer physician extenders.

Appointment Scheduling

The appointment scheduling process is one of the key variables in physician productivity. The goal of the process is to have the physician render medical care as continuously as possible during scheduled hours, while minimizing patient waiting times and staff overtime costs.

There are four basic types of appointment scheduling: standard segment, wave, resource-based, and open-access scheduling. Under a standard segment system, the number of patients the physician sees per hour is divided into 60 minutes and scheduled in equal segments. If a physician sees six patients per hour on average, an appointment is scheduled every 10 minutes. Unfortunately, this system can be inefficient. If an individual patient requires less than the allotted 10 minutes, the physician may experience wasted time during which no patient is available. Alternatively, if an individual patient requires more than the allotted 10 minutes, the schedule will be disrupted. The physician, therefore, essentially has three choices: work through a scheduled break (such as a lunch break), if one is available; try to catch up by spending less than 10 minutes with the next patient(s), which may lead to dissatisfaction; or run the rest of the day behind schedule.

Standard segment scheduling becomes even more problematic if multiple sequential steps are required for each patient. For example, many practices require each patient to be "worked up" by a physician extender prior to the physician encounter. For example, many pediatricians' offices have a technician or nurse measure the child's height and weight. If an individual patient requires additional time during this preliminary step, then the physician's schedule will become disrupted even if the physician is running on time.

Wave scheduling attempts to correct this natural variability by establishing a queue of patients. Under the same assumptions as above, a wave schedule would have three patients scheduled at the top of the hour and three scheduled at the bottom of the hour. Thus, if the first patient takes 5 minutes to be seen, the physician can move on to the next patient, who is already available to be seen. The second and third patients, however, may experience substantial wait times under this system.

A hybrid solution, called the modified wave, combines aspects of segment and wave scheduling. If a physician sees six patients per hour and the minimum visit is 5 minutes, appointments would be scheduled from the top of the hour in six 5-minute intervals until half past the hour. (That is, patients may be scheduled at 9:00, 9:05, 9:10, 9:15, 9:20, 9:25, and 9:30.) This ensures that the physician is always busy, but the fourth, fifth, and sixth patients may experience substantial wait times.

Another alternative scheduling method is based on time units. Typically, the 5-minute exam has characteristics that are distinct from the 15-minute exam. The 5-minute exam might be a routine postoperative exam and represent one unit of time, whereas the 15-minute exam would be an initial new patient visit using three units of time. By determining the type of exam, the number of units of time it will take can be determined. This can help to minimize patient wait times, which are stressful on both physician and patient, while reducing or eliminating periods of physician inactivity.

One of the most complex yet most effective scheduling methods looks at resource allocation. Each component activity of the medical service is analyzed and identified with a corresponding resource requirement. These resource components include technicians and nurses, physicians, diagnostic and surgical equipment, exam rooms, and waiting areas. Resource allocation looks at the availability of each of the resource components, seeking to maximize utilization while minimizing costs and reducing patient waiting times. Additionally, resource allocation requires that you forecast demand; planning includes making decisions about the demand for each type of appointment, whether it be for new patients, follow-up appointments, or surgical cases. Although complex, this sophisticated tool creates the most efficient and cost-effective schedules.

For example, in one high-volume ophthalmology practice the flow for most new patients is as follows:[15A]

- Registration (5 minutes)
- Technician work-up (10–15 minutes)
- Optometrist evaluation (15 minutes)
- Ophthalmologist evaluation (15–20 minutes)
- Surgical coordinator (20 minutes)

Open-access scheduling is an emerging method that seeks to have patients come to the office on the day of their call. By matching provider supply and patient demand, the method, used primarily by larger primary care providers, is designed to expeditiously meet patient needs, resulting in fewer no-shows and higher revenues. Open access has the advantage of providing services to the patient based on the patient's needs and wants, a powerful driver of patient satisfaction in today's competitive healthcare environment. This model presumes, however, that no insurance authorization or precertification is required prior to the patient's visit. Hence, open access is most prevalent in primary care practices, for which authorization of visits is usually unnecessary.

Physician Billing
CPT Coding

In order for both physicians and their patients to be properly reimbursed for services by insurers, the procedure or procedures performed must be identified. Medicare, as well as most insurance companies, utilizes the American Medical Association's Physicians' Current Procedural Terminology (CPT)[16] to describe the services provided to the patient. This process of reviewing the service and categorizing it is referred to as coding. The CPT book (updated every year) contains some basic coding information, as well as thousands of defined services or procedures. Each of the described procedures is defined by a specific five-digit code.

Under some circumstances, a code must be reported with one or more additional two-digit modifiers that identify relevant additional information needed to determine the amount or type of service performed. There are 25 surgical modifiers commonly used for surgical procedures and an additional 6 that refer to the evaluation and management sections of the CPT code. For example, modifier -50 identifies that a bilateral procedure was performed during the same operative session; modifier -54 identifies that the surgical care was provided by the billing physician and that another physician provided the preoperative and postoperative components of the surgical procedure.

Some physician activities require the use of Health Care Financing Administration (HCFA) Common Procedural Coding System descriptors, HCPCS (pronounced "hicpics"). Level II codes are a series of national codes that describe supplies, injectable drugs, and physician and other healthcare provider services not described in the CPT (HCPCS Level I), as well as dental services.[17] A third level of descriptors, HCPCS Level III, includes local codes used by the Medicare carrier to describe services and activities for which national coverage has not been determined. The number of local codes is decreasing as Medicare and other private and governmental insurers move toward a uniform national payment policy. (HCFA was replaced by the Centers for Medicare and Medicaid Services [CMS] in 2001.)

Care must be taken when coding, for many reasons. It is important to accurately reflect what services were provided, and miscoding may result in civil and criminal investigations. Accurate coding is important not only to ensure that the service was provided as described, but also to avoid the unbundling of charges. Unbundling occurs when a procedure is broken down into discrete components rather than being identified by the procedure code that defines the entire service. The reason that unbundling represents an incorrect coding method relates to the way in which the value of procedures is determined. The value of the work performed by improperly componentizing the procedure would be significantly greater than the work value that would derive from the global or bundled procedure. In other words, the sum is greater than the whole. As an example, during the repair of a retinal detachment, a physician may inject medication, use a laser to seal the tear, and drain subretinal fluid. Each of those three procedures has its own discrete CPT code. When taken as a whole, they are regarded as components of CPT code 67105; repair of retinal detachment (**Exhibit 18.1**). The

---

Exhibit 18.1   Example of Bundled Codes

BILLED CODE

67105—Repair of retinal detachment, one or more sessions; photocoagulation (laser or xenon arc) with or without drainage of subretinal fluid

BUNDLED CODES

67015—Aspiration or release of vitreous, subretinal, or choroidal fluid, pars plana approach (posterior sclerotomy)

67101—Repair of retinal detachment, one or more sessions; cryotherapy or diathermy, drainage of subretinal fluid

67141—Prophylaxis of retinal detachment with or without (e.g., retinal break) drainage, one or more sessions; cryotherapy, diathermy

67145—Prophylaxis of retinal detachment (e.g., lattice degeneration) with or without drainage, one or more sessions; photocoagulation

67208—Destruction of localized lesion of retina, one or more sessions; cryotherapy, diathermy (e.g., small tumors)

67210—Destruction of localized lesion of retina; photocoagulation (laser or xenon arc)

67227—Destruction of extensive or progressive retinopathy, one or more sessions, cryotherapy, diathermy (e.g., diabetic retinopahy)

67228—Destruction of extensive or progressive retinopathy, one or more sessions; photo coagulation

67500—Retrobulbar injection; medication (separate procedure—does not include supply of medication)

92504—Binocular microscopy (separate diagnostic procedure)

Source: CPT codes only © 2002 American Medical Association. All rights reserved.

amount paid if the procedure were broken down by components would be significantly greater than that billed under the "global" code.

Evaluation and Management Coding

CPT coding also includes physician evaluation and management (E&M) services. Evaluation and management services is the term applied to what most people would consider "a visit with the doctor." This can take place in a variety of settings, such as the physician's office, a hospital room, a nursing home, or the patient's home. The level of intensity of the visits also can vary from a blood pressure check by a nurse to a comprehensive examination for a life-threatening disease.

HCFA's successor, CMS, continues to work in conjunction with the AMA and other industry groups, expending significant effort in an evolving process to measure the complexity and intensity of these widely variable activities. Major revisions to the process occur every several years; the trend is to make the evaluation and management coding system less subjective and easier to interpret and audit.

The purpose of the coding structure is to accurately evaluate the relative value units (RVUs) associated with the activity. The site of service (e.g., hospital or office) has an impact on costs associated with the provision of service. The premise in this instance is that it is less expensive for the physician to provide services in a physical location that is paid for, maintained, and staffed by another organization, such as the hospital.

Documentation Guidelines for Evaluation and Management Services

Seven components are recognized in defining the level of E&M services: These are:

1. History
2. Examination
3. Medical decision making
4. Counseling
5. Coordination of care
6. Nature of the presenting problem
7. Time

History, examination, and medical decision making are the key differentiating components in the overwhelming majority of evaluation and management services. The other components are important only when the majority of the time is spent counseling and coordinating care.

Four types of patient history can be selected for proper coding: problem-focused, expanded problem found, detailed, and comprehensive. Each type, at varying levels of detail, encompasses the following categories:

- Chief complaint—A concise statement that describes the primary reason the patient presented to the physician, including symptoms, problems, conditions, diagnoses, and physician recommendations for return visit.

- History of present illness—A chronologic description of the development of the patient's current illness from the first sign or symptom (or from the last visit) through the present time. This description should include the location, quality, severity, duration, timing, context, modifying factors, and associated signs and symptoms of the illness.
- Review of symptoms—An inventory of body systems obtained through questions intended to identify the patient's current or previous signs or symptoms. The recognized systems are constitutional symptoms, eyes, ears, nose, mouth, throat, cardiovascular, respiratory, gastrointestinal, genitourinary, musculoskeletal, integumentary, neurologic, psychiatric, endocrine, hematologic/lymphatic, and allergic/immunologic.
- Past, family, and/or social history—The patient's previous experiences with illnesses, operations, injuries, and treatments; a review of medical events in the patient's family, including hereditary diseases and risk factors; and a review of previous and current social activities.

Diagnosis Coding

The International Classification of Disease (ICD), published by the World Health Organization, is used to code a diagnosis or diagnoses applicable to the service rendered. The US Public Health Service and CMS mandate the use of the ICD manual for their programs. Approximately 1300 pages in length, the manual lists thousands of diagnoses. Each diagnosis is given a unique three-digit code, which can be further subclassified with an additional two digits, if necessary. The ICD coding of disorders resulting from impaired renal function, 588, is shown in **Exhibit 18.2**.[18]

Exhibit 18.2   ICD9 Codes for Disorders Resulting from Impaired Renal Function

588   Disorders resulting from impaired renal function

    588.0 Renal osteodystrophy

        Azotemic osteodystrophy

        Phosphate-losing tubular disorders

        Renal:

            dwarfism

            infantilism

            rickets

    588.1 Nephrogenic diabetes insipidus

    Excludes: diabetes insipidus NOS (253.5)

    588.8 Other specified disorders resulting from impaired renal function

        Hypokalemic nephropathy

        Secondary hyperparathyroidism (or renal origin)

    Excludes: secondary hypertension (405.0–405.9)

    588.9 Unspecified disorder resulting from impaired renal function

Source: Reprinted with permission from ICD-9-CM, Practice Management Information Corporation.

Methods of Physician Reimbursement

Usual, Customary, and Reasonable

Many indemnity insurers use (or used to use) what is referred to as the usual, customary, and reasonable (UCR) methodology, or a close variant thereof. Under this method, the insurer collects a database of charges for each service submitted by all similar physicians in a geographic area. The insurer then sorts these from the lowest charge to the highest and limits payment to a determined percentile. Some commercial carriers will pay at the 50th percentile of the charge array, whereas some others may pay as much as the 90th percentile charge. This is referred to as the "customary charge." The fee that the individual physician normally charges for the procedure is the "usual charge." The third fee that the insurer considers is a "reasonable fee." This fee allowance can vary based on documented special circumstances of the case, but generally is considered to be the average of all physician charges for the same service, in the same geographic area. The insurer will pay the lower of the usual or customary charge, unless a reasonable-fee adjustment is warranted. An example of a UCR system is shown in **Exhibit 18.3**.

Relative Value Systems and Resource-Based Relative Value Systems

As early as the mid-1950s, payers began investigating a method of physician payment based on relative values. Under relative value payment methodologies, the economic cost of providing a service is the basis under which it is reimbursed. Physician time and training, the intensity of the service, and practice and malpractice expense components are factors that comprise the economic costs of providing a service. Rather than a reimbursement system based on historic charges, a relative value system quantifies the resources necessary to perform a service.

Relative value systems, when properly constructed, also have value as a management tool. They offer the opportunity for an organization to measure the resources necessary to deliver

Exhibit 18.3 Determination of Allowable Fee Under UCR Method

Table of Historical Charge Data		
Physician	*$*	
Dr. Smith	75	
Dr. Gomez	60	.. 90th Percentile
Dr. Casper	55	
Dr. Felix	50	
Dr. Felix	50	.. 50th Percentile
Dr. Singer	47	
Dr. Alex	45	
Dr. Alex	45	
Dr. Jones	40	

Examples—Insurer pays 90th percentile
- Dr. Smith submits charge for $75. Insurer allows $60. Charge exceeds 90th percentile UCR.
- Dr. Felix submits charge for $50. Insurer allows $50, the usual fee for Dr. Felix.
- Dr. Alex submits charge for $75. Insurer allows $45 based upon his historical charges.

services and to compare them to an independently derived value. An organizational efficiency measurement can then be derived. Services can be measured in terms of both cost and revenue on an individual basis.

Relative value systems also provide organizations with a method to quantify the number of units of service provided. This method provides a productivity benchmark that is unaffected by changing case mix and fee schedules. Many practices track, as part of their financial management systems, the number of patient encounters. Relative value system–based management recognizes that some encounters and services are worth more than others. For example, Medicare has established that a comprehensive consultation with a physician expends 4.86 units of resources, whereas a comprehensive established patient visit expends 2.37 units.

Relative value systems also are useful in the measurement of the costs involved in providing care under capitated systems. The organization can track the number of units of service it provides and the capitated payment to compute the reimbursement per unit of service. By comparing the payer's reimbursement per unit of service to the organization's cost to provide a unit of service, management can make informed decisions about the profitability of managed care contracts.

The most significant relative value system in terms of impact on the industry was adopted in 1992 by Medicare. The resource-based relative value scales (RBRVS) system came into effect because of the belief that the historical Medicare payment structure favored subspecialty and surgical procedures rather than primary care and cognitive medical activities. Many feel that there is a serious inequity when primary care physicians, such as family practitioners, are earning significantly less than subspecialty surgeons.

DETERMINATION OF RELATIVE VALUES

The principal researchers that developed the relative value system used by Medicare and most other payers was a team of Harvard researchers—commonly referred to as the Hsiao Team, named after its principal researcher. They surveyed a cross-section of physicians in multiple specialties to determine the amount of physician work involved in a number of described encounters/services. Physician work took into account the amount of time, intensity of effort, and technical skill required to provide the service. The physicians evaluated the work components relative to other defined encounters, indicating their perception of the amount of work involved in the task. These work values were then cross-linked against all of the procedures surveyed. The intent of the study was to have a uniform scale under which all physician activities could be evaluated. HCFA then adapted and expanded on the work done by Hsiao to develop a schedule of work values for all covered Medicare procedures. Beginning January 1, 1992, the Medicare-approved fee for any service could be defined by calculating the following formula:

$$\text{PAYMENT} = (\text{WORK} + \text{PRACTICE EXPENSE} + \text{MALPRACTICE}) \times \text{CF}$$
$$[(\text{RVUws} \times \text{GPCIwa}) + (\text{RVUpes} \times \text{GPCIpea}) + (\text{RVUms} \times \text{GPCIma})] \times \text{CF}$$

where:

RVUws   = Physician work relative value units for the service
RVUpes   = Practice expense relative value units for the service
RVUms   = Malpractice expense relative value units for the service
GPCIwa   = Geographic practice cost indices (GPCI) value reflecting one-fourth of geographic variation in physician work applicable in the fee schedule area
GPCIpea = GPCI value for practice expense applicable in the fee schedule area
GPCIma   = GPCI value for malpractice expense applicable in the fee schedule area
CF   = Conversion factor (dollar denominated)

After the work components had been valued, two additional values had to be determined: practice expense and malpractice expense. The practice expense component reflects the overhead costs associated with providing the service. Practice expense and malpractice expense components were calculated by reviewing their historical costs, which were based on specialty-specific overhead ratios. The practice and malpractice expense ratios for a particular service were calculated to reflect a weighted average based on all the specialties performing the services.

During the consideration on the OBRA-89 legislation, debate arose over the need for adjustments to the fee schedule to account for variations and geographic costs. Geographic practice cost indices (GPCIs; pronounced "gypsies") were developed to make geographic adjustments against each of the fee schedule components. The practice expense GPCI is intended to account for variations of office rents, employee wages, and other operating expenses. The malpractice GPCI was used to adjust the malpractice component of the cost in order to reflect the varying costs of malpractice liability insurance in different localities. The third factor, the physician-work component GPCI, was the most controversial. Rural physicians complained that it was unfair to reward urban physicians with higher incomes simply because they practiced in areas with higher costs. They persuasively argued that physician cost of living was directly linked to the attractiveness of the location. Compromise was reached where only one quarter of the geographic variations of physician GPCI would be used to adjust the payments.

After the work, practice expense, and malpractice components are determined and geographic costs are adjusted, the sum is multiplied by the conversion factor. The conversion factor is a monetary multiplier and is used nationally to compute the reimbursement level. The conversion factors can be adjusted annually to meet Congress's budgetary goals. For example, Medicare uses a Sustainable Growth Rate (SGR) mechanism to control expenditures for physicians' services.

The Billing and Collection Process

After the task of defining the service and linking it to its appropriate diagnosis is completed, the billing and collection phase of the physician reimbursement process begins. Each physician or group needs to create a billing and collection policy, a written set of procedures under which patients are expected to pay for the services they receive. A number of factors need to be considered when determining the payment policy. Does the group expect payment at the time of service (PATOS)? The advantages of this payment system, one of which is a rapid payment cycle with a low level of accounts receivable outstanding at any point in time, have to be weighed against the potential loss of patients who resent the unwillingness of the provider to bill the insurance companies for their appropriate balances. Patients may choose to obtain their services from competitors who offer more liberal collection policies.

The group or physician also needs to decide whether it will become a Medicare-participating provider. Under this reimbursement option, the physician agrees to undertake the responsibility of collecting 80% of the approved charge directly from the Medicare carrier, making the patient responsible for only the 20% co-payment and deductibles. Again, the socioeconomic characteristics of the target market need to be considered.

Insurance Submission

After the CPT and ICD codes have been selected for the encounter, claims are submitted to insurance companies for payment. Claims can be submitted on paper, often on universal billing forms, or electronically if the practice is automated. Each year, greater numbers of practices utilize electronic billing, because payment often is made more quickly, important management information can be produced, and submission costs can be reduced or eliminated. The payer applies its own rules when processing the claim. It may reject a charge based on inappropriate use, such as billing a follow-up visit as a new patient encounter. The insurer also may apply a fee screen (an automated edit of information). The fee screen will approve payment only for charges with specific diagnoses related to the services rendered. The rationale behind these fee screens is that tests and procedures are valid only for a limited range of diagnoses and appropriate patient types. For example, Medicare will not pay for a fundus photograph (a photograph of the retina) when the diagnosis is cataract (cloudiness of the lens).

Insurance companies often will reject unbundled codes, which represent multiple components of a global service. The insurance companies often adopt their own internally developed fee screens. These screens also may incorporate frequency-of-use limitations. This trend has continued to accelerate in both the private and governmental insurer fields as software is developed to enforce compliance with the insurers' disease management criteria.

The Accounting Process

In order to evaluate the efficiency of the billing process, the physician should establish an accounting system that collects all the pertinent information. One of the commonly used systems is the chart of accounts developed by the Center for Research in Ambulatory Health Care Administration (CRAHCA).[19]

Gross charges are defined as the full value of medical services provided before any adjustment. Gross charges are then reduced by the following items:

- Charity adjustments
- Contractually agreed-upon reimbursement discounts (i.e., the difference between the charge and what the insurer allows on an assigned claim)
- Courtesy adjustments (such as for other physicians)
- Employee discounts

The result is the adjusted (net) gross charges or the maximum amount of payment that could be collected if all payers (insurers and patients paying co-insurance and deductibles) met their obligations. Net gross charges then become the collection goal of a physician practice.

The next step in the collection process is to record all cash payments collected from patients or the amount paid on their behalf by insurance companies and other payers. Noncash adjustments are referred to as payment allowances. These noncash adjustments are composed of bad debts, settlements, and provision for bad debts. Any remaining balance after the deduction of these items would represent a change in the accounts receivable.

The importance of timely and careful evaluation of the collection process cannot be overemphasized. Disruptions of cash flow can have major negative impacts. First, if fees are not collected in an efficient manner, the practice could suffer a liquidity crisis and be unable to meet its ongoing obligations. Second, and perhaps more important, the older a receivable is, the less likely it is to be collected. As the time period between the rendering of the service and demand for payment increases, patients will rationalize reasons why the fee was too high or they didn't receive what was expected. There is a greater perceived value to the service at the time the service is rendered.

Financial analysis and operational measurement generate numeric ratios and values that can be used to benchmark the organization's collection activity. These tools are utilized by well-run organizations, irrespective of the size of the organization.

Billing and Collection Systems

A physician practice has a number of options, manual and computerized, under which it can manage the billing and collection process. There are effective manual accounting systems, adequate for smaller practices that operate under a payment-at-time-of-service collection policy. The two common manual accounting systems used are the double entry system and the pegboard system.

A double entry system uses a charge and payment journal and individual records for each patient that list the individual's charges and payments, referred to as a ledger card. When a charge is incurred, a charge is entered into the charge and payment journal, as well as the ledger card. Thus, there is a double entry for each account activity.

The pegboard system improves on the double entry system by relying on a single-entry system. The ledger card is aligned in such a way that activity recorded in it also is recorded on a day sheet (listing all the day's transactions) by the use of carbon or duplicating paper. The entry also simultaneously creates the bill. Such systems, however, rely heavily on manual clerical functions for repetitive billing and aging of receivables. Both of these approaches are rudimentary and create only limited management information.

The trend in collection systems is toward computerized systems for a number of reasons. Most computerized collection systems are able to generate standard health claim insurance forms efficiently, a process that is very inefficient for manual systems, requiring work that duplicates efforts performed in the charge-posting activities. The overwhelming majority are capable of electronically transmitting these claims to Medicare carriers and other insurance companies. Many systems are capable of posting remittances electronically as well. The net result is faster and more accurate turnaround of claims payments. Computer systems also can be programmed to generate bills to patients without interrupting normal office procedures. Outsourcing solutions that print, fold, and mail statements and collection letters without using the practice's clerical staff can also be used. In addition, most of these systems include computerized patient scheduling capability.

More sophisticated computer systems are able to pre-edit insurance submissions as well. By applying diagnosis and procedure linkages, submission errors due to miscoding or inappropriate unbundled charges can be prevented or corrected prior to submission. This helps to control the costs associated with the processing of denials, manual resubmission of claims, and telephone hearings with the insurer. It also flags inappropriate practice patterns, reduces the inflation of gross charges that can occur through inappropriate and uncollectible charge entry, and speeds the collection of patient co-payments, as well as payments made by insurers.

Of particular importance is the ability to generate an aged accounts receivable and other analyses. These reports categorize the age of a receivable, which is calculated as the number of days since the service was rendered. This is an extremely important benchmark to monitor because of the previously described loss of collectibility over time. Such a system also can be set up to force manual review, followed by the write-off or placement with collection agencies of uncollected debts.

Computerized collection systems also help reduce labor costs associated with manual systems. Submission of insurance claims on behalf of Medicare patients, now required by law, requires the repetitive entry of demographic and policy information. Many individuals will expect the practice to generate commercial insurance claim forms as well. This activity helps to expedite the payment of physician services to the patient. Basic computer and software packages capable of handling small practices are available for less than $5,000, although systems for large groups can exceed $250,000.

The need for information about the practice also makes computerization valuable, particularly in a managed care environment. The data entered in the course of recording account activity can give important insights into the demographics, case mix, and referral patterns in the practice. The ability to identify changes and extrapolate trends allows the physician to react proactively. Increasingly, practices use the demographic and diagnosis information contained in the computer's database to interact with patients through targeted newsletters and other communications calculated to aid patient retention and service utilization of discretionary healthcare purchases, such as cosmetic surgery and aesthetic services and supplies.

Computerized billing and collections systems need not be owned by the practice. The practice can contract with an independent billing organization referred to as a service bureau. A service bureau functions solely to collect payments owed to physicians and other healthcare providers. By providing a collection function for a number of physicians, economies of scale and attention to the collection process can be achieved that may not occur within the physician's practice, with its focus on patient care. Service bureaus typically are paid on a percentage-of-collection basis, and this motivates them to collect efficiently and promptly. This is not to disparage in any way the ability of a physician's own employees to effectively collect patient accounts; many can and do achieve results comparable to or significantly better than those provided by service bureaus. Management oversight, training, and system design always are the keys to a successful collection procedure, whether the activity takes place within the physician's office or through a service bureau. The efficiency of the collection function can be compared to collection data compiled by independent sources. A number of organizations, such as the Medical Group Management Association (MGMA), collect median data indicating gross and adjusted collection rates, as well as accounts receivable aging data.

Evaluation of Managed Care
Contracts and Opportunities

Few physician practices can afford to ignore opportunities presented by managed care contracting. Some specialties, such as cosmetic plastic surgery, are unaffected by insurance requirements because there is generally no coverage. However, nonparticipation in insurance plans limits these specialties' access to patients seeking insured reconstructive surgery following an accident. Physician groups that enjoy a monopoly in their marketplace also can remain relatively resistant to the fee controls that can be a part of managed care contracting, but may suffer a diminishment in patient demand due to higher out-of-pocket costs.

The majority of managed care contracting continues to take the form of negotiated discounts. These may be a percentage reduction in the charge. Most frequently, prices are set at a premium or discount to the Medicare fee schedule or other relative value system. Patients pay a co-payment amount, which may be fixed or a percentage of the amount allowed for the services.

It is important to understand the current or projected market share of the prospective MCOs. The reimbursement that a physician accepts under the contract is often heavily dependent on the projected volume of services that the practice will gain, retain, or forfeit through nonparticipation. Careful intelligence and networking, along with requests for information from the MCO, should include:

- A general plan description
- The number of covered lives in the marketplace
- Affiliated insurance companies
- Sample provider contract
- Financial status of the plan
- Payment terms and co-payments
- Withhold amounts
- Authorization processes and guidelines

Inasmuch as any arrangement with an MCO requires substantial administrative time and expense, the practice should focus its MCO contracting efforts on those plans that offer the best reimbursement terms and meaningful populations of patients.

Management of the patient mix between private pay, discounted, and capitated patient population is essential. A useful analogy is often made between a physician practice and an airplane. Each day planes/physicians roll out to start a schedule. To be maximally efficient, the plane/ schedule has to be full. To maximize revenue, the plane/physician wants to provide as many first-class seats/full-fee patients as possible, followed by business class seats/discounted PPO patients, filling the remainder of the plane/schedule with discounted advanced booking/capitation seats. If the plane/physician books too many advance-booking seats/capitation patients, revenue suffers as first-class seats/full-fee patients and business class seats/discounted PPO patients cannot be accommodated. The mix of filled seats/office appointments is critical to maximize profit. Yield management models can be used to adjust this mix.

Authorization Process

Many managed care contracts require some level of authorization before providing services to the insured. These may be quite limited, as in general indemnity policies where authorization may be necessary only prior to a nonemergency hospital admission. Other tightly controlled plans, such as HMOs, may require preauthorization for any visit to a physician other than a primary care physician, restrictions on approved hospitals and home health services, and authorization for diagnostic testing and office-based surgical treatments. It is important for the physician services organization to set up a system that provides the pertinent information to the appropriate personnel in a timely fashion; that is, before the services are rendered. A practice can incur significant losses through poor authorization control, and every member of the staff needs to be attuned to strong authorization compliances.

Capitation is another method by which MCOs contract with physicians for services. Under capitation, physicians agree to provide a designated list of services to patients for a fixed payment, per member per month (PMPM). Risks are thereby transferred from the insurer to the physician to control costs associated with the listed procedures. In essence, the physician becomes the insurance company for risk associated with the amount and level of care provided.

In order to set capitation rates, the physician practice, utilizing the data derived from actuaries, attempts to project the amount and cost of service the population will require to be served adequately. The age, sex, and employment status of the population can have important cost implications. The cost of providing eye care escalates dramatically in senior populations, whereas the cost of obstetric care is very low in patient populations that are skewed to middle-aged and older individuals. Specialty-specific analysis is necessary to understand fully the population subject to be bid. Frequently, stop-loss provisions are included to protect the physician from extraordinary costs, such as those associated with organ transplants or complications that can require extremely intensive therapies.

Financial Benchmarking

Financial benchmarking, often referred to as ratio analysis, is an important management tool necessary for sound practice management. Benchmarks are numerical indexes, used regularly and systematically, measuring overall performance or the performance of a specific target process (see **Exhibit 18.4**). Although it is a numeric index, the data reviewed may consist of either quantitative or qualitative measures. Two levels of benchmark comparison are possible. First, the organization compares its performance against past or projected performance in order to evaluate trends. Second, the organization may compare and contrast its performance with

Exhibit 18.4   Examples of Ratio Types

Liquidity Ratios

$$\text{Common Ratio} = \frac{\text{Current Assets}}{\text{Current Liabilities}}$$

$$\text{Quick Ratio} = \frac{\text{Cash + Marketable Securities + Accounts Receivable}}{\text{Current Liabilities}}$$

$$\text{Receivable Days} = \frac{\text{Accounts Receivable}}{\text{Net Collections}/365}$$

Profitability Ratios

$$\text{Write-Off Ratio} = \frac{\text{Charge Adjustments and Allowances}}{\text{Gross Charges}}$$

$$\text{Adjusted Collection Percentage} = \frac{\text{Gross Charges – Allowances and Adjustments}}{\text{Net Collections}}$$

Capitalization Ratios

$$\text{Fixed Asset Ratio} = \frac{\text{Total Operating Revenue}}{\text{Fixed Assets}}$$

Activity Ratios

$$\text{Surgery Yield (Specific type of) or Laser Yield} = \frac{\text{Total Patient Visits}}{\text{Surgeries (or Lasers)}}$$

$$\text{New Patient Ratio} = \frac{\text{Total Patients}}{\text{New Patients}}$$

external data compiled by organizations such as the MGMA, covering larger populations of self-reporting organizations. Benchmarks are useful in that they:

- Summarize complex information
- Allow early detection of financial problems
- Help in the management of payables and receivables
- Provide a framework for revenue and expense budgeting
- Allow the monitoring of re-engineered processes
- Provide a method to measure the performance of objectives identified during the practice's periodic goal-setting exercises

For analysis to be appropriate and sensitive, the design of the benchmarking system needs to consider the comparability, consistency, predictability, and relevance of the measure. When comparing ratios, particularly to externally derived benchmarks, it is important to understand the characteristics of the external measure. Is the group in the same specialty? Are there geographic or demographic biases? Is the data set composed of high-performing practices rather than "average" organizations?

Consistency refers to measurement of the item being reported. Are expenses carefully and uniformly classified by the reporting sites? Do all the reporting practices recognize a given expense within the same general ledger account? Predictability is another important feature of good indexing. Does the measure offer insight into future organizational or financial performance? And is that insight relevant or meaningful?

There are four types of practice ratios:

1. Liquidity ratios—The ability of the practice to meet payment obligations
2. Profitability ratios—The difference between the organization's expenses and revenues
3. Capitalization ratios—The relationships between debt and equity
4. Activity ratios—The relationships between input and output

The most commonly used liquidity ratios are the common ratio (current assets divided by current liabilities) and the quick ratio, expressed as the sum of cash, marketable securities, and accounts receivable divided by current liabilities. When the ratio falls below one in either case, the practice will likely experience a cash shortfall in meeting its current expenses, necessitating the use of additional liability financing. When using the quick ratio, care must be taken to value properly the accounts receivable. An unrealistic valuation—that is, one that does not properly quantify the bad debt and contractual allowances—will result in a quick ratio that misstates the ability to meet short-term obligations.

Although not strictly a measure of liquidity, receivable days and payable days measure the effectiveness of the collection process and the time lag in paying expenses. Receivable days are expressed as accounts receivable divided by annual net collections divided by 365 days. The measure determines the velocity at which services are converted into revenue. Gross or adjusted receivables can be used for the calculation, with adjusted receivables providing the best measure of velocity. Receivable days can be impacted by rapid insurance processing and submission, PATOS, and timely bad debt adjustments, all of which will reduce the number of days. Prepaid revenue, such as capitated payments received in advance of rendered services, will also cause a reduction in this important ratio. Rapid growth, whether cyclical or sustained, will, conversely, extend the number of days.

Payable days (current liabilities divided by annual operating expenses less depreciation divided by 365 days) measures the velocity at which expenses are being paid. This ratio is affected by periods of growth as well, because expenses during these periods often exceed the norm. Cash management requires attention to both numbers; a growing number of days in either measure can signal a coming liquidity crisis.

As with many accounting ratios, the best numbers to work with are based on accrual rather than cash accounting. Accrual-based accounting minimizes the effects of seasonality and timing, prepaid revenues and expenses, and other distortions caused by the failure to recognize payables, such as the need to fund retirement plan contributions. The careful tracking of profitability ratios has become increasingly important. The write-off ratio—the difference between gross charges and recognized revenue—has increased dramatically with the growth of managed care associated discounts, as well as Medicare fee schedules. If professional fees are set at a high level to maximize indemnity payments, the write-off ratio will be greater than for a practice with lower fees and equivalent collection efforts.

It is increasingly important to perform analysis on a by-payer basis. A careful review will allow the determination of the actual percentage of total claims paid by the payer. This not only indicates the extent to which the payer is adhering to the negotiated fee schedule, but also allows the observation of the impact of disallowances, bundling, and noncovered services.

It is vital that physicians and managers understand the differences between allowances and adjustments. Adjustments reduce the gross charge to the amount that can be theoretically collected. For example, if a procedure is charged at $125, and the associated Medicare allowed amount is $100, the account is credited with a $25 adjustment. The maximum amount legally collected on the patient's account is $100. In the event the patient failed to make the 20% co-pay, the account would be credited with a $20 allowance for bad debt (**Table 18.3**).

Allowances are the differences between gross charges and net revenues, and include such items as bad debts, settlements, and hardship adjustments extended by the physician after services are rendered. Bearing these issues in mind, the adjusted collection ratio (gross charges less adjustments divided by net collections) is the best measure of collection effectiveness.

Accounts receivable aging ratios also allow the measurement of collection velocity. Aging analysis tracks the proportion of total accounts receivable that fall within 30-, 60-, 90-, and 120-day-old periods since the charge was incurred. Several important factors must be considered. For example, consider similar periods. If the practice experiences seasonality, such as tourism inflows, these ratios will fluctuate a great deal. As the practice experiences an upswing in charges, the percentage of accounts in the older "buckets" will diminish. Likewise, at the end of the cycle, the older buckets will increase in percentage because of the wave effect. Why is it important to track receivables carefully? Consumer payment habits have shown that the longer a bill is deferred, the less likely it is to be paid. Excessive percentages of accounts more than 120 days old may indicate a suboptimal collection effort or a lack of discipline in the review of accounts for write-off or referral to a collection agency.

Table 18.3   Allowances Versus Adjustments

Physician fee	$125
Medicare allowed amount	$100
Adjustment	$ 25
Amount paid by Medicare	$ 80
Patient co-pay*	$ 20

*If the patient fails to make this 20% co-pay, the $20 would be considered allowance for bad debt.

There are also important operational (or activity) ratios that can be either financial or nonfinancial measures. Examples of financial activity ratios are the percentage of nonphysician (staff) payroll expenses expressed as a percentage of revenue. Likewise, many practices track the percentage of revenues paid in the form of payroll and nonpayroll discretionary expenses distributed to the physicians and physician-owners. Other financial ratios include revenue per physician day worked, percentage of revenue generated through surgical codes, and average charges per patient.

Nonfinancial activity ratios are also important. The new patient ratio (new patients divided by total patients) is an often-tracked ratio in surgically based practices. Most surgically based practices experience the highest charges at the initial time period shortly following the new patient registration. Following surgery, there is often a period during which the surgeon provides follow-up care at no charge, or provides low-revenue office visits. The new patient ratio acts as a leading indicator of practice charges and is also sensitive to changes in referral patterns, advertising effectiveness, and patient-to-patient referral.

There are important caveats associated with all ratio analyses. Ratios provide measurement, not answers. There is no "correct" answer, and no single ratio can provide a good measure of practice "health." Some ratios may actually be counterintuitive on face value. For example, it is commonly believed that a low overhead ratio is an indication of a well-run practice. Yet, a citation at the beginning of this chapter showed that group practices with higher overhead ratios generated higher incomes to the physicians and physician-owners, because of higher levels of capital investment and wider service offerings. The physicians are taking home a small portion of a larger pie—but the slice is bigger than the larger slice of a small pie.

Other important factors also impact the ratios. Environmental differences, such as inner city locations and poor local economies, negatively impact collection ratios, as does high managed care penetration. Differences from the norm can be part of a strategic plan. Practices that take aggressive marketing positions, such as high advertising levels, to stimulate the demand for services will have higher expense ratios than the norm. Practices also may offer low margin services in order to provide comprehensive care.

Practice philosophy and strategy also can have important impacts on the numbers. The physicians may have a heavily referral-based practice that has adopted the position that no one is turned away on the basis of ability to pay. Or, the physician may enjoy a more casual, less hurried approach to practice. Conversely, staffing costs might be increased through scribing and dictation costs in order to maximize physician productivity.

Ratio analysis needs to be undertaken carefully with an understanding of the practice, its goals, and the environment in which it practices. It is most valuable as a comparative measure within the practice, an indicator of change in relative performance over a comparable pertinent prior period measure. It becomes relatively less valuable as the measure is applied in comparison to other practices in the same specialty, and increasingly less relevant when compared to practices in dissimilar specialties and markets.

Notwithstanding these weaknesses, it is important to benchmark in order to carefully measure the impact of internal change, as well as performance, against the peer group. Benchmarking and ratio analysis are powerful tools that take data and turn it into information.

References

1A. Centers for Medicare & Medicaid Services. National health expenditure data. Available at: http://www.cms.hhs.gov/NationalHealthExpendData/02_NationalHealthAccounts Historical.asp#TopOfPage. Updated October 28, 2009. Accessed Februrary 16, 2009.

1. Coddington D, et al. *The Crisis in Healthcare*. San Francisco, CA: Jossey-Bass; 1990:38.

2. American Medical Association. *Physician Socioeconomic Statistics*. 2000–2002 ed. Chicago, IL: American Medical Association; 2002:110.

3. American Medical Association. *Physician Characteristics and Distribution in the US*. 2002–2003 ed. Chicago, IL: American Medical Association; 2003:42.

4. Havlicek P, Eiler M, eds. *Physician in Medical Groups: A Comparative Analysis*. Chicago, IL: American Medical Association; 1993:7.

5. Ibid, 28.

6. American Medical Association. *Physician Socioeconomic Statistics*. 2000–2002 ed. Chicago, IL: American Medical Association; 2002:73.

7. Havlicek P, Eiler M, eds. *Physician in Medical Groups: A Comparative Analysis*. Chicago, IL: American Medical Association; 1993:14.

7A. Surowiecki J. *The Wisdom of Crowds: Why the Many Are Smarter Than the Few and How Collective Wisdom Shapes Business, Economies, Societies, and Nations*. Random House; 2005.

7B. American Medical Group Association. 2008 physician retention survey. Newswise. Available at: http://www.newswise.com/articles/view/549601/.

8. Hyman H. *Health Planning: A Systematic Approach*. Gaithersburg, MD: Aspen Publishers; 1975:10–13.

9. Health Insurance Association of America. *Source Book of Health Insurance Data*. Washington, DC: HIAA; 1992:116–117.

10. Hyman H. *Health Planning: A Systematic Approach*. Gaithersburg, MD: Aspen Publishers; 1975:13.

11. Health Insurance Association of America. *Source Book of Health Insurance Data*. Washington, DC: HIAA; 1992:17.

12. American Medical Association. *Physician Socioeconomic Statistics*. 2000–2002 ed. Chicago, IL: American Medical Association; 2002:8.

12A. Kaiser Family Foundation. Kaiser/HRET survey of employer sponsored health benefits, 1999–2008. Kaiser Family Foundation. Available at: http://ehbs.kff.org/?page=charts&id =1&sn=5&ch=564.

13. By the numbers 2002. *Modern Healthcare*. 2002; December:23, 24.

14. Shouldice R, Shouldice K. 1978. *Medical Group Practice and Health Maintenance Organizations*. Washington, DC: Information Resources Press; 1978:10.

14A. Carlson RP. Physician practice management companies: too good to be true? *Family Practice Management*. 1998;5(4):45–46, 49–51, 55–56.

15. Cowan D. *Preferred Provider Organizations: Planning, Structure and Operation*. Gaithersburg, MD: Aspen Publishers; 1984:5.

15A. Miguel MF, Bowen HK. Ophthalmic consultants of Boston and Dr Bradford J Shingleton. Harvard Business School case 9-697-080. Cambridge, MA: Harvard Business School Publishing; 1997.

16. American Medical Association. *Physicians' Current Procedural Terminology*. Chicago, IL: American Medical Association; 1993.

17. Brittenhom J, ed. *1991 HCFA common procedure coding system*. Los Angeles, CA: Practice Management Information Corporation; 1991:1.

18. *ICD.9.CM.* Los Angeles, CA: Practice Management Information Corporation; 1993:270.
19. Schafer E, et al, eds. *Management Accounting for Fee-for-Service/Prepaid Medical Groups.* Englewood, CO: Center for Research in Ambulatory Health Care Administration; 1989.

Biographical Information

Michael J. Kelley, MBA, CMPE, is the Director of Strategic Operations for the University of Miami Miller School of Medicine at Florida Atlantic University, having previously acted as the Director of Satellite Operations and Ambulatory Surgery for the Bascom Palmer Eye Institute, University of Miami School of Medicine. Previously, he served as the Chief Operating Officer of Retina Consultants of Southwest Florida, a tertiary care ophthalmic group practice offering comprehensive medical, surgical, and rehabilitation services in Southwest Florida. Mr. Kelley began his healthcare career in 1980 and has participated as a lecturer in numerous professional educational programs, with a focus on financial management. He has served on the executive committee as president of the Ophthalmology Assembly, Medical Group Management Association, and has chaired the American Academy of Ophthalmology's committee guiding the development of administrator skill levels. He received a BS in Biology as a Faculty Scholar and an MBA with an emphasis in marketing and management at Florida Atlantic University. Mr. Kelley is active as a member of the Medical Reserve Corp., and led a first response team for Hurricanes Katrina and Rita.

Steven Falcone, MD, MBA, is the Executive Clinical Dean for the University of Miami Miller School of Medicine at Florida Atlantic University and Associate Professor of Radiology, Neurosurgery, and Ophthalmology. He has previously served as the Medical Director of Radiology Services in the Department of Radiology and Vice Chair of the University of Miami Medical Group. He also serves as a delegate for the American Society of Neuroradiology to the House of Delegates of the American Medical Association. He obtained his MD and MBA degrees from the University of Miami and is board certified by the American Board of Radiology with added qualification in Neuroradiology.

Stephen G. Schwartz, MD, MBA, is Assistant Professor of Clinical Ophthalmology at University of Miami Miller School of Medicine, and Medical Director and Division Chief of Bascom Palmer Eye Institute at Naples. Previously, he served as Assistant Professor of Ophthalmology and Program Director of Ophthalmology at Virginia Commonwealth University, Medical College of Virginia Campus. Dr. Schwartz is board certified by the American Board of Ophthalmology and is a practicing vitreoretinal surgeon. He received a BS with honors in Biological Sciences at Cornell University, an MD at New York University School of Medicine, and an MBA at Northwestern University's Kellogg School of Management.

Implementing a Physician Practice Compliance Program*

Lawrence F. Wolper

Planning and implementing a compliance plan and program have far greater operational implications to physician practices and physician organizations than are apparent in much of the literature. Before implementing a compliance plan and program, broad organizational and operational issues should be considered by the individual physician, physician group practice, or physician organization (e.g., management services organization, independent practice association [IPA], faculty practice plan, large network, or group practice). Succinctly stated, the question is: Can individual physicians, small physician practices, or even larger physician organizations plan, implement, and operate successful compliance programs within their current organizational and operating structures, "corporate" cultures, management styles, and historical manners of doing business, or do some of these organizational matters need to be addressed and possibly changed before a plan can succeed?

Before proceeding further with this discussion, it is important to note that for the purposes of the Office of Inspector General (OIG) compliance plan guidelines and programs, the term physician is defined as "(1) a doctor of medicine or osteopathy; (2) a doctor of dental surgery or of dental medicine; (3) a podiatrist; (4) an optometrist; or (5) a chiropractor, all of whom must be appropriately licensed by the State."[1]

It is clear from the recent OIG Compliance Program for Individual and Small Group Physician Practices that the intent of a compliance plan and program is to install a working system to reduce or eliminate abusive and fraudulent practices, not only relating to billing and collections, but also, eventually, to other areas of "business" risk. The OIG appears to be sympathetic to the limited resources of small practices and individual physicians: "The guidance

---

*This article originally appeared in Aspen Publishers' *Physician Compliance Resource Manual*, www.aspen publishers.com. Reprinted with permission.

provides great flexibility as to how a physician practice could implement compliance efforts in a manner that fits with the practice's existing opportunities and resources."[2] Significantly, the OIG has loosened the requirement that physician practices implement all seven of the basic components of an effective compliance program derived from the Federal Sentencing Guidelines and listed in previous guidances as necessary for other types of healthcare providers. The OIG acknowledges that full implementation of all components may not be feasible for smaller physician practices and that a practice can begin by identifying risk areas that, based on the practice's history, would benefit from closer scrutiny as well as specific policies, monitoring, and training.

Although sympathetic to the limitations faced by smaller groups, "The OIG believes that written policies and procedures can be helpful to all physician practices, regardless of size and capability."[3] The OIG also appears to suggest a more detailed and comprehensive standard for larger practices: "By contrast, larger practices . . . can use both this guidance [i.e., the recent guidelines for individual physicians and small group practices] and the Third-Party Medical Billing Company Compliance Program Guidance."[4]

In response to the broad range of compliance plans that may be required for physician groups, the scope of this chapter encompasses not only an exploration of the elements of a compliance plan and program, but also the organizational, operational, and managerial challenges that physicians and practice managers are likely to face when planning and implementing a compliance program. It is important to note that sections of this chapter (e.g., auditing and monitoring) present standards and principles that are not OIG requirements or recommendations, although in using terms such as independence, objectivity, and internal controls, one must suspect that the OIG had in mind some of the matters that will be discussed in this chapter.

This chapter is organized into the following topics:

- The compliance plan within the context of a physician practice
- The elements of compliance plans and programs
- A planning and implementation work plan

The Compliance Plan Within the Context of a Physician Practice

Collectively, the Federal Sentencing Guidelines and the OIG Compliance Program for Individual and Small Group Physician Practices refer to processes and procedures that are not necessarily incorporated into the daily operations of many physician practices and physician organizations, regardless of size or organizational setting. For example, they make reference to auditing, monitoring, internal controls, sampling, due diligence, and standards of organizational and employee behavior.

The OIG recommendation that a compliance plan include internal auditing to focus on high-risk billing and coding issues[5] in and of itself necessitates the implementation of a range of organizational and operational changes. This holds true for smaller practices that may select only a simple random sample of 5 or 10 charts per provider or federal payer, but more so for larger physician practices that will select larger samples and use established audit and sampling guidelines.

In addition, the body of OIG compliance guidance refers to responsibility, authority, and lines of communication (e.g., when defining the role of the compliance officer). These elements are not always clearly defined in physician practices because of the frequent duality of management roles between physicians and lay practice managers, as well as other factors that differentiate physician practices and physician organizations from organizations in other industries. Although the OIG compliance guidance does not address these issues directly, they are nonetheless important to the operationalization of a compliance program and the effectiveness of the compliance officer's/contact's position, regardless of the size of the practice.

Planning and implementing a compliance plan and program should begin with an understanding of the organizational contexts into which these plans will be placed, and what managerial and operational changes may be required to accommodate these programs and ensure that they are effective and dynamic over time. This discussion will address a range of managerial and organizational functions that will be affected or will be required to be in place when implementing a compliance plan. The topical areas that will be covered are: delegation, responsibility, and authority; planning, controlling, and conducting evaluation and feedback; human resources management; and management styles, corporate culture, and compliance.

Delegation, Responsibility, and Authority

Management is working with, and delegating functional tasks and responsibilities to, other people in an organization to achieve the objectives of the organization. Responsibility is defined as a duty or activity that has to be accomplished. A high degree of delegation of responsibility and decision making in a physician practice implies that many employees, particularly at senior levels, do not require constant oversight. Generally, in larger and more complex organizations, the need to delegate responsibility is greater. Delegation allows senior staff more time to accomplish tasks that are consistent with their level of experience, education, and areas of direct responsibility. Authority is defined as the power to act on someone else's behalf. The delegation of responsibility should be accompanied by the granting of a concomitant amount of authority to carry out the delegated tasks. Authority also involves the ability to make decisions, often independent of a superior in the organization.

In physician practices, responsibility and authority are not always delegated in parity with one another. Physicians, primarily because they have been medically trained in an apprenticeship setting, generally are comfortable delegating medical tasks to other physicians and clinical personnel, because they assume that individuals who also have been medically trained are capable of a range of clinical tasks. On the other hand, physician leaders often have less experience and comfort when delegating business tasks to lay personnel. Because the nature of medicine and physician practice has both medical service and business elements, it is likely there always will be an overlap in roles between physicians and lay management, even in small groups. This is dissimilar to organizations in most other industries. This overlap in roles—and often the related managerial tensions—tends to increase as the following practice characteristics or combinations of these characteristics increase:

- Practice size (numbers of physicians, other providers, and lay staff)
- Hierarchical complexity
- Range of clinical services offered
- Degree of organizational decentralization
- Involvement in medical education and research

The most notable organizational setting that is an example of all of these characteristics, and in which there are particular challenges to implementing and managing a compliance plan and program, is the faculty practice plan. If the faculty plan is decentralized along departmental and clinical or specialty lines, delegation of responsibility and authority from upper levels of management to lower levels, and laterally, can become difficult. It is not unusual in many faculty plans, as well as large multispecialty groups, for an imbalance to exist between the responsibility and the authority delegated to management, with the authority being more resident in positions held by physicians.

If the amount of authority delegated is not commensurate with the level of responsibility, the ability to execute the tasks necessary to achieve the goals of the organization is hampered. Therefore, to implement a compliance plan and program, the individuals with delegated responsibility for the entire program (e.g., the full- or part-time compliance officer or contact), or for components of the program (e.g., auditors, receptionists, billers, or collectors), also must be given a requisite amount of authority.

When considering the functions of a compliance officer, larger practices may wish to turn to the Compliance Program Guidance for Third-Party Medical Billing Companies, which identifies that the organization "should designate a compliance officer (and/or a compliance committee) to serve as the focal point for compliance activities. This responsibility may be the individual's sole duty or added to other management functions depending upon the size and resources of the organization, and complexity of the task." The Guidance stresses that it is critical to the success of the program that the compliance officer have "appropriate authority," be a high-level official in the organization, and have "direct" access to the organization's governing body (in a smaller practice, shareholders), all other senior management, and legal counsel.[6]

Carrying out these themes in larger physician practices, physician organizations, and faculty practice plans may require that the compliance officer and related compliance functions be centralized, while including the assistance and input of departmental chairpersons and managers. Direct access to the governing body suggests that these individuals should have enough authority to accomplish their responsibilities without being pressured or influenced by physician clinical department heads.

In its Compliance Program Guidance for Individual and Small Group Physician Practices, the OIG takes a more relaxed view of delegation related to the compliance officer/contact for small practicers. Unlike the guidelines for billing companies, small practices may designate more than one employee with compliance monitoring responsibility, and these individuals can be called compliance contacts. The OIG also suggests that a compliance officer can serve that role for more than one practice, or a practice may outsource that function to an outside person. The OIG notes that care should be exercised in making the decision regarding the manner in which the organization fills the role of compliance officer.

For small practices, the issue of independence and potential conflicts of interest can become problematic if assigning compliance roles to an office manager or billing staff, or indeed anyone whose regular responsibilities are activities that represent an area of risk for the practice. The OIG recommendation could, for example, lead to a supervisor auditing the correctness and adequacy of his or her own billing, as well as that of the doctor(s) for whom he or she works. This may be a very difficult task in a small, closely held practice. It generally would require added oversight from the physician, who, because it is his or her records and billings that are being audited, may not be entirely independent either. Further, reliable auditing results require not only a knowledge of correct billing and coding, but also an awareness of correct auditing approaches. In small practices, billing staff may not have the requisite knowledge. An alternative may be to outsource the auditing function, which the OIG recognizes as an acceptable solution.

Planning, Controlling, Evaluation, and Feedback

Planning, controlling, evaluation, and feedback are important to the success of all organizations, and they are at the core of effective compliance programs. They are referred to in OIG compliance guidelines for billing companies and laboratories, in the Federal Sentencing Guidelines, and in the OIG Compliance Program for Individual and Small Group Physician Practices. The three elements of management in any organization are planning, controlling, and conducting evaluation and feedback. Although systems for planning, controlling, and conducting evaluation and feedback cannot completely eliminate fraud, abuse, or waste, the existence of these controls can provide a reasonable mechanism to better ensure that these types of exposures are reduced over a period of time.

These three components of management form a continuous cycle, and they are important to the implementation of a compliance plan and program within a physician practice. It is only in recent years that physician practices have evolved from a "cottage" industry to a consolidating, corporately-oriented industry. Therefore, these three elements, as a continuous cycle, generally are not present in physician practices, regardless of size or organizational complexity. As such, the implementation of a compliance program is likely to require that one or more of these elements be put in place. This may be easier said than done.

Therefore, a discussion of this management cycle (i.e., planning, controlling, and conducting evaluation and feedback) and the tasks within each of these three components can provide the basis for many physician practices to plan and implement a compliance program. As mentioned earlier, these elements are identified in the seven basic compliance plan steps.

Strategic, Long-Term, and Operational Planning

There are three levels of planning: strategic, long-term, and operational. Strategic planning typically has a five-year analytical horizon. This level of planning includes market research; analysis of competition, market needs, and trends; assessment of opportunities and market threats; and evaluation of the strengths and weaknesses of the organization. Strategic planning answers the two-part question, "What businesses do we want to be in, and how do we want to conduct those businesses?" The outcome of these analyses will be an identification of the broad goals of the organization for the next five years. Goals are defined as long-range aims for a specific time period. Some of these goals will be articulated in an organization's mission statement, corporate bylaws, codes of ethics, and other statements of corporate vision. Objectives stem from goals, and they are defined as specific results that are expected within a time period, usually by the end of a budget cycle (typically one year).

Therefore, the commitment to compliance planning and a compliance program, as well as to the ongoing process of reducing and eliminating fraudulent, abusive, and wasteful corporate practices, ideally should stem from the strategic plan of a practice. It is not a government assumption that all groups have a strategic plan, and it is possible to make the commitment to compliance goals without having a written strategic plan in place, but it is easier to execute compliance goals if they also can be stated in strategic terms along with other long-term goals that may support the achievement of compliance planning.

For example, a compliance plan should require that new employees be properly screened and reference checks be conducted to determine if individuals have a record of prior offenses related to fraudulent or abusive practices. It also should require that position descriptions be drafted and regularly updated for employees engaged in the compliance process (as well as all other employees). If these functions have not occurred in a physician practice, or have been performed in too informal a manner, another strategic goal that supports compliance planning and ongoing programs would be to implement a more formal human resources function internally, or to outsource it.

Long-term planning has a shorter time horizon than strategic planning, typically not less than one year and no more than four. It answers more detailed questions about how to execute the broad strategic goals of the organization, and it includes the identification of financial and performance objectives, as well as the human and physical resources that may be necessary to accomplish the strategic plan.

Operational planning has the shortest time frame—typically less than a year—but it can be broken down into shorter intervals such as months or days. Operational planning encompasses assignment of tasks to designated personnel, required budgets, and production timetables.

Controlling

The second stage in the three-stage management cycle is management or internal control. In the Field Work Standards for Performance Audits that are used by federal auditors, the comptroller general of the United States defines management control in its fourth field work standard as the "organization, methods, and procedures adopted by management to ensure that its goals are met."[7] Management controls include systems for measuring, reporting, and monitoring program performance. These field work standards include four categories of management controls, the following two of which are directly applicable to controls in a physician practice:

1. Program operations—"Controls over program operations include policies and procedures that management has implemented that reasonably ensure that a program meets its objectives."[8]
2. Validity and reliability of data—"Controls over the validity and reliability of data include policies and procedures that management has implemented to reasonably ensure that valid and reliable data are obtained, maintained, and fairly disclosed."[9]

Applied to physician practices, this would include controls over the information that is used by physician practices, physician organizations, and physician billing computer systems to bill and collect for services rendered to patients. The application of these types of controls extends beyond the billing system because demographic and insurance information derives from the activities of appointment schedulers, registration personnel, and insurance companies. The absence of data validity and reliability controls, particularly in the appointment scheduling and registration subsystems of a practice's billing and collection process, can lead to incorrect billing at the least, the over- or undercollection of co-payments and deductibles, or patterns of not collecting co-payments or deductibles. Each is an area of risk.

Management texts define internal controls in a similar manner. Management controls are those policies and procedures that:

- Ensure the efficient and effective use of resources
- Involve the development of standards for employee performance
- Design work plans for the implementation and monitoring of internal programs
- Institute methods for motivating employees and appraising their performance
- Solve operational problems, coach, and counsel

In most organizations, many, if not all, of these functions involve human resources management or a human resources department. The human resources management function in many physician practices is informal, or does not exist. Therefore, in implementing a compliance plan, many practices will need to assess the degree to which they use effective human resources management.

Effective internal control over the billing and collection functions in small and large practices generally requires the creation and maintenance of internal operating policies and procedures. Related to the billing and collection cycle only, these policies and procedures should, at a minimum, encompass appointment scheduling, patient registration, insurance, data input, patient checkout, and collection. In practices that outsource computerized billing, vendor manuals provide only one component of this requirement. They are supplemental and generally pertain only to the computer system. They should be used in conjunction with policy and procedure manuals that are specific to the practice and its major operating systems.

Evaluation and Feedback

Evaluation and feedback, the third and last phase of the management cycle, involves both qualitative and quantitative methods for assessing whether the procedures and controls that have been established have resulted in the achievement of the program's goals. It leads to the beginning of the planning phase of the management process.

Methods for assessing the achievement of a program's goals can include analysis of budget outcomes, statistical analysis of the performance criteria that were established early in the management cycle, surveys of senior executives and employees, and retrospective audits. The evaluation and feedback phase of the management cycle is very important because it determines whether modifications need to be made in the planning and controlling phases to better ensure the achievement of the organization's strategic and long-term goals. If plans need to be modified, added, or deleted, the evaluation and feedback phase provides the information and analyses for management to make these decisions. If controls in one or more segments of a practice's procedures or policies are weak and need to be tightened in order to increase the probability of detecting unacceptable practices, it is the evaluation and feedback phase that provides the information to management to make these changes.

The OIG recognizes that the establishment and effectiveness of a compliance plan and program evolve over a period of time, and perhaps, particularly in smaller groups, initially focus only on matters related to accurate and proper billing. The evaluation and feedback mechanism ensures that the compliance process in small or large physician practices remains dynamic, current with changes in regulatory change, and in keeping with the unique characteristics of each physician practice.

Human Resources Management

Particularly for larger group practices, compliance plans and programs should include the following:

- Position descriptions for all employee categories that are involved in compliance (presumably for all position categories)
- Evaluation of employees and performance feedback periodically
- Employee sanctioning for those who do not adhere to the practice's ethical guidelines or policies and procedures related to the compliance plan
- Conformance to applicable labor, wage, and salary and other federal (e.g., Occupational Safety and Health Act) and state laws
- Methods to communicate with and receive communications from employees
- Recruitment and screening of prospective employees and checking of their references
- Compliance training for new and existing employees

Even if effectively used, these functions are not foolproof. Bad hires will occur, as will unidentifiable but adverse employee activities. The government is looking for reasonable and diligent efforts in the recruiting process, the employee evaluation mechanism, training, and other human resources management functions that can reinforce high ethical standards and reduce the possibility of illegal behavior.

Most, if not all, of the preceding functional tasks involve human resources management. Except for larger medical practices with established human resources management departments, many of these functions may not be in place or exist at all. In smaller practices, they may be handled informally. Human resources management, whether resident in a department within a larger practice or performed informally or outsourced in smaller practices, typically encompasses the following six functions:[10]

1. Human resources planning
   - Job analysis and job descriptions
   - Staffing levels
   - Staffing plans and policies and workforce objectives
   - Job evaluation
   - Wage and salary administration and merit and compensation planning
2. Employment
   - Identifying sources to recruit new candidates
   - Interviewing, testing, and performing reference checks of prospective candidates
   - Maintaining records and turnover statistics
3. Induction and orientation
   - Design of staff orientation programs
   - Processing of benefits
   - Performance of follow-up within probationary period
4. Training and development
   - Design and implementation of skills training and management development programs
   - Administration of tuition refund programs
5. Employee training and development
   - Design and administration of performance evaluation program
   - Training of management in management and motivational skills
   - Design and coordination of employee communication methods and programs
   - Administration of employee newsletter
6. Health and safety
   - Physical examinations
   - Occupational Safety and Health Administration (OSHA) requirements

The question that needs to be asked is, "How many physician practices, large or small, have the previous functions in place, informally or formally?" If the answer generally is unfavorable, practices that are implementing a compliance plan should consider which other functions need to be put in place.

To reiterate, the seven basic steps outlined by the OIG contain many principles and functions that are related to human resources management. Most can be accomplished through an existing human resources management department, can be delegated to appropriate personnel in smaller practices, or can be outsourced. Because of the range of functions that involve expertise in human resources management, it is important for practice managers and physicians to ensure that these tasks are monitored and evaluated, particularly in practices with more limited numbers of personnel or personnel without the requisite expertise.

Management Styles, Corporate Culture, and Compliance

In small or large groups, an underlying purpose of compliance activities is to create a culture within the organization that engenders the prevention, identification, and resolution of behaviors that are inconsistent with federal and state law, private insurer program requirements, and the practice's ethical and business policies. These goals and related policies should originate at the governing body level of the practice or, in smaller groups, with the physician owners. As stated earlier, it should be articulated in strategic plans, corporate bylaws, policies and procedures, and other corporate documents. Small practices should have bylaws and other corporate documents in which to infuse these communications. Moreover, they should be reinforced by the actions and attitudes of the physicians in the practice, as well as senior management, on a uniform and consistent basis so as to engender an attitude among all employees that there is zero tolerance for behaviors that are adverse to the prevention, identification, and resolution of activities that are inconsistent with federal and state law and private payer program requirements, as well as the practice's ethical and business policies.

The creation of an organizational culture is easier said than accomplished; it requires time, conscious effort, and commitment of capital. In smaller practices, the culture that exists often is a function of the personalities and management/medical styles of the key physicians. In larger integrated practices, corporate culture is influenced more by the attitudes and actions of the governing body, medical director, and senior management, as well as the ongoing management decisions that support the cultural vision of the practice. In decentralized but organized physician practices and faculty plans, corporate culture arises from the governing board, medical director, and senior management. It also is dependent on departmental managers and physician chairpersons to reinforce the corporate culture. In larger, more complex types of practice settings, the physician clinical department chairs, particularly in large, dominant clinical departments, can create a departmental culture that is not necessarily in harmony with the corporate culture. In these situations, the role of the medical director is even more important.

Culture, therefore, is changeable over time as the priorities of a practice evolve and the medical and managerial leadership changes. Because of the relationship between corporate culture and management style, as it pertains to compliance plans, an overview of major management theories may be useful.

Management Practices

Even in the smallest of organizations and physician practices, there is a relationship between the manner in which individuals manage (including physicians) and the establishment of corporate culture. Each of the management practices discussed has a certain type of management style or attitude, and each may have a different impact on the ease of implementing a compliance plan and motivating employees and physicians to embrace it.

During the mid-1800s through the early 1900s, the classical school of management first attempted to apply scientific approaches to management. Frederick W. Taylor, who is often referred to as the father of scientific management (as opposed to modern personnel administration), was among the first to introduce scientific principles to increase the efficiency of workers. The efforts of Taylor and other classicists were directed specifically at worker efficiency—learning the correct way to perform a task, or series of tasks, as determined by experts such as engineers, scientists, and managers in the field. Work was broken down into a series of standardized tasks, each of which was designed to produce the most efficient process. Taylor claimed that hidden waste in an organization and the resulting cost was a function of worker inefficiency. He believed that workers needed to be won over and led by management, and he was firmly committed to the principle that management was the only force that determined the nature of the work process and the workplace. "Won over" and "led" certainly describe a particularly autocratic and centralized style, with no focus on workers or their needs. This style in a physician practice would not likely create an environment conducive to compliance plans.

Whereas the classical school concentrated on work tasks performed by employees, the behavioral school of the late 1800s to 1950s stressed that sound management arises from an understanding of workers and what motivates them to work efficiently. This acknowledgment created very different, more democratic management styles that were worker inclusive. The genesis of this assertion was an outgrowth of the well-known Hawthorne experiments conducted by the social scientists Elton Mayo and FJ Roethlisberger.[11] These experiments greatly influenced the modern human relations movement in organizations and had a significant impact on our understanding of human behavior in the work environment. During these experiments, Mayo and his colleagues changed certain physical aspects of the work environment, such as lighting. They found that regardless of the intensity of the lighting, or any other changes in the work setting, worker productivity was enhanced. Mayo and associates discovered that the employees were responding not to the researchers' changes to the work setting, but rather to the fact that the workplace was more enjoyable. This stems from the workers' belief that they were taking part in an important experiment and felt a common identity and sense of belonging with the other participating employees. These factors, which related to the relationships among employees and individual employee psychology, were thus called human relations factors. In summary, these researchers observed that employees tended to cluster in informal groups in order to fill voids in their lives in the workplace that arose from an absence of management attention to their basic need for cooperation and comradeship.

Rensis Likert and Daniel Katz later identified that managers play a very important role in the success of an organization. Managers who were employee focused, were cooperative and reasonable, and used a democratic management style were more likely to be successful than those who focused primarily on production.[12]

AH Maslow's work added to our understanding of the needs and motivations of workers. He identified five sets of goals or basic worker needs: psychological, safety, love, esteem, and self-actualization. Maslow further found that these needs not only were related to one another, but also were arranged in a hierarchy of importance. Maslow posited that when a lower-level need was fairly well satisfied, the next highest need in the hierarchy emerged.[13] Other behavioral researchers and managers to this day see the worker as having perpetual needs that are both personal and social. These needs suggest that employees want to satisfy, through their work, their need for security, independence, participation, and growth.

Applying the principles of Maslow and other behavioral scientists, Japanese industrialists innovated quality circles over three decades ago. The outcomes include enhanced self-images of workers, increased quality, improved worker morale, and greater managerial ability. This approach to the worker, the work environment, and management style is what underlies successful human resources management in hospitals and physician practices around the country.

In implementing some or all of the core principles stated in the seven basic elements, most of which require employee cooperation and "buy in" to the compliance plan, the physicians and managers in both small and large practices should consider what type of management style and culture they have in place. It would appear that the closer their management style is to the findings of Maslow and the others who followed his tenets, the more fertile will be the environment for compliance planning and effective management in general. Because physician practices continue to evolve from small independent workplaces to larger, more corporate settings, physicians and management need to be attentive to human resources management, management style, and corporate culture. The principles that arise from the work of Maslow and others point to the hazards of operating a physician practice, large or small, in an autocratic manner.

Many physician practices are high-volume, high-stress settings in which physicians and staff can be "overburdened." It may appear easier in these settings to use an autocratic, production-oriented style, but this approach tends to demotivate employees. The behaviorist approach tends to engender a team concept that is more conducive to maintaining high morale.

The Elements of Compliance Plans and Programs

The previous section places the compliance plan and program into the broader context of general management, operations, organization, and internal controls. One could argue that if physician practices employed the elements that have been discussed earlier in this section, they would already have a significant portion of the framework for a compliance plan in place. This argument generally would be correct, and all the practice would need to do is to infuse a set of guidelines that were specific to the seven basic elements. However, even in today's consolidating practice environment, most physician practices are not large and do not employ the types of organizational, managerial, or formal human resources management practices that one would find in most organizations. The OIG, as evidenced by its recent guidelines for individual physicians and small group practices, appears cognizant of this fact.

A discussion of the managerial and operational implications of implementing a compliance plan should facilitate understanding of the areas physician practices may need to address in implementing any or all of the seven basic components of a compliance program.

Evaluating the Size of a Practice

The OIG guidance for physician practices targets "individual" physicians and "small" group physician practices, and recommends that practice size and resources be considered in designing an appropriate compliance program. The OIG also suggests that larger physician practices may wish to refer, and adopt as is applicable, elements of the more comprehensive guidelines for third-party billing companies. However, the OIG does not offer suggestions regarding what distinguishes a small from a large physician practice. This poses little difficulty to obviously large practices such as faculty practice plans, IPAs, and other physician organizations, but what of the majority of the other practices in the country? How do they determine whether they are small, moderate, or large for the purpose of designing and implementing a compliance program?

Regardless of the lack of guidance from the OIG, there are certain operational and financial characteristics that reliably can be considered in determining relative practice size. Some are quantitative, whereas others relate more to operational or organizational characteristics. It is important to note that for most practices a single criterion will not define a practice as small or large. However, when using a few criteria, a practice is likely to come to a reasonable decision about its relative size. Using many criteria, a few key determinants to size that a practice may wish to consider are as follows (nonhospital-owned multispecialty groups are used as examples, but similar information is available in the cited publication for major single specialty practices):

- Total practice revenues—A broad financial determinant of size is revenues generated per year, either expressed as total practice revenues or revenues per physician. The annual Cost Survey for the year 2000, prepared by the Medical Group Management Association indicates that the mean and median total medical revenue per FTE physician in a nonhospital-owned multispecialty group was $534,961 and $532,485, respectively. The 25th percentile medical revenue generated per physician was $429,209, and the 75th percentile was $619,290. A practice may wish to use this information as a guideline to determine relative size on the basis of revenues generated.

- Medicare receipts—The number of receipt dollars collected by a practice from Medicare also indicates relative practice size. In addition, it can also be used by a practice to determine how substantial they are in terms of the magnitude of payments made to them by the Medicare program as it may relate to audit risk (the relationship between Medicare payments made to a practice and the risk of being audited is conjecture). For example, the survey indicates that the mean and median percentage of gross charges allocable to Medicare in a nonhospital-owned multispecialty practice was 27.99% and 28.00%, respectively. The 25th percentile was 16.77%, and the 75th percentile was 37%. A practice may also wish to analyze its own percentage of Medicare charges and revenues to total collections.

- Operational expenses—The level of operating expenses of a practice can be an indicator of practice size and complexity because payroll costs are typically a majority of total operating expenses. Further, practices with multiple offices and more complex organizational structures generally will sustain larger overhead obligations. For example, the mean and median operating expense level per FTE physician in a nonhospital-owned multispecialty group was $312,034 and $299,758, respectively. The 25th percentile was $244,002, and the 75th percentile was $372,945.

- Numbers of physicians and support staff—The number of physicians and nonphysicians in a practice is a strong indicator of practice size. However, care should be exercised in using these criteria because in certain specialties few physicians and staff are capable of generating substantial revenues. They might then qualify as large in terms of revenues but not necessarily on the basis of expense levels. For example, for nonhospital-owned multispecialty groups the mean and median number of physicians was 42.73 and 24.75 FTE physicians, respectively. The 25th percentile was 12.14 FTE physicians, and the 75th percentile was 45.13 FTE physicians. The mean and median number of total support staff in nonhospital-owned practices was 226.52 and 119.83 FTEs, respectively. The 25th percentile was 62.84 FTEs, and the 75th percentile was 238.04 FTEs.

- Organizational complexity—Does the practice have more than one office, and if so, how many satellite offices are there? The number of satellite offices is an indicator of organizational complexity and relative size. The survey indicates that the mean and median number of satellite offices for nonhospital-owned multispecialty groups was 5.21 and 2.50 respectively (a standard deviation of 7.16). The 25th percentile was 1.0, and the 75th percentile was 7.0.

Another consideration in determining organizational complexity is the nature of the governing body of the practice. The existence of a board of directors that meets regularly or having regular partnership meetings are more common in larger physician practices and physician organizations.

If, in considering all of the preceding factors, a practice generally skews toward the higher percentiles, it may conclude that it contains many elements of larger practices. If so, it should consider implementing all seven components of an effective compliance program, as well as integrating other aspects of the OIG guidance for third-party billing companies.

The Seven Basic Components of an Effective Compliance Program

Although the essence of the seven basic elements in the Federal Sentencing Guidelines can be found in all of the OIG compliance guidances, the manner in which the OIG has applied the seven elements (i.e., examples of what measures can be taken to comply with the seven elements) varies between the guidelines directed to billing companies and those issued for individual doctors and small group practices. For example, the most recent guidelines directed at individual physicians and small group practices appear to apply some of the principles more broadly in recognition of the organizational differences between small practices and typically larger organizations such as billing companies.

The differences between the guidelines for billing companies and those for individual physicians and small group practices appear most noticeable in the requirements for policies and procedures manuals, the suggestion that a compliance officer be used, the recommendations for internal audits and related sample sizes, the assessment of areas of risk, the communication methods for reporting alleged wrongdoing, and the training requirements. In these categories, the OIG occasionally recommends less formal, less costly approaches that are tailored to the resources of individual and small physician group practice. On the other hand, the OIG appears to feel that certain compliance components (such as written standards and procedures and auditing) should be implemented regardless of organizational size or type.

However, the OIG compliance guidance for physician practices does not give any definitive indication about which specific component will be deemed acceptable for a partially implemented compliance program or provide a standard measure of staff or financial resources to indicate when the OIG would expect a practice to fully implement all seven components. Large practices will need to implement a detailed and complete compliance structure, similar to the one outlined in other OIG guidances and in particular, the third-party medical billing company guidance. Individual and small practices may choose to only partially implement a compliance program targeting the areas of risk identified in internal auditing, or as part of a progression toward full implementation of a compliance program. The following section presents all seven elements to address management issues involved in each one, so as to cover the full range of implementation options for physician practices, regardless of size and resources.

1. Standards of conduct and policies and procedures—Standards of conduct and policies and procedures should be developed for employees that include a commitment to compliance by the physician practice and its senior management. The standards should function as a guideline that provides detail regarding the intent to reduce or eliminate the possibility of wrongdoing. The standards should promote integrity, objectivity, and trust and be supported by the board, senior management, and staff. Standards and procedures should be reasonably capable of reducing the prospect of criminal conduct.

2. Designation of a compliance officer—A compliance officer should be hired or designated who is a high-level individual, has overall responsibility for the program, and has the responsibility and authority to ensure that the program is consistently enforced and monitored, evaluated, and modified so that it conforms to changes in regulations. This individual must have direct access to the uppermost levels of management and to the governing board. The compliance officer must have the authority to review all documents and materials that are relevant to compliance activities. He or she must have the authority to review contracts and obligations that may contain referral and payment provisions that could violate statutory or regulatory requirements.

   It is important to note that due care should be exercised to prevent authority from being delegated to those with an inclination to engage in illegal activities. Screening should be reasonable and diligent.

3. Conducting effective training—An educational and training program should be designed and implemented that ensures an understanding of compliance requirements and internal policies and procedures. The program can be provided internally or by outside professional organizations. Initial training should include a review of the company's standards of conduct and employees should sign an attestation that they have a knowledge of and commitment to those standards. Training also should include billing and coding matters, as well as summarize fraud and abuse statutes.

4. Effective lines of communication—Effective mechanisms should be developed that will allow employees and other agents, in good faith, to report known or suspected misconduct without fear of reprisal. The OIG suggests a confidential hotline, e-mail, and a drop box in the practice, although other mechanisms can be used.

5. Auditing and monitoring—Auditing and monitoring mechanisms should be developed that can reasonably detect criminal conduct by employees and other agents. The courts have carefully scrutinized these auditing mechanisms when determining how effective a

compliance plan has been. It is important that these mechanisms be designed and used properly. Documentation of audit processes and findings should be detailed.

At a minimum, these audits and reviews should "be designed to address the billing company's compliance with laws governing kickback arrangements, coding practices, claim submission, and reimbursement and marketing."[14] Techniques that can be considered include testing billing and coding staff on their knowledge of reimbursement criteria, checking personnel records to determine whether any individuals who have been reprimanded for compliance issues in the past are among those currently engaged in improper conduct, distributing questionnaires to solicit impressions of employees and staff, and performing trend analysis or longitudinal studies that seek to identify deviations over a given period.[15]

The reviewers should possess the qualifications and experience necessary to identify potential issues with regard to the subject matter being reviewed, be objective and independent of line management, and have access to audit and healthcare resources and to relevant personnel and areas of operation.[16]

6. Establishing disciplinary guidelines—Disciplinary guidelines and penalties should be developed that consistently and uniformly define actions that will be taken when an individual commits an offense, fails to detect and/or report an offense, or makes a bad faith report that offenses are, or have been, occurring.

7. Responding to detected offenses and developing corrective action initiatives—There should be documented corrective action taken in response to identified weaknesses in compliance standards and procedures. This documentation should include any changes that need to be made to the compliance plan that are designed to prevent any future offenses of the same kind.

Managerial Implications of Implementing the Compliance Plan

The operational implications of implementing a compliance plan in any size practice actually extend beyond the seven basic compliance elements. In fact, many of the seven elements, as implemented (even in their most simple form and in the smallest practices), may represent features and functions that have never existed in physician practices or do exist, but in basic forms. For example, auditing and monitoring to detect breaches in compliance (and the rectification of those breaches) are, perhaps, the most distant from the organizational fabric of most practices. On the other hand, it is one of the more important of the OIG guidelines. Auditing is a high-risk and difficult function if done properly, even if the practice is small and conforms to the recent guidelines for individual physicians and small practices. If an audit, even one involving a small sample, is conducted poorly or by individuals without the requisite knowledge and experience, it may lead to greater liability.

Many of the seven basic elements involve human resources management functions that may never have existed, or may not exist in as formal a manner. Even though the OIG provides for less formal compliance approaches for smaller practices, certain human resources approaches need to be in place to conform to the OIG guidelines. For example, how many practices have personnel manuals or operations manuals that include requirements and mechanisms to reference-check prospective employees, and how many have written annual employee performance evaluations that tie performance to compensation and promotions? How many practices have internal management controls designed to identify and reduce billing and coding errors, and how many have feedback mechanisms to convey changes in billing and coding so that they are no longer being performed incorrectly? Of the practices that may have these types of controls in place, how many discipline or terminate employees who do not adhere to exemplary compliance standards or, conversely, how many have written procedures in which employees are rewarded for exemplary performance? Each practice needs to answer these and related questions in order to determine how it might need to modify existing operations, augment human resources, and implement new procedures and internal controls.

The operational and organizational implications of implementing a compliance plan and program generally can be categorized into two areas of management: (1) those that relate to general management functions, and (2) those that involve human resources management functions. As shown in **Table 19.1**, there are 12 functions that fall within these two categories. All originate from the seven basic elements.

Table 19.1   Compliance Plan and Program—Organizational Functions

General Management Functions	Human Resources Management Functions
Corporate documents, mission statement, and code of ethics	Organizational design, responsibility, authority, and delegation
Operating policies and procedures	Training
Assessment of risk	Personnel policies and procedures
Internal auditing	Personnel discipline, enforcement of policies, and terminations
Communication and reporting systems	
Investigation of wrongdoing	Position descriptions
Program assessment and evaluation	

General Management Functions

Review and Upkeep of Corporate Documents, Mission Statement, and Codes of Ethics

The compliance plan should begin with a statement of commitment from the governing board or shareholders (i.e., in a smaller practice) that underscores their intent that the practice and its employees exhibit a code of conduct that is consistent with preventing, identifying, and reducing or eliminating wrongdoing. These principles, infused into the practice's mission statement, applicable policies and procedures, and other corporate documents, should be simply written, easily comprehended, and accessible to employees. New employees should be given the code of ethics and mission statement, be allowed a reasonable amount of time to read them, and be asked to sign a statement that they have read and understand the code of ethics and intend to diligently adhere to its provisions. It is important to note that these policy statements need not be overly detailed; they should not describe overarching ideals unless the practice intends to initiate and enforce them. Crafting goals that a practice cannot reasonably achieve can lead to demotivated employees and an ineffective compliance plan. There should be periodic updates of the mission statement and code of ethics designed to incorporate exogenous change (e.g., regulations) and internal change within the practice (e.g., new risk factors).

It is important to emphasize here that the OIG compliance guidance for small and individual physician practices does not include the development of a code of conduct in the seven basic elements of an effective program, contrary to guidances the OIG has released thus far for other types of healthcare providers. Larger physician practices that have the resources to implement a full compliance program following the elements contained in the third-party medical billing company compliance guidance should likely include a code of conduct in its program. Although the OIG does not recommend a code of conduct for smaller practices as part of its compliance initiative, a code of conduct can provide an easy-to-develop tool that lays a framework for more specific compliance efforts.

Operating Policies and Procedures

Fundamental to the operating structure of any organization is the establishment of operating policies and procedures that govern what employees do in an organization and how they go about doing it. Procedures set forth the correct and efficient way to perform operational tasks, including the use of internal controls that are designed to detect and correct errors or deviations from established procedures. Applicable policies and procedures in the practice should be reviewed to determine if they are sufficient to meet compliance standards. Where necessary, they should be revised or newly written. Policies and procedures, as noted in the audit section herein, also provide the standards against which an auditor will review a practice. The policies and procedures should be simply written and understandable.

On-the-job training is not uncommon in physician practices. There are both advantages and disadvantages inherent in this practice. One major disadvantage is that the same individual may not train all new employees (because of personnel turnover, dependence on part-time individuals, and so forth). Therefore, that which is "taught" may be someone's interpretation of how to perform certain tasks. The existence of a written procedure manual presents an opportunity to have a resource that will define the manner in which functions should be performed. Therefore, it should be made part of the initial training of all new employees. Procedure and policy manuals are "dynamic" documents and, as such, should always be changed to accommodate modifications in operations, external requirements, new technologies, and other factors that affect what is done in an organization.

A word of caution is in order. The manuals a billing company gives a practice when automating its billing systems define the manner in which the automated billing system should be used. They can affect certain operational processes, but they should not be used in lieu of having operational manuals for the entire practice. According to the OIG, the practice should, however, periodically review the sections of the billing systems manual that describe the manner in which coding edits are used.

Assessment of Risk

The assessment of risk is an important factor in determining the scope of a compliance program. Although the area of billing and collections is an acceptable beginning point, a compliance program should go beyond the prevention, detection, and correction of Medicare and Medicaid billing and coding irregularities, including compliance with regulations regarding anti-kickback and anticompetitive behavior, OSHA, and other requirements. As will be discussed further in this chapter, the assessment of an organization's risks also is important for defining the scope of internal audits.

As discussed earlier, the OIG has identified a number of risk areas that should be considered for small and larger practices. Organizational status and organizational structure also should be considered in determining risk. Practices that are part of multiprovider systems need to consider their relationships with the hospital system and other physicians in relation to Stark law prohibitions against self-referrals, free or below-market space or equipment rentals, or other benefits they may obtain. Likewise, a practice that is part of a large physician network or MSO, or one that has expanded significantly as a result of merger or acquisition, should consider whether it has additional risks. If these are potential risks, the practice should consider a legal audit of contracts.

Practices that use multiple offices (this does not have to be a large practice) may have higher risks related to having weak internal controls or the inconsistent application of correct billing and coding standards. Practices with many physicians within specific specialties may have a higher risk related to not uniformly applying billing and coding standards. Surgical specialty practices may not have as much concern with coding for evaluation and management (E&M) services than would a multispecialty group. On the other hand, there are many surgical specialty practices that derive a great deal of their revenues from E&M services. This only serves to underscore how important it is to define the practice's risks before designing the scope of the compliance plan.

In summary, it is important that the practice place the greatest compliance efforts on those areas that may represent the most significant risk. In addition, to overscope a compliance plan places the practice in the position of possibly not being able to satisfy all plan goals.

Internal Auditing

As stated earlier, internal auditing (sometimes referred to as performance or operational auditing) is one of the key components in a compliance plan and program, whether in a small or large practice. In order to be done well, and to produce reliable information, requisite knowledge of the audit process, proper sample selection, and experience are necessary. Improperly conducted audits can place a practice at greater liability. As such, audits should be properly scoped, and they should be supervised by competent individuals who are independent and objective. Audits can, and usually are, retrospective. They also can be concurrent, in which case they perform more of a monitoring function.

Because of the importance of the audit function within the compliance plan, as well as the expectation that an audit should extend beyond billing and coding matters, this subject will be explored in greater detail. This discussion is not intended to establish a higher standard than the

OIG may require, but rather to acquaint the reader with key principles that underlie sound auditing. If all of these principles cannot be adhered to initially, they provide a series of goals toward which a practice can evolve as its compliance plan matures.

There are various types of audits. Most individuals are aware of financial audits. Financial audits are an independent and objective assessment designed to provide reasonable assurance that the information presented in the financial statements of an organization do not contain material misstatements regarding the operating results of the organization and that the financial statements have been prepared in accordance with generally accepted accounting principles. Accounting firm professionals with expertise in the financial audit function generally conduct financial audits. The American Institute of Certified Public Accountants (AICPA) promulgates comparatively strict accounting and auditing guidelines (generally accepted auditing standards) that govern financial audits. Government audit standards closely follow those of the AICPA.

Operational (performance and compliance) audits are independent, objective, and systematic examinations of evidence for the purpose of providing an assessment of the performance of an organization, a unit within an organization, a function, or a program in order to improve accountability, efficiency and effectiveness, internal controls, profit, and decision making. These audits encompass:

- Assessments of financial performance
- Use of human and other organizational resources (i.e., appropriateness of staffing levels)
- Compliance with laws that affect the organization
- Policies, procedures, and internal controls
- Management structure and internal communications

Performance audits can be broad and encompass all of the preceding and more, or they can be very targeted at specific organizational units, functions, procedures, or personnel in an organization. Often, a baseline or annual comprehensive audit will reveal areas of concern or weakness, but before conclusions can be reached, more specific and intensified audits may be necessary. Frequently, a comprehensive performance audit will reveal areas of weakness in systems and controls or other factors that should be of concern to management. These should be rectified and thereafter reviewed in more targeted audits.

Prior to beginning periodic (minimally annual) audits, the OIG suggests performing a baseline audit. A baseline audit should consist of all of the following; annual audits thereafter should consist of the first two items listed.

- Operational (performance audit)—As previously identified, this type of audit generally consists of a review of all major operating systems (scheduling, registration, billing and collections practices, checkout and payment, medical records filing, general ledger and accounting, physician and nonphysician staffing levels, marketing and practice-building activities, financial analyses). It also would include a review of coding and documentation (Current Procedure Terminology and International Classification of Diseases [ICD-9-CM]) for appropriateness and compliance with regulations and guidelines. In addition, it would include a review of medical record documentation to determine if the documentation supported the codes that were used.

- Legal review—This is a review of all contracts (e.g., space rental, equipment leases, co-ownership/shareholder contracts with institutional or physician providers; any arrangements, formal or otherwise, wherein a practice receives payment from a supplier, vendor, etc.).
- Other compliance areas—This is a review of the practice's compliance with OSHA, the Clinical Laboratory Improvement Act, and so forth.

In performing an audit, auditor independence and objectivity are essential:

Auditor Independence. It is apparent, whether government or AICPA guidelines are followed, that the principles of independence and objectivity should be considered when contemplating compliance audits in a physician practice setting. Therefore, a further review of the meaning of these principles seems warranted.

There are four general standards used by government auditors[17] to describe independence, three of which relate more directly to the auditor's role in physician practice organizational settings. Although these standards for independence and objectivity relate to financial auditing, in principle they apply to all types of auditing. In reality, the last thing a practice wants is to have its audit results invalidated by the government because the practice's auditor was not independent or objective.

The first government principle states that the auditor (internal or external) and audit staff (i.e., the organization conducting the audit) should possess adequate professional proficiency for the tasks required. The second principle states, "In all matters relating to the audit work, the audit organization and the individual auditors, whether government or public, should be free from personal and external impairments to independence, should be organizationally independent, and should maintain an independent attitude and appearance."[18] This standard "places responsibility on each auditor and the audit organization to maintain independence so that opinions, conclusions, judgments, and recommendations will be impartial and will be viewed as impartial by knowledgeable third parties."[19]

There are three general classes of impairments to an auditor's independence—personal, external, and organizational. Personal and external impairments will be discussed because of their relevance to physician practices. Personal impairments can include:

- Official, professional, personal, or financial relationships that might cause an auditor to limit the scope of the review, to limit disclosure, or to weaken or slant findings in any way
- Preconceived ideas toward individuals, groups, organizations, or objectives of a program that could bias the audit
- Previous responsibility for decision making or managing an entity that would affect current operations of the entity or program being audited
- Biases, including those induced by political or social conscience[20]

In a physician practice setting these may include situations in which a compliance auditor may have an ownership interest in a business entity owned by the practice (e.g., an ambulatory surgery center or billing company), may be a close friend or relative of a physician in the practice, may previously have worked in the department being audited, or may have worked closely with one or more of the physicians being audited (e.g., a nurse or technician). In any of these situations, the auditor and the audit results may be in question because of the actual or perceived impairment of the auditor. In large practices that may hire a compliance officer who will conduct the audits, these issues may be of less concern. Practices, large or small that identify someone from within, however, should consider these issues. In small practices in which compliance personnel have responsibility for many functions, it is important that the compliance officer not be someone whose independence is impaired by virtue of the other functions for which he or she is responsible.

The second principle relates to external impairments. These involve impairments to the auditor's independence and ability to have complete freedom to make judgments. They include, but are not limited to, "external interference or influence that improperly or imprudently limits or modifies the scope of an audit, limits the selection or application of audit procedures, appears to overrule or influence the auditor's judgment, or that influences the auditors continued employment for reasons other than competency."[21]

The third principle is organizational independence. The OIG refers to this when stating, throughout many of its compliance guidelines, that the compliance officer should have access to senior management and the board. This principle also states that the auditor should be sufficiently removed from the political pressures that arise from within the organization. If the auditor is an employee, one might speculate that an "organizational" impairment may arise from inside the organization if, for example, the physicians being audited have an opportunity to review their medical record documentation prior to the auditor having access to them, or if the physicians try to modify the scope of the audit. This clearly would be a situation in which the authority of the auditor, and his or her ability to be independent, would be compromised. Another organizational impairment might occur if the physicians who are potentially affected by an auditor's report of findings have an opportunity to review and change the report prior to its issuance.

Auditor Objectivity. The AICPA defines objectivity as "a state of mind, a quality that lends value. It is the distinguishing feature of a professional. The principle of objectivity imposes the obligation to be impartial, intellectually honest, and free of conflicts of interest."[22] Objectivity is theoretically uniformly applicable to any organization regardless of size or ownership. However, physician practices generally are closely held businesses in which physicians often have a direct and dominant influence over the management and operations of the practice. In most respects this is no different from small businesses in other industries except for the fact that the product or service of a physician practice, namely medical or surgical services, perhaps requires that a physician play a role in the management of the practice, certainly in those issues that are clinical in nature. The conventional relationship between a board and management does not exist, as in most industries. Therefore, a tension can arise from the duality of management responsibility in many physician practices.

How this duality affects the compliance officer and his or her objectivity (and independence) is a matter that warrants consideration when assigning responsibility to an individual. In turn, it is something about which physicians should be aware once the audit function is in place.

Other Factors Relating to Auditing. Performance auditing, and indeed compliance auditing, should use accepted standards so that the findings and recommendations are not compromised or invalidated. The following five field work standards for performance audits are noteworthy.

1. Work is to be adequately planned. The scope and objectives of an audit should be clearly defined, as well as the audit, sampling, and other methodologies. Methodologies should be used to provide sufficient, competent, and relevant evidence to achieve the objectives of the audit. Methodology includes not only the nature of the auditors' procedures, but also their extent (e.g., sample size). The plan should consider the internal controls that exist (or do not exist) in the organization, the results of prior audits and management reports, legal and regulatory requirements, and other factors that can affect the audit.[23]

2. Staff are to be properly supervised. Staff who are conducting an audit should be supervised by a senior staff person, and should understand the scope and purpose of the audit.[24]

3. When laws, regulations, and other compliance requirements are significant to audit objectives, auditors should design the audit to provide reasonable assurance of compliance with them. In all performance audits, auditors should be alert to situations or transactions that could be indicative of illegal acts or abuse.[25]

4. Auditors should obtain an understanding of management controls that are relevant to the audit. Management controls are the plan of organization, methods, and procedures that are adopted by management to ensure that goals are met. They include processes for planning, organizing, directing, and controlling operations, and they use systems for measuring, reporting, and monitoring organizational performance.[26] If the auditor believes that management controls are weak, particularly those that affect the reliability of information, then the scope of the audit should be expanded.

5. Sufficient, competent, and relevant evidence is to be obtained to afford a reasonable basis for auditors' findings and conclusions. Evidence is categorized as physical, documentary, testimonial, and analytical.[27] A record of auditors' field work should be retained in the form of working papers. Working papers serve three purposes: they provide the principal support for the auditors' report, aid the auditors in conducting and supervising the audit, and allow others to review the audit's quality. Working papers should contain sufficient information to enable an experienced auditor having no previous connection with the audit to ascertain from them the evidence that supports the auditors' significant conclusions and judgments."[28]

Communication and Reporting Systems

Communication and reporting systems should be available so that employees can report compliance problems. Confidentiality should be maintained, but it is important that employees be aware that it is not being guaranteed. How this is accomplished in a physician practice is a matter of choice, and the methods for communication and reporting that already may exist in the practice play a role. Practices may use a hotline, a designated answering machine, or a suggestion box in a central location. Employees should be encouraged to identify their name and telephone number should someone need to contact them for additional information, and they should be made aware that the practice will not retaliate for information made in good faith.

All reports should be entered into a central log or a secured computer data file. They should be subjected to a preliminary inquiry designed to determine whether a more comprehensive investigation is required. A summary of the results of the preliminary inquiry also should be logged. If the results of the preliminary inquiry demonstrate that a comprehensive investigation is appropriate, that investigation should be planned and implemented expeditiously. Investigations also can arise from audit findings.

Investigation of Wrongdoing

If the compliance officer determines in a preliminary review of a confidentially submitted employee complaint that an investigation is required, the process is similar to an audit. Investigations should conform to the audit principles discussed earlier (i.e., planning, scope, collection of evidence, documentation in working papers). Investigations should be conducted with the input of counsel throughout the process, and they may require the assistance of others in the practice or outside professionals. Interviewing technique is very important in an investigation, particularly if the person being interviewed is suspected of a crime. In these circumstances, it may be useful to have an additional person attend the meeting.

The compliance officer should provide investigative summaries and recommendations to the compliance committee of the board, and to the board when applicable. On a quarterly basis, the compliance committee should summarize all pertinent compliance activities and results (e.g., audits, investigations) to the full board.

Program Assessment and Evaluation

The impact of the compliance program should be assessed on an annual basis, and findings should be used to make modifications to the program. However, acute weakness in the compliance plan and program, particularly in the neophyte years, should be rectified on a concurrent basis. As discussed previously in this chapter, evaluation and feedback is one of three critical phases of good management in general. Therefore, the assessment of the compliance program hopefully will be part of an existing and productive feedback process. The compliance officer should prepare an annual report for management and the board that provides documentation relating to the activities that have occurred during the year, summarizes audit and investigative efforts and actions that were taken, and makes suggestions for change (as required) in the compliance plan and specifically changes that have or will be made to comply with applicable regulations. The documentation, when possible, should refer to the seven basic compliance elements in a compliance program. It should be reasonably, but not overly, detailed. Counsel should review the report in draft form to assess whether the action to disclose and correct the reported problems is sufficient to demonstrate that the program is effective.

Assessment of program effectiveness also can be solicited via group interviews with employees and physicians and through surveys. It is important to include questions that assess whether employees and physicians are aware of the program, the reporting mechanisms, and other features of the compliance plan. If there are new employees who can be interviewed, they often can provide a barometer for how visible the compliance program is and whether employee training is effective in familiarizing new employees with the practice.

Human Resource Management Functions

Formal human resources management departments are not typical in physician practices. Often, the functions consistent with human resources management are shared by a number of employees in a practice, are the responsibility of the practice manager, or are not in place at all. As stated earlier, many of the organizational implications of the seven steps involve functions that traditionally are considered human resources management. This section will discuss those functions.

Organizational Design, Responsibility, Authority, and Delegation

The best conceived compliance program will have little chance of success if installed in a practice in which the lines of authority and communication are unclear or conflict. Likewise, if personnel responsibilities are not well defined and delegation is haphazard, these factors will interfere with program effectiveness. In a well-run practice, all of these organizational elements must be defined and clear. The chain of command should be apparent, communication should be upwardly and downwardly effective, and responsibility and authority should be delegated in a balanced manner.

The compliance plan should be supported by the governing board or, in smaller groups, the physician shareholders. In large practices that can economically justify recruiting a compliance officer, that individual should have access to the board and the chief executive officer and report to one or the other. As discussed earlier, the compliance officer should not have impaired independence or objectivity.

Training

Education and training can assume many forms. Regulations change frequently, government fraud and abuse "alerts" are regularly issued, and many other compliance-related issues change. Therefore, education and training should include updates on internal changes that have been made to the practice's compliance programs. Ideally, training begins with the establishment of a budgeted number of dollars for the purpose of internal and external education. Larger practices may wish to budget for the preparation and presentation of seminars and workshops conducted by their own staff. Smaller practices that do not have a formal budget can earmark a specific number of dollars for external staff and physician compliance training. The compliance officer should organize this effort.

As part of an annual planning process, external seminars and workshops should be identified and prospectively scheduled for attendance. Obtaining continuing education credits provides an added incentive to employees. Participants, including physicians from the practice, should be identified to attend. Attendees should be selected to attend educational seminars that are consistent with their organizational roles (e.g., billers should attend seminars relating to billing and coding issues, an OSHA supervisor should attend OSHA seminars, and so forth). Attendance at compliance workshops should be noted in annual (or more frequent) evaluations. Those who attend outside seminars should be asked to prepare presentations for their colleagues on what they learned.

Other materials such as tapes, disks, and manuals are useful for education. In smaller practices these forms of internal education might be more economically feasible. Newsletters, printed regulatory updates, booklets, and other compliance material should be routed to appropriate staff with a check-off box in which each person reading the material can acknowledge that it was read. Internal management meetings should discuss the practice's policies and procedures related to compliance and proper billing. On a periodic basis the compliance officer should make presentations to the board to keep members abreast of compliance and regulatory changes.

Personnel Policies and Procedures

All policies and procedures should be reviewed, and modifications should be made, as required, to incorporate components of the compliance plan. They should include the following:

- Policies and procedures related to enforcement and discipline (how wrongdoing was identified, documentation of billing errors, and corrective action that has been taken)
- Policies and procedures related to rectifying wrongdoing
- Policies and procedures to avoid the recurrence of wrongdoing, to identify the preventive steps that will be taken, and to document the training that will occur to remedy similar problems in the future

All policies and procedures (whether operating or personnel) should be easy to read and comprehend, not overly detailed, and designed to foster the application of judgment. Personnel policies and procedures should include, at a minimum, the following topical areas:

- Standards of employee conduct
- Disciplining personnel
- Termination
- Recruiting personnel and obtaining references (includes verification of licensure and other credentials and a check for prior government sanctions)
- Retrospective and concurrent performance evaluations
- Confidentiality relating to employee disclosure of knowledge related to wrongdoing

Employee annual evaluation forms should include performance criteria related to the employee's contributions to the compliance process and to upholding exemplary ethics. In addition, supervisors should be evaluated based on their contributions to upholding the compliance process.

Personnel Discipline, Enforcement of Policies, and Terminations

Enforcement is another critical element in compliance plans and programs for at least two reasons. First, if there is no enforcement of the program, then the government will not consider it effective. Second, and more operationally important, if employees conclude that there is no enforcement of the policies and procedures related to preventing, detecting, and remedying wrongdoing, then they will not be motivated to uphold the principles of the program.

The most available method of enforcement is the written annual employee performance evaluation. Employees exhibiting behavior contrary to the compliance plan should receive adverse write-ups in their annual evaluations. If the behavior is adverse but can be rectified, then a memorandum should be placed in their personnel file at the time of the infraction. In addition, problem employees can be moved to a quarterly performance review until their behavior changes positively, or until enough documentation of adverse behavior exists to support their termination. Employees who support the program should receive positive evaluations.

In cases of documented and serious instances of wrongdoing, employees should be warned or suspended from their responsibilities. In certain instances, immediate termination may be justifiable, particularly for repeat offenses. If criminal behavior is involved, the practice should be prepared to involve law enforcement after first seeking the opinion of counsel.

The discipline or punishment should parallel the infraction. The practice is ill advised to terminate an employee for an innocent first mistake. It should refer this employee for more training and implement additional supervision. Continued, but intermittent, errors of the same or similar type should receive more serious disciplinary response. Repeated (i.e., chronic) problems, or those in which the behavior is extremely serious or criminal, may require termination. Counsel should be sought in these situations.

It is important to document all enforcement and disciplinary decisions and actions in the employee's personnel file. Although no two noncompliance problems are necessarily the same, the practice should endeavor to apply its policies uniformly and fairly in order to preserve the credibility of the compliance officer and the compliance program, as well as to avoid wrongful dismissal and other labor law concerns.

Review and Upkeep of Position Descriptions

Position descriptions are the crux of recruiting, wage and salary administration, performance evaluation, authority, responsibility, delegation, and communication. All of these elements of management are affected by or influence the success of a compliance program. Not only does a compliance program require the creation of a position description for the compliance officer (or modification of the position description of the employee who will perform this function part time), but it also necessitates modifications to the position descriptions of all employees who will be responsible for adherence to compliance standards (compliance contacts).

The position description for the compliance officer, for example, should encompass:

- Designing, implementing, and modifying the compliance plan and program
- Hiring or internally using other staff in administering the compliance program
- Ensuring (possibly with the human resources manager or credentialing supervisor) that all clinicians have current licenses and required certifications
- Developing and overseeing educational and training programs
- Designing, participating in, and coordinating compliance audits
- Establishing communications systems for employees to report compliance concerns
- Investigating alleged wrongdoing and taking (or causing to be taken) disciplinary action
- Evaluating the impact of the compliance program
- Preparing reports to senior management and the board (or shareholders in smaller practices) periodically (at least annually)

Patten and colleagues suggest the use of eight principles as a guide to writing a position description:[29]

1. Arrange job duties in logical order. If a definite work cycle exists, duties may be described in chronological order. When work cycles are irregular, more important duties should be listed first, followed by less important duties.
2. State separate duties clearly and concisely without going into such detail that the description resembles motion analysis.
3. Start each section with an active functional verb in the present tense.
4. Use quantitative words where possible.
5. Use specific words where possible.
6. Avoid proprietary names that might make the description obsolete when equipment changes occur.
7. Determine or estimate the percentage of time spent on each activity, and indicate whether the duties are regular or occasional.
8. Limit use of the word "may" with regard to certain duties.

Job descriptions also can include (in the heading) a definition of the position (e.g., the chief executive officer), to whom the person reports (e.g., the board), and the staff members reporting to the person (e.g., all billing staff).

A Planning and Implementation Work Plan

The design and implementation of a written compliance plan are likely to require an appreciable amount of time and resources. In order to ensure that the compliance program eventually extends beyond compliance with billing and coding guidelines (the government's initial intent) and remains an ongoing, dynamic process, human resources such as physicians, management, outside professionals in practice and organizational consulting, coding experts, and attorneys may be necessary.

The general work plan that follows contains suggestions that should be further tailored to the specific needs of the practice. Where applicable, the work plan on page 739 identifies alternatives for both small (shown in italics) and large practices; however, it is important to remember that no one compliance plan is a universal fit for all practices, and it is not certain how the OIG defines a small or large practice. The work plan is not exhaustive in detail, because its purpose is to outline a broad approach that the user can supplement with task detail. In defining a starting point, the work plan assumes that a practice knows little about the federal compliance plan guidelines and is literally starting at the beginning.

Table 19.2 is a Gantt chart, which is a tool generally used for planning purposes. The chart identifies the tasks and subtasks that are required to accomplish a particular project or program; assigns tasks to individuals with responsibility for those tasks; and estimates the number of calendar days, weeks, or months that may be necessary for implementation. As such, the Gantt chart is not only a planning tool, but also a monitoring tool that can be used to assess progress against a predetermined set of timed goals and over a long time period.

Table 19.2 Gantt Chart for Implementing a Compliance Plan and Program

	1	2	3	4	5	6	7	8	9		Staff Assigned
Phase I—Initial Compliance Planning											
1. Board expresses interest											
—Form ad hoc committee											
—Develop compliance knowledge											
—Conduct research											
2. Board hears committee presentation											
—Give subcommittee presentations											
—Have board vote											
3. Develop compliance planning work plan											
4. Make vs. buy decision											
—Solicit proposals from professionals											
—Make decisions											
5. Design position descriptions											
—Design position descriptions											
—Hire compliance officer											
6. Develop code of ethics											
—Incorporate into corporate documents											
7. Identify areas of risk											
8. Conduct baseline audit											
—Have done by outside professionals											
—Receive baseline audit results											
Phase II—Implementation Tasks											
9. Create implementation team											
10. Revise position descriptions											
—Review position descriptions											
—Modify position descriptions											
11. Review/modify operating policies/procedures											
12. Review/revise personnel policies/procedures											
13. Develop internal audit processes											
—Define audit scope											
—Determine sample size											

(continues)

Table 19.2 (Continued)

	1	2	3	4	5	6	7	8	9			Staff Assigned
Develop audit work plan												
—Select sample												
—Conduct audit (field work)												
—Write audit report												
—Involve legal counsel												
14. Establish internal communications/reporting systems												
—Conduct preliminary inquiry												
—Report sensitive findings to counsel												
—Document												
15. Conduct full investigation												
—Define scope of investigation												
—Determine sample size												
—Develop work plan												
—Select sample												
—Conduct investigation												
—Write investigation report												
—Involve legal counsel												
16. Enforce and remedy wrongdoing												
17. Report to compliance committee/board												
18. Educate and train												
—Prepare budget for education												
—Identify seminars/workshops												
—Identify attendees												
—Acquire other materials												
—Disseminate information												
—Educate board												
Phase III—Evaluation and Feedback												
19. Evaluate plan and program annually												
20. Prepare annual report to board												

Sample Compliance Plan and Program Work Plan

All italicized text applies to small practices.

Phase I—Initial Compliance Planning and Fact Finding

Task 1: Board of Directors (Physician or Physician Shareholders) Express an Interest in Compliance Planning

- Subtask 1.1: Form ad hoc committee. Board preliminarily assigns fact-finding responsibility to an ad hoc committee of the board. The committee members are the president of the practice, the physician chair of the quality assurance subcommittee of the board, the chief executive officer (CEO), and the chief financial officer of the practice. The committee is asked to attend appropriate seminars, workshops, and so forth, and to seek professional advice in order to develop a knowledge base that can be presented to the board in writing and in an oral presentation in 6 weeks. *(The president of the practice assigns this task to a shareholder who has been involved in billing and coding matters, and to the practice manager. They are asked to present their findings in 8 weeks.)*
- Subtask 1.2: Develop knowledge regarding compliance. Research and develop an inventory of presentations and workshops that are devoted to compliance plans, and identify professionals who may be available to speak about compliance plans.
- Subtask 1.3: Conduct research and develop reports for the board *(shareholders)*.

Task 2: Hold Meeting of Board of Directors (Shareholders) to Hear Presentations and to Vote

- Subtask 2.1: Present ad hoc committee findings to the board. Presentations are made to the board *(shareholders)*, and a recommendation is made to proceed with the development of a compliance plan and program. A budget is presented as part of the findings of the report.
- Subtask 2.2: Have board vote. Board members *(shareholders)* vote to accept the recommendations to proceed with the development of a compliance plan and to hire a compliance officer. Vote is taken and passed. Ad hoc committee is dissolved, and board votes to create a permanent compliance subcommittee of the board. The compliance officer is to report to the CEO. Responsibility and authority are given to the compliance committee to design and implement the plan and to seek the board's input as appropriate. *(Shareholders vote favorably and establish a working committee to develop a compliance plan. The two members remain the same, and the practice manager is assigned the part-time role of compliance officer. The compliance officer is asked to develop a budget for planning and implementing a compliance plan so that a "make vs buy" decision can be made due to the practice's limited internal resources.)*

Task 3: Develop Compliance Planning Work Plan

The compliance committee asks the CEO to develop a written work plan to ensure that the process of planning and implementing the plan proceeds smoothly and on time. It is assumed that the practice will keep the function of compliance planning internal, except, perhaps, to have a baseline audit performed by an outside company. *(The practice manager develops an informal work plan.)*

Task 4: "Make vs Buy" Decision

- Subtask 4.1: Solicit proposals from outside professionals. Although believing that they will internalize the compliance planning function, the large group practice solicits proposals from outside consultants. Proposals are solicited from attorneys to conduct a legal audit of rental agreements, lease contracts with equipment vendors, and so forth. Proposals also are solicited from consultants to conduct a billing and coding audit and to develop a compliance plan and program after the baseline billing audit is conducted.

- Subtask 4.2: Make decision relative to make vs buy. The costs to internalize the compliance function are equal to the costs to have this function performed by outside professionals. Therefore the practice elects to internalize the function in order to control costs as well as the process. *(Costs to develop the plan internally [hire a senior billing supervisor, as well as practice manager's time] are less than the cost of using external professional support. Nonetheless, shareholders decide to expend the funds for outside assistance because they are concerned that the process might divert too much internal human resource time and might interfere with operations and increase billing and other errors. The high costs associated with outside professional services are determined to be largely a one-time expense that will allow the practice to internalize the majority of the compliance program functions in the future.)*

Task 5: Design Position Description and Recruit Compliance Officer

- Subtask 5.1: Design position descriptions. Reporting relationships are contemplated, and there are two apparent options: the compliance officer can report directly to the CEO of the practice and be a member of the compliance committee of the board, or the compliance officer can report directly to the compliance committee of the board, specifically the chair of that committee. The latter approach is not inconsistent with many other industries that use internal audits. The intent underlying this approach is that the board desires to assess all levels of the organization and to keep the audit function totally independent of management. However, the former option is selected because it is determined that reporting to the CEO will facilitate the resolution of compliance problems that are identified. The human resources department designs the position description and obtains approval from the CEO. The position description is inclusive of, but not limited to, the following:
  - Defines the role to plan and implement the compliance plan inclusive of policies and procedures
  - Develops and plans both internal and external educational and training programs for each category of personnel and tries to obtain continuing education credits for employees
  - Designs and coordinates internal audits in accordance with applicable standards for auditing and sampling

- ° Establishes a mechanism for employees to report suspected violations confidentially and to evaluate those reports preliminarily
- ° Works with the CEO and other senior managers and physicians to evaluate internal controls continuously and to modify them as required
- ° Implements disciplinary measures directly or through administrative channels
- ° Evaluates the compliance plan annually (at a minimum) and identifies areas for change
- • Subtask 5.2: Hire compliance officer. A compliance officer is hired with significant compliance and internal auditing capability. The hiring is contingent on a check of references. The human resources department conducts the reference check and administers a personality test to the compliance officer. *(The practice assigns this responsibility to the practice manager on a part-time basis and increases that person's salary. The practice manager, for compliance issues, will report to a designated physician.)*

Task 6: Develop a Code of Ethics

- • Subtask 6.1: Design a code of ethics and incorporate it into corporate documents. The compliance officer drafts a code of ethics, which is reviewed by the CEO and other members of the compliance committee. It is submitted, as a draft, to members of the board for their informal input. Modifications are made. The final code of ethics is submitted to the board and adopted. Then, the code of ethics is added to the appropriate corporate documents and to the practice's mission statement. The new mission statement is posted in employee areas and patient waiting rooms and is incorporated into the personnel manual and new employee orientation process. The compliance officer designs a mechanism to periodically review and update the code. *(The practice manager drafts a code of ethics and the shareholders approve it. It is added to the practice's general operations manual. New employees are given an operations manual to review when hired, and periodically they attend workshops on manual provisions. The manual is periodically reviewed by the practice manager. A performance question is added to the annual employee evaluation form related to the degree to which the employee cooperates with the principles of the compliance plan.)*

Task 7: Identify Areas of Risk in the Practice

The reports are thoroughly reviewed with particular emphasis on the risks noted. The risks are categorized as follows:

- • Risks related to billing and collections
  - ° Upcoding
  - ° Internal controls relating to billing information
  - ° Billing for services not rendered
  - ° Inappropriate balance billing
  - ° Appropriateness of E&M coding
  - ° Discounts and professional courtesy write-offs
  - ° Routine waiver of co-payments
  - ° Improper "incident to" billings
  - ° Failure to refund credit balances promptly to patients or insurers

- ○ Billing for services rendered by unqualified, uncertified, or unlicensed personnel
- ○ Failure to periodically review the billing software of the practice's automated physician billing company
- ○ Coding without documentation or making assumptions about the appropriate CPT or diagnosis code in the absence of (or due to inadequate) medical record documentation in instances where someone other than the physician defines the code to be used
- ○ Improperly altering existing medical records
- Operational, organizational, and legal risks
  - ○ The number of office sites, physicians, and employees may increase control risks
  - ○ Prior Health Care Financing Administration (HCFA) investigations may increase the practice's risks
  - ○ The practice's specialty may put it at a higher risk *(same for a smaller practice)*
  - ○ Compliance with federal or state regulations such as self-referral, anti-trust, and anti-kickback, particularly for practices that are part of multiprovider systems in which they may rent space and equipment from a hospital or other providers
  - ○ Compliance with the Clinical Lab Improvement Act, Americans with Disabilities Act, and OSHA, as applicable

  (Smaller practices may not face many of these risks. Types of risks that may relate to smaller practices may include a lack of or laxness in applying internal controls over billing and other data)

Task 8: Conduct Baseline Audit

- Subtask 8.1: Have baseline audit conducted by outside professionals. An outside consultant conducts a baseline billing and operations audit. This operations audit is designed to independently and objectively assess the policies, procedures, work flow, data accuracy and reliability, staffing levels, billing practices, and internal controls of the practice. It includes a review of a sample of bills for coding correctness and medical records for documentation appropriateness. Counsel conducts a legal audit of all employee contracts, physician contracts, rental and lease agreements, employee and physician compensation methods, and so forth. It also assesses compliance with federal and state laws (OSHA, antitrust, Clinical Laboratory Improvement Act). Other consultants assess other areas of compliance, as necessary. *(The same audits are conducted for the small practice.)*
- Subtask 8.2: Receive baseline audit results. The consultants issue their reports to the compliance officer and members of the compliance committee. The reports outline weaknesses in internal systems, policies and procedures, internal controls, staffing levels, coding and billing practices, areas of operational risk, and so forth. Although they do not identify any wrongdoing, they do outline new policies and procedures that should be used in the future to report these types of problems internally (and possibly externally on the advice of counsel), rectify those problems, and incorporate methods to assess the effectiveness of the changes. This includes, but is not limited to, changes in policies and procedures, disciplinary measures including termination, documentation investigations that were completed and identification of the corrective action taken, and changes in the curriculum of staff education to integrate new findings.

Phase II—Implementation
Task 9: Creation of an Implementation Team

To implement the applicable changes suggested in the baseline audit, and to begin to design and implement the compliance plan, the compliance officer creates an ad hoc committee of physicians, managers, and supervisors. The committee largely consists of middle managers and existing supervisors in the practice. They meet on a monthly basis. Committee members are assigned specific recommendations with a specific timeframe within which implementation must occur, based on the milestones in the Gantt chart. *(The practice manager/compliance officer is charged with responsibility for implementing the findings and recommendations of the consultants. In smaller practices it requires less effort because there is greater hands-on control of the process, but limited resources result in implementation taking longer.)*

Task 10: Revise Position Descriptions

- Subtask 10.1: Review position descriptions. All employee and physician position descriptions are reviewed. Where applicable, they are modified to reflect commitment to compliance and to assign responsibility for functions related to compliance. *(The smaller practice never has maintained position descriptions. The practice manager prepares position descriptions for all personnel, factoring in responsibilities for compliance. The practice manager obtains the approval of shareholders.)*
- Subtask 10.2: Modify position descriptions as required. Modified position descriptions are forwarded to the employees who now have responsibility for compliance. They are asked to sign a statement acknowledging that they are aware of these new responsibilities.

Task 11: Review and Modify Operating Policies and Procedures

All policies and procedures (e.g., billing and collections, appointment scheduling, registration, personnel) are reviewed and modified as required. The policies and procedures address, at a minimum, the following:

- *Enforcement and discipline (personnel policies)*—How wrongdoing will be identified, how billing errors will be documented, and how corrective action will be taken.
- *Rectifying wrongdoing (billing and collections and other operating areas of a practice)*— Procedures to avoid recurrence, identify preventive steps that will be taken, and document training that will occur to remedy problems in the future. Related to billing and information development processes, the practice should have written internal control procedures.

  (Most, if not all, of the preceding applies to the smaller practice because it does not have the range of written policies and procedures of the larger practice. It is too cumbersome to begin to write new policy and procedure manuals in the short term [this will be designated as a long-term project]. In lieu of expanding its existing general policy and procedure manual, the small practice decides to document changes and additions to policy and procedures in the minutes of its periodic meetings of shareholders.)

Task 12: Review and Revise Personnel Policies and Procedures

All policies and procedures should be easy to read and to comprehend, not overly detailed, and designed to foster the application of judgment. Personnel policies and procedures relate to:

- Standards of employee conduct
- Disciplining personnel and uniformity thereof
- Termination
- Recruitment and obtaining references (verification of licensure and other credentials; existence of prior government sanctions; signed acknowledgments from new employees that they have read the code, were given an opportunity to ask questions, and understand it)
- Retrospective and concurrent performance evaluations
- Confidentiality relating to employee disclosure of knowledge related to wrongdoing
- Employee annual evaluation forms (now include performance criteria related to employee contributions to the compliance process and to upholding exemplary ethics; supervisors now will be evaluated on their contributions to upholding the compliance process)
- Review of all existing and prospective contracts with physicians and outside provider organizations (to ensure they are not out of compliance; perform with CEO)

  (Most, if not all, of the preceding applies to the smaller practice because it does not have the range of written policies and procedures of the larger practice. It is too cumbersome to begin to write new policy and procedure manuals in the short term [this will be designated as a long-term project]. In lieu of expanding its existing general policy and procedure manual, the small practice decides to document changes and additions to policy and procedures in the minutes of its periodic meetings of shareholders.)

Task 13: Develop Internal Audit Processes

Of all the implied requirements in the seven basic elements, that of periodic audits perhaps represents the greatest challenge to physician practices both large and small. Auditing is generally not a function performed in most practices because it requires expertise that falls beyond the technical and experiential base of most professionals in practice management and is high risk if not conducted properly.

The purpose of this task is to design and implement a reasonable audit process performed by internal staff or by qualified external auditors. This decision depends on the human resource capacity of the practice and its financial resources. Auditing is a high-risk area in general, and auditing must be conducted properly and consistently. Individuals with requisite training in the audit process, with a keen appreciation of confidentiality, and with independence and objectivity, should conduct audits.

Although an external baseline audit is suggested by the OIG, internal auditing should be made an integral part of a compliance plan. A broad annual audit should occur (see task 8) and periodic audits, often targeted, should occur throughout the year.

- Subtask 13.1: Define the scope of the audit. When defining the scope of the audit, the following should be considered at a minimum: size of practice; baseline audit findings (did the baseline audit reveal any significant areas of weakness that need to be rechecked, did it suggest the need to implement certain controls, policies, or procedures that need to be tested for the first time?); prior audit history (have there been any prior HCFA or OIG audits?); areas of billing risk based on the practice's specialty; number of offices, staff, and physicians; the degree of employee turnover in operationally critical functions; new or updated automated billing systems; and prior internal audits or reports rendered by management or outside consultants. It is important to note that future audits should consider the findings and recommendations of all historical audits and that the scope of a current audit includes verification that prior recommendations have been implemented and are operating satisfactorily. This type of continuity and due diligence is what the OIG generally looks for, and it is consistent with accepted professional auditing practices. The scope of the audit also would define whether the auditors are targeting only billing and collection issues, or if the scope is broader and includes operational functions (scheduling, registration, internal controls, etc.), compliance with other federal and state regulations, contracts, and so forth.

- Subtask 13.2: Determine sample size. Sample size and type (e.g., random or targeted, retroactive or concurrent) are determined in accordance with the scope and frequency of the audit. Sampling techniques should be selected. Larger groups may wish to refer to the OIG RATSTATS sampling program (www.hhs.gov/progrog/oas/ratstat.html) and other audit and sampling guidelines (e.g., AICPA audit guidelines). *(The recent guidelines for individual physicians and small group physician practices suggest that there is no set formula for how large a sample should be, but acknowledges that larger samples better ensure confidence in the findings. The OIG's basic guide is 2 to 5 medical records per insurer, or 5 to 10 medical records per physician for each audit.)*

- Subtask 13.3: Develop an audit work plan. The work plan is the guide used by the compliance officer or audit team to conduct the audit. It stems from the scope of the audit, and it provides a detailed checklist of the functions that need to occur during the audit, what is being audited, documentation requirements, and reporting needs.

- Subtask 13.4: Select the sample. This effort generally includes the applicable medical records or portions thereof, explanations of medical benefits (EOBs) for those medical records, and billing and collection activity reports for the transactions being audited from the practice's billing system. If the audit scope encompasses more than billing and collections, other internal documents will be sought. When conducting an operational (i.e., performance) audit, the policies and procedures of the organization become the first guideline against which the auditors will hold the organization accountable. Then, further operational standards are applied to determine if there are reasonable policies, procedures, and internal controls in place to prevent and detect wrongdoing.

- Subtask 13.5: Conduct the audit (field work). Field work must be adequately supervised by the compliance officer or other competent individual. It is best that the auditors be independent and objective so that their findings are credible. Audit planners are referred to the Comptroller General Field Work Standards for Conducting Performance Audits that are used by government auditors, as well as the AICPA standards that are used by accountants in financial auditing and consultants in performance audits. The field work generally will consist of reviews and analyses of charge tickets, medical record documentation, and computer records; interviews with staff and, sometimes, patients; certain tests for internal controls; and observations. If the audit extends beyond billings and collections, the field work will review original source documents (e.g., contracts, policies, and procedures) and include interviews. An important field work standard concerns the collection of evidence (i.e., documentation).

Sufficient [Author's note: Sufficient information is not synonymous with excessive detail], competent, and relevant evidence is to be obtained to afford a reasonable basis for the auditors' findings and conclusions. A record of the auditors' work should be obtained in the form of working papers. Working papers should contain sufficient information to enable an experienced auditor having no previous connection with the audit to ascertain from them the evidence that supports the auditors' significant conclusions and judgments.[30]

The text relating to working papers in the previous quote identifies one of the more important contributors to successful auditing; specifically, the ability of an experienced auditor having no previous connection with the audit to ascertain from the working papers what the primary auditors' evidence was in support of their conclusions and judgments. *(Smaller practices can narrow the scope and sample size of audits and increase their frequency in order to reduce the internal staff time required. Alternatively, they may retain outside staff to conduct periodic audits. To the extent possible, they should adhere to the principles of auditing discussed herein, particularly related to ensuring independence and objectivity, developing an audit plan, obtaining evidence, and documenting findings in working papers.)*

- Subtask 13.6: Write the audit report. The audit report should identify the scope of the audit, major findings and recommendations, and suggested follow-up. It should be written by the compliance officer, submitted to the compliance committee of the board, and follow-up resolutions should be made by this committee. Follow-up should be assigned to specific individuals in the practice, and periodic checks made thereafter to ensure conformity. Recommendations also can call for follow-up audits that are more targeted to specific physicians, practice office sites, procedure codes, or operational units within the practice. *(The practice manager should submit findings and recommendations from the audit [whether developed internally or by outside professionals] to the shareholders of the practice.)*
- Subtask 13.7: Involve legal counsel. The practice may wish to share sensitive information with counsel to determine further strategies regarding the manner in which that information should be presented. Counsel can assist in determining whether certain findings warrant reporting to the government.

Task 14: Establish Internal Communications and Reporting Systems

This task refers to establishing internal methods that would allow employees to confidentially communicate wrongdoing that they perceive. It can include a hotline, drop box, designated telephone answering machine, or a standardized form to be submitted to the compliance officer. All communications should be entered into a central logbook or into a secured computer database. It is important that employees be given assurances of confidentiality;

however, guarantees cannot be extended because employees may need to be queried in the future if the investigation yields confirming results requiring further action or reporting. *(Recent guidelines for individual physicians and group practices suggest that an effective open door policy or a drop box are sufficient in smaller practices.)*

- Subtask 14.1: Conduct a preliminary inquiry. A reasonable preliminary inquiry is conducted regarding reported wrongdoing. This inquiry should determine whether no further action is required or further analysis and inquiry are warranted.
- Subtask 14.2: Conduct a full investigation (see task 15). If the findings are suggestive of wrongdoing or behavior that is inconsistent with the practice's code of ethics, a full investigation may be appropriate.
- Subtask 14.3: Report sensitive findings to counsel, if required. This action is designed to address significant areas of concern and to develop appropriate courses of action.
- Subtask 14.4: Document. All steps, relevant information, findings, and corrective action (if employed) should be documented.

Task 15: Conduct a Full Investigation

Based on reasonable preliminary investigations (task 14), the compliance officer may have reason to conduct, or have conducted, a full investigation. A full investigation is similar in process to an audit. It may be more targeted based on the employee's report or the findings of an audit.

- Subtask 15.1: Define the scope of investigation. In an investigation, the scope is likely to be more targeted than in an audit. The investigator should be mindful, however, not to limit the scope such that important evidence or related wrongdoing (similar to the specific complaint that triggered the review) is overlooked.
- Subtask 15.2: Determine the sample size (if appropriate in an investigation). Sample size and type are determined in accordance with the scope and the frequency of the audit. Sampling techniques should be selected.
- Subtask 15.3: Develop an investigation work plan. The work plan is the guide used by the compliance officer or team to conduct the investigation. It stems from the scope of the investigation and provides a detailed checklist of the functions that need to occur during the investigation, what is being investigated, documentation requirements, and reporting needs.
- Subtask 15.4: Select the sample. The sample generally includes the applicable medical records or portions thereof, EOBs for those medical records, and billing and collection activity reports for the transactions being investigated from the practice's billing system. If the scope encompasses more than billing and collections, other internal documents will be sought.
- Subtask 15.5: Conduct the investigation (field work). Field work must be adequately supervised by the compliance officer or other competent individual. It is best that the investigators be independent and objective so that their findings are credible. The field work generally will consist of review and analysis of charge tickets, medical record documentation, and computer records; interviews (staff and, sometimes, patients); tests for

internal controls; and observation. If the investigation extends beyond billings and collections, it will include a review of original source documents (e.g., contracts, policies, and procedures) and interviews. When conducting an investigation, the policies and procedures of the organization become the first guidelines against which investigators assess alleged wrongdoing because they should be reflective of current billing, coding, and collection requirements. If alleged wrongdoing is found, further operational standards will be applied to determine if there are reasonable policies, procedures, and internal controls in place to prevent and detect future wrongdoing. As with audits, the collection of evidence (i.e., documentation) is paramount (see the subtask 13.5 discussion of working papers). An important field work standard concerns the collection of evidence (i.e., documentation):

> Sufficient [Author's note: Sufficient information is not synonymous with excessive detail], competent, and relevant evidence is to be obtained to afford a reasonable basis for the auditors' findings and conclusions. A record of the auditors' work should be obtained in the form of working papers. Working papers should contain sufficient information to enable an experienced auditor having no previous connection with the audit to ascertain from them the evidence that supports the auditors' significant conclusions and judgments.[31]

> *(Smaller practices can narrow the scope and sample size of investigations and increase their frequency in order to reduce the time required of internal staff. Alternatively, they may retain outside staff to conduct periodic investigations.)*

- Subtask 15.6: Write the investigation report. The report should identify the scope of the investigation, major findings and recommendations, and suggested follow-up. It should be written by the compliance officer, submitted to the compliance committee of the board, and follow-up resolutions should be made by the committee.
- Subtask 15.7: Involve legal counsel. The practice may wish to share certain information with counsel to determine further strategies and whether certain findings warrant reporting to the government. If refunds are necessary, they should be made promptly, typically within 60 days. *(The practice manager should submit findings and recommendations from the investigation [whether developed internally or by outside professionals] to the shareholders of the practice.)*

Task 16: Enforce and Remedy Wrongdoing

Policies and procedures for enforcing and remedying wrongdoing are in place. On the basis of audits, investigations, or performance evaluations that reveal personnel that persistently do not cooperate with the code of ethics or compliance plan, steps should be taken. Those steps should uniformly align with the established policies and procedures of the practice. Operational changes should be put in place promptly as well. All actions, whether related to personnel or changes in the operations of the practice, should be documented. *(Same applies to the smaller practice.)*

Enforcement can include counseling employees and physicians regarding improper or illegal practices, probation or suspension if there were prior warnings, and terminations. The employee evaluation should be made part of the enforcement process. If employees are evaluated annually, it should be documented in the yearly review. If an employee already has received an annual review, it is appropriate to place a memorandum to the personnel record in the employee's file. Conducting more frequent performance reviews after an employee has been counseled is not inappropriate.

Task 17: Report to the Compliance Committee (Shareholders)

The compliance committee should meet periodically to report and discuss audit and investigation findings, enforcement and disciplinary action that may have been taken, and any operational changes that may have been implemented to reduce wrongdoing. The committee also should report any changes in operations that may be necessary to reduce wrongdoing or improper behavior, improve employee and physician awareness of compliance requirements, and increase education related to compliance. *(The practice manager should meet periodically with key staff who are involved in the compliance program to report major findings and to suggest ongoing changes in the compliance program.)*

Periodically, perhaps on a quarterly basis, the compliance officer (practice manager) should submit a written report to the board of directors (shareholders) that outlines the activities that have occurred during the prior period. It also should report any recommendations that should be incorporated into future audits designed to determine if there is compliance with new regulations and guidelines, or if there were weaknesses that were detected (and rectified) that need to be re-checked through audit technique.

The compliance officer may wish to speak to counsel prior to discussing certain matters with the board *(or with shareholders at a meeting)*, or have counsel at meetings at which sensitive matters may be discussed.

Task 18: Educate and Train

Education and training can assume many forms. Regulations change frequently, government fraud and abuse "alerts" are issued regularly, and many other compliance issues change. In addition, although the OIG acknowledges that practices (particularly smaller ones) may begin their compliance program to target only billing and coding irregularities, the OIG expects that practices will expand their compliance programs over the years. Therefore, education and training should include updates on internal changes that have been made to the practice's compliance programs.

- Subtask 18.1: Prepare a budget for education. Create a budgeted number of dollars for the purpose of internal and external education. Larger practices may wish to budget for the preparation and presentation of seminars and workshops conducted by their own staff. The compliance officer should organize this effort.
- Subtask 18.2: Identify seminars and workshops prospectively. As part of an annual planning process, external seminars and workshops should be identified and scheduled for attendance. Obtaining continuing education credits provides an added incentive to employees.
- Subtask 18.3: Identify attendees. Attendees, including physicians from the practice, should be identified. They should be selected to attend educational seminars that are con-

sistent with their organizational roles (e.g., billers should attend seminars relating to billing and coding issues, an OSHA supervisor should attend OSHA seminars, and so forth). Attendance at compliance workshops should be noted in annual evaluations. In addition, those who attend outside seminars should be asked to prepare presentations for their colleagues based on what they learned.

- Subtask 18.4: Identify and acquire other materials. Other materials such as tapes, disks, and manuals should be purchased and used routinely, especially for new employees.
- Subtask 18.5: Disseminate information internally. Compliance information should be distributed internally and at periodic office staff meetings. Internal management meetings should discuss the practice's policies and procedures related to compliance and proper billing. Minutes of meetings should be kept. Newsletters, printed updates, booklets, and other compliance material should be routed to appropriate staff with a check-off box in which each person receiving the material can acknowledge reading it.
- Subtask 18.6: Give educational presentations to the board. On a periodic basis the compliance officer should conduct presentations to the board in order to keep members abreast of compliance and regulatory changes. *(The practice manager should keep shareholders abreast of changes in compliance requirements for economic reasons, small practices may elect to make more use of update newsletters, tapes and disks, booklets, and internal meetings to learn and communicate new information. If the practice sends a representative to an outside seminar, then that individual should be responsible for bringing back pertinent information and presenting it to all personnel and, when applicable, to the physicians.)*

Phase III—Evaluation and Feedback

Task 19: Evaluate the Compliance Plan and Program Annually

The compliance plan and program should be analyzed on an annual basis and changes made as required. Changes made to conform to new external requirements should be documented. The practice can conduct internal surveys and interviews to determine if changes need to be made in aspects of the compliance plan. *(The practice manager should prepare a report describing the accomplishments of the program, any disciplinary actions that have been taken, and suggested changes to the plan and program.)*

Task 20: Prepare an Annual Report to the Board

The compliance committee and compliance officer should prepare and present an annual report to the board of directors. The board should consider any recommended changes to the compliance plan, code of ethics, and policies and procedures.

The CEO should conduct an annual performance evaluation of the compliance officer's impact on the compliance plan and the degree to which the level of compliance has been enhanced. *(The practice manager should present the annual report at an annual meeting of the shareholders. Any suggested changes to the compliance plan should be discussed and voted on. Appropriate discussion should be committed to the minutes of the meeting.)*

References

1. Office of Inspector General. OIG compliance program for individual and small group physician practices. US Department of Health and Human Services. Available at: http://www.hhs.gov/oig/.
2. Inspector general issues voluntary compliance program guidance for physician practices [news release]. Office of Inspector General. September 2000.
3. Office of Inspector General. OIG compliance program for individual and small group physician practices. US Department of Health and Human Services. Available at: http://www.hhs.gov/oig/.
4. Ibid.
5. Ibid.
6. Office of Inspector General. Compliance program guidance for third-party medical billing companies. *Fed Reg.* 1998; 13 (63 70, 138).
7. Government Accounting Office/Office of the Comptroller General. September 1994. Field Work Standards for Performance Audits 10.
8. Government Accounting Office/Office of the Comptroller General. September 1994. Field Work Standards for Performance Audits 11.
9. Ibid.
10. Metzger N. Human resources management. In: Wolper LF, ed. *Health Care Administration: Planning, Implementing, and Managing Organized Delivery Systems.* New York: Aspen Publishers; 1999:282–284.
11. Wolper LF. *Implementing a Physician Organization.* Chicago, IL: American Medical Association; 1996:13–15.
12. Likert R, Katz D. *Motivation: The Core of Management.* Chicago, IL: American Management Association; 1953:3–25.
13. Ibid.
14. Office of Inspector General. November 1998. Compliance Program Guidance for Third-Party Medical Billing Companies 20.
15. Office of Inspector General. November 1998. Compliance Program Guidance for Third-Party Medical Billing Companies 21.
16. Ibid.
17. Comptroller General of the United States. 1994. General Standards, in Government Auditing Standards.
18. Comptroller General of the United States. 1994. General Standards, in Government Auditing Standards, Section 3.11 at 3.
19. Comptroller General of the United States. 1994. General Standards, in Government Auditing Standards, Section 3.12 at 3.
20. Comptroller General of the United States. 1994. General Standards, in Government Auditing Standards, Section 3.16 at 4, 5.
21. Comptroller General of the United States. 1994. General Standards, in Government Auditing Standards, Section 3.17 at 5.
22. AICPA. September 1999. Code of Professional Conduct, Section 55, Article IV at 1.
23. Comptroller General of the United States. June 1994. Field Work Standards for Performance Audits in Government Auditing Standards, Section 6.2 at 1.
24. Comptroller General of the United States. June 1994. Field Work Standards for Performance Audits in Government Auditing Standards, Section 6.22 at 7.
25. Comptroller General of the United States. June 1994. Field Work Standards for Performance Audits in Government Auditing Standards, Section 6.26 at 7.
26. Comptroller General of the United States. June 1994. Field Work Standards for Performance Audits in Government Auditing Standards, Section 6.39 at 10.

27. Comptroller General of the United States. June 1994. Field Work Standards for Performance Audits in Government Auditing Standards, Section 6.47 at 13.
28. Comptroller General of the United States. June 1994. Field Work Standards for Performance Audits in Government Auditing Standards, Section 6.46 at 12.
29. Patten, et al. *Job Evaluation: Text and Cases 93–94*. 3rd ed. Homewood, IL: Richard D. Irwin Inc; 1964.
31. Comptroller General of the United States. June 1994. Field Work Standards for Conducting Performance Audits in Government Auditing Standards, Section 6.46 at 12.

Biographical Information

Please find Lawrence Wolper's biographical information on page ix.

Index

Numbers

P

P&T (pharmacy and therapeutics)
    committees, 541–542
Paging system, relationship of quality to
    productivity, 422
Palliative care, 444–445
Pare, Ambrose, 491
PAR-level (pre-authorized
    replenishment-level)
    supply chain management, 575
    types of distribution systems, 591
Partnerships
    impact on competition in healthcare
        market, 330, 332
    legal entities for group practice, 679
    types of ownership in ambulatory care
        services, 448
Pasteur, Louis, 495
Pathologists, 506
Patient care committees, in pharmacy
    management, 540
Patient flow and program spaces, planning
    ambulatory care center, 630–632
Patient movement, studies for increasing
    productivity, 424–425
Patient registration, planning ambulatory care
    center, 638–639
Patient safety. *See* Quality and Patient Safety
    (QPS)
Patient testing. *See* Clinical laboratories
Patient/public entrance, planning ambulatory
    care center, 630
PATOS (payment at time of service), 696
payback period, long-range decision making
    and, 219–221
Payer-based health records (PBHRs)
    description of, 374
    HIMSS recommendations, 364
    patient-centric data management systems,
        372
Payment at time of service (PATOS), 696
Payments
    performance-based payment systems, 57
    planning billing and payment area in
        ambulatory care facility, 632
    prospective payment system (PPS), 68
PBHRs. *See* Payer-based health records
    (PBHRs)
PBM (pharmacy benefits management)
    companies, 567

PDSA (Plan, Do, Study, Act), performance
    improvement methodology, 663–664
Peer Review Organization (PRO), 668
Pegboard system, for billing and collections,
    698
Peña, Jesus J., 497
Penalties, for violation of federal anti-
    kickback statute, 134
Pennsylvania Hospital (est. 1751 AD),
    492
Perceptual maps, analysis of competitive
    position via, 333
Performance
    comparing productivity to performance
        goals, 412–416
    of organized delivery systems, 82–84
    reward systems, 426
    in Scope and Standards for Nurse
        Administrators, 317–318
Performance improvement methodologies
    Failure Modes Effects Analysis (FMEA),
        664–665
    Lean management techniques, 662–663
    overview of, 660
    Plan, Do, Study, Act (PDSA), 663–664
    risk resiliency, 666–667
    Root Cause Analysis, 665–666
    Six Sigma, 660–661
Performance-based payment systems, 57
Person hours per output, measures of
    productivity, 412–413
Personal health records (PHRs)
    description of, 374–375
    HIMSS recommendations, 363
    patient-centric data management systems,
        372
Personal services, safe harbours and Stark Law
    exceptions, 119, 151
Personnel. *See also* Human resource
    management; Staffing
    policies and procedures in physician
        compliance program, 734–735
    requirements of clinical laboratories,
        505–508
    reviewing/modifying policies and
        procedures, 744
Personnel records, limiting access to, 294
Pharmacies
    ambulatory care and outpatient systems,
        558–560
    conclusions regarding, 567–568